MAJOR: A POLITICAL LIFE

'Seldon has written the indispensable historical guide to the Major Government: its triumphs and its failures, its achievements and its shortcomings, its life and its death'
Peter Clarke, London Review of Books

'Anthony Seldon's book is a work of scholarship. It will be visited again and again by serious academics long after the instant histories we have recently been subjected to are forgotten. It is the first building block in establishing John Major' *Financial Times*

'Comprehensive, absorbing ... fascinating reading' *The Times*

'Seldon's life of Major is a considerable achievement, a sympathetic and fair study stopping well short of hagiography'
Scotland on Sunday

'A very impressive achievement ... a pre-eminently fair book ... done with skill and sympathy' Roy Jenkins, *Daily Telegraph*

'Instant history on a monumental scale ... the work of a real historian' *Independent*

'Authoritative ... [the] well-written biography that John Major deserves ... many gossipy myths can now shrivel and die' Douglas Hurd, *Evening Standard*

'Resourceful and highly readable' *Independent on Sunday*

'Mr Seldon is scrupulously fair. He pays as much attention to John's successes as to his failures - an attitude I find refreshing ... When I came to the end of the book, I was strangely moved. It was, I realised, the story of a man who loved his country and did everything he could to serve it' *Daily Telegraph*

'Admirably recounted ... Anthony Seldon is one of the most skilful of the historians of contemporary Britain' *Guardian*

Churchill's Indian Summer (1981)

By Word of Mouth (with Joanna Pappworth, 1983)

Ruling Performance, ed (with Peter Hennessy, 1987)

Contemporary History, ed (1988)

The Thatcher Effect, ed (with Dennis Kavanagh, 1989)

Political Parties since 1945, ed (1989)

Politics UK (with Bill Jones et al., 1990)

Governments and Economies since 1945, ed
  (with Andrew Graham, 1991)

The Major Effect, ed (1996)

Conservative Century, ed (with Stuart Ball, 1994)

How Tory Governments Fall, ed (1996)

The Heath Government 1970–74, ed (with Stuart Ball, 1996)

Ideas and Think Tanks in Contemporary Britain,
  ed (with M. D. Kandiah, 1996)

Contemporary History Handbook, ed (with Brian Brivati, 1996)

The Ideas that Shaped Post-War Britain, ed (with David Marquand, 1996)

Anthony Seldon is co-founder (with Peter Hennessy) and first Director of the Institute of Contemporary British History and Headmaster of Brighton College. He is author or editor of several books on recent history, has founded and edited several historical journals, including *Contemporary British History*, and edits the *Making Contemporary Britain* series. When not writing or teaching he enjoys directing and watching plays and spending time with his wife Joanna and their three children Jessica, Susannah and Adam.

Major
A Political Life

ANTHONY SELDON

with Lewis Baston

Distributed by
Trafalgar Square
North Pomfret, Vermont 05053

PHŒNIX

A Phoenix Paperback
First published in Great Britain
by Weidenfeld & Nicolson in 1997
This paperback edition published in 1998
by Phoenix, a division of Orion Books Ltd,
Orion House, 5 Upper St Martin's Lane,
London WC2H 9EA

A CIP catalogue record for this book
is available from the British Library.

ISBN: 0 75380 145 0

Printed and bound in Great Britain
by The Guernsey Press Co. Ltd,
Guernsey, Channel Islands.

*To my former colleagues and students
at St Dunstan's College, Tonbridge School
and Whitgift School, from whom
I have learnt so much.*

All profits from this book will be divided between
the Institute of Contemporary British History and to help
students at St Dunstan's College and Brighton College

CONTENTS

ILLUSTRATIONS

The loyal deputy: Michael Heseltine.[3]
Michael Howard, Brian Mawhinney, Norman Fowler and Kenneth Clarke.[3]
Welcoming the three tenors to Downing Street, July 1996.[3]
With the author.[7]
A picture of despair? January 1994.[6]
Launching the National Lottery, November 1994.[3]
Announcing his resignation as party leader, June 1995.[3]
Victory in the leadership election, July 1995.[3]
A week before 1997 polling day, with the author.[7]
Conservative election poster.[3]
On the hustings in Brecon, 9 April 1997.[3]
Leaving Number Ten for the last time, 2 May, 1997.[3]
Back where it all began: at the Oval, 2 May 1997.[3]
'When the curtain falls it is time to get off the stage.'[3]

Sources
The Author and Publishers are grateful to the following for permission to use photographs:

[1] Rex Features Ltd
[2] Joanna Seldon
[3] PA News
[4] Gemma Levine, Camera Press
[5] Universal
[6] Ross Parry, West Yorkshire
[7] Sarah King

INTRODUCTION

THREE YEARS AGO, in September 1994, John Major said he would cooperate in my research for what then became a 'semi-authorised' but not official biography. When we first spoke, I said to him that I would endeavour to write an accurate, balanced and fair book, and he told me that was the book he expected.

Writing a biography of the last Tory Prime Minister of the 'Conservative Century' as the Party hurtled to its biggest defeat in 150 years sounded an enticing challenge for one interested in contemporary history. A book about recent history, particularly a period of history so contemporary and so often bitterly contested as the Major government 1990–97, is always a balancing act, between different principles of writing as much as between the clamour of competing versions of history. It sounded a once in a lifetime challenge. Nothing, however, prepared me for the mountain of work it would prove – six and a half years is a long premiership to cover – and I also had a full-time job in the demanding environment of a school. Nor did I fully realise beforehand what a very highly charged exercise it would be.

As a biographer, there must be human sympathy for one's subject, for without it there can be little understanding of that subject's character and motives. With John Major, regardless of the wisdom or otherwise of each of his political acts – and I have tried to show how little room he often had for manoeuvre – I have formed a high opinion of him as an honourable man who retained his dignity through to his very last hour as Prime Minister in an overwhelmingly hostile climate, often with little ground for cheer. His courage, not least for such a sensitive man without great reserves of inner security, was exceptional.

Being sympathetic did not mean being uncritical. My objective has not been to write a pro-John Major book, although that will not stop some from saying that I have done so, nor others from saying that I have been unfair to him. While a biography necessarily concentrates on the subject, and from November 1990 that also meant a Number Ten perspective, my aim has been to try to be fair to all sides. This is a book without heroes and villains. I conducted over 550 interviews with Major's foes as well as his friends in four continents, with interviews lasting rarely less than an hour – the longest single session lasted over four. Drafts were sent out to nearly 200 people for comment. Not everyone agreed to see me, although most did, and not everyone could or did comment on my drafts. But most key actors, and many others, had their chance to have their views represented at some stage. I do not, of course, believe that with such a long and contemporary book I will have eliminated all errors and unfair judgements. I stand open to correction for any subsequent editions.

The book does not have a simple 'thesis' – a dreadful admission – such as John Major good, the right bad, with a cabal of disloyal colleagues precipitating election defeat, still less Major being stupid and weak – as some very intelligent people appear to believe – because he did not lead the country in a wholeheartedly Eurosceptic direction and, had he done so, all would have been well. Alas for the simple explanations and arguments! Books based on such an approach may make great waves and afford much comfort and *esprit de corps* or not, but often make bad history. So what is my verdict on John Major?

The quick answer is to read the epilogue, but the full answer is to read the thirty-nine chapters that precede it. The huge defeat of his party in 1997 happened because the country and the media were deeply bored with the Tories, and fed up with a party that seemed to have no common beliefs or loyalty to bind it together. By the end of the century, the Tories' stock of agreed policies on which the leadership could draw was running dry. There were ideas aplenty, but not ones around which all sections of the parliamentary party could unite, and with a wafer-thin and disappearing majority after 1992 all elements needed to agree if the government were to receive parliamentary endorsement for its programme. Historians will say something like this in 2097, too; they will not say that John Major failed and his party was devastated in the 1997 general election because he was not a Eurosceptic nor sufficiently Thatcherite. Politicians are fundamentally self-interested people. For most of the Party's history, self-interest has dictated loyalty; in the 1990s, with the polls continually showing a huge Labour advantage and the likelihood of a heavy Tory defeat, self-interest was better served by actions other than loyally following the Party leader. Coupled with that, the Tories faced the most creative Labour leader since Attlee, if not Ramsay MacDonald; one who brilliantly exploited Tory divisions while stealing their natural voters.

The book will have two main types of critics: academics, who will say that the account, in as far as they will give it attention, is woefully incomplete in vital respects; and some participants, who will say that I have seriously misrepresented them. The former have my envy for their time and their intellects, the latter my admiration for their self-belief – and my apologies. If indeed there are serious misrepresentations, as opposed to special pleading, then I can only plead lack of time for sufficient checking and admit that my aim of impartiality in this case was not realised.

I have tried to avoid the book becoming an outlet for the poison that entered the soul of the Conservative Party in the 1980s and is still with us – I leave that to the next crop of political memoirs and, dare I say it, some of my reviewers. I have placed worthy and unworthy alongside in the text, just as they sat in Parliament and around the Cabinet table. This is not a failure of judgement, for the wise judge does not lead the jury in his or her summing up. The jury are future historians, and the readers.

Anthony Seldon
Brighton, September 1997

PROLOGUE

AT 5 P.M. ON THE afternoon of Thursday 1 May 1997, John Major was being driven around the committee rooms of his Huntingdon constituency when the phone rang in the Prime Minister's car. The message from Conservative Central Office in London was that the Party was heading for a catastrophic defeat. Exit polls, and the Party's own research, suggested that the figure of 240 seats, which Major had been given only two days before, seriously overestimated the size of the Tory vote. He was heading for the landslide defeat he had always dreaded.

His mood had been buoyant during the day as he joked with Party workers and friends around the constituency, and he had been pleased with reports of how his local competition in Huntingdon was going. He always took particular pride in his constituency result and was on course for the biggest Conservative majority in the country. But the news of the national picture hit him very badly. Those travelling with him describe him as being 'shell-shocked' and 'very, very bleak'. For the next two hours he had great difficulty maintaining his spirits as he visited the remaining committee rooms before returning to his home, The Finings, at around 6.30 p.m.

He had a long talk with Peter Brown, his constituency agent, reflecting on the likely vote, and again with Arabella Warburton, his Personal Secretary from Number Ten, shortly after she arrived from London in a car festooned with flowers and blue balloons from well-wishers. While walking around the garden, Major told her: 'The exit polls are very bad. It will be a very bad night for us. It looks much worse than we thought.' Tentative efforts to cheer Major up, by pointing out how misleading the polls had been in 1992, or hoping that the sunny weather had brought out Conservative voters, fell on stony ground.

The house by now was filling up. Howell James, Major's Political Secretary since 1994, arrived with a handful of personal staff from Central Office and Number Ten. James was deputed to go off to buy fish and chips with James Major to fill everyone up for the long night ahead. As they ate in the kitchen, the mood was sombre, everyone now accepting it would be a crushing defeat. The house was strangely silent. No one knew whether or not to mention the election or the likely result. Major himself ate in almost total silence. One present said it was as if he was in trauma, as if he had been in a car crash.

Part of him was still desperately hoping the exit polls were not true. Only with great difficulty was any kind of conversation maintained. Norma, as ever, was a source of strength. Instructions had been given to the Number Ten switchboard not to put any calls through to The Finings. The group sat round the kitchen eating their fish and chips suspended in time, almost detached from reality.

Seventy miles away in London, the three most powerful official members of the British state dined together: Robin Butler, Head of the Home Civil Service, Robert Fellowes, the Queen's Private Secretary, and Alex Allan, the Prime Minister's Principal Private Secretary. They discussed final arrangements for the now-inevitable transition to a Labour government the next day. As ever, they were clinically efficient, concerned that a day that would be of great fatigue and even greater emotion would run smoothly. Allan was one of the few to speak to Major on the phone that evening. Over the last five years the two men had spoken almost daily, often many times, and had formed a deep bond. They agreed that the likelihood was a huge defeat, and they discussed the mechanism for Major conceding to Blair. Brian Mawhinney, the Party Chairman, and the man who ran the Tories' election campaign, was another to speak on the phone that evening to Major. He asked Mawhinney whether he should phone Blair before he went to the Huntingdon count; Mawhinney felt he had already made up his mind that he should.

At 10 p.m., as the polls closed, they put on ITN's *News at Ten* in the drawing room at The Finings. 'It was like death,' said one present. As the bells of Big Ben chimed, the headline announcement spoke of the likelihood of a massive Labour victory. It was suggested Major might prefer to watch the television alone with Norma. He went off, but then drifted back before starting to draft his notes about what he would say at Huntingdon. He was still undecided when he would say he was standing down. Norma was determined not to break down in tears in public.

At midnight, he withdrew to a quiet room with Howell James to phone Blair, whom Alex Allan had contacted at his home in his Sedgefield constituency. They spoke for five minutes. After all the rancour of their relationship over the previous year, and especially over the previous week when Major had been disgusted by Blair's prediction that the Tories wanted to end the state pension, their conversation was surprisingly amicable and honest. Major told him he had won, congratulated him, and offered him success. Blair thanked him, said that the manner of his concession was typically dignified, and wished him well.

There then followed an agonising wait of over two hours before the Majors could leave for the count at Huntingdon. They watched the television in a desultory fashion. The enduring image of the evening of one present was watching Major transfixed in front of the television mouthing to himself, 'I just don't believe it, I don't believe it.'

Reaction to the string of defeats for Tories ranged from genuine regret, when some right-wing critics who they felt had been loyal, like Michael Portillo, fell, to muffled cheers when others, like David Evans, populist MP for Welwyn Hatfield and a constant thorn in Major's side, lost their seats. Major had formed a particular loathing for some he regarded as trouble-makers on the right, whom he blamed for many of his government's difficulties and hence for the scale of the defeat. At 2.30 a.m. the Prime Minister's motorcade moved off to the count, nobody saying a word.

Peter Brown and John Bridge, the constituency chairman, met him on arrival at the hall, and he was shown into a small holding room, but he had already collected himself and knew what he must do. He went out into the hall with Norma on his arm, and chatted good-humouredly to the Labour, Liberal Democrat and other candidates. His own majority of 18,140 votes brought him some comfort, tinged with disappointment that the intervention of the Referendum Party candidate, the ecologist David Bellamy, who won 3,100 votes, denied him his personal target of a 20,000-vote majority. Before the jostling cameras, and drawing deeply on his reserves of energy, he thanked his constituency helpers, but also ceded defeat nationally. 'Elections always have winners, and they always have losers ... we have had great victories in our time and we have had great defeats in our time.' The words were his own. When he was at his most moving, the words almost invariably were his own. One past error was corrected: he thanked Norma handsomely, whom he had overlooked to thank at the last count in 1992.

At 3.15 a.m. they boarded the convoy, the Majors in the front car, the police back-up vehicle behind, and the Downing Street aides and James and Elizabeth Major in two cars behind. The roads were virtually empty as the cars glided southwards towards London. Major had conceded defeat publicly. That was difficult enough, not least because in making himself so much the focus of the general election campaign, the defeat was so personal. No air raid shelters were available. He had still one chance left to leave office at a time, as he had said four years before, that would surprise people. Some days before, he had decided that if the defeat was heavy, he would announce immediately that he would be standing down as Leader of the Conservative Party. Several figures, notably Lord Cranborne, his chief of staff during the campaign and Leader of the Lords, and Alistair Goodlad, the Chief Whip, tried to dissuade him. Cranborne worked hard, arguing that the time to go would be in the autumn, to maximise the chances of holding the Party together and ensuring that a measured leadership election would take place. Major was adamant. 'I love my party in the country, but I do not love my parliamentary party', he said. If he stayed on, the Party would tear itself apart waiting until the autumn. The leadership election, he thought, had already started. 'It would be terrible,' he said, 'because I would be presiding with no authority over a number of candidates fighting for the crown. It would merely prolong the agony.' Howard and Redwood were already campaigning for him to leave early so they could get on with their leadership bids. He would be trodden underfoot as the leadership race waged all the more intensely.

Norma agreed he should leave at once. She had become increasingly fierce in her anger at the way certain figures in the parliamentary party had treated her husband, and she did not want him to endure one moment more of it than he needed to after he ceased to be Prime Minister. His thought was that Heseltine would take over either as caretaker or longer-term leader (one reason why Cranborne, on the opposite wing of the Party, had been so anxious to persuade Major to stay on). An extraordinary transformation had come over Major's relationship with Heseltine. When he had succeeded as Prime Minister, Heseltine was the figure around his Cabinet table he most mistrusted. Now he loved him, and regarded him as his most trustworthy and powerful ally since the leadership election in July 1995. But Major was to be denied his wish to hand over the leadership to him. Accounts varied as to the seriousness of the angina attack that Heseltine suffered the next day, which led to a statement ruling out his standing for the Party leadership. It was not related to his heart attack nearly four years earlier in Venice and there is some reason for thinking that, as with Macmillan's decision to stand down in 1963, the announcement was precipitous. That said, Heseltine would have been sixty-nine at the time of a 2002 general election and he had been worn down by stresses of the previous few months. He was not sorry to withdraw finally from the fray.

By the time the cars swept into Smith Square at 5.20 a.m., Major knew not only what he would say, but had prepared himself mentally and emotionally for the next few hours. As they travelled south, news came through steadily of one defeat after another, with seven Cabinet ministers losing their seats, and talk beginning of this being the worst Tory defeat for 150 years.

At Central Office Major was greeted by Portillo at the front of the welcoming party. Looking tired and pale, Major clasped his hands warmly. After several such greetings with campaigners, he repaired upstairs with Howell James for consultations with Cranborne and Mawhinney, when he told them he was going to announce later that morning that he would be standing down. With another cheery speech of thanks to Party workers, full of stoical resolution – 'OK, we lost', but they would come back to fight another day – he left for Downing Street at 6.30 a.m. In a gesture of gratitude to Mawhinney for his hard and loyal work as Party Chairman, he invited him to join Norma, James and Elizabeth for breakfast in the flat at the top of Number Ten. They were all drained but talked about what they would do in the future.

At 10.30 a.m., after showering and having subtle make-up applied to disguise his tiredness, he came down to the pillared room on the first floor where the Number Ten staff of some sixty had gathered for coffee, croissants and orange juice. Major made his way around the staff gathered in various groups and spoke individually to them, addressing each by their first name, trying to give them encouragement and strength. He then moved into the middle of the room and addressed them in a steady but quiet voice. He thanked them all, said what a wonderful place Number Ten had been to work in, that it had been not just an office but also their home, and told them how much he would miss them all. By now, everyone in the room either had tears in their eyes, or were openly crying. He said to them that he knew it was the tradition for staff to line the ground floor corridor to clap out departing prime ministers, but he said he would find it difficult enough to face the cameras in Downing Street without a lump in his throat, and he wondered if they would mind saying their farewells there in the room. If he caught the eye of any of them, he was not certain he could control himself.

At 11.10 a.m., he left the room with Norma and the children, and walked downstairs to the anteroom outside the Cabinet Room, where they were joined by Alex Allan, Howell James, Jonathan Haslam, the Number Ten Press Secretary, and Brian Mawhinney to discuss how to position themselves for the waiting cameramen. He had decided some days before that, whatever the result, he would go off to watch cricket at the Oval – the one luxury he told Sue Lawley on *Desert Island Discs* that he wanted to take with him.

At 11.25 a.m., he came out to the spot where 2,347 days and one hour before he had announced that he had accepted the Queen's invitation to form a government, and said: 'It has been an immense privilege to serve as Prime Minister of the United Kingdom.' Congratulating the incoming government, he said they would inherit the most benevolent set of economic statistics since the First World War. There was one final matter he wanted to clarify. He would be advising his parliamentary colleagues to select a new leader. With words that recalled the theatrical tradition of his parents, he said, 'When the curtain falls it is time to get off the stage and that is what I propose to do.' With this most dignified of exits, he and Norma boarded the Prime Minister's official car for the last time for his journey to Buckingham Palace to hand in his resignation. From there, he was driven to watch cricket in south London, where, fifty-four years before, his story began.

ONE

An Unprepossessing Start:

1943–59

JOHN MAJOR WAS born on 29 March 1943, the fourth child of his parents, Tom and Gwen, though only the third to survive infancy. Most other prime ministers this century have either been born to wealthy and educated backgrounds, where letters, from boarding school on, flowed freely – as with Winston Churchill or Clement Attlee – or showed early evidence of future distinction – as with David Lloyd George or Harold Wilson. John Major was bestowed with neither characteristic. His early years profoundly shaped his outlook on life but, for reasons that will become clear, comprehending his inner – and indeed his outward – life with any certainty is difficult.

Major's Immediate Family

Some facts are reasonably clear. His father, Tom Ball, a strong, independent-minded man, was born in May 1879 near Walsall in the West Midlands, the son of a master bricklayer.[1] In the mid-1880s the Ball family set off for the United States in search of employment in the Pittsburgh steel industry.[2] Their mission had only limited success, and in the late 1890s the family returned to Britain, probably back to the Midlands.[3] Tom's career now took an unlikely turn, as he briefly became a trapeze artist, the aspect of his career the press seized upon when his younger son achieved prominence as a politician. Professionally he used the name 'Tom Major'. He married his first wife, Kitty, also in music hall, in 1910 and a busy career on the stage together followed. They had no children. A year after Kitty died in 1928, following a long illness caused by a stage accident, Tom married Gwen, Major's mother, on 4 April 1929.[4] She was already pregnant.

Gwen Coates was the daughter of a grocer's assistant from Gainsborough, Lincolnshire, twenty-six years Tom's junior. A vivacious and strong-willed woman, she joined Tom's travelling variety troupe in the 1920s. When Kitty became ill, Gwen looked after Tom; it was Kitty's wish, the family legend goes, that the two should marry if she died.[5]

Kitty's illness and death took Tom's heart out of show business, and with Gwen's first baby on the way, and cinema displacing music hall, Tom decided to settle down. Their marriage certificate already lists his occupation as 'builder' and hers as 'insurance agent'. Their first child was born prematurely in June 1929, but died at birth. Then, a year later to the month, Pat was born, followed by Terry in July 1932. Terry was christened 'Terry Major Ball', and has been known since as Terry Major-Ball. John's birth certificate eleven years later registers his name as plain 'John Major', though he was christened John Roy Major.[6]

The family settled down in a bungalow at 260 Longfellow Road in Worcester Park, southwest London, a house they initially rented. The road was solidly suburban, a mixture of Victorian and inter-war housing, middle class – just – pleasant and comfortable.[7] The bungalow was a modest, four-roomed dwelling, excluding kitchen and bathroom, with a long garden at the back. It must have seemed a blissful haven to Gwen after years on the road. Tom experimented with various occupations, including selling fuel,[8] before establishing Major's Garden Ornaments, which made cement-cast figures and garden accessories. As the depression eased in the 1930s the company flourished, and by the end of the decade the family with their two young children were relatively prosperous. They owned the only motor car in the road; Gwen had domestic help, and they could even afford to buy the bungalow. When war came in 1939, however, their market and supply of raw materials collapsed. Tom closed down the business and Gwen became the breadwinner, working in the library.[9] With reduced income, Terry and Pat were moved from fee-paying to local state schools. In 1941 Pat won a place to Nonsuch Girls' Grammar School; Terry, to his regret, did not pass the eleven-plus.[10] Both children were bright; Pat, however, was the more studious of the two.

The Majors do not appear to have written many letters to each other; they did not keep diaries; barely any written records remain. There were no nannies, no close relatives who knew the family intimately, nor surviving close friends who saw the family grow up. Tom and Gwen died without leaving written recollections. Thus one must lean heavily on the memories of the three children when reconstructing the events of John's early years. Terry discovered a flourishing career in the 1990s as a colourful memoirist and raconteur, achieving a status in life he felt his failure to go to grammar school had always denied him. Pat has not written her story, but has some vivid recollections of Major family life. Both are reluctant to admit how bleak it must have been for their brother. John's own memory of his first sixteen years is poor, and what he can recall is painted in often dark tones, which accurately reflect his experience of it.

The account that follows of those first sixteen years is thus the fullest that can be written and, *force majeure*, leans heavily on the testimony of the three children.

Major's Early Years: 1943–54

John was born in St Helier Hospital near the family home. By all accounts his was a difficult birth. Gwen had double pneumonia and pleurisy and had collapsed, heavily pregnant, in the kitchen at Longfellow Road. She was taken into hospital with her life in the balance, but gave birth safely to John.[11] Gwen recovered, but John caught a serious infection in hospital and required blood transfusions. He still bears the scars on his ankles.[12]

Pat and Terry were aged twelve and ten when John was born; Tom was two months off sixty-four; Gwen was thirty-eight. Tom had not intended there to be another child: they could hardly afford the extra cost, and he may have worried at his age about his ability to father another offspring.[13] Gwen, however, had secretly planned it, according to Pat:

'It was wartime. Terry and I went off to school in the morning and Mum didn't know whether we'd come back home again. It is times like that when women have the urge for an insurance to make sure there's a child for the future. She was just about young enough to have one. My father wasn't overly keen on the idea, but she wanted another child and that was it. It was a woman's urge.[14]

Pat was close to her mother, and Gwen told her why John was conceived. Terry was kept in the dark and assumed for many years after that his younger brother's birth had been an accident.[15]

The infant Major returned home to Longfellow Road. Gwen made a speedy recovery and was soon back at work at the library, taking John with her and parking the pram amidst the books, where he became, for the first few months of his life, a centre of attention among wartime browsers.[16]

On the same day, as John's birth, 29 March 1943, Hitler approved a blueprint submitted to him by Albert Speer for a massive, reinforced concrete missile silo on the Channel coast, from which London could be bombarded.[17] Though the first V-1 bomb, or doodlebug, was not fired on London until 13 June 1944, London had begun to become a dangerous place again for the first time since the blitz in 1940–41.[18] Earlier in the year a bomb had landed near the Majors' bungalow; shattered glass landed in the cot where John had shortly before been laid.[19] Tom and Gwen had had enough and decided to evacuate the family to the countryside and to safety. The Cowleys, who lived next door, made temporary arrangements for them to live with their relatives in the hamlet of Saham Toney in East Anglia, twelve miles west of Norwich. After a short stay they moved into a mansion nearby, a home for several evacuee families.[20] For Gwen, Norfolk brought peace of mind: the children were safe from bombs and missiles, and Tom had a chance to recover after several years of war work as an air raid warden, during which he had fallen heavily on his helmet during a blackout, damaging his chest and heart.[21]

With the danger of flying bombs past, the family moved back to Longfellow Road in April 1945.[22] VE Day in May was spent at home joining the street celebrations, which was not what Tom felt like doing when Clement Attlee

became Labour Prime Minister that July. Did the young John imbibe a dislike
of socialism then from his father? According to Terry: 'Father had always
been a true blue Tory ... Father would often get involved in heated political
discussions. On one occasion in 1948, I ... heard father in full spate with a
much younger man from up the road who was saying, "Tory bastard. You
need your head punching." ... Father blamed Attlee for everything.'[23]

The tenor of Tom's political views, and the vehemence with which they
could be expressed, must have left an impression on the younger boy. Pat
certainly believes the reason Major went into politics was because of Tom's
influence.[24] Tom had other views, too, which his son might well have
absorbed: he was angry at the way inflation had put up ornament prices at
the start of the war.[25] He had a dislike of interfering bureaucracy: before the
war, Tom had been in trouble with the local council for running a business
from home and had had to find workshops away from Longfellow Road.[26]
His precise moral standards, his dislike of officialdom and of inflation, and
his high expectations, undoubtedly also left their mark on John.

Despite the wide age gap – Tom was older than many children's grand-
fathers – he enjoyed a positive if fairly distant relationship with his younger
son. Tom had been athletic and a great swimmer as a younger man. Too old
now to be the sportsman-father, or to teach the young John to swim, he
contented himself with more sedate, fatherly occupations: card tricks,
memory games, composing limericks and storytelling about his youth and
days as a performer.[27] John was clearly devoted to his elderly and stern father
and would wander off to spend time with him, watching him in his little
workshop at the back of the house.[28] Tom became increasingly blind after the
war, with a degenerative disease in both eyes. According to Gwen, he did not
receive any pension from the state after his sixty-fifth birthday in 1944 and,
despite a small, regular sum from the Variety Artists' Association, he felt
unable to retire.[29] But he found work a strain, which accounted in part for
his bursts of bad temper with his family. Irascibility under pressure is another
John Major trait.[30]

Gwen was less overtly political than Tom, and her instincts were more to
the left. A philanthropist by nature, she was happy to see the bungalow full
with people coming to stay or calling in to unburden themselves. Gwen
busied herself after the war helping the family business, running the home,
and bringing up her young son. In the last task she was helped by Pat, aged
fifteen when war finally ended, who spent long hours reading to her younger
brother in the evenings when she returned from school.[31] Gwen went through
a difficult period just after the war, missed the lack of domestic help with the
housework, and for a time found life hard to manage. While nothing could
displace her central role in the family, in some ways Pat became like a second
mother to John, almost thirteen years her junior. Pat loyally described her
mother as 'like a stake in the ground. Everything was fixed to her, and if she
was pulled up, everything would go wrong'.[32] From his mother John may
well have inherited some of his strong desire to please others.

Family bonds were undoubtedly strong: John Brand, Major's childhood friend, described them as 'very close-knit'.[33] Like most families in Longfellow Road, the Majors were relatively poor in the late 1940s. Terry and Pat had enjoyed a better standard of living as children, but John knew no other life. Although the family could not afford summer holidays or many expeditions, John was never in want of food, or presents at birthdays and Christmas, and was always smartly turned out.[34] Despite the attentions of four loving, if busy, adults, John grew up into a subdued, rather secretive little boy. Pat recalled: 'He contained his feelings, stoical. There was a tendency to find out long afterwards how he'd felt about something inside, as though it all took place around him, without touching him. But it did.'[35]

In 1948 or 1949 – the precise date is unknown – John joined the local state school, Cheam Common Infants' School, moving up to Cheam Common Junior School in September 1950. The school, a half-mile walk from home, was well run and he seems to have flourished there. The only written record that survives about Major's years at Cheam Junior School is the registrar's book, giving the bare dates of his arrival and departure. Christopher Spencer, the Head in the mid-1990s, confirms that there are no reports, attendance registers or photos, and says all those who taught him have either died or can no longer recall him. Major played in the soccer and cricket sides, and was 'probably a quiet, hard-working pupil in what was then a large school with thirty-five or forty per class'.[36] As Major's own memories of his primary education have faded, his early schooling remains a lacuna. More, however, is known about Major's life at home during the years 1949–54, before he reached his teens.

Remaining very much his own person, keeping his own counsel, his favourite occupations were reading (the usual boys' fare, including Robin Hood stories and Anna Sewell's *Black Beauty*[37]), the local cinema on Saturday mornings, and playing sport. Pat taught him the rules of cricket and rugby and the former in particular became a passion, both as a player and a follower of the professional game. John Brand recalls an excitable young boy who, during a test match against Australia in summer 1953, 'was always running in and out of the house, shouting out to the kitchen for the score, where his mother had a radio, and him telling me in the street all about cricket'.[38]

The ornaments business was not reviving. Terry, who left his secondary modern school in 1947 aged fifteen, had begun to work full time for the family firm and, together with Gwen, progressively took over running the business from Tom.[39] Falls at work, and old age, had taken their toll. He passed his seventieth birthday in 1949, and was not young for his age. Like Gwen, he was a heavy smoker: one visitor recalls the house was always full of smoke.[40] Before the war Tom had talked about wanting to retire to South America and, according to Pat, would have done so but for the war.[41] Afterwards his dreams settled on Canada,[42] although he would have preferred the United States. Emigration, however, was much easier to Canada, it being part of the Commonwealth. Tom's degenerating eyesight, however, led to the plan being aborted.[43] He was deeply disappointed, and further misfortune was to follow soon after: in 1954 he suffered his first heart attack.

Rutlish School

Major did sufficiently well at Cheam Common Junior School to pass the eleven-plus exam into Rutlish, a boys' grammar school in Merton, three miles away. Rutlish had just moved to the soulless, red-brick building that houses the school today. Although not fee-paying, Rutlish aped many of the traditions of the public schools; a combined cadet force, a high-profile sports fixture list, an active house and prefects system, a six-day week and Latin were all strong features of the school. Even straw boaters were permitted in summer term. Here, it might have been thought, was the opportunity for Major to blossom, both socially and academically. Most puzzlingly, over five years, he was to do neither.

Major was rarely happy during his five years at the school from 1954 to 1959. His subsequent memories of Rutlish are patchy, and illuminate more his feelings about the school as a mature man, when he clearly resented Rutlish not having done more for him, or recognising his talents:

I didn't like the school ambience, I didn't like the shepherding together of lesser beings who were told that they had to be subservient to and respect greater beings who happened to be schoolmasters. I am not suggesting the school was harsh or unfair in any way. I am just suggesting that to me the innate view that a certain class of people is better than a certain class of other people was absolute anathema. The reason I didn't work at school was alienation from the school. If you had the sort of difficulties we faced at home at the time, you are alienated. I wasn't interested in school. I wasn't stupid at school, I just didn't work. I couldn't work.[44]

Those unsuccessful at school often speak harshly of it with hindsight, and Rutlish offered plenty that Major found disagreeable. The headmaster, John Blenkinsop, had been in office for twelve years before Major's arrival. As a pacifist and a Quaker he held beliefs that might have appealed to Major's later humanitarian side; but Blenkinsop was a rather ineffectual figure, remaining for much of the time in his study. Ridiculed by some of the boys for his horse-like appearance, he was inevitably nicknamed 'Dobbin'.[45] Some staff also found him a weak leader, and wished that he would take more of an interest in their work.[46] Major himself did not rate his headmaster. Nor did he have a high regard for, or form bonds with, other teachers.[47]

The school does not seem to have been tuned to nurturing individuals: many pupils testify to it being rigidly conformist and hierarchical during these years. The ethos of the school remained, despite Blenkinsop, military, sporty and non-academic. Major courted unpopularity among some of the boys by opting not to join the CCF; whether this was as a reaction against its macho image or to spare his parents extra expense is not known. Major had a particular loathing of prefects, who had carved a powerful niche for themselves in the school, throwing their weight around with the younger pupils; Major was one of the boys made to suffer. Colin Brock, the school's historian, is more precise, referring to 'institutionalised bullying'.[48]

John's surname provoked particular ridicule. For reasons that are unclear, though are perhaps connected with the status thought to be attached to a double-barrelled name, he was registered for the school as 'John Major-Ball', which he hated. A contemporary believes Major was bullied because of the 'Ball', which aroused predictable schoolboy humour.[49] Derek Esterson, his form teacher in the early days, recalled, in an episode Major believes apocryphal, that: 'It was more or less a standing joke with the class. I would call the register and ... he would jump up and shout, "Major-Ball, Sir." I'd said, "I'll make you bawl if you don't be quiet", which the boys found very amusing but I suppose psychologically may not have been very kind.'[50]

Sometime afterwards, he managed to drop the 'Ball' from his register entry. Had his parents been in better health, and perhaps more switched on to academic schooling and their child's potential, they might have intervened to enquire why their son's performance was not better. Pat thinks that at home John gave the impression that he was quite happy at Rutlish, and this being the time before parents' evenings and full reports, it was easy for a school not to communicate effectively that a child had been underperforming.[51]

Sport was the one exception. His seven wickets for nine runs in a Colts XI against Royal Masonic in the summer of 1958 remain one of the high points of his entire experience of education. The school magazine described it as one of the 'notable individual performances'.[52] The only critical comment about his parents Pat can recall John making was that they did not come to watch him play: 'Everybody else's parents go, but mine don't,' he confided to his sister.[53]

Old age and increasing ill-health apart, he might have pointed to the family's declining personal circumstances, which necessitated a move to Brixton and cheaper, rented accommodation, the year after Major arrived at Rutlish in 1955. Major remained at the school, but now had an hour and a half's journey each way, sometimes being bullied on the way between Loughborough Junction and the Brixton flat. When, on one occasion, he set on his taunters and hit an attacker, the youths retaliated, saying they would carve their initials on his legs.[54] The incident left an unsavoury impression in his mind. Reduced circumstances also highlighted feelings of social and financial insecurity in the young Major. Justified or not, Major clearly felt his parents were less well off than those of other pupils, and was sensitive, not least for their sake, about coming to school in a cheaper and inferior uniform.[55]

Even at the subjects he enjoyed – history, English and mathematics – he did not shine. His teachers detected his lack of effort: 'Every fortnight the staff met in a "letters meeting" at which every boy could be discussed and allocated a letter grade for effort. Major never rose above the lowest grade available to a boy not in trouble.'[56] Much of the blame for this lack of achievement must be laid at the door of the school. He was in the lower stream, where expectations and quality of teaching were below the standards required for a selective school. The atmosphere was neither sufficiently encouraging nor conducive to bringing the best out of such pupils. Academic standards as a whole were not impressive. Despite attracting only the ablest children, of approximately one hundred boys in each year, only 60 per cent passed four or more O Levels, and roughly half left without going on into the sixth form. Of those who sat A Levels, only a third went on to university, and entrance to Oxford or Cambridge was a rarity.[57]

Major left Rutlish in 1959, sitting his O Levels that summer. Whether he departed at the end of the Lent or summer term, and how many O Levels he achieved at the school, and the grades, is unclear. The school's records for the 1950s were placed in Surrey County Archives in 1988; the following year, Major gave instructions for them to be closed indefinitely.[58] The school's headmaster in the 1990s, Tony Mooney, would not reveal anything about the results, nor would he help with questions about Major's career or even reply to letters. A press release from Number Ten in April 1991 stated that Major eventually acquired six O Levels, in English language, English literature, history, mathematics, British constitution and economics. Some, probably two or three, were acquired at school; others he apparently took by correspondence course.[59] His sensitivity about his schooling remained long after he left.

The decision to leave Rutlish, and miss out on A Levels, was his own. His parents did not seem keen on him leaving, but any objections were insufficiently strong to make him change his mind.[60] Major, despite being reserved and private for a sixteen-year-old, was nevertheless unusually determined, and was quite capable of making big decisions on his own. He had had enough of school; the time had come to make his own way in the world and earn money for himself and the family.

Coldharbour Lane

'My parents ... wanted me to continue at school. But that would have meant continuing hardship,'[61] he later recalled. The ornaments business had encountered a severe cash flow crisis in the mid-1950s. Three thousand pounds, a significant sum to the small firm, had been reclaimed from the business when some key investors backed out. After Tom's heart attack in 1954, he played little further part in the business, and with Gwen suffering increasingly from bronchitis, the burden of keeping the business afloat fell on Terry, employed full time after his return from national service.

The bungalow in Longfellow Road had been sold for £2,150 in 1955. The move to a rented flat with two rooms in a large Victorian house in Coldharbour Lane, Brixton, a far less affluent area than Worcester Park,[62] was a bitter pill for the family.[63] 'No doubt it was a great trauma for my family,' recalled

Major. 'But my mother had the capacity to throw a girdle around the family, and the world could go drifting by ... Any difficulties from that time were shielded from me as much as was possible both by my father ... and by my mother.'[64]

Husband and wife could not even sleep together in one room. Gwen and Pat shared one top-floor room, which converted to a living room by day; Tom, Terry and John shared the other room, which was also no more than twelve foot square. A cooker was situated in the landing between the two, and they shared with other residents a communal bathroom two storeys below.[65] The tenants varied from the respectable to the criminal; Major was warned by his parents to keep his distance from some.[66]

The family's decline in living standards was tangible. Even though they had never recovered their pre-war affluence, by the early 1950s they had been again comfortably off, and were one of the few houses in Longfellow Road to own a television, on which they watched Queen Elizabeth's Coronation in June 1953. They now descended to a level of poverty and insecurity the children had never known. Compounded by Tom's frailty, now all but blind and bedridden, and Gwen's steadily worsening breathing, it was a glum home for John to return to after school. He vividly remembers 'waking up and seeing the water coming through the roof in the morning, and running down the light switch'.[67] But for Terry's and Pat's income, practical work and cheer in the house, their plight would have been worse still.[68] It was all a far cry from Tom's dream of seeing his family grow tall in a spacious, prosperous home in Rio de Janeiro, or in Canada, and a sad place for him to spend the twilight years of his life.

Child and Adolescent: the Making of John Major

John Major's childhood and adolescence may not have been unusual for any ordinary boy growing up in early postwar London, but were exceptional for a future prime minister. His first sixteen years saw scant evidence of the intellectual ability, independence of spirit, intense ambition, confidence and charm with people, which characterised his subsequent career.

His pastimes were the normal boy activities; Subbuteo (table football) in the flat at Brixton,[69] trips to see Surrey play cricket at the Oval and Chelsea play football at Stamford Bridge, and pride in collecting the programmes of all Chelsea's matches he attended.[70] There were odd flashes of initiative. In Longfellow Road, one of his companions recalled how, while not being the gang leader, he would come up with ideas and take part in pranks, playing about at the sewage farm, which was forbidden, or running over local allotments to the annoyance of their owners.[71] At Rutlish he failed in his attempt to organise football, but did manage to arrange a Saturday social side.[72] At Rutlish, also, he was wont to answer back. 'I didn't always agree with decisions and didn't see why I shouldn't say so. I often did say so.'[73]

He had friends, but few of them close, and none seems to have known him intimately. One such at Rutlish, Tony Waymouth, believes he was as friendly with Major as anybody, but says he never got to know or understand him well.[74] Major remembers another boy, Graham Hill, as being his closest friend. To those outside the family, and to masters at Rutlish, he remained an unknown. Most surprisingly, there were no mentor figures at school, no members of staff who took him under their wing, or to whom he felt drawn. The lack is a reflection both of him, and of the school.

With no first cousins, aunts or uncles, his only close relationships were with his immediate family. Much though he loved Pat and Terry, they were too old to be real companions. The loneliness undoubtedly developed his self-reliance, just as the move to Brixton, and experiences at Rutlish, taught him resilience. His parents' ill-health clearly left a deep impression on him: he acknowledges the effect 'if, when you are born, your father is sixty-three and becomes ill when you are quite young, and your mother becomes very ill'.[75]

Trying to make sense of Major's first sixteen years, with such scant evidence, and without falling into the traps of amateur psychology, is difficult. The problem of understanding his early years is all the more troublesome because of the need to disentangle the life he actually led from the one he has subsequently constructed. Nevertheless, some traits and influences were already clearly established by the time of his sixteenth birthday in March 1959. The feeling of being passed over, dismissed, is powerful within him, and owes much to these years. So, too, does the feeling of insecurity, which was to haunt him all his life.

His parents gave little impression of having recognised his quite remarkable talents. How far he felt loved by them is ultimately unprovable, but there is strong reason to believe that, with elderly and frail parents and financial worries, he had neither a particularly loving nor secure upbringing. His potential was also grossly under-estimated by his school, which, as Anthony Storr believes, must have further nurtured in him inner feelings of resentment and possibly engendered a conviction that no one understood him or knew what he was actually like. He was later to develop a brilliantly manicured exterior, but very few people claimed truly to understand him. A polished outer surface and exceptional drive, alongside a restless interior and a strong hunger for affirmation are the keys to unlocking the Major enigma. He might not agree, but he also admits to having little understanding himself of his motives and personality. He was unquestionably more isolated and lonely than many children. His background may well have contributed to his low drive and self-esteem in his childhood and adolescence.[76] Anyone meeting him on his sixteenth birthday would have thought him an unprepossessing young man, and the suggestion he was destined to become one of the youngest and longest-serving prime ministers of the century would have been utterly fanciful.

TWO

Escaping the Chrysalis:
1959–68

JOHN MAJOR'S LIFE divides into two clear stages, before and after 1959. At sixteen, already losing confidence in adults' willingness to help him, he began to take charge of his life. With his decision to leave Rutlish School he resolved that henceforward he would become master of his own destiny.

Work and Family: 1959–64

If he had expected a sudden transformation in his fortunes after Rutlish, he was disappointed. His aspirations and even immediate career plans on leaving school remain a mystery. But what is clear is that at the end of the 1950s, with very low unemployment, especially in the South-East, he could not find work he liked. His first job was as a clerk at Price Forbes, an insurance brokers in the City. His dominant recollections reflected his feelings at the time of social awkwardness. 'I remember I was very nervous, very poorly dressed. I had a suit on that I'd purchased for a very modest sum. It was the first suit I'd ever had. It wasn't a great fit and I wasn't very self-confident. I was in a strange element. I wasn't very sure what to do.'[1] Again, as at Rutlish, he found himself behind a desk with work that bored him given to him by superiors he did not respect, ill at ease in the social milieu. After a few months, he quit.

What he did between 1959 and 1962 remains a puzzle, with his and others' recollections imprecise, and records inconclusive or non-existent. What is known with certainty is that he completed more O Levels. For part of the time he worked for David's Rural Industries, the company which took over his father's business in late 1959; he appears to have been happy with physical work, and enjoyed being reunited with his older brother Terry.

Money from the sale of the company allowed the family to move to better rented accommodation in Brixton at 80 Burton Road on the Minet Estate. The family now had three bedrooms and a dining room, and though they still shared a bathroom with other tenants, their space doubled. It was a vast improvement after the four years of comparative squalor in Coldharbour Lane.[2] A visitor in the early days at Burton Road, Derek Stone, recalls the family home being very tidy, and 'there were books everywhere'. Suburban respectability was again restored, but Gwen was still suffering from asthma and bronchitis, and Tom remained unwell. John thus 'saw himself as having to pull his weight in the family'.[3] Pat also returned to live in the family home, accompanied by her new husband Peter Dessoy, after just six weeks of marriage.

After two years of intermittent manual labour at David's Rural Industries, John left to look for other jobs, signed on for the dole, and whiled away afternoons watching films in local cinemas. He applied to be a bus conductor, passed the tests, but was turned down in favour of a West Indian whom he clearly recalls, down to her name, Barbara Laguerre.[4] The unemployment, the rejections and the feckless existence he was leading left their scar, reinforcing his underlying feeling of insecurity.

Then life at home changed radically. On 27 March 1962 his father died aged eighty-two. Although blind and bedridden, he retained his mental faculties to the end. John was with him when he died: 'It was the most peaceful thing you can imagine.' He walked around the Brixton streets, cried, and then returned home to comfort his mother.[5] His father's death proved a milestone. Looking back one sees that he now realised that in life he was on his own.

At last, in December 1962, three and a half years after leaving school, he moved into stable employment as a clerk at the London Electricity Board's offices in Elephant and Castle, south London. (Another lowly LEB employee, albeit at a different time, was George Carey, the future Archbishop of Canterbury.) Major found the work no more inspiring than at Price Forbes, but his attitude to it, now aged nearly twenty, was more mature. Earning cash, and gaining in respectability, had become his driving motivations and he regularly put in overtime. London Electricity (as it is now called) profess to have no records of Major beyond bare dates.[6] Recollections of his former colleagues contradict: some recall him not discussing politics, others say he liked political arguments; some have him (improbably) in flowery shirts, others soberly dressed in traditional suits; some say he was meticulous in adding up cash sums, others that he was cavalier with figures.[7] He made no lasting friendships: his social life and his interests lay outside. But though he saw the job primarily as a means to an end, his mind did not switch off totally. He disagreed with the accounting system, had his own ideas on improving it, but was reluctant to tell his superiors.[8] He was gaining rapidly in confidence, however, due to his work in a completely different sphere.

Young Conservative: 1959–64

Major's rapidly developing interest in politics was another sign of maturity and ambition. Despite his father's pronounced Tory views, there were not many thoughtful political discussions at home; Tom's were more gut than intellectual convictions. National politics had first impinged upon the young Major in 1956, when he was fourteen. He met Marcus Lipton, the Labour

MP for Brixton, at a local church fête and was offered a tour of Parliament. The visit, coinciding with a debate on Chancellor Harold Macmillan's budget, captivated him, particularly 'the grandeur of it, the size of it and the sense of history'.[9] But it was not until the Suez Crisis later that year that his interest began to crystallise. He recalls going 'pretty much with the majority [pro-government] tide ... I don't think I had an unconventional view of it.'[10] It was not until the October 1959 general election, when Macmillan returned as Prime Minister, that he can 'really remember being caught up in the excitement of politics, with those early black-and-white television pictures of Macmillan and crowds'.[11]

Accounts vary as to exactly how he became a Young Conservative. One version suggests he was recruited by Neville Wallace, a YC member, on a door-to-door canvass in 1959 while the family still lived in Coldharbour Lane.[12] But Derek Stone, who became a YC friend, says he recruited Major when the family lived in Burton Road, when he was promoting a YC dance shortly before Christmas in 1959 or 1960.[13] A third story suggests that in 1961 Marion Standing, the newly appointed agent for Brixton Conservatives, was travelling the streets to build up constituency membership. She recalls meeting Mrs Major and asking her if she would like to join the association. Gwen said that although she had always been a Conservative, she did not want to become more involved, but she wished she could persuade her son to join the YCs. Marion Standing liked the young Major, whom she met the next day. 'He was a clean-cut young man and I thought he'd be useful on the doorstep.'[14]

What is clear is that by the early 1960s he had become an active YC. Stone described what a powerful factor it soon became in his life:

John's life revolved around YC activities. On Saturday night there was a dance, and political meetings were on Wednesdays. They would go to events in neighbouring YC branches. Major was also the main speaker when they went out campaigning. I had to persuade him at first to give speeches but he learnt the courage ... we would set out a collapsible platform outside the Prince of Wales pub [in Brixton] just before closing time in the afternoon and argue with people as they came out. He was argumentative but reluctant to make someone feel small.[15]

Major found a level of companionship, acceptance, and stimulation that he had never before known. Unlike at home or at Rutlish, he no longer felt restricted. His self-confidence blossomed in a way that many subdued, middle-class children of his generation found after they arrived at university, freed from parents and the scripts they and school had written for them. So dominant and confident did he become that he rose through the ranks to become Chairman of the Brixton YCs by 1963.[16]

Why did Major become a Tory, when so many of his embryonic views – on privilege, authority, social advance and race – put him closer to Labour? His attraction to the Conservatives certainly had something to do with the YCs finding him first, but it ran deeper than circumstance. He chose to see

Labour as the party that denied individual expression and treated people as groups. He revolted against their assertion of collective values, and their endorsement of regimentation of the kind that had so discouraged him at Rutlish. Tory philosophy, however, provided him with a way, as he put it, of 'getting him out of the circumstances of life that events had thrown him into'. The Conservatives offered him the passport out of the ghetto; their emphasis on individuality and personal freedom struck a deep chord in the young man. They were also the party of prosperity, of a world he aspired to join.

Like Mrs Thatcher his emergence as a Conservative was a matter of personal experience. But unlike her he was not shaped by the reading of any text – much to the irritation of some Tory intellectuals, he later commented, 'It wasn't a book that made me what I am and what I think.' Nor does he seem to have been unduly influenced by any Conservative politician, though he clearly found Iain Macleod a particularly attractive mentor. Macleod, he says, 'had a gift of speaking directly to young people that I have not seen equalled. And he also had a great presence when speaking because of his physical disabilities. He couldn't move his head; his arthritis had him absolutely rigid ... so his whole body moved.'[17] Something about misfortune, and Macleod's overcoming of it, he found inspiring.

Major's new-found confidence led him to what his sister saw as a change of persona. It was as if he had outgrown his home and wished to make his own identity independent of his associations with it. He became both a far more effective operator in life and a more outgoing personality. Here one can see in embryo the warm, outgoing and winning manner bolted onto a diffident and uncertain core.

Growing Up in a Hurry

No single person was more important in Major's rapid maturing from callow youth to the polished and effective young man he became than a divorcée thirteen years his elder, Jean Kierans. The story of their relationship was kept secret for thirty years, only to emerge in February 1995, to Major's intense discomfort.[18] Mrs Kierans, who herself had remained silent about the affair, was a friend of Gwen Major and her children and later godmother to Terry's daughter. She lived on the other side of Burton Road, at number 123, and first met Major in 1963. Shortly after, they became lovers. Contemporaries describe her as 'terribly nice-looking, nice smile, very intelligent and charming'.[19] Mrs Kierans was confident and sophisticated, part of the Brixton Conservative scene, and it is easy to see why the twenty-year-old Major fell for her.

Two years later Jean Kierans accompanied Major on the holiday he had saved for to take his mother to Spain.[20] Gwen came increasingly to resent Jean's relationship with her son, and to see her influence as sinister and manipulative. She disliked her place being usurped by an older woman, the same age as Pat, who also came to dislike her.[21] Such feelings from close family are understandable. Jean Kierans did take the young John Major, emotionally and physically, away from his mother, sister and brother. She also made Major smarten his appearance, groomed him politically and made him more ambitious and worldly. Their intense physical relationship also helped Major grow in self-confidence and self-esteem, and gave a quality of love and emotional support which he had hitherto lacked.

A measure of Major's new-found confidence was his decision to stand in the local government elections of May 1964, in the Larkhall ward of Lambeth, a safe Labour seat.[22] He hurriedly assembled a sparse curriculum vitae to put on his election address, which read: 'John R. Major is our youngest candidate being just 21. He works in an accountancy department and is studying accountancy and economics ...'[23] He campaigned hard but was defeated heavily, and predictably, by the Labour candidate: 'They counted my votes and weighed my opponent's.'[24] Five months later came the first national election in which Major was actively involved, when after thirteen years of Conservative government Harold Wilson led the Labour Party to victory. The Brixton Tory candidate was Ken Payne, a shipping broker and Surrey county councillor. He has vivid recollections of Major's contribution to his fight: 'When my voice gave out, he would take on the public speaking. He became very good.' Payne found him particularly helpful and knowledgeable dealing with questions from voters, many of which concerned local housing.[25] In the same election, Major delighted in harassing Bob Mellish, Labour candidate in the nearby Bermondsey constituency. 'It was a very safe Labour seat. We followed him around with a soap box and a microphone making speeches attacking his speeches at the other end of a block of council flats, or wherever. He had a better loudspeaker than us, so he won the argument!'[26]

In 1965 Major and some YC friends launched a local magazine, the *Brixton Area Young Conservatives*. Full of youthful exuberance, it aroused the disapproval of Marion Standing, the Brixton agent, when Major published an article on the taboo subject of witchcraft, written by an LEB colleague.[27] In April the Brixton YCs held a private dinner at which Major played a 'typical prank'. The same LEB colleague was passed off by Major as a visiting Middle Eastern dignitary, but the game was up when heavy, black, lace-up shoes were seen beneath the oriental garb.[28] Major's distinctive and subversive sense of humour with intimates was another facet of his character to begin to manifest itself at this time.

The year 1965 saw other important developments in his life. He left the LEB in May and moved to a job with better prospects at the District Bank (since taken over by NatWest).[29] Again, there seem to be no records left of his year there, but he appears to have prospered and he studied concurrently for banking qualifications. Late in 1965 the family left Burton Road for Thornton Heath, a suburb further out and to the south of London. Pat and husband Peter wanted to be nearer to Terry, who had already moved there with his wife Shirley.[30] Pat took Gwen with her, but John remained behind in

Brixton, splitting his time between Mrs Kierans's house and a small *pied-à-terre* in Hanover Flats, Mayfair, rented from Edward and Patricia Davis, two teachers, where he could study quietly.[31] Gwen was doubly upset that John did not join them: she wanted her youngest child living with her, and she did not relish the greater opportunities he now had of seeing more of Mrs Kierans. Major's relationship with Jean Kierans and her two children, Kevin and Siobhan, did indeed deepen. According to some sources, he became like a father to them, especially to Siobhan, who had never known her true father, and was thirteen years Major's junior.[32]

The general election of March 1966 saw another step up in his self-confidence. The Tory candidate in Brixton was now Piers Dixon, the Old Etonian son of the diplomat Sir Pierson Dixon. Gone was Major's reticence in dealing with those older and senior: Dixon found that his young adjutant 'had very definite views about canvassing and he clearly didn't think much of the way that I was planning my canvassing ... He was very polite about it, he's a very polite man, but he was quite firm.'[33]

In September 1966, with the first part of his banking exams behind him, he moved to Standard Bank, a change to a more stimulating job at an international bank. Here his horizons widened enormously. It was another important decision in his life. When accepting the job, he understood it would mean a prolonged posting abroad in the near future, with significant repercussions for his political career and personal relationships. It was a bold decision to accept the challenge. The prospect of the excitement, promotion and increased pay attracted him: 'I reckoned I could then save a hundred pounds a month [nearly £1,000 today], which was a huge sum to me at that stage. I knew that if I was going to go into politics I would need some money.'[34] What he did not know was how soon his call abroad would be, nor how short the stay would prove.

Nigeria: 1966–7

His posting to Nigeria came in the wake of civil unrest the year before. Both Standard and Barclays, the two big British banks in West Africa, called for young employees without family commitments to go out at short notice to replace Nigerians caught up in the domestic unrest. Major flew out from London on 10 December 1966.

The job was to be deputy accounting officer at the Standard Bank of West Africa in Jos, a small town 3,000 feet up a plateau in the north of the country, the main clients being companies mining locally. He lived in a town flat with another bank employee, Richard Cockeram, and struck up a friendship with him and others seconded to the town. In early 1967 Major wrote a letter back home to the vicar of the local parish church, St James, Camberwell, attended by the family.

I have been in Nigeria for three months and now I feel justified in putting my impressions down on paper. I am stationed on Jos plateau, scene of the bloodiest fighting of the coup of last September, but now very peaceful, where the climate varies between 75–95°F. and is consequently very pleasant. I share a flat with a lad from Derbyshire and between us we employ a Hausa [local tribe] steward, one Moses [Dewa] who is extremely competent and looks after us very well ... The most interesting aspect of Jos is undoubtedly the Nigerians themselves. The most intelligent of them have only received a very rudimentary education. The vast majority of them live in small townships, are totally illiterate and utterly pagan ... Unemployed Nigerians, of which there are many in Jos, can be seen sleeping in barrows, ditches or on the roadside ... The salaried rate for employed Africans is extremely low, far too low. Employers explain this by saying that Northern Nigeria is far less developed ... In practice the low wages are simply capitalism paying the market price for labour ... I am enjoying my stay immensely, but I am still looking forward to returning home, probably next Christmas ...

Yours sincerely,

John Major[35]

This letter is important as one of his earliest surviving, and as an indication of his sensitivity to the wages and conditions of the black Africans. Nigeria had become independent in 1962, but colonial attitudes to blacks remained widespread. John Rennie, who worked in Jos for Barclays, recalled: 'The European Club old hands were often overtly racist and proud of it, and got hold of the younger ones and told them that the stewards were always thieving.' Many young westerners sent out from Britain adopted these attitudes about blacks, but Rennie remembers being particularly attracted to John Major because 'he was not a racialist'.[36]

Victor Laniya, an employee at the bank, says Major was unusual in insisting that they should be on first-name terms, a situation he initially found uncomfortable.[37] Racial liberalism is a strong feature in Major's political make-up. Peter Golds, a friend since the previous year and later a close political ally, believes it stems from growing up alongside blacks in Brixton. 'The market in Brixton was a great centre for buying Caribbean food. You could buy yams and pawpaws down Electric and Atlantic Avenues. So everybody knew many, many black people ... [Major] certainly has an abiding hatred of anything to do with racialism or racist views ... If anybody gave a prejudiced view he would really come down like a ton of bricks.'[38]

Nigeria gave Major much. It was the first time he had been away from home on his own: 'I got very homesick,' he later admitted.[39] But it forced him to become more self-reliant. He had his first experience of management: 'You were given responsibilities that you would never have received at that level in the United Kingdom. I enjoyed all that enormously.'[40] The deprivation hit him, as seen in his letter to his vicar: 'It was the first time in my life I really saw grinding poverty, that dwarfed even the difficult circumstances one saw at home ... I remember going right out into the outback and there was a dead body, just rotted. I didn't know how long it had been there.'[41]Dead bodies, severe malnutrition, extreme poverty, overt racism: it was a powerful education for twenty-three-year-old Major.

After five months he was mastering the very alien environment and enjoying himself. Popular with other bank employees from Standard and Barclays, he kept his distance, drank little and avoided the local women. Some thought him rather dull and aloof for refusing to join in the fun.[42] One evening in early May he relented, and went to a farewell party with John Rennie and other British bankers for colleagues whose visas were expiring and who were returning home. Three cars cruised around various drinking establishments. 'They were like these places in New Orleans, with women draped over the balustrades offering themselves,' Rennie recalled.

The version of events that follows leans heavily on Rennie's testimony. When it was time to go home, Rennie travelled by car with three Standard Bank employees, including Major, asleep in the rear, and the driver, Major's flatmate Richard Cockeram, who had been drinking beer (Heineken, Rennie recounts). Rennie was dropped off at his house on the outskirts of Jos, thankful at last to be free of Cockeram's erratic driving. 'They drove off while I was standing there wondering whether to invite them in for coffee. I watched them swaying off into the distance, and went in where my steward had a cup of tea and was waiting to tuck me into bed.'

He found out on the Sunday morning that there had been a nasty crash. Cockeram and the other Standard Bank employee in the front were unhurt, unusually, but Major, in the back, had sustained a serious injury and was lying in the Mission Hospital run by Catholic nurses. It has never been established precisely what happened, but it seems the car had turned over and Major's left leg had taken much of the force, leaving his knee crushed. Major himself believes he was thrown out of the front windscreen; he certainly sustained many glass cuts. When Rennie saw him, Major was lying in bed with his leg suspended. 'A sadder looking boy you have never seen in your life. I was relieved he was alive.'

Major had no recollection of what had happened, in the accident or in the hours leading up to it, but has since exonerated Cockeram of any responsibility for bad or drunk driving. The X-ray showed that the kneecap was broken into pieces and the doctor told Rennie that the job of clearing up the mess was one for London. Major was shocked and upset at the accident: 'This has ruined everything,' he lamented.

When, after some days, it was felt safe to move him, Rennie arranged for Major to be flown back to London courtesy of Barclays. It was a perilous journey, first by light aircraft to Kano and then by VC10 back to London, Major sprawled in great pain across three seats. An ambulance crew came onto the plane when they landed and helped him into an ambulance, where Gwen and Pat were waiting, along with their *bête noire*, Jean Kierans.[43]

Convalescing Conservative: 1967

A Standard Bank colleague who knew him well, believes that the accident changed for ever Major's attitude to banking, tilting him decisively towards politics. The smash certainly destroyed what would have been a conventional career with the bank, entailing three- or four-year spells in West Africa.[44] Without the chance accident, Major would not have become a local councillor, and in all probability would not have begun to climb the rungs of the ladder that led to the premiership. The effect on his leg is beyond speculation. He was lucky not to lose it, and has since suffered from a swollen knee if he exerts himself too much. He was operated on at King's College Hospital in Dulwich before being returned to Croydon's Mayday Hospital, conveniently close for Gwen to visit him from Thornton Heath less than a mile away.

Major was impatient to leave hospital, which he seems to have succeeded in doing by the end of June 1967, when he moved in with Jean Kierans in Burton Road.[45] Her care helped rekindle their relationship, which had looked in jeopardy when he originally left for Nigeria for what they both assumed would be an extended stay.[46] He used his convalescence over the summer to read prodigiously, light novels, crime, but particularly political biography, which he'd scour to glean what might be useful.[47] One favourite pastime, and an important source of self-esteem and prowess for the young man, playing cricket, was terminated by the accident: he had been nominated for a London *Evening Standard* cricket award before his posting to Nigeria, and he was immensely proud of his cricketing skill.[48]

By the autumn of 1967 he was sufficiently fit to begin working for the bank again, though he still walked using a stick. He was impressed and touched by the support he had received from his employers, who kept him on full salary, sent staff to visit him in hospital, and ensured that a job in the London office awaited him.[49] On his return, his conscientiousness impressed his superiors, who judged that he was now on a par with someone who had come in as a graduate.[50] He was also working flat out to complete his banking qualifications. His landlords at the Mayfair flat, to which he returned part-time remember Major as a very earnest young man who worked hard both before work in the morning and after his return in the evening.[51]

Political ambition and the complexity of his domestic arrangements now led Major, strictly speaking, to be less than honest. To stand in the 1968 local government elections, he needed an address on the 1968 electoral register showing residence in Lambeth. He could have given 123 Burton Road, Jean Kierans's address, but to avoid drawing attention to his relationship with her, used instead 14 Templar Street, the house of Rose Olifent, one of his mother's friends.[52] When challenged by *Panorama* in 1991 about this deception – he never stayed even a night at Rose Olifent's address – Downing Street replied that it was well known that he was staying with friends close by in Brixton, and he was using 14 Templar Street as an 'accommodation address' for his post.[53]

An upset that did erupt at the time was Marion Standing's dismissal as Brixton agent in the winter of 1967–8.[54] She had done more than anyone in politics in the early and mid-1960s to groom Major and turn him into a politician.[55] He had now lost his first strong ally at a time he most needed help, for unlike most of his political colleagues, he still had not found a seat, and time was running short. Clive Jones, a Vauxhall activist who became a close friend, recalls that 'he reappeared on the scene in the autumn of 1967 ... when all the decent seats in the forthcoming election had already got candidates selected'.[56] However, he was still adamant he should stand somewhere in Lambeth in 1968, wanting 'to build up my political biography'. He found an important new ally in Jean Lucas, the abrasive yet powerful agent in Clapham.[57] As so often in his political rise, Major was helped by an influential female champion. In March 1968 he was duly selected as one of three Conservative candidates for Ferndale, generally regarded for Conservatives as one of the most hopeless wards in the borough.[58] But Major's gloomy estimation of his prospects in the local elections proved unfounded. The Wilson government was becoming deeply unpopular, and on 20 April 1968 Enoch Powell made a speech in Birmingham which rewrote predictions about the May local elections, and helped propel Major into the first elected public office of his career. The chrysalis had been broken and, once free of it, nothing would hold him back.

THREE

First Rung on the Ladder:

Lambeth Council 1968–71

MAJOR'S GROWTH IN confidence and maturity in the four years since his unsuccessful contest in Larkhall ward in 1964 had been considerable. But he badly needed to be elected to local government if he was to build up his curriculum vitae. A new target now entered his sights: being selected for a parliamentary seat. Leaving state school at sixteen, with no A-Levels or university education, compared poorly with the record of many public school and Oxbridge Tory aspirants on the parliamentary path. With such a modest background, practical experience as a local councillor offered his best hope of further advancement.

Election Victory: May 1968

The Ferndale ward of Lambeth, which was solidly Labour, appeared to offer scant prospect of the electoral success he needed. In north-western Brixton, it was an area of dilapidated terraces and council flats and maisonettes. 'It wasn't a seat we expected to win,' he recalls. 'I wasn't very fit. I couldn't walk very far without sticks and crutches, and I was still in a lot of pain ... But we hadn't got a candidate for Ferndale.' Major at least had more of a track record to boast about in his election address than he had had in 1964. Assiduous work had indeed transformed his profile: 'John R. Major is a Banker who has lived in Brixton since 1955 ... He serves on the Association's Executive Council and is on the Central Office panel of speakers. Temporarily seconded to Nigeria as a Bank Accountant in 1966, he returned after a severe road accident. He is a governor of Kennington School.'[1]

Major campaigned tirelessly in April and early May 1968, but his freak victory at polling day on 9 May owed everything to developments on the national stage. The Wilson government's popularity had slumped soon after its re-election in March 1966. Political humiliation of the 1967 devaluation had sapped voter confidence, and the economic benefits had yet to become apparent. Chancellor Roy Jenkins's budget on 19 March 1968 contained what the Tories claimed were the largest tax rises in peacetime history. Then, on 20 April, Enoch Powell delivered his famous speech in Birmingham in which he spoke apocalyptically of 'the River Tiber foaming with much blood' because of racial tensions. Though Edward Heath, the Conservative leader, promptly sacked Powell from the Shadow Cabinet, the groundswell of white opinion which rallied around Powell boosted Conservative electoral popularity. In May, Labour's Gallup poll rating fell to 28 per cent – a low during the life of the government; Conservative popularity meanwhile reached an all-time high of 56 per cent.[2] It was indeed ironic that Major, whose political career showed him to be consistently anti-racist, should have received his first election boost on the back of such a racially motivated reaction.

The Conservatives were not totally unprepared for winning control of Lambeth. Elections for the Greater London Council the previous year had given them hope, and elsewhere in the borough, in Streatham and the leafier parts of Norwood, there was a solid core of Tory councillors. As the poll closed at 9 p.m. on election day, 9 May, the candidates and their supporters converged on Lambeth Town Hall in Brixton, where the count took place. A mood of cautious optimism turned into mounting excitement as the ballot papers were counted. Events of the evening are remembered vividly by the Tories present as one of the greatest victory nights of their lives. Different wards had their counts in various rooms of the town hall, and increasingly wild rumours began to circulate around the building. 'It was a glorious feeling,' recalled Clive Jones. 'People were saying, "It's not been like this since 1931!" (There were still a few Tories present that night who remembered 1931, when Labour had been routed).' Not only did the Conservatives win previously hopeless seats, they gained overwhelming control of the council, taking fifty-seven out of sixty seats. Major was home, by seventy votes, the smallest Conservative majority in the borough.[3] Across London, the success was repeated: 1,438 out of 1,863 councillors elected were Conservative. Future Major ministers received their first victory at the same time: in Lambeth, Sir George Young; Robert Atkins and Peter Brooke in other London boroughs. In Islington, Liverpool and even Sheffield, Labour was almost wiped out.

The new group of Conservative councillors who assembled for the first full council meeting were indeed fifty-seven varieties. Their politics ranged from ultra-Powellites through mainstream supporters of Edward Heath, to some very liberal figures, especially on social policy, the wing with which Major was to identify strongly. Some were highly able, others less so, and some, surprised to have been elected, disappeared three years later having left no visible mark.

The leadership, which was solidly progressive, had highlighted four themes in the election: a new approach to financial control and administration, a fresh look at Lambeth's housing problems, priority for traffic and transport improvements, and enhancement of welfare and social services.[4] A fairly anodyne programme, it left plenty of room to choose specific policies once in power. Though the leadership proclaimed efficiency to be the priority of their new administration,[5] it was in other areas where the Tories were to leave their mark on Lambeth during 1968–71, with the young Major emerging as their brightest star.

Racial Politics: 1968–70

The election campaign itself had been perhaps inevitably overshadowed by the issue of race and immigration. In Lambeth the local paper, the *Brixton Advertiser*, expressed support for Powell.[6] The three candidates for Bishop's ward in the far north of the borough issued a leaflet entitled 'We Back Enoch, Don't You?'. Their action was strongly disapproved of by most senior Conservative councillors in the borough, and if they had made their views known earlier, they might not have been selected. Major himself won without resort to populist slogans or the race card.

The three 'We Back Enoch' councillors were joined by eleven others, who signed a round-robin letter within days of the election, declaring, 'We the undersigned call for a complete ban on all further immigration to the borough.'[7] The Powellite hard core had pressured some of the younger councillors, including Major's friend Clive Jones, to sign.[8] Major, however, already known to be a liberal on race, was not approached.[9]

The June 1970 general election, at which Heath swept Wilson aside, was the last in which Major did not stand. Still diffident about his blossoming curriculum vitae, he was anxious to avoid being rejected even for the Candidates' List, the first step before adoption. The Lambeth borough contained parts of five parliamentary constituencies.[10] Local Conservative candidates in the general election, sensing the strength of popular feeling, were fairly Powellite on race. In Vauxhall, Clive Jones stood on a strongly right-wing but not racist manifesto. Bernard Black, for Norwood, was a noisy populist concerning law and order themes, while his successor was the left-wing Tory, Peter Temple-Morris. Duncan Sandys, Churchill's son-in-law, regarded by Major as a snob, stood in Streatham on a Powellite platform. William Shelton in Clapham did not, but was still elected on a large swing based in part on prejudice against his black opponent, David Pitt.[11]

Major's own Brixton Conservative Association reflected the divisions on race of Lambeth borough. The prospective candidate, James Harkess, was disliked by many in the association hierarchy not only for his extreme views – he had been one of those who had signed the anti-immigration round-robin but for his arrogant and supercilious manner. Major, who had become Chairman of the association earlier in 1970,[12] took part in a plan to dump him as candidate, and papers were sent out to members of the Executive Committee to discuss it. But time was not on their side. Soon after notice of the meeting was sent out, Harold Wilson announced the general election for June; another note had swiftly to be dispatched to members about adopting Harkess officially as the Brixton candidate.[13] Harkess later accused Major of trying to oust him in order to put himself in the vacant place.[14] That accusation is almost certainly untrue: Diana Geddes, a GLC member, would have been the replacement candidate. With Harkess remaining *in situ*, Major, to his distaste, was duty bound to campaign for him. Harkess did not soften his stance after the attempted reselection: his election address announced, 'I will press for a stop to any further permanent immigration and encourage voluntary repatriation.'[15] Major was not sorry that Harkess lost the election to Marcus Lipton. His stance against Harkess – who later colourfully turned up with his wife and daughters in the diaries of Alan Clark – was brave. His political career thus began as it ended, struggling against the right in his party.

Spreading His Wings: 1968–9

His three years as a Lambeth councillor are thus important in providing the first solid evidence of where Major stood politically, as well as for giving early indications about his political strengths and skills.

As in the House of Commons after 1979, Major began his career in local government cautiously, determined to sniff out the atmosphere, form alliances, and absorb as much as he could from those he admired. He was closest to Clive Jones, Barbara Wallis (who later became his constituency secretary) and Laurie Kennedy, although he was friendly with most of the new entrants in 1968. In the early months, after meetings the more zealous would get together over drinks to discuss politics, local and national, on which they all thrived.[16] Barbara Wallis says what helped draw her to Major was a shared vision of a 'classless society', a harbinger of the term he later popularised.

Major soon came to the attention of the Conservative leadership. The council leader Bernard Perkins, and his deputy Peter Cary, dominated the Conservative Group.[17] Major quickly worked out the key to progressing swiftly:[18] 'By and large, if you are interested in politics, you go for the big issue. In Lambeth, that meant housing.' It was a subject on which he felt he had something to offer. 'I knew something about living in bad housing that other people didn't.'[19]

Major was duly placed on the Housing Committee. He had already shown, at Brixton Young Conservatives and in the Constituency Association, that he knew how to progress through committees, and he was swiftly appointed Vice-Chairman by Perkins in January 1969. One fellow Conservative described Major at this time as more ambitious and more sure of his ability to get to the top than anyone he had ever known before; at the same time, and paradoxically, he was never labelled 'pushy' or gained a reputation as 'a hack'. His shrewdness was nevertheless apparent: one colleague described how 'immediately he found himself on the council he sussed out what the Conservative Group was like, looked at the personalities of his colleagues, who was able, who wasn't so able, looked at the front bench and worked out

iis route to front bench promotion'.[20] Both Clive Jones and Barbara Wallis
estify to Major being the outstanding member of the new council intake,
with administrative gifts and a business know-how (acquired from Standard
Bank) possessed by none of the other newcomers. 'Perkins realised very early
on that he'd got a star and he made very effective use of him,' said Wallis.[21]

Major was coming to the limelight in other ways too. He campaigned to
have meetings of full council and committees tape-recorded, succeeding with
the question period of full council meetings.[22] The transcripts were printed
in the official minutes, and the practice continued after Major left the council.
His advocacy of more open government was also seen elsewhere, as recorded
in the minutes of the General Purposes Committee on 18 June 1969. 'On
the suggestion of Councillor J. R. Major we have considered the possibility
of instituting an Annual Council Report which is debatable and separate
from the Mayor's Report.' The committee favoured the plan and it was
approved in full council on 9 July.[23]

The Soviet-led invasion of Czechoslovakia in August 1968 produced
ripples extending to Lambeth. Many in Britain thought the Soviet military
intervention outrageous. The borough had a twinning arrangement with
Moskvoretsky, a suburb of Moscow, and a vote to maintain the link in the
light of the invasion was just carried by 28–24, with the Conservative Group
split down the middle. Sadly, no record was kept of how Major or other
individual councillors voted.[24] No cold war warrior, in 1969, Major went on
a twinning visit to Moskvoretsky, as well as to Finland and the Netherlands.
He was influenced by what he saw of housing and local government in the
Soviet Union.[25] 'The mayor was a man called Chilikin', he recalled. 'I remember being astonished that Mr Chilikin had so much authority in Moskvoretsky
and he remarked with a smile that it was very cold in Moscow in winter
without a flat.'[26]

Housing Chairman: 1970–71

Major proved such an effective deputy to Peter Cary, the Chairman of
Housing, that he was the obvious choice to take over when Cary became
Chairman of Finance. The promotion, in June 1970, was a tremendous step
up in responsibility and honour for the twenty-seven-year-old. He was the
only councillor of the 1968 intake to chair a committee. The success he made
of his task, and indeed the entire achievement of the Tories' housing policy
in Lambeth from 1968 to 1971, owed much to the brilliant Director of
Housing, Harry Simpson. Simpson was the professional local government
officer who went on to serve Ken Livingstone, who became Labour's Housing
Chairman in Lambeth after 1971, before finishing his career as Controller of
Housing to the Greater London Council from 1974 to 1982. From a similar
social background to Major, always an important factor with him, Simpson
developed a close and enduring bond with his young protégé. Stories abound

of him taking Major back regularly to his house after meetings to eat supper, arriving at 10 or 11 p.m., and talking excitedly about housing until the early hours.[27] Simpson had a consensual style in negotiation that appealed to Major, as did his deep social concern. Most revealingly, Major ascribed more influence on the formation of his political views to Simpson than to any other single figure in politics.[28] Some saw Simpson as a Labour sympathiser, but Major remembers him as 'a Tory with a social conscience'.[29] The admission, in an interview shortly before he stepped down as Prime Minister, is a fascinating statement about Major's political beliefs: whether a Tory or not, Simpson was committed to social provision by the state of housing for the poor and underprivileged.[30] A starker contrast to the 'gurus' and ideas that influenced Mrs Thatcher can hardly be found.

Major's priorities, as Vice- and then full Chairman, were indeed to accelerate house-building, improve the quality of dwellings, and enhance dialogue between the council and those living in the borough. He planned the maximum feasible building, and was able to answer proudly in full council in May 1971, just before the local elections that would oust the Conservatives, that families housed between 1968 and 1971 had been 7,097, compared to 4,276 under Labour from 1965 to 1968; dwellings 'under construction' over the same period were 3,012 compared to Labour's 1,306.[31] Like Macmillan, with whom Major shared many similar views, Major established his political reputation on the back of avid house-building (Macmillan had been Minister of Housing, 1951–4).

Not all Major's projects, as Macmillan's, met with long-term approval. Two developments that have subsequently encountered particular opprobrium are the Moorlands Estate along Brixton's Coldharbour Lane, near his old home, and the 913-dwelling Stockwell Park Estate.[32] Major did not accelerate the pace of demolition of traditional houses in favour of high-rise blocks, but neither are claims that he significantly slowed the pace corroborated by the evidence: he merely continued existing housing policy, when the conventional wisdom of the time still favoured systematic demolition and erection of high-rise flats in their place. Few influential figures in the early 1970s were critical of this practice, which Major and Simpson pushed for humane reasons: they considered housing in new buildings offered a superior lifestyle to the old and often crumbling dwellings they replaced.

The demolition issue inevitably became a matter of controversy as all aspects of Major's career were minutely picked over after he became Prime Minister. Lambeth Council in April 1992, under Labour control, thus voted down a Tory proposal for a plaque to commemorate Major's time in Lambeth, stating that the borough already had 'sufficient monument to John Major in the form of the Stockwell Park and Moorlands Estates'.[33] Major's belief in mass housing is apparent in his last Housing Committee meeting on 6 April 1971, on which funds were voted for officials to be sent on a study trip of housing in Poland.[34] Major has made his own *mea culpa* on the high-rise blocks: 'At the time they simply seemed a good use of scarce space, but we were all wrong about that, as events proved.'[35]

Nevertheless, in some cases he did favour improvement to existing dwellings, as seen in the increasing emphasis he placed upon renovation of old houses, and the expansion of a scheme initiated by Labour of loans to housing associations for purchase and rehabilitation of dwellings.[36] A registration scheme was introduced by Major under Simpson's guidance to try to combat overcrowding – some single houses had forty or more people living in them. The aim was to restrict numbers of people per dwelling; neither landlords nor tenants liked the scheme, which was only a partial success.[37] Another way found to combat overcrowding was to encourage people who were on the waiting list to move out of Lambeth, as long as jobs and houses were available in other boroughs. Major highlighted Peterborough as a particularly suitable destination, and oversaw a 'Peterborough Week' from 27 March to 3 April 1971 and the printing of 60,000 special leaflets extolling its virtues. Some of the people who took up this opportunity would become his constituents after 1979.[38]

Private rented housing remained a particular worry. Some landlords were exploiting the housing shortage by charging very high rents, with blacks particular victims. Peter Walker, Heath's new Minister for Housing, and regarded by Major as a kindred spirit, was invited to see the problems for himself, and on 8 July 1970 visited 142 Railton Road in Brixton. 'One of my first actions as Secretary of State', Walker said, 'had been to look at housing in Brixton. I remember going into one room which housed a West Indian family of a man, his wife and two children. It was without windows ... I expressed my horror and asked how much they paid in rent. When they told me, I pointed out that there was legislation to stop this kind of extortion.'[39] In February 1971 Major launched a twenty-page code of conduct for private landlords.[40]

The third tack of Major's housing drive was improving communication between council and tenants, to which end the main initiative was the opening of a Housing Advice Centre. The idea was not new, and had been proposed initially by the Seebohm Committee (which included Simpson) in 1968; but Lambeth deserves credit for being the first borough to act on the proposal. The centre did not just advise council tenants on how to deal with the housing department; Major was also keen for it to advise private tenants, and help show council tenants how to become owner-occupiers. Major's hand, and Simpson's, can also be seen in taking the Housing Department out to public meetings in various parts of the borough to gain the views of tenants and residents on a whole range of housing issues. 'I saw very clearly that people were actually frightened of petty authority. That is why I took the Housing Advice Centre on tour. Many of the people most in need ... would come into the centre, but people in real despair didn't. That was bureaucracy. They were frightened to come in, didn't know what questions to ask.'[41]

How successful was Major in his first major public office at housing? He did not alter the long-standing policy of replacing existing dwellings with high-rise flats. His stance on the sale of council houses was not radical, certainly not when compared to other London boroughs. Sale of council houses rose from none before 1969 to two in 1970 and twenty-one in 1971. But in 1970 Haringay sales numbered thirty-seven, and Hammersmith 307.[42] A reason for the comparatively slow progress was that Lambeth tenants, with rents so low, saw little gain in purchase.[43] Management problems were also envisaged if only one or two flats in a block were sold.[44] Progress was made to combat overcrowding – figures for the 1960s have suggested 300,000 inhabited Lambeth, compared to 200,000 in the early 1990s.[45] But in 1972, just after Major's tenure, Lambeth still had the longest waiting list in London, with over 12,000 individuals wanting homes.[46] Council rents were put up in 1968–71 to the third highest level in London for larger new flats, and by 1971 spending was increasing at 20 per cent per annum.[47] Labour from 1971 tried different strategies; but they could not prevent the riots in April 1981 in Brixton, provoked at least in part by poor housing. With hindsight, one can see that Major's housing policies, while not original, were certainly in step with the more progressive local authorities in other parts of the country during the period.

Lambeth was indeed acclaimed as one of the jewels in the crown of Conservative local government in the 1971 local elections. The council achieved a reputation for humanity, efficiency and progress in its time, especially in housing – even if, with their overwhelming majority, opposition in the council was virtually non-existent. The work received recognition at the time from Anthony Greenwood, Labour's Minister of Housing until 1970, and subsequently from Ken Livingstone, who said, 'Overall, they were very good. Most people in the Labour party became very fanatical because they were doing well,' and he told Major's biographer Ed Pearce: if they had been messing it up, then Labour would not have minded so much.[48]

Much of Major's work as Vice- then Chairman of Housing was inevitably routine: council records reveal a man ploughing his way through large bundles of documents on individual dwellings, and having to master details of matters such as the layout of new estates, the placing of walkways and the awarding of contracts. This was micropolitics *par excellence*; but, as we will see, his period in local government revealed many of the traits that were to characterise his subsequent career.

Labour Returns to Power: 1971

The Conservative Group in Lambeth realised they were likely to have only one term, then three years, running the borough, and the leadership was consciously determined to make a mark as a very go-ahead authority.[49] As one councillor put it, 'We wanted to go out having done a damn good job.'[50] Their judgement about their short tenure in office proved correct. The Heath government's popularity dropped rapidly during its first year in office and Lambeth fell victim to the national swing against the Tories in the May 1971 local elections. Lambeth's Tory council were rejected almost as decisively as their Labour predecessors, with Labour winning forty-eight seats compared to the Conservatives' twelve.

Major, despite moving to the safe prospect of Thornton ward where he now lived in 1971, was defeated by 411 votes. He had mixed feelings about the result. He had high hopes of succeeding Bernard Perkins as leader if he had been re-elected in 1971 – Peter Cary was the only other contender – and none of the younger Conservatives had risen as high or received such recognition as Major from 1968 to 1971. On the other hand, as he said, 'I wasn't much interested [in being leader] in opposition, to be honest, though I was still disappointed when we lost.'[51] The success he had been on the Housing Committee and the confidence it gave him emboldened him to look beyond local government to Parliament. According to friends, from 1969 to 1970 he began to talk increasingly seriously about his parliamentary ambitions.[52] With a growing reputation as one of the bright hopefuls in the London Tory firmament, he could rest on his laurels: his duties to Lambeth had been discharged.

Lambeth saw the coming to political maturity of Major. Aged barely twenty-eight when his term on the council came to an end, he had nevertheless exhibited what were to be the main traits of his subsequent career in national politics: exceptionally hard work, a determination to master his brief, and courage, seen in his refusal to give in to the pain of his leg injury, which nagged him, especially early on. He clearly enjoyed working with officials, extending far beyond his close relationship with Simpson. Sensitivity to criticism also began to manifest itself; at its grossest, he showed himself shaken when a histrionic lady threw a rat at him in a housing meeting.[53] He combined his ambition for personal advancement with a desire to help others and improve their lot, even if it meant spending public money. Self-doubt remained throughout. He displayed a cautious, incrementalist approach to personal promotion where, initially apprehensive of his ability to perform on the next step on the ladder – at first he would feel sick before speaking in the council chamber – he then realised he could manage it and sought something higher.

Philosophically, he showed his desire to build bridges and reach out to those in need, rather than sheltering behind the anonymity of government. The genesis of the Citizen's Charter approach can thus be traced to the Housing Advice Centre and other initiatives. He also recognised how the press could be enlisted as an ally, and built up a very good relationship with two *South London Press* reporters, in which both sides would help the other.[54] One cannot exaggerate the importance of the time on Lambeth council to the rise of John Major. Above all, it allowed the platform for his considerable latent talents to be realised, bolstering enormously his self-confidence. By 1971 he was ready to offer his talents on a wider stage.

FOUR

Securing the Foundations:

1970–76

THE 1960S HAD opened with Major rootlessly moving from casual job to dole queue, and ended with him an accomplished operator, achieving at a higher level than many young men of his age who had been through public school and Oxbridge. Few by the age of twenty-eight were undertaking as big a task as chairing one of the major committees in a London borough, responsible for a budget of over £30 million a year. Major had still, however, to erect the three foundations on which his career would rest: a happy married life, financial security, and a parliamentary seat.

Family Matters: 1970–75

Major became, in his twenties, suddenly popular with women. They found him charming, tall and good-looking, strong yet also vulnerable, arousing their maternal instincts as well as their admiration. A number of girlfriends flitted across his life, none serious, except Jean Kierans, of whom he saw steadily less after his election to Lambeth council in May 1968. In truth Major, unlike her, had outgrown the relationship, and he found himself increasingly uncomfortable with it. She carried on hoping for a change of heart, but it was only after Major had met his future wife that he finally convinced her that their relationship was at an end.[1]

Norma Wagstaff had also been brought up in south London. Her father, a printer, died at the end of the war and her only sibling, her brother Colin, died days old earlier in the year. Following her father's death, her surname reverted to her mother's maiden name, Johnson. Privately educated until eleven, she subsequently attended Peckham School for Girls, a comprehensive in Camberwell. At eighteen, after A Levels, she took a teacher training course in domestic science at Battersea College in 1960. For five years she taught the subject at St Michael and All Angels School in Camberwell before leaving to concentrate on dressmaking.[2] She had neither particular interest in, nor knowledge of, politics. Apart from family, opera was, and is, her chief love in life. A measure of her passion, and an indication of her determination, is a weekend trip she made in her white Morris Mini to see Joan Sutherland sing in *Julius Caesar* in Hamburg.

They met on the unromantic (to her) occasion of the GLC elections on 9 April 1970, at the Conservative Association office at 332 Brixton Road. Her uncustomary incursion into the world of politics followed a request for help from her opera-loving friend, Peter Golds. She and John felt an immediate attraction for each other. She was a good-looking, self-possessed and accomplished young woman.[3] To him, she seemed sophisticated, yet she also came from a similar social background, a key factor in those with whom he is comfortable. To her, he was successful, suave and immensely reassuring. His indifference to opera being matched by hers to politics did not trouble them, nor has it since. Very soon (twenty days, he later recalled), uncustomary haste for a man normally cautious, he proposed. She accepted, and the date for the marriage was fixed for 3 October 1970.

Less than three weeks before the event, and with plans already far advanced, Major's mother Gwen died at Croydon's Mayday Hospital on 17 September. Aged sixty-five, and living with daughter Pat close by the hospital for the past five years, her smoking-related breathing problems had worsened since the 1950s. Her funeral service was held in the same Variety Artists' Benevolent Fund Chapel in Streatham where, eight years before, the family had bade farewell to Tom.[4] The children absorbed the death of their surviving parent in different ways. Terry, by now with two children of his own, took their mother's loss the hardest, and became 'seriously depressed'.[5] Pat, ever resilient and also with two young children, donned some of the anchor role in the family of her mother, a part she was to play even more strongly after her own husband died two years later. John had already emotionally separated himself from his mother. He was upset, certainly, and spent much time consoling Terry, who was particularly distressed by her death.

The Majors' wedding day was a sparkling affair, made all the more so by June Bronhill, the celebrated opera singer and a friend of Norma, agreeing to sing the Bach-Gounod *Ave Maria* from the gallery of St Matthew's, the early-nineteenth-century church in Brixton where the couple were married. Three features of the day highlight different aspects of Major's character. He invited almost all the councillors of Lambeth to the wedding, many of whom he barely knew, indicative of his gregariousness, and desire to please. His indifference to physical pain was shown by the lack of fuss he made of a severe recurrence of his leg pain, Clive Jones, his best man, helping him minimise the amount of walking required.[6] His commitment to work, and eye for the public image, was seen that morning when he insisted on attending a Housing Department meeting with residents on a Lambeth housing estate. He had also arranged for a *South London Press* reporter to attend his morning housing estate visit, and take photographs of him attending to council business in his morning suit.[7]

On return from honeymoon in Ibiza, the couple settled into Major's two-bedroom flat at Primrose Court, Streatham. Jean Lucas had earlier impressed on him the advisability for his political ambitions of having his own property rather than continuing to live in rented accommodation.[8] Primrose Court became host to many late-night political discussions for Major and council colleagues over takeaway meals. Major could not yet afford furniture; they sat on the floor. Primrose Court was also home to several councillors; graffiti on the wall of the men's toilets in the town hall said, 'I live in Primrose Court but I don't want to be a councillor.'[9] Norma shared the sentiment. She rapidly transformed the flat from spartan bachelor pad to a reasonably civilised home. Relieved when John's defeat in the May 1971local elections ended the need to live in the borough, and with the birth in November 1971 of their first child, Elizabeth, they moved to Beckenham, a leafy south London suburb conveniently close to Norma's mother. Their three-bedroom house in West Oak, a pleasant development backing onto woods, proved a happy place for them to bring up a young family, with other families with children on the same estate.[10]

Of immediate excitement to Major was their next-door neighbour, David Rogers, Iain Macleod's personal assistant from 1964 to 1970.[11] They spent long hours together, talking about politics, and improbably playing Major's records of Macleod's conference speeches. Rogers recalled their odd pastime:

We'd start by listening to a record and reading the transcript and then saying, 'Well what was it Macleod was trying to get across on this particular occasion? How well did he succeed? Where did he put the punch lines? Did he make the important point right at the start of the speech and then keep reinforcing it? Or was it built up to a peroration at the end?[12]

Norma had married an obsessive, a political anorak, in 1990s jargon. Evenings, weekends, even holidays, would be taken over by political discussions and meetings. But she tolerated his obsession. She had her man, and she loved him deeply. And he had at last found the accepting and secure foundation that was to be the *sine qua non* of his long ascent to the political summit.

Standard Chartered Bank: 1968–74

A solid financial base and obtaining a responsible position at the bank were the next requirements. When he returned to work after the Nigeria accident in December 1967, he resumed in the fairly lowly post of clerk in the bills department, a much less rewarding job than he had enjoyed in Africa. Because of his injuries, and political ambitions, it was unlikely he would again be sent on a tour of duty abroad, which placed him in an unusual position for a Standard employee. He found the work back in London drudgery, and stressful to combine with his mushrooming council work. But he saw bank work as a means to an end that could not be ducked.[13] Salaries, even at established banks like Standard, were still not high; the City culture of high bonuses familiar in the 1980s was only just beginning to emerge.

On 1 October 1968 promotion came to the bank's investment and international division.[14] Alan Orsich was Major's boss at the foreign exchange dealing room during the next two years. He described his subordinate's performance in this way:

In those days, the foreign exchange and Eurodollar markets were starting to take off. There were about 20 people in the dealing room, compared to 200 now: the area was embarking on rapid growth and he was a part of it. The dealing room was new to most banks, and the brighter people tended to go through it at some stage. As a dealer, Major was average – but average in the dealing room is better than average elsewhere. You needed to think quickly and come to the right decision, and assimilate new material.[15]

Major's working day was concentrated, but not excessively long, lasting from 9.15 a.m. to 4.45 p.m. In particular, he was required to ensure that the bank's accounts with other finance houses and the Bank of England balanced at the end of each trading day. An exacting job: if he had not been able to make his figures agree, he would not have lasted.[16] His political activities were, however, to prove intrusive, with phone calls from the press, and from people with desperate housing problems, proving irksome to him and his colleagues in the pressured atmosphere of the dealing room. Management began increasingly to be aware of his dual loyalties.

A move was arranged in mid-1970 – when the extra burdens of the chairmanship of Housing were beginning to bite – initially to securities and then, after two months, to the comparatively tranquil environment of the business development division in the bank's King William Street office.[17] The bank itself was undergoing major changes. In early 1970 Standard merged with the Chartered Bank, another British finance house specialising in overseas banking. The combined bank was initially called the Standard and Chartered Banking Group, restyled as Standard Chartered in 1975. With the contraction of the British empire, former colonial banks had to remodel. Standard had extensive interests in Africa, and Chartered in Asia; they were natural partners, with plans to develop into North America and Europe as well as Britain.[18]

Major's new job in the combined bank involved him in another growth area, marketing. His new manager, says Major's work entailed him finding out what existing customers were looking for, and how new customers might be attracted.[19] His particular area of concern was Africa,[20] and increasingly Asia, which necessitated him being sent out to Kuala Lumpur and Singapore in August 1974.[21] His pleasant demeanour and ability to put people at ease were 'ideal for the marketing role', as one colleague put it.[22]

The early 1970s were a golden age for trade unionism in the banking industry, where for many years company staff associations had deterred the growth of the National Union of Bank Employees (NUBE).[23] A branch was founded at Standard Chartered in June 1973.[24] The Heath government had passed the Industrial Relations Act in 1971, widely seen as anti-union, but Major shared none of the suspicion of unions of some of his fellow Tories and he became an active NUBE member, albeit a moderate in a very moderate union.[25] Union officials have clear memories of him being approached to stand for election as Standard Chartered shop steward because people thought him trustworthy and liked his serious approach to personal issues.[26] He was also the person selected by marketing staff to lead a less formal approach to management for a salary increase; his command of the argument yielded the result the staff wanted.[27]

Major's progress at the bank was steady and unspectacular. He exhibited little of the flair, ambition or shrewd analysis of power structures and promotion prospects that characterised his political career. He put his head down, in an approach that can best be described as dogged, achieving the respect, if not the admiration, of management. In 1972 he at last completed his exams on which he had worked part-time for seven years, achieving associateship of the Institute of Bankers.[28] At the bank he remained involved in marketing, while the high-fliers moved around in the mainstream banking divisions.[29] Major baulked at being labelled 'in marketing' in political circles: he preferred to play up his status as an 'international banker'.[30] But he could not escape the fact that his work was handling relations with the general British press and the specialist financial press. Management approved of the way that he dealt with the latter stages of the fallout from a troublesome takeover of the Hodge Group, a controversial Welsh secondary bank operation, which resulted in an Esther Rantzen BBC television probe. He also earned plaudits for his handling of the bank's major investments in South Africa, then exciting the ire of liberal opinion in the UK.[31]

Reward for Major's persistent, unspectacular work at Standard Chartered came when, in August 1976, public relations was set up as a separate department. He was appointed its first manager, with the status of dealing with senior figures externally, and with regular access to the main board. It was here that he encountered the Chairman, Lord Barber, who had succeeded Macleod as Heath's Chancellor of the Exchequer (1970–74). Barber, who enjoyed Major's company and conversation, still took a keen interest in politics, but he fell far short of being a decisive political influence on his development.

The second leg of the tripod was at last in place. The final leg, a safe parliamentary seat, was one Major pursued with a single-mindedness and a zeal that would have astonished his managers at Standard Chartered. But the prize he sought was to prove more elusive than a happy marriage and a respectable job.

St Pancras North: the February 1974 Election

Major would discuss his parliamentary ambitions endlessly with his closest friends, Clive Jones and Peter Golds, but it was Jean Lucas whom he regarded as his mentor.[32] After meetings of the Brixton Conservative Association, she would give him a lift home – he did not learn to drive until the mid-1970s. 'We would sit in my car outside his home in Primrose Court', she remembers, 'and have long discussions about national and local political issues. His heart was set on becoming an MP, but he was not at all confident he would make it. Eventually, with difficulty, he began to ask me about his prospects for a Commons career.'[33]

A key step was to have his name placed on the Candidates' List at Conservative Central Office. His defeat as a local councillor in May 1971, and the winding up just after of the Brixton Association, of which he remained Chairman until the end, gave his search for a seat an extra impetus, but first he needed an establishment sponsor; local MPs like Duncan Sandys he regarded, perhaps wrongly, as 'not interested in people like me'.[34] But he had met and liked Jill Knight, a Birmingham MP who had a house in nearby Vauxhall. Prompted by Jean Lucas, Major wrote to her and asked her to sponsor him for the Candidates' List, and she agreed,[35] Jean Lucas speeding his acceptance with a glowing testimonial, dated July 1971:

In my opinion he is exactly the calibre of person we should be looking for. Since he was 15, he has been active in the Young Conservatives, transferring eventually to the senior Association, and until June of this year he has been Chairman of the Brixton Conservative Association...

When successful in election to the Borough Council in 1968 for an apparently hopeless ward, he quickly made his mark, and within three years was Chairman of Lambeth Borough Housing Committee, and one of the top three leaders of Lambeth. This despite his youth, as I think he is still only 27. His speaking ability is considerable; he does not hesitate, and is persuasive in manner; he does not shrink from harsh words about his opponents; he marshals his facts well, and carries authority.

He comes from a humble background, and has worked his way up ... He has recently married a charming wife who will be a great help to him.'[36]

She also gave him advice on how to buff up his curriculum vitae to make his political and business career sound fuller than the facts strictly merited. Major was attending the Conservatives' 1971 Party Conference in Brighton when news reached him, via Peter Golds, that the St Pancras North Association was looking for a candidate.[37] Though a safe Labour seat, it appealed strongly to his desire to cut his teeth and prove himself as a determined, capable candidate. St Pancras North was a mixed constituency: at each end were pockets of affluence, at the fringe of Regent's Park and in Highgate, but the heart was working-class parts of the London borough of Camden, populated by council tenants with a fair smattering of Irish residents and railway workers. The poverty, racial tensions and housing problems were familiar to Major from Lambeth and before.

The selection panel met in early November 1971 and narrowed the entries down to a shortlist of two. Norma was not invited to the final selection on 24 November, in part an act of consideration to Major's unmarried rival, Peter Watherston. Major spoke up boldly at the meeting, and was dubbed the

'Galloping Major' by one of those present. He did well enough to defeat Watherston by twenty-one votes to eleven with one abstention.[38] Formally adopted as prospective parliamentary candidate at the annual general meeting on 24 March 1972, just short of his twenty-ninth birthday, he felt a huge exhilaration in rising so far.

Major began immediately to work the constituency, he says, 'as if it was a marginal'.[39] Sadly for him, it was anything but. In the 1970 general election, Jock Stallard, the Labour MP, won with a majority of slightly under 6,000. The seat would not go Tory unless there was an enormous landslide victory for the Conservatives at the next general election. Major's belief in his ability to win elections, nourished by his freak victory in Lambeth in 1968, has been one of his leitmotifs. He campaigned on local issues, believing that although 'the vast majority of people [are] disaffected by local politics', there was still something to be learnt from the Liberals' community politics.[40]

The evolution of Major's views in this period can be traced in a column he wrote in the *Camden Journal*, a local newspaper in which he was periodically invited to express his opinions under the title 'In My View'. For his first foray he chose to inveigh against the evils of cannabis (he counselled his readers that it was popularly known as 'pot'), an interesting choice, as the sixties music and culture seemed to have passed him by largely unnoticed, apart from his wearing of flared trousers. He blamed much of the increasing drug use on 'the blaze of publicity that surrounded drugs, particularly cannabis and LSD, throughout the Sixties'.[41] Major regarded the sixties culture as essentially frivolous and self-indulgent, and not something for which, in his earnest life, he had any time.

He wrote the 'In My View' column five more times over the next few months, addressing housing and other issues which were of particular concern to residents in the constituency. He did not pull punches, lecturing Labour's council leader as wrong-headed in her opposition to Heath's Housing Finance Act of 1971: 'Personally, I prefer to consider you a latter day Don Quixote, tilting at windmills, a little confused perhaps, with your denouncing of ogres that do not exist.'[42]

Major's tireless work and exquisite personal manners quickly won the respect of his Conservative Association officers and members.[43] An episode recounted by Roland Walker, the association Treasurer, explains why Major became such a popular candidate. One evening after work, Major attended a home-based constituency event. Only one person attended; Major was charming to her and said to the host after she had left: 'Oh, it was marvellous. She was a genuine floating voter: it's the best thing you could have done.'[44] Such stories entered constituency folklore: Major was astute enough to realise that a petulant response would have done so also.

None of his St Pancras activists foresaw, any more than did Heath's Cabinet, how quickly the general election would come upon them, called in February 1974 in the wake of the breakdown in the government's relations with the National Union of Mineworkers. His work for the bankers' union did not make him squeamish at laying into the Heath government's *bête noire*. Major's election address advocated trenchant resistance to union demands. Local reference was made to the 'decline' of St Pancras during the period it had 'persistently' elected Labour candidates. The address contained a photograph of a very young-looking Norma, carrying a two-year-old Elizabeth holding a fur cat.[45] In an article in the *Hampstead and Highgate Express* he expanded on his attack on the trade unions: 'The power of the unions to effectively veto Government policy is the crucial battleground of this election',[46] and on the themes of inflation, pensions and housing. His cause even received the support of Doris Hare, star of television's popular comedy series *On The Buses*: his team circulated an endorsement from the actress, advising voters to 'Take "Mum's" Advice'.[47]

The campaign hotted up. Two weeks before polling, Major accused the local Labour Party of being 'the extreme left of a party that is itself well to the left of reason'.[48] Jock Stallard accused him of making personal attacks. On one particular issue, Major backed off late in the campaign. He wrote a last-minute leaflet, the exact details of which are sketchy, but which probably involved citing comments about communists by Cardinal Heenan to sway the Catholics in the constituency. As the print deadline approached, he had second thoughts. 'He told us quite openly, "I've had a sleepless night worrying about this thing." We had a hasty meeting and we all agreed to scrap the one he had done.'[49] His caution over election propaganda was an enduring trait still apparent in 1997.

Optimism ran high among his party workers throughout the campaign, but the ground was shifting from under the feet of the Tories nationally in the last ten days of the campaign. Not just Heath, but also Major, was rejected by the electorate.

Stallard	Lab	14,761	52.8%
Major	Con	7,926	28.3%
Medlicott	Lib	4,825	
McLennan	Comm	466	

Due to boundary changes since 1970, precise comparison with the previous Conservative performance in St Pancras North cannot be made. Estimates of the swing to Labour put it at 2.8 per cent, rather higher than the average inner London swing of 2.4 per cent.[50] There was to be no positive 'Major effect' in St Pancras North that day. Major did not like losing. As he drove back to Beckenham with Norma in the early hours of 1 March, the lesson he took away was that he would have to fight even harder in his next parliamentary election. What he did not guess was how quickly that would come, nor that he would be fighting it in the same constituency.

Déjà Vu: *St Pancras North October 1974*

Major threw himself back into the work at Standard Chartered, conscious that he had neglected it for most of February. The St Pancras North Association, grateful for what he had achieved, but conscious he would now be looking for a seat with a better chance of success, released him to fight elsewhere. He was interviewed at Portsmouth North and at Paddington,[51] but with the inconclusive national result in February – Harold Wilson's Labour government lacked an overall majority – he had little time to be successful. With an imminent general election increasingly likely, Major accepted the invitation to become the St Pancras North candidate a second time. With the defeat in the May 1974 local elections of the last Conservative councillor in the constituency, however, Major returned to fight the seat again with few illusions.

The period up to the October 1974 election – only the second time this century when two elections have been held in the same year – was like a prolonged campaign. Wilson manoeuvred to find himself in a stronger position to win a working majority in the coming general election. The political atmosphere, exacerbated by trade union, student and urban unrest, was volatile and tense.

In St Pancras North a steadying hand and distraction came in the form of a vivacious young agent, Sue Winter, sent by Central Office in September in response to appeals from the association for someone to help. Her youth – she was, at twenty, the youngest election agent in the country – and good looks generated a local stir: 'A Major Role for Sue', predictably punned the *Hampstead and Highgate Express*.[52] She goaded a reluctant Major into some publicity stunts: paying for his election deposit in Monopoly money to highlight inflation – a serious issue for him[53] – or canvassing with local journalists, dressed in the then-fashionable polo-neck jumper and duffel coat.[54] He did not enjoy her electoral gimmicks, as he saw them, but was happier addressing open-air meetings on the two Saturdays before the poll, speaking through a megaphone on street corners. Even then, this was regarded as rather nostalgic and quaint: 'Mr John Major ... has brought the proverbial soap box back to street corners,' announced the local paper.[55] An incident that particularly stung him occurred at the local association headquarters, when they arrived one morning to find 'Not A Major Success' painted in big letters on their wall: he was, even then, very sensitive to perceived personal slights.[56]

Compared to the February campaign, Major came across as more confident and at home in north London. His election address for the October election had resonances of a Liberal leaflet, with letters from local residents highlighting his commitment to constituency work.[57] His evolving political views can be traced in a leaflet produced to assist canvassers by explaining his stance on key issues. On social services, he wrote, 'My personal priorities are the people who have no effective lobby – young widows with children;

the blind; the deaf; the physically and mentally handicapped; and the chronically sick.' He favoured two upratings in pensions a year to protect pensioners from inflation. On education: 'I believe parents should have a much greater influence over the type of education their child receives.'[58] His personal conversations revealed more of his priorities. Sue Winter says that he came over to her as a left-wing Conservative, who felt most strongly about those issues which involved the disadvantaged. 'He cared about poor people getting a good deal at a time when Conservatives who talked about that were unfashionable.'[59]

One issue on which he favoured a hard line was terrorism. An acquaintance of Norma had been killed earlier that year by an IRA bomb at the Tower of London. Jock Stallard, who continued as his Labour adversary in St Pancras North, had visited the Price sisters, who were republican prisoners, in jail. Major expressed his 'disgust and contempt' for those who brought comfort to terrorists, mindful of the impact of Stallard's and his action on the large number of Irish voters in the constituency.[60]

For many Conservatives, the October 1974 election was tiring and depressing, fought very much on the defensive, and with most available money used up on the February general and May local elections. The party naturally appeared to have little fresh to offer. Conservative activists thought Stallard personally unpleasant to Major; they also believed the two local papers, the *Camden Gazette* and the *Hampstead and Highgate Express*, were biased to Labour, especially the former.[61] Major's enthusiasm and punctilious personal relations, and Sue Winter's liveliness and organisational flair, did something to lift spirits, though Major himself missed Norma on the trail, pregnant with their second child, to be christened James.[62] Major, as ever, worked tirelessly, held surgeries, followed up all enquiries personally, gingered up party workers, and all but ignored the bank again during the campaign.[63] The count on the evening of election day, 10 October, was recalled by Major's party supporters as rowdy and with a menace evident in the air.[64] All were despondent at the result:

Stallard	Lab	14,155	58.6%
Major	Con	6,602	27.3%
Medlicott	Lib	3,428	

Major had lost 1,300 votes on February's total. The swing to Labour in the constituency was 3.4 per cent: the national swing was only 2.1 per cent, though Labour's swings were generally higher in inner-city areas. Nationally, Wilson failed in his bid to obtain a secure working majority. Labour had an overall majority of just three, but a forty-two seat cushion over the Tories. Unconvincing though the result was, there was unlikely to be another general election in the immediate future, and Major was free to resume his search for a better seat with, in all likelihood, time to spare.

Rebuffs and Doubts: 1974–6

The next two years, until late 1976, was a see-saw period for Major. He felt
at times as if the 'up' escalator that he had been on since the mid-1960s had
shuddered to a halt. His search for a seat was single-minded. Although he
applied for many, including Cambridge, interviews were rare, but he did
succeed in achieving one at Ruislip-Northwood, where his views on housing
went down badly with the selection committee,[65] and also at Dorset South,
where he tripped up on a question about fox hunting, a subject he knew
nothing about.[66] Robert Cranborne, his future friend and senior Cabinet
minister, was the victor there. Norma has vivid impressions of the snobbish
indignities of the selection trail, and the experience seemed also to confirm
his own convictions about being patronised for his humble background.[67]

Mid-1975 found him campaigning in both St Pancras North and Paddington for the June 1975 referendum on whether Britain should remain in
the European Economic Community. Robert Hughes, later a strongly pro-
European Conservative MP, recalls Major being active in the 'Yes' campaign;[68] others have no clear recollection of him being strongly committed
either way, then or earlier in the debates, before Britain joined the EEC in
January 1973.[69]

In Major's quest for a seat, his two most trusted advisers remained Peter
Golds, whom he described as 'an encyclopedia of politics',[70] and Jean Lucas,
who had become agent in Putney in 1971. She pressed his case on her local
association, which was looking for a candidate, but was told his curriculum
vitae was too slight. Surprised, she asked to look at it and was handed the
details of a John *Reveley* Major, also a London Tory activist, but without
Major's distinction of having fought two elections and served as Chairman
of a Local Authority Committee. The confusion sorted out, Putney were
duly impressed by the credentials of the right John Major. As John Reveley
Major commented wryly: 'I suppose there is a limit to how many John R.
Majors the political world can accept!'[71]

The Putney Conservative Association was impressed by Major, and he
stood a strong chance of being selected. But with selection in full train, he
heard that Carshalton was looking for a new candidate to succeed Robert
Carr, latterly Home Secretary in Heath's Cabinet (1970–74), and about to
go to the House of Lords. 'I had to choose,' he says. 'Was I going to go for
Putney, which was a Labour-held marginal, or Carshalton, which was a safe
Conservative seat?'[72] It was a difficult choice. Carshalton, the constituency
of his birth, and with a population with whom he felt at ease, won his
affections, but Major lost in the second round. Carshalton selected Nigel
Forman, and Putney chose David Mellor.[73] Major consoled himself over a
drink with a friend: 'People like us, with modest backgrounds and non-BBC
accents, will always be at a disadvantage in selections.'[74] Some constituencies,
like middle-class Sevenoaks, did not even offer him an interview.[75]

He became disillusioned, and appears to have considered abandoning politics. The string of rejections had undermined his self-confidence and made him seriously question where his future as a father of two best lay. He talked it over with one of his bosses, Derek Pinks. 'John came to me and said that he was giving up all his political aspirations and concentrating on the bank. He seemed quite relaxed about it. It was a sensible decision in a way. He had a young family, he'd spent a lot of time and effort and got nowhere.'[76]

The bank were certainly keen on him committing himself whole-heartedly to them. His appointment as manager of the public relations department had taken effect from 1 August 1976, and he was developing a close relationship with Lord Barber, whom he accompanied to Manila for an IMF conference. According to Peter Graham: 'When Tony Barber came on the scene, he felt the need to have someone to relate more directly to the press, and decided that the chap to do it should be John Major.'[77] Graham was one of the senior Standard Chartered figures, along with Michael McWilliam, the Chief Executive, Derek Pinks and Roy Mortimer, who had been supportive of Major's political ambitions. Middle managers thought differently. By the late 1980s they had risen higher in the bank, and hosted an event for Major when he was Chief Secretary. He turned to his friend Ian Cameron Black and said 'These people wouldn't have given me the time of day when I was here.'[78]

Towards the end of 1976, Major told the bank that he would stay with them and give up politics.[79] But then he heard that Huntingdon was looking for a parliamentary candidate. He asked Peter Graham for permission 'to have one last go at it'.[80] Norma recalls: 'I thought at that point that we had reached the end of the line, if Huntingdon didn't come off. He was quite depressed, and had got to the point where he wondered what on earth we had to do to get a seat . . . I thought at the time that if he didn't get Huntingdon, that would be it.'[81]

Huntingdon and parliamentary life were, before long, to eclipse in import-ance the two other foundations he had erected in the previous few years: the bank totally, and his family, in time certainly – to his guilt – though never in his affection.

FIVE

Into Parliament:

1976–83

Candidate for Huntingdonshire: 1976–9

HUNTINGDONSHIRE WAS NOT the obvious constituency for one whose background and experience of politics had been confined to inner London. The seat, which was solidly Tory, was to be vacated by Sir David Renton, MP since 1945.[1] Major was one of over 250 applicants for the plum job. Relieved even to have been given an interview, he followed Norma's suggestion that they study the constituency, which he had never before visited.[2] The couple met the agent Andrew Thomson,[3] and attended a local council meeting to soak up the local atmosphere and issues.[4]

Thomson impressed upon them that this was far from a standard rural constituency. Though the squirearchy was still dominant, at least in the upper echelons of Tory life, increasingly it was made up of London overspill. Some sixty miles north of London, it contained three towns – Huntingdon itself, St Ives and St Neots – and some seventy scattered villages. The constituents included many former Lambeth residents encouraged to move to nearby Peterborough only a few years before. A more attractive seat for an ambitious Tory was not to be found.

Major sailed comfortably through the first round. Those who were knocked out at that stage included such future Conservative luminaries as Michael Howard, Peter Lilley and Chris Patten. The final round, on Friday 19 November 1976, comprised just four candidates: besides Major there was Jock Bruce-Gardyne, a high-powered intellect who had lost his Angus seat in 1974; the Marquess of Douro, Eton and Christ Church Oxford, a banker and heir to the Dukedom of Wellington; and Alan Haselhurst, a former President of the Oxford Union and National Chairman of the Young Conservatives, who had also lost his seat, in Lancashire, in 1974.[5] It was strong opposition, comprising one of the most brilliant minds in the Party, a top-drawer aristocrat, and a proven speaker and organiser. Major, on paper, was the rank outsider.

The candidates were taken in alphabetical order. Each had to give a speech; the first two candidates flopped, Haselhurst performed strongly, and Major rose to the occasion, as he was often to do under pressure. He spoke passionately about the need to reunite all sections of the constituency, blaming

Labour for worsening the divisions in society. Questions followed the set piece speeches. Major's response to one sceptical farmer made a particular impression: he won over many in the audience by admitting that, though he did not yet know much about farming, he would become an authority within twenty-four hours, if selected.

The questions over, constituency members, numbering some 186, cast their votes. Major won the support of 109, an outright winner on the first ballot.[6] His selection was officially ratified by the association on 3 December. Major's acceptance speech was not adventurous: 'I will do what I believe to be right and what I believe is best in the circumstances,' he announced, somewhat overwhelmed by the occasion. 'Other than that, there is no promise I can make.'[7]

There were strong dissenters to Major's selection, especially among the squirearchy. A key factor that swung over some of the older members was the argument that Major would appeal to the new breed of Huntingdon voter and do more to ensure a Tory future for the constituency than the other three candidates, all public school and Oxbridge products. Renton, not wanting to be involved in the selection process, took off for the United States. On hearing the news on his return, he asked Archie Gray, Chairman of the association, 'But has he ever been on a farm?'[8] Renton quickly grew to appreciate Major's abilities; others of his background continued to regard the Majors as social *arrivistes*, and considered that the rejection of his social betters in the selection ballot had been an act of folly.[9] It was, in fact, those the association had discarded early on, like Patten, rather than his three competitors in the final round, who were to prove the real stars. The rebuff Major felt from some of the social élite in the constituency served to reinforce his own fears of snobbery in the Party against him.

For the next two and a half years, Major worked almost fanatically to win over floating voters, participating in an estimated 450 meetings in the constituency, and attending all eighty-seven branch AGMs in the period up to the 1979 general election.[10] Renton proved to be more generous than many outgoing MPs in the degree of support and tutelage he offered.[11] Several senior members of the association took Major under their wing, like Roger Juggins, the only farmer on the executive, who was prominent in straightening him out about farming: 'An MP does not have to know how to milk a cow, but he does need to know the politics of cows.'[12] Major was later to recall the comment wryly.

He proved outstandingly good at winning people over, coming across as self-effacing, charming, intelligent, and interested in his constituents personally. 'When he met me in 1979 again, he knew my name, remembered where we'd met, and what we had talked about. Very impressive indeed,' recalled one, who had moved to the area in 1977.[13] He proved particularly effective in canvassing among the ex-Londoners in council houses or in cheaper private property.[14] Major was able, by his transparent sincerity and hard work, substantially to reduce the snobbery and resentment of him.[15]

A condition imposed by the association's executive committee was that the successful candidate had to live locally.[16] Housing in the constituency at least was not too expensive, and the Majors bought a house at Hemingford Grey, a village outside Huntingdon. Their home in Beckenham, however, proved difficult to sell, and it was not until December 1977 that their move was completed.[17] The children, Elizabeth and James, were approaching school age, and Norma was pleased to settle down for what they all expected would be a long stay in the village.

With Major's adoption at Huntingdon, his whole attitude to the bank shifted. No sooner had he flirted with the idea of a permanent career in the bank than he was adopted. With his agreement, he was moved to a less demanding, and much less interesting, area dealing with analysis of the bank's customer base. His attitude veered between concern that middle managers were checking up on him, or saying that he was no longer exerting himself,[18] and feeling bored and being prone to occasional flippant behaviour. In the two summers of 1977 and 1978, when he became frustrated with writing reports on companies – a large slice of his job – he was known to announce suddenly, 'I'm off to the Oval.' He would place an old jacket over the back of his chair, spread files across his desk, and invite a friendly colleague to clear his desk and put his jacket away at the end of the day.[19] Frequent telephone calls would be received at work from Huntingdonshire prospective constituents. When the phone went, a colleague would repeat the surname: if Major shook his head, the caller would be told Major was out.[20] He continued to enjoy access to the Chairman, Barber, some compensation for his relative lack of status, away from the mainstream, the high-fliers, the corporate cars and the high salaries.

Not that Major had any complaints about his treatment from the bank's hierarchy. On 1 October 1978 he was moved over to the advances department on a part-time basis.[21] His pay appears to have been kept up fully until he became an MP in May 1979 when, on the instructions of Barber, a complex formula was arranged whereby he was paid a top-up figure in addition to his parliamentary salary, equivalent to what he had been earning when working at the bank full time.[22] He formally left the bank on becoming a minister in January 1983.[23]

Major's heart was clearly firmly entrenched in his political career. While still a candidate, he was assiduous in developing contacts with the Party at Westminster. He cultivated friendships among contemporaries on the Candidates' Association, run by John Watson, several of whom, like Graham Bright and David Mellor, went on to serve under him.[24] Watson recalls that Major worked harder nurturing his constituency than any of the other candidates, despite having probably the safest seat. 'I'd have listed John Major among my five best friends,' Watson recalled. 'Probably there were ten of us who'd have said the same thing! But he probably wouldn't have listed any of us as his close friends. He had that knack of making people feel you were special to him.'[25] He developed contacts in many other quarters, as with the

Conservative Party Research Department, taking one of their staff, Peter Cropper, out for lunch to discuss tax policy. It is remembered as a rare occasion that a prospective parliamentary candidate took this initiative.[26]

When James Callaghan, who succeeded Harold Wilson as Prime Minister in 1976, called the general election for 3 May 1979, Major worked obsessively during the campaign. According to the *Hunts Post*, he had built up a vast team of three to four thousand helpers.[27] Peter Brown, who subsequently became his agent, said that when he arrived he was frequently told of the horrors of the 1979 general election,' when Major was a nervous wreck, and drove everybody to the madhouse'.[28] One reason for the frenzy was his irritation at being told so frequently that he would not win as many votes as Renton. Norma, who carried with her a dread that they would lose the election, admits that they were both irritated, and a little unnerved, by such talk.[29] The result, when it came, staggered them all: his majority was 21,563, over double Renton's October 1974 majority.[30]

John Major (Con)	40,193	53.3%
Julian Fulbrook (Lab)	18,630	25.7%
Dennis Rowe (Lib)	12,182	
Kenneth Robinson (NF)	983	

The constituency had increased in size from 79,800 to 95,000 voters since the second 1974 election. Major had been successful, as some selectors had envisaged back in 1976, in winning over the new voters.[31] The national swing to the Conservatives of 5.1 per cent accounts for most of his 7.1 per cent swing and any personal voting made only a modest contribution at best, but it was an impressive win that silenced any local grumblings.

Major significantly put much greater effort into winning the seat than into defining clear policy positions. He remained cautious on policy, and a trawl through his various pronouncements from 1976 to 1979, and especially during the campaign, fails to provide much of interest about the evolution of his thinking: Labour's 'extremism' and 'hypocrisy' in making promises to increase public spending without tax rises were common targets, and promises to reduce tax on income and capital, extend choice in welfare, and provide stronger police and defence were the main Tory policies highlighted.[32]

Life in Parliament: 1979–82

It had taken Major ten years to realise his dream of becoming a Member of Parliament. Aged thirty-six, he was now one of the youngest MPs and sitting for one of the safest parliamentary seats. For the time being, ever the incrementalist, he had no further ambitions. But he had carefully planned how his career might evolve:

With a majority of 20,000, I knew I was there for a long time, and I knew I would get jobs and I wanted to be prepared for them. I regarded it very much as preparation time ... If you went up too fast you fell down too quickly it seemed to me. I wanted to spread the base across, I wanted to learn how Parliament worked, learn how the committee system worked. If you went on committees you learned what the tricks of the trade were, you could make your speeches and mistakes in private, you found out the way in which Parliament worked ... I knew nothing about policy groups, nothing about lobbies ... I wasn't interested in thrusting myself forward. I just wanted to spread myself as widely as I could and absorb as much of the place as I could.[33]

His ascent was thus plotted with consummate skill. What is perhaps most unusual about this phase of his life is that he had no guide or mentor. Marion Wright and Jean Lucas were in the past; Mrs Thatcher – his mentors were usually women – was to come. Major played his cards close to his chest. Barbara Wallis, who became his Commons secretary,[34] recalls 'he was careful not to ally himself too quickly to any specific group within the parliamentary party'.[35] Cat-like, he listened and took careful note. 'He got it absolutely dead right,' said one colleague. 'He didn't irritate people by trying too hard, but equally he didn't lose any chances to get himself noticed.'[36] All agree he was extremely ambitious, but not in a way that alienated them. 'It was pure instinct,' as he summed it up himself.[37]

His maiden speech was in the debate on Chancellor Geoffrey Howe's budget, on 13 June 1979. Suitably modest, and respecting the House's conventions of praising his predecessor, Renton, he made a constituency case that Cambridgeshire was doing badly out of local government grant payments from the Department of the Environment.[38] Not everything went according to plan. He admitted: 'I made one or two silly speeches that didn't actually reflect what I thought, largely because I hadn't prepared them properly.'[39] On some occasions, as on the US-led boycott of the 1980 Olympic Games in Moscow, he was desperate to be called, and deeply frustrated to be passed over.[40]

His speeches after the first year followed a fairly orthodox government line, though not in an unthinking way. In January 1981, for example, he supported intervention for industries that faced temporary problems, but thought that steel should 'find its own level'.[41] He supported Howe's restrictionist and deeply controversial budget of 1981 ('I thought Geoffrey Howe was absolutely right ... the whole economy was structurally unbalanced')[42] and spoke in favour of government economic policy in July 1981, which he thought, significantly, was the line of 'pragmatic Tory philosophy'.[43] In the economic debate in April 1982, he regretted that the question of public expenditure had become a 'touchstone of philosophy', and stressed the importance of the public sector.[44] At several stages he suggested his unease with high interest rates: 'disastrous' he described them in November 1979;[45] 'usuriously high' in November 1981;[46] and he was still pressing for cuts in November 1982.[47]

His views on the great Europe question before 1979, as seen in his St

Pancras North period, are opaque; it was not an issue that much interested him. In the debate on the Queen's Speech in 1981, however, he uttered the following revealing words:

At the beginning of the parliament recess I firmly believed that Britain should not enter the EMS [European Monetary System]. I have returned to the House, having spoken to firm after firm in my constituency, believing that the sooner we enter the EMS to improve exchange rate stability the better it will be for our exports and our imports generally.[48]

A year later, he made a more general pronouncement on his stance on Europe:

Emotionally I am an agnostic on the subject of a united Europe. I've no longer term vision of a federal Europe and I don't wish to diminish the languages and the cultures of the member states … [I am] a European by logic, not emotion.[49]

Those who spent hours, and pages, agonising over his true beliefs on Europe needed to go no further than look up this 1982 statement, from which he deviated only negligibly over the following fifteen years.

He developed specialisms, in particular two where he felt he had more experience than most, local government and housing. The 1980 Housing Bill absorbed much attention, its aim of introducing the right to buy for council tenants one he had supported as a politician in both Lambeth and St Pancras North. His work on the Bill's standing committee attracted favourable attention from the whips, and his speech in the guillotine of the Bill was characterised by John Tilley (Labour, Lambeth Central) as 'knockabout humour'.[50] His interventions in Queen's Speech debates were a sign that the whips regarded him as loyal and intelligent. A few, such as Ian Lang, were already tipping him for high office.[51]

His first step on the parliamentary ladder came soon after the 1979 election when invited to become one of two secretaries of the Conservative backbench Environment Committee. As far as rungs go, this one was about as low as one could find. But it was a start. Major had come to the attention of Chairman Anthony Durant as a new entrant who he thought was 'an expert on housing'.[52] Backbench committees when the Tories are in power, especially in areas like environment, are low-key affairs and provide a forum for interested backbenchers to discuss issues and to listen to speakers, often ministers.[53] Major served as Secretary until 1981, coming across to colleagues as 'hard working, very keen and not at all bombastic. Everyone liked him.'[54]

His specialism in housing, and social concern, was reflected in his continuing membership of the board of the Warden Housing Association, a Harrow-based voluntary organisation providing low-cost rented housing. He had been recruited in 1975 because of his reputation as a good housing chairman in Lambeth and continued until he joined the Whips' Office in 1983. Although the duties of board membership were not onerous, the

Chief Executive, John Drew, remembers him as someone who 'commanded immediate respect and could grasp problems quickly'.[55]

Politically, from 1979 to 1983, Major tended to the left of the Conservative Party, though he strove to avoid being labelled as belonging to one faction or another. His inclinations were mostly expressed in private, but in July 1981 he spoke in favour of the Private Bill of Plaid Cymru's Dafydd Wigley on disability, and mentioned his father's own physical difficulties. He greeted the doubling of the blind person's allowance warmly.[56] Four months later he spoke in a social security debate about 'the casualties of the social changes ... through which we are passing', the need for them to be 'protected by the state' and 'long-term social benefits must, in our society, retain their purchasing power'.[57] Later in the Parliament, a more right-wing tone is detectable, above all on economic issues, as when he spoke in November 1982 of the need to 'price workers back into jobs'.[58] Colleagues, nevertheless, recall him as, overall, left of centre: to Wigley, whose pair he became in 1982, 'not an instinctive Thatcherite: a different sort of Tory';[59] to Chris Patten, 'slightly left of centre, similar to me on social issues, race and Europe, but I was more left on economic policy';[60] and to John Watson, 'In the early 1980s, John Major was a subscriber to a fairly classic "One Nation" type of Conservatism.'[61] Mrs Thatcher concurred: she wrote in her memoirs, 'John Major was certainly not known to be on the right of the party during his first days as an MP.'[62]

Major's deliberate strategy of gaining breadth of experience led him to join a trip to the Middle East organised in April 1982 by Labour MP Ernie Ross. The party was to meet Yasser Arafat, leader of the Palestine Liberation Organisation, and the Crown Prince of Jordan, on what was essentially a propaganda mission to teach MPs more about the Palestinian plight. Most MPs who went were pro-Arab, including Tony Nelson, the Conservative friend of Major, and Labour MP Ken Weetch. Major was reflective throughout the trip, and calm when a rock thrown at the group almost hit him.[63] Weetch recalled that 'Major listened carefully to all the arguments people made during his meetings with Palestinians and Jordanians. He responded in a cautious and thoughtful way. He kept his own counsel on it and did not identify himself with one line or another.'[64] Major often found himself drawn to divides: his desire to heal, and unite warring factions, is one of his deepest and most powerful instincts.

Friends and Political Groupings

Major's first two years in the House were among the happiest in his life. The week was spent staying in the flats of different friends in London, weekends in Huntingdon. He would talk animatedly to parliamentary colleagues about Norma and his young family, but no sooner did he get home on Friday evening than he would be out again in the whirl of constituency activity on which he thrived.[65] Like many driven fathers, he regrets that he did not spend more time with his young children.[66]

In London, new friendships blossomed. Then, as later, he was more conscious of his modest background than others when assessing him. He was also not as much of a social misfit as he thought: of the 339 Conservative MPs after the 1979 general election, 93 (27 per cent) were non-public school, and 109 (32 per cent) had not been to university.[67] Matthew Parris, who entered the House at the same time, believes there was *some* social snobbery after 1979 about Major and his ilk:

The Members' Smoking Room – with its smell of cigars and port, brandy and whisky – was still the engine room for one section of the Conservative Party, and it wasn't a section to which John Major belonged. One would have found him in the Tea Room, or in the Strangers' Cafeteria. Nobody, to his face, would have made any remark about his accent or his background but he would always have been very conscious that there is a strain in the Conservative Party that does notice and does actually mind about your social origins. It will not overtly discriminate against you, but it will not treat you as one of the boys in quite the way that the boys would be treated. It's a subtle thing, but you know it's there.[68]

Graham Bright, who shared a similarly modest background, celebrates Major as a great Tea Room man, always present in the afternoon, listening to people. 'If anyone wanted to know what was going on, he was the guy you would ask, because he would know.'[69] The early 1980s were a time of wild living for many Tory MPs: according to one, at least half the Conservative MPs were having affairs, and of those at least half did so openly. Major did not belong to either category.[70]

With his social and political background, he was a natural to be invited to join the 'Guy Fawkes' group of Conservative MPs, convened by John Watson for the class of 1979, and so called because it first met on 5 November of that year. It was formed in direct reaction to the exclusivity of the 'Blue Chips', a group of twelve urbane new MPs, many of whom were already marked down as high-fliers, several of whom had worked in the Party organisation up to the 1979 general election. The difference between Blue Chips and Guy Fawkes has been characterised as 'Oxbridge against red brick, public against state school, Londoners against provincial MPs'. More colloquially, Blue Chips had a higher calibre of conversation, more drink, was more witty and formal.[71] They were also to the left of Guy Fawkes. Blue Chips were distinctly, in the parlance of the time, 'aristo and wet'; Guy Fawkes 'self-made men and hard-nosed'.

Guy Fawkes comprised several figures who were later to feature prominently in Major's life, including Stephen Dorrell, Brian Mawhinney and David Mellor. It met monthly and contained many of Major's allies in his early days in the House. On 14 April 1981 members speculated who in the parliamentary party would hold the top jobs in the government (regardless of whether or not they were Guy Fawkes members) in April 1991. Some of their conjectures are instructive (PM, Chris Patten; Chancellor, William Waldegrave; Foreign Secretary, Robert Cranborne), but none more so than the nomination for Financial Secretary to the Treasury – John Major.[72] Neither his friends, nor Major himself, saw him destined, after two years in the House, for the very top. Able, trustworthy, likeable, serious-minded were the Major virtues that struck contemporaries, and the Party hierarchy. A deserving candidate for promotion at some point, certainly, but not one of the stars of the very talented 1979 entry. Mellor, John Patten and Waldegrave shone far more brightly, and all had received ministerial jobs by the end of 1981. Major began to feel left behind. Perhaps his careful master plan had not been well enough conceived.

A Tentative PPS: 1981–3

When a job arrived, it came like a consolation prize: not a minister, but Parliamentary Private Secretary (PPS) to two Ministers of State at the Home Office, Patrick Mayhew and Timothy Raison. More galling, the appointment was to succeed the suave John Patten, appointed in January 1981 Junior Minister at the Northern Ireland Office.[73] Admittedly, Chris Patten was only appointed a PPS at the same time, but his was to serve a Cabinet minister, considered a much more elevated perch.[74] The PPS job, to act as a bridge between ministers and the parliamentary party, came to Major on the suggestion of the whips.[75] Reviews of MPs were conducted each six months. Major, according to Michael Jopling, Chief Whip at the time, came out consistently top of the class of 1979, admired for the quality of his speeches, interventions, and work on the environment and standing committees.[76] Major was being typecast as neither brisk high-flier nor free-market warrior, but as solid citizen. They were not the kind who rose high in the Thatcher government in the early 1980s.

The job of PPS can be marginal, or akin to that of a junior minister in the department. Everything depended on how fully the minister wished to involve his PPS. Home Secretary, and undisputed master of the Home Office, was William Whitelaw, who said of Major: 'I found him shy at the time. Valuable certainly, but very quiet. It was not till after he left the PPS job that he blossomed.'[77] Whitelaw was always concerned to hear the views of Tory MPs, and found Major's feedback on the Commons temperature and views useful, especially on matters like immigration. But the government's parliamentary majority of over forty was considered safe, and the controversial issues for the first Thatcher government were economic rather than Home Office affairs.

Major attended Whitelaw's political meeting ('prayers') each morning, intended to provide the opportunity for ministers and PPSs to go through the day's agenda. Nervous and thin-voiced at first, Major would report back parliamentary opinion with increasing confidence. But he was not one to 'throw up ideas on policy'. Raison thought he performed very competently, 'but no one saw him as a future PM'.[78] He continued, 'some ministers used the PPSs as part of the creative team. Whitelaw didn't use them in that way: he really saw them as a way of communicating parliamentary opinion.'[79] Mayhew concurs: 'Major had a rententive memory, and was good at smoothing things over with backbenchers. He was everything a PPS ought to be, but not an obvious future Prime Minister.'[80]

Realising he would never be considered more than a marginal player at the Home Office, and seeing that there was no grand patron in sight to champion his cause for advancement, Major engaged on purposeful activity of his own, developing friendly relations across the Party, from newcomers to old hands. 'He made sure he knew everyone. He was cementing friendships with everybody. If you talked to those people later, they would remember Major as a young man who was kind, who would listen to them.'[81] This careful nurturing of people yielded tremendous dividends later in the 1980s, and when he stood for Party leader in 1990.

The Falklands War came and went (he supported it, naturally). Then the summer and autumn of 1982 passed, still with no promotion to junior minister. As later, he hid his feelings from the world at large, but inside he became despondent: both Norma and he began to feel he would never receive office under Mrs Thatcher.[82] Typically, he had arrived in the House in May 1979 a little apprehensive, not sure he would make the grade. In little time, he realised he was just as able as his contemporaries, and began to itch for promotion.[83] A colleague similarly passed over in a minor reshuffle in 1982 turned to him and said, 'It really gets up my nose that there are at least fifteen ministers whom I know I can outperform.' Major swung round on him and quipped, 'Really, only fifteen!'[84] His lack of promotion success he blamed on snobbery; he hated being slighted – as he saw it. How much, deep down, he believed that was the reason, and how much he was merely using snobbery as a scapegoat, is difficult to say. In any event, he had not much longer to wait. In January 1983 he was appointed an assistant whip, the lowest form of ministerial life, but still a minister. The eleventh of the 1979 entrants to be appointed, he nevertheless was now a member of the government.[85] After a comparatively slow start, he was moving across to the fast lane.

SIX

Whip and Social Security:

1983–7

MAJOR TOOK UP his job as an assistant whip on 14 January 1983. The last name in the reshuffle to be announced, Major was, nevertheless, according to the *Financial Times*, 'widely regarded as one of the most likely backbenchers to be promoted'.[1] *Private Eye* celebrated his arrival in government by making him the subject of their 'The New Boys' column. Unlike later treatment, this piece was not unkind: 'far from an archetypal or caricature Tory ... He listens without giving much away. That was a quality of another junior whip 30 years ago called Heath and another 15 years ago called Pym.'[2] Appointment to the Whips' Office was not without a certain cachet, as all the whips must agree to a new appointment. Anyone regarded as unsuitable was blackballed. Major was not. 'It was the most flattering job ever to be offered,' he later said, 'because you are offered it by the people who want to work with you.'[3]

Major entered the hidden world of the Whips' Office presided over by Michael Jopling, and containing many future allies in his government such as Tristan Garel-Jones, Tony Newton, Alistair Goodlad, Douglas Hogg and Ian Lang. In his new job, Major's self-effacing manner was seen as a positive attribute. From early on, Major began to impress the traditionalist Jopling: 'The job of a whip is to listen, not to be egotistical or a bore. Being liked and trusted is important, as is intellectual ability, loyalty, negotiating skills and being articulate. Major had all these qualities. "He could charm the birds off the trees." '[4] When Jopling left the job in June 1983 he told Mrs Thatcher that Major, after just five months in the job, was destined for a 'big future' in the Party.[5]

Fortunately for Major, the incoming Chief Whip, John Wakeham, shared Jopling's opinion. Mrs Thatcher had a high regard for Wakeham's skills as Party Manager, and thus listened all the more carefully to his assessment of the strengths of individuals whom, like Major at this time, she barely knew.[6]

During Wakeham's period as Chief Whip (1983–7) the office became less patrician, less a home for retired soldiers and elder solid citizens, and more meritocratic, a launch pad for future careers.[7] He moulded the office into one in which half the posts went to those destined for high office, such as Hogg, Francis Maude and Michael Portillo, and half to the 'solid backbone'.[8]

Major he placed squarely in the first category. 'The key thing about John Major was that he could grasp complex issues. He was also particularly good at spotting the difficulties that lay ahead – the ability to foresee the future is a key skill of a whip.'[9] There were some difficult backbenchers for the whips to handle in the 1983–7 Parliament, chief among them Richard Body and Ann and Nicholas Winterton.[10]

Major's characteristic traits as a whip were to be courteous to all wings of the Party, even when Tory MPs – as did Robert Hayward on the abolition of the Greater London Council – voted against the government. 'For about a year after,' Hayward recalled, 'Major would tease me about being a persistent rebel, but he never took it personally.'[11] The new intake of 1983 was subjected to a Major charm offensive: he took several, like John Maples, under his wing, and would frequently be around the Members' Dining Room or Tea Room chatting, asking questions, offering support and advice.[12] Notes and letters of appreciation would appear after first speeches or notable endeavours. He displayed all the old-fashioned courtesy of a public school headmaster. When he sensed a rebellion, he would move in on the MP, and explain the government's approach to the member, give him the feeling of being on the inside track, and help him to justify supporting the government to his own constituents.[13] Wakeham would bring his Cabinet papers into the office so that whips could know what was going on across the government's whole waterfront. Most whips did not bother to take up Wakeham's offering; Garel-Jones dipped into most, but Major read them all.[14] It gave him a unique purchase on government policy, and an ability to comprehend and explain.

Whips were given both geographic and departmental responsibilities. Major's regional 'patch' was East Anglia, which included some of Mrs Thatcher's core 'wet' opponents: Jim Prior, in office until 1984, and two former Cabinet ministers she had already dismissed, Francis Pym and Norman St John Stevas. Major was felt by Francis Maude, the whip who succeeded him, to have managed these malcontents 'spectacularly'.[15]

His first departmental responsibility was for the environment, chosen because of his local government interests and his secretaryship of the Environment Committee after 1979. With rate capping and the GLC's abolition on the agenda, it was a trying time for the department, though with a majority of 144, blood pressure could be kept within bounds. Major, as usual, began his assignment with self-doubts, but these evaporated as he realised he was rated as businesslike and efficient by the department.[16] Ian Lang thought him 'the first whip ever to understand the local government finance system'.[17]

Major's tactile manner now began to be noticed. 'He was very good at gripping your arm, gently touching you, and just being generally friendly in that open kind of way that people like, and he was popular for that reason.'[18] He became more confident, too, with humour, and developed something of a reputation for reading Mrs Thatcher. A more junior colleague and he were returning after dinner to the Chamber. Along the corridor they saw Mrs

Thatcher and her entourage approaching. Major said, 'Don't go past her now.' 'Why not?' his colleague enquired. 'Because she might stop and talk to you, and you'll either have a conversation over banalities, in which case she'll think less of you, or she will raise a subject about which she knows far more than you, in which case she will also think the less of you. Not a very good idea.'[19]

The media began to start noticing him. Each intake after a general election contains three to six MPs on each side whom a consensus among the media rate highly; 1979 was unusually strong for new entrants, like 1950 and 1970, and by 1984 Major began to be recognised as one worthy of serious attention.[20] Major repaid them by offering useful stories and leads, and began to build up good relations with journalists including Elinor Goodman (Channel 4), Trevor Kavanagh (the *Sun*), Robin Oakley (*The Times*) and Peter Riddell (the *Financial Times*). Major's rise in visibility was aided by the backing of two of the biggest socialites and form-watchers of the day. Tristan Garel-Jones thought Major the consummate whip, with all the skills required to a high degree: he used to say of Major as whip that he was 'magic'.[21] Alan Clark first spotted Major in early 1983: 'He had such beautiful manners. It was quite unusual to find a whip who never bullied, who was immensely courteous. He was different to the sort of reliable person who would get on in the Conservative Party because he wasn't a creep. He was actually rather a pleasant person with a dignity of his own.'[22] Chris Patten was another who talked up Major at this time.

In 1983 he received the ultimate social accolade of being invited to join 'Blue Chips'. Rare indeed was it for the initial dozen members to invite a fresh face to join their ranks, but they did not want to miss out on such a talked-about figure in their ranks. Meetings were held at Garel-Jones's house in Catherine Place, near Victoria, at his expense over dinner. Major, graduate of Lambeth Conservative Party and Standard Chartered Bank, had arrived in the bosom of the Tories' social élite.

General Election: Treasury Whip 1983–5

His increasingly exciting life at Westminster did not lead Major to neglect Huntingdon. He remained extraordinarily assiduous as a constituency member. Almost weekly stories circulated in the local press about how he was defending the interests of his constituents, against British Rail over local trains to King's Cross,[23] against the 'unfair' European Community,[24] and against the county council over their attitude to the siting of Cruise nuclear missiles at RAF Molesworth.[25] Individual constituents were supported on a wide array of subjects, from inadequate service pensions to problems over immigration rules.[26] The pages of the *Hunts Advertiser* were festooned with Major stories, testament also to the efficiency of his media machine.

A boundary review which came into operation for the 1983 general election created extra work as the constituency was lengthened at the northern end, bringing in areas that previously had belonged to the Peterborough constituency. In 1982–3, he worked this new territory relentlessly. Roger Juggins, who had taken over as his association chairman, drove him around to function after function. 'He seemed to enjoy it. He never found the events a bore.' Juggins detected his rapidly growing confidence: 'Major by the time of the 1983 general election had become an assured speaker. And when he knew there were no press around, he would tell parliamentary anecdotes brilliantly.'[27]

Word spread about how quick and personal he was in responding to constituents' letters and enquiries.[28] Norma was popular too, and played an increasing part in the constituency.[29] Factors beyond his control were also moving in his favour. The boundary changes proved to be to the benefit of the Conservatives,[30] in part by removing St Neots which was felt to have 'unreliable tendencies'.[31] The London overspill that had favoured the Conservatives throughout the 1970s continued into the 1980s; the population increased by 20 per cent between 1979 and 1983. The election result in June 1983 was never in doubt. Few, however, expected Major to win so convincingly:

Major (Con)	34,254	62.4%
Gatiss (Lib)	13,906	25.3%
Slater (Lab)	6,317	
Eilorart (Ecology)	444	

The swing to the Conservatives in the constituency of 6.9 per cent, compared to the national swing of 3.9 per cent from Labour to Conservative, gave him, as ever, great satisfaction.[32]

A few months after the election Major moved his weekday London base from a flat in the Temple to the top floor of a house in Stockwell, adjacent to Brixton, belonging to Standard Chartered colleague Stan Hurn. It provided Major with more space, and a location where he felt more at home. He remained there until 1989, when he became Foreign Secretary. He used to drive back from Huntingdon on Sunday evening, leaving his Rover in the Commons car park after someone had put a brick through the window in Stockwell. He would always be anxious to be back in the flat in time to see *Spitting Image* on television.[33]

In October 1984 Major rose another notch in the Whips' Office when he was promoted to a Lord Commissioner. This advance, based purely on the length of service as Assistant Whip, was less significant than the concurrent switch from being Environment to Treasury Whip.[34] Garel-Jones had been the first choice for this most highly prized whip's job, but economics was not his forte, whereas Major particularly craved the job. Garel-Jones had a talk to John Cope, Wakeham's deputy, and Major duly became the Treasury Whip.[35]

Leaders emerge through a mixture of ability, stealth and luck. This appointment was a conspicuous example of the last. It brought Major for the first time into contact with the heart of government business, and allowed him to display his skills and manner to some influential figures, above all Nigel Lawson, Chancellor since June 1983. Major went to Number Eleven or the Treasury three or four times a week for Prayers: Lawson held court over his ministerial colleagues and political advisers at 8.45 a.m. He would call on the whip to give the Treasury team 'a summary-cum-situation report' of Party opinion and recent parliamentary events.[36] Lawson, who had been a whip himself (1976–7), appreciated Major's succinct yet well-informed reports, and approved of his diligence and attractive personal manner.[37] Apprehensive again at first – he found it daunting to have the attention of the Chancellor and the senior Treasury ministers – he was apt to misuse the odd word. But confidence soon grew.[38] Characteristically, he worked hard to master the papers and issues before Prayers began, hating to be caught unprepared on any issue. All those present found him unusually professional, and with 'an inner ear for political nuance'.[39] He would tend to stay quiet during policy debates, regarding his job as watching over the parliamentary party for the Chancellor.[40]

The Finance Bill was a particular task of the Treasury Whip. Major, utilising fully his knowledge of finance for almost the first time since entering the House, excelled at it. Younger backbenchers found him particularly considerate: 'He dished out amendments on the Finance Bill to help train them. He was never the sort of whip to tell people to shut up and go through division lobbies.'[41]

By 1985, Major's reputation was spreading. Having not yet risen high enough to arouse jealousy, or been promoted to positions where he had to take unpopular decisions, he was riding on the crest of a wave. Some critics thought his subsequent career an anticlimax, that in his subsequent career he was always too much a whip and too little a politician: good at Party management, but lacking a clear vision; all tactics, no strategy. No one said this at the time. Major, who was enormously happy and fulfilled as a whip from 1983 to 1985, realises that he learned much from the experience:

If you go into government as a junior minister you get surrounded by civil servants. You never learn how the sewers of Parliament work ... If I hadn't learned parliamentary procedure, parliamentary tricks and a whole range of other things, we would probably have lost the Maastricht Bill ... But two years was enough. I wanted by then to get out and get a job.[42]

He believed he had handicapped his chances of achieving that promotion, perhaps fatally, by a spat with Mrs Thatcher at a whips' dinner at Brooks's Club in St James's in July 1985. Mrs Thatcher was expounding to the assembled company about tax cuts, and argued against high taxes for blue-collar workers. Major interjected that he thought the public had not properly understood the government's reasons for cutting taxes. His concern was with presentation, not the strategy. She jumped to the conclusion, however, that he was attacking the whole tax-cutting philosophy and turned on him. He tried to defend himself, and explain what he meant, but she would not listen. After she left he turned to Wakeham and said, 'Well that's buggered up my political career.'[43] There was clearly no ill-feeling between Mrs Thatcher and Major at this stage. He had complained in the early 1980s that she had never spoken to him and that she would never promote someone like him. But that was the usual frustration of an ambitious young man.[44] Friends cannot recall him expressing any strong feelings about her, positive or negative. But beneath the surface, unexpressed, he had reservations about her, even as early as the mid-1980s.[45]

Junior Minister at Social Security: 1985–6

As the 1985 summer recess approached, Major knew that a reshuffle was in the air, hence his anxiety about the repercussions of his clash with Mrs Thatcher.[46] Wakeham urged the case for his promotion; she probably acceded to push him up a level without much agonising, though claims in her memoirs, which can be inclined to *ex post* judgement, that she decided he should go to Social Security to alert him to 'the realities of social security and the dependency culture', to cure him of his wet views.[47] Their uncertain relationship survived an early episode soon after his promotion. Major had been asked to Number Ten to see her, and he was placed in the waiting room. He was then forgotten about until an attendant reminded the Private Office an hour later that he was still waiting. Nigel Wicks, Principal Private Secretary, alerted Mrs Thatcher, but she was no longer able to see him. Upon being told her news, he responded, 'Parliamentary Secretaries – they are meant to wait', grinned, and walked off without giving any indication he was irritated.[48]

Major's appointment as Parliamentary Secretary to the Department of Health and Social Security took effect from 2 September 1985. The work of the department seemed dull and routine to many Conservative MPs, who saw it as a home for the colourless and punctilious typified by the character of the Secretary of State Norman Fowler (1981–7). To many observers, the department was summed up by its 'dreadful' modern building, Alexander Fleming House in Elephant and Castle, a mile removed from the centre of life in Whitehall and Westminster.

The department ran in two quite distinct halves: health and social security. Major was assigned to the latter, with Tony Newton, Minister of State, as his immediate boss, with whom he formed a lasting alliance. Rather than being repelled, as were many of his fellow Tory MPs, by the intricacy of the work and its humdrum subjects – ordinary people – Major thrived on it. From the outset he attacked the work with gusto, glad that it was a department where parliamentary secretaries had real jobs of work. He was immediately plunged into the passage of the complex Bill which was to become the Social Security Act of 1986, a substantial piece of legislation. The Act, which sought to clarify many of the confusions in the benefit system that had grown up in the previous twenty years, introduced common rules to assess benefit entitlements, replaced Family Income Supplement with Family Credit, and Supplementary Benefit with Income Support.[49]

By the time Major arrived in September, the first part of the Bill was going through standing committee and the technical, latter parts were being rewritten. Major concentrated on piloting the early stages through committee while Fowler and Newton worked on the latter parts in the department.[50] Major dealt with the Bill and with the interest groups with a skill and sensitivity that earned him plaudits from both sides of the House.[51] The Social Security Act was a portmanteau piece of legislation covering a wide variety of subjects. Much of it was not particularly partisan, although withdrawal of benefits from people aged sixteen and seventeen, and the Social Fund, which changed the way in which the poor met large one-off expenses, were highly controversial. Its provisions were introduced in stages until 1988.

Major's administrative abilities now developed alongside parliamentary and man-management skills. Fowler had a massive department to run – Health and Social Security were given separate secretaries of state in 1988 – and he left the running of the latter very much to Newton and Major. The two men were very similar, concerned about the deprived, non-doctrinaire, emollient and popular within the department, and conscientious to a fault in mastering the detail. When not engaged on the Bill, the bulk of Major's work was taking the lion's share of dealing with the 30,000 letters a year from MPs with social security enquiries on behalf of constituents,[52] many of which required individual answers. On one weekend, he was reputed to have taken home to Huntingdon thirteen ministerial red boxes, crammed with letters. He began work early on Saturday morning and did not finish until late on Sunday evening.[53] Newton was also heavily engaged in answering letters, but could be less decisive than Major at cutting through them: he could agonise over individual cases and found some of the decisions very hard.[54] Major was also thought by officials to have the more acute political mind: 'He was very shrewd. He knew how to get things through the House or past Fowler, including some of the more cynical ploys like putting in for more than he knew he would get. He was very sharp at all that.'[55]

On the intricacies of social security policy, however, Major was no match for Newton. Major relied on his civil servants to give him the answers, knowing how to use their expertise. When taking decisions on technical matters, he would ask half a dozen people their views, and choose the one he thought the best without necessarily having a preconceived viewpoint of his own.[56] With difficult decisions he was wont to take a piece of paper, draw a line down the middle and list the pros and cons.[57] Officials warmed to this rather unusual man in their midst, who brought an obvious dedication to the work, and who clearly knew first hand, without mawkishness, some of the personal predicaments in which claimants found themselves.[58] Major reciprocated their positive feelings. Not since his chairmanship of Lambeth Housing, fifteen years before, had he had a group of officials working for him. He enjoyed playing the part, giving his private office presents, inviting them for drinks, and treating them as equals.[59]

His competence began to make an impact on Mrs Thatcher. Jack Jones, the General Secretary of the Transport and General Workers Union (1969–78), and President of the Retired Members Association since 1979, came to Number Ten for an annual visit. Traditionally, he used it as a platform to publicise the iniquities of the government's pensions policy. Thatcher liked to have a junior minister with her. Major duly arrived, and transformed the meeting by showing, in a pleasant, unaggressive manner, that pensioners in history had never been as well off as they were now.[60]

The thaw came at the right moment. To progress beyond junior minister, the support of the Prime Minister was the *sine qua non*. Fowler wanted to move Barney Hayhoe, Minister of State for Health, and switch Newton across to take his place, leaving a vacancy as Minister of State at Social Security. Fowler called Major into his office to pick his brains on Newton's successor. From their conversation it 'became clear that he himself thought he would be the right person to do the job'. Fowler agreed but as Major had only a year's departmental experience, he thought he should consult Wakeham, still Chief Whip. The latter was initially concerned at the speed of Major's rise – 'was his ambition overreaching itself?' – but after discussion they decided to put the recommendation forward to Mrs Thatcher, who accepted their judgement.[61] Major was lucky to be moved up to Minister of State level so quickly. 'He was I think pretty fortunate to make that jump at the time that he did,' recalled Fowler, 'but the cards went his way.'[62]

Minister of State 1986–7

The September 1986 reshuffle was billed as a 'big reshuffle in Thatcher's middle ranks', involving seven dismissals and thirty-three other changes, all below Cabinet rank. Strengthening the Department of Health and Social Security to counteract Labour's attacks was seen as a key part of her strategy. Prominence in press coverage was, however, not given to Major, but to Newton, seen as a high-flier, as well as to Edwina Currie, promoted to Parliamentary Secretary on the health side, whose picture adorned the front page of *The Times*.[63] Peter Riddell in the *Financial Times* described Major's promotion as a reward for his hard work, and to his success in handling the social security legislation.[64]

Aged forty-three, Major had his first big command. With Fowler absorbed increasingly with policy on AIDS, in effect he left Major – as he had with Newton before him – to run the social security department on his own. The main part of the work that interested Fowler was pensions.[65]

Major's stewardship began well. At the annual Party Conference in Bourne-mouth he gave his first major platform speech on 8 October, in what was thought would be the last autumn before a general election. He seized on Labour's plan, announced at its own conference at Blackpool, to increase social security benefits. Calculations made at the department suggested that Labour had seriously underestimated the cost to taxpayers, and if the costs were met by increased borrowing, Major pointed out it would prove seriously inflationary. He poured scorn on Michael Meacher, Labour's Shadow health minister, who 'travelled the country like a peripatetic Santa Claus littering uncosted promises with every speech'. Meacher had made 'unachievable, cynical, bogus and dishonest promises'. Major then turned to defend the government's record on social security spending. 'How dare they say we don't care for these people?' His rebuttal of Labour's charges of indifference were met with sustained applause. The speech was a personal triumph for Major, and gave his confidence a further huge boost.[66]

Meacher's blood was now up. Winding up the second day of the debate on the 1986 Queen's Speech, he said there had been a deafening silence in the government's programme for the coming year about the reappearance of mass poverty. 'We are seeing the re-emergence of an underclass of the dispossessed on a horrifying scale', with a 10 per cent increase in poverty since 1983. 'What is worse is that the government has humiliated and degraded poor people by laying waste the whole of the environment of the social security system.' This was the first sustained attack on a policy for which Major was responsible, and over one, relief of poverty, on which he was particularly proud of his record. The next month, Major was attacked by his own side, as well as by Labour, when he announced plans to limit the amount of supplementary benefit paid for mortgage interest during the early months of unemployment. A backbench revolt threatened, only to fizzle out.[67]

These assaults, however, failed to school him adequately for the 'cold weather' payment row in January 1987. Yet again he was caught in the uncomfortable position where his instincts led him in the direction of being generous with the state's money, but the ethos of the era, and Mrs Thatcher's own predilections, dictated financial stringency. The latest episode was sparked by an article in the *Sunday Times*[68] which accused Major of cutting to 'virtually nothing' the level of government help for the old and cold. 'Investigations by the *Sunday Times* reveal that ministers have devised a scheme which will ensure that special cold weather payments are hardly ever made.' David Hobman, director of the pressure group Age Concern, commented, 'It is very cruel to make old people go through another winter without the confidence to keep themselves warm.'[69] The *Sunday Times* probe came hard on the heels of an acrimonious pre-Christmas period when Labour had pressed for an automatic £5 weekly cold weather payment, and Major had retorted, mocking Labour's record in office, labelling Neil Kinnock as 'the leader of the yobbo tendency'.[70]

The government was then caught out by an exceptional bout of cold weather in early January 1987. The department had worked out a policy over the summer of 1986 for cold weather payments that would be triggered if temperatures fell below a certain point, as measured by regional met-ereological posts.[71] Major met Mrs Thatcher at Number Ten and it was agreed that all those entitled to receive the benefit – one and a half million people – be given £5. Major had found it difficult at first persuading her to overrule the Treasury, who were against the payment.[72] A meeting with Mrs Thatcher and John MacGregor (Chief Secretary) took place in her study at Number Ten. Major recalls walking to her window, looking out over the snow and saying, 'It must be very cold in a two-up two-down at this moment, if you can't afford the heating.' His appeal registered firmly with her. 'When I said that, I knew John MacGregor had lost and he knew he had lost.'[73] Major announced the help in the House of Commons in mid-January, and the next day he told MPs that the government had agreed to underwrite the cost of additional shelters, blankets and hot food.

For some days Major had become the most hated man in Britain, receiving more media exposure than ever before, an experience he found acutely uncomfortable. His television appearances he found particularly unsettling, and he became sensitive about his five-o'clock shadow, taking care to shave at 4 o'clock before appearances. As with the graffiti at St Pancras in October 1974, he hated personal ridicule and attacks, and was anxious at all costs to try to avoid it.[74]

Back at the department, the chief worry among senior officials was that the extra spending Number Ten had authorised had broken regulations. 'Major and the department spent a very unhappy week. We had stepped right outside what we were enabled to do. If anyone had challenged him, we would have been exposed.'[75] The *Sunday Times* maintained its attack on Major, claiming he had agreed to the £5 payment only after he had been 'overruled' by Mrs Thatcher.[76] Matthew Parris offered to Major to 'put it about' that he had been in favour of more generous payments all along, but had been overruled by the Treasury. But Major was adamant that Parris was to do no such thing.[77] Further indignity came later in January when Major had to admit responsibility for a 'technical error' in the 1986 Social Security Act with regard to payment of death and maternity grants. Charles Kennedy, the youthful Liberal MP, said Major appeared to be suffering from 'Ridleyism' (based on the propensity of Nicholas Ridley, Environment Secretary, to make errors).[78]

Major's performance as Minister for the Disabled – another part of his job – attracted far less opprobrium. The main decision he had to take in this area was over the provision of artificial limbs, which had been disrupted by a long-running industrial dispute. Ian McColl (then Professor of Surgery at Guy's Hospital, and as Lord McColl, Major's PPS in the Lords from 1994 to 1997) had been commissioned to write a report on the service. Major delved into the detail of the issue, and implemented the report virtually in full.[79] He enjoyed this aspect of the work, developed productive relations with the various disability interest groups, and took pains to go out and visit them, which is *de rigueur* for the minister with this portfolio, although shirked by some. Generally he found himself very much at ease in this environment, as he had done with the travelling Housing Advisory Centre in Lambeth.

His time as Minister of State was, as he admits, 'a very sharp learning curve'.[80] For the first time in his political life he had taken hard knocks, been accused of incompetence and indifference, and suffered personal ridicule. It toughened him. In the department he became more decisive; 'he would know what he wanted from a meeting: he didn't muck about.'[81] In Parliament he had become a more aggressive, partisan debater, rejoicing in speaking roughly of Labour opponents such as Meacher, Margaret Beckett (a Labour social security spokesman) and David Winnick. Memorable phrases about his opponents – such as his depiction of one Labour backbencher as 'prattling like a constipated parrot'[82] – became a trademark. He took the House very seriously, would demand intensive briefing and facts, 'wanted the House to see that he had mastered the brief and how confident he was with it'.[83] Despite his occasionally barbed tongue, keeping in with Labour was another trademark. After debates he would frequently be found in the Strangers' Bar – unusual for a Conservative minister – and would chat happily with Labour opponents.[84] Politically, his tone sharpened. He made tough noises about scroungers and others who abused the social security system,[85] while also being determined that where people genuinely needed help, they would receive it.[86] He took particular pride in his part in setting up the Social Fund, to help those who fell through the safety net.[87]

To Fowler, Major 'thought similarly to Ken Clarke and myself. Yes, he had a social conscience, didn't want to be in a party driven purely by market forces . . . even more than Ken or myself, who were not public school products, he actually had experience of the social security system. He felt some issues in a very personal way.'[88] Major achieved the delicate balance for a social security minister, a deep grasp of detail with sensitivity.

Successful ministers of state would normally expect to be in office for two or more years before promotion to Cabinet. Committed though he was to the department's work, he also saw it as a means to further promotion. The authority he had developed as minister of state, especially at the Dispatch Box, made him realise he could really do well. He worked assiduously on his ministerial boxes, battled to avoid further mistakes, improve competence, and build friendships, waiting for the next step. It was not long in coming.

Onto Centre Stage: 1987

No one can know for certain when Mrs Thatcher's attitude to Major started to change. Their disagreement at the whips' dinner was soon forgotten, and may even have done him some good. She liked people who stood up to her, especially when it was her personality that prevailed. Major continued to nurse reservations about her, as when he told colleagues he was 'appalled' by how she conducted a Cabinet committee on which he sat. But during the course of 1986 she began to regard him highly. He had several qualities to commend him. Numeracy at budgets and his realisation that costs mattered and must be weighed, were virtues she admired in subordinates. She liked people who mastered their brief crisply, and were successful in what they wanted. But above all she came to like him because he was not a minister crudely jockeying for position or a personal profile, which she found repellent.

She never probed his political leanings, and assumed he was 'one of us', hence her later anger at the feeling that she had been betrayed by him. She clearly thought that, if he did have wet tendencies early on, he had grown out of them at Health and Social Security. She saw a man who was plainly unsentimental and not given to impassioned speeches about hardship, and convinced herself he was on the centre right of the Party. According to Matthew Parris: 'You had only to talk to Major for five or ten minutes to realise how much he cared about the quality of public services, and the importance of the safety net for those who cannot pay. I doubt whether she ever did talk to him in that way, or had any real idea about that side of his beliefs.'[89]

Bernard Ingham (Number Ten Press Secretary 1979–90) believes that she began to talk about him as a man of 'exceptional talent' soon after his move to Social Security, and was tickled by the symmetry with her own ministerial career beginning in the same job (1961–4).[90] Charles Powell, the Private Secretary who became her other closest confidant in her last years at Number Ten, agrees that she first began to speak well of him at this time: 'She clearly identified him as one of the abler members of the government. She saw him as somebody who had come up not from the traditional social roots of the party.'[91]

In the months leading up to the June 1987 general election Major was talked about as the coming man. The Party's leadership gave him more exposure during the general election than was usual for a minister of state. One of a panel for several early morning television press conferences from Conservative Central Office, he came over as confident and presentable, though never taking the initiative. He was also swept up into the exercise forced by Lawson and Fowler on Central Office of costing Labour's manifesto pledges, especially on social security and tax.[92] He had already been entrusted with a special brief on DHSS presentation by Fowler, and impressed both Lawson and Fowler with his calmness and detailed knowledge.[93]

This extra election work in London caused him considerable anxiety. Determined not to let up – or be seen to be easing up – in the constituency, he would often have only four or five hours' sleep during the campaign. He worked fanatically in Huntingdon, but was torn by the new level of commitment in London, such as on 'Wobbly Thursday', when he was at Central Office in the midst of a very tense day.[94] Travelling around the constituency soon revived him after stressful moments, as did the assurances he was receiving from his Party workers about likely voting. Polling day fell on 11 June, and the showing in Huntingdon was his strongest so far.

Major (Con)	40,530	63.6%
Nicholson (SDP/AU)	13,486	21.1%
Brown (Lab)	8,883	
Lavin (Green)	874	

During the campaign, speculation had arisen about the post he might be offered after the election. Major told Nicholas Lyell, his colleague at Social Security, that he hoped he would become Chief Whip.[95] Major had made his own soundings, and saw that Wakeham would almost certainly move on. 'I'd have liked the job of Chief Whip', he said later, adding, without side, 'I'd like to think that if I had been appointed, Mrs Thatcher would not have lost in 1990.'[96] But when the summons came to Downing Street on the morning of 13 June 1987, she had another job in mind.

SEVEN

Chief Secretary:

1987–9

MAJOR'S APPOINTMENT AS Chief Secretary made him the first of the 1979 intake to enter Cabinet, ahead of Chris Patten, John Patten, William Waldegrave and the others who had earlier gained promotion ahead of him. Ahead, too, of Norman Lamont, MP since 1972 and Financial Secretary to the Treasury since 1986, who had been eager for the job, and was destined in later years to fall out badly with Major.[1] The press billed Major as a cost-cutter, an image which bore an inexact relationship to his actual record as Minister of State for Social Security. 'High flyer of benefit cuts lands at the Treasury,'[2] said the *Guardian*, while a *Daily Telegraph* editorial commented, 'We applaud Mr Major's promotion and the signal it gives of the determination to press on with shrewd and successful economic policies.'[3] His stealthy rise from obscurity in 1983 was widely seen now as 'meteoric'. One further appointment received widespread attention. John Moore moved from Transport to the more senior Cabinet post of Secretary of State for Health and Social Security, and was widely seen as Mrs Thatcher's favoured successor. Within two years, Major had claimed that mantle, and Moore was nowhere.[4]

Early Months: 1987

Major was thrilled to be given the post and, by the privy councillorship that came with it, a status he particularly cherished. Norma claims, 'He always said that being made a privy councillor was the only title that was really worth having.'[5]

His Chief Secretary selection had been the subject of heated argument. Mrs Thatcher had held discussions with Whitelaw and Lawson about who should succeed John MacGregor, destined for promotion to his own department. Lawson, as early as February 1987, had made a note that Wakeham was his first choice, and Major his second, to fill the slot. But when the former told Lawson he hoped for a bigger Cabinet job, Major went to top of the list. Wakeham also wanted a job that required little travel, as he was still suffering from the IRA's Grand Hotel bomb attack at the Conservatives' 1984 Brighton Party Conference that had killed his wife.[6] Mrs Thatcher, however, favoured Major for Chief Whip, and promoting Lamont to Chief Secretary.[7] Lawson held out for Major against her. Whitelaw, who initially favoured her choice, then swung behind Lawson, who duly acquired the Chief Secretary he wanted.[8] Lawson, who had resented the way that in 1983 Peter Rees had been foisted on him as Chief Secretary, was determined this time to get his own way.[9] Major had impressed him, not least by his performance as Treasury Whip in 1984–5, and he thought he had shown at Social Security the right blend of mastery of detail with a pleasant yet determined manner that one needed as Chief Secretary.[10]

The Conservatives fought an uncertain election campaign in 1987, and the reshuffle was similarly fraught. The day after polling day, Friday 12 June, was dominated by Mrs Thatcher trying, unsuccessfully, to persuade Norman Tebbit to remain in the government.[11] By the Saturday morning speculation on posts reached a climax. The waiting room at Number Ten filled up, with Norman Fowler, Ken Clarke, John Moore and John Major; it is normally considered bad form to have more than one minister waiting. Major nervously asked the policeman at the front door to see the list of who was due, which only heightened the tension among the group of aspirants.[12] Major's turn came. His meeting with Mrs Thatcher was brief and to the point. Norman Fowler chatted to Major as they left Downing Street together. 'His response was typical of him after promotions, which is neither smugness nor over-whelming delight, but a feeling of "This is good", mixed with, "Am I going to be able to manage it?" '[13] recalled his former boss.

Major's premonitions were well founded. Although the most junior Cabinet job, and one that did not involve him being in charge of a department, it nevertheless demanded a knowledge of economics and finance considerably beyond anything he possessed. 'No one told me he'd only been in marketing at Standard Chartered Bank,' Mrs Thatcher was apt to remark later.[14] Major certainly at times like this felt acutely aware of his lack of financial background. The job also demanded he take on and say 'no' to more senior Cabinet ministers, who in several cases had commanded important posts before he had even entered Parliament. Major went through a rocky inaugural period, and wished he had been made Chief Whip. He was in 'a very shaky emotional condition', Lawson later said: 'he had not been prepared for the workload and for the wide spread of knowledge needed.'[15]

Lawson began to wonder whether he had made the right choice of Chief Secretary, as Major 'would come and see me at Number 11, ashen-faced, to unburden himself of his worries and to seek my advice'.[16] Lawson would be no admirer of Major in the 1990s, and may well have been overstating his undoubted difficulties in coping. Major himself says he never sought out Lawson and believes Lawson's comments are merely *post hoc* judgement. The early months were nevertheless testing for Major. Said one observer: 'When he arrived, he had no idea how the country or the economy were run. Yet he was dealing with Thatcher and Lawson who knew everything there was to know.'[17] John Wakeham had a late-night drink with him after he had been in office a few weeks. 'The sheer volume of work was getting him down.'

To Norma, his first few months as Chief Secretary were, simply, 'hell'.[18] His self-doubt, his complex about his lack of education and his suspicion of the Treasury being filled by snooty Oxbridge graduates who knew little of ordinary life were, however, overcome by his discovering that he possessed skills which were no less useful and were in many ways superior to theirs. Some reticence, however, would remain to the end. Peter Middleton, Treasury Permanent Secretary, said of Major: 'I would put him at the top of the scale for someone who is privately nervous, but almost bottom of the scale for someone whose nervousness manifested itself in public.'[19] The apparent paradox of the assured exterior around an uncertain centre was thus becoming institutionalised.

Several factors helped him win through, including phenomenally hard work, at its peak from 6 a.m. until midnight. Fortuitously, Stan Hurn, his former bank colleague and landlord since 1984, who was a trained economist and director of a merchant bank, was on hand to answer those questions about how the economy and financial markets worked, including some which he would have felt uncomfortable asking Treasury officials. Hurn was amazed by how quickly Major assimilated facts: 'much faster than I had ever seen him do when he worked at the bank.'[20]

Major inherited a remarkably tenacious and able Private Secretary in Jill Rutter, who had already spent a year in the job.[21] Major had earlier formed a valuable relationship with his Private Secretary at Social Security, Colin Phillips, and enjoyed having a drink and discussing cricket with him.[22] Jill Rutter, another cricket lover, was the first of what became a succession of absolutely key and trusting working relationships Major was to have with his private secretaries. The fact that she was intellectually very self-assured, intrepid on the telephone, and an admirer, helped sustain him above all other factors in those first few months. Another piece of good fortune was the timing of his tenure as Chief Secretary. The economy was growing strongly, spending on social security lower, and tax receipts rising. Revenue from council house sales and privatisation was freely flowing and, with Treasury accounting rules, created extra room for spending. Moreover with an election just over, political demand for spending was comparatively manageable.[23]

Major took office shortly before a parliamentary recess. The summer stretched ahead of him and although much of it he spent working, he was able to have a family canal holiday with his Commons friend Robert Atkins. The barge's leisurely pace provided Major with a welcome respite from the fast currents of the previous two months, and an opportunity for good-humoured speculation about where his political career might lead.

Public Expenditure Round: 1987

The Treasury team Major joined was as strong as at any time during the Tories' eighteen years of office. Lawson, in his fifth year as Chancellor, was at his peak. By the autumn, Major proved every bit as deft and tenacious as Lawson hoped. 'They had complementary skills,' said Andrew Tyrie, one of Lawson's political advisers and a shrewd observer. 'Lawson was the brains behind the operation, and gave an air of rigour and intellectual coherence to the whole of government policy. Major had the personal qualities and the ability to fend people off in debate.'[24] Below them, Lamont as Financial Secretary was particularly effective at driving the Finance Bills through the House, and Peter Lilley, who joined the team as Economic Secretary at the same time as Major, rapidly showed his powerful intellect.

Major kept his attention firmly on his public spending task, the *raison d'être* of the Chief Secretary; unlike MacGregor before him he took little interest in wider political and economic issues.[25] By his last two years, 1987–9, Lawson had anyway become little interested in hearing the views of any of his subordinate ministers. Said one: 'Lawson never asked any of us about macroeconomic policy, and would steer ministers away from the subject.'[26] Policy was made by Lawson, with input primarily from Peter Middleton, Permanent Secretary, and Terry Burns, Chief Economic Adviser.[27] 'Lawson did talk to colleagues,' said one official, 'but his idea of consulting them was telling them what he thought or what he was going to do.'[28]

Discussions on the 1987 public expenditure round began in earnest shortly after the election was over. A headline in *The Times* greeted Major on his first day, Monday 15 June: 'Public spending round starts with £1bn election hangover.'[29] It pointed out that pre-election increases, such as on nurses' pay and the European Airbus, had meant that the plans for 1987–8 were well above the level set in the January 1987 White Paper, even taking into account an extra £5.5 billion boost in spending agreed in November 1986. Extra funding would also have to be found for a number of manifesto commitments such as urban development corporations.[30] Major knew that Mrs Thatcher approved his appointment because she thought him 'sound' on spending, and he had no illusions that she meant him to be tough.

In his first speech as Chief Secretary, given at the Royal Commonwealth Society in London on 22 June, he issued an express warning to certain ministers, in particular Health, Education, Environment and Wales, that they should not come to him with 'ingenious schemes' for more cash.[31] He returned to the theme in a speech in Huntingdon on 28 June, when he warned that 'we must not let the growing strength of the economy delude us into thinking that restraint of public expenditure is unnecessary'.[32] Privately, Treasury officials were predicting an acrimonious public spending round; Major's speeches were designed to repeat a clear message to spending ministers that the brakes were now on after the overly generous pre-election increases.[33] There would be no 'blank cheques'.[34] Toughness was also to the fore when, in early July, he refused Kenneth Baker, Education Secretary, the money to employ two hundred extra civil servants to prepare the new Education Bill for the autumn.[35]

Cabinet met on 23 July to consider Major's spending paper, which argued that bids received earlier in the month were far too high and had to be scaled down considerably in the coming weeks.[36] Cabinet reaffirmed the overall spending target for 1988–9 of £154.2 billion, and a statement was issued saying that the annual spending review would come as close as possible to that figure, while continuing to reduce public spending by a projected 1 per cent below the 41.75 per cent of gross domestic product figure projected for 1987–8. Baker and Nicholas Ridley (Environment), however, made it clear they thought their own allowances likely to be far too low.[37] Major swung round on Ridley in a speech on 28 July, arguing that the problems of inner cities could not be solved by throwing money at them – an interesting charge for him to level at the ultra-Thatcherite Ridley – but could be tackled only by direct action to encourage local initiative.[38] Reports suggested that initial departmental bids had come more than £6 billion above the target, with a significant part of the excess taken up with action aimed at the inner cities.[39]

In the few weeks since the election, Major had had to endure personal comments of a new kind. Talk of him being the son of a former trapeze artist became commonplace, often repeated, or interpreted, as a slight on his pedigree.[40] In fact, the trapeze story, even if misleading, was a clever line; talk of him being the son of a variety artist or gnome-maker could have been more damaging. Major's speaking style was next in the spotlight, as ridiculed by Craig Brown in *The Times*: 'Mr Major is grey and tall, but mainly grey ... his delivery is that of a doctor with indifferent news for a patient for whom he has no particular feelings ...'[41] In the same finance debate on which Brown commented, Major had to respond to a fierce assault by Bryan Gould for Labour, who accused the government of cynically increasing spending to win the election, only to bring in cutbacks afterwards.[42] The same accusation had been made in 1983, as it was to be again after the 1992 election.

Parliament went into recess on 24 July, as Major prepared himself for the long series of bilateral meetings with spending ministers to agree their claims. Major had announced in his June Huntingdon speech how he would proceed in his deliberations with spending ministers. He would ask them: was the spending necessary? If so, did it need to be carried out in the public sector? Had clear and consistent objectives for spending been set? And were performance targets demanding enough?[43] The approach often caught the spending minister off guard. 'The way we whittled away at their money was by suddenly asking questions, and the minister didn't know the answer to them, and in many cases his officials didn't know the answers either,' Major recalled. 'Once they retreated, you knew you were going to get your reductions.'[44] A key weapon in his armoury was to ensure that he was better briefed than the spending minister and his departmental team, using to good effect the expenditure divisions at the Treasury, presided over by a succession of powerful officials including Robin Butler, to crunch the numbers while he focused on the interpersonal side.

One particular technique was that 'he used always to try to send ministers out with something that they could show to their officials to demonstrate that they had done well out of the Treasury'. That at least was the view of Chris Patten, who found Major personally sympathetic to his department, Overseas Development.

He showed tremendous self-confidence. He knew the figures as well as anyone, and announced, 'Shall we get rid of the officials?', and we settled the whole thing on our own. While we were doing it, my finance officer turned to his Treasury official in the room outside, which had photographs of previous Chief Secretaries. 'Who was the best of them?' The Treasury official jabbed his finger at Major's room and said, 'He is, and much the nicest.'[45]

Not all ministers had such charitable views of Major's *modus operandi*. The difficult clashes in 1987 came from expected quarters, besides Education. Peter Walker at the Welsh Office fought Major hard, but Major knew he was on weak ground as Walker could always appeal to Mrs Thatcher, reminding her that he consented to become Welsh Secretary in June 1987 only on the understanding that she would give him backing to achieve his aims in Wales. If she would not back him, he would resign. Walker got his way, but also because the sums involved were not large.[46]

George Younger at Defence held out for higher spending, always a sensitive area for Conservatives, but Major brought his figures down in part by superior knowledge on the details of his budget.[47] He had some unpleasant exchanges with Nicholas Ridley, Environment Secretary, rare in 1987 as one who neither liked nor rated Major. Again, it was Major's will that prevailed for the most part. This caused him a flicker of anxiety later, when it was rumoured he would be reshuffled to Environment.[48]

No victory was so convincing as that against John Moore at Health and Social Security. Because both men were seen as favourites, their clash, embellished by Alan Clark's diary entry that Major was out 'to get' Moore, has become part of political folklore.[49] Major, it is asserted, deliberately set out to humiliate his rival in the 1987 round, and even more so in 1988. Such a deliberate attempt to damage a colleague would have been out of character: Major's political weakness was the exact opposite, the lack of the killer instinct.

Moore was certainly naïve in 1987 in having bid for too little money, believing perhaps that his parsimony would impress Mrs Thatcher, and his former Treasury boss, Lawson. 'John Moore really was destroyed by accepting a totally inadequate settlement because the Treasury reminded him where his duty lay, and he still thought as a treasury minister, not as a departmental minister,' said Cecil Parkinson.[50] Major also managed to persuade Moore to agree to freeze child benefit, which the Treasury had long wanted, and which saved a considerable sum, even allowing for the new Family Credit.[51] On the health side, officials were alarmed at another tight settlement after several years of restraint. 'There was a feeling around that it had to be addressed drastically in 1987, it was an opportunity to put things right or face the consequences. But there was no sense that it would precipitate the political trouble it did.'[52]

The summer deliberations in 1987 overall went well for Major. Much of the £6 billion excess bids were reclaimed, sometimes after 'bitter exchanges'.[53] By the end of the round, only three ministers had not settled; Lawson saw them himself and swiftly forced agreements.[54] In this way, the government for the first time in some years managed to avoid having recourse to the 'Star Chamber', the Cabinet committee convened each year to adjudicate on disputes and agree final totals, an achievement that particularly impressed Treasury officials.

Major's performance in his first spending round also made a definite mark on Thatcher, even if she was left with the impression that his views on public spending were more hard-line than they really were.[55] Parkinson confirms that 'it became increasingly obvious at this time that she was putting him in a rather special category, onto what you might call the fast track'.[56] Confirmation of his special status came when Whitelaw retired in January 1988. Major, along with Hurd and Parkinson, received some of the Whitelaw spoils. Major's share included a nebulous role in presentation of government policy and adjudicating in clashes between departments. Robin Oakley in *The Times* commented that 'ministers are particularly intrigued by the new role accorded to Mr Major'.[57]

Growing Pains: January–June 1988

The announcement of his new responsibilities was hailed as identifying Major – improbably – as the new 'white hope of the right', and as Mrs Thatcher's heir apparent.[58] The head-banging adjudicator job does not seem to have amounted to anything; nor was the presentation job ever clearly defined. Bernard Ingham says Major became his 'mentor' after Whitelaw's departure, and briefed him after each Cabinet meeting, so Ingham could then brief lobby journalists.[59] Ingham described their meetings thus:

Major called in to see me in my room in Number 10. He wandered in diffidently, put his head round and asked if it was okay to come in. He would stand up when my secretary came in with coffee. He took me through the Cabinet agenda, quite broad brush, he tended not to brief me on things he didn't think mattered and I sometimes had to pursue him on items ... I soon came to respect him as a minister who is very sharp politically.[60]

The experience was useful for Major, in giving him a wider understanding across the whole range of government policy, from a different perspective from that of the Treasury.

The 1987 autumn statement contained no surprises about future spending, re-emphasising the government's determination to hold public expenditure increases below increases in gross domestic product. After its publication, the focus in the Treasury shifted squarely onto the budget. Lawson invited Treasury ministers and senior officials to the customary 'away day' discussion in January 1988 at the ministerial country house at Chevening in Kent. Ministers and others were asked to offer comments on the economy and the fiscal position, a mere formality some said. Major raised mainly political points on how the budget might be received in the country. Delivered on 15 March, this key Lawson budget was chiefly notable for its deep cuts in income tax, as well as for the interruptions during Lawson's reading of the statement, which is traditionally unchallenged. Labour was incensed by what Lawson said, and argued that the top 1 per cent of the population gained more out of the budget in cash than the bottom 50 per cent.[61] Major, while moving the second reading of the Finance Bill, did not mince his words, and compared Labour to dinosaurs and economic Luddites in opposing the tax reforms and reductions.[62]

The budget distracted attention from the health crisis that had been brewing since early that year. Major adopted a higher profile as Moore was felt not to be handling it well, and achieved notice for the way he clashed with Gordon Brown.[63] The low health settlement in 1987–8 was blamed for working relations and conditions in the NHS beginning to deteriorate. Unrest broke out in early February 1988, with thousands of nurses and other health workers going on a 'day of action' over NHS pay and funding levels. As surgical operations were called off, a confrontation took place in central London as nurses and others filed into Whitehall. Labour threw its support behind the nurses' protest, with Michael Meacher and Harriet Harman joining picket lines. As keeper of the nation's purse strings, Major was square in the firing line. Though he promised that the pay review bodies would in future report earlier in the year, he told the House on 24 February that he could give no pledge that there would be any more money for health salaries.[64] On 16 March, however, came a change of heart, as Major hinted in the budget debate that the government would be generous to nurses out of the contingency reserve when the pay award was announced in April, as indeed occurred.[65]

A ministerial group, including Mrs Thatcher, Lawson, Major, Moore and Newton, had begun to meet concurrently in February to consider the long-term future of the NHS and its finance. The review led to much acrimony between Thatcher, who had a radical vision but was cautious on details, and Lawson, who pressed hard for specific cost-cutting and efficiency measures, a battle that continued into the 1990s in their memoirs.[66] Major's own role in the review was initially on costings, but he became increasingly involved in the detail.[67] Thatcher had a rare early doubt about Major, whom she suspected of toeing the Treasury line.[68] Out of the review's deliberations came a White Paper, *Working For Patients*,[69] and the National Health Service and Community Care Act of 1990, the biggest change since the 1946 Act, which gave hospitals the option of becoming autonomous trusts, and established the purchaser-provider split, and GP fundholding.

Mrs Thatcher became increasingly disenchanted with Moore during the first half of 1988, disappointed at his failure to promote government policy with more vigour and his indecision during the NHS review. She let it be known that his department would be split in two, and he would at best receive the less glamorous part, social security. Major was singled out as the key to her next reshuffle and the expectation grew that he would shortly gain his own department. The talk in the press in the summer of 1988 was that he had become, over the last few months, 'a powerful influence in the government' and, inaccurately, as a minister who 'frequently' argued with her at ministerial meetings.[70] Predictions of Major's promotion were also incorrect. On 25 July a minor reshuffle did indeed occur, relegating Moore to plain Social Security Minister, and promoting Ken Clarke to Health Secretary. Major remained as Chief Secretary. Few, however, expected it to be for more than one further year.

Public Expenditure Round: 1988

When Cabinet met on 14 July to consider Major's second, and final, paper on the public spending totals for the coming year, it agreed to keep as close as possible to the £167 billion total. With departmental bids in at £9 billion higher, Major knew he would be in for tough bargaining when his bilaterals with spending ministers commenced. Fortunately, since the public spending round proved more difficult, he had gained considerably in confidence and experience. Several settlements proved awkward. Douglas Hurd at the Home Office wanted – and achieved – money to build more prisons and improve conditions, as well as for police, and Kenneth Clarke, the new Health Secretary, was anxious to underpin the planned reforms to the structure of the NHS. Major ended up giving big increases to Health (£2 billion), and also to Paul Channon at Transport (£1.4 billion), partly for London Docklands, a pet enthusiasm of the Prime Minister.[71]

Defence again proved a tough challenge. The clear Treasury brief was to hold down the defence budget, yet Younger was anxious to press for the principle which he established in the 1986 round that if inflation again became significant, he would ask for more money. How big was 'significant'? Major argued that the scope for efficiency savings outweighed the pressure of inflation. The matter was still not resolved by the time of the Party Conference in mid-October, and the two ministers and their officials decanted to a quiet hotel to keep the meeting under wraps. Defence officials found Major 'calm, courteous, on top of his brief', and 'ultimately immovable'.[72] He did well enough in the argument for him to feel that he did not need to give any ground, and Younger judged it would be unproductive to refer the matter upwards to Mrs Thatcher. Major was assisted in his struggle with Younger by a tenacious Treasury official, Steve Robson, who would later turn up as a civil servant driving ahead privatisation in the 1990s. Robson was convinced in the late 1980s that British defence spending was too high and proved a formidable ally for Major.

Kenneth Baker came in hard with his education bid, but Major was a match for his bombastic style. Much of the education budget contained local authority current expenditure, agreed earlier in the year. The main items in the spending round were capital expenditure and student loans, where Major saw off Baker fairly easily.[73] Walker had not softened after the 1987 round; in 1988 his big project was the second crossing to the River Severn. Carys Evans, Major's Private Secretary from July 1988, was a Welsh speaker, who drafted a memo in Welsh which Major sent to the non-Welsh-reading Walker.[74] Their personal relationship was not close.

Social Security again proved a tough fight. Moore determined this time to be unyielding, above all on not allowing child benefit to be frozen for a second year. He feared his credibility would otherwise be demolished, especially as the press had billed the 1987 freeze as a defeat for him at the hands of the Treasury. Moore, or his supporters, unwisely leaked to the press that he would not allow a second freeze in 1988, and he told David Waddington, the Chief Whip, that he would be prepared to resign unless it was increased. A meeting at Number Ten was convened on 18 October 1988, with Mrs Thatcher, Moore, Major and Lawson.[75] According to Parkinson, 'The PM very skilfully said she thought Moore ought to go away and think about it more before saying anything further, because you can't threaten to resign to a prime minister to their face. If you threaten it, you have to go, so she didn't allow him to speak the words.'[76] The following day, a formula was found which allowed Moore to accept the freeze, coupled with a compensating increase in Family Credit, duly announced in the House on 27 October.[77]

Social Security was last to settle, but Ridley at the Department of the Environment had been the most acrimonious. The Community Charge – the 'poll tax' – of which he was no enthusiast, enters the Major story in 1988. Major's task with Ridley in the July local authority grant settlement was to achieve a result tight enough to exert 'downward pressure' on local government spending without transferring a huge burden on to the poll tax itself. Discussions went round in circles for some time. Major was all too aware of the leverage Ridley could exert through the argument about the damaging local impact of high poll tax levels.[78] Ridley was in favour of controlling public spending tightly, but in his own department, every item, whether housing or urban programme, always seemed to Major to have a good reason for requiring extra revenue. Ridley also wanted money from council house sales to come back into his own department, rather than go direct into the Treasury.[79] With no sign that Major could square him, it looked as if the matter would have to be settled in the Star Chamber.

Whitelaw's retirement, however, had created a gap in the chairmanship. Mrs Thatcher announced that Parkinson would take Whitelaw's place, a controversial choice considering his unpopularity in some quarters, which played a part in several ministers agreeing to settle bilaterally with Major rather than going to Star Chamber under Parkinson. Ridley in particular had no time for Parkinson, so consented to a bilateral meeting with Lawson to resolve outstanding items. Lawson was well briefed by Major, and settled, very much to the Treasury's favour.[80]

The Ridley–Major relationship had not mellowed over the previous year: Ridley's personal dislike of Major had deepened and he perceived him as untrustworthy and an intellectual lightweight.[81] Jealousy, and contempt for someone he saw as having little ideological depth, no doubt played their parts. Major's view of Ridley was equally unflattering. They were indeed polar opposites: Ridley an ideological politician, Major a process one. Major was sensitive to Ridley's *froideur*, which predated his own, and he came to dislike his aristocratic disdain. Ridley was the shaper of the mould into which Major was to deposit increasing numbers of 'enemies' in the coming years. Major experienced *Schadenfreude* as his career blossomed and Ridley's faded. Major was Chancellor, the job Ridley had always wanted, when Ridley was forced to resign after incautious anti-German remarks in a *Spectator* interview with Dominic Lawson, Nigel's son, in July 1990.

Early concerns about the overheated economy and inflation that were to dog Major's spell as Chancellor began to make their appearance. Lawson issued strong warnings about the need for restraint from those ministers who had still not settled.[82] To dampen concern, Major had to announce – on Lawson's instructions, he played little part in the decision – that there would be no autumn budget in 1988 to reduce demand stoked by his tax-cutting 1988 budget.[83]

The autumn statement, delivered on 1 November 1988, announced that due to the exertions of the previous three months, and extra receipts coming into the Treasury with the economy booming, the books balanced. Major in December identified efficiency savings of £2.3 billion as one of the main reasons which enabled him to keep within the Cabinet's expenditure objectives for the coming year.[84] Much time was spent in the weeks before Christmas explaining and defending the autumn statement, and examining special pleading for funds from the reserve. As the year ended, Robin Oakley named Major 'Tory politician of 1988' in *The Times*,[85] while the *Sunday Times* listed him as one of the 'winners' of 1988 (and Moore one of the 'losers').[86] The second year of his term as Chief Secretary was probably the happiest period of his ministerial career. Major, it seemed, could scarcely put a foot wrong.

Chief Secretary on a Roll: 1989

Major quietly enjoyed the knowledge that his star was in the ascendant, but he was anxious not to promote himself too ostentatiously. He was distinctly uncomfortable when BBC television's *On the Record* filmed a short profile of him,[87] and earlier he had turned down the offer to give the prestigious Conservative Political Centre annual speech in October 1988 at the Brighton Party Conference, renowned as 'a much-prized showcase for setting out one's political stall'.[88] Malcolm Rifkind, Scottish Secretary, delivered the talk instead.[89] Major later justified his refusal thus: 'I was aware it could be counter-productive. I preferred to get the job right first. I actively went out of my way to avoid making speeches that could be described as philosophical because I knew the construction that could be placed upon them.'[90]

His refusal was interpreted as evidence that, compared to many politicians, he was not overly ambitious. Others interpreted it rather as showing that he was very ambitious, but also very subtle about it: it would be much easier to win broad support if he did not commit himself to one wing or other of the Party. Perhaps more realistic is the argument that he did not accept the lecture because he realised it came too early, before he had worked out exactly where he did stand philosophically.

Major opened the February 1989 debate on the expenditure White Paper by claiming that, thanks to firm control of public spending over a number of years, Britain now had the strongest fiscal position of any nation in the world. John Smith, speaking for Labour in his first big debate since his heart attack in the autumn of 1988, argued that Major's attempt to make public spending fall as a percentage of GDP was wrong-headed, and neglected expenditure on infrastructure and the public sector.[91] The pre-budget meeting for the Treasury team in 1989 was held not at Chevening, as was customary, but at the ministerial country house at Dorneywood, where the Lawsons were living. Major and the other Treasury ministers arrived for a day's discussion on 7 January, but there is again little evidence of significant influence by any of them on Lawson's March budget.[92]

Some moments of high tension existed in his relations with Mrs Thatcher, notably over the privatisation of Short Brothers, the large aircraft manufacturing company in Northern Ireland. Government money needed to be put into the company before it could be sold off to the private sector. Major agreed figures with Tom King, Northern Ireland Secretary, but Mrs Thatcher thought his figures overly generous. Strong words were spoken at a meeting at Number Ten between the Prime Minister and Chief Secretary. She refused to back down, and neither would Major, as he was convinced that the figure reached with King was the lowest that could be achieved to make Short Brothers sellable. The meeting ended inconclusively. Major went back to the Treasury and talked about resigning, feeling that he would have lost all credibility with her if he had yielded; but the next day Mrs Thatcher backed down.[93] Major's victory meant a great deal to him: it reinforced his sense that Mrs Thatcher had real confidence in him.[94]

Her estimation of him grew, undimmed by the episode. She convinced herself increasingly that, even if he was not as solidly right-wing as Tebbit or Ridley, he was definitely on the centre-right of the party. As her suspicions of Howe continued to grow, and she became disillusioned with Lawson, she saw Major as the best of the younger generation.[95] Whitelaw confirmed that 'he was seen by 1989 as someone invited to her parties at Chequers. She talked to me about him as a future leader, about how highly she saw him. But she had no plans to go in the short term, and certainly not, as I had thought, in May 1989 after ten years . . . there was no successor . . . she certainly would not have had Geoffrey [Howe].'[96]

Ideologically, Major's underlying views saw little change. Lamont thought that Major as Chief Secretary was very affected by the needs of the dis-advantaged, reflecting his background and experiences, and that overall, 'He was a left-wing Conservative; his heart was with the Blue Chips.'[97] Lawson thought differently, believing that he 'never detected any political beliefs in Major in 1987–9. Beliefs were not important to him. Politics, not ideas, was his game.'[98] Major certainly showed himself to be a minister primarily concerned with tactics and achieving results, rather than pursuing a philo-sophical view about the kind of economy and society he wished to build. He showed as Chief Secretary that he was a technician, not a philosopher. That is not to say he lacked values, which remained those of a free-marketeer on economics who tended to the left on social issues.

Major was also concerned that government money should be well spent, which he articulated in perhaps his most important public statement as Chief Secretary, the first Audit Commission lecture on 21 June 1989. Major was invited because he had been instrumental in expanding the remit of the commission to the NHS. He decided to make performance standards and value for money in public services a personal theme.[99] In the lecture he came to praise the public service, 'an immensely valuable inheritance', not to bury it in further doses of privatisation. It was a most telling exposition of his views – highlighting his differences with Mrs Thatcher[100] – which later found expression in his Citizen's Charter. He had not yet worked out his vision for an ideal society, as had Lawson and Thatcher, but was beginning in a fairly inchoate way to advocate a Britain where public services worked efficiently, where there was opportunity free of snobbery, and which was compassionate without encouraging dependency.

Major played a good political game as Chief Secretary. The job rarely took him out of London, and with a flat in town he could spend time regularly each evening in the House, chatting to colleagues, building relationships, praising and writing notes. 'He excelled at the micro-politics: he was very good at noticing things,' said Francis Maude.[101] Major took pains not to cause offence and appear open to all shades of opinion. At a dinner of the right-wing No Turning Back Group in May 1989, he played the Eurosceptical card.[102] One colleague was given a spare copy by him of the telephone numbers of all Conservative MPs. 'I'd never have needed to carry such a list with me, but it was typical of the whip in him, carrying everyone's number so he could get in touch at any time with people.'[103] He worked his press contacts assiduously, not with the editors, whom he considered too grand for him, but with the 'working press' – political and economic editors, and the lobby, with whom he felt, then, at home.[104] Nigel Lawson said he 'never let up on his instinctive networking; he became a near-universally liked figure in the party'.[105]

Officials echoed the last opinion. At the Treasury he was appreciated because of his competence, diligence and ability to achieve results in a pleasant way. In the informal league tables the civil servants compiled, he was the best Chief Secretary since Leon Brittan (1981–3), possibly since Jack Diamond (1964–70). They liked the way he would go out of his way to invite comments from junior civil servants who worked on particular subjects. 'He was fun to work with' was a common view. 'He would run meetings informally, jackets off. Officials enjoyed that atmosphere.'[106] He was remembered for his friendly manner towards everyone in the office, chatting with the clerks and secretaries in a perfectly natural way.[107] In stark contrast to his often warm and positive relations with officials, his relations with Treasury ministers were distant: he never became close to Lawson, nor indeed to Lamont or Lilley.

Major had learned much since his appointment in June 1987. He impressed officials by being able to focus immediately on the important issues, and for his consummate skill as a negotiator. The Treasury saw Major as destined for his own department, and many saw him likely to go even higher. His job as Chief Secretary was, indeed, his most successful period in office, though he did not show himself to some on the right to be an ardent believer in 'sound finance'. If too much money was indeed spent in 1987–9, with insufficient money being pared off in the upswing, then it is a criticism that he shares with others, notably Lawson and Mrs Thatcher. Besides, the background of tax cuts and public sector debt repayment was not of the best for large cuts in public expenditure.

Political speculation mounted as the summer of 1989 arrived. Norman Tebbit had publicly tipped Major – a man from his social mould – as early as 1987 as a future leader of the party.[108] Patrick Cosgrave, one of Mrs Thatcher's early champions, and with good contacts in her camp, said in a profile in *The Times* in July 1989 that Major was her favoured choice as her successor.[109] Word had spread for some months previously that Moore would not survive the next reshuffle. The decks had suddenly cleared. The hottest speculation as July wore on was 'What promotion would Major be given?'

EIGHT

Foreign Secretary:

July–October 1989

MAJOR'S APPOINTMENT AS Foreign Secretary, aged forty-six, propelled him from the most junior office in Cabinet to one of the three most senior. 'Incredible, bizarre, astounding', was how the appointment struck Geoffrey Howe, whom he replaced. 'There was just a slight feeling that, this time, Margaret had overdone it,' thought Cecil Parkinson.[1] No Tory politician since Selwyn Lloyd in 1955 had been appointed Foreign Secretary with so little experience in Cabinet, and none this century came to the office with less background in foreign affairs. His appointment marked also the point when Major ceased to be everyone's friend – bar Nicholas Ridley's – and began to arouse jealousy from elements in the Conservative Party, and serious criticism in the press. The long honeymoon had come to an end.

Vacancy at the Foreign Office

Mrs Thatcher's relations with Geoffrey Howe had deteriorated steadily since before the 1987 general election. By the end, neither could tolerate the company of the other. 'Bad, bad', was how a well-placed official described their relationship by the summer of 1989.[2] The sourness was in part personal chemistry, but she also resented him being increasingly – as she saw it – the mouthpiece of the mistrusted and Europhile Foreign and Commonwealth Office. 'I think I only realised when I read her memoirs and saw her television series the extent of her contempt for the Foreign Office,' said Patrick Wright. 'I spent five years as Permanent Under-Secretary trying to reassure young entrants into the Diplomatic Service that they shouldn't believe everything they read. It was only in retirement that I discovered the situation was a good deal worse than I thought.'[3]

But whom could she appoint in Howe's place? Lawson was the next in the hierarchy. He was certainly avid for the job, which might explain some of his hardness on Major.[4] But 'she was suspicious, increasingly and sadly' of Lawson, according to Charles Powell. To Lawson, 'She had become paranoid about "plots" organised by Geoffrey and myself.'[5] Hurd, Home Secretary, and also very keen on the Foreign Secretary's job, was the obvious candidate. But she was resistant: as a younger man he had been in the Foreign Office and she thought him hopelessly imbued with its values and outlook.[6]

Major, on the other hand, appealed to her precisely because of his lack of exposure to the Foreign Office. He was untainted. She also believed the job the quickest way for him to receive public recognition.[7] Though she came to deny it later, she saw him at that time as a successor, she looked forward to getting to know him better on the long foreign journeys they would spend together, and she wanted to give him a chance.[8] Major had been tipped for a variety of posts as reshuffle fever mounted in the summer of 1989. '[He] is certain to be shifted sharply upwards,' said the *Sunday Times*. Transport, Northern Ireland, even Party Chairman were all aired, with Environment and Defence entering as late runners.[9] Exactly when she settled on Major for Foreign Secretary is uncertain, but Howe's and Lawson's threats of resignation on the eve of the Madrid European Council in June were a last straw. They pressured her to commit Britain to enter the ERM at a set date, which she refused but agreed to new 'conditions' for Britain joining. 'Something had happened to Geoffrey,' she wrote, 'his clarity of purpose and analysis had dimmed.'[10]

But first she had to rid herself of the turbulent incumbent. The FCO had expected Howe to be moved at some point, but there was surprise at the speed and brutality with which she did it.[11] It took a fraught day on Monday 24 July to prise him out. Summoned to Downing Street at 8.50 a.m., Howe was offered either Home Secretary (the one of the three most senior Cabinet jobs he had not held) or the leadership of the House of Commons. He received the news 'like a bolt from the blue'. He returned, dazed, to his office and discussed the matter with close colleagues, and considered resigning. That moment, however, had not yet come. He declined Home Secretary, but assented to Leader of the House as long as it included the title of Deputy Prime Minister. The reshuffle was going badly: it leaked out that she had offered Howe the job of Home Secretary, without her consulting the incumbent, Hurd.[12] In one swoop, she had antagonised her three most senior lieutenants, Howe, Lawson and now Hurd.

Major was biting his nails all day in his ministerial office at the Treasury, as were many other colleagues anxious for their summons to Number Ten. No one knew what exactly was going on, though Major had had wind before the weekend that he might be offered Foreign Secretary.[13] Norma had made it clear this was the one job she did not wish for him, because of the entertaining and travel.[14] On the Thursday evening before the reshuffle he was speaking in Tooting for his old mentor, Jean Lucas, and was uncharacteristically elliptical to her about the forthcoming changes. 'He knew he was moving, but wouldn't tell me where. He said things are a bit sensitive at the moment, and said, "I don't know if I am ready for it yet." '[15] It was not surprising Major was so jumpy. It was not until late afternoon that the summons came.[16]

The Prime Minister came straight to the point: 'I want you to go to the Foreign Office.' 'Do you think it is a good idea?' he responded. Might it not be interpreted as her wanting in the job her own person who wouldn't argue? 'She brushed all that aside,' he later said. 'Basically, when you are confronting a Prime Minister you either say, "I don't want the job, I am leaving the government," or you take the job. It isn't a negotiating system.'[17] He became Foreign Secretary. 'You had better hang on to your seatbelt,' she advised him, and as he was leaving told him to get ready for his first meeting with the President of the United Arab Emirates, which was imminent.[18]

According to his Treasury civil servants, he returned from Number Ten 'looking like someone who had been used to playing for the fourth team and was going to be on the field for the first team next Saturday'.[19] His first thoughts were how much less knowledgeable he would prove than Douglas Hurd.[20] 'He was in a state of shock,' said Carys Evans. 'It was terribly sad to see him go. People came over from the Foreign Office and took him away. He said "goodbye" to everyone and that was it.'[21]

Stephen Wall, Principal Private Secretary to the Foreign Secretary, and Andrew Burns, Head of the Foreign Office News Department, were the two deputed to collect him. 'When I arrived for him, he was celebrating his appointment. I was immediately struck by the informality of his relationship with his Private Office staff and other Treasury civil servants', recalls Wall. 'The ease with which he did business with people was part of my first impression. He immediately asked what he would say to the press. Being projected into the public arena was his first major concern at being appointed Foreign Secretary.'[22]

What exactly was in Mrs Thatcher's mind? Some, like Howe and Lawson, believe she did indeed want a poodle at the FCO, as Selwyn Lloyd was to Eden and later Macmillan. There is some truth in that, but equally she wanted an outsider of a sceptical background to bring the FCO more into line. Hella Pick caught the mood when she wrote in the *Guardian*: 'The world will be watching closely to see whether Mr Major becomes his own man, prepared to stand up for his views.'[23] Whether or not Mrs Thatcher's plan was to colonise the Foreign Office, she certainly intended him to remain *in situ* for three years,[24] then move him to become Chancellor of the Exchequer after the election.[25]

Major received several briefings from Howe. It was not easy for either man. Howe, bundled out of the job he loved, had further to endure unpleasant stories emanating from Number Ten, including the talking down of his new title of 'Deputy Prime Minister'.[26] He said that Major, who felt awkward about jumping into his shoes, 'conducted himself with great understanding and modesty'.[27] At the end of his first full day as Foreign Secretary, Major came back to his new office from a long meeting with Mrs Thatcher at Number Ten, pleased to be away from her. He loosened his tie. 'I'm back and I can take the lead and collar off,' he announced.[28]

Heavy Weather

Major took over the Foreign Office at a time when the world was on the cusp of momentous changes. In particular, the Soviet Union and its satellite regimes were collapsing, which was largely unforeseen and therefore all the more striking when it happened. Major had taken only passing interest in these great events when Chief Secretary. They were now his direct concern, as was formulating his line on a whole range of foreign subjects: European affairs, with the key inter-governmental conference at Maastricht only two years away; East-West relations, and a common Atlantic line on the emerging democracies, with key questions of nuclear weapons, aid, and Germany's future; the Middle East, especially on hostages with Terry Waite and John McCarthy still in captivity, and the question whether to reopen diplomatic relations with Iran and Syria; Southern Africa, and the sanctions debate in the run-up to the Commonwealth Conference in Kuala Lumpur in October; Hong Kong, especially the issue of the Vietnam boat people and the status of those in the colony who wanted to reside in Britain; finally South America, and restoration of relations with Argentina. It was a dizzy cocktail.

'I can't do this job as it should be done, it is impossible,' he lamented to Douglas Hurd. 'There's a world full of 150 countries, always exploding into bits and pieces, there are boxes full of stuff about places I've never heard of. And I am expected to take decisions about that!' Hurd later reflected: 'Now, most people in that position would have just placed a tick where a tick was required and gradually learned all about it. But he wasn't like that. He found it terribly depressing.'[29]

Major was painfully aware of his lack of background in foreign affairs. His initial reservations – he told confidants he would have preferred to stay at the Treasury[30] – were confirmed when the briefings, meetings and files started to pile up in earnest. Apart from his work at Standard Chartered Bank, which had an international dimension, and a limited amount of travel as a local councillor and MP, he had spent a decidedly insular career. He had been on the parliamentary trip to the Middle East in April 1982, but it was not until he became Chief Secretary that he again came across foreign policy issues, and then as only a minor aspect of his work. The Foreign Office budget had been fairly sacrosanct, but Major had nevertheless had several meetings with Howe, impressing FCO officials by his command of the issues and his good humour. Major had to back out of a weekend visit to the Foreign Secretary's official residence at Chevening. 'I'll forgive you for not going to Chevening if you give me what I want on the spending round,' Howe said. Major quipped, 'If you don't do what I want on the round, you may not have Chevening to go back to.'[31]

But once in the Foreign Office, the quipping ceased. 'I think he thought he was coming into a den of Etonian and Wykehamist scholars, all aristocrats and likely to look down on a boy from Brixton,'[32] recalled one mandarin. Said another, 'I think he was slightly on the lookout for offence, rather as one might expect a Labour Foreign Secretary to be.'[33] He soon lost many of his prejudices, in as far as he ever had them, but never felt as much at home socialising with diplomats as with the more socially mixed Treasury officials. Francis Maude, a junior Foreign Office minister, confirmed that a fear existed among certain officials that he would be 'Mrs Thatcher's man at the Foreign Office'.[34] His style they found disarming: 'Hello, I'm John Major,' he would say on first meeting an official (ministers do not introduce themselves to civil servants). In some respects, he was the most unusual Foreign Secretary since Ernest Bevin (1945–51), though his lack of international knowledge had more in common with Bevin's successor, Herbert Morrison (March–October 1951).

Officials' respect for Major increased rapidly, aided by the job he did for them in the September public expenditure round. 'As Chief Secretary he had written the Treasury's bottom line. Then he came to the FCO and he negotiated the Treasury right down to their bottom line. He was extremely popular in the office for that.'[35] Rodric Braithwaite (Ambassador to the Soviet Union, 1988–92) caught on a visit to London a vivid snapshot of the new Foreign Secretary. 'I came into the Private Secretary's Office and saw this thin, middle-aged figure, looking much like an elderly Under-Secretary, bent over the newspaper display. It turned out to be John Major. He certainly didn't fill a room with his charisma. But he was pleasant, intelligent, quick, easy to talk to.'[36]

Formal banquets Major found a great burden, not least because he abhorred ornate food. He didn't even own a dinner jacket, and got in a state when having to dress up to go to Buckingham Palace to pick up his seals of office.[37] Norma came to London for the occasion, but felt overawed. It was the most difficult time in their married life.[38] She was uncomfortable about the way that, for the first time, security intruded into their lives, turning their new home, The Finings at Great Stukeley, into a high-tech zone. Encounters with royalty were a part of the job he did not relish. 'Surely the Prince of Wales won't be interested in seeing the boy from Brixton,' he once joked to his senior officials. 'Actually, being the boy from Brixton will increase your attraction in the eyes of the Prince of Wales,' one replied.[39]

Rather ostentatiously, or so it was initially seen, he refused to work in the Foreign Secretary's study on the first floor looking out over Whitehall (at the opposite end of the building from the usual grand office, then undergoing extensive refurbishment). Instead, he worked at a large table in a conference room between it and the private secretaries' room, as if to show that he could live without the grandeur and scale of the FCO building (which quite dwarfs the rather homely and *petit* Number Ten).[40] Throughout his working life he favoured having a large table with his papers spread before him.

He would like to work with his officials from the Private Office. The team of three, led by Stephen Wall, worked loyally for him, but they found it a difficult transition. Major had worked long hours into the evening with his private secretaries at Social Security and the Treasury, eased because they did not have young families, unlike those at the Foreign Office. Under Howe, they had been used to arriving home between 9 and 11 in the evening, but in the first days with Major they were not getting back until midnight. They let it be known 'gently but firmly' that such timekeeping was not popular; ever-understanding, he readily acceded to their wishes.[41]

Major found having to deal with several issues at once, with insufficient time to brief himself to his satisfaction, difficult to manage, although the experience proved useful to him when he became Prime Minister, when this was a fact of his life. 'However hard we tried at first to spare him,' said Patrick Wright, Permanent Under-Secretary, 'he had come into a job which has on average something like twelve or fourteen overlapping diary items, all requiring a degree of briefing, and many requiring quick decisions.'[42] His initial attempts at dealing with one issue at a time broke down as a backlog of decisions accumulated, frustrating the FCO departments who were used to answers from Howe within twenty-four hours.[43] His desire, too, to have full briefing papers created much extra work, and had to be abandoned on the grounds of time. He hated, as always, not being briefed to his satisfaction before taking decisions. Further tensions arose because, in order to allow himself time to cover the paperwork, meetings with foreign dignitaries and others were cut back from the fourteen that Howe managed to just three or four a day.

His domestic living arrangements were another early cause of upheaval. His first thought had been that he would carry on living in his top-floor flat in Stockwell, rented from Stan Hurn, his old bank friend. It was smartly pointed out that this arrangement was problematic; 'living alone with another man, could give rise to rumours'. The Foreign Secretary has an official London residence, at 1 Carlton Gardens, but Major did not want to pressure the Howes to leave. So he fell back on living in the resident clerks' attic flat at the top of the Foreign Office, which alarmed officials, who saw the temptation for them to be drawn into late-night briefings now all the greater. A press story about the Foreign Secretary having to sleep in the attic because he had nowhere else to go could have been an even bigger scoop than 'Foreign Secretary lives in house with bachelor male friend', a fact missed by his Foreign Office minders.

Having the Foreign Secretary living over the shop created some unforeseen problems. 'Carlton Gardens was very useful for turfing out the Foreign Secretary into so we could get on top of our work and send over a box or two later to keep him quiet,' recalled one official.[44] Security officers would go off with Major for a takeaway, or be despatched to bring back supper – McDonald's was a favourite – so he could carry on working undisturbed. 'The detectives just loved him,' said one, 'because he would take them to places that served food they liked rather than having to ponce around outside some St James's club or other as for most ministers.'[45]

As in his time as Chief Secretary, his confidence began to grow within a few weeks, when it became clear to him that he could actually master some of the issues. His ministerial team, which included several also new to foreign affairs, like Francis Maude and Tim Sainsbury, were brought far more into decisions than had ever been the case under Howe, and this relieved him of some pressure. He decided to concentrate on Europe and delegate other matters to the junior ministers, such as William Waldegrave, who oversaw the Middle East. He was fortunate, too, in having Stephen Wall, a fiercely loyal and effective Principal Private Secretary, whom Major was delighted to be able to bring into Number Ten in March 1991 to succeed Charles Powell, the last of the Thatcher courtiers to survive into the new regime. Wall was both an intellectual and an operator: 'He made the trains run on time.'

Paris, Spanish Holiday, USA

On 30 July, less than a week into the job, Major was pitched into his first international conference, the twenty-nation peace conference on Cambodia in Paris. Top priority for the British government at the conference was a bilateral meeting Major was due to have with James Baker, US Secretary of State, on the Vietnamese boat people, an intractable Anglo–American disagreement.[46] The British concern was the influx of Vietnamese boat people into Hong Kong, which created severe problems of overcrowding in the colony's camps. Major argued trenchantly that 'it is neither humane nor practical to keep increasing numbers of people in the camps'.[47] The Bush administration, however, playing the human rights card, made it clear that they thought Britain was badly mishandling the issue, arguing that Britain's plans for forcible repatriation were utterly mistaken. Baker forcefully explained, backed up by charts his staff had prepared, that the US was doing much more to help the boat people than Britain.[48] The meeting failed to resolve the impasse, but Major did at least succeed in making a positive impression on the Americans with his quick grasp of the issues.[49] The negotiations were prickly, in part because Major suspected the Baker camp had leaked to the press a highly partisan briefing on the issue.[50] Relations with Baker were not easy. Major locked horns with him again in September over the European Broadcasting Directive, in discussions which struck an experienced official as 'pretty robust on both sides'. However, Baker came to respect and trust Major, and their relationship blossomed when Major became Prime Minister.[51]

In Paris, Major also had a forty-minute meeting on Hong Kong with Chinese Foreign Minister Qian Qichen, the first senior Western politician to meet a Chinese leader since the massacre of pro-democracy students in Tiananmen Square in Peking on 3–4 June, less than two months before. The meeting aroused adverse comment in London, above all over the offer of resumption of talks on the future of Hong Kong at the end of September. It was condemned in a leader in *The Times* as 'premature in the extreme. Six months, not two, would have been the minimum delay that would decently reflect the depth of anger and disappointment at the crushing of China's democracy movement.'[52] Neither Major's forthright condemnation of the killings, nor his call on China to give guarantees on the way of life in Hong Kong after 1997, were enough to soothe the newspaper. Major had neither the time nor the knowledge to change the direction of the juggernaut of British policy on China and Hong Kong[53], although he was instinctively hostile to China's suppression of the democracy movement, and was sympathetic to the position of the Dalai Lama.[54]

A few days' further work in London preceded a holiday in Spain. The Majors went to the home belonging to the Spanish wife of Tristan Garel-Jones, some hundred miles from Madrid. Garel-Jones was one of Major's closer friends at Westminster. The Majors were accompanied by Robert Atkins and his wife (the relationship cooled in the early 1990s and the Majors for the following three years went alone to Garel-Jones's house). A modern villa at the foot of the Gredos hills, it had seven bedrooms, a garden and a swimming pool. 'It's too f——ng hot for anyone in their right mind to use in August,' Garel-Jones had told Major earlier that summer in typical style, 'but if you want it, it's yours.'[55] He stayed with them for the first night, and then went off, leaving the Majors alone with the ebullient Atkinses, a huge number of files and telephones,[56] and strict instructions (duly ignored) to attend a bull fight. While the others relaxed under the hot sun, Major read through the background briefs he had asked to be prepared on the history of all the key international troublespots with which Britain was connected. 'I spent the whole of August cramming in a most astonishing way.'[57] Periodic calls would be made back to his Private Office in London, one being when he asked for clarification over the partition of Cyprus.[58]

In intermissions between working, he became particularly absorbed reading Alistair Horne's *Macmillan 1957–1986*, just published. What particularly caught his attention was Macmillan's views on development in South Africa. Major realised the thirtieth anniversary of Macmillan's 'Winds of Change' speech was to fall in February 1990, and he told Atkins that now he was Foreign Secretary he wanted to make a major speech to mark the occasion. He felt very strongly about South Africa, Atkins recalled, though he had no especial regard for the aristocratic Macmillan himself.[59] News of the *Marchioness* tragedy on the Thames, and a daily visit from the Spanish army, were the only disturbances to routine in what was a relaxing if busy break.[60] The rest of August he spent continuing reading at home in Great Stukeley.[61]

The first few days of September were spent mostly at the Foreign Office before travelling to the United States for the UN General Assembly. He had debated for some time whether to take Patrick Wright on the trip and had demurred lest by taking him he gave the impression that the mandarins did not trust him and were sending their senior figure to keep an eye on the Foreign Secretary.[62] Major overcame his doubts, and later described Wright as 'a gentleman in every way, who could not have been more helpful'.[63]

Major had not been to the US before. The party flew first to Washington, on 10 September, and stayed in the striking Lutyens house presided over by Antony Acland, well-connected Ambassador (1986–91) and later Provost of Eton College. They arrived late in the day, but Major insisted on going for a walk around the garden in the warm evening air with Acland, pumping him with questions about his visit the following day to see President Bush. 'When we go into the Oval Office, who starts the conversation going?' he asked, and other similar questions.[64] Top of the agenda was the need to align British and US positions on the Soviet Union in anticipation of simultaneous talks between Britain, the US and the USSR on 23 September.

The White House meeting with Bush was friendly enough, but the President appeared preoccupied. 'It never really took off,' recalled a British official. Some positive response, however, was generated by Major offering to help in the fight against the Colombian drugs cartel at a time when Bush's 'war on international drugs' was pivotal to his image in the first year of his presidency. The Hong Kong refugees also came up, Major stressing the difficulty of finding a humane home for the 56,000 boat people in the camps, the Americans stressing their opposition to compulsory repatriation.[65] A productive meeting with Vice-President Quayle was deemed more successful than a later meeting on Capitol Hill, 'almost embarrassingly poorly attended'. Lastly, Major faced a *Washington Post* working breakfast hosted by Kay Graham, impressing the top-flight journalists she had assembled, not least with his attractive manner.[66] Before leaving Washington for New York on 12 September, and despite him having shortly to make possibly the biggest speech of his life, Major asked Lady Acland if she could bring together the staff in the Ambassador's house so he could thank them all personally for their service during his stay.[67]

On the flight to New York he was captivated by seeing Manhattan for the first time from the air, yet, recalled one official, 'I was struck by him being extremely solicitous of the secretaries and clerks at the back of the plane: he is simply an extremely polite sort of man.'[68]

Again, he faced a press conference in New York, in which he was found clear-headed and personable, but short on detailed knowledge.[69] Mrs Thatcher was not pleased to hear reports of him saying in his speech that the government believed in a 'stronger, more united Western Europe' and that 'our active membership of the Community is a fixed point in our future'.[70] *The Times*, however, wrote approvingly, and interestingly, that: 'If Mr Major is signalling that he will devote more attention to creating useful alliances in Europe, he is heading in the right direction.' But it also observed that the enthusiasm in the speech for enhancing co-operation with Europe was 'well nigh' incompatible with the fears of a super-state expressed in Mrs Thatcher's Bruges speech of September 1988.[71] Perhaps, Mrs Thatcher thought, she was wrong to think that he would not 'go native' at the FCO.

It was not Europe, however, but what he said on the Falklands that worried Number Ten more. Major's comments on British sovereignty over the islands departed from the standard form of words, and merited a message from

Charles Powell from the Number Ten Private Office. Usually the reply to such rebukes was a Foreign Office-drafted *mea culpa*, but Major was in no mood to apologise for an utterance which he believed had not actually deviated from established policy; 'He was not going to be hectored by Charles.'[72]

Major's first trip, overall, had gone surprisingly well, and the absence of glaring mistakes added to his self-esteem. Peter Stothard, then *The Times*'s man in Washington, wrote that the trip 'has been a decent success', and that he had 'done his bit' well to talk up Anglo–American relations after an unhappy Bush visit to London in July.[73] Major was back in New York later in the month. His speech at the UN General Assembly on 22 September, entitled 'From Cold War to Global Warming' and drafted by the Foreign Office policy planning staff, was then reworked by his Private Office. Major added passages and slants, but the core, involving subjects he had not yet mastered, was not his.

While in New York, he attended an official dinner for representatives of 'The Quad' – the UK, the US, Germany and France. Raymond Seitz, one of the State Department team, was preoccupied with a sister who had been taken seriously ill. 'Major came to my seat at the end of the dinner, took my arm, said how sorry he was to hear about my sister. It was one of those very thoughtful things that are so easy to neglect in institutionalised diplomacy, but it was personal and genuine, and I was very touched by it.'[74] Major's personal touch was later to yield dividends several times over when Seitz became US Ambassador to Britain in the summer of 1991.

No End of History

Other policy areas saw some movement under Major as Foreign Secretary. Talks on Hong Kong's future were to be resumed in late September. Major took a strong line over the colony at the UN on 22 September, requesting China not to station troops there after 1997. On the question of passports, he was anxious to see the Hong Kong people being treated generously,[75] and took their part against the Home Office, though it was left to Hurd as Foreign Secretary to settle the passport question. On the Falklands Islands, Major met Domingo Cavallo on 27 September, the first time that British and Argentine Foreign Ministers had met since the Falklands War in 1982.[76] Mrs Thatcher remained distinctly uneasy that he would be too liberal on the issue of the islands' sovereignty.[77] Over Iraq, he agreed with Thatcher that Hawk training jets were not to be sold to Saddam Hussein.[78]

Major did not arrive at the Foreign Office with any preconceived, or even instinctive, positions on foreign policy, other than wishing to build good relations with Britain's allies. He employed a decision-taking method he had used at Social Security: pro and con columns on a sheet of paper, building up the arguments on either side.[79] It was not the approach of someone with a clear foreign policy agenda of his own. His passion was more engaged by the issue of management reform with which he had become very familiar as Chief Secretary. 'We had great plans for what we wanted to do: cutting out lots of the bureaucracy, cutting out the stuffiness. I was really beginning to feel I got to grips with it,' he later recalled.[80]

On Europe, he avoided committing himself to one side of the argument or another, in what was rapidly becoming a bitter area of division in the Party. He did not, as Foreign Secretary, form any clear view on entry to the ERM, but over his three months he did move in the direction – swallowing the FCO line, critics said – of being more positive about the European Union in general, and began to develop cordial relations with some of the leading European politicians, such as France's Roland Dumas and Germany's Hans-Dietrich Genscher. According to Francis Maude, 'while he did not have very strong pro-Europe views, we both thought that Mrs Thatcher was making the worst of our case on Europe: we thought that her oppositional line was losing us the argument.'[81] Major's New York speech on 12 September knowingly courted her disfavour by deliberately trying to build bridges with Europe, as did his Foreign Secretary's speech to the Conservative Party Conference in Blackpool on 12 October.[82] He reasserted the Tories' traditional claim to be the party of Europe, by drawing attention to what Britain had gained from membership, while opposing the later stages of the Delors plan for monetary union and the Social Charter. To Nicholas Wood of *The Times*, he made 'a determined attempt to heal Conservative wounds over Europe ... [he] delighted pro-marketeers by quietly abandoning the ferocious Bruges rhetoric of the Prime Minister a year ago'.[83]

One vignette from the Party Conference dispels any myth that his initial nerves as Foreign Secretary endured for long. On the evening after his crucial platform speech at Blackpool, he announced to his startled aides and detectives that what he wanted more than anything was some really good fish and chips. Enquiries were made about a suitable venue, and off he was whisked. One of his advisers recalled:

He was just as happy as a sandboy, far removed from all the gladhanding, the networking, the functions he was supposed to attend, sharing jolly light-hearted banter with friendly people, being laddish not in a smutty way, with his pint of bitter and his fish and chips. It was the happiest I ever saw him. I felt I saw more of the essence of the man than at any other time.[84]

Mrs Thatcher's anxieties, off-stage, were a leitmotif during Major's foreign secretaryship, her footsteps behind his back a constant presence. Once only did the occasional tap on his shoulder become something much stronger. The episode occurred, improbably, at the biannual Commonwealth Heads of Government meeting at Kuala Lumpur in October. 'She made him eat manure then,' said one observer.

Out of the Attic

The winds of change were at last blowing through South Africa, which was moving away from Apartheid, steered by President F. W. De Klerk. By October 1989 he had freed all ANC prisoners except Nelson Mandela, with Mrs Thatcher behind the scenes exerting pressure for change. The Foreign Office thought the white Commonwealth countries – Canada, New Zealand and Australia – were trying to curry favour with the black Commonwealth. For their part, they thought Britain, and above all Mrs Thatcher, was giving comfort to Apartheid in going out on a line and appearing reluctant to condemn the South African regime in public.

Major flew straight into this atmosphere on 18 October at the Kuala Lumpur meeting. He arrived exhausted after a twenty-hour flight in the old and uncomfortable RAF VC-10 that survived miraculously into the 1990s. He still disliked overseas travel, and his humour had not been improved by sharing the cabin with Mrs Thatcher. Privately he told one of his officials – and in contrast to one of the reasons for appointing him – that the experience he least relished was sharing a long flight with her.[85] Bleary-eyed on arrival, he spoke in public of the 'British' Commonwealth (very politically incorrect and revealing his lack of familiarity with foreign affairs: it had ceased to be called the *British* Commonwealth in 1946).[86] Despite his apprehensions, Major got on well with Mrs Thatcher; she took her young protégé under her wing, and invited him to lunch with Denis and Charles Powell each day. Major had not expected this level of intimacy. They appeared to be settling down warmly together, away from the tensions of domestic politics, holding their *tête-à-têtes* at Langkawi, the large retreat where the heads of government were staying.

The Commonwealth foreign ministers lived, and met, in less grand surroundings. Their most difficult discussions were over South Africa sanctions. A sixteen-hour meeting, that began on 20 October, dragged on into the night, with Major objecting to point after point, feeling that his opposite numbers were being too negative about progress in South Africa. Tempers became frayed over the communiqué and at about 3.30 in the morning Gareth Evans, the Australian Foreign Minister, exploded and said something on the lines of, 'For Jesus Christ's sake, this isn't the f——ing Koran.'[87] The exact language is lost in the official records; memories, understandably, are hazy.

By dawn they had agreed a text, which said at four or five points 'with one member [i.e. Britain] excepting'. Major felt pleased with the outcome: he had battled hard for Britain's position, which was to offer 'a bit of carrot as well as stick'.[88] As they were walking away, an aide said to Major of his sparring with Gareth Evans, 'Well, you've just had a lesson in the Les Patterson school of diplomacy.' When some journalists shortly after asked Major what he thought of the conversations, guilelessly he repeated the phrase about the comedian, which was duly reported in the *Melbourne Age*.[89] Unlike his initial difficulties with James Baker, Major's poor relationship with Evans was never mended. He thought Evans was a bully who had tried to set him up, while Evans found Major tetchy and negative. When Major was Prime Minister and Evans was passing through London and asked to see him, Major refused.[90]

Major went to bed happy with the outcome in which he had prevailed in persuading the Commonwealth not to increase sanctions on South Africa. Mrs Thatcher at Langkawi, however, was far from happy with the Foreign Secretary's deliberations. According to Charles Powell:

She was increasingly fed up with the Commonwealth on South Africa and had been arguing for some time that there is no point in going with the mealy-mouthed communiqués with separate paragraphs representing the British view. Why the hell don't we just say what the British view is? So I was sat down in my bedroom to draft a separate communiqué.[91]

The evidence differs at this point. Powell, confirmed by Thatcher and Ingham, swears that he read the communiqué over the phone to Major, who proposed one or two changes 'of a fairly minor sort' which Powell then included.[92] But according to Foreign Office officials, Major was 'flabbergasted', 'absolutely gobsmacked' when he heard about the redrafting.[93] Now either Powell remembers incorrectly that he consulted Major or, more likely, Major felt bounced by the news of the redrafting and did not have time to think through the implications on how it would be read by Commonwealth partners or the British press.

For implications there were in plenty. Britain's Commonwealth partners were shocked both by what the Thatcher–Powell redraft said, and even more so because the British had resorted to issuing a separate communiqué, which appeared to undermine and undercut what the foreign ministers, including Major, had agreed.[94] Bob Hawke, Prime Minister of Australia, and Brian Mulroney, Prime Minister of Canada, were outspoken at her action, both in public and in private to her at Langkawi.[95] The whole incident was seized on with glee by the diplomatic correspondents who were attending the conference.[96] Major presented the British achievement at the foreign ministers' meeting as a success, but the correspondents were much more interested in discord.[97] There were suspicions among British diplomats that some of the old guard 'journos' were out to make trouble for Major, whom they regarded as young and inexperienced, a 'whipper-snapper in a grey suit'; frankly, said one diplomat, 'they had an interest in shafting him.'[98]

Labour picked up on the stories, and harassed Major in the House of Commons when he returned on 25 October on his first appearance at the Dispatch Box as Foreign Secretary, with sniping at Question Time on his relations with Mrs Thatcher and Charles Powell.[99] Neil Kinnock declared that 'Mrs Thatcher is double-dealing the Commonwealth and double-dealing her own Foreign Secretary'.[100]

Considerable strides had been made under Major to improve Number Ten–Foreign Office relations from the nadir they had sunk to in Howe's last two years (1987–9). Powell in particular had had contempt for Howe. Powell's own influence on foreign policy had been viewed with growing alarm by FCO diplomats, as his influence over Mrs Thatcher in general had by some in Number Ten. The atmosphere was seething in 'a ghastly network of small betrayals and big shortages of trust which frothed around Margaret and Charles and their relationship with the Foreign Office individually and institutionally', according to Chris Patten.[101]

Major had been appointed in part to re-establish Number Ten's faith in the advice they were getting from the Foreign Office. In the early days he intervened to improve trust. For example, he instructed Stephen Wall when sending letters to Charles Powell to include the pros and cons of why the FCO was taking a certain line, to prevent Number Ten thinking they were being hoodwinked.[102] Major went out of his way to befriend Powell. In such ways, relations began to recover. Some of the senior mandarins welcomed Major's arrival, as it gave the opportunity for a new and more constructive era with Number Ten.[103]

He also had to prove to the Foreign Office that he was going to be neither hatchet man nor Mrs Thatcher's poodle. He soon made it clear he would be neither. An early meeting with David Hannay, Permanent Representative to the European Community, about Britain and Europe convinced him: 'I came out of that meeting feeling that if Mrs Thatcher had appointed him in order to get somebody to do a hatchet job on the European Community, she had made a mistake.'[104] The rumours had irritated Major considerably. On several occasions he snapped that he 'was damned if he was going to be presented as Mrs Thatcher's lackey'.[105]

Any differences were soon overtaken by events. The day after Mrs Thatcher returned from Kuala Lumpur, a crisis blew up that swamped the difficulties over the communiqué. Major called a surprised Stephen Wall into his room and told him, 'By six-thirty, you may have a new Foreign Secretary.' The bombshell was that Nigel Lawson has resigned as Chancellor of the Exchequer. Mrs Thatcher, worn out by her long journey and buffeted by the news, had called Major in to see her. She sat next to him on the sofa and as Major took her hands in his a tear came to her eye.[106] After just ninety-four days, his tenure as Foreign Secretary was about to come to an end.

NINE

Chancellor of the Exchequer:

1989–90

FROM EARLY IN his political career, Major had set his ambitions on becoming Chancellor, the culmination of his political career. Once achieved, however, he found the experience as satisfying, but the duration certainly shorter, than he had ever imagined. He was never as much at ease with the Chancellor's economic management job as he had been with the Chief Secretary's public expenditure work. Neither had he developed an intellectual analysis of the working of the economy or how he wanted to manage it. Major, above all, was a political minister, and the scope for being a political Chancellor was much less than for being a political Chief Secretary. He was also uncomfortable, more than he needed to be, at following the completely intellectual Chancellor, Nigel Lawson.

Rude Awakening

Lawson and Mrs Thatcher had been drifting apart for nearly two years, with disagreements over her increasingly dictatorial style and exchange rates to the fore. For Lawson, a particular thorn was the presence in Number Ten of Professor Alan Walters, who had returned to Thatcher's service as economic adviser in May 1989. Thatcher increasingly began to lose trust in Lawson's, and the Treasury's, advice as the summer of 1989 progressed, with Lawson feeling that he was being systematically undermined. The final straw came when extracts from an article Walters had written in the US were reprinted in the *Financial Times*, arguing strongly against Britain joining the ERM. Lawson later described the article as 'the tip of a singularly ill-concealed iceberg of dispute'.[1] He saw Thatcher the day after her return from the Kuala Lumpur trip on Thursday 26 October to talk about her economic adviser. His presence, Lawson said, was damaging the economy: the markets did not know whose voice to listen to, and the Opposition was happily exploiting the confusion. Either Walters was to go by Christmas, or he, Lawson, would resign. She would not let Walters go. Twice more she saw Lawson that day to persuade him to stay on. Within the Treasury, Lamont was also trying to persuade Lawson that the ERM was not worth a resignation; all efforts failed and his resignation was announced that evening.[2]

It was after Thatcher's statement on Kuala Lumpur that afternoon at about 4.30 p.m. that she called Major to her room in the House, and asked him to become Chancellor. Before finally accepting Lawson's resignation, she had to be confident that she could fill the slot with someone more acceptable to her. She had admired his Chief Secretary's performance; he had not done anything too wrong in her eyes as Foreign Secretary, and she felt he would be dependable and loyal at the Treasury.[3]

The knock-on of the foreign secretaryship vacancy, if she appointed Major, had also to be faced. Her first choice would have been George Younger, but he had left the government as Defence Secretary in the July 1989 reshuffle to become chairman designate of the Bank of Scotland. An appeal was made to try to win him back, to no avail.[4] She toyed with the idea of appointing Tom King, but she had no support for his candidacy.[5] That left Hurd. She had no doubts about his ministerial experience – he had been Home Secretary since September 1985 – or knowledge of foreign affairs, but she harboured the same anxieties about whether he was 'sound', above all on Europe, which was what had deterred her from appointing him earlier in the summer.[6] In the furore such doubts were swept aside, and to his surprise and pleasure Hurd found himself appointed Foreign Secretary.

By the end of the day her three most senior departmental ministers were all new: Major, Hurd, and David Waddington, a safe choice for Home Secretary. Ridley saw himself passed over for the chancellorship, and worse still saw himself beaten by Major. He felt dreadfully let down by his beloved Prime Minister.[7]

A story in circulation at the time ran that Thatcher, who had allegedly squared Major's availability in Kuala Lumpur, contrived the dispute.[8] This is unlikely, and Major himself denies any recollection of it.[9] Howe, who, despite their estrangement, knew Mrs Thatcher as well as anybody, believed that Lawson's ultimatum on 26 October came as a genuine surprise to her. 'I don't think she staged the crisis. She simply expected other people to fall in as she wished.'[10] Deep down, Thatcher was certainly becoming uneasy about perceived threats to her power, and was unwilling to share it with those whose judgements she no longer shared. She had begun to find Lawson an overmighty subject and was looking for a way out, and may well have thought of moving him after the next general election and putting Major in his place then. She, too, was shocked by the violence and speed with which events unfolded.

First priority for Major once *in situ* was to steady financial markets by offering, within minutes of arriving at the Treasury in the early evening of 26 October, reassurances that Lawson's policies would continue unaltered, above all the battle against the rising levels of inflation, and keeping interest rates high.[11] Major had arrived in the job at a time of acute tension, made worse by his having a series of speeches he was bound to deliver.

Major spent a late night celebrating with close Treasury aides, pleased to see him return, and woke very early on the Friday morning. He told officials he had been lying awake in bed since 5 a.m. Prime in his mind was the speech he was due to make that evening in his constituency. He had already worked out some phrases in his head, and decided to issue a press release, anxious to show that the ideas were his, not the Treasury's, still less Number Ten's. His officials were immediately struck by his resolve. 'I was enormously impressed by how he coped with the pressure and by his unflappability,' said one. 'The opposition were gunning for him from the start and would have loved to shoot him down. He was remarkably calm and methodical; "Let's do the first speech first," he said, "the rest of you work on the next speech and I'll come to it when I've tied up this one." '[12]

The first actual decision Major had to take concerned interest rates. Lawson had raised base rates, as a counter-inflationary measure, to 15 per cent on 5 October.[13] Major had to decide quickly whether the gyrations of the financial markets after Lawson's resignation were a temporary 'blip' or a signal of deeper problems. Major insisted on Thursday night, against the advice of some of his officials, that he would not put up base rates. Instead, he told the Bank of England to use currency reserves to stabilise the pound, while he turned up the rhetorical heat against inflation.[14] On Friday evening, after a full day at the Treasury which was not without some wobbles – first he was going to do a *World at One* radio interview, then he was not – he gave the speech at Huntingdon, in which he reiterated that the reduction and elimination of inflation was the government's central task, as well as maintaining a firm pound. This latter nostrum was considered important in view of speculation during the Friday that with 'Thatcher's man' now in charge of the Treasury, the commitment to a firm exchange rate would be lost.[15] Significantly, he emphasised the 'evil effect' of inflation on those on low incomes and without savings.[16] In the Huntingdon speech he also uttered (the words were his own), 'The harsh truth is that if the policy isn't hurting it isn't working', and warned that 'there is a difficult period ahead'.[17]

The Conservative press greeted Major's arrival positively. Several papers spoke of relief that the ambiguity of who was running economic policy – Walters or Lawson – was at an end,[18] because Walters resigned hours after Lawson. Labour tried to keep the issue alive: having castigated Major for being 'Mrs Thatcher's poodle' earlier in the week following the communiqué débâcle in Kuala Lumpur, they now argued that Major would continue as her poodle as Chancellor, all the more so for living next door to her at 11 Downing Street.[19] Ian Aitken caught the atmosphere when he wrote in the *Guardian* of Major as moving 'from foreign lap dog to economic poodle'.[20] His year at Number Eleven was to turn out differently. His star rose as Thatcher's waned, with power ebbing steadily from her to him.

The all-important question concerned whether Britain should enter the ERM, a widening fault-line in the Party. The issue was opened just two days after Major became Chancellor when, on Saturday 28 October, Howe gave a speech in Bath in which he stressed that the government must be seen to be acting in good faith in implementing its commitment, iterated at the

Madrid summit in June 1989, to enter the ERM. Thatcher – who later described the speech as calculated malice[21] – was, he thought, overstressing the obstacles to entry.[22] Over the weekend Major sought a middle way by endorsing Mrs Thatcher's conditions, but declaring unambiguously that the government's position thenceforth on ERM entry 'is not whether but when'.[23]

This commotion aside, the harbinger of the issue to dog not just his chancellorship but his premiership also, Major was delighted to be back in the Treasury. He returned to a department and people he knew, and away from the travel and unfamiliar problems of the Foreign Office. When his former Private Office took him out for dinner a few weeks after his move to the Treasury, they remarked on how relaxed he seemed, and how his humour flowed, unabated by the anxieties that had formerly dogged him.[24]

As at the Foreign Office, he also broke with convention by changing his principal workplace. Howe and Lawson spent much of their time working from Number Eleven. But from his first day, Major made his base the Chancellor's room in the Treasury, working from the vast, long table in the middle of the room. Major felt more comfortable at the Treasury; officials, spared regular walks back and forth to Downing Street, raised no objection.[25]

Initially popular with officials because of the credit he had earned as Chief Secretary, he did not capture the same high standing with all senior mandarins as Chancellor. Major had not changed; his job had. His skills in face-to-face negotiations, so central to the job of Chief Secretary, were not called on so often. In addition, he was dealing with some different officials; he visibly warmed when he came across those he had worked with as Chief Secretary. In place of Lawson's large meetings, where he would hold court over senior mandarins and Treasury ministers alike, flaunting his brilliance and technical command, Major preferred to work with smaller groups of officials, often wanting to call in even those quite junior who were doing the detailed work. Some felt not just intellectual bite, but also some coherence, was lost in the transition from Lawson. For the first sustained time in his official career, he became sensitive about his press coverage. He could snap and become irritable with those around him; he tended to take criticism personally, and was not always comfortable with people disagreeing with him. Critical comments were indeed made in private of his ability and manner in the Treasury. He sensed that he had lost some of the overwhelming approval and aura of success that had been his since he first became a minister in January 1983, and he did not like it.[26]

When he became more confident in the job, relationships with the senior mandarinate improved significantly; he was also doing what most wanted him to do, take Britain into the ERM. Major developed a wary respect for Peter Middleton, the Permanent Secretary, a grammar school non-Oxbridge product who shared a similar view of the world. Middleton also appeared to enjoy having a 'pupil' Chancellor after the magisterial Lawson, who left little room for anyone outside a very close circle to offer much. The other dominant figure in the Treasury was Terry Burns, Chief Economic Adviser (since

1980). Major warmed to Burns's unstuffy style. Major worked particularly closely also with Nigel Wicks, on overseas finance, and Michael Scholar on monetary policy.

As was Major's wont, he ran his Private Office in a relaxed and informal fashion. His Private Secretary was John Gieve, who was recognised in the Treasury as an exceptional Private Secretary to an indifferent Chief Secretary, Peter Rees (1983–5). Major had run into Gieve frequently during the 1987 spending round, and as Press Secretary in 1988–9. Gieve had worked at pushing Major's themes of standards in public services. He was appreciated as a professional and helpful presence, with whom Major established friendly relations; but he never became a personal friend as occurred with Jill Rutter and Stephen Wall or would with Alex Allan (1992–7).[27]

The official he warmed to most as Chancellor on a personal level was his Press Secretary, Gus O'Donnell, who ironically had shortly before turned down Gieve's job.[28] O'Donnell shared with Major a similar south London background, a love of cricket, and above all was loyal and capable, but did not make him feel threatened. O'Donnell's particular contribution was to translate economic jargon into English. As at the FCO, Major gave his ministers – Lamont (Chief Secretary), Lilley then Francis Maude (Financial Secretary), Richard Ryder then John Maples (Economic Secretary) – space and independence. He felt least easy with Lamont. Major disagreed strongly with some of his judgements on public expenditure. Lamont felt that Major was inclined to take an unrealistically optimistic view of the economy, and considered his dislike of open debate in his presence as a weak point in his management of the Treasury. Lamont felt he was not always being trusted.[29] Their relationship, which was never warm, reached a low point in September 1990, with Major becoming frustrated, though perhaps not 'paranoid', as Chaplin recorded in her diary, about their disagreements.[30]

Major told Lawson's political advisers on his first day that they could all stay on with him. Andrew Tyrie, a young Turk, peppered the Treasury with heterodox minutes. Judith Chaplin was another inherited adviser. She missed Lawson's intellect and decisiveness, but grew to like and sympathise with Major, despite being politically much to the right of him, and socially from a different class. He spent his first evening as Chancellor in her home, celebrating.[31] Although Major did not find great use for political advisers at the Treasury, he felt easy with Judith Chaplin and it was no surprise that she was one of the two figures he took with him from the Treasury immediately into Number Ten when he became Prime Minister – the other was O'Donnell.

The Budget: 1990

Major came to the office knowing little about macroeconomics, but he worked hard to make up the deficit, inviting officials into his room and quizzing them on their particular specialism. Like many Chancellors, he did not arrive having fixed views on the mechanics of economic policy, neither did he develop them. But he had clear goals, first to reduce inflation, and second to continue with the free market reforms on the supply side of the economy. Europe was never an area on which he held deep convictions, though he was concerned to take the heat out of the worsening argument within the Conservative Party and to try to restore peace with Thatcher. More than many chancellors, Peter Middleton thought, Major was concerned about the impact of economic policy on 'ordinary people'.[32] Major was responsible for introducing into the Treasury language such as 'the underclass' and 'social exclusion'.[33]

Early November was spent preparing for the autumn statement, which he delivered on 15 November. With eyes on a general election in 1991 or 1992, and with inflationary pressure continuing, he warned that '1990 may not be an easy year', predicting that the economy would grow by only 1.25 per cent in the year ahead, and that the line between that and falling into recession was perilously close. While emphasising that 'we do not forecast a recession' he warned that some slow-down in the growth of GDP was necessary to reduce inflation, then at around 7.5 per cent, down to a predicted 5.75 per cent by September 1990.[34]

The statement contained some of the gloomiest forecasts Tory MPs had heard since Howe's in the dark days of 1981 although the reality turned out to be even worse than the forecast.[35] But the pill was sugared by Major being more willing than Lawson to acknowledge that the trade gap was too big and should be cut, above all by substantial increases in public spending. He added £5.5 billion to total government spending for the following year, including £2.6 billion to Clarke for the NHS reforms, and substantial increases for transport and even for the arts. These increases led Simon Jenkins in the *Sunday Times* to declare that the 'autumn statement ... unquestionably marks the final triumph of the wets over the forces of Thatcherism ... The 1980s are clearly at an end.'[36] They were also to be picked on later by those who claimed that Major was soft on public spending.

Major's speech left John Smith, Shadow Chancellor, with little to attack; Major's skill at subtly pre-empting Opposition criticism, in contrast to Lawson's more confrontational style, was widely commented upon. True to form, it was as much a political speech as an economic one. Not only did it please his own party and stall Labour, but it also helped lay some ghosts: according to Robin Oakley he did enough 'to indicate that he is his own man, neither a Thatcher poodle nor a Lawson clone'. Major felt much relieved by the reception. That weekend was the first real time he took off since becoming Chancellor, not least to enjoy a family party celebrating his daughter Elizabeth's eighteenth birthday.[37]

Pressure for further action to combat inflation continued unabated. On 29 November Judith Chaplin recorded in her diary that officials were 'continuing pressure for a rise in interest rates'.[38] Major agonised about whether to increase rates above 15 per cent. Lamont added his weight to that of officials.[39] But on balance Major argued that the currency problems were short-term turbulence rather than a long-term slide, and that inflation would come down with patience.[40] Thatcher was a powerful force behind him, pressurising against interest rate increases.[41] Major, in fact, underestimated inflation in the autumn statement; the pound's fall in the remaining weeks of 1989 led to inflation steadily increasing.[42]

Little work had been put in by Lawson on the 1990 budget by the time he left.[43] Major could begin from scratch. The pre-budget weekend, which reverted in 1990 to Chevening, was held on 12–13 January. The meetings were split into two parts: discussion of economic background, to form views of the overall size of the budget, then discussion on the theme of the budget.[44] There was general agreement that the fiscal stance should be neutral. The officials present – Middleton, Burns, Wicks et al – however, thought that monetary policy was still too loose. This produced the most discussion, with Lamont and Major disagreeing about interest rates. Lamont still thought, as he had since 1988, they should go up again, or inflation would be intolerably high at the time of the general election. Treasury officials weighed in with gloomy forecasts and warned of nearly double-digit inflation.[45]

Thrift became a theme that united Major's own beliefs with macro-economic priorities. The Treasury had wanted to raise the savings ratio for years and tax schemes to achieve this were discussed every year after 1987. Two schemes were aired, later consolidated into one, to be called Tax Exempt Special Savings Accounts ('Tessas'). Major was keen to extend favourable tax treatment for savers down the income scale. Tax breaks already existed for equities (PEPs) and life assurance, and National Savings, but Major was surprised there were no tax breaks for building society accounts and bank deposits, hence Tessas.[46] Most attending Chevening concurred that encouragement for people to save, as long as it did not put too many distortions into the tax system, was the right move at the time. Lawson had made the big changes in tax in the 1980s, and with policy needing to be tight those at Chevening felt that not much more could be done in the budget.[47]

As 20 March, budget day, approached, Major came under pressure from both the Treasury and the City to be austere, including not raising personal income tax allowances in line with inflation. This move Major resisted, not least because of the impact it would have on average-income earners so soon after the Lawson tax reductions for the higher paid. Major's judgement was probably right; stepping harder on the brakes would have led the budget to be blamed for the recession that followed.[48] The speech-writing was 'very late and disorganised' according to Chaplin.[49] Officials were somewhat thrown by the difference between Major's 'chaotic' approach to speech writing and Lawson's habit of setting a rigid timetable. One reason for the disruption was that just before budget day, newspapers stories appeared about Tom, Major's father, which consumed valuable hours in conversations with his brother Terry to set the family record straight.[50]

Tessas, with the interest on savings held for five or more years within building societies to be free of tax, were the centrepiece of a fairly limited budget.[51] Major dubbed it a 'Savers' Budget'. The biggest cheer from Tory MPs came when he announced a doubling in the upper limit of savings people could hold before they lost their entitlement for rebates on the forth-coming poll tax and other social security benefits. The community charge, or poll tax, was to be introduced in April 1990 in England and Wales, having come into effect a year earlier in Scotland. Major's poll tax sweetener upset Scottish MPs, who interrupted his speech to demand that his poll tax concessions should be made retrospective in Scotland. Major quickly conceded this, and an extra £4 million was found after Malcolm Rifkind, Scottish Secretary, had threatened to resign.[52]

Tax changes were the third element in the budget, with the first overall increase in tax since 1981. Two taxes were abolished – stamp duty on share transactions, and the composite rate tax. The latter change was an important element in the 'Budget for Savers'. The Inland Revenue was opposed and Major took considerable pains to persuade it.[53] The overall tax changes hit the better-off most, in marked contrast to the thrust of his predecessor's budgets. Major the political Chancellor was seen in the £100 million he put into football grounds over five years to improve safety, coming after the Hillsborough football stadium tragedy in April 1989 in which ninety-five spectators were crushed to death.

The budget, the first to be televised, itself an additional stress, was criticised by the City for being insufficiently firm on inflation, predictably singling out income tax allowances rising in line with the cost of living as a particular lost opportunity. Major had prepared the markets by revising his autumn statement forecast for end-1990 inflation from 5.75 per cent to 7.25 per cent, and tried to forestall the criticism by emphasising that the budget was one for the medium term and should not be judged by the reaction in foreign exchanges.[54] Goldman Sachs waspishly commented that the financial markets did not like the budget because 'he was trying too hard to be too nice to too many people'.[55] Tim Congdon concluded, 'The brutal fact is that this government has lost its way on inflation.'[56]

The slump in the pound the next day was followed by the loss of the Mid-Staffordshire by-election on 22 March with a record 22 per cent swing against the Conservatives. The unpopularity of the poll tax was seen as a major reason for the scale of the defeat.[57] Chaplin recorded in her diary how, the morning after, 'Mrs T was in an absolute tizz over the poll tax, demanding fundamental changes and extra money – she rightly sees it as one of the things that could bring her down.'[58] The poll tax contributed significantly to Major's inflation problems, and severely restricted his scope for cutting interest rates. Inflation rose from 8.1 per cent in March to 9.4 per cent in April, and 10.9 per cent in September – 'a figure I had never believed would be reached again while I was Prime Minister', wrote Thatcher later[59] – before beginning to fall after October.[60] Major had resisted City and Treasury pressure to increase interest rates, and Mrs Thatcher's urgings to reduce them. They remained at 15 per cent until October 1990.

International Finance Minister

Perhaps because of the experience he gained as Foreign Secretary, Major particularly enjoyed the international aspects of the Chancellor's work. His confidence in handling international business grew, and he forged several relationships with other finance ministers which were to prove valuable when he became Prime Minister.

He found the monthly meetings of European Finance Ministers (ECOFIN) much more congenial than those of the Foreign Affairs Council he had attended as Foreign Secretary. ECOFIN meetings, held either in Luxembourg or Brussels, had a 'clubbable' feel about them, and even though the ministers were from different political parties, Major quickly developed a good rapport, notably with Pierre Bérégovoy (who became French Prime Minister) and Albert Reynolds (later Irish Prime Minister).[61] Reynolds says their relationship was cemented over lunch at a Brussels ECOFIN in early 1990; Major as a newcomer asked Reynolds to help 'show him the ropes'.[62]

The two big issues under consideration during Major's year were the steps towards economic and monetary union (EMU), of which membership of the ERM was a first step, and the question of tax harmonisation. The latter involved removing the frontiers between the member states for tax adjustments to VAT. Lawson had worked hard to find ways of achieving this without going down the road of fully fledged harmonisation, including common rates of tax, as some members wanted. Major picked up where Lawson left off, and managed to achieve a compromise, which fell short of tax levels being decided by Brussels.[63]

Major prepared meticulously for the monthly ECOFIN meetings. 'He spoke in a rather low, modest way, but one that showed that he had done his homework,' said David Hannay (UK Permanent Representative to the EC 1985–90). 'He showed what a very effective performer he was at these meetings in getting his case across.'[64]

With discussions on EMU heating up throughout the first half of 1990, Major played a leading part in two sideshows. The first, the European Bank of Reconstruction and Development (EBRD), was created to channel investment into the emerging democracies in eastern Europe. Mrs Thatcher was sceptical when President Mitterrand pressed for its establishment in the course of 1989.[65] Major, however, liked the idea, and was keen to see such an important institution set up in London. A deal was struck whereby Britain would 'lend' some of its IMF quota to France[66] so that the two countries would share fourth place in size of quota in return for French agreement that the bank be sited in London.[67] Progress was swift and the bank made a controversial start under Jacques Attali, a Mitterrand protégé, as its first president.

The second sideshow was the so-called 'hard ecu', a Treasury plan supported by Major, and published on 20 June 1990, as an alternative to the divisive EMU. After the 1989 Delors Plan EMU came under serious consideration, but with Britain perceived to be dragging its feet there was the need to come up with a constructive British proposal. Lawson had the idea of selling competing currencies, i.e. making all EC currencies valid in all EC countries, and allowing the stronger ones to drive out the weak. It received little support in Europe.

The 'hard ecu' idea originated in the (now merged) Samuel Montagu merchant bank in London. Michael Palliser (Permanent Under-Secretary at the FCO 1975–82), and then Chairman of the bank, reported to the Treasury that one of his directors, Paul Richards, had hit on the plan. Wicks asked for a paper on it, and found a warm supporter for the plan in Michael Butler, Hannay's predecessor as British Representative at the EC, and now heavily involved in the City.[68] Butler worked up the plan, which was to develop the European Currency Unit (ecu), the unit of account representing all EC currencies, to a common currency, circulating alongside existing currencies, the 'hard' element coming because it would be impossible, as it would be linked to the strongest currency, for it to be devalued. Eventually, it was envisaged, the ecu *could* develop into a single currency, in contrast to the Delors EMU plan, which would without question lead to a single currency.[69] Butler went to see Mrs Thatcher at Downing Street on 20 April and sold the plan to her. She immediately saw its potential for stalling stage one of EMU, then imminent.[70]

Major was not present at the 20 April meeting, but also seized on the idea as a softer, and therefore he hoped a more palatable, version of economic union for Mrs Thatcher and sceptical opinion in Britain to swallow. Hurd, now Foreign Secretary and increasingly an ally of Major against Mrs Thatcher's negative stance on Europe, offered Major warm support on the hard ecu. Major chose to launch the plan at an Anglo–German business leaders' dinner on 20 June (replacing, late in the day, Lamont, who was scheduled to have given the after-dinner speech). Major said, 'The Ecu would become a *common* currency for Europe. In the very long term, it could develop into a single currency.'[71]

The Treasury took the plan seriously from early 1990 until the end of the Maastricht negotiations in 1991.[72] Following the 'launch', Major sent out his ministers and officials all around the EC to drum up support. The French were surprised to see a positive proposal emanating from the British, but still would not buy it. Spain and others at the ECOFIN meetings on 23 July and 8 September offered it a certain amount of support, after intensive lobbying by Major. Chaplin recorded in her diary after the latter meeting, 'Portugal and Greece more supportive. [Major's] trawling around finance ministries has paid off to some extent ... Thatcher delighted at slowing down of Delors Plan.'[73] But Germany, principally, and France, felt it failed to address their full aspirations for the future of Europe, and regarded it as a red herring. The plan hence died.

Had the plan been floated three years earlier, before the Delors plan, it might have worked. As it was, the Franco–German view that it was a typical British 'spoiling' tactic became the accepted wisdom.[74]

Mrs Thatcher's response to the hard ecu after its launch fuelled division between the two. Having endorsed it in April, she appeared to pull back in answers in the House of Commons on 21 June. She then dismayed the Bank of England and Treasury by appearing to distance herself from the implications of the proposal. 'It does not mean that we approve of a single European currency,' she said, in a way that was predicted would increase Major's problem in seeking support for the scheme in Europe.[75] Major thought her changing attitude was because she never properly grasped what the hard ecu plan entailed, but had approved it only because it was a diversion from the mainstream single currency proposal.

The saga of the hard ecu disappeared from the screen in the increasingly acrimonious political disputes over the single currency after 1991. Yet, if Major's 1990 scheme had proved attractive to Mrs Thatcher and the other European leaders, it might have spared him, and everyone else, much trouble. The hard ecu, or common currency as it became known, would also have had attractions for both wings of the Conservative Party. Edward Leigh, a Eurosceptic critic of Major as Prime Minister, proposed just such an idea in 1995 as a way of gaining the benefits of monetary union without abolishing the pound.[76]

The Centre Cannot Hold

Ever since the economic boom of the mid-1980s petered out after the stock market crash of October 1987, problems had been accruing for Mrs Thatcher. The dismissal of Howe as Foreign Secretary in June 1989 and resignation of Lawson in October hacked away at her authority. In the wake of the latter departure, Mrs Thatcher had been challenged in November for the leadership by a backbencher, Sir Anthony Meyer, with her Europe stance and leadership style high on the list of concerns among Conservative MPs. In the end only thirty-three MPs voted against her. EMU was the plague that would not go away. Resignations in 1990 of Fowler (January), Walker (May) and Ridley (July) were further evidence of a government in decay. The by-election defeat at Mid-Staffordshire in March, poll tax riots in London at the end of that month, and a press increasingly critical of Mrs Thatcher, were further de-stabilising factors.

The summer of 1990 marked an interlude of remission for the government. Despite the onset of recession, Labour's poll lead drifted down to the low teens instead of the low twenties it had been in March and April. The expensive 'Summer heat on Labour' campaign, launched by Party Chairman Kenneth Baker, with its direct targeting of Kinnock, and an easing of the poll tax drag played their parts in preventing Labour's lead returning to former levels. With Major's high public profile, boosted by his televised 1990 budget, he was selected to play a leading part in Baker's campaign. He had to be pushed into participating: he had never before been prominent in a party press conference, and was apprehensive about how well he would perform. Baker persisted. He realised Major's importance as Chancellor would be in ensuring that attacks by him on Labour's economic policy would be reported widely.[77]

Major's revised inflation predictions in his March budget underestimated the problem. The principal concern in the Treasury for much of 1990 remained that the economy was still failing to respond to the high interest rates.[78] Inflation, stoked by the poll tax, not the recession, was their primary concern at the time. Even after accumulating evidence of recession over the summer, and reports from industry, both Thatcher and Major at the IMF on 22 September dismissed talk of Britain moving into recession.[79] Tim Congdon wrote that 'unless interest rates are cut, the slowdown will become a full recession next year'.[80] So why did Major not reduce interest rates in August or September? The reason, he told the House of Commons in October, is that cuts in interest rates would have been interpreted by financial markets as a signal that Britain was not serious about maintaining a firm exchange rate.[81] Major agonised in September over whether to cut interest rates, but backed off, accepting Treasury advice.[82] As it was, the cut to 14 per cent in October came too late, with 10.9 per cent inflation that month and an economy moving rapidly further into recession.

Into the ERM

Ejection from the ERM in September 1992, more than any other single event, undermined the second Major government. It is thus peculiarly important to understand why and how Britain entered the ERM in October 1990.

Major, we have seen, did not have deep beliefs about Europe. It did not arouse the gut feelings in him about identity, national pride and sovereignty that it stirred in more traditional Tories, like Mrs Thatcher, Tebbit and Ridley. He had not confronted the European issue first-hand until he became Foreign Secretary in June 1989. His three months at the Foreign Office made him more European-minded, and helped Britain develop a more constructive relationship with its European partners than Mrs Thatcher was prepared to court. But on the merits of entering the ERM, as he told an FCO official, 'I am an agnostic.'[83] So he arrived at the Treasury with generally pro-European views, and believed that as Britain was a member of the EC, which was set on a course towards a single currency, at some stage it would have to join the ERM, then in its eleventh year of existence, as the precursor. He did not arrive with a fully developed understanding of the economic case for entering, but it was to be economic arguments, and the political balance of forces, that were to convert him, rather than any emotional desire to be closer to Europe. To Major, ERM entry was a means to an end, the end being a better-managed domestic economy, and more harmonious relations with Britain's European partners.

When he began to study the briefs, he soon appreciated that most of the establishment was pro-ERM entry. The critical nexus was Burns and Middleton at the Treasury and Eddie George, then Deputy Governor at the Bank of England. Robin Leigh-Pemberton, the Governor, was another supporter. Almost all the senior Treasury officials, including Wicks and others in the overseas finance division, continued to follow the pro-ERM course set out under Lawson. FCO officials, particularly Kerr, viewed it as a useful tool of European policy. Most of the senior mandarinate in Whitehall, indeed, felt similarly. Senior figures in the Conservative Party tended to back entry: Eurosceptics were then in a minority, and strong mainly in the lower echelons of the parliamentary party. Howe and Lawson were obviously ardent supporters, while Hurd, the new Foreign Secretary, was also in favour. Many in the City, Bank of England, and even more so in the CBI and industry, anxious for exchange rate stability, saw entry as the way forward. Britain's trading partners were urging entry, as were the opposition parties in Parliament. So, too, was the great majority of newspapers – *The Times*, the *Daily Telegraph* and *Financial Times* – including some of their most respected financial commentators, not least Samuel Brittan of the *Financial Times*.

With Whitelaw's departure, Mrs Thatcher lost a valuable balancing force. Lord Young, Secretary of State for Trade, had made occasional anti-ERM grunts, but he too had retired.[84] Parkinson was opposed to entry, but he was no longer a heavyweight.[85] Ridley, Tebbit and Walters – off stage – tried to stiffen her resolve. Even her Policy Unit in Number Ten, led by Brian Griffiths, advised her to join. As Charles Powell put it, 'The truth is that she was in a tiny minority in the government always in opposing joining the ERM and she fought off attempt after attempt to do it. Her only support of any intellectual weight in Cabinet had been Nick Ridley',[86] until he left in July 1990, after his ill-judged anti-German remarks in the *Spectator*.[87] Others opposed to the ERM, such as Howard and Lilley, were too new to Cabinet to lend much weight. The balance of political forces was for entry.

Mrs Thatcher, buoyed by Walters, thought she had pulled off a master stroke by insisting on her Madrid conditions against Howe and Lawson. The condition that all member states should dismantle remaining capital controls put the onus on the rest of Europe to move towards proper freedom of capital and the single market; the vaguely defined condition that Britain's inflation should be 'low' enough they thought could delay entry indefinitely.[88]

When Major arrived at the Treasury he commissioned a review of economic policy. It concluded that there was indeed no alternative in the battle against inflation to the use of high interest rates.[89] This left a gulf. Monetary policy, which Major accepted would have to remain the principal economic tool, needed an 'anchor'. Money-supply targets, and shadowing the Deutschmark, had both been discredited in the 1980s; membership of the ERM would provide such an anchor.[90] To sceptical commentators such as Edmund

Dell, the Treasury was searching for an external discipline because it had lost confidence in the ability of politicians to provide domestic discipline. Major was in a box: ERM entry, with the stability it promised for prices and the exchange rate, was the best available way out. It also offered a route out of a political impasse. He took it.

There was no sudden Damascus Road experience in Major's intellectual acceptance of the case for the ERM, which took place over several months between October 1989 and March 1990. He wanted to be fully convinced before he put his weight behind what was becoming politically nearly inevitable. Achieving entry where Lawson had failed was an additional incentive. As the EC Council on monetary union in Rome, scheduled for December 1990, approached, he came to see – urged on by the ever-powerful FCO official John Kerr – that ERM membership by that time was vital to putting Britain in a position to influence the evolving debate on the future of Europe.

But first he had to persuade Mrs Thatcher. Judith Chaplin persuaded him to submit a paper to her before Easter Sunday, which fell on 15 April. Chaplin writes that Thatcher agreed the following week that Britain would join, probably in September.[91] Mrs Thatcher records that at her meeting with Major she held out against him, and wrote disparagingly of him in her memoirs (1993) with the judgement of hindsight that 'I was extremely disturbed to find that the Chancellor had swallowed so quickly the slogans of the European lobby', and 'intellectually, he was drifting with the tide'.[92] She believes her agreement did not come until two months later: 'Only at my meeting with John Major on Wednesday 13 June did I eventually say that I would not resist sterling joining the ERM. But the timing was for debate ... I had too few allies to continue to resist and win the day.'[93]

How did he persuade her? Major was always immensely solicitous of Mrs Thatcher at their regular weekly meetings. 'Major went out of his way to be sensitive to what the PM wanted to do, and the fact he was sensitive meant they got on pretty well. It also meant he got his way on most issues,' recalled one close Treasury observer.[94] He played her with all the skill of a fly fisherman after a big and suspicious salmon. He would raise the subject, then drop it when she objected, then come back to it from a different angle at their next meeting. Another Treasury official commented how 'she could never really get to grips with him like she could with Nigel or Geoffrey'.[95] For all his arts, however, he probably could not have persuaded her alone. Charles Powell was a pivotal ally. Although he found his mission 'very hard to swallow' as he had been 'a convinced opponent of [ERM] for ages', Powell nevertheless set about the task with gusto and not a little apprehension. He employed the external discipline argument. Though 'she was not very receptive' to this line, she was swayed, according to Powell, by 'the trade-off between getting the interest rates down and ERM entry'.[96] She kept the subject away from Cabinet, but as Parkinson, one of her few remaining political friends, said, she realised she could not afford to lose another Chancellor.[97] *The Times* commented perceptively in an article on Mrs Thatcher and Europe in July that Major and Hurd 'are as nearly unsackable as Thatcher ministers can be'.[98] Even then, in her heart she still clung to the belief, or hope, that entry could be avoided.

With Mrs Thatcher's veto effectively removed, there were two critical – and linked – questions: when to enter, and at what rate. Major steadily modified his rhetoric on ERM. His 20 March budget speech said ERM entry was not a case of 'when' only. He told the *Wall Street Journal* in May about the positive benefits of entry,[99] and word leaked out to journalists that entry would be in the autumn.[100] A diplomatic offensive was conducted to persuade them of Britain's earnestness about ERM entry, even if there remained deep reservations in London about EMU.[101]

The domestic economy, and mounting press speculation about entry, were meanwhile providing headaches for Major and the Treasury. Despite the maintenance throughout the year of 15 per cent interest rates, in the summer prices came under new pressures from pay settlements as well as from the aftermath of Iraq's invasion of Kuwait on 2 August 1990, which pushed up world oil prices. Then in September the pound, which had been held high by foreign exchange markets with the carrot of imminent ERM entry, was coming under strain as confidence in early entry waned. Gus O'Donnell had been hyperactive in his capacity as Major's Press Secretary, telling the financial markets, via journalists, that Major would indeed prevail over Thatcher and that entry would take place soon. But it was an uphill struggle. A speech on 21 September by Karl Otto Pöhl, Bundesbank President, fuelled doubts and by the time Major arrived that day at the IMF meeting in Washington, the pound was looking very weak.[102] While still in the US he did his best to rally markets by saying inflation would come down, and intimating entry before the end of the year was very likely. Privately, he told Peter Riddell in Washington that he was determined and was prepared to push Thatcher, if necessary, into accepting entry, but appeared anxious lest she attempt a last-minute block.[103]

The high inflation, economy in recession and falling pound pointed to two conclusions: rapid entry, or deferred entry. The entry date of Friday 5 October was finalised at the last moment. Timing was a matter for Mrs Thatcher and Major. He met her on Wednesday 3 October and told her he had decided to go in before the weekend. She believed that with wide 6 per cent margins within which sterling could move up and down, mitigating some of the disadvantages of a rigid fixed exchange rate system, the ERM might just be palatable. But she held out for a simultaneous interest rate cut of 1 per cent as her final piece of Danegeld.

Major worried to the end that she might wriggle off the hook, so he hurriedly arranged another meeting for Thursday 4 October to pin her down. Major was accompanied by Middleton, Wicks and Burns from the Treasury, and George from the Bank of England. Incredibly, much of the meeting was spent rehearsing the economic arguments with her for the umpteenth time. Middleton, at his most eloquent, carried the day.[104] The Treasury team

explained that with Britain's inflation at 10.9 per cent the Madrid conditions
had not been met, but Treasury forecasts said prices would fall next year and
inflation begin to converge with the EC average of 5.5 per cent. The Treasury's initial entry date was 12 October, but Major pressed for the announcement being made on the following day, 5 October, lest the news leak or
Thatcher prevaricate (with the reason for the swift announcement widely
thought to be to upstage the Labour Party Conference, which had gone well
at Blackpool).[105] It was finally agreed to announce at 4 p.m. on 5 October
that Britain would enter the ERM on Monday 8 October. Discussions
followed over the timing of the interest rate cut: the Bank and Treasury
favoured a delay; Mrs Thatcher wanted it simultaneous with the 4 p.m.
announcement. Major did not fight her on this one, and she had her way, to
the irritation of Robin Leigh-Pemberton and Eddie George at the Bank of
England.[106]

After the meeting she asked Middleton – an official she liked – to stay
behind for five minutes. 'Will it work?' she enquired anxiously. Middleton
replied it would, but cautioned her, first that the news of entry would be
greeted by criticism that the rate of entry was too high, and second, that she
must keep an eye on Germany, and remember that the rate could be adjusted
if necessary.[107] Major had left for the Treasury, where he phoned Leigh-
Pemberton and told him, ' "We're going in on Friday." It was astonishing
news. I hadn't any idea what had been going on,' Leigh-Pemberton recalled.
He congratulated Major on the decision, but said it created a personal
dilemma for him as he was due to go on an official visit to Japan leaving on
that Friday. Major told him to proceed with his trip as planned.[108]

The settlement on the figure of DM2.95, the figure Middleton said might
be regarded as too high, was not in fact a matter of much contemporary
dispute among those involved. DM2.95 was the current rate and was in line
with the average of the previous few years, and would impose the firm anti-
inflation discipline they craved. Some in the Bank of England wanted a still
higher rate, favouring DM3.00 or even DM3.10.[109] The figure of DM2.95
was felt by those present to be the only practical level, and one EC partners
would be thought to find acceptable.[110] Mrs Thatcher believed a high
exchange rate equalled a strong currency, and that it was important to enter
without a devaluation.[111] Major did not dissent. She even intimated to Major
that she thought a higher rate than DM2.95 should be considered as a
tougher counter-inflationary measure.

Whatever the merits of going into the ERM, and there were many subsequently who discovered they had been opponents all along, three possible
mistakes were made. The first was the simultaneous interest rate cut, on
Thatcher's insistence. Few outside the Bank or the Treasury spotted this at
the time, but Leigh-Pemberton did write to Thatcher to say, 'I implore you
not to try and take your dividend before it's been earned. If we join the ERM,
you'll see that the exchange rate will rise and you will have a glorious moment
in which to lower interest rates.'[112] The combination gave the impression that

entry was for the purposes of short-term political gain, and may well have delayed further reductions of the interest rate below 14 per cent.[113] The second error was to enter at the rate at DM2.95. Though sterling could not have joined at a substantially lower rate in October 1990, its value was artificially high because of high interest rates. When inflation eased, recovery from the rates – especially if German rates remained high – would be blocked by the ERM. Thirdly, Mrs Thatcher's insistence that their tight-knit group fixed the rate themselves pre-empted the usual EC consultative procedure which gave its Monetary Committee the task of setting the rate. Britain's unilateral rate declaration did not generate vital goodwill among EC countries to its membership of the ERM.

The press comments on the Saturday and Sunday were favourable. The consensus view was summed up by *The Economist*: 'ERM offers Britain its best opportunity of lasting improvement in economic performance.'[114] *The Times* editorial offered a cautious welcome, but concluded, 'Economic policy is back in the hands of politicians.'[115] Kinnock said he approved of the ERM entry, the rate, and the interest rate cut, but sought political capital by highlighting Mrs Thatcher's ambivalent role. William Keegan in the *Observer* was unusual in arguing that the rate had been fixed too high.[116] Anatole Kaletsky in *The Times* warned that the rate would accelerate the process of deindustrialisation through making British manufacturing even less competitive.[117]

The initial reaction from the foreign exchange markets, too, was favourable, with the pound indeed rising to DM3.08 after the first few days. But talk of splits between Mrs Thatcher and Leigh-Pemberton over the interest rate timing, and of divisions within the Party following Lawson's provocative speech on 23 October, in which he reiterated his strong belief that Britain should have entered in 1985, unsettled the markets and sterling drifted back to DM2.95 by the end of October.[118]

In the debate on ERM entry, eleven Conservative MPs, led by John Biffen, voted against the government. They included Tony Favell, Major's Eurosceptic PPS, who had resigned earlier over the policy.[119] Tebbit withdrew his endorsement of Major as Mrs Thatcher's successor.[120] They were the little-noticed early warning signs of what would be in store for Major when, the following month, to the surprise of all, he succeeded Mrs Thatcher at Number Ten. The need to win the general election – with increased public spending and lower interest rates – was to put the Party under increasing strain during the period of ERM membership.

Major's period as Chancellor was the only protracted time in his career before he became Prime Minister running his own department. How good a Chancellor was he? A year is not long to judge performance. He was not intent on devising a new economic strategy, and anyway lacked the background and the economic training to do so even had he wished to. He was in tune with the conventional wisdom on economic matters, above all in entry into the

ERM. A more experienced Chancellor might have probed the call for ERM entry more firmly. Nevertheless, he displayed consummate political skills in persuading Mrs Thatcher to assent to it. At the same time he improved Treasury–Number Ten relations from the low point of the Lawson years. His one budget was modest in scope, but introduced a sensible change encouraging more long-term savings. The most controversial aspect of his chancellorship was to take Britain into the ERM at the time and at the rate that he did. The history of the 1990s could have been very different had he not done so. Regardless of the broad agreement that it was the right course of action, it was his decision with Thatcher. The consensus in the late 1990s was that entry was a grave error. If it was, it was one which, with his lack of economic theory or strong sceptical views on Europe, he was destined to make. He was prisoner of the *Zeitgeist*. ERM entry aside, his greatest weakness as Chancellor, ironically, was in the very area where he performed so effectively in his earlier manifestation at the Treasury, his oversight of public expenditure which, with a weakening Prime Minister, was beginning its spiral out of control. Major was above all a political rather than an economic Chancellor. His was not at all a bad performance. He emerged with his reputation enhanced, and without damaging his relationship with Thatcher irreparably.

TEN

Leadership Election:

October–November 1990

THE 1990 TORY leadership contest attracted as much feverish interest from the media and writers of books as if it were a general election.[1] On top of the usual fandango of an election, curiosity was aroused initially by the possible toppling of Margaret Thatcher, the longest-serving Prime Minister this century, an extraordinary political figure, who had won three general elections in a row; and latterly by her replacement by a modest and rather opaque man who appeared to have 'risen without trace'.

The focus here will be on John Major: what was he doing and thinking, who supported him, and why did he want so much to win? In particular, did Major plot to remove Mrs Thatcher, as some on the right alleged? As Thatcher experienced her first waves of disenchantment with Major within just weeks of his arrival at Number Ten, rumours grew of plots to prise her from the premiership and of the succession being subject to manipulation. She was not short of courtiers who gave these rumours currency.

Death of a Premiership: October 1990

The announcement of Britain's entry into the ERM provided a favourable backdrop for the Conservative Annual Party Conference. Major's conference speech on Thursday 12 October, had to be redrafted following the ERM decision,[2] and turned out to be one of the most successful platform speeches of his career, mixing serious messages with slapstick, and a new-found passion with an ease of manner at the microphone. Prospects for the economy was his principal theme. Inflation had risen to unacceptable heights, he told delegates, because growth had been too fast in the 1980s. The cure, high interest rates, was admittedly painful, but would result in tumbling inflation during 1991. The speech contained Major nostrums aplenty: the evils of high inflation; his determination to improve standards of living for all, from children to pensioners; his irritation with those people who never 'stopped talking this country down'. He defended the ERM entry rate of DM2.95 against the charge of overpricing British products abroad by asserting that the rate was competitive, and stable exchange rates were exactly what industry needed. He tried to steer tactfully around the divide between Thatcher and

Howe on EMU by saying that joining the ERM did not put Britain 'on a road leading inexorably to a single currency'. Howe appeared to contradict Major, speaking at a fringe meeting an hour later, which led to the lead headline in *The Times* the following day 'Howe opens rift with Major on monetary union'.[3]

Major's best joke in his speech was also his most pointed: 'When it comes to the crunch, the trade unions will put their arms around Mr Kinnock's shoulders and say "Neil" – and he will.'[4] The speech received the most enthusiastic standing ovation of the week so far; media reports abounded with representatives hailing it as the performance of the next party leader.[5] Jeffrey Archer, who had become a recent Major fan, had helped with rewrites on the speech; some in the Major camp felt perhaps unfairly that Archer was even claiming the credit for Major's jokes, 'though they had already been written'.[6]

Mrs Thatcher's own speech on Friday was not her happiest, and included an ill-advised reference to the Liberal Democrats as a dead parrot. She offered Major grudging support, but the defeat she had sustained the week before on ERM entry bit deep, and she was uncompromising: EMU, she said, 'would be entering a federal Europe through the back-Delors'.[7] Her colours were nailed ever more firmly to the Eurosceptic cause. Major, intentionally or not, had emerged as the key figure in the centre ground over Europe, halfway between Thatcher and Howe. He could not have been better placed for the events of the month to come.

On the Thursday after the conference, the Eastbourne by-election, necessitated by the IRA murder of the sitting member Ian Gow, proved a disaster for the government. The result, a Liberal Democrat victory with a swing of 20 per cent, confirmed that the better fortunes the Tories had been enjoying since the summer had come to an end, and that the ERM honeymoon had faded after just two weeks. That night, with figures showing unemployment still rising, inflation above its level in 1979, and productivity stagnant, Major gave his only Mansion House address as Chancellor. A strong attack on EC partners, especially Germany, for attempting to fix a date for progress to EMU was a key theme. It was criticised with some justice for failing to offer a constructive way out of the stagflation into which the economy was heading.[8]

The bonds holding the government together were now fast unravelling. Bad news on Europe – divisions, talk of mistimed ERM entry, overvalued currency, recession – dominated the news until Mrs Thatcher returned, splenetic, from a Rome European Council on 28 October.[9] Press coverage was dismissive: 'Britain was double loser at the Rome summit' said *The Times*.[10] In reply to questions in the House of Commons she uttered her emphatic 'No! No! No!' response to the integrated Europe she thought Delors was envisaging.[11] Her performance was lauded by Major in the corridors of Westminster afterwards; he was scrupulously loyal to her, in public. Her words, however, at last pushed Howe beyond the brink. He had been sitting next to her during her Commons speech, and now retired to consider his position. After two days brooding on the mechanics of detaching himself, he resigned on the evening of 1 November.[12] Losing Howe, the only other member of her 1979 Cabinet still in office, was one resignation too many. As a former Chancellor and Foreign Secretary, his departure unleashed pent-up anger within her Party that was to sweep Mrs Thatcher aside before the month was out.

November Gales

Howe's resignation received a sympathetic reception from a press broadly disillusioned with Thatcher. It was now open season for leadership specu-lation. The Sunday papers on 4 November centred on Michael Heseltine as a successor, a menacing 'voice off' to Mrs Thatcher and convinced antagonist since his Westland resignation nearly five years earlier in January 1986.[13] He tested the waters in a letter to his constituency association chairman on 3 November, but was knocked back by an aggressive counterattack from the Thatcher camp, with Party Chairman Kenneth Baker prominent in the assault. A phoney war ensued between the Thatcher and Heseltine camps, with intense behind-the-scenes manoeuvring. Newspaper surveys were con-ducted which seemed to assure the Thatcherites that a challenge was unwanted by the bulk of Tory MPs, and that if there were an election she would probably win.[14] Number Ten more or less told Heseltine to 'put up or shut up', and simultaneously squeezed his slow but emerging bandwagon by pressing Cranley Onslow, Chairman of the 1922 Committee, to bring forward the date of any leadership election. On 7 November Heseltine's constituency chairman responded with a Thatcher loyalist letter. Head momentarily bowed, Heseltine stated publicly that Thatcher would lead the Party into the next general election.[15]

Not everything was going Thatcher's way, however. Poor showings in the Bradford North and Bootle by-elections on 8 November undermined the impression she endeavoured to cultivate that she was in control of events.[16] Any temptation to play the 'Gulf War card', by asking for unity in the face of threat, was strongly discouraged by those close to her.

Major delivered his second autumn statement as Chancellor on the same day as the by-elections, a date brought forward from later in November in an attempt to overshadow what the Party saw as the inevitability of the by-election defeats.[17] His statement was well received as a politically deft exercise, though involving considerable increases in public spending. 'Resourceful Major tries to square the economic circle,' declared the *Guardian*.[18] Expen-diture was to increase by 4.5 per cent, allowing for inflation, with spending breaking £200 billion for the first time. *The Times* asked whether it marked the end of Thatcherite radicalism: 'Faced with economic recession, a radical Conservative government would have cut spending. This conventional government is to increase it.' But then it went on to commend the statement as not just 'wise politically' but 'right economically', and asked, 'Ought not the government to be planning to spend more?'[19] A warning signal was, however, sounded by Sarah Hogg in the *Daily Telegraph*, who asked whether, without electricity privatisation receipts, Major could possibly balance his budget in 1991.[20]

With the week behind her, Mrs Thatcher had high hopes that she might survive; nominations for the leadership with the accelerated timetable would have to be in by the following Thursday, 15 November. Major remained meticulously loyal to Thatcher in public. He was not a front-line candidate aired by the press in the previous week; the names of Heseltine, Hurd and also Howe were those most frequently cited. At this delicate stage, Howe tipped the scales decisively against her. Following Lawson's precedent the year before, and spurred into action by Number Ten's attempt to make light of his differences with Mrs Thatcher, he had intended to make a speech to the House of Commons outlining the reasons for his departure. Now he considered, and rejected, the idea of standing against Mrs Thatcher for leader; he would make a Commons speech on 13 November, two days before nominations for candidates were to close.

Howe's speech was one of the most powerful and influential to have been given in the House of Commons since the war, his theme that the Prime Minister's increasingly isolated and hostile stance to Europe had forced on him an impossible conflict of loyalty, to her, and to the national interest. He could no longer resolve that conflict, so he had been forced to resign.[21] He said it was for others to consider their response to the crisis, interpreted as a call for a candidate to challenge her. The response was immediate. 'Many Conservative MPs last night believed they had witnessed the undoing of the Prime Minister,' Patrick Wintour observed.[22] Several commentators thought that his speech would result in a new leader before the end of the month. Mrs Thatcher was mortified by Howe's speech; after three years pondering over it, she described it in her memoirs as his 'final act of bile and treachery', and, 'the character he assassinated was in the end his own'.[23]

Heseltine formally declared his candidature for the leadership the following morning, 14 November. Howe was anxious to avoid any impression of collusion between them, even though they did speak on the phone before Howe's speech, and the timing of the attack provided exactly the launch pad Heseltine needed. Mrs Thatcher was at once nominated by Hurd and seconded by Major. Her campaign was organised by Peter Morrison, her PPS, who was widely blamed for her demise. There were to be six days of campaigning among the electorate, restricted to the 372 Conservative MPs, before the first ballot on 20 November. The Whips' Office remained neutral, as it was bound to do, but gave her the assessment that she would win fairly easily.

What was Major's thinking in all of this? Judith Chaplin had recorded in her diary in September that Mrs Thatcher had told Hector Laing (Chairman of United Biscuits) that she wanted to see Major succeed her when she left.

The story was communicated to Major, and she recorded that he 'has clearly thought out who his opponents are and what strategy' he might adopt.[24] For the two months following his agenda was full – ERM entry announcement, 5 October; conference speech, 12 October; Mansion House speech, 18 October; ERM debate, 23 October; autumn statement, 8 November. His mind was more preoccupied by the recession, and by the effect it might have on the election, than by his musings on the future Party leadership. He had nevertheless worked out that he had little serious hope of succeeding Mrs Thatcher that November. Indeed, a contest then seemed likely to worsen his eventual chances: a replacement leader would damage his long-term prospects, which looked much more promising if she remained *in situ* and retired, probably, he thought, after the next general election. All the same, he had rising doubts about tying his body to what he suspected was a mortally wounded carcass. Chaplin recorded in mid-November that 'I get the feeling [Major] isn't that keen' on seconding Mrs Thatcher, and two days after doing so he told Chaplin that he thought she was finished.[25]

On the afternoon of 18 November, Mrs Thatcher flew to Paris for the Conference on Security and Co-operation in Europe, assured by her camp that all would be well. Two days earlier Major had gone into hospital to have his wisdom teeth fixed. Not only had he been taking painkillers for some months, but in Washington, during the IMF conference in September, he had been forced to make an emergency visit to a dentist.[26] Any suggestion, as in some quarters, that the dental operation was a pretext to remove him from the fray while his adjutants plotted his advance, is without foundation. The operation date had been booked several weeks in advance, after his return from Washington, and his constituency secretary Barbara Wallis had cleared his diary.[27] Released on Sunday 18 November, he went home to The Finings on medical advice for a planned week of convalescence.[28]

The Sunday newspapers were not sanguine about Mrs Thatcher's prospects, with editorials in the *Observer* and (with more reluctance) the *Sunday Times* saying she should go. The *Sunday Telegraph* remained staunchly loyalist: its editorial said she had been scandalously treated, and, 'You can find Heseltines wherever you go. But there is only one Mrs Thatcher. Handle with care. This valuable object is irreplaceable.'[29] Michael Jones interviewed both Thatcher and Heseltine in the *Sunday Times*. The poll tax was the main issue dividing them, but Heseltine called also for education reforms and more participation in Europe.

That Sunday was the crucial day in the campaign. A broad realisation grew among Conservative MPs that Thatcher would not beat Heseltine sufficiently decisively in the first round, and a second ballot would be needed. It was assumed (wrongly) that she would stand down at that point, and there was 'a sort of establishment decent chaps' convention' that the man most likely to defeat Heseltine was Hurd, who had on 17 November declared his willingness to stand in a second ballot if Mrs Thatcher yielded. This move to implant Hurd as the beat-Heseltine candidate – and the Tory establishment·

was absolutely determined to see Heseltine beaten – was headed off by various Major loyalists, including Lamont, Ryder and Maude.[30] Monday morning's *Guardian* headline was 'PM's backers almost certain second ballot likely'.[31]

On Monday 19 November, the last day before the election, Jeffrey Archer travelled to Huntingdon to see the Majors, staying for lunch. He aired the idea of Major standing as a stop-Heseltine candidate if the whips reported that he would do better than Hurd in that capacity.[32] Archer had a habit of turning up as a picaresque figure in moments of high political drama, as if his life and novels were merging together. 'Norma, John and I spent the day together. I brought him every newspaper in bed. Lamont called him soon after lunch,'[33] Archer recalled. Lamont raised the same question as Archer: would he stand? Major was interested, flattered, and non-committal.

Voting took place during the day of 20 November, with Mrs Thatcher still in Paris and Major still recuperating in Huntingdon. The result was announced in Westminster at 6.30 p.m., amid confused scenes, by Onslow, Chairman of the 1922 Committee. Thatcher had received 204 votes, Heseltine a very high 152; she was just four votes short of the outright victory that by the complex rules would have avoided a second ballot, and kept her at Number Ten. Just two MPs switching from Heseltine to her would notionally have saved her, but opened the door to a grave political crisis.

The news was broken to her in her room at the Paris embassy by the hapless Morrison. 'Not quite as good as we had hoped,' he intoned, in stark contrast to the encouraging advice he had been offering over the past few days. After a silence between them, Morrison telephoned Hurd in his room in the embassy. Hurd, having called Major, came round to see Mrs Thatcher, who was controlled but upset, and he declared that she should stand in the second ballot, promising her both his and Major's support. Buoyed somewhat by his words, she was able to put on a brave showing in front of the press downstairs to say that, while she was 'disappointed' to have fallen just short of the number to win on the first ballot, her name would go forward to fight in the second round. Hurd followed her, lamenting that the 'destructive, unnecessary contest' was to be prolonged, and promised her his full support.[34] She went off to Versailles with President Mitterrand, her head buzzing.

Enter Major

Conservative circles around Westminster were buzzing also, late into the night and on into the following morning, 21 November. Several meetings took place, the most celebrated being at Catherine Place, home of Garel-Jones. The consensus among both ministers and backbenchers was that many of her 204 first-round supporters were drifting away, and victory over Heseltine in the second round was widely judged unlikely. The questions then to be answered were: how exactly was the anti-Heseltine crusade to be rallied, and what would senior ministers tell Thatcher?[35]

By the time she returned to Downing Street from Paris just before midday on Wednesday 21 November, she was among only a small number of Conservative MPs in believing she could remain as premier. Even Denis told her, 'Don't go on, love.'[36] Meetings with her closest aides – Morrison, Wakeham, Tebbit, MacGregor, Baker – and others were dispiriting for her, but she shouted out to journalists in Number Ten as she went to the House of Commons that afternoon (recalling Cyrano de Bergerac's dying words, had she but known it), 'I fight on, I fight to win.' After her statement on the outcome of the Paris summit, Thatcher toured the Tea Room of the House of Commons to drum up support. The scene was pathetic. Her appearance among MPs had come at least a week too late, and probably much longer than that. But she was adamant: she would not yield. She returned to the PM's room in the Commons and promptly appointed the capable Wakeham to run her team, again a move too late, and saw Hurd, who readily agreed to nominate her formally for the second ballot. She then phoned Major at The Finings and asked him to second her. She claims there was a 'palpable hesitation' before he said he would do so. The pause was in fact longer than she recalled it: fifteen seconds, Major believes. He agreed to back her, but was, as she detected, less than happy about doing so.

In the early evening she saw a succession of senior Tories, including most of her Cabinet. In general they said that, whereas they themselves would *of course* be supporting her in a second ballot, they did not believe she could win. Wakeham further told her that he was having difficulty even putting together a campaign team. She suspected that her Cabinet had all connived together to sing a common tune uttering, as she put it, 'weasel words whereby they had transmuted their betrayal into frank advice and concern for my fate'.[37] She returned to Number Ten, upset and confused, and having slept on it, phoned Andrew Turnbull, her Principal Private Secretary, at 7.30 a.m. on the Thursday morning to say that she had decided to resign. Before going to bed, however, she had stressed to close aides how important it was that Major's nomination papers were ready before the deadline for the second ballot the next day. At Cabinet that morning she announced her decision to go, and urged them to unite behind the figure most likely to defeat Heseltine.

Major had become increasingly agitated as all these events unfolded, stuck at home picking up the news second-hand. That he wanted to become Prime Minister, and was one of the most ambitious men in the House of Commons, there can be no doubt. As early as 1987 he was confiding his ambitions to close colleagues.[38] He was flattered when, in early 1990, MPs had begun to suggest to him that if he stood for Leader after her, he could probably win.[39] For years he had been courting MPs and assiduously cultivating a network of allies; his diary secretaries at the Treasury would express periodic exasperation at his readiness to see backbenchers, thereby straining his diary commitments.[40] But all this falls a long way short of him 'plotting' against her. His lack of enthusiasm for seconding her for the first ballot was, as he admitted to close advisers at the Treasury, because he thought she would have to go, and he was not keen on keeping her as PM.[41] He hesitated before agreeing to second her for the second ballot because he resented the breathless tone of her phone call, which lacked any pleasant preliminaries (such as enquiring how he was after his tooth operation) and in which she presumed without any explanation that he would be willing to back her.

While all the manoeuvrings were going on in London from 18 to 21 November, he was not goading colleagues, but his supporters were at work. On Monday 19 November *The Times* said that Major would emerge as a contender if she lost, and that he could fill the role of 'unity candidate'. A senior MP told the paper 'we are longing for a leader with ease of manner'. But he himself gave no word, in public or in private, that he would stand in a second ballot.[42]

So the main charge, of conspiracy to bring her down, is not supported by the evidence. Chaplin's diary, which is not uncritical of Major and so can be assumed to be relatively objective, says firmly that he and Lamont 'remained loyal until she said she was standing down'.[43]

There is, however, something in a second charge from the Thatcher camp: that he could have done more for her. He could certainly have been more robust defending her from Howe's assault, and spoken up more for her after Heseltine declared on 14 November. He could have issued a statement after the press reports on 19 November saying under no circumstances would he stand. He could have done more when convalescing from 18 to 21 November to stiffen the Thatcherite supporters. But the charge of lack of positive support, while sustainable, was a counsel of perfection, above all for one who had concluded Mrs Thatcher had outlived her usefulness.

Norma drove him to London the next day, too late to hear Mrs Thatcher at Cabinet announce her resignation and that he was her favoured successor. Not only Major, but Hurd announced his candidature in the second round. *The Times* reported that Major's was the bandwagon 'that appeared to be gathering speed fastest'.[44] Other possibles were mentioned, including Norman Tebbit, but in the end he declared that Major was the candidate around whom both left and right should unite. Tebbit believes, with hindsight, that had he stood, Heseltine rather than Major would have become Prime Minister.[45]

The Major Bandwagon

Hurd and Major assembled their teams on 22 November. Hurd's supporters included the two Pattens, Waldegrave, Clarke, Rifkind, Bottomley and Jeremy Hanley. Major received the solid Treasury team backing that Hurd received from his Foreign Office ministers. Major's proposer was John Gummer, the Minister for Agriculture and former Chairman of the Party (1983–5); the seconder, and campaign manager, was Lamont, with support coming also from Ryder, Michael Howard, Lilley, Maude, David Mellor, Ian Lang and

Gillian Shephard. Several press reports commented upon Major still being in post-operative pain on 22 November, hence his team were speaking for him.[46] Lamont's backing for Major's candidature was crucial; but why should a man who did not regard him highly volunteer to become his campaign manager? The answer is probably that Lamont realised that, if his champion was successful, his own career would receive accelerated promotion, as indeed it did.[47] There was speculation over an explicit deal.

Late on 22 November Maude spoke to Major by phone, and said that his initial canvassing suggested he had support from a third of the parliamentary party.[48] With only five days before the second ballot on 27 November, Major's campaign moved quickly, thanks to Lamont, the key figure in selecting and galvanising the team. Some Major loyalists, mindful of their subsequent differences, have tended to make light of Lamont's role and say that becoming campaign manager was purely a cynical move on his part (he had initially toyed with supporting Heseltine in the second ballot). But his political management skills proved critical.

Ryder's role in Major's team was deciding which television interviews Major should accept, and as a former Political Secretary to Thatcher as Party Leader (1975–81), in building up support for the Major campaign in the Party beyond Westminster. He worked hard on the National Union and on constituency chairmen, with the result that local associations favoured Major over the other candidates. Maude was the other key figure in the triumvirate and, with Major's backbench friend Robert Hayward, kept exact records on how MPs were intending to vote. Hayward described it as 'student politics writ large'.[49] Apart from these figures, Mellor played a valuable role packaging Major to the outside world, the ever-loyal Graham Bright massaged egos, and his Treasury special adviser Andrew Tyrie wrote many of Major's articles for the press, assisted by the journalist Bruce Anderson. Non-right-wingers such as Gillian Shephard were used disproportionately to try to show Major had a balanced ticket.

The campaign was based in three locations: Number Eleven, the Chancellor's room in the Commons and Gayfere Street, the canvassing centre. Lamont insisted on campaign team meetings at 8 a.m. and 9 p.m. every day. Waverers would be arm-twisted by a Major loyalist with whom they had strong connections. Major himself played little part on the first day, but warmed up by Friday after he had became convinced he could win.[50] Late on the Saturday afternoon, 24 November, his team had compiled a list of those Major should canvass by telephone. Major hated doing it. The first name on the list, Michael Jopling, had his number dialled by Lamont, who handed the phone over to Major.[51] From the Saturday onwards, and with his vitality recovering, he played an increasing part, above all talking one-on-one to waverers, often at Number Eleven.

Major himself rejected taking a populist right-wing or Eurosceptical line for his platform. At the heart of his pitch – which he had little time to formulate – was a pledge to make Britain a 'classless society' by the year

2000. He wanted 'changes to produce across the whole of this country a genuinely classless society so people can rise to whatever level from whatever level they started'. Other elements included concentrating tax cuts on the lower paid, increasing the status of teachers and further changes as necessary – a middle-of-the-road position – to the poll tax, rapidly becoming the central issue in the campaign.[52] It was a pretty left-of-centre manifesto, but one which accurately reflected Major's own philosophical position.

Major's campaign effort was slick and well organised, unlike Heseltine's and Hurd's. The steam quickly went out of the Heseltine effort once the two Cabinet ministers entered. His team had expected to be fighting Mrs Thatcher again in the second round, and underestimated the force of the anti-Heseltine feeling that welled up in the days before the first ballot, and became a strong tide after it. They rightly saw a concerted effort by the Cabinet to make her stand down, preventing a straight Thatcher–Heseltine fight in the second ballot, which they were sure she would lose. Despite late endorsement on the final Saturday from Lawson and Howe, Heseltine saw supporters drift to the Hurd and Major camps, and his campaign thereafter became half-hearted.[53] As to Hurd, he lacked Major's ambition, and was neither unduly optimistic nor excited about his prospects. He spoke to Major most days, keen to ensure that, on a personal level, they remained trusted colleagues.[54]

Major's supporters were seen as coming very much from the right of the party. Thatcher's vote glided effortlessly sideways to his camp. Even though she declined to 'publicly endorse' Major, she still made it clear that she would vote for him.[55] She worked hard to whip up support for him from the Thursday to Tuesday, rallying those who were suspicious of the part played by Lamont, Lilley and other key Major supporters, who were alleged to have been disloyal to her, in the previous week, and those inclined to think Heseltine carried more weight.[56] She phoned her friends among newspaper editors and pleaded for them to back Major.[57] She further hosted a large dinner for Thatcherites, and lobbied them, telling them, 'You must vote for John.'[58]

Despite all this support, partly indeed because of it, Major reacted against being seen as her successor. 'I am not running as son of Margaret Thatcher. I am running as myself,' he let out on ITV's *Walden* programme, 'with my own priorities and my own programme.'[59] He went on to proclaim himself a 'one nation' Tory, stressing that he saw the welfare state which had twice saved his life (when newborn, true; after Nigeria, an exaggeration) as integral to British instincts. The emphasis on 'one nation' values and independence from Thatcher was a complex amalgam of pique, a calculated bid for the centre-left vote, but mostly a reflection of his own inner feelings.

Major and his team played a good game. Because of his comparative inexperience and lower public profile, Major had much ground to make up, especially with the media. Lamont's aim was, first, to get Major into second position, then to move ahead, but not to announce too early that they were front runners. The turning point came on Sunday 25 November, when several papers indicated that Major would do as well, if not better, at restoring

Conservative electoral appeal than Heseltine. The *Sunday Times* disagreed, and continued to back Heseltine, but the *Sunday Telegraph* in an editorial declared: 'Mr Major represents all that is best ... in modern Britain. Indeed, he is a veritable role model for aspiring youth. Mrs Thatcher might even agree to serve under him ... a Major victory this week would ... send the reassuring signal of "business as usual".'[60] By the Monday, Major had won the press war, being endorsed by *The Times*, *Financial Times*, *Today*, *Daily Mail*, *Daily Express*, *Sun* and *Daily Star*. The *Independent* and the *Guardian* preferred Heseltine, while the *Daily Telegraph* endorsed Hurd.

Sideways Step

On Tuesday evening, 27 November, Major's supporters were in the big state room at Number Eleven. The television was on in one corner; the picture was unclear, but the sound was audible. Their intelligence sources told them he would be comfortably in the lead, but a third ballot would be needed. Major, however, thought by now that he would win, and remained silently confident as the noise died down so they could hear the news. As Onslow's Harrovian tones declared Heseltine's vote at 131, there was an immediate cry of success, as it was about fifteen votes lower than his campaign team had predicted. Hurd's figure of fifty-six was almost exactly as they had anticipated, and Major's figure of 185 was ten or fifteen above what they hoped. The margin was still not enough to guarantee avoiding a third ballot. The party gathered around the television set to await developments. When, ten minutes later, Heseltine came outside his Belgravia home and conceded, followed by Hurd, the atmosphere rapidly became euphoric. Onslow turned up at Number Eleven and confirmed there would be no third ballot. Major was officially the victor.

A constant theme of the betrayal thesis, echoing down the 1990s, was that Major was elected by the right, and then abandoned them. The fullest research to have been conducted on voting was completed by Philip Cowley in 1995. He found that whereas the Thatcherite right voted 80 per cent for Major, and the left voted solidly against, the leadership election was won for him by 'the floating centre of the party': 121 of his 185 votes came from this area. Major was also the candidate heavily favoured by the state-educated, non-graduate and non-Oxbridge elements. Among the factors Cowley gives to explain Major's high level of support are: his assiduousness as a House of Commons operator, the blessing of Mrs Thatcher, and polls showing on 25 November that Major would be at least as likely as Heseltine to win a general election as Prime Minister. The final but unquantifiable factor was Major's undoubtedly better-run campaign, which proved brilliantly effective in mobilising latent support.[61]

'It was too early,' Major recalled five years later, of his accession to premier. 'On a personal level I was not keen to do it.'[62] Such doubts were far from his mind that evening. Francis Maude recalls that after he gave Norma a big hug she anxiously asked him, 'Is it going to be all right?' But Major 'seemed suddenly to have grown into it over those five days. He had just become a Prime Minister.'[63] Mrs Thatcher came over from Number Ten with her entourage; she was visibly emotional and delighted, and danced at the top of the stairs.[64] Tim Bell vividly recalls sensing 'power move across the room from her to him', as people left her side and gravitated to Major.[65]

Major had handled Thatcher with delicacy during the leadership crisis and had retained the reported blessing she had offered him in September. He had done what she asked while she was a candidate, although he had not concealed his reluctance from her when she appealed for support on the second ballot. Whether by accident or design, and the Thatcher camp believe the latter, he had navigated between the Scylla of being dragged down with her and the Charybdis of alienating her through disloyalty, and achieved his ideal result. However, that evening with the prize theirs, the Major team did not know exactly how to handle the deposed leader. This uncertainty, rather than Major's successful management of her in 1989–90, was to be the motif of his premiership.

All hell was breaking loose in Number Eleven, singularly ill-equipped to cope as the house became bombarded by messages. Unlike Number Ten, it is not an office, and the single telephone operator had to cope with calls from the Queen's Private Secretary and President Bush.[66] Major, meanwhile, needed to give a victory statement from the steps of Number Eleven. It was suggested that he and Mrs Thatcher should stand together before the world's media. Major, irritated by her earlier promise to be 'a good back-seat driver', intimated with a gesture that he did not wish her to accompany him, and Lamont intervened to prevent her. Nothing had been prepared, so he retired for thought into a bedroom, and based his words on a text Ryder had given him.[67] He then went outside into Downing Street with Norma, leaving Mrs Thatcher to look down from a window above, and finished his short statement with the declaration: 'We are going to unite totally and absolutely and we will win the next general election.'

ELEVEN

The New Prime Minister:

November 1990

IT TOOK JOHN MAJOR eleven and a half years in Parliament to become Prime Minister, the length of Mrs Thatcher's premiership. If his initial rise had been slower than some of the 1979 entry, from his appointment to his first departmental job in 1985, promotion had been unusually swift. Many since have puzzled over how he managed to emerge so quickly.

Although his lack of connections and self-confidence as an MP counted against him at first, his assiduous hard work and pleasant manner soon brought him to the attention of the whips. Once he received his first job in January 1983, as a whip, his attention to detail, accurate reading of people and congenial personality earned him wide recognition. As Social Security Minister from 1985, he revealed an outstanding ability to master his brief in a department where detail is all, and he proved himself sensitive in dealing with individual cases of hardship as well as a surprisingly effective and occasionally rebarbative parliamentary performer.

Now two patrons, and a fair smattering of circumstance, or luck, intervened to propel his rise. First, Nigel Lawson battled to secure him as Chief Secretary at the Treasury, a job tailor-made for his talents, where he gave the most complete ministerial performance of his political career. His next jump, his steepest, occurred when Mrs Thatcher, in a hurry, needed to find a new Foreign Secretary to succeed Geoffrey Howe, the incumbent she could no longer bear. Major was, she thought, 'one of us': too young in Parliament to have associations with Ted Heath, whom she succeeded as Party Leader in 1975, and socially from the self-made stable she admired. He was masterful at managing her, at relating to her personally in the way she liked, while also being confident enough to stand up to her without causing offence.

Circumstance again ran in his favour when Lawson resigned as Chancellor in October 1989 and when again there was no other obvious candidate available; Mrs Thatcher would have loved to appoint Nicholas Ridley but was warned strongly against by the whips, and Major was a more than acceptable compromise candidate. For his final leap, to Number Ten, Howe's resignation speech came at just the right moment. Major's bouncing of her into the ERM in October 1990 might have led to her becoming disillusioned with him, as happened earlier with John Moore. Major's excellent conference speech in the same month had raised his profile and reputation at exactly the right moment. Her doubts about Major, for his lack of scepticism on Europe and his liberal domestic policy instincts, had yet to form. The three heavy-weights of the later Thatcher years, Howe, Lawson and Norman Tebbit, had all ruled themselves out from standing. After Heseltine's first ballot challenge, Thatcher was removed without fatal damage to Major's relations with her and he remained her anointed successor. The decks were now clear for Major to slink past Heseltine and Hurd in the second ballot, as the candidate of the right and the person best placed to unite the Party.

Ability and circumstance alone are insufficient to explain Major's rise to Number Ten. Without intense ambition Major would not have become Prime Minister. His gift for making people like him, his assiduous building of friendships across the parliamentary party, and his clever and deliberate avoidance of being labelled as belonging to one wing of the Party or the other, enabling him to keep in with all factions from left to right, meant that by the time of the leadership election he had many friends and advisers and very few enemies or outright opponents. Judith Chaplin's comment in her diary hours after he became premier is revealing as coming from a highly perceptive, albeit sceptical, observer who knew him well. Reviewing his prospects at Number Ten she wrote,

He is certainly tough enough. It is possible to understand if you recognise that every decision is taken on how it affects and promotes him. This doesn't mean he is not a very nice man, as everyone says he is but he is ruthless. Is he experienced enough? Difficult to say. What an exciting – and sad – week.[1]

The misleading aspect of her entry is the impression it leaves that Major was more egotistical than most successful politicians. He was not. Neither was he as ruthless as she imagined. His would have been an easier premiership if he had been.

First Reactions

The lights in Downing Street burned long into the night on 27 November. A group of twelve of the campaign team were encouraged to move from Number Eleven, to continue their celebrations in a private room at Wiltons, a Westminster restaurant, where they were mortified to discover Michael Heseltine in the main dining room, staring glumly into his soup.[2] As Mrs Thatcher retreated to the study in Number Ten with Denis and close cronies, in the words of Tim Bell 'to get drunk,'[3] Major spoke with his closest allies, including Gus O'Donnell, his Treasury Press Secretary, and Richard Ryder, one of his campaign managers, to plan the immediate future: liaising with Number Ten about how to organise the transition, which media interviews to accept and how to reunite the Party after the leadership contest. 'When Major eventually retired in Number Eleven', recalled O'Donnell, 'it was for a short and restless night's sleep.'[4]

Next morning Mrs Thatcher was driven from Number Ten to meet the Queen at Buckingham Palace at 9.45, to tender her resignation as Prime Minister. Forty-five minutes later, Major followed and was shown upstairs to the Audience Room where the Queen invited him to form a government. They then 'kissed hands' (in reality, merely a handshake).[5] Major, at the age of forty-seven, had become the youngest Prime Minister to take office since Lord Rosebery in 1894. In the three-minute drive back from the palace, he sifted through the pocket cards on which he had hastily written the text that he would utter to the waiting press on his return to Downing Street.[6] The words are telling about Major the man, about his wish to bring harmony and, reiterating one of his themes of the leadership campaign, of his desire to see the standard of living improve for all. In tone and content, it owed more to 'One Nation' Toryism than to the rhythms of Thatcherism. With his arm around Norma's waist, he told the waiting crowds:

I want to see us build a country that is at ease with itself, a country that is confident, and a country that is prepared and willing to make the changes necessary to provide a better quality of life for all our citizens. I don't promise you that it will be easy, and I don't promise you that it will be quick but I believe that it is an immensely worthwhile job. Now, if you will forgive me, because it will be neither easy nor quick, I will go into Number Ten straight away and make a start right now.[7]

The need for urgent decisions was no exaggeration. Rarely had a Prime Minister arrived at Number Ten with so little ground prepared. The immediate tasks included the construction of his government, the organisation and staffing of Number Ten, as well as responding to the flood of offers, invitations and congratulations that had been arriving in his office since the night before.

Major later said he was too busy to be nervous, to explain why he had no repeat of the self-doubt that had beset him in his first days as Chief Secretary and Foreign Secretary; he enjoyed, as he put it to one official, 'having all the levers now'.[8] This answer is only partly true, however. He did bury himself immediately in the work, but as Norma recalled: 'The transition was a nightmare for both of us.' She herself was overwhelmed with the paperwork, with her new responsibilities, the many public functions both at Number Ten and outside, and with the fact 'everyone noticed whatever I did or wore'.[9] Support from within Number Ten, and sympathetic letters, including one from Harold Wilson's wife Mary, who had spent eight years as Prime Minister's wife, cheered her up.[10] After two or three months' acclimatisation, life became easier for both the Majors.

Major's succession was well received. He drew comfort from the immediate improvement in the polls, which gave the Tories an eleven point lead, apparently confirming the wisdom of Major's election. From the outset at Number Ten, he was a voracious poll and press watcher. Margaret Thatcher announced on his first day as premier that 'he will be a superb leader of this country', while Tebbit called him 'very tough, very dry', proof that his centre-left comments during the election campaign had not disillusioned –

or apparently permeated – some on the right. From the left, David Hunt said, 'We are probably more united now than we have ever been', while Emma Nicholson celebrated that 'Cabinet Government will be back again'.[11] The opposition leaders' response was predictable. Major was merely son of Thatcher, Neil Kinnock declaring him to be 'the no-change, no-majority prime minister', with Paddy Ashdown stating: 'The face has changed, but the politics remain the same.'[12]

The press was overwhelmingly positive. Right-wing papers celebrated his appointment unreservedly, with Sarah Hogg in the *Daily Telegraph* typical in praising him for being 'a fighter and a winner'.[13] *The Economist* was insistent that he was his own man, and said 'Britain's policy towards the EC is about to change sharply.'[14] But there were some prescient warnings from the left. Hugo Young wrote that 'political parties seldom renew themselves when they are in power', but added that Major might well be able to achieve it, being the anointed right candidate but offering a style for conciliatory and inclusive leadership.[15] Will Hutton said that Major would soon be tripped up when walking the tightrope between left and right on Europe; by his pledge to build a 'classless society by 2000', at a time when income disparities were widening sharply; and by his pledges to improve education at a time of spending pressure caused by the deepening recession and the new constraint of having to hold the pound inside the ERM.[16] Michael White, meanwhile, emphasised that as his rise was so dependent on being crowned Mrs Thatcher's chosen successor it is 'imperative for him to stamp his own authority on the government he has inherited, to prove that he is not "son of Thatcher" '.[17] The 'classless society' talk was the first subject that prompted attack from the right. Norman Stone, historian and Thatcher acolyte, rebelled against the announcement that Major would not use Chequers, and his 'classless' pledges which smacked to him of the despised 'social engineering'.[18]

At the very outset of his premiership, commentators had identified many of the constraints that were to dog him: lack of time to prepare, the Europe split, the ERM straitjacket, the recession, the difficulty of finding a post-Thatcherite voice, and Mrs Thatcher lurking in the background. Major was to discover another and more tangible constraint on his premiership immediately. At lunchtime on that first Wednesday, he set out to walk across to the House of Commons for lunch. But the police stopped him and told him gently but firmly that he would never be able to walk there again as long as he was Prime Minister. Such constraints on his freedom hit him hard.[19]

Major's Beliefs

Major began his premiership with two principal disadvantages. As he himself acknowledged, both at the time and since, he came to the job too early in life, with insufficient experience of politics, government or issues.[20] Second and more important, unlike his two predecessors, Heath and Thatcher, he had

had no time to prepare his programme for office, nor any experience of leading the Party in opposition. The most telling criticism of his premiership is that it lacked coherence. Major himself was neither a conceptual nor a strategic thinker; rather he was a tactical operator. He was uncomfortable making pronouncements on ideology and broad policy direction. As a local councillor, MP and minister, it was more reliable to divine his beliefs from his actions than his words, which explains why his brand of Conservatism was so hard to pinpoint. Major's principal Tory hero, Iain Macleod, was admired more for what he could teach him about oratory and overcoming handicaps than for his political beliefs, which in Macleod's case were equally difficult to pin down.

Major had eschewed the opportunity of outlining his philosophy when invited to give the prestigious Conservative Political Centre lecture at the 1988 Party Conference. His beliefs however can be traced from four specific platforms. The first was the speech the following year to the 'Radical Society' at the invitation of the chairman, former MP Neville Sandelson, when he was still Foreign Secretary. The speech, drafted by Maurice Fraser, a bright special adviser he inherited at the FCO, followed several evenings talking politics with Major and encouragement for him to think boldly.[21] From their conversations, Fraser concluded that Major was 'squarely on the liberal/left of the party emotionally and intellectually'.[22]

In the heart of the speech were six criteria to be applied when considering any policy option. Would it extend opportunity? Make providers more accountable and responsive? Enhance individual responsibility? Improve life for the worst off in society? Be environmentally sound? And enable all individuals to make the maximum contribution to society?[23] All except the fifth, on the environment, were core Major instincts, which found practical expression all the way from the Citizen's Charter in 1991 to the 'Opportunity for All' theme in 1996–7. The speech to a packed fringe audience went well, and was followed by a long question and answer session. Major received visible support from Tebbit, standing in the doorway, who liked its anti-establishment tone. The speech was remarkable not least for being the first occasion in public when Major outlined his thinking on 'the classless society'.[24]

To the right-wing Adam Smith Institute, also in 1989, he gave a succinct and revealing summary of his mental outlook. 'Unlike Adam Smith, I am not a moral philosopher, nor an economist, nor an intellectual. I am a practical politician.'[25] At the 1990 Party Conference at Bournemouth, he developed his theme of the Conservatives being the party of opportunity, committed to all sections of society, and all ages, from enhancing their children's prospects of education to security in old age.[26]

Finally came his several pronouncements during the leadership election in the final week of November. On economic policy, he reiterated his long-standing aim to bring the main enemy, inflation, under control. The main new stresses came on social policy: not just a 'classless society' by the year

2000, but more money for education and an enhanced status for teachers, the regeneration of inner cities and a bigger rented sector, with the NHS to receive his very strong support. Finally, on foreign policy, a tough line against Iraq in the Gulf, and on the EC a policy that would ensure Britain being 'absolutely at the centre of Europe'. His line on Europe, however, was not that of a Europhile, as he also spoke against Britain joining the Social Chapter, or moving towards a single currency without sufficient caution. On the poll tax he was similarly undogmatic, indicating he would be in favour of change, but giving no clear idea of how far he was prepared to go.[27]

These Major utterances were all he possessed by way of a personal manifesto. He had not written a book or even a pamphlet setting out his thinking. Nor did he subscribe to a particular intellectual tradition in the Party that would have allowed him to take some of their positions, and policies, off the peg. On one of his first evenings as Prime Minister, he recalls how he sat down in the Cabinet Room and wrote some words which might serve as his aims for his premiership. First came 'inflation', which he saw as the root cause of Britain's decline and loss of competitiveness over many years. Next came 'Ireland', an issue he had encountered as a whip but not studied deeply: 'I always believed Northern Ireland should have been given a higher profile and that it was not acceptable to have any part of the UK engulfed in that sort of bloodshed and treated almost as though it was a matter of course.' A third word was 'unemployment', which he believed had to be reduced. Finally, 'opportunity' and 'class'. By a 'classless society', he explains, he did not mean he was against the existence of separate classes, but rather

I disliked intensely the automatic assumption that if you came from a particular stable you were a certain sort of person. I disliked the different opportunities that gave to people. I disliked the patronising way that the broad mass of people were often treated by bureaucracy. I probably thought I knew more about how those people felt than, if I may be immodest, any Conservative politician for fifty years who was remotely near the top of the party.[28]

No sooner had he arrived at Number Ten, however, than problems requiring his decisions crowded him in and made it hard to find the space to develop these ideas. Not until after Christmas was he able to sit down with advisers at Number Ten to hone these ideas and translate his inchoate thoughts into policy proposals.

Major's First Reshuffle

With Major's first Cabinet scheduled for 11 a.m. on only his second day as Prime Minister, 29 November, his priority was to finalise his choices and see everyone concerned. His main aims were to reward his campaign team and backers, heal the Party after the divisions of the previous months – especially in the run-up to and during the leadership campaign – and to avoid alienating

Mrs Thatcher herself and her followers. As Major sat down with Andrew Turnbull, whom he inherited as Principal Private Secretary from Mrs Thatcher, it became apparent that despite his confidence of success during the campaign, he had done little real thinking as to who would do what.[29]

Of the senior ministers, Hurd was straightforward: he could remain as Foreign Secretary. Heseltine posed his first real problem. A hike too far would have antagonised Mrs Thatcher and her loyalists, who had regarded Heseltine as beneath contempt ever since his walkout from Cabinet over Westland in January 1986. Since that point, his enthusiasms for closer European integration, intervention in industry, and replacement of the poll tax were all anathema to her and her kind. Major had, however, made it clear on his first visit to the House of Commons as Prime Minister that he would unite the Party and have a 'Cabinet of all the talents'.[30] Heseltine had won warm plaudits from the Major camp for the way he promptly announced that he would not take the leadership contest into a third ballot, but would stand aside for Major. Major had debated making him Party Chairman to exploit his campaigning gifts, but ruled this out as too risky.[31] Heseltine himself wanted to be made President of the Board of Trade, but was persuaded that it would be politically difficult at this point, and was half-promised that it would happen later.[32] He did not want to be Home Secretary, but he accepted the job of Environment Secretary, with a brief to decide on the future of the poll tax. Ian Aitken described the appointment, rightly, as 'a master stroke'.[33]

The other key decision was the chancellorship. Lamont was appointed, principally for two reasons: he had been Chief Secretary in the Treasury for the previous year, and had served continually in the department for four years; Major thought he would be the obvious candidate to assure the markets of continuity, especially only seven weeks into ERM entry, and with the recession deepening.[34] Second, he had been Major's campaign manager during the leadership election. Some doubts were expressed in the highest quarters about whether he was up to being promoted from the most junior Cabinet post to the most senior, but Major swept reservations aside.[35] There may well have been an element, too, of Major thinking that he could still steer economic policy to some extent from Number Ten. On the other hand Lamont, and some Treasury advisers, felt that Major had a weaker understanding of economic principles than the new Chancellor. Lamont was certainly a more convinced Thatcherite, and was an incongruous choice given Major's intentions of increasing public spending and building relations with Europe. Ideological differences more than bad personal chemistry led to the deterioration of the relationship between Prime Minister and Chancellor over the next two and a half years.

Other names considered for Chancellor included John MacGregor, Major's acclaimed predecessor as Chief Secretary (1985–7); Kenneth Clarke, an MP since 1970 who had already held three Cabinet posts, most recently Education Secretary since the beginning of November; and Chris Patten, fellow Blue Chip, who had survived the unenviable job of handling the poll tax as

Environment Secretary since July 1989.[36] Clarke was a shade unlucky to be left where he was, though he professes to have been unsurprised, and had barely begun to get his teeth into education reform, a priority area for the government and a challenge his combative nature relished.[37]

Patten, a former director of the Conservative Research Department (1974–9), had a slower rise than his talents deserved under Mrs Thatcher, who distrusted his connections with Heath, and thought him politically too far to the left. Major had no such qualms, and swiftly appointed him Party Chairman. Patten had all the qualities Major needed: knowledge of the Party, administrative ability and force of personality to knock Central Office into shape for the general election campaign, which would have to come within eighteen months and in all probability, Major thought at the time, much earlier.[38] Major also regarded Patten as a good friend (despite Patten backing Hurd in the leadership election); their relationship was indeed to deepen into the closest political friendship of Major's premiership. Patten was called to Number Ten away from a lunch with American correspondents. He was surprised by the offer, and at once determined that, from what he had seen of Prime Minister–Party Chairman relations, 'above all else, I would never allow a piece of tissue paper to settle between me as Chairman and John Major'.[39]

Patten's appointment meant moving Kenneth Baker out of the party chairmanship. Major had not rated Baker's performance particularly highly, a view reinforced when Patten reported on the poor shape of the organisation and finances of Central Office. Major regarded Baker nevertheless as one of the Party's 'big beasts' and in his drive for reconciliation it was important to give this vocal Thatcher loyalist the next most senior Cabinet post in the government, Home Secretary.[40]

Mrs Thatcher had promoted David Waddington Home Secretary in October 1989 from Chief Whip. A solid, experienced Tory, though an unassuming figure, he possessed impeccably right-wing credentials and was thought likely to reassure the Thatcherites. Robin Butler, Cabinet Secretary and Head of the Home Civil Service since 1987, the senior official in Whitehall, had stressed to Major the need to find a disinterested and utterly loyal source of counsel, such as Whitelaw famously was to Mrs Thatcher.[41] Major regarded Waddington as an establishment Tory with 'bottom', and he alighted on Waddington as the man to fit the Whitelaw role, which Major described as 'a comrade away from the hurly-burly to help him manage the business of government'.[42]

Waddington turned down the offer of the leadership of the Commons, combined with chairing several important Cabinet committees, but accepted instead leadership of the Lords, agreeing that he could also chair some Cabinet committees from there. The idea of anchor man was a good one; the choice of individual to fill it, however, was not. Waddington came to regard the move as 'the biggest mistake I have made in my life'.[43] He did not like the Lords leadership job, nor did the 'Whitelaw' role come to fruition.[44]

He became an increasingly marginal figure over the coming months, and to rub salt in the wound, the vacancy at the Ribble Valley seat he vacated when he was elevated to the Lords led to an embarrassing by-election for the government.

For Chief Whip, Richard Ryder was promoted from the relatively junior job of Economic Secretary at the Treasury. A doubly clever appointment, Ryder was trusted totally by Mrs Thatcher (not only had he been her Political Secretary, but his wife Caroline was her personal secretary), and was also discreet almost to a fault, tough and utterly loyal to Major. He had impressed Major during the leadership election by the way he had managed the parliamentary party and the Party in the country for him.[45]

Ryder succeeded Tim Renton, who was perhaps lucky to become Major's Minister for the Arts, a post outside the Cabinet. Mellor, another Major helper during the leadership election and a good friend, was promoted to Cabinet as Chief Secretary, with an unwritten brief to keep an eye on Lamont. Mellor had also entered Parliament in 1979, as MP for Putney, the seat Major had sought for himself in 1976. A grammar school and Cambridge product, he had been a successful barrister before being given a series of junior ministerial posts by Mrs Thatcher, earning a reputation as intelligent, publicity-conscious and an effective debater.

Major's final Cabinet promotion was again prompted by a debt of friendship: Ian Lang, whom the whips rated highly as an unusually safe pair of hands.[46] The obvious position for Lang was Scottish Secretary, a logical promotion from Minister of State at the Scottish Office, where he had served for over three years. This appointment meant moving Malcolm Rifkind from Scottish to Transport Secretary, at best a sideways step for a figure about whom Major then had reservations.

Apart from Mrs Thatcher, two figures left the Cabinet, Lord Belstead, Leader of the Lords, and Cecil Parkinson. Belstead self-effacingly accepted the job of Paymaster-General outside the Cabinet. With speculation that Major might sack him, Parkinson's fate seemed uncertain. Thatcher's final Transport Secretary and one-time favourite opted instead to fall on his own sword. He phoned Major on Wednesday morning, congratulated him, and asked to be released.[47]

Major moved nine of the twenty-two of his Cabinet, leaving thirteen *in situ*. These were, apart from Hurd and Clarke, John MacGregor, Lord President and Leader of the Commons; Lord Mackay of Clashfern, Lord Chancellor; John Gummer, Agriculture Secretary; Tom King, Defence Secretary; Michael Howard, Employment Secretary; John Wakeham, Energy Secretary; William Waldegrave, Health Secretary; Peter Brooke, Northern Ireland Secretary; Tony Newton, Social Security Secretary; Peter Lilley, Trade Secretary; and David Hunt, Welsh Secretary.

Lower down, at minister of state and parliamentary secretary level, Major had neither will nor time to make many changes. Heseltine pressed hard to secure jobs for Mates and others of his backers, but unsuccessfully.[48] Major promoted some of his own favourites: Sir George Young, sacked in 1988 for opposing the poll tax, was made Housing Minister; Gillian Shephard became Minister of State at the Treasury, and Brian Mawhinney, Minister of State at the Northern Ireland Office.

Major was relieved by the speed and comparative ease with which the reshuffle locked into place. His selection came under immediate attack from two perspectives. Less damaging was the charge that its heavy preference for public school and Oxbridge ministers made a mockery of his talk of a classless society. More seriously, he had unwittingly appointed the first all-male Cabinet since Home's in 1963–4, which gave Labour its first chance to claim the initiative.[49]

Gillian Shephard smartly defended his appointments on television, and the whips actively highlighted her promotion and also that of Virginia Bottomley to Ministers of State, hinting that preferment would follow swiftly once they proved themselves. At Question Time that day Robert Hughes (Labour) asked whether the woman in Cabinet would be Mrs Thatcher, acting as back-seat driver. Kinnock sat conspicuously flanked by his Shadow Cabinet women colleagues. One of them, Ann Clwyd, accused Major of sexism, while Harriet Harman, sitting behind Kinnock, said Major was 'lost in an old boys' network'. Clare Short hit harder with 'Mr Major's opportunity society does not extend to women.'[50]

The most damaging critic, however, was on his own benches. Teresa Gorman denounced Major in the lobbies and told the press, 'I am hopping mad. I will go and squat on the front bench and they will have to evict me.'[51] Number Ten suspected Gorman's anger stemmed from her own failure to receive preferment;[52] the animosity was to harden over the years.

The all-male issue stung Major. He told aides that with only seventeen female Conservative MPs to choose from, and no obvious senior women ministers in the wings, his legacy gave him little room for manoeuvre.[53] Of all Tory prime ministers this century, he was perhaps the most convinced of the merits of equal opportunities. But he had another appointment in mind which he hoped would go some way to correct the imbalance.

Sarah Hogg and the Policy Unit

For the senior political appointment in his office he chose Sarah Hogg, to head his Policy Unit in Number Ten. She became the critical, and the most controversial, figure inside Major's Number Ten. Female she was, but classless she certainly was not. Married to Douglas Hogg, Minister of State at the Foreign Office and son of Lord Hailsham (Lord Chancellor 1970–74 and 1979–87), she was herself the daughter of another former Tory Cabinet minister, Lord Boyd-Carpenter. Aged forty-four on her appointment, she had gained a first in PPE from Oxford, and had spent the years following as a journalist, first on *The Economist* and culminating as economics editor of the *Daily Telegraph*. Her strengths were her sharp intellect, formidable appetite for work and fierce determination. Politically, she was in the centre tradition of her father and father-in-law, but not a Thatcherite. Some adverse press comment on her appointment noted that her strengths did not lie in policy-making nor in devising new ideas.[54]

Major had met her through her journalistic work when he had been Chief Secretary at the Treasury, and then Chancellor, and they had formed a bond. She was exactly the sort of economically literate, bright woman he liked and with whom he felt comfortable. During the leadership election they had had breakfast together and discussed policy.[55] Other names for head of the Policy Unit, such as David Willetts, Director of the Centre for Policy Studies, Howard Davies, of the Institute of Directors[56] and Graham Mather, General Director of the Institute of Economic Affairs, were mentioned in the press,[57] but Major was never in any doubt: he wanted Sarah Hogg.[58]

No one expected Brian Griffiths, Mrs Thatcher's head of Policy Unit since 1985, to remain. He offered some help to Major as he planned his government on the first Wednesday, but by the evening attention was already turning to his successor.[59] Griffiths had made some important contributions in education and economics until 1988–9, but was no longer a commanding presence in either Whitehall or even Number Ten, and lacked the clout of some of Mrs Thatcher's earlier Policy Unit heads, notably John Redwood (1983–5).

Hogg's first task was to recruit her team. The Policy Unit, though its salaries are paid from public finances, is made up of civil servants (normally two, seconded from their Whitehall departments), and political appointees (drawn from outside government). She invited the two civil servants *in situ* to continue until the general election, Carolyn Sinclair, a high-flier reputed to have had Mrs Thatcher's ear, who oversaw health, environment and Home Office issues, and John Mills, who oversaw local government, Europe and education.[60] Mills had battled for the Policy Unit to be given a watching brief over EC developments but the move had been 'fiercely resisted' by Charles Powell, Mrs Thatcher's foreign affairs adviser at Number Ten, until she was persuaded to rule otherwise. Only one of Mrs Thatcher's political appointees remained, Howell Harris Hughes, recruited from the City in early 1989 and asked by Sarah Hogg to stay on to oversee the DTI, employment and Welsh affairs.[61] For the first few weeks until Christmas, Harris Hughes, Mills and Sinclair sat rather awkwardly in the second-floor suite of small offices at the front of Number Ten that houses the Policy Unit, with the flow of paperwork and activity limited, while Sarah Hogg completed her recruitment.

Some from the Thatcher Policy Unit, such as Robin Harris, resigned at once. A Thatcher diehard, he had worked there after his period as Director of the Conservative Research Department (1985–9). He departed Number Ten to write Mrs Thatcher's speeches and articles and to begin work organising her memoirs.[62] As her *éminence grise*, he rapidly developed a contempt for Major, and penned some of Mrs Thatcher's most withering attacks on him in the years to come. George Guise, who was an ideologue and also close to Mrs Thatcher personally, was told he was no longer required, and her final Policy Unit member, Andrew Dunlop, left at the same time.

Major wanted Sarah Hogg to bring in Nick True, whom Major had met at Health and Social Security (1985–7) when True had been Fowler's special adviser. Major rated True very highly, and had planned to bring him into his Treasury team, before the leadership crisis broke.[63] True barely knew Hogg. At a pre-Christmas meeting they disagreed about the poll tax (he thought it might still be made to work), but got on well, and their relationship swiftly blossomed thereafter with True emerging as her deputy, a title formally recognised in 1992.[64] True, though to the right of Major on social policy, became a deeply trusted aide and speech writer.

Jonathan Hill, who with Hogg and True became the third figure in the triumvirate of Major loyalists at Number Ten, wrote to Hogg in December to offer his services. After a history first at Cambridge in 1982, and an uncompleted doctorate under Norman Stone, he drifted into working at Central Office in 1985, but his career took off only as Kenneth Clarke's special adviser from 1986. He left in 1989, attracted by the salary offered at Lowe Bell Communications, the public relations agency run by Tim Bell, but yearned to return to the centre of politics.[65] The arrival of Major provided the opportunity, and Hogg grabbed it avidly. True oversaw social security and the Citizen's Charter when it emerged in early 1991, Hill transport, housing, inner cities, and increasingly presentation; both joined formally in the New Year. Hogg's final appointee was Alan Rosling, a young business executive brought in from Courtaulds, who oversaw defence and Scottish issues.

Having built up her team of seven, she set about defining the Policy Unit's new role in Major's Number Ten. She herself took on responsibility for the economy, and overseeing the Prime Minister's relations with the Chancellor and Treasury. Griffiths had failed to keep on top of Number Ten–Treasury relations in the last years of Mrs Thatcher, his efforts undermined by her reliance on Walters, the increasingly cold relationship between her and Lawson, and the latter's determination to keep her, and others, at bay. Hogg rapidly realised that in reasserting the position of head of the Policy Unit, she would need to sit in on all discussions between Prime Minister and Chancellor. Once it became appreciated that she had Major's backing on this, her pivotal place in economic policy duly transpired, to the chagrin of Lamont, who rapidly became suspicious and resentful of Number Ten interference.[66] Hogg became intensely involved also in the replacement for the poll tax and preparations for the Intergovernmental Conference at Maastricht in December 1991, but she also tried to keep her vision broad on government policy as a whole.

The restoration of the Policy Unit to the mainstream of Whitehall life was eased by the Prime Minister's demonstrable backing for the Unit, and for her personally. The emergence was also aided by the part the Policy Unit would play in helping Major develop his own thoughts into a distinctive platform and style for the coming general election.

John Mills, one of the Policy Unit members inherited from Mrs Thatcher, observed:

... she had the Prime Minister's ear ... she was the Prime Minister's woman, selected by him, brought in by him to be a strong arm. She herself was very efficient and bubbling with energy, knew everybody, or so it seemed, had terrific antennae, and we all felt re-energised. The message went around the bush telegraph in Whitehall very quickly that a new force was in town, whereas by late 1990 under Thatcher it was as if the system knew her power was waning and that therefore the Policy Unit couldn't deliver.[67]

Once Hogg had established herself, relations between the Policy Unit and the Number Ten Private Office also improved sharply,[68] although Powell still resisted their involvement on Europe. He would leave Number Ten four months later, in March 1991. Friction with the Private Office also continued, albeit at a reduced rate, over economic policy, finance and local government. Hogg strove to keep the Policy Unit profile high. She attended Cabinet and key Cabinet committee meetings, and was a ubiquitous presence. A Prime Minister is never more powerful, with ministers and officials, than in his first few months. Major stood tall; people did what he wanted.

Hogg's Unit was different from those under Thatcher in other ways too. Its political appointees were less a priesthood of true believers. Thatcher's Policy Unit members have been described as 'gamekeepers, who were there to make sure the rules were being observed'.[69] None of the Major incomers, Hogg, True, Hill nor Rosling, were especially dogmatic, and they spanned a range of Conservative views. Expression of heterodox viewpoints became acceptable again, and papers going up to the Prime Minister were not filtered by Hogg for purity as they had been by Griffiths.[70] The Prime Minister would even drift up to the Policy Unit offices himself, unheard of in Thatcher's day; he would also like to be briefed, as was his style, by the Unit member working on the detail. Hogg was businesslike in the way she planned the Unit's work: she chaired weekly meetings, usually on Mondays, and earned the respect of her team because of her drive, practical know-how, and support for their work.

Sarah Hogg's Policy Unit 1990–92 – the height of its influence and success – was at the heart of government, involved in all discussions key to the Prime Minister and policy. Secretaries of state would phone up asking if the Policy Unit was happy with what they were proposing, anxious to secure its backing, aware of the influence it carried with the Prime Minister. It would not always be that way.

Major's Number Ten

The Policy Unit is just one part of the incredibly small office, consisting of only twenty key players and sixty overall including secretaries, which makes up Number Ten, the office of the Prime Minister.

The pivot is the Private Office, the buckle that joins the Prime Minister to the rest of Whitehall. The Private Office is situated in an inner and outer room through a door off the south end of the Cabinet Room. It is run by the Principal Private Secretary, the third most powerful official in Whitehall, behind the Cabinet Secretary and Permanent Secretary of the Treasury, who, with the Queen's Private Secretary, form the 'inner establishment' guarding the constitution. The relationship between Principal Private Secretary and Prime Minister can become immensely close, as Jock Colville with Churchill (1951–5) or Robert Armstrong with Heath (1970–74). Major inherited Andrew Turnbull, a Treasury product, who had served Thatcher since 1988.

Turnbull, an outstanding Whitehall operator, knew how to deliver what the Prime Minister sought and was respected as a heavyweight, who served Major with great effectiveness until May 1992. His influence was never more important than in the first few months when Major was new, and so were his three principal advisers, Hogg, O'Donnell (Press Secretary) and Chaplin, his Political Secretary. Not afraid to challenge Major, or offer advice he knew would not be welcome, Turnbull was in many ways ideal for Major, courageous, and independent-minded. They shared some common facets too: a grammar school background, and love of football (Turnbull was an ardent Spurs supporter); but the personal chemistry was never quite right. Turnbull was in the mould of John Gieve (Principal Private Secretary to Major as Chancellor, 1989–90); Major respected and valued him, but they were never personally close. Turnbull is a shy man, which Major interpreted as coolness. A shortcoming in Major, and a corollary of his not having close Cabinet friends, was that he liked his closest aides to be loyal almost to a fault, to have an emotional commitment to the work, not to be detached. Turnbull was not of that stamp. Nevertheless, he and Major parted amicably when, in May 1992, he returned to the Treasury, subsequently to become Permanent Secretary at Environment.

Below the Principal Private Secretary were four private secretaries, the most important of whom was the official who dealt with foreign affairs, who shared the inner office with the Principal Private Secretary. The incumbent was Charles Powell, who had figured prominently in Major's life during his brief period as Foreign Secretary in the summer of 1989, and who, abetted by Mrs Thatcher, had defied attempts by the Whitehall establishment to move him on from the post he had held since 1984. Powell's Eurosceptical, Foreign Office-sceptical instincts chimed deeply with Mrs Thatcher's own. From the mid-1980s he was unquestionably the most powerful figure in Number Ten, overshadowing the milder Nigel Wicks (Principal Private Secretary, 1985–8), and having a sparring partnership with Turnbull. Despite the relationship Major had cultivated with Powell when he had been Foreign Secretary, he was wary of working with him when he became Prime Minister, not least because of his reputation for arousing suspicion and fear in Whitehall, particularly in the FCO, and his almost umbilical relationship with Mrs Thatcher.

Major's first quip to Powell when the latter called in to see him in his study on his first Wednesday at Number Ten, was, 'I don't know if I can do this job.'[71] Powell had a gift for making the powerful confide in him, and he rapidly proved his indispensability to Major: his knowledge of foreign actors and issues was *sans pareil*, and the continuity of personnel was all the more important with the Gulf crisis hanging over government. Powell was keen, after nearly eight years at Number Ten, to leave government service for the City, believing he would find no other FCO job as satisfying as his current position, even assuming an acceptable niche could be found for him. But equally he did not wish to leave with Mrs Thatcher, because it would have seemed that as a civil servant he had become hopelessly tarred with the Thatcher brush. Powell proved his worth, and performed an invaluable handholding operation until, in March 1991, he left with Major's sincere regret, to be replaced by Stephen Wall (Major's trusted former FCO Private Secretary).

The other three private secretaries were more shadowy figures: Barry Potter, on economic affairs; Dominic Morris, parliamentary affairs; and Caroline Slocock, followed in January 1991 by William Chapman, on home affairs. Morris was to emerge as a key figure, returning to the Policy Unit in 1993–6, where he handled European issues. The final person with a desk in the Private Office was the diary secretary, a subordinate but important post as the gatekeeper of access to the Prime Minister, with Thatcher's Amanda Ponsonby being replaced by Sandra Phillips.

At night, after the security guards had gone round and closed the wooden shutters in Number Ten, the building became a cavernous place. If Major had no engagements, he would wander down from working on his boxes in the flat, and call in on the Private Office, or invite them for a drink or chat. Even in his first few months, he was often a loner as Prime Minister.[72]

The Press Office, situated on the ground floor at the front of the building, was the organ that linked the Prime Minister to the media. Press Secretary since 1979 had been Bernard Ingham, the most influential figure in Thatcher's Number Ten after Powell. Ingham had been closely identified with Thatcher, and when she resigned he too decided to take early retirement.[73] Major immediately invited Gus O'Donnell, his thirty-eight-year-old Treasury Press Secretary, to succeed Ingham. There was no personal difficulty with Ingham: he swiftly settled down to write his book (published in 1991, *Kill The Messenger*), and happily offered O'Donnell advice for the first few weeks.[74] Indeed, he would have liked to have offered Major more counsel than opportunities permitted and, as a master at handling the press, it was a loss that more notice could not have been taken of him. Robin Butler gave O'Donnell clear instructions that he wanted him to lower the profile of the Press Secretary job after Ingham's high exposure, a process not helped initially by the interpretation put on O'Donnell's being the first Number Ten appointment to be announced, prematurely, by the BBC's John Cole.[75]

O'Donnell stayed in the job a little over three years, and rapidly became one of Major's most trusted and closest advisers. But O'Donnell was an economist, primarily, who became a press secretary only by accident when his domestic circumstances led him to prefer the job of Press Secretary to that of Principal Private Secretary to Lawson at the Treasury. He never entirely settled into the press mould. He arrived at Downing Street with a reputation for having been more accessible to the press than most Treasury press secretaries.[76] Delighted to restore relations with lobby journalists, and welcome back the *Independent*, the *Guardian* and the *Scotsman*, which had left under Ingham, his reception in his first year was positive.[77] Major came to Number Ten an inexperienced media operator, prone to uncertainty, particularly during 'doorstep' interviews. O'Donnell's term as Press Secretary saw him become more assured – perhaps too assured and therefore indiscreet. Major was more willing to accept advice from the mild O'Donnell than he would from more abrasive media professionals such as Christopher Meyer, his next Press Secretary. But O'Donnell was in many ways too guileless and pleasant-mannered for an increasingly cynical and combative press. Though always liked personally, he committed the error of becoming too close and informal with journalists, to suffer when they turned hostile after Black Wednesday in September 1992.

The final main organ of Number Ten, the Political Office, linked Major to the Conservative Party, and was situated in a room off the north end of the Cabinet Room. At its head was the Political Secretary. Again, it was a formality that Mrs Thatcher's incumbent, John Whittingdale, another doctrinaire loyalist, would depart with her. Major could not decide which of his two special advisers from the Treasury, Judith Chaplin or Andrew Tyrie, to appoint. Splitting the job was considered, but eventually he decided on Chaplin, influenced not least by the desirability of having more women in senior posts, with Central Office pressing to make an early announcement of her selection.[78]

A product of the exclusive Wycombe Abbey girls' public school, Judith Chaplin was immensely organised, determined and ambitious. After a degree in economics at Cambridge, she founded a nursery school in Norfolk, which developed from her providing for her own children. In public life she became Chairman of Education on Norfolk county council, and later head of policy at the Institute of Directors before moving to the Treasury as a special adviser. She had set her heart on becoming an MP since the early 1980s,[79] and had been selected for the Parliamentary seat of Newbury, which would have meant resigning her position from the Treasury, a government-paid post. But as the Political Secretary was paid for out of Party funds, she could combine the Number Ten post with that of candidate. She had not reckoned on finding herself in a considerable conflict of loyalty, but her Newbury Association now put pressure on her to spend increasing time in the constituency, just as Number Ten demanded her full attention.

Her absences from Downing Street were increasingly frowned upon, and she was unable to assist in even some core functions, such as providing the political input for the Prime Minister when he prepared for Prime Minister's Questions (PMQs) each Tuesday and Thursday, or liaising with Central Office on manifesto preparation.[80] David Cameron was brought in to help with PMQs, an aspect of the work Chaplin never liked,[81] and Jonathan Hill increasingly came downstairs from the Policy Unit to take over her liaison work with the Party in the country.

With her growing difficulties running an effective Political Office, Chaplin's personal relations with colleagues began to deteriorate. She was jealous of Sarah Hogg's influence with Major, but also found Hogg's style uncomfortable. As her diary reveals, relations had turned sour well before the general election.[82] Some in Central Office viewed the Chaplin–Hogg contretemps as an Amazonian struggle, in which the latter emerged victorious, colonising the Political Secretary's work.[83] Chaplin had little stomach for a turf war: she continued to enjoy a trusting friendship with Major, but with a dense atmosphere at Number Ten, she increasingly withdrew to nurse her constituency, which was under Liberal Democrat attack. She duly won Newbury in the April 1992 general election, and represented it until her sudden death ten months later.

The Political Office also comprised the Prime Minister's Parliamentary Private Secretary (PPS), the bridge with the parliamentary party. Following Tony Favell's resignation over entry into the ERM, Major had asked his old friend Graham Bright to join him as Chancellor's PPS.[84] Major felt comfortable with Bright, who shared his lower-middle-class, non-university background and had the same outlook on life. After Bright had been a zealous presence in the leadership election, it was natural for Major to invite him into Downing Street. Criticised for keeping the Prime Minister too remote from parliamentary opinion, and failing to communicate MPs' concerns sufficiently, he nevertheless remained with Major as a loyal and trusted lieutenant until 1994.

Barbara Wallis, Major's constituency secretary, also came over into Number Ten, and combined the task of keeping Major in touch with Huntingdon with the job of secretary to Norma. When she left in 1992, the job was split into two. She retained the strongest recollections of the first few weeks, not least of her worries coping with the 60,000 letters that arrived between Major's appointment and Christmas,[85] as opposed to the usual weekly diet of three to eight thousand that are sent to Downing Street.[86] The processing of letters was undertaken by a ten-strong correspondence unit. Typing was handled by the thirteen 'garden room girls', situated in a subterranean area at the back of the house, overseen by the redoubtable Janice

Richards. There were ten messengers who kept information and people flowing in the building.

Two final figures were important in Major's Downing Street. Percy Cradock had been appointed Mrs Thatcher's Foreign Policy Adviser in January 1984, and was one of only three senior figures (alongside Turnbull and Powell) to survive the transition in November 1990. The post was created in 1982 and arose from Mrs Thatcher's disenchantment with the Foreign Office during the Falklands War, when she felt she had not been well advised, or warned, about developments in the South Atlantic. She wished to have an alternative opinion to Foreign Office advice. Cradock, a former Ambassador to China (1978–83) and authority on the Far East, notably Hong Kong, took over from another former ambassador, Anthony Parsons.

Typically for Number Ten, with no job descriptions or terms of reference, Cradock had to interpret his role as he thought best. The Foreign Office was unsurprisingly suspicious, and tried to hem him in with self-denying ordinances, such as forbidding him contact with foreign ambassadors or press. But when Powell emerged as a major pro-Thatcher figure in Number Ten, the Foreign Office began to see Cradock less as enemy than as an ally, communicating to it what the Prime Minister was thinking in foreign affairs.[87] Major quickly formed a good relationship with Cradock, who gave him a useful and paternal source of advice on an area, foreign policy, where he still felt weak. He also let Cradock continue to chair the Joint Intelligence Committee, which oversaw the intelligence activities of MI5, MI6 and the government's communications centre, GCHQ. Cradock filtered the information, and briefed Major on it.[88]

The Appointments Office, situated on the first floor at the front of the building,[89] advised the Prime Minister on his patronage powers, which range from Church of England bishops to museum trustees. Robin Catford, the incumbent since 1982, was a conventional and correct official.

Genuine sadness – shock, indeed – had been felt by Number Ten's staff at Mrs Thatcher's departure. They lined up, as custom dictated, to clap and cheer her out on the morning of 28 November *en route* for the palace, and two hours later, clapped Major and Norma as they walked into Number Ten. Although they had found Thatcher always very considerate, the atmosphere in the building became more relaxed after her departure. Many Whitehall officials who dealt regularly with Number Ten breathed a sigh of relief when she left, especially after her bizarre final fifteen months, when Number Ten had resembled the Elizabethan court, with the monarch, flanked by her two favourite courtiers, Powell and Ingham, uttering quixotic decisions while her most senior barons, like Howe and Lawson, lost their heads.

'We'd been having such a mad, wild time,' recalled one senior official, 'we were just relieved to be off the helter-skelter, back on level ground, with a chap who fitted into a normal mould, easy, likeable, who went round talking to people and actually listening to them.'[90] But with issues crowding swiftly in, any honeymoon proved short-lived.

Major's Priorities

With the appointments in place, foreign concerns, above all the Gulf crisis, immediately pressed on the new Prime Minister's attention. Major had given only passing attention to the invasion of Kuwait by Saddam Hussein's Iraqi army on 2 August. Mrs Thatcher had taken the key decisions on committing British troops at her final Cabinet on 22 November and had agreed to double British troop deployment.[91] Major had not been a member of Thatcher's War Cabinet, so had to be taken through the papers step by step, before being briefed by the chiefs of staff. The operation, he was told, could require very difficult decisions, especially if chemical and biological weapons were used. George Bush and the White House were contacted immediately after his arrival at Number Ten to be reassured of Major's commitment to continuity of policy. Major kept the War Cabinet intact, but brought back the Cabinet Office, which Mrs Thatcher had excluded, as the secretariat. As concerns at the prospects of war were being raised by the churches, he invited the Archbishop of Canterbury, Robert Runcie, and Cardinal Basil Hume in for talks.[92]

European Community matters were a second foreign concern. Relations with Britain's partners, Major decided, were to be improved dramatically, as *The Economist* rightly predicted, with a European Council in Rome just two weeks away. Of particular concern was Germany, with bridges needing to be rebuilt with both Chancellor Kohl and Foreign Minister Genscher, who had taken personal offence at recent remarks by Mrs Thatcher in the House of Commons. More generally, her antipathy to German reunification – which she had done her best to block – had left deep scars.[93] With other EC partners, Major's initial concern was to forestall moves, supported in many European countries, to create a 'European pillar' of NATO in opposition to US security interests.[94] The Gulf War had one welcome side-effect: it reaffirmed UK–US relations, which had taken a battering because of disagreements over Germany, Central Europe, and French nuclear tests. Dealing with a collapsing Soviet Union and new regimes in eastern Europe were Major's other pressing foreign problems.[95]

The Tory Party itself also needed attention. By his appointments, above all the binding-in of Heseltine, he had gone some way to heal the Party at Westminster. But the wider Party was sore and confused. Morale among activists was low, with anger widespread at the dumping of Mrs Thatcher. Major was also concerned at the image the Party had gained for being aloof and detached from the aspirations and lives of its supporters. From the outset he wanted to tap into the roots of Conservative voters, and see the common sense, traditional values and concerns of Conservatism restored.[96] Finding a satisfactory way of achieving this, and addressing his growing concerns about the Party's outdated structure, were, however, to defeat him.

Major's early personal initiatives, to unfreeze child benefit allowances and to award compensation to HIV-infected haemophiliacs, were intended to signal symbolic breaks from what was seen as an uncaring Thatcher tone. But they did not please all. No factor was more important in unifying the Party than the prospect of an imminent general election. At Central Office, Patten found no serious preparations, and he reported a lack of fight, and indeed skills, among some senior party officials.[97] Though the poll improvement was a source of hope, election prospects were not being helped by the state of the economy. The *Sunday Times* in an editorial 'The dark clouds gather' summed up the contrast between the promise in Britain and abroad at the start of 1990 with the bleak scenario at its conclusion.[98] Major's was not the easiest inheritance.

Major typically insisted on honouring an acceptance he had given as Chancellor to deliver a speech at Altrincham on 28 November, even though this was now his first full day as Prime Minister. It was the first of many battles over his diary, officials keen to restrict his acceptances, and Major adamant from the beginning that he was not going to duck commitments.[99] The Altrincham speech contained a telling phrase that in the Europe debate he wanted to be played on the pitch, not jeering from the terraces. The passage ironically was Charles Powell's, eager to show that the new Prime Minister was not a dyed-in-the-wool Eurosceptic.[100]

The following morning, 29 November, Major chaired his first Cabinet as Prime Minister. He welcomed the two newcomers – Lang and Mellor – and welcomed back Heseltine after an absence of fifty-nine months. He had warm words for both leadership contenders, expressed the hope that there were no bruises left over,[101] and delivered his now familiar words, 'Who would have thought it?', which eased the tension.[102] Besides the economy, he identified three priorities: the Gulf crisis, preparation for the Maastricht IGC on Europe, and the need to review the community charge. He invited everyone to look at the policy priorities in their own departments, to prepare for a series of meetings he planned to hold with ministers to discuss their proposals for policy and legislation over the coming months.[103] Discussion followed on the Middle East and Europe.[104] Ministers noted the stark contrast in atmosphere and procedure with Thatcher's Cabinets, which were more formal and where discussion was rarely encouraged. They departed for their lunch in high spirits, full of optimism about the new era.

For Major there was no chance to relax: he had to settle down to working on his first PMQs that afternoon. Becoming fluent at Question Time was one of the aspects of the job he found hardest; Hogg and Hill estimate it took him up to two years, well past the general election, to master the technique.[105] His first question that afternoon, however, was easy enough, from a Tory backbencher, 'May I assure the Prime Minister of our total and united support?' Tougher questions followed, on the poll tax and on being Mrs Thatcher's man.[106] He felt dissatisfied with his performance; at the debrief afterwards he said, 'It really wasn't very good at all.'[107] The *Daily Telegraph* was kinder: 'an assured question time debut'.[108] Favourable reports also flowed from the results of two by-elections held that day, in Paisley South and Paisley North, which saw the smallest Conservative vote loss since June 1982.[109]

By-election results would never be so favourable for Major in the future, nor indeed, after a honeymoon period, would the *Daily Telegraph*.

TWELVE

War in the Gulf, Peace in Europe:

November 1990–March 1991

THE FIRST ANXIETIES in London and Washington, on hearing of the Iraqi invasion of Kuwait, were whether Iraq would try to invade Saudi Arabia as well. At US request, British naval and air forces were despatched to protect northeast Saudi Arabia on 9 August. Concurrently, intensive US diplomatic negotiations took place to build up an international coalition to isolate Saddam Hussein. Sanctions were imposed against Iraq and on 25 August, UN Resolution 665 empowered forces to stop Iraqi trade in defiance of those sanctions. The British government came under increased pressure to commit ground forces and, on 6 September, Parliament was recalled for a special two-day debate, approving a tough government line by a 437:35 majority. A brigade group ('the Desert Rats') was duly sent to reinforce the multinational forces in Saudi Arabia, and Peter de la Billière, a former head of the SAS, was appointed Commander of British forces in the Gulf. Mrs Thatcher, chairing the small War Cabinet committee to decide British policy,[1] relished the opportunities that the crisis offered. Her departure from office denied her the chance to relive her role of war leader, as during the Falklands War in 1982, and was a reason, if not the most important, for her great sadness at leaving Number Ten.

The key deployment decision, to commit nearly 30,000 British forces personnel to the Gulf, prompted by Saddam's failure to comply with UN resolutions, was taken by Cabinet the week before Major became premier. This was rapidly followed by the passage of the key UN Security Council Resolution 678 on 29 November, which set the deadline of 15 January 1991 for Iraqi withdrawal from Kuwait, and authorised the use of 'all necessary force' if the resolution was not acted upon. The resolution was passed after intensive US–UK consultations, and an exhaustive mission by James Baker, US Secretary of State, travelling around the world visiting all Security Council member states except Cuba. Hurd also missed Major's first Cabinet on 29 November to attend the UN meeting. From the outset, Major was aware that Iraq was now presented with a very short ultimatum to withdraw, or face the prospect of war.

Britain was unquestionably the junior partner behind the US in the campaign. Tom King, the Defence Secretary, had already conceded in October 1990 that if it came to war, British forces would serve under

US 'tactical command'. The British nevertheless were the keystone in the growing international coalition, which included several moderate Arab states.[2] So the relationship was crucial to the Americans, especially after their disappointment at the Germans' response, on whom they had pinned high hopes. For US domestic consumption the White House needed to demonstrate an international alliance, as war was not proving a popular prospect.

Washington's first reaction on learning of Mrs Thatcher's departure was surprise and just a little irritation. The White House debated whether Major might want a delay, to give him time to settle in,[3] and whether he would have the stomach of Mrs Thatcher for a fight. The British, for their part, wondered whether the resolve to go all the way to war was shared fully by those surrounding Bush, not just in Congress but even in the administration.[4] Initial apprehensions were reduced by a phone call from Major to Bush at the end of November, and by the news that Charles Powell (a key figure in the eyes of the White House) would be continuing at Number Ten.[5] Bush himself had met Major only perfunctorily, but Baker had encountered him as Foreign Secretary and Chancellor, and despite differences over the Vietnam refugees in Hong Kong, reported favourably.[6]

An early meeting between Major and Bush was deemed crucial, in view of the imminence of the ultimatum deadline. Officials at Number Ten and the White House found a space on 21–2 December, when the President would be at his retreat at Camp David. The meeting would bring Major up to date on latest US intelligence and thinking on the crisis, and reassure the Americans finally that Major was totally behind the US plan to attack, at the earliest opportunity. As a subsidiary aim, it was hoped that a personal relationship would be forged between Bush and Major.[7]

Major flew the Atlantic with Norma and Charles Powell (significantly, neither Hurd nor King was in the party). On arrival in Washington, they were due to fly by helicopter to Camp David, but as the weather was misty and inclement they drove. In the first car Bush and Major sat together on the back seat, with Brent Scowcroft, National Security Adviser, and Powell facing them on the jumpseats.[8] For the hour and a half of the journey, they discussed war plans intensively. Bush had asked Scowcroft whether they should divulge the exact details to Major, and he was told they were bound to. So in the car, Bush said 'John, we're going to keep working, joining you on the diplomatic trail, but if all this fails, on or about January 15, we are going to have to commit our force to battle.'[9] Major swallowed hard: there was at the back of his, and everyone else's, mind the hope that it might never come to war, but he offered his assent,[10] without saying – and this was noted carefully by Bush and Scowcroft – that he would have to consult with his Cabinet or Defence Secretary. 'I was very impressed', Bush said, 'by his total commitment, his "we're with you" attitude.'[11] Major, for his part, was struck by Bush's determination to fight, and did not believe the Americans thought that a way out would be found.[12]

It was a trip of bizarre contrasts. On one level two world leaders had agreed to a war that some believed might prove cataclysmic in its repercussions, on another, two families were meeting for a pre-Christmas holiday get-together. Bush liked Camp David: it was less formal than the White House, he could relax, change into casual clothes, and be isolated from the press, who were not allowed within its perimeter. Norma, always prone to carsickness, had suffered on the journey along the snowy road winding up the valley to Camp David. Barbara Bush greeted the cars on arrival. She asked Norma what she would like to do, and was struck by the resolution with which Norma replied that she would just like to go off to their cabin and rest (Camp David has separate cabins for visitors).

For Norma, the trip had loomed large in her mind, not only because it was her first overseas engagement as Prime Minister's wife, but because it was to the President of the United States. She was duly relieved when, on arrival, she discovered how easy it was. Barbara Bush found it refreshing to be with someone who knew her own mind: most of her visitors would defer to her judgement.[13]

The visit marked the beginning of a close relationship between the two families. While the relationship of Major and Bush lacked the longevity and historical importance of that of Thatcher and Reagan, their relationship was no less warm, and much more two-sided; Washington had always been anxious about the extent Thatcher lectured and dominated Reagan. The White House was so keen to avoid another such unbalanced relationship that Bush began his presidency in January 1989 with a determination to be his own man, and not allow Mrs Thatcher to speak for them both.[14] There were other differences. Mrs Thatcher had a deep respect for the office of the American President, and would address both Reagan and Bush as 'Mr President'. Bush, however, much preferred Major's more casual, informal style, his use of first names, and direct way of speaking.[15] Bush, who liked to have close relations with other leaders too, was not particularly sorry to see Thatcher go. His and Major's backgrounds could hardly have been more different, with Bush a patrician Yale graduate, but Major felt none of the aloofness that he experienced with many British men from similar backgrounds.

The immediate rapport at Camp David helped align both countries in the crisis. Talks that had begun in the car continued after they arrived. The main issues, in Major's words, were, 'Would the Iraqis use chemical and biological weapons? How should we respond? Should our soldiers be inoculated? How many of them could be inoculated? What sort of land war was it likely to be? How would we retain public support, which was very strong at the time, for what we were proposing to do? What would we do if the Iraqis decided to attack Israel?'[16] Major was satisfied by US responses on these points; remarkably, no substantive difference emerged, which showed the trust the British had decided to place in the essentially American-directed operation. In reality, even if Major had qualms on any point, as one so new to office he would have been very hard pressed to try to change the direction of the war juggernaut now speeding towards its destination.

In the evening a male voice army choir came up from the nearby base and sang Christmas carols in front of the blazing log fire, with Bush, wearing cowboy boots and a bootlace tie, sitting in a low seat and Major in a sweater leaning against a chair by the fire.[17]

The party broke up the next day. The Americans could not have been more pleased by the outcome. They secured Major's total support, which would be useful for them in obtaining the crucial vote from Congress in early January approving military action. Major left to spend Christmas at Great Stukeley; he and Norma wanted to have as normal a family holiday as circumstances would permit, in the security of their own home. On New Year's Day they assembled a small party of his closer political friends and colleagues – Mellor, Ryder, Lamont, Atkins, Jeffrey and Mary Archer and Sarah and Douglas Hogg – at Chequers.[18] The pattern of Christmas at The Finings and New Year at Chequers was to become a regular feature in his calender as Prime Minister.

Major as Warlord – Desert Storm

The break over Christmas and New Year gave Major his first chance to draw breath since becoming Prime Minister. There was no doubting what weighed most heavily upon him over the holiday: the Gulf, and the prospect of war. The first Prime Minister of Britain since 1945 to have no personal experience of world war, even as a civilian, he had also escaped national service by less than three years. He was apprehensive about his ability to lead the country through war and about the safety of the mushrooming numbers of servicemen and women in the Gulf. He had to consider the horrifying implications if the war spread in the Middle East, or if biological, chemical or possibly even – no one could be certain – nuclear weapons were used. Could he hold domestic opinion behind the war if it did not all go as smoothly as his military planners foretold? Grim contingency plans were being made for as many as 50,000 British casualties.[19] Hospitals throughout Britain would set aside wards for wounded and gassed. Although there was no doubting his readiness, after the US visit, to see war begin, the implications were of a different scale from anything he had ever experienced.

Major decided before Christmas to fly out to see the British forces in the Gulf.[20] Troops had been stationed there since the summer, and some of the senior officers were concerned about the effect on morale of Mrs Thatcher, a staunch defender of the services, and a proven warlord, being replaced by an unknown.[21] The trip was set for early January. On the flight out on 5 January Major was reflective, not least because of his lack of experience of matters military, and how to put himself across to the troops.[22] He had worked hard immersing himself in military language; he had begun by using wrong phrases and misusing technical jargon, and was taken gently in hand to avoid any public infelicity, especially in parliamentary statements.[23]

Major landed at Saudi Arabia's King Khalid Airport in the capital Riyadh on the morning of 6 January, greeted by an impressive number of senior Saudi royal family and ministers. After the ceremonial introductions, he was driven by his guide and minder for the trip, Peter de la Billière, to the British embassy for lunch, where he told members of the British expatriate community how much their remaining at their posts in Saudi was respected at home. After lunch he went to de la Billière's headquarters, to talk to senior officers, and was informed of the military's concerns that the initial air attacks might not be successful in reducing Iraq's fighting power by up to fifty per cent, which was their desired measure of impact before the land war began. Powell passed on to de la Billière in confidence the news that Bush had given Major in the car on the way to Camp David, that the air war would begin on 15 or 16 January. Having the news confirmed came as a big relief to him.

At Major's meeting with King Fahd – the other big event of the first day – the King assented to sign the Host Nation Agreement whereby the Saudis agreed to pay for the upkeep of British forces stationed in his country. Major had no idea how to play someone like the idiosyncratic King Fahd, who often, though not on this occasion, kept his visitors waiting around before seeing them. Charles Powell steered Major gently through this encounter.[24]

On 7 January Major flew to the port of Jubail, to observe naval manoeuvres, visit RAF units, drive a Challenger tank, and address ground troops. His message was clear: the British people were totally behind the servicemen, the cause they were involved in was just, and he stressed how essential their efforts were in evicting the Iraqis from the country they had invaded. He did not attempt to hide the risks. The attentiveness of the servicemen made a very deep and lasting impression on him, as they gathered around him. 'What they really wanted to know', he recalled, 'was were they going to have to fight, within a few days? And I said to them, in all probability – yes. And they were very relieved to hear that.'[25] Major was also struck by how young many of the servicemen were, just eighteen or nineteen, and by the trust they placed in him.

De la Billière rated the trip's effect as 'first class in every way', and was impressed that Major – 'very much his own man' – 'had come out on his own initiative'.[26] Major won the respect of the troops, both by his direct talking and absence of flannel, and by the ease with which he mixed among them, listening to them, joking, and signing autographs. Powell believes he struck just the right note: 'You can just imagine, Mrs T would have done a great Boadicea act with these young men who obviously thought that some of them were going to die. I think they responded much better to his "gather round and let's have a quiet chat" approach.'[27]

Major returned to London late on the evening of 7 January. He phoned his sister, Pat Dessoy, and told her that facing the troops and saying that they would have to fight was one of the hardest things he had ever done.[28] Three days later at Cabinet, following 'very lengthy' discussions on the military campaign, he received total support.[29] Detailed decisions were taken in the more secure environment of the War Cabinet. Major chose four ministers – Hurd, King, Wakeham, and Mayhew, the Attorney-General, who would deal with the international law implications – as well as the Chief of Defence Staff, Sir David Craig, the senior British officer, and Percy Cradock.

Major grew in authority during early War Cabinet meetings. More consensual in manner than Mrs Thatcher, he nevertheless quickly made it evident to all that he was in charge.[30] A committee of officials met after War Cabinet to examine how to implement its decisions, while a third group, chaired by Wakeham, met daily to oversee the news management of the war, with the clear objective of making a better job of it than during the Falklands War.[31]

As the final days ticked away to the deadline, diplomatic discussions heated up, at the UN, with European partners and with Russia. Gorbachev worked hard to avert the war; the allies were equally keen that he did not use his Security Council veto to cause problems at the UN. Major had long telephone conversations with him just before the air war began, and again before the ground war, to convince him that the Iraqis had to be taken on militarily, and that no acceptable compromise was in the offing.[32] Persuading Gorbachev was no foregone conclusion. Although he realised that Kuwait had to be retaken, he had deep reservations about the need to go to war to achieve it, not least because the Russians had huge interests in Iraq.[33] In early January, only days before the deadline, talks took place at Geneva between James Baker and Tariq Aziz, Iraqi Foreign Minister, though Major did not believe, any more than did the Americans, that they would prove successful in averting the war.[34]

Major worked hard on domestic opinion, which was less squarely behind military force than during the Falklands War; the Labour Party, too, was more ambivalent. Several prominent British politicians were uneasy about the prospects of war, including two, Tony Benn and Ted Heath, who flew to see Saddam to argue for the release of his 'human shield' hostages. Major went out of his way to reduce partisan divisions over the conduct of the war. The opposition leaders, Kinnock and Ashdown, were given considerable access to Gulf secrets on Privy Council terms. This won the approval of most of his colleagues: 'good politics as well as in the national interest'. Kinnock was appreciative of Major's actions: 'Unlike Thatcher, he did not pretend that he was a general. He took care to be bipartisan. I felt he would keep things that I told him confidential, while I always felt I had to be wary in what I told Thatcher.'[35]

Charles Powell estimates Major's most important contribution before hostilities commenced was 'firstly his management of British public and parliamentary opinion, which he did brilliantly, and secondly his handling of our own forces'.[36] A rare dissenting judgement came from Joe Rogaly in the *Financial Times*, who described as 'absurd' the growing conventional wisdom that Major was proving an excellent war leader, rather than just a follower of Bush.[37]

On 13 January, with the Sunday papers in London solidly behind war (even the *Observer* was saying 'Saddam cannot be allowed to get away with this aggression'),[38] Major flew to Mildenhall airbase in Suffolk to meet Baker, returning from his final round of diplomatic talks. On a bitterly cold day the two men discussed the predicted evaporation of the diplomatic option and final developments and plans.[39] The next day, the last before the ultimatum expired, Major flew to Paris and had lunch with President Mitterrand and Foreign Minister Dumas at the Elysée Palace, a cordial affair designed to demonstrate close collaboration between two European powers with forces in the conflict. Only after Major returned to London did he learn of a last-minute French initiative for the UN to postpone hostilities. Major responded angrily, saying the French proposal was unacceptable, and the Americans responded in similar terms. The French claimed they had good reasons for not launching their initiative earlier in the day when Major had been in Paris, but to the British it looked as if they had been deliberately misled, and it took some time to restore Major's relations with Mitterrand.[40]

On 15 January, before a packed House of Commons, Major spoke calmly but gravely:

We do not want a conflict. We are not thirsting for war, though if it comes I must say to the House I believe it would be a just war. However great the costs of such a war may be ... they would be less than those that we would face if we failed to stand up for the principle of what is right and stand up for it now.[41]

He was on his feet for forty minutes, with frequent interruptions from the Labour backbenches. Dennis Skinner shouted out, 'You aren't risking your life', to which Major responded, 'I would have been proud to be there with those young men and women.'[42] Red paint was thrown down into the chamber by protesters in the public gallery. Major emphasised that despite twelve UN Security Council resolutions, and dozens of diplomatic missions, Saddam had shown no sign of leaving Kuwait, but had built up his forces there to over 600,000 troops. Though Kinnock and Ashdown supported the deployment of military force, while insisting on full compliance with United Nations requirements, in the vote fifty-seven MPs, mainly Labour left-wingers, voted against an imminent outbreak of hostilities. Shortly after the debate's end, Major held a twenty-minute telephone conversation with Bush, who had received his much narrower congressional endorsement for the war on 12 January. The two leaders finally confirmed the decision to use force the following night.[43]

Operation Desert Storm duly began just before midnight GMT on Wednesday 16 January. After listening at Number Ten to news about the first air attacks, Major went to bed, though a telephone link was kept open to the White House all night.[44] He rose before 6 a.m. and was immediately briefed about developments during the night; a meeting of the War Cabinet followed at 7 a.m.[45] Its members were relieved to hear that among the first targets in the waves of allied attacks were Saddam's Republican Guard, which in the final days before the conflict had been one of their main anxieties, along with whether Saddam would use chemical and biological weapons, the latter, Major confirms, being a very real fear. Surprise was expressed by those present, as it was by the British nation waking on 17 January to the extensive media coverage, at the surgically effective high-tech weapons.

At full Cabinet, Major told ministers that the air campaign would continue for forty-eight hours, followed by damage assessment. He cautioned against any expectation that the Iraqis would be given time to reconsider after a certain point: only if Saddam ordered his troops out of Kuwait would there be any cessation. Ministers were also warned not to make any unguarded statements to the media on the prosecution of the war. Concern was expressed about the risk of terrorist activity in the UK. As Home Secretary, Baker said that while he had no intention of establishing a policy of internment, the movement of Iraqis was being watched carefully by security services, and already thirty Iraqi activists were in custody. The general conclusion was that the campaign had made a good start, but it was early days. With messages continually being passed in and out of the Cabinet Room, it was a most dramatic and stirring meeting.[46]

In the House of Commons that afternoon Major cautioned strongly against members believing that the scale of conflict would be limited, or the duration necessarily brief.[47] The *Guardian* praised him for 'an absence, even perhaps a deliberate repudiation, of that triumphalism, that vainglory, that sense of international centre-stage, which was Margaret Thatcher's hallmark'.[48] An hour-long audience with the Queen and several confidential briefings followed.

In the evening he made a direct television broadcast from Number Ten, a ploy Thatcher had never used. Geared up to it by Sarah Hogg and O'Donnell,[49] it was a risk, but he gave a transparently personal and sincere statement of the sort that had succeeded so well with the troops in the Gulf. His concluding remark, 'God Bless', proved the most memorable part of the broadcast, and struck a powerful chord with the feelings of forces' families. Traditionalists, including some at Westminster, were less impressed; even Judith Chaplin crisply observed that his sign-off was 'downmarket but good'.[50] The direct television broadcast was a formula he was to employ later in his premiership, evidence of his own satisfaction with how it went.

The air war lasted for five and a half weeks. All the time, the steady, advancing beat of what Saddam promised would be 'the mother of all battles' concentrated minds, and kept tension high. Patrick Hine, Chief of UK Air Forces and Commander of RAF Strike Command's bunker outside High Wycombe in Buckinghamshire, says Major was particularly concerned about casualties, but was satisfied by the preparations taken to minimise them, which were for 1–2 per cent overall, with 5 per cent casualties in certain phases.[51] As Major had been told to expect, several British Tornados were lost, news he greeted stoically. The first two Tornado pilots shot down were captured, to be paraded through Baghdad, on world television screens. On 18 January Saddam began to attack Israel with Scud missiles and for a while the world held its breath, waiting to see whether attempts to restrain Israel from counterattacking, which could provoke a war across the Middle East, would prove successful. On the night of the attack on Israel, Major was woken up at 2.45 a.m. to be told the news. Every day, nerves were tensed lest the Iraqis, in desperation, unleashed chemical and biological weapons. Secretly, efforts were made by the allies to kill Saddam, but these were aborted as he was too well protected.

On Thursday 7 February at 10 a.m. an attempt was made by the IRA, equally unsuccessfully, to kill Major and other ministers. Three mortars were launched from a stolen van parked outside the Banqueting House in nearby Whitehall. Only one bomb exploded, in the back garden of Downing Street, thirty metres from where Major was chairing a War Cabinet meeting. After the explosion there was a moment's pause, and Powell grabbed Major by the shoulder and shoved him to the ground. When it became clear that no more mortars would explode, Major calmly announced, 'I think we'd better start again somewhere else.'

First, Major was anxious to check that no one had been injured, especially the telephone operators at the top of Number Ten, while some ministers phoned their wives; after a while, the meeting resumed in the underground Cabinet Office Briefing Room 'COBRA'.[52] Full Cabinet followed, meeting upstairs in the Cabinet Office, the security authorities having by then ensured that all the nearby streets were safe. Long discussions took place on South Africa, and cold weather payments. Hunt recorded: 'It's probably only in the United Kingdom that you get the Cabinet, an hour after a mortar bomb, discussing severe weather conditions in East Anglia and the South East of England!'[53] Snow lay on the ground in central London, too; bitterly cold wind was sucked in through the windows of Downing Street, shattered by the mortar blast.

By 20 February the air war was beginning to achieve its results, and the ground forces were straining for action. Major had taken pains to keep not just Cabinet but also Parliament as fully informed as possible through the air campaign, which he stressed would continue until risks of allied ground casualties were minimised. Gorbachev kept up his pressure to avert the land war, and held tense phone calls with Bush and Major.

On Friday 22 February, with the Iraqis setting light to Kuwaiti oil wells, Bush announced that Saddam had until 20.00 (Gulf time) on 23 February to begin unconditional withdrawal from Kuwait. Saddam tried to use the Russian peace initiative as an excuse for stalling. The Americans were not impressed, and at 04.00 (Gulf time) on Sunday 24 February, Bush announced that Norman Schwarzkopf, Commander-in-Chief of coalition forces in Saudi Arabia, had been instructed 'to use all forces available, including ground forces, to eject the Iraqi army from Kuwait'. The final phase of the Gulf War, the battle on the ground, had begun.[54]

It lasted just four days. Major followed it closely from Downing Street. His worst moment came when he heard that nine British servicemen had died as victims of American 'friendly fire'.[55] The war itself was as one-sided as the allied military planners had hoped. Their firepower humiliated the Iraqis, and the feared Republican Guard was routed. Total British casualties in action numbered just twenty-four, in contrast to an estimated 100,000 Iraqi dead and wounded. A ceasefire was announced by Bush early on Wednesday 28 February, after Iraq had acceded to all UN resolutions.

Exchanges later that day in the House of Commons were not triumphalist but subdued, in marked contrast to scenes after the Falklands War. Downing Street further suggested that there would be no Falklands War-style victory parade.[56] Mrs Thatcher, in her first backbench intervention for almost thirty years, warned that 'the victories of peace will take longer than the battles of war'.[57] She was later to say that the Iraqi army should have been pursued all the way into Baghdad. The Americans, however, would have certainly vetoed her had she still been leader and pressed this option.[58]

Why did the battle finish when it did? The decision to end the war was taken at a meeting in the White House. Bush invited Douglas Hurd, who was in Washington, and British Ambassador Antony Acland, to attend, in recognition of the fact that Britain had been closely involved in the Gulf crisis from the very beginning. The decision produced strong, and mixed, reactions in London. Cradock was one of those who thought it premature:

The US forces had the Iraqis in the bag. I confidently expected that they would be destroyed in that bag. That was the object of the manoeuvre. But then we got this strange report from Washington that in their view it would be 'ungentlemanly' to continue with the slaughter. It was an odd message at that time and in that context. We were simply told the fighting was over ... But it was for the Americans to decide. It was primarily their war.[59]

Before the hostilities, it was the British who had taken the most strictly legalistic line concerning the war's objectives and conduct, whereas the Americans wanted to keep their options open.[60] Now, however, it was Washington which decided to end the fighting rather than destroy the Iraqi army or even invade Iraq. The stated objectives – to remove the Iraqis from Kuwait and restore its legitimate government in line with UN resolutions – had been achieved. The precedent of the Korean War (1950–53) loomed large in US minds, when the initial objectives were expanded, and backfired.[61] They worried that an invasion of Iraq would have looked like Western imperialism to their Arab supporters, and blown the coalition apart, leaving a dangerous legacy of instability and sourness in the Middle East.[62] Finally, with the Gulf being the first war to be broadcast, non-stop and instantaneously worldwide, in particular on CNN television in America, concerns were expressed – not least by the fighter pilots – about killing too many Iraqi soldiers in ways that might look dishonourable. As Major recalls, 'We were faced with an enemy that was not really in any capacity to fight. At the front line were young, relatively untried troops in no position to withstand British and American forces. Commanders at the time were talking of a "turkey shoot", of killing people not able to resist.[63]

One big problem remained. The British and Americans had won the war, but Saddam was still there. They had the hope – no more – that the Iraqis would be so humiliated by defeat that a coup in his army or the Ba'ath party might topple him.[64] UN occupation of Iraq was out of the question. It left Major exposed to the Thatcherite and right-wing criticism that he lacked the stomach to finish the job and oust the dangerous tyrant. The decision to end the war enabled enough of Saddam's army to survive and re-establish control in Iraq.

Major's emotions were on a see-saw as the war finished: intense relief certainly, but also a sense of anticlimax, of depression and exhaustion.[65] Alan Clark was sitting next to Major on the front bench during Defence Questions when the issue of magnanimity was raised from the Opposition benches. As Clark recalls, 'Major muttered, "Not f——ing likely." He was half talking to me, and half to himself, but it was so spontaneous. I thought, Hello, that's more like it.'[66]

The Gulf was to be Major's only full-scale war; Bosnia was a more muted affair. On the diplomatic, military and presentational fronts, he acquitted himself remarkably well, his personal qualities being displayed to best advantage – with the troops, with military commanders, as a chairman of Cabinet, and in bilateral conversations with Gorbachev and Bush. True, the major strategic decisions had been taken before he became Prime Minister, and with Britain very much the subordinate partner to the US, Major carried none of the decision-taking load, nor the ultimate responsibility of Thatcher in the Falklands War. Britain was nevertheless the second force in what ultimately became a thirty-two-nation coalition, and the scale and possible implications of war required considerable reserves of steel and judgement. Major provided a calm, proficient and dignified leadership both within Britain and dealing with allies, in what was the biggest British military campaign since Korea forty years before.

Major's own popularity soared. In mid-February, a *Newsnight/Independent* poll showed him to be the most liked Prime Minister for thirty years.[67] But his personal rating was not to be lastingly affected; the war tended to confirm existing public impressions of him rather than create new ones. As with Mrs Thatcher and the Falklands War, the long-term effect of the Gulf War on electoral politics in Britain – as in the US – was essentially limited. Douglas Hurd believes a lasting impression was made on Major himself: 'The fact he successfully conducted the Gulf War gave him considerable confidence in handling international and security matters.'[68] He would need to draw deeply on all his newly acquired assets in the coming months.

After the War – Desert the Kurds?

On 6 March, on his return from a trip to Moscow to see Gorbachev, Major went for his second trip to the Gulf, to see for himself the devastation the Iraqis left behind. The retreating army had relentlessly pursued a 'scorched earth' policy, destroying all in their wake. Thick black clouds of smoke hung heavily in the air from over 500 oil wells still alight after being torched by the Iraqis. Major flew into Dhahran at 5 a.m., the first western leader to arrive in the Gulf since the war's conclusion. He was due to fly on to Kuwait in an RAF Hercules, but this plan was defeated by the heavy smoke and they had to land on a small coastal strip and drive in.[69] As Major addressed the troops, on his ninety-ninth day as Prime Minister, the mood was very different from two months before. The troops had the same respect for him, and appreciation for his words of thanks, but they now were united by one intense desire – to leave the Gulf at the earliest opportunity. As gentle bribes, the troops presented him with an AK47 rifle, and a Chelsea football shirt.[70]

The Gulf crisis had taken out a huge chunk – at a crucial time – of the Prime Minister's time and energy from December to February. March saw him still involved to some extent on Gulf matters: at a summit with Bush in Bermuda on 16 March he discussed the proposed Security Council resolution on Gulf security, and in Cabinet on 21 March he reported on the desperate conditions for ordinary Iraqis.[71] But with the ceasefire on 28 February his attention could turn to other matters neglected over the previous three months.

Major was, however, to make one last, and perhaps his most decisive, contribution to the whole Gulf episode.[72] Bush had encouraged the people of Iraq to finish off the job the Americans felt constrained from completing, eliminating Saddam. During March the Marsh Arabs in the South and Kurds in the North began armed uprisings against Saddam's regime. Initial success was quickly turned around in the face of stronger government forces, and the Iraqi army began to exact brutal revenge.

Major was spending Easter, which fell on Sunday 31 March, at home at Great Stukeley. He was appalled by what he read and saw in the weekend media, as well as in reports from contacts in Iraq sent up to him in his boxes via Number Ten. Vast numbers of Kurds were being forced to flee to freezing mountains in the very north of Iraq, without food, to escape the brutal repression. 'What was self-evident', he said, 'was that unless some action was taken we may be seeing the genocide of the Kurds, and that we would have to take some action to stop it.'[73]

Pressure to act was heightened by Mrs Thatcher's attack on international inactivity on the Kurds' behalf. John Weston (Political Director at the FCO) had been exploring ideas for the Prime Minister to take a foreign policy initiative to a special European Council at Luxembourg, a week away.[74] The Luxembourg meeting was instigated by France, which had already proposed action to be taken about the Kurds and wanted a meeting to discuss the generally weak EC response to the Gulf crisis. Major latched on to the opportunity. During the week after Easter, two ideas were examined: removing the Kurds totally from northern Iraq, or Weston's scheme of offering them secure areas free from attack; the latter, which came to be known as 'safe havens', was clearly the only runner. The initial Weston plan was entitled 'enclaves', but this word was dropped as it might imply an autonomous area for the Kurds.[75]

Major decided to launch the initiative at the council meeting on 8 April. On the hour-long flight to Luxembourg, Major discussed the idea further with Stephen Wall, who had succeeded Powell as foreign affairs Private Secretary on 20 March, and Michael Jay of the FCO, and they worked it up into a firm plan. Major turned to Jay and said, 'Of course, the Foreign Office won't like it, will they?' Jay replied that they would want him to be aware of the risks. 'Of course there are risks,' Major responded, 'but sometimes one has to be prepared to take a flier at things. If we never take a risk, we'll never get anywhere.' Jay and Wall drafted Major's speech to the council, and the secretaries on the plane were two-thirds of the way through typing it when the plane landed. Their word processors were placed in the boot of a car taking them to the meeting, but having dropped the party off the car drove away with the machines still in the back. It had been agreed with Luxembourg's Prime Minister, Jacques Santer, who was in the chair, that Major should speak first, and with only minutes to spare a new text was hurriedly dictated by Wall.[76]

Meanwhile, officials contacted David Hannay (now UK Permanent Representative to the UN) in New York. Major knew that UN Security Council support would be vital to the plan's success, and was anxious to square the UN position before delivering the speech. Jay told Hannay that the Prime Minister was, in twenty minutes, going to announce the safe haven plan. Hannay, despite some comments, said that he would immediately take the required steps to facilitate the plan at the UN, to allow Major to announce in his speech that action had already been taken in New York. One by one EC partners saw Major's proposal as a sensible and humanitarian way forward, and were pleased to show that the Community was capable of responding unanimously and decisively, albeit late in the day, to the Gulf crisis.[77] Kohl, and also Mitterrand, eager to repair fences after his spat with Major in mid-January over the French peace initiative in the Gulf, gave the plan their support, crucial in generating full backing from the other European countries.[78]

European backing was considered essential if the Americans – initially far from keen – were to be persuaded. The plan originally entailed the Kurds being protected by allied troops in a defined area of northern Iraq. With fears of a repetition of Vietnam vividly in their minds, Washington was concerned about the resource implications and political risks of a commitment to troops on the ground which could become open-ended.[79] The White House was worried further about the likely impact on Turkey, which was concerned about its own, sometimes rebellious, Kurdish population.

The European Community had, however, at Luxembourg begun an international bandwagon that even the US could not derail. As drops of relief supplies to the Kurds began, the US launched an appeal for $340 million to support the operation and appointed a special representative to oversee it. British and Dutch marines were duly despatched. Major was able to tell Cabinet on 11 April that President Bush had denied any reservations about the plan within his own administration, and claimed that both governments were at one on the need to create safe havens.[80] At that stage, however, Bush held out against committing any troops. On 13 April he insisted that he 'did not want one single soldier or airman shoved into a civil war in Iraq that has been going on for ages'.

Three days later, however, after intensive lobbying from Major, and reports from James Baker, after a visit, on the dire plight of the Kurds, Bush committed a *volte-face*, and to the irritation of the British press, not to say Number Ten, claimed parentage for the plan. Some 5,000 American troops were soon deployed on safe haven activity in northern Iraq, joining 2,000 British and 1,000 French servicemen.[81] Ground forces remained in northern Iraq until later in the year.[82]

As a result of the initiative, the lives of thousands of Kurds were saved. Major's motives, as often, were a mix of different considerations. As a sensitive man he responded deeply to the suffering of fellow human beings. Equally, he was anxious that the television pictures had raised questions in Britain about whether the war had been fought in vain. He was concerned also to outflank Mrs Thatcher, who was becoming an increasing worry, and to show he could hold the initiative and avert the charges of dithering which had begun to be levelled at him on the poll tax.[83] A similar ambivalence, as well as Mrs Thatcher's shadow, were evident in the second of the great foreign policy issues that concerned him in his first months as Prime Minister – redefining Britain's stance to Europe.

Major's Thinking on Europe: December–March

Major's lack of a 'gut' instinct on Europe, for or against, meant he shared none of the powerful apprehensions of the sceptics in his party such as Thatcher, Ridley or Tebbit, nor the strongly positive instincts of Clarke, Heseltine or Hurd. Europe, as has been seen, had scarcely featured in his life as an issue until 1989. Then, as Foreign Secretary he was encouraged by FCO officials, and after October 1989 by Treasury officials, into a more sympathetic stance to the Community. The two dominant factors shaping his thinking on Europe were always the balance of opinion in his Party, and the balance of the arguments on the particular issue under review, which is why he led Britain into the ERM in October 1990. Major was above all a Europragmatist, convinced that Britain should be a member of the

Community, and play a central role in its deliberations, but content to go with the flow on how far to travel down the federalist path at different times.

The agenda for the all-important Intergovernmental Conference (IGC), to be concluded at Maastricht in December 1991, had been laid down by the Delors Report of 1989 and confirmed by the European Council in Dublin in the spring and summer of 1990: progress towards economic and political union. When Major became Prime Minister he was open-minded about whether to move beyond ERM entry to full economic and monetary union (EMU), involving a single European currency. During 1991 he did not rule out EMU; only later did he become convinced that it was impractical for Britain to join in the foreseeable future. On political union – always more of an inchoate idea – he opposed further transfer of power to European political institutions. Only a few months before, at the European Council in Rome in October 1990, Mrs Thatcher had felt that she was being prematurely bounced by the Italians, and he did not feel very differently from her in resisting greater political federalism.

Mrs Thatcher's earlier anti-'European superstate' Bruges speech of September 1988, in which Charles Powell was heavily involved, had damaged her standing in the eyes of European partners, especially Germany and France. It spawned the Bruges Group, a 'cross-party' but in reality right-wing pressure group which rapidly became the rallying point for sceptics and opponents of further economic and political union. By December 1990, 132 Tory backbenchers were members, including Ridley and Tebbit, and prominent Thatcherite academics such as Patrick Minford, Ken Minogue, and Norman Stone.[84] The last was a prominent member of the Chequers seminar on Germany for intellectuals that Mrs Thatcher held in 1990. Powell's memorandum on the seminar was leaked, revealing anti-German sentiments from Thatcher, which caused particular offence in the eyes of Chancellor Kohl and the Germans.[85]

Major's intentions, as foreshadowed by his statements on Britain being at the 'centre of Europe' during the leadership campaign, and by his Altrincham speech the night he became Prime Minister, were to rebuild fences with European partners, and to adopt a more constructive tone in rhetoric and substance. He interpreted the political mood within Cabinet, to a lesser extent in the Tory Party, and in the press – a fatal misreading, it proved – as willing him to be more 'pro-European'. Major wanted to restore domestic harmony on an issue which in the previous eighteen months he had seen tear the Cabinet apart, and result in the resignations of Lawson and Howe. He believed a more positive stance on Europe would be the way forward. He did not ask for detailed strategy papers to be drawn up outlining the pros and cons of taking different lines towards the Community. It was instinct.

Major's first European Council was in Rome, from 13 to 15 December 1990. The prime aim was to settle the mandate for the IGC, above all on political union. John Kerr, Hannay's successor as UK Permanent Representative to the EC, who had been influential behind the scenes on ERM entry, warned Major before Rome that the forum would be 'absolutely ghastly' and that he would hate it. Major, in fact, found the Council surprisingly productive and pleasant, although he was no more comfortable with formal banquets than he had been as Foreign Secretary. He only picked at the lavish Italian spread, and when the long dinner was finally over he retreated to the British Embassy for soup and a sandwich.[86]

The press reception after the summit was triumphant compared to Thatcher's dismal reviews after the Rome European Council in October. The *Daily Telegraph* headline was 'PM launches charm offensive and wins summit concessions for Britain', with the consensus among newspaper comment being that Major's new tone would be more likely to be productive than Thatcher's.[87] Major's personal objectives at Rome, of re-establishing Britain as a co-operative player on the European scene, and in particular repairing relations with Kohl, were largely realised.

Major requested a meeting with Kohl, appreciating that if Britain was to regain influence, Germany was the key player. To show willing, he deliberately went along himself to the German delegation's office. His line to Kohl was, paraphrased: I have no hang-ups about Germany. As far as I'm concerned, Germany is a large and a strong democratic country, and I am not in any way bothered about the baggage of history.[88] Despite conversing through translators, their relationship was an immediate success. Kohl, unsurprisingly, was delighted to have such a positive British Prime Minister in place of Thatcher. The chemistry also worked. Kohl very shortly came to regard Major as one of his closest allies among foreign leaders, though the relationship was always more volatile than Major's with Bush. Major and Kohl were surprisingly similar in political outlook and the course their lives had taken. Both had risen from relatively humble origins by singular determination and political flair. They were intensely political animals. Such similarity helped give Major confidence in dealing with Kohl from the outset.[89]

Not just Kohl, but across the European Community, pleasure was expressed at having a more pro-European Prime Minister of Britain. France's *Le Monde* rejoiced in the passing of Mrs Thatcher: 'Interventions, tirades, arguments and footstamping are a thing of the past. In its place there arrived the smiling, softly spoken, amicable new British premier. He talks about his generation's fondness for Europe, his willingness to participate ... all this sounds very good to the ears of the other heads of state.'[90] But whether the honeymoon would last, could last, depended critically upon political considerations, not just in Europe, but at home in Britain.

Despite the Gulf War, Major spent what time could be found in January and February in discussions with pro-Europeans in the party, such as Chris Patten, Garel-Jones and Ryder, to gauge the strength of feeling on EMU and political union. Some deeply negative reactions were being stirred by Major's pro-European line, above all his famous meeting in Rome with Kohl. Notice of the stakes being raised was given by Mrs Thatcher's acceptance, reported on 6 January, of the chairmanship of the Bruges Group. Coming hard on her

acceptance of the chairmanship of the No Turning Back Group, it sent out
a powerful early signal that Mrs Thatcher would remain a political presence.
'Thatcher serves notice: I'll head Europe rebels' was the headline in the
Sunday Telegraph about her Bruges Group chairmanship.[91] But Euroscepticism was still muted in the parliamentary party. Major walked into a
pro-European line in 1990–91, unaware of the hidden icebergs of opposition
that would emerge sharply eighteen months later.

Having decided on a pro-Europe line, alliances needed to be forged.
Whether a close bilateral link should be with the French or Germans led,
however, to tension in 1991 between the Foreign Office and Number Ten.
The Foreign Office saw the Germans as wanting to go further down the
federalist path than Britain could countenance, especially on political union,
and would have preferred Britain to team up with France.[92] Number Ten,
urged on strongly by Kerr, decided that Major's early success with Kohl
could be built upon, and believed emphatically that Germany would be the
more profitable close ally during 1991 in the run-up to Maastricht.

Major decided to go to Bonn to see Kohl on 11 February. With stresses in
the Franco-German alliance over monetary policy, the trip was well timed.
Both Major and Kohl were also anxious swiftly to repair any perception of
damage to their relationship from differences over the Gulf crisis. The leaders
had two hours of conversation, on reforms in South Africa and the Soviet
Union, but above all on the forthcoming IGC and on Anglo-German
relations. Following the meeting, Kohl said that West Germany's freedom
during forty-five years of the Cold War owed 'a lot to Britain' and its allies.[93]
This was just a start.

The Beating Heart of Europe: March

Major sought a serious platform on which to articulate his cooperative stance
on Europe. Christopher Mallaby, British Ambassador in Bonn, concerned
by how low Britain's standing in Germany had sunk, had been pressing for
just such a statement from Britain's new Prime Minister. Where better for
him to give his first speech as Prime Minister outside Britain than in Bonn,
at the heart of western Europe, cementing the new Anglo-German friendship
in the process?[94]

Many hands wrote that speech, which it was decided would be given at the
Konrad Adenauer Stiftung (a Christian Democrat think-tank) on Monday
11 March. Drafts from the FCO, which had been pressing Major for a policy
statement on the European Community since early January, were discarded
as being too bureaucratic.[95] Chris Patten helped with the writing, as it was to
be a Party speech, and because he was Major's most gifted wordsmith.[96]
Patten was also close to the Christian Democrats philosophically and personally; the choice of venue in Bonn for Major's speech was perhaps his.[97]
The speech was then passed to Number Ten, where Sarah Hogg worked on

it further. She shared Patten's pro-European views, but for her the motive was primarily economic, seeing the ERM, and the prospect of EMU, as the best device for keeping inflation down. The text was seen by Charles Powell, who balked at it, believing that in distancing Major's line from Thatcher, the speech went much too far in the Europhile direction of Heath.[98] No one heeded his attempt to interject a more cautious note; while respected for his role in the Gulf War, his views on Europe were regarded by Major as hopelessly compromised. Besides, he was on his way out, with less than two weeks left in Downing Street.

Major's speech in Bonn proved to be the most controversial of his premiership. He later recalled that 'very few speeches in the last fifteen years have been so twisted and distorted as to their real meaning'.[99] The sparks were to fly from the following passage:

My aims for Britain in the Community can be simply stated: I want us to be where we belong. At the very heart of Europe. Working with our partners in building the future.[100]

What exactly did Major mean by '*at the very heart of Europe*'? He later protested:

I emphatically did not mean ever Britain slavishly following on at the behest of whatever the fashionable European majority opinion of the day happened to be. What I meant is that we should engage in the argument . . . and argue the British case from the heart of Europe. There is absolutely no point in . . . going to stand on the sidelines . . . if you wish to win an argument, you have to debate and . . . be in the middle of what is decided.[101]

As he immediately went on to say that Britain was bringing its own proposals on economic and political union to the IGC process, and 'will relish the debate', it was clear that he was not accepting the rest of the Community's agenda in a rush towards greater union. He set out in particular British reservations on EMU, and stressed that Britain could not accept the 'imposition' of a single currency, and would want to reserve its decision, to be taken by the British Parliament at a subsequent point.

Most British newspapers accepted that the speech marked a change in the tone, but not the substance, of Britain's policy towards Europe. *The Times* notably compared the Bonn and Bruges speeches idea by idea,[102] and reached a similar conclusion. Major's words, nevertheless, provoked the first open attack from Britain's Eurosceptics. A warning shot had been fired by Mrs Thatcher on US television two days before the Bonn speech. She railed against German domination, and delivered a blistering attack on European unification (rather 'an embarrassment to the PM on the eve of the Bonn summit',[103] the *Sunday Times* noted). So Downing Street were delighted by the way that initial press reactions regarded the Bonn speech as having dealt a crushing riposte to Mrs Thatcher's weekend remarks. Major sought to reiterate his meaning in the House of Commons on Tuesday. In response to a question by Tory Eurosceptic Nicholas Budgen, Major said that there were only three options for Britain over the Community. 'To leave, which is unthinkable; to stand aside and let ourselves be dragged along by others, which is untenable, or to be at the very heart of the Community and help frame the decisions – which is our policy.'[104]

Major's position, however, provided a clothes-horse on which others would hang what they wanted Major's true attitude to be, or thought it was, or feared it might be. This weakness allowed Leon Brittan, Britain's senior EC Commissioner in Brussels, to say that Major had opened the way for agreement in principle on a single currency and Euro-bank.[105] Warm public endorsements from Kohl and Heath only set fire to the dry tinder. Enoch Powell accused Major of 'waffle' and doublespeak,[106] while Nicholas Ridley criticised Major for his 'all-things to all-men image' which would produce a 'devastating explosion' in Europe.[107] Gerald Kaufman, Labour's Shadow Foreign Secretary, said that Major's speech and the reaction to it showed that the Conservatives were now 'split from top to bottom' on Europe, and that Major was 'the man who came to dither'.[108] Mrs Thatcher added to the atmosphere of division in her first major public speech since leaving office. Later she said she was anxious not 'to undermine her successor' but 'could not in good conscience' stay silent while 'the whole future direction of Britain, even its status as a sovereign state, was at issue'.[109]

Major can be accused of failing to understand fully the depth of emotions involved in his own party. Unlike Mrs Thatcher, with her experience of the 1930s and the Second World War, he was a child of the Cold War. For him, Europe was not an emotional, but a practical or logical matter, which clever negotiation and artful diplomacy could resolve. Tactically, however, his policy of keeping the doors open left him vulnerable to attacks and manipulation from both sides of the Europe debate.

The speech unleashed forces which would all but swamp his premiership. 'We knew there were risks,' reflected a close adviser, although estimates of the danger proved too low.[110] But for the time being, he was oblivious of the genie he had uncorked.

The morning after his return from Bonn, Major, and aides in Number Ten, believed his approach would not only please Britain's Community partners, but hold the middle ground between both poles of opinion in Britain. Their hope and belief was that the Cabinet rows and resignations that had plagued the last years of Mrs Thatcher would now be at an end. In lobby briefings that morning, O'Donnell declared that support for the Prime Minister's cautious, pragmatic approach was steadily growing.[111] How wrong that was to prove.

THIRTEEN

Reversing the Charge:

January–June 1991

WHILE TACKLING THE Gulf crisis and finding a way forward on Europe, Major's first domestic priority was the community charge. The poll tax (as it was known) had been the most unhappy innovation of Thatcher's third government after 1987, and played a significant part in her overthrow. Major's challenge was to find a speedy, yet affordable and practical, solution, which would hold the party together on a volatile issue while keeping Heseltine, the man he charged to review the problem, reined in.

Origins of the Poll Tax

Tracing the originators of a failed policy is rarely easy. The parents of the poll tax, and reasons for its conception, are, however, clearly identifiable.[1]

The Thatcher government was anxious to find a replacement for the rates, the local tax which provided around half local government's revenue. Rates were based on notional property rental values, and with costs of property rising rapidly in the 1980s, regular revaluations, required by law in Scotland, proved politically unpopular. Rates also were borne only by property owners, who were the better off, and predominantly Conservative. The poll tax on the other hand was to be a universal adult tax, applying to some thirty-seven million people (as opposed to only sixteen million under the rates) and was levied on the numbers of people living in each house, regardless of the property's value, or whether it was owned privately or by the local authority. As the poll tax *per capita* rate would be set by the local authority, a key virtue was foreseen to be local demand to keep poll tax rates low, thus exerting pressure on high-spending and allegedly wasteful local authorities to reduce expenditure. The fact that a 10 per cent rise in spending would produce a 40 per cent rise in poll tax was seen as increasing local accountability. To many Thatcherite Tories the poll tax was hugely attractive.

The free-market Adam Smith Institute had aired such an idea, but it was not until Kenneth Baker and William Waldegrave, the principal ministerial initiators, headed a review in 1984–5 that it was worked up into a definite plan. Mrs Thatcher gave the project her enthusiastic backing at a Chequers meeting in March 1985, with Whitelaw's support proving critical. Lawson was a vehement opponent, as was Heseltine.[2] The Cabinet endorsed the poll tax plan at the meeting on 9 January 1986, from which Heseltine coincidentally walked into the ministerial wilderness. Progress subsequently was swift: the Scottish Act was passed before the 1987 election and the Bill introducing the English and Welsh poll tax received the royal assent in July 1988. It became operational in Scotland on 1 April 1989, and in England and Wales exactly one year later. At the same time, the government responded to complaints from the business community at what they saw as often punitive levels of rates imposed by local authorities, by setting a national, uniform business rate.

Major had been persuaded by Lawson's opposition to the poll tax and became a firm critic, although as Chief Secretary after June 1987 he had no choice as a member of the Cabinet but to back the Local Government Finance Bill which introduced it. He oversaw the funding arrangements in 1987–8 before the tax was introduced in Scotland, and was involved in the settlement for England and Wales in his final months as Chief Secretary before July 1989. But it was the Chancellor, Nigel Lawson, who mostly dealt with Nicholas Ridley, the Environment Secretary responsible for overseeing the introduction of the tax in England and Wales. Major can, therefore, be absolved from much of the blame for the 1989 poll tax settlement, which badly misjudged the effects of inflation and the distributional consequences of safety nets and relief schemes. Backbench concern at the size of their constituents' likely bills brimmed up in the summer of 1989 from Rhodes Boyson and others, catching the government unawares.

As Chancellor, Major, in his March 1990 budget, sought to sugar the pill with a small sweetener, but he forgot about Scotland, which meant an embarrassing climb-down within hours and an extra £4 million having to be found for the Scots. Although he came to regard the poll tax as a good form of local taxation in principle, he shared with Thatcher the belief that she had been to some extent misled. At its conception the poll tax was estimated at an average charge per head of under £200, whereas the actual 'headline' figure turned out at approaching double that, a far less sellable sum. Thatcher believed escalating local authority spending was largely to blame.[3]

Anger at the poll tax erupted onto the streets of London with the Trafalgar Square riot on 31 March 1990, the day before the tax's introduction in England and Wales. During the course of the year, as MPs' mailbags continued to be deluged with complaints, and polls showed the extent of disillusionment among Tory voters, confidence in the tax among ministers haemorrhaged. By-election defeats at Mid-Staffordshire (March) and above all Eastbourne (October) further sapped confidence in the tax. The Treasury weighed in with their long-held view that the tax was impractical; the yield, it argued, was not proportional to the effort involved. In many inner city areas it proved impossible to collect a large proportion of the tax due to population mobility and evasion of payment. The levels of the poll tax, the speed of implementation and the hike for many voters from their 1989 rate payments all combined to seal the tax's fate.[4]

In the leadership election of November 1990, the poll tax for Major became an issue to defuse rather than to campaign upon. It would have been impossible for him anyway to outflank Heseltine, whose opposition to the tax was long standing and well known; besides, an outright declaration that the tax was fatally flawed and needed to be replaced would have upset the party's right, and have sat uncomfortably with Major's support for the tax as Chancellor. A pledge to keep the tax, on the other hand, would have alienated much of his support from the centre and left of the party, not least the large numbers worried about their seats in the coming general election. So Major opted for a middle position, and declared a need for a rethink.

Major's appointment of Heseltine as Environment Secretary was a signal that the tax would be, if not totally abolished, at least altered radically. The arch poll tax enemy was hardly going to find a way of making the tax suddenly palatable. The Cabinet on 29 November, after a lengthy discussion on how to respond to Labour's forthcoming motion on the community charge, decided that in the debate Heseltine would take the initiative by announcing a review, which he did, not just of local government finance, but also of local government's entire structure and functions.[5] At that first Cabinet, ministers watched with interest to see how Major and Heseltine would relate to each other. Major himself was apprehensive, then and for the next few months, about how the big beast now back from the jungle would behave. He had already unseated one Prime Minister, and had believed confidently until the eleventh hour that he would take her crown. Might he try to unseat another?[6]

Lancing the Boil

The resolution of the poll tax débâcle had separate, but intertwined strands; but first Major insisted that whatever the long-term replacement, high poll tax levels had to be reduced immediately. Any hope of the Conservatives winning the next general election, which would occur before a replacement tax system could come into force, hinged upon it. He insisted that Tory voters should not suffer from any new scheme, and above all he wanted it killed as a political issue, avoiding repercussions. Having made clear his intent and with the Gulf crisis taking much of his time and energy, he asked Norman Lamont as Chancellor to see what could be done to cut poll tax bills in half.[7]

There were two options for reducing poll tax bills. These were known – in the parlance of the time – as 'Big Bertha', a one-off uniform cut in the headline figure to bring it down to a more palatable level, and 'salami slicer', a series of chippings away at the poll tax liabilities, offering politically sensitive groups special relief schemes.

The one-off cut was the first option to be examined, as described by Sarah Hogg and Jonathan Hill in *Too Close To Call*, the first and well-informed insider account of the years 1990–92.[8] The Treasury, however, was adamant. The strategy would only transfer the problem onto finding alternative sources of revenue; it would drain government reserves, and it would offer no guarantees on containing local authority expenditure. Lamont insisted that the future of the poll tax should be clarified before any big payouts were made, and a meeting in mid-January killed off 'Big Bertha', for the time being at least.

'Salami slicer' was the option left on the table. On 17 January Heseltine boosted a 'transitional relief' scheme, initiated in 1990, by £1.1 billion and renamed it a 'reduction scheme'.[9] By the spring of 1991, such methods had restricted the number of people expected to pay the full headline rate of poll tax by over half. But the incremental approach to reducing the pain was both very expensive, and did not yield sufficient political capital, as the figure that the media and public had latched onto was the undiluted headline figure, approaching £400 per person; it was also the figure that was being used to calculate the politically sensitive inflation rate (Retail Price Index or RPI).

By the end of February Sarah Hogg was losing confidence in the ability of relief schemes to achieve their desired effect, and was concerned about losing the opportunity of doing something dramatic in Lamont's first budget, only three weeks away. Major, as Chaplin recorded, was 'clearly very irritated by the Chancellor. He was not only not lowering interest rates as fast as PM wants but also not discussing the budget with him.'[10]

The problem remained that Major's attention, even more so after the land war in the Gulf began on 24 February, was distracted. But with hostilities ending on 28 February, the pressure eased, and Hogg and Turnbull arranged a meeting at Number Ten after the Prime Minister's return from Huntingdon on the following Sunday evening. Lamont was far from pleased to be told that Number Ten now wanted to revive the 'Big Bertha' option, and that he was to be strong-armed into taking account of it in his budget.[11] He had already constructed a careful, neutral budget, having had little room for manoeuvre, and was now being told that the Prime Minister wanted him to alter the structure and to find a sum of £4–5 billion to finance a drastic reduction in the poll tax. The decision was complicated by Major's departing early the next morning on his Moscow and Gulf trip. Lamont rather curtly replied that he would look at some proposals, and would discuss them with Major on his return.[12]

In the Treasury, Bill Robinson (Lamont's special adviser) suggested increasing VAT as the best way to fund such a large sum quickly, and employed the argument that shoving it up would not affect the RPI because of the technical point that both the poll tax and VAT counted as taxes on spending. In the Treasury his argument was easy to sell, being, in Treasury jargon, revenue neutral and RPI negative.[13] It also fitted the Tory preference for indirect rather than direct taxes. Major returned from the Gulf at 2 a.m. on Thursday and at an early morning meeting, just twelve days before the budget, Lamont agreed that he would indeed find the money by VAT. Shortly after tempers flared when Lamont argued that the poll tax relief should not apply to Wales; Hunt, Welsh Secretary, argued that it should, and won the day.[14] The Environment Department was justifiably shocked when they heard about the plan, which had been kept secret.[15]

Lamont's budget, on 19 March, introduced a number of conservative changes, including £1 billion of fiscal incentives for business and industry, offset by increases in tax on alcohol and on tobacco. Mortgage interest relief was restricted to basic rate tax, which had been taboo under Thatcher, and changes were made to national insurance contributions on company cars. But it was the final passage of Lamont's seventy-seven-minute speech which dominated everyone's perceptions of the budget, when he announced that the average poll tax bill would be cut by £140, two weeks before bills fell due. The £4.5 billion knock-on cost of the switch would be funded by increasing VAT from 15 per cent to 17.5 per cent, the biggest switch in taxes since Howe's 1979 budget (when he increased the main rate of VAT from 8 per cent to 15 per cent). To counteract one of the Treasury's objections to the 'Big Bertha' solution, Heseltine was to guillotine through the House of Commons the following week fresh capping powers on local authority spending.

Kinnock's response was to claim that it was 'the biggest climb-down in modern political history'.[16] But in truth Labour and the Liberal Democrats were caught cold by the switch and their reaction was to label it an electioneering budget, irrelevant to the needs of industry. With the additional constraint of Britain in the ERM, it is difficult to see, however, how much more Lamont could have done to stimulate the economy.[17] Press reception, aided by his typically good delivery, was positive enough.

The reduction in average poll tax bills from £392 to £252 at once solved the political problem for the Conservatives and kept alive the prospects of a June 1991 election.[18] Considerable problems were created for local authorities, however, many of whom had already printed and even sent out their poll tax bills for 1991–2. It also, Chaplin recorded, overestimated by 0.5 per cent the required increase in VAT.[19] A further £1.2 billion could therefore be found later in March for a 'community charge reduction scheme', to protect those households that had already lost heavily from the poll tax. Overall, the government's £4.5 billion palliative took some immediate pressure off Major's increasingly fraught job of deciding what to do with the poll tax itself.[20]

Enter the Council Tax

Responsibility for solving the poll tax dilemma fell on a committee chaired by Major, entitled 'GEN 8',[21] consisting of Major, Heseltine, Lamont, with Lang and Hunt representing Scotland and Wales respectively. Several problems were evident even before it met. Heseltine let others believe that abolishing the poll tax root and branch was part of the understanding given to him on his appointment by Major.[22] He was passionate, as one colleague said, 'to obtain the scalp of the poll tax to place on Mrs Thatcher's grave'.[23] At a meeting at Number Ten a fortnight after becoming Prime Minister Major had 'let it be known' that he would 'consider radical options'. At this point, however, the difficulties of doing just that began seriously to be felt. Some fifty backbenchers as well as some right-wing ministers were keen supporters of it, among them Michael Forsyth and Michael Portillo, who had played a leading role in defending the poll tax in the House of Commons as Minister of State for Local Government.

Strong resentment was expressed at any suggestion of abandoning the universal payment principle of the poll tax, and moving back towards a selective property tax, which many on the right regarded, for all the reasons clearly articulated at the time, as anathema. Part of the reason for the unrest among the more excitable was personal antipathy to Heseltine, which manifested itself as deliberately attempting to sabotage anything he might propose, regardless of merits. From non-Thatcherite quarters, too, some Cabinet ministers such as Lang favoured keeping the poll tax, suitably sweetened with relief schemes: Scotland had initially resented being used as a one-year testbed for the scheme, but now that it was operational, Lang wanted to avoid prolonging the period of unsettling change.[24]

Several initial enthusiasts began to change their mind on the poll tax after Major's arrival at Number Ten. Notable among them was Portillo, whose attitude to tax had become more pragmatic after he had seen the damage it had done to Mrs Thatcher and the Party, and who became open to compromise solutions: 'It was essential that any new system was sold as something different from the poll tax,' he later said.[25] Major and Heseltine found him competent and loyal; Heseltine had been keen on his remaining in post because he knew the detail and he would be useful helping to quell any right-wing revolt against the scrapping of the poll tax.[26]

Lamont, too, who had initially been attracted by the poll tax, now became concerned about its continuation, principally due to the difficulties of collection. The Treasury, not displeased that its opposition to the poll tax was being vindicated, was anxious that the Environment Department did not bring out what it saw as another badly flawed scheme. Encouraged now by Number Ten, the Treasury became increasingly involved in the detail of alternative schemes, leading to an inevitable turf war with Environment. Senior Treasury officials even delved into the minutiae of banding schemes.[27] It was the Treasury's price for the likely bail-out in the budget. The Policy Unit also rapidly established its prerogative to become involved, against Heseltine's initial wishes, and in an area where the Number Ten Private Office traditionally enjoyed exclusive links with the Treasury.[28]

Major let the argument run on into the new year, conscious that there were many cross-currents and the arguments had to be played out. Officials described it as a 'phoney war, very politically confused for the first couple of months. An intense argument was going on about whether and how quickly one could decently bury the poll tax, and how deeply you could bury it: the post-Thatcher fall-out was all about how far we were going to trample on her grave'.[29] Heseltine became impatient to get on with the funeral, and on 5 February advanced the Environment Department's proposal for a new property tax reflecting capital values, with banding for different categories of values of building. At the same time, the community charge would be reduced by about half, modified to knock out difficult cases and to simplify collection. Heseltine envisaged the new scheme coming into effect in 1995.[30]

The Policy Unit immediately gave it the 'thumbs down' at a meeting on 7 February, arguing 'it would enable the Conservatives to be portrayed as the two-tax party, even the three-tax one'.[31] Heseltine was put out by the cool reception from Number Ten. Chaplin recorded on 19 February: 'Heseltine keen on property tax and therefore leaks comprehensively to the press. PM and Sarah not so keen.'[32] Officials complained that, with disagreements to the fore, 'It got to the stage that the first some of us heard about what had been suggested was reading about it in the newspapers'.[33]

Meetings of the Cabinet committee GEN 8, and discussions at the Department of the Environment, Treasury and Number Ten, dragged on into March with no sign of a clear way forward. The Conservative Local Government conference in London on 2 March, in revealing strong support for keeping the poll tax, showed how divided and uncertain the Party still was.[34] The Ribble Valley by-election on 7 March, caused by the elevation of David Waddington to the Lords, was a further blow to the Conservatives. Their thirteenth-safest seat fell to the Liberal Democrats by 4,601 votes, overturning a secure Conservative majority of 19,528. Interpreted as a poll tax-inspired defeat, it increased the pressure to find an alternative scheme. Heat was put on by Thatcher complaining in a US television interview, with the poll tax in mind, of the 'tendency to try to undermine what I have achieved'.[35]

The disagreements between Lang and Heseltine proved to be one of the few divisive Cabinet issues during Major's 1990–92 government. On 12 March Lang asked for a meeting with Major and Heseltine in Downing Street 'in a last effort to save the poll tax'.[36] Events were not moving in Lang's direction, however. A report by the Audit Commission stated that the poll tax was twice as costly to collect as the rates.[37] Two days later, in GEN 8 the balance moved in favour of a banded property tax, which when leaked only made the Tory party more feverish.[38]

Labour could not believe their luck. With the Major honeymoon fast passing, and polls indicating a drop nationwide in the Conservatives' standing, they went on the offensive. In a series of speeches in mid-March, Labour frontbenchers labelled Major's policy on the poll tax 'dithering and indecisive'.[39] The pot was stirred again from the Conservative side by former big beasts now on the sidelines, with pro-poll tax statements from Ridley, and anti interjections from Lawson, who said on 17 March that he had opposed it all along and 'it has to be jettisoned'.[40] Worse, in an intervention to the House Lawson criticised the government (in a way he came to regret)[41] for failure to make its mind up: 'I think it was Pierre Mendès-France who said that to govern was to choose. I agree with that. To appear to be unable to choose is to appear to be unable to govern.'[42]

The media latched on to Lawson's speech as evidence of a personal attack on Major's leadership. Chaplin recorded: 'PM in a state because the papers are saying there should be firm leadership over the poll tax whereas he promised consultation ... PM not unnaturally upset by Lawson speech. Unfortunately had press party that evening and PM lays about him so all the journalists know that he is upset.'[43] The press did indeed report Major's irritation, and his retaliatory boast at passing several measures, not least ERM entry, that Lawson never achieved.

Major's tart response at the Dispatch Box the next day, saying of Lawson 'in the past few weeks a number of decisions have been taken that he would have wished to take in recent years but neglected to take', came across as petulant and undignified for a Prime Minister.[44] David Hughes (*Sunday Times*) wrote that it was 'an ill-judged move that left the Labour benches rolling with mirth and the government benches cast deep in gloom'. Joe Rogaly (*Financial Times*) wondered if his vulnerability to criticism was 'a fatal flaw in his make-up'.[45] It all gave vent for the first time to the great leadership question which was to dog his entire premiership.

In truth, Major was extremely tired, indeed approaching nervous exhaustion. After the land war in the Gulf ended on 28 February, which had been a severely trying experience for him, he had to deal with the great backlog of work that had been accumulating. His diary for the first half of March illustrates his punishing schedule:

Friday 1 March:	Breakfast session with Chancellor. Long ministerial meeting on pension age equalisation. Session with Foreign Secretary. Paperwork and odd meetings. Speech writing session for local government conference to late in the evening.
Saturday 2 March:	Breakfast with Chief Secretary [Mellor]. Completed speech in morning. Addressed local government conference before lunch, stayed for lunch and after. Travel to Finings in Huntingdon. PM boxes.
Sunday 3 March:	Huntingdon. Back to London for dinner and meeting with Chancellor on budget.
Monday 4 March:	Spoke to Kohl by telephone early. Political meeting with Party Chairman [Patten]. Several further meetings, including one on education and training. Straight after lunch flight to the Soviet Union. Arrived 10.30 p.m.
Tuesday 5 March:	Breakfast at 8 a.m. Various meetings, saw Gorbachev, liberal leaders, Baltic representatives,

	TV and radio interviews, Shevardnadze for supper, departed for Gulf. Overnight on plane from 10 p.m.
Wednesday 6 March:	Arrived Gulf 5 a.m. at Dhahran, went by helicopter around, including to Kuwait City, saw sheikh at British Embassy, and various air bases. Back to Dhahran. Left 4 p.m. for Riyadh, audience with King Fahd, left Riyadh at 9 p.m. and got back to Heathrow at 1 a.m.
Thursday 7 March:	Breakfast meeting and debriefing with Foreign Secretary [Hurd]. Cabinet, and meetings before and after Cabinet with Chancellor and others. Another session with Foreign Secretary. Preparation for PMQs. Question time. Further meetings. Hosted a European dinner with Jacques Delors.
Friday 8 March:	Flew to Glasgow. Met families of service personnel. National Farmers' Union address. Flew back from Glasgow.
Saturday 9 March:	Arrived Heathrow 1 a.m. Drive to Huntingdon. Events in constituency.
Sunday 10 March:	Buffet lunch. PM boxes. Speech preparation.
Monday 11 March:	9 a.m. fly to Bonn for Konrad Adenauer Stiftung speech. Lunch Palais Schaumburg. Meetings. Back to London late in the evening.
Tuesday 12 March:	Breakfast meeting with Sarah Hogg, then into press briefing. Six ministerial meetings that morning, followed by various other small meetings particularly with Education Secretary. Session with Foreign Secretary on Hong Kong. Then PMQs. Evening spent working on Cabinet papers.
Wednesday 13 March:	London. Meetings, boxes, Commons.
Thursday 14 March:	Cabinet meeting, then off to The Finings.
Friday 15 March:	Various constituency dealings, then flies off to Bermuda. Met President Bush for dinner.
Saturday 16 March:	Meetings all day in Bermuda. Leave 9 p.m.
Sunday 17 March:	Arrive Heathrow 6.45 a.m. Some sleep in transit. Then buffet lunch at Chequers where Major stayed.
Monday 18 March:	Back to London just after 11 a.m. Meeting with the Chancellor. Reception.

During the Bermuda trip, he unwisely admitted to journalists accompanying him that he was 'weary', which they readily reported.[46] George Bush was perturbed to see Major so tired, and told him, 'You have to take care of yourself, John. You must pace yourself.' Bush prescribed a holiday.[47] Charles Moore (in the *Spectator*) reflected, not unsympathetically, on the extreme workload of prime ministers, and the physical strains that politicians had to endure.[48] The stresses and disorientation of travel heightened his susceptibility to becoming depressed and wounded by the unprecedented wave of criticism now levelled against him, and mounted in a way that inevitably sapped his self-confidence.

The post-budget Cabinet on 21 March at last provided movement on the future of the poll tax. Major reported that GEN 8 had finally agreed that the community charge should be abolished, and that it would be replaced by a local tax (still unnamed) with a single bill per household, based both upon the number of adults *and* the value of the property; it was a classic compromise, on the lines of his proposals of early February, containing elements of both poll tax (*per capita*) and rates (property valuation). Major warned the Cabinet that the abolition of the poll tax would prove controversial, but pointed out that in the final analysis, difficulties of collection rendered it unworkable, and that the government had not been successful in persuading the country that it was a fair tax. Clarke chipped in with 'the sooner it was all put to bed the better'. Much work, Major said, had still to be done finalising the details of the replacement, and he rounded off the discussion by thanking the Cabinet for their 'sober realism'.[49] Heseltine announced in the House that afternoon that the poll tax replacement would be introduced 'from the earliest moment', and that 'extensive discussion and consultation' would take place before producing final hard proposals.[50]

On 23 March neither Major nor Heseltine performed well at the Conservative Central Council meeting at Southport, with unrest at the long-running uncertainty over the poll tax to the fore: 'feverish, unhappy days ... a wooden speech,' according to *The Economist*.[51] Major felt that he would be damned if he did introduce the new tax scheme soon, and damned if he did not. Labour realised he was still on the run, and put down a 'No Confidence' motion in the House on 27 March. The government would easily win the vote, but the debate proved embarrassing. The subject was redefined at the last minute to be on narrow points relating to local government finance. Number Ten had three hours' notice to put together a speech on that specific subject; Major was feeling jaded, and with insufficient time to prepare himself, gave a less than totally convincing performance, although the Conservative benches lapped it up.

Producing the detailed plans proved more difficult than hoped as those involved could not agree on the content of the consultation paper. Major therefore instructed the Policy Unit to find a way forward, which they did by simplifying the way the *per capita* element was to be reflected in the new tax. Accepted by GEN 8 in mid-April, it entailed a property tax using seven bands, as well as a personal element, based on whether there were two or one adults in the house, or whether it was empty.[52] The unified business rate was to remain unchanged. The outcome settled a long-running argument between Heseltine and Number Ten.

Number Ten, anxious to regain political capital, took over the launching of what was now to be called the 'council tax', coordinating the Treasury and Environment Department. The consultation paper, entitled *A New Tax for Local Government*, was launched later in April, with comments requested by the end of June. Some technical reservations were expressed by professional bodies such as the Chartered Institute of Public Finance and Accountancy, but in general the council tax proposals were well received.[53] The only significant modification came from Heseltine in response to criticism that the very affluent were treated too leniently, so he secured agreement for an eighth band for properties valued at over £320,000 (with different figures for Wales and Scotland). Heseltine had long been in favour of banding.

The Council Tax solution did indeed have much to commend it: the single person discount dealt with the 'widow problem' (of an elderly person living alone who had to pay high rates). Banding gave a rough equity and was relatively straightforward. Even though it had some benefits as a local tax over both the rates and the poll tax, it fell some way short of achieving Heseltine's expressed objectives of accountability and fairness, according to the Institute for Fiscal Studies.[54] The Queen's Speech in November 1991 outlined the Bill that would kill the poll tax and introduce the council tax, and the Bill was duly enacted, on Heseltine's insistence, in great haste before the 1992 general election, with the new tax coming into effect from April 1993 amidst a relatively calm reception.

Major had navigated the dangerous rapids of scrapping the poll tax. He had decided, partly deliberately, partly by default, to play it long, to allow dissenters like Lang to be won over. Whereas the warfare over Europe could not be damped down by his emollience, in the case of the poll tax his management style proved successful. As was later to be the case over Europe also, critics saw his prevarication as providing fertile ground for divisions to grow; allies say it allowed a harmonious resolution to an issue which in totemic and substantive terms had cleft the Party. There can be no doubt though that the poll tax was killed as a political issue before the 1992 general election.

The tax was indirectly to claim Major's most important lieutenant, Chris Patten, at the 1992 general election, resentment at the replacement of rates being especially strong in his Bath constituency.[55] Ironically the issue of poll tax, which was widely seen during 1990 and early 1991 as a potentially fatal handicap for the Conservatives, may ultimately have worked to their advantage by keeping some Labour voters off the electoral register (some failing to register hoping to avoid paying the poll tax).[56]

If the political cost for the Conservatives was neutral, however, the economic costs for the nation were high. At least £1.5 billion of public money was in effect lost on setting up, administering and replacing the poll tax. The principal academic study of the poll tax, *Failure in British Government*,

calculated that the total transfer costs to the national taxpayer had by
1993–4 reached over £20 billion.[57] Thatcher and Ridley, unlike Waldegrave,
continued to believe that the poll tax had been the right initiative.[58] The
whole issue significantly damaged local government; the council tax now
raised only 20 per cent of local authorities' revenue, and thus made it more
than ever dependent on central government.[59] Help for local authorities,
however, appeared to be in hand, in the form of Heseltine's grand new design
for local government.

Taming Hezza

Heseltine – Hezza as even those inside Number Ten called him – had big
visions and thoughts about how he was going to transform Britain. Denied the
premiership, and for the time being Trade and Industry, he was determined
to make his mark as Environment Secretary. He would transform local
government. According to one Number Ten source: 'Hezza was on the
rampage in 1991. He wanted great regional policies, elected mayors, dockland
development plans down the East Thames corridor. He was trying to grab
responsibility for everything that moved. He had to be tamed.'[60]

Heseltine had not been idle since announcing his full-scale review of
local government structure and internal management on 5 December.[61] His
intention to have a long-term review in local government had been flagged
in a major article in *The Times* in May 1990, but the surprise element in his
December announcement was his invitation for other parties to participate.[62]
The offer has been described as 'a master-stroke, all the more effective for
being totally unexpected'.[63] Labour chose not to take up the offer; the Liberal
Democrats, who did, made only a marginal impression. Heseltine himself
regarded the offer merely as 'a good joke'.[64]

Major, in approving Heseltine's review, shared his bias for new, unitary
authorities.[65] But many in Cabinet were far from keen at any revitalisation of
local government. Some, like Clarke – no friend of local government –
preferred to see most of its remaining functions transferred to central government.[66] Most Cabinet ministers, while not being as extreme in their views,
were sceptical about any plan to enhance local government prestige or powers.
They made their reservations clear to Heseltine, who at a crunch Cabinet
meeting on 21 March forcefully restated his view that a review of local
government's structure and function was integral to any new formula on
funding to replace the poll tax. One member described the reaction of most
Cabinet ministers as being 'horrified' at his wider 'all singing, all dancing'
proposals.

Major had been briefed by the Policy Unit to tread very carefully and offer
little encouragement. He decided therefore to go round the table, asking
colleagues to express their views. One by one, with varying degrees of
embarrassment, they gave the thumbs down. 'They all wanted to get rid of

the poll tax and lance that boil, but they were horrified by everything else Heseltine had in mind.'[67] A flood of arguments were advanced against his scheme, in particular that reorganisation would inflate local authority staff numbers and salaries, and that elected mayors would give Labour a huge power base. It was feared that it would be very difficult to sell the idea of a rival to local MPs as 'elected squire' of an area.[68] Some support, however, was expressed for his idea of abolishing counties and creating unitary authorities based on districts, and Hunt and Lang imposed such a change by legislation in Wales and Scotland.[69]

Despite his colleagues' reservations, Heseltine announced in the House that afternoon that the internal management of local government would be reviewed, as would the structure of non-metropolitan authorities, with a presumption in favour of unitary authorities, and that a local government commission would be set up.[70] The commission idea had come up from within the Environment Department as a way of selling his wider reform ideals to Cabinet.

Heseltine came back with a watered-down set of proposals at a Cabinet committee on 20 June. These were again shot down by the Policy Unit, for favouring Cabinet-style local government which would enhance local government's power. They thought that the payment for executive councillors would entrench Labour activists, especially in cities, and ran contrary to the views of the mass of Conservative councillors.[71] Memories of the painful and contentious Heath local government reform of 1972-4 were too vividly in people's minds for them to wish to see a repetition. Heseltine was tamed by attrition and isolation; Number Ten, perhaps unduly concerned at the risk of another Heseltine resignation, handled him with great care.[72]

The Local Government Commission was duly set up after long delays in early 1992 under the chairmanship of John Banham, Director General of the CBI (1987–92). A bold if risky choice, Banham was an action man who would fight hard to achieve reform. But in April 1992 Heseltine had his wish fulfilled and became President of the Board of Trade; his successor as Environment Secretary from May 1993, John Gummer, had little time for Banham or his commission. A few changes took place in 1994–7, but in general structural reform broke up on the rocks of political opposition, in both Whitehall and among Conservative local councillors, and managerial reform was becalmed in a Whitehall working party.[73]

Major was the first Prime Minister since Attlee (1945–51) to have been a local councillor. He held strong views on the importance of local representation and the quality and responsiveness of local services. But he was unable as Prime Minister to devote the energy to fight colleagues like Clarke or departments like the Treasury, who were unsympathetic to local autonomy, especially when, after Clarke became Chancellor in May 1993, these principal opponents of local reform marched together.[74] Major's personal enthusiasms, for improving public services, accountability and opportunity, were, however, finding an outlet other than local government.

FOURTEEN

A Majorite Agenda:

January–July 1991

BY MARCH 1991, with the main legacies from Thatcher laid to rest, Major could for the first time give sustained thought to what he wanted, on his own initiative, to achieve as Prime Minister. The question asked most frequently about Major during the leadership election, by the media, Labour, and in secret by some in his own Party, had been whether he was his own man, or merely 'son of Thatcher'. If indeed he was his own man, what exactly did he believe in? He needed urgently to develop his half-formed ideas into a distinctive Majorite platform, different from Thatcherism, to prove his quali-fication to lead.

Authentic Major

December and much of January had passed before Major could find the time even to sit down and think through his own ideas. Heath's five years and Thatcher's four years to prepare for the premiership in opposition struck him as the height of luxury as he tried to cram creative thinking time into snatched moments in a frantic timetable travelling Britain and the world. His avowed eschewing of being labelled on any wing of the Party, or philosophy, or political mentors, did not help those trying to work up his ideas into a strategy.

Major had a brainstorming session with the Policy Unit on the morning of Monday 21 January, from which seven broad themes were extracted: the opportunity society, equality of opportunity, quality of public provision in education, health and transport, 'enabling women', widening the role of older people, wider ownership and encouraging voluntary action. Six key eco-nomic themes were also spelt out: limited government, privatisation, liberalisation/deregulation, 'contractorisation' (contracting out both central and local government functions to the private sector), innovation growth of new business, and free trade open markets.[1]

Apart from the casual jottings he made in the Cabinet Room at the start of his premiership, the Policy Unit session produced the first full listing of his objectives for government as Prime Minister. What was included, and what left out, is instructive. Low inflation was taken as read, having been a constant theme for Major before he became Prime Minister. The classless society is not expressly mentioned, nor is Britain being at ease with itself, though both are implied in much that was recorded. Increasing the rented housing sector, and regenerating inner cities, two themes he articulated during the leadership election, faded from prominence. Looking for a way forward on Northern Ireland, which appears in his initial Number Ten jottings, was outside the collective remit of the Policy Unit. The environment, which he mentioned in his Radical Society lecture of October 1989, was no longer apparently a priority. Law and order and defence issues – traditional Tory heartland stuff – are conspicuous by their absence before, or immediately after, he became Prime Minister.

At the meeting with the Policy Unit it was agreed that the principal emphasis under 'opportunity' would be on education, 'making available to all excellence equivalent to the old grammar school route'. Enabling women was whittled down in a bureaucratic manner to the issue of whether the state should be neutral on the issue of working mothers, which affected policy towards child benefit and tax relief on child care. On contractorisation it was felt that stronger central action would be needed to encourage the Civil Service to shift activities into the private sector, as departments were making insufficient headway on their own initiative.[2]

Sarah Hogg was relieved to have pinned Major down thus far, but a follow-up was urgently needed. At a working supper with the Policy Unit on 29 January, Major thought aloud on some of the themes outlined the previous week. The 'opportunity society' he foresaw at the heart of his agenda, and he outlined his concern to see 'wider avenues' for those lacking privileges. There was, he said, a need to look dispassionately at government policies and to ask what was unfair: common sense should be an 'overriding theme' in assessing the worth of policy. He wanted all policy scrutinised – nothing was to be sacrosanct, and certainly not mortgage tax relief, a Thatcher totem. Perhaps all reliefs, he reflected, should be limited to the same basic rate. On social security, an area for which he had responsibility from 1985 to 1987, he was concerned that all sorts of disincentives to work remained. Finally, on education, he wanted reform of the teaching profession, improved training and professionalisation, which would, he recognised, mean paying teachers more in the long run.[3]

Another two months would pass before Major again had the freedom of thinking time. He had articulated his vision for society in those two brief meetings, but it is bizarre that a new Prime Minister should have so little opportunity to sit back and contemplate. Such time was all the more necessary for an individual like Major, whose ideas, unlike Thatcher's, did not fit into a philosophical niche. Moreover, his political career and inclinations rebelled at the notion of 'a big idea'. Some of his ideas would indeed have benefited from several years of deliberation in opposition before they emerged as legislative proposals. So while the Prime Minister was off on Gulf War business, poll tax and much else, it was up to his policy minders, the Number

Ten Policy Unit, to take his ideas forward. Not the least of their constraints was not knowing how this thinking would fit in with a general election, which could have been called before the summer or in the autumn, and the acute sensitivity, as the poll tax issue had shown, of doing anything overtly that appeared to be critical of what had happened under Mrs Thatcher. With Sarah Hogg's guidance his broadranging thoughts were honed down for the immediate future to two principal themes: education, and improving the public services.

The Prime Minister and Education

Education was a tough area for Major to choose, especially in a pre-election period. It was not a traditional area of Tory strength – unlike the economy, law and order and defence – and he chose instead to stick his flag into ground which was traditionally Labour's. He selected it, moreover, just two years after the passage of the omnibus Education Reform Act, 1988, which introduced the National Curriculum, control by schools of their own budgets and the option of grant-maintained status ('opting out') after ballots by parents, the abolition of the Inner London Education Authority (ILEA) and the transfer of higher education funding from local authorities to a Polytechnics and Colleges Funding Council, and a Universities Funding Council for universities. The most significant piece of education legislation since 1944, its passage naturally constrained the options in the short term for further innovation, and invited the response that any significant prime ministerial initiative in this area was just tinkering. To make a real change to education moreover might not just cost money, but would also mean taking on powerful vested interests.

The departure from the Policy Unit of Brian Griffiths, who had made education a particular specialism, was made up for by John Mills and the newly appointed Nick True.[4] More significant, Kenneth Clarke's appointment as Education Secretary in early November led to a fresh sense of dynamism, and the opportunity for a new rhetoric and some change in substance. Major appreciated Clarke's 'take no prisoners' approach when the going got tough, and Clarke in turn was grateful for prime ministerial support: 'He wanted to become involved in education, and I wanted him to become involved.' Major was a valuable ally for Clarke in interdepartmental arguments.[5]

The quality of education had become a subject of widespread concern and discussion during 1990, sparked by a speech from Sir Claus Moser to the British Association and concern from Prince Charles, and the year saw extensive discussion of education in the media, notably on Channel 4 and in the *Independent*.[6] So in some ways the moment was ripe for a prime ministerial drive. In an interview with Robin Oakley in *The Times* on 30 January, Major was keen to talk about education, although he admitted his ideas were 'not yet fully worked up ... I approach this issue with the instinct that something needs to be done and we are trying to determine exactly what it is.'[7]

Other pressures than lack of time were, however, forcing Major to move slowly on the subject in the first part of 1991. An early intervention was to offer strong support for Clarke for setting up a pay review body, to give immediate teeth to Major's belief that teachers should be regarded and rewarded as professionals. The plan ran headlong into opposition from Lamont and the Treasury, who argued that it ran counter to the policy of encouraging the break-up of centrally organised bargaining systems, and who worried that it might prove expensive in the long run.[8]

To the Young Conservatives' conference in Scarborough on 7 February, Major proclaimed boldly, 'At the top of my personal agenda for the 1990s is education', and after the obligatory praise for the achievements of the 1980s, stressed his themes of quality, inspection and basic learning. He gave a hint of the Whitehall battle over teachers' pay by stating, 'I want to see dedicated teachers rewarded fairly.'[9]

Lamont battled against Clarke over the pay review body at a meeting on 17 January and did so again on 8 March. But Major's weight proved decisive. To Lamont's annoyance, teachers were awarded a 7.5 per cent pay rise in April, rising further in December, and a Pay Review Board was set up under Graham Day, Chairman of Rover, consisting largely of industrialists. Some goodwill among teachers was immediately lost, however, when Clarke told the review body that very good teachers should be offered bonuses.[10]

Further education and training were next in Major's focus, spurred by his own experience of leaving school with few O Levels and then having to struggle through several years of arduous work outside the office earning his banking qualifications. Detailed proposals were already under preparation in the Education and Employment Departments, and the principles were approved at a meeting between Major, Clarke and Michael Howard (Employment Secretary) on 25 March.[11] Clarke agreed to let Major launch the proposals himself. Number Ten was concerned, after the reversals and criticism over the poll tax, to display Major as a policy initiator, above all on a topic he had personally trumpeted.[12]

Flanked by Clarke and Howard, he duly launched his first major domestic policy initiative on 20 May, and insisted on fielding the press questions himself rather than passing them over to his two secretaries of state.[13] The thrust of the initiative was two White Papers. *Education and Training for the 21st Century* announced that sixth form and further education colleges were to be hived off from local authority control, there would be new vocational qualifications for those over sixteen, a system of training credits for all sixteen- and seventeen-year-old school leavers, and the publication of examination results by schools and colleges. *Higher Education: A New Framework* allowed polytechnics to become universities, and to compete for funding with them on equal terms. The White Papers were described by the *Guardian* as 'the biggest further education shake-up for 30 years'.[14]

To maintain momentum, Number Ten now felt that Major needed to make a big education speech. A forum of 'sufficient educational gravity' was sought on a par with Callaghan's choice of Ruskin College for his great education speech in 1976, or the Royal Society for Mrs Thatcher's 1988 environment speech. The Policy Unit suggested the Centre for Policy Studies (founded by Thatcher and Keith Joseph in 1974) and Brian Griffiths, its new head, happily obliged. Major approved, seeing it as a way of rebuilding his credentials with the right and showing them 'continuity with Thatcher'.[15] The date was fixed for 3 July, but the CPS, lacking its own lecture hall, booked the Café Royal as the unlikely venue.

Within Number Ten debate raged over what Major should announce in the speech, and what be left over to the new Citizen's and Parents' Charters, which were being worked on in parallel. Grant-maintained schools, which had been a particular source of disagreement within government, provided a possible peg for a major policy announcement. Clarke had pressed since early in the year for all local education authorities to be wound up and schools to be forced to adopt grant-maintained status, supported by central funding. A frosty reception, not least from Lamont and Chris Patten, led to Clarke modifying his axe-wielding desires towards local government. Major felt that automatic or compulsory opting out would be 'too far ahead of public opinion', in flat contradiction to the rhetoric of choice, and could lead to widespread disruption and bad feeling if schools were forced to change status against their will. Not to be deterred, Clarke bounced back with a proposal for 'educational management trusts' to take over responsibilities for groups of secondary schools in inner cities from LEAs, incidentally making the path to grant-maintained status easier to achieve.[16]

Internal arguments also took place over a proposal to 'hive off' Her Majesty's Inspectorate (HMI). David Hancock, the Education Department's outgoing Permanent Secretary, in 1989 told his successor John Caines: 'HMI is absolutely the heart of the department; without it, the department will have very little solidity. It is the way we know what is happening in education.'[17] The Policy Unit, however, thought that HMI had been captured by the educational establishment, and avoided saying how poor many aspects of school teaching were in practice, for fear of courting unpopularity. This picture, needless to say, was not recognised by Education civil servants and HMI, whose annual reports had done much to focus on standards. Clarke was not to be deterred, and argued for school inspections every three years, and also for schools to be able to choose their own inspectors. The Education Act passed in 1992 did legislate for a mandatory inspection cycle, although three years was considered 'too frequent and too costly' by the Policy Unit.[18]

With so much of the remaining education agenda up in the air, Major decided on a primarily philosophical approach to his speech, which was drafted in the Policy Unit. Clarke was closely involved in the writing, although as his department was not fully trusted, the final draft was sent to his home rather than his office.[19] Major achieved the prominence he sought and the speech was widely praised. He spoke of the nation's deep-seated low regard for education, the mania for equality that had rejected proven teaching methods and debased standards, the disdain for vocational training, 'attacks' on traditional approaches to literature and history, and the low expectations of many pupils by their teachers. Low education standards, he said, had been 'a canker in our education system which spread from the 1960s on', a note that went down well with Thatcherites in the CPS audience. The main proposals included a hardened-up form of testing of the National Curriculum, which he felt had been sabotaged by the educational establishment, fresh legislation to 'smooth the path to grant-maintained status', and a tightening up of written exams at GCSE level with a diminution of coursework.[20]

Major was 'flabbergasted' when the *Guardian* praised the speech in an editorial as 'a trenchant diagnosis of what was wrong with the system and as such it pressed the right buttons'.[21] Others thought Major's CPS speech 'the best of his life' and praised his relaxed delivery.[22] Good news was coming from other quarters too. By the end of the month, with disagreements resolved, Major had much more to say about education when launching the Citizen's Charter on 22 July, including an independent school inspection system, the publication of school results for exams and truancy levels, and regular school reports for all parents.

Many of the reforms might have occurred under Clarke's own initiatives, and were conveniently slotted into the pigeonhole of the Citizen's/Parents' Charters. But the political weight from the Prime Minister was decisive in speeding up the process, pushing reforms through rapidly, and in ensuring that education remained high on the political agenda. As the *Times Educational Supplement* remarked neatly at the end of July: 'The Education Secretary has decided that education is too important to be left to the educationalists ... The Prime Minister has decided that it is too important to be left to the Education Secretary.'[23] It all amounted to an important agenda of educational reform; Major had succeeded in his aim of putting education on the fast burner in his first nine months.

Major gained in both confidence and standing from the positive reception to these education initiatives, his first untrammelled domestic success. Even the education world was mostly positive. Many of the reforms were correcting deficiencies in the hasty 1988 legislation and – typically for Major – had a common-sense, undoctrinaire aspect. With a success in his pocket, Major was ready to draw the dividends on the wider issue of the public service.

The Charter for Citizens

Educational reform was a necessary but not sufficient element for the Prime Minister's pre-election domestic agenda. He still needed to convince sceptics that he had a broad personal agenda, extending beyond just one subject area.

Out of Major and the Policy Unit's all too rushed meetings in January had emerged a clear understanding that abandoning Thatcherism in either rhetoric or substance was neither politically wise nor practical. The belief intensified with the backlash over poll tax abolition early in the year. Rather, the Policy Unit concluded, the need, at least until after the general election, would be to 'calibrate Thatcherism for the 1990s'. This would require a new approach as well as a fresh language. The words 'standards', 'aspirations' and 'value for money' all came to the fore in their discussions. But it would not be easy to advance such an agenda. 'Within the Civil Service', said Sarah Hogg, 'there was a kind of conspiracy that no one wanted to talk about the standards of the public service.'[24]

Ever since Major had chaired Lambeth council's housing committee twenty years before, he had deeply held views about the way that bureaucrats related to the public. He had a strong distaste for the anonymity of officialdom, and the high-handed way he perceived that bureaucrats often dealt with the ordinary public. Major and the Policy Unit decided that as the privatisation agenda had largely run its course – though there would be some more to be done there too – the focus should shift to how well whatever remained in the public sector was delivering its service. Major, in one of his few philosophical speeches as a minister, had broached this theme in his Audit Commission lecture in June 1989. He had praised the public service as 'an immensely valuable inheritance', but stressed that it had to be made to act responsively to its customers, and in a way that ensured value for money.[25] The theme was taking shape, fortified by the political advantage of being able to draw the sting from Labour's long-standing accusation that the Conservatives – especially Mrs Thatcher[26] – did not care about the public services. Rather, the Tories could be portrayed as the party that stood up for the little man against the bureaucrats.

A prototype of what became the Citizen's Charter emerged in the Policy Unit in mid-January with the notion of what was originally called 'contractorisation'. Papers were circulated, by Harris Hughes on its application to central government, and from Mills on local government.[27] In his Young Conservatives speech on 7 February, Major expanded on the objective of achieving an enhanced public service, and at the Conservative local government conference on 2 March he spoke deliberately about contractorisation by local authorities, linking the idea with the Thatcherite concept of the 'enabling council'.[28]

Pressure to produce something bold for Major grew sharply during March. The word 'contractorisation' now came to be seen as an albatross: the Policy Unit busied itself finding a more attractive replacement, produced in a seminal memo written by Nick True on 12 March, in which he came forward with the idea of a grid for achieving service quality in each area of the public sector, and advocated finding mechanisms for raising quality across the whole range of public services.[29]

Major chose to unveil what became the 'Citizen's Charter' in his Central

Council speech at Southport on 23 March. The name itself had been heavily contested, and was finally conceived by Jonathan Hill in an Indian restaurant near Victoria Station.[30] Even the siting of the apostrophe was the subject of debate (the singular Citizen's rather than Citizens' was eventually selected in June on the ideological ground that Conservatives focus on individuals, not the collective).[31] Delegates at the Southport conference did not seem particularly concerned, however, what the name was, or where the apostrophe came.

The Central Council had been a poor affair. Attended by three or four hundred activists and local councillors, a tenth of the number at the Party Conference, the annual Central Council was always a testing forum for the Party's leadership, especially on this occasion, the first time the national party had gathered together since the change of leadership. Heseltine failed to receive a standing ovation for one of the few times in his career. Scarcely more enthusiasm was shown to the parade of Cabinet ministers who appeared over the two days. Disillusion, and resentment at the loss of their great leader Mrs Thatcher, reached deep into the grassroots. Major, exhausted from his exertions over the previous month, failed himself to rise to the occasion.

Delegates contrasted the way Mrs Thatcher milked the occasion shamelessly, whereas Major shuffled up onto the platform almost apologetically and spoke in leaden tones. A less auspicious platform for the unveiling of his big idea could not have been imagined. The Citizen's Charter, he announced, would guarantee better treatment for the users of public services by a system of quality control and penalties for poor performance. 'People who depend on public services – patients, passengers, parents, pupils, benefit claimants – all must know where they stand and what service they have a right to expect.' Financial sanctions for failure to meet standards were threatened, including direct compensation to the public.[32]

The Sunday papers were no more enthusiastic than the delegates, and gave Major's speech, and the conference, a bad press. The repeated personal attacks on Kinnock were found in poor taste. Much was made of the contradiction between ministerial speeches which fell over each other to praise Thatcherism, while Major explained how its manifest failures over the public services needed urgent correction. The right-wing press, sharpening its knives, felt that Major's initiative was a distraction from privatisation and lacked real substance.[33] The left, meanwhile, considered that the Citizen's Charter concept was stolen from Labour. 'Major's Big Idea is so derivative of concepts already generated from within Labour and Liberal Democrat parties as to be indistinguishable,' wrote Patrick Wintour in the *Guardian*. 'If he is now trying to develop them at Chequers, his first call should be to Walworth Road [Labour's London HQ].'[34]

Southport concluded a week that had also seen the budget and the launch of the council tax proposals. A fog of ideological confusion descended on Conservatives and commentators alike, leaving uncertainty about whether the Major government had established a new agenda or was just – in the contemporary vocabulary – dithering.[35]

Major, in the first fight-back of his premiership, was determined not to be disheartened by the criticisms, which his team dismissed scornfully as flimsy. According to Nick True: 'If they had amounted to anything we might have backed off. Instead, huge effort was put into developing the Prime Minister's ideas further.'[36]

Major went straight from Southport to a long weekend on policy at Chequers, from 23 to 25 March. Sarah Hogg had pressed hard since the New Year for such an occasion, not least because it might be one of the last chances for an 'away day' (as these occasions were called) to think through policy before a general election.[37] It was also, incredibly, the first time that Major had been able to sit down with many of his Cabinet ministers and have the policy discussion he promised them at his first Cabinet on 29 November. The home team over the next two days consisted of Major, Hogg, True and Chaplin, plus Lamont, Patten and Ryder as Chief Whip. Ministers arrived at Chequers in groups over the two days and were quizzed by the team on policy options for their departments. Major reaffirmed his determination to press ahead with rail privatisation, the wisdom of which had been probed by ministers.[38]

On their return to London, a minute was sent out from the Number Ten Private Office to nineteen Whitehall departments, repeating what the Prime Minister had said about the Citizen's Charter at Southport, and asking for 'constructive ideas' within a month on improving public service in their areas – without adding to existing public expenditure.[39] Some ministers, including Baker, Lilley and Lamont, thought the charter idea small-minded or un-Thatcherite. On the right, Redwood and Maude were rare enthusiasts. Major's personal stock had rapidly ebbed since the Gulf War high point, ministers and officials in departments did not want to understand what the charter was all about and, to undermine it further, the Treasury let it be known it would prove costly and inefficient. By the end of April deadline, the responses received by the Policy Unit were very thin.

If the initiative was not to fail, it needed seizing and galvanising. In a speech to the Scottish Tories on 10 May, Major spoke strongly about how his Citizen's Charter would transform the country, and about his wish to end the 'bystander mentality'.[40] The Monmouth by-election defeat on 16 May, another Labour gain, proved a big upset, coming just two weeks after poor local election results. It further chipped away at Major's standing, but equally spurred Number Ten into its search to reclaim the initiative. Major himself became irritated by the inactivity in departments, which he interpreted as a slight on his authority. Several initiatives resulted. Major saw Robin Butler and it was agreed that a powerful Whitehall official committee was needed to drive the process throughout the central executive.[41] Butler selected Andrew Whetnall, a mild-mannered civil servant involved in work on Whitehall's Byzantine organisation, who proved an admirable choice, tenacious, meticulous and with an unparalleled knowledge of the tributaries and workings of Whitehall. He oversaw the process for the crucial next three months.[42]

The next spin on the wheel came serendipitously. Treasury ministers had become concerned at maintaining the momentum of privatisation, leading Lamont to ask for Policy Unit input to show the Prime Minister's backing for what was also proving a difficult task. At the same time Sarah Hogg had an inspired idea for breaking down the Treasury's opposition to the Citizen's Charter, by asking Lamont if he would allow Maude, a close supporter of Major in the leadership election, and with spare capacity as Financial Secretary to the Treasury, to become involved by broadening the privatisation enquiry into forcing the pace on the Citizen's Charter. Lamont, less than enthusiastic, assented.

Maude thus by stealth became unofficially Minister for the Citizen's Charter. He articulated his predicament thus: 'Number Ten asked me to do it in-house on the grounds that the Treasury would find it less easy to block it. The Treasury agreed to let me do it on the basis that if it was done in-house at the Treasury they would find it easier to stop it.'[43] Whetnall found himself working in effect for Maude.[44] The young Turk and the older sage proved a powerful team: 'We were told we had six or seven weeks to fill fifty blank sheets of paper with a Citizen's Charter. When we started out, no one had any idea what we would put down.' The team included True, Diana Goldsworthy from the Cabinet Office, and Robin Fellgett, selected by the Treasury, Maude suspected, to ensure nothing was done, but who turned into a keen charter warrior. Maude felt relieved that Peter Middleton had retired as Permanent Secretary in May 1991; his successor, Terry Burns, had yet to establish his grip. 'Peter would have hatcheted the Charter in no time at all,' reflected Maude.[45]

Delayed and obstructed, certainly, but it is unlikely that the Treasury even with Middleton still *in situ* would have succeeded in blocking a determined Prime Minister. For such he was. A battle for control was being waged, and Major knew he had to win if his credibility was to survive. When, by late May, the responses from Whitehall to the Maude–Whetnall committee were still inadequate, the Policy Unit devised a specific set of challenge questions for the group to employ in their bilateral meetings with departments. To focus minds still further, True suggested a Chequers seminar on public services.[46] Major responded positively. Together with Sarah Hogg, he sought to broaden the Charter operation into an exercise for putting departmental ministers across the anvil to extract policy plans for the manifesto.[47]

The public service seminar duly took place on Monday 3 June, with a cast of the great and good: businessmen such as Richard Greenbury (Marks and Spencer), service providers such as Bob Reid (British Rail) and Gordon Lister (Cambridgeshire County Council), regulators including Bryan Carsberg (Director General of Telecommunications), and inspectors like Stephen Tumim (prisons). From the think-tanks came Graham Mather (Institute of Economic Affairs) and David Willetts (CPS), but not Madsen

Pirie (Adam Smith Institute), 'spitting with fury' to have been excluded.[48] The home team on this occasion comprised Major, Hogg, True, Maude and Redwood, appointed Minister for Corporate Affairs within the DTI by Thatcher in July 1989 and retained in that capacity by Major. Redwood, as a former head of the Policy Unit and the leading thinker in the Party on privatisation, was seen as a valuable presence.[49] His falling out with Major was still some way off. The meeting was a particular success; ideas fizzed on quality, performance, effectiveness, and independent inspection.[50] Major liked the seminar format, mixing government insiders and outside experts.

The meeting confirmed Major and Sarah Hogg in their belief that the Citizen's Charter was a big policy that deserved to be thoroughly pursued, leading up to a portmanteau White Paper at the end of the month. Back in London on 4 June, the Policy Unit collated the ideas from the seminar. Departments were instructed to speed their submissions in preparation for the White Paper. In an important shift from Major's Southport speech, the emphasis on rebates and penalties for poor service was changed towards rewards and incentives for good performance.[51]

Hogg instructed the Policy Unit to abandon all other work and concentrate wholly on education and the Charter, while she and True travelled the departments prodding them for workable and better proposals. Hogg set the overall strategy, while True doggedly chased details.[52] Maude kept up the pressure with his committee: 'We consciously did it like a spending round, where I sent agenda letters to all Cabinet ministers, and they trooped into the Treasury by turn with their Permanent Secretary where we had bilaterals, went through the possibilities for their departments and persuaded them of what we wanted.'[53] To True, 'the meetings were like Select Committees. The team from each department came with their responses. It was all taken highly seriously.'[54]

A lunch on 11 June with senior officials, however, revealed that the culture had still not been fully changed, with 'a good measure of scepticism about the underlying aims'. Maude reported back to the Policy Unit that if the White Paper was not to be 'a damp squib' it would have to offer proposals that would make a real difference to past practice.[55] After two weeks he reported to Major on 25 June, and to Cabinet two days later. It became clear to all that many details for the White Paper had still to be resolved, and the new deadline for circulating plans to Cabinet ministers on 8 July looked impossible.

A typical example of institutional inertia came over the issue of hospital waiting lists; the Treasury was most resistant to Maude writing to Waldegrave at the Health Department on its headed stationery suggesting that limits might be set on the length of time patients had to wait before operations. 'The Treasury went bananas about it. They thought it was really selling them out in a major way.' Maude was told, ' "You must not let this letter go out, because if it goes out suggesting the proposal as coming from a Treasury minister, the pass is sold." It was sinister. There was this awful, deadening, defeatist conspiracy.'[56]

Not just the Treasury, but all those departments principally involved in the exercise – Education, Health, Transport – found it hard to accept that improvements in quality would not necessarily require more money.

The first five days of July saw a war of attrition in Whitehall as ministers' and officials' opposition was finally ground down. The Café Royal education speech on 3 July and its reception provided an important boost to Number Ten's authority. Health finally agreed to limits on waiting lists, and to comparative information being supplied on hospitals; the Home Office assented to performance tables for police forces; Trade and Industry to greater competition in postal services; British Rail to a Passengers' Charter; Environment to the final details about Charter points in housing; and Education to reform of the schools inspectorate.[57]

Possibly not since the Wilson government came to office in October 1964 had there been so much resistance and suspicion in Whitehall to a Prime Minister's wishes.[58] Success owed everything to Major's personal backing, the forceful advocacy of Hogg and Maude, official support from two very weighty officials, Butler and Turnbull, and the enthusiasm and drive of several key players on the Maude–Whetnall committee and in the Policy Unit.

At Cabinet on 11 July many ministers were surprised at how swiftly and comprehensively the exercise had been conducted. Major launched the White Paper in the House of Commons on Monday 22 July. With obvious relief and pleasure he outlined seventy proposals, in the most extensive and all-embracing White Paper he was to publish as Prime Minister. Here would be the heart of the Conservatives' 1992 election manifesto.

The White Paper itself included the privatisation of British Rail, the Post Office's monopoly to be broken, and London buses to be deregulated; market testing, contracting out and performance-related pay were also developments of 1980s thinking. But the heart was in the new element: improving the public services, including league tables, independent inspectorates, publication of performance targets and an improved system of redress for unsatisfactory service. It also contained one proposal originated personally by a Secretary of State: Howard's idea of the citizen's right to take legal action against unofficial strikes or unlawful industrial action.[59]

Major was at his relaxed best, most of his Cabinet present in the audience, when he stood for the press conference launch at the Queen Elizabeth II Conference Centre in Westminster. He had reason to feel pleased: he had taken on Whitehall, and several of his own ministers, and beaten them in round one. Further rounds would not go so comprehensively his way.

Reaction to the charter launch was mixed. Labour was initially scornful, Kinnock calling it 'a mixture of the belated, the ineffectual, the banal, the vague and the actually damaging'. From the left, elements of privatisation were naturally regarded with disfavour, although Labour councils such as York had piloted some charter concepts such as guaranteed standards in public services. Right-wing criticism, as foreshadowed at the Southport launch, resurfaced. It continued to anger him, as he explained to his biographer Penny Junor:

Who are the people who are sneering, saying it's a little idea? They are people who wouldn't recognise a public service if it gripped them by the windpipe – they don't use buses, they never use trains, they don't send their kids to primary school, they don't queue in some grotty old surgery, they don't hang around in a hospital waiting for five hours while the surgeon sees forty people ahead of them in the queue. They've got no idea about any of that. They don't understand those frustrations at all because they don't face them.[60]

Charting the Charters

With the White Paper published, Maude proposed the establishment of a Citizen's Charter Unit to maintain momentum from the centre, so that the Policy Unit's attention, overly distracted by the charters in May to July, would adjust back to its traditional focus. An Advisory Panel was also created, with outside membership under the chairmanship of James Blyth (Chief Executive of Boots).[61]

At the Audit Commission, Howard Davies realised he could offer two services. The first was practical advice on how to avoid pitfalls when setting up performance targets. 'If you publish numbers of arrests, then the police will assemble coppers on overtime outside the pubs at eleven o'clock on Saturday and arrest people for drunk and disorderly, and the arrest rate will rocket.' Davies also pointed out that the Audit Commission already gathered data that could be used in comparing local government standards of service, and had a reputation for independence.[62]

Major monitored and spurred on the process. When problems arose, he was more than willing to use his power in Cabinet bilaterals to back up the Unit. Regular 'round table' meetings of ministers and the charter teams were convened by Major and the Unit to push the initiative, the first taking place by February 1992. With an autumn 1991 election a possibility, work was accelerated on the 'three Ps' – patients, passengers and parents – in order to achieve quick results. Fifteen charters were published by March 1992, with the text of each cleared by the Charter Unit. There were some initial problems with the Health Department's draft Patient's Charter, which Number Ten and the Charter Unit regarded as not worth publishing. Major's backing for the Unit on this sent a powerful signal around Whitehall that the initiative would not go away.[63]

A Distinctive Agenda?

Did Major's education reforms and Citizen's Charter amount to a distinctive agenda? While both initiatives gave Major sufficient credibility to propel him through the 1992 general election, the consensus among academics is that it was insufficient to be regarded as anything deserving the label 'Majorism'. Dennis Kavanagh thus has argued that Major amended the Thatcherite agenda, and gave it a more human face, but he did not stake out a radically new direction.[64] But the combination of factors that help produce an enduring agenda change have occurred only rarely, notably after the 1906, 1945, 1979 and possibly 1997 general elections. Nor was Major, by inclination and temperament, desirous of founding his own distinctive brand of Conservatism. He would say that he had not become Prime Minister to do that. A defining moment came early in his premiership, when he refused in a speech to a Women's conference at the end of January 1991 to offer any broad sense of his personal agenda, and ordered the use of the word 'Majorism' to be dropped.[65]

If Major had possessed more time to prepare for his accession to Prime Minister in 1990, or for the 1992 general election, and if so much of his tenure at Number Ten had not been spent reacting to events and striving to hold the balance between left and right, even he might have produced a more cohesive corpus of reform and legislation, built around the proposals brainstormed with the Policy Unit back in January 1991.

The question of whether Major might have proved a strategic thinker if only he had had proper time to prepare for office, and was not buffeted from one crisis to another after he became Prime Minister, must remain.

FIFTEEN

A New Style?

November 1990–April 1992

'IN NUMBER TEN, the change in November 1990 was immediate,' recalled one of the few senior figures who survived the transition. 'When Mrs Thatcher was in the building, everyone knew it; there was an urgency, a sense of electricity about. When Major was there, it was all much more low-key, people did not rush about in the same way, sparks did not fly.'[1]

Charles Powell, better placed than most to observe the impact of the transition, captured the contrast thus:

She was tensed up all the time, highly strung, very active. She would be up at 5 a.m., telephoning all hours of the day and night, meeting this person and that, saying get this done, that done, never stopping for a moment. John Major has quite a placid temperament. He functioned much better with a more regular life. He needed seven hours' sleep a night [whereas she] could cope with three hours a night for weeks at a time and it didn't affect her performance.[2]

Even though Major usually had only six rather than seven hours' sleep, in general high-pressure leadership, the management and use of fear and the development of the mystique of power were not traits that Major liked. Everyman had arrived at Number Ten.

Pressure of a particular kind came, however, not least on his diary. No figure in politics is more in demand than the Prime Minister. His exhaustion in March 1991 helped etch in the lesson which his Private Office had been drumming home to him since the outset, that he would have to limit his engagements and think through more clearly how to utilise the time at his disposal. It was a lesson that he was not to learn fully for several more years.

During the week, he would sleep in the second floor flat at the top of Downing Street, a place he always regarded as a flat over the shop. Norma continued living at The Finings in Great Stukeley, successfully keeping Elizabeth and James away from the media glare that fell on Carol and more particularly Mark Thatcher. Major would rise at 6 or 6.30 a.m. and listen very occasionally to BBC Radio Four's *Today* programme, eat breakfast (perhaps a poached egg on toast made by a steward recruited from the Chequers staff) and finish off any papers from his Prime Minister boxes left over from the previous evening.

First up to the flat, any time from 7.30 a.m. onwards, would usually be

O'Donnell, to discuss the day ahead or overnight news. He would have arrived at Number Ten at about 7 a.m., read the newspapers and prepared the press summary. Depending on what was in his boxes Major would also call up the foreign affairs Private Secretary (Powell, then Stephen Wall) or another official. Graham Bright, his Parliamentary Private Secretary, would arrive at about 7.45. 'I used to corner him in the bathroom. I found that was superb, because when he was shaving, he could not escape.'[3] Bright would disappear at 8.10 a.m. to go to the 'Number Twelve Committee' chaired daily by the Chief Whip. Founded in May 1991, it was attended by the parliamentary business managers (the Chief Whip and Leaders of both Houses) and representatives from Number Ten and from Central Office. On a 'normal' day, Major would come down to the ground floor at or soon after 8.30. By this time, Turnbull had arrived at Number Ten, and was available to discuss any pressing business. By 9 a.m., Major was ready to start meetings.[4] Each day an appointments card, placed before him like a stand-up menu in a restaurant, would tell him what lay ahead.

Major began by working in the Prime Minister's first-floor study, across the corridor from the state rooms, but soon found himself too isolated. Not the type who liked to work in silence, he was happier having people around him. He swiftly moved down to the Cabinet Room, using the same seat, with his back to the fireplace facing out over the Number Ten garden towards Horseguards Parade, from which he chaired Cabinet meetings. It took him back to the known world of being a departmental minister, when he liked working at a spacious desk, with the Private Office on call through a door.[5]

His week inevitably varied according to his diary, but a pattern nevertheless established itself. From Mondays to Thursdays he would be in London, with Fridays put aside for visits to Huntingdon or around the country. Meetings would take place at Number Ten throughout the morning, with much of the first half of Tuesday and Thursday given over to preparation for Prime Minister's Questions in the House, and Thursday mornings to Cabinet. Major would chair the most important Cabinet committees himself, Economic and Domestic Policy (EDP) and Overseas and Defence Policy (OPD), as well as a fluctuating number of other standing and temporary 'GEN' committees.

Lunch in the building would either be a snatched working lunch, or a formal occasion in the smaller or large dining room, where he would entertain groups of MPs, a foreign delegation, or representatives of one institution or another. In the afternoons he would go to the House, attend a debate, or use the Prime Minister's room behind the Speaker's chair to work on papers or see people. In the evenings, there would often be a dinner or outside event to attend, from which he would return any time from 10 p.m. to midnight, calling first on the Private Office, manned twenty-four hours a day, before going up to the flat. Evening receptions would be held at Number Ten on average once a fortnight, taking place in the state rooms, for up to 250 guests. For these, he would stand with Norma in front of a fireplace in the Green Room at the top of the main stairs. They shook hands with everyone. Later, as he then moved around the groups, he proved adept at remembering many of the names from the initial introduction (his short-, and even long-term, ability to recall names correctly was extraordinary).

Major was deft at moving in and out of chatting groups, picking up conversation, making appropriate comments, and moving on, giving people the feeling he was totally absorbed by and interested in them.[6] It was his loss that his social charm and ease in small groups failed often to translate itself onto public platforms or television screens. He was at his sparkling best when making impromptu speeches during these receptions, when he would stand on a box to allow everyone to see him. His gift for off-the-cuff speech-making and humour extended to the not-infrequent retirement parties given at Number Ten, with his words – regrettably unrecorded – during the farewell dinner for Cradock and Turnbull in the summer of 1992 a particular high point.

When there were no events to host or attend, he liked to carry on working or holding meetings in the Cabinet Room until about 9.30 p.m., when he would go up to the flat. Red Prime Minister's boxes had been filling up all day in the Private Office, with papers requiring decisions, comments, or just for information, with comments from the Private Office, Policy Unit or Political Office appended. He was not as quick with paperwork in his first eighteen months as Mrs Thatcher had been. Many issues he was unfamiliar with, and he would mark a paper 'please refer' before placing it back in the box. He and Turnbull would have regular sessions in which they would go through the accumulated 'please refer' papers together. His pace on paperwork picked up considerably over his premiership. He would work away at the boxes on the sofa in his flat, glancing at the television news, often in the company of a trusted aide to whom he would chat and off whom he would bounce ideas.

When he was feeling on top, he was not too fussy about his company. When he felt under threat, as in the spring and parts of the autumn of 1991, he would be much more discriminating: Bright was always welcome, as were Hill, Sarah Hogg, O'Donnell, True and Wall.[7] These were Major's inner circle and most trusted confidants between 1990 and 1992, and the closest he came to having a kitchen Cabinet. They would often call in to see him in the flat in the evening, and if a crisis was on, they might all meet together. Bright was often the last with Major each evening, a totally loyal, comfortable and undemanding presence. He would report on business and gossip from the House, which he attended religiously 'to save the PM having to go over'.[8] One of Major's last acts before turning in was to look at the first editions of The Times and the Sun, which arrived at the front door of Number Ten at any time after 11 p.m. In this, he resembled Harold Wilson, but not Thatcher, who relied on the daily newspaper digest prepared for her by Ingham. When staying at Chequers, he would also see the full run of weekend press; at The Finings – somewhat to the relief of aides – he would usually just take the Telegraph. Like Churchill, he would ring up his ministers after reading newspapers first thing in the morning; if the press was bad, colleagues noticed that this would make him gloomy early in the day, and again at lunchtime when the first edition of the London *Evening Standard* arrived.

Major would retire to bed at Number Ten between 11.30 and midnight, while several private secretaries might still be working away in their rooms adjacent to the Cabinet Room; the later evening was often the first time in the day when they could clear the paperwork. Their dread was in letting papers hang around from one day to the next. Several private secretaries commented that they did not tire, even in a fourteen-hour day (followed by a long journey home for some). Many people exaggerate the hours they work; these times were real. A typical observation was, 'Adrenalin got me through it; you found you didn't need as much sleep as you thought you needed. Only when the pressure was off did I begin to sag.'[9]

Adrenalin was always to the fore over battles for the Prime Minister's time – 'there is never enough,' recalled one private secretary.[10] Regular diary meetings took place over his forward timetable, as well as an annual session with him each autumn when he declared what major engagements, and overseas trips, he would agree to make. In practice, many day-to-day decisions were made, and thus policy steered, without his full knowledge. He tended to accept and trust the diary his advisers gave him. Making claims on his time would be members of the Policy Unit, the Political, Press and Appointments Offices and above all the Private Office itself.[11] Each of the private secretaries would argue their own corner – 'that was where collegiality really broke down,' recalled one – with none arguing more forcefully for time than the Foreign Affairs Private Secretary. Hurd described the pressures:

So many overseas people wanted to see John Major. Why? They didn't really want to talk to him, but they wanted to be in Number 10 having their photographs taken with the PM. If you are the premier of say a Caribbean island, or a governor of an American state, that is what you want. If he agreed to see them you said quarter of an hour will be enough, but you went in there after half an hour and he was there talking about imports and exports and inflationary pressure and so on, because Major insisted on reading all the briefs and getting himself interested in the place. The visitor was of course totally delighted. But then Major would turn to me afterwards and joke, 'It's intolerable that you should wish all these foreigners on me!'[12]

Major would then compound a crowded timetable, with space for thinking always the most vulnerable, by insisting on certain engagements, perhaps to repay a political debt, often at the eleventh hour. Once a visitor had successfully breached all the barriers created to a meeting, Major rarely failed to impress even the sceptical, not least because of his thorough preparation and personal manner. But it meant that arranging short meetings was found to be pointless, which put even greater stress on the guardians of his time.

At weekends he returned to Great Stukeley. Here was another stark contrast with Mrs Thatcher, who would go to Chequers every weekend she could possibly manage with Denis (forty-eight weekends a year was the folklore at

Number Ten). Number Ten initially assumed that the Majors would want to continue with a similar routine.[13] But he did not feel immediately at home in the grand rooms and gardens of Chequers; he was adamant that, unless engaged in official entertaining, or holding seminars, he preferred Great Stukeley. Unlike the Thatchers, who had neither children at home, nor a country residence (except a flat in Scotney Castle, Kent), the Majors had both a home and children, who needed to see something of their father at weekends. New Year would, however, always be spent at Chequers, and by 1994–5 – assisted by the time Norma spent researching her history of the house – the Majors had grown to enjoy and have an affection for the country retreat.[14]

Major was happiest at home in Great Stukeley, sitting outside or 'fiddling about' (his words) in his garden, and enjoying the release of being in his own space. He shaped that house considerably, with extra rooms, a pond and more trees. He loves his family deeply, and has carried the guilt of the busy father who knows he has not spent enough time with his children. Music he enjoys: not particularly opera (despite Norma's best efforts and his listing it in *Who's Who*), nor classical music, but Radio Two-type music, sixties pop and female vocalists like Shirley Bassey. His reading showed a preference for thrillers and political biography. Religion never deeply interested him, beyond a general and under-explored sense of believing in God.

Some insight into Major's taste can be gained from examining his *Desert Island Discs* selections in the fiftieth anniversary programme recorded with Sue Lawley and broadcast in late January 1992. Major came across as personable and relaxed, though the proximity of the general election acted against candour in comment and abandon in choice of record: as Matthew Parris wrote a little unkindly, the choices could have come from a private secretary, responding to his 'requested thoughts on the selection of records best suited to elicit approval from key groups among the electorate and abroad'.[15]

His first and last records were deliberately tongue-in-cheek, Gershwin's *Rhapsody in Blue* and Frank Sinatra singing 'The Best is Yet to Come', but the remainder has personal resonances. After his accident in Nigeria he spent several weeks recuperating, and frequently heard 'The Happening', sung by Diana Ross and the Supremes, on the radio – his sole concession to pop music. Stephen Adams's 'The Holy City', a stirring Victorian parlour song, sung by the Majors' friend June Bronhill, was chosen because they took an 'LP' with it on when they went on an English country holiday (presumably in the 1970s), and he remembered lying on the lawn in the sun listening to it. An early musical experience with Norma, his tutor in opera, accounted for his next record too: Joan Sutherland singing 'The Mad Scene' from Donizetti's *Lucia di Lammermoor*. Norma had taken her new partner to a gala performance of the opera to hear the future subject of her biography sing, but he admitted to dozing off after two sleepless nights as a Lambeth councillor. His next choice, perhaps with an eye to showing he was not a cultural nonentity, was instrumental: Rostropovich playing the little-known Popper *Elfentanz*. He had first heard this from the front row of a concert for the European Bank of Research and Development, which he had helped to bring to London.

His two remaining records went to the core of his personality. A recording of the veteran cricket commentator John Arlott commentating during the 1948 test match between England and Australia when Don Bradman came in for his last innings, and Elgar's first 'Pomp and Circumstance March', confirming his innate love of tradition and all things English.

Sutherland's Mad Scene was his favourite record. Circles were run around a compliant Sue Lawley on his choice of book: he offered *Wisden*, Thomas Armstrong's *Crowthers of Bankdam* and Trollope's *Phineas Finn* before she could stop him, but ended up opting for Trollope's *The Small House at Allington*, confessing that Lily was his favourite heroine in fiction. His luxury? A full-size replica of the Oval cricket ground, where he could improve his batting against the wiles of the bowling machine.

The list was mostly honest, with just a nod or two in the direction of image (Rostropovich's *Elfentanz*, for instance). But he was no more playing to his audience than other party leaders marooned on the island, and in the light of the predictably unpleasant and searching scrutiny he knew his selections would – and did – receive in the press from the cultural and political élite, he had more reason than most to be cautious. Thatcher's selections, which included works by Beethoven, Dvořák, Mascagni and Mendelssohn, and Blair's with its emphasis on soft rock music, were equally tuned to appealing to a domestic constituency.

At New Year Major was perhaps at his happiest, when a group of some twelve Huntingdon friends, centred around Emily Blatch and her husband, met for dinner at Chequers. To enhance the sense of occasion they would wear evening dress and drink champagne, and Major was free to talk in an environment where he knew no gossip would ever find its way back to the media. After a late night, the party would go for a long walk on New Year's Day and find a country pub for a drink. This Huntingdon group constitutes a very clear and cohesive set of family friends, the most stable and closest they had.

By circumstance but also by intent, Major's friends inhabit different compartments – he likes to keep them separate. He would enjoy seeing, and has fond memories of, pre-parliamentary friends such as Peter Golds, Clive Jones and Jean Lucas from Lambeth days, and Ian Cameron Black and Stan Hurn from Standard Chartered, but in practice meetings were rare after he became Prime Minister.

Friends acquired since entering Parliament included Robert Atkins (felt to have compromised his relationship by talking too much about it) and David Mellor, who would call in and have a drink with him at Number Ten, or join him on an occasional sporting occasion, but he saw less of them both as the years wore on. He saw more of Jeffrey Archer and Tristan Garel-Jones, both of whom were generous friends, but again these were irregular relationships. Friends he would speak to on the telephone would be Matthew Parris, the journalist and former MP, and less frequently, on Sunday mornings, Bruce Anderson, who campaigned for him and wrote one of the three biographies in 1991, and later on Sue Tinson of ITN. Friends would say that when they were with him, he would be exceedingly warm and anxious to keep in touch, but then, with pressure of work, appear to forget about them until they initiated a new contact, and many felt shy about proposing meetings to a prime minister.

Major never acquired the equivalent of those media and business figures like Tim Bell, Gordon Reece, Alistair McAlpine, intellectuals like Alan Walters and Norman Stone, or newspaper proprietors and editors like Conrad Black and Charles Moore, who were all part of Mrs Thatcher's court in her last years in Downing Street, though he did develop a number of new friendships after 1992–3, notably the carpet magnate Philip Harris. But he never enjoyed, with one passing exception, intimates in Cabinet, as did Thatcher with Ridley and Parkinson. There were those in Cabinet for whom there was a deep mutual respect, conspicuously Lang, Mayhew and Newton, and early on Ryder, the Chief Whip, but they were not personal friends.

The political ally who stood out was Chris Patten. His close relationship with Major was improbable – Patten was typical of the Oxbridge, suave, intellectually confident Tory who repelled Major. They had been rivals on their way up. As Patten said, 'There was every conceivable reason why he should have mistrusted me, but I don't think I have ever been trusted as much by anybody in my entire life.'[16] Major's confidence and patronage helped transform Patten from an uneven performer as a departmental minister before 1990 (good at the Overseas Development Agency, less so at Environment) into someone capable of acting as lynchpin and troubleshooter in Cabinet, and one of the most effective Tory Party Chairmen since the war. Garel-Jones, who helped initially to develop their bond, said how complementary their intellects were during 1990–92: 'Chris is academically cleverer, but he would say Major is viscerally clever.'[17] Patten cut through Major's defences, and could make him laugh and relax, in a way no one else achieved. Major was often a lonely figure as Prime Minister, an impression not cultivated but equally not one he sought to avoid.

Those closest to Major at Number Ten in his first two years, as later, unsurprisingly perhaps were those with whom he worked most closely, in particular Bright, Jonathan Hill, Sarah Hogg, O'Donnell, Nick True and Stephen Wall, to be replaced after 1994 by a different cast, Alex Allan (Principal Private Secretary), Norman Blackwell (head of the Policy Unit), Howell James (Political Secretary), Roderic Lyne (Foreign Affairs Private Secretary), Ian McColl (PPS in the Lords) and Arabella Warburton (Diary Private Secretary).

'Major liked to surround himself by first-rate women and second-rate men' was a jibe that had a certain currency in the early 1990s. The first part is true. He was very good at bringing out the best in clever women – Carys Evans, Mary Francis, Rachel Lomax, Jill Rutter and Moira Wallace at the Treasury, three of whom (Francis, Rutter and Wallace) later joined him at Number Ten, as well as Hogg and Chaplin. Several of these women were renowned for their sharp tongues, but not employed against Major, to whom they were supportive and loyal, responding strongly to his sensitivity and personality. Not all women were attracted to him, but when he sensed they were, he would be charming, appreciative, tactile (in a very correct manner) and not averse to making complimentary remarks about their appearance. They also responded to the way he treated them seriously and as equals without being patronising.

Highly intelligent men could not feel any such protectiveness, and would be scathingly dismissive of Major. He would evoke a peculiar scorn in many intellectual commentators, notably Simon Heffer, Paul Johnson and William Rees-Mogg, who had free licence, unlike the politicians, to express publicly what they felt, which in the case of the first two was often personally very offensive. He sensed the reserve of such men, and perhaps for that reason preferred the company of those whose personalities were of a less brittle, softer hue, like Hill, True and O'Donnell, all three of whom possessed first-rate intellects. Allan and Lyne were also men of razor-sharp intellect, who would have been rightly insulted to be dubbed second rate. Among politicians, Waldegrave and later David Willetts were men for whom Major had a high regard, both extremely bright. So to return to the adage, he did indeed like first-rate women, but also he wanted to have around him first-rate men, who were unabrasive and above all loyal.

It has been argued that because of Major's insecurity, he felt uncomfortable with heavyweight figures around him.[18] Though there is no evidence of Major not appointing a minister because he felt intimidated by his or her intellect, the contrast between Thatcher's 'cold intellectual eye' to the world and Major's essentially emotional response, his wish to give and receive affirmation, was strong, though Thatcher was herself much more emotional than she let the world generally see.

The different personality make-up of Thatcher and Major helps explain why there was so little continuity from one court to the other. Charles Powell made the transition, to serve Major with consummate loyalty; Jeffrey Archer, a master at befriending the politically powerful, and Ronnie Millar, the playwright who managed the unusual distinction of writing speeches for Heath, Thatcher and Major, gained the confidence of both premiers, as did Woodrow Wyatt, a professional courtier who managed to be a good friend to, and write pleasant articles in his outlets in the Murdoch press about, both of them.

A Bruising Experience

Major's personality thrived on success. When his career was flourishing, as it was almost from the moment he entered Parliament until three months after he became Prime Minister, he would be expansive and self-confident. But when the running was difficult, his confidence suffered, and he became peculiarly vulnerable to criticism.

Major would worry – far too much, Norma thought – about what people were saying about him, especially in the press. Whereas friends in political journalism such as Elinor Goodman and Peter Riddell, who had known him since he had been in the Whips' Office, remained broadly sympathetic, neither he, nor Norma, had been well-equipped by life for the way they would be brought under a critical microscope after November 1990. It may have been the lot of the modern prime minister to be ridiculed, but he still bitterly resented the personal slights and his inability to defend himself against them.

Most unpleasant and offensive to him was probably the association with underpants, which was mainly the work of the cartoonist Steve Bell, who worked for the *Guardian*. Major's sudden rise to power had left cartoonists looking for a suitable motif to sum him up, and Bell thought Major most resembled 'a naff, underpowered Superman' who, instead of shiny red briefs, would sport spotty Y-fronts outside his trousers – 'a metaphor for uselessness and awkwardness'.

The Superman image of a Prime Minister dated back to Vicky's portrayal of Harold Macmillan as 'Supermac' in 1958,[19] and Bell summed up the point he was making in a cartoon in March 1991 in which his Major, flying through the air, celebrated 'a remarkably satisfactory few number of weeks!'[20] Major disliked Bell's caricatures: 'It is intended to destabilise me and so I ignore it.' Bell won Cartoonist of the Year in 1993, and the citation said that his underpant motif for Major had 'all but become the universal standard'.[21]

Whether Bernard Ingham would have restrained the press is a moot point, but the tabloids certainly resented his departure, and the strong leads and practical help he would give them, finding O'Donnell altogether too cerebral and easy-going.

With the change of Prime Minister, *Private Eye* magazine had to find a replacement for the regular 'Dear Bill' page, an affectionate spoof of Denis Thatcher. The *Private Eye* team devised 'The Secret Diary of John Major Aged $47\frac{3}{4}$', based on Sue Townsend's portrayal of the teenage angst of Adrian Mole. The fictional Major, as interpreted mainly by Ian Hislop, was full of petty resentments, with his 'bastard books' and his up-and-down relationships with 'my friend Chris [Patten]' and 'Norma Lamont'. He took inordinate pride in his collection of felt tip pens, and displayed astonishing ignorance of the scheming of his Cabinet colleagues. Robert Harris, in 1992, thought the 'Secret Diary' image was the most damaging piece of political satire around.[22]

As Chief Secretary Major had been an avid viewer of the satirical programme *Spitting Image*. He hardly ever saw the programme as Prime Minister, but loathed the way it portrayed him. For the first few months of his premiership he was depicted with an antenna on his head, controlled by Thatcher. By spring 1991 he was sprayed grey, the antenna had gone, but his monotone and his distinctive turn of phrase were impossible targets to miss. Later, he was shown as a sad and lonely figure, deriving excitement from counting the peas on his plate, and harbouring a hopeless infatuation with Virginia Bottomley.[23]

The satirist who perhaps best captured an image of John Major, to the extent of convincing one backbench Tory MP – Richard Body – that he was the man himself, was Rory Bremner. Bremner's first talent was mimicry on television – easy with respect to Major, less easy for other contemporary leaders such as Ashdown and Clinton – but during the Major years he broadened his range to encompass, in 1996, a comprehensible summary of the Scott Report. Bremner is widely credited with Major's image as a grey man,[24] but his main contribution was to refine an image that was already current.

To the Majors' extreme distress, the press worked hard in his first weeks at Number Ten to ferret out information about Major's family and his schooling, how many O Levels he received, and whether Rutlish placing all records of Major's schooling in Surrey County Record Office amounted to a cover-up.[25] Had the Mrs Kierans story broken then, his embarrassment would have been complete, and it is a measure of her character that she kept the affair secret until prised out of her four years later by the journalist and author Michael Crick.

The right unsettled Major from the outset. Some in the Major camp thought that Number Ten remained Thatcherised, with fifth-columnist photographs of her beaming down from the walls.[26] The names of McAlpine and Robin Harris were mentioned as those spreading stories about the 'plot' to oust Thatcher, with Major's personal sin one of omission (to come out strongly for her). Some of the more volatile Thatcherites were believed to be behind the mutterings about weak leadership and the abandonment of the true flame – 'classless' talk irritated them, as did a host of other 'transgressions' – cuddling up to Kohl in Rome in December 1990, handing out £40 million to haemophiliac HIV victims, unfreezing child benefit, praising rather than lambasting the BBC for its alleged lack of patriotism, attacking racists in Cheltenham, and ending his Gulf War broadcast with the words 'God bless'. All of these 'follies' were crowned by the abandonment of the poll tax and the 'very heart of Europe' speech. Michael White (in the *Guardian*) in a favourable assessment of Major's first hundred days mentioned the suspicions of Forsyth, Parkinson, Teddy Taylor and Tebbit, and anticipated the damage that the Thatcherite right might yet do him.[27]

Criticism mounted through March and April 1991. In the *Sunday Times* Brian MacArthur wrote accurately at the end of March that Major's 'honeymoon was suddenly over'.[28] The *Daily Telegraph*, which thirty-five years before had near fatally wounded Eden (Prime Minister, 1955–7) for not exhibiting 'the smack of firm government'[29] now rounded on Major: the Tories 'want a sense of direction . . . Above all, Mr Major should not apologise for himself . . . He is the Prime Minister. Now is the time for him to play the part.'[30] Press attacks on his 'dithering' reached a high point following his television interview with Brian Walden in mid-April, in which he used the expression about his policy 'wait and see' once too much.[31]

Judith Chaplin was becoming irritated by him, complaining in mid-March that 'hearing about his health gets boring',[32] and having to reassure him in early April not to take seriously the attacks from Bruges Group founder Patrick Robertson, 'some 22-year-old just out of college'.[33]

On Friday 12 April, Major was visiting the West Midlands, was on top and enthusiastic, when out of the blue O'Donnell phoned abut a *Panorama* programme to be screened the following Monday, which included discussion of his 1968 electoral registration in Lambeth. Major was thrown by the news. 'So much of our time is wasted looking at what all types of media say,' Chaplin wrote, rather unfairly assuming that others shared the strength of her reaction. 'He cannot bear to be criticised and takes it as a personal slight. He is obsessed by his image.' She concluded, 'It depresses everyone who works for him and wastes time.'[34] The press, too, started picking up on his sensitivity. Mary Ann Sieghart asked why John Major was 'so concerned to keep his early life private?' She argued he should have been flattered, not undermined, by the *Panorama* programme.[35]

Major never learned as Prime Minister fully to rise above the criticism, or to sift it objectively into fair comment, from which lessons might be learned, and unfair comment, which could be dismissed as the regrettable lot of all heads of government in free societies. Being seen to be affected vexed his aides, and emboldened those in the media who, scenting blood, wanted to go even further in ridicule and criticism. Internalising his anger and resentment at what he saw as injustice and gratuitous unpleasantness further churned him up, and did not aid his equilibrium. One can only speculate why he could not brush off the criticisms from his detractors, but his lack of deep personal security and positive self-image from childhood and adolescence clearly figured large. The affable and capable exterior, developed in his late teens and early twenties, was, now he was Prime Minister, being probed to the very limit. Major had great, almost unnatural, determination and courage, but also at his core a vulnerability which no amount of success after his teens could ever remove, and which remained with him until the end of his premiership.

Norma began to feel more confident as 1991 wore on, but continued to wish that he had remained Chancellor.[36] The more phlegmatic of the two, she learned to discount the hostile media more readily. Her decision to devote herself to her children provided them with a stable and happy home background, which, under the circumstances, was a remarkable achievement. She busied herself as a housewife and mother, and became increasingly involved in charity work, especially Mencap. She organised several open performances in the Great Hall at Chequers in aid of her favourite charities, evidence of her priorities, and organisational ability.[37] After the difficult first few months passed, she grew into her role, and became an increasingly important source of strength and advice to her husband, especially in his last two years. She would attend those functions and trips that both felt were essential, and significantly avoided uttering any statement before the 1992 general election that was seen as political, although in fact her instincts are solidly Conservative.[38] She knew how to defend herself and occasionally gave vent to a biting tongue, as when Hella Pick, of the *Guardian*, came up to her and said, 'Is it not about time we got to know each other?' Norma replied 'Why? I seem to have been getting on pretty well up to now.'[39] Norma, until her last two years, achieved less media attention than any Prime Minister's consort since Elizabeth Douglas-Home (1963–4). Even *Private Eye* failed to dignify her with a diary. They might have thought her too dull. She was more than content to let them think that.

New Boss of Cabinet

So much was made of Major's changed style in running Cabinet – more consensual, informal, deliberative – that some fairly major continuities with Thatcher's management of Cabinet can be overlooked. Ministers fell over themselves to tell the press how liberating Major's first Cabinet seemed after Thatcher. The wisdom that she began by announcing the conclusions whereas he would sum up after lengthy meetings has passed into folklore.[40]

The fundamental truth is that both sought to avoid conflict in Cabinet by avoiding discussion of controversial subjects. She succeeded totally in the case of the single currency: he did until March 1996. To avoid controversial subjects absolutely was, however, difficult for both because, as Cabinet lacks a set agenda, with items coming up under the four standing headings of parliamentary, home/economic, foreign and European affairs, it was often possible for a colleague to raise an awkward matter during the meeting. As a senior official put it, 'Occasions when both Prime Ministers had very troublesome Cabinets, and controversial, divisive discussions, were in fact remarkably few.'[41] Some felt this created an air of unreality. 'There were two debates going on in politics,' said a Eurosceptic, 'the real world where people debated Europe, and the cosy world of the Cabinet, where we avoided discussing what really mattered.'[42]

Thatcher and Major always ensured that the most sensitive decisions were endorsed by full Cabinet, and spent considerable time when needed preparing the ground. Neither used Cabinet as a decision-making body for run-of-the-mill decisions, which would be taken at the lowest level at which assent could be achieved, a kind of subsidiarity in one country. Both Cabinets had fewer formal papers presented to them and took fewer formal decisions than before 1979. The Cabinets of Thatcher and Major could be characterised as 'political allies meeting to review business without papers'. Both chaired approximately forty Cabinets a year, meeting each Thursday when Parliament was in session, but not meeting during August, and only irregularly in September and October.

Cabinets followed the same format, and were of similar average length, despite claims that Major's Cabinets, because of more freedom to talk, lasted much longer.[43] Major had been sensitive to early comment that they were too diffuse; he also wanted to get back to working on Prime Minister's Questions on Thursday afternoon, and he was always aware that the press would say there was a crisis if meetings went on too long.

Both premiers' Cabinets were subject to leaking. In January 1992 Chris Patten criticised his colleagues for their 'endless leaks'; Chaplin recorded that 'Rifkind and Baker, the two great leakers, nod wisely'.[44] Not until after Black Wednesday, however, did Cabinet leaking reach torrential proportions, when a mutual regard and trust was lost, never to be regained. This breakdown, far more than the arrival of Redwood in Cabinet in May 1993, was responsible for the loss of confidentiality. In 1994 an official complained: 'There is now an expectation that anything controversial said in Cabinet will be in the *Evening Standard* on Thursday afternoon. People would be much less inclined to speak frankly because they knew it would come out. It had become a major influence on decision-making.'[45] By early 1997 the Cabinet was not even trusted to be told the full details of the manifesto, so certain was Number Ten that the information would be passed on.

Major kept Thatcher's system of Cabinet committees intact, and continued to chair the same standing committees himself.[46] Both Prime Ministers used the committee network extensively, gave careful thought as to who chaired and sat on committees, and lobbied extensively to ensure that their will prevailed in them. Members of committees under both Prime Ministers would often obtain decisions by writing to the chairman and other committee members to secure their agreement. The public expenditure round was conducted in the same way as under Mrs Thatcher until overhauled after the 1992 election.

Both leaders used the Cabinet Secretariat to help them plan Cabinet business regularly, one week, three weeks and three months ahead. They worked closely with Robin Butler, appointed Cabinet Secretary in 1988, who remained throughout Major's premiership. He sat on Major's right during Cabinet meetings and took notes with other Cabinet secretariat officials from which the Cabinet minutes were prepared: 'Very bland,' said Redwood. 'They will tell historians little about the Major years.'[47]

Butler had been Thatcher's Principal Private Secretary (1982–5), and she grew to know him personally, in consequence, more deeply. Spasmodic accounts of a rift between Major and Butler were, however, without foundation. Despite their very different backgrounds, they succeeded in establishing a productive relationship, cricket, as always with Major, an important *lingua franca*. Butler's support over the Citizen's Charter, and during the Scott and

Nolan inquiries and the search for peace in Northern Ireland, as well as his steady hand during innumerable moments of pressure and crisis, were particularly appreciated by Major. The recent Prime Minister–Cabinet Secretary partnership it resembled most closely was Heath's with Burke Trend, highly productive but not driven by a mentor relationship or a sense of mission.[48]

Major's desire to be a team builder and to get Cabinet's hearts and minds behind a decision constituted the principal difference between his and Thatcher's style. It was important to Major to feel that his Cabinet was united, and that the atmosphere was harmonious. He used free-ranging discussions, as in Cabinet leading up to the Maastricht conference in December 1991, as a way of binding ministers to a collective Cabinet viewpoint. Unlike Thatcher, he did not, before 1992, have a fixed group of ministers, an inner Cabinet, on whom he relied and with whom he took decisions removed from the Cabinet and committee structure – except the 'A team' formed before both general elections, and also on other rare occasions such as Black Wednesday. Major described his style of managing Cabinet thus:

I went to a great deal of trouble to listen and respond to whatever people had to say ... If in the development of policy I could reach a conclusion that I believed to be right with a minimum of noise rather than a maximum, I would do so. If I can soothe wounds, I would do so.[49]

Major strongly disliked tension and unpleasantness; Chris Patten felt 'he almost overdid his wish to carry people along'.[50] Major, after he left office, came to agree that his consensual style of running Cabinet was perceived as weak, although at the time he saw no alternative to keeping a divided Cabinet together without resignations. Major hated being pushed into a difficult decision until the last possible moment. If there was a difference, Thatcher's reaction would be, 'Well we'd better decide what to do, and I say we decide this way.' Major's typical reaction was, 'Well, let's hear what everybody says, and if we can't get agreement, we'd better come back to it next week, and with a bit of luck the ground will have shifted, or passions softened, and we can find a way forward.'[51] His unwillingness to assert himself and bang the table infuriated some, and led to charges of indecisiveness, of letting circumstances and other people determine issues rather than forcing a resolution himself. Thatcher's Cabinets were felt to be more of an occasion, but not as much fun: less laughter and more formality.

Note-passing was another Major trait: if a colleague had suffered in an argument, or had spoken particularly well, Major would pass across a note of reassurance or congratulations. Thatcher would write notes in Cabinet meetings, but they were usually to herself, as an *aide-mémoire*.

By such emollient methods, Major managed to minimise disagreements in Cabinet. Those differences that did occur before the 1992 general election came over the poll tax, rail privatisation, where Major and Patten battled against Rifkind and Lamont,[52] and finally, the embryonic stirrings of differences on Europe, where Howard and Lilley argued for a sceptical stance against Clarke, Heseltine and Hurd. By playing it long on Maastricht and avoiding the temperature rising, Major maintained harmony; his management of Howard and Lilley in particular displayed consummate management skills. But other factors were as important in producing the relative harmony of November 1990 to April 1992: Major's newness and ministers' desire to keep in with him, and above all the realisation that a united front was essential in the run-up to the election. Harmony was helped, as Kenneth Clarke recalls, by the fact that it 'really was a Cabinet of chums ... [it] had no two people who strongly disliked each other and a lot of people who were extremely friendly with each other'.[53] Major was not really part of this network, a reflection of his wish not to have a kitchen Cabinet of close friends whom it would cause him personal pain to sack. Later on, however, Clarke had changed his view: 'John's great strength was collective Cabinet discussion. But by the end, Cabinet was not a place anyone wanted to bring business to because of the deep distrust of other colleagues and fear of leaks.'[54]

The 'big beasts' in that 1990–92 Cabinet were clearly defined: Heseltine, Patten, Hurd and Lamont. Baker and Waddington were early contenders, but faded. Baker in particular, a high-flier under Mrs Thatcher, never chimed fully with the new regime. Heseltine was the man everyone watched, and of whom they were wary. More an Ian Botham than a Joseph Chamberlain,[55] his ability to reshape the political landscape made him *sui generis*. Not everyone was an admirer. Awe turned to irritation for some as Heseltine began to offer an opinion on almost every subject under discussion. Said one colleague: 'We had it impressed upon us that he was by far the most experienced politician around the table, on every conceivable subject. The study of Hurd's face when Michael was telling us about foreign affairs is something I shall always treasure.'[56] Even though he lost some ground over the poll tax replacement, and was outmanoeuvred on his plans for grand local government reform, his power and the respect in which he was held grew.

Hurd was also listened to as one who commanded authority, and he forged a strong working relationship with Major, but with frequent trips abroad he engaged only irregularly in domestic affairs. Lamont carried an authority by dint of being Chancellor and the force of his arguments, but he never developed his own strong power base.

The pivotal figure, without doubt, was Patten. As Party Chairman in the run-up to a close election, his advice was listened to carefully, especially as he was so obviously a perceptive political thinker. Major came to lean heavily on him for brokering disputes between ministers, and he played a particular role as Major's bridge to Heseltine. 'Patten was clearly the most powerful figure in the government after Major,' said Waldegrave. 'The PM is a lonely figure, and Patten was the only person of weight in Cabinet with constant access to him.'[57] Patten played an important role, never to be fully replaced, in filtering controversial issues before they resulted in arguments during Cabinet meetings.

Clarke was the next most powerful Cabinet minister: he carried authority in Cabinet way above what one would expect for an Education Secretary. Major both liked and admired him, but remained wary of his ability to say and do things which rocked the boat. Wakeham, like Baker and Waddington, was another figure felt to have been influential under Thatcher, whose star waned, especially during the general election campaign. As Chief Whip Ryder's opinions were highly regarded by Major, especially as he took a self-denying ordinance about staying out of policy. The tight parliamentary arithmetic after 1992 with the disappearing majority was to change his role, and relationship with Major.

Major held more 'Political Cabinets' than Thatcher, becoming almost weekly after full Cabinet in the immediate run-up to the 1992 general election, as happened again in the run-up to 1997. The Cabinet secretariat withdrew, and minutes were taken by the Number Ten Political Secretary. First names were used (as opposed to ministerial titles) and the focus was on the Party, its performance and preparing for forthcoming elections. Major found them a useful technique in Party management, to help ensure that he had all his Cabinet behind him on party political matters.

Major and Parliament

Major had been an assiduous House of Commons man from 1979 to 1990, an avid networker of Tea and Dining Rooms, a soaker-up of atmosphere in the chamber and committee room, and an effective speaker and a debater capable of cutting repartee. He had never sat on a departmental select committee, but most other facets of House of Commons life were very familiar to him.

It is a surprise, therefore, time constraints acknowledged, that the House did not loom larger in his life as Prime Minister, and that he did not spend much time there picking up the mood. As tension between Number Ten and backbenchers grew after 1992, some Tory MPs blamed Graham Bright for failing to do more to encourage his attendance, for isolating him from the parliamentary party, and even for giving him inaccurate information on its shifting balance of power, especially over Europe. Some felt Major insufficiently entertained MPs at Number Ten or Chequers. Ryder as Chief Whip became similarly chastised after the 1992 election. The neglect is puzzling: Major knew that a principal reason for Heath losing the leadership in 1975 was his failure to do more to court his MPs, and Major was much better and more natural than Heath at doing this. Lack of time must be the chief reason, although high office tends to distance its occupants.

Major made more frequent parliamentary statements than Thatcher,[58] but he did so partly because he was more often away on official overseas trips: two-thirds of the twenty-one statements Major made during 1990–93 were reports on international summits.[59] Major similarly spoke more frequently in

debates than Thatcher (on 3.2 per cent of parliamentary days, not far below
the postwar average). But again this fact did not herald a significant change in
prime ministerial behaviour; nearly half his speeches were due to exceptional
circumstances, such as two on the Gulf War, the no-confidence motion on
the poll tax, and six during debates on Europe.[60] Major made only five minor
interventions in debates during 1990–94, and made no closing speeches after
becoming Prime Minister. He was also much less likely than an earlier
generation of Tory Prime Ministers, such as Macmillan, to remain in the
chamber after he had answered oral questions.

Major's experience of Prime Minister's Question Time was qualitatively
different from that of his predecessors, because he was the first to develop
his style entirely under the glare of television coverage. The Commons
had been televised since November 1989, and Thatcher was never wholly
comfortable with the change. The twice-weekly duels with the Leader of the
Opposition were becoming ever more the central event in media coverage of
politics, 'reinforcing the existing tendency towards soundbite partisan politics', as Peter Riddell put it.[61]

Major invested considerable effort in answering oral questions, which he
regarded as his most important opportunity to show his mettle to the House
and the nation. The format of Prime Minister's Question Time had not
changed greatly since becoming a regular feature in 1961. Most questions
were open-ended enquiries about the Prime Minister's engagements for the
day, which allowed the MP to ask a 'supplementary' about more or less any
aspect of the Prime Minister's responsibilities. The Leader of the Opposition
was permitted two, and very occasionally three, extra supplementaries to
respond to the Prime Minister's answer.[62]

Major's technique for preparing himself for the twice-weekly ordeal rapidly
evolved into a ritual. The Parliamentary Affairs Private Secretary (Dominic
Morris until December 1991, then William Chapman) would comb the
Sunday press and weekend political programmes to sense what the lead items
might be for the coming week. On Mondays and Wednesdays, again, the
media was thoroughly scanned and background briefings on lead stories
would be commissioned from Whitehall departments. These were worked
up by the Private Office with an appropriate Number Ten spin, before being
placed in Major's overnight red boxes. From 8 a.m. every Tuesday and
Thursday morning, the days of the questions, Roy Stone, the Parliamentary
Clerk (a relatively junior official but whose value was shown by his remaining
in situ throughout Major's premiership) would start telephoning around
Whitehall for the official line on key stories.

The first briefing session of the day with Major took place in the Cabinet
Room at 9 a.m., attended by Hogg and O'Donnell, the Political Office, most
of the Private Office and representatives from the Policy Unit. Again they
would go through the newspapers, television and radio, especially the *Today*
programme, and Major would be asked how he would like to discuss the
main issues. Attenders would chip in with what they thought his line on

possible questions might be. The meeting would break up at 9.30 a.m., and the Private Secretary would have three and a half hours to revise the briefing folder in the light of the meeting, and provide background or new lines as different stories emerged, or if Major was unhappy with the overnight brief. Departments could again be telephoned by the Private Secretary or by Stone, and harried into getting responses quickly back to Number Ten. The Private Secretary would battle to have the folder ready and complete, with material ordered under neat departmental subjects, by 1 p.m. prior to a second meeting with Major that would begin in the Cabinet Room at any time between 1.15 and 1.30 p.m.

Major would then have little more than an hour and a half to go through the folder, over a sandwich, in the company of just the Private Secretary. Various aides would call in occasionally with new briefs or leads. At about 2.30 p.m., the 'race card' would be brought in, a summary of the proposed answers to questions listed on the order paper and those Tory MPs had apprised Number Ten about. Morris introduced the technique of giving constituency profiles of all MPs whose names were down on the order paper, so Major could offer a swift retort, relating his answer to the questioner's constituency. Major would go through the paperwork calmly and methodically, committing as much to memory as possible. At just after 3 o'clock, Major would emerge with a small entourage (Morris/Chapman, Bright, Chaplin/Hill, O'Donnell) and speed off to the House; in his room there they would run over the last-minute lines. Said one: 'We would sit down and get him into the best mental state we could for the next quarter of an hour.'[63] Questions lasted from 3.15 to 3.30 p.m., and during that first year he would deal on average with eight tabled questions.[64] The ordeal over, he would leave the chamber smartly for his room where the team would have a ten-minute 'post mortem'. He tended to be self-critical, and the temptation for the entourage to flannel him proved too great for some. When it went well, he would radiate a feeling of tremendous relief and bonhomie.

The entire process of preparing for and participating in Prime Minister's Questions twice a week tied down Major and Number Ten for a disproportionate amount of the four days a week he was able to spend in London. Not for nothing did Howell James, his last Political Secretary, advise Blair's team that little would be lost by cutting PMQs down to just one session per week, which Blair announced as one of his first steps in office.[65]

Neil Kinnock, Major's sparring partner until the 1992 election, described their duels thus:

I saw it through the glass of a sporting metaphor: normally the score would be 2–1 either way, and if you emerged on top you could look back and think you did well. On balance, I probably came out a bit ahead of Major over those eighteen months, winning rather more than I lost. He was frustrating to work against. Your punches would not land; they would pass straight through him. He had his brief ready, with his line to get across, whatever it was, and that was frustrating. Thatcher had done that too.[66]

Major took some time to get the measure of Kinnock, but felt himself he had him mastered by the autumn of 1991; aides felt it took longer for him to feel fully confident with the process. He found Kinnock would talk too much, and did not find the weak point in the argument, unlike his successor from July 1992, John Smith. One aide who helped him prepare for questions in 1991–2 noted that Major, consciously or not, regularly treated Tuesday and Thursday questions differently: 'He always hoped that it would proceed in a rather gentlemanly way on Tuesday, but on Thursday his hackles were up.'[67]

In his first six question sessions before the Christmas 1990 recess, he drew with Kinnock. At the outset he made it clear that he did not like the way that Mrs Thatcher's background papers had been prepared, with her several hundred 'killer facts'. He thought she had sounded like a 'Gatling gun firing off endless statistics', and wanted more information, and to indulge in less point-scoring.[68] There was an awkward transition period when he was expected to know everything, and he had not yet developed the style of the quick, confident repartee, nor the frank answer.[69] During January and February 1991, he was helped by the Gulf War, with both Kinnock and Ashdown taking care to show their backing for the government, often prefacing their questions with supportive comments.[70] That spring and early summer was a difficult period when he felt under fire domestically, and he came across several times as rattled. By June he had recovered his composure, and adopted an increasingly combative and point-scoring style in the mounting pre-election atmosphere.[71]

His initial desire to see Question Time as a part of open government, with honest answers to sincere questions, however, was crushed by the 1991–2 session. His manner became much less polite and consensual, and his answers more evasive and point-scoring.[72] In party political terms, some of his most effective performances came in the six months in the run-up to the 1992 election, notably when, in December 1991, he bashed Kinnock over Militant.[73] Major's Private Office took particular pride in one occasion when they predicted, word perfect, all three of Kinnock's questions and Major answered the third by smiling and showing Kinnock the briefing folder. His strongest performances were to come after 1992, when at times he was masterly, as effective as any prime minister at their best.

On occasions Kinnock clearly humiliated Major. On 23 July 1991 Kinnock made Major angry, questioning him over what he had known as Chancellor about the fallen Bank of Credit and Commerce International (BCCI).[74] Worse was the débâcle in April 1991, when Major tried to score a point off Kinnock. Kinnock had been absent the previous night. David Hunt whispered to Major: 'Kinnock missed the vote on the Cardiff Bay last night. You should kick him with it.' Major stood up and said: 'Although the right honourable gentleman is against unemployment in principle, he supports in practice policies that would create it – not least, as a Welsh member, failing to be here earlier this week to vote for the Cardiff Bay Barrage Bill, which would provide 25,000 jobs.'

Kinnock sprang up and responded, to laughter and Labour cheers, 'The reason why I was not in the House on that occasion was that Her Majesty did me the enormous honour of inviting me and my wife to spend the night with the royal family at Windsor Castle. I thought that the Prime Minister's many advisers might have drawn his attention to the Court Circular.'[75] Kinnock recalls the episode: 'He was really knocked backwards, deflated by that one.'[76]

Major's unhappiest performance during 1990–92 was not at Question Time, but his speech following the State Opening of Parliament, the only annual Commons speech which the Prime Minister is bound to make personally, which fell in 1991 on 1 November. Vulnerable to the charge that the government was merely hanging on to office waiting for the right moment to go to the country, Major had little fresh to say. The speech, drafted by Morris, did credit to no one. Major's light patches at the start fell flat, he lost his place, there were long pauses, and the speech fell apart.[77] Labour backbenchers employed the common parliamentary tactic of talking among themselves to distract him, and noise and jeering rose to a crescendo. By the end of the speech he had lost the House, as his own side sat watching the display sullenly. It was an agonising experience for him.[78]

Major's Social Liberalism

Major is a sensitive man, with strong emotions, hidden for the most part from the public, which was not always to his advantage. His strong social liberalism and detestation of discrimination, whether on grounds of race, gender, class or sexual preference, were unusual for a Conservative Prime Minister. Robin Squire summed it up thus:

He feels very deeply about discrimination. I suspect there is not a vicious bone in his body. His experiences of racism in Lambeth helped hone his beliefs. He reacts very sharply to any suggestion that he is prejudiced, or playing discrimination for political advantage.[79]

Major's most dramatic action in discrimination came not over race, arguably the prejudice on which he felt most strongly, nor over gender or class, but over homosexuality. His liking for thoughtful, sensitive men predisposed him to form close friendships with homosexuals, only one of whom, Matthew Parris, has come out; he had none of the hang-ups about gays of many of his generation and background.

In July 1991 Major visited the Royal National Theatre to see Eduardo de Fillipo's *Napoli Milionara* with Ian McKellen. After the play, Major, accompanied by Sarah Hogg, a member of the Board of the National Theatre, was invited to a supper party in the Richardson Room hosted by Richard Eyre, the theatre's artistic director. After the main course, Mary Soames, the theatre's Chairman and mother of Major's parliamentary friend Nicholas, asked McKellen to sit between her and Major. McKellen bantered good-humouredly with Major, offering him assistance with voice projection on the clear understanding if he did so he would not exploit it to win the election.[80] Changing the conversation, he asked Major if he could talk to him about 'a social matter' (he remembers being nervous about using the word 'gay' with him). Major agreed, but said he would prefer to make it a formal exchange at Number Ten.

During the supper party Major came over to his fellow diners from the theatre as warm, rather touching, but also with little idea about their lives and values. At one point in the meal the voices fell silent as Major said how pleased he was to be with them, and added that he had just met George Carey, newly installed as Archbishop of Canterbury, whom he thought 'a very good chap'. The company murmured responses with lowered eyes, most having a perception of Carey as anything but tolerant and broad-minded.[81]

McKellen followed up their meeting with a letter to Major, which went to William Chapman as Home Affairs Private Secretary. Anxious for the meeting to go ahead, Chapman did not inform the Policy Unit, suspecting that they would advise against it, and with Turnbull's tacit compliance sent up a draft for Major to sign, inviting McKellen to meet him. The visit was arranged for 24 September 1991. McKellen duly arrived, armed with a book and a typed text of what he wanted to say, which he had personally prepared on his old-fashioned word processor. He also had a briefing from Stonewall, the first full-time gay lobby group, founded by him and others in 1988. McKellen began, somewhat apprehensively, by following his text to the letter:

One of my favourite books is a little paperback from the Gay Men's Press called *The Pink Plaque Guide to London* which identifies houses and buildings in London where celebrated lesbians and gay men have lived or worked. I hope it might please you to know that on the cover of the Guide is a photo of this building.

At that point, McKellen handed Major the book. Major asked, himself rather nervous now, why Number Ten was on the cover. McKellen continued:

From the available statistics, it is likely that 10% of the people currently working here are homosexual. But the celebrity in question is one of your predecessors – William Pitt the Younger. He never declared himself as gay and I wonder if the burden of his secret led him to the alcoholism which rapidly killed him. Maybe his benign ghost will hover over this meeting.[82]

Major thanked him for the book, and explained that this was not to be a meeting at which decisions would be taken, but one where he could hear about the issues from McKellen so he could then discuss them with colleagues in a more informed way.

McKellen praised Major for agreeing to the meeting and for the response he had made in July when he accepted the principle of equality in the security service (when he also acknowledged that society's attitude to homosexuality was changing).[83] McKellen then raised his main concerns: criminal law, the age of consent (then set at twenty-one), police harassment of gays, homosexuality in the armed forces and abusive language in the press. He said he would like the outlawing of discrimination on grounds of race and sex in the Citizen's Charter to be broadened to include 'sexuality'.[84]

McKellen thought the meeting 'cordial' and found Major 'a very sympathetic listener'.[85] Major for his part found it moving to learn more about everyday repression and harassment,[86] but the large number of letters sent to him at Number Ten about the visit were critical rather than supportive of the initiative.[87]

The visit was a high-risk move for Major, and one the Policy Unit did indeed try to query; 'perhaps the PM is being led into dangerous waters at a sensitive time?' wrote one member.[88] The Conservative Family Campaign was one of several right-wing groups to go on the attack. 'I can hardly believe that such a meeting is taking place,' said its spokesman, adding that it would risk alienating pro-family and Christian support in the country, and serve no useful purpose.[89] Dr Adrian Rogers, its chairman, demanded equal time to that given to the 'queer actor', and dismissed homosexuality as 'sterile, disease-ridden, God-forsaken'.[90]

The press response, however, was generally favourable. The *Independent*'s editorial 'An open-minded prime minister', praised Major for having done 'a simple and a sensible thing'. *The Times* said it was 'inconceivable' Thatcher would have agreed to the visit,[91] and argued that gay people, the Conservative Party and the nation had all gained from the initiative. Indeed, it could not have been more fulsome in its support for Major's reviving the tradition, 'that was threadbare under Mrs Thatcher', of 'one nation Conservatism'.[92] The *Daily Telegraph* alone of the broadsheets was critical, arguing that most Tories, indeed most voters, 'regard homosexuality as something to be discouraged', and thought the meeting pointless.[93] Most of the press picked up on the coincidence of Edith Cresson, the French Prime Minister, arriving for lunch at Number Ten just after McKellen had left. She had recently castigated British men for their alleged high incidence of homosexuality.[94]

The visit inevitably disappointed the more radical gay activists, some of whom thought the visit to a Tory premier an error. McKellen was criticised in the gay press for the poor dividends from the initiative – there was not even the promise of legislation in the 1992 Conservative manifesto, which McKellen had said would be the litmus test of the meeting's value[95] – and for his alleged gullibility in agreeing to a cynical ploy by Major to win a few more votes. Such reactions were unduly negative. Although McKellen himself thought Major sincere, he was not surprised by the limited results of the initiative.[96]

Some developments did in fact follow: Major told his ministers to respond more positively in their departments to representatives from the gay population; announcements were made about gays in the civil service; and he agreed to hold an age of consent debate (in February 1994), albeit on an open vote, which resulted in the age of consent being lowered to eighteen. The gay lobby was disappointed by the outcome – and Major's own vote for eighteen – but recognised that it had brought the day of full legal equality at sixteen closer.[97]

The McKellen visit gave rise to broader hopes from some that Major would develop a right-of-centre socially liberal agenda for the Conservative Party. Though he drew back from doing so, his instincts took him in that direction. His support for ethnic minorities was limited to early on *ad hoc* interventions, such as supporting the appointment of the first Asian diocesan bishop, Michael Nazir-Ali to the See of Rochester in June 1994. His early enthusiasm on sex discrimination became absorbed into the policy of equal opportunities in the civil service, and the occasional symbolic speech, as to the pressure group Policy 2000 in late 1991.[98] Throughout his time in Downing Street Major was very much at ease with gay people, including members of his staff; he would occasionally invite their partners to social functions at Number Ten.[99]

Major did not go further in the direction of a socially liberal agenda because he was wary of right-wing reaction. Had the majority after the 1992 general election been bigger, he would very likely have returned to the theme. But circumstances ran against him, and the right were on the attack. They took vengeance by trying to bounce his 'back to basics' agenda in the autumn of 1993 in the direction of conservative personal morality. Major's hand extended to gays in 1991 was not forgotten; it was indeed a ghost that haunted him, and was one of the factors that led some on the traditionalist right to believe that he was unsuitable for a Tory Prime Minister and had to quit.[100]

SIXTEEN

High Summer, Low Summer:

May–October 1991

MAJOR DESPERATELY WANTED to win his own general election. He sought his own mandate, he wanted to get Thatcher out of his hair and he wanted an end to the uncertainty.[1] As a passionate and partisan Conservative, he longed to renew the Party's hold on power for another term. The postwar Conservative premier he had been compared to most frequently was Alec Douglas-Home (1963–4), also seen as affable and capable, but without his own agenda. The comparison did not please him, especially as it implied that he, too, would lose a general election (and subsequently the party leadership) after but a brief period in Downing Street. From every point of view, he was passionate about winning the general election.

Election Timing

Though the general election was at most a year and a half away by the time of her fall, Thatcher had given it oddly little thought. By an irony, the only policy committee set up to prepare for the manifesto was the Economic Policy Group, which had met on 15 November 1990, chaired by Major as Chancellor.[2] All election planning activity fell into abeyance during December, while Major settled in at Downing Street and Patten, the new Party Chairman, at Conservative Central Office. Patten in particular had to sack some Thatcher–Baker appointees, and bring in his own, notably Shaun Woodward (the editor of BBC television's *That's Life!*) as director of communications. By early January, Patten gave Major the stark news that 'the cupboard was bare' on planning, money and policy.[3] 'It was a grim inheritance,' said Major. Patten calculated that there were only twelve possible Thursdays between 2 May 1991 and 18 June 1992 on which the election could be called. Should they play it short or long?[4]

On 11–12 January, Patten convened a confidential meeting at Hever Castle in Kent attended by Hogg, True, Chaplin and Central Office senior staff. Polls, strategies, organisation, and timing were the subjects under review. Regardless of whether or not there would be a war in the Gulf, June, or even May, emerged as a favoured time. Inflation was falling, the recession was still not too painful, the future of the poll tax was likely to be resolved but any new changes not yet implemented; it would also be before the IGC at Maastricht in December, thus avoiding the risk of any split in the Party over Europe before the election. The mood was upbeat; according to Chaplin 'all fairly optimistic about results'.[5]

As to the thrust of strategy, their thoughts were still fairly embryonic, little more than that the campaign should offer 'hope' and 'peace of mind'.[6] These buzz words, regarded as 'faintly ludicrous' by some participants, were in fact the product of an expensive polling exercise, which also threw up a more practical finding: that there was advantage to be gained on the taxation issue.[7] The meeting resolved that decisive action was urgently required to prepare the ground: a regular planning group should be set up, and the thematic policy groups that had been suggested by Mrs Thatcher should be rapidly convened, meeting under the appropriate departmental ministers.

No definite decisions were taken, however, on timing, and the subject was discussed again at a meeting on 1 February. Lamont said he wanted it played long, but others present, including Major, Patten, Ryder, Hurd and Waddington, favoured an early election provided they could avoid being accused of cutting and running and of holding a 'khaki election' to exploit credit gained during the Gulf War. (The expression was used of the election the Salisbury government fought in 1900 during the Boer War; the 'Hang the Kaiser election' of 1918, fought after the Armistice, might have been a better analogy.)

Major himself was particularly sensitive to the charge that he would be exploiting the war. 'Major was most reluctant about a snap election as it would look as if he was wrapping himself in the flag and taking advantage of the campaign,' recalled Patten.[8] The meeting also discussed the manifesto, 'but the ideas are very vague as yet: opportunity, education, etc.'.[9] These were of course the two key themes in Major's agenda in 1991–2; both, especially the former, would reappear strongly in 1996–7.

Views on timing had changed little at a dinner Patten held on 27 February, with Hogg, Chaplin and Woodward, who were joined by Gordon Reece and Peter Gummer (another public relations adviser, and brother of John). One of Patten's priorities at Central Office had been to bring new people to the task of party presentation; he was dismissive of Thatcher's and Baker's retinue of Tim Bell, Brendan Bruce and Harvey Thomas.[10] The consensus remained in favour of a summer election because of the problems – potential Europe splits and recession – that might lie ahead.[11] Patten still favoured going very early, to capitalise on Major's popularity and the post-Thatcher upsurge in the polls. Failing that, he favoured, like Lamont, playing it long, so they could campaign on the back of a solid record.[12] The Ribble Valley by-election defeat on 7 March gave Number Ten and Central Office a jolt, but the Conservatives maintained their opinion poll lead over Labour in both March and April.

The Chequers seminar of 24–5 March opened with the manifesto. All the Policy Unit was there, to discuss the reports that had emerged from the policy groups it was shadowing. To Chaplin, Major – for reasons of overburden as discussed – gave the impression of having read neither the reports, nor the precis prepared for him, so discussion was not as productive as it might have been.[13] Ministers were quizzed during the seminar about their manifesto plans, with Major worrying about the high cost of many of the suggestions. Chaplin recorded, 'It is worrying that he has no underlying conviction about the way he wants policies to go – pragmatic to a fault.'

As the seminar wore on, talk of a June election began to fade,[14] and even more so on 22 April when Major, Patten, Ryder, Hogg, Chaplin and True met again to discuss election dates. With Major and Cabinet ministers so distracted, policies had not been thrashed out, nor any clear government strategy confirmed.[15] Heseltine's announcement on the council tax on 23 April, with its promised consultation period, meant that the prospect of a summer election was just about out of the question.

The Conservative Party electoral machine was slowly gearing itself up, but Patten and Hogg found the progress frustrating. Saatchi & Saatchi – thrice midwives of previous election campaigns under Thatcher – had been reappointed by Patten as the agency to guide the Party's general election campaign. Steered by Maurice Saatchi, who took a particular personal interest in the account, they counselled from the outset that the Conservatives should focus on a negative approach, denigrating Labour and their suitability for office, rather than basing their election strategy on the virtues of Major and the Tories.[16] Thus the agency came to the big planning meeting on 26 April to discuss Major's 'vision of Conservatism' with already fairly limited views on any role his vision might play in the election. Chaplin was sceptical from a different perspective. Upon listening to what she described as Major's 'one nation Conservative' vision, she concluded that

many of his thoughts are out of date and from 50s/60s attitudes. He is full of prejudices against some people whom he thinks have had it too easy but he doesn't realise many of them had to fight their way up as well – even Mrs T.[17]

Saatchi's impressions of the role of Major's vision of Conservatism were unchanged by the meeting, but they still saw the potential of capitalising on his personal popularity (his approval rating in April was 59 per cent, down from a 63 per cent peak in February) and the popular resonance of his personal 'back street to Downing Street' life-story. Patten persuaded Major to see John Schlesinger, the Conservative-sympathising director of such popular films as *Sunday Bloody Sunday* and *Yanks*, with a view to making a Party election broadcast.[18] A breakfast meeting with Major was duly arranged for 29 April, where Schlesinger came over as a 'nice and funny man, lots of ideas'.[19] Major, however, was deeply apprehensive about bringing his background into the spotlight, and expressed distaste for the celebratory 1987 election broadcast made by film director Hugh Hudson about the Kinnocks, on which the proposed Schlesinger portrait was to be to some extent modelled. It took a further six months for Patten to wear down Major's resistance and for him to agree that the film should be made.[20]

Poor local election results on 2 May also counted heavily against a summer election. The Party had been expecting at least 400 losses as the seats contested were last fought in 1987, when in a general election year they had performed unusually well.[21] In the event their losses were more than double, at 890, as against gains of 490 for Labour and the real surprise of 520 for the Liberal Democrats. Notable Tory council defeats included Plymouth, Luton and Newbury. Overall, the Party lost thirty-eight councils and took 35 per cent of the national vote, compared to 36 per cent for Labour and 21 per cent for the Liberal Democrats. The bald facts of lost seats were less shocking in the light of the share of the vote. Major described the results as 'disappointing but bearable'.[22]

The press was nevertheless awash with reports of confusion in Tory ranks, and pressure was placed on Major to delay the election until the following spring.[23]

Ivor Crewe, writing in *The Times*, was more sanguine: 'In spite of the headlines,' he wrote, 'Thursday's results should have Mr Major less worried than Mr Kinnock.'[24] The Conservatives' own analysis tended to confirm this impression. They concluded that to be only 1 per cent behind Labour in the middle of a recession was not at all bad, and that there was a 9.2 per cent swing back to the Conservatives from Labour in England from the disastrous local election results of May 1990, with the Conservative vote holding up in key marginals in the West Midlands.[25]

Major himself was particularly alarmed at the Liberal Democrat advances, which he warned might yet damage the Conservatives in a general election.[26] Chaplin had breakfast with Major the day after the polls; she was gloomy about the loss of Newbury council, where she was the parliamentary candidate, a seat to which she had grown attached: 'I like it there!' Neither she nor Major was happy. 'For the first time I think we might lose the next election – we have alienated too many of our own supporters', she confided to her diary.[27] But a summer election was still not finally ruled out. On 9 May Major discussed dates with Patten, Lamont and Ryder; a July election was regarded as possible 'but most unlikely' with opinion polls steadily weakening. Plans were made for a series of initiatives over the summer to try to maintain momentum.[28]

It was the Monmouth by-election on 16 May, won by Labour with a 13 per cent swing from the Tories, that finally killed off the prospect of an election before the summer recess. Anxieties over the future of the NHS were regarded as mainly responsible for the result, though privately several in Number Ten thought a contributory factor was anger over the recession – a word neither Major nor Lamont was willing to use – and the reluctance (on the strong advice of the Governor of the Bank of England and the Treasury) to cut interest rates.[29]

The Monmouth result gave the Tories a powerful kick. Belief in a Kinnock victory now began to grow. Perhaps, some wondered, the replacement of Mrs Thatcher by Major had been a rash and unnecessary move? For *The*

Times reported that Monmouth 'convinced many in the government that there was, after all, nothing inevitable about a Tory recovery, and that Labour could win the election'.[30] The day this article appeared, on 23 May, a Political Cabinet was held after a short Cabinet meeting. Major told assembled ministers to prepare either for a Party Conference, or for an autumn election, or possibly even for both.[31] Number Ten had become frustrated by the lack of punch from several Cabinet ministers, reflected in their desultory response on the Citizen's Charter and manifesto preparation, and Chaplin feared it would take some time before the urgency was widely appreciated:

Interesting watching them all try to be best. Some are completely apolitical. Tom King clearly never thinks in those terms ... William Waldegrave battling on but no know-how in the whole room really. Some heavyweights C Patten and K Clarke agree [they] must get act together.[32]

To galvanise the Party's presentation and co-ordination Ryder proposed establishing the Number Twelve committee, which was to become an important body in the run-up to the 1992 general election. An autumn election for some weeks appeared a possibility, but in his Welsh conference speech on 14 June, with polls continuing to show a Labour lead of 3–4 per cent, Major spoke of the unlikelihood of an election before the spring of 1992.[33] He found decisions over election timing particularly onerous, and would agonise about the consequences of the loss of key individuals as well as the overall result for the Party.[34] With the decision to postpone the election, he was at least freed from worrying about it over the summer, which was just as well as his attention was urgently demanded on a series of domestic and international problems.

Dog Days

Major looked forward to a respite with the arrival of warmer weather and the cricket season. But the summer brought no let-up, and instead saw two new adjectives emerge in the press to describe his government – incompetent and oversensitive to the press.

The dangerous dogs saga set a tone. A spate of attacks by 'dangerous dogs' (mainly pit bull terriers) had been reported in the media. After an attack by two of the breed in early May, which left the face of one adult, Frank Tempest, badly mauled, and attacks shortly after in separate incidents by pit bull terriers on two girls aged two and six, Kenneth Baker asked his Home Office officials to investigate possible legislation.[35]

The department's line had always been cautious, as they regarded legislation fraught with difficulties, not least because it was Alsatians and other so-called 'tame' breeds which were responsible for the largest number of reported bitings. They also found their Secretary of State not wholly consistent. 'Baker veered from moments of masterly inactivity, which had been

the Home Office line on dangerous dogs for years, to in another moment
wanting to do something radical, and then, thirdly, onto a middle course. It
was all rather confusing.'[36]

Number Ten was cautious too, and could see the dangers of not responding
decisively to the tabloid-inspired public outcry, as well as of Baker producing
over-hasty legislation.[37] A Cabinet committee considered the issue on 21
May and decided that legislation could be introduced in the next session,
only to be overruled by Major, who thought delay that long was 'politically
untenable'.[38] Several in Cabinet agreed, one asking 'What would happen if it
was my daughter?'[39]

Baker took the hint and forged ahead. A Bill, which specified that pit bulls
should be either put down, or neutered and registered, was introduced into
the House on 10 June, and became law as the Dangerous Dogs Act on 24
July. Baker was pleased with his swift and decisive action; Number Ten
worried, however, whether the legislation might not be judged precipitous and
ill-conceived. The popular press did indeed change its tune, with mawkishly
pathetic stories of dogs waiting on 'Death Row' replacing those of maimed
children. The impression given from the episode was not one of confidence,
though it was a harbinger of several issues that emerged later where Major's
government was damned if it acted early, and damned if it did not.

Two Bills, legacies of Thatcher's final Queen's Speech in November 1990,
now caused further problems. The Criminal Justice Bill was a liberal measure
initiated in 1988 while Hurd was still Home Secretary, and taken through
committee by his successor from October 1989. Waddington (to the surprise
of many who regarded Waddington as rather a reactionary on such matters).
The Act sought to shift the emphasis in penal policy from custody to com-
munity-based punishment, and to introduce a 'unit fine', a penalty based
upon a combination of a sum based on the gravity of the offence together
with the offender's ability to pay.[40]

Major was puzzled by the content of this piece of non-partisan legislation,
the product of extensive Home Office consultation and Treasury scepticism
of the cost-effectiveness of locking people up. He began to consider the Home
Office as a department pursuing its own agenda. Clarke, later to wrestle with
its implementation when the Act ran into serious criticism, considered the
legislation 'extraordinary ... passed almost unknown to any of us'.[41]
The second Thatcher legislative legacy, the Child Support Act 1991,
which established rules for maintenance payments, was rapidly felt to be
unfair, provoking a stream of headline stories of destitute parents unable
to pay for the upkeep of their children, which again reflected poorly on the
government.

For a Tory premier, Major showed little direct interest in 'law and order'
issues before the general election. Those who knew him well at each stage of
his career, however, testify to strongly held conventional Conservative views
on the sanctity of property, and a disgust for those who broke the law.[42]
But he had other preoccupations during 1990–92 and therefore acquiesced

passively in the setting up of the Royal Commission on Criminal Justice (which the Home Office had sought but could never get past Mrs Thatcher), the acceptance of the Woolf Report into prisons, and Baker's proposals for dealing with squatting and 'joy-riding' car theft.[43] The last provoked the following episode in Cabinet:

Baker outlined a major initiative by car insurers with differential premia and car manufacturers introducing deadlocks, all designed to curtail the theft of cars. Halfway through his rather over the top presentation, Douglas Hogg [deputising for Hurd] intervened to say: 'I have to tell you that they said the same thing when I was at the Home Office.' Baker replied, 'I'm sorry to hear then that you were so ineffective.'[44]Major was more than happy for such banter to take place in Cabinet.

Light relief was totally lacking in the increasingly ugly clash with Labour over health. Major had spoken persuasively during the leadership election of his attachment to the NHS, and how much he owed it personally in his own life. But Labour saw, with the Thatcher health reforms, and the purchaser-provider split coming into effect, that the moment was ripe for attacking the government's commitment to a free and universal health service. A Chequers seminar on health had been held on 27 April to discuss improving the nation's health and physical wellbeing by 2000 (prior to the launch of a Green Paper, *The Health of the Nation*).[45] Care was taken to brief journalists that Major would not be exploring any further fundamental reforms, and that he would be consulting fully with NHS authorities.[46] But neither these reassurances, nor Waldegrave's campaign 'Six Labour Lies' on the NHS, drew the sting from Labour's attack, cleverly orchestrated by Robin Cook, the Shadow spokesman, which had been so successful at the Monmouth by-election.

Then in early July, with the poll gap behind Labour stuck on 3–4 per cent, scandal flared in the City when the Bank of England closed the Bank of Credit and Commerce International (BCCI). In the US, where the bank was popularly nicknamed 'Bank of Crooks and Cocaine International', a prosecutor termed it the biggest fraud in banking history. Major had led Leigh-Pemberton to believe that the Bank of England would have a free hand in dealing with the episode. The Governor was therefore a little surprised to learn that Lamont had set up an independent inquiry under Lord Justice Bingham to examine the supervision of BCCI.[47]

Kinnock attacked Major hard on the BCCI scandal in the House,[48] but as Major did not believe he himself or anyone in his government was guilty of any oversight, he considered an inquiry the best way forward. The Bingham inquiry, indeed, proved a happy solution, and when Major next found himself accused on something where he was convinced of his own innocence, the Arms-to-Iraq affair, he resorted to the same device.[49] With Scott, it did not work out as well.

Peace in Europe: Coups in Russia

After his 'very heart of Europe' speech in Bonn in March, European Community matters ceased to be a priority until June and the run-up to the Luxembourg Council, which was to take stock of progress on discussions on political and economic union. The Intergovernmental Conference (IGC) was at the forefront of everyone's mind.

Major aimed to play down the Europe issue, not least because if there was to be a pre-Maastricht election in the autumn, he wanted it as low key as possible. He had been preparing for a speech to the Welsh Party Conference at Swansea on Friday 14 June, two weeks before Luxembourg. The text, on his domestic agenda, had already been written by Nick True when the Eurosceptic Bruges Group produced a paper saying Major was appeasing the European Community and was taking Britain towards its federal agenda.[50] Ridley raised the temperature still further by saying that Major must not give in to the federalist tide.[51] With two days' notice the Swansea speech had to be rewritten, restating Major's position on Europe, in an effort to calm down the feverish atmosphere.[52] On the morning of the speech the final text had still not been agreed, leaving Sarah Hogg to rush between Treasury and FCO, confirming what Major was to say about Britain's stance.[53] Major duly told the mystified delegates in Swansea, who were expecting a tub-thumping domestic speech, that any move to a single currency would only occur with full endorsement by Parliament. His pragmatic approach earned a rebuke from *The Economist*, for sounding hostile to a single currency while leaving escape routes between the lines: 'he must make up his mind and lead'.[54] But the speech at least succeeded in pacifying the atmosphere in the run-up to the Luxembourg Council.

Councils were held in whichever country was having its six months' rotation presidency. Countries held one major council meeting at the end of their presidency, often in one of their exotic resorts, and frequently held a mid-term council too. Luxembourg, having nowhere more exotic than Luxembourg, held both the April (safe havens) and the June Council in the one location. Jacques Santer, the Prime Minister, was in the chair.

The most pressing subject in the discussions on 28–9 June turned out to be not the EC but Yugoslavia, then in a state of rapid disintegration. Three foreign ministers were despatched to Yugoslavia, securing the appointment of Mesic of Croatia as President of the ramshackle federal government. But as Major told the House on his return from Luxembourg, 'The situation remains very volatile and the Community will need to be closely involved over the coming weeks.'[55]

Yugoslavia provided on one level a useful deflector, as negotiations on the main subject, Maastricht, were not easy. The Luxembourg delegation produced a draft treaty, which essentially became the structure of the Maastricht Treaty itself, and which was duly endorsed at the Council. Major had to yield on some points, as over citizenship, about which he was nervous;

and on the rest of plans for political union he expressed strong reservations. On EMU, he outlined Britain's concerns about a single currency and a single central bank, and reiterated that any commitment on EMU by Britain would require a separate decision by the government and Parliament, not just on when but whether to join.

For Major, the key development was securing agreement on the principle of an opt-out from EMU. Major explained in confidence to Santer, Kohl and President of the European Commission Delors that it was inconceivable that he would be able to sign a legally binding commitment to a single currency at Maastricht. Kohl was instrumental in evolving the opt-out idea, which allowed Britain to participate fully in the discussions on the single currency, while retaining the freedom to decide whether to be party to what was agreed. Nigel Wicks, head of the Treasury's international finance division, advised pocketing the concession until the Maastricht conference in December, whereas the Foreign Office's John Kerr – concerned lest something go wrong in the interim – advised making it public in June, to avoid any backtracking by Britain's EC partners.[56] Major followed Wicks's advice, wanting to tease out the details and give the Treasury time to explore the implications, and allowing him to keep open the option of an autumn election; if he had gone public on the opt-out at that point, he said he would have felt duty bound to see through the negotiations before calling an election.[57]

Back in London, Major plunged into preparations for the Group of Seven (G7) economic summit, when the leaders of the seven most powerful western nations, Germany, France, Italy, the USA, Canada, Japan and the UK, meet every summer, again on a rotational basis, to discuss issues of common economic and political interest. The meeting, in London from 15 to 17 July, would show off national pride not just to the other heads of government but to the world's media. With an election beckoning, it was also an ideal opportunity to display Major as a world statesman. Considerable thought was put into preparing for the occasion, especially as the last London G7, in June 1984, had been considered a damp squib. Journalists were carefully cosseted, with generous free helpings of food and drink, to maximise chances of the most favourable coverage. Norma looked after the heads of government wives, her biggest hosting operation so far, taking them for lunch at Chequers, on a sightseeing boat journey on the Thames, a tour of Kew Gardens, a trip to see the musical *Carmen Jones*, and the obligatory grand dinner.[58] More to her taste was a private dinner with George and Barbara Bush at Number Ten, at which Barbara reported she was 'very comfortable' with her role.[59]

With the G7 meeting following in the wake of the Gulf War and the emergence of the 'new world order' after the collapse of communism, the dominant mood was one of optimism. Important measures to strengthen the UN, to increase its powers over the internal affairs of sovereign states, and to arrange for it to set up a conference on the environment the following year, were agreed. The heads of government committed themselves to the effective banning of chemical and biological weapons, to reinforce the nuclear

non-proliferation treaty, and to see the GATT Uruguay round on free trade
through to a successful conclusion.[60] Major even offered a second G7 summit
if it was necessary for progress on GATT, which the *Wall Street Journal*
called 'the best news for the Uruguay Round in a long time'.[61] He had become
convinced of the benefits of GATT and was to pursue the issue to a successful
conclusion in 1993.

The most striking feature of the summit was the arrival on the second day
of President Gorbachev, cap in hand, asking for aid for his crumbling country.
Gorbachev had been fully briefed weeks before on how to behave during his
visit. Wicks had flown to Moscow at Major's request to 'educate' Gorbachev
about G7 summits, warning him 'no big speeches, no surprises or attempts
to bounce the parties'. Gorbachev's main problem, he was told, would be to
convince the G7 leaders that the constitutional arrangements between the
centre and the republics would hold, and that he had an economic reform
plan that he could actually put into effect. Gorbachev stressed how badly he
needed a success in London, and asked what he might expect to come back
with. No money on the table, he was told, but he could anticipate the first
moves towards partnership and bringing the Soviet Union into the world
economy.[62]

Gorbachev's pleas were met by the offer on the final day of the summit of
limited immediate aid and the opening, as foreshadowed, of dialogue with
the West. He remained in London after the G7 leaders left. Britain had not
been as important to the Soviet Union in the 1980s as the US or Germany,
though Thatcher's personal relationship with Gorbachev from mid-decade
had enhanced the British profile in Moscow. Major was anxious to maintain
that position, which would help keep Britain 'in the big league'.[63] He had
no illusions about Gorbachev's fragile position. His confidential briefing
suggested that Gorbachev was close to being finished; the country was
heading towards break-up and economic crisis, with a key western worry
being control over nuclear weapons.

Major and Gorbachev had spoken several times on the phone, above all
over the Gulf crisis, but had met only once before, in the week after the war
ended. Major had flown to Moscow late on 4 March. He spent the rest of the
evening with the Ambassador, Rodric Braithwaite (1988–92), who thought
him tired, as well as not a little apprehensive about what Gorbachev was
hoping to obtain from the meetings. He found when briefing Major that

[He] was very easy to do business with. He speaks coolly, has an agenda, listens to
what he is told, asks the right questions, and has a sense of humour ... He was
obviously determined to make a success of his first encounter with Gorbachev. He
wanted to know what sort of man Gorbachev was, whom he relied on for advice,
what chance he had of bringing off his reforms. He accepted that change in the Soviet
Union was inevitable in the long run, that as Percy [Cradock] used to say, the old
system was dying, but the new system was indeed struggling to be born, and that it
was in our interests to support the process as best we could.[64]

Major had a hectic day: early breakfast meetings on 5 March with representatives from the Baltic states Latvia, Lithuania and Estonia, morning meetings with 'influential liberals' and his *tête-à-tête* with Gorbachev, as well as the standard wreath-laying ceremony. After lunch in the Aleksei Tolstoy house with officials, he held afternoon meetings in the Kremlin with politicians and then generals, a press conference, supper with former Foreign Minister Eduard Shevardnadze, before a canter to the airport to the VC-10 for his overnight flight on to the Gulf region. Major kept up a strong performance all day, determined to show a positive face, while pressing the need for economic change. 'Without private ownership', he told Soviet officials, 'economic reform cannot possibly succeed: it would be like trying to produce milk without cows.'[65]

Both Major and Gorbachev were much more relaxed when they spent time together in London four months later, after the G7 meeting concluded. Major enjoyed parading Gorbachev, who had a hero's reputation. He took him to tea in the House of Commons, opera at Covent Garden – Rossini's *La Cenerentola* – where Gorbachev was cheered on entering the auditorium and in the streets outside, and to a private, candlelit dinner at Admiralty House. Gorbachev and wife Raisa entered the room hand-in-hand, and at dinner he was in expansive form, holding all the dinner guests' attention cracking jokes about people worrying about whether he would be overthrown.[66]

Gorbachev's comments were recalled wryly when, a month later, he was indeed unseated in a coup. Intelligence reports passed to Major had been forecasting the possibility of such a coup, though expressing doubts whether hardliners would really be able to put the clock back and undo Gorbachev's reforms. Western intelligence had not, however, predicted so sudden a coup, because the plotters had made only minimal preparations.[67]

Early in the morning on Monday 19 August, a message was received at Number Ten; Major was woken up and hastily summoned Wall and Cradock to the Cabinet Room, to discuss what to do. With many foreign leaders away from their capitals, he sensed he could seize the initiative. But deciding what action to take was not easy. At a rapidly convened meeting of OPD (the Cabinet's foreign affairs committee), various options were examined. Not the least of the difficulties was the balancing act between Gorbachev, whose star was in the descendant, and Boris Yeltsin, the Russian leader, who had been gaining in authority throughout the year. Number Ten, indeed, were far from clear about exactly what was happening; Yeltsin had not been seized and pictures of him were on local television. On the other hand Kryuchkov, chairman of the KGB, was among the leaders of the coup, and with the KGB behind it, Cabinet ministers thought that several weeks would pass before any counter-coup had any hope of success.

Major authorised a press statement saying that whatever arrangements might exist for a change of government in Russia, they were not being observed on this occasion, so the coup was unconstitutional. Major was the first western leader to pronounce against the plotters, in notable contrast to

Mitterrand, who, according to a senior adviser, 'was perhaps in a bit too much of a hurry to get on television' and accept the coup as a *fait accompli*.[68] Bush, however, followed Major's line. International leaders besieged Number Ten with phone calls; Major, riding on his success as chairman of the G7, was for a few hours the leading statesman in a crisis on the world stage.

An additional stress for the team in London was uncertainty about what Mrs Thatcher might do. Major wanted to avoid being upstaged by someone whose worldwide influence, especially in matters concerning the Soviet Union, eclipsed his own. Cradock was sent round to see her to keep her fully informed, but in reality in the hope that she would be discouraged from doing or saying anything which might undermine the official British government response. On this occasion she played ball, although her comments advocating citizens to resist the coup caused irritation in Number Ten.[69]

Major tried telephoning Gorbachev, held incommunicado with his family in a villa on the Black Sea, but could not get through. On Tuesday 20 August he tried to phone Yeltsin, under siege in the White House, the Russian parliament building in Moscow. Cradock described what happened:

It was a very long shot. I sat by the Prime Minister as he tried to get through to him and, extraordinarily, we had Yeltsin's voice on the line as if he was ringing from suburbia, a call just down the road. Yeltsin gave a dramatic account of how he expected an attack on the White House that very night.[70]

Following the call, it was suggested that Major give a press conference outside in Downing Street, and with some reluctance he agreed. His dramatic account of how he had been in touch with Yeltsin and of life in the besieged White House proved to be one of his most upbeat performances in front of the media. As many believed a showdown was imminent, the drama was all the higher. But on the Tuesday night, the military in Moscow decided not to attack Yeltsin and his supporters after confused street fighting, and the position began to cool. The phone contact with Yeltsin proved a shrewd and prescient move, helping pave the way for a positive relationship after Yeltsin emerged as the real victor of the counter-coup.

Britain did not, however, want to abandon Gorbachev, and had to maintain its subtle balancing act, courting Yeltsin, while allowing Gorbachev to relinquish power with dignity, and helping oversee the transition of the Soviet Union to the Commonwealth of Independent States (CIS).[71] Braithwaite was eager to capitalise on the head start gained from the swift British response to the coup. With Major and Hurd visiting China ten days later, a serendipitous refuelling stop in Moscow was utilised to the full. Norma was in the party and, bringing her own brand of warmth, gave Gorbachev a big kiss to signal her relief that he was safe. After expressions of pleasure at the outcome of events, Major talked mainly money to Gorbachev, but could promise little more than was on offer at the G7 meeting.

With Yeltsin, Major had a different agenda, focused on growing allied concern over control over the vast Soviet arsenal. He wanted to know who would have control over nuclear weapons, and what would be the future relationship between the centre and the republics? The possibility of republics seceding from the CIS with nuclear weapons on their territory, or of former Soviet scientists selling their nuclear secrets to nations or interests hostile to the west, was a big background concern. Yeltsin was in a self-confident mood; the centre would indeed be able to control the nuclear forces, he replied, making it clear that he was now undisputably master.[72]

The trip to Moscow, the first by a foreign leader since the coup, was important in cementing foundations for a close relationship with the emerging Russian leadership. Major came well out of the episode, having not put a foot wrong in a confusing transitional period, and made timely and forceful public statements.[73] Some diplomatic advisers thought he had proved every bit as forceful and decisive as Mrs Thatcher would have been, and more responsible.[74]

Kennebunkport, Beijing and Harare

Major had been in need of a long holiday. The Moscow coup was sandwiched between two vacations. The first, from 2 to 13 August, was his regular holiday in the Garel-Jones villa in Spain, and the second, from 27 to 30 August, was with Bush at Kennebunkport, his holiday home in Maine. A big party was invited: the Majors and their children were accompanied by Sarah Hogg, Gus O'Donnell and Stephen Wall from Number Ten, and Robin Renwick, who had just succeeded Antony Acland as British Ambassador to the US.[75] Care was taken to lay on an enjoyable programme, including a fishing expedition, an evening boat trip through Cape Porpoise Harbor, and a clam bake, to which Senate majority leader George Mitchell was invited.[76]

The visit was intended to build upon their Camp David meeting in the previous December, and to be of use to both leaders with elections on the horizon. Serious discussion loomed larger than had been intended when the visit had been planned, principally because of the Soviet coup. The Americans were inclined to be cautious about aid until the future direction of the country had become more settled, but they reached agreement on a modest six-point aid package, stressing humanitarian support.[77] At the press conference on 29 August, Bush was happy to play second fiddle to Major, aware of the importance of the trip for Major's electoral prospects. 'Did I want Major to win the election?' Bush said later. 'The answer is, "Hell, Yes! One hundred per cent."'[78] Renwick concurred that Bush made it abundantly clear during the visit that he wanted Major to win.[79] Quite apart from the Bush team's low opinion of Kinnock and Labour, they had also worked closely and well with Major during the Gulf War, and Bush himself had strong personal feelings: 'I just like being with him. I love his humour. I love his honour, his sense of decency. And I love his wife.' John Major, he said, would remain one of his closest friends until the day he died.[80]

In some ways, Major appeared the more worldly-wise character of the two; Bush, despite having headed the CIA, and his three years as President, retained a certain innocence, at least as an affectation. It was the reverse of Kennedy shocking Macmillan during 1961–3 with stories of his womanising; thirty years later, the British Prime Minister would regale the President with stories of Mitterrand's complex private life. 'Gee,' Bush whistled, 'he really does that?'[81]

After fond farewells, Major left the US, via Moscow, for China. The prime purpose of Major's Beijing visit was to sign the agreement on Hong Kong airport, a construction initiative which had been the source of deep mistrust between the British and Chinese. London, however, pushed ahead, regarding it as essential to the future prosperity and morale of the inhabitants of Hong Kong.[82] The Chinese had not initially been consulted on what would be one of the biggest construction projects in the world, and they came to see it as a devious scheme for bleeding money out of the colony before Hong Kong was handed over to them as a bare shell in 1997. A Hurd mission had failed to secure Chinese agreement, but a breakthrough came when Cradock (a Sinologist before becoming the Prime Minister's Foreign Policy Adviser) travelled to Beijing in June. He found the Chinese anxious to encourage a Major visit to their country as a way of helping China's rehabilitation following their international isolation after the Tiananmen Square massacre of 1989, and he was able to use that as a lever for their signing the airport agreement.

The Foreign Office was apprehensive about the propaganda potential that China might seek to extract from Major's stay, and were especially nervous about his attending a parade in Tiananmen Square (which was 'stained with blood') and saluting the Chinese flag. Major fully shared their concerns, and saw how British press criticism might damage his image, but he also saw that much benefit could come from reaching agreement on Hong Kong and raising human rights issues with the Chinese leadership.[83] It was a delicate balancing act: if the human rights card was played too lightly, it would look bad at home; if too hard, the Chinese could call off the airport agreement. Both sides used the trip for all it was worth; the Chinese gave prominent media play to Major's ceremonial meeting with Premier Li Peng and President Yang Shangkun. Major spoke prominently in private and public about human rights abuses, and came armed with a long Amnesty International list. Li Peng responded with a tirade about how the West had brutalised China in one hundred years of imperialism. More constructively, a dialogue over Hong Kong was reopened, and agreement (later rejected in Hong Kong) was reached on a Court of Final Appeal, to replace appeals to the Privy Council in London.[84]

The agreement in the bag, Major flew on to Hong Kong, a visit made more difficult by rumours on the putative sacking of Sir David Wilson (Governor since 1987). With a volatile atmosphere in the colony, and uncertainty about what might have been said in China, it was not the happiest stage of the tour.[85] The travelling party felt hot and exhausted, but on the plane on the way home Major was in good spirits, as he read about the favourable response to his foreign travel in the media, and rising speculation about an autumn election.[86] He spent large parts of the flight at the back of the plane chatting easily to the press corps, who were enjoying unprecedented access to a prime minister and generally writing enthusiastically about him. They were still struck by the contrast with Thatcher: Sue Tinson of ITN recalled that 'he just came across as so different from her. She let us sit in the back, never talked to us, she kept her distance. But on that trip the press corps were amazingly supportive and friendly to the Prime Minister.'[87]

Comparisons strongly favourable to Major were also made by Commonwealth heads of government at the meeting in Harare from 16 to 19 October, for the first biannual meeting since the ill-starred CHOGM at Kuala Lumpur in October 1989. As Stephen Wall put it:

Major's success at the Zimbabwe meeting was down to the way that he couched a fairly similar message to that from Thatcher. People responded to him. Mulroney [Canada] and Hawke [Australia] liked him. Part of it was that after all those years in the 1980s, they could talk cricket and football, and use strong language again. Also, there could be a real dialogue again.[88]

Fortunately for Major this was the first CHOGM for many years not to be overshadowed by South Africa, now on its way towards democratic elections. No bitter taste of the Kuala Lumpur exchanges coloured his relations, and he went out of his way to charm and win friends, including some proud and prickly people like Mahathir Mohamad, Prime Minister of Malaysia. A charity cricket match in Harare, in which Major played, helped him forge a bond with Nawaz Sharif, Prime Minister of Pakistan, as well as Nelson Mandela (still only leader of the African National Congress).[89] Though initially reluctant, Major enjoyed the occasion and relished the good coverage it generated.[90]

Major was keen for the Commonwealth to become significant in fostering human rights and good government, and was closely involved in drawing up the Harare Declaration on democratic principles.[91] He made more approving comments about overseas aid than did Thatcher.[92] But the main benefit of the conference for Britain was the restoration of a good relationship with the Commonwealth. Mrs Thatcher had never put the Commonwealth high on her list of priorities, and until the emergence of De Klerk in 1989 had repeatedly clashed over sanctions with Commonwealth heads of government. Major was delighted to be able to chalk up another area where his own emollient style appeared to be more productive than her strident one.

Autumn of Indecision

Foreign successes over the summer had given Major both a psychological and a popularity boost. 'PM's visits to US and China plus Russian Coup etc have moved us up in the polls,' recorded Chaplin, 'and autumn election looks more likely.'[93] The press agreed; *The Economist* wrote that Major 'had a head-turning summer . . . by building his inner confidence and outer image Major's travels will have been invaluable'.[94] Some commentators wondered if the momentum was now irresistible. Major was juggling the prospects of an election in October or November with one in spring or summer 1992 which would allow him to participate in the Maastricht conference. If an autumn election was lost, he would never have the chance to bring off what he thought would be a coup on the EMU opt-out, which he believed would pacify the debate in the Conservative Party. He was battling with the dilemma on timing on the US–Russia–Far East trip.

Major was still debating the issue in his mind on his trip to Scotland from 7 to 10 September which followed hard on his return. He needed to make a morale-boosting tour not least because the Party had recorded its worst ever Scottish result in the 1987 general election, and he combined political work with the tradition Prime Minister's day-and-a-half visit to stay with the Queen at Balmoral. Major's nervousness about royalty had lessened a great deal since 1989, when he had been anxious about a meeting with Prince Charles. Though disapproving of the behaviour of the younger Royals, which he believed contributed to an atmosphere cynical of authority, Major liked the Queen, revelling in the informal Balmoral atmosphere, and enjoyed cooking a barbecue in casual clothes.[95]

From Scotland he flew on almost immediately to Paris for a European Democratic Union meeting from 11 to 12 September. The Paris meeting involved negotiations over the European centre right's approach to Maastricht, and its collective role in the European Parliament. The presence of several leaders from eastern Europe helped Major's emphasis that the need was to broaden, rather than deepen, the European Community.[96] He returned to London, however, still unresolved about his core domestic concern, election timing.

To clarify his mind, in view of the considerable work needed if he did indeed opt for an autumn election, a meeting was convened at Number Ten on the evening of Sunday 15 September. Patten, Ryder, Hogg and Chaplin debated the options. Major himself – despite the Maastricht enticement – was keen on November if possible (October by now had been ruled out, because of preparations for the Party conferences). Patten favoured November too, but cautioned waiting until the results of a thorough poll in marginal seats, which would be available in a fortnight. The main figure who remained against an autumn election was Lamont, whose views were noted despite not being an attender at the meeting.[97]

Discussion of timing, with fear of leaks, was kept away from full Cabinet, which met on 26 September. With seven ministers abroad, Patten quipped, 'Now I know we're not going to have an election.'[98] The private party polls became available the same day. Both polls appeared encouraging. The general poll showed Con – 43: Lab – 36: Lib – 14, and the poll in marginal seats,

Con – 46: Lab – 39: Lib – 14.[99] But newspaper polls painted a different picture, with Conservatives and Labour neck-and-neck, and even a slight Labour lead.[100] Major still favoured November, and tried to convince himself that it was safe. Patten was similarly keen, but knew it was not wise unless the Party was further ahead than the newspaper polls suggested. Concern was now expressed that if the election were called for November, Labour might launch an attack on the Conservatives for calling an election hastily at that point because they knew bad news would follow shortly afterwards.[101]

With the arguments still nicely balanced, a three-day delay was suggested. Meeting again, on Sunday 29 September, on the eve of the Labour conference, the team knew there had to be the final decision.[102] The weekend polls were disappointing, with four putting Conservatives and Labour level pegging. The consensus suggested a hung Parliament, in which the Party would be at best thirteen seats short of an overall majority. The fate of a November election was duly sealed. Sarah Hogg recalled 'there were newspaper stories which started to talk about an autumn election which we decided had to be damped down. We had very heated talks about when to go, and great memories of Jim Callaghan failing to go for the election in the autumn of 1978, when he might have won.'[103]

The following morning, Monday, it was decided that Wakeham would telephone the editors or political editors of leading newspapers. It was media manipulation plain and simple. By leaking the story to the press rather than the broadcasters, the newspapers would splash with it on the Tuesday, upstaging Kinnock's speech at Labour's conference at Brighton (Elinor Goodman of *Channel 4 News*, however, heard of the scheme, and broadcast the story on Monday evening). The leak was also designed to have left open a crack in the door for Major himself to announce a November election if the polls improved dramatically after the Tory conference,[104] but much to Number Ten's irritation, Wakeham went too far in ruling out a November poll. The press, nevertheless, fell in with Wakeham's plan: 'Major rules out November poll' was the lead headline in *The Times*.[105] Reports stressed the benefits of the spring, when the Party would supposedly gain from continued economic recovery, further Major foreign travel, and from pension increases on 1 April.

The Conservatives needed Labour to have a bad conference. They did not oblige. Kinnock's speech on Tuesday was one of his best. In *The Times*, Peter Riddell said he 'excited party supporters in a way not seen for many years', that there were many echoes of Harold Wilson in 1963–4, and that Kinnock was 'starting to act like a potential prime minister'.[106] A mood of optimism grew throughout the week in a carefully managed and trouble-free conference. Kinnock broke with tradition and made a second speech at the end of the week, declaring 'We have a programme rooted in principle and we shall govern in exactly the same way.'[107] By the end of the week, Gallup recorded a two-point Labour poll lead.[108]

In those four days the Conservatives lost the initiative they had held since

July. In-fighting in the Party now broke out; 'their tensions are showing,' wrote Robin Oakley in *The Times*.[109] Number Ten was critical of Central Office's propaganda campaign, which it felt struck the wrong note. Among Cabinet, in the run-up to Maastricht, the sceptics such as Michael Howard were making anxious noises, concerns were expressed about Waldegrave's failure to win the argument with Labour over the NHS, and Rifkind was locked into an argument with Lamont about the Channel Tunnel Rail Link, a dispute that ran on into the Conservatives' conference.[110] Sarah Hogg began exciting unfavourable comment for the way she bossed Cabinet ministers,[111] which, it was alleged, produced confusion because ministers were never totally certain whether she was speaking for herself or for the Prime Minister.[112] The long-simmering difference between Hogg and Chaplin finally boiled over into the open. Hogg, the more forceful personality, had become increasingly exasperated with Chaplin's work rate, because of the time off she had negotiated to allow her to nurse her Newbury constituency. Chaplin, in turn, began to find it almost impossible to work with Hogg, and increasingly withdrew, further exacerbating the problem.[113]

Hogg was particularly worried by Chaplin's failure to work on the Prime Minister's Blackpool conference speech, exacerbated by his own reluctance to engage with it too. True ended up writing most of it, but concerns were then expressed about whether the speech was sufficiently 'prime ministerial'. So Ronald Millar was called in, on the Friday before the conference, to add spice and theatricality to language and delivery. Major and his advisers had not known Millar before, but his reputation as a wordsmith was *nonpareil* and Millar rapidly felt 'on the same wavelength'.[114] While Millar and True, aided by Sarah Hogg, beavered away on the speech in the Prime Minister's office in the Imperial Hotel, Major did the rounds of the conference parties and meetings, still reluctant to think too much about what he was going to say, and personally making 'less input than [to] most of his speeches'.[115]

A row erupted on the Thursday about the way the BBC had handled Waldegrave's speech, which Central Office considered wildly one-sided in its representation of Labour's campaign that the Tories had plans to privatise the NHS.[116] Chaplin was despatched to phone the news editor of the *Nine O'Clock News*, whom she blasted. The next day, they phoned back and agreed that the report had indeed not been balanced, and Number Ten then blamed Central Office for not following up the admission at once. At Jeffrey Archer's annual conference party, Major was clearly angry, went around being outspoken about the BBC, and made a point of ignoring John Birt, the BBC's Director-General.[117] The next day, Chris Patten attacked the BBC in his speech: 'If you are angry about bias in a programme on BBC, ITV ... write to them, above all phone them on the spot. If necessary, jam the switchboards.'[118] The row between Patten and Birt rumbled on long after Blackpool.

Major became increasingly nervous about his own speech, and only focused seriously on it with less than twenty-four hours to go. Work continued until the last minute on revisions, with Millar offering what advice he could on

John Major in 1979 aged 36 at the start of his parliamentary career.

The house in Longfellow Road, Worcester Park, where John Major lived from 1943 to 1955. Major, standing, third from left, a member of the Rutlish School Colts XI, 1958.

The candidate for Huntingdonshire speaking at a Conservative party meeting, 1979.
Archie Gray (Chairman) and Andrew Thomson (agent) also on the platform.

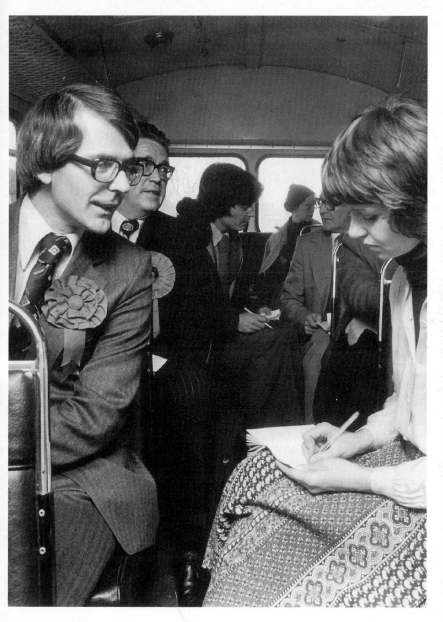

Major being interviewed by Rosemary Whittaker (of the *Hunts Post*) on the way from the count to the declaration at the Town Hall, 4 May 1979.

Huntingdonshire's parliamentary candidate with his wife, Norma.

Returning officer declares John Major elected as MP for Huntingdonshire, 4 May 1979.

With Norma outside the House of Commons, 1979.

The traditional photograph of the newly elected MP, on Westminster Bridge.

In the garden at Hemingford Grey, their first Huntingdon home, with Norma's mother Dee and the children, Elizabeth and James.

delivery. Speeches are always amalgams of different individuals' inputs, but in the main the structure and content of Major's annual conference speeches were True's, the phrasing Millar's and the underlying beliefs and sentiments solidly his own. Using an autocue, and beginning haltingly, he launched into his biggest platform test yet as premier, knowing that he had to expunge the unhappy memory of his last major Party speech at Southport in March.

He summed up his brand of Conservatism as 'the power to choose and the right to own'. Opportunity and ownership were themes that ran throughout the speech, citing his own journey on 'the long road from Coldharbour Lane to Downing Street'. Labour was accused of gutter politics in its allegations of Tory plans for the NHS: there would be no privatisation or charging for doctors' visits or hospital treatment. 'Not today. Not tomorrow. Not after the next election. Not ever while I am Prime Minister.' Families, he said, would be encouraged to own and to save, to create a 'cascade of wealth' that would run through generations. In one of his best jokes, he said, 'A great deal has been written about my education. Never has so much been written about so little', and pledged that he would 'fight for my belief in a return to basics in education'. On Europe, he sought to pacify fears, by saying he would never accept any treaty which imposed a single currency on any timespan, nor would he give up rights of self-determination in defence and foreign policy. Policy for the next election would be based on strong defence, economy and respect for the law, free from the threat of inflation, in which 'taxes can fall and savings can grow'.

A ten-minute standing ovation greeted his speech, which had lasted just under an hour. As the conference sang 'Land of Hope and Glory', the Majors broke with tradition to circulate among representatives on the floor. The speech went down well with the media, the criticisms being confined mainly to its delivery and the lack of detail about his future plans. It marked him out more clearly than ever, as he approached his first anniversary in office, as a consolidator and mild reformer rather than a radical.

The week went well for the Tories, surprisingly in view of the wobbles just before and during it. They did not light up the country with a new vision for the 1990s, but the Party came across as sincere and competent, helped by improved figures on inflation (down to 4.1 per cent) announced on the last day.

Major made a fulsome tribute in his speech to Mrs Thatcher and the legacy she had bequeathed his government. In a delicate piece of stage-management, she had come to Blackpool on Wednesday, being allowed to appear on the platform as long as she did not speak. Delegates had other ideas, and brought chaos to the hall as they stamped and called out for her to offer them a few words, to the visible displeasure of several faces on the podium. The uproar died down only when a message from her was read out saying she wanted the programme to continue – though Matthew Parris was not alone in failing to detect any sign of her volunteering any such 'message'.[119] She had not been so tongue-tied in her views on Major and his government during the previous year, and within a few weeks caution was to be further thrown to the wind.

SEVENTEEN

Maastricht Autumn:

October–December 1991

WITH THE ELECTION postponed until the New Year, Major was free to concentrate on what he knew would be a make-or-break issue, steering a course through the rocks at the Maastricht summit in December. With the promise of top-level backing for the British opt-out from monetary union obtained at Luxembourg in June in his pocket, he could set about banking it in the most advantageous fashion.

Economics and Politics

Hard though Major battled to clear his mind and his diary to focus on Maastricht, domestic concerns kept on crowding in. Foremost was the state of the economy. The government had been slow to appreciate the seriousness of the recession, which had been gathering pace during Major's chancellorship; house prices collapsed and national income and manufacturing output both went into sharp decline.[1] The recession worsened as 1991 wore on, with unemployment rising from 1.6 million in mid-1990 to 2.6 million in early 1992. Unlike the early 1980s, when the recession hit the less well off, mainly Labour voters, most seriously, this time the Tory middle classes, especially in the south, were also badly affected. Exacerbated by the uniform business rate, commercial failures were running at 930 a week by the end of 1991, while house repossessions reached epidemic proportions.

Tensions between Number Ten and the Treasury grew during 1991, heightened by frustration that joining the ERM had put them in a trap: the logic of the recession suggested heavy interest rate cuts to restore confidence and stimulate activity, but sterling's stability within the ERM meant this was the one policy that could not be pursued. Interest rates were shaved to 10.5 per cent in early September 1991, but to have gone any further was deemed unwise, and there they remained until the general election.

The March 1991 budget had done little to ameliorate the recession, and Major resorted to trying to talk up the economy, to some embarrassment from the Treasury.[2] Lamont was not inclined to paint rosy pictures, and in May he upset many with talk that unemployment would be 'a price worth paying' for the defeat of inflation;[3] although in July, he assured the House during a censure debate that recovery would come in the second half of the year.[4] This judgement seemed to be borne out by a bullish CBI survey in September, which produced much optimism in the Treasury and emboldened Lamont at the Party Conference in October to speak of 'the green shoots of economic spring [that] are appearing once again'. Sarah Hogg, who had reservations about Lamont's judgement, put pressure on his speech writers, working in the same hotel in Blackpool, to adopt an optimistic tone.

Patten and Major watched with growing apprehension as the economic bad news continued unabated throughout the autumn. Pressure continued from Number Ten for Lamont to cut interest rates. Lamont saw himself heavily constrained by membership of the ERM, which he asserts he was never keen on – Major says he never shared this – and grew progressively to dislike during the course of 1991 and 1992. Attending ECOFIN meetings he found a particular bane, not sharing the enthusiasm for European integration evident among his fellow finance ministers.

Major's obsession remained the depressing effect high interest rates had on economic activity, even though inflation was tumbling. With interest rate cuts effectively ruled out, Major asked Sarah Hogg in great confidence to prepare a plan for devaluing sterling within the ERM. The preferred scheme, which had been discussed twice in early 1991 and again more seriously in the autumn, became known as the 'Italian option' – letting the pound sink to its lowest permitted level under the existing bands. Major refused to confront Lamont with it,[5] and the Bank of England never knew of it.[6] He did so because he feared it would get out, with adverse consequences on the currency markets. The idea was at best half-formed. When the pound did sink to the lowest exchange rate allowed in summer 1992 it proved most uncomfortable – and in the end unsustainable. It also sat oddly with Major's belief in a strong currency.

But might a full-scale devaluation have been the golden chance passed by that would not only have kick-started an export-led recovery, but also avoided the humiliation of Britain's ejection from the ERM on Black Wednesday the following September? But Major felt it would have been impossible to persuade other ERM countries to allow a devaluation, and interest rates would probably have had to be increased in any realignment to re-establish credibility at the new parity. This would, in turn, have worsened the domestic problems devaluation was supposed to solve, which would have been especially awkward in a pre-election period.[7] The gains from the 'Italian option' would have been too small. So there the issue rested until the summer of 1992, when the question of Britain's membership of the ERM was rudely forced back onto the agenda.

Anxieties about the effect of the recession meanwhile provided irresistible upward pressure on public spending in the run-up to the election. Few actions by Major's government aroused more criticism than the 1991–2 public expenditure round. Labour, as well as many insiders and commentators, interpreted spending levels as a cynical move to gain popularity and buy friends before the general election. Around Whitehall, jokes would fly on the lines of, 'Only thirty-eight more spending days to the election'.[8] The inflated spending, critics were later to allege, had to be clawed back in the 1992 autumn statement, and in subsequent tax increases, posing profound and possibly fatal problems for government popularity.

The 1991 autumn statement forecasts envisaged a borrowing requirement of £19 billion for 1992–3, which turned out to be a serious underestimate. Not until the Treasury produced its forecasts for 1992–3 at the Chevening pre-1992 budget meeting was the severity of the underestimate fully appreciated. Had a more accurate borrowing requirement been available before the 1991–2 spending round, downward pressure on settlements would almost certainly have been exerted. As it was, spending was to increase by 5.8 per cent in real terms, £8.6 billion at current prices; a Cabinet minister later confessed, 'We spent an awful lot. We were the second highest spending government since the war, after Ted Heath.'[9]

About half of the increase was involuntary, caused by social security benefit payments generated by rising unemployment and low incomes. Deepening recession also blew the revenue side of the budget off course by depressing tax receipts. The other half was within the government's control. It was asking much of the government to take a tough line on spending, with the polls balanced, and a general election imminent. 'Spending ministers played the election card for all it was worth,' recalled one Lamont aide.[10] None of the Thatcher governments went into a fifth year, and therefore had to implement two spending rounds under the shadow of a general election. The incentives to buy popularity had applied for a year: 'When you are spending a bit of money to get some credit on the basis that it might only be three months, eighteen months of that sort of spending adds up to a hell of a lot.'[11]

The big winners in the spending round were health, and transport, with a 25 per cent increase going mainly to compensate British Rail and London Transport for depressed fare receipts and safety-related investment. With so many London marginal seats, providing for the London Underground was a compelling argument. Waldegrave had been increasingly agitated by the political capital Labour were making from their attacks on the government's management of the NHS, and concerned at the need for further funding to underpin the reforms that had taken effect in April. He appealed directly to Major, and on this occasion Major chose to overrule David Mellor, his Chief Secretary, and give Waldegrave the money he wanted. Mellor himself was later to receive considerable blame for the lax settlements in 1991–2 from the government's critics on the right. Baker described him as 'a disastrous appointment. He let go of the finances right from the beginning and was very offhand about things.'[12] However, Treasury colleagues recall him as a tough, aggressive negotiator for Treasury positions, who was not afraid to ruffle feathers and cultivated an image in Whitehall as a hard man. His difference with the Department of Health showed that he was capable of dogged resistance.[13] Mellor himself calls the spending round 'intellectually as fine an hour as I have ever had'.[14] Perhaps the most valid criticism of Mellor is that he approached bilaterals like cases taken by a barrister, as separate briefs, and lost a strategic sense of how the entire budget fitted together.

Major himself was the decisive voice in shaping the 1991–2 settlement, and argued consistently for measures to ameliorate the recession, including Lamont's pre-Christmas package to soften the effects of the housing market slump. He later defended the government's actions:

Through the recession, when unemployment was rising as fast as it was, we were predominantly concerned to stop unemployment rising at a rate that would have been unsustainable in a democracy ... We were trying to stop having long-term costs of more firms going bust than would have gone bust, and more people losing jobs, that they would never regain because they were in their forties and fifties, than needed to be the case. It was social expenditure that I will always justify. I am sure it was right.[15]

Norman Lamont was the third figure, alongside Major and Mellor, who must take some responsibility for the spending. He chose to keep the process at arm's length as is customary for the Chancellor. Later he was to reflect, 'Mrs Thatcher thought sound money and control of expenditure was what government was about. Mr Major thought it was about something else, like making people happy.'[16] He felt that, unlike Major, he had a philosophical commitment to low government spending and tax, but was unable to prevail against the Prime Minister.

The verdict must be that, albeit for understandable reasons, expenditure did rise by unnecessarily large amounts before the election.

Spending increases had been foreshadowed in the Queen's Speech of 31 October. The prospect of preparing a legislative programme did not make anyone in Downing Street happy. With an election less than eight months away, and with the manifesto still very far from decided, it was difficult to know how to fill the programme for the coming session. Yet Major announced a 'full programme', admittedly for a half-length session, including legislation to promote the Citizen's Charter, three Bills in education to extend parental choice and raise standards, continuing reform of the NHS, and legislation to enact the council tax.[17] Peter Riddell, in *The Times*, deplored the acrid tone of the Queen's Speech debate, wondering whether Major's harsh partisanship under pre-election tension was risking his 'nice guy' image.[18]

Labour responded in turn by attacking Major for the clandestine way the government had announced (via Wakeham's leak) that there would be no election in November.[19] Discussions of election timing – a leitmotif throughout 1991 – continued at high pitch. On 30 October, Ryder's Number Twelve committee met to consider a Central Office document on plans up to the election. They were critical of the paper, which they felt would have to be rewritten before Cabinet considered it, but proposed few constructive ideas of their own on how to boost the Party's popularity. Heseltine was the most dynamic figure at the meeting, sounding off with, 'If I were PM, I would ...' Lamont pinned his faith on better times next year, while others thought that no one was analysing the real reason for loss of support in the South of England: 'Truth is, it's the recession,' one member wrote, 'and they are furious because their pockets have been hit.'[20]

At a Sunday meeting convened at Chequers on 17 November to discuss the manifesto, a party presentation was given on ownership and account-ability, but there was still a dearth of hard policies. Chaplin recorded: 'PM doesn't have [the] burning desire to change that Mrs T had – [he is] much more political.'[21] Patten decreed that there should be Political Cabinets weekly after Cabinet to galvanise progress. On 21 November ministers duly dis-cussed a paper on election preparation and prospects.

In opinion polls, despite the continuing recession, Labour and Con-servatives were still neck-and-neck. The three by-elections held on 7 December 1991, the last of the Parliament, saw the Tories lose Kincardine and Deeside to the Liberal Democrats, Langbaurgh to Labour, while the third, Hemsworth, remained in Labour hands. But the results were not without encouragement. The swing in Langbaurgh of 3.6 per cent was much less than Monmouth (12.6 per cent) in May. The Kincardine result, however, produced gloom for the Party's prospects in Scotland. At a breakfast meeting with Lang, Mackay and Rifkind, Major came under pressure to say there would be a referendum on the Union after the election. To soothe them down, Major said that they could look at the possibility of a Royal Commission or Speaker's Conference, but it would be a bad idea to raise the prospect of any significant change as it would merely alienate Conservative support.[22]

Against this anxious background to Maastricht came a moment of high farce while Major was working on his pre-conference speech to the House of Commons to be delivered that afternoon. A Number Ten duty clerk inter-rupted Major to say President Gorbachev was on the line and wanted to speak to him urgently. Major said he was busy preparing the speech; could he find out what Gorbachev wanted? The duty clerk reappeared to report it was 'very urgent'; could Gorbachev please speak to him? Major replied that it was bound to be money that he was after, and the hapless duty clerk was despatched to tell Gorbachev that Major would phone him back later. Major returned to the speech. The duty clerk appeared for a third time to say that Gorbachev said it was *not* about money and that it really was very urgent. Major reluctantly agreed to speak, to learn that Shevardnadze was to be reinstated as Foreign Minister.[23] Major listened attentively, and then returned to his urgent business.

The Road to Maastricht

With Maastricht coming before the election, Major badly needed a political success and an absence of party histrionics. The first serious obstacle looked as if it would come from the Dutch themselves, who succeeded to the presidency on 1 July. They did not like the draft treaty for Maastricht produced by Luxembourg, and out of the blue advanced a far more federalist text on political union. Major could not possibly have countenanced this, not least because – as part of the progress towards political union – foreign and defence policy were to come within the remit of Community institutions.

When Lubbers, the Dutch Prime Minister, who was sounding out EC leaders about the proposals, saw Major in The Hague on 18 September, he was told directly that the British government was pessimistic about agreeing to any schemes for political union. Major added, flatly, that the House of Commons would never accept foreign policy passing to the Community. Lubbers was clearly disappointed, and reminded him that Kohl perceived his 'life's work to anchor Germany to Europe'. Major received the same message when Volker Rühe, then General Secretary of the German CDU, talked to him later in the month. Major told him he was not bluffing and would vote against any attempt to bring foreign and security policy under the Commission.[24]

The Dutch proposals were shot down by the foreign ministers' meeting, with only Belgium joining the Netherlands in speaking up in favour. Britain, for once, was not isolated – although one of the reasons the Dutch draft won so little support, even from sympathetic countries like Germany, was because the British would be bound to veto it. In the longer term, the federalist Dutch text served to fuel the fears of Eurosceptics in Britain as well as in Denmark that there was a 'hidden agenda' behind Maastricht.[25]

Left on the table were the proposals for EMU, and the Social Chapter, and it was on these that Major concentrated his attention. Peter Riddell cited an intriguing MORI poll which indicated that half the electorate would increase their support for Major if he stood up more to his right-wing Eurosceptics, and only 5 per cent would decrease their support. He commented that Major had far more grasp of the temperature of the country in his warmer and more open attitude to Europe than had Mrs Thatcher.[26]

The country was not to remain so pro-European during the 1990s, influenced by a heavily Eurosceptic press. Many chose later to forget the public support for the EC at the time of Maastricht. Sensitive to the powerful, if minority, Eurosceptic currents within the Party, Major and Ryder took pains to keep in touch with MPs such as Teddy Taylor and Jonathan Aitken, among the more vociferous, to try to keep their anxieties, and public utterances, to a minimum.

Tebbit, Ridley and Parkinson, each of whom had announced they would stand down at the next election, were making growling noises of differing notes against any concessions. Tebbit was emerging as a key figure among the sceptics, and responded sharply to Major's refusal, at the Lord Mayor's Guidhall banquet on 11 November, to rule out eventual British participation in a single currency.[27] 'The present government', Tebbit wrote in the *Guardian*, 'has no mandate to give away the right of the British people to self-government.'[28] In a series of speeches in November he raised the issue of a referendum on EMU.[29] Mrs Thatcher became equally outspoken, speaking, as was her wont, in the US, damning a single currency and moves towards European federalism.[30]

To build support and gain endorsement for his intended line for Maastricht, as well as bind potential critics, Major staged a debate in the House of Commons on 20 November. In a performance which Peter Jenkins described as 'characteristically moderate and practical, in both tone and substance',[31] Major outlined exactly where he would draw lines at Maastricht. A federal Europe would not succeed, he said, and he would not 'accept a treaty which describes the Community as having a federal vocation'. Pragmatism was to be his keynote, and he reiterated his previous positions of no compulsory EMU for Britain; no surrender of control of NATO or foreign, defence or domestic policy to the Community; no Social Chapter 'that undermined the ability of Britain to compete'. He also said he would press for 'subsidiarity' – the principle where the decisions are taken at subsidiary, i.e. national, level wherever possible – and a commitment to a widening of the Community to include the new democracies in the East.[32]

Kinnock gave a poor reply, losing his temper and calling Conservative MP Robert Adley a 'jerk', but was overshadowed, as indeed was Major, by an intervention by Thatcher. Major had deliberately larded his own speech with references to the Single European Act of 1986. As Hugo Young recognised, Major took 'meticulous, clearly calculated care' to emphasise how much flowed from her act, from the single currency to political union, as a way, he hoped, of reining her in.[33] She would not buy it, and in a tough riposte – in which she accused Hurd of 'going a bit wobbly' – she repeated Tebbit's call that any agreement on a single currency must be put to a referendum.[34] She also, ominously, began to call into question whether Major's trump card, an 'opt-out' on EMU, would in fact be of any real significance, a view increasingly held by Conservative Eurosceptics.[35] Even before the Maastricht conference, the battle lines were being drawn.

That Wednesday morning in Number Ten, when not fending off Gorbachev on the telephone, Major conceded that he could see the logic of a referendum.[36] Number Ten cautiously let it be known that a future Parliament might indeed agree to a referendum before a final decision was made on participation in a single currency. But Major then was so irritated by Thatcher's call for a referendum in the debate that he made Francis Maude, winding up for the government, say 'The government doesn't intend to have a referendum on the outcome of the Maastricht negotiations.'[37]

At breakfast on 21 November, Major was back in two minds on the referendum. He could see real advantages, but Cabinet that morning was adamant that they must not be seen to be pushed around by Thatcher, and that he had to take a lead in ruling out a referendum, which effectively determined the government's line in the Maastricht debate.[38] In an ITN interview the next evening, Thatcher denounced Major as arrogant for refusing a referendum,[39] little realising that it was her own advocacy that had forced Major into a corner, where he felt he could do nothing but.

Thatcher's intervention aside, Major was happy with the outcome of the Commons debate, which gave him a majority of 101. Only six Eurosceptics voted against the government, including Biffen, and nine abstained, led by Tebbit.[40] Major felt it gave him the parliamentary endorsement he wanted for his line at Maastricht, and showed that his opposition in Parliament, if voluble, was small.

With two weeks to go until the Maastricht summit opened, however, Major was still far from confident that he would achieve an effective solution. Patten asked him on 25 November at their Monday meeting what he thought his chances were of securing his limited agenda at the conference; Major replied that he did not know, partly because some countries were determined to push through the Social Chapter and other extensions of qualified majority voting (QMV, a complex formula which meant in effect about two-thirds of member nations had to agree to a decision), and it all depended on whether Britain's EC partners really were convinced he could not carry such a treaty through Parliament. There would have to be a Commons debate very soon after the conference was over, he told Patten, which in effect would be a vote of confidence in the government. Ever the tactician, he saw this as a useful device in rallying dissenters. Major asked Ryder how many he thought might vote against, and was told forty to forty-two; if he lost the vote, which in his heart he probably doubted, Major said he would have to go straight to the country.[41]

Squaring domestic opinion also meant Major ensuring that he had his Cabinet totally behind him. By securing their full-hearted consent, he knew that they could not round on him subsequently and claim that they had not supported the treaty. For some months, Hurd had been chairing a Cabinet committee to prepare the government's line. Major himself chaired the OPD committee, which held particularly important meetings on 28 October and 26 November, Major masterly in coaxing along Lilley in particular, unhappy that too much would be given away.[42]

Major and Hurd met Baker and Howard on 4 December, both of whom also had deep reservations. Baker's principal concerns were to avoid any surrender over Britain's right to control its borders, on which they supported him, nor any loss of British sovereignty over immigration and frontier controls, which they said they would not raise.[43] Howard's particular sticking point was the Social Chapter, which he was adamant that Britain, under no circumstances, should sign.[44] Neither Baker nor Howard was flexible, and Major and Hurd left their meetings gloomy.

The atmosphere lifted dramatically the next day; at the final Cabinet meeting before Maastricht, on 5 December, after some heavy overnight massaging according to Hurd, the atmosphere among ministers was 'serene', with Baker in particular much more supportive.[45] Major achieved the mandate he sought. Major was praised by Cabinet colleagues for the way he had tried to include all concerned departments in Cabinet committee discussions in preparing Britain's negotiating position.

Major had, like Lubbers, also been working the European capitals, trying to bring their leaders round to his position. He held nearly forty meetings with foreign leaders in the run-up to Maastricht.[46] With two weeks to go, Andreotti, Prime Minister of Italy, was arguing against Major that any change in the draft treaties would be used as a 'pretext for not going ahead with full EMU' by Germany.[47] But by the final week, Major was reporting that Kohl was being very supportive, as was Lubbers, but still did not know whether differences over EMU and the Social Chapter could be surmounted.[48]

The relationship with Kohl was of key importance. The Germans wanted, and needed for their domestic audience, a deal at Maastricht which would advance political as well as economic union. Bonn had to be convinced not just that Britain could not sign up to that agenda, but that concessions would have to be made to keep Britain on board. Kohl, for all his camaraderie, also harboured some suspicions that Major might prevaricate simply to get past the general election.[49] Christopher Mallaby, the British Ambassador, worked hard to convince the Germans that Britain was serious about its bottom line. Major exploited his good relationship with Kohl to extract concessions for Britain as the price for not sabotaging Kohl's domestic need to present Maastricht as a big step towards a federal Europe.[50] Major's bond with Kohl was to pay real dividends in the days that lay ahead.

Maastricht: 9–10 December

The British party flew out to Maastricht on Sunday 8 December. The key players were Major, Hurd and Lamont, together with Garel-Jones, the Foreign Officer minister with responsibility for Europe, Sarah Hogg from the Policy Unit, with Kerr, Wall, Wicks from the Treasury, and Michael Jay from the Foreign Office. At stake for Major was Britain's future relationship with the Community, his party's cohesion and performance in the general election, and his personal standing.

The British opt-out on EMU still needed the details to be confirmed and agreed. But could Major secure an opt-out on the Social Chapter, which the Tory Party had convinced itself would saddle employers with a host of dirigiste controls, increasing costs and reducing jobs? There was still little evidence, as the conference opened, that Britain would be able to detach itself from it. Major further had a host of subsidiary objectives which he sought at Maastricht, as he outlined in the House on 20 November and Cabinet on 5 December.

The two-day summit was held in the grim modern Provinciehuis in Maastricht. The heads of government discussed EMU as the first item on Monday morning. Lubbers, the Chairman, opened the discussion, and Major was the third to speak.

'Great Britain is not prepared to commit itself as to when phase three of

EMU [i.e. the single currency] is to start,' he told the conference. However, 'some states have proposed introducing a special protocol [i.e. opt-out] for the United Kingdom', and he went on to outline his dislike of compulsion in the process.[51] After basic positions were stated, Lubbers invited Wim Kok, Dutch Finance Minister, to chair a detailed discussion on EMU with finance ministers. Lamont played the lead part in these negotiations, which suddenly took a turn for the worse, from Britain's viewpoint, when at Monday lunch the French, supported by the Italians, proposed an amendment which greatly advanced the pace towards EMU by stating that in 1999, all countries who met the economic conditions would join a single currency automatically.[52] This was duly written into the treaty, and made a British opt-out all the more imperative.

Since January, Lamont and the Treasury had been piecing together the detail of the EMU opt-out and submitted the text to the meeting. On Major's instructions to avoid giving them too much time to pick holes in it, the text was not released to other finance ministers until lunchtime on Tuesday. That afternoon they began to question the text. Lamont became angry because, in the absence of a general opt-out, the text was specific to Britain and, he insisted, it could not be amended. Lamont led his Treasury team from the talks and the meeting was deadlocked. Lubbers, conscious that without a resolution the whole conference would fail, summoned Major and Lamont to his private office on the first floor. They secured agreement from Lubbers that the protocol granting the UK an opt-out from the single currency could be appended to the treaty.[53] Lamont returned to the meeting and the deal was done.[54]

The long-heralded safety valve for Britain had at last been slotted into place.

The currency opt-out was the easy part, because the principle had been accepted beforehand, but Major badly needed to bring home more from Maastricht. Securing the Social Chapter opt-out would be harder, but was essential. The British bargaining position had not been helped by noises friendly to the Social Chapter being made by a CBI representative. Moreover, since Thatcher had made such a stand against its predecessor at the European Council at Strasbourg in December 1989, it would have been politically difficult for him to have given way now. At the end of the first day, Britain was still being pressed hard to accept, many countries believing that Britain's opposition was merely a debating position.[55]

Back in Maastricht, the pressure on the British delegation was mounting. Both Lamont and Kerr, on Major's instructions, telephoned Howard in London on Monday to see if he would yield in his opposition to the Social Chapter, even in a very heavily watered-down form, which would enhance their bargaining power elsewhere. But Howard was adamant. He told friends privately that he would consider resigning if Britain signed up to the Social Chapter.[56] Howard's strong hostility reinforced Major's view of the need to hold out on the Social Chapter and raised its importance. Sarah Hogg noted that the Social Chapter 'did not have a guardian' present, and was pleased that Howard was taking such a determined line.[57]

The Social Chapter was last on the agenda for discussion on Tuesday, because the Dutch presidency still thought that the British government was bluffing and would be ready to give way rather than wreck the treaty. The British delegates were not unhappy with the timetable, because they correctly predicted that the other countries would not sacrifice a string of done deals just to keep the Social Chapter in the treaty. Also, Major was younger and had more stamina than the other heads of government, and his greater alertness would prove an advantage in the desperate final stages. As can happen at conferences, months of preparatory meetings and thought can concertina into outcomes determined by the vagaries of exhaustion, frustration and the thirst for an outcome.

With no resolution at the heads of government meeting when it adjourned on Tuesday at 6.45 p.m., Lubbers realised he would have to tackle Major on the Social Chapter. After the resolution of the EMU opt-out, those present in the discussion were asked to leave Lubbers's room, leaving just the Dutch Prime Minister, Major and Kerr. Lubbers, who had conducted himself throughout with exceptional courtesy and good humour, now placed a series of tempting proposals before Major, including a watered-down Social Chapter for all, including Britain, to sign, and a plan that the Social Chapter be included in the treaty, with another protocol appended to the end, indicating Britain's reservations.

Major was firm: he would not agree to any inclusion of the Social Chapter in any form whatsoever in the treaty. He simply told Lubbers very directly, 'I am not going to accept your proposals. It's no good asking me. I can't do it. And I won't do it.'

Lubbers, convinced at last that Major was serious and really would block the Social Chapter's inclusion in the treaty if they tried to get it through as applying to all, then produced his own fall-back position, which was an agreement on the Social Chapter to be signed by all the other eleven nations, but outside the formal treaty. This was gratefully accepted by Major; his brinkmanship had succeeded.

In addition, the British were to secure much of what they sought on political union. The 'pillared structure', keeping foreign, defence and security policy in the hands of national governments rather than under the Commission, was enshrined in the treaty. 'Subsidiarity' was the term adopted in the treaty rather than 'federalism', and a number of further objectives were achieved, including a last-minute stand by Major that the research and development budget – a significant slice of Community expenditure – should be decided by unanimity rather than by QMV.[58]

Maastricht was a personal triumph for Major, though it is a misfortune that the comment 'game, set and match', which reeked of atypical triumphalism, should have been attributed to him,[59] especially when the words came from the Press Office.[60] He was the new boy among the heads of government –

eight of the twelve, plus Delors, had been at the previous IGC in 1985 – and many had assumed Major would prove a soft touch.[61] It is a matter of speculation what Mrs Thatcher might have achieved at Maastricht, and whether, even if a less federalist deal had been achieved, she could have carried the Party with her. She would certainly not have worked as well with Kohl, who abandoned some of Germany's treasured positions to accommodate Major. There was to be a *quid pro quo*, however, over Croatia, as discussed below. With Major's gift for personal diplomacy, in months of hard preparation beforehand he managed to persuade Kohl and Lubbers effectively to sideline Mitterrand, which was the essence of British success. At the conference itself, Major's grasp of detail, his negotiating skills, stamina and cool head were the key to Britain achieving so much of what it sought.

He went to bed at 4 a.m. for a brief sleep. When Kerr saw him off at the airport on Wednesday morning, he was feeling extremely happy and enormously relieved.[62] There was no inkling at all of the trouble that the Maastricht settlement would bring his premiership. In the short term, however, his lack of apprehension was well grounded. The reaction in the press and in Parliament was more positive and appreciative than even he could have hoped.

Maastricht Reception

'In almost every sense, it was a copybook triumph for Mr Major, the stuff of Foreign Office dreams,' wrote Boris Johnson, the *Daily Telegraph*'s European Community correspondent. 'The headlines today, and not just in the popular press, will read that Britain has slain the dragon of the social chapter.'[63] The Brussels press corps, judged by many insiders to be shrewder than their counterparts in London, found it hard at first to believe that Britain had indeed managed to detach the Social Chapter from the main treaty.[64] Many agreed with Peter Jenkins, when he said that Major's 'coup' had achieved his twin objectives of ensuring Britain remained at the heart of European affairs while preserving freedom of action in those areas where the UK's sovereignty was deemed to be sacrosanct.[65]

Major made a Commons statement on the day he returned, 11 December. To a crowded chamber, with Tory MPs waving their order papers and shouting excitedly, he stood up to tell them of the deal, the details of which most already knew. Major's peroration, hastily prepared by Wall overnight and completed that morning, went:

This is a treaty which safeguards and advances our national interests. It advances the interests of Europe as a whole. It opens up new ways of co-operating in Europe. It clarifies and contains the powers of the Commission. It will allow the Community to develop in depth. It reaches out to other Europeans – the new democracies who want to share the benefits we already enjoy. It is a good agreement for Europe, and a good agreement for the United Kingdom. I commend it to the House.[66]

The fighting talk of the week before, of Cabinet 'facing down' Mrs Thatcher and her allies if they proved difficult, and ministerial resignations by Eurosceptics, all but evaporated.[67] Helping spike Thatcher's guns was the swift propaganda job done by senior Party figures on what threatened to become an increasingly ugly and undignified fight. Portions of the treaty had been faxed through to the Chief Whip's office in Number Twelve at 3.20 a.m. Ryder and MacGregor stayed up all night coordinating the government's response, with a parallel group working at Central Office. At 5 a.m., despatch riders were sent round to Cabinet ministers and other key Party figures' and opinion formers' homes with a four-page digest of 'bullet points' to assist recipients in dominating the early morning press conferences and media interviews, and in singing a common tune. The *Daily Telegraph* reported one well-placed source saying, 'Mrs Thatcher had been well and truly stitched up.'[68]

The first reaction of the Eurosceptics was that they were happy with the deal struck; one told Colin Brown of the *Independent*, 'We're all breathing a big sigh of relief', and they would be very likely to support the deal.[69] In achieving a settlement all sides could live with, an editorial in the *Daily Telegraph* said, 'Mr Major deserves the heartfelt gratitude of his party for averting a disaster which might have made election victory unattainable.' *The Economist* called it 'the deal that Tory ministers and most backbenchers had been praying for'.[70] Hurd and Lamont spoke at a backbench meeting on the Wednesday afternoon, and experienced no difficulty from Eurosceptics. At Cabinet on Thursday morning, discussion was brief and uncontentious. Ministers calmly examined the meaning of the Social Chapter protocol. Mackay congratulated Major on his success and Baker chipped in with praise for Major's authoritative presentation.[71]

The following week, on 18 December, the two-day Maastricht debate opened. After the excitement at the beginning of the month, and with the histrionics all but played out, it was something of an anticlimax. Major again fully outlined the argument, and Kinnock responded in an effective performance.[72] In place of the forty to forty-two dissenters anticipated by Ryder, only seven, led by Tebbit, rebelled, including Biffen, Budgen, Tony Favell and Richard Shepherd, and three abstained, Thatcher, Gerald Howarth (her PPS) and Teresa Gorman. Some of the prominent Eurosceptics voted for the government, including Bill Cash, the Wintertons, Richard Body, Teddy Taylor and James Cran, and the overall majority was a very comfortable eighty-six.[73]

The Maastricht Treaty was signed on 7 February 1992, in the expectation that it would come into force on 1 January 1993, the same day as the Single European market. First, however, national legislatures needed to ratify it. Thought was given in Number Ten to rushing it through the House of Commons, on the back of the positive atmosphere and the large majority, before the election. The history of the next few years might indeed have been very different if it had been whipped through in early 1992. But several factors militated against, including the parliamentary business managers (MacGregor and Ryder as well as Waddington in the Lords) pointing out the excessive pressure already needed to get existing Bills through in the limited parliamentary time available.[74] More significant, an eruption of Party division whipped up perhaps by Tebbit and Mrs Thatcher, could portray an image of a divided Party which had been worrying Major ever since the summer.[75] Better, it was deemed, to have any internecine battles played out just after an election, leaving ample time for divisions to heal and the public to forget before the following general election in 1996 or 1997.

Such a strategy now appears naïve. The writing was on the wall, as Major saw, though he underestimated, as did many polls and commentators at the time, the depth and extent of the feeling submerged in the Party against further European integration. But there were harbingers. Simon Heffer could not have put the sceptic case more clearly in the *Spectator* just after the Maastricht summit finished: 'Were the Government to be honest,' he wrote, 'it would admit that nothing happened at Maastricht to keep Britain off the conveyor belt to federalism; indeed, quite the reverse.'[76] Even within the portals of Number Ten, Chaplin was writing: 'EMU agreed with British opt-out which we all know is pointless for if [the rest of the EC] have single currency we will have to join.'[77] Ryder and the whips were more prescient to the subterranean shifts in Tory thinking than Major. As early as the late 1980s the whips had feared that Europe was the next big crisis to face the Party, and the result of the election of the chairman of the backbench committee on Europe – in which Eurosceptic Bill Cash was only narrowly defeated by Norman Fowler – was regarded as a shot across the bows.

Ultimately, the trust was lacking for the right to be bound into acceptance of the Maastricht compromise; Major was not trusted, because his stance at Maastricht was seen as more a negotiating position than a position resting on firm personal or philosophical convictions. Eurosceptics warned that Major might make concessions in the future, should circumstances change. Franco-German intentions were viewed with deep suspicion. Thatcher, the right felt, had rumbled Kohl's true intent, whereas Major, under the guise of searching for the chimera of a meaningful new relationship, had been merely gullible, allowing Kohl to subsume a hapless Britain in his grand strategy of a German-dominated Europe.[78]

For Thatcher, Maastricht was a step too far. On the day after his return from the summit, she invited Major to a party at Claridge's to celebrate the fortieth anniversary of her wedding to Denis. When bidding him farewell outside the hotel, she was asked by the assembled press about Maastricht, and she said she thought he had done 'brilliantly'. The statement was taken, by the press and at Number Ten, as indicating she had reconciled herself to the Maastricht Treaty.[79] Yet as she was to write subsequently, 'As I read the newspapers the following day I resolved that there could be no more misunderstandings of this sort, however painful for all concerned the consequences might be.'[80] The headlines proclaiming how she now endorsed Major over Maastricht had given her a shock, and hardened her against any further equivocations on Europe.[81]

The Back-seat Driver: Major's Relationship with Mrs Thatcher

Major, we now know, held ambivalent feelings towards Mrs Thatcher throughout the 1980s. Her doubts about him first surfaced during his chancellorship, particularly over EMU.[82] She endorsed Major in the leadership election, and discouraged Tebbit's standing, but she was more resigned than eager about Major's candidature. He was simply the favoured candidate at the moment when her crown was taken from her. Unlike some of her supporters, she did not think he had plotted to bring about her downfall, but she did believe that when she telephoned him from the Commons, and afterwards, he could have shown more enthusiasm for her at a time when a strong stand from her Chancellor could have rallied support around her.

On his side, once in Number Ten he was sensitive to the 'back-seat driver' charge, but felt caught in a vice from the very outset of his premiership: he needed to show he was his own man, but was aware of the powerful forces in the Party that wanted him to be 'son of Thatcher'. If Major was a mild-mannered Macbeth, she was determined to play Banquo's ghost and spoil his party. Three factors resulted in her antipathy, which he regarded as deeply wounding and destabilising: appointing Heseltine, scrapping the poll tax, and Europe.[83]

Problems between them during the first two months after he became Prime Minister were, however, containable, helped by the presence of Charles Powell in Number Ten acting as a channel of communications. Great care was taken to arrange honours: the Order of Merit (OM) for her in 1990, the gift of the Queen but organised in conjunction with Number Ten, and a most unusual baronetcy for Denis. Turnbull, a respected figure in both camps, proved another key intermediary, taking pains to ensure that her office was kept briefed, and that she was assured she had not been forgotten.[84]

Major and Thatcher met periodically, as on 3 January 1991, when she told him she wanted to see early and large cuts in interest rates. She told him the pound was overvalued in what she saw as a mirror image of the Lawson boom. He responded, no doubt through clenched teeth, that the need was to bring inflation down, and he believed the deficit was shrinking.[85] Even in those first two months, as we know from the diaries of foreign policy analyst George Urban, she was already questioning the judgement of her successor.[86]

By the end of January rumours were starting to circulate about Major and Lamont voting against her in the first ballot of the leadership election.[87] Major, in fact, voted for her. Chaplin, who knew Major had not been enthusiastic about seeing her stay as Prime Minister, became anxious about the stories, and the two instant biographies of Major, by Bruce Anderson and Ed Pearce (as well as Lawson's memoirs), which 'may cause trouble when published'.[88]

During the Gulf War Thatcher became painfully frustrated at no longer being at the heart of things; the war brought the loss home to her more intensely than anything else. When the air raids started she would be found glued in front of the television giving her aides lectures on the merits of Tornado ground attack aircraft, or the accomplishments of other pieces of sophisticated military hardware. Tom King (Defence Secretary) would be phoned regularly about what she thought should be done next.[89] When the war ended, without pressing the advantage home to Baghdad, she became unreasonably angry at Number Ten's 'lack of stomach'. With Charles Powell's departure from Number Ten after the war, another connection ended.

From March 1991 her irritation was to grow, with Europe provoking her first critical comments in public when she attacked the federalist 'Utopia',[90] and spending decisions she thought populist and extravagant. Fresh press reports now began to appear with stories about Lamont and Ryder scheming together before the first ballot.[91] Mrs Thatcher and her supporters claimed they were being cut off, rejected even, by Number Ten and the new Party hierarchy. In early April she made her first public pronouncement since her resignation, trying to influence government policy when she called for action in support of the Kurds, which Major's safe havens plan was wrongly seen as an effort to upstage.[92]

With the pot being stirred by Thatcher friends who, like mediums in a seance, claimed to be speaking for her, Fleet Street became awash with rumours of Thatcher's inner thoughts. The names of those thought to have been responsible included Lord McAlpine, Tim Bell, Nicholas Ridley and Robin Harris. Some other excitable acolytes even whispered in her ear that she could make a comeback; all was not lost.

After eleven years in Downing Street, there can be no doubt that Mrs Thatcher endured a wrenching change in her lifestyle. She was deprived not only of the flow of information that had so fascinated her, but of all sorts of domestic comforts; her daughter Carol records that she had not had to make her own phone calls since 1979.[93] Reports of her being depressed and disoriented in 1991 would, if true, be readily understandable.

There is no doubt that she felt bruised at her dismissal, and that she found the transition emotionally very difficult after eleven and a half years at the centre of events. She had an easy ear for those around her who had no time for Major. An easy voice too: several members of her circle were alarmed at the extent she gossiped and put out messages from her Great College Street base in Westminster, lent her by McAlpine, but were also perturbed at Major's apparent coolness towards her.[94] As the summer wore on she began picking up intelligence, not always accurate, about the government's stance for Maastricht; she had decided she wanted to see the proposed treaty vetoed root and branch, but she heard reports that the government was prepared to go much further than she could stand. She had decided during the course of 1989–90 that she would take on the entire establishment, if necessary, to halt the European federalist juggernaut. It had become her last crusade. Whether she would have succeeded had she remained premier is a tantalising question.

A low point in the Major–Thatcher relationship was reached in early June, when the *Daily Telegraph* reported comments allegedly from her saying he was a 'grey man' who had 'no ideas', to be followed by the Bruges Group paper which nearly sabotaged his Welsh conference speech. A week later she delivered a speech at the Economic Club of New York, written for her by Robin Harris and John O'Sullivan, in which she attacked managed exchange rates, interpreted as an attack on the government's ERM policy.[95] Another speech, at Chicago, produced press reports of 'the Tory party at war'.[96] Major was exasperated, and at moments of high irritation would label her behaviour 'emotional' and her views 'loopy'. After an inconclusive meeting in July to restore relations, his patience completely snapped and he said that if she was going to carry on with her current attitude their relationship would become intolerable.[97]

The Russian coup produced the next serious clash. Her public calls for demonstrations in Moscow against the coup[98] were deeply unpopular in Downing Street. She then became hurt when press stories appeared about Thatcher being an armchair critic encouraging others to risk their lives on the streets.[99]

On her side, it was not until Maastricht that she gave up on his views on Europe. To the last minute, she clung onto the hope that he would not accept the treaty, opt-outs or no opt-outs. After that, the Rubicon had been crossed. Her disillusion was mirrored, and reinforced, by many intellectuals and journalists who held similar views on Europe, and whom Major thought she was encouraging to be critical of him and the government. At her December 1991 Christmas party in her offices in Belgravia's Chesham Place, into which she had moved shortly before, attenders described the atmosphere as like 'a government in exile'.[100] She had gone beyond her earlier, mild fault-finding, 'like an old girl complaining the school wasn't what it used to be', and into a more thoroughgoing critique of a government her friends considered full of detestable left wingers like Chris Patten and Kenneth Clarke.[101]

British 'spineless-ness' as she saw it in the Serb-Croat war had provided yet another parting of the ways shortly before.[102] The feelings against Major amongst guests at that Christmas party had become unequivocal: the Thatcher court had taken to portraying him as simply terribly dull and uninteresting, lacking in flair, a small man letting down Britain, incapable of even understanding the greatness or the mission of Thatcherism.[103]

In the New Year 1992, a measure of quiet came over her relations with Major. She began work in earnest on *The Downing Street Years*, volume one of her memoirs, and she did not want to rock the boat in the run-up to the general election. The Thatcher Foundation, which brought together some of her intellectual allies, such as Norman Stone and Ralph Harris, also began to take more of her interest. Only after the election did normal hostilities resume, with the opening salvo coming just two weeks after polling day in the form of an interview in the US magazine *Newsweek*, which caused Major much personal offence.[104] Over the next three years there were to be many low points, never worse than when the second volume of her memoirs was published in 1995.

Thatcher and Major were both at fault for their poisoned relationship. She was perhaps the more guilty, because she saw the damage she was doing, how divided was the Party, and how small the majority after 1992, and above all because she had suffered herself from similar sniping from her predecessor Edward Heath. The Heath comparison was in her mind but resentment mastered her; as one of her closest friends concluded: 'She behaved very badly at every level: she gossiped, she put out messages, she withheld support. She used all her political cunning to knife him and stab him and demoralise him and weaken him. Above all else she was thinking, "He is doing my job. How dare he?"'[105] According to a Major aide, 'The evil was in the drip feed, the constant gnawing away at him.'[106]

On Major's side, he could have handled her more sensitively, and put aside time to socialise with her and show interest in her advice.[107] But as we have seen, with all the pressures on him, he had not the time, even if he had the will, to spend on her. In the final analysis, apportioning blame is pointless. The fireworks were inevitable. She could not alter her nature – which helped make her the exceptional premier she undoubtedly was – which was to hold forceful opinions and not to hold back. It was small comfort to Major, reeling in Number Ten from the latest Thatcher broadside, to realise that if either Hurd or Heseltine had won the succession in November 1990, the cannon balls from her camp would have been flying across with even more regularity, and perhaps have been even more damaging.

EIGHTEEN

The Long Campaign:

January–March 1992

OVER CHRISTMAS AND New Year Major agonised over whether he had been right to delay the election. The initial rush of blood after his coup at Maastricht, which had encouraged him to think of a January or February poll, had passed. The election would now be held on a Thursday between April and July – March, with the budget, was ruled out. At his New Year's Day party at Chequers, with late December polls showing a Labour lead, the atmosphere was downbeat. Although Major himself appeared in sprightly form, there was no disguising what the Party needed was a good start to the year.[1]

The push came from an initiative, the Near Term Campaign, launched in January. The previous September, a group including Shaun Woodward, the Party's director of communications, visited election specialists in the US, above all those who participated in the Reagan re-election in 1984. The group came back with buzz words and ideas aplenty about the need to be 'proactive' in dictating the election agenda. The solution was to be a meticulously plotted campaign involving the coordination of speeches, conferences, tours, themes and other election paraphernalia.[2] The Party professionals sold the idea to Patten on their return, with their paper on the proposal discussed at Political Cabinet on 21 November 1991. On 19 December the last Cabinet of the year endorsed the Near Term Campaign strategy.[3]

The planners plotted what they claimed would be the most professional and well-orchestrated election campaign the Conservatives had ever produced; with memories of Labour outfighting them in the 1987 election, Central Office was determined to win the organisational, as well as the voting battle. The campaign was to run for eleven weeks, with a new theme for each week. 'Leadership' came first, beginning on Monday 30 December, and profiles duly appeared of Heseltine in the *Sunday Times*, Hurd on BBC's *Newsnight*, with extended coverage elsewhere of Major and Patten.[4] Week two's theme was tax, opening with the unveiling of 1,000 sites displaying a 'bombshell' poster declaring that tax would be £1,000 a year more under Labour, and with an attack by Patten on Labour's tax and spending plans. The 'bombshell' image was the product of Saatchi & Saatchi, and subsequently developed into the 'double whammy' attack on Labour over tax plans and inflation. On 9 January the Tory Party political broadcast announced plainly, 'You'd be worse off under Labour.'[5] A week on defence was followed by a return to tax, with updates on Labour's spending plans.

Though Central Office did not know it at the time, this marked the peak of the Near Term initiative. The strategy probably succeeded in boosting the Party's popularity, and in raising Labour's tax plans as an issue of concern to electors. But after the fourth week, the adherence to rotating themes – law and order, education, agriculture – became a treadmill, and one the media, on whose willingness to co-operate the strategy depended, came increasingly to resent. The later themes, with the exception of law and order, also proved less resonant and faced competition from a Labour election machine in a higher gear. Frustration grew in Central Office at the absence of 'positive' material flowing out of Whitehall because it was being held back for the manifesto.[6]

Most general elections saw tension rise between Number Ten and Central Office. This election was no exception. Central Office criticism focused on Sarah Hogg, considered by some in Party Headquarters to be domineering and insufficiently appreciative of their contribution.[7] Even Patten, a Hogg fan, began to question whether she was not taking too high a profile.[8] From Number Ten, there was irritation at what they considered the mechanistic and inflexible nature of Central Office's Near Term strategy, and at the failure of Central Office to get 'basic things' – like writing the manifesto – done.[9] Sarah Hogg felt that if she was being domineering, it was because she had no alternative.

The role Major was to play in the election had been debated among senior Party figures almost from the day he became Prime Minister. His discomfort at anything that smacked of a presidential contest or personality cult was seen early on in his reluctance to allow the John Schlesinger Party political broadcast based on his life; called *The Journey*, it was screened in March 1992.[10] He simply hated being 'managed' by media specialists.

I didn't take much notice of them, actually. No point in me trying to do something people tell me to do. If it isn't me, it doesn't work. If I am comfortable with it, it will work to the best of my ability. If I am not, there's no point in wasting our time.[11]

Ronnie Millar was the only 'manager' from outside politics to whom he would listen during the 1992 election, and Millar, being a man of the theatre rather than a public relations guru, confined his role to phrase-making.

There was one media 'technique', however, to which Major did agree to subject himself:

I came back from the Gulf very enthusiastic about standing on tanks talking to people. It was direct communication. It was old street theatre: you were surrounded by people ... what I actually wished to do in the election was something that hadn't been done for yonks. That was to hold public meetings, with me just standing in the middle of a large crowd, talking to them, unscripted, and answering questions.[12]

Shaun Woodward at Central Office was keen on the idea, but others worried. Two objections were raised. First, security. The IRA mortar attack on Number Ten the year before had been a dreadful reminder of the problems of protecting the Prime Minister even when secreted in the heart of Whitehall. Second was the problem of control. His advisers worried that 95 per cent of any soapbox session might go marvellously, showing off Major on top of issues and at his relaxed best. But what would be screened on television that night, they feared, would be the 5 per cent where he might be heckled or thrown off balance. Caution prevailed, and the plan was transmuted to a format called 'In the Round' (subsequently 'Meet John Major'), where the audience would consist merely of 'safe' Conservative voters. A trial was held at Bristol in September 1991, and a second at York in January 1992.[13] Chaplin, playing Cassandra to the last, felt that Major was 'tired and answers very verbose and sometimes wrong. Central Office says wonderful, but it is not.'[14]

Conservative confusion over how to present Major was mirrored by Labour's over how to attack him. Kinnock described their dilemma:

Labour hadn't seen Major coming. We had been looking forward to an election against Mrs Thatcher, which we would have won whenever it came because she was very beatable. At the time of the 1990 leadership election, Heseltine was also thought of as a known and beatable candidate, while the worry was over Hurd because his style was so different to Thatcher. Major came up from nowhere and we had no pre-existing strategy that could be used against him. The tactical dilemma was whether to portray him as a Thatcherite, or attack him for the new things he was doing. The choice was made basically for the former because the Tories wanted to project a new image and there was no point doing their work for them.[15]

One advantage which Major had over Kinnock was incumbency. He could play on his status as a leader on the world stage, commanding free television coverage, in the way that Nixon had done so spectacularly in the 1972 US presidential election. Number Ten therefore leaped on an idea which had been floated earlier by Britain's UN Representative David Hannay, that Britain use the opportunity of being in the UN Security Council chair for the month of January 1992 to convene a summit for the five permanent and ten rotating Security Council members.

Such a summit would coincide with Boutros Boutros-Ghali taking up his secretary-generalship, and would be justified by the recent expansion in UN business, including peace operations in Cambodia and Croatia, the need to keep Saddam Hussein under control in the aftermath of the Gulf War, and action being contemplated against Libya over the two indicted suspects for the 1988 Lockerbie plane bombing. The collapse of the Soviet Union and Boris Yeltsin's emergence as Russian President at the end of the year heightened the appeal of the plan. Major sold the special summit involving Yeltsin to Britain's allies as a key way of indicating their support for him.[16] Major realised too that he had neglected his own relationship with Yeltsin since the credit he had gained by being the first leader to denounce the 1991 coup and then visit Moscow afterwards.

Yeltsin had his own reasons, not least financial, for deciding to accept Major's invitation.[17] He came to London on 30 January *en route* to New York and had a day's talk at Number Ten. When discussions reached economic reform, Yeltsin claimed Gorbachev never understood privatisation. On aid, he uttered veiled threats that if the West did not help now they would end up spending many times more money on rebuilding defences against the new dictatorship which would spring up if he fell. On defence, Yeltsin committed himself to further nuclear cuts. At the meeting's conclusion Major and Yeltsin signed a declaration about Anglo–Russian relations, billed as the first since Catherine the Great in the eighteenth century.[18] Braithwaite concluded that it had been 'a most successful visit: much concrete business has been covered in a short time, and there is little of that world-historical philosophising that used to go on between Gorbachev and Thatcher'.[19]

The special UN Security Council summit took place on 31 January, the first, as Major later told the House, in the forty-seven years of UN history.[20] Some positive developments came out of it, including designating the pro-liferation of weapons of mass destruction – nuclear, biological and chemical – as a threat to international peace and security, and categorising international terrorism in the same way, enabling Security Council action against trans-gressors. It gave a powerful signal – though in the event not fully realised – that in the post-Cold War world the major powers were going to make a big effort to work collectively.

The summit was a courageous step, because it could have backfired. Security Council members might not have sent top-level delegations; the meeting could have degenerated into a slanging match; and it might have been difficult to present it as a strengthening of collective security. The press would have been all too ready to slam the summit as a failed and cynical British election ploy. But the gamble paid off. As Paddy Ashdown said in the Commons debate after Major's return: 'Does the Prime Minister realise that many people in Great Britain greatly welcome the fact that the first heads of government meeting in the United Nations' history was chaired by a British Prime Minister?'[21]

Manifesto Difficulties

Major descended from the international heights with a bump in early Feb-ruary. The manifesto had still not been written; campaign plans were not finalised, and worse, the polls, which had turned in the Conservatives' favour in January, now showed Labour again in the lead.

The election date clearly had to be settled once and for all. Over no other subject during Major's first government had there been so much agonising. Lamont continued to press for going as late as possible, in the hope of maximising the chances for his 'green shoots' finally to sprout; against his argument ran the unlikelihood of any such green shoots making much material difference to voters even by June or July, and the deleterious effect on morale of what were expected to be poor local election results in May if the Party hung on. Central Office also had been planning for 9 April. By the beginning of February, Number Ten all but agreed to this date, which meant Lamont having to assent to bringing the budget forward by a week to 10 March, to clear the decks for the campaign.[22]

Lawson wrote to Major with the unsolicited opinion that an election immediately after a budget would be a disaster as things always go wrong.[23] Major continued to agonise over dates, in perhaps the loneliest decision he had to take since becoming Prime Minister. As late as 2 March he was saying, 'I may never forgive myself for not overruling them' (thinking of those who argued for holding the election in autumn 1991). Only on that day did he and senior party figures finally confirm that they would go to the country on 9 April.[24]

When Brian Griffiths had retired as head of the Policy Unit in November 1990, he gave Sarah Hogg one piece of advice: 'Whatever else you do, keep control of the manifesto.'[25] The advice was appreciated but it was unnecessary: she had no intention ever of surrendering control, least of all to Central Office. Yet despite her best efforts to push it forward, manifesto preparations had proceeded throughout 1991 at a dilatory pace, a compound of two factors: the lack of consensus about the government's overall strategy, and ministers' reluctance to make progress with their policy groups and to produce proposals for their departments. To try to galvanise the process, Major convened the Cabinet's five 'big beasts' – Hurd, Lamont, Clarke, Heseltine and Patten plus Sarah Hogg – into a committee given the *Boy's Own* title of the 'A-team'.[26] The Number Twelve committee, which continued to perform a valuable coordinating role, was considered to be far too unwieldy for the task.

Major insisted that the ministers concerned carved out large and sufficient chunks of time in their diaries for the task. The A-team's first meeting, on 9 January, lasted for much of the working day after Cabinet finished. Wakeham joined them throughout, and a succession of ministers were called in and questioned by the group on their proposals. The Policy Unit's idea for the manifesto, to group the entire text around the four themes of choice, ownership, responsibility and opportunity, which Major had been spelling out in speeches during 1991, became an early casualty of the discussions. Conservatism won through, the themes making an appearance merely at the start, followed by the traditional format of sections on different policy areas.[27]

Disagreement arose at that first meeting when Rifkind argued against Major and the Policy Unit over the privatisation of British Rail. Major, joined by Patten, wanted privatisation on a regional basis, recreating the sentimental pride of companies such as the Great Western Railway. Rifkind and the Transport Department produced a plan for splitting InterCity railways from the rest, whereas the Treasury wanted the more complex formula of splitting track and franchises, which was later adopted.[28]

Differences on the manifesto content arose over a wide area, in meetings of both the A-team and Political Cabinet, with Heseltine often in the thick of it. On the use of land, Major, arguing for more building in rural areas (the Treasury line), disagreed strongly not only with Heseltine, but Gummer too.[29] At Political Cabinet on 15 January Heseltine argued for doing more about inner cities, an underlying Major enthusiasm. Lilley took him on over his radical ideas for the use of derelict land. Clarke, revitalised by a trip to Mexico, weighed in with the idea of taking inner city schools away from local education authorities. When Clarke's views were leaked, Patten was forced to give a homily on the subject at Political Cabinet the following day.

On most issues the big beasts seemed to be wandering round in circles, while vital days ticked by. By early February, with Patten too busy on wider election preparation, Sarah Hogg decided she had no option but to take over the writing of the manifesto herself. Elsewhere, January's momentum was lost. The A-team's proposals had failed to produce sufficient detail, while Major himself was reluctant either to impose control over them or insist on introducing his own ideas.[30] With the polls moving in Labour's direction, and the economic news getting worse, Patten commented at the 'Week Ahead' meeting on Monday 17 February that it was 'not the background against which I would wish to fight an election'.[31] With no room left to manoeuvre on timing, it was, however, the only background they had.

The A-team's meeting that week brought a conflict over changes to government departments. Major argued the case for putting the arts, tourism, media and sport into one department under a Cabinet minister, but none of the rest of the A-team was keen, Patten observing that there was 'more scope for [cash] to fall off the back of a lorry if they remained in big departments'.[32] Major was reticent about pushing the idea against them, but A-team members nevertheless yielded when they saw how keen he was; some also surmised that he saw it as a slot for his friend Mellor after the election. Discussions about the name for the new department continued until the day before the manifesto launch. Major complained that most suggestions were frivolous; Lilley boldly retorted, 'That's because the idea is frivolous.'[33] Other decisions on Whitehall structure went through more smoothly: absorbing Energy into the DTI (and Environment); leaving Education and Employment apart for the time being, and setting up a Cabinet post in part for the Citizen's Charter.[34]

Preserve the Union with Scotland

A larger question of governmental structure now entered the frame: Scotland. From the start of his premiership, Major had been concerned about the Conservatives' position in Scotland, where their seats had been hacked in half in the 1987 general election. He had replaced Malcolm Rifkind with his friend Ian Lang as Scottish Secretary in 1990, with the outline brief to stop the rot. Major's instinctive position was against any constitutional change, but he was happy to let Lang placate the considerable pressure, not least from Scottish Tories, to explore devolution proposals.[35]

The very arrival of Major provided a short-lived boost of Tory spirits in Scotland: he was immediately seen as more sympathetic to Scottish opinion than Thatcher. It is easy to caricature Thatcher's attitude to the Scottish as one of exasperation and disbelief that Scotland, the land of Adam Smith and with the sound Scottish character, should not vote Tory. In fact, she tried hard in repeated visits and initiatives to win the Scots over. But her Englishness, and her tendency to preach, grated.

Major's honeymoon, such as it was, did not outlast his first year. The Kincardine and Deeside by-election in November 1991, which reduced Tory seats in Scotland from ten to nine, provided a powerful incentive to focus attention on the issue. Lang by then had ruled out any steps to devolution in a series of speeches. He thought a big speech by Major in support of the existing union between England and Scotland would help to reinforce that stance. Major and Lang decided he should attack Labour's and the Liberal Democrats' devolution plans. The occasion selected was a Party meeting for Scottish candidates at the Moat House Hotel in Glasgow on 22 February.[36] The address was to be exclusively on the constitutional issue.

Major's visit came against a background of a surge in support for nationalism, with polls showing that between a third and half of Scots favoured independence;[37] many commentators agreed with Hugo Young that the devolution bandwagon would prove irresistible for the Conservatives, regardless of what they might protest before the election.[38] Major flew up to Glasgow that 'foul, chill Saturday' morning armed with an uncompromising speech, written mostly by Nick True, who had been instrumental in hardening Major against those voices in the Party arguing for constitutional change.[39] Lang also contributed to the speech, amending some defiant phrases, but more particularly in terms of getting the appropriate tone.[40] In the car from the airport Lang outlined various questions that Major might have asked, including what would happen if the Party won overall, but – as seemed very likely – they lost even more seats in Scotland. They agreed Major should respond, as Lang himself had recently, that he would 'take stock'.[41]

Major spoke passionately on a theme he had increasingly taken to heart. The 285-year-old union between Scotland and England was, he said, facing its greatest threat; if separation occurred the Scots would be far less well off, economically and politically, and he accused the nationalists of misleading the Scottish people about the true costs. Devolution was also the beginning of the slippery slope to independence for both Scotland and Wales.

It is our Party that supports the Union, not because it has always been good for us, but because it has always seemed right to us. Not always in our political interests, but always in that of our Kingdom and the countries within it.[42]

The speech was seminal, yet begged questions. It outlined what was to become for Major a core theme of the general election – preservation of existing constitutional arrangements. It cemented his friendship with Lang, who was relieved that the Prime Minister had been so outspoken in defence of the status quo, over which he had found himself increasingly isolated.[43] The response about 'taking stock' paved the way for the White Paper on Scotland in 1993, which made some limited concessions to Scottish sentiment by enhancing the Scottish Grand Committee.

But why did he see maintenance of the union as so pivotal for Scotland, but not Northern Ireland? The answer requires deeper study.

But not the Union with Northern Ireland?

Major had, in the privacy of the Cabinet Room, identified Northern Ireland as one of the subjects that he wanted to focus on as premier.[44] He finds it hard to pinpoint the origin of his interest:

It had been in my mind for a long time. When we lived in Coldharbour Lane, there were three Irish boys in the flat below us who always used to go home every six months, and they must have talked about 'the troubles'. For a long time, I thought it was silly that we weren't making progress on Ireland and people just seemed to assume that the status quo was right. It was very easy for politicians to make speeches saying that the IRA are trouble and we oppose them, but people were still getting killed. Britain was involved in peacemaking in all sorts of places around the world, and the thought kept running through my mind that if the killing was happening in Surrey it wouldn't be acceptable. But I was never in a position to do anything about it. When I came to Number Ten however I realised that I was in a position to do something about it.[45]

Major decided to leave Peter Brooke, whom Thatcher had appointed in July 1989, at the Northern Ireland Office. Thatcher had achieved an opening with the Anglo–Irish Agreement of 1985, but for the next four years under Tom King there had been little further progress. Brooke had been widowed four years before, had time on his hands, and with strong Irish roots had a passion to try to bring about peace. A bookish man, he read deeply into Irish history and politics. He brought more force of intellect to the problems than any Secretary of State since Hurd (1984–5) and more commitment in time than arguably anyone since the troubles broke out twenty years before.

Brooke's political skills and laconic personality were ideally suited to the Northern Ireland position at that time. His bumbling and genial exterior was deceptive. As he later said: 'I ran risks, but the fact was that the army and the police were losing lives holding the ring for the politicians. If the politicians could not get a move on, then those lives would be squandered.'[46] Movement came in a number of areas. In an interview in November 1989, to mark his hundredth day in office, he said that the government would be 'flexible' and imaginative if IRA violence were to stop. The speech provoked a storm of interest on the nationalist side that he was prepared to countenance a dialogue, and of predictable protest from the Unionists.

In late 1990 John Deverell, an MI5 officer and the head of intelligence in Northern Ireland, came to see him to confirm something Brooke had been learning from other sources, including from John Hume, the SDLP leader, who was in secret talks with Gerry Adams of Sinn Fein. A line of communication was open to the IRA leadership, and Deverell wanted Brooke's permission to explore it further. Such a channel had been operative in 1974–5, and again in 1980–81 during the hunger strikes, but had since been dormant. Brooke gave the permission Deverell sought, while Thatcher was still Prime Minister, on condition that if questioned he could publicly deny that he was talking to terrorists. (He considered that, as a go-between was being employed, he could say with some truth that there was no *direct* contact.[47])

Brooke's urgency in exploring a dialogue with the IRA was prompted by the escalation of violence on both sides of the sectarian divide, with the number of deaths in 1990 rising to seventy-six compared to sixty-two in 1989.[48] Some senior army officers concluded that the war against violence was not being won, and they predicted even worse bloodshed in the years ahead.[49] Equally, Brooke learned from the covert channels that a faction in the IRA had begun to think the war unwinnable on their side and unlikely to achieve their political goal of a united Ireland.

Brooke was urged by Hume to make a clear statement that, contrary to Sinn Fein/IRA beliefs, Britain was not remaining in Northern Ireland to advance their own interests. Brooke duly delivered his seminal speech in his Westminster constituency less than three weeks before Thatcher's fall, in which he declared: 'The British government has no selfish strategic or economic interest in Northern Ireland ... Britain's purpose ... is not to occupy, oppress or exploit.' The way forward for a new phase in policy towards Northern Ireland could not have been more clearly paved.[50]

John Major's arrival at Number Ten provided another fresh impetus. Sinn Fein and the IRA had long concluded that, while Mrs Thatcher was in Downing Street, the chances of any movement were remote. Major seemed to them a more pragmatic figure, and they greeted his arrival with a three-day Christmas ceasefire, the first for fifteen years.[51] In February 1991 Gerry Adams wrote to Major, asking him to talk to Sinn Fein about peace. He was regarded as open-minded by others as well; Northern Ireland Unionist MPs such as Jim Molyneaux had grown to like and respect Major when he was a whip (1983–5). 'He was exceptional', Molyneaux recalled, 'in that he didn't take bureaucratic attitudes to problems: he used his own initiative to get results.'[52] His friendly persona and his abhorrence of lecturing others appealed to Albert Reynolds, then Irish Finance Minister but later to be

Taoiseach, whom Major met when Chancellor of the Exchequer.

The Northern Ireland Office, too, was eager to capitalise on Major's arrival at Downing Street. In December they made a pitch to convince him that the problems of Northern Ireland would be taken forward only if they had a high degree of consistent prime ministerial involvement over several years.[53] For his first Christmas he took to Huntingdon a great stack of papers on Northern Ireland, and returned to work in January eager to start discussions.[54] He visited the province on 22 February, and met a wide cross-section of the community, though in private he had expressed anxiety about whether he would be recognised on the streets of Northern Ireland.[55] Major was sufficiently impressed by Brooke's enthusiasm that he backed his Secretary of State's initiative to hold all-party talks with Northern Ireland's constitutional parties – the Ulster Unionists, Democratic Unionists and the nationalist SDLP – announced in the House of Commons on 26 March.

The talks alerted Major further to the potential for real progress in Northern Ireland. Throughout the talks he was in close personal touch with the Taoiseach, Charles Haughey, anxious to keep him on side and reassure him that the Unionist parties did not agree to the talks as a cynical way of sabotaging the Anglo–Irish Agreement of 1985 (under one of its terms, regular meetings of the Inter-Governmental Conference would not take place while the talks process was active).[56] The talks focused on what became known as the 'three-stranded' approach – internal Northern Ireland matters, north–south relations, and overall Anglo–Irish relations. Despite Brooke's energy and enthusiasm, however, the talks ran out of time in early July with neither side willing to make the compromises necessary for meaningful dialogue. Hopes were high, however, that they could be resumed after the summer.

The IRA, scrutinising developments carefully from the wings, played a dual strategy during 1991: a channel was established between the Provisional Army Council and the British government (albeit not very active until 1993), while on the other hand they still tried to kill and maim ministers and soldiers. Their coup in 1991, which gave them much pleasure and solace, was the February Downing Street mortar attack. Conceived against the hated Mrs Thatcher, to complete the task they had failed to achieve with the Brighton hotel bomb in October 1984, they were not going to abandon the meticulous plan after Major's succession. By breaching security in Whitehall, and achieving a 'spectacular' at the heart of British government, with none of their own operatives captured, they felt they had proved their invincibility and won the right to be taken seriously.[57] They maintained the pressure in their mainland campaign, including firebombs in Manchester in April, a bomb at a band concert in St Albans in November and a series of firebombs in London and elsewhere in the run-up to Christmas.

The slow rate of progress during the first half of 1991 frustrated Major. As with all prime ministers, Northern Ireland impinged on him daily through the security under which he laboured and which he hated. The Bush administration – though not as involved as Clinton's was to be – was anxious to see progress; the economic cost of the troubles, not least on mainland Britain, was a real factor, and he rapidly found that his open, non-patronising way of dealing with Irish politicians, North and South, was liked and could be more productive still. Everything pointed to taking Ireland even higher up the priority list than he had at first contemplated.

When, in the autumn of 1991, it became clear that the constitutional parties in Northern Ireland would not return to the Brooke talks, Major became impatient. 'It is quite wrong, with people still being killed,' he told his Northern Ireland Secretary, 'that they are not prepared to talk.'[58] He urged Brooke over that winter to give even higher priority to finding ways of moving forward; Brooke thought that with a general election approaching Major was being unrealistic, and told him so.[59]

Brooke played little part in the Major–Haughey summit of December 1991. The media wrongly treated it as a non-event, with the uncertainty as to whether either leader would be in office for long. The talks were especially significant to the Irish government, who had what one senior British official described as a 'heightened arousal' about possible breakthroughs ahead.[60] Haughey briefed Major about the Hume–Adams talks, and the two premiers discussed a possible change in strategy by the IRA and Sinn Fein. Major, who knew more about the talks than he let on, appeared interested and positive.[61] It was agreed that Prime Minister and Taoiseach should meet at six-monthly summits, to help ensure maximum priority was maintained at the highest level.

Any undue optimism was punctured, however, when the 1992 New Year opened in particularly bloody style. A bomb in Whitehall Place, less than three hundred yards from Downing Street, on 10 January was timed to remind the Conservatives to include the 'occupation' of Ireland in their talks on the manifesto.[62] A week later, on 17 January, eight building workers were killed by an IRA bomb in Northern Ireland.[63] Extra troops were at once ordered into the Province. After further tragedies, the *Guardian* opened an editorial, 'Twenty-six deaths in 30 days: if the New Year continues as it has begun we will be back to the level of violence which prevailed in Northern Ireland in the early Seventies.'[64]

Brooke now committed a regrettable lapse of judgement. Within hours of the bomb that killed the building workers, he appeared on a television chat show hosted by Gay Byrne in Dublin. Asked to sing 'Danny Boy', he declined, but after prompting he at last agreed to sing, 'Oh My Darling Clementine' to camera.[65] Various Ulster politicians at once called for his resignation for his insensitivity so soon after the outrage. Brooke himself was mortified. He offered his resignation over the weekend to Major, who declined to accept. The House of Commons felt a deep personal sympathy for Brooke when he made his statement the following week and rallied to him. If it had not been so supportive, he would have gone immediately, regardless of Major's view.[66]

General election uncertainty, and speculation that the Conservatives, fearful of a hung Parliament, were trying to woo the Unionists, acted against any resumption of the Brooke talks. Major seized the initiative the day after loyalist gunmen killed five people in Belfast on 10 February. He invited the leaders of the four main constitutional parties in Northern Ireland – Paisley (DUP), Molyneaux (UUP), Hume (SDLP) and John Alderdice (Alliance Party) – to talks in Downing Street. Although these talks, as expected, produced no breakthrough, Major promised all four regular meetings at Downing Street, and urged them to extend their informal contacts in Belfast. The talks, the first since 1976 to bring all the constitutional parties together with the British Prime Minister, provided further evidence of Major's personal commitment to finding a way forward.[67]

The ground was also continuing to shift in Dublin. Haughey fell after scandals and failing energy sapped his credibility and, in the same week as the Downing Street talks, was replaced as leader of Fianna Fail and Taoiseach by Reynolds. Major phoned Reynolds after he was elected party leader, but before he finally became Taoiseach, to congratulate him, and say they should meet.[68] This they did in Downing Street on 27 February. According to Reynolds:

There was no set agenda: we were picking up personal links where we had left off. I said my first political priority would be to end violence in Northern Ireland, and economic growth the second. Before the meeting was over he said that he was equally concerned with trying to reach a solution, to use his position to search for peace, a formula. The trust and understanding between us, that neither would sell the other short, was a very good starting point. We agreed at that first meeting to do everything possible not to condemn another generation in Northern Ireland to sectarian killing. His own humanitarian response to the situation led him to try. He wouldn't let it be said that he didn't try: he would rather try and fail than not try at all. We certainly had some optimism that together we could do it.[69]

The accession of Reynolds, and his meeting with Major, were key events in the evolving political momentum. Dick Spring, Irish Foreign Minister since 1993, described their relationship thus: 'It helped that they had worked together well in the past as finance ministers. In that respect, they knew each other, they could pick up the telephone and talk, and it does help. There was an affinity: they are both unpretentious people, who want similar ends and to get on with it. At the end of the day, they had to do business. That was the key to it.'[70] Major made Reynolds aware right from the outset of his political beliefs.

He said he was a Unionist, but not I thought one in any narrow sense. He saw that you couldn't reconstruct the old Northern Ireland on the majoritarian principles. We had to find structures to recognise identities and differences, and he was prepared to let people work towards new structures. If people decided in the end that they wanted to live in an all-Ireland structure, fine, he was clear he would legislate for that. A broader view than Thatcher, who considered Northern Ireland part of the UK, full stop.[71]

Throughout, Reynolds found, Major was conscious of the way he would be attacked for his initiatives in Northern Ireland from a Scottish viewpoint. Reynolds could only speculate on why Major saw Northern Ireland differently from Scotland: 'To save human life, he took a risk going in that direction. He knew it. It maybe was that he saw Britain as a unit that could not be broken up, but Northern Ireland was "over there".'[72]

No further progress could be made ahead of the election. Major, however, decided that a fresh face was needed at the Northern Ireland Office, and that his former mentor, Patrick Mayhew, would be the right successor. Although Brooke had obtained a consensus to resume talks after the election, he had lost the confidence of many in the Unionist community, as seen in their harsh reaction to the Gay Byrne programme. Brooke was also mentally exhausted. Few jobs in Cabinet are more stressful, and the strain had begun to affect him severely. There was little more that he could give.

Clearing the Decks: Manifesto and Budget

By early March, although the tempo of election preparation was rising, still incredibly, and despite Sarah Hogg's urging, there was no sign of a finished manifesto. At Central Office's 'Week Ahead' meeting on Monday 2 March, it was clear much was still up in the air.[73] The A-team met for their final meeting on the evening of 5 March; with the polls still showing a Labour lead, the mood was not optimistic. Worse, with the election less than five weeks away, and the manifesto needing to be sent to the printers the following evening, many issues were still left unresolved.

The A-team had continued to be a potent source of dispute, main battles revolving around Heseltine's visions for regenerating local areas, including his proposal for an English Development Agency; money, with the Treasury, already alarmed at the size of the public deficit, putting pressure on for the elimination of costly manifesto commitments; and transport, with Rifkind still battling over the form of rail privatisation as well as over the Channel Tunnel Rail Link.[74]

The A-team meeting on 5 March continued after a working dinner in Number Ten's small dining room, but with midnight approaching, attenders realised that little more could be achieved. After they departed Major was left alone with Sarah Hogg, a small Policy Unit staff, and a mass of text spread over the table which needed pulling together. After a moment of awkwardness, Sarah Hogg said to Major that he could leave it all to her and her team. Major went to bed and they stayed up all night working in her office. Most felt exhausted, but Hogg's stamina drove them on. By the morning of 6 March the text had been threaded together. The document was checked and rechecked with Major, and individual sections with relevant

Cabinet ministers.[75] It was due to have been handed over to Andrew Lansley, the bright Director of the Research Department, at midday, but not until evening was she able to give him the disk with the manifesto on it. Lansley drove immediately up to the security-approved printer in Derby, where the disk was converted into proofs. Now it was Lansley's turn to work through the night checking the proofs, which came in at 7,000 words longer than had been planned. He found a large number of typing errors, which he corrected, but says he did not change the substance of the text.[76]

When he drove back with the corrected proofs on 7 March, Sarah Hogg was 'furious'[77] and demanded changes he had made be reversed: 'Ministers had not agreed them. The Party Chairman had not agreed them. The Prime Minister had not agreed them.'[78] This worried her all the more because Major had made it plain he wanted to ensure all ministers concerned felt involved and had approved the final text on their sections.[79] Though she did not mention him by name in her memoirs, she was incandescent with rage at Lansley; it marked a further and decisive stage in the deteriorating relationship between the Party's two policy chiefs.[80]

Lansley was despatched to Derby again, this time with Rosling from the Policy Unit acting as 'minder' to guard against 'further flights of fancy', as Hogg wrote later.[81] Lansley does not recognise the picture she painted. 'If I was so mistrusted,' he asked, 'why was I sent back up to Derby?'[82]

The final manifesto, at 27,000 words, was considered long. Finally approved by Cabinet on 12 March, it had a foreword by Major and a conclusion by Patten. Sarah Hogg had been determined, however, to show that the government was still bubbling with ideas, and had plenty of steam for a fourth term. True to this intention, and to Major, it was stronger on detailed and incremental policies than philosophical declarations. Lansley recalls, 'It was a conscious decision that we were offering a different style of government, one that was managerial and competent, with the Conservatism downplayed.'[83] Critics felt that in its haste and reconciliation of different ministers' strong views, the manifesto lacked overall cohesion and imparted insufficient sense of long-term direction. Hogg had nevertheless caught faithfully Major's wishes and outlook, and had laboured hard over the previous sixteen months to extract from her boss the essence of his beliefs:

The purpose was to arrive at a document with which all members of the Cabinet were happy marching forward. This put two constraints on us. The first was to spread the philosophical range to keep ministers with different conceptions of Conservatism happy, and for the rebuilding of unity within the party which John Major achieved between 1990–92, this was an enormously important objective. Second, making sure there is enough in the manifesto on their subject for departmental ministers, so that the views of the various pressure and lobby groups can be met. It prevents them saying in the campaign that the government is not interested in X or Y, because it is not in the manifesto. It is a terribly important part of manifestos, and one not fully understood probably by journalists.'[84]

The 1992 manifesto was, in many ways, Hogg's finest achievement at Number Ten.

Horsetrading between Lamont's budget and the manifesto had been not the least reason for delay. The National Lottery, a core Major enthusiasm but one which the Treasury never liked, was held over from the budget to the manifesto, and help for pensioners via income support – a policy favoured by the former DHSS double-act of Major and Newton – inserted into the budget.[85] Room for manoeuvre by the Chancellor was again slight; monetary policy was locked in due to ERM membership, and fiscal policy also offered little scope. Pressure for a tax-cutting budget grew following the impact made by the Near Term Campaign's attack on Labour's tax plans, but Treasury officials reminded Major of the sobering news of the size of the deficit, which he was at first inclined to play down.[86]

At Political Cabinet on 20 February, when discussing the fiscal position, Lamont nevertheless argued for a reduction in tax. Baker supported him, arguing for 1p or 2p off the 25p basic rate.[87] Major himself was inclined to agree; Sarah Hogg and Patten also saw the advantages.[88] Against the tax cutting budget were various Cabinet ministers who favoured raising tax thresholds. The argument that tax cuts could backfire as being cynical and electioneering carried force, especially with Treasury officials emphasising their deep concern about the state of public finances.

A compromise emerged late in the day from Jeremy Heywood, Lamont's brilliant Principal Private Secretary (1991–4), who produced the idea of a new 20p income tax band for the first £2,000 of taxable income, to benefit four million low-paid people.[89] Some, like the Treasury special adviser Alastair Ross Goobey, leaped on it as a way of appearing to promise movement towards a basic rate of 20p, while costing the Exchequer very little; others in the Treasury were adamantly against.[90] Major judged it a happy compromise between the protagonists of higher thresholds and lower basic rates, and one that could be sold as in line with the policy of reducing tax on the least well off. The plan was unveiled at the Budget Cabinet on 10 March, to general satisfaction. Chaplin, however, in one of her last diary entries before leaving Downing Street, recorded, 'Some clever ideas that shoot Labour's fox but are not right in themselves eg lower band ... PM's track all over it – political but not right. Massive PSBR £28 bn – [Treasury officials] clearly horrified.'[91]

So newsworthy did the new tax band prove that it largely took attention away from other items in the budget, including income support raised for pensioners, the halving of tax on new cars, and measures to alleviate the effect of business rates on the revaluation of commercial properties.

Lamont delivered the budget that afternoon in typically stylish form, billing it as a 'budget for recovery'. It did, indeed, catch Labour unprepared. Kinnock had prepared his response expecting a 1p cut in the basic rate, and was so taken off-guard that he made no reference to the new tax band in his reply to the budget speech. The decision that Labour would reverse it was only made by John Smith, Shadow Chancellor, later in the day,[92] a mistake, as it could have been sold as the Tories stealing Labour's policy; a similar proposal had been in Labour documents for over a year. At the time, Lamont's budget was well received,[93] but the shine was soon taken off when the markets, unprepared for the high borrowing levels announced, wiped nearly £20 billion off share prices, and the pound tumbled to levels that ruled out any imminent cuts in interest rates. By the Thursday, with polls showing a widening Labour lead, the BBC was saying, 'The budget has bombed.'[94]

Lamont and many other Tories continue to believe that, with hindsight, it was the factor that 'won the election'.[95] Such an assertion can be supported by arguing that the budget helped highlight tax as a key election issue, on which the Conservatives were strong; but Smith's 'Shadow budget' did far more in that direction, by making the classic error of drawing attention to an area of party weakness.[96] Tax experts said the 20p tax rate was an inefficient and untidy way of proceeding, and more critically that it made a nonsense of the tax system. Geoffrey Howe, when Chancellor, had previously abolished such a tax band. However, lower tax bands were retained by Lamont's successors, Clarke and Brown.

The budget did perhaps less than it might have done to address real economic needs of the country, especially coming after the package of measures in late February/early March, including pay rises above inflation of teachers and GPs, new funding for roads and help for Manchester in its bid to host the Olympic Games in 2000, all of which added an extra £4 billion to public spending.[97] With expenditure rising, and revenue falling in the continuing recession, the government deficit after the election was soon heading for £35 billion, or nearly 6 per cent of national income.[98] The government had nevertheless resisted the temptation to cut tax even more, which would have compounded the deficit still further, and it was not as cynical as some pre-election budgets, notably R. A. Butler's in April 1955.

The day after the budget, 11 March, Cabinet met briefly at 11 a.m. Major carefully rehearsed with ministers a rather selective view of his reasoning on election timing. He had thought of a general election in the previous autumn, he said, but did not want any distractions from Maastricht, and it was also uncomfortable to legislate for a community charge replacement with an election in the offing. The choice was then between spring or summer, as the government would be accused of running away if a general election was held before the budget. Decisive shifts in public policy on the NHS had occurred and most if not all of the legislative programme was in place. For that reason, he told ministers, he had decided to hold the general election on 9 April, with dissolution on 16 March.[99]

Major then went to see the Queen, and on his return from Buckingham Palace at 12.30 p.m he told the media crowds gathered outside Downing Street:

There is a lot I want to do in this country. There is a lot that we can do to make this country an even better place to live in ... We have a stack of new ideas to take government closer to the people and make sure that people have more choice, more opportunity. Those are the themes we will be putting forward to the people.[100]

The general election campaign had begun, as Michael White wrote, 'in the least favourable circumstances for a sitting government since Harold Wilson ended the last 13-year tenure in 1964'.[101]

NINETEEN

General Election: A Mandate for Major:

March–April 1992

AFTER HEARING HE had won the leadership election in November 1990, Major concluded his first public statement with the words, 'We will win the general election.' Whether or not he would achieve that goal had preyed daily on his mind over the ensuing fifteen months, but now the election campaign had at last begun and the outcome would soon be known.

The Struggle to be Heard: 11–28 March

Major enjoyed elections. Oddly for a normally mild-mannered man, the rough and tumble of debate appealed to him; he drew energy from meeting voters, and he enjoyed getting out of Number Ten. He also believed, bar one Wednesday evening late in the campaign, that he would win:

I didn't believe what the polls were telling us. I had this instinct that we wouldn't lose. It was also a bit of blind faith. I couldn't actually believe that I had come from where I came from, up to where I was, to be cut off after just eighteen months. It somehow didn't seem historically right.[1]

This belief in his own destiny was a powerful factor in his self-confidence. It was not always well founded. He also said later with complete conviction that he could never imagine Tony Blair in Number Ten.[2]

The first two weeks of the 1992 campaign did not find him at ease with himself. He felt hemmed in and 'packaged' by the party machine, which prevented him firing on all cylinders. Upon his return from Buckingham Palace on 11 March, he capitalised on the presence of the media for his statement outside Number Ten to chat to schoolchildren who had gathered, and was looking 'calm but uncertain', according to Nicholas Wapshott.[3] Any uncertainty he felt stemmed from the enormity of the process which he had unleashed, and anxiety about fighting an election during a recession. The polls placed Labour ahead on 41 per cent, Conservatives 39 per cent and Liberal Democrats on 15 per cent.[4] Not since Clement Attlee in 1951 had a Prime Minister voluntarily called an election while his party was behind in the polls.[5] The City greeted the election news nervously. According to conventional wisdom Major had failed to achieve lift-off for the campaign with either the budget or the timing of the election.[6] Major, however, was bolstered on that first day by messages of support flooding into Downing Street, not least from his friend George Bush, saying he thought Major 'a superb leader' and 'the respect I have for the prime minister knows no bounds'.[7] He spent the rest of the day giving media interviews and working on election plans.

At Cabinet next morning, only trivial points were raised when final approval was given to the manifesto. Judith Chaplin, *en route* to her Newbury constituency, called in to see Major to say goodbye, Jonathan Hill having taken over formally as Political Secretary the week before. Major gave her flowers, a bottle of champagne and a kiss; but deep down both knew that her appointment had been less than a complete success.[8] Major was upset later when he saw what she had written in her diary: 'If she felt those things she never said them at the time.' Indeed, like Alan Clark and some other diarists, the words were written down to let off steam and did not always reflect the balance of what the diarist felt at the time.

In the final Prime Minister's Questions that Thursday afternoon, Major clashed with Kinnock over why he would not agree to a television debate. Major knew that as incumbent, he had more to lose, and a debate would only confer dignity on his challenger. Hence his refusal, of which he tried to make light, quoting Shakespeare, from *Love's Labour's Lost*, that the Labour leader 'draweth out the thread of verbosity'. Kinnock retorted with Thatcher's taunt, 'he's frit'.[9] The House was noisy and excitable, with both leaders claiming victory in their dispute. Parliament met for a further three days, speeding through much of the programme outlined in October's Queen's Speech. The controversial Education (Schools) Bill and an Army Bill were rushed through in truncated form, with the Asylum Bill being the only significant casualty, to be reintroduced in the autumn.[10]

On Saturday 14 March the Conservative campaign was effectively opened at the Party's Central Council meeting in Torquay. Major outlined what he wanted to become the core themes of the campaign: the battle against inflation, Britain's place in the world, where he felt he had a strong record to boast, and preservation of existing constitutional arrangements, especially the union with Scotland. The Conservatives, he reminded the audience, uniquely blended a commitment to freedom and choice with care and welfare. He had some good lines, notably that PR stood for Paddy [Ashdown's] Roundabout, but 'we won't be joining him for the ride'. There was also homespun Major. 'I want to bring into being a different kind of country, to bury for ever old divisions in Britain between North and South, blue-collar and white-collar, polytechnic and university. They're old-style, old hat.' But he squandered some of his best lines, notably about a fourth Trident nuclear submarine: 'So let's hear it from Labour. Will you, won't you, will you, won't you build the boat?'[11]

His peroration – 'I want Britain to be seen as the best – not only in our eyes, but in the eyes of others. First and first again – a world leader – that is where I want us to be, and to stay. And that is where Britain will stay – under the next Conservative Government' – was well written, but his delivery seemed to lack some passion and self-belief.[12]

Major's election speeches were written by Nick True and Ronnie Millar, the latter brought back into the team after his success at the Party Conference the previous autumn. They would sit at a desk together in the bowels of Number Ten, sparking each other off while writing nine main speeches and a host of lesser offerings.[13] As a speech-writing team, they were formidable. Major had total trust in them; in True for his Conservative instincts and grasp of policy; and in Millar because, as he said: 'Ronnie can turn a mundane sentence into a catchy one, by turning it around, re-shaping it. Ronnie doesn't write on a blank sheet of paper – Ronnie picks up a written piece of paper and recasts it. And at that he is a genius.'[14]

Otherwise Number Ten was a subdued place for the four weeks of the campaign; the official machine wound down in both Private and Press Office. For Number Ten's civil servants, constitutionally prevented from engaging in Party activity, the general election marked a period of comparative tranquillity. The concern, under Turnbull's and O'Donnell's watchful eyes, was to ensure that the official machine ticked over, with Major being distracted only by the most essential government business, as they themselves prepared for possible scenarios ahead, including the distinct likelihoods of a hung Parliament or outright Labour victory. The Majors did not feel, however, that Number Ten was a particularly hospitable home for them during the campaign. To them it seemed almost that a Kinnock victory was being anticipated. For this, rather unfairly, Turnbull was blamed.

Major travelled from the conference at Torquay to Huntingdon, where on Sunday 15 March he gave his first 'Meet John Major' show, with Jeffrey Archer as warm-up artist. Major sat on a bar stool in Sawtry Village College, and took questions from a friendly, invited audience of his constituents, many of whom he knew personally, in front of television cameras. The initiative was not well received by the media, who felt the affair was overly stage-managed, and because expectations of 'Major's secret weapon' had been built higher than the reality could bear.[15] The presentation was variously compared to comedian Dave Allen, or to Val Doonican without guitar. Andrew Rawnsley could scarcely contain himself: here was the Tory leader displaying 'his famous small scale charisma' in 'an intimate chat' with 'a few hundred voters, a few hundred camera crews, satellite transmitters, policemen and sniffer dogs'.[16] After reading the press the next day, Major's team concluded that the formula was unlikely to succeed well in providing a platform for Major's most attractive qualities, and those who had always had reservations about 'Meet John Major' felt privately vindicated.

Major canvassed in Huntingdon on Monday morning – he was keen as always to show his personal commitment to the constituency – and was driven down to Central Office to take delivery of the official campaign bus in early afternoon.[17] This was the same armour-plated 'battlebus' that had served Thatcher in 1987, now resprayed in a lighter blue and with Major's name emblazoned on the side. Within, the bus boasted several Apricot computers, a paper and disk fax, a scrambler telephone (for secret calls) and other high-tech devices in what was billed as the mobile 'nerve centre' of Major's campaign. Initially it had been hoped to dispense with the bus, because of its Thatcher associations, but Major's insistence on campaigning and meeting voters throughout the country necessitated its reincarnation.[18]

Norma travelled with the bus throughout, working hard by her husband's side. The bus became not just a practical but also an emotional lifeline for the small team of just seven, including Jonathan Hill and Norman Fowler, present throughout as senior adviser and minder for Major. Debbie de Satge, one of the Political Office secretaries, described the atmosphere:

Everyone was tired, everyone was working at full stretch and was uptight and tense. It would have taken very little to have sparked off an explosion. But in fact it was wonderful, because people really did not lose their tempers. There were no cross words and the Prime Minister, despite the anxieties and getting so little sleep, steadied everyone.[19]

Tuesday 17 March saw Major chairing the opening press conference at Central Office (of the nineteen held there, he attended all but two).[20] Major's day varied little throughout the next three weeks. He would stay in Downing Street during the week, waking soon after 6 a.m. Any government business would be despatched in the flat with Turnbull, Wall and O'Donnell by 7 a.m.[21] At 7.30 a.m. came the morning briefing at Central Office with a large cast, too large, of ministers, advisers and Party officials, preparing Major and other ministers to appear in the press conference at 8.30. Afterwards Major's closest advisers met for a post mortem, to settle any big issues on the campaign and to confirm the plans for future press conferences (which only half the time followed the precise battle plan agreed between Central Office and ministers). Major then set off for his day's tour, and Patten, after chairing a large coordination meeting, would fly by helicopter to Bath to fight what appeared an increasingly forlorn struggle for his own constituency. Major would return to London late in the evening, usually too tired for the planned late-night round-up meeting at Downing Street.[22]

The main concern that first Tuesday was the response to John Smith's Shadow budget the day before; in a televised debate that evening, Smith was felt to have outclassed Lamont. Though Lamont had ordered an immediate refutation of the Shadow budget, it was not ready until Friday. Lamont had to take the blame in campaign meetings, but his supporters say that the delay was caused by an aide who felt that the first figures might have been inaccurate. In the vacuum, Labour won the propaganda war in the first full week.[23] Lamont came to be regarded by Number Ten during the campaign as not strong on television, and after the Monday broadcast was kept away from the limelight. Major's 1990 leadership rivals, Heseltine and Hurd, proved the Tories' star television performers, with Patten, Clarke and Mellor as first reserves.

Education was the other main story that Tuesday. The Party decided to launch a one-off mini-manifesto, *Better Schools Better Standards*, partly to reflect Major's own priority for education, but also to prevent the main manifesto being launched on the same day as, and possibly upstaged by, Smith's Shadow budget.[24]

Wednesday 18 March was manifesto launch day. Entitled *The Best Future For Britain*, it was, as we have seen, the product of careful management of ministers, and the Policy Unit's heroic attempts to extract Majorism out of its unwilling progenitor. The leader in the *Independent* summed up the majority reaction: 'Margaret Thatcher's third-term manifesto, *The Next Move Forward*, was a revolutionary statement of intent. *The Best Future For Britain* is, for all its verbal flourishes, a consolidating document.'[25]

The manifesto sported a smiling John Major on the cover, in recognition that he was the Party's strongest electoral asset. Major was uncomfortable at the choice, worried lest it smacked of a personality cult.[26] That emotion was magnified by the Schlesinger Party political broadcast, *The Journey*, screened that evening, which showed Major retracing his early footsteps in Brixton. Patten later said that Major's attitude to the film was the only time he had known his behaviour to suggest poor grace.[27] Major put it stronger himself: 'I hated it. I didn't want to do it, it was wished upon me. Nothing against John Schlesinger at all ... but I didn't feel comfortable doing it.'[28]

The broadcast certainly raised Major's profile, as did a near riot the following day in Bolton, where Major was jostled by rowdy elements alleged by his team to be Labour supporters. The walkabout was cut short as the party retreated under heavy police escort back to the battlebus, which then received the first direct hits from eggs. Major was not intimidated. Both he and Norma had clearly enjoyed the experience: 'We found it rather exhilarating,' he later said.[29] Described as 'the roughest scenes' of the entire campaign,[30] it provided the opportunity for Major to say, 'What we saw in Bolton was the ugly, intolerant face of the Labour party – a mob, obscene gestures, ugly chants and a return of the political flying picket. If that is what we are fighting against in this election, I will relish the fight.'[31] *The Times* reported that Major was energised by the experience, and that 'top Tories' relished the new bite it emboldened him to inject into the campaign.[32]

New bite was certainly in evidence when he gave his first campaign 'rally' speech, using a circular theatre set inspired by Andrew Lloyd Webber, one of the Tory celebrities recruited for the duration. Major's speech contained his most memorable passage from the campaign, parodying Neil Kinnock's warning in the 1983 election, 'I warn you not to be old ...' Turning the tables, Major said that, were Labour to win:

I warn you not to be qualified. I warn you not to be successful. I warn you not to buy shares. I warn you not to be self-employed. I warn you not to accept promotion. I warn you not to save. I warn you not to buy a pension. I warn you not to own a home.

George Jones wrote in the *Daily Telegraph*, in the event prematurely, 'The Major campaign had at last come alive.' The 'air of relief tinged with excitement'[33] that Jones detected that evening was soon to disappear with the next batch of polls. 'The opinion polls were constant low points,' Major later recalled. 'Every Saturday lunchtime to 4 o'clock you knew you'd get a batch and you knew that the whole of Sunday's and Monday's headlines would be dominated not by anything you did but by those artificial opinion polls.'[34]

The headlines that Sunday after the first full week were not encouraging. The general verdict, in the words of the *Sunday Times*, was 'Round One to Labour'.[35] Thatcher acolytes were also warming to a new comparison: 'For the first time since the political assassination of Margaret Thatcher the Tories realise what it is like to be without her imperious will and her fierce determination to win,' wrote Paul Johnson.[36]

The second full week of the campaign saw familiar patterns: morning press conferences, regional tours to Yorkshire, Scotland, Wales and the Northeast, a 'Meet John Major' in Wales, and rallies in London and Sheffield. The week opened with the Candidates' Conference in London on Sunday, with a carefully planned platform speech from Thatcher received rapturously by the audience. Major went out of his way to praise 'Margaret's legacy', before giving what Patrick Wintour described as a 'passionate and angry speech littered with vocabulary uncharacteristic of him'.[37] He inveighed against 'the politics of the socialist stone age, the politics of envy – economic illiteracy with a dash of calculated malice'. Charles Moore, suppressing a wry smile at the sight of Major and Patten praising Thatcher's achievements, said that only at this event had the Conservative campaign begun in earnest.[38] Major did indeed speak persuasively, but he had still to find his voice.

During the following week, however, Major was to discover both his voice, and a mode of communication. Typically for Major, both developments came when he was on the back foot, reacting to attacks. On Tuesday evening his team flew to Edinburgh, on the evening of a Labour Party political broadcast. Two portraits were offered, based on real examples, of children's treatment for a blocked ear canal, one under the NHS, where the child had to contend with repeated delays, the other private, where the child received immediate treatment. The broadcast was intended to launch Labour's strongest theme, the future of the NHS, on which they had been waging a war for many months. But it quickly degenerated into a slanging match, to be known as 'The War of Jennifer's Ear', after a child in the broadcast.[39]

Major had just completed an 'ill-tempered' interview from a Scottish studio with Jeremy Paxman for *Newsnight* when he was doorstepped about his reaction to Labour's broadcast. With no briefing, he was at a loss, and all next day debate about the broadcast followed him on his Scottish trail, with Labour marginally winning the argument.

Major was irritated and unsettled by the hubbub as he prepared for his speech that evening. But out of this background noise came an emotionally charged and powerful performance, reducing many in the audience of loyalists to tears as he approached the peroration: 'Let us stand together. Stand for what we believe ... Proud of Scotland, yes. And proud of the Union too. Let us go out from this hall and tell the world.' Because he was moved by the theme, he spoke with whole-hearted passion for the first time in the campaign.[40]

At the end of the week he found the means of communicating for which he had been searching, and for which 'Meet John Major' proved such an inadequate substitute. Against most advice, and against a background of continued adverse polls and stories in the press about growing nervousness in the Party at his conduct of the campaign,[41] he went to speak in Graham Bright's constituency in Luton armed with packing case and loudhailer. The packing case was to be his soapbox, from which he would harangue or charm his audience. He had made his decision the day before when travelling back from Cardiff, where he felt yet again frustration at his failure to get through to electors in the street. He later explained his thinking:

I learned my politics standing on a soapbox in Brixton. I feel at home. I don't like speaking to an audience on a platform, the audience seated down there at a distance ... there is no contact, no humanity, no relationship. So I was looking to get on the soapbox all the time. People kept saying 'no, you mustn't do it, too dangerous, won't work, not prime ministerial'. Eventually, events pushed us in that direction and I just did it.[42]

He was right: it was viewed as un-prime ministerial. The Socialist Workers' Party had a bigger loudspeaker and drowned out Major, who was forced to beat a retreat. The Sunday papers contained reports of Thatcher saying the campaign lacked 'oomph', and right-wingers complaining about Major's ineffectiveness as a leader in the election.[43] Faxes arrived at Number Ten from former Thatcher aides calling for the old guard to advise on strategy or risk losing the election.[44] But Major himself had been rejuvenated by the Luton experience. On that soapbox, surrounded by the shouting and confusion, he felt uniquely himself and in command of his destiny.

In Search of the Crown: 29 March–8 April

Major spent Sunday 29 March trying to relax and enjoy himself at Chequers. It was his forty-ninth birthday. The Chequers staff, sensing that it might be his last visit as Prime Minister, were especially attentive; the chef had baked a cake, thoughtfully adorned with blue candles. A second birthday cake followed later that day after the Majors arrived at Central Office for a party.

The bonhomie masked divisions, evident before the election, between Number Ten and Central Office that had grown over the campaign, with tension and tiredness exacerbating any difficulties. There had clearly been

poorly managed areas, as Stephen Sherbourne found when he had to move
to Central Office from Number Ten to organise Major's media schedule.[45]
Errors were not helped by Patten's long absences at Bath each day. Losing
sides tend to bicker, and a growing minority in Central Office expressed in
private the belief that the Party would, indeed, lose. Major did his best to
smooth over the differences, which had also grown over strategic direction.
He lost the argument, especially in the last ten days, of fighting the campaign
on his favoured themes of opportunity, choice and the constitution, the
government's record, not least on inflation, and plans for the future. Central
Office advisers, principally Maurice Saatchi, largely succeeded in making the
Party adopt a negative stance – to which Major himself was not immune –
especially on Labour's tax plans. The biggest dispute, which continued after
the election, concerned the importance of tax and the budget in determining
the election result. Lamont, as Chancellor, believed that the budget and
campaigning on tax had won it, but others regarded Major's personal appeal
as more significant.[46]

On Monday and Tuesday of week three, good and bad news in the press
vied with each other. Major received credit for his line 'Nightmare on Kinnock
Street', which came in a hard-hitting speech against Labour, adjudged by
Philip Webster of *The Times* his most assured of the campaign so far;[47] but
reports of Tory divisions and poor morale rumbled on. The news on Tuesday
evening, 31 March, with just over a week left until polling day, was uniformly
bad. The next day's polls showed the Labour lead over the Conservatives
lengthening to between 4 and 7 per cent. Major at the Wednesday morning
press conference acknowledged for the first time that the Conservatives
might not win the election outright, with the rise of Liberal Democrat
support as shown by opinion polls chipping away at the Tory vote.[48] Later,
on 1 April, standing on his soapbox – now a regular feature – Major attacked
the Liberal Democrats at Bristol as 'Mr Kinnock's Trojan horse with yellow
posters'.

Major returned from his travels that Wednesday evening to find his team
in gloomy mood, even though advance word of the next set of polls was less
discouraging. Patten, himself under the shadow of a local newspaper poll
pointing to defeat in Bath,[49] came to the flat in Number Ten to join Major,
drinking whisky late into the evening.[50] Next door at Number Eleven, Lamont
and some of his close staff had a gloomy supper together, convinced the
Party would lose, and discussing how quickly he would have to leave the
building after polling day.[51]

Kinnock spent the Wednesday evening in more ebullient form. The polls
had provided an excellent backdrop for a Labour campaign rally at Sheffield,
planned as Britain's biggest political assembly since the war, subsequently to
be mythologised as a disaster. Kinnock acknowledged wild applause with
cheerful cries of 'We're all right!' His exuberance, which he later bitterly
regretted, damaged the statesmanlike – even staid – image he had worked
hard to build up, and compounded a perception of the rally as vulgar,

premature triumphalism.[52] The reaction to 'Red Wednesday', and the attendant fall on the stock market, among Tory waverers led to a recovery in their determination. Strategists felt that the next two days were among the best of the campaign.

The Sunday papers on the final weekend nevertheless made depressing reading for Major. Andrew Neil wrote that the decision to focus on Major had been a mistake for the Tories, as his diminished popularity rating showed. The *Sunday Times*, like many other newspapers, thought a Labour victory or a hung Parliament the likely result.[53] Several senior columnists, including Peter Jenkins, had also begun to question whether Major could win. Flattering profiles of Heseltine appeared in several newspapers during the week, suggesting that the Tories might have been in a stronger position had the Environment Secretary been the leader.[54] The Thatcherite right, meanwhile, were irritated to hear Major say on BBC1's *On The Record* that the poll tax 'went wrong in practice', which was the closest a minister had come to making an apology, according to Michael White.[55]

Contrition was far from Major's mind when that afternoon he delivered his speech at the traditional final weekend campaign rally at Wembley. 'Wake up my fellow countrymen, wake up before it is too late,' he cried, warning of the dangers of Labour's plans for devolution and a federal Europe. His spirits were boosted by increasingly firm Central Office predictions of a majority between fifteen and thirty-five.

Major had warmed to the threat to the constitution as a core election subject, especially preservation of the union with Scotland, about which he had spoken in Edinburgh two weeks before, and about which he had insisted on speaking at the press conference on Saturday 4 April, judged by Robin Day his best and most fluent performance of the campaign.[56] Central Office, however, had been briefing the media not to take the subject too seriously, but to focus instead on the 'main issue' as identified by Saatchi & Saatchi, namely Labour's tax plans.[57]

Major exploded when he found out what had been going on, and against Central Office advice, shifted the focus of the final press conference back to the constitution, outlining the four principal threats faced from Labour and Liberal Democrat proposal: breach of the union with Scotland; an unwanted layer of regional government; a federal Europe; and proportional representation. With the polls pointing firmly towards the likelihood of a hung Parliament, and hence the Liberal Democrats holding the balance of power, he stressed that he would make no deals with Ashdown, and warned against the dangers of electoral reform as the price for Liberal Democratic support for a Labour administration. In the circumstances, it was a brave line to take.

Major had shown a different form of bravery with his insistence on mixing with crowds, in contrast to Kinnock, who was neither an IRA target nor the subject of such venom on the streets. At Southampton that Monday Major received his hardest direct hit from an egg, struck with such force on his cheekbone that he was nearly knocked over; for a few seconds he thought it might have been a bullet.[58]

Tuesday saw the final Conservative rally, again at Wembley, inserted into the programme only six days before.[59] Major again delivered his set-piece speech strongly: 'I want a Britain that offers dignity and security to older people. I want a Britain where there is a helping hand for those who need it. Where people can get a hand up, not just a hand out. A country that is fair and free from prejudice, a classless society at ease with itself' – vintage Major sentiments.[60] But the timing was muffed so that it missed BBC1's peak audience *Nine O'Clock News*. That evening the final Party political broadcast was screened, Major talking solo to camera, no razzmatazz, his Gulf War television broadcast the inspiration. It was judged to be the best broadcast of the campaign.[61]

That same evening, at a meeting in the flat at Number Ten, Major learned that Party polls had come to the inescapable conclusion that Patten would lose Bath. Deeply vexed at the prospect of losing his closest lieutenant, he turned to Patten, willing him to deny it: 'Chris, is that right?' To which Patten responded, 'Absolutely, Prime Minister.'[62]

Major devoted most of the final day before the election to interviews for the media. A last, brief trip in the battlebus took Major to south London marginal constituencies. He arrived back in Downing Street at 8 p.m. for what might have been his last visit as Prime Minister. As civil service procedures dictated, Norma had packed away most of their personal belongings in the flat, either having taken them to Huntingdon, or left them in boxes stacked neatly in the hall. Should they have lost, their possessions would have to have been cleared out of Number Ten by midday on Friday to make way for the Kinnocks. Their car was waiting outside to take them to Huntingdon, but Major lingered on his way down from the flat to the front door, his head full of thoughts and emotion. Eventually, by 10 p.m., he was prevailed upon to leave for the journey back to his constituency, where he would learn his fate.

Polling Day: 9 April

Alistair McAlpine wrote that 'The heroes of the campaign were Sir David English [*Mail*], Sir Nicholas Lloyd [*Daily Express*], Kelvin MacKenzie [*Sun*] and the other editors of the grander Tory press', who, he believed, tipped the scales in favour of the Tories.[63] Certainly the *Sun*'s front page headline on 9 April, 'If Kinnock wins today will the last person to leave Britain please turn out the lights', with a vulgar montage of the Labour leader inside a light bulb, helped the Conservatives' cause. At the reflective end of the market, Philip Stephens wrote in the *Financial Times* that 'In personal terms Mr Major has fought a brave election. He has been as energetic and determined as could be expected of any leader.' If Major were to lose the election that day, Stephens believed it would be because he had an 'impossible task' in freeing himself of his legacy.[64] Major's attention was taken, however, less by the praise than by the paper's tentative endorsement of Labour, which made him angry.[65]

Major spent election day, which was warm and sunny, touring his constituency. As was their custom, he and Norma split the committee rooms and polling booths, with each of them covering roughly half. Major himself was accompanied in the morning by Archer, who thought Major was convinced that he would win.[66] Peter Brown, Major's agent, thought him abnormally confident also, very relaxed and buoyant all day.[67] Major did indeed discount the final polls, which claimed that the parties were neck-and-neck, believing the Conservatives had a lead sufficient for an overall majority.[68]

At 8 p.m. he was driven back to The Finings, to bath and change. Just before the polls closed at 10 p.m., the phone rang and Major was told that the exit polls put the Party slightly in the lead, ITN predicting the Tories would win 303 seats to Labour's 298. Major believed this an underestimate, and thought that the Party might win 317, nine short of the 326 the Party needed for a secure majority. 'For an hour or so', he recalls, 'I was wondering about minority government, Ulster Unionists, and so on.'[69] Jonathan Hill, Sarah Hogg and Tim Collins, who had handled the press on the battlebus, all came to The Finings to watch the results unfold on television. Hogg had a more doleful reason: she carried a black box with confidential briefings for Major prepared by the Number Ten Private Office for every eventuality from victory through hung Parliament to loss. She had kept the documents from Major during the campaign for fear of disheartening him. Only that evening did she show him, but after a five-minute glance he passed the documents back, apparently amused.[70]

Shortly afterwards, at 11.23 p.m., David Amess's result at Basildon appeared on the television screen. Major leaped to his feet, went over to Norma and said, 'You may not know it, but that's it, we have won.'[71] His joy and release were mixed with sorrow a short while later as he watched the pictures of Patten at his unsuccessful count at Bath.[72]

Peter Brown telephoned from the Huntingdon count at about 2.30 a.m. to say that their local declaration was approaching. Brown recalls an unusually dull count in the soulless sports centre. Major's arrival enlivened the atmosphere, above all when another of the candidates, 'Lord Buckethead', introduced himself. 'I'm pleased to meet you. I've never met a lord like you before,' Major responded.[73] Elated already by the picture emerging nationally of a Labour swing smaller than any poll had predicted, his spirits rose still further when it transpired that he had held Huntingdon by a margin of over 35,000; Brown thought him 'stunned by the size of his majority'.[74]

Major had always put great store by his personal standing in his constituency. During the campaign he had felt guilty that he was unable to be more in evidence on the streets after the first 'Meet John Major' on the opening Sunday. But as he was in Huntingdon each weekend, his constituency activists ensured that the local, and in the main weekly, press had a new set of photographs and stories for each issue. The Labour candidate Hugh

Seckleman detected a high level of affection for his adversary and only very rarely encountered personal criticism. The 1992 campaign marked the high point of Major's personal standing in the constituency, with the additional pride at having the sitting Prime Minister as its member.[75] Major's majority proved to be the biggest in the country – helped by the constituency, with 93,000 voters, being significantly over-sized.

Major's relief at his personal result faded after his acceptance speech. Irritated at himself for forgetting to thank Norma, he appeared to close observers, for the first time in the four weeks, emotionally drained.[76] At 3.30 a.m., Jonathan Hill bustled him into the Prime Minister's Daimler for the journey back to London for the traditional celebratory party at Central Office. The convoy sped along the largely empty roads; in the back seat of the first car sat Major and Norma. He finds it difficult to recall exactly what they said to each other on that journey south, but remembers asking her if she thought she could bear another five years. She replied that she thought she could. Major then began to reflect on what he might want to achieve with his new lease of life, and they talked through what victory would mean for their children.[77]

Shortly after 5 a.m., the convoy entered Smith Square and drew up at Central Office. After the obligatory glass of champagne, handshakes and thanks, Major and Norma returned to Downing Street as dawn was breaking. Up in the flat, in an unreal atmosphere, they had further drinks with Sarah Hogg, Hill and Patten. Major then persuaded his Party Chairman to come outside and face the lights and cameras, standing side by side to acknowledge that victory was indeed theirs.

The Reckoning

The campaign was one of the longest this century. Yet it probably did little to change the overall result. Labour gained ground over the second weekend (28–9 March), but lost it again shortly after. The last two days saw a detectable late swing to the Conservatives. Academic opinion has focused on four influential factors to explain the result: the Conservative-inclined 'don't knows' and soft Liberal Democrats returning to vote for the Tories, fearful of a Labour victory; the tabloid press, especially the *Sun*, influencing some of the more impressionable with their increasingly bold offensive against taxes, immigration and Kinnock; some voters being alarmed at the prospect of tax increases under Labour, as the Near Term Campaign and aggressive advertising had suggested since the start of the year; and finally, the relative leaders' images may have been a significant influence. Despite Major's personal popularity declining, his clear line on the Union and the constitution contrasted with Kinnock's equivocations over pacts and proportional representation.

As for manifestos, despite the blood spilled over preparing *The Best Future*

For Britain, the principal academic study of the election campaign by Butler and Kavanagh concluded that they had 'rarely made less impact'.[78] Also surprising was how the election concentrated on such a narrow range of themes, tax and spending, the NHS and constitutional change, all but ignoring defence and foreign policy, Europe, the environment, the poll tax and its replacement, race and trade unions. The Tories – in stark contrast to 1997 – succeeded in ensuring the agenda of the campaign was mostly fought on ground chosen by them.[79]

The polls gave a false impression of the state of opinion throughout the campaign, but probably gave a broadly correct picture of the movement of Party support. Despite his obsessive interest, Major did not allow himself to be depressed by the published polls, in part because the regular projections from Central Office based on their own soundings showed the Party's prospects always as much better than polls published in the press.[80] The Conservatives were indeed probably 2–4 per cent ahead throughout, with a mid-campaign peak for Labour bringing them to level pegging or slightly ahead, before falling away at the time of, but probably only partly caused by, the Sheffield rally.

The final result, declared late on Friday 10 April, gave the Conservatives 336 seats to Labour's 271, and the Liberal Democrats 20, earning the Tories an overall majority of 21. They secured the largest vote, over fourteen million voters, in British electoral history, though the electorate had increased by a quarter since the previous peak in 1951. All the same, the majority of only twenty-one was a poor reward for such a large lead over Labour. The electoral system operated against the Conservatives because of tactical voting; if the swing had been uniform across the country, they would have won a seventy-one-seat majority. The history of the next five years would have been very different had that been the case.

On the level of individual results, Major suffered doubly. Three of his most loyal and able supporters lost their seats. Patten's defeat took away Major's best troubleshooter, strategist and friend. It can best be compared to Thatcher's loss of Whitelaw in January 1988; neither Prime Minister ever found an adequate replacement. Francis Maude, another to lose, would have been promoted to Cabinet with a brief to oversee the Citizen's Charter. Finally, John Maples, also destined for high office, would have supplied a cutting edge the government often lacked after 1992.

But the election can also be seen as detrimental to Major through bringing in fifty-four fresh members, many of the more articulate of whom, like Iain Duncan-Smith, Alan Duncan and John Whittingdale, were Thatcherite and Eurosceptic. The impact of the exchange of 'Major's Friends' for 'Thatcher's Children' was not, however, to be fully appreciated for some months. Though a twenty-one-seat majority seemed an adequate cushion in the afterglow of victory – Churchill had led a successful government from 1951 to 1955 with an initial majority of four fewer – it was nevertheless the first time a Tory government had returned to power with a reduced majority since mass democracy came to Britain. Backbench critics, emboldened by the 1992 intake, were numerous among those Major was later to call 'the dispossessed and the never-possessed', the casualties of thirteen years in power.[81] In the 1980s hardcore rebels could be ignored; one (Nicholas Winterton) was abruptly dismissed by Tristan Garel-Jones – then a whip – with the words, 'I'm too busy to waste my time with a tosser like you', and an invitation to make himself scarce for the rest of the Parliament.[82] In the 1992 Parliament, the tossers – as Garel-Jones would call them – now had the whip hand.

In the short term, however, there was ample cause for celebration, not least for Major personally. Andrew Neil thought he 'emerged as his own man – and the man of the match', while his paper, the *Sunday Times*, said in its editorial: 'So John Major turned out to be Clark Kent after all ... Under John Major, Britain is in for an Iain Macleod government. The *Sunday Times* has waited a long time for this.'[83] The *Daily Telegraph* declared him 'the unquestioned hero of the hour'.[84] As to the tabloid headlines, the *Sun* opined, 'It's The Sun Wot Won It', and the *Daily Mail*, in a headline penned by editor David English, 'Nice Guys *Do* Finish First'.[85] Neither Major nor the editors – Neil, Hastings, MacKenzie and English – knew how brief the honeymoon from these quarters would prove, or how speedily their praise would turn to anger and contempt.

In defeat, Labour needed to regroup. Kinnock promptly resigned as leader, with an election for his successor to take place before the summer recess, saying Britain deserved better. Major bore no grudge, and they had a lunch *à deux* at Number Ten that July. They had had a wary relationship, but it was not without warmth or regard. 'I rather liked Neil Kinnock,' Major said, two years later.

I think he did more to organise and revolutionise the Labour Party than anyone else, and he did it when it was most difficult. If he gave me his word, I would trust him implicitly. I never had any reason, in the backstairs deals we did, and on the occasions we met, to doubt his integrity. I felt very sorry for him when he lost. I know how I would have felt in his position.[86]

Kinnock, in return, found Major personable and trustworthy in their dealing. Their mutual interest in sport – Kinnock for rugby and Major for cricket – ensured they had no shortage of small talk. And despite the brutality of his own treatment at the hands of the Tory press, Kinnock felt some sympathy for Major when he faced what he regarded as the sneers of *his* snobbish persecutors.[87]

In victory, Major characteristically displayed no triumphalism. There were no culls, as had been predicted, at Central Office. Number Ten–Central Office tensions during the campaign were swiftly downplayed; 'It really wasn't at all bad,' said one party official.[88] In a way he was right: sparks always flew during elections, and 1987, with Tebbit Chairman, had seen far greater mistrust between Number Ten and Central Office.

It was victory, but at what price? Patten felt that 'the electorate didn't really want us to win. We won by default, but they didn't really think we deserved it. From the moment we won, the press and people at large were looking for things to criticise us for: we gave them plenty of opportunity to do just that.'[89]

Patten is surely right, especially when the issues on which the Conservatives campaigned to defeat Labour – lower taxes under the Tories and superior managerial competence, in particular over the economy – became so rapidly open to question. Major himself put it succinctly in 1997, when he reflected that a fifth term was to 'stretch the elastic of democracy too far'.

The Reshuffle

Only seconds after hearing the Basildon result on election night and knowing the Party had won, Major started to think about the make-up of the new Cabinet: 'My heart just sank a little. Reshuffles are painful business.'[90] After a brief sleep on Friday morning, 10 April, he turned to the reshuffle in earnest. He hated dismissing people against their will, so was relieved that several spaces became available without unpleasantness. King was keen to retire as Defence Secretary. Waddington knew he had not been a very effective Leader of the Lords, so was happy also to leave. Brooke left of his own free will, but would not have objected if he had been asked to stay.[91] The main sourness came over Baker. Major had not held a high opinion of his administration of the Home Office; half-heartedly, he was offered the Welsh Office, which he declined. He left to write his memoirs, and to become a tribune of the Eurosceptics, to the resentment of Number Ten.

Two further spaces were created by increasing the number in Cabinet by one and by Patten's defeat. Major tried desperately hard to persuade Patten to stay on, either with a seat in the Lords, or by the offer of creating a by-election; Nicholas Scott's seat in Chelsea was mentioned. Patten spoke to Tony Garrett, the candidate supremo in Central Office, who put his chances of winning at no more than 50–50. Patten did not want his wife Lavender and his family involved in another close election, especially as, remembering the case of Patrick Gordon Walker in 1965, there was no guarantee of success. The prospect of elevation to the Lords, meanwhile, with a vague promise of succeeding Hurd as Foreign Secretary at some future point, Patten thought ill-advised and allowing friendship to overwhelm political judgement. The idea of becoming a hanger-on seemed anathema to him. These are his declared reasons.[92]

Hurt pride may also have played a part in his decision to quit the political scene. A life peerage in the House of Lords, too, would have been a one-way ticket for a man still with ample political ambition. So came about the governorship of Hong Kong in the run-up to the handover to China in 1997. Contrary to Cradock's advice,[93] Major had decided on his September 1991 trip to the colony to make the next Governor a political appointee.[94] Brooke had been offered the job in late 1991, but had declined, with David Owen another possible candidate, but it was decided to leave it to the patronage of the victorious Prime Minister after the general election.[95] It provided an admirable peg for Patten, though one that was to arouse considerable controversy, not least with Cradock. Garel-Jones fought a rearguard action to persuade Patten to stay in London, arguing that he would not find Hong Kong a sufficient challenge. 'It's a big job, but not *that* big,' he told Patten.[96] Patten went to France to think it over, and when he came back he was determined to accept.

To fill the Cabinet vacancies, Major chose two women, both allies and one from each wing of the party. Stung by the criticism of the lack of women in his first Cabinet, he was pleased to end that anomaly by promoting Gillian Shephard to Employment, reprieved as a separate department for administrative as well as presentational reasons, and a somewhat reticent Virginia Bottomley to Health. Patrick Mayhew, who had long wanted to take on the Northern Ireland Office, was told by Major that he wanted to make Northern Ireland his top domestic priority.[97] Finally, John Patten from the left became Education Secretary and Michael Portillo from the right was promoted to Cabinet as Chief Secretary as a reward for his competence and loyalty as Minister for Local Government (to be replaced in that job by another rightwinger, John Redwood). Norman Fowler was appointed Patten's successor as Party Chairman. A trusted aide – proven most recently during the campaign – he was felt to be a steady and utterly reliable presence.

Major's decision which aroused most comment was leaving Lamont at the Treasury. Their relations had worsened during the campaign, Lamont believing that the budget and taxes were crucial issues that were receiving insufficient attention. His advisers also considered that Major had moved during the campaign from being uninterested to being irresponsible on tax, giving hostages to fortune through phrases like tax cuts 'year on year'. Major had doubts over Lamont's political views and his presentational ability. Some in the Cabinet believed that Major had had plans to replace Lamont with Patten, moving Lamont perhaps to the Home Office had Patten held Bath. The absence of another candidate for Chancellor who might not prove just as awkward, and the difficulties of where to place Lamont if he was moved, all weighed heavily in favour of keeping him at the Treasury, as did the argument that, having seen Britain through a very hard period economically, Lamont was entitled to preside over the upswing. The election, moreover, had just been fought with tax, and trust in the Conservatives' management of the economy, key issues; ousting his Chancellor under the circumstances would have appeared odd.

Three ministers who were thought not to have performed especially well received new jobs: Malcolm Rifkind was perhaps lucky to get Defence, William Waldegrave, who had failed to win the propaganda war on the NHS, went to the Office of Public Service and Science, not least to nurse the Citizen's Charter, and Peter Lilley, who was not at ease at Trade and Industry, moved to Social Security. The strong performers received promotion. Kenneth Clarke became Home Secretary; Michael Heseltine achieved his long-standing ambition of taking charge of the Department of Trade and Industry (DTI). Previous DTI Secretaries, notably Nicholas Ridley and Peter Lilley, had even doubted whether such a ministry should exist at all, but Heseltine saw it as a power base for his ideas on how to revitalise British industry. His first move was to restore the old title of 'President of the Board of Trade' for himself, which earned a certain amount of jest about 'Prezza Hezza'.[98] Michael Howard, thought to have performed well at Employment, particularly in pressing Labour over the costs to jobs of their minimum wage proposals, was elevated to Environment. John Wakeham became Leader of the Lords and Tony Newton Leader of the Commons. David Mellor, as expected, went to the new Department of National Heritage.

As with all reshuffles, Major kept largely his own counsel. The key figures were Richard Ryder, Andrew Turnbull and Robin Butler. For one normally open, reshuffles saw Major at his most secretive.[99] His changes were conservative, and judged as such by the public. But Major at last had his own team, and what appeared to be a safe majority of twenty-one, to build the Britain of his dreams.

TWENTY

Indian Summer:

April–August 1992

JOHN MAJOR WAS to enjoy the most tranquil working period of his six and a half years at Number Ten in the two months following the 1992 general election.[1] Socialism had been defeated, and once the immediate relief and exhaustion wore off, he felt upbeat and confident. The country, he argued, would benefit from a period of relative tranquillity from politicians. His first year and a half had been like a juggling act. But freed from the legacy of November 1990, he now had space and the opportunity for rest.[2]

With hindsight, a measure of both momentum and initiative were lost in those first weeks of post-election glow, but no one at the time was urging greater activity.

Riding on the Crest of a Wave

Major opened his first post-election Cabinet with the words, 'Well, here we are.'[3] Such banalities and sweet reveries – which he later regretted uttering – were rudely interrupted less than one week later by Mrs Thatcher, who gave an interview whipped up into a widely discussed article in the US journal *Newsweek*. No sooner had Major begun to luxuriate in having achieved his own mandate than she rushed in to remind him of his debt to her:

I don't accept the idea that all of a sudden Major is his own man. He has been prime minister for seventeen months and he inherited all these great achievements of the past 11½ years which have fundamentally changed Britain, ridding it of the debilitating, negative aspects of socialism . . . There isn't such a thing as Majorism . . . Thatcherism will live. It will live long after Thatcher has died, because we had the courage to restore the great principles and put them into practice.[4]

The article was all the more surprising as she had been – apart from the standard background noise of reported criticisms – publicly loyal during the election, and had campaigned herself in over thirty constituencies. Although not a fully considered piece, the text faithfully reflected her thinking. Alarmed by some of Major's Cabinet promotions, her concern was to warn against growth of spending and borrowing (with 'one nation' Tories like John Patten now in spending departments), against industrial intervention (with Heseltine at Trade) and any enlargement of the public sector. But she also wanted to fire a warning shot over the bows that her legacy was not to be ignored or dismissed in the new Parliament. The piece aroused much anger from Conservatives; it wounded and irritated Major.[5] Bernard Ingham and other allies went to see her and said quite vehemently that she had better stop such articles or she would lose all influence with her party.[6] Even they must have realised their mission, well-intended though it was, would prove forlorn. Ingham himself tried on at least one further occasion to advise her to keep quiet about Major.

The Queen's Speech, announcing the government's programme to last for eighteen months, was delivered on 6 May. Major had agreed to the inclusion of nearly half the manifesto commitments – too much, it transpired, as it left too little for later sessions – less to distract attention from the passage of the Maastricht Bill, than to show how busy the government's agenda was. With a small majority, the advice of the new team of business managers (Ryder, Newton and Wakeham) to put the controversial Bills in the first two sessions also made sense. The programme announced sixteen Bills, including the privatisation of coal, many of the rail services for franchise, a National Lottery, curbs on trade unions and an expansion of the Citizen's Charter, health, education and housing reforms, the Asylum Bill, as well as the ratification of the Maastricht Treaty.

In the debate following the Queen's Speech, Major produced the biggest surprise of the programme when he announced legislation to put the secret intelligence service (SIS or MI6) on a statutory basis, to make it more accountable, and he named the head as Sir Colin McColl. He promised to 'sweep away the cobwebs of secrecy which needlessly veil too much of government business', and said he had asked Waldegrave to identify areas of 'excessive secrecy'.[7] Within two weeks, responding to pressure from Peter Hennessy and other academics, as well as reflecting his inclinations, it was announced that details of Cabinet committees and *Questions of Procedure for Ministers* would be published for the first time.

The programme was busy, but not radical, with the exception of the rail and coal proposals. Peter Riddell thought his speech, with its talk of 'no barriers, no glass ceilings' to the progress of an individual to reach his potential, 'came as close as he ever does towards offering a vision'.[8]

Bills that the whips expected would be controversial were the reintroduced Asylum Bill, to exclude 'bogus' asylum seekers, the trade union Bill, requiring unions to give seven days' notice of strikes, to be preceded by postal ballots, and the Bill to implement Maastricht. Major maintained the no-nonsense line which he adopted in the election campaign: 'We will resist any pressure from Brussels to reimpose handicaps on our industry that we removed, one by one, in the 1980s.'[9] Resistance to the Bill was expected to come from 'a small core of Tory rebels', and hence the business managers hoped to push the Bill through before the summer recess, to enact it as quickly and painlessly as possible.[10]

The speech and debate were a defining moment in the premiership; never again would he have so much power and so much ability to establish his own agenda and tone. His tone was non-triumphalist and moderate. In almost his only piece of self-satisfaction, he observed that 'for the first time since 1826, a government has returned for a fourth successive term'. He radiated quiet confidence. His supporters on the benches behind him, believing that Labour, with Kinnock retiring, would be a lame force for some time, and that the Tories would be in power for many years to come, expected rather more swagger. Kinnock himself showed no bitterness, and his counterattack on the government's plans received little enthusiasm from the Labour benches.[11] With a half-point cut in interest rates earlier in the week, there were even hopes in some quarters that the recession, which failed to sink the Tories in the election, would gather momentum on its way out.

The spirit of high optimism was enhanced by the local election results on 7 May, the best for the Conservatives since 1977. The Party gained two hundred seats on the last time they were contested in 1988, while Labour lost over three hundred. The most notable result was Basildon, where the Conservatives managed a clean sweep, thereby taking control of the council. Michael Howard, the new Environment Secretary, spoke of a 'sea change in British politics'.[12]

At a European reception later in May Major was being spoken of as pre-eminent among European politicians: Mitterrand was ill, Kohl and Gonzalez looked likely to lose their forthcoming elections, the Italian Christian Democrats appeared in terminal decline.[13] Major's stock, in both Britain and the European Community, was never to be higher.

Chill Wind from Denmark

No one could have foreseen that Major's brief weeks on the crest of a wave would be ended by news of events in Denmark, and Mrs Thatcher.

A week after the Queen's Speech, and prompted by the Bill to ratify Maastricht, as well as by the Queen addressing the European Parliament at Strasbourg, which infuriated Eurosceptics, Thatcher delivered her most important speech since leaving office, setting out a vision for the future of Europe radically different from the government's planned Maastricht Bill. Drafted by Robin Harris, John O'Sullivan and Norman Stone,[14] it argued for a looser, multi-track Europe, based not on a centralised bureaucracy but on a market of competing individuals, companies and governments, with the power removed from the European Commission. The speech was delivered abroad (at The Hague), she later wrote, so that Major would be free to lead the Party and the country in his own way.[15]

Although the Maastricht Treaty had been signed by EC heads of government in December 1991, it needed to be ratified by member states. In the second-reading debate on 21 May, Major set out to reassure MPs that with the treaty 'for the first time we have begun to reverse the centralising trend', and that fears of a federal Europe were thus misplaced, especially as the timing and nature of EMU remained uncertain.[16] Major's personal stake in the treaty was immense. Believing that he had achieved as much as could possibly have been expected for British interests while preserving his party's unity, both he and Hurd, as well as the whips, worked hard behind the scenes to persuade their backbenchers to support the Bill. In the event, twenty-two Conservative MPs voted against in the biggest revolt over Europe since British entry into the European Community twenty years before. Some commentators saw the twenty-two opponents as but the tip of an iceberg; Philip Stephens wrote of 'a corrosive factionalism which would wreck the foundations of Major's government'.[17] Ryder had long predicted that the new Parliament would be much harder to manage, but few had heeded his warnings: most senior figures in the Party chose still to see the vote in the debate as a protest by malcontents, best soon forgotten.[18]

Enter the Danes. Each of the twelve EC countries had to agree the treaty before it could take effect. Some, like Denmark and Ireland, were obliged by their constitutions to throw the issue open to their electorates to decide in a referendum. The Danish government told the British that the answer would be a secure 'yes', and that if they had not been confident, they would not have been the first country to put it to the popular mandate.[19] The Foreign Office readily endorsed this view. Several British sources, including the *Spectator*, cast doubt on whether they were right, but were ignored.[20]

News of the wafer-thin Danish result – the treaty was rejected by only 48,000 votes – percolated into Downing Street on the evening of 2 June. Major had three quick thoughts: first, he quite admired the independent spirit of the Danish people, voting against their government's wishes; second, it might mean Denmark being sidelined by the rest of the EC; third, but only fleetingly, it might be used by his own Eurosceptics as a pretext for renegotiation of the treaty or raising again the question, aired by Thatcher before the election, of a referendum. But as the treaty had received the overwhelming endorsement of Parliament the previous December, he did not believe at first such a line would get anywhere.[21] The realisation that it might dawned only slowly on Major as the night wore on; the press quickly rumbled that Number Ten had been caught 'on the hop' by the result.[22] Later, as the options were considered, a Downing Street adviser tentatively suggested that the Danish vote might open a real, constructive debate on Europe and thus be a blessing in disguise. Major responded with a rare Churchillism: 'If it is a blessing in disguise, it is very well disguised.'[23]

Officials worked throughout the night on the implications of the news. Major telephoned Hurd first thing in the morning, before Hurd appeared on the *Today* programme, and advised him, 'Don't give an actual date when we are going to introduce the Maastricht Bill, but stress of course that the policy remains unchanged.'[24] Next door, in Number Eleven, the news was greeted differently; Lamont told an adviser at morning prayers, 'It's the best result ever.' Was it better even than the election result? he was asked. 'Much better!' came the reply.[25] Major and others in his camp express incredulity that he held these views: 'If that was his opinion, he kept very quiet about it at the time.'

Lamont was one of several Cabinet ministers – the others were Howard, Lilley and newcomer Portillo – who believed that Major should seize the opportunity to reject a treaty they had never liked, and substitute it with a looser agreement with the EC which they believed would be much more acceptable to the Party as well as to the country.[26] Major convened an emergency meeting that morning with Hurd and Ryder. The latter's advice was unequivocal: the Bill, then in its committee stages, would have to be delayed, or the Party would be defeated. Hurd agreed strongly, provoking a rare row with John Kerr, the British EC Representative, who thought it should continue through the House. Major, seeing no practical alternative, took his Chief Whip's advice, and did not even call a Cabinet meeting as the decision was so clear cut.[27] He told the House in a statement that afternoon that while the committee stage of the Maastricht Bill would be temporarily suspended, he had no intention of abandoning the treaty, as the House had already three times endorsed the policy. Nor would he consider holding a referendum in Britain: 'I am not in favour of a referendum in a Parliamentary democracy, and I do not propose to put one before the British people.'[28]

Major's statement did not go down at all well with the Party. One sceptic later said, 'It was the very moment we realised that Major was not one of us.'[29] FCO officials were shocked as they sat watching the change that had come over the House. One of them, Michael Jay, later recalled:

The day after Major had returned from Maastricht, there was tremendous roaring and cheering and waving of order papers from the Tories who were fully behind the PM. But his statement after the Danish referendum was greeted completely differently. Behind him there were rows of sullen faces. He had virtually no support. Suddenly, we had the sense that whatever goodwill and pro-European feeling there had once been, was gone, and that the atmosphere from then on was going to be ugly.[30]

Several ministers below Cabinet rank too were secretly, and some increasingly openly, contemptuous of the Maastricht Treaty, but were bound by convention to vote with the government. At a meeting of the No Turning Back group strong opinions were voiced against continuing with the treaty, and Portillo was asked to convey the message to Number Ten, where predictably it was badly received.[31] On 3 and 4 June nearly one hundred backbenchers – in the biggest display yet of Eurosceptic feeling – signed an Early Day Motion calling for a 'fresh start' for the government's European policy, before the whips cracked down.[32] Thatcher was active behind the scenes, emboldening the waverers and agreeing to become head of a new group pressing for a referendum in Britain.[33] At Cabinet on 4 June, Douglas Hogg (in Hurd's absence in Oslo trying to pick up the pieces with European Foreign

Ministers) said, 'My FCO brief says we must forge ahead immediately with the Bill. I say that would be quite mad – the horses have broken out of the stable and are careening all over the field.'[34] Major found himself in a rut, with increasing divisions among backbenchers and ministers.

After Hurd returned from Oslo he related that Ellemann-Jensen, the Danish Foreign Minister, said the Danish government would get the treaty through another referendum, and he begged to be given 'time and allies with strong nerves'.[35] But when Mitterrand decided that day to call a referendum in France, to help him handle his domestic opposition, Major was forced to admit that the treaty might not succeed, especially if the Irish or French referendums went against. The Commons debate on the treaty, he announced, would not now take place before the autumn, at the earliest.[36]

What had gone wrong, and why had the number prepared to defy the government quadrupled since the second-reading vote two weeks before? The answer is that the Danish referendum provided merely the catalyst for many Tory MPs, perhaps two-thirds of backbenchers, and a half in the government, to be more open about their opposition to the Maastricht Treaty. Two broad historical movements occurring in conjunction explain the upsurge in Euroscepticism in the Party. With free trade achieved, the nature of the European project had been changing as the 1980s wore on. Conservatives saw the next stages – social policy, monetary union and more 'federal' political institutions – as, in Thatcher's words in 1988, 'socialism by the back Delors' and cooled accordingly; Labour, meanwhile, became more enthusiastic, opening the door for a clear Party difference on an increasingly popular cause. The Tory change had been masked by the need for Party unity, and respect for Major as new leader after November 1990, but now bolstered by the influx of the new MPs in 1992, the balance within the Party had tilted heavily towards scepticism.[37]

Major's refusal to countenance abandonment, or to accept a referendum (which he though he might lose) was due to more than proprietorial feelings towards a treaty of which he was proud. He had negotiated in good faith with European leaders, especially Lubbers and Kohl, and with Britain's six-month presidency of the EC beginning in July, he wanted to be, and be seen to be, a trustworthy and good European, rather than backsliding in the face of – what appeared to him then to be – fickle parliamentary pressure. Moreover, his three most weighty Cabinet ministers – Heseltine, Hurd and Clarke – were all convinced that they should fight to save the Maastricht Treaty once the heat died down rather than risk a renegotiation. All three, in public or in private, admit that they underestimated the depth and breadth of feeling in the parliamentary party about the treaty.[38]

In between them and the three Eurosceptics in Cabinet were seventeen ministers, and the balance of opinion, while generally Europhile, was in favour of delaying, believing there would be less objection if the Bill was taken later.[39] Newton, as Leader of the House, was also cautious and advised against 'making any precipitate decisions to carry on with the Bill'. Newton also reported pressure for an extra Commons debate prior to the Bill's committee stage, and recommended conceding this. In doing so, he was aware that such a course had its risks, and required a government effort to calm parliamentary opinion.[40]

Given that Major would clearly not accede to renegotiation, or a referendum, delay was the preferred outcome for the Eurosceptics in the Cabinet. This was the first occasion when the presence of Chris Patten might have made a difference on a key issue; a convinced European, Patten believed strongly in pressing ahead with the Bill before the summer recess, before opposition had time to harden. Failure to do so he regarded as a 'major mistake'.[41]

Major's reaction to the Danish referendum is one of the turning points of his premiership. He had the authority, domestically and in Europe, to impose his will. Many in his parliamentary party, possibly a majority, though not in Cabinet, favoured renegotiation along other lines. But he never considered this: 'Before I went to Maastricht, I set out my objectives to Parliament and got their approval. At the conference, I threatened to wreck the negotiations unless they gave in on the opt-outs. After the conference I achieved a huge parliamentary majority on my return on the treaty. No international partner would ever have believed in Britain's word again if, having obtained concessions and secured agreement, we had then tried to reopen negotiations.' A meeting in Central Office the morning after the Danish referendum, with Fowler and Lansley in attendance, had recommended renegotiation, not that Central Office (which was becoming steadily more Eurosceptic) was heeded on such matters.[42] While any attempt to loosen Maastricht by a putative renegotiation would probably have invited bids for him to go further and further, a referendum might have been different. Had Major agreed to a referendum at this stage to achieve a popular mandate (or not) for Maastricht, many of the turmoils of the years that followed might have been avoided, and his premiership would have turned out very differently. But Major believed he must honour commitments, and was too proud and perhaps stubborn to abandon the treaty which ultimately lost him his premiership.

No Escape from the ERM

Questioning the wisdom of Britain's membership of the ERM, though increasingly not the DM2.95 parity, had been a minority pursuit since entry in October 1990. The record of membership was mixed; in its favour, interest rates had fallen from 15 to 10 per cent, and inflation from 11 to 4 per cent. But from early June 1992, fuelled by the machinations after the Danish referendum, the ERM came to be seen increasingly as a scapegoat for interest rates regarded, with business confidence and industrial output still depressed, as still far too high.[43] Thatcher was one of several prominent figures calling for interest rates to be reduced, even if it risked a devaluation of the pound within the ERM.[44] Keynes's *Economic Consequences of Mr. Churchill* (1925) was republished as a pointed critique of high fixed exchange rates.[45]

Sarah Hogg became extremely concerned. The Bundesbank was keeping interest rates unusually high, while US interest rates were at a thirty-year low. Investors sold dollars and bought Deutschmarks, increasing the stress on the pound, which fell to below DM2.90 for the first time since the general election. The Treasury looked forward to the result of the French referendum on 20 September, which would remove a major element of uncertainty. A 'no' would have meant, it was widely accepted, a general realignment or even suspension of the ERM, and a 'yes' would calm the markets. The second way out would be for the Germans to give precedence to the needs of sterling and other currencies above their domestic requirement for high interest rates. Major spoke to Kohl to ask him to pressure the Bundesbank into reducing or at least holding their interest rates steady. But neither escape chute offered a way out.

Major's optimism plunged in early July, as he came under pressure to take action to ameliorate the recession, which showed no sign of lightening. Tentative signs of recovery after the election seemed to have been snuffed out by July, with falling retail sales and construction still in a deep slump.[46] For the first time in his premiership he became the subject of personal ridicule and criticism not just from backbenchers, but by ministers too. For the moment, most of this criticism was voiced privately or anonymously, with threats of later trouble should interest rates not come down quickly.

Major's reputation on his backbenches fell further on the last day of Commons business before the summer, when the government lost its first division of his premiership on the perennially tricky issue of payment of MPs. By 324 to 197, on a very low Tory turnout, office expenses were increased from a little under £29,000 to nearly £40,000, despite a government plea for restraint. Major compounded the error by ostentatiously promising not to collect all his extra expenses. Backbenchers pointed out that Major had the Number Ten office – and a very rich constituency party – to help him, and that he had tried to overrule the recommendation of the expert committee set up to decide such matters. It was a sour end to a session that had begun so promisingly.[47]

The government's European policy – increasingly identified as his own – and above all ERM membership, was blamed for the economic problems for which MPs were being constantly chided by their constituents. Major asked for a Treasury presentation on the ERM, and was convinced by their arguments. His Chancellor's response bore public fruit in a speech to the European Policy Forum on 10 July, which reflected the newly reinforced conventional wisdom of the leading Treasury figures on currency issues, Terry Burns, Nigel Wicks and Alan Budd, who had succeeded Burns as Economic Adviser in 1991. The Treasury consensus was that a unilateral devaluation would only heighten pressure on sterling, produce even higher interest rates, and would not thus be a route out of recession.

Lamont's speech was a strong defence of existing policy, and became the government's point of reference in the stormy waters of the next two months. Lamont systematically examined the options available to the government, including sharp cuts in interest rates within the ERM, as well as leaving the mechanism, but ruled all roads out as resulting in the pound losing credibility on foreign exchanges and as less desirable than holding to the present course. Devaluation within the ERM was firmly expunged as an option, but a general realignment of the ERM based on a revaluation of the Deutschmark, he said, could be considered at a future stage.[48] The crucial element was a concurrent devaluation of the French franc.

For a convinced Eurosceptic, it was a brave speech. Lamont knew he was a prisoner in the ERM, and he had to make the best of it, but from then on his own position was unequivocally hitched to non-devaluation within the ERM. In both the House and to Cabinet, Major reiterated as articles of faith that Britain's commitment to the ERM, and at the existing parity, were non-negotiable. By July, Major was seen as having nailed his colours to the mast, and sanctioned much more lurid proclamations than the measured EPF speech.

To underline the seriousness of Major's intent to defend sterling's value, he resorted to making excessive claims for the pound. At a Downing Street party on 16 July, Major spoke to Philip Stephens (of the *Financial Times*) and Gordon Greig (of the *Daily Mail*) and trailed his thinking about making the pound the strongest currency, thinking, he said, of the long term. Stephens did not write it up, thinking it too fanciful; Greig gave it a couple of paragraphs.[49] At a dinner on 29 July in Kensington at the private flat of Andrew Neil, the *Sunday Times* editor, he speculated even more brazenly on sterling becoming one of the strongest currencies in the world, stronger perhaps than the Deutschmark.

Neil, an early supporter of the single currency, had been growing irritated with the government's inability to lead the country out of recession. Neil blamed the level of taxes, and increasingly the high interest rates dictated by membership of the ERM. The dinner was convivial and, Major believed, off-the-record. Neil subsequently mentioned the occasion on television, which Major regarded as betrayal. It left him with an enduring hostility towards Neil.[50]

The dinner also produced a headline in the *Sunday Times* on 2 August: 'Major aims to make sterling best in Europe'. The front-page article said that Major had set himself against any drop in interest rates or devaluation as a way out of the recession, but was determined to show the markets that he was serious about conquering inflation and to bring about a permanent change in the attitude to sterling. Political tough-talking mirrored his financial message: rebels who threatened his policy on Europe could risk a vote of confidence, his own resignation and a general election. Inside, an extraordinary editorial penned by Neil said that Major, in ruling out any prospect of devaluation, realignment or interest rate cut, against the wishes of many in his Party, had 'embarked on one of the most dangerous gambles in recent British political history'. Nevertheless, in response to Major's call for a ceasefire from the press, who he believed were damaging prospects of recovery by disturbing the markets with calls for interest rate cuts, Neil said the *Sunday Times* would mute its criticism until the end of the year.[51] According to Neil, this was in response to a specific plea from Major at the dinner to the effect that continued criticism was making it more difficult for the government to cut interest rates.[52]

The *Daily Telegraph* was another organ re-evaluating its position. A series of disagreements had taken place in the summer about whether the government's ERM line was sustainable. The editor, Max Hastings, remained broadly supportive, following the line of his influential City Editor, Neil Collins, that Britain's membership of the ERM, which he initially opposed, was now beginning to yield dividends. But then, in August, Collins came to see Hastings to tell him he had changed his mind, and had come to the conclusion that the position was no longer sustainable, and Britain would be driven out of the system. Collins's news shook Hastings to the core.[53]

Major, following the Treasury line as stated by Lamont to the European Policy Forum, had no way back. With neither the French nor German escape routes coming to his rescue, and with currency speculators chipping away at his position, he was on a collision course. Eddie George at the Bank of England had developed a series of strategies to defend the pound from attack, but like the fortress rings surrounding a child's sandcastle, they were destined to be washed away by the incoming tide. When Major went to Garel-Jones's house in Spain for the summer holiday, he was kept in almost daily touch with news of the weakening pound by Mary Francis, who had replaced Barry Potter as Economic Affairs Private Secretary in Number Ten.

In early August, sterling dipped below the lowest permitted level of DM2.77 in the ERM. George and Hogg kept in daily touch about the deteriorating position. At the Treasury, officials were beginning to get 'really bothered' about the pound.[54] After Major's return, his bilaterals with Lamont became more frequent and focused on the currency, with the Bank spending more and more supporting the pound. A witness recalled that the atmosphere in August and early September in Number Ten was one of despairing anxiety.[55]

Contributing to the general level of anxiety was the temporary relocation of Major to Admiralty House (between the Mall and Trafalgar Square), five minutes' walk through Whitehall corridors from Number Ten, where the windows were being replaced and strengthened (in response to the IRA mortar attack). In his new, cramped and claustrophobic surroundings, Major felt displaced and disoriented. On one occasion, when unauthorised people wandered into his area, he exploded with the tension. Officials, meanwhile, found it a nightmare. With the Private Office remaining in a boarded-up room in Number Ten, and with inadequate secure communication, they had to waste valuable time travelling back and forth themselves. Stephen Wall felt that having Major in Admiralty House was a real drag on effective decision-taking and contributed significantly to the difficulties fast enveloping them.[56]

Adding to Major's woes was political gossip he was hearing about the amorous activities of his new National Heritage Secretary, Mellor. It caught Major in one of his vulnerable areas. The opposite of ruthless in matters of patronage, Major displayed exceptional loyalty to his ministers, above all, as was the case with Mellor, when he had known them a long time. When news of Mellor's affair with an actress, Antonia de Sancha, was disclosed by the *People* in mid-July,[57] the story made front-page headlines for a week. Major rushed to show support for his minister, by altering his plans in order to attend a reception hosted by Mellor, and spending thirty minutes chatting to him and his officials. Mellor's personal life, Major was reported to have said, was a private matter and he would not listen to suggestions that Mellor should resign. Major was riled by the episode: if he was to succumb to pressure over Mellor, his credibility might be damaged over the government's commitment to the pound.[58]

By Major rallying so strongly to him, Mellor survived, for the time being. But the episode led to a questioning of his judgement of people. Mellor was seen by some to be flashy and not wholly reliable, the very opposite of Major, who was seen to be expending a good principle, loyalty, on a less than worthy subject. Major, like Macmillan over Profumo, was also seen to be naïve in trusting the word of his more worldly minister. When press pressure eventually did succeed in forcing out Mellor in late September, it emboldened them to hunt and press even more persistently in later 'scandals'. It took Major another two years before he learned how to handle such episodes.

Summer Travels

Between May and August, Major embarked on six overseas journeys, besides several foreign day trips, some connected with Britain's EC presidency, which began in July.

In between the Queen's Speech and the Danish referendum, he undertook a four-day tour to eastern Europe, for his first visit to Poland, Czechoslovakia and Hungary as Prime Minister. The trip sought to encourage the leaders of post-communist countries along the path of reform and privatisation, as well as, importantly for Major, to discuss possibilities of EC enlargement eastwards, again with the British presidency in mind.[59] He flew out first to Warsaw, which he had last visited when a Lambeth local councillor, and signed an agreement to abolish visa requirements for Poles travelling to Britain. In Prague, he signed a treaty on security with President Havel,[60] before travelling down to Budapest to hold talks with Hungarian leaders.[61]

The excitements of the Danish referendum behind him, he embarked on one of his longest overseas trips, to North and South America from 6 to 13 June. But events back in Britain kept on intruding. The *Sunday Times* had serialised Andrew Morton's sympathetic biography of the Princess of Wales, *Diana: Her True Story*.[62] Major condemned it as 'unsubstantiated rumours' and emphasised the deep roots of the monarchy.[63] But rumbling dissatisfaction within his Party over Europe could not be so easily quenched. Press reports during his absence spoke of parliamentary divisions and a loss of authority (the trip had been planned on the supposition the Danes would vote 'yes'). At one stage, after Lilley had made a statement on Europe deemed to be 'unhelpful', Ryder in London had an anguished telephone call with Alex Allan (who had succeeded Andrew Turnbull as Principal Private Secretary in May 1992), speaking from an airport building in a remote part of Colombia, with flies, dogs and policemen with machine guns buzzing around him as he tried to phone through Major's response.[64]

The trip had begun happily enough with what was planned to be a part-holiday weekend at Camp David. Some work was undertaken with George Bush, but it was also an opportunity for friendly conversation, walks, and relaxation, which included a video of *Patriot Games*, the film about the IRA's attempt to take revenge on an American serviceman, played by Harrison Ford; the script, with a terrorist called O'Donnell and a treacherous Private Secretary, produced plenty of banter about the security of Major's entourage.[65]

Bush was genuinely delighted at Major's election victory, and was hoping that some of his winning formula would rub off on him; he was particularly interested in hearing how Major thought he had achieved the feat when so many had written him off. Bush still thought he could win his election, and told Major, 'I have known Bill Clinton all my life. In my view he would make a very good president, but I regard Ross Perot [the third party challenger] as a nasty little man.'[66]

Major was not so convinced of Bush's prospects; he toned down a press release prepared by O'Donnell and Wall which spoke of his warmth about Bush, just in case he did not win. In this, he was reflecting the views of the British Embassy, which by June had concluded that Bush had but a slim chance. Accordingly, British Ambassador Robert Renwick attached one of his younger diplomats, Jonathan Powell, brother of Charles and later to be Blair's chief of staff at Number Ten, to travel around the campaign trail with Clinton, forging close relations.[67]

On Monday, back in Washington, Major attended a dinner at the British Embassy. Flushed with the aura of electoral success, he was at the peak of his standing in America, reflected by the number of Senators who attended the dinner – seventeen. 'That's more than attend an average debate in the Senate,' George Mitchell, Senate majority leader, was heard to say.[68]

Major travelled to the Earth Summit via Colombia, the first time since the war that a British prime minister had set foot in South America, where he gave BP a boost by visiting one of their installations, before arriving in Rio de Janeiro on Wednesday evening. The first UN Conference on Environment and Development (or 'Earth Summit') was attended by over one hundred heads of state and delegates from over 170 countries. Britain had led the way when Major was the first of the G7 leaders to promise to attend; subsequently Michael Howard, the new Environment Secretary, proved himself an improbable supporter in helping to secure an agreement between different Washington departments, whose squabbling threatened to jeopardise US backing.[69]

Thatcher had become converted to the environment cause late in her premiership, prompted by the diplomat Sir Crispin Tickell. Major came for the last two days of the summit, tired, but eager to make an impact. Two conventions were signed, on climatic change, committing signatories to cut emissions of 'greenhouse gases' to 1990 levels by the end of the century, and on biodiversity, a cause that proved more problematic when the US suddenly refused to sign. Major and Howard, however, decided that they would sign regardless of the Bush administration.

Major's personal contribution to the environment issue showed itself on his return. Reporting back to the House of Commons, he took particular pride in policies he had launched, including the Darwin initiative, which offered international access to British botanical science facilities.[70] More than ever before, environmental policy in Britain was to be subject to external influences, an erosion of national sovereignty to which Major and Howard were happy to assent. David Hannay said, 'Major strongly supported the view that you had to have a world effort on the environment, because pollution by individual nations affects others.'[71] Howard's successor at Environment from 1993, John Gummer, proved himself particularly committed to advancing the green agenda, in which he was supported, albeit at arm's length, by Major.

Three more international conferences followed in quick succession after Rio, leading the *Guardian* to comment acidly that 'summit conferences are just about the only growth industry at the moment' as world leaders escaped from recession and turmoil at home.[72] First came the European Council in Lisbon from 25 to 27 June, which rounded off Portugal's EC presidency, and at which Hurd believed the IGC would have only been completed had Thatcher remained premier. Despite the Danish vote, all heads of government reaffirmed their commitment to Maastricht, Major emphatically so both there and in the Commons afterwards. To the *Independent* Lisbon showed Major's 'emergence as a determined advocate of the Maastricht treaty', demonstrating 'impressive leadership in his dealings with potential rebels in his party'.[73] Major's staunch line pointed to the British presidency, beginning on 1 July, as the unlikely saviour of the treaty.

However, there was no such harmony on the issue of the speed of admission of new member states, nor on the EC's financial arrangements, a hot potato Major and Lamont picked up with the presidency. The EC was 'more divided than before' according to the *Guardian*'s experienced Brussels reporter John Palmer.[74] A lowest common denominator statement on Yugoslavia was agreed, but it was overshadowed by Mitterrand's dramatic visit to Sarajevo.

Major also assented to the reappointment of Jacques Delors as Commission President for a truncated third term. He did not, however, appoint Neil Kinnock as one of the British commissioners: Kinnock, on top of Maastricht and Delors, was considered too heady a brew for his backbenchers.

The G7 summit, hosted by Kohl in Munich from 6 to 8 July, followed swiftly on the heels of the council, and was not a success, although a new credit line was extended to Yeltsin's Russia. Major went to Munich with high – and well-advertised – hopes of resuming progress on GATT, stalled because of militant French farmers and US electoral politics, but retreated 'licking his wounds', with a limp communiqué expressing only the hope that agreement would be reached before the end of 1992. Diplomatic correspondents considered Major's tactics in trying to pressurise the wily Mitterrand were 'ham-fisted' and easily seen off.[75] The US team even wondered whether it was worthwhile to continue with annual G7 meetings, and Major agreed that there were too many international meetings but not enough international discussion.[76]

The treadmill of diplomacy took Major straight to Helsinki for the Conference on Security and Co-operation in Europe (CSCE). Even more than Lisbon and Munich, it was overshadowed by the war in Bosnia, whose President Izetbegovic had escaped the siege of Sarajevo to plead for help. The conference only produced better naval enforcement of sanctions on Serbia and an increase in the aid effort in Bosnia.[77]

After so much business travel, and stresses over Europe and sterling, Major took to the skies again, but this time on holiday. On 7 August he travelled once again to the Garel-Jones's Spanish villa via a day in Barcelona spent watching the Olympic Games, which he found a delight. Humour and a touch of the ridiculous came in an urgent phone call to Bush on Bosnia. The only place Major could find to make the call was a general office behind the Olympic stadium's VIP suite. Every few minutes Major would interrupt the conversation: 'Wait a minute George, one of your chaps has just won a medal.'[78] The Olympics proved a perfect start to his holiday; he began to unwind, interrupted only by calls from Downing Street on the deteriorating sterling position, until Bosnia finally intruded. Major decided that he had no alternative but to cut short his holiday, and on the night of 17 August he returned to London.

Bosnia

The problem that had been brewing for the last year, the break-up of Yugoslavia, had now reached crisis point. The first war in mainland Europe since the 1940s was to continue for most of the period that Major was in power. The complexity of the situation, and the strains it created within the European Community and NATO, militated for a succession of short-term tactical responses to problems as they developed, and against long-term strategic thinking. This said, Major was never comfortable with the broad moral and geopolitical issues involved, but did take control on two occasions in reaction to sudden crises, in 1992 and 1995.

Yugoslavia, ruled by Tito from liberation until his death in 1980, had always been one of the more decentralised and pluralistic states behind the Iron Curtain. The bonds that held the disparate Yugoslav republics together began to unravel in the 1980s, speeded by the fall of communism and the adoption of nationalist slogans by former communists. As late as the presidential succession crisis in June 1991, Major was among international leaders pressing for Yugoslavia to remain unified, but it was well past the time when such exhortations could have any effect. Slovenia seceded from the federation and the crisis degenerated that autumn into a nationalist war between Serbia and Croatia, the two largest republics, for control of those areas of Croatia inhabited by Serbs. In between Serbia and Croatia lay Bosnia, a multi-ethnic republic on which Serbia also had designs. The Serb-Croat war, particularly the atrocities after the Serb capture of Vukovar in Croatia in November 1991, was a foretaste of the larger disaster in Bosnia.

The European Community, optimistic about the prospects for a common foreign policy, appointed Lord Carrington (Foreign Secretary 1979–82) as an intermediary in September 1991, with the onerous task of devising constitutional arrangements in former Yugoslavia. His talks process, aimed essentially at an orderly dismantling of Yugoslavia, with protection for ethnic minorities and possibly some confederal arrangements for republics that wanted them, proceeded slowly. Its proposals were blocked by Serbia, and the international community became impatient; other actors now entered the scene.

The United Nations responded to the war by imposing an arms embargo on all former Yugoslav republics and, when a ceasefire in the Serb-Croat war had taken hold, appointing Cyrus Vance (Secretary of State 1977–80) to oversee the introduction of the United National Protection Force (UNPROFOR) in the Serb-held areas of Croatia, and broker a deal between Serbia and Croatia.

Percy Cradock, Major's foreign policy adviser, wrote a minute detailing how he was

uncertain and unhappy about our policy – its hand to mouth quality. Did we consider that the republics were independent entities? If they were, then the Serbs were committing aggression in the same way that Saddam committed aggression against Kuwait.[79]

The Carrington process, such as it was, was destroyed by Germany's decision to force recognition of Croatia through the EC's foreign policy structure. At a Foreign Ministers meeting on 16–17 December it was decided – against only token British opposition – that Yugoslav republics should be invited forthwith to apply for recognition. Though no linkage with German helpfulness to the British at Maastricht was ever committed to paper, diplomats close to the process do not dissent that there was an informal understanding.[80] Genscher, the German Foreign Minister argued, 'we did our best to help you in Maastricht – please listen to me on this one.' Hurd and Dumas thought he would have gone ahead regardless. In January 1992 Croatia was recognised, even without the guarantees of minority rights that the EC agreement in December, a compromise Hurd cleared with Major by telephone, had proposed as a condition. How much damage this decision did to the future of Bosnia is still debated.

In April 1992, fighting broke out in Bosnia, and by the summer the Serb offensive had conquered about 70 per cent of the republic and had driven out or killed the mainly Muslim inhabitants of eastern Bosnia in an 'ethnic cleansing' programme. The issue came to a head for the West when in early August a number of journalists and a television crew (with the *Guardian* and *Channel Four News* in the vanguard) sent back reports and film of the Serb-run detention camps in northern Bosnia. With distressing pictures of emaciated prisoners at the Omarska Camp staring blankly through barbed wire, analogies with the Nazi concentration camps were soon being conjured up, and moral indignation reached fever pitch.[81]

The UN, which had known about the camps for several months, felt impelled to act, and decided that a further peacekeeping force needed to be sent into the area. The British government had declined to commit troops earlier in the year; would they commit troops now?

Influencing policy in the background was Thatcher, who had become incensed by the West's failure to act to protect the Muslims in the face of Serb aggression. For her, the issues were black and white, and morally of a piece with the Falklands and Gulf Wars. News of the camps was for her the final straw. Advisers like Norman Stone were of the same mind. He had been appalled by the ignorance and indifference among the British establishment: 'You could hardly go into the Beefsteak [a Whitehall club] without someone coming up to you and saying what a gentleman Johnny Serb was.'[82] Thatcher had to speak out. But where? Believing that the FCO, following 'many fruitless conversations', was feeble, or even, as some of her advisers put it, pro-Serb,[83] she launched her attack on the West's inertia in the US. 'Serbia will not listen unless forced to listen,' she wrote in the *New York Times*. 'Waiting until the conflict burns itself out will not only be dishonourable but also very costly: refugees, terrorism, Balkan wars drawing in other countries, and worse.'[84]

Thatcher was naïve if she hoped to persuade the Bush administration to act, which, with an election in sight, was no keener on foreign adventurism in the Mediterranean than the Eisenhower administration had been over Suez in 1956. They recalled their 1980s Lebanon experience, when American soldiers were prime targets because of the news and propaganda value of killing them. Nor did they wish to do anything in Europe that would suggest to the Russians that they were taking strategic advantage of their turmoil.[85] Brent Scowcroft (National Security Adviser) and Lawrence Eagleburger

(Secretary of State) were especially sceptical of the ability of intervention to make any impression on what they saw as the ingrained desire of the Balkan people to kill each other.[86] Bush and James Baker, who had moved aside as Secretary of State to mastermind Bush's re-election, professed themselves to be in favour of tough action against the Serbs, but with no domestic support for US involvement they concurred that this was one for the Europeans.

Major and Hurd were incensed by Thatcher's intervention. But on the other side, there were powerful voices in the Cabinet, notably Clarke, Lamont and Rifkind, and some prominent backbenchers, who opposed any British military involvement. Major worked hard to master the issues quickly. Peter Hall (Ambassador to Yugoslavia) was called in to see him. 'Prime Minister,' he said, 'the first thing you have to know about these people is that they like going round cutting each others' heads off.'[87]

The day after his return from Spain, on 18 August, Major chaired a meeting of the Cabinet committee OPD which lasted six hours, discussing both the Bosnian position and extra air protection for the Marsh Arabs in southern Iraq, on which it was decided to impose a no-fly zone.[88] Meeting in the Cabinet Office briefing room in the basement of Number Ten – the Cabinet Room was being refurbished – Major listened carefully to the military advice. Two decisions needed to be taken: should troops be sent to Bosnia and, if so, in what form? Deep reservations were expressed about British soldiers getting sucked irrevocably into the area; now the British were citing American analogies, this time Vietnam. But a consensus emerged: the refusal to commit troops to UN peacekeeping operations was untenable.

The initial military advice had been for a light force of 800 men. Major himself was quite clear that Britain must send a force that could look after itself if the position moved towards all-out war, rather than let the size of the British commitment be dictated too much by money.[89] The meeting thus decided that 1,800 men from the Cheshire and Prince of Wales regiments would join forces sent by other nations, notably France.

A week after the decision, Britain hosted the first London Conference, jointly sponsored by the EC and UN and attended by thirty nations, including representatives of the Yugoslav republics. With Britain holding the presidency of the EC, the conference was good both for Britain's profile and as a way of trying, despite American lack of interest, to achieve a concerted European and world response.[90] At the meeting, which he jointly chaired with UN Secretary-General Boutros-Ghali, Major announced at the outset that world opinion would not forgive anyone who tried to impede efforts to stop the war: 'The people who we represent have been appalled by the destruction, the killing, the maiming, the sheer cruelty which has disfigured Yugoslavia.' The conference, he continued, must mobilise international pressure to prevent force being used to alter frontiers, as with Bosnia, and to protect minorities, refugees and human rights in general.[91]

Major was adamant. He had received reports that up to one million people might die of exposure and starvation in Bosnia that winter, and he was determined to reduce the risk of such a widescale tragedy.

Major was the dominant personality. He deployed all his considerable negotiating skills, taking the individual Yugoslavian leaders into a private room to persuade or cajole them, or offer compromises, and driving the plenary sessions through with his blend of force and charm. In an atmosphere of extraordinary tension he achieved at the eleventh hour a number of agreements. At the end of the second day, Major and Boutros-Ghali announced that the warring parties had assented to virtually all demands for a swift end to fighting, UN supervision of heavy weapons, recognition of the borders of Bosnia, a no-fly zone over Bosnia, and return of refugees. The parties also agreed to set up tribunals to investigate possible crimes against humanity. Negotiations between the three parties in Bosnia – the Bosnian Serbs, Bosnian Croats and the Muslim-led Bosnian government – were to begin in Geneva under the chairmanship of David Owen for the EC and Cyrus Vance representing the UN.[92]

The Times called the conference 'a triumph for international diplomacy'. It was also a coup for Major, though he had no illusions about the difficulty of holding the Serbs to their promises, and for that reason he announced that existing sanctions would be tightened.[93] The conference was a serious attempt to reactivate the peace process that had become bogged down in the fighting in Bosnia; the solution of neutralising Serb aggression and reversing ethnic cleansing 'appeared to provide the basis for a lasting settlement'.[94]

The problem came, however, with the implementation of the conference's agreements. The Serbs did not stop their aggression, the sanctions and the no-fly zone were not enforced, and though the UN troops (numbering nearly 8,000 by the end of the year) helped protect lives and ensure safe distribution of humanitarian aid, their precise role remained unclear. The Vance–Owen Plan, negotiated from October 1992 to May 1993, eventually foundered on Bosnian Serb intransigence and American ambivalence.[95]

The war rumbled on and the London conference that appeared to have achieved so much quickly became but a footnote; the blame for failing to make the agreements work being laid variously at the doors of Britain, for not committing more troops, the EC for failing to provide a more concerted response, and the Bush administration for keeping away. The international community had not developed the cohesion and powers to impose its will. Another three years were to pass before in 1995, with the all-important US influence at last forthcoming, a more lasting settlement could be implemented.

The seeds of Major's 'long night' from September 1992 until 1995 were all in evidence following the general election. Yet despite Party divisions over Europe, Thatcher unrestrained in her criticism, the first green shoots of sleaze and press vindictiveness, an agonisingly slow recovery from recession, divisions within Cabinet, and the effect of the reduced majority, Major was still seen, both at home and abroad, to be in command.

The afterglow of his personal election success still hung on. The day after the election itself, Patten came to Number Ten, where Major presented him with a bottle of champagne. As they went outside to see the cheering crowds, Major reflected that within a year they would be the most unpopular government for a very long time.[96] Events were about to unfold that were to make Major's prescience come true, and far more quickly than he had predicted.

TWENTY-ONE

Black September:

1992

WITH THE AWFUL inevitability of a Greek tragedy, the Major premiership crashed on its 160th day in office after the 1992 general election. His hubristic talk of the summer duly brought its nemesis. Several billion pounds – the exact figure has never been disclosed – were lost from the reserves as the keystone of the government's economic policy was knocked out of position. Major himself regarded it as the biggest single setback he faced as premier.[1] Major's own authority was damaged for two or three years after, and perhaps never fully recovered from the blow; neither did the Party. The Conservatives' popularity plunged that month, and thereafter remained bumping along at about 30 per cent until the 1997 general election. Among postwar events, only Eden's handling of the Suez Crisis in 1956, Labour's devaluation in 1967, and Heath's management of the miners' dispute in 1973–4 compare with it.

The day Britain was ejected from the Exchange Rate Mechanism was swiftly dubbed 'Black Wednesday', 16 September.

Sterling in Trouble

When the London Conference on Bosnia concluded on 27 August, Major was preoccupied by a series of domestic concerns, including preparations for his Party Conference speech at Brighton, and thinking about how and when to pilot the Maastricht Treaty through Parliament. For a few days, too, when preparing for and chairing the Bosnia conference, he had been freed from anxieties about the currency and state of the economy. But the underlying position was worsening, notably after a French poll on 25 August suggested that the country might vote 'no' to Maastricht in their referendum on 20 September. Pressure on the weaker ERM currencies, including sterling, increased markedly. With the Bank of England being forced to sell $1 billion from reserves to support the pound, Lamont issued a statement about the government's intention to do 'whatever is necessary' to protect the parity.[2]

Privately, Major had some sympathy with the ERM's growing band of critics. He believed that the system he had led the country into as Chancellor in October 1990 had been a flexible one, with wide bands for the currency to move within, and devaluations a practical possibility. But with the Germans and French moving towards EMU, the flexibility had been compromised, and the government found itself locked into what had become a rigid system in which there was no give. Domestic needs for high interest rates in Germany after reunification were forcing the individual monetary policies of ERM members to dance to the tune played by the Bundesbank. Major and other leaders tried repeatedly to persuade Kohl to reduce German interest rates so other countries could follow, and accelerate recovery from recession. But, to Major's mounting annoyance, the German government washed their hands, and professed impotence concerning the Bundesbank. 'They just hid, and said it was all up to the bank, nothing they could do about it.'[3] For Major, it was a critical moment. He concluded that other EC countries would put self-interest before the interests of other states. 'It removed any illusions.'

At a meeting on 1 September Major and Lamont discussed the remaining options. As with the sterling crises of the Wilson government in 1964–7, devaluation, or even leaving the ERM, became unmentionables. Major and Lamont, at this stage, reacted tetchily at the merest hint of such ideas. Hopes were pinned instead in the 'informal' ECOFIN meeting that weekend, which might just come up with a general round of interest rate cuts.

At the end of the week, Friday 4 September, the Bank of England announced a £10 billion ecu credit, to demonstrate that it had ample reserves to resist any devaluation. The markets responded favourably, with sterling rising above the DM2.77 floor within the ERM mechanism. That evening, EC finance ministers and central bank governors travelled to Bath for the standard six-monthly informal ECOFIN. Lamont was the host, but the convivial dinner at the Royal Crescent Hotel on that Friday evening gave no hint of the tension that was to explode on the floor of the conference in the eighteenth-century Assembly Rooms the following day.

Lamont and Major were more united over the three months leading up to Black Wednesday than at any point since 1990. With Helmut Schlesinger, President of the Bundesbank, attending the conference, and Britain in the chair, could Lamont not bring pressure to bear on him – and surely receive support of other EC finance ministers – to reduce German interest rates?[4] The Italians and French, and indeed others, were certainly happy to join in any arm-twisting of Schlesinger during the nine-hour conference on Saturday. Lamont – with Major's agreement, urging even – opted to bounce rather than caress the German banker, asking him directly four times to cut German rates; after the fourth request Schlesinger had had enough, slammed his folder and made to leave, to be restrained only by the intervention of a colleague by his side.[5] Another central bank governor thought it 'the most ill-tempered meeting I have ever attended'.[6]

Messages were sent to Major in London, where he was watching cricket at Lord's: 'no realignment, no interest rates cut, lots of bad blood', and to the Treasury's Terry Burns, enjoying a weekend game of golf, contacted on his mobile telephone. Burns immediately abandoned his clubs to drive to Bath in time to ensure that a final communiqué could at least be salvaged, to display some positive benefit from the conference.[7]

Schlesinger had been deeply offended by Lamont's pressure, and agreed only with some reluctance to a communiqué which affirmed the rejection of realignment within the ERM, and stated that the Bundesbank had no intention of increasing German interest rates 'in present circumstances', a weak statement he further qualified in a BBC interview.[8] Continued pressure on Bonn to reduce German rates, whether from Major or the British Ambassador Christopher Mallaby, had had no effect. Robin Leigh-Pemberton, Governor of the Bank of England, overheard Schlesinger talking to German Finance Minister Theo Weigel. They were saying: 'In 1948, remember we had nothing, and look at what we have now. We achieved it by pursuing our own line of policy. We mustn't weaken now.' To Leigh-Pemberton, that conversation encapsulated the German attitude at the time, and explained why they were not prepared to do more to help the British.[9]

Some, like the financial commentator Philip Stephens, see Bath as a missed opportunity, where finance ministers could have discussed realignment of currencies within the ERM.[10] Lamont is widely seen as the principal culprit for his uncompromising chairmanship and *idée fixe* about pressuring Germany rather than exploring multilateral realignment options. But his tactics in Bath had been agreed with Major, and also reflected the desperation of Italy, France and Ireland, which had been communicated to Lamont before the meeting, to see a general reduction of interest rates. The Italians feared, correctly, that the lira would be the first currency to go under, but were unwilling to contemplate devaluation.[11] If Bath's Assembly Rooms were indeed the last chance saloon, then blame for the policy must be laid as much at Major's door, because he helped create it. Major was later to recall that he had high hopes of interest rate reductions coming out of Bath.[12]

Years later Treasury officials remained unrepentant, believing that a general realignment would not have solved the main problem, which was the impact of German monetary policy on British interest rates and thereby the recession. There had been no case of a devaluing country in any fixed exchange rate system being able to reduce its interest rates below those applying to the anchor currency of the system. The principal miscalculation admitted by the Treasury was the extent and rapidity of non-inflationary interest rate reductions that proved to be possible after leaving the ERM.[13] If the writing was on the wall that weekend, people could only see it when they were able to step back and look at it with a longer perspective.

Enough of such conjectures. Back in the real world, with the escape route of a German interest rate reduction frozen out, hopes were pinned on the French referendum, to take place on Sunday 20 September. If the French voted 'no' – and polls continued to show it was in the balance – it would spell the end not just for the Maastricht Treaty, but probably for the ERM. Britain could return to floating exchange rates, free to set interest rates according to domestic priorities. If the answer was 'yes' discussions of an orderly realignment and any consequent interest rate reductions could proceed in a calmer climate. However, storm clouds were gathering. On Wednesday 9 September the Finnish markka (which had been pegged to the ERM although Finland was not technically a member) succumbed to the pressure from the markets and fell in value by 15 per cent. As Will Hutton reflected in the *Guardian*, 'The hunt was now on for bigger game, with banks' foreign exchange departments around the globe who had not made a killing holding inquisitions, and those who had, scenting blood.'[14]

With the Italian lira now coming under heavy pressure, Major welcomed the Cabinet back on Thursday 10 September for the first meeting after the summer. Life, he stated, had to be toughed out within the ERM; no realignments or devaluations were on the agenda. He praised Lamont for his handling of the currency turmoil. Ministers accepted the news stoically, none doubting – in public at least – their ability to hold on for ten days until the French vote.[15]

That afternoon, Major flew to Glasgow to give what one can see with hindsight to be the most fateful speech of his premiership, in which he chose to commit himself wholly and irrevocably to defence of the pound at the existing parity. The *Financial Times* said 'he has put his own reputation and maybe his political future on the line'; *The Times* that he 'staked huge personal credibility on the defence of sterling and the defeat of inflation, apparently to the exclusion of all other economic goals'.[16] Major, addressing the Scottish CBI that evening, chose, as was his wont, to couch his message in personal tones:

All my adult life I have seen British governments driven off their virtuous pursuit of low inflation by market problems or political pressures. I was under no illusion when I took Britain into the ERM. I said at the time that membership was no soft option. The soft option, the devaluers' option, the inflationary option, would be a betrayal of our future.

Critics of the existing policy were dismissed as 'quack doctors peddling their wares. Miracle cures simply don't work – never have, never will.'[17]

Why did he choose to identify himself so totally with the policy? The decision was his own. Sarah Hogg had tried to dissuade him from going as far: 'Be softer, less definite.'[18] John Kerr, perhaps the only other figure who could have restrained him, asked him if he was really sure of what he was saying, and whether he thought his line tenable. Major looked startled and cross, and told him they only had to hang on for another ten days until the French referendum.[19]

Major was in the proverbial box. He was determined not to devalue, although he was less adamant against suspending Britain's ERM membership. Loss of face played a part; devaluations, he said, were something that only Labour governments went in for. The manifesto had also pledged to tame inflation by maintaining sterling's parity in the ERM. Figuring also was his personal reputation: he had taken the pound into the ERM with the central rate at DM2.95 in October 1990,[20] and he had been speculating only six weeks earlier with Andrew Neil and others about making the pound the strongest currency in Europe. There was also the prevailing Treasury wisdom that a devaluation within the ERM might not necessarily achieve the goal they all sought, a reduction in interest rates; some like Alan Budd argued that higher interest rates might result.[21]

A debate was occurring within the Treasury. Whereas its leading figures were united that current policy should be maintained – 'the best thing to do was simply to hang on with grim determination and just try to get through it'[22] – some less senior officials were thinking seriously of the only realistic alternative, a general realignment, and were unconvinced by the argument that such a realignment was neither manageable nor would it be accompanied by a reduction in interest rates.[23]

Major, screened from such thoughts, was free from doubt. His mind was set as he sat down to finalise his Glasgow speech. He had to support the existing policy, knowingly staking his personal reputation on it, wedding it rhetorically to his deeply held distaste of inflation He knew the risks. As one sage observer put it: 'There is something about fixed exchange rates that turns politicians into liars.'[24] Any expression of doubt would be seized on in the financial markets as a sign that devaluation was on its way and thereby cause greater pressure, even if rationally an exploration of the options was desirable. Major realised that he and Lamont were boxed in, as Callaghan had been before devaluation in 1967, and had no choice but to stress support for the existing exchange rate.

Major was pleased with his speech and its press reception, which reflected exactly the message he sought, his deep personal commitment to defending the pound. As relieved as under the circumstances he could be, he left for his annual weekend with the Queen and Prince Philip at Balmoral. Alex Allan, his new Principal Private Secretary, stayed with the Queen's Private Secretary, Robert Fellowes, in a house on the estate. Major and Norma enjoyed the clement September weather, having a barbecue cooked by Prince Philip, with the Queen laying the table, and walking in the large grounds. The Queen said, at a formal meal in front of several guests, that she had been gratified by Major's championing of the Union in February and again during the election.[25]

On Sunday morning, Major received a call from Italian Prime Minister Giuliano Amato to say the Italians were devaluing, and what would Britain do? Major said without hesitation that Britain would stick to their parity.[26] Treasury officials that Sunday morning attended a rapidly convened meeting with Lamont; the possibility of a British realignment was raised only to be dismissed. Major then spoke to Lamont on the telephone, and both expressed hopes that the small cut in German interest rates two days before would relieve some of the pressure on the pound.[27]

Major flew back to London on Monday 14 September, and that evening held a top-secret meeting with Lamont, Burns and Hogg. Lamont raised the issue of a possible British withdrawal from the ERM if there was no improvement before Christmas; he made a point of recalling this suggestion in his resignation speech on 9 June 1993, and he went on to tell the House that Major had refused to countenance the proposal. Accounts of the meeting vary, principally over the seriousness of Lamont's proposal, and the strength of Major's denial. Major distinctly recalls saying that without significant easing, they might have to act 'a good deal before' the Christmas deadline. Lamont recalls nothing remotely like this proposal.[28] It may never be possible to reconstruct the exact details of that meeting wholly satisfactorily.[29]

The endgame now began. Nervousness at Westminster and in the City was heightened on Tuesday 15 September by the announcement from Number Ten, which they later regarded as an error – the pressure was apparent – that Major would not be flying to Spain the next day for EXPO 92 at Seville. The decision for Major to remain in London was taken only in part because of the volatile position of sterling. Such a motive was naturally denied; but with the pound dropping to within a hair's breadth of its permitted floor of DM2.77. the decision of Chancellor Denis Healey to return from Heathrow to tackle the sterling crisis in September 1976 was a popular if unhappy comparison conjured by the media.[30] Neil Collins in the *Daily Telegraph* wrote that the government was now very close to a full currency crisis.[31] Lamont, who had also cancelled a lunch engagement on the Tuesday, watched 'resignedly' while pressure on the pound continued to mount. That afternoon the Deputy Governor of the Bank of England with responsibility for monetary operations, Eddie George, told him that further attacks on sterling were expected, as speculators continued to turn their attention from the now-devalued Italian lira to sterling, and he asked for approval for further intervention to prop up the pound.[32]

The safety valve of the French referendum, however, remained. Major had been optimistic about limping through until Sunday, when news reached Number Ten that Tuesday evening of remarks by Schlesinger in Germany implying that the pound should have been devalued alongside the lira. Major, with masterly understatement, regarded his comments as 'deeply unhelpful', and he believes they played a significant part in pushing sterling over the brink.[33] Lamont would later refer to Schlesinger's remarks as 'the trigger'.[34] It was clear that the Bundesbank was prepared to leave sterling to its fate, and within hours of Schlesinger's comments sterling fell through the DM2.77 floor on New York financial markets.[35] As Major spent that evening presenting awards to long-serving Lambeth councillors, he realised he was facing the biggest crisis of his premiership.

Black and White Wednesday

The most difficult day in Major's political life began ordinarily enough, with Downing Street basking in a day more summery than autumnal. At his pre-

7 a.m. meeting with Allan, he was given news of overnight activities, when foreign exchange officials had been monitoring the grim picture of a wave of selling of sterling in foreign exchange markets – New York, Tokyo – gathering momentum as it moved towards London. The question that morning was, should interest rates be put up then, or might further intervention just work? The Bank, however, spent millions of pounds before the opening of the London market, but to no effect.[36]

Shortly before 9 a.m. Major and Lamont spoke on the telephone. As the intervention had failed, Lamont said that an interest rate hike was the only alternative. It had been the news Major had dreaded hearing: any interest rate rise would play straight into the hands of Eurosceptics as evidence of why Britain should not become any more closely involved in Europe.[37] Major was anxious to involve his three most weighty Cabinet ministers – Heseltine, Hurd and Clarke – in the evolving decisions, not least – as was his style – so that the big beasts felt bound into any outcomes. It so happened that all were at Admiralty House that morning for a meeting to discuss contingency plans after the French referendum result. Major was called out of the meeting at 10.30 a.m. to talk to Lamont, and returned to say he had agreed to a 2 per cent interest rate increase to stem the run on the pound.

The mood of those present was one of nervous gaiety. The press had been full of louche stories about the Princess of Wales and the Duchess of York, and one remarked that it was a pity they could not produce a third royal princess in a scandal to deflect the media's attention. Another offered David Mellor's antics as a possible diversion. The suggestion fell very flat.[38]

After the meeting broke up, Major told Kohl and Pierre Bérégovoy, the French Prime Minister that, despite the interest rate rises, Britain intended remaining within the ERM, if it was at all possible. The rise took effect at 11 a.m., but sterling failed to respond immediately. Lamont was glued to the money market screens and realised within seconds that the battle was lost.[39] Leigh-Pemberton even phoned his fellow central bankers to see if they could do anything to ease the pressure on sterling, hoping against hope that the Bundesbank might relent with an eleventh-hour meaningful interest rate cut.

Major did his best to maintain a semblance of normality. At around midday he kept an appointment with a group of backbenchers including Stephen Milligan, to Number Ten one of the most highly regarded members of the 1992 intake. Milligan recalled Major as 'calm and courteous' despite the pressure. Major asked their opinion about the sterling crisis, Milligan replying that it was a fight worth fighting. Major said, 'That's all very well, but do you think I should raise interest rates to 15 per cent, 20 per cent, considering the effect on millions of people with mortgages, the small businesses ...?' With Treasury officials waiting impatiently at the door, Major chose to extend the meeting to twenty-five minutes rather than ushering out the backbenchers at the end of their allotted ten minutes.[40]

Heseltine, Hurd and Clarke, understandably distracted by the morning's events, returned to their departments where they anxiously watched events unfold on television. At 12.30 p.m. all three were recalled to Admiralty House, where they met Major and Lamont in the dining room, lined with portraits of former naval heroes, now used as the temporary command centre. The news was not good. A wave of gloom had swept across British business and home owners that morning, as they faced interest rates they could not afford. Billions were wiped off share prices as the stock market shed another thirty points.[41] The Chancellor was in a state of understandable anxiety: 'We are losing tens of millions of pounds for every few minutes that we are going on talking,' he burst out. Speculators, sensing the kill, were locked into selling sterling in the knowledge that they could, after the inevitable devaluation, buy it back more cheaply, thereby making billions of pounds of profit at the government's expense.

At 12.45 p.m., the ministerial group was joined by Treasury and Bank officials. Major's chairing of the meeting was described as slightly rattled, but undeniably authoritative. As the morning interest rate rise had failed, the options now were fourfold: to increase interest rates to 15 per cent, to let the Bank continue to intervene until all reserves were exhausted, to realign sterling within the ERM (i.e. devalue) or to suspend Britain's membership forthwith. Major announced that if further intervention failed, as was likely, the Chancellor and Bank favoured withdrawal. Lamont and Treasury officials were adamantly against a further increase, believing that only more damage would be done as speculators lined their pockets even more. (Talk immediately after Black Wednesday was of some £10 billion lost that day to speculators, including some £1 billion to one, George Soros.) But Hurd, responding first, supported by Clarke and then Heseltine, won the day, arguing that they should go – and be seen to go – the last half yard to remain within the ERM. If they did indeed have to suspend membership temporarily, they said Britain should play exactly by the rules to facilitate re-entry. They thus favoured the further interest rate increase, at least until 4 p.m., when European trading officially closed.

The meeting on the surface was calm and orderly; beneath, there were extremes of tension. Major faced one of the most important decisions of his life: back his Chancellor and the Treasury, and suspend ERM membership now, or follow his most senior Cabinet ministers, and give it one last heave?[42] He chose the latter. The meeting broke up at 2 p.m. and at 2.15 p.m. the Bank announced the rates would rise to 15 per cent the next day (the delay a concession to the Treasury) – reversing all the hard-fought cuts since October 1990.

Speculation in Whitehall had been rising to a crescendo all day. Many Cabinet ministers knew little of what was going on. John Wakeham, Leader of the Lords, was due to go to Charterhouse school to see his son play in a 1st XI football match, but spoke to Robin Butler before leaving, saying he thought it odd that he had not been involved. Butler replied that he himself only found out what was going on when he happened to pass through Number Ten.[43] Butler joined the group when they reassembled before 4 p.m.

in Admiralty House, waiting for the Governor and Chancellor to return from the City to report on the effects of the second interest rate increase.

The three heavyweight ministers were all tetchy at not being better informed. Butler joked in the waiting room that here were some of the most influential people in the country during a decisive moment in its history, sitting around with no form of access to any market information whatever;[44] no one had thought to install any Reuters monitors or a computer network in the Prime Minister's quarters in Admiralty House. There they sat in a cocoon, isolated from the outside world, reliant on information pumped via Whitehall from the drip feed in Number Ten.

When the Chancellor and Governor returned, Lamont first had a private meeting with Major, and then the large meeting was reconvened. Sarah Hogg had been prominent in urging Major to include all his senior ministers in the final decision.[45] Major was resigned and calm. The day had so obviously been lost; the conversation revolved around how best to handle and present the news. Lamont, it was agreed, should announce the reversal of the rise to 15 per cent back to 12 per cent. Heseltine and Clarke pressed for a return to 10 per cent, but the Treasury and Bank agreed that such a move was precipitous and might put the pound in too much jeopardy.[46] Lamont duly appeared outside the Treasury at 7.30 p.m. and announced, 'The government has concluded that Britain's best interests can be served by suspending our membership of the exchange rate mechanism.' Britain would rejoin 'as soon as circumstances allowed'.[47] Norman Fowler was despatched to do the rounds of the television studios, presenting the news as favourably as he could under the circumstances. Perhaps over-cautiously, Fowler was deputed to speak because as Party Chairman he was not a government minister and therefore would not be speaking prejudicially before the meeting of the EMS Monetary Committee in Brussels later that night.[48] But Lamont, too, conducted several of the early media interviews before returning to the Treasury and debating, over takeaway pizza, what should be done about interest rates and what line Wicks should take at the Brussels meeting.

Stories soon bubbled through the grapevine that Major had variously cracked, lost his nerve, or 'wobbled' on the day. There is no truth in any of these rumours: too many witnesses testify so. Some suspected Lamont's supporters put the rumours about,[49] an accusation he denies, and he does not believe this occurred.[50] Major had periods of irritation, particularly against the Bundesbank. He complained that the Bank of England, especially Eddie George, had not done enough earlier to remedy the position.[51] But throughout the key meetings and in all the decisions he was almost inhumanly calm and self-possessed. Though obviously under heavy stress, he elicited opinions from everyone, asked the questions, listed pros and cons, summed up, and took the final decisions.[52] Sarah Hogg had sat by his side throughout the meetings, his closest aide and confidante.

That night, mulling it over, Major was the first of his team – Hogg, Hill, Allan and O'Donnell – to take on board fully what a devastating blow it would prove to the government, and his own position, as well as to Party unity.[53] He had regarded ERM entry as probably his finest achievement as Chancellor, and he regarded the Maastricht Treaty as perhaps the greatest achievement of his premiership. Suddenly, the ground had been swept away from underneath him. Leigh-Pemberton went to bed that night feeling he had suffered the worst defeat of his life. A sensitive man, his thoughts turned to Major; in some ways he regarded himself as the younger man's mentor. During the day he had witnessed Major's demeanour change, as the policy that he had battled so hard for, and staked his reputation upon, was sliding away from under him.[54]

A Devalued Government?

The day after Black Wednesday – already dubbed 'White Wednesday' by Eurosceptics as it meant the end of the hated ERM – Lamont saw Max Hastings, editor of the *Daily Telegraph*. The newspaper had taken an uncompromising view towards Lamont that morning, saying Major had to sack him.[55] Hastings told Lamont to his face that he should resign, because nobody had confidence in him any more and someone should take the rap for a disaster of the magnitude of Black Wednesday. Lamont disagreed, and the meeting broke up in a chilly atmosphere. It was a moment of truth. Lamont saw it as the start of a media campaign to hound him from office; Hastings, in turn, never felt able to trust or respect the Major government again.[56]

The facts and motives behind Lamont's continuation in office are exceedingly muddy. Nine months later Lamont claimed in his resignation speech that Major had told him in writing on the evening of 16 September that he himself had no intention of resigning, and that Lamont should not do so either. While Major certainly was not keen for Lamont to go, Philip Stephens says there is no record of correspondence between Major and Lamont in Whitehall archives, and that senior officials at the time do not recall the exchange.[57] Whatever the truth, Lamont certainly did not see why he should take sole responsibility, and did not thus insist that he resign. He consulted various allies, including Howard and Portillo, and asked their opinion. They said he should stay.[58] He had made no secret to those in the Treasury in recent months that he was opposed to the ERM, preferring floating exchange rates. He felt, rightly, that he had loyally followed government policy and done his best to make the ERM work, and that if anyone was primarily responsible for the débâcle, it was Major, who as Chancellor had taken the country into the mechanism (though the weakest part of Lamont's case is that he should not have accepted the chancellorship if he did not support the ERM). Major had also overruled him and, against Lamont's advice, decided to raise interest rates to 15 per cent on Black Wednesday, which some regarded as the worst decision of the day. Some in the Treasury think that this pivotal decision was the reason Major did not ask for Lamont's resignation. He almost certainly did say to Lamont that neither of them should resign, and Number Ten made it clear on the evening of Black Wednesday that he was safe.[59] It would be quite understandable if Major felt that, if Lamont went, it would make his own position more, not less, vulnerable. Criticism might grow that he had sacrificed his Chancellor when the policy, which he had supported in such ringing terms at Glasgow less than a week before, was more his own, and he should thus have made the ultimate sacrifice instead. Alastair Ross Goobey, Lamont's former adviser, was a rare voice among his allies saying he should resign. Had Lamont done so, he believes he could have achieved almost a hero's reputation.[60]

Reaction in the Tory Party, not least at the temporary hike of interest rates to 15 per cent, was every bit as angry as Major feared. There was muted speculation for the first time since his entering Downing Street that Major would face a leadership challenge that autumn.[61] Lamont also came into the firing line. Unlike Major, he had not built up a personal following among his colleagues during his rise up the ministerial ladder. He was less assiduous – his friends would say less cynical – in nurturing a network of contacts. Unusual, too, for one on the right, Lamont did not have the blessing of Mrs Thatcher, and hence her supporters. Thus when Lamont fell on hard times, as he did in the wake of Black Wednesday, few spoke up for him and those who did were often malcontents, anxious to exploit the predicament to put the spotlight on Major.

William Rees-Mogg wrote in the *Independent*: 'Yesterday was one of the most grotesque days in the history of British finance, a day of crisis, disorder, confusion and mismanagement.' Press comment in general was sharp, but not unduly hostile to Major personally. The *Daily Telegraph* was not atypical, saying that although Major's personal credibility was shaken, he would survive in office 'because the overwhelming majority of his party wishes it and sympathises deeply with his troubles'.[62] *The Times*, where the editorship had just changed from Simon Jenkins to Peter Stothard, was more astringent: 'Yesterday, Major showed the courage for which he is famous without also showing the common sense that made him prime minister. The result was sadly ridiculous.'[63] It is indeed surprising that the press reaction was not more personally critical of Major at the time.[64] Perhaps this was in part because most of them had supported the ERM.

On Thursday 17 September the Cabinet's meeting to discuss the situation lasted a reported three hours. The mood was sombre and there was a bunker mentality, which is why Major may have chosen the inappropriate metaphor when defending Lamont in public, that he 'should not be seen as an air raid shelter', taking all the criticism for a policy the full Cabinet supported.[65] Major's remarks were more a restatement of the doctrine of collective Cabinet responsibility for decisions, though in reality the Cabinet did not properly discuss, nor indeed did several fully understand, what had been happening before and during Black Wednesday, nor whether devaluation was ever an option. Tentative though Cabinet support might have been in the past for sterling policy, each member of Cabinet that Thursday now pledged his or her support to the Chancellor. Emboldened by their affirmation, Lamont came out of the Cabinet and told the waiting media: 'I am not going to resign. I have been operating the policy of the whole government and I know that I have the support of the prime minister and the full support of my Cabinet colleagues.'[66]

Number Ten were emphatic: 'We will resume membership of the ERM as soon as conditions allow.'[67] The reason for this stance, Number Ten say, was Lamont's insistence in Cabinet that morning that they must not exclude the possibility, but return was most unlikely because it would be not only politically impossible, it made no economic sense unless the system was radically restructured. There were some hopes of persuading other member countries of the British government analysis that there were 'fault lines' in the system that necessitated reform. But to admit that a return was in doubt would have brought the pound under renewed pressure. In Cabinet that Thursday, Howard, still the boldest Eurosceptic in meetings of the new Cabinet, reminded his colleagues of the political unlikelihood of ever obtaining Conservative parliamentary support for such a move. Indeed, even as they were meeting, Eurosceptic MPs were gathering in huddles to whip up support for a 'no return' strategy.[68]

Labour demanded, and achieved, recall of Parliament and a Commons debate on 24 September. Attitudes in the intervening week hardened. Polls showed that more than half the country (54 per cent) thought Lamont should resign, showing his position to be considerably weaker than James Callaghan's following Labour's devaluation in 1967 (when he did go as Chancellor).[69] The Eurosceptic right hardened their stance another few notches. Their faces 'positively glowed' at all the bad news when they reconvened from their summer break for the emergency debate.[70] Charles Moore was in the vanguard of Eurosceptic right-wing commentators, calling the withdrawal from the ERM a defeat 'almost as complete as it is possible, in peacetime, to conceive'.[71]

News of economic indicators brought Major no relief: the jobless total of 2.8 million was the highest for five years. Tebbit, moreover, was on the war path, repeating to all microphones and journalist pens available that it was Major who had dragged a reluctant government into the ERM, although some noted that the ultimate responsibility for that rested with the prime minister of the day. With Thatcher deeply immersed in her memoirs, only occasionally lifting her head above the book's parapet for a round of rapid fire, it was Tebbit who moved into the vanguard of the Thatcherite right's attacks on Major.

The long-heralded French vote duly took place on 20 September, recording a small 'yes', the worst conceivable result for Major. Either a 'no', with its possibly deadly impact on the Maastricht vision for Europe, or a strong 'yes', imparting a more emphatic sense of momentum, would have been preferable. As it stood, Eurosceptics could claim that two-thirds of the French did not vote in favour of ratification.[72] Major gathered a team of close advisers around him that Sunday evening to consider the government's response. A laborious drafting session ensued, with too many present finding the need to speak. Major went out before the media to announce their conclusion, and rather nervously enquired of those present at a buffet supper afterwards whether he had done all right. Everyone said of course he had, but they knew he had been humdrum. So, too, in his heart did Major.[73]

Economic policy had now to be reconstructed. A meeting took place at Admiralty House to consider the way forward. Officials recall the atmosphere as 'passing the parcel', with no one keen to open the discussion. The lead at that meeting was taken very much by Terry Burns, calm, creative and very practical.[74] Burns was to spend a remarkable twenty years at the very heart of Britain's economic policy, first as chief economic adviser and from 1991 as Permanent Secretary at the Treasury. For him, as for all other senior officials involved, the events surrounding Black Wednesday were a harrowing experience.

Major's mood was at its lowest ebb in the days between the French referendum and the Commons debate of 24 September. He repeatedly pondered the idea of his resignation, floating it with several colleagues, including Fowler on the evening of Tuesday 22 September.[75] Despite finding no support, he would not leave the subject alone, and came close to putting it into practice on the Wednesday. He went as far as to write out, by hand, the script for a resignation broadcast, and tip off his preferred successor, Clarke, that he should prepare himself for a leadership election. That evening, in the gloomy surroundings of Admiralty House, he tried to show the text to Stephen Wall, who refused to read it or to accept that he should resign. Instead, Wall and Major talked for two hours. Major subsequently regarded this conversation as crucial to his decision to carry on.[76]

Once he had decided to stay, Major determined his strategy for the debate. This was to assure the House that policy outside the ERM would remain tight on both inflation and on public spending, reaffirming his commitment to seeing through the Maastricht Treaty in Britain, while ruling out an early return to the ERM. But all the trumps were held by John Smith, in his first appearance in the House as Labour leader since taking over from Kinnock. With the core plank of Major's economic policy splintered, and as yet nothing very clear to replace it, Smith had him at his mercy. Tory Eurosceptics sat opposite for Smith to exploit. The Mellor saga, rekindled after the August holiday, continued to sap the Prime Minister's authority.

Major was determined to put in a strong performance, and came with a well-drafted speech, which began promisingly.[77] He reminded the House of a fact many would have sooner overlooked, that entry into the ERM had been supported by Labour, the Liberal Democrats, industry, the City, the TUC and most trade unions. He, perhaps unwisely, ridiculed Tebbit. The government, he said, still stood for a low-inflation, low-tax economy. But he then began to struggle when discussing future policy: 'Outside the exchange rate mechanism, the conduct of monetary policy cannot, indeed should not, be exactly the same.'[78] But it was the onslaught not from Smith but from his own Tory Eurosceptics that undermined him. Teddy Taylor, Nicholas Budgen, John Wilkinson and Michael Spicer all intervened during his speech. Bill Cash tried to break in, but Major would not yield for him. Major was particularly unsettled by Spicer's question, asking whether a free vote could be permitted on the Maastricht Bill. Major responded sharply: 'I believe that my Hon. friend stood at the general election supporting the Conservative manifesto, which indicated that we would bring the Bill before the House.'[79]

With Major already apparently in trouble, the stage was set for a humiliation. Smith's response was emphatic, with his own side willing his success. Opening to roars of Labour support, he delivered several hard punches, above all to Major – 'You don't know what your economic policy is – that was startlingly clear in your speech' – and accused Major of being 'a devalued prime minister of a devalued government'. Hard questions were asked about why Britain did not realign within the ERM once the extent of the sterling crisis had become clear. Major gave no convincing answer. Major was taunted for his comments to the *Sunday Times* about the pound becoming the strongest currency in Europe.[80] Although the government secured a comfortable majority in the debate, carrying it by 322 votes to 296, no one could doubt that the day was Labour's.

Lamont's own speech, fortified by earlier reductions of interest rates to 10 and then 9 per cent (at Major's insistence), was better received than Major's. After Black Wednesday the early sympathy in the Party had been all for Major, but the position began to shift, as Lamont was liberated from the constraints of the ERM. Lamont was given an enthusiastic reception by eighty MPs at the meeting of the Tory backbench Finance Committee, where he took the unusual step of asking MPs to show loyalty to the Prime Minister in his current predicament. Critics were taking increasingly to the air waves; even Marcus Fox, chairman of the 1922 Committee, told BBC Radio 4's *The World at One* that the Prime Minister bore responsibility for the last two bad weeks, and 'tougher and new' policies and more 'panache' would be needed to restore confidence at the Brighton Party Conference.[81]

The world was never the same after Black Wednesday. Eurosceptic feeling, which flexed its muscles in the debate after the Danish referendum, would from now on be unrestrained in its attacks on the leadership. In the government, middle-ranking ministers like Redwood became more open in their criticism, and in Cabinet Howard, Lilley and increasingly Portillo, felt more confident in their ability to speak out. The balance of power in Cabinet began to tilt away from Major. The Tory press would never return fully to the fold. The Conservative Party lost its image of managerial competence in the eyes of the electorate; thereafter, Major's government was operating against a public perception at various stages of wariness, contempt and boredom.[82] The wisdom of re-electing the government in 1992 was suddenly being questioned. Major's personal rating went into a steeper decline than Conservative voting intention. He was never wholly to lose a public perception of lack of grip and distance from reality acquired at that time. Relations with other EC countries, especially with Germany, were also to suffer.

How culpable was Major over the entire ERM saga? Critics such as Edmund Dell give him a hard verdict. They say his professed belief in 1990 that he was entering a flexible system was flawed, as the Delors report, seeing the ERM as an inevitable precursor to a single currency, had already been published. The writing was already on the wall by October 1990 that Germany, with impending unification, would be in for a rough ride, with high German interest rates inevitable because of monetary union with East Germany. Major's discussion with Sarah Hogg in 1991 on a possible devaluation sits uneasily with his stated dislike of devaluation as something only Labour governments did, while his belief that Kohl and the German government could pressure the Bundesbank to reduce interest rates revealed a fundamental misapprehension of the German constitutional position, whereby the Bundesbank resists pressure from any political figure.[83] There is truth in these strictures, but Major must share some of the responsibility with others.

The government never apologised for ERM, and there was no official enquiry into what went wrong. The line remained that the government was right to enter, as most agreed at the time. It then became the victim of circumstances, above all German reunification, demanding the maintenance of high interest rates; Spain, Italy, France and others, it was stated, all fell victim. Each entered the system in good faith only to find that the ERM had become a different club from the one they thought they had joined.[84]

No one can know for sure the inner effect the events had on Major. Even the very strongest figure would have found it shattering. Major rarely talked about the experience, or how he felt about it. But he had acted on what he regarded as the best advice in the country, and had taken what he thought were the brave and right decisions. Now he found himself widely reviled. He had never felt so lonely or exposed in his working life.

Mellor Postscript

Major's black September was not yet over. In mid-month he hoped that the Mellor episode might die down when it transpired that some of the more lurid claims about Antonia de Sancha's relationship with Mellor had been made up.[85] Unfortunately for Mellor, an old story came back to haunt him. He and his family had been on holiday to Marbella at the invitation of a friend, Mona Bauwens, who was the daughter of the treasurer of the Palestine National Council. In a libel action brought by Bauwens against the *People*, George Carman QC, for the defence, said Mellor had been behaving like an ostrich with his head in the sand 'exposing his thinking parts'.[86]

Pressure built up on Major to sack Mellor, but Mellor now showed little sign of wanting to resign. He now admits that the catalyst for his eventual decision to go was on discovering that Marcus Fox was about to tell Major that he had lost the support of the 1922 Committee, and that 'It would have been embarrassing if the 1922 Committee had met and had in effect advised the Prime Minister to get rid of me.'[87] Mellor insisted. Despite all that he wanted to achieve at National Heritage, he was going to leave the government. The announcement was made on 26 September.

After Major bowed to pressure and accepted his resignation, it was Major's, not Mellor's, conduct which attracted the criticism. *The Times* accused the Prime Minister of being over-influenced by his personal friendship.[88] The ever-willing Peter Brooke was smartly drafted back into government to fill Mellor's place. But the impression, given first when the scandal broke in July, and reinforced in September, was of Major defending the indefensible. Only now it was compounded by the impression that Major had been forced to abandon his man not on principle but bowing to media and Party pressure. The outcome for Major could not possibly have been more unfortunate.

TWENTY-TWO

'The Worst Period By Far':

October–November 1992

MAJOR BADLY NEEDED a quiet autumn to allow the Party to regroup, for nerves to be steadied, and for economic policy to be calmly reconstructed. He suffered precisely the opposite, with divisions laid bare at the Party Conference – over the subsequent pit closure plan and the introduction of the Maastricht Bill – and with the atmosphere anything but steady to allow his authority to recover. He later described the autumn as 'the worst period by far' of his premiership.[1]

Brighton Conference: 6–9 October

One person had been conspicuous by her absence during the immediate crisis over the ERM in late September. She reappeared on the scene with a vengeance mid-conference: Lady Thatcher, now like Tebbit ennobled by Major and in the House of Lords. So widespread had Euroscepticism become, however, that her attack was almost lost among the noise of the volleys being fired at the government.

For one usually so good at bouncing back after reverses, Major found getting his second wind after Black Wednesday more difficult than expected. He had barely paused since his summer holiday was cut short: the London Conference, currency troubles and party splits then rose to the top of his agenda in rapid succession. Running through it all was Britain's presidency of the EC.

Major flew to see Mitterrand on Wednesday 30 September. Struck by the narrowness of his French 'yes' vote ten days before, the French President agreed that the role of national governments needed to be further safeguarded within the EC to counteract the anti-Maastricht bandwagon. Reassured by his intention, Major felt emboldened to bring the Maastricht Treaty back into the House of Commons 'sooner rather than later'.[2] The news did not please Eurosceptics, nor the Tory press.

The attack on Major personally, detectable in the week between Black Wednesday and the emergency Commons debate, intensified. Stories started to appear of Major personally phoning newspaper editors after Black Wednesday to highlight German responsibility in sterling's retreat from the ERM.

He admitted later that this was one of the rare occasions when he did call editors over a story. He got more than he bargained for at the *Sun*. Its editor, Kelvin MacKenzie, responded in his own words: 'I've got a large bucket of shit lying on my desk and tomorrow morning I'm going to pour it all over your head.'[3] These stories may have grown in the telling, and Major himself has no recollection of MacKenzie resorting to any such language. The damage was done by the widespread circulation given to his alleged conversation with MacKenzie, showing a Prime Minister over-concerned by the press and prepared to compromise his dignity to lobby it.

Not that any such phone calls helped. Peter Stothard, the new editor at *The Times*, was a strong Eurosceptic, as was Conrad Black, owner of the *Telegraph* papers and the *Spectator*, whose editors independently shared his views. The *Spectator* was particularly scornful, with its regular columnist Simon Heffer in the vanguard. Major's old foe, Nicholas Ridley, was given space in the journal the week before the Party Conference in early October to rail against Major's economic and European policy. Hastings at the *Daily Telegraph* meanwhile intensified his pounding, and Charles Moore at the *Sunday Telegraph* wrote ominously that, since the election, Major had lost 'two of the props on which he most relied, the Germans and the press. Next week will show whether he has lost the third and most important – the rank and file of the Conservative Party.'[4]

Most serious of all to Major was the loss of the *Daily Mail*, whose new editor, Paul Dacre, was unashamedly anti-Maastricht, and not too keen on Major personally, which led to a rapid cooling of the warm relations with Downing Street, so recently underlined during the general election.[5] Dacre lent his columns to Tebbit who, apparently locked into an increasingly personal criticism of Major, wrote that he 'should reflect that he became prime minister only because Heseltine and his supporters brought down Mrs Thatcher'.[6] Watching the spectacle amazed, Andrew Marr of the *Independent* wrote: 'Rarely, if ever, can a recently victorious Tory prime minister have faced a party conference with the Conservative press so hostile, so vitriolic, so apparently implacable.'[7]

Major's task as he went into the conference was to show he still had the initiative, with a clear way forward on both Europe and the economy. At a Cabinet meeting on Thursday 1 October he presented ministers with three options on the Maastricht Treaty: abort, which he said was not a real option; delay, which would fuel charges that the government was drifting; and press ahead now. He went around the table to secure their agreement to the last. Said one afterwards: 'He took on all the villains on both sides of the European argument and picked them off. They are all locked in now.' An up-beat lobby briefing followed the meeting. 'The government is pressing ahead on Maastricht. The Cabinet are ranked behind it. The PM is back on the front foot,' was the message given.[8]

The news inflamed Tebbit, who – he claims – had not initially intended to speak at the conference. But on Tuesday 6 October, the opening day, he put in a request to do so, making it swiftly clear that if not called, he would go public on the fact he had been gagged.[9] Tebbit spoke. As his name was announced to be called up to the rostrum, representatives stood up to applaud.

Alluding to the Brighton bomb eight years before, when his wife was paralysed, he said that when he retired as Party Chairman in 1987, for reasons everyone would understand, he never intended to make another conference speech. But the need of the hour called him unwillingly back. He could not do less than speak his mind on the crisis over Europe. Lamont, he said, should not be sacked when the policy to enter the ERM had been Major's. 'This conference', he said, 'wants policies for Britain first, Britain second, and Britain third. Politics, like charity, begins at home.' Whipping some representatives up to fever pitch, while the platform looked stonily on, Tebbit, revelling in the affirmation, invited audience participation, evincing shouts of 'No' to a succession of questions: did they want to be citizens of a European Union, to see a single currency, to let other countries decide Britain's immigration controls? Nationalism was what Tebbit wanted. Major should launch a Maastricht Two, with none of the federalist ambitions of the Maastricht Treaty itself: 'John Major should raise the flags of patriots of all the states of Europe.'

After his rallying speech, he walked into the body of the hall, waving amid prolonged cheering.[10] He told BBC television later, 'I have offered a hand of friendship.' Number Ten were not so sure that an offer to back Major if he renegotiated Maastricht merited this description. 'An ageing and slightly pathetic figure', and 'a ridiculous, triumphalist, stomach churning speech' was how they saw it. Major himself thought Tebbit's behaviour and intemperate rhetoric disgraceful, and that he had deliberately misrepresented the Maastricht Treaty.[11]

Hurd responded for the government, in what aides thought the most important speech he had ever delivered to a Party Conference. Major, sitting beside him, scribbled a brief note and passed it over: 'Good luck! Give 'em hell, and don't worry about causing offence. How can they expect us to break our word [to Britain's EC partners about seeing the Maastricht Treaty ratified]?'[12] The atmosphere was exceptionally volatile when Hurd stood up; earlier pro-European speeches had been hissed and barracked from the floor.[13] Hurd began gravely. Bemused delegates were told that the Party's splits over the Corn Laws and tariff reform had cost it on each occasion ten years in opposition. Europe must not become a third such issue; 'Let us decide to give that madness a miss.' He then launched into a passionate defence of Britain playing its part in the European Community, which was not the federalist juggernaut that its critics alleged. His calm authority succeeded in restoring a sense of shared purpose to the Party delegates, and a sense of perspective. Donald Macintyre wrote that the speech was 'lucid, passionate – even, dare it be said, prime ministerial'.[14] Hurd was indeed rarely more impressive; against the odds, he turned the conference back to the government.

Two additional boons came Major's way: the conference tangibly showed Britain's EC partners how constrained Major was by his own backbenchers – a position some of the EC was disinclined to acknowledge – and it upstaged Ken Baker. The former Party Chairman delivered a fringe speech in which he declared that he would vote against the Maastricht Treaty; with a display of regret, he cited Martin Luther, 'I can do no other.' Cabinet ministers fell over themselves to pour scorn on Baker and accused him of sour grapes at being dismissed as Home Secretary after the general election.[15]

The conference was Fowler's first big test as Party Chairman. He had served Thatcher loyally as one of her Cabinet ministers for nine years and had made an agreement with her that she would appear on the platform but not say anything.[16] That was the plan. But Thatcher was a prima donna not susceptible to *sotto voce* stage management. Silent in speech, yes, but not in print. She had written an article which was faxed to the *European* newspaper early on the Tuesday evening, with publication timed to coincide with her arrival the next day. One of her court let slip, 'We knew it was dynamite.'[17] The conference organisers were not consulted, and were furious at her obedience to the letter, but breach of the spirit, of the deal. To the Major camp, it was nothing less than a declaration of war.

Thatcher described the Maastricht Treaty as a 'ruinous straitjacket' which would damage 'our constitutional freedoms' and put Britain 'on the conveyor belt to a single currency'. Talk of Britain remaining at the 'heart of Europe' was 'even less rational than our discussion of exchange rates'.[18] Worse, in a simultaneous interview for the Spanish *ABC* newspaper she said the Tories were 'deeply divided' on Europe and repeated her call for a referendum in Britain. Anthony Bevins described the impact in the *Independent*: 'Deep Conservative wounds over Europe were kept open last night by Baroness Thatcher in a double-barrelled blast.'[19]

Many Party faithful felt that this time she had overplayed her hand, and the ovation when she reached the platform, while still wildly enthusiastic, was noticeably more subdued than in 1991. Some stayed seated; even a few boos were audible. She and Major kissed; 'the most touching display of genuine affection since Judas planted one on Jesus,' considered Andrew Rawnsley.[20] Some steadier voices in the Thatcher camp later regretted the timing of her interventions and thought them an error of judgement.[21]

A reaction was setting in at Brighton. Thatcher's words, following Tebbit's, rekindled sympathy for the leadership. Heseltine's speech received an enthusiastic response, twice bringing delegates to their feet as he defended government policy on Europe.[22] He deliberately incited, then crushed, the more extreme Eurosceptics, and recovered his mantle as a conference darling for the first time since his departure from office in 1986.

Lamont was principal speaker on Thursday. Still smarting from the post-Black Wednesday fallout, and locked into an increasingly acrimonious relationship with Major, he tried to downplay the seriousness of Black Wednesday, considering talk of a 'national defeat' overdone (a contrast to Clarke's talk in the media of a 'disastrous setback' the previous Sunday). He went as far as he could to belittle the EC and its institutions. His speech cemented his long-standing reputation as a Eurosceptic, and stilled for the time being some of those voices on the right calling for his resignation.

Lamont had little to say about economic measures, however, and in terms of drama his speech was soon eclipsed by an incident at Jeffrey Archer's Krug and shepherd's pie party that evening in the Grand Hotel. Clarke had been incensed by Tebbit saying – truthfully – that he, Clarke, had not read the entire Maastricht Treaty. Clarke, in a highly charged state, accused Tebbit of declaring war on the government, and trying to take the conference by storm. Tebbit, equally roused, responded that he was being ganged up on and labelled as anti-European. Journalists swooped in on them 'like a cock fight'. Major himself was in the bathroom talking to David English about the *Daily Mail*'s criticisms at the time. Ryder and Archer watched the Clarke–Tebbit row with growing alarm before Ryder decided he should separate them with a tap on Clarke's shoulder. Major appeared in the room after they had parted to be told, half-annoyed and half-amused, what had happened.[23] The press had seen enough to reproduce an almost verbatim transcript over the next few days. The dispute served as an emblem for the state of polarised Tory opinions.

In Major's conference suite, long discussions had been taking place all week on the content of the Prime Minister's speech for Friday. Nick True drafted the bulk of it, with big inputs from Major and finishing flourishes as usual from Ronnie Millar. One of the open questions was whether to have a passage attacking Tebbit, but it was felt Hurd and Heseltine had done enough. Major's reference to Tebbit in his speech in the emergency debate on the ERM was felt to have provoked him, and Major's aides worried lest further personal attacks inflame him even more. Instead of attacking him and Thatcher by name, Major delivered a glancing blow citing Don Quixote, fighting imaginary battles: 'He tilted at windmills in the belief they were giants. He saw things that weren't there.'

Europe constituted the bulk of the speech. The Maastricht Bill, as he had indicated the previous Thursday, would be swiftly proceeded with in the Commons; if it was abandoned, Britain's future influence would be broken for ever and the country would be left 'scowling in the wings'. Major did, however, come across as more sympathetic to Eurosceptic concerns than Hurd had been on Tuesday. Policy would be based, he said, on 'a cold, clear-eyed calculation of the British national interest', steps towards a federal Europe would be resisted, and he ended by saying that Britain's interests would come 'first, last and always'.

The biggest hole was on economic policy; he spent more time than Lamont on sympathising with a repeated cry during the week, of business suffering from the recession. But he offered goals alone, low inflation and tight public spending controls, rather than specific measures to boost the economy. Any return to the ERM was neatly side-stepped. Other items were secondary in his speech: Heseltine would scrap red tape strangling business; 'hit squads' would be targeted at inner-city sink schools and, for the gallery, 'new age travellers' came under attack. The Citizen's Charter brought the promise of court action if public services were disrupted through unlawful strikes (Millar regretted its inclusion. 'I couldn't imagine anything more offputting than a Charter to start with, and Citizens makes me think of Robespierre,' he later commented).[24] Improving motorway toilets and facilities received a brief mention, which became a convenient object of ridicule for those seeking to deride Major and the speech.

Unusually for a Major speech, delivery outran the content. But he did enough to remind the Party about their common destiny, and their success in the general election, a very long six months earlier. In the most volatile and disunited Conservative Party Conference since 1963, when Macmillan's succession had been the story, Major had at least succeeded in reasserting his authority.

As his car sped away from Brighton on Friday afternoon, Major felt intensely relieved that the conference was behind him, and pleased by the affectionate reception given to his speech. The press at the weekend soon reminded him how much further he had to go. *The Times* offered hope: 'If anyone can unite the Conservatives, it is Mr Major.' But MacKenzie's *Sun* and Dacre's *Daily Mail* thought Major had not addressed the nation's anger and anguish over the recession.[25] The *Daily Telegraph* editorial line was personally sympathetic to Major, while critical of much he said; Bill Deedes, its former editor, used its columns to ask damagingly whether Major was up to the job.[26] Most hurtful of all was Frank Johnson in the *Sunday Telegraph*. Motorway service station toilets were symbolic of the aimlessness of his speech, he wrote, chiding Major for 'making wee-wee jokes when his economic and European policies had simultaneously collapsed'.[27]

The Pits

Major was restless that weekend, pacing around The Finings for other reasons than the hostile press. He was worried, deeply, that news of wholesale pit closures to be released the following week would backfire badly. 'I feared it would blow up in our faces. I said to Norma, "I can't do anything about it, because I have no economic arguments that cannot be easily knocked down. Economically, we should close the pits. But politically I am sure this will go wrong." ' Major's premonitions proved well-founded. He regarded his failure to give more thought to this issue as one of his biggest mistakes as Prime Minister.[28]

The plot is straightforward. British Coal wanted to close down thirty-one pits with the loss of 30,000 jobs, leaving just 25,000 coalminers employed in

Britain. The main market for coal was the electricity generating system, which had been privatised in 1990. The private generators inherited contracts for British coal stretching the other side of the last possible election date, and were now itching to replace coal with gas power. Energy Secretary John Wakeham had rejected all pre-election 'big bang' pit closures. If the Conservatives won the election, so the theory went, they would be politically strong enough to proceed with a closure scheme;[29] had Labour won, Tory insiders speculated that one of the first acts of the incoming Labour government would have been to emasculate the British coal industry.[30]

British Coal subsequently put the plan to Heseltine, who as President of the Board of Trade had absorbed the Energy Department into his fiefdom. He ordered a review of the closures but the economic arguments seemed convincing enough. Plans were discussed and tuned with colleagues in the DTI and the Cabinet committee on the economy over the summer. Heseltine battled with the Treasury for £1 billion, sufficient to give the miners a £23,000 redundancy payment each, which he thought generous enough to buy off any discontent.[31] Major agreed that the redundancy deal should be as generous as was available in earlier rounds of closures to NUM miners. Heseltine's victory over the Treasury came at the cost of agreeing that the redundancies would be in the 1992–3 financial year, thus in something of a hurry. Number Ten officials put some of the blame for the fiasco on the Treasury's rearguard action, which had led to exhaustive discussions of detail and not enough of principle or strategy.[32]

Heseltine saw the dangers of mass closures and lobbied for economic aid for the affected areas. He had grand ideas to regenerate the areas with new enterprise, and even dreamed of being seen as the white knight who rescued the mining areas from terminal decline.[33]

Heseltine thought the ground had been well prepared. A widely leaked report from the merchant bankers Rothschild two years before had stated the economic case for the pit closures. The likelihood of closure had been frequently aired, and just after Black Wednesday Arthur Scargill's release of a leaked government letter listing thirty doomed collieries had aroused little public response or surprise. At a meeting with the Prime Minister on the Friday morning of the Brighton conference, all was finally agreed.

Major's political antennae were normally so acute. Why did he not foresee earlier the storm that was about to be unleashed? On this occasion he had been preoccupied on other matters – ERM, Mellor, EC presidency, Party splits and recession – and he also possessed great faith in Heseltine, particularly in his political judgement, as seen in Brighton where the Party faithful took him back into their embrace. Major, despite some reservations, on which the DTI gave him reassuring answers, thus saw no reason to hold Heseltine back, not even when he said that they had to forge ahead and not delay the announcement.[34] One Number Ten insider said, 'We were mugged by Hezza', whose insistence on immediate release prevented detailed preparation and costings being completed.[35]

Throughout the process, Heseltine's apparent certainty and his reputation (subsequently revised in Whitehall and Downing Street) as a skilful political operator gave others the sense that there was nothing to worry about. When Wakeham casually told Ryder's first Number Twelve Committee meeting after the conference that an announcement on coal was imminent, he assured those attending that all angles had been covered. Some, however, did not have their apprehensions quelled.[36]

The announcement came on Tuesday 13 October via two press conferences, the first by British Coal emphasising the government's role in the decision, the second by Heseltine, who found himself on the defensive and facing considerable anger.[37] The Labour opposition, Tory rebels, the press and the country responded as one. Over 20,000 letters were received in Number Ten the week after the announcement, in contrast to the usual few thousand. Even normally loyal backbenchers made their protest clear. Winston Churchill offered a celebrated gesture of support with fellow Conservative MP Elizabeth Peacock at Silverhill colliery, to be cheered by miners in front of cameras. The reason for Tory anger was clear. Many of the thirty-one pits to have been closed, especially in Nottinghamshire, were represented by the Union of Democratic Mineworkers (UDM) and had stayed open during the NUM strike of 1984–5. The government was now seen to be betraying its allies among the miners of that epic struggle.

The spectre of whole mining communities going into decline pricked the nation's sense of justice. Many disgruntled MPs on the Eurosceptic right jumped on the bandwagon, especially as their old enemy Heseltine was the minister responsible for initiating it. The timing of the announcement could not have been more unfortunate: figures released that week showed a further fall of 0.3 per cent in manufacturing production, with unemployment figures up another 32,000 to their highest level in five years. A reduction in interest rates to 8 per cent did nothing to deflect the heat away from the government. Labour demanded, and achieved, a debate on the mines for the following Wednesday after Parliament returned following the recess, while Marcus Fox, Chairman of the 1922 Committee, publicly called the closure programme 'unacceptable'.[38]

Disquiet erupted in Cabinet on 15 October. The key decisions on the closures had been taken in Cabinet committee, and many members felt they were being blamed for decisions to which they had not been a party. Nor, unusually, had the matter gone up to be rubber-stamped by full Cabinet, as happened normally with key or contentious Cabinet committee decisions.[39] The concerns were listened to attentively, but Cabinet still decided not to back down on the closure programme.

The press response was the angriest yet, worse even than after Black Wednesday, and was not assuaged by a package of measures Major announced – including retraining for miners made redundant – to try to regain the initiative. Peter Riddell wrote recalling the chilling 1956 leader about Anthony Eden in the *Daily Telegraph*, and said that now it was Major who needed to deliver 'the smack of firm government'. He wrote of the 'impression of shambles' being given by government in 'the worst week of its life'.[40] The charge of dithering, last heard seriously in mid-1991, now made a reappearance. The *Independent on Sunday* was not alone in calling for Major to go; even the loyal *Sunday Express* called the pit closure announcement 'the most maladroit piece of government this country has seen for many years'.[41] The dominant mood was one of incredulity that Major, whose chief attribute was seen as his ability to empathise with the aspirations of ordinary people, should have so misread the public mood as to be now adding to the jobless total.[42]

The whips worked on discovering how widespread was the concern within the Party, and reported that they could not be confident that the government would defeat Labour's motion in Wednesday's debate on pit closures, which had been carefully crafted to scoop up Conservative waverers. The whip David Heathcoat-Amory brought the unwelcome news to Major, who called an emergency meeting on Sunday evening, 18 October, attended by Heseltine, Lamont, Wakeham, Clarke, Portillo, Ryder and Shephard, the Employment Secretary. Though Heseltine resisted a climbdown to the point where one Number Ten observer thought he was 'virtually ready to walk away',[43] it was now clear that a U-turn had to be made.

Mindful of resentment by those Cabinet ministers who had been excluded from the earlier discussions on closures, Number Ten contacted them all on Sunday to summon them to a special Cabinet meeting the following morning, 19 October. An extra £165 million, it was agreed, needed to be thrown at the problem, and twenty-one pits would be subject to a full review of their viability. Armed with this, he hoped, attractive new proposal, Major followed Cabinet with lunch at the Carlton Club with the executive of the 1922 Committee. He was in expansive form in his speech after their first course, outlining the new package and his views on the economy. Indeed, so loquacious was he that the executive became concerned that their roast lamb would arrive cold. Major was gently asked to break his speech, to be continued after the Tory bellies were filled with their red meat.[44]

But Major was still not in the clear. Heseltine in the House that afternoon appeared to go back on what had been agreed at Cabinet hours before, with talk merely of the twenty-one pits having a three months' stay of execution. 'We were in headless chicken territory,' according to one official.[45] Heseltine relented before a meeting of the 1922 Committee executive next morning, and agreed to a thorough review of the government's entire energy policy and of the future viability of the twenty-one pits, subject only, he said, to Cabinet agreeing. None present thought for one moment that he would fail to receive that support. Major confirmed the further U-turn at Prime Minister's Questions that afternoon.

Victory in the vote on Wednesday 21 October looked more likely. Heseltine was lucky to escape. The debate was rowdy, with the fury of Labour MPs in the areas affected very evident. To the relief of watching officials he was not confronted with detailed questions on individual pits: 'That could have destroyed him,' thought one. Sullen Tory backbenchers were rallied by Labour's baiting of Heseltine, and by his own stirring but crudely partisan speech. Only six Tories rebelled, five abstained, and the government had a majority of thirteen.[46] Even though it still left difficult decisions to be taken the following year, the heat was off the government. Victory in the debate also took the sting out of the march in Hyde Park that day by 50,000 miners and their supporters, brandishing posters declaiming, 'Sack Major Not The Miners'.[47]

The same message was repeated increasingly by the press, with a new twist – 'was Major having a breakdown?' An article in *The Times* posed the question. It alleged that Major had been leading a solitary life in his temporary flat in Admiralty Arch, while Norma spent much of her time in Huntingdon. It expanded a question Simon Jenkins, the recently retired editor, had posed in the newspaper two weeks before, about whether Major had cracked up on Black Wednesday, when he suffered apparently from some kind of 'nervous setback'. Unable to relax any more, or to know whom he could trust, he was reputed to have made emergency calls to Patten in Hong Kong (but he recalls a Prime Minister 'cool as a cucumber'[48]). His inability to sack anyone because he feared unpopularity had explained in the eyes of some commentators his dithering over Lamont and Mellor.[49]

Number Ten strenuously rebutted the charges in *The Times*, but Peter Stothard refused to retract.[50] Simon Jenkins, however, distanced himself from those who claimed Major was wobbling and of unsound mind. 'Some of the stories were ridiculous. He did not flip that day, but he had no idea what hit him and he was very upset.'[51] Meanwhile, on the day *The Times* article was published, a MORI survey in the *European* revealed that Major was the most unpopular Prime Minister in the history of polling.[52]

Number Ten let it be known that they blamed Thatcherite, anti-Maastricht elements for spreading the rumours. The wobble story was picked up by television's *Newsnight* and was being screened in the Whips' Office at the very moment when Major dropped in to see them. One of the whips rushed to turn the television off, but Major insisted on them all, leaden-faced, watching it. They were more careful when Major called in on subsequent occasions.[53]

Whereas there is no truth that Major had a nervous collapse or even had his judgement clouded by anxiety during Black Wednesday, by late October part of his spirit was crushed. In front of outsiders he would always put on a show. But there were some dark moments, shared only with those closest to him: Norma, Sarah Hogg, Hill, Allan and Wall. What is remarkable is not his loss of confidence, but the courage and resilience he showed in surmounting it and rediscovering his self-esteem. Many people would have been crushed by what hit him. One has to go back to Heath in 1973–4 to find a premier operating under so much duress.

It was not the decision to close the pits that had been at fault, but the presentation and timing, and Major knew it. He did not spend time looking for scapegoats. David Poole, the Policy Unit member directly responsible, still blames himself for not sounding the panic button. 'It got as far as it did', he said, 'because like lots of things in government, it took on an inevitability, a life of its own.' After the episode subsided, he wrote an *aide-mémoire* which he called 'Seven Lessons from Coal', now hanging in his home. It listed the questions which should have been asked, such as: 'Will those the policy affects understand it? Will they find it risible?' Or, for short: 'How will it play in the pub?'[54]

One issue playing strongly in pubs across the country that autumn was, 'What is the government doing to end the recession?'

New Economic Policy

The underlying reason for the malaise in the Tory Party was not just Europe, but the state of the economy, and in particular the belief that the government was insufficiently acknowledging the widespread discontent. The Party had promised during 1991, and again in the 1992 election, that the effect of the recession would soon pass; Major bore much of the blame for sticking by the ERM, widely seen as responsible for excessively high interest rates. The spike in interest rates briefly to 15 per cent on Black Wednesday caused widespread horror and incredulity.

Major and Lamont pressed for interest rates to return to 10 per cent the day after Black Wednesday, against Treasury caution, and again for it to be cut to 9 per cent five days later.[55] Some of the work on establishing a new monetary framework had been put in place before the Brighton conference. Reconstructing monetary policy was the first priority.[56] The pound was weak, falling to a new low the Monday before the Party Conference opened, while the government came under heavy pressure before and during it to do more to stimulate growth. A meeting was convened in the Grand Hotel in Brighton with Major, Hogg, Allan, Lamont, and Treasury officials Burns and Budd. Major brought them under heavy pressure to have a further interest rate cut to give some practical encouragement to the conference delegates, but Lamont, taking the Treasury line, on this occasion prevailed: there were to be no further cuts to be announced for the time being, because of the risk of building inflationary pressures.[57]

Their meeting was frequently interrupted by a speaker van going up and down the front at Brighton, unwittingly offering the Prime Minister support. The messages 'bring down interest rates' and 'end the recession' were chimed out at opportune moments. So telling were these chance slogans that the official Number Ten record apparently alluded to them in the minutes.[58] Delegates at Brighton would, indeed, have preferred the secret Grand Hotel meeting to have followed the advice of the slogans rather than the Treasury. Nothing announced about economic policy during the conference altered the immediate impression of the government fiddling while Rome burned.

The outcome of the Brighton meeting was written up in a letter, dated Thursday 8 October, to the Chairman of the Commons Select Committee on the Treasury and Civil Service, John Watts.[59] This announced that the government would adopt an inflation target of 1 to 4 per cent over the next four years to replace the exchange rate anchor of the ERM.

Sarah Hogg was prominent in urging Major to announce measures to show that the government did have an economic policy for growth. A relaxation of economic policy was discussed in broad terms in the emergency coal Cabinet of Monday 19 October, but few ministers expected Major to act so fast.[60] Prompted perhaps by the criticism that he had been too withdrawn from the limelight during the coal crisis, Major gave a very rare lobby briefing himself, around the Cabinet table in his room in the Commons. He told surprised journalists about his new thinking on economic policy, speaking in similar terms in a recorded interview on *News at Ten* that evening, when he announced, 'A strategy for growth is what we need, a strategy for growth is what we're going to have.' The next day's headlines were consequently changed from 'New U-Turn on Pits' to 'Major Goes for Growth'.[61] The substance of the apparent new policy was, however, thin, and the Treasury – to whom the announcement came as a surprise – wondered whether he was talking up growth too far.[62] Major's announcement was also interpreted as implying an imminent further cut in interest rates.

Relations between Major and Lamont were becoming increasingly tense again, with disagreements across the range of economic issues, from interest rates to public spending, compounded by Major's suspicion of his Chancellor's motives. Lamont insisted that with the pound out of the ERM, no further stimulation was needed. Major told him that he must protect those projects with job-sustaining potential in the public spending round to be announced the following month.[63] To Lamont, this confirmed his view that Major did not understand public spending issues.[64]

More flesh was put on the government's economic policy in Lamont's Mansion House speech on 29 October, with a two-pronged strategy which bore evidence of some form of compromise being hammered out between Chancellor and Prime Minister. Growth was to be supplied by protection for capital projects in what would be a tough autumn spending round, and by a new partnership between private finance and public sector projects called the Private Finance Initiative (PFI). The first had been strongly pressed by Heseltine and Major, although Portillo as Chief Secretary was also sympathetic to reprieving the Jubilee Line extension to the London Underground. The second prong bore Lamont's imprimatur, although Major was an enthusiast for it. Additionally, in the wake of the ERM exit there was to be a new era of more open policy-making. This commitment to visibility would assist in achieving the new inflation target, which Lamont now announced was to be towards the *bottom* end of the 1 to 4 per cent range by the end of the current Parliament. Several fruits of the new thinking were announced.

A monthly monetary report of the regular Chancellor–Governor of the Bank of England meetings to set out the basis of policy decisions; clear explanations for any changes in interest rates, to reassure the markets about what the government was thinking; a forecasting panel of seven independent economists (dubbed 'the wise men') to assess the economy and supplement the Treasury's forecasts for the economy; the Bank to publish a quarterly assessment of the progress of counter-inflationary policy. Lamont also announced that when the first new unified budget – bringing together the spending round with the spring budget – took place at the end of 1993, government accounts would separate capital and current spending.[65]

The Treasury had wanted to institute much of the programme for some years; it took the new atmosphere of post-Black Wednesday *perestroika*, and Lamont's efforts, to allow the *glasnost* to proceed.[66] Lamont would have gone even further, and favoured an independent Bank, but that was for Major a step too far.[67] Here were the building blocks of the government's new economic policy, and they were to prove remarkably successful.

Birmingham Summit

Europe was the other large ball Major was having to juggle. He had said he would reintroduce the Maastricht Bill. So much was clear. But when, exactly? Judging the right time, and dovetailing it with the EC Council at Edinburgh in December at the culmination of Britain's EC presidency, were constantly in his mind.

The right to convene mid-term summits for heads of government was one often exercised by those holding the EC presidency. Major decided on such a meeting for 16 October at Birmingham, on the advice that the Danish and French referendums and the ERM crisis put Europe in a difficult position requiring stabilising action. He sought a clear statement on curbing the powers of the EC Commission and to enhance 'subsidiarity', to try to win over Eurosceptics to the Maastricht Bill by showing them that talk of federalism was much exaggerated, and to reassure Danish public opinion. But Birmingham proved significant only as a stepping stone to further talk on the subsidiarity principle at Edinburgh. In important respects Birmingham weakened Major's position too. News stories of him consorting with European leaders discussing European business played badly in the public eye when miners and their families were facing grim future prospects; quite erroneously, it gave the impression he cared more about Europe than the plight of his own countrymen. Eurosceptics, too, were not impressed. Birmingham failed to allay Eurosceptic fears, said Michael Spicer: 'I could not see the point in holding it.'[68] Others on the right felt Major had missed another vital opportunity to exploit the cool response in Denmark and France to the Maastricht Treaty to press for a new, much looser form of association between the twelve member states.

Several factors militated against Birmingham's success. Major was distracted, and had not had time to conduct his usual pre-conference lobbying. In the midst of the conference itself, he even had to abandon his chair for vital minutes on receiving a telephone call that Lamont had angrily walked out of EDX, the new Cabinet committee on public expenditure, and no one knew where he was.[69] Lamont reacted badly to expressions of opinion on economic policy from other ministers, especially Clarke, seeing such statements in the volatile atmosphere as manoeuvring for his job. EDX was not usually the forum for a consideration of wider economic policy: its focus instead was the limited issue of public spending. Lamont's mood was angry that Friday because he thought himself particularly isolated on public spending, which he felt he was fighting a lonely battle to constrain.[70] Major and his entourage spent some time in frantic telephone calls to London, trying first to discover where Lamont had gone and how deep his disaffection went, and secondly to make sure the story did not leak to the press.[71]

Not that the episode made any significant difference at the summit. The core reason Birmingham failed to achieve the results that Major sought, despite his brisk chairmanship, was because of a fundamental lack of sympathy from the other eleven EC countries for his objectives. The other delegations arrived in Birmingham suspicious that the British government would do little to save Maastricht, and would enjoy the benefits of competitive devaluation. They left only a little reassured.[72] Some of the more hardline member countries were irritated by Britain's delays over ratifying Maastricht – though there was a growing realisation of Major's parliamentary difficulties – and by its reluctance to plan for re-entry into the ERM. Germany felt, in particular, it had fallen over itself to help Britain achieve what it wanted at the Maastricht conference, yet Major still seemed to be dragging his feet and asking for more. Delors was not willingly going to allow any surrender of the Commission's powers, and smaller countries like Luxembourg and Portugal were only too happy to support him, seeing the Commission as a defender of their interests against the strongest EC members. The love-in that Major had enjoyed with EC leaders, and Kohl in particular, was seen to have cooled considerably.

Sporadic chanting from angry miners protesting outside Birmingham's International Conference Centre provided a constant reminder to Major of his domestic difficulties. At the press conference at the conclusion, questions on the summit were quickly despatched and Delors left the platform gratefully while the media focused on what they were really interested in: not more Euro summitry and carefully crafted diplomatic statements, but coal and the economy.[73]

Crazy Paving

Birmingham may not have helped Major with the Eurosceptics, but it made him all the more determined to conclude the passage of the Maastricht Bill to restore his standing with heads of government before his Edinburgh summit. On Thursday 22 October it was announced, therefore, that a 'paving debate' on the Maastricht Treaty would be held on 4 November, followed by the committee stage, with completion by late November. Some in Cabinet, like Howard and Lilley, favoured delaying the Bill's reintroduction until the New Year. Major overruled them. The 1922 Committee, however, which had not been consulted about the timing beforehand, exploded when it met that Thursday evening, and launched a full frontal attack on the government's entire Maastricht policy. After Marcus Fox reported the strong feeling to the Prime Minister, Major backtracked and said that, whereas the paving vote would take place on 4 November, he would not 'railroad' the rest of the Maastricht Bill through the House, using the argument that to do so would squeeze time for debate on other matters, above all the economy.

In private, Major began to talk about resigning if pushed too far on Maastricht.[74] News of his dejected statement percolated outside Downing Street. Tebbit urged Eurosceptics not to be intimidated; finding a replacement would not be 'too difficult'. The stakes were rising. Major was obliged through duties overseas to leave the bubbling pot of speculation briefly unattended, but not before contributing a further scrap of meat for the stew. At a lobby briefing, the Sun's Trevor Kavanagh, trying to gauge the importance Major attached to the paving vote, obtained an answer that at least suggested the possibility of 'taking it to the people' (i.e. calling a general election) rather than his resignation.[75] Kavanagh wrote up the story as a threat to call a general election should the government lose the paving vote but, unconvinced whether the threat was for real, the normally headline story was relegated to page two.[76]

Major, and a journalistic entourage, then spent the weekend of 24 and 25 October in Egypt, the occasion being the fiftieth anniversary commemoration on the battlefield of El Alamein. Kavanagh's piece aroused the curiosity of Andrew Neil, the increasingly anti-Major editor of the Sunday Times, who wondered what such a significant story was doing on page two of the Sun. Anxious to obtain a stronger commitment, or else a denial, Neil arranged for a journalist in the prime ministerial party to question Major and Gus O'Donnell further.[77]

Kavanagh's piece had also aroused strong reaction in Number Twelve, where Ryder was put out to hear of such a scheme emerging out of the blue. He found the election threat an unhelpful device for whipping through the paving vote, and tried to persuade O'Donnell to kill the idea. Major, however, had suffered enough that week from accusations of U-turns on coal and the economy, vividly describing his recent experience as 'like hot coals with poisonous snakes coming through it', and in expansive mood on the flight to Egypt became more attracted to the idea of a dramatic showdown. He told O'Donnell not to knock the story down,[78] and Neil's correspondent and other journalists reported that, far from being dismissed, the election story had been 'stood up and amplified' on Friday night at the Cairo Carlton, where Major was staying. Number Ten sources believed this was mischievous invention. Neil was incredulous that the Prime Minister and the government were on record as threatening to commit the Tory Party to mass suicide for losing a treaty 'that nobody cares about', and decided to put the story on the front page of the *Sunday Times*.[79]

Neil's reaction was far from unique. Discontent with the prospect of a Maastricht-inspired election, and a leadership which was prepared to make such a threat so apparently lightly, reached ministerial ranks. 'Petulant, silly and pathetic' was how one Tory critic described Major's stance to Anthony Bevins.[80] The new MP Alan Duncan gave voice to the increasingly discussed opinion that, although the right had most of the parliamentary party, the government was run from the centre left. Most of his 92 Group audience agreed. To the Labour whips, the election threat was exactly what they needed to ensure a full turnout against the government motion. The prospect loomed of both the Maastricht Treaty and the government falling at the same time, despite the existence of (different) Commons majorities in favour of each surviving.

Major returned from Alexandria, where he had given a sensitive and gracious speech to the veterans of the desert war, on Sunday morning. He was on relaxed form on the plane journey, and journalists travelling with him were convinced that his mind was settled on his strategy for the paving vote.[81] On his return to work in London on Monday morning, he found his colleagues up in arms about his threat. Fowler was as horrified as Ryder at the idea of calling a general election, and there was very little support for it among the Cabinet. Major bowed to their combined opinion,[82] and briefings now suggested that his threat amounted to nothing more than a 'flyer' to test out one of several ideas. The Major camp within Number Ten had not stopped considering other options. One, as reported by Andrew Marr, was the scheme that Major could resign the Party leadership if the paving vote was lost, and promptly stand again. It was hoped that this would flush out a standard bearer for the Thatcherites, who would then be defeated. The plan in embryo was the leadership election triggered by Major in spectacular circumstances in June 1995.[83] The leaking of drastic schemes in the autumn of 1992 was intended to pressurise the Eurosceptics, and the absence of an unambiguous withdrawal of the general election threat was designed to prey on the minds of some waverers.

As often when his back was against the wall, Major gave some of his strongest performances at Prime Minister's Questions, crucial in reminding his Party of his qualities as their leader. Rarely did he speak better than to 200 backbenchers of the 1922 Committee on the evening of Thursday 29 October, when he declared himself – in a phrase that was to be oft-repeated against him – to be the Cabinet's 'greatest Euro-sceptic'. He said it to try to reassure his audience that he was fully aware of their concerns about federalism, which he shared, but equally he argued that inward investment opportunities would be sacrificed if the treaty was not ratified by Britain, and the country would be marginalised by an increasingly federal Community. His pleas won over several waverers. Press reports stated that Major received eight rounds of desk-banging (the traditional 1922 Committee way of showing approval) during his thirty-five-minute speech.[84]

Lobbying of MPs continued at an even more furious pace at the start of the following week, in the run-up to the paving vote on Wednesday 4 November. As during the general election, Major cast caution aside to operate at 'street level' with his Party's backbenchers, using all the charm and persuasive tricks on sceptics that he had acquired in thirty years of politics. Heseltine and Clarke were prominent among Major's senior adjutants working on backbenchers, while Tebbit and others worked hard to lobby backbenchers to vote against. Ryder's team of whips was felt to have conducted the most intensive and tough campaign since the Labour whips battled to keep James Callaghan in power during his minority from 1977 to 1979. Given the size of the Thatcherite general election majorities (43, 144, 102), it is unsurprising that her whips did not have to resort to such strong-arm tactics. Now both Conservative and Labour whips employed practices that were considered manipulative and heavy handed, causing much enduring offence.

The Major camp knew that they stood little chance of winning over the twenty-two diehards who had voted against the second reading of the Maastricht Bill back in May. Instead, they concentrated on the remainder of the eighty-four Conservatives who had signed the post-Danish referendum 'fresh start' early day motion in June.

Eurosceptics have been divided up into four basic groups.[85] The 'all-out' anti-marketeers opposed the EC from the outset in 1972, and included John Biffen, Richard Body and Teddy Taylor. The constitutionalists, like Bill Cash and Richard Shepherd, stressed the threat to national sovereignty. The free-marketeers took the Thatcher line that the EC was an unwelcome interference in Britain's capitalist endeavours. Numerically the largest group, prominent members included Michael Spicer, Nicholas Budgen, George Gardiner, Teresa Gorman and several of the new entrants in 1992, including Iain Duncan-Smith, Bernard Jenkin and John Whittingdale. Finally came the populist nationalists, such as Ann and Nicholas Winterton, Rhodes Boyson and Tony Marlow. Such a categorisation is not wholly satisfactory, in part because many people belonged to more than one group. But it does help to show why European issues excited such widespread antipathy, because it touched so many deep Tory nerves. In the case of the diehards, it transcended their concern to keep the Party in power.

Two Maastricht votes took place on 4 November. A Labour amendment proposing to delay consideration of the Maastricht Bill until after the Edinburgh summit was defeated by 319 to 313 votes. A second, more borderline, vote on the paving motion itself, inviting the Commons to resume progress on the Maastricht Treaty, was carried by 319 to 316 votes. Twenty-six Tory MPs voted against the government, and a further seven abstained. Four of the twenty-two diehards who voted against the second reading came round to the government's side – Rupert Allason, Michael Carttiss, Harry Greenway and Andrew Hunter. To win over Carttiss, and another, Vivian Bendall, promises were made – though Number Ten alleged it had been implicit for some time – that the third reading would be delayed until after the result of the fresh Danish referendum in May 1993. The rationale of the paving motion, to show Britain's EC partners evidence of real progress towards passage of the Bill before Edinburgh, was thus heavily compromised.[86]

Even with the support of all but one Liberal Democrat, it had been a perilously close episode. MPs, much given to hyperbole, said they had never before witnessed pressure on MPs, or tension in Parliament, quite like it. On this occasion, for those who joined in 1979 or after, they were almost certainly right. Labour, who had boxed themselves into a corner of opposing Maastricht in the belief they would win, were livid with the Liberal Democrats for propping up the government: 'We are going to hound them from one end of the country to the other,' a Labour spokesman responded angrily.[87] The Eurosceptics, too, were angered. They would not forgive Major for the paving vote: 'It was a totally unnecessary step,' said one.[88] Others considered it a declaration of hostilities. While the *froideur* between Labour and the Liberal Democrats went away, that between Major and his Eurosceptics would not.

Major had taken a back seat in the debate to a smooth Douglas Hurd performance. But he had survived. Relaxation, however, bar a quick glass of champagne with the whips, was out of the question. His personal authority, damaged further by calls from Tory journalists like Simon Heffer and Paul Johnson for him to stand down, had to be restored.[89] As Hugo Young perceptively observed, 'Insulting the leader, in public and in private, has entered the recognised protocols of Conservative political conduct.'[90] And he had two further crises to handle: an increasingly acrimonious battle with Cabinet colleagues over public spending, and the threat of a world trade war following the breakdown of GATT talks. 'Another day, another crisis,' sighed a Downing Street insider.[91]

TWENTY-THREE

Deep Winter:

November 1992–January 1993

THE WEEKS FOLLOWING Black Wednesday saw Major's leadership under sustained pressure. Had Heseltine, his only serious rival at the time, not been so Europhile, and not had his reputation so severely damaged by the pits closure débâcle, Major's leadership might have been even more strongly called into question. Even the realisation of this did nothing to raise his spirits. Peter Brooke, returning to Cabinet in September to replace Mellor, found the mood utterly different from six months before. He ascribed the demoralised feeling in part to the Cabinet Room being out of action as part of the Number Ten refit: 'meeting in that dreadful Cobra Room under Number Ten, with a ceiling not much over six feet. It all was incredibly depressing.'[1]

Once the paving motion had been carried, Major felt a surge of anger: these rebel MPs, he felt, were only where they were because of his winning the general election, and this is how they thank me. The experience hardened him – not the reaction of a man chronically depressed. He became more determined than ever to take the Maastricht Bill through the House, and show his critics the quality of his leadership. In this he was helped by evidence of slight poll recovery in December 1992 and January 1993. Perhaps, he wondered, the corner had been turned.

Cuts, Arms and Bruises

The 1992–3 public spending round was always going to be tough, following the high and controversial pre-election settlement in 1991–2. Although the economy in fact began, tentatively, to recover as early as the second quarter of 1992, this fact was neither obvious, nor were the benefits widely felt at the time. Pressure on spending ministers was further increased by Major's insistence that cuts must fall not on capital projects, but rather on current expenditure, which Major thought would not cause damage to jobs.

Much was changing not just to the content but also to the structure of economic policy. The advent of the unified budget in December 1993, announced by Lamont in his March 1992 budget, meant that the 1992 autumn statement on public spending would be the last of its kind. In addition, in an idea traceable to Lamont and Bill Robinson, the Treasury in

1992 adopted a new procedure for deciding public expenditure allocations. In place of the former system where one worked 'bottom-up', with spending ministers putting in bids and then having them hacked down to arrive at an acceptable public spending total, a 'top-down' system was instituted, where an overall 'control total' figure was arrived at by Cabinet, and individual ministers had to vie with each other to gain their slice of it. The process was designed to make it easier to achieve the elusive aim of gradually reducing the public sector's share of national income.[2] In a further development, the old 'Star Chamber' was replaced by a new Cabinet committee called EDX, chaired by the Chancellor, and containing six other ministers (Clarke, Heseltine, Newton, Wakeham, Waldegrave and Portillo).[3] With a heavy preponderance of non-spending ministers on the committee, the group could be more impartial in adjudicating on the merits of each case.

The Cabinet in July decided the control total for the following year would be £244.5 billion. After the summer holidays, EDX met regularly, with Portillo, the new Chief Secretary, working hard to trim ministerial ambitions. Most work was required on Howard (Environment), Shephard (Employment) and Bottomley (Health).[4] The conclusions of EDX were brought to a special Cabinet on Monday evening, 2 November, where Portillo outlined his recommendations, and ministers haggled for four hours. Public sector pay was a source of particular dispute, some ministers even wanting it frozen to make way for their own projects. The Cabinet continued deliberating on Tuesday and again at the regular Thursday meeting. Eight hours were spent reaching agreement.[5]

The autumn statement, delivered on 13 November, hit the figure of £244.5 billion precisely, omitting 'cyclical' spending items such as unemployment benefits, which the target excluded as they rose and fell with the state of the economy. Capital spending, as Major intended, was indeed protected, with hospital building and the Jubilee line extension to Canary Wharf being two of the areas reprieved. Public sector pay was the main victim, with pay rises for most limited to 1.5 per cent, provoking a predictable uproar, especially as higher increases went to senior civil servants, judges and others in the upper strata, who received 2.8 per cent.

Lamont's presentation of the statement was deliberately cheerful in tone, reflecting the government's new-found commitment to going for growth. It was well received by backbenchers, Philip Stephens noting that 'a collective cheer from Tory MPs for Lamont's recovery package' led to the government's hopes being raised that it might at last 'have a chance to draw a line under the political turmoil of the last two months'.[6] Major, helped considerably by Portillo, who proved himself a tough-nosed cost-cutter, thus succeeded in steering Cabinet through the difficult spending round at a time when his own standing remained in question.

At this point, to Major's chagrin, an issue landed in his red boxes, the Arms-to-Iraq episode, which heaped even more trouble on his beleaguered government. Concern over British arms trading with Iraq had emerged before the Gulf War. Suspicions grew during the course of 1991 that illegal shipments of machine tools had reached Saddam's regime with ministerial knowledge. A machine tools company, Matrix Churchill, was being prosecuted for breach of the trade restrictions with Iraq when the trial suddenly collapsed on 9 November. Alan Clark, the former Minister of State at Defence, admitted in his evidence to giving encouragement to the company in its trade with Iraq.[7] A storm broke as Clark's statement seemed to lay the government open to the charge that it was happy to stand by and see innocent men, employees of Matrix Churchill, sent to prison to cover up its own secret promotion of arms sales against its own official guidelines.[8]

Major was barely aware of this ticking time bomb. Tom King, when still Defence Secretary, had sent a minute to Major querying 'the wisdom of letting Clark appear in the witness box', but Major was content for him to proceed.[9] When the furore broke out on a day when Major was preoccupied by hosting a banquet for Yeltsin, Major consulted the Lord Chancellor Lord Mackay, Robin Butler and Alex Allan, among others. Those involved recall Major's approach very clearly: 'I am absolutely confident that the government has not behaved improperly, and it will not take any time once the facts are out in the open to establish that the government has not done so.' The meeting with Butler and Allan agreed on a judicial inquiry with a single judge as the best forum to ascertaining the truth; Major, who had made open government one of his causes, readily endorsed this. Fresh in his memory was the Bingham Report on official supervision of the corrupt bank BCCI, which had been successfully published on 22 October. While critical of the Bank of England's easygoing approach to City regulation, it dismissed the allegations that had so offended Major in summer 1991.[10] Mackay put forward some names, of whom Richard Scott was the front-runner.

Scott had presided over one of the 'Spycatcher' appeals in the late eighties and was known as a liberal judge. He was deliberately selected as one who would carry credibility with centre-left opinion, alert for any official whitewash or cover-up. One Number Ten insider commented: 'Major accepted the advice that an enquiry was the best way to kill it off. He knew he had done nothing wrong himself, and he had no reason to suppose anyone else had. As far as Scott personally went, to be frank, he wouldn't have known him from Adam.'[11]

But Major was impressed by Scott's impeccable credentials, and he saw at once that Scott would lend peculiar authority to the clean bill of health that he was confident would be delivered.[12] In the highly charged atmosphere, and with deep scepticism in the press and among the public about the government's integrity, Major was convinced that he had acted decisively, and taken not just the honest but the morally right course of action.[13] He had been accused of dithering and being indecisive on several occasions over the previous few weeks; on this occasion, he was going to react swiftly.

Neither the announcement of the inquiry on 10 November, nor the choice of Scott, however, were to quieten the storm. 'Day by day the accusations and revelations generated by the collapse of the Matrix Churchill case grow more grave and far-reaching,' said an editorial in the *Independent*. 'They now involve the honour and integrity of the Prime Minister', as well as several ministers.[14] The *Sunday Times* concluded at the end of the week: 'This government has become so inept that when it tries to cover up its own conspiracies it succeeds only in exposing them ... Like Watergate, the cover-up is even worse than the conspiracy.'[15]

The fire burned on and on, with Major's decision to set up an inquiry seen by his right-wing critics not as wise and fair-minded but as weakness and folly. Major thought he was initiating an inquiry merely into whether ministers had conspired to put innocent men in prison.[16] Scott interpreted his brief in a far more free-ranging manner, and spent three years producing his over-long and under-analysed report.

Lamont's reputation meanwhile continued to be badly bruised by a whole series of embarrassing and often untrue stories that appeared in a press which had not forgiven him for the recession. Stories about him buying champagne and Raffles cigarettes at a Thresher's off-licence, with hints of secret assignations, turned out to have been made up. Further damaging stories, of his NatWest bank account, leaked to the *Sun*, showing him frequently to have been in debt, and the use of public funds to pay legal bills to help him evict a 'sex-therapist' from his rented London home, sapped his authority and gravitas. United again exactly two years after the leadership election, Major rallied to his embattled Chancellor and refused to demand his resignation.[17]

Lamont was having almost as bad a time as Major. The most choleric of the 'Cambridge Four' who had been at university together (the others being Clarke, Gummer and Howard), Lamont was under huge strain, looked very drained, and felt he was being insufficiently supported by his colleagues while the press tried to drag him down.[18] The irony was that he was embarking on his most successful six months as Chancellor, beginning with the autumn statement, for which he later felt he was denied much of the credit. Many in Central Office and elsewhere felt he should have been moved immediately after the statement.[19] When the end came, in May 1993, all the bitterness Lamont felt inside him towards Major welled up into the open.

Annus Horribilis

Major's attention was being absorbed in the last weeks of 1992 by yet another intractable problem, the royal family. Reports percolated through in the autumn that he was spending an unusual amount of time on royal matters.[20] Though insiders are notoriously cagey in divulging details of Prime Minister–monarch relations, it seems clear that he set greater store by the relationship than Thatcher, and devoted more attention to the monarchy – though his focus on royal issues is down mostly to the greater royal turbulence in the 1990s than in the 1980s. His regular Tuesday meetings at the palace lasted on average an hour to an hour and a half; Major would go with his Principal Private Secretary, Andrew Turnbull then Alex Allan, who would sit drinking sherry in one room with Robert Fellowes, the Queen's Private Secretary, while monarch and Prime Minister talked upstairs in the Queen's sitting room with no record made.

When both were under pressure, as they were that autumn, their meetings took on the role of a joint confessional. A constitutional conservative, Major strongly admired the Queen, whose coronation, when he was aged ten, he still remembered. He also believed that the troubles of the royal family and the troubles of the nation and government were linked, and reflected national morale including a pervasive cynicism.[21] He felt irritated that the behaviour of the young royals did not just detract from the sanctity of the institution of monarchy, but also reinforced a climate of scepticism towards those in positions of authority.[22]

The royal cord of distress had several strands. But it took the publication of Andrew Morton's *Diana: Her True Story* in June 1992 to chronicle the detailed cracks in the crumbling edifice of the marriage of the Prince and Princess of Wales. The tabloids locked onto the story, especially when it was revealed that Morton's book had been written with Diana's tacit approval.[23] Major held discussions with the Queen before the summer, and again at Balmoral.[24] He met both Charles and Diana, Diana separately on several occasions. They were frank with him and she wrote him several grateful personal letters.[25] But any support and guidance Major could offer was to no avail. After it became clear that the marriage was unsustainable, his prime concern became the constitutional position.[26] On 9 December Major told the Commons that the Prince and Princess were to separate, though the constitutional position and the succession to the throne would in no way be affected, a statement greeted with some gasps of incredulity.[27] He appealed for 'a degree of privacy and understanding' for the couple from the media. Major deliberately sought the sympathy of a sombre House, realising how important it would be with the future of the monarchy at stake.[28]

The failed marriages of Princess Anne and Prince Andrew led to a further erosion of popular support for the monarchy, especially when lurid details of Diana's private life emerged to reinforce the sleazy impression left by revelations about the Duchess of York's liaisons.[29] Half-naked pictures of 'Fergie' with her financial adviser John Bryan, and the 'Squidgy' and 'Camillagate' tapes, fed the nation's appetite for sex and intrigue in high places but caused deep depression at the heart of Buckingham Palace and Whitehall.

1992 'is not a year on which I will look back with undiluted pleasure', said the Queen with not a little understatement at a lunch at Guildhall in the City of London on 24 November. In contrast to Dryden's 'Annus Mirabilis', she spoke of the year turning out to be an 'annus horribilis'. Dryden's poem, published in 1667, spoke of the fire of London the previous year, and was prefaced by verses to the Duchess of York. The Queen's speech, 325 years later, had no desire to honour the current Duchess, nor did she refer directly to the marital problems of her children, nor the rising demands for her to pay tax, though she did refer to 'the tragic fire at Windsor', which had severely damaged the castle earlier in the year. But all her travails were well understood by the audience, which gave her a standing ovation to show its support and sympathy.

The government's decision that the state and not the Queen would pay for the damage to Windsor Castle produced, however, not approbation, but a storm of protest, which resulted in Major announcing at the end of November, some weeks earlier than intended, the news that the Queen would pay income tax on her annual private income, estimated at around £5 million a year. At the same time, another principal source of public dissatisfaction with the monarchy was to be scrutinised: the size and scope of the Civil List, which refers to those members of the royal family who receive support from the public finances.[30]

Major rounded off the year with a staunch defence of the monarchy: 'I believe [it] will weather the difficulties it has had in recent months and emerge strengthened. I detect no enthusiasm in this country for anything other than a continuation of the constitutional monarchy.' Alan Hamilton in *The Times* wrote – with some foundation – that not since Churchill (1951–5) had the Queen enjoyed such a close relationship with a Tory Prime Minister.[31]

Edinburgh Summit

Major needed above all two boons as his own demi-*annus horribilis* drew to a close: to boast of a success for his leadership style, and movement in Europe to achieve the difficult balancing act of satisfying domestic and Community aspirations. He achieved both with the outcome of the Edinburgh summit on 11 and 12 December, described by one admittedly partisan FCO spokesman as 'possibly the most successful EC summit ever'.[32]

A positive result was far from certain, even up to the last minute when Sunday's headlines were being rewritten at the conclusion of the conference. Talk at the unsuccessful Birmingham summit had been of a flawed British presidency. Major's self-confidence was low before he turned in late November seriously to plan for the EC Council meeting, only three weeks away. Unlike in the run-up to Birmingham, he read himself in thoroughly – as usual complaining at the size of the briefs, but absorbing them all nevertheless. Systematically he worked his way through seeing the Community's heads of government, flying to nine capitals in little more than a fortnight. The travel seemed to lighten his mood, and he became increasingly animated and confident as the conference approached.[33] The two capitals Major did not visit as part of his preparations were Paris and Bonn. He did not see Mitterrand again after Birmingham, but they spoke on the telephone and on the evening before the summit opened they dined together.[34] He found the ailing President noticeably more frail than at Maastricht, but more willing to be supportive.

A key meeting took place with Kohl at Ditchley Park, the conference centre in Oxfordshire, on 11 November (by coincidence, the anniversary of Armistice Day). Truce was much in the air during the day, which took on an atmosphere of reconciliation between the two leaders after the bitter feelings surrounding Black Wednesday and aftermath, and the blame Major and Lamont placed to Bonn's annoyance on the Bundesbank. Much time was spent smoothing over Germany's irritation, shared by other Community countries, about Major's announcement in the paving debate the week before that the third reading would not be held until after the new Danish referendum. At the press conference afterwards, Kohl referred several times to 'John', with Major frequently touching the German leader as they self-consciously displayed to the media how close their relationship had again become.[35]

The main sticking point in the preparation for Edinburgh came from Felipe Gonzalez of Spain, who fought hard both before and during the conference for the 'poor four' (Spain, Portugal, Ireland and Greece) receiving more money from the EC budget to help them move into line with other member economies as they prepared for EMU. At his meeting with Gonzalez in Madrid on 1 December, Major picked up a piece of paper, tore it in two, and let both pieces drop to the ground. The gesture was meant light-heartedly, to indicate Gonzalez's likelihood of success unless Spain fell into line and accepted Britain's much more modest budget proposals.[36]

The suggestion for a large increase in the Community budget had been made in March, but ducked at Lisbon in June. Lamont favoured avoiding the issue during Britain's presidency on the grounds that, as Britain was pressing for the lowest figure, it would be better not to do so when it had the chair. He favoured passing it on to Denmark, who were to take over the presidency in January 1993, as Portugal had passed it to Britain. The matter was resolved in October, when Lamont and Nigel Wicks from the Treasury and Hurd and John Kerr from the Foreign Office met Major to decide the way forward. Kerr's advocacy won the day, employing the argument that the very fact of being in the chair could be used to tip the argument of a low budget decisively in Britain's favour.[37]

Major's whirlwind diplomatic round had not been able to clear up several key points at issue, notably Denmark's demand for opt-outs to maximise its chances of a successful outcome in its second referendum, and the EC budget. However, his task was eased by a change of heart by EC heads of government since Birmingham: there was now far more willingness to concede that blaming Britain for being deliberately difficult in ratifying the Maastricht Treaty was not constructive, and that sacrifices all round and a spirit of compromise would be necessary if the European project was to be put back firmly on the tracks. Kohl was conspicuously helpful on the budget; he came to Edinburgh determined to offer Major maximum support to achieve his financial objectives.

To tweak the goodwill of the visitors even more, Major had obtained the agreement of the Queen to borrow the Palace of Holyroodhouse, one of the Queen's royal residences. Major was keen to follow the tradition of having the final council away from the host country's capital, and a Scottish venue also served to emphasise the tautness of the Union. The FCO spent £6.4 million converting the palace to a conference centre and on hospitality for the five hundred delegates, with no expense spared to show off British largesse, thereby highlighting, not wholly unintentionally, the contrast with the drab conference facilities and hospitality at Maastricht the year before.[38] Lunch on the Friday would be held at Edinburgh Castle, and dinner that evening on the royal yacht *Britannia* in nearby Leith harbour. Protocol and diplomatic sensitivities resulted in twenty-five seating plans before the nautical placements were finalised. The two biggest beasts in the EC duly had their status recognised, with Kohl placed next to Prince Charles, and Mitterrand between the Queen and the Princess of Wales.[39]

Major appeared throughout at the peak of his powers. He opened the conference on Friday 11 December with some history, saying that the palace had been founded in 1128 by David I, who had miraculously escaped from an enraged stag, the story being traceable, he told delegates, to general amusement and guffawing from Kohl, to a legend of St Hubert of Maastricht. His successful use of levity would be employed on several occasions as the conference wore on.

Major's strategy was first to reach agreement on Denmark, which he did with a complex formula obtained by noon on Friday, whereby Denmark obtained opt-outs on defence and EMU *it* regarded as legally binding, but other EC countries did not.[40] Having secured this, Major then made it clear that failure to reach agreement on all other items being discussed at Edinburgh would not only prejudice this Danish agreement, but also jeopardise the entire Maastricht momentum.

Gonzalez continued to hold out for more money for the 'poor four'. At lunch at Edinburgh Castle, Major played for high stakes; the British figure for the EC budget was a take-it-or-leave-it offer. On Saturday morning Major kept up the front, repeating that if Gonzalez refused to accept the British figure, he would be remembered as the man responsible for killing the Maastricht Treaty. Gonzalez meanwhile banked on Major backing off first because he would not want to see Britain's presidency end in a deadlocked council.

Major was irritated to learn that Mitterrand and Kohl, who had breakfasted on Saturday with Gonzalez, now appeared to support the Spanish demand. Major switched some funds from Commission salaries to help win Spain over, but Gonzalez held out for still more until eventually succumbing in mid-evening when it was clear he lacked further support from other heads of government. The British delegation thought the Spaniards probably obtained more money than they deserved, but that the sum was far smaller than would have occurred had Britain not been in the chair. The agreement spread the burden of funding EC spending wider, with Italy and the Netherlands now joining Britain, France and Germany as net contributors.

By 10 p.m. on Saturday evening exhaustion was setting in. Major rattled through the final conclusions at such a speed that he achieved a weary consent from the company without all the heads of government totally taking in to what they were agreeing. Kohl and Mitterrand, who had indeed been helpful throughout, both burst into applause at Major's chairmanship, which had cajoled and charmed heads of government into agreement. Many other EC leaders echoed their sentiment. Albert Reynolds described the final settlement as 'an excellent deal and an excellent result for the presidency'.[41] It was all a far cry from the comments about Britain's presidency being a failure and one of the worst in recent memory heard in European circles in the wake of Black Wednesday and at the time of the Birmingham Council. Douglas Hurd believes that Edinburgh was Major's greatest single negotiating triumph,[42] while those like Simon Heffer, who wrote of Edinburgh that if it 'reflects the British Presidency that has preceded it, it will be a shambles',[43] were forced to revise their judgement.

What had been achieved? On top of the Danish and budget solutions came the decision to begin enlargement negotiations with Austria, Norway, Sweden and Finland, a 'subsidiarity' deal to define more clearly the scope of national powers, eighteen extra seats for Germany and smaller boosts for most others in the European Parliament, final agreements to clear the way for the single market in the New Year, an agreement on the future siting of EC institutions, and measures to open up EC procedures. Britain even retained its annual £2 billion budget rebate, which had come under attack from other EC countries, in the treaty – an important victory. When Major outlined the conclusions in the Commons the next day he was given an easy ride by both wings of his party. Showing all his former confidence for the first time for several months, he looked and sounded like a man who had returned from a long nightmare journey and was glad to be alive.

At Strasbourg on 16 December for the traditional end of presidency debate at the European Parliament, Major's stock was high; the man blamed by many for almost pulling the European project apart had now stuck it back together again. Patching up the Maastricht Treaty at Edinburgh had been the easy part. Major now had to secure passage of the Bill through the British Parliament. He continued to regard it as at the heart of his policy, and that it was vital for Britain's economic and political interests to see it ratified.[44]

Although Major refused to be drawn in the Commons debate the Monday after Edinburgh on the timetable for the Maastricht Bill, there could now be no excuses for delay after the Danish referendum, assuming it was affirmative. The Eurosceptics were subdued, biding their time, their hostility undimmed. They knew their day would come when the Bill came before Parliament and in the meantime, stealthily, they made their preparations. For the time being, however, there was relief, and even laughter. In Cabinet on Thursday Newton led the congratulations on the successful summit, and then brought Cabinet to a state of hilarity by saying, 'And you all remember what happened to the person who last congratulated the PM on his success at Maastricht, Ken Baker.'[45]

Christmas and New Year

Major flew out of London after Cabinet on Thursday 17 December, bound for North America, with Newton's words and the good humour in Cabinet still warming him. But he could not get away from the Community, literally, because Delors was due to accompany him on the flight to report to Bush and Brian Mulroney of Canada on progress during Britain's presidency. But the EC Commission President was held up by fog in Brussels, and Major was left waiting in a Tristar on the Heathrow tarmac for over an hour. The flight across the Atlantic proved exceptionally turbulent even for winter, with 200 mph winds buffeting the plane. So thick was the fog over eastern Canada that the plane had to divert to Montreal, entailing a two and a half hour car journey on to Ottawa.[46]

The long journey on top of the recent exertions took its toll on the Majors. Norma, never a good car passenger, felt too unwell after the long drive to attend a glittering banquet organised by the Mulroneys at the Canadian Museum of Civilisation. Major, his internal clock telling him it was the middle of the night, struggled through the banquet and the official conversations. Feeling better the next day, and anxious to combat stories of his exhaustion, he used the flight to Andrews Air Force Base near Washington to talk to journalists, telling them, 'I am well, *very well*', and with a smile, 'I am sorry to disappoint you.' Norma, he explained, also felt restored by her night's sleep, though she was still looking pale when they arrived. Official cars swept them into central Washington, where Major and Delors had a 'rather perfunctory' meeting with President Bush on progress in the EC.[47] Major was not sorry to see Delors depart; he liked Britain's unofficial role explaining Europe to the US to be unsullied by outsiders. Then, with their wives, Bush and he went up by helicopter to Camp David for the pre-Christmas weekend.

Before leaving Washington Major had a thirty-minute phone call with President-elect Clinton. Had relations been better, the two men would have met, as Major wished, but the Clinton entourage was still aggrieved by two incidents during the summer. Two party officials from Central Office had travelled to Washington to assist the Republicans in the presidential campaign. They preached the success of negative campaigns in their defeat of Labour, and then on their return boasted about their help for the Republicans. More damage had been done when it emerged that the Home Office had searched its files for information on Clinton, to see if, during his year at Oxford in 1968–9, he had applied for British citizenship at the time of the Vietnam War to avoid the draft. By implication, Major's government had been trying to find dirt on Clinton which might be of use to the Republicans. Not so, the Americans were informed; the search was made only to clear up the record because of accusations regarding Clinton's conduct while in England.

The Clinton camp was told that Major did not instigate either the Conservative Party help for Bush's re-election or the file search, but the damage had been done. Jonathan Powell monitored a negative reaction at Little Rock (Clinton's campaign base) when news of the Home Office search broke.[48] The British were unsure exactly how it affected Clinton, but Raymond Seitz (US Ambassador in London) later confirmed the damage done:

Imagine you have gone through a campaign for two years, and you finally win a race to Washington. You have a ledger in your mind as to who was with you and who was against you over all that time. And the idea that 'foreigners' were involved in the game against you just pisses you off.[49]

Clinton himself was fairly phlegmatic about it; others, like his wife Hillary, James Carville (chief campaign strategist during the election) and George Stephanopoulos (his first communications director) more angry. It seemed to them that the Home Office was doing exactly what the US State Department had done under Republican control to try to rake over Clinton's past, and it reinforced a latent anti-British prejudice among several key figures surrounding Clinton.[50]

Such background invested the phone call that Friday with a peculiar importance. Official reports, inevitably, described it as an 'easy and friendly' conversation. The war in former Yugoslavia, the GATT talks and the state of the world economy were the main topics of conversation.[51] The talk was indeed convivial, because both were highly political men, eager to make a good impression. In their see-saw relationship over the following four years, there was rarely a cross word when they talked together; the difficulties always arose when they were apart.

Major never achieved the same rapport with Clinton as he had with his predecessor. Official business with Bush at Camp David focused on measures to enforce the 'no-fly' zone over Bosnia and ways of preventing the spread of fighting in former Yugoslavia, in particular to Kosovo and Macedonia.[52] Differences had welled up with the Bush administration in the last few weeks. Spurred on by Clinton's hawkish stance towards Serb aggression, Bush's team, notably Dick Cheney (Defence Secretary) and Lawrence Eagleburger (Secretary of State), had adopted a more belligerent posture themselves, above all wanting to enforce the no-fly exclusion zone. The British, mindful of their 2,700 troops on the ground should Serb planes be shot down and the war escalate, were cautious. The Bosnian Serb leader Karadzic had reinforced British anxieties by sending Major a letter saying that any shooting down of Serb planes would be regarded as an act of war and would endanger the safe passage of humanitarian convoys and UNPROFOR troops on the ground.[53]

Business aside, nostalgia was to the fore over the weekend. Bush was still in a state of some shock after the election result seven weeks before. He had not expected to lose, and was finding the bereavement acutely painful. At dinner on Saturday he rose to make a farewell speech, but when he came to the word 'John' he broke down and could not continue. Barbara Bush filled the pause saying, 'Trust you, George, to mess it up.' Christmas presents were exchanged, hugs and more fond words.[54] Bush told reporters before the Majors left on Sunday morning that their stay had been 'a very wonderful visit with a very distinguished world leader'.[55] Three years later the occasion was still vivid in his mind: 'That visit was very emotional for me,' he confirmed.[56]

Back in Washington, Major had lunch in the British Embassy with Vice-President-elect Al Gore and other key Clinton players. In contrast to the Major–Clinton phone call two days before, tensions were evident at the lunch, especially over former Yugoslavia. The British Ambassador, Robin Renwick, working hard to mend fences, had no illusions about the difficulties. He had at least extracted a promise from Clinton that Major would be the first European leader to be seen by him, as indeed occurred in February.[57]

Given his goodwill with Bush, Major was surprised to land back at Heathrow on Monday 21 December to reports of Anglo–American disagreement. 'Major and Cheney clash over Bosnia Deadline' was the headline in *The Times*. Without Bush's knowledge, and against his wishes, Cheney had spoken on television the day before of the need to impose a fifteen-day deadline for the Serbs to cease all flights over Bosnia.[58]

The Number Ten and White House press departments worked overtime to talk down any sense of a difference of thinking between both governments. Major opportunely had a pre-Christmas trip to Bosnia planned for the Tuesday. Armed with presents (pop music cassettes), he wanted to see the troops and reassure them that their safety would be given his highest priority if the no-fly zone was enforced. He also assured them that their endeavours were saving many lives and were appreciated by those at home. Ever since his first Gulf visit in January 1991, he had discovered a taste for meeting troops in the field; photographs of him with servicemen were also helpful in enhancing his image, as they had been for Mrs Thatcher, especially so now after the battering of the previous three months.

Flying by VC-10 to Split, the party was ferried by helicopter to a scrubby field by the side of a mountain on the Bosnia/Croatia border. As it was considered too dangerous and time-consuming to travel any further to see the Cheshire Regiment at their base in Gornji Vakuf, he was met there by the commanding officer of the 1st Battalion, Bob Stewart, who later commented on how tired Major seemed, though he did his best to disguise his exhaustion. Major addressed members of the Cheshire Regiment, destined to spend their Christmas in Bosnia, and inspected the work of the Royal Engineers. 'You may think you are on your own here,' he told them, 'but many people at home are thinking of you too.'[59]

Major was more than usually drained when he arrived at Chequers on Christmas Eve. He needed a break. His old friends Robert and Dulcie Atkins and their children joined the Major family for a week in and around Chequers.

Major was able to reduce the time spent on government business to an hour a day.[60]

As he greeted his Huntingdon friends for the now-traditional New Year party at Chequers, he hoped the worst was behind him. The newspapers' annual reviews were scathing about the second half of 1992, but 1993 held out the prospects of economic recovery, the end of the argument on Maastricht, and the turmoil of the autumn fading into history. Even Joe Rogaly closed an article with an appreciative benediction:

Once the unknown Mr Nice Guy, Mr Major has become the all too well-known flawed politician. He cannot be cast in the heroic mould of his predecessor, which is a great relief. He is down to size: an ordinary chap who made a dreadful mess of his extraordinary job a month or so ago and is now recovering. We are getting to know him better. That is just as well. He could be around for many Christmases to come.[61]

Any hopes of an easier New Year were called into question as he came to be assailed on several fronts. The opening salvo hit him in the area where he felt at his most sensitive and vulnerable, his private life.

Unpleasant Taste in Bombay

Preying on Major's mind over the summer and autumn had been rumours of an affair with the cook Clare Latimer while he had been Chancellor of the Exchequer. Her catering company, Clare's Kitchen, in Primrose Hill, north London, numbered Parliament and the government among its clients. Major had first met her when she catered parties for the Whips' Office, and then employed her when he went to Number Eleven in October 1989. Rumours about an affair started soon after: she was single, they enjoyed each other's company, they were both tactile, and Norma was living at Great Stukeley during the week.[62]

After he became Prime Minister the gossip died down, but tongues began to wag again after the general election, with stories appearing in Simon Hoggart's *Observer* diary and the 'Mr Pepys' column in the London *Evening Standard*.[63] The latter declared: 'The problem is our politicians have no style. I heard of one the other day – more eminent than Mr Mellor – who contented himself by ravaging the cook!' The innuendo and snide comments unsettled Major. He discussed the matter with close advisers, none of whom believed there had been any impropriety, but they advised that he could do nothing.[64]

With no benefit to be gained by contemplating the issue further, Major tried to dismiss it from his mind. In late January 1993, he set off for an export-boosting mission to India, returning via Oman and Saudi Arabia, the first of several such trade expeditions with leading industrialists. Howard Davies, Director-General of the CBI, accompanied him on the journey, along with the chairmen and chief executives of British Gas, British Aerospace and Rolls-Royce, among others.[65] They appreciated the initiative, responding to Major's now-renowned personal charm with small groups, as well as to the business opportunities.[66] The trip, initially suggested by Indian Prime Minister Narasimha Rao, who had struck up a good relationship with Major at the Commonwealth Conference at Harare in October 1991, was built around attendance at India's most august national occasion, Republic Day. Major became the first British Prime Minister to have been invited to the celebrations since independence in 1947. Mrs Thatcher would never have been so honoured. Major was also helped by the Indians' own needs: they felt exposed following the collapse of the Soviet Union, and were anxious to renew friendships.[67]

Major hugely enjoyed seeing India, though he felt constrained from achieving one desire, visiting the Taj Mahal, as the Princess of Wales had been famously photographed there alone before her separation, which led to widespread speculation, 'Where's Charles?' With the image so strongly in the public mind, it was thought wiser for Major to leave the Taj Mahal for another visit. At the end of the first day, which the *Guardian* correspondent called 'supremely amicable', several new business ventures were announced, including a £100 million deal with British Gas. Major claimed that Anglo–Indian relations 'are closer and deeper than at any time since 1947'.[68]

While Major was saying these words, the finishing touches were being put on an article by Steve Platt, editor of *New Statesman and Society* (*NSS*), describing the gossip in the press over the previous two years about the alleged Latimer affair.[69] Platt, a serious journalist, had been told of a right-wing conspiracy to discredit Major, which he investigated. Although he could find no evidence, he discovered that various right-wing Tory MPs and writers – whom he will not name – had avidly been spreading the story to discredit Major and try to bring him down.[70]

Platt's article referred to a piece in a down-market satirical magazine, *Scallywag*, which dared Major and Latimer to sue, and which alleged that Major's indecision about sacking Mellor was due to anxiety about his own extra-marital affair. Platt was dismissive of *Scallywag*'s piece, and concluded that 'no one has produced a shred of evidence' to suggest that Major and Latimer had an affair.[71] The *NSS* nevertheless made a big splash of Platt's article, putting a montage of an eating John Major with Clare Latimer cooking behind him on their cover, which bore the words 'The curious case of John Major's "mistress"'. No doubt unwisely, they used the story to boost sales as part of an aggressive remarketing drive.

Number Ten had received word that the *NSS* was going to run such a piece. With Major in India, Allan discussed the matter with Lyell, Attorney-General, and with private solicitors. Major was told about it just after he concluded a speech to 200 guests at a state dinner in Bombay.[72] He went into conference in his suite at the Taj Mahal Hotel with O'Donnell, Wall and Bright, and decided that the article, and in particular the cover, were defamatory. Number Ten had decided earlier that suing *Scallywag* would only give the story, and the magazine, publicity. That view changed; they now felt that if they did not sue *NSS*, the press would make a major splash of the story, given credence by having appeared in a respectable political organ.

For Major, the *NSS* article was the last straw. He exploded in rage at the story. The decision to sue was not one he took lightly or willingly, and the issue was eventually settled in July 1993, with no admission of libel and both sides able to claim victory. The episode had cost the *NSS* £250,000, which they could barely afford, in legal costs and lost revenue; the weekly journal felt understandably aggrieved that it had borne the brunt of rumours that had also been peddled in far richer daily newspapers. There was indeed some irony in a left-wing organ suffering because of rumours circulated primarily by the right.[73] Major found the whole business harrowing and unpleasant; insiders testify to how much it took out of him.

Major's party flew on from India to Oman, where they were taken by helicopter into the desert for lunch with the Sultan in his tent. Every year the Sultan, like a feudal magnate, travelled the desert – admittedly in his superior tent, with gold taps in the bathrooms – to meet his barons. Major, despite only two hours' sleep the night before, rose to the occasion and promptly sold the Sultan eighteen tanks; British officials were a little uncertain how useful tanks built to combat the Soviets in central Europe might prove in Omani terrain. Major was then flown on to Riyadh after dark, where he listened courteously to an hour-long monologue by King Fahd, after which the King agreed to buy forty-eight British Tornado aeroplanes. This rounded off the entire trip very happily.[74]

Before Major left on his travels the trip had been criticised for being ill-judged, especially as it was unusual for a Prime Minister to make such a lengthy expedition when the House was sitting. The trip was compared to Callaghan's visit to the Caribbean during the 'winter of discontent', and to Bush's ill-starred expedition to Japan with his country in the grips of recession.[75] Financial deals and diplomatic talks in India had made the critics appear precipitous, but the *NSS* story dented the positive momentum. According to one report, 'Most of the journalists treated Major with something approaching contempt during the Indian trip ... [they] were not interested in contracts for electricity-generating turbines – they had gone hoping to witness prime ministerial gaffes.'[76] Major's attempt to chat to the press in the specially chartered 747 on the flight back home received not their appreciation but their scorn. Major loved India and later was to claim that it was one of his three favourite trips abroad.[77] But the Latimer story and the press corps's demeanour were unpleasant elements. Far worse was to come from travelling journalists later in the year.

TWENTY-FOUR

Broken Spring:

January–May 1993

MAJOR HAD BEEN groping towards various conclusions about what had gone wrong in the autumn even before he took the Christmas break, and had told a meeting of parliamentary private secretaries that he had failed to listen sufficiently to the Party since the general election, which was even more necessary with a majority of but twenty-one. His agenda in the new year, he said, would see a determination to 'go back to basics'.[1] On the plane on the way back from seeing Bush before Christmas, he told journalists that with the EC presidency behind him, he wanted 'to spend a great deal of time on the domestic agenda in 1993'.[2] As Andrew Grice commented in the *Sunday Times*, in Bush's defeat 'Major had a graphic reminder of what can happen to a leader who spends too much time on foreign affairs'.[3]

A series of New Year interviews saw the fruit of his rethinking. He admitted on television to David Frost, in what became an early January ritual encounter, that in the nine months since the election he had failed to offer a sufficiently clear vision of where he was leading the country, and that he had indeed given those crying out for 'strong government' some cause for complaint. The cornerstone of his philosophy would from now on be the creation of an efficient and accountable free enterprise society, with the extension of 'choice and opportunity' – old Major chestnuts – at its centre.[4] He saw his Citizen's Charter as the engine for his reform package, and defended it against those on the right who saw it as 'worthless and meaningless'.[5] On Radio Four's *The World at One* and elsewhere he was more gung-ho, holding out the prospect of a decade of growth that would re-create the prosperity of the 1980s. The language he employed in this, his first post-election relaunch, struck many commentators, however, as just as hubristic as when he talked about sterling before Black Wednesday, and provoked headlines such as 'Major heralds start of a new golden era' in the *Daily Express* which could only result in disappointed expectations.[6] His remarks also produced alarm in the Treasury, and profound irritation in Lamont, who had been far more cautious in an Anatole Kaletsky–Peter Riddell interview in *The Times*.[7]

Where is the Agenda?

The need for clarity in Major's programme came squarely back on the agenda over the new year. For all the government's proclamation of improvements to the public services, and of rapid progress towards implementing the 1992 Queen's Speech programme, the lack of cohesion and direction was felt widely, not least by ministers, who had been talking of little else during Major's prolonged absences on Europe business and in the United States during December. A plan was even aired of holding a general election in 1995, or at least talking about it, to have a target within sight to rebuild a common sense of purpose.[8]

Major knew what he had to do. To refocus attention and to clarify thoughts on the domestic agenda, he convened a Policy Unit seminar at Chequers on 10–11 January. Departments had been asked the previous summer to prepare ideas for a medium-term programme, to provide momentum after manifesto proposals had mostly been enacted. Ideas were presented, not by ministers, but through Policy Unit members or Norman Fowler, the only senior figure other than Major to attend. Major expressed irritation that the government was not receiving sufficient credit for its education and health service reforms, and urged that emphasis be given to further steps in deregulation and to training for sixteen- to nineteen-year-olds, as well as to forging ahead with the Citizen's Charter and measures to combat crime. Stimulating economic recovery also lay at the heart of Major's concern, as it had in the autumn, and coded messages were sent to Lamont, at his budget planning meeting the same day at Chevening, not to take measures which might depress economic activity.[9]

The Chequers seminar was a key moment for Major, an opportunity for him to stamp his mark afresh on government and retune his message. However, the seminar failed to make the desired impression, and within two weeks talk of U-turns and drift were again being heard. Thatcherites were brazenly talking in front of journalists about a new critique of Major's administration: a reincarnation of the Heath government, doomed in the eyes of true believers for its policy on Europe, U-turns and high public spending.[10]

Why did Major's attempt to impose order and direction seem so easily swept away? Lack of time for thinking again lay at the root of his difficulties, as it had done before the election. The onslaught of problems in the months running up to Christmas prevented him standing back sufficiently and asking himself fundamental questions about what he was really wanting to achieve as Prime Minister. But that was not all. His own authority and standing with his Party and the press had been damaged more severely than many had appreciated. A strong assertion of will from the centre was always likely to fall on a sceptical and resistant audience. The Number Ten Policy Unit, moreover, the closest the Prime Minister had to strategic planners and troubleshooters, lacked the numbers or the power to command departments to obey, and Sarah Hogg herself, the one heavyweight in it, was heavily preoccupied on economic and trade matters, leaving little chance, even if she had the will, to focus on the long term.[11]

The relative lack of resources available to a modern prime minister in advancing his own agenda was all too obvious. A strengthened Prime Minister's Office, or even a return of the Central Policy Review Staff, abolished in 1983,[12] might have helped, above all for a prime minister like Major, not naturally given to thinking in strategic terms.[13]

Major's leadership style, of leniency with Cabinet ministers, and leaving the whips to strong-arm recalcitrant backbenchers, was not ideal in building unity and loyalty. Above all, Cabinet ministers were in no mood to follow a central lead: they had their own agendas, personal and political, to be weighed against pleas from Number Ten to behave and toe the line.[14] Reports began to circulate that some on the right in Cabinet thought the Citizen's Charter, which had to be driven through a generally resistant government in 1991, was a 'spastic' idea, suggesting how deep the divide had become.[15]

From the beginning of January 1993, leaking and reports of Cabinet infighting burgeoned in the press.[16] Major had had enough, and in Cabinet on 21 January 'read the riot act' over leaks. He said some reports in the papers were so accurate that they could only have come from ministers[17], which while useful to historians was not conducive to smooth conduct of government business. After Cabinet some ministers went into a private cabal and concluded that the leak had come via a junior minister.[18]

Personalities and Politics

Two kinds of battles were in progress in Cabinet. Personality clashes were becoming more unrestrained, inevitable perhaps with any enterprise in trouble. Shephard was not happy with Heseltine for springing the pit closure plan on her, but he was also the bogey figure with the right – Lilley, Portillo and Howard. Clarke irritated increasing numbers of Cabinet ministers for 'offering us his opinion on everything',[19] and aroused suspicion because he was seen to be front-runner in the jockeying for Lamont's succession: few thought the Chancellor could last out the year.[20] Howard was the favoured candidate on the right, and MacGregor the compromise candidate. But more serious than personal tensions were differences over policy. Divisions over Europe lay at the heart, with the Eurosceptic four (Howard, Lamont, Lilley and Portillo) ranged against the more numerically strong and dominant Europhiles (Clarke, Heseltine, Hurd, Gummer and Hunt). On the economy, Heseltine joined Major in favouring expansion against the Treasury's caution from Lamont and Portillo.

Cutting across the left–right divide was the argument between radicals and consolidators. The radicals, including those on the left like Clarke and Heseltine as well as those on the right such as Lilley and Shephard, wanted to see the domestic agenda driven forward. They thought the best way to manage the Party and distract attention from splits on Europe was to exhibit a dynamic range of fresh policies. The consolidators – with the business managers at the core, Newton, Ryder and Wakeham – felt that the 1992 Queen's Speech was plenty busy enough, and that ministers should concentrate on steady administration and avoiding stepping on banana skins.

Disagreements among Cabinet ministers over the first three months of 1993 arose over many issues: the future of the thirty-one pits; the form of privatisation of British Rail; whether to have a nationalised police force, or just fewer forces; the amalgamation of some English and Scottish regiments; the reorganisation of hospitals in the wake of the Tomlinson Report; the future of naval dockyards at Rosyth and Devonport; Britain's role in Bosnia; and whether to have tax increases in the March budget. Details of discussions on all these and other disputes were spread across the nation's broadsheets.

Major himself tried several gambits to regain the initiative. The views he expressed at the Chequers policy meeting formed the basis of his party political broadcast on 20 January: a new emphasis on growth and jobs (he established a Cabinet committee on unemployment), improved public services, education and training, and measures to tackle crime.[21] But his ideas were not always taken as seriously as he would wish. When questioned in the House about poor economic performance, his response – 'I propose to hold a seminar at the beginning of February ...'[22] – provoked hoots of laughter and derision.

As often when under pressure, he decided to deliver a keynote speech. The Carlton Club on 3 February provided the forum. The speech contained some nostalgia, repeating his vision of Britain with its local bakers' shops, Rotary Clubs, 'meals on wheels', and traditional villages. His concern for the monarchy was emphasised, and he said that Britain needed 'more than ever ... those institutions that give continuity and framework to our national life'. In a telling phrase, he stated his brand of Toryism would have 'an ear for history and an eye for place'. But it was not all about tradition and sentiment. Several fresh policy ideas were outlined, including widening training opportunities for the young, tougher measures on crime, a new 'right to buy' campaign, proposals for 'road pricing' including tolls on motorways, and reform of the honours system to eliminate 'old class-based distinctions' and to place a greater emphasis on rewarding voluntary work. He also said that the new Cabinet unemployment committee had been looking at an idea which the Americans called 'workfare': 'I increasingly wonder whether paying unemployment benefit without offering or requiring any activity in return serves unemployed people or society well.'[23]

Unfortunately for Major, however, the speech turned into a public relations mess-up which muddied the overall message and contributed further to the general air of confused leadership. Gillian Shephard's Employment Department had not been properly briefed about the 'workfare' elements, and so the day after the speech, Number Ten was saying that measures to force the unemployed to undertake some work were being positively considered, while

Shephard spent the day speaking dismissively of the scheme.[24] She was perturbed by the idea of such a scheme applying to large numbers of unemployed people, and found Cabinet allies. The Treasury was worried by the cost implications, while the right, which might have been expected to like it, regarded it as dangerously close to a government guarantee of a right to work.

The main outcome of the discussions that followed Major's Carlton Club speech was the lifting of regulations prohibiting unemployed people from taking full-time education, and a small-scale 'workfare' pilot scheme. As Andrew Marr remarked, the sound of ministers rowing back was audible all week after the speech.[25] Labour made effective political attacks: Smith accused Major of lurching hopelessly from one muddle to another, and taunted him with, 'Can you not get one simple objective and stick to it?'[26] The speech, and the 'workfare' muddle that followed it, were perfect illustrations of the lack of time for Number Ten to develop fresh ideas on the wing, and of its lack of authority and respect.

What also continually undermined Major's attempts to stamp his authority on the government was the state of the economy, and the general lack of confidence in the government's economic management after Black Wednesday. The question of unemployment and the recession was a constant subject of Cabinet discussions in the early months of 1993. On 11 February Shephard said unemployment would shortly rise above three million, and in Cabinet a week later Lamont gave the startling opinion that he thought it would be unlikely to fall again before 1995.[27] Despite the cut in interest rates to 6 per cent at the end of January, belief in recovery remained low, with no sign that the financial markets were recovering confidence in the government's policy. 'Confidence will not be restored until there is a new Chancellor and the government resolves contradictions in its economic strategy,' said *The Times*.[28]

Recovery was also threatened by the prospect of the breakdown of trade talks between the USA and the EC. Obtaining reassurances from Clinton that he was not going to take his country in a protectionist direction – which would have cost many British jobs and significantly added to Major's problems – was at the forefront of Major's mind when he set out in late February to see the new administration in Washington.[29]

Progress with Clinton

A trip to the United States is always an opportunity to display prime ministerial leadership, especially when he is under pressure at home. Major travelled out by VC-10 with Sarah Hogg, who had become his personal emissary on GATT, Rodric Braithwaite, Cradock's successor as the Prime Minister's foreign policy adviser, and Stephen Wall, as well as Robin Butler and Alex Allan, keen to forge links with the new administration in Washington.[30]

Since that first tentative pre-Christmas phone call with Clinton, much bridge-building had been in train, with Raymond Seitz and Robin Renwick, Ambassadors in London and Washington respectively, to the fore. Renwick's cultivation of the Clinton camp during 1992 was paying off. In January he had been invited to dinner with Clinton and had, with some prescience, impressed on him that despite all the domestic criticism and problems about which Clinton had been briefed, Major would survive and be Prime Minister throughout his first administration, which would last until the end of 1996.[31] To help usher in a new atmosphere of cordiality, Major offered his 'warmest best wishes' to Clinton via the American television channel ABC during Clinton's inauguration speech on 20 January.[32] While not having close emotional links with any foreign leader, nor country, unlike Bush, by the time of his meeting with Major the ghosts had been largely laid to rest.[33]

Major flew out on Tuesday 23 February. Breakfast on Wednesday with Lloyd Bentsen, Treasury Secretary, was followed by a trip up Capitol Hill to meet congressional leaders. Over lunch he talked to more members of the administration, including Tony Lake, the National Security Adviser, and Colin Powell, Chairman of the Joint Chiefs of Staff. Clinton greeted Major warmly when he arrived at the White House that afternoon. They sat down at 3 p.m. in the Oval Office for the first of their two meetings that day. They discussed Bosnia and the Gulf, but much of the session was devoted to talking about trade, and the need to get an agreement on GATT.

When Clinton had been elected in November, trade talks between the EC and United States were threatening to collapse, and some feared his inauguration as President might finally kill off any prospect of agreement. Major and his team had prepared their ground thoroughly; they were to sell the argument to Clinton that the G7 summit in Tokyo in July was to be the first big international engagement for his administration. If he wanted to get something out of it, and see the GATT talks resolved, Britain would help him achieve it, in particular by mediating with the European Community.[34] So successful were they, and others in the Major party in singing the same song with their opposite numbers, that they acquired the broker position they sought, and under Sarah Hogg's guidance played a pivotal role in the trade negotiations.

Clinton and Major intentionally avoided talking about Ireland in that first session, knowing it would prove a difficult subject. Throughout the Major–Clinton relationship, two issues were repeatedly to divide both administrations: Bosnia and Ireland. On the latter, Clinton had upset London the previous year by promising a 'special US peace envoy' to be sent to the province if he was elected President. Clinton had been energetically briefed by Renwick, as well as by several of his own staff, that the idea made little sense if the British were so opposed to it.[35] The President, however, was locked into the proposal, and was under heavy pressure from some powerful figures in Congress, not least Edward Kennedy, to buck the British.

The person tipped for the envoy assignment to Ireland was Tom Foley,

Speaker of the House of Representatives. Seitz, who had flown over to Washington ahead of Major's party to brief the administration, went to see Foley, but was surprised to hear him say he had no wish to become special envoy, and thought it a 'cockamamie' idea.[36] Seitz found the administration in a state of high confusion over the envoy plan. One British diplomat observed: 'It normally takes six months for a new administration to work out what it is doing and normal business starts to resume. With the Clinton administration it was nearer to two years.'[37]

Clinton and Major broke their first session at 4.30 p.m. for a press conference in the East Room. Despite their hopes, questions on Northern Ireland did come up. Twice Clinton parried by saying that they had not yet discussed the topic, but it came back a third time. 'Mr President ... do you share the view expressed by some members of Congress that there are abuses to human rights in Northern Ireland that need to be addressed?'

Before Clinton could respond, Major leaped to speak: 'Well, I'll address that point first. The real abuse of human rights in Northern Ireland is the abuse of human rights of people who find bombs in shopping malls when they go about their ordinary, everyday business.'[38] By seizing the initiative, he left Clinton no space to disagree or demur. After the conference concluded, Clinton withdrew for a few minutes with his aides. He turned to Seitz and said, 'Did you see the way that Major handled that question on Northern Ireland?' Even though he knew he had been outmanoeuvred by Major, he was admiring of Major's political skills.[39]

The whole press conference had been good-humoured, to the irritation, it was noticed, of some of the British press avid to find evidence of snubs. Clinton made reassuring noises about the US commitment to free trade, made a point of saying he was one of only two presidents who had lived in England, and made a joke of how grateful he was that the British had managed to keep information on most of his time in the UK classified. Major, for his part, offered public support for Clinton's controversial Bosnian initiative of air drops of food and medical supplies, which the British privately thought unworkable. Major called the move 'imaginative'.

Before a working dinner that evening, the two men talked alone. Clinton offered, in effect, to abandon the special envoy idea, though for reasons of face neither side was to say so directly. Most of their conversation, however, was personal. Clinton mused on the election and, to Major's surprise, he heard Clinton express fond memories of his year in Britain. Both men were encouraged by their *tête-à-tête*, and felt they had achieved a good foundation for future discussions.[40] British officials noted that Clinton was more direct, and a much better listener than they had expected. He was particularly interested in hearing what Braithwaite, who had recently retired as British Ambassador in Moscow, had to say about Yeltsin and Russia. Clinton was found by Major's team to be highly intelligent, and he impressed them by his willingness to take account of British positions. Both leaders struck officials as similar, not just in terms of their personal style and mastery of detail –

'they were both policy wonks' – but also in their ideological positions and mastery of tactical politics.[41]

On one issue, Bosnia, the meeting papered over the cracks. The Clinton team came to office with a desire to do more than Bush to take on Serb aggression, but no plan of action. The British tried to sell them the idea of a US troop commitment to implement the Vance–Owen peace plan, which proposed a federal Bosnia divided into ten cantons. Before Major's Washington trip his aides believed the idea had been accepted,[42] but Clinton had become sceptical about Vance–Owen in the interval, believing it to reward ethnic cleansing.[43] The British had been hoping to see progress towards a joint policy with the Americans, as in the Gulf, and were disappointed to be told in Washington that the administration was not yet ready to spell out their policy, beyond air drops.[44] Major then became more irritated when, during an extended round of television interviews beginning at 7 a.m. in Washington on the Thursday morning, he faced a stream of hostile questions about the problems in Britain, rather than allowing him the platform to digress on what he wanted to portray as a highly successful summit.

When ITN's cameras stopped rolling, he vented his spleen at the British media for jeopardising the prospects for economic recovery. 'You talk about confidence,' he said sharply. 'You spend half your time wrecking it by projecting just the negative things.'[45] Though the press was positive on the Thursday – the *Guardian*'s headline was 'Clinton and Major pull old alliance together' – by Sunday 28 February the trip had become swallowed up in the usual diet of gloom about economic prospects and Tory divisions. The US press meanwhile regarded the summit with some indifference: the only British story to make the front page of the *New York Times* was the tragic murder of two-year-old James Bulger. The lack of interest underlined the truth that whereas Mrs Thatcher had film star appeal in the US, Major was just another European leader.

For Wall, it was his last overseas trip, exhausted by the excessively taxing demands of the job of Foreign Affairs Private Secretary. On the plane on the way home Major said he thought Clinton one of the most political people he had ever met.[46] Wall turned to him and said he still did not fully understand what type of person Clinton was. Major commented simply, 'Nor do I.' Indeed, he never did work him out in the four and a half years they had dealings together.[47]

Angst over the Economy

No sooner had Major returned to Britain than his nose was rubbed again in the dirt. Bad party and personal opinion polls were exacerbated by worrying economic forecasts. Press hostility was by now unremitting. The *Daily Telegraph* repeated the 1956 call for the 'smack of firm government', while the *Sunday Telegraph* invited a range of the great and the good to respond to the view put forward in an article by Roy Jenkins that Major was unfit for the job.[48] The heavyweights, who included Alan Walters, Rees-Mogg and an 'anonymous Cabinet minister', responded in a damaging, even insulting, fashion. Praise from those like writer Jilly Cooper and Graham Leonard, the former Bishop of London, stressing his 'niceness', did little to redress the balance.

Major was quick to counterattack. Downing Street fired off a volley of statistics to support his contention that the corner had been turned on the economy, providing figures on inflation, interest rate levels and retail sales.[49] On 4 March Major introduced his policy on honours, having aired it to Cabinet that morning. The response was positive, particularly on the widening of access, though some worried about the effect in the City on the ending of an automatic knighthood for a Lord Mayor of London. The ending of distinction between ranks for military honours had been resisted by the MOD, but he and Waldegrave, drove it through. Major was very proud of the reforms, very much his own initiative, which were hailed as the first significant changes to the honours system in seventy years.[50] Reactions were predictable: many were pleased, but the right thought it egalitarian tinkering, the left that it did not go far enough, and some felt it a trifling distraction from the real problem, the economy.[51]

Finally, Major gave a hard-hitting interview to Andrew Marr in the *Independent*. He insisted that his government was in the process of introducing a revolution, yet people could not see it because they were so 'bedazzled' by the Party squabbling. As a fightback interview outlining a positive agenda it made a good case, but what caught the media's attention was not the fresh initiatives Major outlined, but his criticism of governments in the 1980s for promoting the service sector too highly at the cost of ignoring manufacturing. He did not, in the recorded part of the interview, mention Thatcher by name, but Marr regarded the implication as unmistakable. More controversial, and more difficult for him to sustain, was his statement that he had been in a 'minority' opposing this policy.[52] Marr thought Major's historical revisionism was an important news story, that he had been given a strong steer that Major was distancing himself from Thatcher's record on manufacturing. Major thought he had been stitched up and used by Marr as a stick to beat Thatcher. Next day, he was furious when he saw a series of 'Major attacks Thatcher' headlines.[53] In the Commons, he distanced himself from suggestions that he had been critical of Thatcher and was in turn harshly critical of Marr. It led to a welter of comments about more U-turns, Major lacking the courage of his convictions, and being afraid of his predecessor.[54] As so often happened, initiatives launched by Major to reassert his control did not just backfire, but did so spectacularly.

Even in Number Ten the pattern of one step forward and two steps backwards was being recognised as a fact of life.[55] But in terms of gravity, such episodes were pinpricks compared to two other events, the budget and the passage of the Maastricht Bill.

At the pre-budget Chevening meeting on 9 and 10 January, the conclusion became inescapable that the heavy budget deficit was caused by more than the economy being near the bottom of the business cycle, and that stringent action would be required to make amends.[56] The public sector borrowing requirement for 1993–4 had risen dramatically: in the spring of 1991 it was estimated to be £8 billion; the estimate on which the 1991–2 round was based put it at £19 billion; by the time of the 1992 budget the figure had risen to £32 billion; by early 1993 it was projected to rise towards an extraordinary £50 billion, which represented 8 per cent of national income. The financial markets reacted predictably to the burgeoning total, with the pound in early March 1993 falling to DM2.35.[57] Lamont readily became a convert to the need to raise taxes dramatically to bring the budget closer to balance. Once his mind was made up, he became a powerful advocate of a tight fiscal policy.

The public spending round in the autumn of 1992 had already been quite tight, but had made little impression on the overall deficit. Further drastic cuts were ruled out as politically unacceptable. The Treasury probed deeply into a number of options for raising revenue, and produced a rolling package of tax increases spread over three years, with the heaviest burdens coming in 1994–6, when economic recovery was expected to ameliorate its worst hardships. Lamont decided that the budget should announce higher national insurance contributions, restrictions on mortgage tax relief and VAT on domestic fuel (an idea that was accepted only very late in discussions after a broader extension of VAT had been rejected) at 8 per cent from April 1994 and the full 17.5 per cent from 1995. There had been some debate over whether to phase VAT on fuel or not, with Hogg arguing strongly for the phased solution.

Major was deeply troubled about the tax increases. In a series of bilaterals over the spring, he and Lamont talked through the options. Major, who had forced the pace of interest rate reductions, was worried about the effect tax increases might have on economic recovery, and on the Party's political fortunes, especially as the rises would severely hit middle- and lower-income households. Major also knew that the Party could be attacked for breach of promise: the Tories' 1992 manifesto had pledged unequivocally 'to continue to reduce taxes as fast as we prudently can',[58] and was all too aware that he had himself promised specifically that there were 'no plans and no need' for an extension of VAT.[59]

But equally Major realised the desperate state of public finances, and after initial jibbing accepted the need for the measures Lamont and the Treasury had devised. Treasury estimates of the deficit, which leaped £7 billion over two months, finally persuaded him. The sessions with Lamont were tense, and on one occasion, when they disagreed over national insurance contributions, the Chancellor picked up his papers, prepared to storm out.[60] Once convinced of the inescapability of heavy tax rises, Major had to be sold the particular forms of increase. VAT on fuel he found the hardest to take, but accepted it on the argument that there was no particular logic to fuel being zero-rated, and that a fuel tax would conserve energy and hence fit in with the Rio Earth Summit undertakings. Protection was also to be offered for those on low incomes – though in the haste, insufficient consultation had taken place with the Department of Social Security, with the Treasury wanting to put off designing a package until autumn. The result was a post-budget U-turn when compensation was increased, which led to much of the tax being given back in lopsided measures.

If the economy had been as strong as Major had hoped, and the ERM commitment sustainable, his tax strategy might have been acclaimed as politically brilliant and an economic risk worth taking. In the event, Major had fallen into the trap familiar to politicians of believing that the best would happen, through luck or the effect of previous good judgement. His reputation for honesty and competence depended on a spin of the roulette wheel of economic prediction: Major bet it all on black, but the outcome was deeply in the red.

Lamont's budget on 16 March proved not just the last spring budget, but also his personal swansong. The reception was surprisingly positive at the time, with his determination to tackle the deficit through a programme of tax increases being generally praised for restoring confidence without endangering the recovery.[61] The political whiplash was, however, far stronger than expected. The slogan 'Labour's Tax Bombshell' was thrown back in the government's face by Labour, while for disillusioned Tories, VAT on fuel became a target of anger, longer-lasting and deeper than that over pit closures the previous autumn.

Angst over Europe

Major's other running sore in the first half of 1993 was the passage of the Maastricht Bill, the European Communities (Amendment) Bill, to give its full title. He found the whole saga exceptionally frustrating and often felt angry and puzzled by the way the Eurosceptics held up government business and perpetuated the impression to voters of a Party at war with itself.[62] Indeed the parliamentary dissent over the Maastricht ratification process has been described accurately as 'without parallel in postwar history', during which the government sustained 'the most serious Parliamentary defeat suffered by a Conservative government in the twentieth century' before achieving eventual success.[63]

A high proportion of Major's time in the first half of 1993 was devoted to Maastricht-related matters. Participants recall an apparently endless series of meetings with whips on handling, with ministers and special advisers plotting strategy and lobbying for support, and with legal advisers offering advice on amendments. Major was also handicapped by losing Stephen Wall in March, halfway through the proceedings. For all his successor Roderic Lyne's prodigious energy and talents, he was, unlike Wall, not a specialist on Europe.[64]

The paving debate on 4 November had served notice of the depth and bitterness of feeling among the Eurosceptics. The paving motion was carried only by Major promising to delay the third reading until after the second Danish referendum. The Edinburgh summit made a Danish 'yes' vote far more likely, and in January 1993 it was announced that their referendum would be held on 18 May. There was thus no urgency in pushing the Bill through. Major was also acutely aware of the risk that excessive haste would increase the possibility of a defeat. Yet any defeat, or concession on the text of the treaty, would entail a renegotiation of the entire treaty itself, scarcely a viable option.[65]

The committee stage of the Bill to precede the third reading, as required for bills of its scope and importance, was taken on the floor of the House. A symbolic start to the committee stage had been made after the paving vote, but consideration began in earnest on 13 January. Some 500 amendments had been tabled, in addition to 100 proposed new clauses. Attempts by government whips to speed the process by curtailing debate were thwarted by their own backbenchers, who for the first time began to vote against the government 'business' motions. Even in 1972 during the passage of the treaty of accession to the Community rebels had not defied the government's business managers.

However the struggle over ratifying Maastricht proved less bitter than the confrontation over the paving vote the previous November. The government whips had grown accustomed to the existence of a separately organised Tory faction on this issue, with its own headquarters (McAlpine's Great College Street house), unofficial whips and 'briefing books'. Ryder would have regular meetings with the leaders, who found him courteous and professional: 'Bill, you've got your job to do and I've got mine,' Cash recalls him saying.[66] Ryder had taken care to appoint Eurosceptic whips, David Davis and David Heathcoat-Amory, to help his cause. The government could also strike bargains with the Liberal Democrat, Ulster Unionist and Plaid Cymru MPs to offset the rebels' votes, and even cut occasional deals with Labour. Support from the Liberal Democrats and Nationalists was usually enough to preserve the government's majority.

Many difficulties were encountered before the committee stage was completed on 22 April, having taken a total of 163 hours of deliberations over twenty-three days of Commons' time. The government in particular was forced to accept two concessions which later were to cause it trouble. On 8 March the government incurred its only defeat on the Bill itself, by twenty-two votes, on the method by which UK members of a new Committee of the Regions should be chosen. The defeat caused Eurosceptic jubilation; although it did not threaten ratification, it did mean that a report stage would be necessary, which would add several weeks to the Bill's timetable. More seriously, after prolonged machinations in February and March, Labour's clauses 74 and 75 were accepted for debate, requiring a specific vote on the

Social Chapter after the completion of the Bill, but before it became operative. It was this vote that was to cause the government so much trouble in July.

To pre-empt defeat in the final phases of the committee stage, the government on 20 April accepted further Labour amendments requiring ministers and the Bank of England to report to Parliament on progress towards EMU. Two days later, on the same day the committee stage was completed, the government, with opposition support, successfully fought off the Eurosceptic demand for a referendum, with a vote of 363–124.

Major celebrated the end of the committee stage with an address to the Conservative Group for Europe at the InterContinental Hotel in London, written with the help of Dominic Morris, who had joined the Policy Unit (having earlier served in the Private Office) to beef up presentation of its European policy, 'The most pro-European speech of his premiership' was the verdict of the *Independent*.[67] It featured not just praise for Heath, the right's *bête noire*, for taking Britain into the EC, but also acknowledgement of the role of Europe in expanding trade. Major's irritation with his backbench tormentors was apparent in his choice of words: the Maastricht Treaty was the 'scapegoat for many and nameless fears' held by the sceptics, and a newly discussed idea from Lady Thatcher of a North Atlantic free trade organisation was dismissed as a 'sugar coated turnip'.[68] The speech was remembered best not for its highlighting of the positive case to be made for Europe, but for its concluding phrases, which sought to remind Eurosceptics that his concern to see Britain part of Europe sat side-by-side with a deep love for his own country: 'the country of long shadows on county grounds, warm beer, invincible green suburbs, dog lovers and pools fillers, and as George Orwell said, old maids bicycling to communion through the morning mist . . . Britain will still survive, unamendable in all essentials.'

Major's words brought ridicule on his head: 'What a lot of tosh' thought the *Independent on Sunday*. Major's lyrical vision of England (critics pointed out that county grounds are in short supply in Scotland) was deliberately nostalgic, looking back to the era of the 1950s, the first decade of which he was conscious, and before the war, even, to Baldwin, who had delivered himself of strikingly similar sentiments in 1924: '. . . the sight of a plough team coming over the brow of a hill, the sight that has been in England ever since England was a land, and may be seen in England long after the Empire has perished and every works in England has ceased to function . . .'

Major was not put off by the criticism, which he thought penned by those with little direct experience or knowledge of ordinary British people, and returned to the theme in his 'back to basics' conference speech in October. The sentimentality of his words reflected a yearning within him for simpler, more decent times, although the ramifications of an appeal to traditional values were to lead him not into the pleasant lands of his memories but into altogether different and hostile territory.

Following the report stage of the Maastricht Bill in early May, Labour support was again significant in the third-reading victory for the government on 20 May (two days after the Danes recorded their expected 'yes' vote in their referendum) by a margin of 292 votes to 112. Forty-six Tory MPs rebelled, however, the largest number so far to have voted against the government.[69]

The Bill now went on to the House of Lords, but the government was far from out of the woods, with further key votes to be taken before the summer recess. After 210 hours of debate and five months of fighting, the government might have won for the time being, but it had been forced into a number of tactical retreats, agreeing to amendments and ducking procedural motions it regarded too risky to put to a vote, and providing the unedifying spectacle of the party's most senior figures, including Major, Hurd, Heseltine and Fowler, frequently having to appeal for loyalty, as at the Conservative Central Council meeting at Harrogate from 5 to 7 March. In the North Yorkshire spa, the rank and file were far from happy. There were many grumbles about Europe, as well as the Party's parlous financial position.[70]

May Elections

The elections on 6 May, for local government in England and Wales and a by-election in Newbury, had been seen for some months as the first real test of government popularity since the general election. The May 1992 local elections occurred too soon after it to be a reliable barometer of opinion and, unusually, there had been no by-election in the intervening year.

The Newbury election had been caused by the tragic and unexpected death of Judith Chaplin. Since her election, she had spoken to Major by phone on Sunday mornings at regular intervals, the tensions of their last few months together at Number Ten all but forgotten. Shortly after her Newbury election she became worried about the return of cancer from which she had suffered at the start of the 1980s. She went into hospital in March for routine keyhole surgery, but died from a freak complication two days later.[71] Probably the ablest female Tory MP, she would have seen rapid promotion, perhaps even to Cabinet, before 1997. Major was telephoned with news of Chaplin's death in his car on the way back to Huntingdon.[72] It was another cruel blow.

Fowler believes the defeat at Newbury was the worst by-election result in his two-year period as Party Chairman (1992–4). The Party had a strong candidate and fought a good campaign, with the press believing that they could win. Yet they lost spectacularly. The Liberal Democrat majority was 22,055, with a 28.4 per cent swing from the Conservatives, the worst by-election defeat since the Tories had come to power in 1979. The county council elections, which saw 500 Conservative seats lost across the country, were a similar rout. The Conservatives held only Buckinghamshire, but lost overall control of Kent and Surrey, and incredibly came third in Berkshire and Devon. Several authorities lost had been Tory ever since their creation under Lord Salisbury in 1888.

Before the elections it had been possible to maintain the belief that the Party was merely suffering from transitional difficulties and bad luck, and that the Party's electoral position would not be affected. The 6 May results exposed the full extent of the government's plight. It also brought peril to Major's position. Rumblings about whether he was up to the job intensified.[73] A MORI poll stated that only 17 per cent of voters thought him a capable leader, while 8 per cent believed he had sound judgement. The heavyweight press continued to be almost universally disparaging about his personal performance.[74] Westminster buzzed with 'persistent gossip', mostly emanating from Eurosceptics, about whether he would be challenged for the leadership in the autumn.[75]

The election defeats caused the discontent to climax, epitomised in a Rees-Mogg article in *The Times*. Major, he wrote, 'is not a natural leader: he cannot speak: he has a weak Cabinet which he has chosen: he lacks self-confidence: he has no sense of strategy or direction ... His ideal level of political competence would be deputy chief whip, or something of that standing.'[76] Rees-Mogg had been an early admirer of Major as Prime Minister. Major's detestation for Rees-Mogg dates from that article, though before the summer was over he would have still more reason to dislike him.

Clarke's public admission that the government was in a 'dreadful hole', and open talk by Cabinet ministers the weekend after the elections that Major had lost his authority and a major relaunch was needed, did little to restore confidence.[77] Major came back fighting at the Scottish Conservative Party Conference in Edinburgh on 14 May. His response to critics that he or the government should give up was that they should 'Give over!' He acknowledged that the government had been hurt by the recession, but the government had four years of determined policies ahead to win back the doubters. His support for his beleaguered Chancellor had never been as forthright, with praise for his 'determination, skill and guts'.[78] These words were remembered when, only two weeks later, Lamont disappeared from the ministerial screen.

Lift and Strike

Rumbling through the first half of 1993 was the continuing war in Bosnia, and western infighting about how to respond. The Vance–Owen plan was collapsing, and vicious fighting was breaking out between Croats and Muslims, uneasy allies against the Serbs in 1992. These events strengthened the hand of those in Britain who wanted to keep out of the conflict entirely. Marcus Fox warned Major in January that backbenchers would not be supportive if British military involvement got any deeper, and the service chiefs were unwilling to send more forces there with unclear objectives or an open-ended commitment. In Cabinet, Clarke argued rumbustiously against involvement whenever he had the opportunity to do so, usually backed up by Lamont. Rifkind, the Defence Secretary, was deeply sceptical, and most of the rest of the Cabinet were similarly edgy or believed that nothing good could come out of it. If Major and Hurd had not been united, the anti-intervention forces might have carried the day. As it was, there was even reluctance to enforce agreed no-fly zones in Bosnia. Debates in Cabinet concerned the extent of troop commitments for peacekeeping and aid delivery. The Labour leadership were unwilling to push the issue, and supporters of a more assertive policy were too scattered and too far apart politically, from Lady Thatcher through Conservative MEPs and Paddy Ashdown to Ken Livingstone on the Labour left, to form a powerful pro-intervention lobby.

Major had already decided to commit troops to Bosnia the previous summer, but what to do next proved frustrating. The government policy was examined in a series of meetings in the first part of 1993 while the position on the ground shifted constantly. The tone was set by Major in the first meeting of the year of the relevant Cabinet committee, OPD, on 12 January, when he announced that, 'We are not here to take decisions.' At a seminar on 22 January, to which he invited David Owen, one present recalled, 'Everyone wanted to grab the bull by the horns, but no one knew where the bull was or whether it had horns.'[79] Major, according to Owen, was always committed to UNPROFOR as a way of ensuring that humanitarian aid got through, while very resistant at this stage to being edged over into combat.[80] He feared the risks of a wider Balkan war involving Kosovo and Albania.

By April, however, Major had firmly decided against lifting the arms embargo on the Bosnian government. The argument was expressed vividly by Hurd, who inveighed against the creation of a 'level killing field'. Thatcher called this 'a terrible and disgraceful phrase' and it was certainly a reversal of the Cold War theory of deterrence.[81]

Major's response contrasted starkly with the Clinton White House's simple verities that Europe was being weak in former Yugoslavia, and tough action was required. The warm glow of the February visit soon wore off, and with the Vance–Owen peace plan discredited in American eyes, pressure built up on Clinton to get tough. The thinking was summed up by one close White House observer: 'They operated just like people from Think Tanks, perhaps because many of them did come from Think Tanks: they were all theory, no practice. They said, "We'll start with a clean sheet of paper, and let's come up with a really bold solution." '[82]

'Lift and Strike' was the plan: lift the arms embargo on the Bosnian government, and use air power to strike Serb targets. Various senior White House aides, including Tony Lake, the National Security Adviser, had become convinced of the Muslim cause, and thought that the Serbs must be deterred.

Renwick thought the plan unworkable, and told the administration so, because of the jeopardy in which it would place the lightly armed and exposed British and French troops on the ground.[83] Nevertheless, the administration had become so wedded to it that Secretary of State Warren Christopher was despatched to Europe, ostensibly to talk to EC governments about the plan, but in reality to tell them what the Americans were planning to do. The scheme had obvious advantages to the Americans. It satisfied congressional opinion that something needed to be done, while falling short of committing US ground troops, as Clinton – like Bush before him – was painfully aware that foreign disasters had helped bring down two previous Democrat administrations (Johnson's in 1968 over Vietnam and Carter's in 1980 over Iran).

Christopher flew first to London and held talks with Major, Hurd and Rifkind at Chevening on Sunday 2 May. Seitz drove down from London to the Kent residence with him. With a British driver, for security reasons Christopher handed Seitz the 'talking points' he was planning to employ. Seitz communicated across the back seat in writing, along the lines of Renwick's doubts, that the British would be horrified by the plan. Although Hurd had warned Cabinet on 22 April that it might prove difficult to resist US pressure for intervention, when Christopher presented the plan at Chevening the three British ministers were dumbfounded at how far the White House was prepared to go. They fired back at Christopher a series of questions – about what would happen if British troops were attacked; what would happen if the Croats blocked the supply of weapons; what exactly would provoke an air strike on the Serbs – which he was unable to answer. The meeting was restrained, but the gulf between both groups – with Seitz embarrassed to be on Christopher's side – was unbridgeable. The formal meeting over, Seitz suggested to Major that he have a quiet personal word with Christopher to explain how domestic opinion would never allow British acquiescence in such a plan. Major duly sat in the alcove with Christopher for twenty minutes in Chevening's big sitting room, but made little apparent headway.[84]

Christopher flew on to Paris, Bonn, Moscow and Brussels, but found similar lack of enthusiasm for the plan. After his return to Washington, the administration even considered putting 'Lift and Strike' direct to the UN Security Council, but were deterred from doing so when it became clear that the British would veto it. For months after, the British were unsure whether Christopher's scheme was sincere, or whether it was simply a ploy so that Clinton could turn round to Congress and the American public and say, 'We tried to be more vigorous, but the Allies blocked us.'[85]

The failure of the Lift and Strike mission – and Christopher's affront at the tone of press coverage after British briefings – cast a temporary blight on transatlantic relations. A minimalist agreement, the Joint Action Plan, was reached on 22 May, setting up missions to the UN 'safe areas' containing beleaguered Bosnian Muslims, and calling for containment of the conflict to Bosnia itself. The flimsy nature of the 'Action Plan' perturbed some in the US administration, and on 25 July National Security Adviser Lake came to London and met British officials in secret at the Goring hotel to try to work out a fallback position in case the situation on the ground became even worse. The meeting paved the way for US enforcement of what was essentially the

Europeans' solution, *de facto* partition of Bosnia on ethnic lines. But there were to be two more years of bloodshed and diplomatic intrigue.[86]

Sack the Chancellor

Few events in Major's premiership are so open to rival interpretations as Lamont's dismissal on 27 May. Major's critics say that he hung on to Lamont after Black Wednesday because to have lost him then would have jeopardised his own position, as entry into and remaining within the ERM, against an increasingly opposed Lamont, was Major's policy. But by May, Lamont had become a liability as he became the scapegoat for the tight decisions in the autumn statement and the tax increases in the March budget; his unpopularity, heightened by press smears, meant for the first time that he could be sacked without dragging Major down with him.[87]

Lamont's political base had collapsed despite a good economic record as Chancellor which attracted support from commentators such as Peter Jay, whose verdict on 1992–3 was 'the age of enlightenment in economic policy making'.[88] Lamont's innovations in monetary policy were an important step towards Bank of England independence. He unified the tax and spending aspects of the budget, and oversaw the introduction of the EDX committee system. In the early 1980s Major had enjoyed teasing Labour by pointing out that Denis Healey had said that there is a lag of eighteen months to two years between an economic policy decision and the outcome. If so, Lamont was the Chancellor most responsible for the recovery.

Lamont's critics state that Lamont was never up to the job, and Major unwisely appointed him, to the surprise even of some officials, in November 1990 out of loyalty for his role in the leadership election. He was never industrious or very able, and was carried by his civil servants. After Black Wednesday, it is alleged he became even more erratic and Treasury morale slumped towards the end because of his lack of firm leadership. By May, the rumours and lack of confidence had become chronic, and Lamont's critics felt that neither economic nor political recovery would occur until the chancellorship was occupied by someone who could command more authority.[89]

The truth is difficult to ascertain. It is true that Major was not anxious to see Lamont resign immediately after Black Wednesday, as it would have made his own position more exposed. Equally, had Lamont chosen to fall on his own sword, Major would have been powerless to restrain him. Those close to Major assert that he dismissed Lamont as Chancellor eight months later because of an accumulation of factors that had made his position, in Major's eyes, untenable: he had lost the confidence of the City and industrialists, as well as many of his colleagues; the farrago of stories, including his credit cards and legal bills, even if partly untrue, had made him look ridiculous; and Number Ten believed his attempts to underpin his position by securing support from the Eurosceptic right, as seen in his speech to the Party

Conference in October, were becoming increasingly divisive.[90] Their relationship had indeed become so poor after Black Wednesday that they rarely spoke to each other outside strictly official business. At their regular bilaterals, the atmosphere was chilly.[91]

Lamont's remark, 'Je ne regrette rien', made in Newbury during the by-election campaign in response to a question at a press conference, even if quoted out of context, was considered by Number Ten to have been ill-judged and smacking of arrogance. But a week after the disastrous 6 May results Major spoke very warmly in support of Lamont to the Scottish Tories. So what suddenly went wrong over the next two weeks?

Major sought advice of senior Party figures about what to do with Lamont in an impending reshuffle. The results seem to have spelt Lamont's fate. Party Chairman Norman Fowler came to see Major to say that canvassers in the Newbury and local elections had been told that Lamont was a deeply unpopular figure with voters, and was an important factor in the disastrous results. A significant opposition weapon in the Newbury by-election was the slogan, 'A vote for the Conservatives is a vote of confidence in Lamont'.

Ryder reported that Lamont's standing with backbenchers was weak. Major's advice further from within Number Ten was that the rot would only stop and confidence be restored if Lamont was replaced. He was also led to believe that unless he acted decisively now to dig out the spreading rot, a leadership challenge in the autumn would be very likely.[92] Dissenting advice came from *The Economist*, which said that 'to sack Norman Lamont now ... would smack of prime ministerial panic and cheap populism'.[93] Major found himself in a no-win situation, with which he wrestled for those two weeks.

Even those closest to Major say they did not always know why or when he became decided on certain difficult matters. But once he was clear on what he wanted to do, he acted swiftly, determined to make the changes before the parliamentary Whitsun recess, which began on 27 May. Lamont sensed his impending doom very late, when he returned to Number Eleven on the evening of Wednesday 26 May from a champagne party at the Spanish Club in London's West End – where he was reported to be looking very stressed – to celebrate Portillo's fortieth birthday.[94] Major had been invited, but did not turn up. Instead, on his return to Downing Street, Lamont saw official cars parked outside Number Ten and was immediately suspicious.[95] His fears were confirmed when the next day he received a summons next door at 9.15 a.m., and held a ten-minute conversation with the Prime Minister.

Major offered him a move to Environment, in place of Howard, and the offer of continuing to live in Dorneywood, the Chancellor's house that the Lamonts liked. Lamont did not even consider the offer and made it clear he would be returning to the backbenches.[96] Major could at best only have half hoped Lamont would accept: if he had, there would have been little opportunity to 'freshen' the Cabinet, the stated intention of the reshuffle.

Lamont was deeply hurt, and very, very angry, as was his wife. He had, he says, told Major that he wanted to continue until the unified budget in

November and would then go.[97] He believed he had been given a 'nod and a wink' that he could stay until then, to be moved to another job after three years, which would not have been an unreasonable stint for a Chancellor.[98] So to be removed in May, after he had taken the flak for the recession, but before the plaudits could be received for the recovery which his policies had put in place, was deeply galling for him. He also felt his dismissal was dishonest. Lamont mulled over his position with William Hague, his Parliamentary Private Secretary, and just four years off becoming Party leader, and with David Cameron, his political adviser, whom he took to lunch at Toto, the Italian restaurant in Knightsbridge. Lamont made it clear that there would be no pleasantries between the Prime Minister and himself.[99]

When Major's letter arrived thanking him for his outstanding achievement and regretting his decision to leave the government, Lamont instructed David Cameron merely to issue a statement to the Press Association, rather than the conventional 'My dear John' letter of appreciation. Lamont's short statement omitted any reference to Major or promise of continuing to support the government: 'I have always been willing to be judged on my record. I believe that the success of the policies I have put in place will become increasingly clear.'[100] To maximise Major's discomfort, Lamont promised 'further comment' in a few weeks' time, with the ominous undertones of an assault on the lines of Lawson's or Howe's against Mrs Thatcher in the offing.

Major had already decided that Clarke would become Chancellor rather than Howard, the only other serious contender, although he considered springing a surprise by appointing John MacGregor. Both men, especially the former, were felt in some quarters to have been manoeuvring for the chancellorship over the previous few months.[101] Clarke was more eager for the job; Howard – who flatly denies he manoeuvred for the job[102] – was pleased instead to be made Home Secretary, a significant promotion.[103] John MacGregor was the only other possible candidate. Various figures such as Michael Portillo thought he might sneak through, because in choosing Clarke or Howard, Major would be giving out such a powerful signal for or against Maastricht, with key votes still pending, and the single currency.[104] The principal reason for Clarke's preferment over Howard was that Major felt more personal and political affinity for the pragmatic Clarke; after his increasingly distant and uncertain relationship with Lamont over the previous two and a half years, he wanted someone with whom he felt he could work in harmony.[105]

The appointment of Clarke was nevertheless a risk, because he was the current favourite in media leadership speculation, and a man with his own independent Europhile agenda. The Eurosceptics see this as another key turning point leading ineluctably to the divisions of 1996–7 and electoral defeat in 1997. Had Howard been appointed, the single currency could have been ruled out, which the great majority of the parliamentary party increasingly wanted, and the Party could have unified around a popular policy. Clarke was at the height of his popularity in the Party. Major might have worried more if he knew that for the next two years until July 1995, Clarke's presence and position as a possible alternative leader detracted from Major's authority as premier. The Eurosceptic right were not, in the main, antagonistic to him during 1993–5, despite his views on Europe. Nevertheless, Clarke's preferment in other ways alarmed them, especially because Europhiles now held the dominant five positions in Cabinet: Major, Hurd, Heseltine, Clarke and Fowler. Major was aware of this anxiety, and had sought to mitigate it by balancing Clarke's appointment with Howard's promotion to Home Secretary, and by bringing Redwood into Cabinet as Welsh Secretary. Other changes to Cabinet had less ideological significance: Gummer to Environment, Shephard taking his place at Agriculture, and Hunt moving into her job at Employment.

Overall the reshuffle was not notably well regarded. In particular, unfavourable comment was directed at promoting Gummer, seen as an unexciting minister, at leaving Patten at Education, where he was having difficulties putting across the government's case, and at sacking Edward Leigh as a junior minister. 'Is it for disloyalty or incompetence?' Leigh asked. 'Disloyalty', Major replied, but he did not say that it was to send the signal to others on loyalty. The message was not heeded. Leigh became an active critic from the backbenches – particularly as brother-in-arms with Lamont.[106]

The reshuffle was billed by Downing Street, rather limply, as 'refreshing the Cabinet to put the right people in the right jobs'. Few swallowed that line, which was interpreted immediately as Major's way of exorcising his turbulent Chancellor, the first time a Tory Prime Minister had sacked his Chancellor since 1962, when Macmillan fired Selwyn Lloyd in his major Cabinet facelift. Lloyd was deeply hurt, but held his counsel. Lamont exploded forth two weeks later, in a stinging twenty-minute speech to the Commons on 9 June. He stated to the House that Major had told him not to resign after Black Wednesday, and he had thus provided a shield that deflected criticism from Major personally; when the polls turned adverse, he was the scapegoat. He then moved from the particular to the general. Major was too ready to listen to pollsters and to the Party's business managers. Most damaging, Lamont asserted, in a series of piercing phrases, that 'There is too much short-termism, too much reacting to events, not enough shaping of events. We give the impression of being in office but not in power.'[107] There is no doubt that Lamont was dealt a difficult hand and that he was justified in some of his anger. He did not perhaps help himself subsequently by stating a strongly negative position which was to upset even some of his friends and admirers.

Lamont's speech touched several raw nerves, not least because many accepted the force of the criticism that, since the general election, the government had been insufficiently in control of the agenda. The speech came at a time when Major's personal satisfaction rating according to Gallup was at the lowest for a Prime Minister since polling began in the late 1930s, and the Conservative Party rating, too, fell by 5 per cent. As Michael White correctly pointed out, the poll torpedoed any claim that the reshuffle, which aimed to freshen the government's image and restore Major's personal authority, had any positive effect.[108]

Major found it difficult to respond effectively to Lamont: his speech was frequently punctuated by Labour jeers. Number Ten had not been anticipating a full frontal assault from Lamont, and when it came there was no time to rewrite Major's speech. The contrast with John Smith's own response, his wittiest since he became Labour leader, was stark. Many of the faces of his party behind Major betrayed their lack of support. It was left to Paddy Ashdown to give the knife its final twist: 'What we have seen is the beginning of the end of your premiership ... I have to tell you that if you had bothered to turn around you would have seen your fate indelibly written on the faces of Conservative members.'[109] *The Times* believed, 'The fall of John Major came closer yesterday ... Downing Street is not working. He needs different eyes and ears and minds to aid him ... He must heed the truths that came yesterday from so close to home. Or he is going, almost gone.'[110]

Lamont's speech may not have been as damaging as Howe's November 1990 assault on Mrs Thatcher – Lamont claims he did not mean to be the cause of trouble – but it plunged Major into the worst crisis of his career so far. Had there been a popular challenger for the leadership acceptable to both wings of the Party, he would have been unlikely to have survived beyond the autumn.

TWENTY-FIVE

Pyrrhic Victory:

June–September 1993

The Danger Passes: June

MAJOR SPENT WHITSUN at The Finings, in real need of recharging his energy. He took time off in the pleasant, early summer weather to work in the garden and plant delphiniums. Refreshed, he hit back hard at his critics when he addressed the Conservative Women's Conference in London on 4 June. The speech pitched directly at the Tory right, which he saw as his main danger. Offering a staunch defence of monarchy and the constitution, he pledged to fight the EC move to enforce a forty-eight-hour working week through the European Court, a convenient way to display his Eurosceptic credentials. Departing from his prepared text, he took the leadership question head on:[1]

I will tell you what I am tired and weary of: I am weary of gossip dressed up as news, malice dressed up as comment and fiction reported as fact. But I have news for some people. I am fit, I am here and I am staying . . .[2]

He had been stung by yet another William Rees-Mogg article on Whit Monday, blaming primarily him for the longest and deepest recession since the 1930s and calling for him to go.[3] Leadership speculation was whipped up even further by Lamont's resignation speech on 9 June. The authority of the 'Party managers', Ryder, Newton and Fowler, was also called into question by Lamont's criticism of their dead hand. Fowler let his anger rip when he rounded on Lamont for 'thrashing around' in his resignation speech, which was 'dud, nasty, ludicrous and silly'. Judged by some to have been petulant and undignified, several commentators believed that Fowler's outburst led to his even replacing Lamont as 'public enemy number one'.[4] Major's Number Ten team – principally Hogg, Hill, O'Donnell and Bright – were also increasingly brought into the line of fire by a Party desperate to find scapegoats for their continuing woes.[5]

Oh, for there being this government's equivalent of the 'Prime Minister's Willie' – a widely respected figure with 'bottom', preferably a big one, such as Whitelaw, capable of giving wise counsel, pouring oil when required and keeping the Prime Minister out of trouble. Accepting the prevailing wisdom that Thatcher had progressively lost touch after Whitelaw retired in 1988,

Major spent much of his premiership after Chris Patten's departure in search of a similar loyal and effective presence. Wakeham after 1992 proved to be that figure no more than Waddington before him, and by 1993 he was casting his net wider. On 18 January he suggested to Hurd – who, though a leadership challenger in November 1990, was no longer remotely interested in the crown – that he might take such a role at a future reshuffle. After mulling it over for a few weeks, Hurd declined.[6]

In the summer it was seriously proposed that the man Major had called 'my Machiavelli', John Kerr, could be recalled from Brussels to bring his diplomatic cunning to the troubleshooter-cum-chief of staff task. The idea of giving a senior civil servant such a political role caused great fluttering in Whitehall, and by the end of the summer the plan had been seen off (though, ironically, Tony Blair appointed the former diplomat Jonathan Powell chief of staff at Number Ten after May 1997).[7] So great did the need become for a 'Willie' figure in the face of continuing woes that Major even considered bringing back Chris Patten from Hong Kong.[8]

The *Sun* and other tabloids had had their knives out for Major since Black Wednesday, capped by the VAT on fuel announcement in March. Fed by loquacious Tory MPs, by early June the media was holding open house on whether Major could, and should, survive as Prime Minister. Several events coincided to rescue him. As so often when his back was against the wall, he dug in hard, coming over strongly at Question Time on Thursday 10 June. Cheered by his performance, and by the table-banging that greeted him at the meeting of the 1922 Committee that evening, his morale began to improve. Marcus Fox emerged after the backbenchers' meeting to declare: 'The message is that we are fully behind the Prime Minister. He will be our Prime Minister for a very long time to come.'[9]

Why did the threat to his leadership begin to wane? Fox was a wily Chairman of the 1922 Committee: he knew that whatever reservations MPs may have had about Major, he was the leader most likely to hold the Party together. That the only other serious contenders, Heseltine and Clarke, were Europhiles weighed heavily with Lady Thatcher when she spoke in mid-June of the need for the Party to unite behind Major, and appealed for an end to sniping against him. Though the great lady ringmaster qualified her views by saying she did not favour a leadership challenge 'at the moment', her call for no 'stalking horse' candidate against Major that autumn was undoubtedly influential in persuading the right-wing 92 Group to offer Major almost unanimous backing.[10] Had the right had a well-placed candidate, Major's outlook in mid-1993 might have been different. But Lamont's credibility was too damaged, Portillo and Redwood were still too junior, and Howard had also yet to make a mark in a frontline office, having only been at the Home Office since May. Their time, Thatcher and others knew, would come.

Major's immediate safety was secured when Heseltine, the favoured leadership challenger, suffered a minor heart attack in Venice on 21 June. Pictures of him in a dressing gown boarding the plane home, looking tired and frail, significantly damaged his credibility as a man capable of standing up to the stresses of the highest office.[11] Heseltine's illness removed the most plausible leadership rival – even with his pro-European views and error over pit closures. For the next few months Clarke would be the only serious potential challenger, but for the time being Major was through the danger.

Enter Sleaze

One of Heseltine's closest supporters, Michael Mates, junior minister at the Northern Ireland Office since 1992, now caused Major concern. He had decided, unwisely as it transpired, to befriend to Asil Nadir, the Cypriot businessman who had given large donations to the Conservative Party in the 1980s, and whose business operations had since come under investigation by the Serious Fraud Office. Mates's next unfortunate move was a birthday present for Nadir, a watch inscribed 'Don't let the buggers get you down'. Mates's gift seemed much worse when Nadir, facing thirteen charges of fraud and false accounting involving £13 million, fled the country to Northern Cyprus to avoid trial. In the House in early June Major rebuked Mates, but insisted the present was not a 'hanging offence'.[12] Mates by now agreed 'it would have been better if he had not done it',[13] and with the Party rallying behind him, the matter appeared to rest there.[14] Major in private thought Mates had behaved foolishly but did not want to sack him, not least as he enjoyed Heseltine's patronage;[15] instead he was cautioned to avoid further embarrassing contacts with Nadir or his associates.[16]

The press had Mates in their sights, however, as they had had Mellor and Lamont earlier, and were not going to let matters rest. In this quest they were helped by Mates himself who, before the watch story had broken, had asked Nadir's public relations adviser if he could borrow a car for his estranged wife. Major now became seriously irritated with the distracting saga, especially when 'doorstepped' on arrival at his hotel in Copenhagen for a European Council on Sunday 20 June by reporters, who demanded to know what he intended to do about the latest allegations. Major conspicuously failed to offer him support.[17]

Major's attention on the Monday was absorbed by the fairly low-key Danish Council. Passion at Denmark's end-of-presidency conference did not come over Europe, where the pace of the federal train – to Major's relief – appeared to be slowing. The Danes had only endorsed the Maastricht Treaty in their second referendum by securing similar safeguards to Britain, and continental Europe was also facing the recession later, which allowed Major to lecture fellow EC leaders on the benefits of Britain's competition policy.[18]

Explosions came instead over Bosnia. The Germans sided with the American line that the Bosnian government should be armed by lifting the embargo, while Britain and France, with troops on the ground, argued that such a move would only escalate the killing and endanger their soldiers. Tempers frayed late on Monday evening with Kohl and Major clashing loudly in the banqueting hall, the mood so thunderous that coffee had to be abandoned. Kohl described his uncharacteristic exchanges with Major as 'completely undiplomatic'. It was Major, nevertheless, who won the day. Helped by a reluctant Mitterrand, he persuaded the Council to reinforce safe areas rather than lift the arms embargo.

Major returned to London on Tuesday to find the Commons embroiled in an acrimonious dispute about Conservative Party funding. The 'sleaze' question was beginning to gain momentum. The *Guardian* claimed that the Conservative Party had received £7 million from Saudi Arabia, while Margaret Beckett, Labour's deputy leader, alleged that £15 million of the £26 million spent by the Party at the general election had come from unknown sources. Major was angered by these charges of misconduct, into which Mates's relationship with Nadir inevitably became caught.[19] Mates's fate was sealed when, on top of a letter leaked to the press to Lyell, the Attorney-General, interceding for Nadir, he had dinner at the Reform Club on the following evening with Nadir's public relations adviser.

Major's humour was not improved by Thatcher's address at Nicholas Ridley's memorial service, in which she pointedly said, 'It was sometimes said that Nick was short on presentational skills, but he was never short of policies *worth* presenting – a much more difficult and creative side of politics.'[20] Even from beyond the grave, Ridley, with Thatcher as medium, appeared to undermine him.

Major was on the point of asking for Mates's resignation following his Reform Club dinner, but was pre-empted when they both decided late on the morning of Thursday 24 June that it was no longer tenable for him to stay. For Major, the episode was unwelcome and damaging. The press accused him of vacillation and poor judgement, the *Sunday Telegraph* on 27 June weighing in with 'the vacuum left by the lack of leadership'.[21] The ledger from the Mates affair revealed a considerable deficit. 'Tory sleaze' established itself firmly on the agenda; with another scalp, the press would now become more brazen. Major suffered from appearing to have caved in to the Party's right, who had never liked Mates, not least because of his closeness to Heseltine. Speaking that weekend in Huntingdon about the recent crisis, Major responded tartly, 'It is closed. It is finished.'[22] But he knew it was not.

In an interview earlier in the week in the *Los Angeles Times*, Major had produced a graphic image to explain the problems in the Party since the general election: 'You have a number of backbenchers in the Conservative party forming a circular firing squad and opening fire.'[23] As a description of the previous year it was accurate, if over-dramatic; but as a statement about what was to unfold in the month to come, it was powerfully prescient.

Maastricht End Game

After the third reading of the Maastricht Bill in late May, Eurosceptics, thwarted in the Commons, hoped to hold up the Bill in the House of Lords until after the summer recess. Their strategy was to make it an issue again at the Party Conference in October, where a popular rising might finally kill it off.[24] Skilful business management in the House of Lords, however, offered critics of the Bill a full twelve days to debate it in return for an agreement not to filibuster or sabotage it. The principal hope for Eurosceptic rebels in defeating the Bill lay with a call for a national referendum. The idea had first emerged at the time of the Maastricht conference, but the Private Member's Bill that followed was defeated in February 1992. After the general election the device re-emerged as the Eurosceptic rallying cry.

Major had declared himself against a referendum on the grounds that Parliament itself had voted in favour of the Maastricht Treaty, so a plebiscite was not necessary. Eurosceptics, convinced that they had a winning case, pressed on undeterred. When, in the debate on the Bill in the Lords, Thatcher claimed that she would never have signed Maastricht, she placed herself at the head of those demanding a referendum.[25] The argument in the normally sedate House of Lords was heated on both sides, but with the government unusually imposing a three-line whip, and heavy drumming up of support from backwoods peers who rarely attended the upper house, the referendum proposal was defeated by 269 votes on 14 July. The Bill duly passed out of the Lords and received the royal assent on 20 July.

Before the Act could come into force one high hurdle remained. During the committee stage the government had had to accept a vote on the Social Chapter. Now two votes had to take place on Thursday 22 July, on Labour's amendment preventing ratification without the Social Chapter, and on a government motion simply to 'note' the opt-out policy on the Social Chapter secured by Major at Maastricht.

Cabinet had been anticipating a torrid time in these votes, and at their meeting on 15 July had moved the date of the debate forward by a week to distance it from the Christchurch by-election on 29 July, and to give them more time before the summer recess to make amends lest anything go awry.[26] Cabinet ministers decided that Major should take the lead in the debate. For some weeks he had been toying with the idea of making the final Maastricht debate a vote of confidence. His conviction had been strengthened when he read in the newspapers the previous weekend that the Eurosceptics would call his bluff by voting with Labour for the Social Chapter – which they did not want – to be included, merely as a ploy to sabotage the hated Maastricht Treaty.[27]

Speculation and rumour washed back and forth across Westminster and the media in those hot July days. Positive government actions, such as the White Paper on Open Government, released on 15 July, became lost in the morass. Major, though desperately tired – as he often was in July and

December – steadied himself before the week of the vote. He admitted on BBC television's *On the Record* on Sunday 18 July that it had not been a good year so far, with recession at home, the 'very bitter dispute' over Europe, and a series of 'funny stories'.[28] At Jeffrey Archer's annual summer champagne party at Grantchester outside Cambridge that afternoon he was reported to be in good humour, and confident that Labour's motion would be defeated outright.[29]

Bad news came on Monday 19 July with William Rees-Mogg, an arch-Eurosceptic, being given leave to proceed to question by judicial review the ratification of the treaty – a challenge the government had not been anticipating – accompanied by a toughening of resolve by Tory rebels. Euro-sceptic MPs met in Committee Room J to discuss tactics and then repaired for refreshment to their unofficial headquarters, Lord McAlpine's house at 17 Great College Street, to drink English wine and eat 'Maastricht pie', prepared by Bill Cash's butcher from all-English ingredients.[30] Ryder's 'pri-vate' advice to Major, spread across the newspapers the next day, was that he expected a defeat that Thursday.[31]

At Number Ten on Tuesday, the mood swung one way then the other. Various schemes were picked up and discarded. One such had been a Hurd plan for a face-saving compromise to put the Maastricht process on hold to allow the Eurosceptic rebels to come back on board. Major pounced on the flaw: there would follow – as indeed the rebels wanted – months of indecision, dragging on throughout the party conference season and the autumn, with the media creating havoc with tales of Tory divisions.

That evening, Major held a dinner at Number Ten for an informal group of Party elder statesmen brought together periodically by Graham Bright – Paul Channon, Michael Jopling, Tom King, Cranley Onslow and Tim Renton. It was their turn now to devise an escape route for the government in the event of a defeat. Bright very excitedly passed their 'wheeze', as it was called – the exact details of which remain obscure – to Number Ten officials. The atmosphere was feverish and Major became caught up in some of their excitement; but after he had consulted Geoffrey Fitchew, head of the European Secretariat in the Cabinet Office, he decided that this plan, too, would not fly.[32]

Major's mood on the Wednesday was bleak. It was known that twenty-five Tory rebels would defy the whips and vote for the Labour amendment. But one arch-sceptic, John Carlisle, gave Major some small comfort by announcing that he would side with the government. Cabinet rallied strongly to Major, with a round of meetings taking place at Number Ten and elsewhere involving principally Hurd, Clarke, Newton, Ryder and Hunt.[33] Howard, an avowed Eurosceptic, also helped. Heseltine was still on sick leave, and the talk was that both he and John Patten, who in the midst of a turbulent period at Education had been admitted to hospital the week before, would be wheeled into the chamber to vote.[34] All day Major's spirits could not be lifted. After nine of the worst months of his life, he visualised defeat, followed even perhaps by political oblivion. In the evening a series of emissaries were sent across to the House to continue working on rebels, and to report back on the latest predictions. Major settled down in the Cabinet Room, worrying away at his speech for the next day, until at midnight he was eventually persuaded to go up to the flat to get some rest.[35]

The sleep transformed him, and even though the news was no better in the morning, he was in a much brighter, more steely mood. Aides thought it was as if he had spent the day before turning inward, conserving energy for what he knew was going to be one of the most testing days of his premiership. At morning Cabinet at 10.30 a.m. at Downing Street, the first of three that day, Major revealed the current whips' assessment that the government would be defeated, and said Cabinet should meet that evening once the actual result was known. He repeated that the treaty had been endorsed by Parliament and the electorate, and that setting the treaty aside was not an option he would consider.[36] Major let ministers talk freely, and then moved on to discuss other urgent matters that had to be cleared before the summer break.

The Ulster Unionist Party was also meeting that morning, under the chairmanship of their leader Jim Molyneaux. They had still to decide which way to vote. Major knew their votes could be crucial, so was delighted when the UUP agreed that Molyneaux should see him. A hurried appointment was arranged at 2.30 p.m. Molyneaux found Major at the Cabinet table putting the final touches to his speech and brushing up for Prime Minister's Questions that afternoon; he appeared surprisingly relaxed. Molyneaux recalls their conversation vividly, along the following lines:

When I arrived, Major asked me, 'Did you have any tea after your lunch?' I answered that I had been at the meeting of the parliamentary party and had little time for lunch.
  'Right, we'll remedy that.'
  'No, for heaven's sake, get on with completing your speech – don't worry about tea.'
  'No, tea it will be.'
  So over tea, I said, 'I think we can deliver nine.'
  'Nine abstentions?'
  'No, nine with you.'
  'But that's eighteen!'
  'That's right enough,' I said. 'I don't think we should engage in anything of a sordid deal because it's not in either of our characters to do that. I think we simply did what's best for the United Kingdom, and Northern Ireland in particular.'
  'But that's what we've always been doing anyway.'
  'Yes it is. Why don't we leave it at that?'
  'What am I going to say if someone asks me during my speech what deal I did to get you on side?'
  'How about telling the truth?' I looked at the picture rail behind him and intoned, 'Nothing was asked for, nothing was given.'
  'Nothing was asked for, nothing was given. Hmm. That's all right!'[37]

As they thought, there was indeed speculation that Major had given the Unionists a deal in return for their support. Both men deny any such agreement. What finally decided the Unionists to back the government, however, despite their reservations on Europe, was when Labour revealed that they would use the Social Chapter vote as a way to defeat the government; nor were the Unionists enamoured with a recently and conveniently leaked policy paper by Kevin McNamara, Labour's Northern Ireland spokesman, which they regarded as favouring the nationalists.[38]

With the Unionist votes in his pocket, but still unsure whether he could win the vote that evening, Major went down to the House and at Question Time delivered a scathing attack on Smith. Major's speech opening the debate at 4 p.m., for all his agonising, was powerfully delivered; Michael White judged it 'one of his most effective performances'.[39] The vote was still to come when Major, at his most persuasive, addressed the end-of-term meeting of the 1922 Committee at 6 p.m., buoyed by the cheers when he entered the room.

Marcus Fox was unequivocal: with most of the rebels pointedly absenting themselves, he told those attending the meeting, 'The prime minister has earned the loyalty and respect of the entire Parliamentary party.' Major admitted to backbenchers that it had been a bumpy year, but nevertheless he said the economy was recovering, and a third of the manifesto commitments had already been enacted. To placate waverers and affirm those on the right who had decided to back the government, he held out the promise of a busy 'traditional Conservative agenda' for the autumn.[40]

Major and Ryder met at 6.30 p.m. to review the position before the second Cabinet of the day met at 7 p.m. in the House. Even with the confirmation of Unionist support, the Chief Whip's verdict was that the government would still lose, and Cabinet discussed whether to hold a confidence motion. They divided into three. Redwood, Portillo and Lilley, who would have been content to see the Bill fail, were against. The largest group of ministers was for the confidence motion, but did not want to link it to the Bill. This would have kept the government in office, but left the Bill to be resolved in the autumn, when, it was argued, further pressure could be applied to win the rebels back over. A third group, led by Major, argued for carrying the Bill on the confidence vote. Major wanted to call the bluff of the Euro-rebels, but doing so carried a much higher risk.

Almost everyone spoke in the discussion. Major – at his most commanding – articulated a clear high road (his strategy) and a low road, and argued forcefully that the latter would perpetuate the infighting and increase charges of dithering. In the end Major won over the Cabinet, with none of the reluctant Eurosceptic ministers resigning over his handling of the vote.[41] Ministers then debated when to hold the confidence motion: with the recess due to begin midweek, the choice was either the next day, Friday, or the following Monday. Delay over the weekend, they agreed, would only allow the rebels more time to regroup, to the sounds of further damaging speculation. As one minister aptly put it, 'We have decided to play the king. It's not an ace – the rebels hold that. What we don't know is if they will play it' – which would have forced a general election in the autumn.[42]

The vote was called at 10 p.m., making it a sensational live television story. The first vote was on Labour's amendment. Not only the nine Unionists, but also Nick Winterton, James Cran and John Biffen backed the government. The result was announced at 10.16 p.m.: the Ayes – 317, the Noes – 317, heralding the first tie since 1976, the night Heseltine waved the mace.[43] Although it was revealed the following day that there had been a miscount, and the government had won by one vote. In line with convention the Speaker's vote was used to decide the vote for the government that evening. The second vote, on the government's motion to 'note' the opt-out, was, however, defeated by 324 to 316 votes, with twenty-six Tories voting against. One Labour left-winger was seen giving a clenched fist salute. It was the most dramatic parliamentary occasion since cameras were let into Parliament in the 1980s. Major, showing no emotion, then delivered the government's decision to call a vote of confidence the following morning.

The third and final Cabinet was held at the House that evening. Major, in commanding form, ordered colleagues into battle the next day. Ryder, asked for his advice and commented Delphicly, 'At the Charge of the Light Brigade the regimental sergeant major galloped up to Cardigan and said, "Same again, sir?" ' The Cabinet were reasonably confident – no more than that – that the rebels would return to the fold and avoid bringing down the government, so provoking an autumn election which, on current polls, would certainly have resulted in a Labour government, and one far more Europhile than Major's administration. If the rebels held an ace, this was Major's trump.

Hunt recorded in notes at the time how those of his Europhile persuasion viewed the events: 'JM was driven by his inner determination to get Maastricht through. When all this is looked back on within the Party, we will see that it was his determination to drive that through that enabled us to survive.'[44] Major's skills in holding Cabinet together were indeed rarely better displayed than over the closing phases of the Maastricht Bill.

In the event the confidence motion on Friday 23 July proved an anticlimax. Major, drained by the events of Thursday, spoke adequately, no more, and promised better times ahead after a year of misfortunes. Smith, who recovered the form that had deserted him the day before, completely upstaged him. But the Conservatives still carried the motion by a convincing majority of thirty-eight votes. The Eurosceptics had made their point. They had blocked and humiliated the government, but they were not ready, yet, to bring it down. Only one Tory MP failed to support the government, Rupert Allason (the spy writer Nigel West), who was absent, and had the whip withdrawn. Central Office, which had tentatively pencilled in the date of 2 September as an election day in the event of defeat, stood down from battle stations.[45] Magnanimity was the order of the day. Both Fox and Fowler, heads of the backbenches and Party machine respectively, issued statements that there should be no reprisals against rebel MPs, the clear determination being to draw a line rapidly under the divisions, and to hope that by the time Parliament returned after the summer, all could be forgiven and forgotten while the Party turned all its attention on Labour.

After more than a year of discussion, seventy parliamentary votes and sixty-one days of debate, the Maastricht Treaty had finally been ratified by Parliament.[46] But at what cost? The impact on Major's authority is difficult to gauge. He won plaudits for his single-mindedness and coolness under pressure. *The Economist* even considered the July days 'showed at last that he might, after all, have what it takes to be king of the political jungle'.[47] But his reliance on a confidence motion to give the Maastricht Bill the last heave through Parliament exacted a price. The rebels had developed bonds of shared adversity, and the virtual party within a party was not to be disbanded as the leadership hoped. They resented the methods that had been used against them, from the whips' bullying in the paving vote and after to the ultimatum of the confidence vote. The 'bullying' entered the folklore as evidence of Major's alleged nastiness, to be recycled whenever a critic sought to expose Major's true character.[48] The rebels went on to form a hard core of plotters, posing the threat of a leadership challenge every autumn, and the next time the confidence vote technique was used it was to show how deep Eurosceptic disaffection ran.

But could Major have acted differently? He had staked his leadership on the Maastricht Treaty, and that meant putting it through Parliament. Bar abandoning the treaty, which he was not prepared to do, he had little alternative but to act as he had. If he had won a Pyrrhic victory, it was perhaps the only victory on offer.

Bastards

A mixed bag followed in the backwash from the week. The most exotic came on the Friday evening of the confidence vote. Major had been interviewed by ITN's Michael Brunson about the drama. When the television lights were turned off, Major unclipped his microphone and, believing he was now having a relaxed private conversation with a journalist he liked, said, 'What I don't understand Michael, is why such a complete wimp like me keeps winning everything.' He continued:

The real problem is one of a tiny majority. Don't overlook that. I could have [sic] all these clever decisive things which people wanted me to do – but I would have split the Conservative Party into smithereens. And you would have said I acted like a ham-fisted leader.

Brunson asks about the three Cabinet ministers reputed to have been willing to resign if Major had agreed to the Social Chapter. Major:

Just think it through from my perspective. You are the prime minister, with a majority of eighteen, a Party that is still harking back to a golden age that never was, and is now invented. You have three right-wing members of the Cabinet who actually resign. What happens to the Parliamentary party?

Brunson suggests Major could find replacements. Major:

I could bring in other people. But where do you think most of this poison is coming from? From the dispossessed and the never-possessed. You can think of ex-Ministers who are going around causing all sorts of trouble. We don't want another three more of the bastards out there.[49]

Brunson did not know that while they were talking, all their words were being taped. He realised only when a lobby journalist greeted him a couple of hours later with the words, 'Great interview, Mike!' He felt genuinely embarrassed about the leak, made initially to the *Observer*. ITN blamed the BBC, as facilities for the interview were being 'pooled', which meant a number of studios, including some of the BBC's own, were receiving recordings from Number Ten.[50] It later transpired that, though the cameras had been turned off, one of the microphones used for the interview was still 'live'. Brunson believes that Major had been letting off steam with him because he had been frustrated by the tone of his other 'on the record' interviews from Number Ten that evening; even in his hour of triumph, he felt the media's carping still continued.[51]

In the short term, the leak was felt to have endangered the truce after the confidence vote. Backbench Eurosceptics leaped on the words – taken to refer to Lilley, Portillo and Redwood – as evidence of Major's true feelings about them. Edward Leigh, dismissed at the same time as Lamont, said, 'It is rather distressing for a British prime minister to start swearing at Cabinet colleagues. It smacks of the Nixon era.'[52] John Redwood agreed: 'I was called a bastard just a few weeks after being appointed to the Cabinet. You can imagine what a shock it was to hear on the airwaves that that was how the Prime Minister saw me.'[53] In fact Major's use of such language was usually brought on by frustration and a raw passion which he had learned to hold back in public. Right-wing critics, though, suggested colourfully that he did so merely to emulate the behaviour, as he saw it, of the upper classes. In the long run, while the use of the word 'bastards' may have helped marginally in combating the grey image with the public, it further damaged his relations with the right.

The words 'inspired' Teresa Gorman to write her book *The Bastards* on the Eurosceptic battle against Maastricht.[54] Gorman, like fellow travellers Cash, Carlisle, Gill, Leigh and Marlow, Major did not care for, whereas with other entrenched Eurosceptics, such as Taylor and Shephard, he respected their deep-held opinions, even though he disagreed with them.[55]

The threat from Rees-Mogg's judicial review case – believed by Number Ten to be Goldsmith funded – rumbled on for a few more days, but the former *Times* editor abandoned the challenge on 2 August, ironically the same day that the ERM, buffeted beyond endurance by the financial markets, finally capitulated, with wider fluctuations permitted. The virtual ending of the mechanism, over which so much blood had been spilled, passed largely unnoticed by the chattering classes sunning themselves on their summer holidays. Unfortunately for the government, the loss of the Christchurch by-election five days earlier took place under full glare. Defeat had been expected; its scale had not. The 35 per cent swing against the Tories was the highest against a government since the war.

Robert Hayward, the Conservative candidate, had been MP for Kingswood until defeated at the general election, and was a member of proven quality. Major had been most solicitous towards him, speaking to him twice on the phone during the campaign.[56] On top of the 'bastards' comments, the result meant the government went into the summer in bad shape. It was a bad blow for Major personally, aggravated by his own backbenchers speaking to the media about how the government needed to change policy, principally on VAT on domestic fuel; Gorman said that unless Major changed his policies, he would find himself out of a job. A MORI poll published in *The Times* showed a further slump in Major's popularity, even among Tory voters, only 25 per cent of whom thought he was doing a good job.[57] Major was as relieved as anyone in Cabinet that the summer holiday had at last arrived.

Summer Trips: Japan, Sweden and Portugal

Major had never visited Japan before, but the summer of 1993 saw him there twice within ten weeks. The G7 annual summit, held in Tokyo in early July before the Maastricht vote shenanigans, was a stiflingly formal occasion, with official hospitality reaching new heights of generosity. Twelve thousand press passes were issued as domestic audiences placed excessive expectations on the outcome.[58] Major was backed by Clinton in another bid to make the meetings more like the brief 'fireside chats' for heads of government alone, which the summit had been in the mid 1970s, leaving foreign and finance ministers to get on with their business at home.[59] However, they were successfully opposed by Kohl and Mitterrand, who argued that countries with coalition governments faced peculiar problems in slimming their delegations down to just one representative. Major and Clinton did manage to move a little towards informality, cutting down the media circus at the next talks and producing briefer and punchier final declarations.[60]

The main business of the summit was the unblocking of the General Agreement on Tariffs and Trade (GATT) round which had started in Uruguay in 1986. The aim of the treaty was to increase global trade by removing tariffs and restrictions. The Uruguay round aspired to bring farming and textiles into its remit, and set up a body, the World Trade Organisation, to police the treaty. It was a cause particularly close to the heart of Sarah Hogg, to whom Major was happy to delegate the negotiations. She was able to form a strong axis with Mickey Kantor, President Clinton's Trade Representative, to ensure that the free trade agenda did not get lost with the change of administration in Washington or the interest group politics of European agriculture. Major's personal impact, and sensitivity to the political limits of other leaders, was most apparent when he and Clinton succeeded, in a meeting at the Akasaka Prince Hotel that dragged on until 3 a.m., in disposing of many of the remaining items of contention.[61]

With Parliament in summer recess, Major managed a few days away from Number Ten, attending cricket matches and relaxing at Great Stukeley. But on 11 August it was modestly back to work, two days on the first official visit by a British Prime Minister to Sweden for thirty years. Carl Bildt, Conservative Prime Minister, had invited Major to help persuade a sceptical Swedish population of the merits of joining the EC. Major used the visit to highlight his long-held belief in EC enlargement, that the Community should be widened rather than deepened.[62] Norma went too, and business played a minor part.

Just before leaving Stockholm, the case of five-year-old Irma Hadzimuratovic hit the headlines. Wounded by shrapnel in her back, her pathetic picture, clutching a Barbie doll, touched a deep spring of compassion and resulted in a flood of letters and phone messages calling for the government to take action. Damned if he acted – cynical; damned if he did not – callous, Major opted for the former and ordered an RAF Hercules transport to be sent to whisk Irma off to hospital. Being in Stockholm, he was happy to make the evacuation of the intensive care unit at the Sarajevo hospital, which followed the help for Irma, into a joint initiative with Sweden. The press had a field day, dubbing 'Operation IRMA' 'immediate response to media appeal' and pointing out that other countries like Italy had taken many more patients, with less fuss.[63]

The Majors' annual overseas holiday was looming. After four years at the Garel-Jones villa at Candeleda in central Spain, they wanted a change. They had become local celebrities, their annual visits well publicised, and they felt their seclusion had become compromised.[64] Stephen Wall, now Ambassador in Lisbon, offered a cousin's farm on the Douro.[65] In relaxed and happy mood, Major had already unwound from July's exertions in an unusually tranquil August, and enjoyed exploring the Portuguese countryside.

His mind did not fully switch off politics, however, particularly the question of Europe, and how to accentuate the common ground with his party's Eurosceptics, which continued to prey on his mind. After detailed discussions with Wall, with whom he stayed two days *en route*, he set down his thoughts on Europe's future direction. His draft, initially intended for a speech, was sent to Downing Street. Roderic Lyne, Wall's successor as Foreign Affairs Private Secretary, thought the content was sound, but worried lest some passages appear unnecessarily hostile to the Community. Lyne faxed back some ideas, which Major mostly agreed to adopt.

On his return to London on 5 September, the text was debated at Number

Ten. No suitable opportunity for a speech immediately presented itself.[66] Sarah Hogg felt a keynote speech on Europe before the Party Conference in early October might upstage his conference speech, so she suggested turning it into an article. Why not try her former journal, *The Economist*, which would be the ideal medium for a reasoned, longer article than could comfortably fit within a newspaper format?[67] It was agreed. Rodric Braithwaite was given the task of converting the speech notes into an article, but when Major saw his draft he thought the language too much Braithwaite and not enough Major. With Sarah Hogg he transferred the text back into his own words, and resisted all official attempts to 'smooth its edges'.[68]

Published at the end of September under the title 'Major on Europe – Raise your eyes, there is a land beyond',[69] the article offered a fresh vision for the future development of the European Community, and revealed quite how far he had moved in a sceptical direction during the bruising two and a half years since his 'very heart of Europe' speech in Bonn. He advocated a European Community of sovereign national governments, which protected national and cultural differences, to embrace the whole of democratic Europe, in a single market which enhanced the economic opportunities and freedoms for all member nations. To achieve his vision he wanted greater subsidiarity, a streamlined Commission and emphasis on Maastricht's 'intergovernmental pillars', which extended collaboration on foreign, defence and some domestic policies'.

One particular passage caused upset in the Community, with Kohl above all angered by the words: 'I hope my fellow heads of government will resist the temptation to recite the mantra of full economic and monetary union as if nothing had changed. If they do recite it, it will have all the quaintness of a rain dance and about the same potency.'

The Foreign Office had become alarmed at what Major was hatching, but failed to rein him back any further. They thought such passages insufficiently statesmanlike, and knew they would cause trouble. Typical comments from officials were 'a silly article'; 'a serious misjudgement to spit on things that were important to people like Kohl'; 'acceptable if it had been in a traditionally Tory paper like the *Daily Mail*, as people in Europe would have understood it then, but the folly was to put it in a serious international magazine where it gave the world outside the impression that this was his new platform for Europe. It set us back. European leaders felt affronted by it.'[70] Hurd's reaction was more reasoned: 'He obviously enjoyed writing it, but it was perhaps a bit ahead of its time and jarred a bit as far as I was concerned.'[71]

After all the currency turmoil, and the effective termination of the ERM in early August, Major's intention had been to hold the Community back from forging ahead with EMU, which he correctly saw would be the next battleground with his Eurosceptics, and make the EC reflect more on where it should be going.[72] He was not unduly troubled by the rumblings in Europe following publication.[73] The article did indeed serve substantially to delineate his thinking on Europe for the following four years. The tragedy for him was that relations with the Eurosceptics had been so damaged that *The Economist* article made little impact on them. The truth was, as Major was shortly to discover, that trust in whatever he now said about his views on Europe had been lost.

Far East: Journey to Hell

The ground for a difficult second trip to Japan had been prepared over the two weeks before his departure on 17 September. Scent of future trouble was evident at a Political Cabinet on 9 September, where Major gave a stern warning for Cabinet ministers – he was thinking principally of the three 'bastards' – to unite behind the leadership, or 'face the consequences'. Fowler echoed that the grassroots in the country, reflected in letters and messages received at Central Office, were fed up with a bickering parliamentary party.[74] Kenneth Baker's memoirs, published at the end of August with an accompanying BBC television programme, contained passages critical of Major, especially his half-hearted support for Thatcher's effort to fight off the Heseltine challenge in November 1990. They stirred up a few embers, but created less damage, ironically, than Penny Junor's sympathetic biography, *The Major Enigma*, which began newspaper serialisation on 5 September. In this highly critical account of Thatcher's style of leadership and policies, Junor said the former Prime Minister deserved to fall, whereas Junor championed Major's role and behaviour during the leadership election. According to Michael Jones, 'The authenticity of Ms Junor's claims to represent Mr Major's views is not in doubt. Ms Junor tells me he read her book twice before she sent it to the publishers.'[75] Even via a proxy, the words riled the Thatcher camp.[76]

There is no proof that the two books provoked the leadership speculation that began in earnest on Monday 13 September, with talk of stalking horses and a November contest. It may simply have been that the Eurosceptic right, who were behind the stories, and who were still smarting after the confidence vote and the 'bastards' remark, were merely awaiting a critical mass to return from their summer holidays. But the week that followed was a bad one for Major. Talk of challenge to Major from Clarke backed by Portillo became widespread: in return for Portillo's endorsement (and offer of a top job, probably Chancellor) Clarke would become leader but would agree to soften his pro-European line. Here was a dream ticket: with no right-winger yet credible enough to challenge outright, this was the next best alternative. As if to confirm the impression of a new-found Euroscepticism, Clarke's lecture to the Swiss Bank Corporation on 13 September warned Britain's EC part-ners not to rush to reconstruct the ERM.[77] Clarke's closest advisers, however, vehemently deny he was scheming then, or at any time, for the leadership: 'I have never met a politician who plotted or planned less,' said Tessa Keswick, his political adviser and confidante.[78] But her comments, while fair, do not mean that Clarke did not *want* to become Prime Minister – he did, badly.

Unrest was further inflamed as a result of an article by Lamont in *The Times* and an interview in the *Sun*, on the first anniversary of Black Wednesday on 16 September, calling for 'the right leadership'.[79] A former Chancellor belittling his Prime Minister added legitimacy to the discussion of a successor. Lamont vehemently denied on BBC television's *Question Time* that he was trying to bring down the Prime Minister – as many believed him to be doing – saying instead that his motives were entirely honourable and he was merely trying to offer 'fresh perspectives' on the crisis of the previous autumn.[80] Polls published the same Wednesday, revealing Labour were eighteen points clear of the Conservatives, and voters' trust in Major to run the NHS was even less than it was for Thatcher, caused further damage.[81] As the specially chartered plane left Heathrow for Tokyo the next day, many at Westminster and in the media thought Major would not survive until the new year.[82]

The DC-10 flew eastwards with thirty political reporters at the back of the plane, twelve top business leaders (led by Michael Perry, Chairman of Unilever) in the middle, and the Number Ten staff in the front cabin. The main aim: promoting British business on the lines of the Indian trip in January. The main problem: insufficient stories for the British media, beyond demands by British prisoners of war for compensation from the Japanese for their suffering during the Second World War.

Errors made during the trip flowed in swift succession. On the long flight out Major, still smarting after the bruising week that had just gone by, spoke to journalists at the back of the plane on the record, and when asked about the Eurosceptics and the leadership challenge, spoke disparagingly of both. Major appeared guilelessly unaware of the headline news his remarks would create in a highly volatile atmosphere back in Britain.

John Sergeant, the senior BBC figure on the trip, became alarmed that as soon as they touched down in Tokyo his press colleagues would gleefully begin to file their stories about Major's comments, but he would have no film as Major had declined to be interviewed on camera. On the drive in from the airport, Sergeant explained his concern to Gus O'Donnell who, typically sympathetic, said that Major would say something on camera, but he added that Sergeant should ask questions about the trip itself first as Major did not want another overseas trip overshadowed by stories of domestic unrests.

As he arrived at the Embassy Sergeant duly asked Major two questions about the Party divisions. Major responded tersely. But once in the building he exploded at the way he thought the BBC was trying to sabotage the trip. O'Donnell, clearly ruffled, on top of being exhausted, came out and snapped at Sergeant, calling him a 'jerk' in front of others from the press. Despite O'Donnell's apology, his rebuke to Sergeant, and Major's anger at the media, were widely reported in Britain.[83]

Major was still angry when he appeared before an audience at the Japanese Press Club. The 200 Japanese reporters stood up and applauded respectfully when he came in; the British press contingent remained conspicuously seated.

Again, questions came from the British about the leadership challenge, specifically about Clarke, who had been speaking out widely to the media in a fashion reminiscent of the ambiguous style of one of his predecessors as Chancellor, R. A. Butler (1951–5). Major snapped back, as he did repeatedly during the Japanese visit, that he was fed up seeing an important overseas trip demeaned: 'It is time to cut out this stupid internecine squabbling and get on with the job.'[84]

A tape-recorder had been brought into the television conference at the Embassy and placed unseen on the chair of the *Independent*'s Colin Brown, directly in front of the Prime Minister. Fatigue and general irritation made Major forget the lesson he thought he had learned from his off-the-cuff 'bastards' remarks two months before. On this occasion, he said he could hear 'the flapping of white coats' when his 'barmy' Tory critics poured out their bile on his leadership, and indicated he would be tackling them head on at the Party Conference in October. Not surprisingly, these remarks were avidly seized upon by the media. The trip was rapidly turning into a nightmare. Rather than headlines in the press about the Prime Minister leading British business successes abroad, the news was full of stories of the leadership challenge, Lamont's threats about further ERM revelations and Major's anger with his critics.[85]

The increasingly fractious party flew on 21 September to Kuala Lumpur. Major arrived suffering from lack of sleep, having spent much of the previous night in contact with developments in Russia, where a confrontation was developing between Yeltsin and a parliament dominated by his opponents. Alongside worrying away at final tuning of his *Economist* article, he also had to decide what line to take on Russia. Badly needing a turn of good fortune, he went straight from the airport to a banquet only to have British policy in Bosnia lambasted by Dr Mahathir Mohamad, Malaysia's Muslim Prime Minister, who demanded effective British action to end 'this ongoing holocaust'. Major was so angry he thought of leaving at that point. But wiser counsel prevailed, and he merely added a paragraph to his own speech. Despite his tiredness, he revised the text of his lunchtime Chamber of Commerce speech the next day to deal with the Russian situation. The first news of the confrontation in Russia breaking was coming through and, just as in August 1991, Major was the first western leader to come out with a statement of support for Yeltsin.[86] Mahathir, having made his point, was more emollient with Major the next day. But details of a £1 billion trade deal signed in Malaysia were mostly buried on newspapers' business pages, blamed by the media on Major's press team supplying them with inadequate information to write front-page stories.[87]

The last leg of the 'journey to hell', as it came to be described, was a brief stopover in Monte Carlo. This was a final gesture of support for Manchester's bid to stage the Olympic Games in 2000, as the International Olympic Committee made its choice of venue. Ever since the Manchester bid had been approved by British sporting bodies, Major had taken a personal interest in its success. He set up a civil service team at home, promoted the bid through government offices abroad, entertained IOC delegates in Number Ten, and instructed Cabinet ministers to drum up support. The government was also willing to underwrite up to £2.5 billion of costs. It was all to no avail: his final destination proved no happier than Tokyo and Kuala Lumpur, as Manchester's bid was, to huge dismay, to come third.[88]

Matters were little better on his return to London. Upon arrival, Major learned that Richard Body was threatening to resign his seat (Holland with Boston), believing he was on Major's list of 'barmy' rebels. Calls were also made by several senior Party figures for Bright and O'Donnell to be replaced, to allow Major to be presented more effectively to the Tory Party and to the country at large.[89] Stories reappeared about him being lonely and isolated from trusted lieutenants. Privately, many of his supporters were dismayed by the way he had lowered himself in front of journalists, and believed it would have been much better to have been more detached and statesmanlike.[90]

The week of the trip was one of the worst of his premiership. Among his own party, Teresa Gorman said, 'He must be totally out of touch with reality', and even Marcus Fox opined that, 'He is going to have to improve his performance. I have no doubt at all.'[91]

Major's recovery was helped by a twist on the Richard Body episode. Body's threats to resign were withdrawn after he said he had spoken to the Prime Minister and was assured all was well between them. Number Ten did not react until another backbencher told Bright that he, too, had received a conciliatory call from Major. At this point Number Ten stated that Major had not in fact made any such telephone call. Body, however, asserted that he had. The mystery took baffled civil servants a day to unravel – the comedian Rory Bremner had carried off the most successful piece of premier impersonation of his career.

TWENTY-SIX

Regaining the Initiative:

October–December 1993

How DEEPLY IN trouble was Major? No one knew for sure. The turbulence in September, however, showed that the hopes that the animosity which peaked during the Maastricht debates in July would subside after the summer were in vain. If Major's *Economist* article had been intended in part to cement a new truce with the Eurosceptic right, it failed. What direction to take the government to rebuild a common sense of purpose was at the forefront of his mind as summer turned to autumn.

A New Agenda?

Major's two new initiatives in his first eighteen months had been education and the Citizen's Charter. By mid-1993, although there was much he still wanted to achieve in each, neither was sufficient for his domestic agenda. Something fresh was needed.

Education reform, his core concern in the first months of his premiership, still inspired him. He saw himself as the champion of the child from the ordinary home, and his determination that the state school system was meeting the needs of its students spurred on his pursuit of more testing and league tables. After the 1992 election, John Patten had been appointed to the Department for Education (DFE) with a brief to force the pace on reform. His Education Act of 1993 covered two broad areas. It merged the two education bodies NCC and SEAC into the combined School Curriculum and Assessment Authority (SCAA). It also continued to take functions away from local education authorities by encouraging schools to 'opt out' and by setting up 'hit squads', formally called Education Associations, to take over 'failing' schools.

Despite the passage of the Act, Patten's term at the DFE was marred by clashes with education groups and a deteriorating relationship with Number Ten. Major's Number Ten had been hostile to the official culture at the DFE from the beginning, and considered that the government's difficulties had enabled it to engage in 'a huge reassertion of control, making it extremely difficult for the Education Secretary'. But Patten himself was increasingly criticised for failing to handle the department with sufficient grip. One move that particularly angered Major was when he argued what the Policy Unit saw as the DFE line of offering the abolition of the Assisted Places scheme as an economy measure.[1]

Patten's determination to drive through policy alienated many in the education establishment, and the hitherto disunited teaching unions organised a successful boycott of the June 1993 tests. Shortly afterwards, Patten fell ill. Ron Dearing, chairman-designate of SCAA and troubleshooter in chief, worked to resolve the impasse. His final report, published in December 1993, reduced the compulsory elements of the National Curriculum, simplified tests and marking, reduced attainment targets and called for a period of consolidation and stability.[2] It was a painful defeat for Major. Patten was dismissed in the 1994 reshuffle; he felt that he had an impossible task in clearing up a legacy of poor legislation, and was given insufficient backing to achieve it.[3]

The Citizen's Charter had also hit some difficult times. After the launch in 1991 there followed the routine work of the Charter Unit in monitoring and extending the charters throughout the public services, which took place to little acclaim. Major's loss of authority in Whitehall hampered the effort to get meaningful charters out of many departments, and he was disheartened by the scorn of some of his Cabinet, and even more by the extent to which the Citizen's Charter had come to be seen by many as a symbol of the ineffectiveness of the Major government. 1993 had been a particularly bad time, with the fiascos of the underemployed 'Charter Line', and the 'Cones Hotline' meant to reduce driver frustration with motorway roadworks, which degenerated into a national joke. He 'fell out of love' with the charter project,[4] and his confidence was only gradually rekindled after the introduction of the publicly nominated 'Charter Mark' awards and by growing public acknowledgement that the charters were of value in improving public services. Even foreign governments began sending delegations to Whitehall to study the initiative. He took considerable pride in the achievements of the charter programme, and it proved possibly his most significant innovation in domestic policy.

Major's other initiatives in public service reform were also experiencing difficulties by 1993. Market testing, whereby functions carried out by the civil service were compared with private sector operations for value for money, had caused ructions in Whitehall. These culminated in a one-day strike in November 1993, which was the biggest civil service industrial action since 1981, but this did not prove as obstructive as the teachers' boycott, and reform continued in 1994.

Also continuing, but making depressingly little impact on the public, were the moves to open government contained in the July 1993 White Paper. This set out a new code of practice on access to information held by the government, and of more current and historical documents. The measure had encountered some resistance in Cabinet on grounds of *realpolitik*. The decisive voices in favour were Waldegrave, whose White Paper it was, and

Mackay, who countered the argument that everything leaked out anyway by saying that it would be better to publish it all properly. On the other hand, it fell well short of a Freedom of Information Act demanded by open government enthusiasts or indeed by those who had high hopes of Major's promises of 1990 to open up government. Whitehall insiders continued to dismiss the cry for open government as largely confined to a small group of obsessives among the chattering classes living mostly in affluent areas in north London.[5] There was indeed little take-up for newly accessible information; whether this was because the cynics were right, or that people were not made sufficiently aware of the initiative, remains to be seen.

The parts of Major's initial agenda that had yet to be put into practice by autumn 1993 consisted only of odds and ends of policies such as Whitehall reform and the tail end of privatisation (coal, rail, parts of the nuclear power industry), that had little public appeal or resonance. There was certainly no organising principle there which could be used to give a coordinated rather than departmental thrust to policy and refute the charge that the government had run out of steam.

Urgency for the quest for an organising mission for Major's government was given by a paper Sarah Hogg produced at the end of the summer, which argued that whereas the economy was set on its course away from recession, it would not translate into support for the Party. A new term thus entered the political lexicon: 'voteless recovery'. Frustrated by the lack of opportunity to plan strategy, and with Chequers out of action for redecoration and repair, Hogg had taken the Policy Unit away for an overnight stay in July to her home in Lincolnshire.[6] Plenty of interesting individual proposals were heard, and resentment expressed at the failure of the media, and the Party, to acknowledge that a significant part of the 1992 manifesto had already churned through the House. But there was no single, big idea on offer.

In the absence of suggestions for a portmanteau domestic idea, Major increasingly saw the attraction of the platform he outlined to the end-of-session 1922 Committee meeting on 22 July, of 'a traditional Conservative agenda', focusing on the economy, law and order and education. He had also promised 'a very substantial criminal justice bill' in the 1993–4 session.[7] The proposals may not have won over many Tory rebels during the Maastricht debates, but Major's growing conviction was that this was what the Party wanted, and that such a menu would offer the best prospects for healing the Party's divisions. Intensive regional tours in September to meet the Party faithful, arranged by Jonathan Hill, further showed that such a programme would be popular with the Party's core supporters, who felt that it had drifted too far from the issues that concerned them.[8] Major was prepared to downplay his own personal agenda – classless society, Citizen's Charter, and advancing his liberal beliefs – if a traditional Tory platform was going to prove a stronger rallying cry around which his government could unite, restore Party morale, and thereby strengthen his own position. He did so against some resistance from Central Office, which had settled on 'Building on the Recovery' as the theme of the Party Conference.[9]

The truth was that Major had been too distracted by the Maastricht saga and by dramas over the summer to put sufficient thought into this new platform. As one observer noted: 'The new agenda, such as it was, was fashioned by the Policy Unit and Political Office at Number Ten, which meant that interdepartmental ministerial consultations and meetings failed to take place before it was rushed out in a hurry.'[10] Neither the Number Ten Private Office nor the Cabinet Office machinery were involved in working up the theme. Nor was the Whips' Office consulted beforehand.[11]

Cabinet on 30 September contained an upbeat report by Major on his Far East trip – the Japanese government, ministers were told, regarded Britain as their leading European partner – and was followed by a Political Cabinet to prepare for the Party Conference the next week.[12] Presenting a unified image was the main instruction to Cabinet ministers; but detailed briefing about what the image was to be was overlooked.

Major, meanwhile, was still pondering in his own mind whether to strike out hard against the Tory rebels in his end of conference speech, on the lines of Kinnock's celebrated 1985 Bournemouth speech where he lambasted Militant Tendency, as he had intimated to journalists on the Japan trip he would do, or whether to be forgiving and constructive. The dilemma, whether to be harsh or forgiving to those who stray, is one familiar to any parent, or leader: for a Prime Minister, it opened up the charge of indecision, and it was a strategy Major never resolved satisfactorily from 1991 until the end of his premiership.[13]

Blackpool Party Conference: October

Considering all that had gone before, Major was in surprisingly good spirits when he went into his third party conference as premier, and it proved to be one of his quieter and more successful weeks. Two books threatened to upset the harmony: Gorman's *The Bastards* and the first volume of Thatcher's memoirs, *The Downing Street Years*.[14] The former was all but ignored, the latter had considerable disruptive potential. Writing the 900-page book with Robin Harris and a small team had absorbed her attention and accounted for her lower political profile since early 1992. The finished draft was submitted to Robin Butler, the Cabinet Secretary, as was normal practice. A number of cuts and amendments were agreed between Butler and Thatcher, but even so Major – who was entitled under the rules governing ministerial memoirs to make his views known – was disturbed by the tone of several references to himself, and disputed her account of his views on Europe where she spoke of him 'intellectually ... drifting with the tide'.[15]

Thatcher disliked the perception which she believed had gathered strength over the summer that she was jealous or petulant about Major, and had no wish to become entangled in a confrontation with him during the conference week. She followed the advice of Norman Fowler and other party colleagues and insisted that the *Sunday Times* begin serialisation of her book only after the end of the Conservative Party Conference. The memoirs nevertheless proved significant noises off throughout the week. Thatcher reluctantly agreed to a pre-conference interview with Andrew Neil, while the *Daily Mirror* kept the story bubbling in the run-up to the conference by publishing a series of purported leaks from the text.[16] The potential for damage to Major was, however, largely neutralised by Thatcher's unusually pro-Major comments in Blackpool on 6–7 October. All week Cabinet ministers lined up to endorse Major's leadership, the most eye-catching being from Kenneth Clarke that 'Any enemy of John Major's is an enemy of mine', a firm signal to the right, and to Number Ten, which had grown suspicious of him, that he was not prepared to become a focus for attempts to unseat Major.

The week also witnessed a drumbeat of right-wing populist slogans and speeches, at both conference hall and fringe meetings. Lilley's conference speech was seen by some of the media as a crude attack on foreign benefit 'scroungers'. Sailing close to the wind, he also pointedly claimed his mother's authority that he was not fatherless, *pace* Major's off-the-cuff remark about 'bastards' – indicative of how raw the feelings of the three were, not least at what they saw as Number Ten's failure to make amends after the highly publicised comments after the Brunson interview. Howard, adding to a twenty-seven-point list for tackling crime, further criticised the 'erosion of responsibility' since the sixties and, using new research, linked adverse social trends to single-parent families. Portillo, along similar lines, presented the Tories as the 'decent majority of ordinary Britons', returning the country to traditional values.[17] Hurd's gentlemanly and restrained speech stressing 'One Nation' values was all but in the face of the thunder from the right.

What was the right doing? The media interpreted their actions as jockeying for position to claim a vacant seat of right-wing heir apparent. Howard denied any such positioning. 'Why is it', he later observed, 'that when Tony Blair made a speech about the causes of crime everyone said "how marvellous". When I did, they said it was a leadership bid?'[18]

Leadership jockeying may or may not have been a motive behind part of their speeches during the week, but more important was the right's frustration at what they saw as an insufficiently clear lead from Major, amounting almost to a policy vacuum, and their desire to push the Party decisively into taking a strong stand on family values and law and order. To an American observer there were 'intriguing parallels' with the ill-fated Republican convention in Houston in 1992, where the well-meaning platitudes of President Bush were upstaged by the right-wing moralising of Pat Buchanan.[19]

The content of Major's speech, drafted as usual by Nick True with significant Hill influence and redoubtable Ronald Millar phrasing, was debated until the last minute. Major could not decide exactly how to play the Eurosceptics, trapped still twixt carrots and sticks, and asked for advice from

Sarah Hogg, Norman Fowler and Tim Collins. Fowler he summoned from a dinner on Thursday evening to show him the draft speech, which had a long opening passage attacking the rebels. Fowler strongly advised that, while understandable, the attack would inflame divisions and Major took the point. The speech duly limited the hardline material to the opening paragraphs, and it was played down subsequently in briefings.[20]

The emphasis on back to basics, however, produced a fresh set of problems that none of Major's team had properly envisaged. It sounded as if it was pressing all the right Tory buttons, but what exactly did it mean? The public was not sure. More importantly, neither exactly was the government. Most worrying of all, neither was Major's entourage.[21] Major had sensed the dangers of investing his speech with a personal morality or a 'moral majority' flavour. Nick True argued strongly in favour of staking out a moral agenda, reflecting his own religious views, as well as his judgement about what Major needed to be saying at this time. True conceded some ground when Major made it clear that he intended to concentrate on reform of education and social work, and basic economic priorities.[22] However, sufficient purple passages on traditional values remained in the margins to allow the speech to be linked with the right-wing personal morality theme of the week, and this development was encouraged in the spinning of the speech by Tim Collins, which led to talk of a 'war on permissiveness' and 'making liberalism as dirty a word as socialism is now'. Alarm bells were already ringing from the whips, whose daily work gave them a clearer insight into human frailties than the Number Ten staff who came up with 'back to basics'. Ryder and his whips knew that any initiative with even a hint of moralising about it would give the press an excuse to hunt down Tory MPs. The speed with which the initiative had been devised, without passing through the usual bureaucratic machinery, had not given Ryder and his colleagues time to warn about its dangers.[23]

In the short term, however, Major's speech could not have been better received. Dispensing for the first time with teleprompters, he received the longest standing ovation of his premiership so far, notably warmer than Thatcher had received earlier in the week, with many delegates, irritated by the memoir leaks, refusing to rise to applaud her. Major spoke of 'The old values, neighbourliness, decency, courtesy ... They are still alive ... yet somehow we feel embarrassed by them.' In a line deliberately inserted to defuse the danger of moral posturing, he asserted that governments could not make people good: 'That is for parents, for churches, for schools, for every single citizen.' Fashionable theories had done great damage to society, he said, whether by erecting tower blocks, rejecting teaching of spelling and tables, or preaching that criminals needed treatment, not punishment. 'Fashionable,' he said, 'but wrong, wrong, wrong.' And then the punchline:

We must go back to basics, we want our children to be taught the best; our public services to give the best; our British industry to beat the best.

The audience in the Winter Gardens loved it; the message was judged exactly right. Feet were stamped, arms waved as the Party faithful burst into 'Land of Hope and Glory'.

Major's and Ryder's instincts that the back to basics theme should not become a personal morality crusade was prescient. How prescient, Number Ten would not learn for another three months.

The Fog Lifts

'Back to basics' now became – out of a blue sky almost – Major's most important domestic initiative since the Citizen's Charter two years before. Both were turned into portmanteau ideas to be applied across the range of government departments. Both met resistance in the field. There was, however, a core difference. Whereas the Citizen's Charter was worked up from scratch, beginning with Major's own beliefs and then the detail filled out laboriously by the Policy Unit, back to basics, a vague slogan that had been in currency for three years, emerged in new centre-stage guise before Number Ten had discussed, still less tuned, it fully, or won backing for it from key lieutenants in Cabinet.

Major spent a week back in London after the conference while the Policy Unit set to work developing the theme. At Cabinet on Thursday 14 October, Howard briefed ministers on English football supporters who, as if on cue, had run amok in Rotterdam and Amsterdam, leading to a thousand arrests. Major said he had been in touch with Lubbers, the Dutch Prime Minister, to apologise for their behaviour. A lengthy discussion followed on economic prospects as a background to the budget on 30 November; Clarke pleased them with evidence that sustained non-inflationary growth was gathering pace as the recession was passing. The mood was confident, buoyed by the reappearance of Heseltine, whom Major welcomed back after four months of convalescence.[24] Tangible evidence of a new, calmer atmosphere was the absence of stirring when Major was out of London from 20 October for the biannual Commonwealth heads of government meeting, held in Cyprus.

As the autumn nights drew in, three matters preoccupied him. Public spending cuts and European Community business were ever-present concerns, but his attention was increasingly focused on a subject that had hitherto occupied him only irregularly, Northern Ireland. An IRA bomb in a shop in Shankill Road, Belfast, had killed ten people on Saturday 23 October, and there was every indication that the Loyalists were about to respond with similar ferocity. While the province held its breath, the response followed a week later at Greysteel, of which more in the next chapter.

On 27 October apprehension struck the Tory Party at the fate of Canada's Progressive Conservatives when election results came in. Kim Campbell, the Prime Minister, lost her seat and saw her party reduced from an overall majority to a token presence of two MPs. Talks of a 'Canadian wipe out' entered British political discourse, while Major supporters pointed out that getting rid of the previous incumbent Brian Mulroney – a leader for whom Major had considerable sympathy – could hardly be said to have restored the Canadian Tories' fortunes.[25]

Cabinet sat down on 28 October for three hours to debate spending cuts. Clarke sought to contain spending below the £253.6 billion control figure and said that encouraging though the recovery was, economic growth did not obviate the need for deep savings if the deficit was to be reduced. Gummer (Environment), Lilley (Social Security) and MacGregor (Transport) particularly objected to the proposed cuts in their departments' budgets. Dissent also came over the compensation package following the imposition of VAT on domestic fuel. Should aid be restricted to the poor on income support, or the 'nearly poor', including many elderly Tory voters (such as in Christchurch) who would not qualify because they exceeded the £8,000 savings limit?[26]

The toughest decisions came over defence. Since the era of the Cold War, defence spending had suffered heavily. The 'Options for Change' programme of 1990 foresaw 20 per cent cuts. A rearguard action had been led by the Commons Select Committee on Defence, which resulted in part in Rifkind's reprieve of some regiments earlier in the year. Throughout 1993 Whitehall was awash with rumours of the Treasury's plans to make deep cuts on defence spending, with anger erupting into the open at the Party Conference in Blackpool and in the House in later October.[27] Rifkind fought hard in Cabinet to resist the Treasury's planned annual £1 billion cuts over three years, to the annoyance of other ministers, and teetered on the verge of resignation.[28]

The service chiefs were, not surprisingly, unhappy at the prospect of further cuts, which fell heaviest on the RAF. Chief of Air Staff Michael Graydon, spoke out against the Treasury's plans on 8 November. The service chiefs believed its officials had little understanding or even respect for the job that the armed services were doing. The chiefs liked Clarke personally but suspected that he did not believe Britain any longer had a world role to play.[29] Shortly before Graydon's speech, on 27 October, all three service chiefs, led by Chief of Defence Staff Peter Harding, went on a secret mission to see Major at Number Ten. Harding set the scene:

We were all getting worried that dogma was overcoming common sense and that we would find ourselves badly off when the first war came along. I told the Prime Minister at that meeting that we had come in suits, there were no swords or medals, we had come at night, so nobody could see us, and we had come in different entrances because we felt it would detract from the message if the press heard about it.[30]

Major, flanked by Rifkind, listened sympathetically to his senior military officers, and asked penetrating questions as the chiefs explained their worries that the cuts in personnel would have a serious impact not just on efficiency, but also morale. The mission may have led to some marginal gains, but Major was not prepared to stand in the way of the drive towards defence savings. Politically, there was no longer any great attachment in the Conservative

Party to high defence spending. Even Portillo as Chief Secretary argued strongly for cuts – as he would be reminded when he later became Defence Secretary. The service chiefs were disappointed but not surprised that their unusual mission to see the Prime Minister had not produced greater effect; they had their own powerful constituencies resisting cuts, and they could at least demonstrate to them that they had taken their cause right to the top.[31]

At the interim Belgian European Council on 29 October Major had his own cause to advocate. *The Economist* article had epitomised to many European leaders what they saw as an obstructive British attitude. George Brock wrote of the 'bile and anger' in Europe towards him, and how he was loathed, not least because his comments on a looser Europe had caught the tide of events.[32] Major did not allow himself to be affected by the iciness in Europe, nor by the reservations of FCO mandarins. Major's rethink on Europe did not end with *The Economist* article.

A month before, on 30 September, he had convened a small seminar of officials to meet over dinner at Number Ten: Michael Jay, John Kerr and Roderic Lyne attended, as well as Geoffrey Fitchew from the Cabinet Secretariat. Kerr was in typically dominating form: he launched into a brilliant exposition of all the arguments against moving closer towards the European Community, before concluding that a pro-European Community policy was in Britain's best interests.

Major became progressively less easy with the pungent opinions expressed; he became somewhat impatient with such abstract thinking when his own course of action was unclear.[33] Nevertheless, in a BBC interview just before leaving for Brussels, he appeared to rule out a single currency 'in this century'.[34] During the summit, he hit out at the plans produced by Delors to increase spending to boost employment across the Community. Such dirigiste policies, he said, had resulted in the EC's share of world markets declining by a fifth since 1980. Ambitious plans such as EMU needed to be superseded by plans to boost growth based on deregulated markets. Delors retreated on the jobs package, but Major also gave ground by allowing an increase in Community investment spending. In some ways Major seemed to be increasingly the reincarnation of Mrs Thatcher, or so he appeared to Community leaders, if not to his own Eurosceptics.[35]

Back to Basics Takes Shape

Major's recovery of authority and confidence now turned to domestic policy. He was acutely conscious of the local and European elections in the early summer of 1994. Some recovery at the polls was essential if he was to avoid a repetition of the personal humiliations earlier in the year. The Policy Unit had proceeded apace on the back to basics agenda, and following their discussions were confident that they had a resonant core Tory theme that could be used to reimpose central control over Whitehall departments, much as the Citizen's Charter had done in 1991.

Number Ten had two problems with the theme, however: whether it was purely reactionary, raised by several commentators, including Simon Jenkins, who had tried to present it as a backward-looking, nostalgic message of 1950s suburbia; second, they continued to worry that some ministers, notably Redwood and Lilley, were persisting in trying to divert it into a moral crusade.[36] To counteract both, Major sent a confidential strategy document in early November, drafted by the Policy Unit, to all ministers asking them to frame new back to basics policies based on 'traditional values, common sense and a concern for the citizen'. Individual ministers were then to be summoned to Number Ten for progress sessions. Deliberately leaked to the *Sunday Times* to publicise the new momentum in Number Ten, and to increase pressure on ministers to conform, the document spelled out that 'The Prime Minister wants to create a better future, not re-create the past. Respecting tradition does not mean indulging in nostalgia.'

The Number Ten document made it clear that back to basics had nothing to do with sexual morality, but an individual's responsibility for his own and his family's behaviour meant 'expecting and respecting personal responsibility'. The battle against socialism had been won, it said; the new enemies were liberalism and permissiveness, with the nostrums of the sixties in the firing line. The doctrine was to be applied to education, where testing was to be fully implemented despite teacher union opposition; and law and order, including legislating for the twenty-seven point crackdown on crime announced by Howard at the Party Conference.

The leaked document came consecutively with heavy ministerial quotations about Major regaining control after a 'horrendous' period that was compared to Thatcher's difficulties with economic policy in 1981 or over Westland in 1986.[37] Heavy briefing by Gus O'Donnell also sought to focus the media's attention away from back to basics being about a personal moral crusade.[38] Hurd and Clarke became alarmed by the right's still seeking to shift the meaning in that very direction, and urged Major to combat their efforts still further.[39] They were pressing at an open door.

Major's Guildhall speech to the Lord Mayor's Banquet on 15 November focused on education, law and order, and a strong economy, making no mention of family values, still less of single mothers, despite recent remarks by right-wing Cabinet ministers to play up that issue.[40] In ministerial meetings Major would react angrily when generalisations were made about single parents. On one such occasion he exploded: 'I will not have you speak like that until you know what you're talking about. My sister's husband died when she was young leaving her with children to look after and I was too young and too poor to help out. But until you've had that happen to your family, you just shut up.'[41] His widowed sister, Pat, was not the type of single mother the right had in mind; whether that was pointed out to him is unrecorded.

The back to basics campaign continued to have few friends, the right regarding it as a lost opportunity, the Tory left as caving in to the right, while progressives believed it reactionary. Edward Heath thus savaged it with, 'Who on earth could have landed us with back to basics? ... No one has ever captained an advance by shouting to his troops "Back, boys, back". There is nothing for the future in that.'[42] Matthew Parris, in a rare public attack on Major, wrote, 'Do homosexuals detect (I think we do) a new frost in Tory thinking?'[43] *The Economist* considered that the search for a big idea would have to continue, and that even in its repackaged form, back to basics was 'comically uninspiring'.[44] Whitehall departments regarded the Number Ten initiative with a degree of cynicism: some responded to Major's memorandum with their current list of priorities, with minor textual changes genuflecting in the direction of the slogan, and sent them back to Number Ten with 'back to basics agenda' written at the top.[45] One Cabinet minister put it plainly: 'Why should I change what I was doing to fit in with some stupid relaunch?'[46]

For the time being, however, back to basics continued to succeed in reasserting the authority of Number Ten and reuniting the Party. But if a popular chord had been struck, this had only a temporary effect on Party popularity. October's polls, on average, indicated a drop in Labour's lead from nineteen to fifteen points, but by December it had risen again to twenty-one points.

A pervasive popular sense that 1993 was a bad year cut across Major's attempt to mobilise support. The murder of two-year-old Jamie Bulger, and the trial of his two young killers cast a tragic pall. On a lighter note in April John Smith cruelly mocked Major for incompetent stewardship of a country 'where even the Grand National doesn't start'. Although the Prime Minister could do nothing about the performances of England's football and cricket teams, their dismal efforts appeared to rub off on him; and by a strange quirk of misfortune Graham Taylor, the unsuccessful England football manager, had a dog called Major.

Back to basics fed powerfully into the Queen's Speech, on 18 November. The Cabinet had discussed possible contents on 13 May, and agreed it should contain a number of prominent measures on crime and deregulation which Howard was pressing, as well as a Sunday Trading Bill.[47] Cabinet returned to consider the Queen's Speech on 4 November. Measures to privatise the Royal Mail and deregulate London buses were put on hold. MacGregor and Portillo argued strongly for the latter, but they were overruled because of the damage it might do to the Party's prospects in the local elections in London the following May.[48] The sharpest debate was over whether the Deregulation Bill should include general privatisation powers so that the government could privatise anything without having to pass new legislation. Clarke and Heseltine fought hard for it, with Tony Newton opposed. Caution won the day. Major, summing up, accepted that a strong case had been made for including general privatisation powers in the Bill. However, on balance, the Cabinet accepted Newton's view that this would risk making the Bill unmanageable.[49] Free market enthusiasts had to satisfy themselves with merely a coal privatisation Bill.

Back to basics was seen principally in a new Education Bill and bumper criminal justice legislation to add to the Police and Magistrates' Courts Bill already agreed. Howard had been battling hard as Home Secretary to shift the ground on law and order, as Tony Blair, his opposite number, kept moving Labour's policy in a more hard-line direction. Howard's response was to outdo Labour by the sheer range of legislative action. With no budget for the first time the following March to provide a focus, the aim was also to make law and order legislation, considered vote winners, dominate the political agenda in the spring in the run-up to the elections in May and June.[50]

The Queen's Speech confirmed how far the government, with a majority reduced, after Newbury and Christchurch, from twenty-one to seventeen (counting the whipless Rupert Allason as a supporter) and with deep divisions below the surface, was having to trim its policies to maintain unity and avoid electoral damage. Back to basics, even in the limited Major sense, was a mission of a kind, but it was one primarily electorally driven rather than motivated by Major's personal beliefs – though the reaction against intellectual fashion, the desire to boost personal responsibility, and to see a return to traditional teaching methods were heartland Major.

Attention now shifted to the budget. Clarke had settled in quietly at the Treasury. Though initially knowing little economics, he was quick to learn, and was found to be sparky and decisive, in contrast to the mercurial Lamont.[51] Improved Number Ten–Treasury relations were a welcome bonus. Major made a point of discussing budgets with his Chancellors, the example of the mistrust between Lawson and Thatcher etched in his mind. Clarke's two main problems when planning the budget were the drawn-out end to the recession, with output still only growing slowly and house prices on average 30 per cent below those in early 1990, and the projected £50 billion deficit. To boost the former, he cut interest rates from 6 to $5\frac{1}{2}$ per cent in November, a move supported by the Bank of England Governor since May, Eddie George.[52] Clarke aimed to reduce the deficit by cuts in expenditure of £10 billion over three years, and by raising tax revenue of nearly £5 billion in the 1995–6 financial year.

On top of Lamont's March budget, it was the largest percentage annual tax increase in history. The bulk of the reduction in spending came from hitting defence, education and road spending projects particularly hard. The political battle over compensation for those hardest hit by VAT on fuel was won by those arguing for political expediency: a package to compensate fifteen million pensioners was announced. The extra tax revenue came from reducing the value of mortgage tax relief, new taxes on insurance premiums and air travel, and further taxes on motorists and smokers. Back to basics ingredients were provided by Peter Lilley the next day in his statement on social security, when he announced a replacement of unemployment benefit by a 'Jobseekers' Allowance', to be means-tested after six months, and a clamp-down on invalidity benefit, superseded by a taxable incapacity benefit. Coming on top of the Home Office proposals, Lilley's announcement sent a chill through some on the left of the Party. It had also led to a long and acrimonious battle between Lilley and Shephard's Employment Department over which department should oversee it, which ended in a compromise.

Although in content and in presentation Clarke's budget received nothing but praise, it did little to hasten the return of the feel-good factor among Tory voters, as events in the new year were to show.[53] Major was, however, pleased enough. Having interfered heavily in economic policy in Lamont's last nine months, he was anxious to give Clarke a freer hand; encouragement for the VAT compensation package, and support for Clarke with ministers, such as Rifkind, reluctant to accept cuts, were his main inputs into the budget process.[54]

Danger, however, loomed for Major in the glory with which his new Chancellor was now showered: as Joe Rogaly observed, 'A chancellor with *grip*, standing confidently beside a seated PM who has been accused of lacking in that commodity.'[55] Hopes of immediate preferment for Clarke had moved on to a back burner following the rally to Major at the Party Conference, and Clarke's ignoring the right's pleas for no more tax increases. But his independent spirit welled up again at the final European Council at Brussels on 10 and 11 December, when his comments on the Delors employment plan jarred with Major's more constructive tone. A modified version of Delors's plan was agreed, and an apology given to him for the behaviour of Clarke.[56] What was Clarke up to? Michael White and John Carvel wrote: 'To the consternation of mainstream Europeans but the likely satisfaction of the Tory right which he is wooing, Mr Clarke took every opportunity to play the boisterous Eurosceptic rather than the long-standing Europhile he was widely taken to be.'[57]

Major's continued temperate sceptical line may not have won Eurosceptics over, but it played its part in the truce with the Tory rebels. They had not succeeded in blocking the Maastricht Treaty, which came into force on 1 November, with the title 'European Union' or 'EU' officially taking over from 'European Community'. But the right did not dislike Major's language in the Queen's Speech, stressing subsidiarity, enlargement, fiscal discipline and the intergovernmental pillars.[58]

International developments provided drama in another quarter, too, at the tail end of 1993. The deadline for the final settlement of the GATT round was 15 December. Major had insisted that this date should not be allowed to slip, or else the parties to the deal would never focus on it. Several issues, including film subsidies, had proved particularly intractable, and went right down to the wire. The round was settled with only hours to spare, and, parodying Mrs Thatcher's statement that 'we have become a grandmother', Major threatened to go out before the cameras and announce that 'we are a GATT mother'.[59] Parentage of the deal was a truly collective matter, with Peter Sutherland (Director-General of GATT), Mickey Kantor (US Trade Representative) and Leon Brittan (the EU Trade Commissioner) core players. But Major and Sarah Hogg played a critical role too; it was her most significant achievement in her last two years at Number Ten.

The year ended on a high point for Major. Sarah Hogg wrote an upbeat paper for him before the Christmas break, highlighting the reasons for optimism, despite the continuing shyness of the feel-good factor: unemployment coming down, the economy growing, GATT at last resolved and Maastricht through. She listed one further reason for applause on which Major had been working, and to which we now turn: Northern Ireland.[60]

TWENTY-SEVEN

A Breakthrough in Ireland:

April 1992–December 1993

MAJOR'S BRAVEST INITIATIVE of his premiership came not in a purely domestic policy area, but in Northern Ireland. Progress was all the more remarkable because he had to overcome the deep-seated suspicions not just of the Unionist, Nationalist and Republican constituencies in Ireland, but also the right of his own party, which became all the harder once the government's majority began to disappear, and the right was gunning for him.

End of the Old Road: Constitutional Talks April–November 1992

Within three weeks of Patrick Mayhew's appointment as Northern Ireland Secretary in April 1992, constitutional talks started in earnest. Mayhew's appointment, intended by Major to signal his personal commitment to progress, caused some initial apprehensions on both sides of the border in Ireland. The Irish government in the South and the Catholic SDLP in the North had been antagonised by his decision, when Attorney-General in the late 1980s, not to launch a prosecution of RUC officers in the alleged 'shoot-to-kill' incidents, while Unionists were concerned by his earlier links with a series of Cabinet ministers – notably James Prior and William Whitelaw – not known for their sympathy to their cause.[1]

Mayhew's personal skills and tangible sincerity chipped away at such reservations, but he had no illusions about the mountain he had to climb. It was not just mainstream opinion that balked at his appointment; from a target list found concealed in a flat in Clapham, he knew that he was high on an IRA assassination list.[2]

The talks duly opened with Mayhew in the chair on 29 April at Stormont, in an atmosphere of some optimism. Earlier meetings under Brooke had helped prepare the ground by disposing of some procedural matters. According to one commentator, politicians participating had thus been introduced 'into a culture of negotiation'.[3] Progress could soon be made on the so-called 'Strand 1' discussions involving the four main Northern Ireland parties: James Molyneaux's UUP, Ian Paisley's more hardline DUP, John Hume's SDLP and the Alliance Party. Gerry Adams's Sinn Fein was excluded from the talks because of its association with the IRA. But sticking points emerged

Chancellor of the Exchequer John Major announces Britain's entry into the ERM to the House of Commons, under the disapproving gaze of the Prime Minister, 5 October 1990.

The Prime Minister triumphant on 10 April 1992.

Top left: Sarah Hogg, head of the Policy Unit, 1990–95.

Top right: Judith Chaplin, Major's Political Secretary, 1990–92.

Left: Jonathan Hill, Major's Political Secretary, 1992–94.

With Chris Patten on election night 1992.

Norman Lamont announcing sterling's suspension from the ERM on Black Wednesday, 16 September 1992

Major presented with a captive rifle by Gulf war troops, in Kuwait, 6 March 1991 ... and a bat from Wes Hall, Barbadian minister of sport and tourism, Lord's, 22 June 1991.

The 'Cabinet of chums', 1991.

Cabinet with 'bastards', 1993.

Major visiting Ian Paisley's constituency, 21 December 1995

In mourning, Dunblane, 15 March 1996.

Remembrance Sunday 1991: the only appearance together of Major and Kinnock at the Cenotaph.

Major hosting the G7 meeting in London, 17 July 1991. From back left: Jacques Delors, Giulio Andreotti, Brian Mulroney, Toshiki Kaifu, Ruud Lubbers. Front: George Bush, Mikhail Gorbachev, John Major, François Mitterrand, Helmut Kohl.

With Boris Yeltsin after signing a treaty of friendship with Russia, 9 November 1992.

Major giving President Clinton a wary welcome to London, 29 November 1995.

to dent the early hopes of progress, notably the Unionist parties' eagerness to reduce any influence in Northern Ireland politics from Dublin, institutionalised by the Anglo–Irish Agreement of 1985, which Hume, anxious to see a greater all-Irish dimension, resisted.

Strand 2, which would bring the Northern Ireland parties into discussion with the Irish government in Dublin, thus began on 6 July in an atmosphere of some apprehension. However, progress was made; when representatives of the two Unionist parties attended the opening of Strand 2 at London's Lancaster House, it was the first time in seventy years that all the constitutional Northern Ireland parties had sat down around a table with Irish government representatives. The British government could barely disguise their relief: 'We weren't sure whether it would work,' recalled Mayhew, 'especially whether the Unionists would agree that it was now time to bring in the Irish government.'[4]

Nationalist and Unionist differences over the future role of the Dublin government, however, became steadily more apparent, an uncertain backdrop for Strand 3, which brought in the British government, and which opened on 28 July. Two papers tabled in September 1992, one by Mayhew – described in the Unionist press as 'lethal as an IRA Semtex bomb' – and another by the Irish government, caused deep unease. With the Unionist parties on one side, and the SDLP on the other, drifting further apart than ever, the end of the talks without a conclusion on 10 November came as little surprise. No party felt they wanted to go any further with the talks at that stage, while Hume was anxious for Gerry Adams, with whom he had been in dialogue intermittently since 1988, to become involved before the talks made any further progress.

Major had taken particular interest in the Lancaster House conference during Strand 2. Links between London and Dublin had become more productive after Albert Reynolds succeeded Charles Haughey as Taoiseach in February 1992, and from the end of the year Major's personal interest stepped up a gear. The failure of the constitutional talks provided a spur. But other factors, too, lay behind Major's decision that now was the time to make Northern Ireland a priority concern. With his old sparring partner Reynolds back as Taoiseach he sensed that his personal diplomacy might achieve a breakthrough where the constitutional talks appeared to be stalled.

The continuing cost of the troubles in both human and economic terms vexed him greatly. 1992 was a particularly bloody year, leaving eighty-five dead from terrorism in the province and with the symbolic figure of the 3,000th victim being passed. The IRA's bombing campaign in mainland Britain cost not less than £800 million over the year.[5] Just one bomb, at the Baltic Exchange in the City of London, detonated in April, the day after the British general election, caused greater financial loss than all the bombs exploded in Northern Ireland over the previous twenty-five years. Internal reports indicated that a repetition of such a bomb could damage the City's standing as a centre of international finance.[6]

Early 1993 had seen a change of personnel in Number Ten. Roderic Lyne, who possessed both great appetite and acumen in managing the Irish connection, succeeded Stephen Wall. Number Ten's loss over Europe was its gain on Northern Ireland, and Lyne went on to stamp his mark on the conduct of relations over the following three years.

With Major's greater interest, the focus of top-level decision-making on the British side shifted within Whitehall to Number Ten itself, though the Northern Ireland Office (NIO) remained a prime mover, above all due to the work of two key officials, John Chilcot, Permanent Secretary, and Quentin Thomas, Deputy Secretary. The Cabinet Office continued, too, to be involved on the inside track, with Robin Butler taking something of the part that his immediate predecessor, Robert Armstrong, had played in the Anglo–Irish Agreement of 1985 and after. The close involvement of the Cabinet Secretary was also prompted by the central part played by Butler's opposite number in Dublin, Dermot Nally, and by the very sensitivity of the discussions to the British state. Martin Mansergh, the Taoiseach's personal adviser, was to be another key figure in the evolving peace process. The son of a distinguished academic, and a historian himself, Mansergh was educated at King's School, Canterbury, and Oxford, and had an unusually clear understanding of the British mind and sensibilities.

The close relationship between NIO and Number Ten was a conspicuous feature of the London end: papers would come into Number Ten from the NIO at a far earlier stage in processing than from any other Whitehall department. Major's personal relationship with Mayhew was to prove vital; the driving role by a Prime Minister in a department's work might have been resented by a less secure or more ambitious Secretary of State.[7] Major, indeed, did not enjoy such a trusting relationship with any other of his departmental ministers.

The time was certainly ripe for fresh thinking on Northern Ireland. On 16 December Mayhew delivered a speech in Coleraine which he regards as one of the seminal initiatives of his political career. As he recalled:

A time comes in any Secretaryship of State when one needs to get people to lift their eyes, to show what the future could hold, to set out a strategy. I thought the time had come. We needed to persuade the various parties to look forward, not backwards, and to do it in such a way that avoided frightening anyone into retreating behind their familiar battlements.[8]

Mayhew reiterated Brooke's key phrase that the British government had no selfish strategic or economic interest in Northern Ireland, and acknowledged that the British bear responsibility for much that was tragic in Ireland's history, a significant admission. But he also lamented that the IRA had excluded themselves from the talks by their refusal to 'renounce unequivocally the use and threat of violence'. The British government would be merely a facilitator in any future peace process, with no separate political agenda of its own other than helping with the expression of the democratic will of the people of Northern Ireland.[9]

The Back Channel: January–November 1993

While the constitutional Strand talks were in train, the British government was meanwhile involved in contacts of an altogether different kind. A renewed dialogue with the IRA, authorised by Brooke in 1990 on the advice of MI5, had been successfully hidden from the public eye. Conducted through an intermediary, in a process known as the back channel,[10] the contacts made sense as a means of finding out about new IRA thinking, as well as a possible way of influencing them. Messages passed back and forth, on a fairly low-key basis, until early 1993.

The nature of the exchanges changed significantly, however, when, on 22 February, a message was received in Downing Street (via the NIO) from the IRA suggesting that they were seeking help in winding up the armed struggle. Major has a recollection of Stephen Wall bringing him the information in the Cabinet Room, where he was working in the afternoon.[11] The exact content of this and subsequent messages passed between the government and the IRA over the rest of the year has been the cause of disagreement, with the IRA denying the veracity of much of the British government's account of events, which they disclosed following newspaper revelations of the back channel in late November. The main events are, however, reasonably clear.[12]

Mayhew followed up the IRA message with a minute to Major that they should take it seriously, but cautiously. On 26 February the government duly passed a message back to the IRA indicating that a full British position was being prepared. A week later on 5 March, the IRA responded by saying that they desired a meeting with the government, and nominated Martin McGuinness and Gerry Kelly, both prominent Sinn Fein members, to speak for its side. At the beginning of March the wheels were oiled when Mayhew reiterated in public that the British government would facilitate the province joining the Republic in a united Ireland, as long as this was the wish of a majority. But on 11 March the government complained bitterly, through the back channel, that it was finding it difficult to produce a constructive response to the IRA overture of 22 February as long as acts of violence continued. The IRA had convinced themselves that individual acts of terrorism, from small-scale acts to 'spectaculars', such as the Warrington bomb on 20 March which killed Jonathan Ball, aged three, and Timothy Parry, aged twelve, increased pressure on the British government to make concessions. The government, meanwhile, continued to assert that precisely the opposite was true.

On 19 March, the day before the Warrington bomb, the government sent the IRA a key message in which it stated unequivocally that, 'The position of the British government is that any dialogue could only follow a halt to violent activity.' It continued:

The British government cannot enter a talks process, or expect others to do so, with the purpose of achieving a predetermined outcome, whether the 'ending of partition' or anything else. It has accepted that the eventual outcome of such a process could be a united Ireland but this can be only on the basis of the consent of the people of Northern Ireland.

An accompanying note, callously disregarded assuming that the IRA high command had the ability to abort the Warrington bomb, warned them that continuing atrocities would jeopardise peace prospects.[13]

The British response of 19 March was the product of prolonged deliberations principally between Major and Lyne from Number Ten, and Mayhew, Chilcot and Thomas from the NIO. Their concern was to go some way to meet the IRA's wish for a dialogue, by offering exploratory discussions – as opposed to political negotiations, the distinction was important – as long as there was a genuine and established ending of violence. But equally the government was emphatic that if the IRA was hoping to trade a ceasefire for some form of political solution favourable to themselves, then the British were not interested.

On 23 April the British government sent another message asking for clarification of the Republican position. The IRA response was immediate. Despite the wave of revulsion sparked by the Warrington bomb, including a march of 15,000 in Dublin, they opted to detonate another 'spectacular'. This was in Bishopsgate, again in the City of London, on 24 April, killing a freelance photographer and causing an estimated £350 million of damage (half the cost of the Baltic Exchange bomb the year before).[14] Anger and frustration welled up in Whitehall. One of those on the British side later commented: 'We found their sincerity hard to believe when acts like Warrington and Bishopsgate continued to happen; they were creating a situation where news of even an exploratory dialogue would not be acceptable to public opinion.'[15]

The IRA were, however, apparently serious about talks. They established a small committee, chaired by Gerry Adams, to coordinate their response to the latest British message, duly received in London in early May: 'Some time has passed since we both agreed to proceed to delegation meetings. Are you still serious about this? Are there problems?'[16] The British replied swiftly on 5 May, repeating their disapproval of continuing IRA violence and hoping that private assurances of a ceasefire would soon be forthcoming. Two days later, in response to an IRA query, they said that any dialogue must follow, not precede, private IRA assurances of an end to organised violence.[17]

The Republicans' full response to the key British message of 19 March was received by the government on 10 May. It stated that the IRA appreciated the personal contacts with the intermediary, and continued: 'We wish now to proceed without delay to the delegation meetings.' They asserted that Sinn Fein should enter the peace dialogue by right, and demanded answers to a number of specific questions, including who exactly would represent the

British government, when would talks start, and where was the proposed venue? The IRA also said that, as discussed with the British representative, they agreed to a two-week suspension of violence. Their clear assumption was that political talks would be opening shortly, and that merely the logistics needed refinement. The IRA were thus disappointed when they learned that, contrary to their beliefs, or hopes, the British had no immediate intention to proceed towards a conference with delegates from both government and Republican sides.[18]

The British government was at this point in a quandary. How far should they go to meet IRA wishes? Major and Mayhew were cautious: eager to proceed with any talks if it meant finding a way out of the bloodshed, but wary of the complex risks involved. A British message on 17 July reflected the differences of opinion: while criticising the IRA for continuing with their violence, it suggested that progress was still possible. The communication stated: 'The peace process cannot be conditional on the acceptance of any particular or single analysis. Can you confirm that you envisage a peace process which is aimed at an inclusive political process and that a lasting end to violence does not depend upon your analysis being endorsed as the only way forward?' This latest British rejoinder disappointed more impatient Republican voices. A series of bad-tempered exchanges flowed back and forth over the summer and early autumn, the British emphatic about a permanent end to violence being the necessary precursor to any peace talks, the IRA complaining about press leaks and British prevarication.[19]

Major was not prepared to change the position of the British government. On 29 October he met Reynolds on the fringes of a European Council in Brussels and hammered out a common line. The fruit of that meeting was consistent with an uncompromising message sent to the IRA on 5 November, which refused to shift from the government's public position, that talks could only commence if there were a total end to violence. But it stated that, with the necessary reassurances, the first meeting in the peace dialogue could take place 'within a week of the Parliament's return in January'.[20] It continued: 'There could be no secret agreements or understandings between governments and organisations supporting violence as a price for its cessation ... It is the public and consistent position of the British government that any dialogue could only follow a permanent end to violent activity.'[21]

This unequivocal message effectively brought to an end the back channel phase. What had it achieved? From the British side, they learned that the IRA were at least considering a renunciation of violence rather than just a short-term ceasefire in return for an offer of participation in peace talks. Despite repeated requests, however, the British failed to elicit a clear confirmation from the IRA that a permanent ceasefire was their unanimous intention. So concerned were the IRA to deny in public that they were considering just such an option, that they went to lengths to deny that the initial message of 22 February, asking for advice on how to end the conflict, had ever been sent.[22] But this strange back channel interlude was not without value: when, in May 1995, an exploratory dialogue was opened between ministers and Sinn Fein, it was on the basis of the British messages of 17 July and 5 November.

One can only speculate on the IRA's motivation for exploring a peaceful way forward. Twenty-five years of violence since the late sixties had brought them no closer to achieving a united Ireland. Neither was their cause winning fresh supporters in the South; indeed, the opposite seemed to be occurring. Meanwhile, economic changes in the North were transforming the prospects for Catholics in Londonderry and even Belfast. Prosperity meant both were becoming far less propitious seedbeds for hard-line terrorists. If the British government was indeed sincere about having no selfish economic or strategic interest in the province, then Sinn Fein/IRA reasoned there was at least a prospect of achieving their ends by deliberation rather than by violence.[23]

The Third Avenue: Declaration Discussions

A third thread in the complex tapestry of the Anglo–Irish dialogue – alongside the constitutional talks and the back channel – were the private discussions that had been taking place in Ireland towards the achieving of a 'joint declaration' on the future of Northern Ireland, with both Dublin and London setting out their aims and principles for developments in the North. This approach had originated in talks between the Irish government and John Hume of the SDLP, with irregular inputs from Sinn Fein/IRA. Major had first discussed the initiative with Haughey in the course of a routine summit in December 1991.[24] During 1992 both Hume and the Irish government sent London drafts of such a declaration document, and by January 1993 three versions were on the table. London, however, was unmoved. While it told Dublin that none of the drafts was within 'a million miles' of being acceptable,[25] the end of the constitutional talks in November 1992 nevertheless encouraged the British government not to dismiss the declaration option completely out of court.

In June 1993, London learned that Reynolds had become excited about the latest draft of the joint declaration, negotiated with Hume and the Republicans, over which he himself claimed a large degree of paternity. The document subsequently acquired the somewhat misleading title the 'Hume–Adams' text,[26] and stated that the British government would legislate to introduce self-determination – a principle of great symbolic importance to the Republicans – 'over a period to be agreed by both governments'.[27]

In Reynolds's initial idea, he would fly incognito to London and put this most sensitive draft into Major's hands personally at Number Ten, on a take-it-or-leave-it basis. Wiser counsels prevailed, and it was agreed that Robin Butler would fly on a covert mission to the military airport at Baldonnell outside Dublin, to take receipt of the document. Reynolds drove out to the airport, had a cup of coffee with the British Cabinet Secretary, and placed a sealed envelope for Major in his hands. When doing so, Reynolds stressed that for the first time he had managed to make the IRA agree to the 'consent principle', i.e. that the North would only join a united Ireland with the active consent of a majority of those in the province, and he stressed that in his opinion the joint declaration route would lead to a far better chance of a permanent end to violence than any resumption of the constitutional talks. The consent principle was most significant, as it would reassure Unionists – in a clear majority in Northern Ireland – that they could veto any attempt to force unification with Eire upon them.

Reynolds was singing the same tune when, later in June, he flew to London to see Major, highlighting the bargaining and brinkmanship that had gone into the document which he had handed Butler. Major was not overly impressed. He did not rule out a joint declaration, but refused to negotiate on the Reynolds text because there were still far too many points to which he objected. The British government did not like the way it could be seen as an advocate of Irish unity; it felt the document was 'fuzzy' on the question of self-determination for Northern Ireland; and that it paid insufficient regard to sacred British positions such as its constitutional guarantee to the people of Northern Ireland. Discussions between officials from both governments took place over the next few months, although in the jaundiced view of one British observer, 'the joint declaration proposals were not even a starting point'.[28]

In a complicating factor for Britain they were also being lobbied hard and separately by Hume who, within two weeks of the Reynolds document being received in London, produced one of his own, and openly disparaged Reynolds's efforts. Over the summer the Dublin government vied with Hume for being the better channel for London in discussions of the declaration proposal. Hume asserted that he, uniquely, had managed to persuade the Army Council of the IRA to agree to the consent principle, and thus London would have no hope of being a party to any future discussions unless they accepted his approach.

But London appeared to key segments of Irish opinion to be dragging its feet. The Dublin government, as well as Hume and the IRA, interpreted British caution as dictated by the need to appease Unionist opinion, especially with the Unionists playing a pivotal role in the knife-edge Maastricht debate in late July 1993. In particular, they believed – as we have seen, wrongly – that Major and Molyneaux had concluded a deal to secure Unionist backing in the key Europe vote on 22 July. Might this be a reason for British tardiness, they asked? By September, irritation and despair at London's caution was growing among all shades of non-Unionist opinion in Ireland. Reynolds felt impelled to write a passionate personal letter to Major, imploring him to keep the declaration proposal on the table:

Peace will be an achievement worth striving for. After 25 years of violence it would be on a par with any of our predecessors in this century ... The principle of consent

on which you laid so much stress is not an issue. The Nationalist proponents now
fully accept the idea subject to the sort of framework set out in the paper ... I will
therefore ask you in all sincerity to continue to give the process your full and
enthusiastic backing ... Time is not on our side. Finally, if the Arabs and Israelis can
do it, why can't we?[29]

Hume also sought to maintain the pressure. On 17 September, he went to
Downing Street to see Major but, disappointed by the cautious response, he
decided to issue a joint statement with Adams on 25 September about their
dialogue. The leaders of the SDLP and Sinn Fein duly declared that: 'We
are convinced from our discussions that a process can be designed to lead to
agreement among the divided people of this island which will provide a solid
basis for peace.'[30] Hume's bilateral statement angered both London and
Dublin: in publicising his understanding with Adams, both governments
felt – because of strong feelings about talking to terrorists, and being seen to
allow such bodies to dictate terms – that Hume had retarded the peace
process.

London had anyway come to the conclusion that it had too many objections
to the Hume–Adams declaration of June. Dublin then produced a new draft
of their joint declaration, which London thought more promising than the
June document.[31] A series of meetings took place in London in October to
work out the British response to the Reynolds draft. Mayhew was pessimistic,
however, about these new proposals providing a way forward, and MI5
reports were sceptical about whether the IRA could deliver on a ceasefire.
Major wrote Reynolds a letter in which he stated that, after giving his new
declaration document prolonged consideration, 'We have very reluctantly
concluded that it will not run at the present time.' On 19 October, Butler
flew to Dublin again in secret suggesting that other ways forward must be
explored, even proposing, to Dublin's chagrin, a revival of the constitutional
talks.[32] Michael Ancram, the minister in charge of political affairs at the NIO,
had spent much of 1993 engaged in talks with the four main constitutional
parties in the North, though progress in that forum seemed as remote as
ever. None of this went down well with Reynolds and Dublin, who thought
constitutional talks not the way forward and who were dismissive of what
they saw as a very negative response from London.

Terrorist outrages before the end of October appeared to make the prospect
of progress via the joint declaration route further away than ever; in fact,
though no one at the time foresaw it, the declaration idea was the very
platform on which, within two months, a major breakthrough would occur.

Progress on the Joint Declaration

On 20 October the death toll for the year was 'only' fifty-one, an unacceptably
high figure, but lower than for some of the worst years of the conflict. Three
days later, on a Saturday afternoon, the IRA planted a bomb on the Shankill

Road in an ultra-Loyalist area of Belfast. The bomb was placed in a fish and chip shop beneath a headquarters of the Protestant paramilitary group the UDA, with the intention of the blast killing everyone upstairs. No one, however, was in the office, but bystanders there were aplenty, the bomb blast killing nine men, women and children, as well as one of the IRA bomb-planters. The IRA plan of assassinating leading paramilitary Loyalists had backfired spectacularly. It was the worst IRA misjudgement since the Enniskillen bomb on Remembrance Sunday in 1987. Some crumbs of comfort came when Adams reacted to the Shankill Road bomb in unusually strong language. But any optimism was crushed when he shouldered the coffin at the funeral of the IRA bomber. Loyalist paramilitaries reacted with predictable and indiscriminate anger, killing six Catholics at random over the next week, and a further eight at a bar in the village of Greysteel the following Saturday. Suddenly, October became the worst month for casualties since 1976.[33]

Movement, however, was in the offing. As a mark of respect following the Shankill Road bomb, Dick Spring, the Irish Minister for Foreign Affairs, postponed the Anglo–Irish Intergovernmental Conference planned for 27 October, which was unpopular with Unionists. The same day he announced in the Dail six democratic principles for a sustainable peace, including no change to occur in Northern Ireland's status without freely given majority consent, with such consent even to be written into the Irish Constitution. This was movement indeed on the Nationalist side, with Molyneaux describing the principles as a 'great improvement'.

Two days later, Major and Reynolds met for an hour's private consultation during the Brussels European Council meeting. They were alone, without officials, which helps explain the different understandings of what was said by each. Major told Reynolds that if any progress was to be made on the joint declaration initiative – and the British, he stressed, were far from committed to such a way forward – then it had to be seen to be utterly divorced from the Hume–Adams dialogue. Reynolds understood, and the communiqué after the meeting duly acknowledged such a distancing, but also offered the carrot of talks with Sinn Fein, as long as these were preceded by a renunciation of violence.[34]

Major had been sickened by the sight on the television news of Adams shouldering the coffin of the Shankill Road bomber. Anger in the Loyalist community, too, made it even more imperative for him to distance himself from any suggestion of being influenced by the Hume–Adams initiative. Major nevertheless set up an ad hoc Cabinet committee, including Mayhew, Clarke, Hurd, Howard and Rifkind, to discuss the way forward.[35]

November saw a dramatic easing in sectarian violence, but also political reversals which seemed set to derail progress towards peace. On 4 November, Hume, under pressure from both critics and supporters of his dialogue with Adams, again visited Major in Downing Street. The SDLP leader was in adamant form: Adams 'had the Provisionals committed to the principle of consent and dialogue', he told Major.[36] The meeting over, he emerged to tell the waiting media that there could be peace 'within a week' if the Prime Minister followed his advice and accepted the Hume–Adams declaration.

Major became increasingly absorbed by Ireland as November wore on. His political antennae told him that, contrary to all the public signs, a breakthrough could be achieved. Reynolds was becoming desperate for progress – too desperate, London thought. Dublin produced yet another declaration draft – accompanied by what one source described as 'Reynolds's heavy breathing' – about how short the time was, how the opportunity would not recur, how failure to agree on a way forward would be a disaster for Anglo–Irish relations.[37] Major was unmoved by all of this. He stood firmly on the ground that he was not going to discuss any document that bore any Hume–Adams fingerprints, which he reiterated would be viewed to be rewarding years of terrorism. Nor would he consider any proposals from the Irish government under any threat or ultimatum. Reynolds's retort was that his latest proposals had been drafted in his own office, with 'some input' merely from Hume, stressing that the original Irish government's joint declaration initiative predated by some way the Hume–Adams document.[38]

On 10 November Reynolds told two journalists at a concert given in Dublin by Whitney Houston, the American pop singer, that 'if it comes to it, I will walk away from John Major and put forward a set of proposals myself. I am not prepared to let the opportunity pass.' Reynolds subsequently claimed he was speaking off the record, but his comments were widely reported, with predictable reactions among Unionists, as evidence that Dublin was actively considering an all-Irish solution.

London was becoming exasperated with Reynolds's press leaks. 'We were pretty displeased with the way Reynolds incessantly raised expectations in the press,' recalled one British observer. 'He talked obsessively to the media: when he did it off the record, his trail was all over it. He was spinning the press like mad, hyping up the situation, trying to put pressure on us through the media. This was particularly foolish because it caused a negative reaction in the North who thought the Taoiseach was trying to browbeat them.'[39]

A meeting took place between officials of both governments on 10 November – the same day as what became known as Reynolds' 'Houston Declaration'. Robin Butler explained that John Major recognised that there was a real opportunity for peace, and said that London had unspecified 'independent evidence' (from the back channel) that the IRA were thinking seriously of peace. But the Cabinet Secretary stressed the depth of anxiety and suspicion within the Unionist community about political developments, and the inescapable need for any proposal to carry them forward with it.[40]

The British government had in fact been informally testing Unionist opinion for some months. Molyneaux of the UUP was a particularly useful sounding board, but links were also kept open with Paisley's DUP. To widen the government's knowledge, frequent communications took place with Dr Robin Eames, Archbishop of Armagh and head of the Church of Ireland, known and trusted as one with close and wide contacts with leaders of the Unionist community. The aim was to find out exactly what the Unionist community would bear if they decided to go ahead with the joint declaration. As a British insider observed: 'The lesson we learned from the 1985 Anglo–Irish Agreement was that we were not going to move anything forward in Northern Ireland if the Unionists rejected the initiative. We were very keen not to be in that territory again.'[41] To the British government's relief the soundings were not discouraging: moderate Unionist opinion was felt to be quite open, and among the paramilitaries even the UVF (though not the UDA) was willing to consider propositions seriously if they would lead to peace.

Major's optimism found public expression in his speech to the Lord Mayor's Banquet in London's Guildhall on 15 November. He restated clearly that Sinn Fein was welcome to join in political talks as long as the IRA gave up violence for good. He emphasised the need for courage, the real opportunity for peace and the need to take risks. The speech raised expectations of progress, though he would not budge from his insistence on a cessation of violence prior to Republicans entering talks.[42]

Events in later November, however, served to dampen expectations of a breakthrough. On 19 November Emily O'Reilly, a Dublin political journalist, published a leaked draft of an internal Irish government document on the future of Northern Ireland. By revealing Dublin's far-reaching aspirations for a role in the future administration of Northern Ireland, the report played straight into Unionist fears in the North. The following day, Hume and Adams released another joint statement, calling for the British government to respond to their initiative. London considered this step provocative, undermining the line that Reynolds had been taking in stressing the distance between them and the stance of the British government.[43] At this delicate point, news of the back channel communications with the IRA leaked out. Number Ten was unsure at the time who was responsible: the information came via Willie McCrea, the DUP MP, who passed it on to Eamonn Mallie of the *Observer*, co-author with David McKittrick of a well-informed account of the peace process *The Fight for Peace* (1996).[44]

When details of the back channel appeared in the *Observer* on 28 November, all hell let loose. Major's personal integrity came under scrutiny, especially as he had told the House earlier in November that the idea of talking to Adams or the IRA 'would turn my stomach. We will not do it', and he had said two weeks before in his Guildhall speech that he would 'never talk to organisations which did not renounce violence'. Major believed that what he was ruling out on these occasions was face-to-face talks, but such subtleties were lost in the political row. Mayhew called a press conference that morning, at which he appeared awkward and wrong-footed. He performed better in the House the next day when he made a statement about the affair. With the exception of the excitable Paisley, who was ordered from the Chamber for accusing Mayhew of 'falsehoods', MPs mainly supported

Mayhew or offered only mild criticism. Molyneaux, who had known of the back channel since July, was considerably more matter-of-fact than his DUP opposite number: 'If anyone asked me if I was shocked if the British had been in secret negotiations with the IRA, I would have said I would be more surprised if they hadn't,' he later recalled.[45]

Mayhew announced that he would be placing a copy of all correspondence via the back channel in the Commons Library to illustrate that everything the government had done was in line with their own pronouncements and did not amount to negotiation, and was in response to the IRA's initial message of 22 February searching for a way out of the armed struggle. The Republicans responded furiously, releasing their own dossier of documents to the press, which purported to show that London's disclosures had been less than the whole truth. To general astonishment, Mayhew announced on 1 December that typographical and transcription mistakes had indeed been responsible for no less than twenty-two errors. Mayhew offered his resignation to Major who, though irritated, did not 'for one moment' consider sacrificing him.[46]

The right in Britain were particularly angered by the contacts with the IRA. The *Sunday Telegraph*[47] as well as some Tories fulminated against any dilution of the Union, as well as against dialogue with Republican terrorists. Many of the critics were the same right-wingers – for whom British sovereignty was all – who opposed Major's European policy. One prominent former Cabinet minister thought such contacts were 'treason'.[48] Major was dismissive of those who questioned the wisdom of dealing with the IRA. In seeking a way out of the impasse in Northern Ireland, he believed the government was morally right to explore all options, however distasteful it might have found them.

Revelation of the contacts brought relations with Dublin to the lowest point of the year. 'Neither IRA–Sinn Fein nor the British government told me that they were talking to each other,' complained Reynolds. 'I made it clear to both sides that this was anything but desirable. I put it in strong terms.'[49] Indeed he did. Reynolds had an angry forty-minute phone call with Major on Monday 29 November.[50] He considered it hypocrisy for Dublin not to have been briefed on the exchanges while at the same time Number Ten had been remonstrating against any taint of a Dublin relationship with Adams. Major made soothing noises, but underneath London was unapologetic: 'If you have a secret channel operating, you don't go and tell other people about it. We were under no obligation to brief the Irish government. We didn't feel we had done anything for which we had to apologise,' recalled one observer.[51]

A Major–Reynolds summit was scheduled for 3 December. Major sensed that, despite all the turbulent groundswell, a real opportunity might be opening up. As his position continued to strengthen over the autumn, he felt ready to take a bold initiative. But whose document – if a joint declaration was indeed to be the way forward – would provide the basis for talks? Reynolds was scornful of a British redraft of his declaration document sent to Dublin at the end of November. Major wrote to Reynolds that 'there is clearly no hope of securing even tacit acceptance by the Unionist mainstream of a joint declaration along the lines of your draft . . . as we've agreed all along, association with Hume–Adams is a kiss of death'. The new British document took Unionist opinion more fully into account than any Dublin draft, and in Major's words, 'goes as far in my judgement as the market will bear'.[52] Butler was despatched again to Dublin to present it to Reynolds and his advisers. One recorded in his diary: 'Albert gives him hell. Tells him he doesn't have a clue. He also tells him that Major's proposal, which involves the two leaders finding some kind of middle way, won't wash.'[53]

Reynolds now told Major directly that he would agree to their summit going ahead only if the British document was withdrawn. With both sides issuing threats, tension ran high in both camps. The 3 December meeting, to be held in Dublin Castle (the former seat of British power in Ireland), was one of the twice-yearly summits between Prime Minister and Taoiseach. Agendas were often decided late, but no one could recall one before on such a knife edge. Major and Reynolds spoke again by phone on 1 December.[54] A compromise seemed to be hammered out, which allowed the summit to proceed, but, not untypically, there was disagreement about what the compromise was. So when both delegations arrived for the summit it rapidly became clear that the Irish thought the new London draft would not be discussed, the British government team – Major, Mayhew and Hurd – that it would.[55]

The Downing Street Declaration

The two delegations sat across a table in the Dublin Castle drawing room known as the King's Bedroom glaring at each other. Strong words were exchanged. To unlock the bolted door, Major suggested that he and Reynolds retire to a separate room alone. Other ministers with their large official troupes went off in another direction for separate discussions, while one adviser to each leader sat outside the room in which Major and Reynolds argued for an hour.

Major went in armed with a dossier of press cuttings. Systematically, he went through the alleged leaks contained in them, criticising Reynolds for what he considered underhand and self-defeating tactics.[56] Reynolds came back just as strongly with what Dublin considered British duplicity and hypocrisy in proceeding with the back channel without informing Dublin. It was an uncomfortable few minutes, but both men felt they had cleared the air. Reynolds's remark to his team on leaving the one-to-one dialogue was typically robust: 'It went all right – I chewed his bollocks off and he took a few lumps outa me.'[57]

The mood music might have been less jagged, but little progress had yet been made on the substance of the joint declaration they had come to Dublin Castle to discuss. The remaining period up to lunch saw a tense forty-five-minute conversation between both delegations, with exchanges described as 'hot, frank and argumentative'. Still agreement eluded them on whose draft declaration would be used as the basis for discussion. Which side would be the first to back off? Which government would look worse if talks broke down and both blamed the other side to the media? Fear and brinkmanship were rarely more strongly in evidence at any of Major's international conferences; his sang-froid was of similar quality to that which he displayed at Edinburgh in December 1992. By lunchtime, a consensus of a kind was emerging. Both sides appeared to want to find a way forward, though the British would still not commit themselves to proceeding with a joint declaration, still less to any fixed timetable.[58]

Over lunch the atmosphere lightened considerably, with both delegations sitting together to eat. With the 1994 Five Nations rugby tournament to commence the following month, and both Prime Ministers keen followers of the game, they proudly boasted of the merits of their national sides.[59]

In the afternoon session they turned for the first time to considering the joint declaration in detail. The British delegation at this point declared that, to make progress possible, they would put their own draft on one side and allow the Irish document to be the focus for their deliberations. Major went through the entire Irish text, and laid down a number of amendments, on top of the changes the Irish had already made following their own exchanges with Protestant leaders to accommodate Unionist feelings. He also made it clear there were five or six sticking points on which the British were not prepared to move. Ritual war dancing continued as the two leaders, proud of their command of detail, were eager to show off the depth of their understanding. Tempers again rose, and failure again seemed possible. Reynolds was adamant that he could not sell Major's proposed changes to his Irish audience; Major was equally clear that he could not carry the Unionists with him unless the document was changed in the ways he specified.[60]

Reynolds threatened to break up the conference. 'Well fine, John,' one witness recalled him saying, 'you go ahead, off you go home. We'll go out and tell the journalists that there's no point in talking any more because the Brits won't do business.'[61] Major in his frustration broke the pencil in his fingers, and threw both bits on the table.

An adjournment was suggested so both delegations could meet in private. The British party believed it quite possible that the Irish would throw in the towel, and that they had pushed them too far. The minutes ticked by, and the British debated what they on their side would say if the conference did indeed stall. To their relief, the Irish came back to them with a compromise formula, though with a number of points, including an all-Ireland dimension to any formula, that they said were non-negotiable. Realising they had all pulled back from the brink, the atmosphere lightened. Both parties agreed that they were indeed working towards a joint declaration.

The press conference at the end of the day was decidedly optimistic. Concord seemed to be underlined symbolically when a question addressed to both Prime Ministers led to them both responding simultaneously, with almost identical words. The relief, however, while understandable, was premature: the Dublin conference had done little more than bring both governments back into negotiations. Many of the tough decisions on what the joint declaration would say, and what it would omit, had yet to be taken.[62]

Both leaders emphasised their intention to hold further talks during the EU Council in Brussels the following weekend. In the meantime, intensive exchanges took place at official level between London and Dublin. The British continued to take soundings with the Unionists, and in great privacy began to show selected individuals, including Molyneaux, parts of the text. The message began to filter back to Number Ten that the Unionists wanted further concessions and guarantees to be made. While they were not prepared to say that they welcomed the exercise, equally – and this was the key point – Number Ten learned that the Unionists were not going to commit themselves to opposing it. The exercise helped them to delineate those amendments that were vital if indeed the joint declaration was to be accepted by the Unionist community.[63] Whether Dublin would accept all these points was still, however, an open question.

The Brussels meeting, on 10 and 11 December, showed how much work still had to be done. At Major's bilateral meeting with Reynolds, and various meetings between officials, the Irish protested that the British were pushing them too far, and threatened to pull the plug on the whole enterprise. Wednesday 15 December had already been identified tentatively as the date for launching any joint document, but the date began to look balefully premature. An Irish Convention was one of the sticking points on which Reynolds insisted; the British eventually accepted this idea in watered-down form, as the 'Forum for Peace and Reconciliation', operating only in the Republic. Discussions continued between officials by fax and telephone over the next three days. Major and Reynolds spoke at 10.30 a.m. and again at 3.30 p.m. on the Tuesday 14 December. Final agreement was only reached by 8 p.m. on that Tuesday.[64] A senior British observer recorded: 'The deal is done. The Irish are confident that it stands a chance of doing the trick with the IRA.'[65]

While Major could heave a huge sigh of relief, the work of officials was still not over. Alex Allan and Roderic Lyne decided that their preparations for the following day needed far more attention. So they worked together throughout the night on Major's parliamentary statement, the press statement, question and answer briefings, a television broadcast and other responses that he would be called upon to make. As dawn rose the next morning, they went up to the Number Ten flat and went through it all with him.[66]

The Irish party flew to London later that morning. They were all deeply conscious of occasion, and talked on the journey about the treaty negotiations that led to the creation of the independent Irish state seventy years before. Reynolds recalled: 'There was a great sense of history attached to it. We had

finally come to agree upon a declaration that was going much further than
the British Prime Minister or British government had ever gone before, and
indeed than an Irish Prime Minister on behalf of an Irish government had
ever gone before.'[67]

Major was at the door of Number Ten to greet the party, and ushered
them into the Cabinet Room, where he sat on one side of the table with Hurd
and Mayhew, and Reynolds and Spring on the other. Officials sat at either
end of the coffin-shaped table. Some time was initially spent checking for
consistency what had finished up as a twelve-point declaration. Every sentence checked, formal speeches were then made by Major and Reynolds,
followed by the clink of champagne glasses, a photo opportunity in Downing
Street, and the press conference in the State Dining Room. The venue for the
declaration should have been Westminster's Queen Elizabeth II Conference
Centre. By a strange stroke of irony, the plan had to be aborted as it had
already been booked by a prime mover in another divided land, Yasser
Arafat.[68]

In the House that afternoon, Paisley launched a predictably unpleasant
attack on Major. The Prime Minister was able to undercut the DUP leader
by talking eloquently of his dream that there should be 'no more coffins
carried away week after week because politicians don't have the courage to
sit down and try to find a way through'.[69] John Smith, Hume and even
Molyneaux, albeit tentatively, offered support. 'Bold and brave' was how
Hugo Young, not untypically among press commentators, described the
declaration.[70]

Everything hinged now on how the declaration would be received by the
Unionist community in Northern Ireland and by Republicans. The text itself,
for all the heartache that went into its composition, was both brief and to a
degree opaque. It certainly bore the scars of heavy-duty lobbying by a whole
range of constituencies: Number Ten and the Taoiseach's office, the NIO,
John Hume and Gerry Adams, James Molyneaux and Robin Eames, as well
as a range of other Unionist and Nationalist leaders sounded out in the crucial
two-week period prior to 15 December.

The document itself spoke of the need to develop an agreed framework
for peace to remove the causes of conflict and to overcome the legacy of
history. It repeated Brooke's and Mayhew's dictum that the British government had 'no selfish strategic or economic interest in Northern Ireland'. In a
tortuous phrase, the document stated 'the British government agree that it is
for the people of the island of Ireland alone, by agreement between the two
parts respectively, to exercise their right of self-determination on the basis of
consent, freely and concurrently given, North and South, to bring about a
united Ireland, if that is their wish'. This statement skilfully enshrined both
the consent as well as the self-determination principles. Equally, the Irish
government accepted that 'it would be wrong to attempt to impose a united
Ireland, in the absence of the freely given consent of a majority of the people
of Northern Ireland'.[71]

Nearly all the points or guarantees insisted upon by Major at Dublin were indeed present in the final document. Number Ten ascribed this success in part to Reynolds having all but staked his premiership on achieving a joint declaration with London: failure to agree would have exacted a higher political cost for him than for Major.[72]

The Unionist community looked at the joint declaration long and hard. Molyneaux, who knew what was in it, managed, if only just, to bring his UUP into line. Initially they saw it as a very green document, heavily influenced by the IRA as a bribe for a ceasefire. But when Molyneaux persuaded his senior party figures to read the text, they accepted that their position was in fact protected. Paragraph ten, which called for a commitment to exclusively peaceful means, and which invited only those parties fully wedded to the democratic process into talks, was a particularly important clause in swaying them. Molyneaux recalled:

John Major talked to me maybe three or four times a week immediately before the declaration. The last one was on the Monday before the signing at around midnight. I made one last effort to get rid of the phrase about 'no selfish interest' because it would make life more difficult for me. But his refusal to take it out confirmed my belief that it was there for a special purpose. I had to sweat it out. But it was a smokescreen for the key statement about 'exclusively peaceful means'. Those last three words are the most important in the declaration.[73]

Molyneaux was convinced by Major. He saw the political need to include the statement about 'no selfish interest'. He also saw the sense in it: after the Cold War, there were no longer Russian submarines and trawlers off the west coast of Ireland, so the strategic aspect was now largely nominal. As for the economic interest, 'there is no extraction of mineral wealth. All we have is soggy lignite coal.'[74] The phrase, however, had great symbolism not least to the Americans, showing that Northern Ireland was not an imperial outpost being milked by the British, but a province where the British remained only as long as they were wanted. To the Republicans, also, it was a most seminal statement of intent. Molyneaux's support was pivotal not just in placating Unionist opinion in the province, but also the Tory right at Westminster. Major's meticulous courting of Unionist leaders paid dividends. But not all were won over. Paisley continued to huff and puff, but, for the time being at least, his brand of rejectionism had lost the day.

Another target audience, the IRA–Sinn Fein, reacted more slowly. The Joint Declaration wrong-footed them. Their long-term objective was to come into direct negotiation across the table with the British government alone. They did not want to have the Ulster Unionists present, preferring to assume that the British government represented the Unionists and hoping that it would then deliver the Unionists on whatever was agreed. The objective of the back channel communication for the Republicans was to achieve bilateral talks with the British, which was one reason why Reynolds reacted so negatively when he heard about it.

The declaration nevertheless went further than many in the IRA thought possible of Major, with him acknowledging Irish self-determination and formally repeating the 'no selfish interest' principle. Hence the IRA's dilemma: to reject the declaration might marginalise them and look bad internationally as well as across Ireland; to endorse it would mean accepting hitherto rejected positions as well as risk splitting the movement. So they resorted to the classic tactic of playing for time, and asking for 'clarification'. Number Ten interpreted this ploy as another attempt to bring the British government into bilateral talks with the Republicans. What they were after, Number Ten believed, was to have the document renegotiated and parts they did not like removed and other bits dating back to the Hume–Adams document of June reinserted.[75]

On his regular pre-Christmas visit to Northern Ireland on 22 December, Major responded forthrightly to the IRA–Sinn Fein demand for clarification: 'There is a gauntlet down on the table. It is marked peace. It is there for Sinn Fein to pick up. The onus is on them. There is no need for fresh negotiation ... I am not playing that game.'[76] The government spent the first quarter of 1994 repeating the same message. Pressure mounted for a breakthrough. The Dublin government opted for a conciliatory tone, responding to questions from the Republicans, and removing the twenty-year ban which kept Sinn Fein off the airwaves in the Republic. Hume urged Adams and the IRA to respond positively, pointing out that the Joint Declaration had much in common with the Hume–Adams text. Adams, sensing that he needed to broaden the pressure on London, went to the USA in February 1994 to try to bring the Americans into play on his side.[77] Sinn Fein promised a decision by the end of January 1994, then it was posted back to St Patrick's Day on 17 March, then April, then June. The story is picked up in later chapters.

The Downing Street Declaration was a most significant text in the tortured history of Ireland. The Joint Declaration route, which began as an Irish peace initiative, addressing the concerns of the Republicans and Nationalists, ended up meeting also the fundamental concerns of Unionists in such a way that a very wide cross-section of opinion across the divide could support it.[78] The primary aim of the Joint Declaration, in the eyes of London and Dublin, was to present a united front which the paramilitaries could only respond to by laying down their arms.[79] It had yet to be seen whether this aim was to be realised.

As the IRA ended its three-day Christmas ceasefire sixteen minutes after midnight on 27 December with a mortar attack in County Tyrone, no one could be certain what the future would hold.[80]

TWENTY-EIGHT

Back to the Bad Times:

January–May 1994

THE DOWNING STREET Declaration and the optimistic three-month period leading up to Christmas had imparted a new spirit of hope into Number Ten. But as so often in Major's premiership, when the corner appeared to have been turned, events boomeranged against him. Rarely did they do so with more force than in the early months of 1994.

Moral Backlash: January

Boxing Day newspapers traditionally provide light relief and a gentle return to reality after Christmas excesses. They brought neither to Major on Sunday 26 December 1993, with the *News of the World* revealing that Tim Yeo, a married middle-ranking minister in the Environment Department, had fathered a child with his mistress, a Tory councillor called Julia Stent. The news had not been unexpected. A meeting at 12 Downing Street had been convened before Christmas, attended by Major, Fowler, Ryder and Gummer, to consider their response to the story, if the newspaper went ahead and published. Their conclusion, fatefully, was that it was a 'private matter', with no bearing on Yeo's fitness as minister. Gummer, known as a committed Christian, agreed that his junior minister should be retained.[1]

There were clear precedents for toughing it out. Steven Norris, the junior minister at Transport, had ridden out revelations of his exotic love life, which had surfaced, moreover, during the October Party Conference, and had rumbled on with successive revelations in the weeks thereafter. Paddy Ashdown, the Liberal Democrat leader, had the year before also survived news of an affair with his former secretary. Yeo believed it not unreasonable to hope that the story would go away. At this point he had a long-standing commitment to take his family on holiday to the Seychelles. Confident that the story was containable and he had done all he could, he saw no need to stay in Britain.

The pre-Christmas meeting at the Chief Whip's house miscalculated the mood badly. The media had a field day over the scandal, and it became the dominant political story of the Christmas holiday period, crowned by photographs of Yeo covering his face in the back of his car as he returned from the Seychelles. Major's response to the episode appeared uncertain. He supported Yeo in public, but not as robustly as he might have done if he had deeply believed in saving his man. Yeo's outspoken opponents within his Suffolk South constituency association compounded the problem.[2] On Wednesday 5 January, after a bruising ten days, he was summoned to meet Ryder and Fowler, and was told the game was up.[3]

The wheel had been given a powerful turn by David Evans, the voluble right-wing MP, and a member of the 1922 Executive, who kept the story going. He castigated Major and Fowler for trying to defend Yeo. The right in general had little sympathy for Yeo, a left-of-centre Tory with few strong allies on the opposite wing. Evans played the back to basics moral card forcefully: 'You cannot [excuse] people bonking their way around London,' he said.[4]

Major's insistence on 6 January, the day after Yeo's departure, that back to basics was never intended as 'a crusade against [sic] personal morality' fuelled the flames. The right liked the personal morality dimension to back to basics, as articulated by their champions, Lilley, Portillo and Redwood, the previous autumn. Now the Prime Minister appeared to be disowning that very element, and the aspect moreover that Lady Thatcher herself had lauded. To make matters worse, the Party leadership had decided to dump Yeo only when it became clear that his constituency officers failed to give him unequivocal support. As with the Mellor and Mates cases, accusations of indecision and weak leadership were levelled at the Prime Minister. The headline in the *Sunday Telegraph* on the eve of Parliament's reassembly after Christmas, 'Tory chaos as back to basics backfires', gave the worst possible start to the New Year as MPs returned.[5]

As one of Major's aides later admitted: 'We did not handle it well. It was a quiet time for political news, and it raised to the fore again the question of who was running Britain; it played straight into the weakness of the PM over it.'[6] Another insider revealed the corner that Major found himself in:

The Yeo episode was one of those occasions when there was strong pressure from a number of senior party figures that here was a good minister doing a good job, and it would be wrong for him to resign over such a personal issue. The Prime Minister accepted their advice. He understood that there are human failings. Then the media pressure built up, and it became very difficult for the Prime Minister to distance himself. Inevitably, calls came into the Number Ten Press Office demanding to know the Prime Minister's position and there was no choice but to say that he supported all his ministers. Then when Yeo did resign, like others after him, he appeared to have backed down. Eventually we ended up with a rather ruthless regime in which it became clear that defending ministers was a mug's game and it was better that they quit quickly.[7]

Number Ten's apprehensions that the press were unleashing a vendetta against the government, and Major in particular, appeared to be confirmed by the episode. A number of alleged cases of personal misconduct that had been in circulation for some time exploded into print in close proximity, with back to basics providing both the text of double standards and the opportunity to divide left and right within government.[8] The press, from tabloid to high Tory, were united in their condemnation of what they saw as hypocrisy. The strongest attack came from the pen of the former Labour supporter and now arch-Thatcherite, Paul Johnson, in the pages of the *Spectator*. Under the title 'A New Year curse on John Major and all his mendacious administration', he penned an article, which Simon Heffer believed 'understated',[9] dripping with bile. Johnson labelled the government 'the most disreputable of my lifetime' and concluded 'This is a government born in treachery, surviving by sub-terfuge, double-dealing and fraud, Janus-faced and brazen, slippery and underhand, a dismaying blend of incompetence and low cunning, doomed to end in shame and recrimination.'[10] The *Sun* meanwhile declared baldly, 'What fools we were to back John Major.'[11]

Just as the Yeo issue was dying down, Alan Duncan, the right-wing 'million-aire' Parliamentary Private Secretary to Brian Mawhinney at Health, resigned after publicity over his purchase of a Westminster council house. With Conservative-controlled Westminster Council already under investigation for its policy on the sale of council houses, the story was a tabloid, and Labour, dream. Bob Cryer was one of several Labour MPs into the fray, calling it 'an example of the filthy rich taking advantage of the ordinary poor'.[12]

On the Saturday evening after Duncan's resignation, a distraught Lord Caithness, Minister for Aviation and Shipping, telephoned Major to say that he had just discovered his wife had shot herself. Caithness was in deep shock, some of it rubbing off on Major, who began to wonder when the woes would end. Caithness resigned the next day, but the following week stories appeared that his wife's suicide on the eve of their wedding anniversary had been sparked by fears that he was on the verge of leaving her for another woman.[13]

Before the week was out, yet another morality story came to light, with the admission by David Ashby, a backbench MP, that he had shared a French hotel room with a male friend. Ashby described newspaper reports that he was having a homosexual relationship with the man, for whom he was supposedly leaving his wife, as 'nuts'. The stories about Ashby may have been distorted, but the impression left was merely to add to the impression of sleaze.[14]

With the leadership question, dormant since September, now thrust back to the surface, Major felt the need to crack the whip. On BBC TV's *Breakfast with Frost* on Sunday 9 January he restated what *he* had intended by back to basics. It was, he said, a programme in defence of traditional institutions and values in the face of a rapidly changing world. To try to defuse the moral backlash, he appealed for tolerance towards ministers and MPs who might have behaved foolishly in private. The government was not seeking to preach on morality, and the need for personal responsibility was but 'one part' of a wide patchwork of back to basics.[15]

In Cabinet on 13 January, the first of the year, he echoed the same theme.

He told ministers emphatically that when he had used the phrase the previous October at the Party Conference, it was a useful description to unite a number of themes and policies then in train. For the umpteenth time, he said, he had not intended it as a crusade about personal morality. He wanted nevertheless to persist with the theme, not least because opinion polls showed that back to basics was popular with the country as a whole. Ministers were firmly warned off any implications that it was linked to personal sexual morality, or against any suggestion that the government was targeting particular groups. Those around the Cabinet table were reminded to read the papers from Number Ten circulated after his party conference speech and to ensure that what they said in public was consistent with what was in those documents.[16]

That evening it was the turn of the 1922 Executive to listen to the Prime Minister. They were given a similar message to Cabinet, and learned that errant ministers would be despatched more quickly in the future.[17] Heseltine and Hurd, meanwhile, were given prime responsibility to relaunch the policy on the right lines. In public, the right fell into line. Howard and Portillo both swiftly made loyalist back to basics speeches, though to some Portillo's read like the manifesto of a leader in waiting. If the right-wingers were left in no doubt that their wings had been clipped, someone – not from the Cabinet – soon exacted revenge. A passage from the Policy Unit's autumn *aide-mémoire* on back to basics, which stated, 'Going back to basics means expecting and respecting personal morality', was leaked to the press. The right also let it be known that any show of unity after Major's reading of the riot act would be skin deep. One told *The Times* that they saw no point in precipitating a leadership crisis at this stage, when the increasingly distrusted Clarke was heir apparent. 'We are not yet ready.'[18] The principal players from the right were busy, however, stamping in the wings waiting for the right moment to come into the limelight.

The scandals, however, would not die down. One Central Office apparatchik recalled: 'Every Saturday night, I would have a conversation with Norman Fowler about who was going to get it next. It got to the point where I would phone the Fowlers' home, and his wife Fiona would answer, and she would ask, "Who is it this time?" not what was I ringing about.'[19] At the high point in mid-January the stories were indeed breaking daily. On Thursday 13 January Westminster City Council and its former leader Dame Shirley Porter were alleged to have rigged votes to hold on to power; the next day Teresa Gorman was accused of having made £1 million from council houses bought from Westminster Council; twenty-four hours later it emerged that Wandsworth, another Tory council, was under investigation for gerrymandering.[20]

John Smith mercilessly exploited the government's woes, making standards in public life a particular theme. Extending the attack beyond the moral standards of Tory MPs, he embraced the morality of civil servants, sale of honours and the selling of arms. Two further ripe plums dropped into Smith's lap. The Scott Inquiry had been conducting hearings since May 1993 in pursuit of its investigation into the Matrix Churchill/Arms-to-Iraq affair. The temperature rose when on 12 January former Foreign Secretary Geoffrey Howe voiced the concerns of increasing numbers of Tories when he criticised the conduct of the inquiry. The next day, Hurd spoke to Cabinet about Howe's attack. As the government had set up the inquiry under Richard Scott, he said it was not for it to comment upon, still less to criticise, the way it was being conducted. Howe had not given advance notice of his attack, and he wanted to clarify that Howe was speaking in a purely personal capacity.[21]

Major had had to spend several hours preparing his own evidence for the inquiry – 'a ridiculous waste of a Prime Minister's scarcest resource' in the eyes of some in Number Ten.[22] His appearance on 17 January before Presiley Baxendale, the inquiry's tenacious counsel, gave his critics little to bite on, bar some surprise that he did not know more about the episode considering that he had served in three relevant posts, Foreign Secretary, Chancellor and Prime Minister. Robin Cook, Shadow Trade Secretary, said that in denying he knowingly misled Parliament, Major revealed a worrying lack of grasp: 'The departments through which he passed appear stuffed with documents he never saw or which he saw but did not read to the end, or which he read but did not act on.'[23] Most, however, thought he had acquitted himself openly and fairly, and few believed he was personally culpable. In Cabinet on the following Thursday, Wakeham congratulated him on the way he had given his evidence, a view echoed enthusiastically by his Cabinet colleagues.[24]

The second issue that leapt up from the past was the Malaysian Pergau Dam affair. In 1988, the then Defence Secretary, Lord Younger, gave an assurance during a visit to Kuala Lumpur that Malaysia was eligible for British aid 'alongside' – a key word – a £1 billion-plus arms package. The following March, Mrs Thatcher promised Dr Mahathir Mohamad, Malaysia's prickly Prime Minister, to provide financial help to fund the Pergau Dam construction. The costs escalated by one third, and at those prices the Overseas Development Agency (ODA) concluded that the project was uneconomic, and should not be funded at that cost. The issue came to a head when, in early 1991, the Malaysians, who had bought the British arms, asked for the funding. Tim Lankester, Permanent Secretary of the ODA, advised the aid would not be an economic use of taxpayers' money, but Hurd, who consulted Major, authorised the payment to go ahead, on the argument of prior commitment by Mrs Thatcher and Britain's wider national interest.

A National Audit Office report in October 1993 brought the episode into the open. In the subsequent hearings by the Commons Public Accounts Committee, Lankester revealed that his advice had indeed been overridden by Hurd and Major. The Foreign Affairs Committee concluded that in linking aid to the arms sales, guidelines had been broken, and the courts later found that the Pergau payments were unlawful. Major never denied that he had had the chance to reject Hurd's recommendation. Hurd for his part admitted after his retirement that the Pergau decision was one of the mistakes he had made in office.[25]

The government's weakened moral authority was now being compared with the early sixties, when the Profumo scandal dented the Macmillan government's credibility. Major certainly shared with his predecessor a tendency to be over-trusting of those whose personal standards were less exacting than his own. Major was left hurt and puzzled by the barrage of accusations against him and his government. He could not believe that the public, nor even the media, thought that he or his ministers were corrupt. Yet the charges kept on accruing.

Labour chose this moment to launch a new offensive on tax and public spending, accusing Major of lying in his promises about tax during the 1992 general election. John Smith used a clever theme, as it served to further highlight Major's differences with his right-wingers, who were antagonised by the tax increases and by the high public spending. In private, Major admitted that mistakes, based on Treasury estimates of the deficit, had indeed been made in 1991–2. But there was no conscious effort to deceive. Over Scott, meanwhile, he found it incredible that anyone should think ministers tried to put innocent men in jail. Over Pergau, he had no criticism of Lankester; but equally, he argued that it was right and in Britain's interest not to override the pledge made by Mrs Thatcher to Mahathir. On private morality, he disapproved of infidelity, and he refused to believe that it was widespread among his government. His anger was directed rather against John Smith and Labour, as well as against the media. By harping on so much about the alleged decline in moral standards, he felt that the media for commercial interests and Labour for party political reasons were giving a wholly distorted impression to the public at large and were damaging public confidence in government and public officials. It was a very long way from his dreams of the kind of country he wished to create.[26]

A telling example of what he saw as the deplorable standards of the press came at the farewell dinner in January for Gus O'Donnell. It was planned to be a touching and intimate occasion for a man who was regarded warmly by lobby journalists. While guilty of being occasionally too easygoing in his handling of the media, especially on overseas trips, O'Donnell had run an effective press operation at Number Ten through some difficult years. O'Donnell's wife and parents were present, also senior Number Ten staff, and selected journalists (including Nick Lloyd and Stewart Steven, the loyalist editors of the *Daily Express* and *Evening Standard*). But a feeling of resentment existed amongst those who had not been invited, among them Trevor Kavanagh of the *Sun* and Gordon Greig of the *Daily Mail*, whom Number Ten had labelled as the two hatchet men in the vanguard of turning the press against Major.

At pre-dinner drinks, Major chatted to Michael Brunson, political editor of ITN, whom he liked, and allegedly said, 'I am going to f——g crucify the right for what they have done and this time I will have the party behind me.' The actual language is in dispute. Number Ten denied he uttered these words and Brunson will not discuss the matter, regarding it as private. Others present cast doubt on whether he used this language. But the sentiments were ones he certainly felt. Major was in expansive form at the dinner itself, and talked about how he thought the worst of his problems were over.[27]

After the dinner, which had indeed been relaxed and convivial, Brunson returned to his room, which ITN share with the *Sun*, in the press gallery at the Commons. Despite the late hour Simon Walters of the *Sun* was still there, and Brunson chatted to him about what he had heard at the private dinner. Walters passed what he heard to Kavanagh, who told Greig. Simultaneously stories appeared in the *Sun* and *Daily Mail*. For the third time Major's unguarded comments (after 'bastards' and 'flapping white coats') came out into the open, not only rekindling the right's animosity against him, but also focusing dissatisfaction with the government's performance onto Major's own head.

O'Donnell and Major were both appalled when they heard the news next morning about the reported remarks. O'Donnell was left wishing that they had never had the dinner, so marred had the farewell been by the subsequent press stories. He was not sorry to return to the Treasury. Major's view of the standards of wide elements of the media meanwhile sank to even lower depths.[28]

The Right in the Ascendant: February–March

The turbulence in January did not produce an overt challenge to Major, but it detracted significantly from his authority, as did reports circulating that Cabinet ministers – not confined to the 'bastards' – were privately disparaging him. A further hack at his standing came in an interview in *The Times* with Lamont, seen widely as bitter, alleging that Lamont said he had been misrepresented, that he had described Major's leadership as 'weak and hope-less', an exceptional statement from a former Chancellor and serving MP about his party leader.[29] Press reports and Labour's attack showing how the tax burden had risen continued to undermine claims that the Tories were the low tax party, a charge only lamely countered by Kenneth Clarke.

Backwash from the Lamont interview swamped coverage of a fight-back speech Major gave to the Leeds Chamber of Commerce on Friday evening, 28 January, into which much work had been put by the Policy Unit, and which contained a reasoned statement of government strategy on the economy, education and law and order. As he sat listening to earlier post-dinner speeches, he jotted down some doggerel, with which he opened his speech:

> Life all tonight is clear and bright,
> don't worry boys, the country's all right.
> Interest rates down and inflation low,
> exports up and we're ready to go.
> Things are better, and they won't get worse,
> if we can accept the grace in verse.[30]

The audience appreciated his spontaneity and his wit, and he spoke well. He relaxed so much that at one point later in the evening he doubled up and was photographed head in hands, an image to be endlessly recycled in the press thereafter as evidence of a man at the end of his tether.[31] Formalities over, he retired with aides and some of the dinner guests to a private room. So much was he enjoying himself, that it was decided to abort the plan to return that night to Huntingdon. Rooms were rapidly arranged, overnight necessities procured, while the conviviality and drink flowed long into the night.[32]

The Prime Minister's party awoke early next morning to the papers full of speculation about Major's successor. The following day the *Sunday Times* quoted William Hill, the bookmaker, giving odds of 8–11 that Major would be out of office by the time of the next general election, with Clarke favourite to succeed (4–5), then Howard (4–1), Portillo (5–1), Hurd (10–1), Heseltine (oddly, at 20–1), Redwood (20–1) and even Lady Thatcher making an appearance (100–1).[33] It was much more than press mischief-making, there being a widespread assumption that he would not survive disastrous local election results in May and European Parliament elections in June.[34] The corridors at Westminster were awash with talk of who should succeed Major and when he might go.

Portillo was seen by Number Ten as a main *agent provocateur*, in that others plotted on his behalf, although they believed that his 'Spanish sense of humour' kept him from being part of any disloyal conspiracy.[35] He was slapped down by Major in Cabinet in his attempt to prevent approval of a Crossrail London link from Liverpool Street to Paddington stations.[36] Then Portillo's keynote speech on Europe in Gloucester, which his aides had promoted heavily to the media, was doctored by Number Ten.[37] George Gardiner, whom Number Ten were glad to see voted off the 1922 Executive – to be replaced ironically, by David Evans – promised Portillo the support of the 92 Group of right-wing MPs (which he chaired) 'when the time came'.[38]

Major's retort was to dismiss Gardiner peremptorily after a two-minute audience.[39] The put down was seen by some as being on the advice of Christopher Meyer, the former Head of FCO News Department in the mid-eighties, who succeeded O'Donnell as Press Secretary in late January with a reputation for being a no-nonsense press manager.[40] Not so. Major had told Meyer before he took up his appointment that from now on he was going to come out of the bunker, and would be blazing from all guns.[41] A strong rallying performance before the 1922 Committee on 4 February, which was well received, suggested that a corner might have been turned.[42]

Just when a mini-revival seemed in place, scandals resurfaced to knock Major off his new-found perch. On Monday 7 February, as he was preparing to give an upbeat speech at the Conservatives' Winter Ball at London's Grosvenor House Hotel, the grandest event in the Party's social calendar, he learned that the body of Stephen Milligan, the former journalist and MP for Eastleigh since 1992, had just been found.[43] Major looked shaken when he arrived for the ball, but gave a forceful speech on the need for Party unity, especially with the elections coming up in May and June; he said they should all feel confident with 'the best economic prospects in front of us that we have known for many years'.[44] Lurid stories circulated in the press in the following days about the bizarre circumstances of Milligan's death. Major did not know Milligan particularly well, but was shocked by the reports; he began to feel 'Good God, who will it be next?' He did not have to wait for long. Within days, Hartley Booth, Mrs Thatcher's successor as MP in Finchley since 1992, had offered his resignation as Parliamentary Private Secretary at the FCO after the *Daily Mirror* was sold a story about his feelings towards a female researcher.[45]

Polls in the press showed a big drop in public support for back to basics since the autumn.[46] Major was determined to show that he would not give way to public pressure, and returned to the theme in speeches in the Midlands, and in Scotland on 18 February, when he said, 'Back to basics is a series of very hard-edged policies that meet the concerns of ordinary people.'[47]

The theme, however, was to be effectively abandoned shortly afterwards. No sudden event snapped his confidence in it, rather the cumulative attrition of press stories, and the practical difficulty of detaching the theme in the media's and public's mind from the private behaviour of his party's MPs. The effect of dropping it produced its own difficulties. Having been forced to alter his economic agenda after Black Wednesday, it now appeared that he had been forced to abandon his social theme as well, in the face of events which critics said could have been played to his advantage. The fact that the wheels of fresh government policy kept turning, with a heavy legislative programme not least on law and order and deregulation, was largely obscured. Public perception was dominated by the collapse of Major's initiative. He felt the blow deeply and shied away from any further policy initiatives with a 'family' dimension for fear of reigniting back to basics.

Why had Major been unable, despite reading the riot act, to command the agenda on back to basics? Why, moreover, had the ground made during the autumn been so speedily lost? The answer to both questions is the same, and it is that the strengthening of Major's position from October to December was just a veneer, covering the deep underlying weaknesses. The enemies he had made on the right over Maastricht had not forgiven him, and he was unable to find any common ground between left and right around which to unite his party. Back to basics, intended in part as a sop to the right, ended up pleasing no one, while the Joint Irish Declaration further antagonised the right. With many of his backbenchers and even Cabinet contemptuous of him, only the lack of an agreed right-wing challenger kept the flak within manageable proportions.

With so much turbulence at home, Major was not sorry to board the plane on 14 February with Hurd, bound for Russia. It was only his second foreign trip so far that year. The first had been to Brussels for an unhappily timed NATO summit on 10–11 January as Parliament was reassembling. While at the NATO summit, he discussed with Helmut Kohl his concerns, shared by the German Chancellor, that President Yeltsin was being poorly treated by western leaders. Each time they met him it seemed, they effectively put him in the dock, interrogating him about his economic reforms and demanding to know why the Russian economy had not performed better, before reluctantly agreeing to the next slice of western aid. The impression had crystallised at a bad meeting with Yeltsin, also in Brussels, in December the previous year. Major, who had led international support for Yeltsin in earlier crises, was keen to see a more positive tone adopted. Particular urgency was given to the need to outflank Vladimir Zhirinovsky, the neo-fascist Russian leader, who claimed that his country was being treated as a second-class citizen on the world stage.[48]

Major arrived in Moscow armed with the offer, confirmed with Bill Clinton in a phone call on 12 February, that Britain and the USA were ready to offer Russia a permanent place at the political discussions held each year at the G7 summit. A further motive was to wean Yeltsin from continuing to block NATO's new-found determination to mount air strikes against the Bosnian Serbs besieging Sarajevo. Only a week before, a Serb mortar landing on a market in Sarajevo had killed sixty-eight people, and led to an international call for action.

Meetings between Major and Yeltsin on 15 February at the Kremlin followed a ceremonial welcome and mannered formality seemingly little changed from the days of Communism. Yeltsin was very agitated about the bombings in Bosnia. An unsuccessful phone call with Clinton had done little to calm him, so Major was able to do some useful peacemaking. Although Yeltsin continued in public to take a tough stance, in private he became more reconciled to the NATO proposals.[49] To bolster the show of mutual friendship, both leaders stressed to the press that relations were closer between their countries than at any point since the end of the Second World War. A largely symbolic gesture was an agreement to stop targeting strategic nuclear missiles at each other's cities. In addition, joint military exercises were announced, to take place from 1995, the first cooperation between both armies since before the Cold War.[50] Major's successful rapport with Yeltsin was reflected in the invitation to him and his wife for a weekend at Chequers later in the year.[51]

On the final day of his trip, on the suggestion of Braithwaite and Lyne, Major toured the city of Nizhny Novgorod (the former Gorky), a closed city until three years before, to which dissident Andrei Sakharov had been exiled. But now, under a dynamic governor, Yeltsin protégé and future Deputy Prime Minister Boris Nemtsov, it was a showcase for the Russian free enterprise spirit. The fleet of fifty cars with wailing sirens arrived in sub-zero temperature, Major's visit – the first to the city by a western leader since its foundation in 1220 – beginning at a privatised truck factory and finishing with a question-and-answer session with local businessmen.[52] He appeared visibly relaxed, and stimulated by the experience, and returned to London in high spirits. Nizhny Novgorod, he told Cabinet the next day, had been a high point.[53]

Major was encouraged by the press coverage, even if the praise was grudging: 'For the first time since the General Election', wrote George Jones, 'he has completed a gaffe-free trip.'[54] Credit was given to Meyer for the success of his strong-arm tactics handling the media. Major heeded his new adviser's counsel that he should not wander to the back of the plane to chat to the travelling press corps, especially with the domestic scene continuing so negative. Neither would Meyer permit questions on domestic politics during the trip's press conferences. Fresh stories were fed to the press day by day, thus ensuring that the Prime Minister's party retained the initiative. Meyer had learned much from watching Bernard Ingham operate as Press Secretary in the eighties, and regarded him as a mentor.[55] To cap Meyer's textbook operation in media management, he announced as the trip was ending that the Queen was ready to accept an invitation to visit Moscow, which, splashed across front pages, allowed the trip to finish on a high note.[56]

Back at home, the main legislative priority of the government in the run-up to Easter (and beyond) remained law and order, with two major Bills, the Police and Magistrates' Courts Bill and the Criminal Justice and Public Order Bill both introduced by Howard into Parliament in late 1993. Here at least was red meat for the right, the popularity of the Bills being reflected in Howard's enhanced prospects as a leadership contender. Major was heavily involved with the new emphasis on taking a tougher line on crime. Nick True recalls how 'Law and order became increasingly a preoccupation of the Prime Minister. He had a strong sense of what life was like for the underdog: he would say that crime doesn't bite on the middle class, but on the people he used to know in Brixton.'[57] He wanted to emphasise crime as something felt by the victim, and reduce the concern given to the criminal.[58]

In his monthly bilaterals with the Home Secretary, Major began to make clear from soon after the general election his dislike of the drift of Home Office policy since the early 1980s, criticising what he saw as the department's liberal ascendancy, which bore fruit in the 1991 Act. He believed the pendulum had swung too far in favour of the criminal suspect (with the cutting down of the number of people including juveniles sent to prison), and against the police.[59]

When Kenneth Clarke was appointed Home Secretary in April 1992 he was thus given a mandate from Major to take a grip on the department, and attack the liberal status quo. Major was pressing at an open door, given Clarke's appetite for challenging vested interests. Clarke lost no time in attempting to reform the police through the Sheehy Report, although the proposals ran into determined opposition. Some progress had been made under Clarke, but the pace speeded up considerably after Howard succeeded him in May 1993.[60] Howard was instinctively more inclined to make peace with the police and attack the 'liberal' judicial establishment than Clarke, his drive for tougher law and order policies reaching an early climax in the twenty-seven-point plan he announced at the 1993 Blackpool conference. Clarke's supporters were quick to point out in private that twenty-three of those twenty-seven points had previously been agreed between Clarke and Major. Howard was apt to be suspicious of the Home Office, and was grateful for whatever backing Major and the Policy Unit could give him.

Major's support for Howard's policies, and for a host of other policy initiatives relating to juveniles and crime prevention, remained in contrast to his relative liberalism on race and homosexuality. He granted a free vote on the age of consent for homosexuals, and in the vote on 21 February opted for the compromise age of eighteen, disappointing those who wanted it reduced to sixteen, but adopting a more liberal position than that chosen by many of his party, including four of his Cabinet, who voted for the age to remain at twenty-one.[61] He was heavily criticised by the right for going as far as he did.[62] It can only be a matter of speculation as to whether he would have been more active on the rights of both ethnic minorities and homosexuals had he received a larger majority in 1992 and did not need to pay so much attention to his own right wing.

Bringing the two blunderbuss law and order Bills forward in early 1994 should – as intended – have dominated the political agenda with popular measures.[63] The plan did not work out as hoped. The passage of the Police and Magistrates' Courts Bill proved exceptionally stormy. In February a House of Lords revolt attacked the central clauses of the Bill which sought to tip the existing structure of police accountability towards central government control. Two Conservative ex-Home Secretaries, Lord Carr of Hadley and Lord Whitelaw, spoke powerfully against so much authority being given to the Home Secretary. The government was forced to introduce compromises, which, though largely cosmetic, damaged public perception before the Bill received the royal assent in July. Tory peers in general were far from happy at the rightward drift in government policy, although were far less scathing of Major than their counterparts in the Commons.

'The Tories were given an open goalmouth on crime and disorder,' declared a leader in the *Sunday Times*. 'To be left floundering with a Police and Magistrates' Courts Bill that is almost friendless in the House of Lords requires self-destructive skills of a high order. Who would have believed it possible for a right-wing Tory Home Secretary such as Michael Howard to earn the public wrath of chief constables and the police federation alike?'[64]

The passage of the Criminal Justice and Public Order Bill, which boosted police powers, particularly in the realm of public order, generated less disturbance, though on civil liberties it too aroused considerable disquiet outside the House. Newton and Waldegrave were prominent among those who argued against Howard's more punitive measures, though disagreement in Cabinet was kept behind closed doors.[65] But Conservative divisions blunted any hope that the legislation would provide a rallying focus, or of clearly differentiating Tory policy from Labour. Tony Blair, Labour's skilful frontbench spokesman, who was beginning to make a real impact on popular perceptions, played a clever and successful shadowing game, ensuring that Howard could not portray Labour as the party soft on crime. The blunting of Howard's spearhead drive on law and order had its upside for Major: had both Bills sailed through with widespread party and popular support, the Home Secretary, in a more senior Cabinet job than any other of the potential right-wing challengers, could have become a favoured hero for the right to rally behind at a time in mid-1994 when Major was highly vulnerable.

Fireworks Over America

For some days before Major left for his trip to see Clinton on 28 February, it was being billed as what might be 'his most difficult overseas trip since becoming Prime Minister'.[66] It was not difficult to see why. Differences over Bosnia and Northern Ireland, the two constant irritants between London and Washington, were running at a high level, with the latter causing more tension than ever before during Major's premiership. By early 1994 Major was spending an estimated 10–15 per cent of his time on Irish affairs, more than he devoted any other single policy issue.[67] Matters came to a head when Gerry Adams applied for a visa to enter the United States. His motives were clear: with the IRA in a stalemate on how to respond to the Declaration, he hoped to bring in United States support to put pressure on London to amend the Declaration in the direction of the Hume–Adams document, while strengthening the position of Republicans in favour of a ceasefire.

Irish Republicans, via supporters in the USA, had early in 1992 identified Clinton as more likely to be helpful if elected President in place of Bush, and were delighted when he made campaign promises to give Adams a visa, and to send a peace envoy to Ireland. They were thus dismayed when British lobbying partly led Clinton to drop both pledges. In November 1993 Clinton rejected a request for a visa, again on British advice, saying that 'Credible evidence exists that Adams remains involved at the highest level in devising PIRA strategy. Moreover, despite his recent talks with John Hume, Adams still has not publicly renounced terrorism.'[68] Number Ten therefore had little doubt that Adams's latest request, in January 1994, would be similarly rejected.

They had not reckoned on the influence exerted by some powerful advisers inclined to the Nationalist cause who were close to Clinton. Number Ten responded with some alarm when they received early warnings about Clinton's change of heart on the visa request. Several phone calls passed between Number Ten and the White House, principally between Lyne and National Security Adviser Lake. Lyne argued that if Adams was granted a visa, the pressure on Sinn Fein to respond positively to the Declaration would be sacrificed. London wanted to squeeze the IRA from all sides to emphasise there were no benefits from continuing with violence. The advice to the White House was unequivocal: 'Tell Adams that if there is a cessation of violence, then he can have the visa.'[69]

In December the White House had reappraised its Irish policy, egged on by Nancy Soderberg, a senior figure in the National Security Council with special responsibility for Irish affairs. Other powerful voices in the greening of the White House were the man for whom Soderberg had worked for seven years, Senator Edward Kennedy, as well as his sister, Jean Kennedy Smith, appointed by Clinton as US Ambassador to Dublin.[70] Influential Irish–American figures also included Senators Christopher Dodd and Daniel Moynihan. The advice was by no means one way. Warren Christopher and the State Department, the Department of Justice, the CIA and FBI, which had some intelligence linking Adams to terrorism, were all opposed to the granting of a visa.[71]

Robin Renwick, the British Ambassador in Washington, intensified diplomatic pressure on the administration and Congress. Adams was told to meet the US Consul in Belfast, Val Martinez, who would say he could have the visa but only if he renounced violence and supported the Declaration. Adams's reply was that he wanted to see 'an end to all violence and an end to this conflict'. The meeting with the Consul was exactly what Number Ten sought, and again they were convinced that Adams's equivocal response would be rejected by the White House. Martinez phoned Raymond Seitz, US Ambassador in London, and told him that after an hour's conversation Adams had failed to meet either condition. Seitz went home content that Adams had failed to meet the criteria.[72] But a change of heart came over the White House. Adams, through intermediaries, convinced them that if he came to the US it would encourage him to make a big step towards a ceasefire and peace in Northern Ireland. Clinton met Soderberg, George Stephanopoulos and Lake in the Oval Office. A hoax 'IRA' bomb in California provided the opportunity for them to ask for Adams to issue a condemnation of the bomb in return for the visa, with which he willingly complied. Soderberg explained that even without it, they were resolved to give Adams the visa: 'It was a win-win for the administration because if we gave the visa to him and he did deliver a cessation, fine. And if he didn't, he would be exposed as a fraud.'[73]

Number Ten was deeply affronted at the news, the more so when Adams made the trip and was given VIP treatment by the American media and many influential figures in the establishment. A massive propaganda coup was indeed notched up for the Republicans. The White House was to claim subsequently that granting the visa was vindicated by the ceasefire, which came eventually in August 1994. Number Ten thought differently. An aide responded: 'That claim is an absolute load of rubbish. There isn't a shred of evidence or intelligence to back it up, and we know an awful lot more about what goes on inside Sinn Fein than the Americans do. It took the pressure off Adams rather than keeping it on him. Without it, we'd have had the ceasefire sooner.'[74] Was not this exactly what the right had maintained would follow the foolish Joint Declaration? Major indeed found the visa embarrassing, and vented his anger in Cabinet on 3 February, at which he let ministers know how let down he felt by the Clinton administration. Ministers were told to emphasise in public that Adams had never made a commitment to cessation of violence, nor, contrary to the hopes of some, had he done so on his US trip.[75]

Clinton, too, was put out by the way Adams exploited the propaganda potential of his trip, without coming any closer to agreeing to a ceasefire. The President was doubly upset when, in the course of a routine plane trip, he was shown a fax, sent to the National Security Council from Number Ten, drawing their attention to an article from the *Sunday Times* of 6 February.[76] The piece quoted an anonymous White House official who claimed that Clinton 'didn't like' Major.[77] In the heat of the Adams furore, harsh words had indeed been uttered by both leaders in private about the other. But having any words that might or might not have been spoken by the President leaking out into the open was a serious matter, as articles on both sides of the Atlantic playing up the gulf between both leaders served to illustrate.[78] In a dramatic change of tone, Clinton decreed that he would go out of his way to fête Major when he came over at the end of that month, and kill stories of a rift with the British Prime Minister.[79] More attention, briefings indicated, would be lavished on Major than on any other foreign leader to have visited the USA so far during his time as President.[80]

Major and his party arrived in Washington on Sunday 27 February. Next day, meetings took place with leading figures in the administration and in Congress before the Prime Minister and his party, with Tony Lake as escort, flew to Pittsburgh to meet Clinton. The National Security Adviser was relieved to find Major clearly harbouring no grudges.[81] Intensive last-minute discussions had taken place between the White House and Number Ten, constructing an itinerary that would please the Prime Minister. Major's grandfather and father Tom had for a time lived in Pittsburgh, where there dwelt a sizeable Irish–American community considered unlikely to embarrass both leaders by staging a demonstration, unlike their compatriots in Boston and New York.[82] In his official welcome at Pittsburgh airport, Clinton made all the right noises about the USA's relationship with Britain, and about Ireland: 'I'm supporting, very strongly supporting', the President said, 'the initiative that Prime Minister Major and Prime Minister Reynolds have undertaken in the Joint Declaration.'[83]

The Pittsburgh visit concluded with a fireworks display and a dinner for four at a small restaurant, The Tin Angel, high above the town, with just the two leaders and Lyne and Lake. Since neither Clinton nor Major wished to discuss business, they chatted with intimacy and emotion about their own lives. The similarity in their backgrounds became increasingly evident, and a bond. Major was intrigued to hear Clinton talk about his alcoholic stepfather and his mother, who had died shortly before their meeting, of whom he was tremendously fond. Her death clearly still affected him deeply. He aired his lack of family wealth, and his struggle to get himself to Oxford as a Rhodes Scholar and on to Yale Law School. The lack of financial means in their backgrounds provided another touchstone, encouraging Major to talk about his own origins and his parents in a way he rarely did with intimates, let alone with comparative strangers. Further similarities became apparent, as Clinton discussed his concerns about poverty, race, health and education in America, and how best to direct public money, in a way that echoed much of Major's thinking.[84]

Dinner over, the party flew back to Washington, where, with the enthusiasm of a schoolboy wanting to show off his toys, Clinton suggested a late tour of Washington in Marine 1, his official helicopter. They flew three times around the Washington Monument before landing on the White House lawn at midnight. Clinton had insisted that Major spend the night at the White House – the first world leader to be his overnight guest there, and the first British Prime Minister to stay since Churchill.[85] Once inside and with Hillary away that evening, Clinton insisted on giving Major a tour. Despite it now being near his normal morning rising time in London, Major happily fell in as Clinton showed off every room in the executive mansion, talking excitedly about every significant piece of furniture and painting, before leaving the exhausted Major at the Lincoln Bedroom.[86]

The following morning Clinton wandered down at 8 a.m. to collect Major and take him upstairs for breakfast with Hillary and for a more cosy chat before the hard negotiations began. The White House felt that their differences over the Adams visa helped Clinton be more sympathetic to British positions than would otherwise have been the case. 'I don't think that we understood at the time fully British sensitivities on the issue,' recalled Lake.[87] On Ireland, soothing words were uttered, though Clinton fell short of saying that the Adams visa had been a mistake; in private, however, White House officials let it be known that they felt let down by Adams, and that any further visa applications would be unlikely to be successful.[88]

Differences over Bosnia had been the other principal source of friction, with long-standing resentment by the British government for the Clinton administration taking the high moral ground in supporting the Muslim-led government, but failing to back this up with practical help on the ground. Britain had approved the NATO ultimatum to the Bosnian Serbs on Sarajevo, about which it had had qualms, earlier in the month, and the Clinton administration now agreed to a joint Anglo–American civil planning mission to assess the civil position in Bosnia and determine what needed to be done to restore power, water and other utilities to the besieged city.

Before leaving the United States, Major flew to New York to see Secretary-General Boutros Boutros-Ghali at the UN, and to make a speech to the British/American Chamber of Commerce. Before several hundred businessmen, he argued that Britain had changed out of all recognition in the previous fifteen years: 'How many in America get a view of modern Britain from downbeat films of inner-city life or recreations of a bygone age? A world of Miss Marple or Middlemarch, a hide-bound, class-ridden society. My more cynical advisers say: why not leave the image like that? Let our American friends see us as still living in *The Remains of the Day* while we get on with running Brooks Brothers, Burger King or BP. But I want our image to match up with reality.' Yet again, he told his audience how strongly Britain had come out of recession, with low inflation, an enterprise culture and an open economy.[89]

Major felt bolstered by the visit. There had been also several media coups, including his humiliation of some pro-Republican Congressmen over Ireland, and the shooting down of four Serb planes by NATO aircraft gave him some precious soundbites, in which he proved more alert in his response than Clinton.[90] He told Cabinet on his return to London on 3 March that it had been a constructive, friendly and informal visit, and that he had the definite impression that Adams would not be granted another visa without very detailed prior assurances.[91]

Within days, an *aide-mémoire*, drawn up by officials in Number Ten and the White House, listed twenty-five 'points of agreement' between both governments.[92] Number Ten, for all their pleasure, were not dewy eyed about the state of the relationship. They had been stung by the change of mind on the visa; as one British official wryly observed, 'There are two key features of Clinton. One, he hates to be disliked, so he shies away from personal confrontation. Second, he can shift his position more quickly than anyone in American history.'[93] Subsequent events showed they were right to be cautious.

Bosnia took increasing prominence throughout March. After much discussion it was agreed to send more troops, following the UN request from Sir Michael Rose, the British commander of the UN troops (UNPROFOR) in Bosnia. In the House on 10 March Rifkind announced, following Cabinet agreement that morning, that a battalion group of 900 men from the Duke of Wellington's Regiment would be sent for an initial period of four months. Major flew to the region on the evening of 17 March, for his first visit since December 1992, to see conditions on the ground for himself, and to boost morale among the British troops after a difficult winter.[94] He spent the night in Split on the Croatian coast, before being shown around by helicopter the next day, visiting Gornji Vakuf, Bugojno, Vitez, as well as Sarajevo, where he spent three hours. He inspected the restoration work as had been agreed with Clinton earlier in the month and the steps being taken to repair the war-torn city. The trip was seen as an important show of support for the work of General Rose, from whom he had a briefing. Major's visit coincided with a pause in the two-year-old siege of Sarajevo, which had benefited from a ceasefire since February in response to the NATO ultimatum.

Throughout his trip, Major stressed the need to safeguard the ceasefire and maintain the momentum towards peace.[95] A £12 million aid package for Sarajevo was announced, and he had praise for the 'fabulous performance' of the British troops. He returned to London encouraged that the worst might be over, and satisfied by the success of the British troops, now numbering 3,300 men, in policing the new ceasefires and in promoting peace across wide areas of Bosnia.[96]

March Hares: Greek Tragedy

Peace, however, proved as elusive as ever for Major on the domestic front. The success of the Russian and American trips, and the high profile Major was playing over Bosnia, did nothing to quell the leadership speculation. An interview arranged with Jimmy Young on BBC Radio 2 on 7 March provided a platform for him to champion his leadership. Yet again he took the leadership question head on: 'I was elected at the last general election with the largest vote any party or any party leader has ever had. I was elected to remain Prime Minister of the country at least until the next election.'[97]

Circumstances were, however, stacked against him. Continuing disappointing performance in opinion polls did nothing to dissipate the alarm about the prospects for the forthcoming elections: further talk of a Canadian 'wipe-out' became common.[98] Mortar attacks by the IRA on London's Heathrow airport, though not detonating, appeared to have jeopardised not just the peace process, but also Major's judgement in thinking the IRA might be amenable to argument.[99] The continuing economic difficulties many experienced, coupled with tax increases, including the long heralded VAT on fuel, lay at the heart of the malaise, with claims that 'the public faces the biggest tax increases in Britain's peacetime history'.[100] Disagreements on spending continued to leak out of a Cabinet where ministers' tongues wagged over anything they considered would advance their position. Yet pinning down the leakers was notoriously difficult for Major, as it is for his biographer: when asked, Cabinet ministers, as over leadership jockeying, admit it was ubiquitous, but point the finger always at others.

Manoeuvring for advantage among putative contenders in a leadership contest reached new heights in March, with the Scott Inquiry providing a new ingredient. Clarke pledged he would resign if shown he had acted improperly, while Heseltine – making a comeback after the heart attack – denied that his evidence should be interpreted as a bid for the leadership. This denial, like those of Clarke, Howard and Portillo cut little ice with the media.[101] Waldegrave later that week brought forth some ridicule and suspicion on the government by his honest if ill-judged admission to the Treasury and Civil Service Select Committee that ministers lie in exceptional circumstances.[102] All the time, the fury of the Party – especially the right – at what was seen as Major's naïveté in setting up the inquiry, not least with Scott at its head, mounted. Then on 14 March came the re-election of George Gardiner to lead the hundred-strong right-wing 92 Group. Number Ten made no secret of its wish to see Tony Durant, a former whip, elected in the place of the troublesome Gardiner. His defeat was seen as a direct rebuff by the right to Major.[103]

The underlying malaise was given a near-fatal twist by an episode which, after the ERM departure, was the biggest single blow to have befallen Major so far in his premiership. The Maastricht Treaty, now ratified by all member countries, had passed into law. With it, the name of the EC changed to

European Union (EU). But this did not, to Number Ten's regret, free Major from divisive issues spilling over from Europe into domestic politics. This particular difficulty arose over Qualified Majority Voting (QMV), an episode from which none of the key players involved were to emerge with much credit. The issue originated with the imminent enlargement of the EU. Major had always been an enthusiastic supporter of further enlargement, but it brought a need to rethink structure and procedures within the Community. QMV involved the size of the 'blocking minority' needed in the various councils of ministers to overrule Brussels legislation. With the EC consisting of just twelve members, the blocking minority had been twenty-three votes (equivalent to the votes of two large and one small country). Once the four new nations (Austria, Finland, Norway and Sweden) joined in 1995, should the figure remain on twenty-three, or be increased to twenty-seven in proportion with the increase in total number of votes? In truth, it should have been a relatively minor issue.

The British government began to focus on the matter in the summer of 1993. The advice from John Kerr was that the British should insist that the number of votes each country had should be related more closely to population, an issue made even more pressing by the proposed entry of four more relatively small countries. It was already possible for a group of small states representing 12 per cent of EU population to cast a blocking minority, while two large states representing up to 40 per cent could not. Initial FCO advice was that other 'large' countries, Germany, France and Spain, would also back reweighting, or keeping the blocking minority of twenty-three votes. But the attitude of the German government, prompted by Kohl, began to change in early 1994, and France followed suit.[104] Major felt that it was another example of Germany and France changing their policy having first led Britain to believe that an agreement had been secured. 'That was our mistake,' he later said.

At this point, the government, with just Spain to support them, an uncertain partner, should have backed off, and accepted a compromise put up by Hurd before it became a *cause célèbre*. But despite Major's antennae alerting him to possible dangers ahead, he failed, as with the pit closures, to call 'halt'. The official advice that he received throughout January continued to be that Britain could win if it fought sufficiently hard.[105] So Hurd, despite his qualms, reiterated the government's position, and on 7 March was all but isolated at a Foreign Ministers' meeting, with Spain his sole supporter.

Since Christmas, stories about QMV leaked out increasingly to the press, and by March, what was a technical issue beyond the understanding of all but the most dedicated Europe-watchers became blown up into a question followed even by the tabloids where Britain's national pride was at stake against the European juggernaut. Successive attempts to resolve the matter at Foreign Minister level during March left the issue to be resolved at a special Foreign Ministers' meeting in Ioannina in Greece on the weekend of 26–7 March. The stage was set for a drama of epic proportions.

At a critical meeting in mid-March of OPD(E), the European sub-committee chaired by Hurd, Clarke and Heseltine came out forcefully for remaining with the British position of twenty-three votes rather than reweighting. Their uncompromising stance was interpreted as motivated by personal ambition. George Jones thus wrote: 'With their leadership ambitions rekindled, neither was anxious to be seen causing offence to the Tory Right wing – whose support would be vital if a leadership contest was triggered later this year.'[106]

At full Cabinet on 17 March Major adopted the technique he used before the Maastricht conference and invited all ministers present to contribute, to reduce the risk of ministers disowning the outcome.[107] The remit that Hurd was given duly left him only a little room for manoeuvre in trying to rally support during the coming negotiations at Ioannina, with instructions that he had to 'preserve the substance of the existing position', and reject the twenty-seven-vote proposal.[108] Gummer and Shephard were both in favour of going with the majority in the Community and accepting twenty-seven votes, but with the Cabinet's European champions otherwise engaged, their views were easily swamped.[109]

What of Major's views? Having accepted the FCO's advice, he was reluctant to change course even after Britain's early allies on the issue in the EU began to melt away. At the height of the negotiations, he aired his thoughts in private: he believed that keeping the blocking vote at twenty-three was going to be important for Britain, as there would be key issues coming up in the Social Chapter in the next two years. Enlargement, he believed, would not serve as a brake on measures that would increase social costs, and he was conscious of Britain's relative lack of solid allies in the EU. Allowing the blocking vote to rise to twenty-seven was more than a totemic issue: it was an issue of substance, without which Britain's ability to veto measures it disliked would be much harder.[110] But he acknowledged there were also political reasons for a tough line. It was not just the arch-Eurosceptics Cash and Marlow who demanded 'no surrender'. Normally moderate MPs like Terence Higgins and David Lidington in a backbench meeting with Hurd on 16 March also insisted that the Foreign Secretary not back down.[111] Major was deeply conscious of the need to hold the Party together in the run-up to the elections. By mid-March, he was locked into a course from which he could not escape.

In this atmosphere of inflated expectations, Major's judgement let him down in the House of Commons on Tuesday 22 March. Speaking just after the latest European Foreign Ministers' attempt to break the deadlock had failed, he said, to loud cheers of Tory MPs:

We aren't going to do what the Labour party do, which is to say 'yes' to everything that comes out of Europe without any critical examination. We will not be moved by phoney threats to delay enlargement.[112]

In a question from Labour MP Giles Radice he went further, and derided

John Smith as being 'Monsieur Oui, the poodle of Brussels'.[113] The moment he returned to his room in the Commons he knew he had gone too far. The expression had been discussed and rejected in Number Ten that morning, but it had stuck in his mind. It was considered for use in face-to-face exchanges with Smith himself; the words when spoken to a third party came across as aggressive.[114]

When Major saw the headlines next day he realised how far he had allowed himself to become boxed in by events.[115] Particularly upsetting were suggestions that his words made 'a mockery of [his] talk of being at the heart of Europe'.[116] Meyer summoned Peter Riddell, author of one of the critical articles, to see Major at Number Ten on Thursday. The Prime Minister banged the Cabinet table and protested that everyone was being unreasonable, with other countries promising help that never materialised.[117] Number Ten tried to back-pedal, and soften expectations of the Ioannina weekend conference, but they were swimming against the current. The *Guardian* published a Hugo Young interview with Major on Friday 25 March, but recorded before the Commons attack on Smith, in which Major said be would even be willing to delay the British objective of enlargement to get his way on the twenty-three votes.[118]

Hurd, conscious of the difficulties that lay ahead at Ioannina, was upset and worried when he heard what had been said in the House on the Tuesday. The next day, he and Major had a thirty-minute meeting in Downing Street, exploring a possible compromise. But Cabinet on Thursday 24 March 'officially' decided against any such compromise, though Hurd let slip to *Independent Television News* that he had been given some flexibility and room for manoeuvre, a line amplified in leaks to the press.[119] Just before leaving for Ioannina, Hurd gave a speech, described as 'gloomy and irritable', to the Conservative Central Council meeting in Plymouth on Friday,[120] in which he made clear his distaste for '*Britannia contra mundum* – Britain against Europe – [which] cannot in our saner moments be our rallying cry', and went on to rail against the 'divisive nonsense' within the party over Europe, which was 'yesterday's game. Those are yesterday's battered toys.'[121]

Hurd flew off to Greece determined to achieve his best deal: 'I didn't have any officials with me, just my private secretary, so I didn't have any back-up,' he later recalled. 'It is a very remote spot. Communications were not that good.'[122] Britain found itself friendless, despite all the respect for Hurd personally, with foreign ministers arguing that Britain had even been prepared to delay enlargement to achieve its ends. His back to the wall, Hurd came away with the best deal he could secure – what became known as the 'Ioannina compromise', a complex formula which gave to any member states whose votes totalled between twenty-three and twenty-six the concession that the Council would do 'all in its power', within a 'reasonable time' to reach an acceptable solution. Hurd had to fight hard to achieve it, but when he told Major about it after his return on Sunday, the Prime Minister was gloomy, knowing at once that it would be seen as a climbdown, as indeed it was played in Monday's newspapers.[123] To heighten the pressure, the other ten EU countries insisted that the British and Spanish governments confirmed their agreement of the Ioannina compromise by the Tuesday evening (29 March), or risk delaying enlargement for the four new entrants by up to one year.[124]

The fuss distracted attention from yet another keynote speech by Major, this time to the Plymouth Central Council meeting on Saturday 26 March. He defended the government's record, and told critics of his European policy to 'grow up', in a speech which contained 'little more than hopeful prediction'.[125] Worse, Heseltine's 'barnstorming' speech outshone his own, with the result that the Sunday papers reported widely on how the President of the Board of Trade had rehabilitated his leadership prospects.[126]

Heseltine had arrived in Plymouth in some style, by helicopter at midnight from Leeds, where, significantly, he had been addressing the constituency association of Giles Shaw, a member of the 1922 Committee Executive.[127] Andrew Marr reflected a common mood when he wrote 'the balance of probability is that Michael Heseltine will be Prime Minister by the end of the year ... Clarke, who only a few months ago seemed unchallengeable as the crown prince, has been losing ground fast to Mr Heseltine.'[128] Number Ten did not think that Heseltine was actively plotting, though as one aide put it, 'He is rather like a professional lady, strutting the boards, setting out his stall.' Any suggestion that he could actually do the job, however, was dismissed as mistaken as 'his health is not up to it'.[129]

At this point Major found himself locked into a crisis with his staunchest supporter in Cabinet, Hurd. He did not want to accept Hurd's Ioannina compromise. Loyalists claimed that Major himself would have achieved more had he, as at Maastricht and Edinburgh, not Hurd, been in the lead. The newspapers on Monday morning were not sympathetic: a leader in *The Times* said that nothing could be worse for Major than for him to be seen 'as a latter-day Grand Old Duke of York, marching his troops to the top of the hill, and marching them down again',[130] a phrase to be recycled about Major's leadership *ad nauseam*. Hurd gave a polished defence of the compromise in an emergency Commons session to discuss the issue on Monday afternoon. But 'the mood was turning black' as one Tory official remarked, and whips began to report very deep anger at what was being seen – however positively it was sold by Hurd – as a sell-out. Marcus Fox relayed to Number Ten the sinister atmosphere among MPs in a hope of stiffening Cabinet's resolve to reject the compromise when it debated the issue the next day in special session, called so the government could give the EU its response in advance of the 5 p.m. deadline that evening.[131] Major spent much of the rest of Monday seeing individual Cabinet ministers, testing the water.[132]

By that night Major was still reluctant to accept the compromise, even if it meant that Hurd would resign in the summer; he was too loyal to have resigned immediately.[133] He spoke to Hurd that evening on the phone, and invited him to talk before the Cabinet on Tuesday. Hurd found Major's mood was despondent. A crisis point had been reached. With no agreement between them, Major suggested calling in the Chancellor of the Exchequer. To Major's surprise, and disappointment, he heard Clarke say that he thought they should back the Foreign Secretary's judgement.[134]

The mood in the ensuing Cabinet was sombre. Hurd opened by explaining the compromise, and saying that in his judgement it was not now possible to obtain any improvement or further significant concessions. Major said that Hurd's negotiating position at Ioannina had been weakened by the leaks about his ability to compromise, and again he offered the floor to ministers, encouraging all to express a view. Ministers later spoke of 'great tension' at this moment, as opponents of Hurd's deal could have held out and split the Cabinet.[135] Howard led the criticism of the deal, suggesting they reject it, and proposing a special summit of the EU's twelve prime ministers and presidents. Portillo and Lilley both supported Howard. Redwood was even more outspoken, coming back a second time to question the promise given as part of the deal not to impose the Social Chapter on workers' rights on Britain.[136]

It became clear that these four were the only ministers to oppose Hurd's position. Those who supported the compromise, including Clarke and Hurd, were clearly predominant, and Major summed up by saying they would accept the compromise, insisting emphatically that every member of the government supported the Foreign Secretary.[137] Howard, Lilley and Portillo were all willing to defend the Cabinet's decision in public, though Redwood let his opposition be known the next day when confronted by a BBC camera crew.[138] But leaks were soon made to the media about the anti-compromise position taken by the three other sceptics in Cabinet. It was shortly after this that a senior Cabinet Office official decried the lack of loyalty and the leakiness of this Cabinet.[139]

Major was left to defend the line in the House that afternoon. In these circumstances, he often reached within himself to find inner strength. On this occasion he could not manage it. He put up a staunch defence, admitting that the government had not achieved all it sought, but it had still obtained some valuable concessions. Little impression was made by his overtures on a deeply sceptical House. The opposition possessed all the cards: Smith said it had been a humiliating climbdown and mocked his 'vainglorious assertion of no surrender', while Paddy Ashdown said he had made rather 'a fool' of himself.[140] Worse by far came from a Conservative, Tony Marlow, who said the experience showed the Prime Minister had no credible policy on Europe, and he should 'make way for somebody else who can provide the party and the country with direction and leadership'.[141] It was the first time since 1963 that a Tory backbencher had called on the Prime Minister to resign. But when ultraloyalist Peter Emery tried to come to Major's support saying that he had the support of his backbenches, there was almost complete silence. Many of those backbenchers who normally supported him could not bring themselves to let their support be known, and Major knew it.

Major jabbed back hard at Marlow. An aide later commented, 'I don't think Tony Marlow gets to him. Marlow is clearly in barking mad territory.'[142]

Many Tory MPs felt that Marlow was 'beyond the pale', but the wound left a deep mark on the Prime Minister.[143] With Westminster awash with Tory MPs saying they now believed that Major could not survive,[144] Major returned to Downing Street that evening, his mood bleak. To make matters worse it was his fifty-first birthday. Some of those close to him described it as his 'absolute nadir'.[145] A birthday cake, drinks and an impromptu party were held in the Cabinet Room for Number Ten staff. Norma rallied everyone present. 'How long have we been here now, three and a half years?' she asked. 'When do we overtake Ted Heath?' 'She was absolutely magnificent,' recalled one of the guests. 'She made it absolutely clear that they were there for the duration and no one would budge them. It was one of the times one saw how sensible, acerbic and tough she really was.'[146]

The press the following morning was as bad as after Black Wednesday. *The Times* said in its editorial that 'John Major is closer than ever to the Downing Street back door', and went on to consider the leadership challengers, as did much of Fleet Street.[147] With Heseltine reinstated as the frontrunner against Clarke, the latter said on Wednesday night, 'I intend to succeed John Major when he, of his own volition, goes.' Rees-Mogg wrote that only twice in his life had he seen a Prime Minister inspire so little confidence, Eden after Suez in 1956 and Wilson after devaluation in 1967, and on neither occasion 'did the withdrawal of confidence seem so absolute, or last so long'.[148]

The departure of MPs on Thursday 31 March for the Easter recess brought temporary respite. That day, Major's position was further undermined by a MORI poll published in *The Times* showing Labour on 49 per cent and the Conservatives on just 28 per cent.[149] That weekend's *Sunday Times* conducted a poll of one hundred Tory MPs, out of which Heseltine emerged as the clear front-runner.[150] Various moves to arrest the Heseltine bandwagon emerged over the Easter recess, by Clarke's supporters as well as by the right wing. Portillo's backers flew a kite about their man being perhaps willing to serve as Heseltine's Chancellor, as the autumn before they had floated a 'dream ticket' with Clarke. But the word from on high was that their champion was not yet ready. Lady Thatcher let it be known 'privately' that another divisive leadership election would be a mistake – at this time.[151]

It was the most comfort Major had that Easter. The QMV episode had been an unmitigated disaster. Internationally, it damaged Britain's standing in the eyes of her EU partners, who were irritated at her letting domestic politics interfere with one of her long-stated objectives, enlargement.[152] On top of *The Economist* article the previous September, it lowered the opinion some heads of government had for Major personally. But the greatest damage was domestically. Hurd described it as 'the worst episode' during his time as Major's Foreign Secretary.[153] It was the most serious difference between both men, though their relationship swiftly recovered. Major's authority with his party did not heal so quickly. Now the Europhiles were disillusioned as well as the Eurosceptics; both were united in seeing his handling of the affair as uncertain. Now more than ever before he was engaged in a struggle for survival.

Local Difficulties

The five weeks after Easter were dominated by the local elections on 5 May, and by the leadership speculation surrounding the prospects of three Cabinet front-runners, Clarke, Heseltine and Portillo. The two currents interacted: the worse it appeared the government would perform in the local elections, the more febrile became the succession game. Within Number Ten, the atmosphere was one of grim determination, remembered with little affection by those who lived through it as a time when nothing seemed to go the Prime Minister's way.[154]

Tactics for the local elections and European election had been discussed in Political Cabinets on 20 January and 24 February. Norman Fowler presented Party polling evidence to show that it would be an uphill struggle, and ministers decided they would have to go 'all out' to restore confidence in the government.[155] On 3 April an NOP poll in the *Independent on Sunday* gave Labour a twenty-four point lead (50–26) over the Conservatives.[156] Two more Tory MPs now joined Marlow in his call for Major to stand down, John Carlisle and Nicholas Fairbairn, the latter detracting from the gravitas of his attack by saying, 'He is *vin ordinaire* and he should be château-bottled.'[157]

Against this background, Major concluded that he should take a higher profile. At the official launch at Central Office of the local election campaign on Wednesday 6 April, Fowler duly announced that the Prime Minister would be touring all the main target regions. The press interpreted this as part of a carefully thought-out strategy for the Prime Minister to take personal charge of the campaign, investing it with a coherence and prominence that had never been fully intended. Number Ten and Central Office were not unhappy at that construction.[158] At the same time, party officials were keen to emphasise that the focus of campaigning in the local elections would be on issues of local concern, and that they should not be seen as a referendum on Major's leadership or the performance of the Party nationally – a forlorn hope.

Fowler tried to stoke up morale by announcing that the Party had assembled the largest team ever to fight a local election, with every minister drafted in for regional tours, daily press conferences, and all Tory MPs instructed to 'pull their weight'. Saatchi & Saatchi, which still held the Tory account, were to be 'closely involved' throughout. The Party Chairman was in confident mood, predicting a net gain in the election – for a third of the seats on district councils in England and Wales, twelve Scottish councils and thirty-two London boroughs.[159] His forecast, against the run of the opinion polls, was based on the fact that most of the seats in contention had last been fought in 1990, at the height of the poll tax controversy, when the Party was unpopular at local level, and hence performed very poorly. It was thus not unreasonable to think that from a low base, the Party would make up ground. To achieve that end, the Conservatives opened the battle with a party political broadcast ridiculing Labour-controlled councils in London and the West Midlands for wasting money, not least on 'mobile phones for gravediggers and recycling paper clips'.[160]

Major's personal tours sought to emulate his visits during the general election two years before. Once out electioneering, he was in ebullient form, beating the drums of Labour extravagance and the improving economy. But the crowds were smaller than had been hoped, and their ardour less. Party activist reports to Central Office painted a picture of voter apathy, and discontent with the performance of the national party. Worse, the attempt to focus on local issues was repeatedly undermined by a succession of episodes that damaged the government's national standing. Good stories for the government, such as inflation reported as the lowest for decades (16 April), or hopes of economic recovery (21 April) were eclipsed by Party discontent, not least at the disappearance of long-established military regiments.

The government's reputation for expertise on military matters was further knocked in mid-April over its preparations for the fiftieth anniversary of the D-Day landings in Normandy that June. Major was keen on the event being appropriately commemorated, but the anniversary became enmeshed in controversy. The press, thoroughly alienated from the government, seized on any error of judgement and blew it up into further evidence of an incompetent administration. A 'spam fritter' competition thus became the emblem of a crass government willing insensitively to cash in on recent history involving widespread loss of life to boost its flagging reputation. When popular folk hero Dame Vera Lynn publicly criticised the plans, Major had had enough. He decided to bring in Lord Cranborne, a junior minister in the Lords, to take control of proceedings and thereby defused the mini-crisis.[161] Some well-grounded suggestions were even made that Cranborne had been involved in whipping up the 'spam fritter' fuss to secure sole control over the anniversary.[162] Anyway, by then it was too late to prevent the government's image being tarnished.

European battles of more recent vintage erupted later in the month. A visit to London by Chancellor Kohl on 27 April produced little for the government to boast of diplomatically, but provided a catalyst for divisions in the party to come to the surface. Lord Young of Graffham, the former Cabinet minister and favourite of Lady Thatcher, chose the day of Kohl's visit to announce that Britain was 'wasting its time in the EC'. The next day, the *Sun* claimed Major was contemplating a referendum on withdrawal if the 1996 Inter-governmental Conference proved unacceptable to the government. 'Completely bogus and dishonest' was Number Ten's opinion. The *Daily Telegraph* responded with an article claiming that 'the fragile truce' on Europe within the Party had been destroyed,[163] while Tory Eurosceptics began openly canvassing the option of an eventual British withdrawal and a referendum on a single currency, the next big issue over which the European battle in the Tory Party would be waged.[164]

The Sunday papers on 1 May, the last weekend before polling, reverberated with the debate within the Party, which was fanned still further that very day when Portillo in an interview on GMTV overrode government policy by insisting that Britain would never sign up to a single currency. These remarks followed a speech ten days before which was seen as a veiled attack on Major's consensual style of leadership.

Portillo's television remarks were seen as going too far, breaching the doctrine of collective Cabinet responsibility, where all ministers refrain from criticising agreed government policy, in this case on the single currency. Major, although angry, decided against sacking him because of the damage it might do to Party unity as well as to his own position at such a volatile time.[165] Instead, the errant Chief Secretary was given a dressing down by Clarke on 3 May, while Major rebuked him during a difficult Prime Minister's Questions the same day.[166] But Portillo, though he apologised, felt that similar deviations from the government line by pro-Europeans had gone unpunished. He and his supporters did not forget the humiliation.

As polling day approached, Fowler's prediction of gains appeared wildly optimistic. Opinion polls showed no improvement in the government's popularity over the month-long campaign – quite the reverse. A MORI poll in *The Times* on 28 April confirmed the Tories' rating at 26 per cent, its lowest ever.[167] To Major's chagrin, the Conservative councillors in his own Lambeth Council discouraged him from visiting the borough. Peter Evans, deputy leader of the Tory group, said, 'We cannot afford to have John Major come here. It would backfire.'[168]

David Evans, rapidly becoming a leader of the backbench critics, said there were 'perhaps fifty' Tory MPs who 'still would not accept' Major's leadership 'at any price', and urged him to sack Fowler as Party Chairman, six Cabinet ministers, his 'kitchen Cabinet' and other advisers in Number Ten. John Patten, embroiled in conflicts with teachers, and Virginia Bottomley, who was causing widespread disquiet with her plans to close St Bartholomew's as part of her plan to rationalise London's hospitals, were two popular targets for Tory ire. As Don Macintyre observed, Evans's salvo startled MPs, not least because his 'estimate of 50 dissidents exceeds by 16 the number required under party rules to force a leadership contest this November'.[169] With John Carlisle also openly admitting in public that a significant number of Tory MPs hoped for a heavy defeat in the local elections as it would provide the impetus for them to get rid of Major, the Praetorian Guard launched their counter-attack.[170] Hurd, Garel-Jones, Archer and Gillian Shephard all spoke up strongly for Major, but the last was to fuel leadership speculations even further. In her attack on those campaigning for the 'two Michaels' (Heseltine and Portillo), she confirmed to the world beyond Westminster that such campaigning was indeed taking place.[171]

Major worked at Number Ten during polling day on Thursday 5 May, and that night watched the results on the television in the top floor flat with Jonathan Hill, his assistant George Bridges and Graham Bright.[172] Major tried to put a brave face on the results, but there was no disguising their awfulness for the Party. The Tories had a net loss of 429 seats, the Party recording its worst national result of the century, with just 27 per cent of the vote (equivalent to the Liberal Democrats', and in contrast to Labour's 40 per cent share). No Conservative councillors at all were elected in some cities, including Manchester, Newcastle and Oxford, and in Basildon the party was wiped out. Although the Party retained Westminster and Wandsworth, it lost control of Croydon and Enfield. Birmingham was comfortably held by Labour, which gained middle-class Edgbaston; other core bourgeois citadels were also lost to the Party, notably Tunbridge Wells and Worthing. Major's personal prominence during the campaign served further to channel blame onto him.

Major awoke early on the Friday morning. Listening to the radio shortly after the 7 a.m. news, he was startled to hear John Carlisle on BBC's *Today* programme offering himself as a stalking horse candidate in a leadership election: 'If I do not force an election, others will,' he declared.[173] As feared, a bad result would indeed cause deep problems. After hearing Carlisle, Major conferred with Chris Meyer. They decided it would be better for him to seize the initiative himself, or the media would hound him relentlessly until he responded to Carlisle's challenge.[174] So Major appeared on the steps of Downing Street at 9 a.m., to deliver a sombre but unequivocal message before leaving for the official opening of the Channel Tunnel. He conceded candidly that the election losses were the result of national, not local factors, including 'deep bruises' from the recession and Party disunity – the admission, he hoped, would draw some sting from Party activists' anger. A leadership challenge in the autumn, he then acknowledged, was quite proper under Party rules, but he declared, 'I will meet a challenge whenever it comes.'[175]

Carlisle provided the catalyst for Major to throw down the gauntlet. But it was his own Cabinet ministers, Heseltine, Clarke and Portillo, who were the serious threat to his leadership. All three would no doubt declare their loyalty to Major, and how they would never stand in a first round ballot against him. Reports were widespread of discontented MPs lobbying for the thirty-four votes needed to trigger an election, at which a stalking horse candidate would come forward and acquire enough votes against Major to make a second round heavyweight challenger an inevitability.

The *Sunday Telegraph* that weekend listed five such possible stalking horses apart from Carlisle – Baker, Biffen, Lamont and Leigh, as well as, ominously for Major, an 'unknown Cabinet minister'.[176] Heseltine retained his place as the favourite after the local elections. On Channel 4 the day following the results he spoke warmly of Portillo's spell as his deputy at the Environment Department in 1990–2, called him 'extremely able' and said 'I get on extremely well with him.' Coupled with Heseltine's refusal to condemn Portillo for his remarks on the single currency, this was interpreted as Heseltine keeping afloat the balanced ticket with Portillo in the hope of uniting both wings of the party.[177] With opinion polls still placing him as favourite to succeed in a leadership election it was to prove the high noon of Heseltine's leadership prospects.[178] But his star was shortly to wane, as Clarke's, mired by presentational errors in economic policy and refusal to trim more to the right, had waned earlier in the spring.

Portillo remained the only serious challenger from the right of the Party in the first half of 1994. His carefully crafted interview appearances and speeches kept his profile high and reminded the right of his soundness – on Europe, finance and public morals. 'He behaved like a man with an acute sense of his own destiny,' wrote Andrew Grice in the *Sunday Times*.[179] Two keynote speeches had made a particular mark: in January, when he spoke of a 'new British disease' of 'the self-destructive sickness of national cynicism', and in April, when he spoke up for the 'still small voice of Britain's quiet majority' which wanted the government off their backs. Portillo's motives were double-barrelled: putting his marker down lest Major fall that autumn, and putting his name at the head of the pack of putative right-wing challengers after the general election. With his remarks on the single currency on 1 May, all the more audacious as he was leading the party's local election campaign in London, he realised he had gone too far, though, as Simon Heffer wrote, 'Most of Mr Portillo's faction regarded his remarks about the single currency as wonderful, and an act of long-overdue leadership.'[180]

Portillo's relationship with Major was at its lowest ebb during the 1994 local election campaign. They had worked together reasonably successfully until Black Wednesday. But the events of that day had a profound effect on Portillo. Not just did he feel resentful as a Cabinet – and Treasury – minister that he had been excluded from the events of the day; he also felt it peculiarly personally as a national humiliation. His followers were divided over the merits of a 'devil's pact' with Heseltine, but most concluded that Portillo's youth (aged forty) and comparative inexperience would count against him if there was to be an early leadership campaign, so perhaps a Faustian pact was the best option.

No direct challenge to Major's leadership, however, was to follow the local election débâcle – from any quarter. Major's prompt Downing Street assertion of his intention to fight helped rally support and won grudging praise.[181] A consensus emerged in Party circles by the weekend that it would be better to await the results of the Euro-elections on 9 June before deciding on a challenge. With Major again leading the Party's campaign from the front, the election would inevitably again be seen as a reflection of his personal standing. Michael Jones wrote, 'The private opinion of senior Tories I have consulted this weekend is that Major will not survive a week if the Euro-elections are as bad as they expect.'[182] But before polling day for the European Parliament arrived, an event was to occur which transformed the entire political landscape.

TWENTY-NINE

A Kinder Summer:

May–September 1994

'I FELT LIKE we were granted a one month's stay of execution,'[1] said one insider after the local elections, with four weeks leading up to the European elections on 9 June in which to improve performance at the polls or face a near-certain leadership challenge in the autumn. The week after the local elections remained uncomfortable, with Labour mounting a sustained attack on the conduct of Nicholas Scott, the long-serving Minister of State at Social Security, over his handling of the Disability Bill. No let-up seemed in sight. Then, shortly after 8 a.m. on Thursday 12 May, exactly a week after the local elections, a message was picked up by the Number Ten police over their radio network: John Smith had suffered a heart attack.

Death of a Leader: May

The Private Office told Major, who was stunned, as Smith's health had recently been good. Alex Allan promptly phoned Murray Elder, Smith's private secretary, who had not heard the news.[2] Quickly they learned that Smith's heart attack, in the bathroom of his flat in London's Barbican, was life-threatening.

Smith's first heart attack more than five years earlier had warned of his vulnerability, and though he had refused to lighten his load, there were no indications that a repetition was likely. Doctors and paramedics battled to revive him on the ambulance journey to St Bartholomew's Hospital, but at 9.15 a.m. he was pronounced dead.[3] Major had been preparing for Cabinet and Prime Minister's Questions when the confirmation came into Downing Street. He was much moved and became very thoughtful, asking to be left alone for a few minutes.[4] Cabinet ministers learned about the heart attack while assembling in the anteroom outside the Cabinet Room. Major called them in and announced, with deep regret, that the Labour leader had died. He told them he had decided that the Commons should be adjourned as a mark of respect. All present readily concurred, and agreed that a public statement should be issued recording their united deep sadness at the news. The mood in Cabinet, witnesses recall, was very sombre and shocked.[5] However, the more politically astute were already realising, as one senior civil servant put it, that Major was 'lucky' and that the tragedy would spare him an immediate leadership challenge.

Major decided that questions that afternoon in the House should be abandoned. In their place were to be tributes. In a chamber where many MPs did not conceal their tears, Speaker Betty Boothroyd, her voice breaking with emotion, used the standard form of words to declare, 'I regret to have to report to the House the death of the Right Honourable John Smith QC, Member for Monklands East.'[6] Major then spoke. He had already won respect for his decision to suspend proceedings, and Labour listened all the more solemnly as he delivered one of his best-judged and most moving parliamentary performances:

John Smith was one of the outstanding parliamentarians of modern politics. Even for those against whom those skills were deployed, it is hard to bear that we will never see or hear those skills in this House again ... When I think of his premature death, I shall think of the waste that it has brought to our public life; the waste of a remarkable political talent; the waste of a high and honourable ambition to lead our country; and the waste of a man who in all his actions retained the human touch.[7]

His language may not have been Churchillian, but he spoke from the heart, and often extempore, and he judged the mood perfectly. So, too, did Matthew Parris capture a mood when he wrote next day about the sad ending to 'the coincidence of [having] two more decent political leaders than our political system has thrown together for decades'.[8]

Major spoke warmly in his tribute of his 'frequent' behind-the-scenes conversations with the Labour leader to discuss political business. They would share a drink: 'sometimes tea, sometimes not'.[9] But in reality their relationship was never as friendly as Major understandably painted it that Thursday afternoon. Major had regarded Kinnock as basically a decent man, who was harshly treated by the media, but who struggled. For Smith he had much more respect as Leader of the Opposition, and he liked him personally, though he had become affronted by his harping on about sleaze during the last few months. Number Ten believed that Labour had deliberately set out after 1992 to discredit Major's reputation for trustworthiness; Major himself thought that much of it made the Labour leadership guilty of humbug.[10] There was little love for Smith on the political side of Number Ten. One noted, 'Smith's death saw him achieve a standing he never achieved in his life.'[11] Smith had not turned out to be as effective at Question Time as Number Ten had feared, though he proved better in debate than they had anticipated. The Number Ten Political Office even had to ask the Whips' Office to discourage backbenchers from intervening in Smith's speeches, because he would invariably turn such interventions to his advantage.[12]

One Number Ten aide described the thought process that flashed through all their minds after hearing the news of Smith's death:

Our first thought was, 'How awful, a man only in his mid-50s.' Another second later the next thought followed, 'Well, that's stuffed Hezza then' – a moment of satisfaction. But then a new idea struck. 'Oh my God, it'll let Tony Blair in. He'll be even more difficult.' It's what we all thought.[13]

Heseltine was certainly jolted by the widespread comment that Smith's second and fatal heart attack diminished his own chances of reaching the highest office. In interviews on Sunday, which could be viewed as in poor taste, he insisted that his own heart attack in Venice would not be an obstacle to his succeeding.[14] The apprehensions about the identity and potential of Smith's successor were also well grounded. Central Office was even more pessimistic about the long-term prospects than Number Ten. They had not rated Smith's performance as leader as highly, and had written a paper in 1993 arguing that he would be challenged for the leadership the next year. It also struck them as 'absolutely obvious' that Blair would now step into his shoes, and would cause the government far greater problems than ever Smith had achieved.[15]

Major's immediate task was to rethink what had been planned as a hard-hitting speech for the Scottish Conservative Party Conference at Inverness on the following Friday evening. Designed to launch the European election campaign, his text contained direct attacks on Smith personally, and on Labour's European policy for planning to sign away the national veto. With the speech to be given, moreover, in Smith's home country, Scotland, Major was emphatic that he had to deliver essentially an apolitical message. With twenty-four hours' notice the text was heavily rewritten, even as they journeyed northwards. But in a passage whose words and sentiments were his own, Major said:

The reaction to John's death tells us much about our country. It shows the priceless asset of the essential decency of the British. We can weep for a good man, even as opponent, because we recognise his qualities. This reminds us that there are things higher than politics and across all divisions, common bonds of humanity that unite us ... I often have little taste for the politics of point scoring or for belittling others. I have none today. I care passionately for what I believe in, but I don't care passionately for damning what other people believe in ... Sometimes I feel – and I don't only mean in the reporting of politics – that there is too much knocking, too much carping, too much sneering.[16]

The media latched on to his theme to suggest Major was exploiting the mood of mourning to speak to his own Party tormentors. There was an element of that. But it also spoke deeply of a powerful strand in Major's political outlook – no less real for his not always following it – to be consensual, and in his essentially unideological approach to politics to strive to find common ground with the opposition. Not all politics was exorcised from the Inverness speech. It contained a powerful defence of the government's record since the 1992 general election on the economy, on education and on fighting crime; it also told critics to suspend their judgement for the next three years – when he fully intended to remain as Prime Minister – until his programme was complete. On Europe, he advocated a 'middle way' between Eurosceptic and Europhile positions. 'Europe is absolutely fundamental to this country's national interest. We cannot turn our backs on that.'[17]

Major returned to Scotland with Norma a week later for John Smith's funeral at Cluny Parish Church in Edinburgh on Friday 20 May. The following day, Smith's body was laid to rest in a private ceremony on the Western island of Iona, a place he favoured during his life. Major's return trip from Edinburgh was enlivened by the presence of Tony Benn, to whom he offered a seat on the private plane because Benn had missed his own flight. Benn was talkative, and Major, still full of the spirit of cross-party harmony, was entertained by his company; 'There's a man who never makes personal attacks on people,' Major told Norma.[18] He had also begun to sense that the tide of political fortune was beginning to run again in his direction.

Euro Elections: May–June

Major was later to claim that the European elections went much better than the local elections 'because we had a campaign and there was substance. There was also interest, because people thought we would be completely wiped out.'[19] There is something in this view. Together with the fillip of Labour being distracted with its own leadership concerns and resulting adjustments, a new sense of purpose was evident at Number Ten and Central Office.

Lessons had been learned by the Tories from their poor 1989 European campaign, when the Party appeared disunited and suffered badly in the polls. Major and Fowler were adamant that, above all with the temperature so recently raised by the QMV row, all elements of the Party had to remain in step. A preliminary statement to align Cabinet on Europe had been agreed and circulated earlier in the year.[20] Planning for the election had been under way for many months. A strategy committee, chaired by Fowler, had met first on 14 June 1993, initially at monthly intervals, then weekly, and daily once the campaign proper began. Composed of MEPs and party officials from Number Ten, Central Office, the FCO and the party's National Union, it had heated debates on the substance and tone to be adopted. The MEPs, led by Christopher Prout, managed to prevent the adoption of the negative 'diet of Brussels' line of 1989, though a principal thrust of the Conservative campaign was still to be on the absence of any veto on EMU and on the Social Chapter in their opponents' policies.[21]

A further committee, to draft the manifesto, had met from October 1993 to February 1994 under the chairmanship of Douglas Hurd. So overtly 'political', with no civil service presence, officials even refused to serve its members tea paid from taxpayers' money when it met in the FCO.[22] While Eurosceptics such as Tim Collins and Andrew Lansley from Central Office, and sceptic FCO minister David Heathcoat-Amory and PPS David Martin were included, care had been taken by Hurd, to the right's mounting suspicion, to exclude more extreme Eurosceptic members. They need not have worried unduly: the document produced was cautious, so anxious were the Europhile drafters to avoid inflaming divisions. Ammunition was to be directed at the idea of a centralised European superstate, but not at the word 'federal' or at European institutions, which would have placed Tory MEPs in difficulties in the EU and upset Europhiles at home.

'Major trusted Douglas totally to get on with the job,' recalled Maurice Fraser, the secretary of the committee and chief drafter of the manifesto.[23] Not until early April did Major see the 18,000-word draft, when it was examined by a committee including Hurd, Clarke, Howard and Heseltine. Major liked the draft, but thought it too long and charged Sarah Hogg with giving it more of a campaigning edge.[24] Rumours circulated that the manifesto was being given a Eurosceptic wash, but it was the background history and padding that she excised while the policy line remained unchanged, some window-dressing notwithstanding, added to placate Eurosceptic hyper-sensitivities.[25]

The final document of 12,000 words was discussed at a Political Cabinet on local election polling day, 5 May. As part of the drive to mend relations between MEPs and the party at Westminster, which had been unsatisfactory for at least five years previously, Prout was in attendance. Howard had taken upon himself the role of tribune of the Eurosceptic right, and was particularly argumentative, but Major, in unusually authoritative form in Cabinet, gave firm instructions that all the Cabinet were to unite behind the reworked manifesto.[26]

The right, sensing that Major had already moved, wanted to give one last heave, not least to emphasise further an attractive campaigning difference on Europe with Labour. But Major would not be persuaded. *A Strong Britain in a Strong Europe* was duly published shortly after the Cabinet, the title indicative of the careful balancing act undertaken by the drafters. With a foreword from Major, and an afterword by Prout, it was short on commitments. But it did at least provide a platform on which the Party could, to the extent it ever would, unite on Europe.

Major, even more deliberately than for the local elections, and despite the mixed success of his involvement, led the Conservative campaign from the front. The contrast with 1989, when Mrs Thatcher had only campaigned on two days, and appeared at only two press conferences, was deliberate.[27] Smith's death delaying the campaign's start for a week led to Major being even more ready for the fight. As he knew, even with Smith's death, his own survival to some extent still hinged on the results.

Major's own campaign was more focused than in 1992; his aides felt they had to strike a balance between the way that campaign hustings renewed Major's energy and the risk of wearing him out with a long tour. Major took the deliberate risk of running a high-profile personal campaign, knowing that he would take the blame if it was a disaster. His gut feeling for elections, that only deserted him in 1997, told him that it was going to be better than expected and that he would earn credit, not blame, for the outcome.

Despite his 'don't push it' message to the Eurosceptics in Cabinet on 5 May, the Euro campaign was to mark another key staging post in Major's slow boat journey towards Euroscepticism, with the 1993 *Economist* article a key port on his voyage. On the eve of the campaign he repeated the 'middle way' line of his Inverness speech to the *Independent*: 'I'm not going to get into the "Eurosceptic" or "Euro-enthusiast" argument. I am a Euro-realist. I think that is the position of most people in the country.'[28] But Major's definition of his middle way, or 'Euro-realism', became more sceptical over the Euro campaign. The shift in his position was in part a sop to his right wing, as well as a calculated bid to entice disaffected Tory voters back to the polling booth. He was, after all, fighting for his political survival, and it was easier for him to change course once the campaign was in progress, and the delicate balancing of the various constituencies and the policy groups was over. But there was more to it than just that. As Hurd put it:

John Major's own experience was turning him in a sceptical direction, especially on a single currency. The more he read and thought about it, the less likely and desirable he thought it was. On the other hand, although he felt increasingly sympathetic with that kind of scepticism, he was increasingly fed up with the Eurosceptics in his party. He had no time for them.[29]

Major himself later acknowledged his increased scepticism over his premiership, seeing Britain's leaving the ERM as the turning point.[30]

A sceptical tone was evident on his first tour of the campaign, to the West Country, culminating in an evening speech on Monday 23 May in Bristol. Keynote speeches, often drafted by Nick True and Ronnie Millar, were chosen as a major plank in his personal campaign strategy. Major delivered a frontal attack on Labour and Liberal Democrat policy on the veto for their failure to offer adequate safeguards for Britain's prerogatives in Europe. He told his audience that:

This British nation has a monarchy founded by the kings of Wessex over 1,100 years ago. A parliament and universities formed over 700 years ago, a language with its roots in the mists of time ... I cannot believe that the people of the West Country would vote in the election for a party whose central belief on Europe is to dilute our national identity.

His peroration was even more unashamedly patriotic:

I must say that I never leave Britain without the spirits sinking just a little. And it always lifts the heart to set foot here once again ... I believe this is still the best country in the world in which to live ... our most basic belief is the integrity of the nation.[31]

The Party's opening election broadcast was also screened that evening.

With nostalgic images of English countryside and Britain's 'heritage' – a castle, a steam train – and the strains of Purcell's music, it became clear that the nationalist card was being played hard, albeit in rhetoric.

Major's 'kingdom of Wessex' established a pattern for the campaign, with Labour and Liberal Democrats being forced to react to the Tories' agenda. That Friday, the *Bristol Evening News* carried an interview conducted with Major when he had been in the city on the Monday. Achieving one of its biggest ever scoops, the local paper recorded Major saying, 'The problem about begging is as old as the hills. It is very offensive to many people.' The interviewer asked him whether he found beggars an 'eye-sore',[32] to which he responded 'yes'.

Number Ten had known begging was a local issue in the Bristol area, and had asked the Home Office for a briefing; the remarks were pre-planned to that extent, but Major's expression of his personal view was off the cuff.[33] The weekend media, however, invested them with a significance that he had never intended, portraying them as an attempt to steer the agenda onto the domestic front in order to distract attention from Tory divisions over European policy.[34] While Major's comments certainly touched a chord with Conservative voters in the shires,[35] they also allowed Labour to portray Major as heartless, and upset some of the Tory Party's liberal supporters. The *Independent* nevertheless exaggerated when it portrayed the remarks as a turning away from Major's belief in 'Conservatism with a human face' and an abandonment of his 'One Nation' Toryism.[36] Portillo helped ensure the story remained high on the agenda by linking the begging issue to an attack on Labour's social security policy.

The media was still debating the merits of Major's remarks when, on Tuesday 31 May, he delivered an evening speech in Ellesmere Port, Cheshire, his most important policy statement on Europe during the campaign. Major employed a phrase held over from the week before so as not to become swallowed up in the manifesto launch:[37] 'multi-track, multi-speed, multi-layered Europe'. Hurd had spoken similarly of a 'multi-speed' Europe in a speech in Warsaw on 6 May, but had done so in a descriptive way. Now Major was using the terminology prescriptively, and the words were seized upon as potentially explosive, especially as Major's speech included a staunch attack on European centralisation. He concluded: 'Only the Conservatives are pledged unequivocally to stand up for our vital national interests by protecting our veto.'[38]

Added import was given by the speech being delivered on the same day as a summit between Kohl and Mitterrand in Mulhouse, the French Rhineland town, in which the two leaders discussed the future of the EU.[39] Major's Ellesmere Port speech, on the Mersey, was portrayed as his response on Britain's future progress in the EU. The speech had been drafted in Number Ten and was not shown to the FCO until late in the day. Unsurprisingly, it was less than happy, but the speech went down well with the right.[40] Tebbit referred to it as a 'turning point in this election' and one which would persuade many Conservative voters not to abstain (a big worry in Central Office).[41]

Europhiles were dismayed: Hugh Dykes, who accused Major of indulging in 'propaganda and fantasy', spoke for those who felt let down by what they saw as an increasingly negative campaign. But Hurd loyally came to the rescue, saying the speech had usefully refocused the discussion on European issues. Number Ten felt satisfied by the spotlight coming back onto the veto and the threat to the country posed by the opposition parties' policies on Europe.[42]

Number Ten was also happy that Tebbit, albeit grudgingly, was back on side. Long discussions had also taken place among the Party hierarchy about how to handle Lady Thatcher during the campaign. Her role was discussed at a meeting just before the first press conference in which Major asked how they should react if they were asked what she was planning to do during the campaign. No one knew. Fowler suggested they say she was playing an 'active role' in support of the candidates. Major asked what if she were abroad? Clarke chimed in suggesting they reply that she was playing an active role supporting the candidates abroad. Major was alone in failing to find the Chancellor's joke amusing.[43] They need not have worried about her intentions. The former Prime Minister, busy writing the second volume of her memoirs, was in fallow mode. Not until after the summer was she to stir again from her lair.

Major began to relax as the shortened, three-week campaign ground on. His spirits rose as always when on the beat, with six and a half days of the campaign spent on tour. On 1 June he spent a day visiting East Anglia, which included a closed meeting with selected Tory supporters, considered a successful evolution of the 'in-the-round' meetings during the general election. Another innovation was 'personalised' letters from Major to over one million target Tory voters.[44]

The tempo of the campaign was interrupted for three days, from 4 to 7 June, by celebrations to mark the fiftieth anniversary of D-Day. Major had been angered in the spring by the way that the government had been accused of trivialising and even demeaning history, but the fuss had all but died down since April.[45] The preparations proceeded smoothly under the oversight of Cranborne, who drafted in Lord Bramall, a former Chief of Defence Staff (1982–5), to help reassure veterans that their views would be taken into account.[46]

President Clinton flew over on Saturday 4 June, and held two hours of talks that morning at Chequers with Major, covering Bosnia, the conflict in Rwanda, and the forthcoming G7 Naples summit. It was Clinton's first visit to Chequers, and Major was pleased to reciprocate something of the hospitality of his highly personal spring visit to the US by showing the President around the house and, despite the rain, the grounds.[47] After a brief press conference they separated, Major to go to Portsmouth, flown there in 'a grotty helicopter that leaked', as 'Royalty had secured all the best helicopters'.[48] Despite the continuing rain, which led to the garden party that evening taking place indoors, Major, and the millions of his countrymen following the events in their homes, revelled in the atmosphere. He was moved by the veterans and the sense of occasion, and always enjoyed showing off Britain's historic places to full advantage.[49]

The next day, after seeing the ships putting out to sea from Southsea Common, Major boarded the royal yacht *Britannia*, in the company of the Queen, senior royals and over fifteen heads of state, including President Clinton, for a review of the ships. Clinton was duly ferried across the choppy waters to a US Navy boat, before *Britannia* steamed across to France. The mood on board was cheerful and nostalgic, and Major enjoyed having the chance to chat at some length to foreign leaders, including Paul Keating (Australia) and Jim Bolger (New Zealand).[50]

The anniversary day itself, Monday 6 June, was spent in France, with Mitterrand, nearing the end of his presidency, ordering lavish celebrations. The British government saw the affair as a 'huge PR opportunity' to build on the goodwill of the opening of the Channel Tunnel the month before and to remind the French of how vital had been the British involvement in the liberation of their country. Encouraged by British Ambassador Christopher Mallaby and his staff in Paris, regional papers across northern France carried special historical supplements.[51] Puffing the entente cordiale was only one of the gains of the celebrations, which were widely seen as appropriate and tasteful, confounding the initial sceptics.

Back in the fray on 7 June, Major's official day began with a combative interview on the Radio 4 *Today* programme with John Humphrys, and ended in London with another of the Party rallies in Hammersmith, with 500 loyal supporters packing the conference hall of the impersonal Novotel Hotel. The audience was kept waiting, listening to the standard fare of Henry Purcell's string music, and to Norman Fowler. Major rounded off a witty speech with an attack on Brussels, Delors, and the 'seven deadly sins' of Labour and Liberal Democrat policies on Europe. In a last-minute plea, he urged Tory voters not to stay at home, which would only allow 'a socialist majority at Strasbourg' to create a centralised federal state with high spending and taxes.[52]

A final press conference at Church House, Westminster, the last of three he chaired, saw him on his best form of the campaign. Rumours of reservations from John Gummer and other colleagues on the Eurosceptical campaign were swept aside. He reiterated his clear hope of seeing the EU succeed: 'I passionately hope it will.' He returned to the same theme throughout the last full day, spent in Yorkshire and giving further interviews.[53]

The European results were not to be declared until after voting had been completed in other EU countries on Sunday, so the first results to be announced were the five by-elections also being held on Thursday 9 June. Only one of the contests saw a seat defended by the Conservatives, Eastleigh, vacated as a result of Milligan's death, the loss of which reduced the government's majority to fifteen. The four other contests all witnessed a collapse of

Tory support, but the Eastleigh defeat, in a prosperous, safe, southern seat, utterly eclipsed them in scale. The Labour vote increased, while the Tories won just 25 per cent of the vote, falling from first to third in only the third such by-election result since the war (after Rochdale in 1958 and Brecon and Radnor in 1985). The *Sunday Times* called the by-election results 'the grimmest moment in Tory fortunes for 15 years'.[54]

Eastleigh was a moment of truth. Talk of a Labour landslide in a future general election, of his parliamentary party losing confidence in him, and of a large Cabinet reshuffle as his last remaining gambit, led to an anxious three days in Number Ten waiting for the European results.[55] Fighting messages were passed out about Major's intention to carry on at all costs, of his pride in his record to date, and his unique qualifications to lead the Party into the future.[56] But underneath there was apprehension, heightened by intelligence that George Gardiner was going around MPs collecting pledges from thirty-four of them to trigger an autumn leadership challenge.

Enormous relief was the reaction in Central Office and Number Ten when the news came through on Sunday evening that the Party had held eighteen seats in the Euro election.[57] Remarks by several commentators that the Party might only win three or four seats had been etched into their minds: eighteen seats could be sold by the Party's media team as a bonanza.[58] Never mind that it was the worst ever share of a vote recorded by a major party in a national election this century,[59] nor that Conservative majorities in five seats were less than 1 per cent, and in another nine less than 5 per cent, nor indeed that the Party lost almost half the thirty-two seats it had won in 1989. Disaster had been avoided, if only by a few hundred votes in key constituencies. Due to a poor Liberal Democrat performance, the Conservatives moved firmly back into second place. Eighteen seats was also comfortably above the figure cited in the press that Sunday as the minimum Major would have needed to avoid a leadership challenge.[60] As a leader in Tuesday's *Daily Telegraph* noted, Major had been granted a respite.[61] Several heavyweight commentators, including Anthony King and Peter Kellner, lent support to Major's cause, arguing on poll evidence that changing the leader was not the answer to Tory unpopularity.[62] The continuing evidence that the Tories would be unlikely to fare better under any other leader was to prove a significant factor in bolstering Major's position in the months to come.

The result was indeed not as bad as it might have been for the Tories, considering the disarray that preceded the campaign, as well as a stream of bad news that peppered it, including the Chinook helicopter crash which killed twenty-nine people including army, police and intelligence officers involved in counter-terrorism in Northern Ireland, and electorally sensitive reports that the gulf between rich and poor had grown over the last ten years. The competitiveness White Paper, launched on 24 May, was upstaged by a tabloid scare over a 'flesh-eating killer disease' which broke on the same day. Competitiveness was a particular obsession for Michael Heseltine. He had long been concerned with 'national efficiency' and had arranged for copies of the historian Correlli Barnett's *The Lost Peace* to be circulated to illustrate his point. His discomfort was met with mixed feelings in Number Ten, as it had been feared that he was trying to use competitiveness to grab control of the domestic agenda. Meanwhile, talk of a 'voteless economic recovery', as predicted by Sarah Hogg before Christmas, was prevalent.

The feeling in Downing Street on the Monday after the Euro results rose to one of near euphoria. Major thought that with another week in the campaign – the time lost due to Smith's death – another seven or eight seats might even have been won.[63] 'The Prime Minister's self-confidence came roaring back,' recalled a Number Ten official.[64] When chatting in Downing Street with aides that morning, with the sun pouring in through the windows, he seized on the idea of holding a press conference in the garden that afternoon.[65] He had been toying with such an idea since Meyer had become Press Secretary, and the success of his front door statement the morning after the local election results encouraged him to think the moment had come.

The press pack was bemused when the summons came to the back garden of Number Ten that afternoon, some speculating that Major would be announcing his resignation.[66] They duly trundled into a garden few had ever visited and sat down in the scorching heat on gilt chairs with red seats. Standing at a makeshift lectern before his shirt-sleeved audience, Major had, in Andrew Marr's words, 'no information of great moment to communicate',[67] bar his intention to remain in office. He answered questions for half an hour, appearing quite at peace with the world, a central part of the message he wished to convey. Before disappearing through the french windows back into the house, he offered advice for the man who had by now emerged as the certain Labour successor, Tony Blair: 'Don't believe what they say about you now … and don't believe what they say in eighteen months.' Major's conviction was that the media would turn on the new Labour leader after a honeymoon, just as they had turned on him. That the media did not act as he had predicted was to prove a heavy burden, but for the time being Major was riding high. After all, he had come through a hellish period to fight a campaign even his Party critics praised. And before the month was out, there would be further successes.

European Councils: June–July

With the Euro elections out of the way, the next big event on the European calendar was the choosing of a successor to Jacques Delors, President of the European Commission for the last ten years, to be decided at the summit on the island of Corfu over the weekend of 24–6 June. The front-running candidate was Jean-Luc Dehaene, the Belgian Prime Minister. Championed by Germany and France, Dehaene had emerged as their favoured candidate after Kohl and Mitterrand's Mulhouse summit on 31 May. But the right in Britain had pounced on Dehaene as too much a federalist, and the Eurosceptic press, typified by a scornful article by Nick Assinder headlined 'The Belgian Bruiser who will use his weight to rule Europe' in the *Daily Express*, ran a campaign against him.[68] His Belgian nationality and even his appearance counted further against him in Fleet Street and Westminster.[69]

For more rational reasons, Major's advisers counselled against Britain accepting Dehaene. John Kerr spoke out forcefully at a meeting at Number Ten on the morning of Saturday 11 June; Major, in morning suit in preparation for Trooping the Colour, was only too happy to concur that Dehaene must not be appointed.[70] Kerr was sent back to Brussels to inform the Belgians that their man was unacceptable to the British, and did so.[71] Cabinet's OPD committee met on 20 June and happily confirmed the outright rejection of Dehaene.[72] But Major, learning from the QMV experience, was careful in the week leading up to the Corfu Council not to raise expectations of success.

Major promoted the candidacy of Leon Brittan, the former Conservative Cabinet minister and one of Britain's two EC Commissioners. But opposition from the French, who resented Brittan's role over GATT, and from the powerful group of Socialist MPs in the European Parliament because of his lack of support for the Social Chapter, effectively undermined Brittan's prospects.[73] Major, however, remained quietly confident of his ability to block Dehaene as he flew to Corfu. He had breakfast with Silvio Berlusconi, the Italian Prime Minister and another opponent of Dehaene, to coordinate strategy before the dinner that evening where the succession was to be decided. Berlusconi, like Major and some other heads of government, resented the way that Kohl and Mitterrand had appeared bilaterally to have decided on Dehaene. With his own Eurosceptics and press at home goading him on to prove that his talk of a 'multi-speed' Europe was not just election posturing, Major knew he had to thwart the apparent Franco–German *fait accompli*.[74] The British delegation worked frantically throughout the day to stiffen opposition to the Dehaene candidacy.

Bonn and Paris countered with equally heavy behind-the-scenes diplomatic arm-twisting, which continued up to the last minute. Dehaene's team thought that Kerr was bluffing when he told them that Major would use his veto, but as the Prime Ministers assembled, it seemed that those countries opposing Dehaene, led by Britain and Italy, would lose the argument. When the leaders gathered for dinner at Corfu's grand Achilleion Palace, Dehaene was still the clear favourite.[75] Both Dehaene and Ruud Lubbers, the Dutch Prime Minister and the alternative front-running candidate, excused themselves from the meal to avoid embarrassment, sending their foreign ministers instead.

Andreas Papandreou, the frail seventy-six-year-old Greek Prime Minister and holder of the EU presidency, opened the discussion. As a way out of the impasse, he proposed each of the twelve countries nominate their preferred candidate. Kohl immediately protested that this was the wrong way to proceed, but Reynolds disagreed, and suggested they wrote the names of their first and second choices on slips of paper. This tactic was followed, producing eight first preferences for Dehaene, three for Lubbers (Italy, Spain and the Netherlands) and one (Britain) for Leon Brittan. Second preferences revealed six countries supporting Lubbers.[76]

With midnight approaching, and the bonhomie of dinner rapidly fading, Major declared that there had never been a proper discussion of the merits of rival candidates. Papandreou had had enough, and abruptly quit, leaving those remaining with the impression that the matter was to be held over to the next day. Motorcades were summoned, and the premiers began to drift away to their hotels. Some had already reached their hotel bars when frantic phone calls summoned them back to the Achilleion. Spain had declared itself willing to switch their support from Lubbers to Dehaene. But Wim Kok, the Dutch Foreign Minister, refused to budge from his opposition to his Belgian neighbour, and an increasingly blunt Major made it clear that he had no intention of following suit either. 'I've told you once and I'll tell you again for the umpteenth time that I cannot back Dehaene,' he pronounced.[77]

With no break in the deadlock, Major and the other leaders retired to bed after 2 a.m. While he was asleep, his officials arranged an early morning meeting on Saturday with his Italian, Spanish and Dutch counterparts, and at 3.10 a.m. Chris Meyer raised the temperature among those still at work when he uttered the word 'veto' for the first time in public.[78] In the morning, the odds remained stacked against Major. When Lubbers announced he was withdrawing his candidature, Major found himself isolated against the other eleven heads of government. Comparisons were made with 1984, when Mrs Thatcher similarly isolated had used the veto to block the French Foreign Minister Claude Cheysson from becoming President, ironically letting in the great European centraliser Delors. Major saw no alternative but to follow suit, as had been foreshadowed in the early hours, and employ the British veto, thereby scuppering any prospect of a solution being reached at Corfu. A deeply frustrated Mitterrand snapped that they were now in a position of crisis: 'The situation is only a crisis if everyone wants to make it one,' retorted Major.

Major subsequently explained in public that whereas he liked Dehaene personally, he came from 'a tradition of big government and of intervention. That's not my position ... We need a Commission president whose instincts are for enterprise, openness and subsidiarity.'[79]

Germany, which was to take over the presidency from Greece on 1 July, summoned the heads of government to Brussels on 15 July to reopen discussions on a successor to Delors. Ominous unattributable press briefings were given in Europe suggesting the contempt EU leaders felt for Major pandering to Eurosceptic opinion at home, and how he would be humiliated and outflanked at Brussels.[80] Though they had not said so at Corfu, in private several heads of government were, however, relieved that the Franco–German attempt to steamroller Dehaene on the rest of the EU had been defeated. Even Kohl did not resent Major for his stand; according to one official: 'I think there was if anything increased respect from Kohl when Major stood up over Dehaene. Although he had been a personal choice of Kohl, the German Chancellor according to aides regarded it as a fair cop. Their relationship did not suffer.'[81]

The excitements over Delors' successor overshadowed what had otherwise been an important summit, albeit coming at the end of a weak Greek presidency. Closer links with Russia were discussed, though its membership of the EU was ruled out for a long way ahead. Accession treaties with Austria, Finland, Norway and Sweden were signed, and agreement reached on the closure of Russia's Chernobyl nuclear plant.[82] Major flew back to London on Saturday night to a rush of applause from those who normally condemned him, many of whom had expected him to cave in. Arch-critics George Gardiner and John Carlisle both had positive words to say of his stance,[83] while Simon Heffer applauded his performance in the Commons on Monday 27 June, as his best day since the general election – adding 'an honour for which there was, admittedly, little competition'.[84] Lady Thatcher let it be known that she thought Major's action at Corfu had been an 'excellent example' of standing up for British interests.[85] The affair had indeed significantly improved his chances of avoiding a stalking horse challenge to his leadership in the autumn.[86]

A backlash from the Europhile left was only to be expected, above all after Major praised a bullish Portillo speech on Europe delivered in Barcelona. Clarke's response came in Bonn two days later to the Konrad Adenauer Stiftung: in words echoing Major's own, he said, 'We Conservatives intend to be at the heart of Europe', and spoke positively about the prospects for the single currency.[87] That night, at a private dinner of the 92 Group attended by Ryder, the Chief Whip came under heavy pressure to silence Clarke – or jeopardise the new sense of unity.[88] If the right was trying to suggest Major's continuation at Number Ten was only on sufferance, Europhiles had different ideas. Hurd gave an uncompromising speech to the Conservative Positive European Group denying that the use of the veto at Corfu had anything to do with appeasing Eurosceptics, and asserting that Britain's essentially pro-EU line was to continue unchanged.[89]

Over the next ten days, the political spotlight temporarily moved away from the Tories onto Labour, with much speculation about how Tony Blair, set to be crowned Labour leader on 21 July, would perform once elected. The economy, meanwhile, was steadily if slowly improving, with Clarke telling David Frost on 3 July that, 'I think we are about halfway up the hole.'[90] Dividends from the behind-the-scenes lobbying, and the acceptance by the right that there was no widespread support for a stalking horse challenge that autumn, set the scene for Major's 'end of session' speech to the 1922 Committee meeting on Thursday 7 July, into which Number Ten had put considerable thought.

Speaking for thirty minutes, Major admitted to assembled backbenchers that 'we have missed a few tricks in recent months and years. Our message has been too diffuse and needs to be concentrated and repeated and repeated and repeated so when people hear the word "Conservative" they know what we stand for and why.' He recalled his comments when he had been Chancellor that if policies were not hurting, they were not working. 'It did hurt – but it has worked,' he said, foreshadowing a theme the Party was to revisit two years later. A line should now be drawn under the Party's performance of the previous two years, he continued, and the Party should focus on placing 'clear water' between themselves and Labour.

Mindful of the imminent coronation of Blair, he lambasted Labour's policies, yet warned that a fifth Tory election victory would mean further spending cuts that autumn as the price of tax cuts before Britain went to the polls in 1996 or 1997. To prepare for that election, a series of manifesto groups, which were to include backbenchers, would be set up after the summer recess. But in a full-frontal attack on what Number Ten saw as a creeping defeatism, he said that to suggest the Party needed a period in opposition to regroup was 'a load of rubbish'. The first rule of government was to win and the second was to want to win.[91] Marcus Fox – increasingly under fire for being too subordinate to Number Ten – closed proceedings with a 'ringing declaration' that Major would indeed lead the Party into the next election and beyond.[92]

The speech echoed many of Major's own cherished themes, and displayed the confidence in victory and in himself which he had rediscovered on the campaign trail during the European elections. Unusually far-seeing, his promised creation of policy groups could also be read as an admission that much of the 1992 agenda had been fulfilled, and fresh ideas and initiatives were sought. The speech received a four-minute standing ovation, and achieved his aim of raising spirits and re-establishing his authority. Praise too came in the press. A leader in the *Independent* noted that 'the about-turn in John Major's fortunes over the past six weeks is a resurrection, and a miraculous one at that',[93] while Tony Bevins wrote in the *Observer* that 'he is now, perhaps for the first time since he assumed the leadership in 1990, in command of his party and his government'.[94]

Such talk was, of course, over-stated. Aside from the great divide on Europe, the government was under heavy fire from a number of quarters, notably over its administration of the NHS, to which piquancy had been added by a well-publicised critique from the Bishop of Birmingham.[95] Public dissatisfaction with the government remained high, reflected in a July MORI poll, in particular over job prospects and the continuing lack of a 'feel-good' factor, and over the government's crime, child support and education policies.[96]

Aside from these issues, two further internal discussions underlined the lack of strategic clarity. The division within Cabinet between consolidators, such as Hurd, Lang, Newton and Ryder, and creators, such as Lilley, Portillo and Redwood, who wanted to forge ahead with the Thatcherite agenda, was manifest in two White Papers published that month: that on the BBC bore the consolidators' imprimatur, while the Civil Service White Paper showed the creators' influence.[97] A third July White Paper 'Front Line First', which proposed defence cuts, was not a clear victory for either faction, though it split the right, some of whom wanted cuts, while for others defence spending was sacrosanct. The lack of a clear left/right split in Cabinet was also seen in Heseltine and Clarke being in the creators' camp, especially on privatisation. It served to show the fragmentation that had occurred in the Tory Party in the 1980s. In the post-Thatcher world, consensus about the direction of Party policy at home, and abroad, was not to be had. Even the standard fall-back of denigrating the opposition was about to be denied the Tories because of the second strategic uncertainty that became apparent at the time.

Discussions were taking place in Downing Street and Central Office on how to handle Blair. Should the Party attack Blair for being, beneath the 'Bambi' surface, an unreconstructed Old Labour man, who would impose socialism on the country? Or should he be portrayed as a closet Tory, of impeccable public school attitudes, mouthing Conservative policies in a desperate and cynical search for middle-ground votes? Clarke and John Patten favoured the latter, but Major preferred the former, and for the time being won the day. The two debates were linked. The position that said that Blair had stolen Tory clothes tended to be followed by an argument that the way to deal with the situation was to re-establish 'clear blue water' between the parties by shifting to the right.[98] Ambivalence over how to play Blair and 'New Labour' was to continue all the way up to polling day in 1997. It was never satisfactorily resolved.

On Sunday 8 July Major flew to Naples for the annual G7 summit. His criticism of the Munich G7 in 1992 bore fruit in a smaller, less glitzy affair. The turning point for many had been the 1993 Tokyo meeting, in which the size of delegations and showiness of the itinerary all but squeezed out purposeful dialogue between the heads of government. So for Naples, the twentieth G7 summit, Berlusconi had given instructions for a table so small that the heads of government would be placed elbow to elbow, as if in a restaurant. Even then, some of the flummery proved too much for Major, with discussions taking place in one grand palace location, and meals in another.[99] The southern Italy July sun also proved oppressive, and a distraction from serious dialogue, but not as much as the power cut in the hotel the British delegation shared with the Canadians. The Italians had failed to provide sufficient current for all the electrical equipment the delegations required, so the building was plunged into darkness. One small bulb per room was permitted until the authorities found out how to boost the power supply.[100]

The serious business of the summit revolved around measures to alleviate third-world debt, end domestic recessions and provide a united front to maintain sanctions against Serbia until a peace agreement was in place. Threatened divisions over Clinton's bullish remarks on the falling dollar did not transpire, and the summit discussions proved surprisingly consensual.[101] The expansive mood extended to conferring on Yeltsin virtually equal status to the other seven leaders, as well as to consideration of reform of world institutions, including the IMF and UN, approaching the fiftieth anniversary. Major particularly enjoyed the free-ranging discussion on how existing institutions would have to adapt under the changed circumstances they would face early in the next century.[102] He spoke with some passion about some of the idiocies of the current UN system. The Germans, anxious for a permanent Security Council seat, had not wanted to rock the status quo, but Kohl was so impressed by what Major said that he turned round to his officials and indicated his support.[103] The heads of government vowed to return to the topic at the G7 the following year, in Halifax, Nova Scotia.

Some edge was taken off Major's concentration by an unwelcome intrusion of domestic politics. News was received from London on Saturday that the *Sunday Times* would the next day be running a story under the banner headline 'Revealed: MPs who accept £1,000 to ask a parliamentary question'.[104] The article detailed how two Conservative MPs, David Tredinnick and Graham Riddick, had been set up by the newspaper's investigative team into accepting cheques for asking questions in the Commons. To test widespread rumours that some MPs were asking parliamentary questions in return for cash, ten Labour and ten Conservative MPs had been chosen at random, but only the two named MPs fell into the trap.

Major's reaction was described by an aide: 'He felt it was really appalling that the *Sunday Times* had deliberately set out to entrap people. But he thought it equally appalling that MPs had been foolish enough to accede to this type of activity. He thought it indefensible. It came as a great shock to him.'[105] Major had several phone conversations from Naples with Ryder, and decided there was no alternative but for the two MPs to be suspended from their jobs as Parliamentary Private Secretaries. Once back in London, Major gave public backing on Monday 11 July to an inquiry to be set up to investigate the 'cash for questions' affair, and he let it be known he was deeply concerned to maintain standards in public life.[106] That, he hoped, would be sufficient for the issue to die down over the summer.

The issue of Delors's successor had still to be settled, and occupied much of the week leading up to the special Brussels summit on 15 July. Tough noises had already been made from Downing Street about Major's willingness to use a second veto should another front-running candidate prove no more acceptable than Dehaene.[107] The name of Jacques Santer, Prime Minister of Luxembourg since 1984, was not even on the list of seven or eight possibilities a week before the special conference, convened to resolve the issue. When Santer's name did emerge, teased out as a compromise candidate after last-minute exchanges between the twelve capitals, he was immediately dismissed by British Eurosceptics as 'almost indistinguishable from Dehaene'.[108] Major nevertheless made it clear he would back Santer's candidature as the least objectionable compromise. Briefings poured forth from the Whitehall machine about how Santer had helped devise the 'pillared' structure to the Maastricht Treaty in 1991, which acted as a shield against Brussels's federalism. After lobbying and reassurances, the Eurosceptics – in as far as they had a collective view – made it clear that 'the choice of Mr Santer is not something to waste our ammunition on',[109] and Major flew off to Brussels with British support assured.

In the event, Santer's selection proved a formality, and the Brussels summit passed off uneventfully. Major declared of Santer, 'He's the right man for the job in the right place at the right time.'[110] The truce over the new EU President, however, was to prove remarkably short-lived; after Santer made widely publicised remarks within a week of the Brussels meeting pledging his support for the single currency, deploring Britain's opt-out on social policy and calling for a weakening of the national veto, the right felt they had been all but deceived.[111] But despite grumblings from Cash, Budgen *et al*, no revolt occurred, and the story was soon overshadowed by news nearer home.

Major Reshuffle: July 1994

An imminent government reshuffle had been the political talk for the past two months, fuelled by Major's announcement at the garden press conference in June that one would almost certainly come in July. Sarah Hogg and Jonathan Hill had pressed for it to take place after the European elections, but Major opted to follow Mrs Thatcher's custom of announcing it just before the summer recess. It gave incoming ministers time to prepare, and sacked ministers time to recover, while avoiding their making mischief until after the holidays, by which time the media's agenda had moved on.[112] Major reflected on his style in government-making:

I had these criteria when I put people in position ... I tried to bring on young talent, irrespective of their philosophical bent; I tried to put people in jobs that I thought they would fit and for which they would have an aptitude ... I switched people around maybe, in the first couple of years, too much, in order to give them a broader experience. Increasingly, I left people a little longer, so they would have a longer memory span than the officials who served them.[113]

What proved to be the biggest reshuffle of his premiership was announced on Wednesday 20 July, timed to upstage the appointment of the new Labour leader the day after. To spare those being dismissed the ordeal of the cameras in Downing Street on the morning of the reshuffle, Major asked them to come to Number Ten late on Tuesday evening, after a cocktail party for Tory MPs and their wives. One insider told Colin Brown of the *Independent* the evening ploy was 'Typical of the man. He has shown great sensitivity. It can be very distressing.'[114]

Five key figures were to depart in the reshuffle. Fowler's intention to go had already been posted earlier in the year. Patten was the most distressed to leave, delivering a terse and brief letter of farewell, believing he had been unfairly treated after carrying out his difficult brief at Education to the

Prime Minister's wishes. His friends felt he was the scapegoat for difficulties not of his making that he had encountered with teachers and that he had had insufficient support from the centre. His detractors said that he was accident prone and had shown insufficient sensitivity and judgement, and as a result had provoked the education world to oppose government reforms.

MacGregor, who had had a difficult year clashing with Labour over rail privatisation and with signalmen over strikes, was not unhappy to return to the backbenches. Wakeham, on whom such high hopes had been pinned after the 1992 general election, had failed to spark either as Cabinet fixer and head-banger, or as Leader in the Lords, where he had been confronted by rebellious peers during a contentious legislative programme, above all on the two major law and order bills. Brooke, the final casualty, brought back into Cabinet in September 1992 to fill Mellor's place, had held out against the right who wanted to dismantle the BBC, but had not expected to stay long *in situ*.

In considering new appointments, Major turned once again to the possibility of summoning his old ally Chris Patten back from Hong Kong. Hurd had made tentative overtures to Patten in summer 1993 about returning as Leader of the House of Lords, but Major refrained from asking him directly then. In summer 1994 Major himself offered Patten a triple role: Leader of the Lords, Foreign Secretary and the title of Deputy Prime Minister. The attractions for Major were obvious; the analysis that the government was suffering from infighting, poor presentation and coordination because of the loss of Patten's guiding hand of 1990–92 had become commonplace. While there is some scope for doubting the serious intent of Major's suggestion – he was prone to speculate about such things – Patten took it seriously. The plan was also music to the ears of Patten's opponents in the Foreign Office, Hong Kong and Beijing. But Patten declined, primarily because he felt he could not abandon Hong Kong at a difficult time, but also because tethering himself to a government in deep trouble, and taking a seat in the Lords, were not appealing prospects.[115]

In the end, five new Cabinet appointments were made. The most surprising and the highest profile was Jeremy Hanley as Party Chairman. A comparative unknown at Westminster and in the country, and a minister since only 1990, Hanley's appointment was a calculated gamble. A personal choice of Major, Number Ten sources say that the role model was Cecil Parkinson, who, appointed Party Chairman in 1981, brought the Party to a spectacular election victory in 1983. 'What we knew about Jeremy was that he was big, he was cheerful, he was funny, brilliant with people, a superb worker of a room, very good with Party faithful, utterly loyal,' said Jonathan Hill.[116] An accountant by training, and from a theatrical family (son of the popular actors Dinah Sheridan and Jimmy Hanley) he had proved himself in his jobs at Northern Ireland and Defence. His brief was clear if demanding: restore morale, unify the Party and rebuild finance, as the platform for winning the general election.[117]

Another selling point of the reshuffle was David Hunt's elevation. Initially pencilled in for Hanley's job, late in the day Major heeded the whips' concern about Hunt's ability to inspire trust in all wings of the Party, above all among the Eurosceptic right. The whips also feared, somewhat implausibly, that Hunt as Party Chairman could become a Trojan Horse for his close philosophical ally, Heseltine. Hunt was surprised and disappointed not to get the chairmanship, and had a difficult forty-minute interview in Downing Street with Major on Wednesday morning. Appointed to the sinecure post of Chancellor of the Duchy of Lancaster, initially it could have been seen as a demotion until Number Ten made it clear to the media that Hunt was to have a high-profile if imprecise role as Cabinet 'chief of staff' – much discussed inside Number Ten for the previous year – and chairman of some key Cabinet committees, including industry, environment and local government, but not EDH, covering social and home affairs, which would go to Newton.[118] Hunt's instructions were also clear: he had to help provide the coherence and coordination to government policy that Wakeham had been unable to achieve. Major was particularly concerned by contentious issues not being settled before they reached Cabinet. With his proven political skills, Hunt's appointment seemed like the perfect solution to a problem that had become increasingly apparent since the general election.

Aitken's appointment was another selling point of the reshuffle: a nephew of Lord Beaverbrook, the newspaper proprietor, he had glittering connections in business as well as in politics. A Eurosceptic, the right had been pressing for his elevation.

The three other new Cabinet appointees aroused less interest: Mawhinney succeeded MacGregor at Transport, Dorrell replaced Brooke at National Heritage, and Cranborne became Lord Privy Seal and Leader of the Lords. Cranborne, known to Major since Blue Chip days in the early 1980s, had been an unpromising backbencher. He had left the Commons in 1987, to be later appointed a junior minister in the Lords. His silky political skills and high standing with the Party's 'grandees', as well as the conspicuous success he made of the D-Day celebrations, commended him to Major. Their relationship intrigued observers at Westminster. It was indeed paradoxical that Major, a decidedly modern Conservative, should grow so dependent on this most visible symbol of ancient Tory history. It also cast a curious light on his feelings about class. He retained his disgust at snobbery, but was fascinated by, even deferential towards, some of the most traditional trappings of the British aristocracy. Delighted now to be offered the job of leading the Lords – the job once held by his grandfather – after just two years in the upper House, Cranborne asked to be shown the other changes planned for the upper chamber. Not all of them were to his liking. He asked to take the list away, which held up progress on the reshuffle, and returned with his own list of appointments; Major was only too happy to give Cranborne the ministers in the Lords he wanted.[119] Three Cabinet ministers were moved: Gillian Shephard to Education, with a brief to restore harmony as she had done to the farming community, Portillo given his first department at Employment, and Waldegrave to fill the gap at Agriculture.

Chris Meyer sold the reshuffle as the team to take the Party into the next election, with extensive clearing out and changes at lower levels.[120] Some long-serving middle-ranking ministers such as Peter Lloyd, Tim Sainsbury and Nicholas Scott felt they had had their day, while some ambitious and able younger figures such as William Hague and Ann Widdecombe, and some longer-serving figures like George Young, were appointed as Ministers of State.

How does it rank in scale as a mid-term reshuffle? None of the four big Cabinet beasts (Hurd, Clarke, Heseltine and Howard) were moved, as those holding their posts had been in Macmillan's great reshuffle of 1962. Nor was a clear new ideological direction imparted to the government, as it was in Mrs Thatcher's 1981 reshuffle. So it does not rank as one of the big facelifts.[121] Nevertheless, twelve ministers and four whips dismissed or departing voluntarily made it a dramatic reshuffle in Major's terms. It also bore all the hallmarks of Major the Party manager. Care was taken not to antagonise either wing of the Party: the right was pleased that Redwood and Lilley remained, at Portillo's and Jonathan Aitken's promotions, and the advance of David Davis and Michael Forsyth just below Cabinet level, while the left were happy at Dorrell's and Hanley's promotion, and the central position afforded to Hunt, and George Young's return to ministerial rank.[122] Major kept his thoughts very much to himself, apart from confiding closely in Ryder, whose influence was also heavily evident in the changes.

Changes at Central Office and at Number Ten were designed further to provide vigour and purpose. Two new deputy chairmen were brought in under Hanley, both considerably more experienced politicians. John Maples, the former Treasury minister, was joined by Michael Dobbs, who had served as chief of staff under Tebbit as Party Chairman during the 1987 general election. Dobbs took the job that his fellow best-selling author of political thrillers, Jeffrey Archer, would have loved to have been given. But Archer was, insiders say, considered too risky to bring back, for all his flamboyance and appeal to the Party faithful. The hope was that he would remain a key rallier and charmer of the Tory flock in an *ex officio* capacity.[123] For all their wisdom of hindsight, few in the media or in politics identified the one real danger appointment – a far greater risk than anything Archer might have provided – in the reshuffle, promoted to the Cabinet's spending job: Jonathan Aitken. Only after his fall from grace in mid-1997 was the full extent of his deceit made public.

Within Number Ten, the reassuring if undynamic Graham Bright was replaced as Parliamentary Private Secretary by an equally homely figure, the largely unknown John Ward. To bolster his intelligence in the Lords after the bruises of the previous year, Major created a new job of Prime Minister's

PPS in the Lords, appointing Lord McColl, professor of surgery at Guy's Hospital. When the telephone call from Number Ten came, McColl was in the middle of an operation; he was told that this call was special and he might want to take it immediately. The Private Office, not wanting an open body to be left lying on the operating table, suggested that the patient be sewn up before McColl came in person to Number Ten. At the suggestion of Cranborne,[124] McColl was also given the task of looking after the MEPs, which he did assiduously.[125]

The reshuffle was greeted as sensible if safe. Radicals were disappointed that trouble-prone or uninspiring ministers, such as Gummer, Bottomley, and even Ryder, an increasingly isolated Chief Whip, were not replaced. Some dead wood was hacked away from the middle and lower ministerial ranks, but much remained. But was there much more that could have been done? Even taking into account some promising Eurosceptics being ruled out as too disloyal or too much of a risk, the pool of talent to draw on after fifteen years in government was still not broad, as the failure of the three most adventurous appointments, Hanley, Hunt and Aitken, was to show. Moreover, Dorrell's appointment to a department about whose work he professed to have little knowledge was not a success. Portillo at Employment and Shephard at Education proved capable administrators, but the star Cabinet appointment of the reshuffle was a figure little noticed at the time, Robert Cranborne. A direct relation of the Prime Minister who saw in the Conservative Century, and the first Salisbury in Cabinet since his grandfather, he was to show that even in a classless society, political nous might still be inherited.

One final domestic initiative before the summer break was an upbeat speech Major made on 27 July to the European Policy Forum, a think-tank directed by the MEP Graham Mather, formerly of the Institute of Economic Affairs. Major was determined to build on his speech to the 1922 Committee three weeks before and to produce further evidence that his refashioned government would put 'clear water' between it and Blair's Labour Party, thereby shoring up his own position against attacks from the right that momentum had been lost. As if on cue, Gardiner called the speech's timing 'not a moment too soon'.[126] Major outlined a range of legislative measures for the next parliamentary session, including Bills to reduce bureaucracy in the NHS, 'commercialise' the Post Office, curb pension fraud and liberalise the laws on agricultural tenancies. In the longer term, when public finances permitted, he wanted to widen the 20 pence income tax band, and to expand the provision of nursery education. When in future ministers wished to spend public money on new projects, they must first convince the Treasury there was no private finance alternative.[127] The speech reaffirmed many of his core beliefs.

I expect my ministerial team to put government on the citizen's side, to control public spending, cut back on regulations, deliver on their Charter targets, listen to ordinary

people and give them greater ownership of their own lives ... Over the years the role
of the state grows almost imperceptibly unless it is deliberately kept in check ... We
must resist the clamour for Government action, magnified by pressure groups on
every item of news. It is one of the greatest follies of the late 20th century.[128]

It was the first in a series of pronouncements intended to be a stock-take on
policy. Andrew Marr noted a paradox that while the Party was 'ceasing to be
the party of Europe', Major had little to say on the subject bar a reminder
that 'the individualism of an island race' would be a major theme in the
coming battle with Labour.[129] Within a month, however, Major was to give
his most important lecture on Europe since his Bonn speech in March 1991.

Winds of Change: Ireland, Europe, South Africa

Another Second World War commemoration saw Major make a trip to Poland
on 1 August for the fiftieth anniversary of the Warsaw Uprising. The revolt
against Nazi occupation broke on 1 August 1944: RAF planes flying from
Brindisi dropped some supplies on the besieged city but failed to prevent the
uprising being brutally crushed by the German army. Major, accompanied
by RAF veterans, laid wreaths. With awareness of Britain's wartime role to
the fore, Major was well received, and he spoke movingly about building on
ties forged during the war.[130] The trip to Poland is remembered by Major's
staff less for its programme than for the fact that it had the worst weather of
any of his foreign trips. The tour party laboured first under unbearably hot
and sticky skies, only to be drenched by rain once the commemoration
began.[131] The following day Major paid a brief visit to the Lithuanian capital,
Vilnius, a happy occasion despite his disappointing the leaders of the three
Baltic states who had hoped for rapid accession to NATO.[132]

Back in Britain from 3 August, he saw some of a test match against South
Africa on their first visit to Britain since 1965, before flying out to Portugal
with Norma on 6 August for a two-week holiday. They spent a couple of
nights with Stephen Wall in Lisbon and the remainder in the Douro valley,
as in the previous summer. This year, they found the sun too hot and the
press beginning to intrude, but their friends the Symingtons, as ever, 'superb'
hosts. Again, day trips were organised, and the rest of the time was spent at
the house in the company of the detective and Number Ten Garden Room
girl support.[133] Though Major had relaxed by the end of the fortnight, he
became restless to be back in London, with an important speech on Europe
in the pipeline, and tantalising reports coming through on the secret communication network of a possible breakthrough in Northern Ireland.

Over nine months had passed since the Downing Street Declaration in
December 1993. The Republicans had repeatedly put off making their
response, demanding further 'clarifications' of the text, while the IRA mortar
attacks on Heathrow in March had done nothing to warm opinions in London.
But Major was prepared to sit back and play the long game. His line on the

Declaration remained that he would not take it off the table: it was a set of principles that would stand, but it was up to the IRA to take the next step, which was to call off violence; he was not prepared to enter into any negotiations with them to pay a price for peace. At Easter, the IRA declared a three-day ceasefire, and Adams wrote to Major demanding a direct dialogue and asking for a meeting to clarify the Joint Declaration.[134] Major refused, and repeated publicly the terms for exploratory dialogue following an end to violence that the government had spelt out in their private message of November 1993. His aim in going public was to show the world that the British government was prepared to offer a dialogue to the IRA, and was not being merely negative, as the Republicans alleged. London also encouraged Dublin to prod Sinn Fein about clarification of the Declaration, which Number Ten always regarded as a red herring as it did not believe any points needed clarifying.[135]

Sinn Fein's response was to pass a letter through Dublin to the British government in early May asking twenty questions that they said needed clarification. The Northern Ireland Office promptly responded in a press statement that they had received the letter, and would reply quickly. A rushed series of meetings was held in Downing Street, where it was agreed that only one of the twenty questions genuinely merited clarification, which they duly provided. The other nineteen questions were given replies which either cited the Declaration's words, or were outside the Declaration but where the government's position was well known. Number Ten felt its reply, given on 19 May, had done the trick. One insider believed it had 'burst the IRA's clarification balloon. We heard no more about clarification after it.'[136] The IRA considered the British reply was phrased in measured, non-confrontational language, and it now felt under greater pressure to respond.[137]

By June, London began to receive reports from various sources that a cessation of violence was becoming increasingly likely. Adams tried to go back to the United States. Number Ten again strongly advised the White House to reject his visa request and to tell him that, as he had failed to deliver with his first visit, he could not have another visa until there was a cessation of violence. On this occasion, the British advice was followed. With the temperature in the Republican community still unclear, Sinn Fein delegates from across Ireland met in the County Donegal town of Letterkenny on 23 and 24 July. The media, which had talked up the conference as a prelude to a ceasefire declaration, then tended to be overly pessimistic about the result. The truth was that the Republican movement was deeply split, but the forces favouring a ceasefire rather than a continuation of hostilities were beginning to win the day. With the Loyalists also countenancing a ceasefire in July and August, there was speculation about which side would declare first.[138]

A series of reports in August, including telegrams from the British Ambassador in Dublin, heightened the belief in London that there could be a ceasefire by the end of the month – albeit one which fell short of the permanent end to violence they wanted.[139] Reynolds insisted that the Republicans' prevarication on the ceasefire be settled before September began. 'No two Prime Ministers had ever given so much time and energy, nor had their officials, to the problem before, and we couldn't go on indefinitely.'[140]

So diplomatic channels were buzzing when Major returned from Portugal on Saturday 20 August. He was delighted to read a brief prepared for him by his Private Office which collated the diverse reports on the likelihood of an early IRA ceasefire. On 28 August Hume and Adams issued a statement saying they believed significant progress to peace was being made. That day, a Sunday, Major and Reynolds spoke by telephone, having learned that the ceasefire was indeed imminent. The two leaders coordinated their reactions when the news came. In an undignified breaking of ranks, Reynolds was later to maintain, after leaving office, that the news was a shock to Major, who was disinclined to believe it. Major was irritated by Reynolds's assertions, which tried to show that the British were less well informed about ceasefire progress than in fact they were.[141]

On 31 August the statement was published that the IRA had declared that, as from midnight, 'there will be a complete cessation of military operations'. The news, after twenty-five years of conflict and over 3,000 deaths, more than 1,700 at the instigation of the IRA, made a deep impression throughout the length of the British Isles. But rejoicing aside, the announcement also left the British government with a most searching question. It had offered to start exploratory talks within two and a half to three months of a cessation of violence. Had the IRA now met this requirement? Reynolds maintained that the ceasefire was indeed permanent, and within days invited Hume and Adams, without notifying the British, for a trilateral meeting. Major was more cautious, engaging in a semantic argument over what qualified as 'permanence'. As well as this point, it was also clear that the idea of a cessation of violence was understood differently by the IRA, who continued 'punishment beatings' and tracking of targets during the ceasefire period.[142]

Major was in a vice. Had he possessed a larger majority, and not needed to be ever mindful of his right wing, who abhorred any dealings with the IRA or weakening of the Union, history might just possibly have been different, though Number Ten sources deny Major would ever under any circumstances have entered into talks with the IRA on the basis of the conditional ceasefire they had offered. That said, having pacified the Tory right in June and July, he was deeply concerned to do nothing again to jeopardise the new mood of unity. Lamont had written threateningly in late July in the *Sunday Telegraph* under the title 'Good Riddance to the Downing Street Declaration'.[143] Far more important, the Unionist community in Northern Ireland was deeply suspicious of developments, and Major knew he had to carry their leaders with him. As he had always made clear over the last two years, Unionist compliance was the *sine qua non* of any proposed way forward.

Early Unionist response to the ceasefire was all the more untrusting as the IRA had brought its supporters out onto the streets to celebrate. A celebration for the IRA, Unionists reasoned, meant a defeat for them. Unionist leaders, some of whom should have known better, continued to spread rumours of a secret deal between the IRA and the British. Meanwhile the government worked hard behind the scenes to reassure the Unionists. The role of Robin Eames, Archbishop of Armagh, was again pivotal, with Major reassuring him by telephone of the sincerity of the British case. Eames then did much to calm the Unionist community.[144]

It soon became clear to Number Ten that Adams, having helped lead the IRA towards a ceasefire, lacked the influence and perhaps even the will to persuade his fellow leaders to go the final leg and make it permanent. The British strategy was to steer the IRA towards the point at which the disadvantages of going back to terrorism would outweigh the disadvantages of not achieving all their objectives. As one insider put it, 'It was a question of seeing if we could ease them into permanence over a period of time, until they reached the point at which they, as a movement collectively, decided to give up.'[145]

Major visited Belfast on 16 September for the memorial service for the victims of the Chinook helicopter crash in western Scotland. While there, he put forward a package of carefully constructed measures, worked out with the NIO, which included a commitment (his own idea) to hold a referendum on the outcome of the talks process, seen as a crucial reassurance for the Unionists.[146] He also reiterated his core point on the ceasefire that 'he needed to know it's for good'. On the other side of the equation, he lifted the (entirely counter-productive) broadcasting restrictions on Sinn Fein, and announced an imminent relaxation of other security measures. He also spoke, bravely in view of hostility from arch-Unionists in his party, including the newly promoted Cranborne, of his approach being 'scrupulously fair to both traditions ... it does not favour one side or the other'.[147]

The ceasefire as it stood was good enough for the Clinton administration, who let Adams visit the US on 24 September. Number Ten this time did not oppose a visa, but felt the White House transgressed good judgement by letting Vice-President Gore telephone Adams to inform him that the American government had lifted its ban on official contacts, while Tony Lake gave Adams what London considered an obsequious letter inviting him to come and begin a dialogue with the Americans.[148] Downing Street thus felt a degree of *Schadenfreude* when Adams again seemed to betray the administration's trust by saying in public that violence might under some circumstances start again (though Adams maintained his remarks had been misrepresented). The next month, six weeks later than the IRA, the Loyalists began their ceasefire. A wind of change, it seemed, was blowing through Northern Ireland.

A similar spirit was evident in Major's thinking on the EU. He knew that Europe was the most important domestic and foreign issue, not just for his party but also for the country. For some months he had been searching for a platform to outline his evolving thinking about the EU, which had crystallised further during the European elections, and he took the opportunity when invited to give the second William and Mary Lecture at Holland's University of Leiden on 7 September. 'It was absolutely his point of view,' said one aide. 'He wanted to set out a coherent strategy, a vision on Europe that he himself believed in, and that all reasonable people could agree with.'[149] The Leiden lecture was conceived as a successor to the 1991 'heart of Europe' speech. Major, his staff and the relevant departments considered his words very carefully, and it was certainly more closely argued than *The Economist* article of the previous year.

The speech was well received in the Party and in the press, and did not cause ructions with other European governments. It was the longest expression of Major's views on Europe, and remained the set text whenever Number Ten or anyone in Whitehall wished to refer to the 'thoughts of Chairman Major' on the issue. However, its public impact was blunted by the lack of a catchy phrase like 'heart of Europe'.[150] In markedly confident form, he dismissed as outdated the original vision of the founders of the European Community in the forties and fifties, such as Jean Monnet. In its place, he sought a new vision and a new role for Britain, free to select those areas of policy in which it wanted to participate fully, while retaining its status as one of the EU's most senior and influential members. Thus he dismissed Franco–German notions of a permanent hard core of 'inner' EU nations as 'a real danger' because of the risk of countries like Britain being marginalised, while praising flexibility as 'perfectly healthy', with some member states free to integrate more closely than others. He went further than hitherto in laying out his agenda for the planned IGC beginning in 1996 on the future of EU institutions, including wholesale reform of the Common Agricultural Policy, curbs on some Commission powers and reform of the qualified majority voting system.

In a passage that drew comparisons with Mrs Thatcher's 1988 Bruges speech, he spoke dismissively of the democratic claims of the European Parliament to speak for the peoples of Europe. Deriding the 'pitiable low turn-out' for the European Parliament elections that June, he asserted that it was the twelve national parliaments alone which conferred democratic legitimacy on the Council of Ministers.[151] These remarks brought forth a public letter of complaint from Henry Plumb, who had succeeded Christopher Prout as the leader of the Conservative MEPs.[152] Realising his remarks might have been insensitive in attacking too easy a target, Major made amends subsequently to reassure doubters that he did value the work of the European Parliament.[153]

While waiting to see whether his Leiden speech would indeed succeed in becoming the framework around which 'all reasonable people', not least in his own party, could rally, his mind turned to another Parliament, in Cape Town, where he was to deliver a keynote speech to both Houses as the high point of his visit to South Africa from 20 to 23 September.[154]

South Africa had always held a special place in Major's affections. Since his Nigerian experience in 1968 he had formed a deep affection for the continent, and formed an easy bond with black people. While holidaying in Spain as Foreign Secretary, he had been moved by reading about Macmillan's famous speech in Cape Town in February 1960 on the last occasion a British Prime Minister had visited the country. But since becoming Prime Minister his opportunity for influencing the transition from Apartheid to democracy had been limited, and the nearest he had come to visiting the country was his visit to Harare in October 1991.

No abrupt policy change regarding South Africa was apparent when Major became Prime Minister. Mrs Thatcher had, despite appearances, welcomed political reform, and Britain's influential Ambassador before he went to Washington was Robin Renwick (1987–91), whose home would frequently be filled with those from a wide spectrum of opinion, from people connected with right-wing militias to those to the left of the ANC.[155]

One of Major's first initiatives in the country as Prime Minister was to help secure Mandela's agreement in June 1991 to the lifting of the sporting ban. After his general election victory, Major gave South Africa a higher priority: his Private Office ensured they put telegrams on South Africa into his boxes if reporting anything his officials deemed interesting, when comparable telegrams from countries of greater size might be omitted. When South African leaders passed through London, he would see them at lower levels than those from most other countries.[156] One such visit was by Mandela in May 1993, when he visited Major at Number Ten and forged a close personal bond.[157] They would then discuss matters every six to eight weeks on the telephone. It seemed to Number Ten that Mandela, after nearly twenty-five years in Robben Island prison, still regarded the phone as an exciting toy.[158]

Mandela was inaugurated President in May 1994, in succession to F. W. De Klerk who became Vice-President. Major would have liked to attend to show his enthusiasm for political developments, but it was impossible to schedule in the midst of the local and European elections. So the invitation had to be postponed, and Mitterrand became the first western leader to visit President Mandela's new South Africa. But when Number Ten learned that Mitterrand's visit had not been a wholesale success, the attraction of a September visit, when Major moreover would be fresh from his holiday, became obvious.[159]

A visit to Saudi Arabia and Abu Dhabi had to be fitted in on the way south. Following the precedent of earlier trips, a party of British businessmen and scientists accompanied the Prime Minister. Major wanted to build on the contracts signed on his last visit to Saudi Arabia in March 1991. On the evening of Sunday 18 September, while the business leaders explored export opportunities with their Saudi counterparts, Major had an audience with King Fahd, followed by a banquet.[160] Meyer, the ever watchful Press Secretary, felt uneasy about this Middle Eastern leg of the trip, fearful, as occurred with the Japan trip the September before, that news of business deals would hold insufficient attraction to deflect the press corps from making mischief. So the idea was born of Major making a major economic speech in Saudi Arabia.[161] He duly delivered on Monday his most upbeat assessment yet of what was to become his leitmotif over the next two and a half years, Britain's economic performance. 'We are standing on the threshold of an economic recovery unlike any we have seen since the Second World War ... based on sustainable growth, low inflation and sound public finances.'[162] With talk of Britain's economic miracle still reverberating, the party left Jeddah and, after a brief stopover in the United Arab Emirates, flew through the night to Cape Town.

The itinerary in South Africa was the fruit of intensive planning by Anthony Reeve (Renwick's successor as Ambassador), Rod Lyne and Meyer. They studied the Mitterrand trip and listened carefully to those like Hurd and Heseltine who had paid recent visits. Meyer followed his trusted formula of a story a day and strong television pictures. Lyne drafted the speech and realised Major's wish of including leading British sportsmen in the party: Rob Andrew, the rugby player, Bobby Charlton, the former footballer, Judy Simpson, the former Olympic athlete and Alec Stewart, the cricketer. Colin Cowdrey represented the Lord's Taverners, a cricketing charity. Number Ten was delighted by the self-effacing and dignified way the four sportsmen conducted themselves; for Major, their inclusion in the party was a highlight of the trip.[163]

Major's first assignment, the address to both Houses of Parliament, came shortly after he stepped off the plane. The invitation was an unusual honour for a head of government: South African precedent dictated that only a head of state could address a joint session. The last British Prime Minister to speak in the Parliament had been Harold Macmillan with his 'wind of change' speech, which infuriated the Verwoerd government by predicting the end of white rule. Number Ten knew that Major's speech would generate high expectations. 'So we worked very hard on it,' recalled one aide, 'more than for any other foreign policy speech, putting it through something like nineteen or twenty drafts.'[164] Another cause for anxiety was the warning London received from Cape Town that the speech could have a difficult reception from left-wing representatives, with hostility being whipped up in the radical ANC communities, and equally the possibility of hissing or even walkouts from the far-right Afrikaner representatives.

As with speeches on Northern Ireland, a carefully balanced final text was produced, deferring to both sides. But the script was long. Major had to read it rather than extemporise, and the microphones amplified his voice thinly. Nevertheless, it went down well enough, with the audience and in the world outside. Learning from Mitterrand's speech, Major included red meat in the text, such as a three-year £100 million assistance package, and mentioned sport, considered a deft touch. He urged South Africa to play a more prominent role in preventing regional conflict throughout the continent, while also warning the country off adopting socialist measures in the running of its economy. Flattery was part of his repertoire, telling the parliamentarians they were 'the wonders of the world', making not just today's headlines but 'the stuff of history and legend'.[165]

Gratified by his reception, Major went for lunch in the parliamentary dining room. Speaking after the meal, he opted for the personal touch, telling guests that Norma had said, 'If you go on too long, I'll throw a bread roll at you.' Michael White in the *Guardian* seized on an analogy with Macmillan's visit, but not in a way that caused Number Ten concern: 'Macmillan never pretended to understand Africa or to be at ease with its people. Mr Major showed every sign of doing so.'[166]

That afternoon, Major went to visit Mandela at his office. Number Ten had been told that the new President was tired, and should not be over-extended during the talks. The British had expected a meeting between both leaders with their advisers present; instead, Mandela took Major off to his study, without any note-takers. Both delegations, including senior African figures like De Klerk and Thabo Mbeki, the First Deputy President, sat down and waited outside. More than an hour later the two leaders emerged, arm in arm, having obviously communicated well. They announced to their subordinates that their joint meeting would now begin, which was equally harmonious: 'The final record of it tells absolutely nothing,' recalled one present, 'it was all atmosphere.'[167] Agreements were signed and Mandela was presented with a cricket bat by Major, autographed by both nations' cricket teams, who had recently been playing against each other in England. This gave him deep pleasure. The leaders then appeared on the doorstep, a euphoric moment for Major, with the sun shining down, Table Mountain overlooking them and the media friendly.[168] If Major were to pick just one high point of his premiership, that might well be it.

The rest of the day was taken up by a long meeting with Chief Buthelezi, leader of the Zulu-based Inkatha Freedom Party, which, in contrast to an unhappy earlier meeting in London, went smoothly, and by an official dinner. At its conclusion Mandela delivered a very warm, emotional speech to the television cameras about the visit and Anglo–South African relations, and then stayed talking until late into the night.[169]

Wednesday morning saw the focus shift to sport and education. The party flew to Johannesburg, where Major went to Alexandra township, accompanied by his sporting ambassadors. Together with Colin Cowdrey, who had done much to bring South Africa back into international cricket, Major launched a sporting initiative designed to promote coaching and the training of coaches. He toured the Alexandra Oval, which had been transformed from a rubbish dump with British funds, then rolled up his sleeves and bowled in the nets. Knocking over with his first ball the stumps of Steve Tshwete, the South African Minister for Sport, showed he had not lost all his prowess despite rarely playing since his Nigerian accident. Surrounded by a sea of black faces of schoolchildren, he felt utterly at home, shooing away his security men anxious for his safety.[170]

At Ivory Park, another township, he unveiled a fully equipped library paid

for by British funds,[171] and announced another initiative, this time to help
combat South Africa's burgeoning law and order problems with a British-
style community policing project. Over lunch he addressed the Johannesburg
Chamber of Commerce, highlighting Britain being South Africa's second
most important trading partner. Given the opportunity to build on that base,
with the country on the verge of a new horizon, Howard Davies, CBI
Director-General and unofficial head of the business team, expressed himself
very pleased with the links forged.[172]

The final official visit was on Thursday morning, to the training camp at
Wahlmanstaal, north of Pretoria, where thirty-four British army officers were
helping integrate the former ANC and PAC guerrillas into the new South
African national army. Douglas Hurd laid great store on the symbolic as well
as the practical importance of having a British army team at the heart of this
delicate but vital work.[173]

The trip exceeded all the hopes of Number Ten. Major himself regarded
it, with his two Indian trips, as his most enjoyable overseas visit.[174] The only
threatening shadow were comments Lady Thatcher made on a tour to India,
where she said that fears of violence coming to South Africa might deter
investors, as they had in Rwanda and Somalia.[175] Her words were relayed
from India to Number Ten and on to the party in South Africa. Major was
briefed on it when in Alexandra township, so was prepared for the Chamber
of Commerce lunch, where he refused to be drawn on her comments, but
denied there was any risk for foreign investors. Major's advisers, knowing
Lady Thatcher's support for progress in South Africa, were disinclined to
believe she had deliberately undermined Major. A message went back from
them to Number Ten, who contacted Lady Thatcher's private office which
willingly and speedily issued a statement speaking positively about the opportunities for investment in South Africa.[176]

A mishap thwarted, both camps then flooded the media with honeyed
comments on the other, with Major praising her role in encouraging the
development of South Africa in the 1980s.[177] News was also released about
a private dinner on 4 September at the St John's Wood London home of
Lord Wyatt of Weeford, described as a 'veritable orgy of reconciliation' in
which she had assured her former protégé that there was no one she would
sooner see lead the Party, and that she would play no part in any campaign
to get rid of him.[178] This reconciliation was now in the open.

For all the euphoria, and uncustomarily positive press, had the trip achieved
anything? On one level, the visit paved the way for the Queen's official visit
to South Africa in 1995, and Mandela's visit to Britain in 1996. Obtaining
the trust of all elements of the new regime had not been a foregone conclusion.
Pik Botha, the former Foreign Minister who continued to serve in Mandela's
government, highlighted Major's achievement. 'He spoke sincerely, categorically against Apartheid and for the new deal, but he also in a very subtle
and effective way made it clear he would stand for certain principles, freedom,

economic liberalism, the promotion of economic growth. So he pleased us, and he pleased the ANC, which is quite remarkable.'[179]

De Klerk, too, had high praise for Major's 'skilful balancing act', while also acknowledging the difficult task in binding both sides of the divide into a common picture of the future.[180] While there is no doubting the strength of goodwill towards him across the political spectrum, Major's importance in South Africa overall has been little more than that of a supportive, candid friend. That said, in South Africa, as in India, if not in the United States or even his own country, he was hailed as a world leader, who eclipsed his predecessor.

Major's diplomatic-orientated month ended with a visit by Yeltsin to Chequers over the weekend of 24 and 25 September, the first time any Russian leader had stayed at the Prime Minister's country retreat. The informality of the occasion was demonstrated by both leaders going to the pub together, the Bernard Arms at Great Kimble, Major in casual jumper and Yeltsin wearing trainers. On arrival at RAF Brize Norton, the Russian leader praised previous meetings with Major 'which gave wonderful results' and spoke highly of the value he placed on Russian–British relations. Conversations at Chequers covered a revised plan for Bosnia and the Queen's visit to Russia the following month, and arrangements to share in each other's VE Day anniversary celebrations in the summer of 1995. As Yeltsin left for the UN General Assembly in New York, he said, 'I consider we have never had such wonderful relations as exist now between Great Britain and Russia.'[181] The words were in part diplomatic niceties, but all the same Major could not have asked for a better ending to a golden September.

THIRTY

The Lieutenants Fall:

October–December 1994

IF THE PERIOD from early June to late September had marked the most settled and optimistic period for Major in the entire middle phase of his premiership, within two months the carefully woven strands were all to be unpicked, and Major's leadership plunged into a new crisis from which it only properly recovered after his re-election gambit in June–July 1995.

Why did this happen, when Major's rejection of Dehaene, his Leiden speech, his tough line on the IRA ceasefire and his promise of future legislation all pleased the right? Even Lady Thatcher had sworn allegiance, while the rail dispute that had dogged the summer ended in late September. The answer was that three ticking bombs – Euro divisions, 'sleaze' and continuing poll unpopularity – assaulted Major's new status quo. Had the superstructure been stronger, it might have rebuffed their force. But not since 1992 had Major's premiership had the vital firm underpinnings of a loyal Cabinet and parliamentary party, a confident party machine and a shared sense of purpose. Major's problem was now compounded by the deft work of Blair in making Labour less frightening to floating voters, and several of his lieutenants failing one after the other, leaving him exposed and with insufficient resources to fight back effectively.

Conservative Party Malaise

In November 1990 Major had inherited an ailing Conservative Party. Ideologically, it was already divided over Europe, and between 'One Nation' Tories and economic liberals; membership, both in numbers and activism, was in long-term decline; it lacked a clear management structure; and finance was depleted.[1] The primary aim of the party under Chris Patten had been to win the general election. Victory boosted morale, but further damaged solvency, and did nothing to arrest organisational decay. A survey conducted shortly before the election revealed that the average age of Party members was a staggering 62.[2]

Norman Fowler's chairmanship of the Party (1992–4) saw considerable organisational reform but a continued slump in membership and morale under the assault of repeated by-election and local government election disasters.[3] Weak local organisation and coordination led to the fumbling of the opportunity presented by the Boundary Commission review of parliamentary constituencies. At the start of the process, it was estimated that it was worth an extra forty on the Conservative majority, but after a series of Labour successes at local public inquiries, the outcome was a net increase of only five.[4]

The core problem at Central Office, however, was financial; the Party had been living beyond its means at least since 1987. By 1992 the position was desperate – if the Party had been a public company it would have ceased trading. Fowler himself described the organisation as 'ramshackle and bust. We were struggling just to keep solvent.'[5] Major trusted his former ministerial boss at Social Security to handle the situation. By 1994 the finances had stabilised and the deficit was being reduced.

Party morale and depleted membership were becoming topics of wide public discussion during 1994.[6] Surveys as well as the Party's postbag revealed that, despite the blows of 1992–4, Major was still widely regarded positively by Conservative members.[7] Nevertheless, Major and Jonathan Hill realised the damage his standing had sustained, and that relations with grassroots were in need of repair, hence Major's regional tours as well as a mini-consultation exercise with questionnaires to 3,000 party faithful in summer 1994.[8] Although his overseas timetable that September did not permit so many tours, Hill managed to get Major out as much as was possible, including a successful visit to Aberdeen early in the month. Hill had only a few weeks left in Downing Street, but was at his most forceful, not least in ensuring the Prime Minister received and gave upbeat messages.[9]

After Fowler, the Party was in deep need of an ebullient optimist as Chairman, hence Hanley. At his appointment, he questioned whether he was really the right choice.[10] Others close to the Prime Minister also queried the wisdom of appointing someone so inexperienced, at such a high-risk time.[11] For his first seven weeks, such doubts were stilled, as Hanley took to the job with gusto. He toured the country, and spoke to over 500 constituency chairmen. Party members did indeed, as expected, respond warmly to him; his personal charm and optimism were just the tonic needed for jaded sensibilities. Favourable comparisons with the remote Fowler were immediately drawn. Hanley was more than just a smiling suit. Employing his accountant's skills, he slimmed down the Party hierarchy and began to move the Party's finance into the black. Some unguarded comments about Lords Archer and Tebbit hinted at a certain naïveté, but they were largely discounted.[12] His chairmanship might indeed have shaped up well, but for an event on the morning of Sunday 11 September.

Despite the early hour, Hanley was in good spirits when he arrived at BBC studios for an interview on *Breakfast with Frost*. Nobody from Central Office press office went with him. Nor had he looked at the weekend papers, which had been full of a speech the Prime Minister had made to the Social Market Foundation that Friday. In it, Major had said, 'Let us make a real national effort to build an "anti-yob culture" ... We must build a huge national partnership against the criminal – in every city and county, every workplace, every school, every home.' The speech was a core plank in a series of talks Major was giving to assert his authority and bolster morale in the run-up to the October Party Conference.[13]

The Sunday newspapers were stiff with indignation about unprovoked violence at a boxing match the night before in Birmingham.[14] Hanley had heard a snippet about it on the radio, but the significance did not register. So when Frost bowled him what he thought was a friendly opening question about the episode, Hanley dismissed the fighting as mere 'exuberance'.[15] His apparent soft-pedalling on an issue which the Prime Minister had brought to the top of the agenda immediately became the top news story. Hanley admitted on Sky Television that evening that, 'I was caught on the hop. I am new to this game. I have only been in the job a few weeks. Yes, I have made a mistake.' Charmingly honest, it was but further red meat to the media. *The Times* lead headline on Monday was 'Hanley gaffe knocks Tory fightback bid'.[16]

Hanley never fully recovered. Not that the gaffe itself did the damage; many Cabinet ministers survived worse. But according to one aide: 'It sunk him, because it undermined his confidence ... He felt very stupid about it, and he felt he had let the Prime Minister down. It destroyed his fundamental confidence that was the cornerstone of his strength as a public performer.'[17]

Labour capitalised fully on the windfall. David Blunkett, then Labour Party Chairman, pointed the finger at the top. 'It amply demonstrates John Major's mistake and continuing ineptitude in having appointed Hanley to such a senior position.'[18] The error also gave the media their chance.[19] Hanley began to cave in under the pressure. As he later reflected:

There is no doubt that the press decided that if they could not get the Prime Minister, they would get someone else ... They became extremely intrusive. The *Sunday Mirror* searched out my ex-wife in Tucson, Arizona, and greeted her with the line: 'We've tracked you down. We'll get the filth.' There was none, and they couldn't forgive me that there was no story there. Then the *News of the World* went for my son over a mortgage foreclosure. They hounded me for days and said that if I didn't give them quotes and photographs, they would just make them up.[20]

At the worst time of the assault, just after Major's South African trip, Hanley sought solace from the Prime Minister. 'He put his arms around my wife and me, and told us to keep strong, and that he knew what we were going through.'[21]

Not even the prime ministerial embrace, however, could save him from further assaults. Further slips, including saying there would be no further interest rate increases, led to the nickname 'the gaffer'. A report conducted by one of his new Deputy Chairmen, John Maples, into disaffected Tories completed by the end of September, which said that the economic upturn was not yet affecting them, was leaked to the *Financial Times*, to Major's great displeasure.[22] By October it was clear that Hanley was unable to pull himself out of the mire. But he was so obviously Major's choice as Chairman, indeed, to some he was in the image of Major, that early release was impossible. Hanley continued as best he could, sustained by his regular Monday morning meetings at Number Ten with the Prime Minister. But good though Hanley remained as a morale-raiser in the Party, Major had no illusions that he could rely any more on him to be a big hitter, or as one to present a confident face on government policy to the media.[23]

Bournemouth Party Conference

As if to underline the new consensus about Hanley's vulnerability, a leader in *The Times* on the day the Party Conference opened at Bournemouth declared Hanley 'should leave the task of being the Prime Minister's spokesman on television and radio to his deputies' because 'by staying off the airwaves ... he will save his government from embarrassment'.[24] Hanley was only partly to blame for the optimism of the summer fading, which it surely was. MORI polls published in September showed a record collapse in support for the Tories among professional and managerial people; satisfaction ratings for Major too, despite his diplomatic successes, fell to an all-time low.[25] The 'voteless recovery' became accepted in the conventional wisdom, with growth being led by investments and exports, and the benefit of the recovery not being felt by consumers. The government realised that by reducing inflation, salaries and wages stood almost still, while house prices stubbornly refused to rise, leaving those trapped in negative equity to simmer. Clarke's decision in mid-September to edge up interest rates (to 5.75 per cent) further dampened hopes. Plaudits from commentators were scant compensation.[26]

The strategic debates, on how to play Blair – as dangerous socialist or closet Tory – and whether to continue with radicalism or consolidate, resurfaced in September. At his end-of-term 1922 Committee appearance, and at his European Policy Forum lecture later in July, Major had promised a radical forward momentum. Now he was not so sure. A political session after the first post-holiday Cabinet on 15 September did agree, though, on an 'autumn offensive' against Labour. Ministers expressed their confidence that Blair's honeymoon would fade, and applauded an attack by Heseltine on the Labour leader for being 'irresponsible, young and inexperienced'.[27] The Labour debate was revisited in Political Cabinet on 6 October, by which time the Maples Report and other polling research had been completed.

These pointed to a widespread sense of betrayal among middle classes at the tax rises, and anxiety about house prices and job security. This did not suggest that the extensions to the free market, in health, education and elsewhere, as the radicals urged, was what was wanted. Rather, steady, competent administration was in demand.

The new evidence played a significant part in tipping the scales in favour of the consolidators, whose strategy was thought better able to connect with the concerns of disaffected Conservatives.[28] Ministers were told at the 6 October meeting to inject economic realism into their conference speeches, not to pretend, in Macmillan's words, that voters had 'never had it so good' when transparently many were still suffering, despite the upturn. Hanley stressed that the conference would have to demonstrate the 'credibility of government policies' by diverting attention from the difficulties since 1992 and reminding delegates of the concrete achievements since the general election.[29] The government was now halfway through its span, the pain had been taken, and most manifesto pledges already fulfilled; glamour and high promises were out, pragmatism was in.[30] This mood was reflected in the adoption of the tempered conference slogan, 'Britain Growing Stronger'.

The backdrop to the Tories' Bournemouth conference was Labour's the week before, in which Blair delivered his first, highly praised, speech as leader. In it, he foreshadowed far-reaching change to the Party, which aides confirmed meant the replacement of Clause Four of the Party's constitution, thereby ending Labour's commitment to nationalisation, and further bringing the Party into the political centre ground.[31] As the Tory conference approached Major's own mood remained optimistic. Over the summer he had begun to take stock of his own premiership, and had come to believe that history would judge him more kindly than his predecessors, not least because of the economic turnaround and the progress in Northern Ireland.[32]

An ominous harbinger of things to come appeared, however, in the eve of conference Sunday papers, with revelations about Mark Thatcher's involvement in a Saudi arms deal. There was no suggestion that Major might have done anything wrong over it. But it put Tory 'sleaze' back on the agenda.[33] Not that the danger was heeded that evening when Major dined with Hanley, finalising plans for the week ahead. Europe remained a primary concern, with Number Ten already having to hack passages out of a Portillo speech: under no circumstances did they want to see Europe upset the conference or the new equilibrium.[34]

Major sought to steady nerves in his traditional speech to Conservative agents on the first Monday evening. No great initiatives should be expected during the week, he told them. Instead, they should hold tight together and unite behind their 'national' Party, because, repeating an earlier phrase, 'Britain has taken the pain and is poised for gain.'[35]

Major, staying at the Highcliffe Hotel, made frequent forays to Party events, radiating confidence and optimism, assisted by unusually sunny and warm autumnal weather. The conference had a curiously inward-looking quality to it: 'like having drinks on the *Titanic*,' as one delegate described it.[36] The principal challenge came not from Lady Thatcher, who arrived on Tuesday, still fending off sleaze accusations against her son, nor from Lamont, despite an outspoken attack on the EU, nor even from Tebbit, who mouthed the same mantra. The threat came from Portillo, to the deep irritation of Number Ten.

The new Employment Secretary's salience had already been raised by Blair, referring to his political vision the week before as 'Planet Portillo'. The description did him no harm, and in his 'barnstorming' speech at Bournemouth on Wednesday, Portillo won the most enthusiastic applause of the week, pledging to 'stop the rot from Brussels' and declaring, 'If ever there is a conflict between jobs in Britain and toeing the line on Europe, jobs in Britain will win with me every time.'[37] Andrew Marr noted that, though he had always had a group of fanatical young supporters, 'his support seems far wider now – yesterday white-haired ladies were whooping and roaring alongside the moist-faced maniacs'.[38] To the embarrassment of the platform, the latter band, spread strategically throughout the audience, helped ensure a four-minute ovation for their hero.

At a fringe meeting of the right-wing Conservative Way Forward Group, however, Portillo disappointed his more fervent supporters by refusing to endorse Lamont's call to consider leaving the EU. Despite the Eurosceptic audience, and being flanked by George Gardiner, he stuck to the Number Ten line and refused to rule out of court Britain's entry into the single currency. Was this at the insistence of Number Ten, or evidence of growing political maturity? The answer is a bit of both. He realised that in his speeches earlier in his *annus mirabilis*, appearing too radical had allowed his judgement to be called into question. Copies of his *Clear Blue Water* were on sale at Bournemouth and much in evidence; the very title contrasted provocatively with Major's own cry for merely 'clear water' between the Tories and Labour. Even in tempered form, Portillo's express train outshone other speeches and figures during the week.

With his illness keeping him away in 1993, Heseltine made his first appearance at conference for two years. He was well received, though the reaction was only lukewarm, not least when he declared, as if to try to halt Major's drift to Euroscepticism, 'The prime minister is right to talk of a Britain at the heart of Europe.' Clarke, following the Cabinet briefing, called for sobriety in economic policy, and delayed tax cuts, while Hurd gave a 'we need to live in the real world' vision of Britain's future. Howard provided some meat, albeit thin-sliced, for radicals with his promise of identity cards. By following their brief so closely, Cabinet ministers all helped provide a united, if unexciting, message, with only Portillo standing above the parapet. Don Macintyre thought he had 'launched himself as the undisputed champion of the Party's new right'.[39] By the end of the week, just he and Clarke, as well as a new figure on the left, Dorrell, were being discussed as future leadership challengers.[40] Heseltine's prospects had, with Smith's coffin, disappeared from view.

Expectations duly lowered, Major stood up to speak on Friday. Nick True, as usual, had drafted the speech, though much of it was written by Major himself, with Ronnie Millar once more in the team.[41] A boost was given that morning by the Loyalists in Northern Ireland declaring a ceasefire. Hanley helped design a set which brought Major's lectern closer to the audience, a well-judged move that played to his leader's strengths. Major looked calm and unruffled as he delivered his text, which lasted a little over an hour.

It was a consolidator's and unifier's charter *par excellence*. The battle of ideas had, he said, been won by the Party, and he advised delegates in future to 'look for achievements not always in bold plans or crude conflict'. Governing, he asserted, was difficult, and involved 'small steps', and trust. One area in particular where the Party should trust him was over Europe: it was an area best left for him to wrestle with (a growing conviction, to flower fully during the 1997 general election). Reference was made to his Leiden speech, which must have eluded most delegates, though they understood his drift. Steadiness was required across the range of government policies; the NHS and state education would remain high priorities; the economy was set on course for ever greater gains, with living standards perhaps doubling in a generation, and everyone should feel reassured that all would turn out well. Passion, jokes and rhetorical flourishes were almost absent in what Hugo Young described as 'the ultimate in anti-speeches'.[42] Blair as well as Portillo were delivered snubs when he said, 'The time is ripe for grown-up politics.' The peroration, written by Major himself, and peculiarly personal to him, was also a veiled attack on Labour's new slickness:

No windy rhetoric, no facile phrases, no pious cliché, no shallow simplification, no mock-honest, mock-familiar, adman's speak can conceal the infinite complexity of Government ... The glib phrases, the sound bites, the ritual conflicts – all these may be the daily stuff of life for the upper one thousand of politics. But to fifty million other people in this country, they are utterly irrelevant. My interest is with them ... My trade had never been in adjectives. I shall be patient. I shall be realistic. I shall ask for patience and realism in others. And I shall put my trust in results.[43]

With his downbeat peroration ringing in their ears, delegates, satisfied if not excited, picked themselves up to leave the hall. Tony Bevins's end of conference verdict on Major, that 'they do not love him as they love Michael Portillo'[44] may have been correct, of the delegates at least if not of the wider Party. But overall the conference had been a significant success. Delegates bought the message of 'consolidate now, jam tomorrow', and left Bournemouth in better heart than had seemed possible back in May. First indications were that the strategy had worked.

Après *Bournemouth: Division and Sleaze*

Not all elements of the Party, however, were prepared to swallow the 'safety first' line. The right, both inside and outside Cabinet, was disenchanted, arguing that Blair's marching of Labour to the centre dictated the Tories' move further to the right. Portillo, adamant that the Party needed certainty and firm leadership, and that he could provide it, had debated over the summer whether to push until the point he was sacked. Some close to him, like his unpaid adviser David Hart, believed he should resign and make his opposition clear.[45] Portillo refused, believing it would weaken his position, as had happened to Heseltine after he walked out of Cabinet in 1986. Lamont, too, was seen as a weakened figure brooding on the backbenches. Portillo continued to be prodded by his lieutenants, some of whom felt his new job in the reshuffle was insufficient reward, others incensed by Major's put-down at the conference.[46] Redwood became notably more antagonistic to Major after the Party Conference, as did several non-Cabinet ministers and back-benchers.

A strong hand beneath Major driving through the consolidation policy might have warded off the dangers. But it rapidly became clear that Hunt was as out of place in his chief of staff role as was Hanley at Central Office. Hunt was constantly undermined by the right, who never trusted him, and he lacked the clout to pull rank on the big beasts, Clarke, Heseltine, Hurd and Howard.

Sarah Hogg, too, who had battled tirelessly for four years to assert the Prime Minister's authority throughout Whitehall, was growing very tired, and was eager to leave. Clarke and Heseltine, who could have brought solidity and helped shore up Major's position, were preoccupied with their own agendas, while Hurd, heavily engaged on foreign policy, was losing some of his appetite for domestic politics, and was looking forward to retirement. Relations between Major and Ryder were also growing more distant as, handicapped by back pain, Ryder was no longer such a forceful presence at the centre, and he too was looking forward to the day he could retire. Major was a sitting target, and it was only a matter of time before he was knocked down.

It was ironic that 'sleaze' should have provided the blow. He deeply resented the way that his party became saddled with the 'sleaze' label, and found it a very difficult issue to manage. His beliefs and leadership style did not particularly equip him for handling the issue in a decisive manner; indeed, it is possible that no tactic which was politically possible for him could have dealt with the whole sleaze saga in a completely satisfactory way.

After its early manifestations, the issue had faded until early 1994 and the backlash against individual Tories on personal morality. At the same time, concern began to grow about oversight of the burgeoning number of un-elected, unaccountable bodies, or quangos, set to double to over 7,000 by 1996. A Public Accounts Committee report in January 1994, 'The Proper Conduct of Public Business', had revealed a great swathe of mismanagement, incompetence and waste by these bodies.[47] On the back of the report, Margaret Beckett condemned the government as the most 'devious, dishonest and sleazy' in the European Union.[48] In a debate at the end of February, the charge was of the Tories filling these unelected quangos with their own placemen.[49] Even normally sympathetic commentators felt that the government was guilty of acting in a high-handed manner.[50]

Throughout the spring of 1994, John Smith had made the attack a personal crusade against the government, rising to a pitch during the local election campaign in May. The 'cash for questions' inquiry by the *Sunday Times* in July re-awoke the issue when Number Ten hoped it had died away. By September and October, rumours and accusations of misconduct were again widespread, with Mohamed Al Fayed, the Egyptian owner of Harrods and many other businesses, prominent in making allegations. On top of questions about Archer's share deal in Anglia Television and Mark Thatcher's arms sales trading, information filtered into Number Ten that further MPs, including Aitken and Howard, might have behaved improperly. Major, who found it all most distasteful, asked Robin Butler to investigate the charges, and a clean bill of health was at least given to Howard and to other Cabinet ministers whose names were being mentioned.[51]

On 20 October the *Guardian* ran a story that two ministers, Neil Hamilton, Trade and Industry Minister, and Tim Smith, a junior Northern Ireland Minister, had taken money to ask questions on behalf of a lobbying company. Smith immediately resigned, but Hamilton issued a libel writ against the *Guardian* declaring that he had done nothing improper.[52] The issue appeared to be spiralling out of control. A widely cited Gallup poll that month found that nearly two-thirds of people in Britain believed the Tories gave the impression of being sleazy and disreputable.[53] The 'revolving door' whereby former ministers joined the boards of companies or merchant banks that they had dealt with in office, often for high salaries, was another line of attack.

Hamilton, still denying any personal impropriety, now became the focus of attention. Major's initial response was to dismiss the allegations against him as 'unfounded'. Hamilton might have been able to hang on to office if he had not antagonised Downing Street by claiming that, if Major could stay in office and fight a libel action (over the Clare Latimer charge), then so could he. He compounded his error by joking in public about declaring the gift of a ginger biscuit. According to one insider, his brazen behaviour was deemed 'political suicide'.[54] Over the weekend of 22–3 October, David Hunt distanced the government from Hamilton, though Portillo made a public declaration of support for his fellow right-winger. On Tuesday 25 October Hamilton was summoned to Number Twelve Downing Street, for a meeting with Ryder and Heseltine to suggest that he should stand down until the matter was cleared up.[55] Hamilton and the right viewed this as a dismissal and criticised Major for making Ryder and Heseltine do his dirty work for him. Major's motive was, aides say, to make it easier for Hamilton to return to government should he be cleared, because a personal interview with Hamilton would have been more easily construed as dismissal.

But his departure only fanned the flames. Hamilton's right-wing supporters were not only antagonised over his isolation, when Downing Street seemed to be leaning over backwards to protect Aitken (albeit another right-winger), but also by the manner. Rather than do the job himself, Major employed his lieutenants. The right were in high dudgeon when they met for the annual dinner of the 92 Group the night after the sacking. Major had created a 'nasty precedent' by dismissing a minister for unsubstantiated allegations, announced George Gardiner, the group's chairman.[56]

How should Major respond to the rising public concern on standards? He had been toying in private with the idea of setting up a public inquiry, on the lines of Bingham into BCCI and Scott into the Arms-to-Iraq affair. The sleaze charge had run on for so long without his being able to offer an effective response. Bringing the issues out into the open appealed to him: it would show the government was taking the initiative, and it might silence the daily 'sleaze' headlines. Major was reluctantly having to accept that there was a lot of questionable behaviour by those on his own side, and he felt no desire to protect those caught up in such activities. He believed that the charges were becoming a poison that was contaminating the whole role and perception of public life, and he wanted it rooted out.[57] One aide who understood his thinking put it thus:

He started off from humble beginnings and worked himself up to what is considered the highest office in the land, earning only modest sums, never having taken anything for himself, living a modest life for a prime minister but finding himself leading a government that was accused of being sleazy and condoning the kind of behaviour he personally finds completely repugnant. He was deeply outraged that he was being associated with this, and the damage it was doing. He wished to see it cleared up.[58]

Once his mind was made up, he moved swiftly, causing some surprise in Number Ten by the pace ('in a blink' said one) of his reaction. Major called in Butler and Allan, and they decided a judge was needed to head the inquiry. Lord Mackay, the Lord Chancellor, was asked who might be spared. He produced a very brief shortlist, which included Nolan, a Lord of Appeal, who was invited to Number Ten and accepted the assignment.[59] It seemed a very neat way out of the box. Major duly announced on the afternoon of Hamilton's dismissal that the government would be setting up a 'far-reaching' independent inquiry into 'standards in public life'.[60] Major and officials had notified Cabinet ministers before the announcement; when Waldegrave was told, he groaned, 'Not another judge!'

But in the longer term, the decisions of 25 October would return to haunt Major. The right's anger at the treatment of Neil Hamilton did not abate: Portillo continued to think it 'outrageous',[61] while the *Spectator* and both *Telegraph* newspapers fumed.[62] Yet again, Major was open to charges of bowing to media pressure in his dismissal of Hamilton. Blair taunted Major in the House, to the satisfaction of some of the Prime Minister's own side, for being capricious and inconsistent in picking and choosing which minister he would dismiss for sleaze, and which retain.[63] Hunt became even more of a marked man from the right. The setting up of 'Nolan' (as the committee came to be known) caused even more damage to Major's position. Bitterly

resented by the right in Parliament and in the media, more even perhaps than
Europe, it was the issue that was to undermine his position over the following
nine months. Without giving any convincing idea themselves of how they
would deal with the issues, the right condemned the setting up of Nolan, as
they did Scott, as the action of a weak and indecisive man.

The more immediate manifestations of sleaze died away, with the *Guardian*
being forced onto the defensive over how it had obtained evidence about
Aitken and the Ritz by concocting the celebrated 'cod fax'. But the damage
had been done. The fortnight of sleaze that followed the Bournemouth
conference undid completely the ground gained not just during that week
but over the previous four months.

Return to Sender: Post Office Privatisation

Major now ran headlong into another issue which he found similarly difficult
to manage. Major was never a privatisation zealot, although his government
nearly completed the disposal of the nationalised industries. Coal, following
the crisis of October 1992, was sold off in December 1994. Rail privatisation,
a complex technical exercise involving a considerable amount of continuing
public subsidy, was passed into law in November 1993 and the first private
trains started running in 1996. Rail was the borderline privatisation of the
Major government, and that it was proceeded with at all was a sign that Major
could override unease in the Commons and bureaucratic inertia despite
unfavourable circumstances. The Post Office, however, was a privatisation
too far.

Privatisation of the Post Office had been considered by the Policy Unit
early in 1991. Although the Treasury had been keen to see it privatised, the
decision taken in the 1991 Citizen's Charter White Paper,[64] and repeated in
the election manifesto, was merely to boost competition and to free up some
of its commercial operations. Heseltine in his new job at the DTI became an
enthusiast for full privatisation, making it an issue of personal pride. Only
weeks into his new post, he initiated an internal DTI review on the Post
Office's future.

Cabinet debated the issue on 13 May 1993, when discussing the legislative
programme for the next session, but decided against including it on the
grounds of privatisation being too sensitive with the electorate, especially
pensioners, concerned that they might be compelled to receive their pensions
via banks rather than at their local post office.[65] The decision was thus
received with widespread Tory cheers.[66] With the Union of Communication
Workers voting unanimously at their annual conference at the end of May
1993 to consider industrial action if privatisation went ahead,[67] the issue went
onto the back burner. But with Heseltine back in harness after his heart
attack, it re-emerged with a vengeance in the spring of 1994 with him keener
than ever, and Clarke now equally enthusiastic. Though on the left, neither

was in the 'consolidators' camp; both men were behind the battle to persuade Cabinet that a portmanteau privatisation and deregulation Bill should be passed.[68]

Heseltine was determined that this time he would not lose the argument over Post Office privatisation, and have it included in bills for the 1994–5 parliamentary session. His objective was boosted by a Commons Trade and Industry Committee judgement in February 1994 that the 'Post Office cannot be retained in its present form', and that it would face a spiral of decline if not freed to compete against growing foreign competition, notably from Dutch, German and Swedish post offices.[69] Further support came when Bill Cockburn, Chief Executive of the Post Office, declared its latest results were the best ever, and commercial freedom was urgently needed to allow it fully to compete internationally.[70]

One of the options Heseltine floated was to retain the counter division, which ran the network of 19,000 sub-post offices, in public ownership, to allay fears among some MPs that privatisation would lead to the closure of many sub-post offices, particularly in Tory-voting rural areas.[71] Lilley, another enthusiast, went out of his way to appear conciliatory when he spoke to the Federation of Sub-Postmasters in early May, reassuring them that their own businesses would remain secure even if the rest of the Post Office was privatised.[72]

The issue came before Cabinet committee on 19 May. Heseltine was reasonably confident that he would win the day. But deep reservations were expressed, above all from the business managers, about the prospects of winning parliamentary backing with such a small majority. Ministers agreed that when Heseltine made a statement in the House that afternoon, launching a consultative Green Paper, the government should still not commit itself.[73] Though the Green Paper's favoured option was selling 51 per cent of the Royal Mail and Parcelforce,[74] the very act of issuing a consultation paper indicated that the government was still undecided, and might have to dilute, or even abandon, privatisation.[75]

Heseltine was now in effect given five months to try to show the cautious voices in Cabinet that he could allay fears of Tory backbenchers and win over sufficient of them to ensure a parliamentary majority for legislation.[76] With Labour and Liberal Democrats pledged to oppose privatisation in any form, the margin for dissent was paper-thin. Patrick Cormack, the traditionalist Tory MP for Staffordshire South, underlined the difficulties when he said in the House that afternoon: 'There are many old-fashioned Tories, of whom I am proud to be one, who view the prospect of Royal Mail PLC about as favourably as they would view your old regiment being replaced by Group 4 at Buckingham Palace.'[77]

Major's own stance was ambivalent. As he later recalled: 'Instinctively, I was modestly in favour of privatisation. Intellectually, when we looked at the case, I was much more strongly in favour of privatisation. There was no doubt that the Post Office could really capture international markets, but it needed the freedom of a private sector organisation and the capacity to borrow.'[78] But he did not play the strongly positive role pushing Post Office privatisation that he had done over rail, or even coal. Some questions were asked in Number Ten about Heseltine's motives: was he seeking to advance himself as the champion of privatisation, pushing free enterprise into an area from which even Mrs Thatcher had shrunk, in an attempt to build bridges to the right for any future leadership election?[79]

While there may well have been something in their suspicions, Major's own cautious approach had much more to do with a strong wish to avoid a parliamentary defeat on what would be bound to be seen as a central item in the government's legislative programme.[80] Said one insider: 'He felt the government could not afford another parliamentary humiliation after the problems it had had with VAT on fuel and Maastricht, and thought it just not worth the gamble.'[81] The Party's late summer research had been another influence, suggesting strongly that further radicalism was not what was needed to win back disillusioned Tory voters.

Major had high hopes that Hunt could manage to resolve the impasse. When given his new troubleshooting post on 20 July, Major had told him that he thought the government had been taking too many decisions without exploring fully the consequences. Whereas Major thought they might be too far down the road to stop Post Office privatisation, he wanted Hunt to prevent other similar situations from arising.[82] Hunt interpreted his brief as to block the privatisation. He discussed it with Newton, whose importance as a behind-the-scenes troubleshooter had grown since the retirement of Wakeham in July, and found a ready ally: neither man thought privatisation a feasible step at this time, and concluded that pushing the idea would lead to trouble. Hunt accordingly called Heseltine and Clarke into his office to ask for a rethink. Unsurprisingly, they brushed him aside.[83] In his Party Conference speech, Heseltine endeavoured with some success to allay the Tory fears. But heavy behind-the-scenes lobbying, with the assistance of Tim Bell's public relations agency Lowe Bell, was winning new converts to the anti-privatisation cause.[84]

With time ticking away before the contents of the Queen's Speech had to be finalised, crucial days were now lost while Heseltine went on a trade mission to Korea. He returned to a meeting of a key Cabinet committee at the end of October. Hunt in the chair asked him about progress on converting dissenters, to which Hunt believed he had no convincing argument. Hunt then asked Ryder to comment. Ryder, despite supporting the principle, had never thought it would get through the 1992 Parliament, and he said it was still his opinion that a Bill would be defeated. Heseltine spent some desperate days at the end of October and very beginning of November trying to lobby the hard core of twenty opponents, and proposed a series of increasingly desperate amendments to appease them. The key Cabinet, to agree the content of the Queen's Speech for the 1994–5 session, was to meet on Thursday 3 November. Heseltine was forced to report back to Hunt's committee that he still could not guarantee the necessary support in the House.[85]

Cabinet on 3 November proved the most heated since the three Cabinets on 22 July the previous year at the climax of the Maastricht Bill process. The Commons business managers, Ryder and Newton, expressed again the view that any Post Office privatisation Bill would be voted down at the second reading because their own soundings showed no change of heart among the opponents. Cranborne also had doubts about how it would be received in the Lords. Severe embarrassment would be caused if they went ahead.[86] Prominent also on the anti-privatisation side were Howard and Redwood – which provided further evidence that the issue did not polarise.[87] Keenest for privatisation were Lilley and Portillo, in addition to Heseltine and Clarke. Passions ran high in a three-hour meeting finishing at 1.35 p.m. – embarrassing for Major as it kept the recently vetoed Belgian Prime Minister Dehaene waiting for his lunch with Major.[88]

Ministers revisited the whole question of whether they should consolidate, or push ahead with a radical agenda. Heseltine and Clarke argued for the high-risk strategy, and to face down opposition, recalling that all privatisations had been unpopular before they took place.[89]

Heseltine tried one last ploy to persuade his colleagues: he would make it clear to rebel MPs, some of whom had supported him in the 1990 leadership race, that if they voted down the Bill in the Commons he would resign. But he could not persuade colleagues to let the Bill be included even on those terms, a critical intervention against him coming from Howard, and Major weighed in at the end to say that they should not proceed in any form. The government, Major said, should not be apologetic, as its view had not changed: consultation had merely revealed that there was not a parliamentary majority for privatisation.[90] Clarke was later to reflect: 'Post Office privatisation was the turning point. We were seen off on it; after that, we became a consolidating government.'[91]

No matter how much Major intended otherwise, the news was still received as a 'humiliating retreat'.[92] The fallout was considerable. Hunt, already a hate figure for the right, was now blamed by the leaders of the left, Heseltine and Clarke, and their supporters for engineering the downfall of the plan. Heseltine, in particular, never forgave him. But Hunt was small fry; it was Major for whom the knives were out in earnest. Lamont lost no time to express his 'immense disappointment' at the 'absurd' failure of nerve and the muddle in policy direction.[93] Angry right-wingers became progressively more outspoken against their leader at his apparent abandonment of Thatcherite radicalism. According to the *Sunday Times*, 'In the eyes of many Tories, Major has emerged as a man of straw from last week's débâcle.'[94] For David Martin, Parliamentary Private Secretary to Hurd, disillusioned over the direction on Europe, the decision was the last straw and he resigned. Major was blamed for letting Heseltine run with the idea for so long, then using intermediaries like Hunt and Ryder to bring him down, only to reveal his own hand at the last moment.

Heseltine's reputation, however, was enhanced by the Post Office episode;

his leadership prospects, fallow since his heart attack, dramatically revived. Whether an intentional strategy or not – and with Heseltine, even those close to him found it hard to tell – he had now achieved support from the right as well as from the left.[95]

Major continued to believe a Bill would have failed to achieve sufficient parliamentary support.[96] Not all agree. The rebels were mainly those on the left such as Hugh Dykes, with a handful of populist right-wingers like Rhodes Boyson; they were not a homogeneous, united rump. Had the whips come in and used their resources to persuade MPs, as they did with the Maastricht Bill, then the twenty might well have been whittled down to a handful, and the Bill might have squeezed through. But Major knew there would be tough battles ahead in the next session, above all on the European budget, and he wanted to keep parliamentary turbulence to a minimum if the image of a disunited Party was not to continue to jeopardise the Conservatives' electoral recovery.

Post Office privatisation, coming hard on the heels of Hamilton's dismissal, gave the right just the issue they needed to move back on the offensive and galvanise opposition to Major's leadership. The week following the critical Cabinet, names began to be collected to trigger a contest in November, which had to come within fourteen days of the new session which began on 16 November. By the weekend before MPs returned, twenty were claimed who were willing to spark a contest, still short of the thirty-four (10 per cent of Tory MPs) required. Lamont was being cited as one willing to put himself forward as a stalking horse candidate, paving the way for Clarke and Heseltine on the centre left, and Portillo as the main right-wing challenger.[97]

The unsettled background made Major and his advisers all the more determined to show in the Queen's Speech, on Wednesday 16 November, that the government had not run out of reforming zeal, especially with widespread talk that its 'keystone' had been knocked out of place with the removal of Post Office privatisation.[98] Major had moved onto the front foot in his Lord Mayor's Banquet speech in the Mansion House on Monday 14 November, warning MPs off allowing Parliament to become a 'hiring fair'.[99] The speech had preoccupied Major and his speech-writing team at Number Ten until the last minute; now, with less than forty-eight hours to go, they turned their attention to his text for Wednesday. The Prime Minister's speech always followed the Leader of the Opposition's; bar a few sparring rounds with Blair in the October spillover session, it was Major's first major encounter with his new opponent, and he was determined to make a strong impression.[100]

The Queen's Speech outlined thirteen well-trailed bills: continued radicalism with plans to abolish British Gas's domestic monopoly, privatisation of Crown Agents and the Atomic Energy Authority's technology division, as well as the introduction of a Jobseekers' Allowance to encourage the unemployed to find work. The European Community (Finance) Bill was included, and so were less controversial measures, including Bills to improve disability rights, equalise retirement age at sixty-five by 2020, introduce new environ-mental protection agencies and abolish regions to cut back on bureaucracy in the NHS.[101] Equalisation of pensions had caused particular agonising. It was strongly backed by Lilley and supported by Major (who knew the issue as a former Social Security minister). The measure, thanks to some deft handling, did not in the end prove the trouble that had been feared.

The shock element came in Major's speech when he said that he would call a general election if defeated in the European Community (Finance) Bill; it was, he said, 'inescapably a matter of confidence'.[102] The background to this gambit, which caused widespread anger, is discussed below, but early indications were that the tactic had outflanked the likely rebels on the Bill. To reinforce the government's intent, Newton stressed in a television interview that the Prime Minister would without question seek a dissolution if defeated, and the Queen would grant it.[103]

On Friday 18 November, Major left for his Anglo–French summit, this year in the small cathedral town of Chartres. The week, he reflected on his return flight, had turned out surprisingly well. On Monday, an early start saw him attend a 6.30 a.m. launch party and firework display at the Tower of London for a pet scheme of his, the National Lottery. He himself bought £5-worth of tickets at a newsagent in London's Victoria, declaring that – if he won – he would donate his prize to Mencap. He did not win, but over £7 million was raised in the first twelve hours of ticket sales, which augured well.[104] His big speeches on Monday and Wednesday had been well received.[105] And now the summit, Mitterrand's last as President, had gone down smoothly. Major's foreign policy advisers had sought out new areas which would keep both nations closely aligned to build on and eventually take over from the harmony they had enjoyed over Bosnia.[106] Mitterrand and Prime Minister Edouard Balladur stressed their common view that the EU should consolidate rather than rush ahead to further integration: 'I do not believe there is going to be a great leap forward [at the IGC] in 1996,' capped Major, keen to pacify Eurosceptic apprehensions at home for what lay ahead.[107] Agreement on military cooperation sealed the entente cordiale, ninety years after the famous Entente Cordiale between Britain and France signed in 1904.

Major Loses Control

Relations with his own Party, and Cabinet, were now to become anything but cordial. Within days of his return from Chartres, the European Finance Bill brought all the underlying tensions out into the open. The six weeks to Christmas were to be one of his worst spells as premier.

Confused reports had begun to leak out about a dinner at Downing Street on 13 November, Remembrance Sunday, attended by the Cabinet 'big beasts' – Clarke, Heseltine, Hurd and Howard – as well as Ryder and Rifkind, but indicatively not Hunt or Hanley. Major had called the dinner to talk tactics for the vote and gain a consensus for tough action. Cabinet on 10 November three days before had decided a firm line must be taken on the Bill. Both Major and Hurd spoke strongly about Britain's obligations to pass it, which – though further Euro legislation was the last thing they wanted – was inescapable to implement agreements on EU funding made at the Edinburgh summit in December 1992.[108] But what if the Eurosceptic MPs rebelled? This was the primary concern of ministers at that Sunday evening meeting.

Clarke pressed hard for a brutal policy. Why not threaten to call a general election to put pressure on the potential rebels, some of whom, like Marlow, had narrow majorities and who might thus back off? Hurd had mentioned such a recourse at Cabinet three days before. All now agreed the government could not afford a repetition of the prolonged Maastricht saga during 1992–3. This time, rather than be pushed around, they should deploy the ultimate deterrent at the outset, not at the end.[109] Other ministers solemnly concurred, that it was better to get the unpleasantness over in one go, rather than drip feed, in what became known as the 'suicide pact'.[110]

Despite the Eurosceptics' view that Clarke was to blame for the tactic, his gung ho approach reflected the views of Major and Hurd, who were less outspoken but just as keen on a hard line. Hurd made it clear he was duty bound to resign if the Bill was defeated, feeling that he could not honourably face his European counterparts if it went under. He was in no mood to go gently on the Eurosceptics.[111] Close aides thought rebels should 'be put up against a wall and shot, otherwise they would keep doing it'. Ryder's advice, too, was that up to forty-two might rebel against the Bill, and the only way to win was to threaten them into submission. Neither could they fudge the issue. Robin Butler's advice also was pertinent – that the government had given its word to EU partners and that it would be perfectly proper to make the Bill an issue of confidence.[112]

Hanley was distressed when he learned on Monday morning about the meeting, but readily agreed with Hunt to the decision. With no Cabinet meeting scheduled before the Queen's Speech on Wednesday, when Major was to announce the vote of confidence, every Cabinet minister was contacted to ensure they were fully signed up to the strategy. Delegated to sound out colleagues were Major, Clarke, and Howard – a subtle move given his Eurosceptic credentials.[113] Those close to Portillo, Lilley and Redwood lost no time, however, in leaking that they had not been at the Sunday meeting, had doubts about the wisdom of 'bouncing' the right into supporting the Bill and, ominously, that they had given no pledges not to head an alternative government if Major himself resigned.[114]

Number Ten tried to play down the Sunday dinner as merely one of a series of routine meetings between Cabinet ministers. But Eurosceptics' hackles were up. The early headway made by the shock announcement of the confidence motion on Wednesday began to slow down as the rebels regrouped by the end of the week.[115] The Sunday newspapers on 20 November revealed that Cedric Brown, Chief Executive of British Gas, was to receive a £205,000 pay rise, which heightened cynicism of another key element in the Queen's Speech – its free enterprise drive. But it was on Monday 21 November that things began to go seriously off-beam. The *Financial Times* blazed in with news of the leaked Maples research, thought to have come from a source at Saatchi & Saatchi, revealing the extent of popular disillusion among Tories with government performance.[116] The next day, the right-winger Nicholas Bonsor challenged Marcus Fox for the 1922 chairmanship. For the right, Fox's support for the confidence motion was a last straw, and Bonsor's challenge was seen – not entirely accurately, as some Major loyalists were also dissatisfied with Fox – as a proxy for one by the right on the Party leadership itself.[117]

Wednesday's news – blows were coming daily – was of a lobby briefing given by Clarke, which served to publicise and fan divisions within the Cabinet.[118] He confirmed that the rumoured Sunday evening dinner had indeed happened, and stated that, 'The entire present Cabinet agreed to make this a vote of confidence.'[119] But he went too far, as he was prone to do, when – to counter the right – he stated that there was 'no credibility' to claims that Major could simply resign if the Bill was defeated, and that another figure could take his place as premier. BBC reports of Clarke's briefing implied that every Cabinet member had agreed that none of them would take over from Major if he resigned after the vote was lost. Portillo, still unquestionably the most vocal leader of the Eurosceptics within Cabinet, was incensed, and demanded to know why Clarke had talked of a non-existent Cabinet agreement on such a matter. Clarke's response was that he had said no Cabinet minister could 'honourably' take over as Prime Minister.[120] But the harm had been done.

Number Ten was irritated with Clarke for opening wounds in public. In Cabinet on Thursday 24 November, Major cracked the whip.[121] He secured unanimous agreement that the passage of the Finance Bill 'in all its essentials' was to be an issue of confidence, and defeat would result in a request to the Palace for a dissolution. 'Action' would, moreover, have to be taken against any MPs who voted against the government, though it was judged counter-productive to labour this point in advance of the debate.[122] Portillo, Lilley and Redwood all fell into line, with varying degrees of reluctance; the last later said he would have preferred to have seen a free vote on the Bill, and even came close to resigning.[123] Nevertheless, all three agreed to issue statements confirming that defeat would result in the government falling. A release from Number Ten put the matter beyond doubt: 'There is no question of the Prime Minister resigning and an alternative Conservative Prime Minister being found.'[124] All these assurances merely underlined how Major's authority over Cabinet was weakening. Clarke was heard saying that any rebels should 'be crushed like beetles'.[125]

Major's authority in the House suffered similarly that afternoon when

Eurosceptic MP Christopher Gill said during Question Time – to 'gasps across the House' – that he would rather resign the whip than vote for a Bill with which he, and dozens of his fellow Tories, strongly disagreed.[126] Bill Cash escalated the tension by tabling an amendment to the European Finance Bill. Blair, who could scarcely believe his luck at the speed with which the Tories' legislative programme had become derailed, claimed that Tory backbenchers were 'in a state of anarchy', and accused Major of leading an 'ill-disciplined rabble incapable of governing this country'.[127] Eurosceptics took heart from an article by Lamont in that morning's *Daily Mail*, in which he was scornful of 'an unpopular Government threatening itself with electoral extinction for the sake of increasing the taxes we pay to Brussels'.[128] The newspapers were also full of the resignation of Party Vice-Chairman Patrick Nicholls, for an error of judgement writing an article lambasting Germany and France.[129] The only good news during the day came from the 1922 Committee when Marcus Fox defeated Nicholas Bonsor, albeit by only thirteen votes, and from the confirmation that any MPs who lost the whip if they rebelled against the government would be prevented from putting their names down with those calling for a leadership election. Nominations were due to close the following Wednesday.

The outlook in Number Ten was extremely bleak and bitter. One aide told Colin Brown of the *Independent* that those backbenchers planning to rebel were 'totally nihilistic ... They aren't even proper Conservatives. They just seem to be intent on voting down the Government on this one issue. It's complete madness.'[130] Major's own mood was grim. One Cabinet minister recorded: 'The PM is in virtually constant pain. At some meetings he has had to get up and walk around, pulling a face. It is possibly psychological. But he just looks like a man in pain.'[131] In fact, Major had a trapped nerve in his neck and had been receiving medical attention for the pain. Number Ten avoided letting this be known because of the obvious puns that would appear in the headlines. The thought crossed Major's mind that he should gain the initiative and trigger the leadership election himself. But calmer counsels prevailed.[132]

With the vote on Monday 28 November, the weekend before was awash with rumours and speculation about who might rebel and about the leadership challenge. Lamont and Edward Leigh were two of the most frequently cited plotters.[133] Lamont was reported seen with Cash, Leigh and Carlisle in the Commons Smoking Room brazenly drinking champagne ('because our numbers are going up'), and discussing backers for a leadership challenge. By the weekend before the vote, numbers prepared to sign were estimated to be between twenty-five and thirty, just short of the required thirty-four names; but there were still four days to go.[134] Overtures were made to the supporters of Heseltine, known to be still angry at the Post Office decision, in an effort to secure the extra names.[135]

Two other allied arguments were raging. Was the Prime Minister in fact entitled to declare that a particular vote is one of confidence, and if defeated, ask the Queen for a dissolution? If so, what was her constitutional position? Would she have to grant it? Could she not, on advice that Cabinet was far from united on the matter, call for another minister who might be able to lead the government in the Prime Minister's place? Number Ten continued to assert that Major was perfectly within his rights to insist on the course of action he outlined.[136]

Much air and print was also expended, with Clarke and Cash the principal protagonists, debating whether the increase in the European budget was 'modest' (Clarke) or 'pouring money into a bottomless, fraudulent pit' (Cash). The differences in their figures were not trivial, with the former's only 10 per cent of the latter's.[137] Those on either side believed the figures they wanted, further inflaming the divide in what one newspaper called 'a state of near-permanent hysteria'.[138]

The mood in the House on Monday 28 November was certainly fevered. Lamont's speech, 'dripping with barely concealed contempt' according to Michael White, warned that the Commons would be reduced to a European 'rubber stamp'.[139] With the expected Unionist support, however, Major won a majority of twenty-seven for the Bill against the Labour attempt to defeat it. So that removed any question about the government having to resign. But all the attention was taken by eight Tory MPs – Budgen, Carttiss, Gill, Gorman, Marlow, Shepherd, Taylor and Wilkinson – who refused to vote with the government. They nevertheless had not expected to have the whip withdrawn: according to David Willetts, then a whip, it was Budgen who persuaded his fellow rebels that if they merely *abstained*, they would call the government's bluff.[140]

Major and Ryder considered how to respond. It was pointed out that the government would technically lose its majority of fourteen if all eight were to have the whip taken away; its control of committees might also be put in jeopardy. But no one present dissented from the course of action that had to be taken. Ryder wrote tersely to the eight rebels that evening to say, 'You have knowingly failed to support the government on a vote that is an issue of confidence. Therefore the whip has been withdrawn.'[141] A ninth MP, Richard Body, voluntarily resigned the whip in disgust at the treatment meted out to the rebels. The number could have been much larger; many bitter opponents of the Bill, including Carlisle, Cash, Gardiner and Leigh, fell in reluctantly behind the government. There appeared little support for the tough action taken against the now 'whipless' that night among the parliamentary party, but there was much speculation whether Major could survive a leadership challenge. Though George Jones may have exaggerated when he wrote of Major that 'it was probably the grimmest day of his leadership',[142] it was certainly the unhappiest anniversary – his fourth – of his election to Prime Minister.

Why had he acted as he did? Never in the twentieth century had as many Conservative MPs received this, the most severe punishment open to the Party's discipline machine. Those expelled could no longer call themselves

'Conservative' MPs, and could even be unseated as candidates in their constituencies if not readmitted by the next general election. Major was taken aback by the number who rebelled: the advice he had received initially was that calling a confidence vote would bring all the dissidents into line, as had the strategy when last employed at the end of the Maastricht passage, when only one Tory MP (Rupert Allason) had failed to support the government.

It was partly a matter of pride for Major. He believed with some justice that he had negotiated at Edinburgh a very good deal for Britain. As Hanley recalled, 'He was affronted by the Eurosceptics saying the budget deal was not good enough, which it clearly was.'[143] The undermining of his leadership that had begun over Maastricht was exacerbated, in the eyes of several insiders, by the failure to punish Carlisle and Marlow when they had called for him to stand down after the QMV débâcle. A persistent feeling of rebellion on the backbenches meant his authority was being ground away. If he was to restore his credibility and counter the view that it was dribbling away, he had to 'go in and hit, and hit hard'.[144] Many agreed with Peter Riddell that contempt for Major personally was as important in the rebels' action as hatred of the EU.[145] Before finally deciding, he consulted a few close colleagues, but they felt his mind was already made up that on this issue he had to take on the Euro-rebels.[146]

With so many distractions, budget day on Tuesday 29 November crept up almost unnoticed. That suited the government, as it was a cautious, low-key budget. Clarke, who had opened on the European Finance Bill the day before, announced a £24 billion cut in public spending, the largest reduction since 1982, to be phased over the next three years. The economic background was favourable: it had become apparent over the summer that with prices lower than the Treasury had been predicting, the departments could have more money shaved off their allocations in the spending round – Aitken's only one as Chief Secretary. Further reductions in departmental spending, however, had still to be found.

Cutting education was the most risky part of the settlement, with leaked disputes between Gillian Shephard's Education Department and the Treasury heightening tension. It seemed possible that the turbulence which had characterised John Patten's period as Education Secretary would return. But the numbers of authorities that carried out threats to sack teachers to keep within budget proved smaller than expected, and the discontent more manageable. The combination of economic recovery and public borrowing (now at £46 billion) coming down provided an optimistic platform.

The budgets in 1993–6 all had borrowing requirement reductions as a prime aim. Officials observed that Clarke felt more confident in 1994 than he had for his first budget the year before, and was able to give it far more of his personal touch.[147] Differences in emphasis between Number Ten and the Treasury were minor and could be readily accommodated. Political pressure to reflate and to advance the feel-good factor, they agreed, had to be resisted. Sarah Hogg vividly recalled the panic over the voteless recovery. The battle was to say that this was the wrong time, and we should cool down now to position ourselves for a 1996 or 1997 election. The party pressures were unfocused, they were not thinking long term, and it took nerve to say we had to tighten a bit more.[148]

Measures to encourage employers to take on long-term unemployed by granting full national insurance rebates and other incentives to encourage people back to work were Clarke's own;[149] supply-side measures on private finance bore Number Ten's imprimatur.[150]

The deadline for the leadership challenge, Wednesday 30 November, came and went. Best estimates suggest the rebels, with the whipless nine excluded, had collected only twenty-four names, ten short of their target. Major's would-be assassins had to lick their wounds and return to their tent. George Gardiner, often singled out as plotter-in-chief, says that despite his wish to see Major toppled, he had not participated in this attempt because it was never going to gain enough support. He and his allies muttered that next year would be different.[151] Number Ten was happy meanwhile to see Portillo look somewhat ridiculous when a tenth anniversary party organised by his constituency association at Alexandra Palace flopped. By the time the embarrassed Portillo had found out about the surprise party, it would have cost too much money to cancel. The press poured scorn on the event, above all when they heard that a short film – little more than a few clips – was to be shown before dinner. The film idea was vetoed by Portillo, and invitations to Lady Thatcher and Norman Tebbit were also withdrawn. But the damage had been done, and the impression of Portillo being both vain and immature lingered long after the evening was over. As his biographer wrote, 'Prudence had given way to hubris.' To a rueful Portillo 'it was a nightmare from beginning to end'.[152]

Any satisfaction in Number Ten at Portillo's discomfort, and the failure of a leadership challenge that year, was quickly erased by a new row emerging early in December over VAT on fuel. Despite pressure from some in Cabinet, including Hanley and Lang, Clarke refused to delay the unpopular doubling of VAT in his budget (from 8 to 17.5 per cent) to come in from the following April.[153] Though Number Ten had to dismiss the idea that Major had opposed the rise as 'demented rumour mongering',[154] it is clear that he had serious misgivings about the increase. He worried greatly about its political and economic effects but he did not restrain Clarke, in part because he did not like to override his senior ministers, having unpleasant memories of being brought under pressure from Number Ten when he had been Chancellor.[155] So he did not pull rank when Cabinet had discussed the increase on VAT the previous month. Redwood, alert as always to warding off tax rises, was one of the few to question whether, in the light of economic recovery, it was still necessary to proceed with the increase. But Clarke was adamant. If the rate was kept at 8 per cent, where it had been put in 1993, the government would not get credit from a U-turn. It was, moreover, important to show financial markets that the government really was determined to restore healthy public finances.[156] The VAT increase would raise an extra £1.5 billion, and coincide with energy undertakings made at the UN Rio Earth Summit in June 1992. There were some hopes too, no doubt naïve, of cross-party support for the increase, as the Liberal Democrats had previously espoused it, and Labour was interested in an energy tax. The general feeling in Cabinet was that Parliament had voted three times on the increase and, whatever the repercussions, there should be no retreat.[157]

The crucial vote on the VAT increase was to take place on Tuesday 6 December. With whips reporting that a backbench revolt was brewing, Major flew off to Budapest on 4 December to attend the fifty-two-nation Conference on Security and Co-operation in Europe (CSCE). It was a trying affair, and Major did not relish being there, not least with their discussions so fractious. Yeltsin launched an outspoken attack on Clinton for his administration's proposals for expanding NATO into central and eastern Europe. Russian–American tension was also to the fore in the other dominant issue of the conference, Bosnia. President Izetbegovic of Bosnia accused the West of a 'mixture of incapability, hesitation and ill-will' for their failure to save Bihac or to come to his government's aid. London and Paris were singled out by him as having 'taken on the role of Serbia's protectors'. Late on the Monday afternoon, Major warned the warring parties that Britain was on the brink of withdrawing its troops, and joined ranks with Yeltsin in pinning his hopes on the Contact Group finding a solution. Major warned further that an American lifting of the arms embargo would lead to a 'significant escalation of the war'.[158] It seemed that a resolution of the long-running Bosnia saga was as far away as ever.

The end-of-conference state banquet that evening was hosted by President Goncz in the beautiful neo-Gothic Parliament building on the Danube. After five bilateral meetings, including a snatched fifteen minutes with Clinton, and the stresses of the conference floor, Major was in no mood for a formal dinner. He made his excuses. After looking in at a more congenial supper for 'interesting Hungarians' at the British Ambassador's residence, Major retired to his quarters where he took a phone call from Clarke, updating him on his own warring parties. With the VAT vote the next day, the news was not encouraging.[159]

Major flew back early on Tuesday morning to meet Clarke, who in his absence had issued warnings that defeat would simply lead to further tax rises elsewhere. The opponents remained unmoved by his reasoning, so together with Major he now agreed a package of an extra £100 million compensation for retirement pensioners to try to lure the disaffected back into the fold. Ryder told Number Ten that they had done enough and would just win. He was wrong. The government was defeated by 319 votes to 311. The House erupted in scenes eclipsing any drama of the European Finance Bill vote, and recalling the atmosphere in the Commons during the tied vote on the Maastricht Treaty in July 1993.[160] The whips later claimed that they had been tricked by the rebels, and had been told direct lies by some, as indeed they had.[161] With the 'whipless' MPs at their core, the rebels were unrepentant, and boasted that they would exact similar defeats in future.[162] Major's surprise at the result, and his profound anger at the backbenchers, provoked one of his rare recorded episodes of bad temper. Approached for comment by James Blitz of the *Financial Times* after the lost vote, he snapped, 'Don't waste my time.'[163] Arguably it was Clarke's standing which suffered more, though he gained credit for the commanding way he responded over the next forty-eight hours.

Interest rates were promptly raised to 6.25 per cent the following morning. Clarke then sat down in the Treasury with his team and agreed rises in the three 'sin taxes', covering alcohol, tobacco and petrol, to fill the gap in public finances left by the VAT on fuel not being increased. The proposals were then put by Clarke to a group, dubbed the 'inner Cabinet', of Heseltine, Hurd, Howard, Rifkind and Ryder, who met in emergency session under Major at Number Ten that evening.[164] Duly approved by them, Clarke presented the plans to the House as a mini-budget on Thursday 8 December.

Major himself attempted to regain the initiative in an interview on *Channel 4 News*. Talk of leadership challenges was dismissed as being like 'Billy Bunter's postal order: widely talked about, but it never actually arrived'. He would not be deflected from what he thought was right by an unrepresentative minority, and he appealed for MPs to unite behind him in 'the national interest'.[165] But the damage done could not be easily eradicated. While Andrew Marr spoke of 'authority bleeding away', Joe Rogaly compared Major's position to Callaghan's during 1978–9.[166] A Gallup poll in the *Daily Telegraph* put Labour's lead as the largest ever recorded in polling history, an extraordinary 39.5 points ahead.[167]

Further trouble seemed in store when Major attended the EU summit at Essen from 8 to 10 December at the end of the German presidency. Predictions were that discussions would be as vexed on Bosnia as they had been at Budapest.[168] The Cassandras underestimated Kohl's desire for a smooth finale, and his wish to project the EU, in contrast to CSCE and other multinational bodies, as a dominant world group. The Germans went to extraordinary lengths to achieve his ends, with conspicuous overtures to accommodate Britain. 'Throughout the conference in almost embarrassing profusion, the leaders of Europe stood up to agree with every British policy,' was Christopher Lockwood's verdict.[169]

The decisions included steps to prepare six East European states for membership, cutting benefits to reduce unemployment, endorsement of the UN's role in Bosnia, a fight against fraud and waste in the EU, and a £236 million grant for inner-city jobs in Northern Ireland. As George Brock wrote, 'Federalism was in retreat.'[170] Not surprisingly Major described the Essen summit as 'the most productive and good-humoured' since he became premier. He joked to the press corps, 'I hope the lack of a row is not a disappointment.'[171]

He spoke too soon. While he sat down to Delors's 'last supper', an event he had not wanted to attend but ended up enjoying, the pot was being stirred back in London.[172] Eurosceptics were angered by an article in the *Mail on Sunday* where Major wrote in uncompromising terms about there being no appeasement of the whipless.[173] The *Sunday Times* carried a front-page headline 'Heseltine and Clarke unite against Major', though the cause of their purported pact was little more than a mutual distaste for Major's statement in Essen that he 'had not ruled out the prospect of a referendum'.[174] Both men felt disgruntled with Major, but neither was actively plotting to thwart him. Heseltine's backers were not, however, displeased at the events of the previous weeks, which by discrediting the Chancellor had advanced their own man again as the front-running successor.[175]

The Christmas recess brought relief, but not until after another disastrous by-election, at Dudley West, won by Labour with a swing of 29 per cent, reducing the government's majority to thirteen if the whipless supported it. Major was exhausted, and did little over the Christmas holiday, bar putting his feet up at The Finings and enjoying the company of family. Unguarded comments to a friend when he felt despondent before Christmas duly found themselves relayed in the *Independent*,[176] that his disillusion with the way politicians were continually undermined encouraged him to think about what he might do after politics – perhaps return to a career in banking.

The Principal Lieutenant Departs

The end of the year saw the last days of Sarah Hogg as Head of the Policy Unit. For over four years she had been Major's most reliable and effective aide in Downing Street. Her leaving was all the more significant because it coincided closely with that of Major's two other loyalist aides in Number Ten, Jonathan Hill, Political Secretary, and Nick True, officially Hogg's deputy in the Policy Unit since the 1992 general election. Over the summer of 1994, they had all decided the time had come to leave, to give Major a chance to put in place a fresh team to lead the Party into the next general election. Hill left at the end of November, Hogg at the end of January 1995.

Hogg's was the most significant departure. Criticised for being domineering before the 1992 general election, akin to Marcia Williams under Harold Wilson, she became still more controversial afterwards, with the core charge that for a head of Policy Unit, she was short on long-term strategic thinking. The collapse of back to basics in early 1994 was a nadir. Criticism from the Party and the press of Major, but also of her, was unrelenting during this second period, stretching from Martin Jacques's comment in late 1992 that 'This is a government which is undecided on what it stands for or what it really wants to do',[177] to the *Sunday Times* in late 1994 that 'His has become a government without a clear policy or credo.'[178]

Given that her task was not aided by Major not being an ideological or programmatic thinker, and by the lack of thinking time that dogged them both, how much at fault was she? She herself uses the analogy, in describing her last two and a half years at Number Ten, of 'keeping on hammering in the tent pegs around Whitehall while the storm tried to take the tent off the grass'.[179] The storm raged, she believes, principally because of the loss of opinion poll-based authority and the enormous expenditure of energy and political capital on the Maastricht Bill. Coupled with the loss of self-confidence among the parliamentary party, the forces of conservatism, within Whitehall as well as within the Tory Party, were able to reassert themselves.

She accepts that the long term was often sacrificed for the short: 'I wouldn't defend hard against the charge of short-termism. The circumstances of 1992–4 were inevitably firefighting. It was the nature of the circumstances at the time.'[180] She also had fierce supporters within Number Ten. Typical was:

She fought magnificently. Yes, much of her time between 1992–4 was spent firefighting, but if she hadn't done it, and she did it very well, there would have been even greater crises to distract the Prime Minister. The fact she wasn't more successful in her attempts to focus ministers' minds on the longer term is also partly the responsibility of the ministers, and ultimately the Prime Minister himself. It was always open to him to demand a higher priority be given to long-term strategy.[181]

The last was never uttered by Sarah Hogg, even if she thought it. She was to the end utterly loyal to her leader.[182]

Not that the short term always did predominate during 1992–4, though the almost constant atmosphere of crisis, and the media, helped create the impression that it did. Important long-term thinking nevertheless occurred in economic and fiscal policy, law and order, education, privatisation, GATT, EU policy, sport and the lottery, and Northern Ireland, all of which saw direct inputs from Number Ten.

The disdain with which ministers treated attempts to turn back to basics into a strategy served to show how difficult Number Ten found it to exercise control after 1992. One Policy Unit member reflected:

You could see what was happening. Back in 1991, we had just to phone a Whitehall Deputy Secretary and say, 'The Prime Minister is determined to drive on this one', and things happened. But by 1993 a lot of people were sharpening their knives around Whitehall and saying, 'Let's not take notice of this. We'll play for time because he may not be around much longer.'[183]

The lack of thinking time – which even prevented an out-of-town seminar for the Policy Unit in her last eighteen months – and the lack of a coherent ideological thrust or even a consensus among senior figures on the way forward, were Sarah Hogg's core difficulties in producing longer term strategy. Not that she can be absolved from blame: unlike the Policy Units under Mrs Thatcher and Tony Blair, intellectuals were not imported or even regularly consulted, while think-tankers, with the exception of Madsen Pirie of the Adam Smith Institute and Graham Mather of the European Policy

Forum, rarely made an input into government thinking. Major's contacts with intellectuals tended to be on the basis of personal friendship, as with Martin Gilbert.

But the not inconsiderable policy legacy, with much of which she was closely involved, and her shrewd political skills, meant that when Sarah Hogg did leave Number Ten a big hole remained behind, which Major would find hard to fill.

For the moment, Major returned to the fray with renewed energy. In discussions at the margins of the Central Office Christmas party, it had been agreed between his Political Office and Central Office that he should open a new offensive against Labour on tax and the constitution and start 1995 on the front foot. In his New Year message, and a lengthy end-of-year interview with James Naughtie on BBC Radio 4's *Today* programme, Major held out the prospect of a 'golden prize' of the most prosperous economy for generations after 'four years of suffering', up to 5 pence off income tax, and success in the general election provided divisions were not allowed to 'destroy us from within'.[184] He reopened the devolution debate with an attack on Labour's plans for a Scottish Parliament as 'one of the most dangerous propositions that has ever been put before the British nation'.

Defence of the constitution might yet prove a rallying cry around which to unite the Party, and if the tide of European federalism was indeed on the ebb, and economic recovery on the flow, there might well be some real grounds for optimism in the New Year.

THIRTY-ONE

Governing Without a Majority:

January–April 1995

THE RECOVERY OF John Major's authority over the two years from 1995 to 1997 was a painfully slow process, and an uneven one, as might have been expected given the continued hostility to his leadership at all levels of the Party, and the continued failure of the vital elixir, electoral popularity, to materialise. The period from November 1994 to June 1995 marks the low point of his premiership; but signs of recovery were in evidence from New Year 1995, some months before the significant boost in the leadership election in the summer.

A Gap in the Fog: January

A Number Ten position paper in early January 1995 reflected several grounds for optimism. Economic recovery was continuing, Maastricht and the European finance debate were out of the way, and there was progress in Northern Ireland.[1] As important, the first signs were appearing that the Blair honeymoon was coming to an end. Major was not unappreciative of the boost at this particular time: by the end of 1994 three members of his 'kitchen Cabinet', his closest advisers at Number Ten – Hill, Bright and O'Donnell – had gone, and two, Hogg and True, were shortly to depart, leaving him to adjust to a new team. Allan and Lyne in the Private Office provided continuity with the *ancien régime*, but Major, like Thatcher before him, liked to retain familiar faces around him.

The new Political Secretary, Howell James, nevertheless imparted a sense of a fresh start, taking over from a very tired Jonathan Hill. James had been a director of corporate affairs at the BBC and then the telecommunications giant Cable and Wireless. As a special adviser to Lord Young in the mid-1980s, he was no stranger to government, and had begun work at Number Ten on 28 November, the day of the European budget vote.[2] Aged forty, James was six years older than Hill. He brought a steady hand and a new sense of humour into Number Ten deliberations. He drew an analogy with his former job: 'The role I had at Cable and Wireless was advising the Chairman and Chief Executive about what they were doing, and how it was being received. That role of a counsellor and internal consultant who was allowed to speak candidly is what I sensed was needed at Number Ten.'[3] Low-profile in December, while he learned the job, his impact was felt in the more assertive messages over the New Year, such as the prospect of tax cuts dangled by Major, a ploy worked up between the Number Ten Political Office and Tim Collins at Central Office.[4]

James gave more scope to George Bridges, the twenty-four-year-old researcher brought into the Political Office as an assistant from Central Office in January 1994.[5] Bridges's particular gift was for Prime Minister's Questions, when he supplied some of Major's strongest lines.[6] Over the months, Bridges began to fulfil some of the liaison functions with the Tory Party performed by Hill, while James became more of a chief of staff at Number Ten, acting as a troubleshooter for the Prime Minister in a not wholly dissimilar way to Sarah Hogg until her departure. Unlike Hogg, however, James did not sit in on ministerial bilaterals, was not involved in formulating policy, and did not have the same presence in Whitehall. James was a man-manager and public relations figure *par excellence*, and had been the favourite to succeed Tim Collins as the Party's Director of Communications, until Central Office learned he had been captured first by Number Ten.[7]

A new positive spirit was felt in an upbeat television interview with David Frost on Sunday 9 January. The whipless MPs and the government's vulnerability on Europe had been identified as likely sensitive issues on which he might be quizzed. Major had been encouraged by the lack of enthusiasm shown by European leaders at the December Essen Council to further integration. He also spoke in private of his hope that once Kohl ceased to be Chancellor, the drive for unity in the EU would dwindle, as Balladur of France was not a force, and the smaller European countries, he felt, were just following Germany's lead.[8]

On *Breakfast with Frost* Major considered the moment ripe to put down his first marker since his Leiden speech in September on his road to scepticism. He pledged himself to block constitutional changes, including any new powers for the European Parliament or any extension of QMV. Moreover, there would be 'no question' of a single currency by 1996 to 1997.[9] A referendum, he said, could always be deployed if necessary. An olive branch was held out to the whipless MPs, described approvingly by him as 'very Conservative'; he hoped they would return to the fold in the 'weeks ahead'. *The Times* judged it 'a well-timed conciliatory gesture to the Euro-sceptic Right of his party'.[10] Rees-Mogg thought it an excellent performance, praised him for learning from his mistakes, and said his leadership position was now 'impregnable'.[11]

The wisdom in the short term of the overtures to the whipless MPs was shown three days later, when five of them supported the government in a vote called by Labour on the composition of standing committees in the House. Had the government been defeated, the Conservatives' built-in majority on crucial committees would have been lost, the fear voiced when Major debated whether to remove the whip in November.[12] Anxious to maintain momentum, Major told ministers in Cabinet on 12 January that they were to start work immediately on preparing their ideas for the Conservative manifesto for the general election. Secretaries of state were told to report back by the summer, though he stressed he had no intention of calling a general election for at least two years, in order to capitalise fully on the economic recovery.[13] To help ministers trawl a wide range of opinion and ideas, some fifteen policy groups were to be set up. Members of these groups were to consult widely and to report back to the Policy Unit.

Major laid great store by the thorough nature of the policy preparation exercise, in part to counter the charge that policy in the past had been ill-considered[14] or, as a leader in *The Times* put it, 'formulated on the hoof in an atmosphere of barely suppressed anxiety'.[15] Long-term thinking was suddenly in vogue. The day after the Cabinet, Major chaired a Chequers summit with some of his most senior ministers to discuss Britain's long-term defence and foreign policy, a follow-up to a conference at Chequers on Britain's overseas priorities which had taken place the September before.[16]

Number Ten described the atmosphere since the New Year as 'exhilarating'.[17] Major gave some of the strongest performances at Question Time of his premiership. On 12 January he returned to the devolution theme he had discussed in a BBC *Today* interview four days before, accusing Blair of 'running scared of the Scottish Nationalists'. He said of Labour's plans, 'Every single aspect of what you now propose will lead inexorably to the circumstances where the UK itself might break up.'[18] Blair visibly blanched at Major's responses. Major was on even stronger form for the following Tuesday's questions,[19] pouring scorn on the federalist agenda proposed by Santer, the incoming EU President, and mocking the Labour leader's apparent contradictions: 'I'm rather surprised at what Mr Blair has to say about handing more powers to the European Parliament in view of the low opinion he's recently expressed of some members of it.' Of Blair's stance on renationalising British Rail, he said, 'Unlike the Right Hon. gentleman, we have not changed our policy on Friday, Saturday, Sunday and Monday.'[20]

As he left the chamber, Major was cheered by Conservative backbenchers waving their order papers, and he received an equally warm reception from his MPs when he later visited the Commons Tea Room. Major told them, 'We have got to start getting our teeth into Labour. Their honeymoon is over.'[21]

The Tories also had Labour on the run over its policy on VAT in schools and Clause Four of its constitution. Major was in high spirits that evening, saying he thought the previous week had been the turning point. 'There must be something wrong. Even the BBC are saying I am doing well,' he jested.[22]

Everything did, at last, seem to be going Major's way. A Downing Street news conference on 16 January, his first since the garden conference in June, was designed to show to all that he now had the political initiative. The pronouncements – reaffirmed pledge to privatise British Rail, staunch support for the monarchy – may not have amounted to much, but his tone was what mattered, aiming, as Peter Riddell wrote, 'to show he is no longer a leader in trouble, beset by party divisions and government mistakes'.[23] Some bridges were rebuilt when all eighteen members of the 1922 Executive were invited to lunch at Chequers, and Major further signalled his intention to invite backbenchers to Downing Street in groups, and to spend more time talking to MPs in the Commons Tea Rooms and lobbies.[24] On 18 January the government survived by nine votes a difficult vote on controversial EU rules to allow Spanish fishing boats access to traditional British waters.[25] At Cabinet on 19 January, Clarke reported that the latest economic indicators were 'very encouraging'; such a combination of strong recovery and low inflation 'had not been seen for years'.[26] A week later, MORI poll figures showed a five-point rise in Tory popularity to its highest level since May 1994.[27]

Below the surface, some strains were audible. A series of Home Office stories, including the break-out from Parkhurst prison and the suicide in captivity of mass-murderer Frederick West, led to demands for Howard's resignation, but blame did not particularly attach itself to Major.[28] Cracks in Cabinet unity appeared over public spending, after Redwood openly declared that it was a 'myth' that spending was being reduced, and disagreement surfaced over the introduction of identity cards.[29] The right became excited by the beginning of the new session of Congress that month which reflected the success of Newt Gingrich and the Republicans with their radical right 'Contract for America' agenda. The lesson to Portillo *et al* was clear. The turn in the direction of consolidation the previous autumn had been in error: radicalism, not caution, would bring back disillusioned Conservative voters. In a lecture given by Portillo in Liverpool, he called for a similar 'Contract for Britain'.[30]

But these creaks alone were insufficient to sacrifice Major's new position. What, then, went wrong? The immediate answer again was Europe, the beast that refused to lie down. Neither Leiden nor his broadcast comments in early January were enough to pacify the right. It became clear that it was the single currency that was agitating Eurosceptics, along with their keeping the salience of Europe high as a way of bashing down the leader they held in contempt. Tebbit had stirred the pot by declaring that the whipless MPs had his (and Lady Thatcher's) full backing, and goaded the rebels on from his regular column in the *Sun*.[31]

Encouraged by such high-level support, and by what their postbags were telling them was a Tory Party in the country supportive of their stand, eight of the nine Euro-rebels gave a swaggering press conference at the Commons.[32] Their demands, given prominence by a sympathetic Tory press, were a straight rebuff to Major. They declared that they would only come back as a group, and listed eight proposals which together amounted, in the eyes of *The Times*, to 'a call for outright withdrawal from the EU'.[33] Their stance made an early return of the whip unlikely, and led some commentators, including Tony Bevins and Boris Johnson, to inquire whether their statement might become the episode which would provoke a permanent division in the party.[34] The press conference and the impression it gave of an institutionalised split indeed caused widespread concern in the Party.

Responsibility for the self-inflicted wound of this press conference, however, was placed by the right-wing press less on the whipless MPs themselves than on the Party's leadership, for the 'cardinal tactical error' in making the European finance vote one of confidence.[35] Little thought was given to what other tactic Major could have employed to get the vote, vital to Britain's membership of the EU, through the House. To the right, it was the leadership that had provoked the whipless MPs to resort to the only option open to them. Clarke and Ryder continued to be blamed more for the decision than Major personally. Sensing the initiative was slipping away, in a move to show the right that he was not in hock to his Chancellor and other Europhiles, he announced that he would cease regular meetings of the 'inner Cabinet' of six, which in reality was never a forum of great importance, and would consult Eurosceptic ministers more.[36]

The day the story appeared, on 22 January, Clarke unpicked another thread of Major's authority when he declared his support on *Breakfast with Frost* for a single currency and for Britain being at 'the heart of Europe'.[37] Major was all the more angry because on Thursday the full Cabinet was to discuss a paper circulated by Hurd on Britain's stance for the seminal 1996 Intergovernmental Conference (IGC) on the future of the EU, prior to a committee, OPD(E), under Hurd's chairmanship being delegated to consider Britain's position in detail.[38] The problem of the whipless, Number Ten reasoned, was containable as long as they were not provoked; it would be unsustainable, however, if inflammatory statements and infighting broke out at the top. But Major had not calculated on the ire felt by the Cabinet's pro-Europeans to his apparent move to the sceptical wing starting with his Frost interview a fortnight before.

Major insisted in Cabinet on 26 January that all ministers be bound to complete secrecy, and under no circumstances whatsoever, he said, should they leak their own, or anyone else's, positions to third parties. He might as well not have spoken. A lead story in *The Times* the very next day, under the headline 'Hurd's brief on Europe is rejected', finally brought the momentum of the three previous weeks to a halt, and the fog came swirling back.[39] Number Ten was told that Lilley was responsible for the leak, who had been seen talking to Peter Stothard, editor of *The Times*, in a corner at a party.[40] The newspaper's story, widely picked up across the media, was all the more worrying for Number Ten because of its accuracy.

Hurd's introductory paper to Cabinet outlined in a rather scholarly fashion three different positions that could be adopted with regard to the IGC. But his approach was criticised by Cabinet ministers for being the product of Foreign Office Europhile thinking and for taking insufficient cognisance of the more sceptical tone – a clever line – in Major's Leiden speech and Frost interview. The overwhelming opinion, and not just of the usual sceptics, was that the government's position needed to be more robust in defence of British sovereignty, including a veto on significant constitutional changes and no acceptance of a single currency in 1996 or 1997, both positions articulated by Major to Frost.

While the Europhiles still had a majority, the balance in Cabinet on Europe, with Aitken and Cranborne joining the Eurosceptics, had tilted to the right and was never again to be so overwhelmingly pro-Europe. Hurd, Clarke and Gummer were now the three principals who could be relied upon to speak out strongly in favour of the EU; Heseltine remained Europhile, but was moving more with the wind. Significantly, both Hunt and Shephard spoke in favour of a tough stance at the IGC. The right was reassured by the presence of three of their number, Howard, Portillo and Redwood, on Hurd's OPD(E) subcommittee, and by Major's reassurance that full Cabinet would periodically be able to comment on the debate as it unfolded in the committee.[41]

Hurd, usually very level headed, was furious at the leak. He demanded an immediate and categoric denial, said he had not been 'rebuffed', while his friends claimed it was part of a right-wing plot to replace him as Foreign Secretary by a Eurosceptic. Number Ten was in a dilemma. Major described the report in *The Times* as a 'travesty', but at the same time did not want to undo the progress and come across as too Europhile. Edward Heath and Geoffrey Howe roared into the counterattack, while Clarke let it be known that he would be making a major pronouncement on Europe in ten days' time.[42] Before he could do so, however, considerable turbulence was to be caused by another leak, also to *The Times*.

The Framework Document: February

An anxious peace had come over Northern Ireland with the IRA and Loyalist ceasefires in the second half of 1994. But any cessation of violence could only be a prelude to a constitutional settlement which alone would make peace permanent, binding all factions within the province into democratic politics.

With Dublin wanting to hold off constitutional talks until Sinn Fein was able to join, the Northern Ireland Office went ahead on its own under junior minister Michael Ancram, and in February 1994 produced a short document exploring what might be discussed in constitutional talks, quaintly called the 'Notions Paper'.[43] By April 1994, however, the Irish government became more positive, and its Foreign Affairs Department began to work with the NIO on detailed proposals for a constitutional settlement, to become known as the joint 'Framework Document'; John Chilcot and Quentin Thomas were the key British officials involved in the drafting.[44]

Major was not himself involved in the detail, but dealt periodically at prime ministerial level with Reynolds, as he had during their summit in May and at Corfu on 24 June. While there, Major defined what became known as the

'Corfu questions', the two key issues from the British viewpoint that would need resolving in any framework document: was the Irish government prepared to amend their constitution to the point where they would say their territorial claim over the North had been removed, and would they in public recognise the legitimacy of British rule in Northern Ireland for as long as it reflected the consent of the majority?

Publication of the joint Framework Document was repeatedly postponed. The IRA and Loyalist ceasefire announcements made little difference, and the hope of having the document finalised for discussion at the Anglo–Irish Conference in September 1994 appeared forlorn. Unionists knew that secret negotiations were in train between London and Dublin, and they were upset not to be informally consulted, as they had been over the Joint Declaration in 1993.[45]

When, by September, it became clear that work on the document was still not completed, Molyneaux asked if he could see work in progress. As he recalled: 'Every time I enquired about it, they told me it wasn't in anything yet like readable form: it was merely collections of pages and paragraphs.'[46] The NIO argued that it would be an error at that stage to let Molyneaux see it, even though he was regarded as a sympathetic Unionist leader, because they were only working to produce a discussion paper, not a final document. To show it to some parties but not others, they reasoned, might lead to entrenched positions being taken before any talks began. Although Molyneaux did learn later what the text contained, some in London bitterly regret that he was not involved earlier, and had a chance to make his reservations known.[47]

Sensing he might be losing ground among the Unionist community, Major emphasised to them in October that the Framework Document was merely a discussion paper for a future constitutional settlement, not a blueprint which would then be imposed on them. He also committed the government to publish all three parts of the proposals simultaneously, covering Strand One (relating purely to Northern Ireland), Strand Two (on relations north and south of the border) and Strand Three (bringing in the Republic and the United Kingdom). But apprehensions in the Unionist community were not allayed, and with it hardline opposition to Molyneaux's moderate leadership of the UUP began to grow.

With Unionist opinion hanging in the balance, Number Ten was distressed to hear in mid-November that Albert Reynolds was to resign, having been caught out misleading the Dail, the Irish Parliament. Reynolds's last words as Taoiseach reflected his own dismay at the events: 'It's amazing. You cross the big hurdles, and when you get to the small ones you get tripped.'[48] Vital weeks were lost before John Bruton emerged as his successor in December. A visit by Adams to the US, his third, threatened further to upset the equilibrium, especially as on this occasion the Sinn Fein leader was invited inside the White House, to see Tony Lake, National Security Adviser. The Unionists were angry, as were the right in the Tory Party. Heavy lobbying by

Number Ten did at least result in the White House maintaining their ban on Sinn Fein's fundraising within the US, which caused Adams to cancel planned trips to New York and Chicago.[49]

By January 1995 opposition to the joint Framework Document became a unifying symbol around which Molyneaux's Unionist opponents in the province were rallying. To put pressure on him to quit, the hardliners locked the UUP into a rejection of anything the document might say whenever it was published. With the Framework Document nearing completion that month, it was seen as a most regrettable time for the Unionists to be veering towards such rejectionism.

At this delicate point, Peter Stothard of *The Times* got wind that his newspaper might be able to acquire a draft copy of the Framework Document. Stothard assigned his high-flying young leader writer Matthew d'Ancona to follow up. D'Ancona, a fellow of All Souls' Oxford, was known as a sceptic about the direction the peace process was taking, having contributed to a Unionist report published in 1994 called *Ulster after the Ceasefire*, and was judged likely to make a success of the story. While to Stothard 'it was just a story', to d'Ancona it was more than that. On seeing the document he found it not to his liking and by publicising it he hoped that the government might be induced to abandon some of the proposals in it which he saw as sweeping concessions to the Nationalists.[50]

At 4 p.m. on the afternoon before Wednesday 1 February, the day Stothard chose to run the story, Meyer took a call from Stuart Higgins, editor of the *Sun*. He wanted to know whether the Prime Minister had any plans to meet Adams. Meyer was puzzled: why did Higgins imagine such a scenario? The editor replied that the Irish print run of *The Times* the next day was huge, and he assumed the broadsheet was running a major Irish story, and had taken a guess at what it might be. On putting the telephone down, Meyer promptly contacted Lyne, who had already picked up rumours that a version of the Framework Document was about to leak. Meyer confirmed from the political desk at *The Times* shortly before 5 p.m. that they had a big Irish story, but that the editor was keeping it very tight. A little later the desk called Meyer back to say that there was indeed a very significant story coming and that perhaps he should speak to the editor about it.[51]

After a number of conversations, Stothard by early evening admitted to Meyer that *The Times* did have a copy of the Framework Document. Like it or not, they were going to run with the story, saying that the government was giving ground to Irish nationalism. Meyer promptly went into the Cabinet Room to see Major, who was livid. He at once saw the entire peace process being put in jeopardy. The havoc that might be caused if the Unionists withdrew their support in Parliament was an added anxiety.[52] They agreed they would have to act immediately to stop the story. Meyer phoned Stothard again and argued furiously with him that *The Times* had the wrong document, their interpretation was wrong, that the government was not preparing for a united Ireland, and that if he published it 'the shit would hit the fan'. Meyer further explained that the Unionist reaction would jeopardise lives and the prospects for peace. He concluded with a lecture about his responsibilities as an editor.[53]

Stothard was not impressed. He did not blame Meyer for trying to bludgeon or for trying to pretend the document *The Times* had was false: 'He was just doing his job.' But he did not believe that the consequences would be as apocalyptic as Meyer portrayed. Besides, he told Meyer, the first edition of the newspaper had already been put to bed. He subsequently stated, however, that, had Major phoned him and said, 'Peter, in the interests of saving lives, in the national interest, I would like you not to run the story', then he might, possibly, have reconsidered.[54]

Meyer also tried and failed to contact d'Ancona.[55] He went back to Major, and together they decided to give *The Times* a statement, denying that joint authority between London and Dublin over Northern Ireland was even an option, and asserting that when published the Framework Document would only be a consultation text about which all Ulster parties would have full chance to comment. If the majority in the province was opposed to the proposals, they would be rejected. Stothard agreed in subsequent editions to place a box in heavy type in the middle of the front-page story, headlined 'No 10 says deal will need consent'.

Meyer eventually spoke to d'Ancona after midnight. According to d'Ancona: 'Chris Meyer was initially very polite and genial. He began by questioning the authenticity of the document I had seen and told me that a samizdat version had been working its way around Ireland. I told him I was absolutely convinced I had the correct version. When his initial line failed, he led me to believe I had been taken for a ride. The conversation ended pretty abruptly after that.'[56] Number Ten continued to believe that d'Ancona had been chosen by the leakers because they thought he would give the story a sympathetic twist.[57]

Having obtained Stothard's agreement to the boxed statement, Major, Meyer and Lyne repaired to the House for a 10 p.m. meeting in the Prime Minister's office attended by Mayhew, Ryder and NIO ministers. After months of work on the document, the mood was grave; those present concurred that the peace process might indeed be put at risk by the *Times* story. Mayhew thought it a deliberate attempt to end the peace process. Major produced the idea that he could address the nation directly on television the following evening to try to calm nerves. A statement to the House the next day was also mooted. But who should give it? Major or Mayhew? And what could they say? They decided that they should all sleep on it and meet early the following morning to agree the way forward.[58] More immediately, they agreed that a further meeting should take place in the Prime Minister's office at the House that very evening, for any Tory MPs who could be found. About sixty duly turned up at 11.30 p.m., unsure why they had been summoned.

Major stood before them with a faxed copy of *The Times'* story, and spoke of 'black deeds at the crossroads of peace'. In a thirty-minute question-and-answer session he said that by this time last year twenty people had already died at the hands of terrorists. This year, no one had so far been killed. D'Ancona's leak was compared to an action in an Agatha Christie thriller. Major, flanked by Mayhew and John Wheeler, the Minister of State, assured MPs that he would not allow the peace process to be derailed. Consternation spread when it was reported that Molyneaux that evening had condemned the document. But crucially, Cranborne, an influential Unionist sympathiser, pledged his full support for the Prime Minister at the meeting.[59] Mayhew also spoke powerfully and emotionally of the need for calm, later describing the meeting in the Prime Minister's room as 'an extraordinary occasion, like a Victorian print with people's faces illuminated standing all around the cramped room'.[60]

'Anglo–Irish Plan for powerful joint body' was the front-page headline above d'Ancona's story in *The Times* the next morning. The first paragraph declared boldly: 'The British and Irish governments have drawn up a document that brings the prospect of a united Ireland closer than it has been at any time since partition in 1920.' The article said that the document in their hands included a joint North–South all-Irish authority with 'radical executive powers', and gave the opinion that 'the new cross-border institution will be seen by many on both sides as the engine for the reunification of Ireland'. The proposals 'go further even than the 1973 Sunningdale Agreement', brought down by a strike by Unionist workers. The article mentioned the poor state of relations between Ulster Unionists and the British government, and commented rightly that they felt excluded from the Framework Document process.[61]

As predicted, there was outrage among the Unionist community at the reports of the leaked document. David Trimble, one of those anxious to see a new Unionist leadership, accused the government of a 'shabby trick'. The Ulster Unionists threatened to withdraw their support from the government and precipitate a general election.[62]

Back in London, the ministerial meeting reassembled that Wednesday morning under Major's chairmanship. Arguments against a television broadcast were put, on the grounds that it might be seen as an overreaction and could prove counterproductive. Such reservations were swept aside. Major was emphatic that a direct appeal to the country was the right course.[63] That afternoon, Major and Mayhew arrived in the Commons chamber looking 'grim and anxious'. Mayhew spoke solemnly and very quietly about the events, emphasising that no final joint framework text had been agreed, so the document leaked to *The Times* had no real status. Whatever text finally emerged would only be carried forward if it had the 'triple-lock' assent of 'parties, people and Parliament'. A referendum in Northern Ireland, he repeated, would take place on any proposals. Mo Mowlam for Labour responded, offering total backing. According to Matthew Parris, the House was almost completely behind the government. Had a free vote on the government's strategy been put to the House, 'more than 600 of the 650 MPs would have voted for it'.[64]

That evening, Major exercised his right to deliver a non-partisan television address (he had made similar broadcasts during the Gulf crisis and after the Downing Street Declaration). He spoke calmly and with a concern that avoided sentimentality.

The horrors of Enniskillen and Greysteel are behind you. After five months of peace, surely it is time to look ahead. Judge our proposals as a whole ... nothing is going to be imposed on Northern Ireland. New arrangements will only work if they are agreed by the people of Northern Ireland, supported by them and operated by them ... Northern Ireland has come a very long way since the Downing Street Declaration. It must not drift backwards ... it is up to the people of Northern Ireland to decide whether fear can give way to hope.[65]

With the heated events of 1 February over, and the immediate crisis passed, attention turned to who had fed the story to *The Times*. Number Ten never traced the leaker, and d'Ancona and Stothard have always refused to reveal their source.[66] Possible culprits included, implausibly, a Cabinet minister, a member of the Irish government, which had been dribbling proposals from the document to Unionists to judge reactions, or a pro-Unionist civil servant. Mayhew's verdict was that 'it was leaked by someone with an agenda, written up by someone with an agenda, with the intention of maximising shock among Unionists'.[67] Major believed that the report had been planted by someone with hard-line Unionist views in an effort to unseat Molyneaux from the UUP leadership and substitute someone with 'sounder' views.[68] D'Ancona commented: 'I still don't know why I was singled out as the person who should be shown the document, other than I was known to have doubts about the peace process. I wrote the story up in a way that I hope was a fair summary of the framework document, though I was accused of distorting it. Major himself I must say behaved very well to me subsequently.'[69]

If he did, then it showed his powers of self-restraint. While d'Ancona believes the leak made little or no difference to the outcome of events, Major regarded the leaking of the document as a key step that led ineluctably to the IRA's resumption of violence in February 1996. Molyneaux never recovered his ground, and was unseated as leader in August 1995. Molyneaux himself believes: 'The leak was exploited by people in Northern Ireland to do me down. They claimed I had been betrayed, led down the garden path. They forget I had been excluded from the drafting process by the NIO ... They kept on about me having had the wool pulled over my eyes.'[70] With Molyneaux no longer leader, Unionist opinion, on which any future constitutional settlement hinged, would be less biddable. And without a willingness on the part of the Protestant community to yield, no lasting settlement would be found by Major's government.

Cabinet considered the framework text at its Thursday meeting on 16 February. Ministers, including Heseltine and Mawhinney, fired questions at

Major and Mayhew about whether the document was sufficiently pro-Unionist. It was scrutinised paragraph by paragraph and repeated reassurances were given about the safeguards for the Unionists. Cabinet agreed to return to the text at a special meeting on 21 February, the day before publication, to discuss the Framework Document again in detail.[71]

Massaging and lobbying were to the fore in the interval, with the result that the mood was less sceptical, and everyone agreed that the best opportunity now existed for progress, which 'should be grasped and pursued with all vigour'.[72] Howard, mindful of the depth and width of pro-Unionist feeling in the Party, a cause for which he had a strong affinity, was the strongest voice in Cabinet urging caution. He stressed that the government should not be seen as a 'persuader' for the Framework Document; Major was later to state this point in the House. Cranborne, who had himself resigned from the Commons in 1987 after the Anglo–Irish Agreement, had unhappy moments, but was reassured by the 'triple lock', and soothed, according to one account, 'by sympathy and periodic glasses of whisky from Mayhew and Ancram'.[73]

The Framework Document was duly published on 22 February, three weeks after the leak. The night before, Major flew to Hillsborough Castle in Belfast for final agreement of the text with Bruton and his team. Smiles and bonhomie that cold February night belied the fact that tough negotiations had taken place on the document up to the last minute. Major had drawn up a list of forty-three amendments, and at the eleventh hour Dublin accepted most.[74] As a bait to the Unionists, the document stated that there would be a new Northern Ireland elected Assembly. But it also proposed a North–South body of elected representatives, in addition to a Parliamentary Forum of representatives from the North and South to hold 'wider discussions'.

A 'greener' document than many in the Tory Party and elsewhere had been expecting,[75] the document's substance bore a close similarity to d'Ancona's report, though he did not emphasise the 'triple-lock' guarantees that no proposals would be forced through without majority agreement, nor the end of the claim in the Irish constitution to Northern Ireland. His use of emotive language and his highlighting of the all-Irish dimension of the document, coupled with a highly charged leading article in *The Times* the same day, lent support to Number Ten's view that the newspaper's action had been ill-considered.

Major's reception in the House on publication day was encouraging. The negative reaction from Unionist MPs was overshadowed by a generally warm cross-party welcome.[76] Major underlined that he was a 'Unionist' and not a persuader for a united Ireland. He spoke about his hopes for breaking the 'spiral of despair' in Northern Ireland, and about his belief that 'any Prime Minister of the United Kingdom could or should [not] sit in Downing Street without actively trying to find a way out of the problems that have existed for so long'. MPs cheered as he spoke of his hopes of ending violence in the province so that 'the next generation may not face the privations, the murders, the sorrow, the hardship, the deaths and the funerals' endured in the twenty-five years since the Troubles began.[77] Blair and Ashdown welcomed the document, but ominously, if predictably, Paisley condemned 'the monstrous and hideous Irish mutation', while more worryingly Adams commended the document's 'all-Irish character'.[78]

Major's achievement was to carry his party, and Cabinet, with him, without the resignations and protests that followed the Anglo–Irish Declaration of 1985. In another gesture, in part to placate the right, Major travelled to Scotland two days after the document's publication to offer a passionate defence of the Union of England and Scotland, to criticise opposition proposals on devolution as a 'Trojan horse to independence' and roundly to deny any inconsistency between his policy towards Northern Ireland and Scotland.[79]

Open House Revolt

Whatever the longer term difficulties in finding a way forward in Northern Ireland, Major's high-profile handling of the Framework Document in February brought him short-term political capital. He needed every pound of it. With the gains of the much-vaunted economic success still not apparent, he clung to the peace process as a principal personal achievement of his premiership. By the end of February, the main leadership contenders, Clarke, Heseltine and Portillo, gave the impression of exhibiting scarcely concealed disdain for what Number Ten wanted. One figure close to Major described it as 'an utterly ghastly time. Things had got completely out of control. There was internecine warfare between different Party factions. Hacks would phone up Downing Street and ask, "Portillo said this, Clarke said that, who does the Prime Minister support?"'[80] Major, however, refused to believe that Heseltine was personally culpable. He had phoned him when he had had his heart attack and had kept his job open when some thought he might move someone else into the DTI. He had, moreover, brought Heseltine back into government in 1990. Major's faith in Heseltine can be seen either as touching, or naïve.

The row precipitated by the leaked discussions of the 26 January Cabinet on Europe refused to go away. For some weeks, advisers at Number Ten had been pressing Major to give an *ex cathedra* speech setting out his position on the EU, to develop more fully his passing broadcast comments of early January. Sensing a whiplash from the left, Major was reluctant to do so, and refused to commit himself. He had, however, accepted an invitation to give a speech to the Thatcherite Conservative Way Forward Group on 3 February and had yet to decide what to say. Might this be a suitable forum for such a speech? The first draft prepared in Number Ten was about the domestic agenda. But as the date of the lecture approached, and with the right still pressing, Major realised that he had little alternative but to use the opportunity to reclarify his position on the EU.[81] The speech was rewritten, with Europe to be the primary focus.

By this strategy, the product of extensive discussions with Clarke, Major was to set out in broad terms Britain's position on a single currency, and Clarke was to fill in the details in a speech the following week.[82] Major duly told his Tory audience on 3 February that Britain was to set new conditions for joining a single currency beyond those laid out in the Maastricht Treaty. He repeated that Britain would not join a single currency in 1996 or 1997. In a delicate balancing act, he refused to rule out joining the single currency at some point in the future, as the whipless MPs demanded, and his Cabinet Eurosceptics sought, but equally he refused to be tied down to a definite date for joining: 'The right for our Parliament to take the decision that it wants, when it wants, is undoubted.'[83] He pledged further to veto any moves to make the EU more centralised at the coming IGC, and said he would press to change the voting system within the EU to give those countries with the largest populations, like Britain, more influence. The briefing to the lobby stressed that the text had been agreed with Clarke and Hurd,[84] although the clarity of the message was obscured by the diplomat Meyer at Number Ten spinning the speech one way, and the Eurosceptic Collins at Central Office spinning the speech the other.[85]

Heath fumed, and the Euro-rebels expressed, in varying degrees of strength, their 'disappointment'. But in the short term the speech gave every appearance of having been a success, stilling discontent, as intended, among the 'reasonable' right, and staking out the Prime Minister's own ground against charges that his position on Europe was being determined by reacting to others.[86] The right also became excited that Clarke had at long last been squared.

A splutter of minor incidents broke in the week following the speech. News of Major's youthful affair with Jean Kierans appeared in an article by Michael Crick in *Esquire* magazine on 6 February. The media loved details of this 'least scandalous sexual revelation ever unearthed about a British Prime Minister'. Even the *Daily Telegraph* gave the story half a page, under the headline 'And here's to you, Mrs Kierans', a reference to the 1960s Simon and Garfunkel song and the film *The Graduate*, in which the twenty-some-thing Dustin Hoffman is seduced by the older woman and family friend Mrs Robinson, played by Anne Bancroft.[87] Revelations about the affair probably boosted Major's public profile, but he found it all irritating and deeply embarrassing. He barely referred to it and for the next few mornings he appeared uncomfortable and avoided his usual practice of calling into the Private Office for a cheery few words.[88] Meanwhile Allan Stewart, a junior Scottish Office minister, was forced to resign after he raised a pickaxe, reportedly drunk, at anti-motorway campaigners in Glasgow. By now, Major had become 'fairly robust' about the action erring ministers had to take.[89]

The same day as Stewart's resignation, 7 February, Major allowed his tension to break through at Question Time. Pressed four times by Blair – realising he had found the Achilles heel – to say when the government might agree to joining a single currency, Major replied that 'only a dimwit' would ask him to provide an answer before he could assess 'the economic circumstances of the day'.[90] It was the most stormy exchange between the Party leaders since Blair had won the succession to Smith seven months before.

Major had further reason for unease that afternoon, as another ministerial resignation was simmering. Charles Wardle, a junior minister at the DTI, had for fifteen months been in discussion with Number Ten about his anxieties over the immigration implications of the EU's abolition of internal border controls and the legal status of the UK's 'opt-out' in such an eventuality. Major had no doubts about the sincerity of Wardle's views, but was irritated that he chose this moment to resign, a timing seen by some pundits as designed to maximise the government's embarrassment and further raise apprehensions on the right about the EU.[91] Andrew Marr asked whether Wardle resigned 'wittingly to inflame the xenophobia rising in his party and his country?' and said he had rarely witnessed such 'cold contemptuous anger' among the higher circle of government as over his resignation.[92] Major responded in public saying he prized Britain's recent record on race relations, and warned that 'raising fears about immigration does put that at risk'.[93] Wardle, usually regarded as on the left of the party, considered he was doing no such thing, and was raising a legitimate policy issue.[94]

These were all trivial distractions, however, compared to the damage done to Major's position by Clarke's eagerly awaited speech on Europe, delivered on 9 February. Clarke had spent time with Major before his Conservative Way Forward speech, agreeing how the single currency issue was to be handled, including what Major would say, and what he would say. Clarke's task was to elaborate exactly on how the Maastricht criteria were necessary but not sufficient for Britain's entry, and specify what additional criteria would be required for Britain. However, they both left their meeting with different impressions of what had been agreed.[95]

In his speech to the European Movement that Thursday, Clarke did indeed set out new economic and monetary hurdles before Britain would agree to join. The conditions of convergence were unlikely to be in place for 'a long time', and 'there is not a snowball's chance in Hades of Europe embarking successfully on economic and monetary union in 1997'. So far, he was in line with Major's understanding. But he went on to say – contradicting Major – that it was quite possible to have monetary without political union, and he set out a robust defence of the principle of both the single currency as well as political union.[96]

Portillo could barely restrain himself. The next day, in a BBC interview, he castigated Clarke's comments. Portillo's motive was seen as confirming himself as the leading leadership challenger on the right, after Aitken had gained some limelight for claiming he would wait 'an eternity' before voting to join a single currency.[97] When the headlines duly followed about Cabinet divisions, and the Prime Minister and Chancellor at war on Europe, Clarke insisted that he had stuck to their agreement. A subsequent view from Number Ten was that 'what Ken liked to do was to stretch the envelope that held the minutes'.[98] The truth is that Clarke stuck to the letter but not the spirit of his agreement with Major.

But why did Clarke go as far as he did, precipitating his biggest row with Major in their four years so far together in Downing Street? Clarke wanted to make a big pronouncement himself on Europe and, encouraged by Hurd's comment that they should have a full and open debate, he readily seized on the European Movement's invitation as a suitable forum. The first drafts from the Treasury were rejected and the speech was rewritten. Number Ten then demanded deletions, with Major himself spending a long time with Clarke trying to persuade him to tone it down. Tessa Keswick, Clarke's special adviser, also pleaded for him – three times – to cut out certain inflammatory passages.[99] Cabinet Europhiles did not encourage him, but pro-Europeans like Hugh Dykes, Tim Eggar and Jim Lester, a close friend, made their views plain. Then, at the last minute, Clarke became irritated by Number Ten and Central Office's pre-speech briefings that he would be delivering a more Eurosceptic tone on the single currency.[100] As one of his aides said: 'He knew exactly what he was doing in the speech. He did not set out to rile Number Ten but he was going to make his own views plain and no one would stop him. He has always said since he had not regretted doing it.'[101] Major later said that he and Clarke agreed about more or less everything except the single currency, but on this occasion he believed that Clarke had deliberately misrepresented their understanding.

For all the harm done, Major's ire soon ebbed away. One Number Ten aide characterised their relationship thus:

Despite their periodic rows, there was never a loss of confidence in Clarke. The Prime Minister was periodically seriously pissed off with him during the day, but they can then be sitting drinking whisky at 10 o'clock that night. There has never been lasting *froideur* between the two men, occasional clashes, at times pretty heated and steamy, but no sense of a true distancing.[102]

By the following Wednesday Clarke was back at Number Ten with Major, called away early after a dinner at the Savoy, for just one such late-night drink and get-together.[103]

In Cabinet on 16 February, Major felt it necessary to deliver another lecture on discipline. He told ministers that he had attended a meeting of the 1922 Committee executive two days before, where dismay and anger at reports of Cabinet differences over Europe had been put to him in 'the bluntest terms'. He felt he had to insist Cabinet gave the 1922 Committee no cause for similar concern in the future. He referred again to the leaked discussion on 26 January, when 'virtually verbatim' reports had found their way into the newspapers. In future, everyone had to confine themselves to agreed policy and not be tempted into offering comments or responses which went further. If this rule was not followed, power and influence would be handed over to the Opposition.[104] No one could accuse Major of not cracking the whip often enough. The problem was that his homilies were casually disregarded.

Major's position now seemed to become almost intolerable. For the next few months, his standing among Cabinet was the lowest of his premiership. The 'big three', Clarke, Heseltine and Hurd, remained disillusioned over his rightward turn on Europe, while the right, including Howard, kept wanting him to go further. With his new Number Ten still finding their way, he was virtually alone. Although the right were divided among themselves, on Europe they but felt content with how they were manoeuvring the Prime Minister. For the time being, he was 'the best bastard they had got' as Alan Watkins memorably put it.[105]

Major's predicament was underlined at Prime Minister's Questions the afternoon after his latest Cabinet dressing-down. Blair asked three times whether he agreed with his Chancellor that a single currency was no threat to the nation state. Major repeatedly evaded the question, as his MPs around him sat glumly; 'a bad and dangerous moment for the Government,' as David Wastell wrote.[106] The headlines that evening were all about the Prime Minister failing to support his Chancellor. A letter from Major to Gordon Brown was released, signalling his joint agreement with Clarke that 'A single currency would raise significant political and constitutional issues', a clear slapdown to Clarke. To round off a terrible day, the Islwyn by-election (Kinnock's former seat), saw the Conservatives achieve one of their worst shares of the vote ever, at just 3.9 per cent, with their deposit lost. But it was the divisions between Major and Clarke that continued to take the attention of the media.

Ghosts from the past were conjured of Thatcher's clashes with Lawson, and whether Clarke was on the verge of resignation following his rebuff from Number Ten.[107] Lamont, sensing the chance, was reported to be set to deliver a lecture on Prime Minister–Chancellor relations. Instead, he contented himself with a high-profile and solitary vote against his party on the government's policy towards the EU on 1 March.[108] Major had taken personal charge of ensuring that the government was not defeated, including the unusual and high-risk decision for him to speak in the debate. The nine whipless MPs either abstained or voted with the government, allowing it to scrape home by five votes. Although he survived on the day, the assumption was growing, even among loyalist MPs, that he would not survive another such knife-edge vote and that before the end of the year he would be ousted as Prime Minister.[109]

Phoneless in Gaza, Foreign Interludes: March

After a February dominated by squabbling, it was hoped that domestic politics would move into a more tranquil period. Foreign business and trips – described by some cynics in Downing Street as like dinner parties, with little substance or impact – might just provide the opportunity to steady nerves before local elections in Scotland in April, and England and Wales in May.

The diplomatically dominated month opened with a two-hour visit to Downing Street on 1 March by Viktor Chernomyrdin, the Russian Prime Minister. Major was keen to maintain a special relationship with Russia, and ensured that the Russian Prime Minister was well looked after on his three-day visit to Britain. Major was pleased to hear that Russia had deposited the first tranche of £65 million of the £350 million of interest arrears owed to British commercial banks, while new Russo–British trade deals were discussed. On political matters, Chernomyrdin repeated his opposition to NATO's expansion eastwards, while Major made clear his unhappiness with the Russian military operation in Chechnia.[110]

Israel was another country where Major was anxious to foster a close relationship, and it was fortunate that political developments within the country – notably the ending in 1993 of the Palestinian Intifada – allowed him to oversee a significant improvement in Anglo–Israeli relations. Hurd spoke of Major 'always wanting to go to Israel. He has a basic sympathy for Israel and what it is trying to do. It never, as sometimes happened with Margaret Thatcher, who had the same sympathy, distorted his judgement about the British interest.'[111] During a speech to the Jewish Board of Deputies on 25 March 1993 he had spoken with warmth of the two countries' relations, and at a Joint Israel Appeal dinner in late 1994 he announced his trip the following March.

The aim of the visit was to show British support for the Middle East peace process, as well as to boost trade. To that end, Major asked two men close to the Jewish community in Britain, Trevor Chinn (Lex) and Richard Green-bury (Marks and Spencer) to help put together a team of leading businessmen, as had occurred on some earlier trips.[112] Major stressed that the industrialists would also visit Palestinian businessmen in Gaza, in the hope of facilitating peace by economic development of the Palestinian areas. Twenty-eight businessmen duly flew out with Major on Sunday 12 March.[113]

The *Jewish Chronicle* pronounced that Anglo–Israeli relations were at their closest for forty years.[114] At a banquet in Jerusalem on that first evening, Major took the opportunity to affirm his intention that sanctions remain against Iraq until all biological weapons had been destroyed. On Monday, Major laid a wreath at the Yad Vashem memorial to the Holocaust victims, and flew by helicopter over the Golan Heights on the border with Syria. The highlight of the trip was the visit to Gaza on the Tuesday, the first by a western leader to see Yasser Arafat of the PLO in his Palestinian heartland. The Palestinian lobby had noted Major's visit and previous meeting with Arafat in 1982 with some optimism and were hopeful of a positive response. Major's emotional side was engaged by the poverty he saw everywhere around him, and his announcements included a £550,000 aid package, £1 million-worth of police vehicles to help Palestinian police patrol the Gaza strip, and that Arafat had agreed to EU monitors to oversee the forthcoming election in Gaza.[115] Major had secured Israeli Prime Minister Rabin's approval for the proposal, even though he had yet to put it to his EU partners.

Major was intrigued by Arafat, and was gratified by the friendly reception the PLO leader offered him. But it was Rabin who made the biggest impression on him. He admired the way that the Israeli Prime Minister was dragging his country into an accommodation with the Palestinians. They felt a common kinship in their struggle against extremists. Rabin told Major that Israel had done it the other way round from Major and Northern Ireland, with the Palestinian settlement first, followed by the peace.[116] Major was devastated when a right-wing Jewish extremist killed Rabin a few months later.[117]

It was precisely Major's different treatment of Arafat and Adams that threatened at its outset to upset the trip. A journalist from the *Sun* asked Meyer on the plane why the Prime Minister was happy to see the Palestinian, but not the Sinn Fein leader. Meyer's first reaction was that there was no case to be answered. The BBC's John Sergeant insisted in private to Meyer that the comparison, however, was valid, a point that became irresistible when the same question began to be raised in Washington. Meyer saw that a British response was required, and put heads together with Major and Lyne to greet the question if it arose in Jerusalem.[118] They had a ready answer. Major hit back that the comparison was invalid, 'mischievous' indeed, because Arafat had renounced terrorism and signed a declaration of peace, while Adams was still associated with a fully formed terrorist organisation.[119]

Greenbury unwittingly provided another source of controversy. For some time, Blair had been pressing Major about the high levels of pay and bonuses awarded to executives of privatised industries, such as Cedric Brown of British Gas. At the end of February, Major wrong-footed Blair (and angered the right) by admitting the truth – that he found the high levels of these awards 'distasteful' – and he drew attention to a CBI committee set up that month under Greenbury's chairmanship to look into executive pay. The media, on discovering Greenbury was on the trip, repeatedly asked him to comment on his committee. His patience cracked on the Monday evening and he called them 'a bunch of shits, without an ounce of integrity'. After mediation, the *Sun* and some other newspapers agreed not to report his remarks, but *Today* did, repeating his unguarded comments, and hounded him for the next few months.[120] Major consoled him on the flight home with, 'Don't take any notice of them. You just have to learn to live with them.'[121]

More civilised curiosity was also aroused by the presence on the trip of Martin Gilbert, the historian and Churchill's official biographer. Was this Major's Boswell? Gilbert, a lifelong friend of Israel, went to provide Major with historical and political background, and to help with speeches. The two men became friends, and Gilbert continued to be called on periodically to provide a historical dimension to Major's speeches over the next two years.[122]

With the peace process in train, no new political initiatives were needed. A show of British support was sufficient. Major maintained his pro-Israeli policy after the trip. He encouraged Rifkind to visit and give the Balfour

Lecture; he lifted the arms embargo on Israel, and he pushed G7 summits, and spoke individually to Gulf leaders, about lifting the Arab boycott.[123] Trade between both countries grew after the trip, with Israel becoming a fashionable place for business links in the new optimistic atmosphere. While not attaining the euphoria of his South Africa trip, the mood of a fresh political opening was similar, and Major returned to London via Jordan on 15 March refreshed and heartened.

For once the background noise during an overseas trip had not been the antics of his parliamentary critics, but the White House. Clinton, to Major's irritation, had now agreed to lift the ban on fundraising by Adams. The British government's position, argued at many levels in Washington, was that such a step was premature until the IRA announced that the ceasefire was permanent. London had been pressing Sinn Fein–IRA hard for some months to begin the decommissioning of its estimated ten tons of weapons, to show that their ceasefire was permanent. By January, five exploratory sessions between Northern Ireland Office officials and Sinn Fein had failed to achieve an agreed way forward. The fifth meeting broke up when Sinn Fein claimed that the room where they were meeting the officials was being bugged.[124]

Earlier in March Mayhew had gone to Washington for talks, articulating the three conditions for decommissioning and the commencement of talks. The British government believed that, with their intelligence telling them that IRA covert military actions were still going on, and a 'considerable likelihood' that the ceasefire would break down, there was a need to insist that an explicit commitment was made to permanent peace. Any sums raised before then, London argued, would not be used for democratic purposes and electioneering, but to build up further military strength. Rather than confer status and favours, now was precisely the moment for Washington to put the pressure on the Republicans, to force them to make concessions on disarmament.[125]

Hence Clinton's lifting of the ban was greeted in London as a slap in the face. Washington argued that Adams's statement on 8 March that he would be prepared to *discuss* decommissioning was sufficient as a step forward. Worse, Clinton agreed, before any agreement had been made to renounce violence, to meet Adams personally at the White House during St Patrick's Day celebrations on 17 March. This was too much for Number Ten: 'The White House having done the wrong thing, typically the next thing they did was to try getting on the phone to say they were sorry.'[126] Major sent Clinton an angry letter on 10 March, explaining why he thought the administration had been in error, and urging him to confront Adams on the issue of disarmament at the meeting.[127] Clinton tried phoning Major the next day, 11 March, the day he left for Israel. A Number Ten source confirmed: 'It is true, we did not rush to return the call. As Clinton had made his decision, there was very little for the Prime Minister to say to the President.'[128]

News of the failure of Major to return Clinton's call seeped out of Washington, producing headlines such as in *The Times* 'Could you ring back a bit later, Mr Clinton?'[129] Official suggestions that no secure line could be arranged while the Prime Minister was travelling were roundly ridiculed by technology 'experts' in the press. Major's remarks about the comparison between his meeting Arafat – a man who had renounced terrorism – with Clinton meeting Adams, a man who had not, were duly reported as a 'thinly-veiled' rebuke to Clinton.[130]

As Major's party travelled around Israel and Jordan, they received several messages about the President's wish to speak. But Major decided there was still no urgency for the telephone conversation. Lyne explained to Lake that it would be easier for the conversation to take place after their return. Number Ten, still incredulous at Washington's action, may have won a propaganda battle in snubbing a President still weakened by the mid-term election results, and by no means sure of re-election in 1996, but its action appeared to some, not least in Washington, to have been petulant.

Clinton faxed a 'conciliatory' letter to Major, which tried in some detail to set out why he had agreed to meet Adams and to allow him to raise funds.[131] On 16 March Adams and Clinton duly shook hands and chatted briefly at a congressional luncheon; those in attendance, who included John Bruton, broke out in applause.[132] On 17 March the long-awaited meeting between Adams and Clinton, with Lake in attendance, took place at the White House. When Clinton had his delayed phone call with Major, back in Huntingdon, on Sunday 19 March, the President assured him that he had pressed Adams to begin 'serious talks on decommissioning', and that Adams had agreed as long as they could talk to a minister (as opposed to officials) about it.[133] When he returned home to Ireland three days later, however, Adams flatly denied that Clinton had pressed him at the meeting on the issue of disarmament.[134]

Much patchwork had been done before Major's visit to the United States from 2 to 5 April, his seventh and final visit as Prime Minister, and his third while Clinton was President. The chartered Boeing 747 being out of commission on the day of travel, British Airways offered the Prime Minister and his party a cut-rate trip on Concorde instead. Major, who was becoming disenchanted with the noisy and cramped VC 10, leaped at the opportunity of showing off Britain's flagship aeroplane.[135]

Supersonic travel aside, it was a low-key visit, with both men's domestic political standing at low ebb. Clinton signposted his conciliatory stance when saying that progress with the peace process was due 'in large measure to the vision and courage of John Major', and his willingness 'to take risks to himself, his party and his government'.[136] Major spent an hour talking with Newt Gingrich on Capitol Hill. He was interested to meet the man who for the time being carried more influence in the US than Clinton, and who was so exciting his own right wing. Said one aide of this meeting of opposites: 'Major was puzzled by Gingrich, who seemed to him to be talking in cyberspace, in a strange, nutty, post-Thatcherite, zany, planetary kind of language, that left Major cold. But he also came across as sparky and warm, and immensely personable.'[137] Gingrich professed himself impressed by Major. He apparently felt 'a special kinship' and said that it had been 'a special thrill' to meet the British Prime Minister.[138]

Attempts by Ann Ingram, the mother of a British-born murderer, to see Major were made repeatedly during the trip, and achieved widespread publicity. Her son was facing the death penalty in the state of Georgia, but Major refused to plead on his behalf. He sent a handwritten letter to the mother saying how sorry he was, but that there were no grounds for intervening in Georgia's legal system.[139] The episode was a further reminder to Major of how life hung, or seemed to hang, on his decisions. The lives of British soldiers in Bosnia weighed heavily with him always. Disagreements with Bob Dole and other congressional leaders over their pressure to lift the arms embargo against Bosnia's Muslim-led government was the main cloud in an otherwise successful series of interchanges on Capitol Hill. Major repeated his line that such a move would only fuel fighting, and endanger British troops.

Vice-President Al Gore proved the key go-between in brokering Clinton's more conciliatory stance on Ireland. He came to breakfast at the Washington Embassy, where the Prime Minister's party was staying. Gore was full of jokes and funny stories, which surprised the British party who, until that point, thought that mostly he 'worked off autocues'. Gore asked what he could do to repair relations. Major and his advisers outlined three responses they wanted Clinton to give on Ireland. Gore took notes and read them back to check they were correct. Later that morning Major's party went to the White House, where Clinton greeted them in the Oval Office. Clinton, who hated confrontations, spent the first few minutes talking about the basketball he had been watching on television the night before, as if to avoid the subject.

With delay no longer possible, he turned to them and said, 'Al said I need to say A, B and C, and I'll do that.' Major and his aides were delighted, and after a working lunch, mainly on Bosnia, Clinton delivered his agreed script on decommissioning at the White House press conference.[140] The Prime Minister's party, however, no longer harboured any illusions about the President: 'It was typical of Clinton to come out firmly on our side when we were there,' was the jaded recollection of one. 'But after we had gone, he would change his stance without often recognising or acknowledging that he had done so.'[141]

Clinton's willingness to placate a leader who had so recently and so publicly snubbed him was evidence of the still not insignificant place of 'Britain in the world'. That indeed was the title chosen for a high-profile conference for 700 specially invited delegates on 29 March at Westminster's Queen Elizabeth II Conference Centre, organised by the Royal Institute of International Affairs (Chatham House). The idea of bringing together foreign policy practitioners and the great and good from around the world had first been mooted by Douglas Hurd in 1994, as part of a series of initiatives to round off his long foreign secretaryship. He wanted to examine Britain's overseas role, and boost Britain's cultural and trade profile. A similar impulse to explore fundamental questions had led him to call his two seminars at Chequers on Britain's overseas priorities, and how they might be realised.[142] The latter in particular had been a productive and far-seeing meeting, but Clarke had irritated FCO officials by creating difficulties about an extra £50 million sought for a revamping of foreign policy, which to cynics had been the point of the entire exercise.[143]

A far more expansive mood was in evidence at the Queen Elizabeth II Conference Centre. Prince Charles, Henry Kissinger and David Puttnam, the film director, were just three of those invited to speak. Major opened the conference with a wide-ranging speech. Britain should not adopt a 'Little Englander' mentality, nor should the domestic debate focus too heavily on the 'internal workings' of the EU. He spoke of Britain's relationship with and positive influence upon Russia, South Africa, China and NATO, and raised some profound long-term questions including the future of the UN and other international bodies, relations with central and eastern Europe, a 'new transatlantic community' between the EU and the USA, and the problems of terrorism and tackling world poverty.[144]

The whole affair may have been little more than national grandstanding and a farewell jamboree for Hurd, and Major's speech may have raised more questions than it answered. But his was still one of the more impressive speeches of the day, and a reminder of how far he had travelled in conducting foreign policy from the callow Foreign Secretary of six years before. Indeed, for the time being, his conduct of international relations exceeded any success he was encountering in domestic politics, where his position doggedly failed to improve.

The Failed Fight-back: March–April

While Major's attention was on foreign affairs for much of March, he needed his lieutenants to offer steady management, and his parliamentary party to provide loyal support. But that failed to materialise. Clarke followed a gaffe of praising Consett steelworks in County Durham – which had closed fifteen years before – by admitting that it would take 'two years at least' before the electorate felt more secure and prosperous. Worse, he spoke positively of a disposable nappy factory that had closed down in 1991, after which the *Daily Telegraph* dubbed Clarke 'Britain's unofficial minister of gaffes'.[145] It was a title for which he had to compete with the Party Chairman, after Hanley caused dismay by saying that Labour councils tended to be 'corrupt'.[146]

Discontent was stirred by Lord McAlpine, the Thatcher acolyte and former Party Treasurer, who claimed that 'a spell in opposition' was needed to revitalise the Tories.[147] McAlpine held a deep loathing for Major – 'the stupidest Prime Minister we have ever had – a bitter, nasty man'[148] – and was pleased that his comments about opposition appeared to touch a popular nerve in the Party. Major had managed to 'stuff' the Party, McAlpine said, with splits over Europe, dire financial straits and depression in the polls: 'If that doesn't constitute stuffing up a great political party,' he said on the Radio 4 *Today* programme, 'I don't know what does.'[149]

Major was equally dismissive of McAlpine, and considered him an embittered figure because of the financial misfortune that had befallen him. McAlpine's remarks spilled over onto the floor of the House. Dennis Skinner predicted Major would be 'kicked out like a dog in the night', to which Major responded, not wholly convincingly, that there had been leadership election talk last year, and it would probably be around 'next year, the year after and the year after that'.[150] It was not enough to put out the fire, with fresh rumblings about a leadership challenge coming if the local election results in May were poor.[151]

Realising that a fresh attempt to regain the initiative was required, Number Ten identified the annual Central Council at Birmingham on 31 March–1 April as the launch pad.[152] The small Number Ten team had been refreshed at the start of February by Norman Blackwell, a consultant with McKinsey and Co, as head of the Policy Unit in succession to Sarah Hogg.[153] Finding a successor, suitable and willing, had taken time the previous autumn. Candidates considered included Francis Maude and Michael Fallon, who had both lost their seats at the 1992 general election, but they wanted to return to the Commons – a quest in which they were successful.[154] Blackwell was the surprise appointment, chosen in part on the recommendation of Howell James whom he had met when James had been at the BBC in the late 1980s. Also commending him was his work in the Policy Unit under Brian Griffiths in 1986–7, where he specialised in employment, inner city regeneration and NHS reforms.[155]

Blackwell had called in to see Major over the Christmas holidays. 'What was clear in my mind was that we had to start talking about the future. I sat down at my computer and typed out all the thoughts in my head. My training taught me to structure things. I came to him with those ideas.' Major liked what he heard, and he felt he could work well with the mild-mannered Blackwell. He had grouped his ideas for a future agenda under seven headings, which included restructuring and creating an enterprise economy, boosting small firms (a particular enthusiasm), education and opportunity, and law and order.[156]

By the time Blackwell arrived on 1 February, the ideas were beginning to crystallise. Anxious to involve a wide ministerial group, he organised two brainstorming sessions, one for ministers of state and another for parliamentary under-secretaries. Major was present at both, and was interested and invigorated at how fertile the ministers were when invited to roam away from their departmental briefs. Over the following month, a number of seminars for Cabinet ministers took place in the first-floor study at Number Ten, with a different subject, including the family and enterprise, per session. It was left to Blackwell to arrange the details of how the policy groups announced by Major in Cabinet on 12 January were to function, how the Party was to link in, and how they were to report.[157]

On Thursday 16 March, the Policy Unit made a brief presentation to a group of ministers in preparation for the Birmingham Central Council. Drafts of Blackwell's ideas for a fresh Tory agenda were circulated to Hunt's Presentation Committee. However, the initiative cut across a theme that Central Office was developing which was known as the 'reassure the middle classes' strategy. Major's abandonment of this approach in favour of new initiatives caused inevitable difficulty with Central Office.[158]

A 'media blitz' was decreed necessary in the run-up to Birmingham. An interview in the *Daily Telegraph*, in which Major gave a clear statement that he would stay in office and not be 'distracted' by leadership talk, was a first shot. 'We have not run out of things to do or ideas', he insisted.[159] The day the conference opened, 31 March, Major was put on the Anne and Nick morning television show, in which talk of an early election was again dismissed: 'This Parliament can go on until nearly the middle of 1997. We've got a great deal to do.'[160] Although mocked for the insipid nature of the interview, 'popular' television and indeed radio was a forum that Major – with his common touch – could have exploited more fully as Prime Minister, as Mrs Thatcher had done with Jimmy Young.

Number Ten pre-briefed some of the friendly press about what Major would say at the Central Council, which helped produce two days of good headlines. The speech was to show voters that they should renew their trust in the Tory Party, and reject Blair's 'New Labour'. Major admitted that the Party had achieved its 1979 objectives, and he offered them a twenty-five-point 'new agenda' as 'the next phase of Conservatism'.[161] These 'new developments' included the introduction of compulsory identity cards, wider rights for tenants to buy homes, more money for education, new measures to encourage small business, and the promise of tax cuts. He then set out his stall, drawing on work in progress on Blackwell's 'five themes' – a sound economy, opportunity and choice, firm law and order, first-class public services and pride in the nation – and denounced Blair and his colleagues as sloganising. He concluded with a rousing peroration:

I didn't fight my way from a small terraced flat to this platform for the hell of it ... You don't just drift into Downing Street, I'm here because I care ... It may indeed be a monumental scrap. But I have never run away from a fight in my life.[162]

True, many of the twenty-five promises, as was pointed out, were not new, but together they made it look as if the Party was on the move.[163]

The five themes were developed further in a paper that Blackwell circulated to Cabinet ministers before a Political Cabinet on 6 April.[164] Some thought the themes overly prescriptive. Others welcomed Blackwell for bringing a new sense of structure to core government policy.[165] The Political Cabinet also discussed a key speech Blair gave the day before on Europe, with Hurd commenting that the Labour leader would come to regret having given such a positive statement, and it considered a paper that examined ways in which the Party could move towards a 20 pence standard rate of income tax.[166] Major's pronouncement at Birmingham promising tax cuts had caused some consternation, compounded by comments from Hanley in favour of a 'rolling programme' of cuts, and Political Cabinet tried to find a way out of the fiscal box.[167] Inside Number Ten it felt like the clouds, that had descended since the end of January, had at last begun to lift.[168]

But not for long. Within a week of the Birmingham relaunch, the mood of despondency returned with the local election results in Scotland hitting on the night of Thursday 6 April.[169] The Tories polled just 11 per cent of the vote, coming fourth in terms of seats, and failing to win control of a single one of Scotland's new all-purpose councils. Michael Hirst, Chairman of the Scottish Conservative Party, with understatement called it a 'huge disappointment'. Other Tories in Scotland spoke of their great bitterness against the leadership and disunity at Westminster. Hurd led those in Cabinet who leaped to Major's defence – 'he is more popular than the Party' – and warned of the folly of a leadership challenge.[170] Major blamed the poor results on continuing divisions, while those on the left rounded on John Redwood for being publicly critical of Virginia Bottomley's policy of closing London hospitals including the historic St Bartholomew's in the City.[171]

The biggest impression the Scottish elections made on English voters came when, after legal action by opposition parties, Scottish judges prevented a BBC television *Panorama* interview with Major being screened in Scotland three days before the poll. Sensitivities between government and BBC were running high, following criticisms by Aitken in March that it stood for 'Blair's Broadcasting Corporation'. It was now Aitken's turn to be in the spotlight, however, with legal action on 10 April over his involvement in the arms company BMARC.[172] Bit by bit, Aitken's star was burning out as one story after another about his past came back to haunt him.

The Scottish results jolted Major, and he began to worry about the trouble that would follow upon a similarly bad result in the local elections in England and Wales in May. His mind over the Easter weekend (15–17 April) turned to what he could do to reduce the image of a divided Party, which he had convinced himself was causing the rot. His solitary musings found an echo when four officers of the 1922 Committee wrote to him over the Easter recess warning him that restoration of the whip was vital if morale was to be lifted before the May elections.[173] The right was overwhelmingly keen to see the whipless MPs return. Major also felt that the media's continuing focus on the whipless detracted from the impression he wanted to convey of the government being tougher on EU issues. So, he resolved, the time had come for the readmission of the whipless. But when?

Number Ten had been receiving messages for some weeks, often from MPs who had visited the constituencies of the whipless, indicating that for all their bravado, they wanted to return to the fold.[174] The notes were passed on to Ryder, who replied curtly from the Whips' Office that the Prime

Minister had set out very clearly the terms for restoration, and when the MPs were willing to comply with those terms, they could return. Ryder, who had not been among the hawks in pressing for the withdrawal of the whip back in November, despite being blamed for it, had become an entrenched hardliner about readmission. Only if the rebels were willing to give a clear pledge to toe the government line in future should they be readmitted. The whips to a man had been deeply antagonised by the havoc wrought by the rebels since November and were in no mood for any action that smacked of surrender.[175]

With other senior figures agreeing with Ryder, Major kept his own counsel. 'The Prime Minister would very occasionally launch into a project about which he is hugely secretive, and this was one of them. He almost didn't let his own left hand know what the right one was doing,' recalled one Number Ten aide.[176]

Michael Spicer, the Eurosceptic former minister, spoke to Major and said that he would be willing to act as a go-between, and in the weekend after Easter Spicer secured the agreement of eight of the nine whipless MPs (but not Richard Body) to accept the whip. Major then told Ryder that they were ready and should be readmitted. Ryder, 'in a huge hump' about it according to one witness, then carried out his distasteful task in a perfunctory manner. A terse two-paragraph letter simply told the MPs that they were back in the Party. The letters were sent on 24 April, on a day that Major was at Chequers for a Policy Unit seminar, and were dispatched without even informing Hanley, the Party Chairman.[177]

The story for the media was to have been about Party unity. But with Ryder's action catching everyone off-guard, including the rebel MPs themselves who had not even responded before the story broke, the government line could not be properly spun. The media were frantically trying to find spokesmen to comment. Ryder, as was his personal rule, refused to say anything, neither would Newton, and many of those who might have commented, including Hunt, had little idea what was happening.[178] It was a classic example of media mismanagement. The whipless eight, antagonised by the way the restoration was presented by Ryder almost as an ultimatum,[179] seized the initiative with a crowing press conference in which they showed no sign of repentance, and the headlines the next day duly became 'Major surrenders to rebel MPs'.[180] Number Ten were outraged about the rebels' behaviour – 'by nature they are emotional shits to a man and woman,' said one aide[181] – while the view of one loyalist Cabinet minister was that 'we were too trusting. Major and Ryder always felt at the end of the day that the rebels could be trusted and that there was some inner good in them. But some of them had no inner good in them.'[182] Major indeed felt that the implicit understanding he had received via Spicer was that, once readmitted, the backbenchers would be on-side. Not for the first time, he considered himself betrayed.

Number Ten's dismay was compounded at Question Time in the House that afternoon, Major's worst as Prime Minister. Blair said that Major had failed to secure even a minimal guarantee of loyalty from the rebels. Major pointed to Labour's divisions on Europe, to which Blair's response was, 'There is one big difference. I lead my party. He follows his.' Following uproarious cheering, Blair continued, 'After all his tough talk in the beginning about no unity through appeasement he has caved in, his party is still divided and the white flag flies over Downing Street.'[183] Peter Riddell called the return of the rebels 'an exercise in cynicism and insincerity'.[184] Most informed opinion, including many of Major's own followers, agreed with that verdict. The whipless saga was one of the unhappiest episodes in the Major premiership.

THIRTY-TWO

'Backs to the Wall':

May–June 1995

BY THE BEGINNING of May 1995, Major was beginning to run out of options. The January and April relaunches had faltered. His personal initiative to reunite the Party by readmitting the whipless MPs had rebounded on him and further diminished his authority. Their return had seriously damaged his already weakening relationship with one of his crucial mainstays in a divided Cabinet, Chief Whip Richard Ryder.[1] Other allies, such as Hurd, Hunt and Hanley, were either on their way out or, like Lang, Newton and Mayhew, were unable to do much to bolster his position. Redwood was apparently immune to appeals to Party loyalty. Clarke, Heseltine and Portillo may not have been personally campaigning, but their backers were constantly testing the water. On the backbenches sat seventy former ministers, sixty of whom were critical of Major, and some like Lamont, Hamilton and Leigh openly dismissive of his leadership. Never this century had a Conservative Prime Minister been so little supported by his government and party.[2]

Defeat in Britain; Victory in Europe: May

Major badly needed a success in the local elections. Every English borough and district council outside London had at least a third of its members up for election, and every seat in the new Welsh councils had to be filled. The seats were last contested in 1991, a mediocre but not a disastrous year for the Tories, when they lost 920 seats but polled 35 per cent of the vote compared to Labour under Kinnock polling 36 per cent. The Conservatives in 1995 were defending 4,000 seats. At the outset, Central Office was braced for losing a thousand, a figure that drifted upwards as the election became nearer.

The Conservatives decided to run a seven-week, local issues campaign, in contrast to Labour's snappy two and a half weeks, focusing on national issues. In contrast to the 1994 elections, Major decided not to lead from the front, although he did launch the campaign on 14 March with the message to disaffected middle classes that it was 'time to come home to the Conservatives',[3] and set out to reinvigorate the Party's appeal in his Birmingham speech a fortnight later. Regular receptions were held at Number Ten for

constituency chairmen to raise spirits and to drive home the need for loyalty
and to rally support behind Tory candidates in the coming local elections.[4]
But the strategy did not go according to plan. Ministers made excuses not to
follow the lead from the centre; some were openly contemptuous of the
attempts by Central Office and Number Ten to involve them in their coordination of the campaign.[5] Hanley's allegation that all Labour councils 'tend
to be corrupt' rebounded against the Party when John Gummer, the Environment Secretary, conspicuously failed to endorse his comments at the first
campaign press conference.

Rather than following their lead and explore examples of Labour local
maladministration, as the Tories hoped, the media seemed more interested
in reporting national politics, in particular Cabinet divisions over hospital
closure plans and education, with Cabinet effectively overruling Major's
plans, as highlighted in his Birmingham speech, to give the latter more public
money. Protests over losses of teachers because of the tight 1994 settlement
provided an unsettling background for the local elections. Gillian Shephard
said £80 million would square the teachers and avoid trouble. Major supported her, anxious not to take on the teaching unions.[6] Clarke and Aitken
came out strongly against any more spending and the consensus was that
they should not dip into the reserve to find the money. Major warned Cabinet
to remember how they had lined up on the matter.[7]

In mid-April, wide publicity was given to the news that many Tories were
planning to stand for local office as 'independents' because they believed that
they would stand a better chance than under the 'Conservative' label. Anger
towards the government was at a high point, with concern at mortgages going
up with the cut in mortgage tax relief a common complaint.[8]

Major's principal intervention during the campaign was a speech on 26
April on housing and inner cities to the Social Market Foundation. Rather
than replay well-worn themes, Major deliberately chose to 'set out a vision in
a new area'.[9] He felt strongly about social deprivation and poor housing, and
in a speech in which he drew heavily on his boyhood in Brixton, he made a
passionate promise to renew the effort to tackle urban decay. He condemned
the 'essentially socialist' planners of the recent past for following fashionable
theory and bulldozing rows of terraced streets and rehousing their inhabitants
in 'soulless' tower blocks. These 'monuments to the failed history of socialist
planning', he said, had wrecked too many young lives.[10] He wanted 'to
improve the inner cities' and their 'concrete wastelands', working with town
halls and the private sector to revivify these neglected areas. Although imprecise as to exactly how the revitalisation would take place, it was a speech
which deserved wide attention as a prelude to a programme of action.[11]

Labour, however, was quick off the mark with its spoiling tactics. Frank
Dobson, Shadow Environment Secretary, recalled Major's time on Lambeth
Council's Housing Committee, when he had voted for modern housing
developments that he alleged had destroyed the traditional character of the
area. Dobson also recounted how Major had rebuked council house tenants

for painting their doorways without consulting the council. Number Ten's rebuttals repaired some damage, while a White Paper on extending home ownership and stimulating private sector investment in urban regeneration followed in June.[12] But Major himself realised that any progress in this area fell far short of his ambitions, which explained his enthusiasm for making inner-city development a core priority – involving 'billions and billions of pounds' – if re-elected to government in May 1997.[13]

Labour cleverly seized the initiative the Saturday before the polls on 4 May by holding their special conference approving, by a two-to-one majority, their new Clause Four, ending the party's seventy-seven-year commitment to nationalisation. Week by week, Labour was becoming more safe and appealing to Tory voters, helping to ensure that Tory middle-class voters remained disaffected. Blair's speech, reported widely, was compared in impact to Harold Wilson's 'white heat' of technology speech of 1963.

Blair's mocking of the Conservatives was masterly. 'They are split on everything, even identity cards. Half of them want their cards. The other half want an identity. And can you imagine the nightmare values that might descend in a new Tory constitution agreed at a special conference in Thatcherville, the capital of planet Portillo.' The comparison with the young Harold Wilson was indeed apposite, and was being increasingly noted. Blair came to the leadership with the looks, charm and quick wit; the Clause Four conference showed him to have real organisational flair, courage and judgement also.

Major counterattacked in an interview in the *Sunday Times*, when in a stinging diatribe he said that New Labour dealt in 'sneers, half-truths and untruths', and that the Party was too slick for its own good – 'Everything is pre-packaged as though you were selling a soap powder.'[14] The attack reflected Major's growing dislike of New Labour, which he considered lacking in political principles, as well as his mounting personal antipathy to Blair, whom he found insincere and sanctimonious. The jibe about following his party – which reflected Blair's disdain for his capitulation to the rebel Eurosceptics – had wounded him deeply. Downing Street aides confirmed that Major's stance in the interview was merely the first public airing of feelings he had hitherto kept to himself.[15] He had never felt the same degree of personal antipathy to Kinnock. For his part, Blair was, Alastair Campbell says, puzzled by Major's antipathy: it was, he said, as if 'Major regarded Blair's ambition to be Prime Minister instead of him as somehow not legitimate'.[16] The interview also provided the chance for Major to make a pre-emptive attack on any putative leadership challengers by saying that, in the event of a Labour landslide in the local elections, he would not be 'blown off course' but would stay to fight the general election.[17]

The last three days before polling day went badly for the Conservatives. News that the papers of Sir Winston Churchill had been purchased from his descendants with lottery money for £12.5 million, in direct contrast to the hope of a chorus of approval at a fitting memorial to a national hero on the fiftieth anniversary of the ending of the Second World War, provoked widespread anger. Only 8 per cent of those polled believed the Churchill papers were a reasonable use of the first significant awards of lottery funding. To the majority, the Churchill family should have donated the papers to the nation. Though it was not the government's decision, it added to the impression of greed in high places, and tarnished the promise that the lottery, one of Major's pet schemes, was to be a boon for arts and sports.[18] The impression of government culpability was emphasised by a report that Lady Thatcher was 'deeply dismayed at the government's handling of the Churchill papers', and said that she herself would donate her papers to the nation.[19]

A further pre-poll tangle was provoked by a report in *The Times* that mortgage insurance pay-outs were liable to tax, with apparently contradictory statements given during the day by Major, Hanley and others, while the cavalier dismissal of the issue by Clarke, dressed in his dinner jacket, bellowing out that the mortgage tax issue was 'nonsense', contributed to an eve-of-poll public relations nightmare for the Party.[20] In contrast, Labour's media profile, boosted by the 'triumph' of their weekend Clause Four conference, was lifted further by a series of well-judged interviews with Blair.

Some ground was regained by Major's visit to Northern Ireland on 3 May. While visiting Londonderry, supporters of Sinn Fein created a riot that led to twelve RUC officers being injured. An angry Major demanded an apology, which Gerry Adams pointedly refused to give. Piling Pelion on Ossa, Adams said he would be marking the anniversary that day of the death of Bobby Sands, the H-block hunger-striker, and denounced the Second World War as 'an imperialist adventure'.[21] The opinion at Westminster was that the government had been handed a propaganda weapon in its war of words with Sinn Fein. Number Ten announced on 4 May that Michael Ancram would be demanding 'substantial' progress in decommissioning of IRA arms before Sinn Fein was admitted to all-party talks.[22]

Major gathered some of his closest allies to Number Ten that night – Emily Blatch, Howell James and George Bridges, his PPSs John Ward and Ian McColl, and former PPS Graham Bright. Together they watched the local election results on the television in the sitting room in the second-floor flat. It did not make for happy viewing. The party lost 2,042 seats, while Labour gained 1,799 and the Liberal Democrats 495. Control was lost over strong-holds including Hove and Bracknell, and with the Tory share of the vote estimated at 25 per cent, it was left with control of just thirteen of Britain's 407 local councils. The resurgence of Labour in middle-class strongholds including the South was a particularly worrying feature; some pointed to the low turnout, 38 per cent, as indicating that many Tory voters had stayed at home. There could be no disguising the extent of the disaster – the worst national result so far of Major's premiership.

Major tried adopting a brave face the next day. In discussion with Clarke, he supported the high-risk strategy of not raising interest rates, still at 6.75 per cent. The decision may have helped rally some Conservative spirits, but it sent the pound tumbling. Invoking the Dunkirk spirit, Major said that the Tory Party would act as the British nation acted when its back was to the wall: 'turn round and fight for the things it believes in, and that is what I shall do'.[23] He apologised to the 2,000 councillors who had lost their seats and admitted that, despite the intention of the campaign, the Party's national, not local, policies were again to blame: 'We have thus far failed to persuade people that the long-term policies I am following are right for the country.'[24]

The Party faithful were, apparently, no longer interested in candour. Many MPs found that their constituents began to turn on them after the 1995 results, and demanded to know why changes were not being made at the top.[25] Anger from dispossessed Tory councillors filled the media. Tony Bevins wrote that throughout the election, 'Canvassers returned from the local election campaign with a message from the doorstep that the whole Cabinet was stuffed with nonentities, bunglers and time-servers.'[26] *The Times* spoke of the loss of '2,000 loyal Tories who have given years, sometimes decades of service to local government, and who now find themselves not even in opposition, but out of local politics altogether because of the mess that their masters in Westminster have created'.[27] The weekend papers were predictably gloomy. Several picked up Blair's comment: 'John Major isn't the Tory Party's problem. The Tory Party is John Major's problem.'[28] Labour's strategy, Blair's aides say, was not to criticise Major directly, but to emphasise his weakness with respect to an undisciplined and 'sleazy' political party.[29]

Major was left to nurse his wounds. He felt as if he was locked in a box, the key to which had been lost. He avoided blaming himself personally for the bad results, believing that he uniquely could undo the impostor Blair. But the cards were held by Labour, above all Blair's fresh image, toasted by the media, and his successful repositioning of his party which, for one of the few times in its history, was an easier ship to manoeuvre than the Tories.[30]

Major's rumination on all this was overtaken, to his relief, by the celebrations to mark the fiftieth anniversary of VE Day. The largest assembly of world leaders since Elizabeth II's Coronation in 1953 met in London on Sunday 7 May for a service of 'remembrance, thanksgiving and hope' in St Paul's Cathedral. After lunch at Buckingham Palace, the heads of state travelled to Hyde Park in coaches. King Hussein of Jordan amused everyone by announcing 'this is the first time I have been by bus.' In Hyde Park the Queen led a symbolic procession of heads of state to a giant globe containing an eternal flame and book of remembrance. Visiting monarchs and presidents walked hand-in-hand with groups of children dressed in white as a climax to the spectacle. Major was moved by the occasion, as he had been the year before by the D-Day celebrations. The death of Norma's father at the end of the war moved him, and he was acutely conscious of the debt he, as head of government, owed all those who had taken part.[31]

While commemorative street parties and fêtes were held across Britain on an unusually sunny Bank Holiday weekend, Major flew to Paris on the Sunday evening, spending the night at the British Embassy, plugs in ears to shut out the noise, not least from Parisians also celebrating Chirac's election in succession to Mitterrand in the nearby Place de la Concorde. On the Monday morning, after a bilateral with Chirac and commemoration in central Paris, he attended an official lunch at the Elysée before flying on to Bonn.[32] Under great pressure of time, he was driven in convoy into the town centre to meet Kohl and Yeltsin, where he spoke sensitively about remembering 'all sides who fell in the last war', and gratified Germans with a flattering formal reference to Helmut Kohl in the rebuilding of modern Europe. 'Many have contributed to this: Churchill and De Gaulle, Roosevelt, Truman and Kennedy, Gorbachev, Konrad Adenauer who rebuilt Germany and you, Herr Bundeskanzler, who saw it reunited in peace and freedom.'[33]

Absenting himself from the official dinner, he flew on late on Monday evening to Moscow for further commemorations, arriving at 1 a.m. local time, and went to bed in the British Embassy tired out by 2.30 a.m. Up very early the next morning he had a bilateral with Yeltsin, saw the Red Square parade and spoke at the opening of a Second World War memorial, going out of his way to reassure Russian leaders that Britain would not allow new divisions to damage relations between both countries again. In contrast to Mitterrand and Kohl, who made clear their opposition to Russia's continuing war in Chechnia, Major expressed merely 'concern' at the conflict. Major's softer words did not go unnoticed by Yeltsin, who greeted him, 'Welcome to old friends.'

Yeltsin continued to see Major as a vital ally in influencing decisions in Washington and Brussels about not hurrying the eastward expansion of NATO into former Warsaw Pact countries. To show the esteem in which he held Britain, Yeltsin made particular reference to Britain's role in the Second World War, and promised to have school textbooks rewritten to reflect that contribution. Gifts were exchanged: for Major a silver commemorative medallion, and for Yeltsin a replica of a sword presented fifty years earlier by Churchill to Stalin.[34]

Open Gestures and Closed Minds: May

When Major flew back into London on the night of Tuesday 9 May, he and his advisers knew that he would be facing a battle for his political survival. After the 1994 election disaster, there had been the European election and then Smith's death to provide a focus and a fresh challenge. This time there was nothing. Major, James and Blackwell knew that they desperately needed 'to pull something out of the bag'.[35] But what?

A reshuffle was an option on the table. Why not put one in place for the Whitsun recess at the end of May? Would it clear the air, they asked, and would it provide the sense of momentum the Party needed? They were faced by a small number of key facts. They could not fault Hanley's loyalty or determination, but he did not carry the weight they badly needed, and continued to be badly roasted by the press.[36] 'How are we going to seize the initiative', asked one insider, 'when we have a Party Chairman who is seen as a dead duck by the media and not highly regarded by his colleagues?'[37]

Thoughts in Number Ten began to turn, as in 1993 and 1994, to the idea of a Deputy Prime Minister. For all Hunt's personal qualities, it was clear that he lacked the clout or the presentational verve to be the coordinator of government policy, and play the role that Major had lacked in the three years since Chris Patten had left.[38] Dissatisfaction was rising with another core part of the government's coordination apparatus, the Number Twelve Committee, chaired by Ryder: 'Absolutely ghastly,' was the verdict of one attender of its daily meetings.[39] Hunt himself had been increasingly aware of his and the machinery's inability to coordinate and present government policy effectively, and began to press for a new structure.[40] Ryder's relationship with Number Ten had failed to recover in the weeks following the return of the whipless MPs; while Ryder fought manfully against severe back pain and remained loyal to the last, his Whips' Office was no longer seen to be as effective. Torpor was beginning to grip the central machine, and if it was allowed to continue could become chronic.

If the centre was becoming sclerotic, little success was coming from ministers in the field, who seemed to be similarly ensnared. 'There was a sense around the Prime Minister in the weeks following the local elections', recalled one insider, 'that the ministers who should have been most effective working on his behalf to coalesce and give shape to the Party and to government at the centre were not there.'[41] Virginia Bottomley at Health was facing the prospects of strikes from both doctors and nurses, while the press was full of high-profile stories of patients dying because of insufficient intensive care beds, of dangerous mentally ill people walking the streets and committing acts of violence, on top of popular hospitals closing. The government carried, with a majority of twelve, a vote on the future of London hospitals after Heseltine warned rebels that they risked handing the next election to Labour. Former Cabinet minister Peter Brooke, who was the local MP, however, refused to support the government.

At Transport, Mawhinney was finding rail privatisation and bus deregulation provoking a chorus of protest. Gillian Shephard may have proved a smoother figure mollifying the education world than her predecessor, but cash shortages aroused predicted public unrest and threats of resistance. Concern about crime remained high, but so too were the crime figures, and increasing the prison population led to the system coming under immense strain, tensions with prison officers and high-profile misadventures.[42] Opinion polls during May unsurprisingly reflected the low level of public confidence in the competence of government performance.[43] Tony Newton was one of the very few ministers at the time with whose performance Number Ten felt totally happy.[44]

While the economy remained Major's principal hope that the government would recover its popularity, the energy and direction provided by Norman

Blackwell was a more immediate focus – though this, too, tended to be treated dismissively by some ministers, as had every Number Ten attempt at strategic coordination since the Citizen's Charter. In an effort to make ministers think collectively and strategically, the use of Blackwell's 'five themes' in campaigning, and capturing opinion-formers, was discussed for a second successive Political Cabinet on 27 April.[45] More needed to be done to regain the initiative, he argued, beyond their discussions and the policy groups which had been established.

Number Ten and Central Office had been inundated by letters in the spring saying that the leadership was out of touch with the thinking of its Tory supporters. These letters came from activists in constituencies, as well as from senior figures in the Party, and were often abrupt in tone. Might not there be scope here for a fresh approach? Blackwell reasoned that the government had become like the board of a major corporation which was out of touch with its shareholders and its customers.[46] Something needed to be done to rebuild bridges between the Party at the centre and its supporters. Blackwell's thinking merged with that of Hanley, who had been working up a proposal at Central Office for consulting the Party in the country under the title 'Operation Disraeli'.[47]

In the absence of an early reshuffle, which Major decided he would hold over to July, Number Ten seized on the 'consultation exercise' idea as a way of demonstrating it held the initiative. Hence the theme for Major's speech to the Scottish Conservative Conference at Glasgow on 12 May, derided by Labour as the fifth 'fight-back speech' and the fourteenth relaunch.[48] Not to be deterred, Major announced that he and his Cabinet colleagues were to embark on a grand tour to consult Tory activists and the public over the next Conservative manifesto. His aim was 'To meet you, to talk to you. To build a people's policy to bridge the gap between the doorsteps of Britain and the corridors of power' in a consultation exercise to be spread over the following twelve months. He would be 'the first leader in the Party's history' to give every Party member the chance to shape its policies. Lest anyone think, however, that the government was stale, his response was that it was 'still fizzing with ideas', and before the summer was out it would publish new housing proposals, launch a national volunteers programme, and invite 'a bold expansion of nursery education'.[49]

According to initial indications, the speech and the fight-back were well received.[50] Some shine was taken away, however, by two speeches, one a misfortune, the other deliberate. Within an hour of Major's robust defence at the conference of the Union against Labour's plans, the media were abuzz with Rifkind saying he had 'no problem' with the principle of devolution.[51] The Defence Secretary was furious at what he believed was a mis-representation of his views, and told John Humphrys of BBC Radio 4's *Today* programme: 'You really are a remarkable lot. The BBC are becoming a real menace.'[52]

No similar denial of wrongdoing came from far more serious up-staging remarks made by Lamont at a speech in Cheltenham to the Freedom Association the same day as Major's speech. The party was doomed, the former Chancellor argued, unless it could rediscover the radicalism of the 'golden decade' of the Thatcher era, including big cuts in government spending and taxes.[53] Lamont, whose behaviour was regarded in Number Ten as unbecoming, was believed to be nakedly angling for a leadership challenge later in the year.[54]

Major's Glasgow speech was followed up with a letter to all Conservative backbenchers inviting them to participate in the meetings in the constituencies preparing ideas for the next manifesto, and to submit their own proposals either to the policy groups or to Number Ten direct. It seemed a sensible and constructive way forward in rebuilding relations. To raise morale further, Major pledged a political offensive based upon the nation state, the constitution and the free market, all themes dear to the hearts of the right.[55]

Robin Harris, Mrs Thatcher's Svengali, remained one right-winger unimpressed by Major's grand design for openness and consultation, and wrote a withering attack on 'listening' being – he believed – at variance with Tory notions of democracy.[56] His attack caused considerable apprehension in Number Ten about whether the openness and willingness to listen might be seen generally by the right as indicating that there was a vacuum of ideas and leadership at the top, a fear which was only quelled when it became apparent by the summer that the consultation exercise was being well received.[57]

The right, in general, pined for what they saw as strong and certain leadership, where prime ministers, conspicuously Mrs Thatcher, provided the lead and others followed (overlooking the fact that the whole ideological thrust of Thatcherism came from her adopting the ideas of others). But if the Party's consultation exercise was seen by the right as unnecessary and weak, Major's actions over the previous three years in setting up the Scott and Nolan committees were seen as extreme folly. As one Number Ten aide recalled: 'The impression created was of Number Ten failing to take decisions itself. It merely compounded the "pressure cooker" atmosphere.'[58]

The long-awaited report from the Scott Inquiry into the Arms-to-Iraq affair, established in November 1992, was seen as a time bomb waiting to explode. The Greenbury committee's investigation into the issue of top-level pay in the privatised industries – whose establishment had been supported by Major – had been described by the *Guardian* as 'the pivotal moment' in the retreat from Thatcherite ideology into pragmatism,[59] while the right saw it as an unhealthy attempt to regulate capitalism. But it was Major's decision in October 1994 to create a committee to investigate standards in public life that caused the deepest fury. The committee of ten, under Lord Nolan, began work with a missionary enthusiasm, convinced – rightly – that the 'cash-for-questions' and other 'sleaze' issues that led to its inception were casting a real blight on public confidence in government and Parliament. As with the Scott Inquiry, Nolan cast its net much wider than Major had initially envisaged.

To prepare the government's response to Nolan's thoroughgoing investigation, an *ad hoc* committee was set up under David Hunt.[60] Hunt himself thought setting up Nolan had been an 'inspired move' by Major, unlike, he later claimed, '80 to 90 per cent of the Cabinet'.[61] He shared the Prime Minister's conviction that the stories of wrongdoing in high places, whipped up by the media, were damaging the perception of public life in Britain and had to be either squashed or verified.

When Nolan presented his first report on 11 May, Major – blissfully unaware of the boomerang that was about to hit him – immediately announced that he accepted its 'broad thrust'.[62] There were grounds for reassurance. Nolan himself stated that his committee had found no evidence of 'systematic corruption'. However, Nolan also said 'urgent action' was necessary in certain areas to allay public fears. Cabinet debated the report that morning. Ministers agreed to accept Nolan's recommendations on a 'quarantine period' before Cabinet ministers left to outside jobs in the private sector, and to the establishment of a public appointments commissioner to scrutinise ministerial appointments to quangos. Hunt told Cabinet that his committee concluded acceptance of Nolan's recommendations was 'a unique opportunity for us to rebuild public confidence'.[63]

Ominous rumblings of discontent were heard on the Tory backbenches that Thursday evening, echoes of apprehensions voiced in January when Nolan had declared that the rules on MPs' business interests would have to be tightened up, and suggested the need for an independent element to oversee Parliament's activities. Now the Nolan report was going even further and proposing a ban on MPs being paid by multi-client lobbyists. Tory MPs saw this as an attack on parliamentary sovereignty, and on their own freedom of commercial activity. The issue was put on hold for a week, with Parliament set to debate it on 18 May, and the government to announce its full response.[64]

On Monday 15 May, at a meeting of the business managers, Ryder informed Major of the strength of feeling among his MPs against Nolan's parliamentary proposals. With so many angry Tory MPs – mostly, but not exclusively, on the right – threatening to rebel, far more than over Europe, the leadership question was placed firmly back on the agenda.[65] The right-wing press was also highly critical of Major, and in the words of Simon Heffer, regarded the report as 'explicitly anti-Conservative [it] threatens to end the parliamentary Conservative party as we know it'.[66]

This was a bleak moment for Major. He believed he was right to have responded in the way he did to the widespread public concern and set up Nolan. He allowed the committee to have a wide-ranging brief and did not try to influence its proceedings; now its report had landed him in the biggest purely domestic crisis of his premiership. At Hunt's committee on Tuesday, meeting in the office of Tony Newton in the House, it was decided that the government propose referring those parts of the report dealing with Parliament (as opposed to government) to a new committee, to consist of MPs. Allowing the Commons itself to decide its response to that part of the Nolan report that dealt with the legislature seemed a neat way out of the predicament, and full Cabinet gratefully accepted the Hunt committee recommendation on the Thursday just hours before the debate began.

In the Commons, one Tory backbencher after another rose to attack Nolan's proposals, the loudest cheers being unusually reserved for Edward Heath, who said, 'We have now reached a stage where every man and woman in this House is an object of suspicion.'[67] The tone had been set by the Conservative MP Alan Duncan, who badgered Lord Nolan as he made his way to the House to listen to the debate, reportedly saying: 'You are about to obliterate the professional classes' representation in the House of Commons. It is a very, very dangerous game.'[68] Major himself was a sitting target for Blair. The Labour leader asked him at Question Time whether he agreed with Nolan's recommendation that MPs disclose details and earnings from consultancies. Major was forced to respond rather lamely that he wanted to hear the views of the House before reaching decisions himself.

Only at the end of the debate, to an almost empty chamber, did Newton, as the Leader of the House, announce the proposal of a committee of 'senior and respected backbenchers' to consider how to implement the recommendations relating to Parliament. Labour and the Liberal Democrats, sensing that they had the government on the run, then sought with a degree of cynicism to extract maximum embarrassment by threatening to boycott Newton's committee. The six-hour debate was indeed unedifying, self-interest and party interest obscuring the real issues and the validity of public concern. Peter Riddell commented on good report that 'Lord Nolan and his colleagues must have been appalled at how their report was misrepresented'.[69]

Labour moved towards accepting the Newton committee proposal after Major wrote to Blair, making clear his commitment to the highest standards of public life, and stating that the new committee's objective would be 'to consider on behalf of the House the Nolan recommendations and how they might be implemented'.[70] Labour skilfully created the impression of a self-interested government in disarray, procrastinating in the face of its greedy backbenchers who were calling the tune.[71] Further accusations of greed were heaped on the Tory Party when Sir Jerry Wiggin was caught, in the midst of the Nolan furore, putting the name of an unwitting Sebastian Coe to an amendment on behalf of a lobby group for which he was a paid consultant.

Tory anger in May was easy to understand. 'Morale among Conservative MPs has never been lower,' declared a leader in *The Times*.[72] The local election results had led to many 'contemplating defeat at the next general election and wondering what they would do with their lives afterwards'. Then the Nolan Report meant that the prospect of 'earning a decent amount of money' thereafter receded still further.[73] Self-interest did indeed lie behind much Tory anger at Nolan and at Major. More respect might have been earned if they had acknowledged this more and the deep public concern rather than dressing up objections to Nolan as defence of Parliament's integrity, or the risks of putting off able aspirants from becoming MPs. The failure to look outward and acknowledge criticisms of their behaviour did nothing to enhance the standing of Parliament, or indeed the Tory Party. Not for the first time, Major had acted in a principled and courageous manner, to find himself the target of abuse.

Major's response to Nolan had pleased neither his party, nor the public wish for an unambiguously positive response. He had been taken aback by the strength of feeling on the backbenches. He initially underestimated that he would damage also himself by adopting the halfway house position of setting up a committee. He was angry with his backbenchers, and angry that circumstances had combined to put him in a position which even critics like Andrew Rawnsley admitted was impossible: 'damned by the public if he does not act; damned by his backbenchers if he does'.[74]

Major determined that he would exact revenge. Meanwhile, with the news continuing all bad, he would bide his time. The death on 17 May of popular MP Geoffrey Dickens meant another by-election and the virtual certainty of a lost seat. On 25 May the Conservatives went from first to third in the Perth and Kinross by-election, reducing the government's majority to eleven. At the end of the month, a MORI poll suggested that the modest Tory revival seen in the spring had been reversed, as Tory support dropped to 22 per cent, near its lowest-ever levels in its traditional strongholds in the South and among the middle classes.[75]

Hostage Crisis in Bosnia

Major was looking forward to a quiet Whitsun weekend holiday in Huntingdon. For some days, however, he had been keeping an anxious eye on reports from Bosnia, where the lightly armed UN forces including British troops had come under increasing threat from Bosnian Serb forces. NATO airstrikes had unnerved the Serbs, and they took 250 UN personnel, including British soldiers, hostage until the air strikes were lifted. On Saturday 27 May the UN Security Council met in emergency session to discuss developments, and with concern rising for the safety of Britain's 3,500 troops in Bosnia, Major decided to cut short his holiday for an emergency meeting of the Cabinet's OPD committee on Sunday evening. Rifkind's opinion as Defence Secretary was that the mounting crisis was one of 'unprecedented gravity',[76] while Nicholas Bonsor, chairman of the all-party Defence Select Committee, echoed the views of many MPs when he said that the government must consider withdrawing the troops.[77] In an interview in the *Mail on Sunday*, Major reiterated his position that 'I do not want them to leave ... They have saved an awful lot of lives and their presence has held the amount of fighting there has been.'[78]

By the time that OPD met for a three-hour meeting later that Sunday, the position had deteriorated badly with the taking hostage of thirty-three British soldiers, Royal Welch Fusiliers, who were guarding UN observation posts in the eastern protected enclave of Gorazde. Major was in determined mood when he chaired the meeting, attended by Hurd, Rifkind, Heseltine, Aitken and Peter Inge, Chief of Defence Staff.[79] Major had earlier resisted pressure in OPD for withdrawing, but now the mood was changing: Rifkind, backed by Inge, agreed that British reinforcements should be sent.[80] Major said strong resolve would best be displayed by sending in a brigade rather than by sending support apparatus while the soldiers stayed on stand-by, as the Ministry of Defence had originally suggested.[81]

Constant contact was maintained between Number Ten and the Elysée, to allow Major to keep in step with President Chirac, anxious to illustrate that the two largest UN contributors in Bosnia were united in putting pressure on the Bosnian Serbs. Major was at his calm best throughout the Sunday, talking to Clinton and helping bring about a coordinated response from the West. The decision was also taken to recall Parliament, for only the eighth time in twenty-five years during a recess,[82] the following Wednesday. While Hurd was dispatched to Brussels for meetings with the new French Foreign Minister, Hervé de Charette, the first British troops left for Bosnia on Tuesday. Major warned the Bosnian Serb leaders that they would be held personally responsible if any harm came to the thirty-three British hostages.[83]

Major spoke powerfully in the emergency Commons debate, arguing that the prevention of cold-blooded racially based murder was the *raison d'être* for the presence of British troops. To further assuage the doubters, he restated the strategic case for preventing the Bosnian dispute escalating into a wider Balkan war, with all the risks for British financial and military interests that would pose. 'Withdrawal is not a policy. No one should believe that leaving Bosnia would end the UK's interest in this conflict ... Could the West stand really by and let such actions take place in south-eastern Europe? I doubt it. I truly doubt it.'[84] Terror, widespread before UN troops arrived in 1992, would again prevail: 'If we depart, I remind the House those dangers return.'[85] Blair and Ashdown, while implying that British policy had not been faultless in the past, gave their full backing. Against the government was ranged one of the odder coalitions of Major's premiership, including left-wingers like Benn, middle-ground pragmatists like Heath, and right-wingers like George Gardiner, who favoured withdrawal because he believed no British interests were involved.[86]

Having piloted the policy through Parliament, and seen hostages released on 6 June, Major had to see off arguments from the Treasury about the cost of any increased commitment, and from the Ministry of Defence, which began to develop doubts after its support at the OPD meeting.[87] At Cabinet on 8 June, the despatch of the 24th Air Mobile Brigade based at Colchester was discussed. Concerns were expressed about the dangers of the drift towards deeper military involvement, with the United States' experience in Vietnam being again cited as evidence. Nevertheless, Cabinet agreed that the brigade should be sent, and that Rifkind be given authority to deploy it once discussions with the UN over the practical arrangements had been satisfactorily concluded.[88] Major believed that his Bosnian policy had put national above Party interest;[89] to have held out for the policy he believed to be right when his standing in the Party was so low, had indeed taken both skill and courage.

The Vultures Gather: June

For Major, the Bosnian crisis ironically was the calm in the middle of a typhoon. For a few days, he was in control of his party, Parliament, Cabinet and armed forces, and marshalling the western alliance as he wished. But three fresh events were now to crowd in on him in rapid succession and bring him to the point of greatest despair in his premiership.

On the day MPs returned to Westminster after the Whitsun recess, Tuesday 6 June, the headlines were full of a leak of the draft conclusions of the Scott Report. The story was broken by Graeme McLagan, a BBC journalist, who had been told about the contents by a former diplomat.[90] The leak caused multiple difficulties.

Criticism, both open and covert, was now levelled at Major from all levels of the Party. Why had he set up the Inquiry? Why had he not set up a committee of Privy Councillors to investigate the alleged misconduct? Why, above all, had he allowed the increasingly controversial Richard Scott, known for his liberal views, to head the Inquiry? Why, Tory MPs asked, more generally, did the Prime Minister not lead from the front rather than rely on the political expediency of setting up an inquiry which only stored up problems for later? The Scott leak put the leadership question back to the top of the agenda. Lamont's name became widely discussed as the most likely stalking horse candidate. Heseltine emerged from the leak free of any ignominy. Some MPs on the right toyed with the earlier idea of a balanced ticket, with Heseltine becoming Prime Minister, and right-wing Cabinet ministers being put in key posts.[91]

Blow number two was delivered by Lady Thatcher. A shadowy presence in the nearly two years since the publication of volume one of her memoirs in the autumn of 1993, she now exploded back on the scene. The second volume, *The Path to Power*, was to be published on 12 June. In essence the story of her life until the moment that she became Prime Minister in May 1979, she had, in discussion with her publishers, HarperCollins, agreed to include what became a 150-page 'Part 2', outlining her life and thoughts since November 1990. HarperCollins were anxious for her to highlight contemporary elements to give piquancy to a book which would otherwise appear as an anticlimax after *The Downing Street Years*. From the moment she agreed, this section of the book was bound to be either anodyne, or explosive.[92] By mid-1995, despite some more positive utterances over the previous two years, Lady Thatcher's scorn for Major had not abated: she thought he was 'wavering around all over the place'.[93] Voices both inside and outside her immediate circle urging restraint were brushed aside as she threw caution to the winds. 'If Volume 1 of the memoirs was the decree nisi,' said one friend, 'then Volume 2 was the decree absolute.'[94]

The *Sunday Times*, another branch of the Murdoch media empire alongside HarperCollins, serialised the book. Extracts were to commence on Whit Sunday, 28 May, but whetting appetites, a front-page taster appeared on 21 May, under the headline 'Thatcher launches savage attack on Major's misguided policies'. The article detailed her attack on Major for 'dodging key problems, splitting the Tory Party over Europe, causing a needlessly deep recession [by trying to maintain Britain in the ERM for so long] and pursuing misguided social and taxation policies'. The newspaper outlined how she would be setting out her own radical agenda for 'putting these things right', including a return to British sovereignty over EU institutions, rejection of the Maastricht Treaty and an immediate declaration of sterling's independence outside a single currency.[95] Michael Jones considered that her 'caustic' savaging of Major's record would make the breakdown between them plain for every Tory to see, further encouraging Party infighting. Lady Thatcher's own public words, that it was 'for others to take the action required', meanwhile cast a chilling spell.[96]

Supporters of both sides rushed to defend or attack. Bruce Anderson, friend and biographer of Major, retorted that many of Major's 'unresolved problems' had been inherited from his predecessor, that it was she who had signed the Single European Act, a far more interventionist step than the Maastricht Treaty, and he cited her acolyte Charles Powell, who had said that he believed that had she still been in power in 1991, Mrs Thatcher would have 'agreed a deal akin to Maastricht'.[97] Echoing the feeling in the Thatcher court that Major made a cardinal error in 1990–92 by appearing to spurn her, Rees-Mogg wrote, 'When he became Prime Minister, with Margaret Thatcher's support, John Major's first big mistake was to distance himself from his predecessor.'[98]

Lady Thatcher exacerbated tension in a series of interviews to publicise her book. Her praise for Blair, at a time when the Conservatives were trying to dismiss him as insubstantial, was all the more damaging because his popularity and the success he was making of transforming Labour gave it a ring of truth. She called Blair 'probably the most formidable' Labour leader for thirty years, a tribute Blair was to reciprocate.[99] Prominence was given to the remark of a well-placed Thatcher 'confidant' who said that – though she would of course deny it – she had come to the view that Major had to go.[100]

If a cold hostility characterised the feelings in the Thatcher camp towards Major, the dominant mood in Number Ten towards her was one of resignation and despair. Major's response was to remark bitterly that many of the problems over which she was now pontificating had their origins in her premiership. Scant comfort was offered by psychological explanations for her actions, notably from her own biographer, Hugo Young, who described her feelings towards Major as the 'classic hatred for an usurping son'.[101] It was also noted that her treatment of her successor as the Finchley MP, Hartley Booth, bore some of the jealous hallmarks of her dismissive attitude to Major.[102] The Thatcher camp equally believed that Major had been envious of her, which was why he wanted to marginalise her.[103] The knife was twisted a further time with Lady Thatcher's fifty-minute television interview with David Frost to mark the publication of the memoirs, when she said she disagreed fundamentally with the 'absurd' withdrawal of the whip from the eight MPs, said public spending had gone up too far, and attributed the Party's unpopularity to the erosion of her political legacy, including help for home owners, saying 'yes' to Europe, and for not being Conservative enough.[104] This last admission was more lethal than anything she wrote in her book.[105]

The third and final blow came on Tuesday 13 June, at a meeting Major attended of the Eurosceptic Fresh Start Group the day after the Thatcher memoirs were officially published. Major arrived flustered, fifteen minutes late and in a 'chippy' confrontational mood at a windowless conference room in the Commons, and was surprised that the meeting had attracted between fifty-five and sixty MPs.[106] The meeting was convened by Michael Spicer, chairman of the group, and a right-wing conciliator who believed Major's views should be listened to respectfully, not least because of his growing Euroscepticism.[107]

The meeting began amicably enough, with attenders banging desks, albeit perfunctorily. Spicer welcomed Major, and said that the group wanted to discuss two issues, the single currency and how to reclaim powers from Brussels. Major was invited to open the discussion. Speaking for a little over ten minutes, he talked of his determination to maintain the veto obtained at Maastricht, how he would prevent further encroachment from the EU at the IGC, and of his concerns about the practicalities of EMU. Attenders sat there stony faced, resenting Major for lecturing them. An aide said: 'Nine-and-a-half times out of ten, Major instinctively judged the mood of a meeting correctly. This time he didn't.'[108]

The meeting came to life when John Townend, chairman of the Party's backbench Finance Committee, asked whether it was not time for the Prime Minister to come off the fence, and pronounce that as long as he was at Number Ten he would not advise the Commons to accept a single currency. The cheers that echoed around the room were the first indication that Major was losing control of the meeting.[109]

Known enemies of Major then joined in, including Lamont, who said that if a single currency was wrong in principle in 1999 it was wrong now, and George Gardiner, who said people yearned for a clear lead; 'wait and see' was not a clear lead. Bill Cash, Iain Duncan-Smith and Bernard Jenkin all spoke bluntly and dismissively of Major's stance. Major, losing his patience, angered his audience by saying that he did not believe the public cared that much about Europe, and before long MPs were shouting out their disapproval of points being made, and roaring out their approval when each new Eurosceptic arrow landed home. In an increasingly undignified meeting, it was Sir Ivan Lawrence, chairman of the Home Affairs Select Committee, and a respected elder statesman, who delivered the most damaging blow when he stated that if Major did not change his line on the single currency, the Party would not be around to decide in 1999 because it would have already been voted out of office.

Major had had enough. After an hour, he walked out of the room to the sound of half-hearted applause, looking, according to several reports, shattered by the most unruly and disrespectful meeting he was to attend as premier.[110] He immediately regretted his decision to have attended. Even his friends felt it had been an error of judgement to expose himself to so many of his greatest critics. The consensus was that he had convinced none of his case, but rather had unified and strengthened his opponents.[111]

Ironically, developments in Europe were making the adoption of a Eurosceptic position by Major easier. He had had a successful bilateral meeting with Kohl in Bonn on 26 May. Still warmed by Major's listing of him as a great leader alongside Churchill *et al*, the German Chancellor smiled benignly on Major's insistence on vetoeing any further powers for Brussels.[112] On 10 June Major met Chirac, and again pressed hard. The new French President admitted that the EU had failed to give sufficiently serious thought to a single currency that would include just five to seven members, and conceded that studies should take place about the effects of Britain, Spain and Italy all being excluded.[113]

Major felt he was pressing the Eurosceptic button as hard as he dared, with both EU partners and with his own Cabinet Europhiles. He knew the single currency was the nub of the issue – but his efforts earlier in the year to downplay the prospects of Britain joining had provoked the destabilising row with Clarke which undermined earlier headway. He did not see what more he could do without exacerbating underlying splits. His mood swung as on a see-saw. He switched between believing he could win over the sceptics by adopting what he believed was the most Eurosceptic position it was possible to take, to wishing to see the leading sceptic MPs crushed. A Number Ten aide described how they began asking themselves, after the Thatcher memoirs and the Fresh Start humiliation: 'Does the Party still want to win? Is the Party determined to tear itself apart? ... Many MPs had become more interested in promoting their views on Europe than on Party loyalty. Any sense of community and loyalty had departed the camp. We were left asking "who's on our side?".'[114]

Several other camps within the Conservative Party had also begun asking who was on their side. Clarke's chances of succeeding Major had plummeted since earlier in the year. His series of gaffes, culminating in his eve of local election poll remarks on mortgage insurance tax, had led to even the left questioning his suitability for the top job. Setting himself up as champion of the Europhiles – principled to some, self-centred folly to others – on top of his opposition to tax cuts, killed off his prospects. The right had become thoroughly disenchanted with him, while some like Kenneth Baker demanded that he be moved.[115] Heseltine, on the other hand, by trimming his Europhilia, while taking pains to be an ultra Major loyalist, was picking up increasing support from the right of the Party. One Thatcherite MP said in mid-June: 'People are now past the point of being so frightened of Heseltine as leader that they will not rock the boat.'[116]

Number Ten's worries centred on Portillo and Lamont, then Redwood (not Howard and Lilley, whom they did not regard as plotting). While Lamont continued to be more of a lone wolf, a small pack followed Portillo. Major's aides had been watching him and his supporters for some months. 'We knew they were having meetings, outside suppers, conversations. We used to monitor who was going to them, so we knew what was going on. Sometimes we received feedback on what was being said. They would also inflame areas where there was difficulty, to make things even more difficult.'[117]

Number Ten regarded David Hart, Portillo's special adviser, as the Machiavellian figure at the centre of the Portillo drive for the leadership, which was at its height in the spring and early summer of 1995. Edward Leigh was another who Number Ten believed hated Major, and was a figure pressing for a leadership challenge and hoping for Portillo.[118] 'They were very skilled at leaking ... their organisation was so good that they delegated people not just to leak, but also to spin,' recalled another Major loyalist.[119] But for all the efforts of Portillo's followers, and despite, on balance, being the favoured successor of Lady Thatcher, she still considered the moment not ripe for him to succeed, which explains her (albeit reluctant) statement in mid-June that in the event of a leadership challenge, she would advise MPs to vote for Major.[120]

A potential new candidate, who according to a Cabinet colleague 'was putting herself about a lot, and who let it be known in the months leading up to June that she would be interested in being a compromise candidate', was Gillian Shephard,[121] a long-standing friend of Major. As speculation fever gripped the media, William Hill, the bookmakers, were in mid-June offering the following odds: Heseltine, 7–4 favourite; Portillo, 2–1; Clarke, 11–4; Shephard, 10–1, and Dorrell fifth on 16–1.[122]

News of Gillian Shephard's interest came as a particular hurt to Major. He had been disinclined to believe all that his friends had been telling him about the unrest in the Party. According to Graham Bright: 'The Fresh Start meeting was the straw that broke the camel's back. Having been through it, he decided that everything his friends had been telling him, however much he tried to discount it, was true.'[123]

Number Ten had tried one last time to rally Cabinet's spirits. At Political Cabinet on 8 June, Blackwell had outlined the four conditions for winning the next general election: demonstrating unity and purpose, receiving credit for the economic success story, popular fresh policies, and fear of Labour. To try to encourage ministers, they were shown figures on how, using Gallup's figures, previous mid-term lows had been transcended: 23 per cent during 1979–83, rising to 44 per cent eighteen months later at the general election; 24 per cent during 1983–7, rising within twenty-four months to 43 per cent at the election; and 28 per cent during 1987–92, climbing again to 43 per cent. Fairer winds could blow the Party out of these mid-term doldrums too, it was reasoned, with at least twenty-three months possible.[124] The truth though was that a significant majority believed that a factor had been omitted far more important than Blackwell's four points, and it was the one they cared about most: a new leader.

Halifax and Decision Time: June

Major was a troubled man when he flew to Canada on Thursday 15 June for the G7 meeting at Halifax, Nova Scotia. He had spent a miserable forty-eight hours since the Fresh Start meeting, turning over in his mind an idea that he had ruminated on the previous year when he felt under great pressure, but had decided against after consultations with Hurd and Sarah Hogg.[125] This was the plan of advancing the leadership election from the end of the year to before the summer recess, by triggering the contest himself.

Accounts differ on when he finally made up his mind. He had sounded out his most trusted friends, Sarah Hogg and Graham Bright, over the previous months, and although neither still worked at Number Ten both continued as confidants. On the whole, friends thought it would be an error to force the issue.[126] Major himself is not certain what the exact spur was, but it would seem the Fresh Start meeting proved the last straw. According to Graham Bright, 'It really pissed him off.'[127]

So when he boarded the chartered British Airway Boeing 767 that Thursday his mind was largely made up. He was quiet on the flight, due in part to the tiredness towards the end of a long and trying parliamentary session, and also to neck pain, exacerbated by tension and fatigue, which required physiotherapy after he arrived.[128] The press corps at the back of the plane, bubbling with leadership fever, was asking to see him, but he and Meyer decided that any appearances should be left to others. Not improving matters was Major learning on the flight of reports that the Executive of the 1922 Committee was demanding the government change its policy and smarten up its presentation on tax, home ownership and Europe.[129]

The contrast on arrival on the quiet Atlantic coast of Canada to the noise of London could not have been starker. Major's party were greeted by warm weather, fresh air and a view of the small Halifax harbour. The crowds cheered the leaders whenever they saw them. Major was particularly popular, as the British were seen in the Canadian port as on their side in their fishing dispute with Spain. Within hours of his arrival Major's tension had lightened visibly. So far, indeed, did he let his guard down that he was overheard joking to Kohl about his problems with the Tory Party; his comment, 'I am a coalition government on my own' was widely reported back in the United Kingdom.

The din was crescendoing back home. Carlisle declared that 'high noon for the Prime Minister is probably approaching in days now rather than weeks'.[130] Reports also came through that Heseltine was reported to be acting as a prince-in-waiting, declaring his unswerving loyalty for Major while not alienating the right over the single currency – in contrast to Clarke, who branded Eurosceptics as 'right wing xenophobes'.[131] Major decided that he would have to comment, and gave an impromptu 'doorstep' interview on leaving his hotel on Friday morning for the opening session. He warned rebellious MPs that there was no 'magic ingredient' for producing a Tory recovery, and rebuffed the 1922 Committee's calls for changes in policy. The government would not be served by driving him from office.[132]

There was plenty of G7 business to distract him from his leadership concerns. Following the precedent set at the 1994 Naples G7 meeting, the Canadians dispensed with most of the razzmatazz, and concentrated on allowing the leaders opportunity to talk among themselves. Dinner on the first evening was dominated by discussion of Bosnia. The UN had decided to increase the size of the peacekeeping force, but the Republican-dominated Congress refused to support the funding, despite Clinton's protestations. In consequence, Britain's 24th Air Mobile Brigade had to wait on Salisbury Plain, told to undertake extra training, while it was decided who would pay for them. The world leaders, to the horror of their officials, then tried drafting a new UN resolution themselves, until the matter was taken out of their hands.[133]

Reform of the UN, the IMF and the World Bank fifty years after their creation was next on the agenda. The financial crisis in Mexico earlier in the year gave added momentum to the need for change. Major argued persuasively the case for reform, as he had done at Naples, and felt the debate was moving in the direction of slimmer structures.[134] He had made his dislike of international bureaucracy something of a crusade, and seemed at Halifax to make further converts of Kohl and Chirac.[135]

Major was also pleased by his bilateral meeting with Clinton, when they discussed the President's visit to Britain that autumn. Some swift diary work was required by officials as his favoured date would coincide with an autumn leadership contest, were one to occur. In their discussions, Major seized the chance to put across that the IRA had enough Semtex for a hundred bombs of the kind that had been detonated in America's worst act of terrorism at Oklahoma on 19 April, a tragedy still vexing the Clinton administration.[136]

A breakfast meeting between Major and Yeltsin could not be accommodated amidst British concern for Yeltsin's health. Yeltsin was not having a good summit. After being told by other national leaders that they did not consider Russia yet ready to join the economic disciplines required for members of the G7, he left early on the request of the Russian State Duma to tackle the hostage crisis in southern Russia.[137] Less than four weeks later, on 12 July, he suffered a heart attack.

Another source of tension on the second day was the issue of the Brent Spar oil platform. Shell, the owners, wanted to sink it in the deep water of the northeast Atlantic, arguing that this was a cleaner option than dismantling it. Greenpeace activists had occupied the platform at the end of April, and following their publicity, ministers from several EU countries condemned the plan to dump it as 'environmental vandalism'.[138] Kohl, responding to intense pressure within Germany, formally protested to Major about the dumping. Major, however, in effect told Kohl not to be silly, and insisted that Shell was within its rights under international law.[139] On his return, Major again said he believed that dumping at sea was the right course, and less environmentally damaging than disposal on land. Within hours of his announcement, however, Shell bowed to the pressure.[140] Cabinet duly expressed its disappointment at Shell's 'capitulation'.[141]

Not Brent Spar, nor other distractions, took away from what those present remember as one of the more convivial G7 meetings of the early and mid-1990s. Relations between the seven leaders were relaxed. Major, one of the elder statesmen among them, produced two cricket bats on the Friday which he asked his fellow heads to sign, to general mirth.[142] That evening, laughter was more formalised when the leaders trouped down to the waterfront for a special circus performance of the Cirque du Soleil, one of Canada's prize cultural exports. For the final press conference the next day, Major had wanted to appear flanked by Hurd and Clarke. But the latter could not be found. He had seized the opportunity for some bird-watching, his great obsession. When he returned to the hotel, he found his smart clothes had already been packed and were *en route* to the airport. He calculated quickly, and decided that an empty seat beside Major would arouse less comment than his appearance clad in casual clothes.[143]

As Major boarded the plane to return on Saturday afternoon, his mind began to refocus on the leadership question. He had ruminated on it with Lyne and Meyer before dinner the previous night. He outlined three possibilities. He could resign in a 'bloodless transition', and hand over the baton in the interests of Party unity. He saw the attraction of this as an option, but memories of 1976, when Harold Wilson suddenly resigned, was a discouraging precedent: the media would assume that there was a hidden reason or scandal lying behind his departure, as had been recycled endlessly about Wilson. Second option, he could continue, as his intimates advised. No challenge had emerged in 1992, 1993 or 1994: why should one in 1995? If he soldiered on, the seasonal truculence would subside, as it generally did, over the summer. The third course was to trigger the election himself and stand for re-election. The strongest arguments for this last course were that 1995 was the last likely year that a leadership challenge could be mounted, the whips were telling him that backbench unrest was at a higher level than ever before, and that if he did not act the unrest would dominate the period from June to November, detracting significantly from all the work and ideas that had been in train since January. As he put it:

I looked forward to the important events, the summer recess, the Party Conference, the Queen's Speech, the autumn budget, all critical things moving on the new agenda. But all of them would have been wiped off the map by nothing but speculation that would get worse and worse during that period. So I thought, 'I am not prepared to tolerate this. If they wish to have a change, then they must vote for a change.' So I decided to go for a leadership election.[144]

On the flight back home, while the party dozed, Major was seen in long conversation with Hurd, who strongly supported the plan.[145] He had a briefer conversation with Clarke, who also signalled support. Major himself said, less than three months after the event, that 'I made the decision finally flying back from Canada'.[146]

The plane landed at 2 a.m. on Sunday morning, 18 June, and waiting cars drove Major back to Huntingdon.[147] After a sleep, he mulled over the plan, and discussed it with Norma, who was a key figure supporting his decision. He spoke again to his old stager Graham Bright, who told him not to rush into it, but to reason it through calmly. Major's conviction remained unaltered.[148] The leadership gossip in that Sunday's papers further convinced him his decision was correct: the Sunday Times in an editorial seemed to anticipate his thoughts, and said the uncertainty was so damaging the government that he should follow the precedent of James Callaghan and 'challenge his critics to put up or shut up'.[149]

He returned from The Finings to London on Sunday night and on Monday talked it over with Howell James and John Ward in Number Ten. By now it seemed highly likely to them that Lamont would be challenging Major in the autumn, which further suggested the wisdom of his plan of seizing the initiative himself.[150] A report by journalist and future Tory MP Julie Kirkbride in Monday's Daily Telegraph said that seventy names had accumulated behind a leadership challenge in the autumn and that 'plans are being laid to deliver a knock-out blow to Mr Major'.[151]

On Tuesday, he invited Sarah Hogg to call in to Number Ten. They sat together in the Downing Street back garden and he showed her the statements he might make announcing his decision. She put the arguments against quite forcefully, including the likelihood that someone would stand against him, with the risk that MPs would then vote for a change, antagonising people who might feel they were being bounced, and causing an unnecessary contest when experience showed he normally gained authority in the autumn, especially as he would be boosted by a fresh ministerial team after a reshuffle, already pencilled in for July. She gave advice on presentational matters if he did stand, where she said he must stress that he was fighting for re-election and meant to win, and practical questions, such as his campaign team and strategy. He felt that her advice on balance was not to take the risk; she left feeling uncertain whether he would go ahead with the plan or not.[152] It was a particularly tense day for Major, as he was still not absolutely clear whether to go ahead. Sarah Hogg, the consistently most trusted aide of his premiership, had fuelled doubts in his mind.

That evening he was a guest at a twenty-fifth anniversary Commons dinner for Tory MPs first elected to Parliament in 1970. Winston Churchill, sitting next to Major, advised him to follow his grandfather's example in 1942 when under fire from backbenchers and to go into their midst and challenge them to sack him. Inspired by this example or not – and Major, unlike Mrs Thatcher, never regarded Churchill as a particular hero – Major delivered an eloquent after-dinner speech, moving his arch-critic Tebbit to pronounce that anyone who thought of replacing Major by Heseltine needed to 'lie down in a dark room until the feeling goes away'.[153]

By Wednesday morning he felt back on top. All doubts had been expunged from his mind. He had breakfast with Norma in the Number Ten flat, and planned with aides the telling of Cabinet ministers. Maintaining surprise would be key if the ploy was to work, which meant that only most trusted colleagues could be told before the public announcement, timed for the following afternoon. Several, like Hurd and Clarke, already knew, while Mayhew – who wrote a letter to *The Times*, published the following morning, deploring the damage being done by the 'commotion against the Prime Minister'[154] – Lang and Newton, three of his most loyal colleagues, were told soon after. Howard, too, was told early in the week. The Home Secretary believed that Major would never again have as much power if he succeeded, and pleaded with him to take the opportunity to rule out the single currency not just up to 1996–7, but also for the life of the next Parliament.[155]

During Major's absence abroad, Whitelaw had become very disturbed by all the unrest. He told Cranborne on the Monday that it was very bad, and asked if he could see Major with him. Fitted in at 10 o'clock on Wednesday evening, Whitelaw said it could not carry on as it was, and that Major would have to 'do something'. Major replied he had indeed something in mind, but would not say what. After further chat Major saw Whitelaw to the door of Number Ten, but asked Cranborne if he would stay behind.[156] Cranborne sat next to Major at the Cabinet table with Ryder sitting opposite, while Major explained the three options open to him – give up, keep going or trigger the contest himself. He turned to Cranborne and said, 'You are going to have to be pretty persuasive if you are going to dissuade me from the third option.'[157] Cranborne said he would give Major any support he wanted from him.[158] Only at this stage did Major call Meyer out of a dinner he was hosting at Number Ten for regional press editors and tell him.[159]

Major still did not have a campaign manager. By 8 a.m. on Thursday morning, he had asked a surprised Cranborne to take on the task. Major had known Cranborne for sixteen years, trusted him, admired his organisational flair, shown recently at the VE Day celebrations, and above all knew he would carry real weight in the Party.[160] Cranborne loved the limelight and was delighted to take on the task, promptly chairing a meeting at Number Twelve, with Newton, Lang, Ryder and Hunt, at which they decided when remaining Cabinet ministers would be told.[161] Cranborne asked Major if he could miss Cabinet to see Marcus Fox and square all the arrangements with the Party.

As he walked over to the House with Ryder to see Fox, they passed the lobby journalists *en route* to the morning briefing at Number Ten, and were relieved that it occurred to none to enquire why they were missing Cabinet.[162]

The day was unusually busy at Number Ten. Prime Minister's Questions were that afternoon, and Major was determined to perform at his best. He did. Matthew Parris and Andrew Marr both commented how outwardly relaxed he appeared.[163] He saw various Cabinet ministers individually to tell them, including Heseltine – who supported the idea – but mentioned nothing at Cabinet itself; experience had taught him that he could not trust them to keep quiet.

The meeting had a slightly unreal atmosphere. Half the ministers roughly knew what was to happen that afternoon, others did not. Routine business was discussed: Gillian Shephard announced that the National Union of Teachers' ballot had come out four to one against a one-day strike, Mayhew told of progress in Northern Ireland, Hurd on Bosnia; almost all ministers had trips or business to report. The main topic, however, was public expenditure. The PSBR for 1994–5 was £35 billion, down from £46 billion the year before, but still too high. Aitken said that departmental bids were £41 billion over expectation, which was untenable. Major praised spending ministers for their largely 'leak-free' discussions with the Chief Secretary the previous autumn, and said he hoped he could rely on similar discretion in the bilaterals just about to commence.[164]

Those ministers Major had not seen were phoned or seen personally by Cranborne and Lang over lunch. At least one was not contacted until even later, namely Redwood. Howard let him know just after Question Time. 'I've just had a terrible shock,' he remarked to an aide. 'Michael Howard has only just told me what is about to happen.'[165] Redwood confirmed that he resented not being trusted enough to have been informed at the same time as others. It was, he later said, not a decision with which he agreed and he would have liked time to comment.[166]

At 4.15 p.m., following Question Time and a meeting with close aides, Major met the officers of the 1922 Committee in his room behind the Speaker's chair. Solemnly, he delivered his carefully prepared text and handed over a letter announcing his resignation and decision to fight an immediate leadership election. In contrast to the meeting of backbenchers he had addressed the week before, he was listened to in silence and with respect, indeed awe. His message over, he left smartly to be driven back to Number Ten.[167] The 1922 Executive retired to their own room and discussed what Major had said. At 5 p.m., the usual weekly meeting of the 1922 Committee was held, unusually well attended. Marcus Fox read out Major's letter and, in response to a question, said this would be the only election that year.[168]

It was a glorious summer afternoon as Major walked across to the waiting press corps, none of whom knew exactly – some guessed, others had picked up the broad story – what they would hear. ITN's Michael Brunson recalled: 'As we stood around in the garden waiting, one or two asked, "He couldn't possibly be going, could he?" The rest of us almost laughed them out of court, and said, "Good God, no, he wouldn't go that far." It was a genuine bombshell.'[169] To avoid the risk of any of the press hearing from a member of the 1922 Executive, they had been summoned sharply at 4.30 p.m., even though Major would not be ready for them until 5 p.m. at the earliest. He stood before them, as tense as many had seen him before, and said:

Let me just make a brief statement to you. I've been deeply involved in politics since I was sixteen. I see public service as a duty and if you can serve, I believe you have an obligation to do so.

I've now been Prime Minister for nearly five years. In that time we've achieved a great deal, but for the last three years I've been opposed by a small minority in our party. During those three years there have been repeated threats of a leadership election. In each year, they have turned out to be phoney threats. Now the same thing again is happening in 1995.

I believe this is in no one's interest that this continues right through until November. It undermines the Government and it damages the Conservative Party. I am not prepared to see the party I care for laid out on the rack like this any longer.

To remove this uncertainty I have this afternoon tendered my resignation as leader of the Conservative Party to Sir Marcus Fox, the chairman of the 1922 Committee, and requested him to set the machinery in motion for an election of a successor.

I have confirmed to Sir Marcus that I shall be a candidate in that election. If I win, I shall continue as Prime Minister and lead the party into and through the next election.

Should I be defeated, which I do not expect, I shall resign as Prime Minister and offer my successor my full support.

The Conservative Party must make its choice. Every leader is leader only with the support of his party. That is true of me as well.

That is why I am no longer prepared to tolerate the present situation. In short, it is time to put up or shut up. I have nothing more to say this afternoon. Thank you very much.[170]

THIRTY-THREE

Leadership on the Line:

June–July 1995

WITH THE LEADERSHIP contest triggered, Major felt a surge of excitement. Though he sensed some of his senior colleagues thought he might be defeated, he never doubted he would win.[1] The question was: by how much? The size of his margin was everything, which put great stress on the quality of his campaign.[2] He made no secret to his intimate circle that he was prepared to go if he felt insufficiently supported by Tory MPs, an intention that his team took seriously, all the more so because he never revealed what margin he had in his mind.[3]

A Challenge Emerges: 22–5 June

Major was pleased with the garden press conference on Thursday 22 June, and the all-important initiative gained. 'His stunning strike threw his enemies into confusion', said *The Times*, capturing the consensus opinion.[4] 'He's wrong-footed us quite cleverly for about forty-eight hours,' a Eurosceptic MP admitted to Michael White on Friday.[5] Now Major had to ensure that he capitalised on his advantage, to be prepared when the anticipated challenger emerged. Marcus Fox decreed that nominations were to close on Thursday 29 June, and the first round would be on Tuesday 4 July, American Independence Day. Cranborne would have preferred a shorter period for the campaign, over one weekend, but Fox at their private meeting on 22 June was immovable. The votes necessary for victory would be a simple majority of the 329 Tory MPS, i.e. 165, as well as being 15 per cent ahead of any rival if a second round was to be avoided.[6] But any vote less than 200 might fatally weaken him.

A base for campaign operations had to be found, and a team. Number Ten and the civil service staff could not be used, the leadership contest being Party business. While Alex Allan liaised with Robert Fellowes, the Queen's Private Secretary, over the possible outcomes, Number Ten's Private Office kept a low profile and focused their attention, as during a general election, on government business.[7] Although Central Office had to remain neutral, Hanley made his pro-Major partisanship apparent, whereas Ryder, to the regret of some Major loyalists, took the view that the Whips' Office and its members would be there to serve any victor who emerged, and thus should be scrupulous about being seen not to be taking sides.[8]

Major gave Cranborne, his campaign manager, virtual *carte blanche* to pick his team, but said he wanted it to represent all sections of the Party, and that he had already asked Lang and Mawhinney to help.[9] Cranborne, always impatient to run his own ship, quickly began enlisting those he could trust, and he knew carried weight. He had definite views on teamwork. 'There needed to be a small group of five or six people maximum, each of whom was responsible to the rest of the group for a segment of operations.'[10] The third and last general in the battle alongside Cranborne and Lang was to be Alistair Goodlad, the ebullient Foreign Office minister tipped for higher things – the Whips' Office. He effectively became Cranborne's deputy campaign manager, looking after what Cranborne called the 'black arts', keeping the books on the voting intentions and lobbying of MPs. In this he was assisted by two former prime ministerial PPSs, Archie Hamilton, who had served Thatcher, and Graham Bright.

Others who worked closely with Cranborne were Tony Newton and Michael Howard, who proved himself totally loyal, and aligned himself with Cranborne about trying to persuade Major to rule out the single currency. Cranborne's group operated from Goodlad's house in Westminster's Lord North Street, conveniently near to what the media assumed was the nerve centre, the close-by 13 Cowley Street, designated the official campaign headquarters, and home of former Tory MP Neil Thorne. 'The real decisions were taken by the grandees under Cranborne. They were the ones who really knew what was going on', said one who worked in the NCO's mess.[11] Had the media rumbled the importance of Goodlad's house, Cranborne had other 'bolt holes' on standby, including the flat of Nicholas Soames.

Relative seclusion was deemed essential by Cranborne if the operation was to run calmly and efficiently. His group met twice daily: at 8 a.m. at Goodlad's house, and in the evening there or in the Commons.[12] Lessons had been learned from the previous leadership contest, as the Party's premier historian, Robert Blake, spotted: 'Cranborne . . . has a far abler team to run his campaign than the shambolic crew who mismanaged Margaret Thatcher in 1990.'[13]

Cowley Street became the cramped, crowded and initially chaotic executive centre of operations. Howell James was the obvious choice for chief of staff, supported by a group of mainly youthful volunteers. Damian Green, latterly of the Policy Unit, ran the press office, while Tim Collins was delegated to be the spinner in the lobby. A host of special advisers followed their ministers into battle behind Major, Michael Simmonds (Mawhinney's), Gregor Mackay (Lang's), Sophie McEwan (Cranborne's) and Rachel Whetstone (Howard's) helped staff the office, while Debbie de Satge ran the secretariat in the basement.[14] As with his 1990 team, a broad ideological spectrum was represented among the staffers. Their initial concern was that if the media rumbled that Major's campaign effort was inefficient, it would be reflected in their coverage of the operation.[15] Many others flocked to Cowley Street to offer their help, including ministers such as David Davis and David Maclean, anxious to support the cause.

Among Cabinet ministers, the team soon distinguished those who were utterly loyal and dependable, like Gummer, who in a self-effacing way agreed to take on a lot of the regional media, from others, like Gillian Shephard, whom some suspected of hedging their bets.[16] Major was later extremely surprised when he learned about her aspirations.

The assumption throughout would be that a challenger to Major would emerge. But who? Lamont was believed in the Major camp to be the most likely candidate, and the one Cranborne initially favoured.[17] Beating him, after all the damage he had inflicted on Major over the previous two years, would have given one of his aides particular satisfaction.

Lamont had often been talked about as being prepared to stand against Major, but had been reluctant to take the plunge during the year before. By 1995, however, he realised the time had come to decide. Edward Leigh was ready to propose him, and Teresa Gorman to second him. Lamont summoned Leigh on the morning of Friday 23 June and gave Leigh the impression that he wanted to stand. Leigh proposed that the announcement be made early the next week.[18] While Lamont tested the water by writing an article in *The Times* that was critical of Major's European policy,[19] Major's team prepared various ripostes in the event of his challenge.[20] But over the weekend, the Lamont bandwagon failed to move off. Though an undoubted heavyweight, as a former Chancellor, and with strong views on the right, it was clear that he lacked popular appeal. By the Sunday, the campaign team was getting wind that another challenger was preparing to emerge, and one, moreover, who was in the Cabinet. Major had claimed in the *Daily Express* on Friday that he had the 'full and unequivocal' support of every Cabinet member. Now his team were not so sure.[21] The 'Lamontery' pieces were put away, never to see the light of day, while fresh texts were composed and sifted to deploy against a new challenger.[22]

John Redwood had spent Friday at the Lord's Test Match with his anti-Major PPS David Evans, watching England play the West Indies. Major was at Lord's also: when his picture appeared on the big view-screen, a large cheer went up all around the ground. Redwood refused all day to put out a statement supporting Major, but let it be known that he would issue one on Monday, when he had reflected further.[23] Suspicions were confirmed when Major's team, including Cranborne and Newton, failed that weekend to contact him. Said one, 'It became increasingly apparent, when he refused calls from people like Michael Forsyth, what he was up to.'[24]

Redwood was in an agony of indecision. He had come to the brink of open revolt once before, over the EU Finance Bill vote in November, but had pulled back.[25] This time, he was determined not to let the moment pass, though he later said he did not particularly want to become Prime Minister, not the least with a young family. Said by that morning's *Sunday Telegraph* to be standing, he spent the day at home considering his options with his wife

Gail, who was not particularly keen, and talking to his constituency chairman, who agreed he could stand. He was being pushed strongly by his special adviser Hywel Williams, as well as by David Evans. On BBC's *On the Record* that lunchtime Evans expressed his irritation at Marcus Fox saying that the 1922 Committee's executive, of which he was a member, backed Major's decision to stand down, and said he would not himself be supporting the Prime Minister.[26] Lamont made it clear he was happy to move aside to make way should Redwood stand.[27] By that evening, Redwood had, however, still to decide whether he would challenge Major, and says he made up his mind to resign only when he spoke to Major on the telephone on Monday morning and was still uncertain about standing.[28] Accounts of the conversation differ. Redwood said no assurances Major would give satisfied him and it was only then he told him that he would be resigning from Cabinet.[29] Major's recollection is quite different: 'After the weekend press, and the fact that it was impossible to contact him on Saturday or Sunday, I was in no doubt that Redwood would stand. He had an eye to the main chance, to become the standard bearer of the right, and he took it.' At 11 a.m. Redwood went to the Commons to meet Portillo, and said, 'Join me.' Portillo declined, but said he would come in on the second round and, according to Redwood, said that should it go to a second round, he would want Redwood to stand aside. Redwood responded that if it went that far he would not make way, 'having done the dirty work', but would be standing himself.[30]

Pique at not being consulted by Major personally prior to the garden announcement was put out as the reason for Redwood's action.[31] The story annoyed him. In his own words:

I waited two or three days after the extraordinary declaration by Major. What made me stand was his friends briefing the press, saying no one on the right had the guts to stand, and that the right wing case was merely a straw man. I couldn't take that. I resigned because I thought he was wrong to take the private arguments from the Cabinet into the public arena. Once he did that, I had to take him on in public.[32]

Redwood set out his reasons for his challenge fully in a resignation letter and in interviews. But speculation inevitably continued that it had been an opportunist act, because he sensed that Portillo – who had entered Cabinet a year before him – had gained more of the limelight over the previous two years as the heir to the Thatcherite legacy. Friends say he thought himself cleverer than Portillo, whom he considered a bit flaky and hot-headed.[33] He frankly considered himself the better man.

Major's camp were pleased at first. Although they knew Redwood would be harder to beat than Lamont, he was a real candidate, not a stalking horse, and victory against him would prove far more emphatic. Redwood was also considered an easier man to beat than Portillo, who for a few hours they feared might emerge in the lull after Lamont's star faded.[34] Redwood's decision proved not a bad one for him: he emerged with more credit from the leadership election than Portillo, who neither attacked nor came out wholeheartedly for Major. Redwood was also considered by Cranborne and Major's camp to have acted honourably throughout the election, and that he played it totally straight.[35]

What, then, of Portillo? He agrees that he never considered himself a first-round challenger, but he admits he would have become a candidate if it lasted to a second round. Major had seen Portillo himself at 1.30 p.m. on the Thursday, and told him about the plan, asking him not to tell anyone. At 7 p.m. that evening he made a statement of support to the Press Association. Over the weekend he tried phoning Redwood to discourage him from standing, but Redwood would not take his calls. On the Monday, he says he became alarmed when he heard that Major was being defeatist and might throw in the towel before the first round even took place, so he took steps 'to get ready to stand in case the Major cause collapsed'. He therefore gave instructions that a house be prepared, but expressly advised against the putting in of telephone lines.[36]

Major had spent the weekend one step away from the fray, looking calm and confident for the cameras. He talked to supporters and visited friends, trying to ignore the press. On Sunday the Majors had lunch at the home of Philip Harris, the Party Treasurer and carpet millionaire, in Westerham, Kent. Despite the pressure Major made time to come. He arrived late although Norma was already there.[37] The conventional wisdom in the media that Sunday was changing from the 'bravery' of his action to it being an 'unnecessary gamble'. There was now talk of the likelihood of his defeat, with the prospect in the first round of widespread abstentions with MPs being motivated in the second round by the candidate they thought most likely to save their seats at the general election: 'With 135 Tory MPs with majorities under 10,000 and 80 under 5,000, the chief concern of most is simply survival.'[38] On Monday morning, Major attended a ceremony to mark the fiftieth anniversary of the United Nations, before flying off to Cannes for an EU Council. His apparent composure was not shared, however, by his team: 26 June was also Black Monday, when many close to him thought that victory was already slipping away from them.[39]

From Black Monday to Cannes: 26–8 June

The wisdom of Major going to Cannes had been hotly debated by Cranborne *et al* over the weekend. The analogy vividly in everyone's mind was Mrs Thatcher's Paris trip during the leadership election in November 1990. Surely, doubters argued, they would not permit the same mistake of having their champion withdrawing for two critical days, above all when they learned of a challenger's hat just thrown in the ring? A visit, moreover, to a meeting of the EU – hardly the thing to please the right? Here was real danger. Sarah Hogg, remaining an influential counsellor behind the scenes, suggested Hurd could lead the British delegation.[40] Cranborne, however, was impressed by

Lang's counsel, that the Redwood fire needed time to rage and burn itself out.[41] Lang himself remained confident throughout, believing that the trump card would be the constituency association chairmen, who would come out powerfully for Major – as indeed occurred – and persuade their MPs into loyalty. 'They were fed up with the way Margaret Thatcher had been treated and they were not going to have another leader shot out from under them by partisan MPs.'[42]

It was therefore agreed that Major go to Cannes, where pictures would show him conducting himself on a world stage, unmoved by the domestic squabbling.[43] Lang seized on another analogy – Mrs Thatcher attending the G7 summit at Williamsburg during the successful 1983 general election.[44] It struck the team as a happy precedent.

With Major abroad, all eyes turned on his principal lieutenants. What were they thinking? The intention of one at least was clear. Douglas Hurd announced his long-expected retirement as Foreign Secretary the day after Major's press conference announcement. His sixty-fifth birthday had passed in March, and he had said the previous summer and again earlier in 1995 that he wanted to go in the July 1995 reshuffle.[45] Major tried to dissuade him, but saw the force of the argument about having a new Foreign Secretary in place well before the next general election.[46] Hurd and Major agreed it was better to make the announcement at the outset of the leadership contest. Although the imminent departure of someone who for twenty-five years had been at the heart of the Tory Party caused some jitters at Westminster, it also bloodlessly created a space at the top of government, thereby increasing the ministerial openings that ambitious politicians could be offered.[47]

Clarke and Heseltine both rushed to declare their allegiance, and worked throughout the election period to support, and to appear to support, the Prime Minister. Clarke's own prospects had still not recovered from the setbacks earlier in the year, and he knew it. He had little reason to dissemble, though he still wanted the leadership. But Heseltine remained a very serious second-round contender. 'If Heseltine offers Portillo foreign secretary, Major is finished,' opined one Eurosceptic.[48] The dream ticket floated up again before MPs' consciousness but Portillo says he knew of no understandings along those lines. Heseltine certainly craved the premiership. But after his role in bringing down Mrs Thatcher, he was not going to risk appearing disloyal again, which would demolish for ever his prospects, and his repu-tation. The idea that he would go down in history as a double regicide appalled him. His allies pondered best chances of seeing a second ballot occur, when they knew he would stand. Should Heseltine supporters vote for Redwood, and risk seeing the right-winger win, or should they abstain? Keith Hampson eventually met Evans, who had become Redwood's campaign manager, and discussed tactics.

Much shady manoeuvring was indeed going on between the backers of the likely second-round candidates. David Hart, Portillo's adviser, was actively testing the water, as was Hywel Williams, Redwood's special adviser. In contrast to Portillo's lukewarm support for Major, Heseltine remained stead-fast, interested to know what his lieutenants were up to on his behalf, but giving them no active encouragement.[49] Nevertheless, the impression con-veyed was one which contradicted Major's statement about total Cabinet backing. The most he could hope for was an absence of public posturing by his Cabinet until the first ballot was over; the consensus was that, thereafter, it would be open warfare.[50]

Of more immediate concern to Major's team on that Monday were the statements being put out by Clarke's and Hurd's offices, which made Major's platform sound as if it was centre-left, while his team had been labouring from the first hours to assert that the appeal was cross-Party. Clarke had thus dismissed Redwood – with whom he was to stand for the Party leadership in June 1997 – as 'ultra right wing' and his ideas would not win the Tories an election in '1,000 years'. This was too much for Cranborne. Messages were sent out pleading with Clarke and Hurd to desist.[51] Reports came back to Lord North Street and Cowley Street that Redwood appeared to be gaining ground. Lord McAlpine made encouraging sounds about him, while Tebbit caused further apprehension by speaking out in favour of a right turn. One Cowley Street campaigner recalled: 'Monday was the nadir. Redwood was going to launch a new platform, full of fresh ideas. We thought it might get difficult, because he is a clever man, he'd worked as the Head of the Number Ten Policy Unit under Mrs Thatcher. We were worried.'[52] Meanwhile, in Cannes, Major gave a listless interview to the British press. Toby Helm noted that 'he failed to rid anyone of the dominant impression at the time – that he was finished'.[53]

In Major's absence, Redwood launched his campaign in the Commons Jubilee Room – the only space available at the last minute – that afternoon. As he later said: 'I had no money, no campaign team, no structure.'[54] With hindsight, the launch lost Redwood support, and he would have done better to have assembled more supporters, and a more clearly thought-out, and costed, manifesto. The errors were tangible. Being flanked by Tony Marlow and Teresa Gorman on the Monday, regarded as over-excitable, and both dashingly if unsuitably dressed, did not convey the impression of gravitas. Redwood, still planning on the hoof, knew the moment he entered the room what image would be created by the appearance of some who had arrived before him.[55] Gorman and Marlow were removed in future appearances.

Redwood's programme was released the following day. Hastily put together, he offered a solid right-wing diet of policies he had long advocated: deep cuts in public spending to pay for tax cuts, tougher law and order policies, a war on official bureaucracy, not least in the NHS, a resounding 'no' to Britain's entry into a single currency, and, for good measure, saving the royal yacht *Britannia* from planned decommissioning.[56] With it, tension in the Major camp began to ease. 'We ended up laughing when we heard Redwood's proposals,' said one. 'It sounded exactly like what Neil Kinnock had said in 1992. It was just not plausible. From that moment on we felt actually this man is not as clever as he thinks he is. The launch and the programme are two bad things he's done in a row. We'll be fine now.'[57] Tim Collins, meanwhile, ridiculed the challenge by dreaming up the name 'the barmy army' to describe the Redwood team. The tag chimed with Major's unguarded comment two years earlier about 'bastards' and 'flapping white coats', and stuck. 'Vulcan' was another tag used to discredit Redwood's public image: 'It wasn't very pleasant', he later said. 'I never made personally offensive remarks about Major.'[58] To be fair to Major, the smears were neither uttered nor authorised by him.

In the short term, however, the media reaction to Redwood's candidature was favourable, not least because they were delighted at last to have a challenger, and therefore a real contest. Lady Thatcher declared from the US that Major and Redwood were both 'good Conservatives'. She was being powerfully lobbied in both directions – Robin Harris as ever was determined to see Major finished, but Julian Seymour, who ran her office, a close friend of Cranborne's, was giving countervailing advice. In the event, she did not abandon Major.[59] McAlpine recalled there was a heated debate among Thatcherites at the time on the line she should take; McAlpine, however, like Tebbit, had no doubts whom she should support.[60]

What of Major at Cannes? He made it plain he was not going to be distracted from the important EU work at the meeting.[61] The two principal issues were comparatively specialised, the replenishment of the European Development Fund (EDF) and the Europol convention. On the first, Major argued successfully against France to limit figures on multilateral aid, Britain preferring bilateral aid, and on the second he made a stand against Europol having an appeals procedure. The issue was held over for decision at a later point.[62] Major was heartened by the inroads he was making at the summit, and was even managing to enjoy being on the French Riviera. One aide vividly recalls him sitting around, drinking and eating grapes, and laughing in his pink room in the Dirk Bogarde suite at the Carlton Hotel.[63] The Redwood candidacy, however, injected a domestic dimension into the trip, however hard he tried to avoid it.

Howell James accompanied Major to Cannes, to keep him up to speed with leadership developments. Early on Monday evening he received updates over the phone from Jonathan Hill, back to help out from the public relations agency Lowe Bell for the duration, and running Cowley Street in James's absence. James had secured the offer of an article in the London *Evening Standard* the next day. Should they take it, James asked his predecessor? Hill, aware of the need to deflect attention from Redwood, said they should. James and Norman Blackwell, also in Cannes, faxed some ideas back to London to Hill, who then worked on it with Nick True to produce a draft, which they faxed back to Cannes after midnight.[64] Blackwell, who like James read it first thing in the morning, saw it as the opportunity to parade Major's manifesto by inserting many of the policy ideas on which he had been working. The script was duly rewritten around Blackwell's 'five themes'. Major was having breakfast on Tuesday morning with Hurd and Clarke when he was shown the text. They all thought it good, and the text was approved.[65]

The article missed the first edition of the *Evening Standard*. Members of the campaign team waited anxiously by the Cowley Street fax machine for the article, under the title 'How I can unite the Tories and win again', to come back, arriving just in time to make the second and subsequent editions. With some meaty passages about cutting capital tax and reducing public spending below 40 per cent of national income, it was spun as Major talking the enterprise language prevalent in the mid- and late 1980s, and received wide coverage.[66]

Major now came under pressure to 'hype' the Cannes meeting in a Euro-sceptical direction, to win right-wing supporters back from Redwood. On the flight back to London on Tuesday evening, Major read over a draft of the parliamentary statement on the summit that he was due to make the following afternoon. Fairly routine stuff, Major duly signed it off, and prepared himself on the short flight for the challenge awaiting him in London.[67] He felt pleased by the conference, by the coverage it had received, and by a bilateral on the Tuesday with Bruton on IRA decommissioning and progress on peace.[68] In Ireland he seemed to be bringing a peace he had not yet achieved with his own parliamentary party.

Cranborne was awaiting Major on his return to Downing Street. From now on, he was told, the campaign must take precedence over all other activities.[69] Next morning, following a broadcast announcement for the arrangements for VJ Day in August, a party delegation, including Tim Collins, arrived to see him in the Cabinet Room. Its members wanted Major's Commons statement on Cannes, which they had read, turned into more of a Eurosceptic rallying call. Crucial votes, he was told, could be won over. Major felt very uncomfortable. Cannes was government business, and should not, he felt, be confused with Party, still less personal, objectives. He neither wanted to crush nor alienate his lieutenants, however, and promised to think further about their suggestions over lunch.[70]

Major duly delivered the original text in the Commons that afternoon, and in general was praised for eschewing the chance to make party political capital. The *Sun* took a different view, and was no more amused than some of Major's camp by his slapping down of Bill Cash for 'talking through the back of his head'. The newspaper reported incorrectly that the chamber was almost empty, and declared Major dead in the water.[71] Other newspapers were reaching a similar conclusion; several talked in terms of 'after the battle next Tuesday between the two Johns will come the real battle, between the two Michaels' (Portillo and Heseltine).[72] While the lobbying of MPs at Westminster may have been going in their favour, the battle in the press was being lost.

No Change, No Chance? 29 June–3 July

Thursday was the day that nominations closed for the first round. Once Redwood had declared, any further first-round candidate appeared improbable. Such a figure would only split the anti-Major vote, preventing a second round, and thereby saving him. The focus of Cranborne *et al* was on who might support Redwood, while the media and Westminster were aslurp with speculation about second-round candidates should Major be fatally wounded the following Tuesday. Redwood's camp kept on promising big names coming out in support of their champion: Kenneth Baker and John Patten were the two who Major's team most suspected might declare for him. Heavy lobbying took place, and neither they nor any further heavyweight figures pledged support for Redwood.[73]

Question Time on Thursday was to be Major's key parliamentary test of the campaign. Tuesday's questions had been missed while he was still in Cannes, and it was believed that by Questions the following Tuesday, polling day, most MPs would have already decided, and many indeed have voted. Major thus prepared particularly carefully that Thursday morning at Number Ten, with James and Bridges joined by Hill and True helping Mark Adams from the Private Office. Their mood was confident, though they imagined to their regret that Labour would stay clear of the leadership contest, a topic on which Blair's grip had not so far been sure, reflecting an ambivalence about whether they wanted Major to continue.

The House was packed that afternoon, anticipating a real scrap. All present knew that this would be perhaps the most crucial single parliamentary test of Major's premiership. Austin Mitchell spoke first, asking if Heseltine had been consulted about the resignation. Major's response, that he 'informed' his Right Honourable friend, was dispatched in a way that created the impression of Heseltine's relative subservience in the process. Blair next asked about whether Redwood should not have resigned earlier if he disagreed with government policies as much as he said he now did. Major, with impeccable timing, responded, 'I understood that he resigned from the Cabinet because he was devastated that I had resigned as leader of the Conservative Party.'[74] Tory MPs could not contain their mirth. Simon Hoggart thought it 'probably the funniest thing Mr Major had ever said in the Commons'.[75] His response was not just witty: it pricked Redwood's peculiarly ambiguous pretext for standing as a challenger.

Better still was Major's response to a question from Labour's George Foulkes, who enquired about Cabinet ministers installing extra phone lines in anticipation of a second round of the leadership contest. News had broken the day before that Portillo's advisers had been ordering in extra telephone lines to handle the calls that would be necessary if he stood. Major had anticipated this question. In a line provided for him by Lang, he replied that the swift installation of the phone lines could only be put down as a tribute to privatisation. Again, much laughter.

Major's whole performance was masterly: not only had he paraded his oratorial skills under duress, but also belittled his principal antagonists. According to one close aide, 'We knew after that Question Time that as long as we didn't have any disasters, we would be all right.'[76] Sensing the danger, Redwood tried to diminish the achievement on the next day, the hottest in June since 1976, by unfavourable comparison of fifteen minutes' good performance at the Dispatch Box to his five years' performance in government. It was a good line, but Redwood's supporters were felt to have damaged his cause by putting out a leaflet to MPs which was considered by many to be over the top: 'The choice is stark. To Save Your Seat, Your Party and Your Country, vote John Redwood.'[77] More telling was his slogan 'No Change, No Chance'.

Major, meanwhile, was on his best behaviour, acting to instructions from his campaign managers. He addressed meetings of Eurosceptics and Euro-enthusiasts, dispensing soothing balm in all directions. To the Positive European Group of MPs he caused widespread mirth by beginning: 'What shall I start with? The saving of the Royal Yacht or £5 billion of spending cuts?', ridiculing Redwood's platform.[78] He invited known critics to meet him, a process he always loathed, and sweet-talked them in his room in the House of Commons. He went on walkabouts in Kent, creating the type of crowd photographs that had served him well during the general election. Articles written under his name were cropping up everywhere. The most advantageous broadcasting interviews were accepted for him by his team, television's *Breakfast with Frost* that Sunday being the most important and successful.[79] But he would not agree to what some of them said would not just sew up the first round, but pave the way to general election success after it – ruling out a single currency.

Major's team employed a variety of arguments to win over right-wing waverers in the last few days before polling. Responding to the strong pressure from Cranborne and Howard, strong 'hints' were given of an imminent ruling out of Britain joining a single currency until 1999 or later, and of a Eurosceptic replacing Hurd at the Foreign Office, understandings which were not forgotten by those to whom they were conveyed. Portillo's supporters were told that a strong showing for Redwood in the first ballot would ensure he replaced their man as the more powerful figure on the right. Better to wait, back Major now, and let their man succeed when, as Lady Thatcher had said earlier, he was a little older. Hints were also given of a senior job for Portillo in a reshuffle. Finally, to win over sceptics regardless of faction, they told MPs that Major would be bound to secure a winning figure. Much better to give him a massive poll endorsement which would enhance unity and morale in the run-up to the general election than see him splutter home.[80] By the weekend, Major's backers were convinced that any Heseltine bandwagon had stalled, and that their support was increasing.[81]

The press remained unbiddable, despite the increasingly frantic efforts of Lang, Collins, Damian Green and others deputed to phone and intercede with political journalists, editors and proprietors. Neither Murdoch nor Black were amenable. Rothermere (*Daily Mail* and the *Mail on Sunday*) was almost equally negative, but did at least allow the *Evening Standard* to be supportive. Major's team had not foreseen this dramatic loss of press support, some of which was never to return on side.[82] The *Sun*, steadfastly anti-Major, dubbed the contest 'Redwood vs Deadwood'.[83] While the tabloids were turning their focus increasingly to the ado about the actor Hugh Grant's entanglement with a Californian prostitute, a poll in *The Economist* on Friday caused upset by saying that Heseltine could save fifty-two Tory seats.[84] Nor were the weekend papers encouraging, with the *Sunday Telegraph* supporting Redwood, and the *Sunday Times* saying that no fewer than 230 votes from MPs would be sufficient for Major to regain authority, which seemed a forlorn hope.[85] The only cheer was from the *Sunday Express*, which as well as lending its editorial support led with a more favourable survey stressing that Major would win well enough (224 to 60 with 45 abstentions) to remove all doubts.[86]

A Major article appeared in Monday's *Daily Telegraph*, in which he employed an argument being used by his campaign team, that Tory MPs had an option on Tuesday. They 'can jump into the abyss', or they could vote to 'get on with working for a better future for our country and turn the spotlight on Labour'.[87] His article was placed next to a strongly anti-Major editorial written by editor Max Hastings: 'Mr Major has held together in government through recent years at the price of ceaseless fudge, muddle ... It is time for Mr Major to go.'[88] The talk was that Hastings had come under pressure from Conrad Black, especially after Simon Heffer threatened to resign if the paper did not come out against Major.[89] In fact, Hastings still wanted Heseltine to be Prime Minister.

A growing worry among Cranborne and acolytes over the final forty-eight hours was Major himself – what was in his mind? When loyalist MP Andrew Bowden had suggested the previous Thursday that Major needed to win three-quarters of the vote (over 240) for the win to be hailed a success, he was roundly slapped down and wheeled out of sight.[90] The truth was that none of Cranborne's team knew what their man would do. They had all invested too much in a Major first-round victory to see him bow out if the numbers supporting him in the Tuesday ballot did not reach his expectation. By Monday evening, Goodlad's book told them that at least a hundred MPs would either abstain or vote for Redwood. That left Major's support at between 200 and 230. If it was closer to the former, might he quit?[91] Major had told the *Financial Times* in an interview just before the weekend that the belief that he did not take risks or take action that surprised people 'is simply not right'. Retiring after the first round was a possibility he refused to rule out.[92] Major's spirits, high for the four days after he returned from Cannes, appeared now to be more volatile.

On the final night before polling, Major and Redwood appeared before the right-wing 92 Group. With memories of his Fresh Start pasting before the Halifax G7 meeting fresh in his mind, Major found it an ordeal, and in contrast to Redwood, he came across as 'low-key' and passionless.[93] Before going to bed, he learned that even the *Daily Mail* was abandoning him. With a front page headline 'Time To Ditch the Captain', it advised MPs in its editorial that it was 'the last chance' to save the Party from 'electoral disaster'.[94] Some individual journalists, among them Matthew Parris, who wrote the most sparkling journalism of the campaign, supported Major, but the majority of columnists – right and left – favoured a fresh start.[95] Editorially, only the *Daily Express* stayed loyal to Major out of the Tory national daily newspapers. When it became apparent, however, that the press antipathy was having no discernible effect on MPs' voting intentions, Major, if not his team, relaxed a degree on the final day.[96]

Independence Day? 4 July

Major was edgy on Tuesday morning. His campaign team gave him their revised range of expectations: a vote for him of 205–215. He scarcely responded. He discussed with James what he might say to the media just after the result.[97] But his mind was not fully on it. Questions in the House that afternoon had to be prepared. A meeting with Heseltine had also been written into the diary, to discuss his future job in the reshuffle. Heseltine had now accepted that a second round was unlikely, and his leadership kite was not going to fly, so he turned to consider how to maximise those spoils that could be had. It was clear Heseltine merited promotion from President of the Board of Trade to a more central position. Major had been thinking about it for some time, and had held outline discussions with Heseltine a month earlier, returning to the subject when he saw Heseltine just before announcing the leadership election on 22 June, seeking to bind him in as far as he could.[98]

It had long been the conventional wisdom in Number Ten that a big-hitter was needed at the centre to chair Cabinet committees and coordinate presentation of government policy. Proposals that Heseltine remain as President of the Board of Trade with an enhanced role, or become Party Chairman, were swept aside. Heseltine wanted more, and the Deputy Prime Minister job was agreed by both men that Tuesday. Heseltine was concerned that the title, last held by Geoffrey Howe, should have substance and not be a mere sinecure. How could he ensure it was a real job? For thirty minutes, they discussed what it might entail, as well as other planned Cabinet changes, with the Number Ten Private Office taking notes. Heseltine became curious about where his office would be. The Cabinet Office was the natural place, close to Number Ten and at the heart of government. Alex Allan took him through the connecting door to the Cabinet Office and left him with Robin Butler, holding discussions about the remit and operation of his new job as well as about his accommodation.[99] Further meetings took place in the inner sanctum until, two hours after his arrival, Heseltine emerged into the sun in Downing

Street to endless speculation that he had done a secret deal with Major to deliver the votes of his supporters in return for a top job and possibly even – the stories varied – the pledge of the succession when Major retired.[100]

Major's spirits were not high when he left Number Ten for the House for Prime Minister's Questions. Being stuck behind a van and almost arriving late added to the tension. Blair attacked him over top people's salaries (a good subject to drive a wedge between Major and his right wing), and over the release on Monday of Private Clegg, a British soldier in prison for killing a Belfast joyrider.[101] It was widely believed that the announcement of his release had been fixed to win support for Major the following day. There appears to be no truth in the accusation. Major had already refused on several occasions during the campaign to gain personal capital out of government business, and Mayhew was also a stickler for correct procedure.[102] For the rest, Major performed adequately, but he did not spark, and he knew it.

The fear that Major might quit was beginning to spread among Tory MPs. He was lobbied hard throughout Tuesday afternoon, from backbenchers, from ministers including Cranborne, Goodlad and Mayhew, and even Norma. Many MPs left notes on his desk in the Prime Minister's office in the House imploring him to stay, whatever the margin of victory.[103] At 4.20 p.m., forty minutes before the poll closed, Major cast his vote, and returned to Downing Street, deep in thought. A select group was invited to Number Ten to hear the news. Cranborne also asked Mayhew and Hurd, the 'tall men' as he called them, to join him, Lang and Mawhinney, to exert pressure lest Major had a change of heart when the results were announced and decided to quit.[104]

They assembled in the anteroom before the 5 p.m. announcement. Major appeared and Cranborne asked if he would prefer to see the results in the flat alone with Norma. 'No, come on up,' he called from the stairs. Up they trouped to the second floor, where Major fussed around the flat, worrying whether everyone had a chair and a drink, while the tension continued to mount.

It was planned that when the 1922 Committee's tellers had counted the votes, Number Ten would be phoned before any public announcement was made. John Ward took the phone call from Marcus Fox just after 5.10 p.m. and wrote the numbers down on a piece of paper, wordlessly showing them to Major. Major studied them for about ten seconds – which seemed an age to the campaign team who were waiting to hear – and then read them out: 218 Major, 89 Redwood, 20 abstentions.[105]

Jonathan Hill, who had grabbed a sneak preview of the result which Ward had written down, was studying his master:

He didn't react at once. He didn't say, 'That's it, we've exceeded my hurdle, I've won, fantastic.' He didn't in fact show any positive pleasure at all. He was very quiet and thoughtful as he composed himself, and while he simply hugged Norma.[106]

Frantic activity, however, was in train among his supporters when, at

almost 5.20 p.m., Marcus Fox announced the result in front of the cameras
and microphones. Cranborne's estimate – known only to Goodlad and Archie
Hamilton – was only two out. 'It was clear it was not going to be the most
overwhelming of victories seeing he was an incumbent Prime Minister. So it
was important we got people out there to say that it was convincing,' said
Cranborne.[107] The folklore about the November 1990 contest was that Mrs
Thatcher lost the contest in the hour after the first ballot vote was declared.[108]

Lang had been busy during the day preparing a table of numbers and
victory margins, and how each should be spun. He also nominated people to
approach the two big political editors, Robin Oakley (BBC) and Michael
Brunson (ITN). 'It had to be a line that was plausible, that they would be
willing to accept. We got a big roll of ministers and trusties out onto College
Green [opposite Parliament] to approach other key media people too. It was
bedlam but it worked.'[109]

A 'media guidance notice' compared the result with previous Tory leadership contests – 'the largest share of votes that any Conservative leadership
candidate has received in any seriously contested election' – and with Blair's
share of the vote when he became Labour leader the year before.[110] Mantra-
like, before the world's media, the same message was repeated in the most
successful media management exercise of the Major premiership. Jeffrey
Archer, one of the selected spinners, recalled: 'It was sealed up on radio and
television in the twenty minutes following the result, declaring it one of the
greatest Tory victories for any leader. We said it was more than Blair had
against Prescott, which frankly was irrelevant, because Major was putting
himself up for re-election.'[111]

Robin Oakley was praised in some quarters – and not just Tory – for
sealing the victory by pronouncing on the BBC that Major had won a great
contest. In fact just over one third of MPs had not voted for him, and
assuming that almost all his ministers backed him – which cannot be taken
for granted – then up to half of backbenchers failed to support him. As
Redwood later realised, had he made that point, rather than conceding
gracefully, then the shine at least, and possibly more, would have been taken
off the Major victory.[112]

It is impossible to tell for certain how the votes were cast, but it seems very
likely that the hard core on the inflexible Eurosceptic right and a sprinkling
of Heseltine backers voted for Redwood or abstained, while the loyalist right
and centre-left MPs backed Major. Redwood believes that several of Portillo's
supporters pulled back from voting for him at the last minute, worried that
he might be doing too well,[113] which is likely. Goodlad, who had strong links
on that side, was particularly important in winning over the left, and while
Heseltine's supporters were certainly high among the abstainers, the failure
of Heseltine to do more to embolden them led many to conclude that it would
be safer to back Major than risk triggering a second round with the possibility
of a right-wing victor. 'Game theory' is not a science with which the Tory
MPs are familiar, but in their calculations of how to vote, or how to position

themselves, they came as close to understanding it over these ten days as at any point in their recent history. Major received five or six fewer votes than Lang had estimated, due to the twenty abstentions being more than he had thought.[114]

But win Major did. Norma thinks winning the leadership election probably gave him as much satisfaction as any event during his premiership, though she added that he was not wholly pleased by the result: 'But I don't know that he ever really is fully content.'[115] Major himself was disappointed – he had hoped for 220 or more – but had no intention of resigning. He came down from the flat, and announced on the doorstep of Number Ten:

Some days ago I called a leadership election and I did so in the knowledge that it would be very likely to be an election that was contested ... We have now seen the verdict of the parliamentary party. It is a very clear cut decision ... I believe that has put to rest any question or any speculation about the leadership of the Conservative Party up to and beyond the next election ... the election is now over. The message that I would give to every Conservative ... is that the time for division is over.[116]

Time alone would tell whether this last sentiment would hold. He had few illusions, however, that his travails would all be over, in particular with the Party still at least 25 per cent behind in most opinion polls.[117] But for the present it was time to say thank you and celebrate. At his insistence, his personal helpers joined him for the press statement outside in Downing Street. Then he went on to Cowley Street to thank more campaign workers, and back to a large party at Downing Street.[118] In addition to MPs and other supporters, a sprinkling of editors attended, Nicholas Lloyd of the *Daily Express*, Brian Hitchen of the *Sunday Express*, and Stewart Steven of the *Evening Standard*.[119] Jonathan Holborow of the *Mail on Sunday* was also an invitee.[120]

The editorial response to Major's victory continued to be fairly negative. Of the Tory newspapers who campaigned against him, only the *Daily Telegraph* sought to make amends, an editorial saying that it is good for democracy when the press is flouted.[121] Some commentators had praise for Major, including Simon Jenkins, who thought Major had emerged a bigger and a strengthened Prime Minister, and Ferdinand Mount, who drew an analogy with the position of the last Tory premier to come under so much fire from the Conservative press: 'Stanley Baldwin must be chortling in his grave to see the advice of newspaper editors so contemptuously ignored by Conservative MPs.'[122]

The Quarrelsome Reshuffle

In his victory statement, Major had promised an imminent reshuffle. He had debated within Number Ten whether to hold it over to later in July, as in 1994, but decided to illustrate his new resolution by announcing it the day after the contest concluded. As a result, it was executed without his usual full preparation.[123] Over the previous months, as was his wont, he had accumulated a large pile of scrap paper, hoarded in the Private Office, on which he had written down ideas for the reshuffle – he might go up, who had had his day. Major had been thinking about it in particular during the leadership campaign. He completed the changes after the Tuesday night parties, and invited ministers in to see him at Number Ten from 9 a.m. on Wednesday 5 July.[124]

The expectation was that he would make his Cabinet reshuffle a move to the right.[125] It turned out rather to be, in the eyes of the right, some of whom never forgave him, a shift to the left. Nicholas Wood commented in *The Times* that 'a mood of sullen anger gripped the Tory Party last night as John Major took his revenge on the faction that has made his life a misery for the past three years. Privately, leading Eurosceptics were livid.'[126] Just one day into his 'bigger and stronger' premiership, some of Major's aides realised how little had changed.

Heseltine's appointment as Deputy Prime Minister and First Secretary of State was the centrepiece of the reshuffle. The first holder of these combined titles since another putative Tory premier, Rab Butler, in 1962, Heseltine's job was to combine the chairing of several Cabinet committees with a central role alongside Major coordinating and 'selling' government policy. Roger Freeman, new to Cabinet, and based also at the Cabinet Office, was to be his second-in-command. Several senior men did not move, including Clarke, Howard, Cranborne and Newton, but over half the Cabinet posts were shifted or redesignated. Most senior among them was the non-Eurosceptic Rifkind, appointed Foreign Secretary,[127] dashing Howard's and the right's hopes of seeing the Home Secretary become Hurd's successor. Howard was disappointed by the news: he had been led to believe that all the speculation about him becoming Foreign Secretary had come from Number Ten. Though he was not displeased to have to complete his 'unfinished business' at the Home Office, his desire to oversee Tory foreign policy had to wait until Hague appointed him Shadow Foreign Secretary after the general election.[128]

Portillo was the most senior right-winger to receive promotion, to the post of Defence Secretary vacated by Rifkind. He had long coveted the job, and Major was anxious to provide political balance to the reshuffle. Some detected a debt repaid for his not doing more to incite his supporters, others a Machiavellian subtlety in moving him away from a job overseeing public spending to one where he would be placed in a dilemma of wanting to cut expenditure against upholding Britain's traditional defence. Portillo's former department, Employment, was submerged into the Education Department, and brought under the responsibility of Gillian Shephard.[129]

Campaign loyalists were generally rewarded. Lang moved up from Scotland to President of the Board of Trade, Mawhinney became Party Chairman, and Goodlad Chief Whip. The vacancies in the territorial departments were filled by two young men of the right, Michael Forsyth to Scotland and William Hague to Wales.

The latter had been in the public eye since 1977 when as a schoolboy he had taken the Tory Party Conference by storm in praising Thatcher and attacking the Callaghan government; at thirty-four he now became, after just two years as a junior minister, the youngest Tory Cabinet minister of the century. In a clever move, Bottomley and Dorrell swapped their jobs at Health and National Heritage. At Clarke's request, Waldegrave became Chief Secretary. Two final newcomers to Cabinet were steady men, George Young to Transport, and Douglas Hogg to Agriculture, both Major's personal choices. Young had been a friend since the days of Lambeth Council; Hogg was seen as an ally, not least because he was married to Sarah.

Such an extensive reshuffle was made possible for Major by Jonathan Aitken departing mired in legal action which he felt was absorbing too much of his attention, and Hunt, pencilled in as Health Secretary, deciding that he would prefer to leave government altogether.[130] Ryder's departure had long been expected. On top of the distancing of his relationship with Major, his back, originally damaged during a tennis match with Simon Jenkins in February 1991, had caused him frequent pain and needed surgery. Ryder's pleasure in the job of Chief Whip, which he had held for almost five years, had long since begun to evaporate. Major had on several occasions offered him a Cabinet post, but Ryder had stressed ever since his appointment as Chief Whip in November 1990 that he wished it to be his last job in government. In the July 1994 reshuffle, Major had again offered him the choice of becoming a Secretary of State, remaining as Chief Whip or retiring, but with parliamentary trouble ahead on the EC Finance Bill, Ryder elected to stay on for one year. By mid-1995, he felt the time had come to depart.[131]

Jeremy Hanley accepted his demotion to the non-Cabinet post of Minister of State at the FCO with typically good grace, but inwardly he was hurt.[132] Major told him about the change at the victory party in Number Ten, concerned as always to let ministers down gently: 'You will be moving from the hardest job in politics to the best,' Major said.[133]

Was it, in fact, the move to the left that the right said it was, or were they merely mischief-making to exact revenge for Major's victory? Portillo, Forsyth and to a lesser extent Hague were the main Cabinet right-wing promotions; at lower levels, Nicholas Bonsor, Eurosceptic and attacker of Major at June's Fresh Start meeting, was promoted to Minister of State at the Foreign Office. Hunt, bane of the right, departed from his job at the centre of government. But it was the change at the top that most deeply hurt the right. Heseltine was thought by some of Major's campaign team like Cranborne and Howard to have been ambiguous during the election campaign, yet was rewarded with a job almost, they thought, as powerful as Major's himself. Together with Clarke, they suspected that the government would be run from a centre-left axis. Other changes displeased them further. Clarke was to be joined at the Treasury by the 'wets', Waldegrave as Chief

Secretary and Angela Knight as Economic Secretary, and the other economic departments were all to be run by the centre-left loyalists – without a free-marketeer in sight. The one policy they cared most about, the single currency, looked set in stone.

The loyalist right were further annoyed that their champions, Howard, Lilley and Cranborne, received no elevation, and that others, such as David Davis, were not promoted to Cabinet, nor indeed were able sceptics like James Cran and Alan Duncan given junior ministerial jobs. David Maclean, the right-winger whom Cranborne wanted to go to Transport, turned down a Cabinet job. The right believed that their labours and votes had saved Major, and that he had now betrayed them. 'We had been reassured by Major's team that he was going to lead from the right and was solid on Europe, now this,' said one right-winger.[134] Cranborne, who had agreed initially to be campaign manager to keep Heseltine out, and who had no forewarning of Heseltine's job, was shocked and angry.[135] Central Office had organised what was to be a triumphal victory rally at the Queen Elizabeth II Centre two days after the election. He did not attend. He departed per-emptorily for his home in Dorset, pleading ill-health.[136]

Major had not anticipated the right's reaction, and any thought of offending his team had been far from his mind. His whole effort, before, during and after the leadership campaign, was aimed at holding the Party together. But both loyalist and hard core right briefed the media against the reshuffle, and against Major's prospects of success. They spoke to journalists, usually off the record, about their 'humiliation' and anger at Major's alleged 'revenge', and how there would be no peace in the Party, merely a truce.[137] Redwood was talked up as a prince-in-waiting, and threats were made about the new agenda he would be offering.[138] One of Major's most outspoken backbench critics told Toby Helm only days after the contest, with an ominous pres-cience: 'We will continue to put our arguments forward but we are stuck with him until he loses us the election. Then, when we get Labour, we will be back in business.'[139] Quite what business the right-winger had in mind remains unclear.

THIRTY-FOUR

Back in Command:

July–October 1995

WINNING THE LEADERSHIP election, and producing a ministerial team very much to his liking, were not the only grounds for Major's optimism in early July. Redwood's departure removed a figure who had become a scapegoat, in part unfairly, for much of the leaking and dissension in Cabinet since May 1993.[1] For all the right's muted threats, Marcus Fox had decreed that there could not be another leadership challenge until after the general election.

No major European legislation was in the parliamentary pipeline to provide an opportunity for a right-wing ambush, and the assumption was growing that the IGC beginning in 1996 on the future of the EU, unlike Maastricht, would have a minimalist agenda.[2] After Cannes, the prospects anyway for an early single currency appeared as if they might be receding. The economy looked on course for tax-cutting budgets in November 1995 or 1996. Norman Blackwell was telling Major that the manifesto, whose first draft he was completing, had many exciting ideas to carry momentum forward. Major appeared visibly refreshed and more buoyant than he had done since the bright days early in the New Year.[3]

But worries were not far below the surface. A key by-election – Littleborough and Saddleworth – was coming late in July, which threatened to reduce the majority of eleven. Further instalments of Nolan and Scott were scheduled for the autumn and early spring. Labour was continuing its forward march, and was looking almost daily more plausible to middle-class voters, while polls were still predicting a very significant Blair victory in the general election. Without poll improvement in the fairly near future, the morale of Tory MPs and confidence in the leadership would be bound to wane. Public borrowing, although halved over three years to £23 billion, remained a formidable drag on government spending and tax-cutting options: the ridiculing of Redwood's campaign pledge, to cut £5 billion off spending, showed how difficult further reductions would prove.[4] Most ominous of all for Major was the right's anger after the reshuffle, and their belief he had missed a real opportunity during the campaign to rule out the single currency. Now they were expecting strong, certain leadership from him, and a right-wing agenda.

Whether the leadership victory would prove a cosmetic or a substantive change had yet to be proved. Meanwhile, Major's attention was temporarily distracted by unforeseen events abroad.

Bosnian Interlude

The Bosnian hostage crisis in May and the Anglo–French force sent sub-sequently had done little to resolve the long problem of Serbian aggression. The UN recognised this in June, when it sent in the Rapid Reaction Force and augmented UN troops by 12,500. The Serbs responded in early July with increased shelling of UN bases and convoys, and by aiming to take the three 'safe areas' in the east – Gorazde, Srebrenica and Zepa – a prelude to fresh offensives in mid- and northwest Bosnia, including an attack on Sarajevo itself. On 8 July the Bosnian Serbs attacked Srebrenica. Three days later it fell, accompanied by mass slaughter and ethnic expulsion unseen in Europe since 1945. Photographs released by the Americans revealed four mass graves holding 2,500–4,000 adults and children. Gorazde and Zepa came under threat.

The response in London was divided. Tory backbenchers expressed concern about the 300 Royal Welch Fusiliers near Gorazde. Thatcher called for a tougher line, but was in a minority. The conventional wisdom was that any military solution would be futile without a major commitment of troops, which could have extra hazards. The French and American governments had few such reservations, and called for a strong military response: Chirac wanted Srebrenica to be retaken. The Russians continued to urge extreme caution.[5] Major had been following developments in Bosnia since May closely, and now decided that the situation had deteriorated so much that the time had now come for his personal intervention. Fearful that international harmony was at risk, he decided early in the morning of Friday 14 July to convene an international conference in London a week hence to try to establish a coordinated response.[6] A mid-morning meeting was called for key officials from the FCO, Defence and Cabinet Office to make plans, and that afternoon the conference was duly announced.[7]

The initial reaction from Paris and Washington was disparaging. They questioned what any conference could achieve, and favoured immediate action rather than further talk. Chirac absurdly likened Major's cautious response to Neville Chamberlain's appeasement of Hitler.[8] Warren Christopher, US Secretary of State, would not even at first commit himself to attending. Major persevered; a tense thirty-minute telephone conversation with Chirac was followed by similar exchanges with Washington, and a significant cast was invited or cajoled to attend the conference at Lancaster House on 21 July.[9] With Zepa under attack from 15 July, the week leading up to it saw mounting tension, with Chirac keeping up pressure for Zepa and Gorazde to receive immediate protection.

Relations that Friday were thus very tense when the London conference opened. Intending initially to deliver the opening speech and then depart, Major stayed until early afternoon, and in a series of bilaterals brokered a deal between the delegates. After the horror of Srebrenica, firm guarantees were given to the 'safe area' of Gorazde. The British acceded to an ultimatum against the Bosnian Serbs threatening 'disproportionate' punitive military attacks if they continued their aggression, while the US abandoned their previous insistence on generalised area bombing, and the French dropped their plan to land highly armed troops to defend the enclaves. The results were initially communicated through military channels, meaning that the public impact of the conference was less important than the real retribution that hung over the Serbs for the first time.[10]

Two days after the conference, an Anglo–French force of 1,700 was despatched to defend Sarajevo. Were Sarajevo to have fallen, as the British Ambassador in Washington, Robin Renwick, had warned Clinton earlier in the summer, the reputation of no western leader would survive unscathed.[11]

By the end of July, the conflict had turned in a significantly different direction with the launch of a Croatian offensive against the Bosnian Serbs in the northwest. In early August, the Croatians, with US connivance in their breach of the arms embargo, were sweeping all before them. The Clinton administration, principally Tony Lake and Richard Holbrooke, toured European capitals in later August with US plans for a resolution of the conflict. Atrocities continued to be committed throughout the month, notably on 29 August when a Bosnian Serb mortar attack on Sarajevo's main market killed thirty-seven people and injured more than eighty. It was this attack that triggered the ultimatum and led to large scale air attacks and UN artillery assaults threatened at the second London conference, involving RAF and USAF fighter planes as well as British gunners based on Mt Igman, firing against the Bosnian Serbs until they withdrew.

The British government was not unhappy to see the US, after three years of squabbling over Bosnia, become more directly involved through NATO. The government realised that such a presence would be a far more forbidding deterrent than could ever be forthcoming under the UN.[12] The decisive moment in the Clinton administration's change of line on Bosnia came with the realisation that it was no longer tenable to keep castigating Europe for not becoming involved militarily, and that it had to commit forces itself.[13] Yeltsin was predictably angry, accusing the West of being judge and jury, and of double standards in punishing the Serbs while ignoring ceasefire violations by Croats and Muslims. Peace talks opening in Geneva on 8 September paved the way for NATO air strikes being called off indefinitely on 21 September, and Portillo announcing British troop reductions of 500 (leaving, with 8,000 troops, Britain still comfortably the biggest military presence).[14]

On 5 October Clinton announced that a ceasefire would take place, and on 31 October discussions opened at the Wright-Patterson air force base in Dayton, Ohio. After a month of fraught talks, driven single-mindedly by Holbrooke, the Dayton Peace Accord was agreed, ending the war, with Bosnia-Herzegovina to be preserved as a single state, to consist of a Bosnian and Croat Federation and a Bosnian Serb Republic. Peace would be overseen by 60,000 NATO troops, including a substantial British commitment, second only in size to an American force.

Amidst a certain amount of grandstanding between Washington, Paris and London to take the credit and the political spoils in the endgame, an implementation conference in London, the second conference at Lancaster House on Bosnia in the year, was convened by Major in December to focus on civilian issues.[15] In mid-December, Major flew to Paris to witness the official signing of the peace treaty. The war at last was over.

The conclusion the British government drew, rightly, was that American military and political might had been essential precursors to a settlement. Holbrooke thus succeeded where Owen without US troops had earlier failed. The whole episode showed that Europe was neither united nor powerful enough to deal with a relatively contained if complex regional crisis like Bosnia. Major's personal backing throughout 1992–5 for British troops on the ground had been important in saving lives, at a time when many in the Conservative Party were demanding the withdrawal of troops, and when he would have been shown little mercy had there been significant loss of British life. Major was keenly aware of the cross he had borne over Bosnia, which explains his livid response when in the House on 7 November 1995 Ashdown appeared to imply that the government had connived in the fall of Srebrenica, with all the attendant loss of life.[16] The Anglo–American alliance had come under severe strain during the three years of the crisis. Now they were at one, but other issues were shortly to arise driving the White House and Number Ten apart again.

Summertime of Ease: July–September

Major had used the victory parade at the Queen Elizabeth II Centre on 6 July to outline future policy proposals. Expanding on the London *Evening Standard* article sent in from Cannes, it contained plenty of nuggets, but fell short of the radical agenda some sought. The following week he launched a policy paper on sport, *Raising the Game*, an initiative peculiarly his own. A senior mandarin described the battle he had to wage: 'Sport is one of those areas where the Whitehall machine is rather resistant and regards it as somewhat frivolous, while he saw it as an absolutely critical part of British life, essential for a healthy and balanced education. So he had very much to drive that through himself.'[17] A draft of the policy paper had been produced by junior minister Iain Sproat and officials at the Department of National Heritage. They put this to Major at a meeting at Number Ten on 7 June, but he was far from satisfied with it and asked them all to return that evening at 8 p.m., when he went through the entire text, bringing it in line with what he wanted. His Cabinet colleagues were variously indifferent to, amused or irritated by, his passion for sport.[18]

The paper was launched by Major and Sproat at a breakfast meeting with sports writers at Downing Street, and at a training session for children at Millwall Football Club in south London with Bobby Charlton. The proposals

included the setting up of a £100 million British Academy of Sport, to be
funded by National Lottery money, in a bid to boost Britain's sporting pre-
eminence internationally. Schools would also be required to offer six hours
of sport a week, and to publish for parents details of sporting facilities and
achievements. Team sport was to receive a particular boost. In a veiled attack
on teachers opposed to competitive sport, he said, 'If you put any group of
youngsters together they compete and they have fun.' Of Britain's place as a
sporting nation he declared, 'We invented the majority of the world's great
sports and most of those we did not invent we codified and helped to
popularise throughout the world.'[19] The initiative aroused mixed feelings in
the press. While the *Independent on Sunday* designated it as a 'vapid exercise
that will not change anything', *The Times* concluded it was the biggest shake-
up in school sport for fifty years: 'at last the government has served an ace'.[20]

Storm clouds were beginning to gather as the unusually hot month of July
wore on. A loyalist parade in Portadown, County Armagh, erupted in violence, putting stress on the ceasefire as it approached its first anniversary,
while Sinn Fein insisted that the peace process was in crisis. Displeased by
the reshuffle, Lady Thatcher exhorted the government to 'raise their sights'
and learn lessons from Newt Gingrich in America, who within six months
had ceased to be such a vogue figure.[21] Heseltine's new role of imparting
competence and coherence to government policy could not prevent a series
of unfavourable public relations stories, including a row between Clarke and
Archie Norman over share options tax, solved when Clarke climbed down at
the end of the month, a controversial £55 million lottery handout to the
Royal Opera House, and a released killer sent home, where he murdered
another victim. Worse, at the end of the month, the Tories moved from first
to third place in the Littleborough and Saddleworth by-election, reducing
the majority to nine.[22] It was New Labour, not the renewed Conservatives,
who made the running in July, with Blair's Australian speech on 16 July,
addressing senior executives of Murdoch's News Corporation at the Queens-
land resort of Hayman Island, where he spoke admiringly of Mrs Thatcher
as a 'radical, not a Tory'.[23]

Major was relieved when the parliamentary recess finally came on 28 July.
He and Norma packed their bags swiftly and departed for the south of
France, where they stayed in the Riviera villa of Philip Harris. It was to prove
their most enjoyable of the premiership. In France the Majors could meet up
with a number of friends and acquaintances with houses close by, including
Nick Lloyd of the *Daily Express* and Andrew Lloyd Webber.[24] Harris's large
house and garden were relatively secluded, but the paparazzi photographers
still penetrated the defences, and bombarded London-based newspapers with
their wares, demanding high prices to print them. Several editors phoned the
Number Ten Press Office asking whether Major would object if they were
used. The response given was: 'It is up to you.'

The reason for the editorial enquiries was neither deference nor tact, but
concern that if the photographs appeared, Major might issue a press com-

plaint about the intrusion from long-range cameras which could hamper them in the future.[25] No photographs appeared – though editors felt no such constraint two years later when the Majors spent a post-general election break on Paul Getty's yacht. Blissfully untroubled by such concerns at the time, the Majors returned to London in mid-August feeling thoroughly refreshed, and brimming with self-confidence.[26]

Several events imparted a nostalgic mood to this period. Harold Wilson's memorial service in July was followed by the death of his predecessor, Alec Douglas-Home, after the summer. The death of a prime minister was always a big event for Number Ten. Wilson had died on 24 May. Mark Adams, the long-serving Home Affairs Private Secretary, had fortuitously been reading Ben Pimlott's biography. Phoned with the news at 1.30 in the morning, he immediately came to Downing Street to draft the Prime Minister's statement, giving it to Major shortly after 6 a.m. Major worked on it over breakfast, made changes, and suggested it be shown to Martin Gilbert and to Lady Falkender, who as Marcia Williams had been Wilson's Political Secretary throughout his period at Number Ten. She was deeply moved by the text, especially by the sensitive way his surprise retirement in April 1976 had been handled.

For Major's oration on Home, the text was sent for comment to Conservative historian and former MP Robert Rhodes James. Major had found his Wilson tribute, which was well received in the House, easier than Home's, in part because he found it easier to be magnanimous about an opponent than a predecessor in his own Party. But he regretted that, as he scarcely knew either man personally, he found it difficult to enrich either speech with personal recollection and colour. The Private Office always kept a wary eye out for signs of ill-health of Ted Heath, who was seventy-nine that July, and the Queen Mother, ninety-five that August.[27]

For Alex Allan, Major's keystone official aide, on holiday in Australia, the period had its own solemnity. The only call he had from the Private Office was asking him to write an obituary of Jerry Garcia, the Grateful Dead lead guitarist who died on 9 August. Allan, one of the group's serious fans (known as 'Deadheads') possessed all the band's records and, a first for a Prime Minister's Principal Private Secretary, attended every concert that the cult rock group had played in Britain.[28]

The reflective mood continued with the VJ Day celebrations over the weekend of 19–20 August. The build-up had been complicated by the servicemen associations wanting compensation for former prisoners of war, as well as a full apology from the Japanese government. Major handled the issue with sensitivity, meeting veterans' representatives, and explaining his limited room for manoeuvre because of commitments entered into by previous British governments.[29]

The weekend of celebrations, overseen again by Cranborne, included on Saturday afternoon a service of remembrance in Buckingham Palace forecourt, two minutes' silence and the dropping of poppies from a Lancaster bomber and a flypast of RAF planes. The evening was spent watching a fireworks display aboard the royal yacht *Britannia* moored in the Pool of London. Sunday's highlights began with Evensong at St Paul's Cathedral, followed by Beating the Retreat on Horseguards Parade, a moving address from the Queen, the Last Post and a sunset ceremony from Buckingham Palace.[30] As the final event in a year and more of commemoration stretching back to the D-Day anniversaries the previous June, the finale was a suitably spectacular occasion. The finest of British actors, including Joan Plowright, Judi Dench and Edward Fox, read from patriotic texts, bands played music by Ralph Vaughan Williams, Edward Elgar and Gustav Holst, while choirs sang 'I Vow to Thee My Country' and 'Abide With Me'. 'Anyone ... without a lump in their throat and a tear in their eye must be devoid of emotion' said Major, who found himself very moved, especially by the parade past of thousands of Burma Star veterans.[31]

On a lighter level, curiosity was aroused by a photograph appearing in many newspapers of all three Party leaders laughing together, a rare sight. Paddy Ashdown subsequently revealed that Major had been telling them about how a gardener had been applying suntan lotion to a koi carp in the fish pond at The Finings. Upset at first that Ashdown had told the press the possibly belittling reason behind the merriment, Major was placated when an aide told him that the nation possessed many fish lovers who applauded his kindly act.[32]

In the first prolonged break of his premiership, Major spent the three weeks after the VJ Day events relaxing in Huntingdon and at Chequers, and mulling over his conference speech and future policy ideas. Several cricket matches were devoured, a highlight being a long talk with former fast bowler Wes Hall, now manager of the West Indies.[33] His only heavy political meeting of the month was with Heseltine, his new Deputy Prime Minister, and Party Chairman Mawhinney, on 19 August at Number Ten.

Major had decided in July that they needed to have weekly meetings slotted into the diary, to improve the government–Party axis in the long run-up to the general election, to be held on Monday mornings from the autumn. The August meeting was a foretaste to those weekly meetings, at which the three men, joined by Blackwell, debated how best they could, in Major's words, 'hit the ground running' in the autumn. They agreed that they needed two or three core themes which captured an excitement or mood, and which would be widely picked up. Blackwell produced the phrase of Britain being the 'enterprise centre of Europe', and with Heseltine's enthusiastic backing they decided it should be employed at the conference.[34]

On 23 August Bruce Anderson came up to Chequers to interview Major for *The Times*. Major seized on Anderson's last-minute suggestion of an interview – they were due originally just to have lunch – to provide evidence that he was not resting on his laurels and that he had the ideas to take the Tory Party, and the country, forward. He trailed the 'enterprise centre of Europe' theme by expounding on Britain's deregulated domestic economy, and outlined his plans to expand grant maintained schools, for Northern Ireland, and for travelling around the country in September to put the government's case across to 'ordinary people'.[35] Looking further into the future, he sought to show, in line with discussion at Political Cabinet earlier in the summer, that there existed an historic opportunity to put defeatism and decline behind, and move forward to a new era in which Britain could be both a global trading nation and a global power.[36]

Anderson found Major in a far more relaxed state of mind than he had seen him for many months, convinced that his decision to call the leadership election had been vindicated.[37] For the interview photograph, Norma persuaded him to appear in an open-neck, casual light blue shirt. He was pleased with the result, so much so that one of the photographs taken that day, of him leaning against a garden arch, appeared in Norma's book on Chequers.[38]

Major's 'meet the people' tour took place early the following month, under the banner 'Our Nation's Future', and was conceived as part of his promise in the spring to consult activists and the country at large about the next manifesto. In Bedford on 8 September he announced, 'We have to look to Conservative philosophy through to the next century', taken to be a call for others to stop judging policy by the yardstick of Thatcherism.[39] After his traditional Balmoral stay with the Queen, Major went to Birmingham on 12 September, where in his first keynote speech since July he announced a '12-point plan' to raise education standards. Grant maintained schools, he declared, would be free to select children, and church schools that wished to opt out would no longer require parental ballots.[40] Major's anxiety to accelerate the pace of schools opting out brought him into direct conflict with Gillian Shephard, who had a far more positive view about local authority schools than either of her predecessors, Clarke and John Patten and whose staff were thought to have been briefing the press against Number Ten's line. In another difference, Major felt she was not going quickly enough over the publication of test results and monitoring the performance of teachers.[41]

The two once-close friends had drifted apart over the year, but their relationship reached a nadir with this speech, about which she had only been consulted in a perfunctory way. She particularly opposed what he said about church schools, because it interfered with the principle of individual choice, about which she felt strongly. Although they were to have further disagreements, such as over the popularity of grammar schools, their relationship began to recover after the autumn.[42]

But it only did so after Major's anger subsided at a leak from her department of a memo which made clear her support for the view that 'insufficient resources threaten the provision of education in the state school sector'.[43] Additionally galling for Major was that he had been unable to persuade Cabinet earlier in the year to give education more money. The leak was deliberately timed to maximise attention before a widely flagged all-day Political Cabinet at Chequers on 14 September, set up to discuss the Party's policies up to and beyond the general election. During August, Blackwell had produced a first draft of the manifesto, based upon the policy groups which had all reported by July.

The day was divided up under a number of headings: education, law and order, welfare, the economy and enterprise. Shephard, Lilley, Howard and others made presentations using an overhead projector. As they discussed their strategies for the critical areas of concern in their departments, Labour's position and how they planned to deal with it, one witness described the day as 'the nearest thing I have seen in government to a modern management meeting'.[44] The businesslike tone was seen further in ministers being asked to send their planned announcements for the conference the next month speedily to Number Ten, with Major and Mawhinney determined to schedule announcements more carefully than in the past.[45]

All was going well until a message was received just before lunch about the education leak. Proceedings were delayed while Major, Heseltine, Mawhinney and Shephard discussed media damage limitation.[46] 'It was very disruptive deciding how to handle it, who should go to the pub to brief the hacks,' said one Number Ten aide. 'By the *Six O'Clock News* it was clear that the story lacked any limiting factor without Mrs Shephard, and she went back to London to appear on later evening broadcasts.'[47]

The leak took the shine off a day which was important not least for being the first occasion in over six weeks that Major's new Cabinet had sat down together to be enthused with *esprit de corps* and a new sense of purpose. Some now wondered whether the jinx that had bedevilled the government so often in the past had really been exorcised in the leadership election.

Major was back on his best form for the EU summit at Majorca on 22–3 September. Its genesis had been a discussion at Essen in December 1994 about the future shape of the EU. Major created a minor stir by saying he thought the subject so important that heads of government should devote an entire conference to the one theme. The Spanish, whose presidency fell in the second half of 1995, agreed and the Majorca meeting was the result. There would be no agenda and no conclusions, and no delegation was allowed more than three people. The leaders stayed in a small hotel on the tip of the Formentor promontory, conveniently removed from the press corps.

Major spoke early on and argued the case for more competitiveness, keeping social costs down and labour markets flexible. In the privacy of this debate, it was Major's views, rather than the high spending and regulation arguments prevalent three years before, which carried weight. At the end of that first session, Felipe Gonzalez, no particular admirer of Major, asked him to lead again in the next day's discussions, on the political future of Europe. Major responded that Kohl should open the debate, but others insisted that he do so. Overnight, he discussed with Lyne and Meyer what he might say, and the next morning conveyed his views on defence, eastern Europe and the place of Russia. The impression gained by many of those present on both days was that Major, for all the upsets he had caused, was one of the clearest and far-seeing thinkers of the EU leaders.[48] He received support even from

Jean-Luc Dehaene, who endorsed his view that monetary union be viewed in the wider context of making Europe more competitive. The Number Ten note-taker recorded the 'surprised laughter' that erupted from other EU leaders at that delicate point.[49]

Press reports in general failed to reflect adequately either the substance of the discussions, or Major's own role. One or two of the more friendly journalists, as was the way, were selected for especial briefing, but the press's main interest lay in the single currency and divisions in the run-up to the IGC, due to open in just seven months.[50] The *Independent on Sunday*, however, said that Major had persuaded his EU partners to halt the drive towards integration, and to re-examine the risks in EMU. There was a peace dividend for Major at home. In response in part to his stronger line on the single currency, the former 'whipless' MPs agreed to end public hostilities with Major on Europe.[51]

Shortly after his return to London, the Majors hosted an advance party at Number Ten on 26 September for Lady Thatcher's seventieth birthday, which fell on 13 October. Norman Tebbit and his wife, Margaret, paralysed by the 1984 Brighton bomb, and Kenneth Baker were among the guests at the small dinner celebration. Major spoke warmly of her after the dinner, and was 'hugely happy' to be hosting the dinner, and to make a fuss also of Denis Thatcher, whose eightieth birthday had fallen in May. Although planned since the spring, the party containing so many former foes could now be billed as the latest sign of the improving relationship between both leaders, and indeed their camps.[52] As one guest wryly noted: 'The birthday party gave them both the chance to bury the hatchet – and not in each other.'[53]

Labour now appeared the party that was more disunited. A memo from a close Blair aide, Philip Gould, leaked to the *Guardian*, argued that Labour needed a new command structure around Blair if it was to be ready for power. Then Kevin McNamara resigned from Labour's front bench in protest at Blair's support for Major's Northern Ireland policy.[54] At the end of the month, a MORI poll showed Major's personal rating rise from 26 per cent among Tory supporters to over 40.[55] It all helped to set the seal on Major's summer of ease.

The Heseltine Gamble

'Major had never been under any illusion that the most important factor in Michael Heseltine's mind was to keep open and eventually achieve the office of Prime Minister.' So spoke one aide.[56] Major claimed subsequently that, although he assumed, if an opportunity arose, from the moment he brought him back into government in November 1990, that Heseltine would want to be Prime Minister, but he was never manoeuvring. By giving him in the July reshuffle potentially more power than any politician other than the Prime Minister had possessed in thirty years, might Major not be placing too much trust in his deputy's better nature?

There was no shortage of people warning Major of just this risk when the appointment was first announced, especially when they saw how much treasure he had placed in Heseltine's trove. Howard, a particular critic of the appointment, did little to conceal his anger when the new Deputy Prime Minister summoned one of his officials to see him, without consulting the Home Secretary. Press reports that 'Major cedes an empire to Heseltine', and charts purporting to show Heseltine had far more jobs than Major, added to the impression of 'President turned Emperor', and to the suspicion of the right.[57]

In addition to Heseltine chairing Cabinet committees on the environment, local government, industrial affairs and regeneration, and the economic committee EDC, he took the competitiveness and deregulation activities across from the Board of Trade into the Cabinet Office.[58] Along with the Prime Minister, he had the right to attend any Cabinet committee of his choosing. The efficiency unit, machinery of government group and Citizen's Charter programme all became, through Roger Freeman, his responsibility. Heseltine's core job was to chair a reformulated Cabinet committee on coordination and presentation of government policy, EDCP, which met every morning at 8.30 a.m. in his room in the Cabinet Office. Attended by ministers, party officials and civil servants, it considered day-to-day response to media interest, and coordination of policy in both the short and longer terms.

The lack of a sufficiently strong capability at the centre had been Major's constant problem, especially since 1992. The new EDCP replaced the Number Twelve Committee, which had been set up in 1991 and which had met daily from Monday to Thursday under Chief Whip Ryder's chairmanship to try to bring focus and clarity to government policy. The run-up to the 1992 general election saw it operating at its best, but shortly after concerns about its efficacy spread. Its very size, with over twenty attenders by the end, was part of the problem – five or more from Number Ten, the business managers, senior Central Office figures and whips – 'every special adviser and his dog,' according to one cynic.[59] Most present thought it ripe for reform. Some of the criticism focused on Ryder's chairmanship, while he, too, felt the group had lost its way. His frustration with Number Ten reached breaking point on occasions in 1994–5; he wanted it to enforce his committee's decisions, and was often discontented by its failure to act quickly. One Number Ten aide remembered: 'It was ghastly. We were being told, "You go away and do this", by someone we didn't work for. It was just a terrible way to start the day.'[60] While Ryder's temperament was 'action this day', Major's was to play for time and try to bring all players on board.

Adding to frustration and confusion was the creation of a 'Presentation' Cabinet committee in early 1995 under Hunt (the first body to be given the initials EDCP), to improve coordination at the centre, not least between Number Ten and the Cabinet Office, and to keep an eye on the longer term.[61] After discussions with Major and Robin Butler – and with opposite numbers in the US and Canada – Hunt concluded that a figure of no less weight than a Deputy Prime Minister would be essential if the central coordination problem was to be cracked.[62]

Butler and Allan, too, had considered various ways of strengthening the centre and enhancing coordination after the plan to bring in a chief of staff figure fell through.[63] Hunt's appointment in July 1994 as Cabinet committee coordinator was one of the responses, but it became obvious, not least to Hunt, that the arrangement was not working, and by the end of May 1995, Major agreed that the way forward was indeed to appoint an official deputy who would operate from the Cabinet Office and work closely with Butler as Cabinet Secretary.[64] In the weeks leading up to the leadership election, discussions within Number Ten intensified, out of which emerged the idea of merging the Number Twelve and EDCP committees, with civil servants to expedite the decisions, under one powerful figure. Heseltine was approached, but initially was non-committal: he had bigger things in mind. Only on the morning of the leadership election, 4 July, did he focus fully on what Major had offered him.

The new EDCP began to meet daily from within a week of the July reshuffle. It got off to a storming start, Heseltine proving himself a tough and decisive chairman. The Heseltine-Newton-Mawhinney combination was demonstrably more effective than the battered Hunt-Newton-Hanley one had been earlier. Ministers and officials soon learned that Heseltine could speak and act as if he was Major, as Whitelaw had done for Thatcher; as one observer put it, 'They had to appear so close that there was not a scintilla of difference between them.'[65]

Contrary to the predictions of many, Heseltine became a stabilising influence after 4 July. He proved himself utterly loyal from that day until the general election in May 1997. Neither in public nor in private did he undermine Major. Every day, officials recount, Heseltine would call into Number Ten, wanting to know what Major wanted. Of that strange, fraught twenty-two-month period, one Number Ten aide said: 'Heseltine, of all Major's Cabinet colleagues, became the closest to him. Major knew and understood Michael's strengths, and those areas where Michael's judgement was less sure than his own.'[66] Jonathan Hill's view was: 'The truth of their relationship has been that each realised their interdependence. Heseltine realised that his best chance of gaining the leadership was by sticking with Major; Major recognised the huge campaigning skills and fighting force of Heseltine.'[67] Again, contrary to some expectations, his energies were complementary to Mawhinney rather than cutting across his role as Party Chairman, and this partnership underpinned Major's leadership. On one issue alone could Major not wholly rely on Heseltine to support his own political judgment: Europe.

Blackpool Lights: October 1995

A successful party conference was an essential prerequisite to a revival in popularity in 1996 and electoral success in 1997. Major knew it. Never had he put so much thought into a party conference speech.[68]

The Blackpool conference message was to be the party's new-found sense of unity and purpose, the successes of the three years since the general election, and the fresh ideas to be announced by ministers and Major himself. Danny Finkelstein, the new director of the Research Department in succession to Andrew Lansley, arrived at the end of September concerned that insufficient strategic thought had been put into the overall message the Party wanted the conference to convey. Previously director of the eclectic 'think-tank' the Social Market Foundation, Finkelstein was to become a key intellectual presence at the heart of government policy and Party strategy. Early evidence of his timbre came at a meeting with Mawhinney and other Central Office directors on Monday 2 October, when he expounded his ideas that the conference should emphasise the 'millennium challenge' for Britain, focusing on the rise of the Asian tiger economies, the demographic time bomb of world population doubling by 2020, the rise of dependency, and the double risk of supra-nationalism in Europe and regionalism within Britain.[69] Even so late in the day, some of this broad-ranging agenda found its way into the conference message. EDCP met twice on 3 October, and a brief Political Cabinet was held after Cabinet the following day to confirm arrangements and to add the final touches.

Everything seemed set fair: the pre-conference press briefings went according to plan, with stories appearing about Major's pleasure in his strongest Cabinet to date, of Central Office being brought to order by Mawhinney, and measures to ensure that public squabbles in the autumn spending round would be hobbled.[70] What none of the careful planning and stage management had prepared the Party for, nor indeed had the whips under Goodlad foreseen, was that one Tory was far from happy and was about to break ranks.

Alan Howarth had been MP for Stratford-on-Avon since 1983. Previously himself a Director of the Research Department, he rose to become minister responsible for higher education, a post he held until 1992. His unhappiness at the rightward drift of government policy, especially policies pursued at the Department for Social Security and the Home Office, reached a climax in early 1995, when he spoke against the government's Jobseekers' Allowance Bill. Policy pronouncements after Major's re-election proved the final straw for him: 'I wanted to see the opportunity taken to redefine Conservatism and what did we get? Abolition of capital gains and inheritance tax. A crackdown on DSS fraud and more sport in schools. It was simply inadequate.'[71]

A curious phrase had been used by Prescott during Labour's successful conference in Brighton in the first week of October. He spoke of the 'One Nation' appeal of Labour, and invited people from all parties to come over and join them.[72] The phrase was indeed a coded reference to Howarth, who had already had discussions with Blair and his aides Jonathan Powell and Alastair Campbell, and had decided that he had to cross the floor. He had lost hope in his efforts to stop what he saw as the rightward drift of the Tories, and firmly decided that New Labour were closer to his values. The Labour leadership were keen to ensure that the defection made the biggest possible splash, and Campbell prevailed upon him to make his announcement over the weekend between the Labour and Tory conferences.[73] Howarth says he tried to speak to Major on Saturday before the news broke in the Sunday papers, when Anthony Bevins wrote up a carefully orchestrated exclusive interview in the *Observer*.[74] Howarth's letter to his constituency chairman spoke of 'an arrogance of power and a harshness within government which is damaging to our democracy and to the quality of relationships in our society'.

Howarth eventually spoke to Major on Sunday. 'We talked for about twenty-five minutes,' Howarth recalled. 'It was a conversation of two people who wanted to respect each other. I spent a significant part of the conversation explaining my very, very strong feelings about the Home Secretary's policies. He seemed stung by that, and said "You can't believe *I* hold those views?"' Major said that he tried to explain that neither did Howard hold the extreme views attributed to him by Howarth.[75]

Unlike many of his close lieutenants, who spoke out against Howarth's 'treachery', and the cynical way he timed his announcement to maximise damage on the eve of the Conservative Party's conference, Major held his counsel. He was upset and very disappointed, but recognised that Howarth was driven by his social conscience, and could see that he had been through a 'long night of agony'.[76] Major simply issued a public statement saying he was 'very sorry' about the move.[77] Others were not so forgiving and thought Howarth's action was shaped by frustrated ambition. For forty-eight hours the story of the 'first Tory MP ever to defect directly to Labour' remained top of the news agenda.[78] While the whips fired into life counselling potential defectors in an effort to deny Labour another propaganda coup, reports appeared of thirty to forty left-leaning Tory MPs who shared Howarth's concerns about the direction of party policy.[79] Howarth himself let it be known ominously that one or two more Tories might be persuaded to join him on the Labour benches.[80] Having been told that it was the right who were agitated by the tone of pronouncements since the leadership election, it was ironic that the upset came from the opposite quarter. The experience reinforced Major's extreme sense of caution and need to maintain his balancing act.

A nervousness was evident when the conference got off to an uncertain start with a speech by the new Agriculture Minister, Douglas Hogg. But the conference came alive, and the shadow of Alan Howarth was expunged, that afternoon with Portillo's explosive anti-Europe speech, in which he railed against Brussels controlling Britain's defence policy, and adopted the SAS motto in his call to the Tory faithful 'We dare. We will win'.[81]

The initial reaction was that Portillo had repeated the success of his anti-Europe speech the previous year. Major had been gratified by Portillo's loyalty and performance since July, and rose by his side, clapping

Norma Major unveils Peter Deighan's portrait of her husband at the National Portrait Gallery, 9 May 1994

Major shares a joke about a goldfish with Tony Blair and Paddy Ashdown, 20 August 1995.

The loyal deputy: Michael Heseltine at the party conference, 10 October 1996.

The 'big beasts': Michael Howard, Brian
Mawhinney, Norman Fowler and Kenneth Clarke.

Norma and John Major welcome the three tenors to Downing Street, 4 July 1996.

Looking over his shoulder? The relationship between biographer and subject is never easy.

A picture of despair ... but his mind was on comic verse rather than the cares of the world, 29 January 1994

Launching the National Lottery in a newsagents' near Victoria, 7 November 1994.

Announcing his resignation as Conservative party leader, 22 June 1995. Ian McColl in background.

Announcing his victory in the 1995 leadership election, 4 July 1995, his campaign team in the background.

YOU CAN ONLY BE SURE WITH THE CONSERVATIVES

THE CONSERVATIVE MANIFESTO 1997

A week before polling day in 1997, Major contemplates the timing of his decision to resign as party leader (with author, back to camera).

On the hustings in Brecon, 9 April 1997.

Leaving Number Ten for the last time,
2 May 1997.

Back where it all began: watching cricket at
the Oval, 2 May 1997.

'When the curtain falls it is time to get off the stage.' Norma in background, flanked by
Elizabeth and James and their partners.

enthusiastically. The audience loved it. But the secondary reaction was heavily adverse. The pro-Europe left of the Party seethed. Factions on the right, who still could not forgive Portillo for his hesitation during the leadership election, saw it as a crude bid to reclaim pre-eminence from Redwood, who was busy winning over friends in a frantic round of fringe appearances during the conference. While Redwood had made his peace at a 'convivial meeting' with Major, and gave signs of preaching a message of loyalty, it was Portillo who appeared to be rocking the boat, calling into question the new truce on Europe, and possibly encouraging further MPs to defect.

Number Ten had been shown the speech, in common with those of other ministers, although Major himself read the speech only thirty minutes before it was due to be delivered, when it was already typed and going out to the media. Neither he nor, indeed, Portillo anticipated how it would be received; even Rees-Mogg wrote that Portillo should 'grow up'.[82] The services were also angry at a Defence Secretary behaving so inappropriately as to use a regiment for a party political objective. To make amends, Portillo called the service chiefs into his room the following week, and apologised abjectly to them for his error of judgement.[83] Duly accepted, they came to regard him highly. The speech proved a turning point in Portillo's growing political maturity: never again during Major's premiership did he so let his guard slip.

A reasoned Eurosceptical tone was adopted by another minister new to his job, Rifkind, who explained on the first day that ministers would be prepared to be unpopular and isolated in Europe in the pursuit of British interests. Wednesday saw Lilley announce tougher measures on benefits for asylum seekers, Gillian Shephard give a traditionalist speech on education, and Heseltine deliver an old-style tub-thumping rally in which he declared that the conference would be a turning point, like the battle of El Alamein in World War Two.[84]

By Thursday, the Party's nerve had recovered; by consensus the conference was on course for a big success. Lady Thatcher's seventieth birthday ovation was advanced by one day so as not to upstage Major's speech on the Friday. Clarke gave a broad hint of tax cuts, which he regretted instantly for the expectations it stoked up. Howard, with Major's backing, had secured Cabinet support for an announcement of tougher sentencing, including the abolition of automatic early release. Using the slogan 'If you don't want the time, don't do the crime', he claimed his plans would deter criminals.[85] As Mayhew had, however, warned, Lord Taylor, the Lord Chief Justice, within two hours launched a strong attack on Howard's proposals saying, 'What deters [criminals] is the likelihood of being caught, which at the moment is small.'[86] Major was not surprised at Taylor's reaction, and had a response already written into his speech.

The prospect of Major winning the Nobel Peace Prize for his work on the Irish peace process threatened to overshadow his own speech, to be delivered on Friday 13th. Number Ten tried to play down the rumours and when the news came through that he had been unsuccessful, he was not unduly upset.

He knew how much further there was still to go, and he was not sorry that the media would not be distracted from a speech into which he had invested so much of himself.[87]

The text was very much his own, with important contributions from his Number Ten team, and late inputs from Danny Finkelstein, seen in the passage where Major discussed the millennium challenges, and Ronnie Millar, in a phrase about Major understanding the aspirations of European leaders, an expression he liked and wanted expanding.[88] By cherry-picking several pronouncements that would otherwise have been delivered by his ministers earlier in the week, what Major had to say was intentionally more substantial than his earlier conference speeches.[89] He fussed over the speech all week, adding passages, reading it out aloud, striking bits out, until he was confident that he could deliver it without autocue and extemporise extensively, projecting across to the audience better, perhaps, than he had done before.[90]

His reference back to the leadership contest was positive. 'Today we meet united, healed, renewed and thirsting for the real fight with Labour.' In a passage that pleased the centre left and soothed any putative Alan Howarths, he spoke of his commitment to the Tory tradition that those who were not 'thrusting and confident and fit' could always be certain of being protected under his government. A highly personal passage stated:

When I was a small boy, my bread and butter was paid for by my father's small business. He made garden ornaments forty years ago and some people have always found that very funny. I don't. I see the proud, stubborn, independent old man who ran that firm and taught me to love my country, fight for my own and spit in the eye of malign fate. I know the knockers and sneerers who may never have taken a risk in their comfortable lives aren't fit to wipe the boots of the risk-takers of Britain.

On education, he talked of his commitment to the 'One Nation' tradition, and invoking Iain Macleod, announced plans to expand the assisted places scheme to provide more choice, in contrast to the message of the public school-educated Blair of 'no choice for the poor'. The right liked the phrase about making Britain 'the unrivalled enterprise centre of Europe', hence high spending and high tax were 'no longer an option'. His aim was to reduce state spending to below 40 per cent of national wealth. On Europe, 'If others go federalist, Conservative Britain will not.' On Labour's plans for Scottish and Welsh devolution: 'I will not trade easy votes today for constitutional chaos tomorrow.' To counteract the claim, not least from Lord Chief Justice Taylor, that not enough was being done to reduce crime, he announced 5,000 more police 'on the beat', coupled with more closed-circuit cameras in shopping precincts, and an increased effort against organised crime and the 'sheer evil of the drugs trade'. He concluded:

We are building the greatest success for this nation that we have known in our lifetime. We will not surrender it to a lightweight alternative. We carry the scars of battle, but they are honourable scars. We know no other party can win the battles for Britain that lie ahead.[91]

Major knew immediately that it had gone down well. According to Howell James: 'His instant reaction as he comes off the platform is realistic. He is not taken in by people rushing up to him and saying he was marvellous when he knows it wasn't.'[92]

As Major was whisked away to the airport, his aides phoned the Central Office briefers, who gave them the readout from Michael Brunson and Robin Oakley on the lunchtime news programmes. Their positive response was passed on to a thoughtful Major. The team had been nervous because it was the first time the Party leader had spoken in the morning, which gave the whole afternoon for opponents to attack the speech and put their gloss into the evening broadcasts and next day's newspapers.[93]

Anxieties were misplaced. Praise came from all quarters. The *Daily Telegraph* said, 'The skill of the speech lay in the way Mr Major managed to put clear blue water between the Tories and Labour while at the same time retaining the Government's claim to the middle ground.'[94] Andrew Marr said the speech reminded 'all of us what a fighter he is',[95] while Hugo Young said that it proved he was 'the only man fit to lead' the Tories, and that, 'He made his colleagues look like strutting pygmies. Even that famous deputy prime minister must sink below the salt.'[96] The weekend press reflected a belief that the conference had seen the Party triumph over the Howarth affair, and over the divisions that had dogged it in the past.[97]

The speech marked a decisive shift for Major. Shortly after the leadership contest, as in the Bruce Anderson interview, he had surprised and pleased his aides by starting to talk about his vision for the future.[98] This fed through into the conference speech; in contrast to his pragmatic and safe speech at Bournemouth in 1994, he was now looking forward. As he received plaudits after it was over, he remarked, 'Well there you are. People might even think we can win the next general election.'[99]

THIRTY-FIVE

Into a Box:

October 1995–February 1996

WITHIN DAYS OF the party conference, challenges emerged to upset the new mood of unity and confidence. As Parliament returned, the question being asked was, would Major be able to maintain the momentum from the leadership victory and the conference? Would the smaller majority, and proximity of polling day, lead the Party to rediscover its hunger for office and its desire to put divisions behind it? Or would Alan Howarth's defection, by reducing the Tories' majority from nine to seven, make MPs even less manageable, and call into question the whole strategy of playing it long and waiting until the last moment to call the general election?

No Way Out: Prisons and Nolan

When Parliament reassembled in the week after Blackpool, the government was immediately faced with the first of two time bombs which had been ticking throughout the summer. The handling of the first provided grounds for optimism. A break-out from Parkhurst prison on the Isle of Wight in January 1995 led to the governor, John Marriott, being moved to non-operational duties in the Prison Service and the launching of an official inquiry into prison security headed by General Sir John Learmont. His report at the end of September was heavily critical of the management of the Prison Service, which was headed by the Director-General Derek Lewis.[1]

Howard decided that he wanted Lewis sacked, prevailing over his junior minister Ann Widdecombe. She says she spoke to Major in the afternoon of Sunday 15 October, who told her that Howard said the decision on Lewis was 'irretrievable'. She disputed this, as Howard was still waiting to hear from Lewis about whether or not he would resign.[2] The episode became one of the many contested events of the premiership, and the spur for Widdecombe to castigate her former boss just after the 1997 general election for having 'something of the night' about him.

Howard met Major at Number Ten on Sunday evening. Prisons were not a subject Major knew much about, but he realised there would be an explosion whatever way the decision went, and wanted to consider the implications carefully. If Lewis was allowed to stay, the accusation would be lack of accountability and no one ever resigning; if he was sacked, Howard would come under fire for passing the buck. Major was concerned that the sacking, if it went ahead, be honourable and fair, and they discussed the financial cost and other implications. The decision never came to Cabinet, but other ministers, including Forsyth and Clarke, had reservations, and the issues were considered at further meetings on Monday morning. Howard won through. In the House that afternoon he announced that, following the official publication of the Learmont report that day, Lewis would go.[3]

Buoyed by the ostentatious appearance of their new convert Howarth on their benches, and with a swelling public outcry over the sacking, Blair sensed he had the government on the run. Labour put down an emergency debate for Thursday deploring Howard's 'unwillingness ... to accept responsibility for senior operational failures of the Prison Service'.[4] Labour's confident start was dented, however, by an indifferent performance in the debate on rail privatisation that Wednesday, when lack of clarity in its re-nationalisation plans showed through. The same day, the results of the Shadow Cabinet elections were seen as a rebuff to Blair, in particular with Jack Cunningham being voted off, while Tom Clarke, supported by the left-wing Campaign Group, was re-elected.[5]

The debate on Thursday, a damp squib, had some similarity to Kinnock's failure to press home the advantage against a vulnerable Mrs Thatcher in the Westland debate in 1986. Jack Straw, Shadow Home Secretary, floundered, above all when Bernard Jenkin intervened to ask if he thought Lewis should have been sacked. Labour's fundamental argument, about whether Howard could justifiably draw a distinction between 'policy', for which he was responsible, and 'operational matters', for which he was not, was not put across convincingly. Neither was the issue about whether Conservative ministers would ever accept responsibility for an error and resign. Howard had probably won the debate before he even rose to speak, when he unsettled Labour by his self-confident and apparently effortless dismissal of Labour's case, which brought an angry Blair jumping to his feet to intervene. The government won the division by forty-nine votes. Howard had been helped considerably by noisy support from Tory backbenchers, still pleased by the hard law and order measures announced at Blackpool the previous week. He was the hero of the hour, as reflected by David Wastell: '[for] almost the first time since Britain was forced out of the ERM, the Tories looked as if they had got their act together.'[6] Indeed, one week into the new Parliament, and Labour was on the run.

Foreign concerns took much of Major's attention the following week. On 22–4 October he was in New York for the fiftieth anniversary celebrations of the United Nations. His flight arrived too late for him to be included in the 'family of nations' opening photograph of 140 heads of state or government, although he had a front seat reserved. Wry comment was made of the fact that other absentees included Saddam Hussein, Colonel Gaddafi and the leaders of Iran.[7] The visit was notable for Major extending a tentative hand of friendship, thirteen years after the Falklands War, to Carlos Menem, President of Argentina.[8] On the UN, he argued that it urgently needed to reform itself. Security Council membership must be expanded, to reflect the changes in relative power in the last fifty years. 'The threat to the future of the UN will not come from change,' he said. 'It will come from inertia.'[9] Pointed reference was made to the US debt to the UN: inverting the battlecry of the American colonists before 1776, he said, 'It is not sustainable for member states to enjoy representation without taxation.'[10] Overall, Major was not alone in seeing the meeting as fatuous.

On Major's return to Britain, the Queen hosted a state visit from President Chirac. The disagreements over Bosnia in July were put completely behind them; a Number Ten source said their relationship had taken off 'like a rocket'.[11] In contrast to Prime Minister Balladur, whom he found more detached and donnish, Major felt very much at one with the new French President, described by an FCO source as 'a great big expansive, backslapping, very friendly, sandwich-eating ploughman-an-hour man, who speaks English; they had it made together'.[12] Major's gesture in meeting Chirac in January, when he was only Mayor of Paris and not the front-runner for President, had helped pave the way. Their friendship developed through the year. As with Kohl, however, the relationship was volatile. Major's open support for France's unpopular nuclear testing only added to the warmth of their dinner at Chequers on Sunday 29 October and talks at Number Ten the next day.[13]

At Westminster, however, Major's authority was about to be called seriously into question for the first time in four months. In the final debate on the Nolan saga, the impression of governmental competence, so carefully nurtured since July, was about to be unravelled. The government had bought time with the setting up in May of a committee of MPs to consider the question of MPs' outside interests. On 31 October the Commons committee decided by the casting vote of Newton, the chairman, to recommend rejection of the Nolan proposal that MPs reveal payments for providing parliamentary service to outsiders, coming out instead in favour of a ban on paid advocacy, a seemingly clever compromise.[14]

Major was in a dilemma. In setting up Nolan in October 1994, he had made much of his belief that Parliament needed to expunge its growing image of 'sleaze'. Now he had to either back the entire Nolan recommendation on disclosure of earnings, antagonising the majority of Tory MPs from across the political spectrum affronted at the prospect of having their financial affairs revealed, and thus jeopardising the new truce and unity in the Party, or follow the Newton committee's proposal and go for the halfway house of banning paid advocacy, with the risk that he would be seen to be backtracking, and handing to Labour the mantle of moral purists on sleaze issues. A Number Ten insider described how they saw the Nolan disaster approaching: 'We were transfixed. We watched with gory inevitability where the train was going but we couldn't do anything about it.'[15]

In one of the critical decisions of his premiership, he decided to follow the advice which focused on damage limitation and handling the Party rather than on how it would be seen by the country at large. At a morning meeting on 1 November at Number Ten with Heseltine, Mawhinney and Newton, he announced his backing for Newton's Commons committee.[16] The decision lost him the respect of liberal opinion,[17] as well as losing him much moral capital which he had made so many sacrifices to build up over the previous years.

Major had convinced himself that forcing MPs to declare their income was an intrusion too far into their lives. He did not favour a House comprising only full-time professional politicians who lacked working contact with the world outside Westminster.[18] He argued that in choosing to support a ban on paid advocacy, he was in fact going further than Nolan. Only with hindsight did he realise that he may not have made the right decision and, given the expectations aroused in establishing Nolan, the disillusion many would feel at his decision to fall short of full acceptance. Neither did he foresee the encouragement it would provide to others in his party to fudge on the sleaze issue in the future.[19]

Blair capitalised swiftly, calling Major's refusal to back full disclosure 'a stain on his prime ministership', and amid indications that Tory MPs would break ranks and side with Labour, served notice that he would force a debate at the start of the next week. Major had several conversations with Newton as well as Goodlad in the run-up to the vote on Monday 6 November. It was decided to make it a free vote, with no whipping. But it was made clear to backbenchers that they should vote on the same side as the Prime Minister and government ministers and reject Nolan's recommendation on disclosure. Several backbenchers complained that, despite it being made a vote of conscience, the Tory whips were still in action. Emma Nicholson, MP for West Devon and Torridge, was later to claim it was the final straw in her decision to quit the Conservatives for the Liberal Democrats.[20]

Reaction against the whipping explained in part the crushing fifty-one-vote defeat. Twenty-three Tories, including five former ministers, broke ranks and voted with Labour, and twenty-nine abstained. Blair and the Labour front bench had brilliantly managed the whole Nolan issue. They all but denied Major any credit for establishing Nolan, and for accepting the other Nolan proposals such as curbs on former ministers taking jobs in the private sector and appointing a parliamentary sleaze-buster. He was portrayed as caving in to his greedy backbenchers, and lacking the courage of his convictions. The leadership was slow to realise what a cardinal error it had made. An editorial in the *Sunday Times* summed it up. Monday's vote, it said, 'was a crushing defeat and a demonstration that this Tory leadership is hopelessly out of step with public opinion'.[21]

Deaths in Israel and Nigeria: November

Major was at a wine and cheese function on Saturday 4 November, trying to take his mind off the Nolan vote two days away, when the detectives asked to speak to him. Yitzhak Rabin, Prime Minister of Israel, had been shot at a peace rally.[22] A short while later a second phone call said he was dead. Many thoughts rushed through Major's head: grief at the loss of a friend and someone he regarded as a kindred spirit, and concern about how he could pay his respects. He had been due to fly to New Zealand on Tuesday; how could he fit in the funeral? He was not surprised when he heard Rabin had died; he said after the first phone call that he did not think a seventy-year-old would have been able to survive a bullet fired at close range.[23] Number Ten hastily ordered a plane, and contacted Blair and Ashdown, who would also attend the funeral. 'He gave his life for peace,' said Major in a statement, 'His best memorial would lie in achieving it.'[24]

On Monday morning, a small jet from the Royal Flight flew out of London, with Major, Blair and Ashdown sitting rather self-consciously in the front alongside Rifkind, Lyne and Meyer. As the three party leaders chatted during the flight – made even longer by a refuelling stop in Rome – they admitted to a fellow feeling that Parliamentary Questions were an ordeal. Blair, new to the Prime Minister's plane, had his first prolonged opportunity to talk to Major, who found him younger, more nervy and ambitious than Kinnock and Smith, and less easy to establish a rapport with.[25] Although their relationship had hit some lows in the spring there was still a bond between them: only subsequently did real ill-feeling intrude.

The funeral itself was an extraordinary affair, not least because it saw the largest number of world leaders to attend a burial since that of Emperor Hirohito in February 1989. Standing between Prince Charles and Chirac, Major watched thoughtfully as Rabin's coffin was laid to rest in a simple grave in Jerusalem's Herzl cemetery, where his seventeen-year-old granddaughter said to mourners: 'Forgive me if I do not want to talk about peace. I want to talk about my grandfather ... the pillar of fire in front of the camp and now we are just a camp left alone in the dark and we are so cold and sad.'[26]

Major flew straight on from Israel to the biennial Commonwealth Heads of Government Meeting (CHOGM) in New Zealand, arriving on 8 November. Unsettled by the news coming through of the Commons Nolan vote and its backwash, Major had to contend with now being made an international outcast for supporting France's nuclear testing at Mururoa Atoll.[27] The world's newspapers and broadcasting networks had been ablaze with stories of the environmental hazards caused by France's underwater explosions, the third of which was detonated on 28 October. Major was not going to be moved. Intellectually, he accepted the case that France should be allowed to complete its series of tests to acquire the scientific data it needed. British national interest, he believed, would also best be bolstered by standing in support of France.[28]

Greeted on arrival in Auckland by a protest from a hundred nuclear demonstrators waving placards labelling him an 'environmental traitor', he delivered a statement which said that it would have been hypocritical to have taken the 'free ride' and join the chorus of disapproval against Chirac. 'I know the responsibility of being a nuclear power. I understand the difficulties that face the President of France. I am not prepared to condemn him for discharging those responsibilities ... upon this issue, to my regret, we must agree to differ.'[29] He did, however, agree to sign the following year the Treaty of Rorotonga that banned nuclear testing in the South Pacific.

Nuclear testing dominated the first day of the conference. Although Britain was castigated over the issue, with Major compared to Mrs Thatcher in the 1980s for being in a minority of one among Commonwealth leaders, a degree of cynicism had developed in the Prime Minister's camp; all was not in fact as it appeared. The host, New Zealand Prime Minister Jim Bolger, with an election coming up the next year, and with passions still alive from the French secret service sinking Greenpeace's ship *Rainbow Warrior* in New Zealand in 1985, was seen as having domestic reasons for protesting strongly. Paul Keating, equally, had an election the next year, when he had to face an Australian electorate which had similar strong anti-nuclear sentiments. The British saw Keating as worried about being seen as softer in his condemnation than Bolger, and thus driven to make some very strong criticisms of Major before leaving Australia. On arrival, Keating let it be known he wanted an early bilateral meeting with Major. Anxious to avoid a further torrent of abuse, Major's staff stalled. Keating's office prevailed, and a meeting was rapidly convened at which Keating apologised, explaining his strong language was for domestic consumption.[30] Major found that many other Commonwealth leaders did not feel strongly on the issue, so was all the more irritated by the way that the conference's statement on testing was phrased, which forced him into issuing his own version unilaterally setting out Britain's position.[31]

The appropriateness of comparisons with Mrs Thatcher's isolation at CHOGMs was shortly to be put to the test. An issue arose on the second day in which Major sought to take the lead. Would it be followed, or would he be shunned? Nigerian leader General Abacha had imprisoned Ken Saro-Wiwa, the writer and political activist, along with other Ogoni activists who had been protesting against the environmental damage to the Niger delta caused by Shell's drilling. They were now faced by the death penalty. Major, who had strong feelings on the Nigerian action, not least as he had lived in the country, felt increasingly concerned through the summer about the deteriorating political position. He spoke twice by phone to Abacha, the Nigerian President, and sent personal messages, as did other international leaders. Major thought the interventions had made an impact, but as Auckland approached London sensed that 'a wholly irrational atmosphere began to surround Abacha. He became more and more reclusive and closed to contact.'[32] Ken Wiwa, the Tonbridge School-educated son of the dissident, was in Auckland to lobby for his father. On 8 November Major appealed again to Abacha for compassion. 'It seems to me', he said, 'that the sentences are not just and I believe that Nigeria should exercise clemency.'[33] But Major, like others in Auckland, did not expect events to unfold so quickly.

At 7 o'clock in the morning on 10 November, Number Ten phoned Rod Lyne, who had just gone to bed for an hour's sleep after working through the night. Reports had been received in London that Saro-Wiwa had been hanged. Major, Allan, Lyne and Meyer conferred. While in no doubt that Nigeria should be condemned and suspended from the Commonwealth, they thought it unwise to say so ahead of a black African leader.[34] Downstairs in the hotel they learned that Mandela had just given an interview calling for suspension, which paved the way for Major's statement that the trial was 'fraudulent, the verdict bad and the sentence unjust ... I don't see how Nigeria can stay in the Commonwealth without a return to democratic government.'[35]

Commonwealth leaders were due that morning to fly up to Queenstown for the customary retreat. On the coach on the way to the airport, Major's aides phoned Bolger's team, told them about Mandela's and Major's state-ments, and suggested they convene at the front of the plane to produce a coordinated response by the time they landed in Queenstown. With Britain and South Africa playing leading roles, the Commonwealth unveiled a package of measures designed to challenge Nigeria's military regime, and officially suspended it from the Commonwealth for defying the pleas for clemency. Major announced that Britain had imposed an arms embargo on Nigeria, and called for a worldwide ban on Nigerian oil exports. He said: 'We have agreed upon a ladder of measures of increasing severity to encourage and persuade governments to return to acceptable behaviour ... The measures are designed to tackle military regimes which have overthrown a constitutionally elected government.'[36]

Despite the odds, the CHOGM had proved a successful conference for Major. Sticking by France over nuclear testing had not prevented him helping to cement a new sense of moral will among Commonwealth leaders, building on the 1991 Harare Declaration, nor exerting pressure on an unacceptable regime in Nigeria. Relief at his achievement was short-lived, however, after he began to reimmerse himself in domestic politics, where the government's authority was slipping away.

Domestic Upsets: November–December

'The prime minister's remarkable leadership victory should have put the Conservative Party on course for a dramatic comeback against Labour,' announced Hugh Colver, in an article for the *Sun* shortly after his surprise resignation as the Party's head of communications at Central Office. 'Instead,' he continued, 'everything has turned sour and ministers have been seemingly unable to do anything to stop it.'[37]

Colver had been recruited by Hanley to the Party's top press job in May, with a brief to match Labour's artful media management and to prepare the Tories for the general election. But with a background in Whitehall and industry, he was seen as no match for Labour's Alastair Campbell and Peter Mandelson. A press officer rather than a 'spin doctor', Colver felt uncomfortable with the attacks he was being asked to make on Labour, and on 8 November he walked into Central Office at 1 a.m., cleared out his office, and left his resignation letter.[38] The article he wrote for the *Sun* caused far more damage than the fact of his resignation. He said: 'Why with all the advantages of a well-oiled government machine at our fingertips did we continually snatch defeat from the jaws of victory . . . The Tory party behave as if they are in office by divine right.' The precise targets of Colver's attack were not clearly stated, but the impression of incompetence that it created was damaging.[39]

Colver's departure coincided with Gallup showing Labour an extra-ordinary 39.5 per cent ahead of the Conservatives, while the polls also revealed that any fear the voters had of New Labour was less than their fear of the Tories being re-elected.[40] The Nolan defeat, and Colver's utterances, led the *Sunday Times* to pen the lines the leadership hoped would be for ever expunged after the arrival of the new guard at Number Ten and the summer leadership victory: 'There is an alarming drift at the heart of government.'[41]

Mawhinney himself came under attack in the autumn, for his abrasive style, and for his effect on morale at Party headquarters. Low spirits, where they existed, owed more to the continuing bad polls, and were only in part due to the uncertainty caused by Mawhinney's changes. It took him some months to build the team he wanted at Central Office; several senior figures from Fowler's and Hanley's periods were asked to leave. In came Danny Finkelstein, and the MP Michael Trend, a popular and calm administrator, to oversee day-to-day management of Central Office. To replace Colver he wanted to find a journalist like Alastair Campbell (formerly of the *Daily Mirror*), and after several weeks looking hired Charles Lewington, political editor of the *Sunday Express*, who had the first-hand knowledge of the lobby and the party political skills that he wanted.[42] Martin Saunders, finance director, and Tony Garrett, director of campaigning, were the main top figures to survive from the pre-1995 *ancien régime*.[43]

Mawhinney's new brush extended also to outside consultants. On one level, he brought in ICM as the Party's pollsters, but far more significant was the change to the Party's public relations and advertising advisers. In December, the Party paid off its debts to the Saatchi & Saatchi company, whom Mawhinney initially favoured, and took on M. and C. Saatchi (the part of the empire retained by the brothers Maurice and Charles) as their advertising agency, thus paving the way for Maurice Saatchi, Tim Bell and Peter Gummer to become the troika to guide the Party through to the general election.[44]

The first approach came from Tim Bell, Chairman of Lowe Bell Communications since 1987, who contacted Mawhinney after hearing his speech at the 1995 Party Conference. Bell had felt for some months, years even, since the fall of Mrs Thatcher, that the Party had been missing tricks and failing to put its message across. He liked Mawhinney's style, and sent him a fax to congratulate him on what he had said at Blackpool. Could he help? Bell saw Mawhinney in the House of Commons on 31 October and outlined his vision of how, in association with Saatchi and Gummer, brother of John and Chairman of the PR company Shandwick, he might be able to contribute in the run-up to the election.[45]

Bell and Saatchi had last combined on the successful 1987 general election campaign, but Patten thought Bell too tainted with the brush of Mrs Thatcher and dispensed with him for the 1992 election. The pungent duo, who had fallen out in 1987, were now eager to join forces again, linking up with the genial Peter Gummer. The latter had worked with Major during 1992, and came to act as the fixed point between the politicians and the advisers, providing a reassuring balance for Major to the pyrotechnics of Bell and Saatchi.[46] It was Saatchi in particular who worried Mawhinney. The Party Chairman had qualms about his role during the 1992 general election, and about how well he and Bell would work together, but thought on balance that if their skills could be properly harnessed they could prove a major asset.[47]

A contract was thus signed between Central Office and M. and C. Saatchi, with Bell and Gummer making their own arrangements with Saatchi. Bell had fears that, with his close relationship with Lady Thatcher, he would be *persona non grata* in the Major camp. Any apprehensions were eased by Jonathan Hill, who now worked for Lowe Bell, and by Howell James, a former boss of Bell's wife Virginia at Capital Radio, and a close friend of the couple.[48] Bell and Heseltine made clear, despite their differences over Thatcher, that they would work together, while Heseltine had a long-standing and close relationship with Saatchi. A dinner at London's Horseguards Hotel on 28 November went well. Mawhinney and Heseltine said in effect: 'We are the amateurs. You are three of the most professional PR/marketing men in the world. We want you to tell us what to do.'[49] The course of their relationship did not, however, turn out to fulfil the constructive tone of this initial dinner. As the months wore on, Mawhinney, supported fully by Heseltine, became increasingly clear about what he wanted and what was, or was not, acceptable. The question was whether Saatchi, the victor of four election campaigns, would be happy to take instructions.

Dividends from the Party's restructuring could not be felt in the short term, where hopes of a recovery of initiative were pinned on the Queen's Speech on 15 November and the budget on 28 November. Though the leadership hoped it would be able to hold out until May 1997, to maximise chances of economic-based poll recovery, it treated the legislative programme announced in this Queen's Speech as likely to be the last of substance. Bills were promised for nursery vouchers for all four-year-olds for banks and other finance institutions to allow them to offer subsidised loans to students, for state-funded mediation in divorce, a new regulatory framework to promote the development of digital television, and for the right to buy to be extended to housing association tenants. Howard's impetus was again felt in a raft of legislation on law and order, including tougher asylum procedures to root out bogus immigration claims, the security services to be involved in the fight against organised crime, and tougher requirements on disclosure in criminal law cases.[50]

Major hoped to produce a balanced programme, appealing to both wings of the Party, while also being seen to transcend mere Party concerns and respond to national needs.[51] Reception of the Queen's Speech was, however, coloured by Mawhinney's briefing to journalists that it would 'smoke out' Labour. By his reasoning Labour, which had been working so hard to draw close to Tory policy in the centre ground, would be unable to support some of the more populist measures. Mawhinney's words gave the impression that the entire government programme for the coming year was motivated by a desire not to legislate in the long-term interests of the country, but to embarrass a far too successful opposition party. Further damage was done by spinning the Queen's Speech so as to make it appear overwhelmingly right wing (which it was not), thereby antagonising many on the left of the Party. Several MPs anonymously spoke about leaving the Party.[52] Blair cleverly inflamed these divisions by dubbing the programme a 'lurch to the right', and demanding that immigration and asylum matters be taken out of party politics altogether.[53]

Major, stung by how the legislative programme was being interpreted, responded of Blair's speech: 'It was humbug at its worst, and juvenile in its style of criticism. It was what we have come to expect from the Right Hon. Gentleman – cheap soundbites and no sign of his real policy substance, if he has any ... "lurching to the right" ... is the week's approved soundbite from the thought merchants who govern the Right Hon. Gentleman in his back room.'[54] But Labour's media management skills proved again almost effortlessly superior, reflected in the *Financial Times*, which declared that the government 'had put tactical political advantage before serious legislative purpose.'[55]

The 1995 Queen's Speech was indeed a strange affair, owing little to the 'five themes', the main agreed strategy possessed by the government at that time, and bearing all the hallmarks of being determined by Cabinet ministers fighting their departmental corners producing a disparate bag of policies, rather than one reflecting a common strategy. 'Ministers might well have found the five themes dry,' remarked one Number Ten source wistfully, 'and they may even have had trouble remembering them. Some of them may well have had difficulty getting past the first three. But one thing we became conscious of that autumn was our vulnerability to the charge from serious commentators that we had no vision of where we were going. We had one, but we didn't stick to it.'[56] 'Frankly, there were four themes too many,' said a senior Central Office executive, illustrating the lack of consensus in Tory high command.[57] The contrast with the tight discipline of Labour's front bench and party machine, who mouthed the mantras at the drop of a hat, showed that it was not just in media management that Labour had the advantage.

The government was similarly unable to capitalise on any opportunity provided by the budget. Despite Major's and Heseltine's hopes that they had put in place a tough ministerial team on the Cabinet committee EDX to ensure there were no public divisions on spending, many stories spilled out in late October and early November of ministers battling over their allocations. The maximum public sector target had been set at £263 billion, while Major had declared his intention – repeated at the Lord Mayor's Banquet – to reduce spending to below 40 per cent of national income.[58] The main battles came with Shephard (Education), Dorrell (Health) and Lilley, who held out against cuts in benefits for single mothers.[59] A tight settlement in 1995–6 might leave more room for manoeuvre in 1996–7, so it was reasoned. Major helped Clarke and Waldegrave achieve their spending target by seeing some ministers to persuade them to settle at lower figures.[60]

Economic figures published in mid-November increased the pressures on Clarke; the biggest fall in living standards for nearly fourteen years and a sharp rise in unemployment increased the expectation of a giveaway budget.[61] When Clarke announced merely a 1 penny cut in the standard rate of income tax to 24 pence in the pound from April 1996, it appeared a disappointment. 'You Ken not be serious' said a *Sun* headline.[62] Anatole Kaletsky observed in *The Times* that the tax cuts would allow Blair to argue that the average taxpayer was still paying the equivalent of 6 or 7 pence more in standard rate income tax than in 1992–3.[63] Number Ten thought Kaletsky's analysis was wrong and that Clarke should have summarily knocked it down. An NOP poll found that even with the announcement of the tax cut, only 26 per cent of voters trusted the government on tax.[64] The right, who had been pinning great hopes on Clarke to produce election-winning tax cuts, were disillusioned: David Evans and Rhodes Boyson went on the record to say that Clarke should have done more to reduce tax, while Iain Duncan-Smith called for a large interest rate cut as the next best alternative.[65]

Budget day was also the fifth anniversary of Major becoming Prime Minister. With the political atmosphere souring in November, they hoped temporarily, Number Ten and Central Office decided to downplay the anniversary, especially as Mrs Thatcher's tenth-year celebration in May 1989 had backfired.[66] A foretaste of how the anniversary could be portrayed appeared in the *Independent on Sunday* in mid-month; under the title 'the blunder years' it provided a catalogue of the lows and troughs of the period since November 1990.[67] It was decided that television interviews and retrospectives would have 'an obituarist's air', and that any trumpeting of the anniversary would be 'an indulgence: we decided to play it low key'.[68] Thus little was made of it, bar an interview in the *Daily Telegraph*, in which Major said that his experience uniquely qualified him to lead the Party to the general election.

He had much he still wanted to achieve, and much more of the government's evolving programme would be made manifest at the Central Council in March 1996, when the results of the Party's consultation exercise and Policy Unit's plans would be unveiled.[69] For the rest, commentaries on his first five years awarded him scant credit, but developed a fresh angle to explain his longevity: he was above all a 'stubborn' man.[70]

December was a bleak month domestically. Heseltine and his EDCP committee were having little success in controlling the agenda. Major exploded mid-month at the 'inactivity' of his ministers. 'We haven't been doing and saying enough. I want a bigger effort over Christmas when the Opposition has gone home.'[71] Royalty dominated the month, following Diana's *Panorama* interview in late November in which she discussed the problems in her private life. The programme clashed with the Lord Mayor's Banquet, so had to be videoed: they watched it avidly in the flat on their return. Major had to rebuke his minister Nicholas Soames, a close friend of Charles, when he accused Diana of 'being in the advanced stages of paranoia'.[72] Delicate discussions between Number Ten and the Palace had also to take place when Diana was seen as overstepping the mark in her self-appointed ambassadorial role on a trip to Argentina.[73] Clarke exacerbated tensions by saying that those right-wingers who wanted to scale down the welfare state were 'living in cloud-cuckoo land'.[74]

The goodwill gained by a successful bridge-building lunch at Chequers with senior figures from the Telegraph group was dispelled within a week after a story in the *Daily Telegraph* led to cross words being exchanged.[75] 'Like many of our initiatives, it seems to have withered because of time pressure and general dyspepsia,' recorded one Number Ten aide shortly after.[76] In mid-month, Tory MP David Lightbown died, reducing the government's majority to six.[77] A two-vote defeat on European Common Fisheries policy on 19 December ended the Commons session on a low note. The Eurosceptics sensed their cause was becoming ever more popular: both Redwood and Cash published separate anti-federalist pamphlets.[78] Major resolved that it could not go on. At a confidential meeting at Westminster's St Ermin's Hotel, plans were made for a New Year blitz by Central Office.[79]

By the end of the parliamentary session, Major was exhausted and his spirits, raised so high by a promising late summer and early autumn, were downcast. An unwillingness to follow the lead, at every level from Cabinet down to backbencher, combined to thwart Major. 'What lead?' said some high-up figures on both wings of the Party, who had looked for something much more dynamic from Major after the leadership election. But he could not change who he was, even if he wanted to. Neither would a leadership victory change the habits of disobedience that the Party had acquired over three years. The heart of the malaise returning in the autumn was the cumulative disappointment of MPs worried about re-election as the opinion polls failed to recover, resentful over the Nolan threat to their incomes and the size of the public sector deficit, meant the cutback of popular programmes and the inability to offer significant tax cuts to kick-start the 'feel-good' factor. The writing was on the wall, and a party with low prospects of success and in which the incentives for loyalty were not apparent would always be difficult to lead. It was, after all, MPs' concern about their own futures which had been primarily responsible for their dumping Mrs Thatcher five years before.

The End of the Ceasefire: October–February

Major's achievement that even his harshest critic could scarcely deny was the truce in Northern Ireland and the prospects offered of a lasting peace. Now this, too, was to be snatched away. The ceasefire, declared by the IRA in August 1994, had never been a settled or a stable peace, more an uneasy truce which brought relief and a revival of economic fortune to the province, but which left the hard questions on the table. But for the ceasefire to become permanent it required underpinning through political settlement. Sinn Fein first met British officials that December, followed in May 1995 by government representatives, Michael Ancram and then Mayhew himself, in the improbable venue of a suite in Washington's Sheraton Hotel.

Throughout the rest of 1995, the IRA complained that the British government's insistence on prior decommissioning of arms before political talks was cynical or insincere because it knew that for the IRA to do so before any talks opened would be tantamount to surrender. They claimed the issue had been raised to delay all-party talks. They were also angered by London's refusal to release IRA prisoners early and to repatriate those held on mainland Britain to the province, by Lee Clegg's release in July.[80] The Unionists, meanwhile, inflamed feelings during the marching season in the summer, which provoked riots and further acts of violence. Unionist opinion in the North hardened when, as expected, Molyneaux stepped down as UUP leader in September to be replaced by the less amenable David Trimble.[81]

Major was anxious to see progress, but was held back by his awareness that he would need to keep the UUP and DUP on board if constitutional talks, after the publication of the Framework Document in February 1995, were to succeed in capturing the hearts and minds of the Unionist majority in the province. Without that support, any settlement would be valueless. He was further restrained by the right-wing element on the Cabinet's Northern Ireland committee, especially Cranborne and Howard. The right could all too easily point to the government's disappearing majority as the grounds for insisting on decommissioning, on taking a hardline view on IRA prisoners, and in general not doing anything to alienate the nine Unionist MPs.[82] Howard was especially firm about resisting Mayhew's efforts to introduce remission for IRA prisoners on equivalent terms to normal criminals.

To try to break the deadlock, the government discussed a fresh idea with the Irish government to launch what became known as a twin-track approach. The plan was for an international commission on decommissioning to be set up *at the same time* (hence 'twin-track') as ministers from both London and Dublin governments holding talks separately with all political parties to lay the foundations for future constitutional talks. The commission idea had been discussed between Major and Bruton at Cannes in June, and Chilcot of the Northern Ireland Office and Dalton of the Irish Department of Justice were charged to work up proposals. London's concern in part was that Dublin was coming under increasing pressure from Sinn Fein/IRA, causing divisions within the government between Spring, who was viewed as increasingly 'green', and Bruton, who was sticking more closely to the British government's cautious approach. Early signs were that Sinn Fein/IRA would go along with the commission proposal, until late August, when they attached certain conditions, including British arms to be decommissioned alongside those of the IRA, which were unacceptable to London.

Bruton nevertheless agreed on 1 September that an Anglo–Irish summit to discuss 'twin-track' should go ahead. The next day, however, a Saturday, two senior Irish officials were summoned to a secret meeting in Belfast with Adams and McGuinness and told that if the summit and the commission proposals went ahead on the lines proposed, then the IRA would return to violence, and that it would be on the conscience of the Irish government. London reacted strongly to Dublin being blackmailed in this way, and in meetings on 4 September Mayhew appeared to persuade Spring that the Anglo–Irish summit should still go ahead. But shortly after, on 6 September, the Irish government pulled out, with the lobbying of Hume, who carried great weight in the Republic being a decisive factor.[83]

By the autumn Major was becoming restless to see progress. He seized on a surprise initiative that came from Trimble in late September, saying he would be prepared to sit down in an elected assembly alongside Sinn Fein representatives, even without prior decommissioning.[84] Major discussed the proposal with Bruton on a walk in the hotel garden during the Majorca summit. If the proposal came from Trimble, a hardline Unionist, then he would be able to carry the Unionist community with him. Major prevailed on Bruton not to dismiss Trimble's proposal out of hand.[85] Paisley, even more resistant than Trimble, was also thinking creatively, and was working on ideas for an elected assembly.

But before anything could come from this uncustomary bout of Orange constitutional activism, London and Dublin again returned to the twin-track proposals.[86] Various drafts were exchanged in October and November.

The catalyst was a visit by Clinton to Britain and Ireland at the end of November, both governments being anxious to make an announcement before his arrival.[87] Throughout 1995, the White House had been reviewing its stance on Sinn Fein and the IRA, and had become much more sympathetic to the British government's position (similar to the way it had changed stance over Bosnia, the other long-standing point of difference).

Washington's change of heart on republicanism was a product of a number of convergent forces, not least irritation at Adams repeatedly failing to honour pledges, and Vice-President Gore, sympathetic to London's position, proving an increasingly influential voice in the debate. Admiral William Crowe, the new American Ambassador to London, also carried weight in Washington and was critical of the position of Sinn Fein and the IRA, while Hume came to be regarded by Washington with increasing coolness. London regularly fed the White House information on the IRA's continuing underground activities, including punishment beatings, while the Oklahoma bomb gave terrorism a different complexion for the Americans. Finally, Clinton's aides were briefed heavily that he would have to appear scrupulously fair to all factions in Northern Ireland if his November trip was to be successful, which he needed it to be with the election season already warming up in the US. He had, he was told, to do a lot more to convince the Unionists of his goodwill than the nationalist community.[88] By November, London was able to ask Washington to put pressure on Sinn Fein to accept their latest proposals.

Intensive discussions between London and Dublin reached a climax on 28 November, when at 7.30 p.m. Major and Bruton agreed a communiqué announcing the international commission.[89] Bruton told Major he would catch a plane immediately and fly straight over to London. At a hastily convened press conference at 11 p.m. that evening, he and an elated but tired Major (besides everything else, it was budget day) announced that a three-man international body would be set up to report on the decommissioning of arms. It would be chaired by former US Senator George Mitchell.[90] The other members, it was announced later, would be Harri Holkeri, former Prime Minister of Finland, and a Canadian general, John de Chastelain.[91] The commission was scheduled to report in mid-January. The press statement further announced that, if the commission found an acceptable way around the weapons impasse, 'they plan to start full-scale, all-party negotiations by the end of February.'[92]

Clinton's plane was already airborne by the time the press conference was over. The next morning he delivered a speech, much of which he had written himself, to members of both Houses in Parliament's Royal Gallery. Full of apt historical allusions, and personal reflections, it was well attuned to a British audience, not least when he said that the special relationship between Britain and America 'stands alone, unbroken, above all the rest'. Major and Bruton were praised for being prepared to 'take risks for peace'. Standing outside Number Ten, he said the twin-track initiative 'is the best opportunity I have seen to resolve all the issues and I think it should be embraced'.[93] The President held a two-hour talk at Downing Street with Major, and paid a courtesy call on the Queen. At a dinner that evening at Number Ten, Tony and Cherie Blair made their first much-photographed visit through the doors of the building. Clinton then flew to Belfast, Londonderry and Dublin, exuding a 'Kennedy-like charisma', in a tour which exceeded the hopes of even his most optimistic aides and which won him many new friends in Ireland – and among the US electorate.[94]

Four days before Christmas, Major himself went to Ireland to help keep all parties bound into the twin-track approach. Major was initially reluctant to go; he was exhausted, and believed that trips to Ireland to meet the public on both sides of the border tended to go wrong.[95] Nevertheless, 21 December found him in Paisley's North Antrim constituency, where he was warmly received, not least by the DUP leader and his wife.

Relations between Major and the leadership of both the Unionist parties had improved markedly since the low point when the Framework Document was published, and Major was taken aback by his welcome in the very heart of Orange country. His reception was no less positive in the predominantly nationalist town of Downpatrick, Co. Down. He announced that he looked forward to permanent peace in 1996. 'It is an opportunity which we have not had for many years, which may not readily reappear, and I will do all I can to carry it forward.'[96]

Later that day he flew to Dublin for talks and dinner with Bruton. They were due at a performance of Handel's *Messiah* at Dublin's National Concert Hall. Dinner overran, and the second half of the performance was held back. The audience knew that some VIPs were expected, but for security reasons did not know their identity. When they saw Major and Bruton appear on the balcony, the whole audience rose and applauded. Major was still talking about the warmth of the reception when he returned for the night to the British Ambassador's residence, and indeed for several days afterwards. He returned to Number Ten still elated, a mood that carried him through to Christmas and beyond, until brought down with a bump by more and particularly vexing domestic news.[97]

George Mitchell's three-man body published its report on 22 January. Its way out of the impasse was to say that decommissioning could take place in parallel with all-party constitutional talks, not as a prelude to it, as the British had argued, nor in the wake of it, as the IRA demanded. The report set out six principles which it recommended all engaged in negotiations should formally accept, including verifiable and total disarmament of all paramilitary organisations (but not the British army), renunciation of all use of force as a device to influence the political debate, and punishment beatings and killings to stop.[98]

Mitchell's group had worked intensively in the first three weeks of January, talking to all parties. Major himself, Number Ten and NIO officials all spoke to Mitchell during the consultation process, putting forward the British government's viewpoint, and trying to get them to write more into the report about all-party elections, which they argued was the way to help the Unionists accept the new talks process. Number Ten was given a copy of the report a couple of days before publication. It was broadly in line with what they expected. They were pleased by the six principles, though disappointed that it did not stipulate prior decommissioning, and that, on the insistence of Sinn Fein, the consent principle had not been stated explicitly: 'It was a big omission, very regrettable,' said one government source.[99]

The day before publication, Major had a telephone conversation with

Bruton, the content of which became a matter of dispute with the Taoiseach. Major mentioned – as the British records of the conversation show – that the British were keen on the all-party election idea which appeared fleetingly in the report. Bruton claimed subsequently that he had not been forewarned that Major would come out in public in favour of elections.[100]

Number Ten had to prepare their response to Mitchell swiftly. They knew they had to be seen to be reacting positively, and Major in the House on 22 January duly welcomed the report, thanked Mitchell and said the government accepted all of it. He said the British government obviously would have preferred to see a prior start to decommissioning, and if the IRA were serious about peace he did not see why it posed a problem, but he also seized on the minimal reference in the report to the elective process and pointed out that an alternative way forward also existed, via elections. His concern was to prevent the Unionists, who had talked about all-party elections in the autumn, dismissing the report and jeopardising the process.

The reaction in the nationalist and Republican communities, as in Dublin, was one of fury. It seemed to them that the British government had climbed onto the election idea as a way out of rejecting Mitchell's report outright. Bruton accused the British government of bad faith, while Hume, in the Commons, said Major was motivated not by a desire to see peace in Northern Ireland but by the hope of winning Trimble's nine votes to prolong the Tories' period in office. Major responded angrily: 'If I had been concerned about the short term electoral considerations on this issue, I would probably not have embarked on this process in the first place.'

The next two weeks saw a flurry of activity. Hume's SDLP were resistant to elections, believing the proposal yet another time-wasting device, and that if the strategy was adopted, the Unionists would want a new Stormont Parliament which had operated to the Nationalists' disadvantage until its suspension in 1972. Anxious to avoid a loss of momentum, Major became involved in talks with both Nationalists and Unionists, trying to persuade them to work together. The Irish government, meanwhile, set a deadline of the end of February for agreement on an acceptable way forward.[101]

Major was in his Huntingdon constituency on Friday 9 February when, shortly before 6 p.m., Number Ten received a message saying that RTE, the Irish broadcasting company, had been told by the IRA that the ceasefire was over. The codeword used was authentic. The White House phoned to say they had heard the same message via Adams, who appeared to be in a state of panic and surprise. Major's detectives were phoned. 'Had they heard the news?' 'No.' They immediately increased their surveillance of Major himself while everyone waited to see what would happen. Just before 7 p.m. the Metropolitan Police phoned Number Ten to say they had identified a lorry in Canary Wharf in London's docklands, but they did not know whether or not it was a cause of concern. Just after, a political journalist on the *Daily Mirror* phoned the Number Ten Press Office. 'Had they heard about the bomb?' The official tried to play it down; it was only a rumour so far. 'No it isn't', came the reply. 'It has just exploded.' The bomb was, indeed, in the lorry the police had identified, and it claimed two lives, maimed several more, and caused millions of pounds' worth of damage.[102]

Major felt a rush of emotion when he heard the news: shock, horror, anger and frustration. He was sufficiently realistic to know that the ceasefire might well break down at some point; intelligence reports had been keeping him abreast of the mounting impatience among the IRA's hardline activists, and their covert military operations. He knew that the likelihood of an early peace was remote, with the difficulties of reconciling all parties to any constitutional settlement. But he, no more than anyone else in London or Washington, had expected the ceasefire to break down as soon as it did.

Number Ten and the NIO spent a long time trying to discover why the IRA had detonated the bomb. Intelligence reports told them that Adams probably did not know exactly when the bomb was to have been detonated, and was surprised when it happened, although he was probably aware that an 'operation' was planned in the first part of 1996. According to an early theory the bomb had been the work of a rogue unit, acting unilaterally. This was rapidly ruled out. Next they mulled over whether it had been caused by the government's response on Mitchell, or to Major's subsequent rejection of Spring's proposal for Dayton-style 'proximity talks' involving all parties. It became apparent, however, that the planning for the bomb began the previous October or November, and that they wanted to hit the British where they knew from the success of earlier operations that it would hurt them most, in the financial centre of London.[103]

Brushing aside the idea that the whole peace initiative was naïve and doomed from the start, Major spoke on television, repeating his determination that 'peace does not have to be a dream', while in the Commons the following Monday he said: 'If we are pushed back, we will start again. If we are pushed back, we will start again. If we are pushed back a third time, we will start again.'[104] Three further small bombs, including one on 18 February, when a terrorist blew himself up on a bus near London's Aldwych, did not deter him. Major remained adamant that the peace process did not die at 7.01 p.m. on 9 February with the Canary Wharf bomb, but that peace was still a prize that could be grasped.[105]

New Year, New Thinking: January–February

As Major's weary lieutenants in Number Ten and Central Office took stock over Christmas they came to the conclusion that they had become derailed in the previous two months in part because not everyone was agreed where they were heading and which enemy they were attacking. An article by Michael Jones in the *Sunday Times* on the Party Conference had been a considerable influence in focusing the discussion. Jones noted the lack of consistency in ministerial speeches about Blair and New Labour, an ambivalence in the Party's thinking which had indeed been evident for over a year.[106] Some ministers said Blair had no policies, others that he had stolen Tory policies, and still others that while Blair was 'New Labour', the rest of his party were unreconstructed old Labour.[107]

Within the Party, the main creative input came from Norman Blackwell, Danny Finkelstein and Tim Collins, who decided that Labour had changed, that four election defeats and the collapse of Communism had convinced Labour that winning the general election must become their overriding objective, and hang ideological purity. As Finkelstein put it: 'Blair had a single-minded purpose, which was to get rid of the Tories. Luckily for him, it was a purpose that was not merely good for him politically but one the public shared. We had yet to show we were united behind any single-minded purpose, except vaguely to be re-elected, and it was not a purpose shared by the public.'[108]

Maurice Saatchi produced a proposal that New Labour spelled 'New Danger'. His idea was bolstered by the findings of Central Office polling which showed that Tory supporters thought Labour had indeed changed since the days of Kinnock and Smith. Saatchi argued that 'New' needed to sound risky and dangerous, rather than safe and exciting. Another core strand came at the prompting of Bell, who was convinced of the enduring power of an earlier Tory slogan used on posters in the 1959 general election, 'Life's better with the Conservatives. Don't let Labour ruin it.' It was decided to run with the 'New Labour' and 'Life's better' slogans, in place of the 'Millennium Challenge' and 'Enterprise Centre of Europe' strategies.

On Tuesday 23 January, at the Mayfair offices of Shandwick, Gummer's public relations firm, Saatchi, Bell and Gummer presented their preliminary conclusions to the senior Conservative planners. The strategy was to say initially that life is better under the Conservative government, and once that notion had been established and accepted, come in with a campaign saying, 'Don't let Labour ruin it', based on the 'new danger' approach. The ideas were greeted enthusiastically, and Major too expressed himself content with them. It seemed that the conjurors of the Thatcher election victories were producing more of the same magic.

Political Cabinet the next day had been planned initially for Chequers but, with Major heavily involved with the aftermath of the Mitchell report, transferred to the State Dining Room at Number Ten. The discussion opened with Mawhinney reporting on progress on 'Our Nation's Future', the consultation exercise. Finkelstein presented the line Cabinet should take on New Labour: that it had changed and now faced the country with new dangers, although he held over on that occasion from using the phrase 'New Labour, New Danger'. Blackwell, building on his presentations the previous year, spoke about the areas of Conservative strength on which the Party would be campaigning – the economy, education, law and order, welfare, the constitution – and those areas of weakness where Labour could be attacked, including inflation, mortgages, local government, tax, unions, the Social

Chapter and devolution. Discussion followed on the need to focus more exclusively on those core areas where the Conservatives were strong and Labour weak. Most Cabinet ministers were impressed by the proposals, and by the energy and imagination being put into strategy.[109]

In the final part of the session, Mawhinney and Charles Lewington discussed more effective public relations. Lewington had been in his job only a month, but was soon proving he had the full support of the Party's top brass even if some of his former colleagues in the lobby still queried whether he was sufficient of a heavyweight for the job in the run-up to the election. One sympathetic journalist nevertheless said that 'he transformed the relationship between Central Office and the press gallery. He was always around, dishing us out titbits. He had been a respected journalist, that helped. He looked and sounded a bit like a head waiter, but he is a subtle man.'[110]

In a follow-up meeting at Chequers on 26 January the Policy Unit updated Major on progress under the five themes for the manifesto. The consultation exercise was also reviewed: it was on course for reporting at the March Central Council, but under Mawhinney's pushing, and to Blackwell's regret, it was decided that Major should not himself host all of the planned Saturday meetings with Party activists. The aim had been to show a Party leadership actively listening, but the Party apparatchiks, responding to a criticism voiced by Simon Heffer and others the year before, decided the meetings could be portrayed as a vacuous leader desperately scraping the barrel for any new ideas. Accordingly, Heseltine and Mawhinney took over many of the assignments.[111]

In pursuit of Tim Bell's 'Life's better' strategy, a number of initiatives were launched by Central Office, including inviting those in the business community to sponsor a widely circulated document of quotations from around the world about Britain's glowing economic performance. But a newspaper, *Look!*, which gathered together good news stories associated with government policies, backfired when some in the media – dishonestly, Central Office asserted – claimed that pieces had been included without permission.[112]

Good and bad news stories had in fact been dominating the national headlines in equal measure since New Year. Major's New Year message to constituency chairmen opened, 'I have an overriding message for 1996; our country is now an outstanding success.'[113] It failed to swamp Emma Nicholson's surprise announcement on 29 December that she would be joining the Liberal Democrats. 'It hit us that Friday night. We had no advance intelligence,' said one Major aide. 'It knocked us badly after a good Christmas. Her reasons were, we thought, hugely thin.'[114]

Stung by accusations from Central Office that she had left due to 'ambitious careerism' as well as 'personal pique' at not receiving promotion in the July reshuffle, she responded that it was really that Major was 'relying increasingly on the worst, hard-faced, populist instincts of people'.[115] She was particularly affronted by his handling of Nolan. Major was seething at her defection, and was disinclined to think as well of her motivation as he had done with

Howarth.[116] But he kept his own counsel and avoided being involved in any slanging match, calling her instead a 'nice person' on his ritual early January interview on *Breakfast with Frost*.[117] Her defection directly to an opposition party reduced the Conservatives majority from six to four. Peter Thurnham, Tory MP for Bolton North East, caused added anxiety by announcing on 8 January that the government could no longer rely on his support in votes.[118]

Further bad news came with Lady Thatcher's Keith Joseph Memorial Lecture on 11 January. Although she had indicated to Number Ten that the speech would avoid undermining Major, she struck another blow against his authority.[119] In an apparently accidental response to Major's positive estimation of 'One Nation' values at the October Party Conference, she contemptuously dismissed Tory Europhiles as standing for 'No-Nation Conservatism'. The reason for the current unpopularity – a Gallup poll had just put Labour twenty-six points ahead – was because those aspiring to join the middle classes 'feel they no longer have the incentives and the opportunities they expect from a Conservative government'. Howard, Lilley and Portillo, and the exiled Redwood, were picked out for enthusiastic endorsement by the former leader. The only way forward, she said, was to adopt a fully right-wing, anti-federalist agenda.[120] Drafted by Robin Harris, the speech was designed to shake the Party into realising that only a shift right could save it from electoral disaster.[121] Two Cabinet ministers were in the audience, Forsyth and Portillo, and were shown on television rising to clap enthusiastically at the end.

Deep anger greeted the speech on the centre and left of the Party, as well as in Number Ten.[122] Thatcher's words came as a direct rebuff to Major's plea on television four days before that electoral recovery depended on unity, because 'The British electorate does not like parties that squabble with itself.'[123] The irony of Emma Nicholson defecting because the government had become far too right wing, and hearing Thatcher castigate it for not being nearly right wing enough, was no less real for being missed by most commentators. But it still further highlighted Major's trap. He was riled by the Thatcher speech, and by the way it ignited talk of leadership challenges, dormant for the previous six months. Again, photographs began to appear in the press of those considered the main successors: Portillo, Redwood, Heseltine, Clarke, Shephard and Dorrell. The consensus was that the Thatcher attack had 'undermined Major's authority' and depressed the morale of Tory MPs as they returned to Westminster after the Christmas recess. Very few, it was reported, believed they could win the general election.[124]

A new twist was given to the plotting stories, a so-called 'toffs' plot', which had Major being asked to step down if the local elections were bad to be replaced by a 'grandee-approved successor'.[125] Cranborne and Archie Hamilton were alleged to have been at the heart of it. Although both were disappointed by some of the government's pandering to the centre left, and some of their friends may have talked wildly about him having no grip, there is no evidence that a concerted plot was being hatched. Cranborne himself, the king of the 'toffs', was no Stauffenberg: 'A figment of some lobby journalist's imagination. If there were toffs plotting, I was not one of them.'[126]

Major, as so often happened, climbed his way back from the setbacks and came up fighting. The turning point was Harriet Harman's decision, made public on 21 January, to send her son to a Kent grammar school, St Olave's, a decision Blair, to the anger of many in his party, supported. At Prime Minister's Questions on 23 January, the following exchange took place:

Major:	Perhaps I may offer my sympathies to the Rt Hon. Gentleman on his current predicament?
Blair:	I thank the Prime Minister for his kind words of concern over pressure. The difference between us is that I will not buckle under it.
Madam Speaker:	Order! Let us have order on both sides of the House.
Major:	The Rt Hon. Gentleman should not be so sensitive about his difficulties. I just want to be tough on hypocrisy and tough on the causes of hypocrisy.[127]

His last sentence was a mocking reference to Blair's celebrated phrase about being 'tough on crime and tough on the causes of crime'. It was Major's best performance in the House since his cracks during the leadership contest about Redwood's resignation and Portillo's debt to telephone privatisation. It delighted his MPs who bellowed out 'more, more, more' as he left the chamber.

The newly assertive Major was evident in an upbeat interview in that weekend's *Sunday Telegraph*, in which he employed much of the language and argument heard in the Political Cabinet on Wednesday 24 January. The interview concluded, 'I like elections, and clearly we are within fifteen months of an election, so I am beginning to sniff the wind and feeling much happier about it.'[128] Major announced that his long-term aim was to see public spending cut to 35 per cent of national income, while in a stinging Conservative Political Centre speech on 29 January he said that Labour at last was revealing its true colours, 'And the colour they reveal is not soft focus blue. It's the colour of envy and hypocrisy.'[129]

A further boost came on 1 February when the 1922 Committee executive announced there could be no further leadership election before the general election.[130] Hugo Young found that Cabinet enemies were beginning to realise that Major had started to take control of his destiny as well as theirs.[131] One *Telegraph* journalist complained: 'It made things very difficult. The change of heart in some of the rebels was tangible. One could usually rely on someone like Bernard Jenkin for an on- or off-the-record mischievous comment. Not at that time.'[132]

Against this favourable background, the long-awaited Scott Report was finally published on 15 February. Three years had passed since Major set up the inquiry in the wake of the collapse of the trial against directors of Matrix Churchill for breaches of export controls in shipping machine tools to Iraq.

Leaks of the report in the early summer of 1995 had destabilised the government, and few expected it to survive unscathed when the full report was published. Five volumes long, and over 1,800 pages, it lacked any summary, which Richard Scott thought would only distort the truth the report sought to convey.[133] In brief, though, the report found that the policy of selling arms to Iraq had tilted and that an adequate account of this change was not given; and that the Matrix Churchill prosecution should not have been brought. The report did, however, absolve ministers of some of the more extreme allegations current in 1992, did not denounce Major, and said that ministers had not been engaged in a conspiracy to jail the defendants.[134]

Major, who had set up the inquiry in good faith, had become progressively disillusioned as the months wore on, and at the way, hydra-like, Scott went about his work. It absorbed a huge amount of ministerial and senior officials' time, and brought upon Major's head not approbation at his commitment to open government, but opprobrium, from right-wing press and politicians, for letting it be established with such a wide-open brief.[135]

Major's irritation turned to anger when he saw the way that the report, as trailed in the press, was being used as a platform to attack the iniquities of government, especially his own Conservative government. Cynicism about Scott indeed pervaded Number Ten and some of the upper echelons of the Civil Service. In a widely held view Scott was naïve, and had little understanding of the pressure on ministers and officials in their daily lives.[136] Some regretted a more weighty figure had not been appointed, like Lord Franks, who had chaired the inquiry into the Falklands War, and who had had first-hand experience of the way that government was run. Some of the more partisan figures in Central Office thought that Scott was deliberately setting himself up as the person to bring down the Major government.[137]

Months before publication Major decided that neither of the two principal figures highlighted in the leak, William Waldegrave and Attorney-General Nicholas Lyell, had committed any offence worthy of resignation.[138] The issue then became one of warding off Labour's attack and of damage limitation. One Number Ten source summed up the approach. 'The Prime Minister had decided some time before that, while there might have been the odd mistake made, he believed that Lyell and Waldegrave had acted with integrity, and that he was going to give them his backing. There was no doubt about the objective. It was to win the vote.'[139] Another put it even more baldly. 'Scott? Simple. It was just arithmetic.'[140]

Number Ten received an advance copy of the report on 7 February, although Major's own weekend reading was severely disrupted by the Canary Wharf bomb. Lang, as President of the Board of Trade, was asked with David Willetts, a whip recruited for his intellectual and debating skills, to 'cherry-pick from the syrup of ambiguity that was Scott's prose' the lines of defence against probable Labour attacks.[141] They were helped by Scott's avoidance, in the final report, of the words 'misleading Parliament' which would have been fatal. To Labour's anger, Robin Cook, Shadow Foreign

Secretary and leading for the Opposition, was given scarcely three hours in a solitary room to preview the massive report and to prepare his attack. The Cabinet did not trust Labour not to leak it; a sign of how bad relations had become. The squabble created an undignified atmosphere for the opening of the debate, and an impression of unfair government use of power.[142] Blair considered it a government blunder.[143]

When Lang opened for the government in the House on 15 February, it quickly became clear that there were to be no resignations or apology and that the government would be brazening it out. Attacking those who had been making 'reckless and malicious' charges, there had been he said 'no conspiracy . . . no cover-up'.

This was true, but it overlooked the concerns expressed in the report about ministers misleading Parliament, and the government failing to stop an unfair prosecution.[144] Lang came under attack from even normally sympathetic or neutral commentators in the press. Riddell responded that 'the more time people had to read the report, the more partial the version presented by Ian Lang looked',[145] while Philip Stephens found Lang's reading of the report was imbued with 'half-truths'.[146] Blair responded on 20 February by saying that if no minister took responsibility for Scott's criticism, the Tories would remain 'knee deep in dishonour', a phrase that encapsulated for many a growing perception of the Tory Party.[147] It was clear that Scott's hope of the report being taken on its merits was woefully innocent, and that it would be used as a football by two sides, one desperate to score goals, the other determined to kick the ball not just into touch, but preferably out of the ground.

A motley collection of Tory MPs, including Euro-rebels Teddy Taylor, Richard Shepherd and Christopher Gill, and the maverick MP Rupert Allason, but also loyalists Quentin Davies and John Marshall, voiced concerns about the government's defence on Scott. Peter Thurnham, who had indicated his unhappiness with remaining a Tory MP in January, now resigned the whip on 22 February. His decision 'hugely disappointed' Major, who had spent two hours talking to him and his wife, and who had left him with the impression that they would spend the week thinking over his decisions. Within hours, he had left the Party.[148] As with Nicholson, ministers dismissed his action as 'personal pique'.

The full debate was scheduled for Monday 26 February. Lang, opening again for the government, came across notably more emollient, while Cook gave an excoriating performance. Much uncertainty hung over the intentions of the Unionist MPs. Paisley's DUP decided to abstain, while Trimble and his UUP decided to vote with Labour, despite a last-minute appeal from Major and Mayhew. After a weekend of anxiety, Taylor, Marshall and Gill opted to return to the government side, while Shepherd was adamant he would not, and with Thurnham's departure reducing the majority to three, there was no margin for error left.

The outcome of the vote was uncertain until the closing stages of the

Commons debate. Trimble offered Major a deal an hour before the vote but it was turned down flatly. Whichever way the vote went, Major was determined to hang on to Lyell and Waldegrave, and his contingency plan if the government was defeated was to call an immediate confidence vote. If this was won, the ministers would stay on; if it was lost, a general election would result.[149] Such tactics proved unnecessary; Allason, after claiming he had extracted a concession on Public Interest Immunity certificates, sided with the government with only minutes to spare. The vote was won by 320 to 319.[150]

The government had survived, and within a day or two moved on to different matters. Important issues raised by the Scott Report were largely mothballed. The executive had responded defensively, the judiciary had been other-worldly while the adversarial system in the legislature had seen party political considerations triumph over the search for objective truth and concern for the functioning, and the perception, of public life. Scott was not a glorious episode in recent British history.

There was a cost in the government's response on Scott, as there had been with the side-step over Nolan. The public impression, albeit shaped by a partisan press, was of a government which would not accept responsibility for its errors, and of a Prime Minister unwilling to bring erring ministers to book. Again, any credit and goodwill he gained for the establishment of the inquiry was swept away in a torrent of critical judgement.[151]

There can be no doubting that Major believed it would have been unjust to dismiss his two ministers, least of all to satisfy the media's and public's desire for blood. Private morality therefore dictated that Lyell and Waldegrave remained in office. Public morality, and the regard in which politicians were held, however, dictated that with public expectations aroused as they were, some heads should roll, either through suicide or execution. In the longer run, it was not government, but the Government, which lost out more. In saying that, it is difficult to assert with confidence that another government in the same circumstances would have behaved differently. The government was in a box. And it was one which was about to become even more constrictive.

THIRTY-SIX

Mad Cows and a New Party:

March–June 1996

Squaring the Circle: March 1996

NOT FOR THE first time did Major, with domestic politics perilously poised, have to wrench himself away. He always grumbled about long overseas journeys, especially when they fell in the middle of a busy parliamentary session, but in spring 1996 there was no alternative: he had to go to the Far East. He had not visited Hong Kong since September 1991; he wanted to show the people of the colony how seriously the government was taking the handover to the Communist regime in China on 30 June 1997, and this might be the last opportunity for a British Prime Minister to do so. The FCO and DTI had exerted pressure on Number Ten for a visit to Korea, where he had never before been. The country was an important export market and over half of Korean investment into the EU was in Britain. But the centrepiece of the trip, and the first port of call, was Thailand for the Asia–Europe trade conference in Bangkok.[1]

This summit, the first of its kind, may have produced little of substance, but it reminded Major of the immense challenge of competition from South-East Asia. There were also opportunities for him to have useful bilaterals, notably with Li Peng, the Chinese Prime Minister, about Hong Kong. With his Commonwealth links and personal relationships, he was more at ease and on terms with Asian leaders than other European heads of government. While they held back diffidently, Major was in the midst of the sea of faces, drawing dividend from his years of courting foreign leaders. He travelled out with the aim of suggesting London as the location for the second Asia–Europe summit, an offer which was readily accepted.[2]

Major enjoyed the Hong Kong leg of the trip the most, not least because he stayed with Chris and Lavender Patten. He was determined to do what he could to defuse the antipathy building up in some quarters over the way that Britain would be leaving in fifteen months without stronger guarantees under Chinese rule. Britain had no choice on the handover, he said, but 'the United Kingdom will be with you in the future as in the past ... you will not face the future alone'.[3] The sincerity of his message made a good impression on the Legislative Council and others, and he was able to announce changes on immigration of holders of Hong Kong passports into the UK which went down well, and to relay that he had spoken firmly to Li Peng in Bangkok about the need to maintain confidence in Hong Kong.[4]

There could be no disguising, however, that British policy towards Hong Kong, for better or worse, was not primarily Major's but Patten's. Major and Hurd had declared that Patten had in effect *carte blanche* to determine British policy, and the FCO was to do as he instructed. Patten duly developed his strongly independent course of action over the summer of 1992 without significant input from London. Cabinet committee oversight over Hong Kong policy, as had existed in the 1980s, also ceased, with a key OPD meeting in September 1992 to debate Patten's controversial line abandoned. Many in the FCO thought it was quite wrong, 'that policy was being made on such a sensitive and important subject purely by the Governor and his advisors on the spot.'[5] While Douglas Hurd endorsed the line, while others like Geoffrey Howe and Percy Cradock made their reservations clear, Patten's policies of exploiting gaps in Sino–British agreements to extend the franchise won considerable sympathy in Britain and were championed in a sympathetic biography by Jonathan Dimbleby (1997). However, the foreign policy establishment feared that by acting unilaterally, the reforms would be reversed after June 1997 and thus against the long-term interests of Hong Kong.[6]

These tensions lay mostly beyond the media's gaze. The press, restless on a trip devoid of much surface political excitement, made much of a response by Patten that he could 'certainly' see circumstances in which he could return to British domestic politics. Coupled with a Gallup poll showing that Labour's lead was widening again as the Harriet Harman affair subsided, and renewed expectations that the Conservatives would lose and Major depart as leader, it sparked off a flurry of articles about contenders waiting in the wings, now with the added glamour of a late-runner from the Orient. According to Ladbroke's the favourite was Heseltine at 7–2, then Portillo and Redwood at 6–1, Clarke at 10–1 and Hague at 12–1, Patten still being too new to merit a ranking.[7] The media played up Major anointing his favoured successor in an interview on the way home. Neither man, however, seriously envisaged a straight succession, not least because of the difficulty of Patten winning a by-election – the transfer of power in Hong Kong falling two months after the last possible date for the British general election.[8]

Events were moving swiftly while he had been away. The IRA followed up Major's and Bruton's announcement of all-party talks on Northern Ireland by declaring that they would not reinstate the ceasefire. Lord Chief Justice Taylor made a harsh attack on Howard's changes to sentencing rules, while the multimillionaire financier James Goldsmith threatened pro-European Tory MPs and Tory marginal constituencies with his new Referendum Party's candidates.[9]

The tide was moving powerfully anti-Europe. Coupled with the increasingly hostile editorial line in *The Times*, the *Daily Telegraph*, the *Sun*, and the *Daily Mail*, all newspapers that needed to be won back over before the general election, and the growing conviction among Tory MPs and Central Office that a more Eurosceptical stance could consolidate the Conservative electoral base, Number Ten came under renewed pressure to move in a sceptical direction. With Europhile and Majorite intellectuals thin on the ground, the overwhelming proportion of Tory commentators and opinion-formers by 1996 were deeply Eurosceptic, including economists Alan Walters and Patrick Minford, political scientists Ken Minogue and Bill Letwin, historians Norman Stone and Andrew Roberts, commentators William Rees-Mogg and Christopher Booker, and disillusioned former insiders like Bernard Connolly, whose powerful anti-federalist tract *The Rotten Heart of Europe* (1995) won many admirers but lost him his job as an EU official. It all imparted a spicy atmosphere for a crucial Cabinet on Thursday 7 March.

The main item on the agenda in Cabinet was discussion of Rifkind's White Paper on the government's position for the IGC. This fifteen-month conference to reform the EU's institutions and revise the Maastricht Treaty would be formally opened at a Turin summit three weeks hence. But the very decision to produce a White Paper had caused some disagreement. Clarke, at the head of the Europhiles, had tried but failed to block the publication of the government's position.[10] Number Ten and Rifkind disagreed, believing such a statement would 'tell a good story and differentiate the government's view from Labour'.[11] Despite forecasts of infighting, discussions in the Cabinet Committee OPD(E), chaired first by Hurd and now by Rifkind, on the White Paper had proved surprisingly good-humoured. At one OPE(E) meeting Gummer raised the problem of sewage pollution from Holland washing up in East Anglia: 'Yes, we must stop the shit hitting the fens', chimed in Lang. Differences which had threatened to become serious with Howard, Lilley and Redwood, arguing early after the committee began its deliberations in February 1995 for a repatriation of policy areas, and Clarke, who argued against enlargement on ground of cost, had been cleared up by the summer of 1995, with all parties agreeing to accept only minimal modification to the Maastricht arrangements.[12]

Rifkind's committee circumvented prolonged argument in Cabinet; it was made clear that the proposals for the White Paper were not to be altered significantly. The committee concluded that the pillared structure for the EU established at Maastricht should be retained, with foreign affairs and justice remaining a matter for intergovernmental cooperation. The European Parliament should not be given any fresh powers, nor was majority voting in the Council to be extended, while the Common Fisheries Policy was to be reformed to curb 'quota hopping'.

It was far from a Europhile agenda, and the committee knew that the programme would lead to battles with EU partners, but they also realised that the IGC discussions would extend beyond the general election to the Amsterdam Council in June 1997, and that the adoption of a position which resisted further moves to federalism could embarrass Labour – if victorious – as the party of Brussels.[13]

Disagreement in Cabinet on 7 March did not come over the substance of the Rifkind committee proposals, but on a subject which was not the concern of the White Paper, the single currency. As the decision on the currency had already been taken at Maastricht, it was not officially to be part of the 1996–7 IGC discussions. Hence the omission of this most sensitive of issues from the committee's proposals. Major, however, had been making his reservations increasingly clear, and had been trying for some months to deter his European partners from any rush forward in 1999. At various meetings he explained his doubts about the practicalities of a single currency, and tried to deter his fellow leaders also from moving rapidly to further political union.[14] None of his actions, however, was sufficient to placate the increasingly insistent anti-federalist, particularly anti-single currency, ardour in his party.

Major's mind turned again to consider an idea that he had discussed with Hurd in 1994, namely to announce that the government would hold a referendum before deciding whether Britain would join the single currency. Major had asked Hurd in confidence to test the water among Cabinet ministers to see if they would buy this idea, but Hurd advised him that, with opponents ranging from Clarke to Portillo, it would not acquire the necessary support.[15] The idea resurfaced during and after the Madrid summit in December 1995, though again was dropped after Clarke made plain his outright opposition. Mawhinney returned to the subject in the New Year, arguing that Goldsmith's Referendum Party could cost the Tories up to twenty seats in the general election. Other key figures in Central Office, like Finkelstein and Lewington, thought similarly. Offering a referendum would cut the ground from under Goldsmith's party, and outflank Labour which, Major was warned, might even pre-empt the Tories by offering one first itself.[16] The Tory press, moreover, could be won back. Within Cabinet, the Eurosceptics like Howard, Forsyth and Lilley (but not Portillo) had long supported a referendum, and were joined by those in the middle like Newton and Shephard. Blackwell and many in the Policy Unit thought similarly. The balance in favour was overwhelming.

Major began to think it should be driven through against those who opposed it. He also worried about the government in Britain falling out of step with the electorate on the Europe issue, as he saw happening in France and Germany.[17] The referendum would be the way to ensure the electorate 'felt connected'. There remained, however, the principal stumbling block: the Chancellor. Major raised it at a bilateral meeting with him, but he made it plain that he would still not accept it. Some extra leverage would be needed to budge him. But what? The way out of the impasse came from an unlikely source. Douglas Hogg, much to Major's surprise, stepped in and brought up the matter at the 7 March Cabinet meeting. Surely, Hogg asked, the single currency should be considered also in their discussion of the White Paper?[18] Clarke tried to prevent such a discussion but Major persisted, and invited ministers to make contributions. A referendum was mentioned, to Clarke's discomfort. He repeated the arguments he had put when Hurd and Major had raised it earlier, that referendums were dangerous politically, and subversive to the constitution in a representative democracy. Heseltine, too, raised reservations, but the balance among Cabinet was overwhelmingly that a referendum would be a pragmatic and politically expedient way forward. Major summed up: he made his sympathy for a referendum clear, but to avoid the risk of Clarke being overruled in Cabinet, he asked Rifkind to prepare a paper for further discussion examining the arguments on either side.[19]

That afternoon in the House, to ensure that he put the matter on the record before it leaked, in response to a planted question from Marcus Fox, Major replied: 'I have made clear to the House on previous occasions that I believe a referendum on a single currency could be a necessary step ... At present, the government are considering the circumstances in which a referendum might or might not be appropriate.'[20] The government's intention was now in the public domain.

Clarke fumed and his mood never fully recovered from the way he considered he had been bounced on the referendum. If he could see the dilemma that Major was in, and the pressing need to reconcile wings of the Party, he never acknowledged it. For him, the issue was not one of Party management; it was one of principle (as indeed it was to the Eurosceptics). Clarke's concern was that Major's instinct was always to reach a fresh compromise with the sceptics, who then would only push for more. 'If you give half an inch to those characters, they'll end up taking a foot,' he was heard to say.[21] When he felt at his most angry over the issue, he let an aide speak to a newspaper editor about his closeness to resigning.[22]

The Eurosceptics wanted nothing more than for Clarke to resign. Number Ten doubted how serious he was about quitting over the referendum, but accepted he was very unhappy.[23] The White Paper, *Partnership of Nations*, was duly launched on 12 March by Rifkind, its principal begetter. The question about the single currency referendum, however, remained open.

The issue was not finally resolved until early April, after Clarke's return from southern Africa. Major, too, had an overseas trip, to Sharm el Sheikh in Egypt, for a summit on terrorism arranged at short notice for Wednesday 13 March. The catalyst had been two bus bombs in Israel, and the Egyptian and Kuwaiti governments had agreed to participate in the conference, which was symbolically important, not least for the Israelis and Arab states sitting down together. Major was at the summit when a message came through from Number Ten.[24] It spoke of a terrible tragedy that had occurred in Scotland at Dunblane Primary School where a psychopath, Thomas Hamilton, had killed sixteen children and their teacher Gwen Mayor, wounding many more.

As prime minister Major did not normally visit the scene of a tragedy: to do so could risk the charge of exploiting a public sorrow for political ends, as well as, conversely, raising expectations that prime ministers would turn up personally at every disaster. Dunblane was different: the scale of the tragedy, the fact the victims were children and helpless before the evil of an armed murderer. The Prime Minister, moreover, had been due to undertake political engagements in Scotland on Friday 15 March. Michael Forsyth (Dunblane's constituency MP) and George Robertson, the Labour Shadow Scottish Secretary (a Dunblane resident), were both in favour of the Prime Minister visiting the school, and Blair too. Major was initially hesitant about them going together, but changed his mind and after Question Time on 14 March it was agreed. They flew up on Friday morning on the most harrowing visit of his premiership. Norma came too.

With Forsyth and Robertson, they visited Stirling Royal Infirmary to talk to staff and some of the wounded children, as well as meeting police and members of the emergency services who had been involved. But it was the visit to the school that shocked them all the most, especially the gymnasium where the deaths had occurred, and which still bore all the human marks from the tragedy. They could not withhold their emotion as they heard exactly what had happened, and met teachers and parents.[25] Major's call for a minute's silence at 9.30 a.m. on Mothering Sunday two days later touched a chord in a nation deeply shocked by the events.[26] On 14 March Lord Cullen was appointed to head an inquiry into the question of school security, and on 21 March an amnesty was announced on the possession of illegal guns.

In domestic politics, the single currency referendum remained the most pressing issue. Clarke, joined by Heseltine, had several meetings with Major, culminating in long discussions in Downing Street on Wednesday 3 April. The picture that leaked was that Major was using Heseltine as an intermediary to persuade Clarke. It was 'a light fiction' that Number Ten did not discourage. The truth was that Major also had to work hard to convince Heseltine of the referendum's need.[27] After the 7 March Cabinet, it had become obvious to Clarke that he had lost the argument, but he wanted to ensure that he minimised the referendum's scale. He extracted two concessions: the referendum offer would apply only to the life of the next Parliament if the Tories won, and thus would not bind the Party beyond the subsequent election likely to be in 2001 or 2002, and that no further concessions after this one were to be made to the sceptics. It was, he thought, 'a done deal'.[28]

With Clarke's compliance in the bag, Cabinet met on 4 April, when they agreed to release a statement that 'Because we will be keeping [the Maastricht single currency opt-out option] open at the next general election, we have decided to make a commitment in our manifesto that, if the government decided to join a single currency during the course of the next parliament, that decision would be subject to confirmation in a referendum.'[29] In any normal Cabinet this agreement would have been sufficient to hold ministers together, above all with a general election only a year away to focus minds and deter dissent. There were, indeed, high hopes that the agreement would stick. Major had always clung to the belief that there existed a magic formulation on Europe that would allow all sides of the party to unite around.[30] Perhaps he had now found it.

Discussions over Europe since the leadership election had seen Cabinet crystallise into three clear groupings. On the Eurosceptic side was the solid core of six – Howard, Lilley, Cranborne, Portillo, Forsyth and Hague – and a further four who were less 'whole hog' or were emerging sceptics: Dorrell, Shephard, Waldegrave and Mawhinney (although as Party Chairman the latter tended to keep quiet on Europe and lean towards the next group, despite the scepticism at Central Office). In this middle group, the 'Prime Minister's party', were those who, regardless of what they thought on Europe, were first and foremost loyalists. They included Major himself, Lang, Mackay, Newton, Bottomley, Mayhew, Freeman, Hogg (who could be helpful to the sceptics) and Rifkind, although as Foreign Secretary he was always tugged by the FCO in the direction of the third group, the Europhiles, led by Clarke with Heseltine a powerful if increasingly conciliatory second, and consisting also of Gummer and Young. Although there was always movement, as a rule of thumb it meant Cabinet had six 'whole hog' Eurosceptics and four confirmed Europhiles, with the ratio of sceptics to pragmatists and Europhiles at 10:12. In the referendum discussion on 4 April, however, the overwhelming majority of the 'Prime Minister's party' backed the idea of a referendum, leaving only a handful of opponents.

At a press conference at Central Office, outlining the Cabinet's agreement on the referendum, Rifkind went out of his way to reassure the Europhiles: 'The government made quite clear some considerable time ago that we are not going to rule out the possibility of joining a single currency in the next Parliament.'[31]

When the Cows Come Home: March–April

Momentum for the general election planning was to be provided by a Political Cabinet, scheduled for the morning of Wednesday 20 March in the State Dining Room, and a keynote speech by Major that afternoon. In the event, the Political Cabinet was switched downstairs to the Cabinet Room, and less than an hour was devoted to Party political matters, with Mawhinney making a brief statement on the imminent local election campaign and giving an update on communication strategy. The hopes for a full morning on Party strategy had to be abandoned because two days earlier a far more pressing issue had come to the fore.[32] Not for the first time did long-term planning suffer at the hands of crisis management.

On 18 March a fateful memo had been written jointly by Douglas Hogg and Stephen Dorrell, who as Health and Agriculture Ministers were the two Cabinet members most directly involved. It stated that the government's Spongiform Encephalopathy Advisory Committee (SEAC) was shortly to pronounce on new evidence about a link between the spread of BSE among the nation's beef herd and ten new cases of Creutzfeldt-Jakob brain disease (CJD) in humans. The problem of BSE had arisen some years earlier, but had not been dealt with satisfactorily by government in the late 1980s, and several countries, including the USA, had long refused to import British beef.[33]

The fear was that there was a causal connection between BSE and CJD. Major was chatting to Mawhinney in the Cabinet Room after a Monday lunchtime meeting with the business managers, when Heseltine and Alex Allan came in and presented him with the Hogg–Dorrell BSE memorandum.

Major sensed at once that this was a serious issue – how serious no one knew – and a hurried meeting on the implications took place, attended by Major, Heseltine, Mawhinney, Blackwell, and staff from the Number Ten Private Office.[34] The group was uncertain how sweeping SEACs recommendations about the BSE-CJD link would prove, which could range from removing offal from the food chain to killing every cow in Britain, at a cost of many billions of pounds and thousands of jobs.[35] It was decided to break up and to reconvene the next day, 19 March, when they had more information. Officials and scientists from the Agriculture and Health departments met long into the night that Monday and again on Tuesday to consider the correct response. As one member of SEAC put it, 'If you're faced, as I was on Tuesday, with the consequences of your decision meaning the possible destruction of the national herd, mass panic of people being scared half to death, you are determined to get it as right as you can.'[36]

Dorrell and Hogg reported on the expert conclusions to Major and his advisers on the Tuesday. Professor John Pattison, the government's chief adviser on BSE, was questioned intensively by them: was he certain about the link between BSE and CJD? As the number of CJD victims was not rising, might the scientists on SEAC be overreacting? Some ministers, including Mawhinney, questioned whether going public would be the right action at this stage.[37] Mawhinney, the only scientist in the Cabinet, felt a premature public announcement could be a grave error. But the decision was taken, not least on Heseltine's and Waldegrave's urgings, to make an early announcement.[38]

A leak in the *Daily Mirror* on Wednesday 20 March about the links between CJD and BSE added to an atmosphere of panic, with a statement to be made that afternoon in the House already planned.[39] At Political Cabinet that morning, ministers favoured a reasonable, science-based approach, which was the tone duly adopted by Dorrell in his statement. The morning meeting was attended also by Pattison and by Kenneth Calman, the government's Chief Medical Officer, who took Cabinet ministers through the scientific evidence. Ministers raised three particular questions: might families of victims sue? Were children especially vulnerable? What should ministers say about their own beef-eating?[40] The afternoon announcement – that cases of CJD might be linked to the eating of beef before the introduction of the specified bovine offal ban in 1989 – caused an immediate public panic, of a scale which had not been fully anticipated.

It was precisely the type of issue Major had been so anxious to avoid. He quickly made himself a master of the mass of technical detail, but the BSE crisis, as it was to be known, was to distract him and Number Ten for a vital three-month period, and before it was over to inflict lasting damage to the government's credibility at home and abroad.

In the midst of the crisis, Clarke bemoaned the government's predicament: 'Why the bloody hell we should suddenly get a scientists' report on mad cows coming out of the wide blue yonder right now just has to be put down to incredibly bad luck, of a quite extraordinary kind.'[41] However hard the government tried to assure consumers that the measures taken to eradicate BSE after 1989 meant that beef on sale in shops was now safe, alarm spread. Within days, the lack of trust in the government's statements, and general hysteria, manifested itself in a widespread domestic boycott of British beef, not least by schools and restaurants (including the McDonald's burger chain). Worse, on 25 March, following the example of the French the day after the parliamentary statement, the import of British beef and bovine by-products (including gelatine, semen and tallow) was banned by a committee of the European Commission, not just into EU countries but worldwide. The impact on the Tories, the party of agriculture, was devastating. The possible economic and health consequences were Number Ten's most urgent concerns, but the impact on the electorate's confidence in the government could not be ignored.[42]

Major was determined not to be thrown off-balance. Putting a brave face on events, he delivered the Social Market Foundation lecture after Wednesday's Commons statement. His focus on education and opportunity, the third lecture on the 'five themes', was aimed to display the government's evolving thinking in an area of key policy difference to Labour. There should be, he announced, greater selection and choice for parents, and he outlined his aim of moving towards a grammar school in every town.[43] But if his party, and the media, were convinced by his vision for the future of Britain, or his calls for unity behind his lead, they showed little sign. The government's policy on the future of the EU was what many cared more about. Thus, when Rifkind discussed his White Paper on the IGC in the House the next day, 21 March, he was, said *The Times*, 'mauled by many of his back-benchers'.[44] It emerged that Bill Cash had set up an 'IGC Monitoring Group', whose aim was 'to coordinate sceptic attempts to stiffen Major's backbone in the IGC bargaining'.[45]

The following week, on Monday 25 March, right-wingers staged a Commons rebellion on Mackay's Divorce Bill. Major had wanted it included in the legislative programme because he believed the Bill would help families and work for the benefit of children.[46] The right saw the Bill as an attack on family values. Some of them had little time for Mackay's judgement, blaming him for suggesting both Nolan's and Scott's names to chair their respective and detested inquiries.[47]

The irritation Major felt towards his right wing was sublimated during the week as he concentrated on the beef crisis, and in preparing for two important conferences, one foreign, one domestic, at its conclusion. The government machine had still not found the best way to manage the beef issue, whose scale and possibly far-reaching implications were only beginning to sink in across Whitehall. Major began by chairing meetings in Number Ten to which came all relevant ministers and senior officials until they rapidly became so unwieldy that he delegated the central coordination of the government's response to Newton. He set up a reconstituted committee, which in turn became too large and unfocused.[48]

Number Ten sources say it was the most difficult single issue to have occurred during Major's premiership and they accept that the central machine did not organise itself sufficiently quickly or efficiently to give him the support he needed.[49] Certainly, the tentative government response and shifting policy pronouncements suggested a lack of firm control at the centre. The beef crisis was the main item at Cabinet on 28 March. Ministers ranged over how public confidence could be restored. Several expressed anger at the way that 'mad cow' hysteria had been whipped up by the media, opposition parties and EU governments. A ban on the sale of beef from high-risk cattle was agreed as a step to regain trust in the industry.[50] Major grew particularly irritated with the performance of the Agriculture Ministry during the crisis, and had difficulty at times in preserving a calm façade for meetings with its officials. In private, he did not rate Douglas Hogg's performance highly, while acknowledging he had a very difficult hand to play.[51]

Later that day, Major flew to Turin for the summit to open the IGC. Proceedings, as far as the British were concerned, were inevitably overshadowed by the crisis. The European Commission, which had been in the lead in the worldwide ban on British beef exports, had felt angry that they had received no prior warning before Dorrell's parliamentary announcement. Although they were not informed because the British government feared a leak, it was still an error.[52] There was further irritation among EU leaders that the launch of the IGC process should have been hijacked by another British-led upset. But their frustration was mostly sublimated, and they determined to mend fences, giving Major unexpectedly warm support at the conference. They promised him substantial financial help for a range of measures, including the destruction of thousands of older cattle. Jacques Santer expressed his hopes that the Commission's veterinary committee would lift the ban once measures acceptable to the EU had been agreed.[53] Major was grateful for these responses, but they did not stop him venting his displeasure at the ban for creating a 'crisis of confidence' in the entire European beef industry, as well as for helping create an atmosphere of 'collective hysteria'.[54] On the main IGC issues before them he also made it plain to his partners that he would stand firm against any federalist moves, such as limiting the use of the national veto, that would deepen integration.[55]

Satisfied that he had done enough to promote the likelihood of lifting the ban, he left Turin for the party's Central Council in Harrogate on Saturday 30 March. Long heralded as the forum for announcing the response to 'Our

Nation's Future', the Party's consultation exercise, Major found himself too exhausted to spark. He delivered a speech which was notable more for its 'anti-Brussels' rhetoric than for being a pre-election rallying cry or distillation of Party thinking. The year-long consultation exercise, by arousing considerable interest in the constituencies, had confounded its critics.[56] The results, not least in their hostility to a single currency and their indifference to greater choice in education, were not always what the leadership wanted.[57] Nevertheless, the rank and file had been given a chance to speak and to reconnect with the Party at the centre. Rather than exploiting the mass consultation, for a variety of reasons – the beef crisis, new personnel at Central Office who had not initiated the exercise and never felt wedded to it, and Number Ten losing some confidence in it – the potential of the initiative was squandered. What was billed initially as the most extensive consultation in the Party's history finished as little more than a public relations exercise, with only a few proposals, such as on tax relief, finding their way into the manifesto.

The Easter recess, which followed the Cabinet on 4 April where the referendum deal was struck, came as a welcome break to Major. As he rested at The Finings after one of his most difficult springs, worse even than 1994 after QMV, he collected his thoughts, and girded himself for the challenges ahead. He knew that the Staffordshire South East by-election on 11 April and local elections on 2 May would be difficult, and that he was not yet over the worst of the beef crisis. But the economy was continuing to improve, and the planning for the long-term election campaign was well in train – if only he could find the time to concentrate more upon it.

He was right to be wary about the Staffordshire South East by-election, which served notice that the long session up to the end of July would not be easy. Despite fielding a good candidate in Jimmy James, this solid middle-class seat that several Cabinet ministers, including Clarke and Portillo, had said could be won, was lost to Labour on a 22 per cent swing.[58] The timing of the election had been the source of some recrimination: Major had insisted against the advice of Central Office that the three-month period under the Speaker's Convention be adhered to, which meant calling it before the local elections.[59] The morning after polling, Major warned the Party not to over-react to the disappointment, and insisted more would be done 'to get our message across'. Mawhinney tried to make light of it. All next day he cited the example of the Ribble Valley by-election, lost to the Liberal Democrats in 1991 only to be regained at the general election. But the reassurances carried less weight than was hoped. It was a bad blow for the Tories, not least because their Commons majority was reduced to one. Barely one in four Tory backbenchers surveyed the following weekend believed that the Party could still win the general election.[60] Restlessness among Tory MPs, and discontent with the leadership and current policy, were inevitably heightened with each successive election defeat and opinion poll blow.

Tony Blair had been particularly keen to claim the Staffordshire seat. At a speech at Tamworth during the by-election campaign, he said a Labour victory would make an early general election 'much more likely', and show there were no 'no-go' areas for Labour. Blair wanted an early general election to capitalise on the huge poll lead and pre-empt the benefit to the Tories of any return of the 'feel-good' factor. Blair was celebrating in Washington at a British Embassy party in his honour when he heard the news: 'Today's Labour Party,' he said triumphantly, 'new Labour, is a party of the centre as well as the centre left.'[61] To the New York Chamber of Commerce, he staked Labour's claim to the 'radical centre' of UK politics.[62]

Talk of further Tory MPs about to defect in the wake of Howarth and Nicholson, and Labour's calculated appeal to Tory MPs 'with a conscience' to come over to join them, pointed to the need for the Tories to appeal to floating voters in the centre. Such was Major's view, and it was also the conclusion drawn by the centre-left Conservative MPs who gave him an 'unequivocal message' after Staffordshire South East that if the Party could not reclaim the centre ground it risked 'going over the cliff'.[63]

Redwood read the result differently, leading the right-wing calls for a change of direction.[64] The hardline right in fact had all but given up caring whether or not they went over the cliff. The general election was lost. The battle for the next Party leader was on. The war against the EU must be stepped up. The fact that these were all short-term strategies was seldom heard.

The Staffordshire South East by-election marked a point of no return for many on the right. Intelligence began filtering into Number Ten and Central Office of talks, plots even, among the hardline anti-Europeans. Lamont and Redwood were thought to be talking to Goldsmith and to Charles Moore, editor of the Daily Telegraph. The 'plot' was to unsettle Major by goading the sceptics into ever greater acts of defiance, so that when the local elections went badly, or another disaster happened subsequently in the year, Major would be ousted in favour of another leader – any, they thought, would be acceptable, as long as it was not Clarke.[65]

As if on cue, a withering leader in the Daily Telegraph on 18 April written by Moore himself appeared under the title 'Get off your knees'. 'Overall, the government is a disaster ... The fact that Mr Major does not stand for anything', wrote Moore, 'is an invitation for everyone else to fight.' Regarded within the upper levels of the paper as the 'crossing of the Rubicon', Moore had exploded after the by-election: he thought the handling of the beef issue incompetent, and Major's style so weak and lacking in any fixed principles that he was destroying the Tory case. Moore felt he had given Major a fair wind after the leadership election: no longer.[66]

The editorial delivered Major a hammer blow. 'When the flagship of the Tory press dumped that on him, there was nowhere to hide,' said one aide.[67] Major reacted furiously: 'No fixed principles – what about Ireland, the fight against inflation?'[68] Major considered that Moore had never given him a fair chance, but had been hostile from the outset, setting himself up as a great

Tory mandarin pronouncing judgement, when he was pressing his own anti-EU agenda.

With leadership speculation returning to levels unseen since June 1995, Major and his new Foreign Affairs Private Secretary John Holmes, who had succeeded Roderic Lyne at the start of 1996, departed for a four-day tour to eastern Europe.[69] The primary reason was to attend the nuclear safety summit in Moscow. *En route*, he spent an overnight stop on 17 April in Prague, holding conversations with Prime Minister Klaus. Major had promised him a visit at the Blackpool Party Conference the previous October; Vaclav Klaus was a conservative free-marketeer, and the two men enjoyed each other's company.[70] The next day Major toured the Ukraine.

Duty done, he flew on to Moscow, arriving late on 18 April.[71] The summit itself was of no great value, though agreements were reached on support for Russia's ageing atomic reactors, and on the control of the spread of weapons-grade fissile material.[72] After a formal dinner, an unusual late night meeting on BSE took place in the Ambassador's sitting room with Santer, Kohl, Chirac and Dini, all propped up awkwardly on armchairs. Chirac was determined to be helpful. 'Let's be guided by the science,' he said but Major's hopes of smooth progress were dashed. Major was pleased with his conversations with Yeltsin, visiting him on 19 April in his newly restored office in the Kremlin, statues of Peter and Catherine the Great prominently displayed in place of the Communist icons. Yeltsin seemed to Major to want to portray himself as a new Tsar. He found Yeltsin's health restored after the heart attack the previous summer, and he was apparently in command of his material. Major registered his concern about the continuing war in Chechnia, but pulled back from saying how incompetent and appalling the British thought the Russian handling of the problem had been.[73]

Major seized the chance of bilaterals with various other world leaders, notably Clinton, whom he met in the Kremlin to discuss Northern Ireland as well as Russian politics. So relaxed had they become about security in the post-Cold War era, that only subsequently did Major wonder whether anyone had bugged their conversations, and what the leadership would make of the transcript if they had.[74] Major and John Holmes held talks with Russian opinion-formers on the looming election in Russia, and on the threat to Yeltsin from the Communists. When they met the Communist leader, Gennady Zyuganov, they did not believe he had the makings of a leader, and so it proved.

For once, Major had enjoyed being away from the domestic turbulence, but he returned over the weekend into as grim a period as he had experienced. Goldsmith was charging forward. The *Sun* endorsed him after he announced he would be spending an astonishing £20 million on the campaign, and would be fielding 600 candidates.[75] The leader of Britain's newest political party held a highly publicised series of meetings and media interviews from his fifth-floor suite at the Dorchester Hotel, including one with Redwood on 24 April.[76] The purpose of the meeting, according to Redwood, was to discuss the wording and timing of the referendum. He managed to reach an agreement on a fairly innocuous form of words, with the referendum to be held on election day. Redwood wrote to Number Ten and hoped they would accept his mediated deal, but says he was rebuffed. Redwood came to regard Major's failure to take Goldsmith seriously as one of the three ways, alongside the ERM and the Maastricht Treaty, that he destroyed the Tory Party.[77]

Major had misjudged Goldsmith. He had hoped that the 4 April announcement of the single currency referendum would be sufficient for him to back off. Now he realised that Goldsmith had merely banked this concession, and was playing for higher stakes: he wanted a referendum on Britain remaining in the EU. He was enjoying himself, and wanted to use his money to be seen as the champion of British national interest against foreign intrusions into British freedoms. Though no one knew it, he had only a year more to live before cancer was to claim his life. He was a man in a hurry, who wanted to develop his political party and to hold a high-profile conference. It was fun mixed with ideology and passion, and he was not to be deflected.

While some in Number Ten thought Goldsmith an unpleasant distraction which would go away, Major became concerned about the impact Goldsmith's party might have on the general election. An aide summed up his fears:

He was not deceived into thinking that the most visible supporters for the Referendum Party, the chattering classes and twinset lot, were the extent of their support. In the constituencies, some tried to tell him that the anti-French, anti-German, pro-British vote which the Referendum Party would seek would come from Labour's traditional support. He did not believe it wouldn't tap deep into the Conservative working class vote.[78]

Attempts by Archer and others to broker a compromise were rebuffed. While Mawhinney and Heseltine counselled having nothing to do with him, messages filtered into Number Ten that Goldsmith sneered at any suggestion of him calling his bandwagon to a halt.[79] An intermediary was even sent to Mexico, unknown to Major, said McAlpine, to offer Goldsmith a peerage. Goldsmith apparently saw it merely as a further sign of weakness and desperation,[80] though it has to be said that any peerage would never have got past Major and the story is probably apocryphal.

News also reached Number Ten of Party plots reaching up to the Cabinet. Major told John Gummer that he knew perfectly well that a small group had decided the election was lost and wanted to win the Tory Party for themselves after the election. He was at a loss to know how to act. He found their machinations both despicable and futile.[81] In a highly charged atmosphere, some actions, which might or might not have been innocuous, could be viewed as acts of defiance, as when some Cabinet ministers, including Forsyth and Portillo, remained in the chamber for Iain Duncan-Smith's anti-federalist Bill to give Parliament power to overrule decisions of the European Court of Justice. Sixty-six Tory MPs supported the Bill in direct opposition to government policy. One Eurosceptic MP rounded on a pleading Chief Whip Goodlad the night before the vote and told him publicly, 'You are a waste of space.'[82]

When a key plank of Mackay's Family Reform Bill was heavily defeated on 24 April after it had been decided to take it as an issue of conscience on a free vote, Major became angered that it was seen in the press as a humiliating defeat for the government as well as for himself:[83] the *Daily Mail* thus called it a 'stunning rebellion', to the protests of Number Ten.[84] Major was further exasperated by the talk, referring back to the 'so-called secret pact' with Heseltine during the leadership election, about how he would hand over if the local elections went badly.[85] While Major felt secure that his understanding with Marcus Fox was that there would be no pre-general election leadership contest, a symptom of the tension was Number Ten being involved in an embarrassing spat with Redwood over income tax reduction.[86]

Major tried to recover ground in the run-up to the local elections with a speech to the Institute of Directors in which he warned of the use of the UK veto and a policy of non-cooperation if EU leaders did not relent on the beef ban; but he antagonised the right by saying that politicians calling for withdrawal from the EU were living in 'cloud cuckoo land'.[87] Then on 29 April, Downing Street let it be known that he had told Kohl at a meeting at Number Ten that day that if there was an immediate British referendum on joining the single currency, the motion would be defeated. The German Chancellor was famously dished up with British beef and ostentatiously referred to Major as 'Lieber John'.[88]

The government's handling of the beef crisis, local government canvassers told Central Office, was proving a big problem on doorsteps as polling day on 2 May approached.[89] Central Office had estimated the Tories would lose between 650 and 700 seats from those gained at the Party's last high point in the spring of 1992. Some late crumbs of comfort came from Clare Short's statement that people 'like her' should pay more tax, and the Wimpy hamburger chain announcing that it was again to buy British beef.[90]

Major watched the local results come in on his television at the Number Ten flat with Howell James and George Bridges, and his past and current PPSs, Bright and Ward. He worked on his boxes sitting on the sofa while his four aides avidly watched the screen. By midnight it was clear that while the results were poor they would not be a meltdown, and at 12.30 a.m., relatively happy, Major retired for the night.[91] Although the Party had won only 27 per cent of the vote, it had lost just 567 seats.[92]

A resoundingly upbeat message was to be delivered the following day, Number Ten and Central Office decreed. Major was in confident form the next morning, although not quite the 'new man', as one aide described him for the media. Contingency plans for Cabinet ministers to insist in interviews that Major must at all costs stay on, and for whips to contact potential troublemakers, were stood down.[93] Instead, the order of the day was discounting the result, optimism and defiance, a mood sceptically caught in the headline in the London *Evening Standard*, 'Phew! It's only a disaster'.[94] While ever-loyal lieutenants, Heseltine, Mawhinney and Lang, were deputed to say the results were less bad than the 1991 local elections, Major himself gave a series of self-confident media interviews, announcing that he had pencilled in 1 May 1997 for the general election, that he had approved a £1 million poster campaign to begin later in May, and that he had an 'action-packed programme' for the following twelve months, including a White Paper on long-term care of the elderly, tougher discipline in schools and in prisons and new-style family doctoring as well as, he added, another budget.[95]

On a deeper level, strategists at Number Ten and Central Office were less sanguine. The local election was the second-worst national result for the Party in thirty years, leaving it, after four bad contests in successive years, almost a minor player as a party of local government, with only half the number of councillors of the Liberal Democrats.[96] The Tories had had a clear message for the local elections, that Conservative councils ran more efficiently and economically than Labour and Liberal Democrat councils. But from the moment that the campaign began, with Mawhinney attacking Sue Mac-Gregor on the *Today* programme for asking about the leadership speculation, one misfortune had overlain another. For all Heseltine's prowess at managing EDCP, and Mawhinney's tough leadership at Central Office, the impression repeatedly given was of a government not in control of events, nor one able to fight even a local election campaign without divisions. Frustrations between Number Ten and Central Office had spilled over into the media, such as Mawhinney's belief that some ministers, particularly Douglas Hogg should at least be moved. But Major thought it would be seen as a sign of weakness to reshuffle.[97] The party had to work, and be seen to be working, closer together to fare better in the general election. Time, moreover, was running out. There was now less than a year until the last date when the election could realistically take place, 1 May 1997.

Beef War: May–June

Within days of the announcement of the beef crisis, Whitehall departments were asked to produce ideas for possible retaliation against the EU if the ban was prolonged. These ideas were sifted by the FCO and the government's law officers to ensure that they were legal, and would not invite even more damaging countermeasures. Four options were on the table: leaving Britain's seat in EU discussions empty, dismissed as it would prevent the government from exercising their veto; withholding payments, judged by Lyell to be illegal; restrictions on EU meat imports, dismissed because of the risks of retaliatory measures and also questions on legality. That left only one option, which was still only partially formed: obstruction of the EU's decision-making in every case where unanimity was required.[98] The Turin Council on 29 March had, however, put any immediate thoughts of retaliation on the back burner. Major spoke for several days after about the 'spirit of Turin'.

Though he was under no illusions about EU leaders' self-interest, he remained touched by the warmth of the understanding, by the practical offer of financial help for the slaughter programme, and by the firm reassurances he felt he had been given that the ban would not be long-lasting.[99]

As April wore on, however, with no end or easing of the ban in sight, pressure built up for a tough line. In mid-month, Rifkind, on this matter a hawk, was authorised by Newton's beef committee to warn Britain's EU counterparts that 'other options' were being considered in London to get the ban lifted.[100] Rifkind's threats were made known by Downing Street and picked up in excited newspaper headlines with inevitable raising of expectations among Eurosceptic MPs.[101] Several, like Marlow and Richard Shepherd, began calling for withholding of contributions, even if it was illegal. Howard pressed in Cabinet for a hard line, against Clarke and Waldegrave. With Heseltine believing speculation was swirling out of control, he obtained Major's permission, to Rifkind's annoyance, to dampen it down.[102] The Eurosceptics were outraged, having had their appetites whetted, at what appeared like yet another climbdown on Europe after early fighting talk. But the tide was moving their way. With ministers like Dorrell believing some form of retaliation was inevitable, the Cabinet's centre of gravity over the beef crisis tipped towards the Eurosceptics.[103]

Major became increasingly impatient as the days passed with no lifting of the ban by the EU. He believed that the unwillingness of EU member states to deal with irrational fears was causing unnecessary damage to the beef industry, not least on mainland Europe itself. Major's bilateral meetings with Santer, Kohl, Chirac and Dini in Moscow during the nuclear safety summit and in London with Kohl (29 April) and Chirac (15 May) were not translating into any more practical movement than had the sympathetic words at Turin.[104] He began to prepare the ground for tougher action at the Scottish Conservative Conference at Aberdeen on 11 May,[105] but still hoped that strong measures against the EU could be avoided, and was encouraged by optimistic words from Douglas Hogg about an easing of attitudes in Europe.[106]

Major's patience finally broke when on 20 May, to the accompaniment of headlines speaking of 'humiliation for Britain', the EU's veterinary committee voted against lifting the ban on British exports of tallow, semen and gelatine. 'A breach of faith' was how he described it: rightly or wrongly, he believed he had been given undertakings, as had Douglas Hogg, that had been reneged upon. Major was livid with Kohl in particular. One Cabinet minister said he could never recall seeing him as angry as on hearing the news from the veterinary committee, which he thought was them merely playing politics.[107]

With most of his Cabinet now behind tough action, Major knew only one of his ministers would seriously need squaring. The next morning, he called Clarke into Number Ten. With big hitters on the centre and left of Cabinet demanding strong action, and even many Europhile MPs from farming constituencies up in arms, Clarke knew, as on the referendum, that he would have to concede. But he wanted to hear Major spell out the circumstances

under which any retaliatory steps would be lifted, and to satisfy himself that
any action taken would be wholly geared to ending the beef dispute, rather
than to fulfilling a more general anti-EU objective.[108] It proved another of
those occasions where Major and Clarke had different understandings of
what had been agreed.

Major had no intention of letting Hogg make the statement in Parliament
on 21 May about the veterinary committee's decision. Instead, he took
personal charge, and announced that Britain would be pursuing a policy of
'non-cooperation' with Europe. Major's successful statement was aided by
Blair giving his 'weakest Commons performance as Opposition leader'.[109]
Conservative backbenchers were delighted by the news, with Blair and
Labour wrong-footed, and the Tory press generally ecstatic: 'Major goes to
war at last,' declared the *Daily Mail*.[110]

The rush, however, meant that little thought had been given to what exactly
'non-cooperation' in the EU meant. Did it apply just in those areas that
required unanimity? Number Ten and the Cabinet Office were flooded by
questions from Whitehall departments, and from the EU, to find out exactly
what issues were being blocked. It took fully a week before there was detailed
clarification. Even more important, no clear agreement had been reached on
the terms that would satisfy Britain for cooperation to be restored.[111] Major
said there had to be a 'clear framework' in place for lifting the ban before
non-cooperation would end. Although he himself did not use the word
'timetable' for the lifting of the ban, Downing Street, to his annoyance, did.[112]

Once the immediate furore died down, the repercussions of the policy
began to strike home. Ironically, one might think, it made the Conservative
Party not more but even less manageable in the long term. The Eurosceptic
right had taken the retaliation almost for granted, and began to look for the
next turn of the ratchet, while some Europhiles reacted strongly against. The
increasingly disillusioned Tory MP George Walden threatened to resign the
Party whip over Major's 'silly and cynical' behaviour and thereby wipe out
the government's majority. Heath fulminated, while David Hunt set up a new
political organisation called 'Conservative Mainstream', bringing together
various Tory left ginger groups, to combat the 'xenophobic hysteria'.[113]
Within Cabinet, it led to turbulence, with Waldegrave as well as Clarke
distressed at the policy and the reaction in Europe. Various parts of Whitehall,
especially the FCO, were opposed to the policy, though they loyally executed
it, in some instances with gritted teeth.[114]

The reaction in the EU was one of anger and surprise. Britain's relations
with EU partners plummeted to the worst point since it joined in January
1973; Major's personal authority in Europe never fully recovered, nor did
his relations with various leaders including Kohl, and even Chirac, although
normal diplomatic contact continued as before. Many figures in the European
Commission felt that they had already done sufficient to help Britain, at
Turin and after, and it seemed to them that the non-cooperation policy was
an act of pique, designed for British domestic politics, and that Britain

threatened to derail the IGC process. Instead of coming up with clear proposals for eradicating BSE, several EU countries, especially Germany, believed the British government's handling of the issue to be vacillating and uncertain. After seeing British ministers block more than seventy measures, including anti-fraud action that they themselves had been demanding for several years, Santer's patience snapped, warning Britain that 'l'heure de vérité' was approaching.[115] Were it not for Blair offering qualified support for the 'non-cooperation' policy, so questioning the growing belief in the EU that all would be well when Labour came to power, the reaction from Europe would almost certainly have been stronger.

Cash's response was to introduce a Bill calling for a referendum on Europe: in defiance of the government, seventy-eight Tory MPs voted on 11 June for it. Major and Goodlad met and decided that they would have to become much tougher with recalcitrant MPs. Goodlad went on to slap down two MPs, Hugh Dykes and John Gorst, for protesting over the closure of Edgware hospital, for lacking 'honour'. Now the top brass moved in on Cash. He was strongly urged not to accept any more money from Goldsmith's foundation for his 'think-tank', the European Foundation. Cash acceded, but refused to resign as chairman of the organisation. Incensed at what she saw as an unwarranted show of strength, Lady Thatcher summoned Cash to lunch at her Belgravia office. Within twenty-four hours of the ban on Goldsmith money, Cash was brandishing a letter from his former leader saying that she herself would make a substantial donation to his foundation. When Major was told about her donation on Thursday, he uttered three words: 'This is treachery.' Overruling the advice of Number Ten advisers and Goodlad to ignore her action, he delivered a sharp public rebuke to her, that 'Everyone must choose what to do with their own money. Lady Thatcher must answer for her own actions. Personally, I would have given the money to the Conservative Party.'[116] It was the most severe public exchange in their long-running six-year difference.

Expectations, meanwhile, were rising of what Major might achieve at the forthcoming Florence summit on 21 June at the end of the Italian presidency. Pressure built from backbenchers and the Tory press that Florence must not be another 'Grand Old Duke of York' saga, as over QMV. This time, there could be no backtracking. While Eurosceptic MPs trooped into the Whips' Office to make their views plain, Europhile MPs, heartened by a rallying Mansion House speech on 12 June from Clarke on the benefits of EU membership, were preparing to stake out their ground as rumours about further defections from the Party continued to circulate. Wild talk, about the Tory Party splitting after the general election, and Britain planning for a life outside the EU, began to enter the political mainstream, with the Party's historian and guru Robert Blake considering a division quite possible, and with increasing numbers of opinion-formers flocking to Goldsmith's banner.[117] Major's frustrations broke through in an interview recorded during the Welsh Conservative Party Conference at Porthcawl on Friday 14 June.

At the end of a dreadful week, he declared, that he had had a 'bellyful' of European divisions in the Party.[118]

Behind the scenes of this swirling froth, much work on unscrambling the beef problem had been in train. The Newton committee, wound up at the time the non-cooperation policy was announced, had been replaced by a small 'War Cabinet' (as it was inevitably dubbed by the tabloids) chaired by Major, which met to consider overall policy, a supporting committee under Robin Butler, as well as a mixed implementation committee of ministers and officials from the nine main departments concerned, chaired by Roger Freeman. Britain's task was to put in place a clear BSE eradication plan that it could put to EU member states; not until 31 May did it have one. With it, Britain sought a framework agreement with EU partners, Rifkind taking charge of official negotiations while Mawhinney drummed up support from centre-right political parties. The process speeded up considerably when Rifkind met Italian Prime Minister Romano Prodi in Rome on 7 June. As the chairman of the forthcoming EU summit, Prodi pledged himself to securing a deal at Florence and adopting in outline Britain's framework proposals.[119]

By early in the week beginning Monday 17 June, an agreement was in place between Britain and the EU. A progressive lifting of the beef ban, subject to European scrutiny of the cattle slaughtering programme, was to take place. Final decisions would rest with the Council on the advice of the EU veterinary committee, but with the guarantee that its decisions would be taken 'only and exclusively on the basis of public health and objective scientific criteria'.[120] Major was pleased with the deal secured, and by the assurances he received that the Eurosceptics would not create difficulties with it. But on 19 June, the draft of the agreement found itself in the hands of the Labour Party. From 9 a.m., Robin Cook, Shadow Foreign Secretary, was briefing the media that it represented a 'massive climbdown', a line most broadcasts and newspapers were shortly to reflect.[121] The agreement to slaughter an extra 67,000 cattle, the failure to achieve an automatic lifting of the beef export ban to the rest of the world, and indeed to achieve a precise timetable for the lifting of the beef export ban into the EU, were all factors advanced by Labour to show that Major had been defeated.

Major had planned to deliver a calm and reasoned statement of Britain's vision for the future of the EU that Wednesday morning to a City audience. He hoped his lecture would command the headlines in the twenty-four hours before the Florence summit, and that it would show his government to be following a responsible, middle way between both wings of the debate. The speech referred back to and built upon his Leiden speech of 1994, and spoke of the EU as a 'partnership of nations', outlining his vision of the 'flexible' Europe he wanted to see come out of the IGC.[122] But, when Central Office and Number Ten realised in the afternoon of 19 June what Cook had been doing, it was too late. Not for the first nor last time would the Tories' media team be upstaged by the slick and single-minded Labour machine. A last-minute press conference by Roger Freeman later that day failed to change the balance of media opinion.

Major read the headlines in Thursday's press stories with considerable disquiet. 'After British bravado comes a hasty retreat,' said the *Independent*, while the normally sympathetic Riddell wrote in *The Times* that the 'ill-judged beef policy leaves Major with lasting damage'.[123] Major gave a short-tempered live television interview and was still fuming at the one-sided coverage when he arrived at Florence's Excelsior Hotel at 11.30 p.m.: 'Some of the stories in the last twenty-four hours', he said, 'are from *Alice in Wonderland*. There is no question of a climbdown.'[124] Adding to his anxiety, a message arrived at the hotel from London that, with exquisite timing, a story was to break in the *Guardian* that David Davis, the FCO minister angered not to have been promoted to Cabinet, had asked to resign,[125] because, he said, he was disenchanted by the Florence deal.[126]

Major and Rifkind's counterclaims were reflected in Saturday's headlines: 'Major given just enough to claim victory,' now said the *Independent*.[127] While every side found a reason to play up or to belittle the deal, the British public had little idea what to think. The settlement was in fact a qualified success for the government, and was probably as much as they could have achieved, though falling short of some of the more far-fetched hopes of the non-cooperation policy. Major settled when he did because he was satisfied with what he had been offered, and felt that to extend the policy beyond one month would serve to exacerbate unnecessarily relations within his party and with EU partners, which were facing a flashpoint if non-cooperation continued any longer. The British government announced an ambitious timetable for culling cattle. Major was determined after Florence that the cull should go ahead speedily, and pressed Freeman to see the slaughter rate rise to 60,000 a week. The cull hit problems with evidence that cows might pass on BSE to their calves, and there were problems with abattoir capacity and political trouble with the National Farmers Union. The turning point came at the October Party Conference, when Major personally met farmers' representatives and gained their support for the resumption of the culling programme. Thereafter, the worst of the beef crisis was over.[128]

The government's handling of BSE was widely criticised. But he faced tremendous difficulties, with the scientific evidence not always consistent, with his own party at war with itself, and with EU leaders not always remaining unmoved by the highly agitated reactions among their own electorate, nowhere more severe than in Germany. The beef issue was tailor-made to extract maximum damage on a vulnerable Prime Minister and government: it raised the temperature over Europe, divided his party further, and distracted him for three months at a critical juncture in his premiership. Campbell and Mandelson could not in their wildest dreams have devised an issue which would have caused as much disruption.

No Constitutional Progress

One of the casualties of the distraction the BSE issue caused was Major's
plans for constitutional reform. He had intended to deliver a keynote lecture
during the summer setting out his views on the constitution, the fourth in the
series of speeches on the 'five themes', and summing up the results of his
own musings and the work of his advisers.

In an interview with Andrew Marr in November 1995, Major had claimed
that 'I believe in doing things in an evolutionary, not a revolutionary, fashion.
I would defy any dispassionate judge to go over any single parliament in
recent years and find as many moves from previously fixed positions on
constitutional issues' as he had achieved. He listed reforms to the Scottish
Grand Committee, changing parliamentary procedure and the Northern
Ireland process. He told Marr that he had been thinking about the issues for
some months and that more announcements would be forthcoming.[129] Major
wanted to be considered a constitutional reformer. Had the opportunity now
arisen?

An important source was work emanating from one not normally considered a constitutional innovator, Lord Cranborne. But like his grandfather,
the fifth Marquess of Salisbury, who had tried to introduce reform of the
House of Lords in the early 1950s, he wanted to see an evolutionary approach
to reforming Parliament and, more generally, the constitution. The need to
devise a distinctive Tory policy became all the greater when it became clear
that Blair was making constitutional reform a central plank in New Labour's
platform. Rather than just block all Labour's proposals, Cranborne thought
the government needed to offer something more positive of its own, albeit
less radical and mechanistic: Burke rather than Paine, for short.[130]

Major's response to Cranborne's enthusiasm was to suggest a supper to
discuss it, duly convened in the kitchen of Goodlad's Westminster house,
with Lord Strathclyde, Chief Whip in the Lords, and Douglas Slater, a former
Private Secretary to the Leader of the Lords, also in attendance. The date
chosen for the occasion, 19 December 1995, was the day the government
was defeated in the EU fisheries debate. Major soon relaxed after the tense
day and became swept up in the argument over the philosophical grounding
and the practical politics. So excited was he by the tenor of discussions that
he effectively gave Cranborne and his helpers *carte blanche* to come back to
him with proposals they could draft into the manifesto.[131] As Cranborne put
it: 'I thought that if the constitution was properly and imaginatively handled,
it may not have been an election winner, but it would help our cause. I was
keen to be reasonably radical, particularly over reform of Parliament.'[132]

From January 1996, a group began to meet in the Cabinet Office, including
Alex Allan and Dominic Morris from Number Ten, and David Willetts from
the Cabinet Office, to work up proposals. Departments were asked for
changes in their sphere since 1979 reflecting on the constitution, and what
ideas they had for further reform. But then the beef crisis struck on 18

March. Not only were some of the best brains like Allan and Morris distracted from the project, but Major himself was able to devote far less time. Two seminars on the constitution for ministers attracted little interest, while Howard, who as Home Secretary considered matters constitutional in his own bailiwick, was not a fan. The committee began to lose its way, and its proposals were far from clear-cut. The initiative still had its enthusiasts, who favoured adding to the impact of the constitution speech by finding a venue away from the London policy circuit, as Callaghan had done with his Ruskin College, Oxford, education speech in 1976 and Thatcher with the Royal Society lecture on the environment in 1988. All Souls', Oxford, was approached but Major was reluctant to appear in such a formal and high-powered setting and vetoed the idea.[133] The idea of putting the proposals into a White Paper was also shelved. Major duly delivered the speech, drafted by his Private Office, to the Centre for Policy Studies on 26 June, but it proved a damp squib. As so often with his speeches, and this one was made just after Florence, insufficient time and thought could be put into what he wanted to say. Rather than offering a positive prospectus, the lecture became more a peg on which to hang his criticisms about Blair's plans. As for reform, he said:

I'm all for practical change that would solve real problems or improve the way our constitution works. But pointless fiddling with our constitution won't solve any problems. It would just create new ones. In the end, it would begin to unstitch our way of life. I'm a Conservative and I reject change for change's sake.[134]

The satellite ministerial speeches were made, but were swallowed up in the general noise of the period. Cranborne later in the year gave a speech to a new 'think-tank', Politeia, outlining some of his thinking, and Dorrell was appointed by Major to an unspecified job of watching over the constitution. But the great reform impulse, that might have linked in with Major's own instincts in favour of open government, accessible and responsive to the electorate, was swallowed up by the forces of conservatism and reaction. Even with Cranborne's backing, it was judged unwise to upset the right, rattled by Nolan, with such radical thinking. Besides, constitutional reform was becoming one of the 'new dangers' of New Labour. But for the beef crisis, Major might still have driven it through. It was a classic example of the problems of a central machine and of a prime minister under an excessive degree of strain.

Constitutional progress proved every bit as pained in Northern Ireland. After the Docklands bomb, Major came under increasing pressure from those on the right of the Party, such as David Wilshire, not to cave in to 'men of violence'.[135] In early March up to twenty-four Tory MPs threatened an 'ambush' on concessions to Sinn Fein and the nationalists.[136] Major nevertheless pressed ahead with plans for all-party talks in Northern Ireland and following a summit with Bruton set a firm date of 10 June for their opening.[137]

The next concern was to agree about elections. Construction of an electoral system that satisfied all parties in the province was an intellectual and political conundrum. A hybrid monster was eventually devised, allegedly on the back of an envelope, a combination of proportional representation and a constituency system which allowed the small parties to gain seats in the assembly. Much of Major's time was spent persuading Northern Ireland parties to abide with the process, until on 21 March agreement was reached and it was announced that elections would take place in May. From that point on, Number Ten handed over the running to the Northern Ireland Office to put the election together and then start the talks off in June. Reports meanwhile kept coming in to Major of continuing IRA activities. Various responses were considered, including a reintroduction of internment. But without Dublin agreeing to internment as well, and it was considered they would not consent to it, the idea was rejected. Doing so would have handed a propaganda weapon to Sinn Fein/IRA, and the propaganda war, after months of success, was one the Republicans at last were losing.[138]

On 10 June, all-party talks duly opened under Mitchell's chairmanship at Stormont. Sinn Fein, with the IRA still refusing to disarm, protested forlornly at their exclusion. Major was pleased by the momentum building up again in the peace process. On Saturday 15 June, in a week that had included the Thatcher donation to Cash's European Foundation and his statement in Wales that he had had a 'bellyful' of party division, he was relaxing, watching the Trooping of the Colour on Horseguards Parade. A message was passed to him at his seat in the auditorium. A bomb had been detonated in the centre of Manchester. Shocked, he returned immediately through the garden of Number Ten where his staff briefed him. No one knew how many casualties there were, but he was told that the bomb was one of the largest ever to have been exploded in mainland Britain.[139] He feared the worst.

THIRTY-SEVEN

'We'll Win':

July–October 1996

New Labour New Danger: July

WHILE MAJOR'S ATTENTION was distracted by BSE and European business in the spring and early summer, planning for the general election had been moving ahead steadily. The strategy group that met at Central Office at 5 p.m. on Monday evenings was the forum where decisions were taken, or sometimes not taken. Chaired by Mawhinney, it included the three senior Central Office directors – Danny Finkelstein, Tony Garrett and Charles Lewington – together with the emollient and popular Deputy Chairman Michael Trend, Howell James and Norman Blackwell from Number Ten, and the 'three musketeers' as they became known, Bell, Gummer and Saatchi.

The combined efforts of Philip Harris and Charles Hambro had provided a treasure chest of some £10 million.[1] Amid allegations in May of the Party obtaining money in 'sleazy' ways, including 'stolen money' from Asil Nadir, and 'blood money' from Bosnian Serb leader Radovan Karadzic, it had also managed to clear an overdraft of £19 million from 1992–3.[2]

The 'Life's better' opening blast of their communications strategy had been in train since the spring, with posters, *Look!* and a Maurice Saatchi-devised party political broadcast during the local election campaign, exhibiting Major in a series of cut-away shots talking about how Britain had improved. Recognition that Conservative voters would return to the Party only grudgingly helped prompt a series of posters which declared of the strengthening economy, 'Yes it hurt. Yes it worked', the closest the government came to admitting culpability for the hardship inflicted since Britain's withdrawal from the ERM.[3]

Bell, Gummer and Saatchi all wanted the upbeat first phase of the campaign to continue until the party conference season, to allow time for the electorate to become imbued with the fact that life was, indeed, better. Only by entrenching this belief, they reasoned, would people feel there might be anything to be put in jeopardy by abandoning the Conservatives. It was a logical argument. But pressure built up, not least from backbenchers, to get on with attacking Labour. Within Central Office, Garrett argued strongly to begin this attack before the summer recess, and gained support from Mawhinney and Number Ten.[4] There was also a risk that delaying the assault until the

Party Conference would open the Party to the charge that it was more concerned to attack Labour than to proffer its own programme, a charge levelled at the 1995 Queen's Speech. So in June, the advice of the three outside advisers was swept aside, and it was decided to initiate phase two, the attack on Labour, on Monday 1 July.[5] The irony that it was the eightieth anniversary of the opening day of the Battle of the Somme, the worst day for casualties in British military history, seems to have escaped their attention.

The advance in the date meant that Cabinet had no time collectively to discuss the New Labour, New Danger campaign before the offensive began, although Central Office senior staff had been briefing individual Cabinet ministers.[6] A Political Cabinet scheduled for 19 June had to be delayed because of Major's speech on Europe slotted into the diary late in the day for the eve of his departure to the Florence summit. The first day available for the rescheduled meeting was 1 July itself.[7] Although it had been standard practice in the last year to have a ten-minute Political Cabinet at the end of each Thursday Cabinet meeting to discuss the political messages of the week, this was the first full Political Cabinet since 20 March, which itself had been a truncated event.

Peter Gummer opened proceedings in the Cabinet Room, followed by Saatchi, then Bell, who presented the advertisements on a screen at the end of the table. Some hard-hitting parts of Bell's presentation, which implied that the election might be lost unless Cabinet ministers started to demonstrate that they were improving the lives of voters, were toned down or even removed at the request of Mawhinney.[8] Ministers were told that New Labour's policies, rather than being fresh and exciting, were untried, untested, even sinister. Though some time – predictably – was spent disagreeing about whether Europe should appear in the campaign, the tenor of the meeting was positive about the strategy, and glad that the attack on Labour had begun that day. To the amusement, or irritation, of some among the campaign's planners, not all ministers could yet grasp the thrust of the 'New Labour, New Danger'. 'Does this mean that we can still attack Labour for being socialists?' piped up one.[9] The inability of some in the Cabinet to engage with the strategy or to employ the terminology accurately in speeches, reaching right to the top, would prove a growing worry as the months ground on.

Since the spring, Central Office had been delving into Labour's policies, teasing out its weak points and preparing lines of attack. An early target was Blair's enthusiasm, later modified, for Will Hutton's vogue idea of 'stake-holding'. This aroused a smart rejoinder, penned by the Party's top brains, Finkelstein and Willetts. At a press conference on 2 July, Heseltine and Mawhinney performed a double act launching the fruit of Central Office's research, a spoof manifesto *The Road To Ruin*, an attack on Labour's document, *Road To the Manifesto*, to be published the next day. Heseltine played the role of funny guy to Mawhinney's straight man.

The Tory Chairman introduced the 24,000 word document to anticipating journalists and asked the Deputy Prime Minister what 'struck him' about it.

Heseltine responded with the spoof manifesto's gloss on John Prescott's views on taxation: 'Under a Labour government, quite a lot of people would pay more tax. Beyond that, we would prefer to keep our tax plans secret. After all, we are not stupid.' And on it went. Neither man looked entirely comfortable with either the script or his role. The media were not amused, the consensus being that whatever the value of the document as propaganda, the attempt at humour backfired. 'Tories' Two Ronnies raise few laughs', in the *Daily Telegraph*, was a typical response.[10]

The underlying strategy was spelled out by Mawhinney: 'The issue is not whether Labour had changed. It is now clear that it has. The issue is whether Labour is fit to govern. It is not.' But, and this was the key message, Labour's plans for the constitution, for new taxes and the Social Chapter were now the 'new dangers' of the Party's platform.[11] The decision to read out the passages in the double-act was a last-minute proposal, which had not been part of the original planning. By inserting it, the serious message the Party was endeavouring to put across of 'new danger' was partially eclipsed.

The advertising campaign associated with new danger was based around the idea of 'demon eyes', taken from a photograph of a male model's eyes, turned around 180 degrees and retouched by designers at M. and C. Saatchi. The impression the eyes were meant to convey was of New Labour intruding into every aspect of people's lives. The eyes duly appeared in the press and on 1,500 poster sites up and down the country, peeping out of a purse and from behind curtains. The surprise and boldness of the campaign made a wide impact. They became one of the most striking images that July.

The assumption remained that the election would be held in the spring of 1997. The dwindling majority, however, called that aim into question. At one stage, after Emma Nicholson's defection at the New Year and with talk of further MPs crossing the floor, it seemed that a summer election might be forced on the Party.[12] When nothing dreadful followed the reduction of the majority to one after the Staffordshire South East by-election by early summer, it appeared that possibility had been avoided, but contingency planning took place for an autumn election, not least in case another MP died; at least one Tory MP, Barry Porter, was known to be seriously ill and was being watched anxiously. There were positive arguments too in favour of going then: if the Party had an excellent summer on the back of the 'new danger' campaign and opinion polls showed a dramatic improvement, an autumn election could be an attractive proposition.[13]

For an autumn election, the manifesto, as well as the detailed planning of the campaign in Central Office's 'war book' needed to be ready. Blackwell had been working intensely on the former. In the winter and spring, a series of discussions over dinner were held at Number Ten for representatives from the established think-tanks, the Institute of Economic affairs, Adam Smith Institute, Centre for Policy Studies and the Social Market Foundation. These were followed by a Chequers seminar for ministers of state on 13 May, and for Parliamentary under-secretaries on 20 May. Blackwell was keen to spread a feeling of ownership over the policy-formulation process, as well as wanting to trawl for fresh ideas.[14]

A series of meetings were then held with an inner core, Major, Heseltine, Mawhinney, Clarke and Blackwell, to tune the ideas that emerged. They had agreed by mid-July that they favoured a slim document, to be structured around the 'five themes', and that there would be separate manifestos for Scotland and Wales.[15] Blackwell convened a series of meetings before the summer recess for individual ministers to talk through with the same inner group of Cabinet ministers their manifesto ideas in their departmental area. If there was to be an autumn election, then Blackwell believed he could have the manifesto ready.

Preparations for the campaign, however, were not as advanced. Weekly meetings of the election planning committee continued throughout the spring and early summer. Urgency was given to preparation of election publications and to press releases for MPs. A War Room, set up in the autumn of 1995 to combine elements of both the communications and research departments, was made to run at full stretch. More focus groups were convened, which found significantly that Blair was less attractive to target voters on his personal trustworthiness and sincerity beside 'honest John' Major.[16] The quality and range of the Tories' polling, focus groups and other electoral arts, however, lagged some way behind Labour, which was ensconced in its new high-tech media headquarters in Westminster's Millbank. Labour were several steps ahead, not least in election readiness. That was not the reason, however, why the decision was taken to revert to the long-term strategy and delay the election until 1997: no further MP died, nor defected. The polls did improve in the summer, but nothing like dramatically enough. Hopes were thus pinned on the improving economy, the autumn budget, and for long-wished-for divisions within Labour to appear.

July Roller-Coaster

July traditionally proved a month of high excitements, in which Conservative MPs could be relied upon to produce an indiscretion, a rebuff to the leadership, a series of damaging headlines or a resignation. July 1996 did not disappoint. The only seasonal problem the Party was spared was a sex scandal, which came one month earlier in June with the resignation of the unfortunate Rod Richards, a junior Welsh minister.[17] June also saw the final match in 'Euro 96', the four-yearly European football competition hosted on this occasion by England. For the domestic audience, no match was more passionate, exciting and painful than the semi-final between the home side and Germany, which the latter won in the penalty shoot-out.

Major had become swept up in the whole competition, finding it welcome relief from the beef war and Party problems. He saw three live matches, but was sorry to miss the high-scoring England/Holland game on 18 June, insist-

ing that a dinner at Number Ten be interrupted for news of each fresh
England goal. At the semi-final at Wembley on 26 June, he was so caught up
in the match that he leapt out of his seat when Paul Gascoigne narrowly
missed making contact with a goalmouth ball in extra time. Walking out of
the tunnel after the defeat, he passed some of the England players and said a
few words to them. When a Football Association official told him that one
had been Gareth Southgate, who had missed the final penalty, he rushed
back to him, and told him that he should not feel too badly, and that he had
done his best.[18] It was a spontaneous action and he spoke from the heart. In
a subsequent sporting article, Major wrote, 'For me – and, I am sure, for
many, many others – the magic of Euro 96 will live long in the memory.'[19]

Major's sixth and final G7 meeting at Lyon at the end of June was an
anticlimax after the excitements at Halifax the year before and some earlier
G7 summits. Discussion revolved around the same issues – restructuring the
UN, IMF and World Bank and debt relief for the poorest countries – and
the same earnest communiqués were released that few subsequently read.[20]
A certain piquancy was given to discussions on terrorism by an IRA bomb
blast on 28 June at Osnabrück British army base in Germany.[21]

Irish unrest was proving a problem, too, closer to home. For months
considerable effort had been put in by the NIO to try to defuse conflict
during the summer marching season in Northern Ireland. In particular, with
Trimble emerging as the strong-willed victor during the Drumcree stand-off
at Portadown in July 1995, it seemed sadly likely that this year would see a
trial of strength too. The flashpoint came again at Drumcree. The Orange
Order was unwilling to compromise with the Catholic residents' association,
believing them to be controlled by Sinn Fein. When the Orange marchers
arrived in early July at the predominantly nationalist community, they found
their path blocked by the police.[22]

Management of the march was in the hands of Hugh Annesley, Chief
Constable of the Royal Ulster Constabulary, who decided on 6 July to reroute
the Orangemen's march away from the Catholic area in the interests of
public order. The Orangemen failed to comply. As pressure built, with both
communities reinforcing their numbers, and riots and disruption spread
across the province, Drumcree became a hugely symbolic totem, from which
only one side could emerge as the victors. A deputation of Unionist leaders
was received at Number Ten, including Trimble and Paisley, who expressed
grave concern at what might happen if Major did not overrule Annesley and
allow the march to proceed. The Catholics' barricades would be forced down
before long by the marchers, he was told, with untold bloodshed. A rushed
ministerial meeting was convened on 10 July to consider the problem. The
tenor of the meeting was that there would be greater risks if an attempt was
made to sustain the Chief Constable's decision. This conclusion was duly
conveyed to Annesley.[23] The next day, on 11 July, he announced that the
march should proceed, and his police force moved in to clear the barricades.
A whiplash reaction from the thwarted Catholic community was inevitable.

Rioting broke out in several Catholic areas, including Londonderry and Strabane, resulting in widespread damage to property and loss of one life.[24]

Major found the episode profoundly depressing. It showed him that the centre ground in Ulster politics – despite his earlier hopes – barely existed. When a crisis occurred, both communities retreated into their tribal loyalties. Bruton attacked both the RUC and the British government for caving in to pressure, while Loyalist paramilitaries, after a Republican bomb in Enniskillen, issued dire threats that they would end their ceasefire.[25] In an effort to prevent the breakdown of the two-year Loyalist ceasefire, Major met at Number Ten representatives associated with their organisations, to expressions of unease.[26] In a passionate interview in BBC's *Panorama* in mid-July, he urged the people of Northern Ireland: 'Don't look to the extremes, don't turn in temptation to the voices of extremism ... Turn to the centre, to the political leaders who are looking for a peaceful future ... Do we want to return to the twenty-five years of murder, mayhem, slaughter, indiscriminate bombings ... or is it my job, everyone's job, to try and get that put behind us for ever?'[27]

The truth was that the centre was desperately weak in Northern Ireland. Major tried for the remaining months of his premiership to work away to bolster the peace process, but he found Trimble weak and unreliable, and thought that Hume could not deliver on the other side. For a man like John Major, for whom a desire to unite and make concessions for the sake of a common end were second nature, the polarised Northern Ireland mentality was hard to accept. He continued to look for a way forward, but the months before a general election are a difficult time to achieve political progress in Northern Ireland. In November Hume came to see him and suggested that a new ceasefire might be possible if a route for Sinn Fein to enter talks, and a timetable for such talks, were to be mapped out. Major was not convinced that it would work, and felt that giving Sinn Fein a date for entry to talks after a ceasefire was a hurdle too far.[28] In the changed circumstances after the election, with the Unionists less constrained by electoral pressures and a government with a secure majority, the formula brought a restoration of the IRA ceasefire in July 1997.[29]

The centre was proving equally weak in his own Tory Party. To protect the government's majority in the Commons, he let Mawhinney and Goodlad prop up maverick right-wing MP George Gardiner, facing deselection by his Reigate constituency.[30] Such were his negative feelings about Gardiner that Major himself would have been quite prepared to let him sink, even with the impact it would have had on the majority.[31] On 4 July Cabinet considered the 26 per cent pay rise recommended by the independent pay body for MPs and ministers, which Major asked for after the clampdown on outside earnings following Nolan. They urged MPs instead to accept 3 per cent, but on 10 July MPs rejected his own personal plea, and voted for the full increase, worth an extra £9,000 p.a., for backbenchers.[32] Tory MPs, still riled by Nolan, were angered by Major's attempt to restrict their pay. They failed to accept the value of the argument that the sight of MPs voting for huge pay increases for themselves would not be well received in the country nor do anything for the image of Parliament. Major was always rather an innocent about money: he had never earned or owned much, and failed fully to understand the strong feelings of his MPs about it.

He decided to let rip at his end-of-term address to the 1922 Committee on 19 July.[33] They had to stop fighting each other, he told them, and turn all their guns on Labour, which 'doesn't have a single policy born out of strong conviction – everything is born out of what would resonate with the electorate on a daily basis'. The Party had to win back the 'hearts and minds' of the fourteen million people who voted Conservative in 1992. He warned, 'Don't book a holiday next spring', because of the election, and urged them to consider two questions, '"Have I done something today to help win the election?" and "Have I avoided doing anything today which would increase the risk of losing?"'[34]

The Paymaster General, David Heathcoat-Amory, either did not read the passage, or chose to ignore it: three days after Major's speech he took the course he had long been debating and resigned because of his dissatisfaction with the government's 'compromise' position on the single currency.[35] His high profile raised the temperature on the issue again. The right in the Party and in the press increasingly brought Clarke into their sights for preventing the government changing the policy. As a leader in *The Times* said, without his intransigence, 'Mr Major would most probably have agreed by now that he could and should rule out joining a single currency during the next Parliament'.[36] Many key figures in Central Office had been thinking similarly, while Maurice Saatchi believed that ruling out the single currency was the one core magical step Number Ten could take which would both transform the Party's electoral prospects and reunite it.[37]

Because Major had for three years been modifying his position on the EU in a sceptical direction many thought, or hoped, that he would feel little compunction about abandoning the referendum pledge compromise hammered out in Cabinet on 4 April, and rule out the single currency altogether in the life of the next Parliament. But this was a shift he was not prepared to make, for reasons of genuine conviction, and he felt the need to say so boldly in an interview in *The Times* on 25 July. The decision about whether to join would be the most important the country would take for 'fifty years or more'. If Britain was to rule out joining, it would mean that the other fourteen EU countries would plan the future operation of the currency, which would affect this country greatly, with no British input: 'For us to opt out of the debate now would be a dereliction of responsibility.'[38]

Major's position was honourable and sensible in diplomatic terms, but in political circles it won few admirers. On Europe, it was Mrs Thatcher who had the last word in July: she would not, it was suggested, be campaigning for any Conservatives in seats where they were being opposed by a candidate from Goldsmith's Referendum Party.[39] Major's restatement in *The Times* had done nothing to quell those seeking to increase the pressure for the government to come all out against a single currency.

July had further trials. In an effort to pacify Cornish fishermen, receiving widespread public support for their plight under the EU Common Fisheries Policy, he travelled to the port of St Ives to listen to them.[40] The BSE scare continued: numbers of cattle to be culled were raised to 120,000 to speed up agreement on the lifting of the ban, amid new fears of BSE spreading to sheep, and evidence suggesting a hereditary BSE risk in cattle. Strikes plagued the London tube, and the post, leading to Lang announcing that the Post Office's monopoly on letters would be suspended.[41] Progress in the Northern Ireland peace talks was halted for six weeks in the volatile post-Drumcree atmosphere.

Attempts to improve the Tories' prospects in another part of the Union were faring little better. Major's and Forsyth's decision on 3 July to return the celebrated Stone of Scone, which had resided in Westminster Abbey for 700 years, failed to achieve the desired reception when it was portrayed, in another example of the propaganda war being lost, as a publicity stunt.[42] The gesture was followed two days later by Major addressing MPs on the Scottish Grand Committee in Edinburgh – the first time a prime minister had done so – with the dangers of Labour's devolution plans as his text.[43] July also saw Britain's poor showing in the 1996 Olympic Games in Atlanta, with only one gold medal, which prompted his announcement of £100 million of lottery money being available for a National Sports Academy.[44]

There were some bright moments, not least Nelson Mandela's state visit. Major's admiration for the South African leader was undimmed, and he was proud of his association with such a popular and respected figure, who was greeted with an extraordinary ardour throughout his stay. For his meeting with Major at Number Ten on 10 July, the Downing Street staff lined both sides of the corridors to clap him in, Mandela insisting on shaking the hand of every person in the line.[45] Another highlight was Major's visit as guest of Classic FM to the 'Three Tenors' concert (Luciano Pavarotti, Placido Domingo and José Carreras) at Wembley on 6 July, when he received a great cheer from the audience.[46] A July reshuffle provided him with the opportunity of some minor changes to impart a fresh complexion to the government. In particular, he was pleased to promote Willetts, a rising star, to Paymaster General, and to appoint Jacqui Lait as the first-ever female Conservative Whip.[47]

The summer holiday, however, could not come soon enough, and he was happy to fly off to the south of France with Norma in early August to stay again in Phil Harris's house overlooking the Mediterranean, and to put the state of Britain behind him.[48]

Demon Eyes and Rainbow Peers: August

Clare Short could never have imagined that her words in a holiday season interview in the *New Statesman* would provoke such a reaction. Smarting from her demotion in Labour's Shadow Cabinet in July, she was critical of Blair's style and advisers. 'There should be less modifying everything we stand for, pruning it down and down to be acceptable to the *Daily Mail*,' she said, 'because I don't think the *Mail* will ever support us.' There were, she suggested, two Tony Blairs – one nice and decent, the other a creature of New Labour's marketeers and spin doctors, and she spoke of manipulation by forces 'of the dark'.[49]

The article, which appeared on Friday 9 August, immediately gave Steve Hilton, an advertising agent, an idea, which he aired with Finkelstein and Lewington. Why not produce an advertisement in which Tony Blair was portrayed with a black strip across his eyes on which were placed the red demon's eyes from the 'New Labour, New Danger' campaign?[50] They discussed the idea with Mawhinney and Tim Bell, who thought it tremendous. The advertisement was sent to the *Sunday Times* and the *News of the World*, as well as to Jonathan Holborow, editor of the *Mail on Sunday*. Holborow telephoned Mawhinney later on the Friday to say several of his executives did not like it, but on balance he would still run it. Mawhinney also had a difficult two-hour telephone conversation with a sceptical Maurice Saatchi on Saturday morning, on holiday in France, who did not want to personalise the attack by putting the eyes on Blair.[51]

The advertisement, when it appeared on Sunday 11 August, caused an explosive reaction. Labour wanted to create as big a row as possible to put the Conservatives on the defensive over negative advertising. Mandelson condemned it as a 'threat to the political life of the country', while Church leaders condemned the use of 'satanic imagery', and the Advertising Standards Authority began an investigation, which rejected the more serious charges against the advertisement but decided before the month was out that the image was still 'offensive' and broke the advertising code of practice.[52] It was the first time a political advertisement had been subject to a ban, but as the Party and its advertisers were quick to realise, the very notoriety of the image led to it being reproduced free of charge many times over, gaining millions of pounds' worth of free exposure, in a similar way as happened with the celebrated Saatchi & Saatchi poster for the 1979 general election, 'Labour isn't working'.[53]

Major was in the south of France when the advertisement appeared. He did not like it, and it helped to shape his growing dislike of personal attacks on Blair, which was to cause so much discord during the general election campaign, as well as to confirm his apprehensions about the whole Saatchi–Bell approach. He had been stimulated and excited by several of their ideas, but remained wary of two of the 'three musketeers', especially when their minds moved as quickly and explosively as Saatchi's and Bell's were prone to do.[54] Even during the general election, he would still in unguarded moments talk as if Labour remained the unreconstructed party of old. The soapbox was the election world he understood and liked; the world of campaign strategies and subliminal messages was, he thought in his heart, for the birds.

He did not, however, feel so strongly that he resisted nominating Maurice Saatchi for a peerage, along with Peter Gummer, the safe musketeer, in the honours list announced on 21 August. Frank Dobson, Labour's Shadow Environment Secretary, railed against their nomination, saying both men had dragged 'British politics lower than the gutter'.[55] John Taylor, the Tory candidate for Cheltenham who lost in the 1992 general election after his local party split on whether to support him, was another to be ennobled. The Tories' first peer of Afro-Caribbean descent, he was thrilled with the distinction; 'This is the rainbow after the rain,' he said. 'This has more than made up for 1992.' His elevation reflected Major's own prejudices, recognised unusually in the *New Statesman*, in an article by Darcus Howe: 'John Major has courageously set things right. First it is clear that he is compensating John Taylor for his public humiliation. And rightly so. John Major, with roots in Brixton and in Lambeth council, is instinctively anti-racist and has struck a blow for racial harmony in sending a young Afro-Caribbean to the Lords.'[56]

Life Really is Better: September

After his return from France on 19 August, it was a peaceful period for Major, a chance for some cricket matches, having his portrait painted by June Mendoza, some quiet reading and recharging of batteries for what he knew would be the last prolonged rest until election day.[57]

Blair's media operation continued putting pressure on the Tories, achieving a number of coups, such as a conversation by satellite link between Blair and the British Olympic team in Atlanta at the end of July, and a visit to the set of Granada television's *Coronation Street* a month later, both of which attracted wide publicity.[58] Major's team moved into counterattack. In a move seen as a riposte to the high-profile exposure of Cherie Blair, or Elizabeth Dole and Hillary Clinton during the US presidential race, Norma took a step towards the limelight. The hook was the publication of her book *Chequers. The Prime Minister's Country House and its History*, which she had spent the last four years writing, and which was to be published in September. Dedicated to John, to her children Elizabeth and James, as well as to her mother Dee, who was seriously ill, it was a lavishly illustrated and well-written book which proved, to the Majors' delight, a significant critical and publishing success.[59]

On 3 September, Major and Norma embarked on a two-week nationwide tour, under the title 'Life's better' (a name which raised some hackles from purists among the Party's strategists who said that the 'Life's better' phase of the pre-election strategy had finished on 1 July).[60] The Majors were both exceptionally cheery. The tour opened with a dinner in Bristol, then a visit to Bristol docks and on to Weston-super-Mare and Barnstaple, on a day he made a widely publicised comment that Norma had been 'his secret weapon for twenty-six years'.[61] Sheila Gunn, a journalist on *The Times*, drafted into Central Office earlier in the year but now increasingly a personal media adviser to the Majors, was blamed for over-selling Norma and the trip, especially when some of Norma's words were repeated implying she thought Blair would win the election.[62] But the evident success of the trip meant any disapproval was shortlived. Major began to joke about Norma's high profile, telling Party activists, 'I am so pleased that Norma has allowed me to accompany her on this tour.'[63] In Weston-super-Mare a visit to a shopping mall saw the Majors treated as if they were pop or film stars: with everyone crying out for autographs or to shake their hands, it took over an hour to move just three hundred yards. On the Friday at the end of the first week the tour party went to the Majors' local Indian restaurant in Huntingdon at 10 o'clock, Major happily talking about football, the people they had met, anything but politics.[64]

Momentum built during the tour. The following Monday, 10 September, the party travelled by helicopter to Hereford, and then to Buxton in the Peak District, where again they were received with tremendous enthusiasm. The tour finished in Scotland for two days, beginning with a lunchtime speech on Thursday to the Glasgow Press Fund, in which he urged an end to 'soundbite' politics and called for more 'mature debate' in British politics.[65] The party then moved on to stay the night at the Ballathie House Hotel, overlooking the River Tay, just to the north of Perth. Hopes of a quiet stay with walks along the river banks were suspended when it was made clear that the Party's senior officials and businessmen wanted to spend the evening with them and join them for a five-course dinner. Major was typically charming, and stayed talking politics with them until after midnight. The next morning was a beautiful September Scotland day, with the air crystal-clear. Alex Allan and his wife joined the Majors at the hotel to accompany them for the annual Balmoral visit.[66]

While staying with the Queen, on Sunday 15 September, a pre-recorded television interview was screened between Norma and David Frost. Unusually, the interview was filmed at The Finings, in the conservatory overlooking Major's beloved fishpond. Her performance showed how much she had grown in authority and poise over the nearly six years that she had been at Number Ten. Her stylish, unaffected performance gave even the most jaded critic little meat to chew on. Norma had become, particularly since the leadership election, a significant influence on her husband.[67] But it was her veiled criticisms of over-intrusive media rather than her reflections on Chequers which caught the attention of a self-reflecting media.

'A change in atmosphere is becoming apparent everywhere, up and down the country,' declared Major in Avon towards the end of the tour, adding, 'it is a while before it is reflected by the fashionable opinion formers'.[68] The opinion polls were at last beginning to move the government's way. An ICM poll in mid-September had Labour's lead cut to only 15 per cent, with the Conservatives up to 32 per cent.[69] In any normal period this century, such an Opposition lead so close to a general election would have caused panic; but these times were not normal. The key question the Tories were asking was the strength of Labour's vote: their research gave them hope that Tory defectors might well be on the verge of returning to the fold. Hopes were raised by Prescott deliberately calling himself a 'democratic socialist' in contrast to Blair's description of himself as a 'social democrat' and by Labour abandoning its plans to hold a second Scottish referendum on taxation powers, an apparent U-turn which could be cheerfully exploited.[70] Some apprehension was caused by the news that Major and Heseltine might be subpoenaed to appear at the Hamilton–*Guardian* libel case during the week of the Conservative Party Conference. But in general it was a glorious first half of September,[71] and the last time the Majors were truly relaxed and happy until some weeks after the general election.

While the 'Life's better' tour had been in progress, disagreement had been brewing amongst the Party's election strategists about the theme to be adopted for the annual Party Conference and for the autumn campaign. Finkelstein and Lewington in mid-August went to the Republican Convention in San Diego on a fact-finding mission. The former found Jack Kemp's ideas for extending market forces into social policy areas and on 'empowerment' chimed with his growing conviction that more needed to be done to tell, or to remind, the electorate about why they needed the Conservative Party.[72] His thinking crystallised around the slogan 'Opportunity for all', a message he correctly judged would appeal to Major. This theme, however, cut across the convictions of Maurice Saatchi, that antipathy to Europe held the key to the Party's recovery. At a number of 'cold towel' evenings, as Saatchi called evening sessions at his home where the aim was to think the unthinkable, the difference with Finkelstein's approach became increasingly clear.[73]

The crunch came at Chequers on the evening of 17 September. During the day, Major had invited the Policy Unit to join him. The morning was spent hearing about Central Office's latest findings on changing voter attitudes and then examining announcements to be made during the Party Conference. In the afternoon, they worked on ideas for Major's conference speech.[74] Exploiting the opportunity of a walk in the garden with the Prime Minister, Finkelstein, who had also been invited for the Policy Unit's discussions, raised his theme of 'opportunity'. 'You've got to let Major be Major,' the young research director told the Prime Minister.

Finkelstein talked about how he felt Major's own ideals of a classless society harmonised with the opportunity theme, and would provide him with the platform to speak about what he wanted to achieve in politics. Major was interested, and responded that he had indeed not been able to fully to realise his hopes since he became Prime Minister.[75] That evening, the 'three musketeers', together with Mawhinney, Lewington, Howell James and George

Bridges, arrived for a strategy meeting. Maurice Saatchi launched in with a presentation about his 'big D' theme – the big danger, i.e. Europe. Major appeared quite attracted, though mostly out of good manners, and the discussion continued over dinner about the benefits and risks of adopting an overtly anti-Europe tack, and the extent to which any European dangers, for example of tax, could be quantified.

The problem with the 'big D' was that Major's aides felt that it would be impossible to convince voters – even including George Bridges's mother, so her son said – that criticising Labour for supposedly copying from Europe was not in itself an 'anti-European' or 'petty nationalist' position. Saatchi's argument, they feared, was too subtle and risky to hold together through the rigours of a general election campaign.[76] After dinner, Major was presented with three rival slogan boards for the Party Conference: Saatchi's 'True to Britain', Finkelstein's 'Opportunity for all', and 'It matters more than ever'. The last, without a strong champion, being hardly a starter, Major saw the attraction of the first two, but when the guests departed that evening, he had still not decided which he preferred.[77]

The next morning at breakfast he showed the boards to Norma, and to the Wrens who were in attendance at Chequers, and who loved 'True to Britain'. Aides watched in horror as they imagined the entire Party's Conference slogan being determined by the ultra-patriotic Wrens.[78] Major, however, was moving the other way. Back in London, he discussed the selection with Mawhinney in the Cabinet Room. Mawhinney told him he preferred 'Opportunity for all', which was duly adopted. Both men agreed at the same meeting that the words 'for all' should be written on the conference slogan in Major's handwriting.[79] This duly became the theme presented to Political Cabinet on 26 September, accompanied by a résumé for ministers of the latest thinking on election strategy.

Ministers, refreshed by the summer break, were in a positive frame of mind.[80] They accepted with apparent good humour the line from Major and Mawhinney that they were to aim to make two policy announcements and to be positive and forward-looking in their Conference speeches, a point later underlined in a memo from Blackwell the week before the Conference opened, saying that the last portion in particular of their speeches should be devoted entirely to plans for the future.[81] To ensure that there was no mis-understanding, Finkelstein also made personal visits to all Cabinet ministers to ensure that they referred to the opportunity theme and took an optimistic line in their conference speeches.[82]

Some pre-conference antics, however, appeared to disturb the steady atmosphere. A successful Major *Spectator* lecture on 18 September on public services was the last in his series of speeches on the 'five themes'. But the lecture, in which he claimed that the Conservative preference for freedom of choice and a small state was more moral than any alternative model, and a pre-emptive strike by Mawhinney against the Liberal Democrats, were both upstaged by a letter written to the *Independent* by six senior Tories, Brittan,

Carrington, Heath, Howe, Whitelaw and Hurd.[83] The 'grandees' wrote that 'Britain's future lies as a committed member of an interdependent Europe, as a country which sees the European Union as an opportunity, not a threat'.[84] Major was disconcerted by the letter, which he found 'unhelpful', and was particularly surprised to see the last-named a signatory: having been his Foreign Secretary for nearly five years, he thought Hurd would have realised the risks of rocking the boat as the party conference season was about to begin.[85] But the signatories knew what they were doing. There had been an upsurge of Euroscepticism at every conference since 1992 and the letter was a deliberate attempt by the Party's senior Europhiles to head off a repetition in 1996 that could threaten the Cabinet deal on the single currency.[86]

The letter sparked off the now predictable zigzag response from both camps. The right were, as Major feared, riled: Lamont weighed in calling the signatories 'dinosaurs, not grandees'.[87] Tebbit's response on 21 September was even more pointed: the resignation of Clarke and Heseltine would be a 'price worth paying' to change the policy on the single currency.[88] Rifkind, meanwhile, had stirred the pot and caused puzzlement as to his motives when he said in Zurich that a single currency would be divisive within the EU.[89]

Clarke was angry not to have been consulted about the speech, and felt that his reputation as an 'unguided missile' was unjust given what other Cabinet ministers were doing. He reacted injudiciously when, on 22 September, he was asked about the 'wait and see' policy and snapped that it would be 'pathetic' for Britain to stand back only to join later. In his irritable mood, he had mistaken a question about official government policy for one about a Eurosceptic demand to rule out joining the single currency for a fixed period. Damage control was hampered because, almost immediately, he had to fly to an international finance ministers' conference.[90] These remarks came only a week after he had told Anna Ford on BBC's *Today* programme that he thought Labour no longer such a threat to the national interest.[91] Nicholas Bonsor, the Eurosceptic Foreign Office minister, announced on BBC Radio's *World at One* the next day that Clarke was 'out of line with government policy'. Major was forced to support Clarke against Bonsor's attack, but privately he was fuming.[92] The *Independent*, a pro-Clarke newspaper, bolstered him – perhaps – with a front-page picture of a pair of brown suede brogues with the headline 'Can anyone fill this man's shoes?'[93]

Clarke, as ever, knew what he was doing – firing warning shots to show that he was not prepared to accept any further distancing from Europe. Even though his remarks were smoothed over in public, they marked a significant step in the estrangement of the Chancellor from Central Office and to some extent from Number Ten. The former had increasingly identified a new target for their ire, Clarke's special adviser Anthony Teasdale, who had performed a similar influential role with the Europhile Howe. Teasdale was seen as a Machiavellian figure goading on the amiable Clarke to ever greater acts of defiance and a rough equivalent of Redwood's adviser, Hywel Williams.[94] Others, and increasingly his Cabinet colleagues, rightly blamed

Clarke himself: he was not the type of person that even the most seductive of aides could 'goad on'.[95]

Deft behind-the-scenes footwork took place to pacify Lady Thatcher. An article in the *Guardian* by Michael White on 31 August claimed that she was 'ready to cut ties with the Conservative Party' and to support the Referendum Party, while the talk about town was growing of her admiration for Goldsmith.[96] Cecil Parkinson was asked to interpose and discover what was going on, and found out that the Referendum Party story had no firm foundation. Whatever her feelings about Europe, and Major, this close to the election she had decided the time had come to play the loyalist card. She agreed to put out a statement of strong support for Major, rendered all the more necessary by diary extracts from the diplomatic specialist George Urban being serialised in *The Times* in September. Urban quoted Mrs Thatcher saying that within three weeks of Major succeeding her, his government 'want to undo many of the things we have accomplished'.[97] Mawhinney, who had been keeping in regular touch with her, went to her London office to discuss the role she would play at the Party Conference, and persuaded her that it would be best if she and Major spoke generous words about each other; Tim Bell, one of Thatcher's closest allies, had also played a powerful brokering role behind the scenes.[98] Whatever Bell's criticisms of the lack of fire of the Major government, he viewed the alternative, a Labour government, with enormously more apprehension.

To clear the air before the Conservative Party Conference opened in Bournemouth, a reiteration by Major of the government line on the single currency was thought necessary. In Cabinet on 26 September, he made it clear that he would not be moved from the 'wait and see' policy they had agreed in April.[99] The next day, when in Reading, he agreed to be interviewed in a phone-in radio programme. An aide caught his mood: 'He was nervous on the way to the studio as he often was, worrying that the BBC would stitch him up. When he arrived, as always happened, he breezed in and there were glad hands all round the office. Everyone was dazzled and the secretaries went around saying "Isn't he tall?" And he enjoyed doing it and was very persuasive.'[100] He followed it up with a strong reiteration of his 'wait and see' policy to the Reading *Evening Post* of 27 September.

Foreign issues also distracted his preparation for the Conference, particularly the backwash from a storm in Iraq earlier in September. When Saddam Hussein joined forces with one of the Kurdish factions in northern Iraq, the Clinton administration felt it must retaliate, calling for British support in its attacks on missile sites in the south, all the more important because the US was virtually isolated internationally in taking the action. Major felt very strongly that Saddam was evil and had to be punished: 'He's a dictator and he's going to take what we give him,' he told Portillo, the Defence Secretary.[101] RAF planes were on the tarmac on standby, waiting for orders to attack. Major backed their use. Had the administration called for this help, Major would have found himself in conflict with Lyell, who as

Attorney-General argued that there was no base in international law for a military response. But it did not come to that.[102] British backing was limited to offering public support and help in the debate at the UN, and some logistical support.

On 5 October, on the eve of the Party Conference, Major flew to Dublin, for a mid-presidency council convened by the Irish. He found it a fairly pointless exercise; as he stepped off the plane he quipped, 'We're here because we're here because we're here', and the meeting produced so little of substance that Stephen Wall opened his report on the Council with the First World War motif still alive, 'Lest we Forget'.[103] While other EU leaders rallied together to reinvigorate the IGC talks on the future of the EU, Major was made to feel, in the words of a Belgian official, 'like an awkward cousin who may soon be leaving the family'.[104]

On the flight home, Major's thoughts turned back to the Party Conference. The pressure was on as Labour's conference the week before at Blackpool had proved a significant success – Blair's third in a row. Cracks in Labour unity did not appear, boundless self-confidence was ubiquitous, and there was a triumphal Blair speech. Major did not see it, but he read the transcript. He was irritated, and even more so by its press coverage the next day. He found the speech overblown, almost Messianic.[105] Sleaze was another background anxiety. Neil Hamilton, together with Ian Greer, the lobbyist, withdrew their libel action against the *Guardian* newspaper the week before, prompting a fresh series of claims in the cash-for-questions issue.

Major's new Paymaster General, David Willetts, came under attack for trying to block a parliamentary inquiry into Hamilton, while Major himself was accused of only holding on to Hamilton to preserve his majority. Sensing they had a strong issue to undermine the Conservative conference, Prescott said of Hamilton: 'John Major cannot afford to lose him can he? Why? Because this man is his Parliamentary majority of one. He is John Major's immoral majority of one.' They were good lines, but left Major frustrated as Hamilton had repeatedly professed his innocence to him, and he did not believe he had the right to take further action until and if he was proved guilty.[106] It made him even more determined to ensure that Bournemouth was not swamped by the issue and that it proved his most successful conference as leader.

Bournemouth Conference: October

As Major, Norma, Howell James, Norman Blackwell and Ian McColl settled down into their first-class compartment at London's Waterloo station on Monday 7 October awaiting departure for Bournemouth, they had reason for satisfaction. Major had spelled out in an article in *The Times* on Saturday that he would not be pushed before the election into ruling out the single currency, and Clarke, the chief object of their anxiety, had been puffed and reassured by Major in Sunday's *Breakfast with Frost*. So much for the praise. The Chancellor had also been spoken to by Major and Mawhinney, while Blackwell had vetted his conference script. Conscious of the need for stage-management, a number of tactics had been devised to detract media attention away from the several Eurosceptic fringe events.[107]

As Major's party sped southwest in their newly privatised train, a mobile telephone rang in their compartment. It was Lewington, who told them that the BBC Radio 4's *PM* programme was running with a story in the early evening based on that night's BBC television *Panorama* programme, alleging that Redwood hesitated to recommend that voters support the Conservative Party at the general election. Redwood was the figure Major most blamed for causing division, and the mood in the carriage was quickly deflated as visions were conjured up of the former Welsh Secretary blowing the entire conference off course.[108] On arrival at Bournemouth station, Major gave an interview brushing the story aside, and Redwood, who felt he had been misquoted and was anxious to repair the damage, worked with the Party's spinners, quickly killing the story.

With angry farmers protesting outside the conference hall, BSE was another issue which could have upset the conference, but Major and Agriculture Minister Angela Browning talked to the farmers' representatives in private and the issue was defused. Sleaze headlines, too, rapidly faded after the first day; so did any resonance from McAlpine's eve-of-conference defection to the Referendum Party: the media failed to pay much attention to the deliberately timed departure of the former Deputy Chairman and Treasurer of the Conservative Party.[109] The Referendum Party's hopes for widespread, high-profile defections to scupper the conference also failed to materialise.

By Tuesday, a feeling of cautious optimism was beginning to spread among the leadership. Not even the Eurosceptic MP James Cran's resignation as PPS to Mayhew was managing to knock the conference off course. Mawhinney, delighted at his brokering of peace between Major and Thatcher, himself delivered a strong speech, saying, 'Mr Blair, you are no Margaret Thatcher.' He had high praise for his leader. 'This man, this tough fighter, this compassionate, decent man, this true Brit, this is the best man to be our Prime Minister.'

Lady Thatcher's appearance on the platform, greeted by Major with a kiss, led to wild cheers from delegates. Later that day, the two figures made a joint appearance at a reception for Greater London Tories. She had taken great trouble over her speech, and had accepted that it should be unequivocally emollient. To the upset of purists among the Party's strategists, she went completely 'off message' and attacked Labour in old-style trade union terms, rather than for its new dangers. But this did not unduly concern the high command at Number Ten and Central Office. It was her praise for Major that was important, and it was this that caught the attention of the media: 'I have fought more elections than I care to recall. But it has never been more important to see the Conservatives returned to office – and you, John, to

Downing Street.'[110] Her enjoiner 'let's get cracking' was seized on as such a timely message that Deputy Chairman Michael Trend at once turned it into a conference badge.[111] Major was equally fulsome about her and her contribution as the 'architect' of the revolution.

The strategists – Finkelstein, Lewington and Bridges, principally – continued to worry when Lady Thatcher started to say that New Labour had stolen many of the Conservative Party's policies. They had noted the damage done in the US elections in 1992 when Bush claimed that Clinton was stealing his policies: they concluded this tack had strengthened Clinton for his eclecticism, not diminished him as a mere plagiarist. They were even more concerned about Major's recidivist tendencies in abandoning the 'new danger' approach: they termed it his 'jackdaw' tendency.[112]

But they had no need to worry at Bournemouth, where on Wednesday he gave one of his strongest performances in a shirt-sleeved question-and-answer session with delegates. Mawhinney had proposed the form to Major, having been impressed by how well he fielded unscripted questions at a similar meeting for Tories in Bristol in March.[113] Major gave himself the briefest of preparations, with James and Bridges scripting a few points for him to make, and a walk onto the set where he would be talking the evening before. One of his few pre-prepared passages was a story he had told before about Boris Yeltsin. The Russian leader had come to stay at Chequers in tracksuit and trainers. His security men had knocked on the locked door of the pub near Chequers shouting, 'It's the President of Russia.' A voice inside replied, 'And I'm the Kaiser.' But Major was equally concerned to put across serious points, which included the possible privatisation of the Royal Mail, and a 'firm' response on the ownership of hand guns in the wake of Cullen's Dunblane inquiry. His statement about the possible privatisation of London Underground had not been pre-planned and, as happened, came out of the blue, to the surprise of his listening Cabinet ministers. Major concluded the seventy-five-minute session at Bournemouth with 'same time, different place, same job, next year'. Boris Johnson thought 'it was a triumph'.[114]

On Wednesday the leadership became exasperated with the BBC for leading their lunchtime bulletins on Europe splits, whereas the rest of the media had moved away and paid little attention to the fringe speeches of Tebbit and Heathcoat-Amory on Tuesday evening. The BBC's emphasis persuaded Mawhinney to complain to its management about 'distorted coverage'.[115] Whether in response to the complaints or not, the BBC's reporting was felt by the Tories to have improved from that point onwards.

The speech on which the success of the conference, perhaps even the Tories' election fortunes, most rested, was Clarke's. With his strong feelings on Europe, his unpredictability, and the highly charged atmosphere, the question being asked was how would he decide to play it? Adding to the tension were warnings, or threats, that he might be shouted down by angry Eurosceptics.[116] Would he react against it, as he had done in the past? He played his cards close to his chest, and was determined to disappoint the right-wing journalists who he thought had come to Bournemouth to write his political obituary. More time than usual for him was spent finessing and practising his speech.[117]

The ground had been carefully prepared. Clarke and Rifkind, whose own speech had been advanced up the conference agenda, had worked together to 'dovetail' the passages on Europe. It proved the speech of the conference, helped along by its low-key humour. 'Gordon Brown bases his policies on the Dolly Parton school of economics: an unbelievable figure blown out of all proportion.' More important was his urging, 'Let us spend the next six months uniting behind that policy, attacking the Labour Party, talking about the economy and winning the next election.'[118] During Clarke's rapturous ovation, Major came down to the front of the platform to raise aloft Clarke's arm, a hugely symbolic and powerful image. After the applause died away, Major burst into the VIP room backstage and announced, 'That's it. After that speech I *know* we're going to win.'[119]

Major's own Friday speech was always going to be difficult after the success of his Wednesday performance. He opted to be deliberately downbeat and sincere in a speech drafted by Bridges, with much personal input from Major himself and the usual polishing by Ronnie Millar. Major had worked on it most mornings during the conference. On Thursday evening, he discussed it with his speech-writing team over fish and chips in his suite, before departing for the Treasurer's party at 10 p.m. While he was away, both Heseltine and Sarah Hogg came in and scribbled a few words on the text. Major returned after midnight, and worked on the script again until 3 a.m., adding passages and changing others. He then went to bed and his team processed the changes, waking him up at 6 a.m. with the final revision for his approval.[120] His aim of showing that the Tories needed a fifth term in office was achieved by reference to the pronouncements made during the week by his ministers, to which he added one new initiative, electronic tagging curfew orders to juvenile offenders. The speech contained some sharp rhetorical flushes:

It simply won't do for Mr Blair to say, 'Look, I'm not a socialist anymore. Now can I be Prime Minister please?' Sorry, Tony. Job's taken. And anyway, it's too big a task for your first real job.

With an IRA bomb at Lisburn army base near Belfast earlier in the week, there was particular poignancy in the words, which he dictated that morning from his bath, 'I don't believe you, Mr Adams. I don't believe you.' Major had been particularly outraged by the fact that a British soldier had been killed. The phrase that achieved most attention was another late addition to the script: 'New Labour, old school tie'. He finished simply, with the now almost mandatory reference to his origins.

In less than 1,000 days, Labour would vandalise nearly 1,000 years of British history. I didn't come from two rooms in Brixton to 10 Downing Street not to go out and fight with every fibre of my being for what I believe in. So at the election where will I be? I'll be out in the towns and streets. Where you are. I'll be the one talking to the people in the middle of the crowd. So come and join me. And I promise you – we'll win.[121]

The speech was well received in the hall and also by much of the media, although his delivery did not spark in the way it had done on Wednesday. The *Guardian* nevertheless said that it confirmed that Major had now become the Tories' 'chief electoral asset'.[122] Major was annoyed, however, when he saw the Saturday newspapers by the way that the Party's officials spun the speech, focusing on the contrast between 'honest John' and 'smarmy' or 'phoney Tony', picked up strongly by the *Daily Mail* and the *Express*.[123] He felt uncomfortable that the personal attack on Blair had been given precedence over the policy substance in the speech, a harbinger of a debate to recur during the election campaign.

The conference had been a great success. It was Mawhinney's finest achievement as Party Chairman. Although it was the most carefully and professionally planned conference of Major's six years as premier, it also gave the impression of being less stage-managed and authoritarian than Labour's Blackpool conference. Said one party official: 'For once, we did what New Labour did all the time, which was to have a purpose and a project, and all the speeches talked about it.'[124]

Best of all for the Tories, peace seemed to have broken out, too, on Europe. The Eurosceptic bandwagon, despite having the carts all hitched up and ready to go, failed to move off. It was Major, Clarke and Rifkind who won the argument, not Redwood, Lamont, Tebbit and Cash with their talk about a European superstate. Major changing the rhetoric that he used to describe the April referendum pact, from 'wait and see' to the more positive and understandable 'negotiate and decide', helped put the single currency policy across. His exposition of the government's case on EMU had, indeed, shown him at his most clear and eloquent.

Not even the long-heralded news that the disenchanted independent Tory MP Peter Thurnham was joining the Liberal Democrats upset the consensus that the Tory Party was back in with a chance.[125] Stephen Glover best summed up the impact of the conference. Most commentators went to Bournemouth believing they were going to witness the death throes of a party, and anticipating, hoping even, for open warfare, above all on Europe. Instead, 'Major seems widely admired, even loved by the Party faithful ... The thought is going around Bournemouth that this odd, resilient man might pull it off again.'[126]

THIRTY-EIGHT

Can the Centre Hold?:

October 1996–March 1997

Taking the Bricks Away: October–November

Major's own doubts about winning, expressed again in the week before the Party Conference, had been dispelled at Bournemouth.[1] An NOP poll in the *Sunday Times* on 20 October saw Labour's lead tumble from 23 to 14 points.[2] So when he saw the Party disintegrating before his eyes after the conference, his mood turned at times to despair and deep anger, although he clung to the belief until almost the end that a miracle might yet save them.[3]

How did the Party manage to squander its advantage at the very time, six months out from the likely election date, when harmony was never more vital? It is an intriguing study in self-inflicted damage, because by presenting again an image of a disunited and querulous party to the electorate, many more Tory seats were lost than would otherwise have been the case. The depth of the ideological divide on Europe and to a lesser extent on other issues was not in doubt: why the attempts to paper over the cracks failed to be sufficient until after the election is the issue. A series of individually unfortunate episodes should not have been enough to upset the equilibrium.

Thurnham was one such irritant: he sought to inflict maximum damage on his former party when he joined the Liberal Democrats. The final straw, he said, was the Hamilton case: he could no longer support a party that had lost touch with 'basic values of decency'.[4] In private, the leadership thought Thurnham's action petulant and cynical.[5] In public, Central Office's response was to sweep the issue aside: 'It doesn't change anything,' it said. 'Our majority is still the same, which is two.'[6] Thurnham's lasting damage was to help bring 'sleaze' back onto the autumn agenda. Morality was going to be a significant issue in the pre-election period, and Labour's polling told it that it had a clear advantage whenever 'sleaze' came up. His decision also raised fears that others would follow and wipe out the majority.

External factors helped raise the salience of moral issues. On 18 October Frances Lawrence, widow of north London headteacher Philip, murdered outside his school, launched her 'moral crusade' while the Catholic Church published 'The Common Good', also addressing issues of public behaviour. Both main parties fought hard to claim the upper ground, while regarding the other side as seeking to score cheap points. In April Blair had agreed to be interviewed in the *Sunday Telegraph* about his religious convictions.[7] On 20 October some earlier comments by Major, in which he spoke about his religious commitment, were published: 'I do believe. I don't pretend to understand all the complex parts of Christian theology, but I simply accept it', adding enigmatically that he prayed 'in all circumstances'.[8]

Morality was becoming a needle subject in the increasingly personalised and acrimonious relationship that had developed between both Party leaders over the previous six months. Blair believed that Major had behaved pettily over the arrangements for their joint visit to Dunblane in March, seeking to emphasise their different status. In Stephen Castle's opinion Dunblane proved the turning point in the souring of their relationship, a view Blair's aides confirm.[9] Major was then angered when, at Labour's Blackpool conference, a speaker representing the Dunblane 'Snowdrop' campaign addressed delegates, which he believed was exploiting the tragedy for Party advantage. Blair, who thought the 'demon eyes' a juvenile insult, was annoyed the following week by the Tories' talk about the 'old school tie' and 'phoney' jibes. From the outset of the 'sleaze' allegations in the summer of 1992, Major hated the way that his party was being denigrated over moral issues. He now projected his anger on Blair himself, whose portrayal of his own party as beyond reproach compared to the avaricious, dishonest and sexually immoral Tories he found unrecognisable and contemptible.[10]

The heightened moral climate provided the background for the fuss caused by the government's handling of the Queen's Speech for the 1996–7 session, delivered on 23 October. With a wafer-thin majority, and at most half a year until the general election, it was thought unlikely that the government would produce a full or controversial legislative programme. Newton and Goodlad, the Commons business managers, despairing of being able to get many Bills through smoothly, counselled for the bare minimum in the Queen's Speech. There were costs with a minimalist approach, however, of which Newton in particular was equally aware. It would make it easy for critics to say that the government had nothing left to offer and give the appearance of the government merely reacting to Labour, as had overshadowed the Queen's Speech the year before.

Cabinet therefore decided there had to be some substantive Bills, and that they should highlight significant areas of policy difference with Labour, above all over education, and law and order.[11] Thirteen Bills were duly announced by the Queen. Omitted were two widely trailed beforehand, on stalking and child sex offenders. Howard, one of the most activist of Major's ministers, already had three Bills in the Queen's Speech, and accepted that the stalking and child sex legislation could be passed quite happily as private Bills. Uproar ensued, brilliantly exploited by Labour, who claimed that their omission as public Bills from the Queen's Speech revealed a government insensitive on issues of deep contemporary concern. Major, stung by this charge, which had more to do with party politics than substance, at once accepted Blair's offer on the floor of the House that Labour would speed the two missing items through the Commons as public Bills, and said they would be added immediately to the government's legislative programme.

Major's response stunned the chamber. The *Daily Telegraph* caught the atmosphere: 'As an example of policy-making on the hoof, instantly endorsed by senior ministers on the bench beside him, MPs had never seen anything like it.'[12] But was his action a brilliant tactical coup, or the product of muddled thinking? Some senior colleagues thought Major's acceptance of Labour's offer displayed too much of a taste for the grand gesture, and would have preferred him to have challenged the Opposition to cooperate with Private Members' Bills to introduce the legislation.[13] Major defended his gesture robustly the next day on the BBC's *Today* programme, as an example of responsive and responsible governing. But in his heart he had doubts about his action, and it looked to many, not least in the press, that his anxiety not to be upstaged by Labour in the new game of moral climbing had prompted the U-turn.[14] The damage the incident did to Major's authority was difficult to register, but the impression given was not one of strength and resolve.

The next awkward episode again stemmed back to the Queen's Speech. Gillian Shephard's Education Bill did not, contrary to the urgings of the right inside and outside the government include an option for schools to restore corporal punishment.[15] But right-wing pressure in the Party grew via a backbench amendment to the Bill to allow a free vote to restore caning.[16] On the BBC's *Today* programme, Gillian Shephard stated that she was personally in favour of corporal punishment.[17]

When reports of her interview reached Major, he at once said he wanted to phone her to find out what was going on. The Number Ten switchboard, as ever superbly efficient, tracked her down on a mobile phone while she was on the stage at a school. Major's request that she did not reignite speculation about caning in schools became a 'slap-down' from the Prime Minister. Number Ten had, to journalists' surprise, briefed them about the episode. Despite heavily staged rapprochement with a joint photo session the next day, it came over as further evidence of a government at odds with itself, and Labour used it to keep 'Tory split' stories alive.[18] Major subsequently apologised to Shephard for flying off the handle, although his personal dislike of caning was sincere.

Labour's leadership was biding its time, waiting for the right moment to strike the ultimate blow. As soon as Donald Dewar, the Party's Chief Whip, was confident that Labour could win a 'no-confidence' motion, which would trigger a general election, he would recommend one. The most likely circumstances in which such a no-confidence vote would succeed was over a vote on Europe, where sufficient Ulster Unionists and Tory rebels, especially the former whipless MPs, might be incited to vote with Labour or abstain to force an election.[19] Failing a successful outcome of a no-confidence vote, Labour still hoped for an early poll to minimise the chance of any Tory recovery on the back of a return of the 'feel-good' factor.

The Tories survived these post-conference ripples without too much damage, while the all-important European divisions remained submerged in the first few weeks after Bournemouth, although Clarke was happy the way his conference speech had been received, and critics confounded. But within hours of delivering the speech, he was up in arms when he was told that Party officials were reassuring worried Eurosceptics and Tory columnists 'not to worry. It's only Ken. The policy would change. There would be a "Huntingdon declaration" and a brave new policy at the general election.'[20]

The story is still divisive: Clarke's allies are totally convinced that there was an effort on the part of some in Central Office and Number Ten to undermine his policies,[21] while such a ploy is dismissed as paranoia by those supposedly involved. Distorted or not, and the top leadership deny any knowledge of such briefings, the point is that Clarke believed such messages had been given out. 'It was just ridiculous,' he later said. 'It put me in a very bad frame of mind.'[22] But for the time being he held his counsel.

Goldsmith's Referendum Party Conference, for all its glitter, came and went on Saturday 19 October causing barely a ripple.[23] Major was able to make good play of his tough anti-federal stance expressed during a meeting with Chirac in Bordeaux on 8 November. He threatened to disrupt the December Dublin summit unless there were concessions on the EU's moves to impose a maximum forty-eight-hour week on Britain and on its fishing quota.[24] That went down well with the Eurosceptics. The prime need for Party unity was usefully underlined when, on 13 November, after the Ulster Unionists voted with Labour, the government survived a vote on BSE by just one vote.[25]

The week beginning Monday 18 November was to see the launch of a Tory offensive against Labour. Since September, Central Office had been costing Labour's spending plans, emboldened by the belief that the same exercise had inflicted much damage on Labour in 1991–2. That Wednesday, Waldegrave, the Treasury Chief Secretary, announced that Labour's policies would cost an estimated £30 billion on top of what taxpayers were already paying, entailing the average family in spending an extra £1,200 a year in tax.[26]

Waldegrave's claims were the occasion for a full-scale demonstration of the expensive computer software and the skills of the spin doctors both parties employed. By lunchtime, Labour's Millbank unit had prepared a rebuttal of every one of his eighty-nine claims and a denunciation of the use of civil servants for drawing up costing. By teatime the Conservatives had produced a document called 'Labour's Rebuttal Rebutted'. The outcome was 'a messy draw' rather than the direct hit scored by the 1992 'tax bombshell'.[27] The Tories' offensive on spending was planned to be followed by a Commons attack the next day on Labour's proposed £5 billion windfall tax, and by a Tim Bell-mediated speech by Lady Thatcher at London's Dorchester Hotel on the Friday, in which she would praise the government and attack Labour.[28]

At this point, when the Tories were nicely poised, the Europe issue reared its head. It not only destroyed any impact of the November offensive, but reduced the government to its weakest point since before the summer recess. Why did the boil burst at this point, with such obvious and inevitable damage?

Eurosceptics in and out of Cabinet blame Major 'for complete failure to provide leadership'.[29] What they had in mind, in particular, was failure to stand up to Clarke and rule out the single currency in the life of the next Parliament. Eurosceptics for some weeks had been becoming agitated about the imminence of the single currency decisions in the EU, which they argued would force the British government into adopting positions before the general election. The great hazard of Major, Heseltine and Mawhinney 'going long', delaying the election for as far as possible, was that IGC and single currency decisions might force themselves onto the domestic agenda.[30]

Pressure for further moves of government policy in a Eurosceptic direction was heightened considerably by Labour's clever, some might say cynical, announcement on 16 November offering its own referendum on a single currency. Where was the blue water between the parties now on Europe? A storm whipped up just after the announcement, stirred still further by Eurosceptic predictions that Labour might scoop the Tories by ruling out their joining the single currency in the life of the next Parliament.

Major and the business managers were anxious to avoid the public spectacle of Tory MPs clashing, and still more concerned to avoid a confidence vote over EMU. They therefore agreed that it would be best to avoid a Commons debate on EU documents on the single currency, which Eurosceptic MPs were anxious to do before a key ECOFIN meeting that Clarke would attend on 2 December. The documents revealed as part of the 'stability pact', it was put around, indicated that Britain's monetary freedom could be curtailed even if it did *not* enter the single currency. Temperatures rose, whipped by Redwood, Cash and Heathcoat-Amory, until 150 backbenchers from across the Party had signed a demand – some later claimed they did so for a quiet life – that the debate on the documents and on the stability pact take place on the floor of the House.

The decision on whether to recommend a debate fell to the special Commons Standing Committee which monitored EU proposals, and which considered the matter on 20 November. Tory MPs on the committee were lobbied intensely by the whips; they were told that if they voted in favour of a debate on the floor of the House, they could begin a train of events leading to a general election.

The Eurosceptics lobbied equally hard the other way, saying that the very right of Parliament to monitor Brussels, above all in the run-up to the single currency, was under threat: to act to prevent this threat was their greater duty. All eyes turned to this arcane, some thought ridiculous, issue about how a committee few outsiders had heard of would jump. The pivotal vote on the committee was to be cast by John Whittingdale, Political and Private Secretary to Mrs Thatcher from 1988 until he became an MP in 1992, and a Eurosceptic. After intensive pressure from Cash and Duncan-Smith, he opted for a debate.[31] To Eurosceptics like Redwood, he was a 'hero'.[32] To the other side he was wilfully shortsighted.

'What *do* they think they are doing?' Major snapped in Cabinet the next morning, furious with the MPs who, he believed, had driven the government's offensive off course. Worse, at Prime Minister's Questions in the House that afternoon, an embattled and uncomfortable Major received hostile questions from his own side as well as from Labour MPs about his refusal to accede to a debate. Commentators recounted that Tory MPs had not been so angry since the Maastricht debates in 1992–3. The *Sun's* headline was 'Major out in 10 days: We'll force elections, warn Eurorebel MPs'.[33] David Wastell cited one senior official bewailing the sudden collapse of Party cohesion since the Party Conference: 'It's as if you're trying to build a house, but whenever you leave it unattended you find someone's taken the bricks away.'[34]

Labour's spin doctors added to Major's and Clarke's troubles over the weekend. They had got hold of some further, unpublished, Treasury documents on the stability pact and passed them on to the *Sunday Times*, which splashed the documents and alleged that Clarke had tried to cover them up.[35] The demands for a statement were impossible to resist and the Treasury announced that next day, Monday 25 November, Clarke would appear before the Commons to correct the *Sunday Times* story.[36] It fell short of the full debate the backbenchers had wanted, but they would have to settle for it.

Clarke gave a sure-footed Commons performance, in which he repeated many of the points he had made in a letter sent to MPs on 22 November, reassuring them that no binding decisions affecting the British economy would be taken at either the Dublin ECOFIN on 2 December or Council on 13 December, and that Parliament would be able to scrutinise all relevant measures. At his reassuring best, Clarke gave 'copper-bottomed' guarantees that Brussels would not interfere in the British economy if Britain did not join the EMU.[37] After all the steam generated in the week before, the danger passed, and Labour were denied their no-confidence motion.

On Clarke's budget had been pinned the hopes of a powerful kick-start to restore the 'feel-good' factor and boost the Tories' prospects. Despite attempts to talk them down, expectations had become all the higher because his 1995 budget had been cautious, while the 1996 Queen's Speech had also failed to provide much lift to the Party's spirits. Clarke had no intention, however, of letting his budget become an electioneering one, as he saw had happened to Lamont, and indeed in several earlier pre-election budgets, notably R. A. Butler's in 1955.

Clarke's first task as he sat down to ponder in earnest what he could do, in what he realised might well be his last budget, was to make a budget judgement; he concluded that more still needed to be done to tighten policy. Public borrowing, which had been falling since 1992–3, was still too high, with drains such as BSE costing the Exchequer £1 billion which could not be used to cut tax. Interest charges had also proved higher than expected, while the forecasts of tax revenue appeared disappointing.[38] Clarke alerted Major earlier in the autumn that he would not countenance a giveaway budget. Major asked Clarke to do what he could to satisfy the hopes of the Party but, though he felt very torn, did not bring him under greater pressure. They agreed, however, that there would have to be, largely for Party management reasons, some income tax cuts.[39]

Clarke took a fairly world-weary view of this need:

My own conviction was that there was no particular gain in tax cuts and I didn't think we would win many votes by doing so. At most levels of income, people no longer felt overtaxed in the country. There was no great pressure out there for tax cuts: the pressure came from the backbenches of the Conservative Party, which contain some noisy people who are obsessed by the idea that the only way the Conservative Party ever won votes was by tax cuts.[40]

Gordon Brown, the Shadow Chancellor, would certainly have been very quick to attack Clarke if it had been a giveaway budget. With Brown's skilful courting of the business vote, and his declared financial orthodoxy, anything that smacked of a lack of fiscal rectitude would have been shown up and punished very severely.[41]

A tight public sector spending round, moreover, was essential if there were to be any tax cuts. Clarke and Waldegrave came under intense pressure from spending ministers, as Lamont and Mellor had done in 1991–2, to ease spending in electorally attractive areas. Late areas to settle were education, health and social security. Dorrell at Health and Rifkind at the FCO proved particularly intransigent. Both Major and Heseltine had to be brought in to knock heads together to achieve a settlement within the agreed limits.[42] At Defence Portillo had been savaged by the Redwood supporters over cuts and by the privatisation of Ministry of Defence married quarters. He was determined that in the complex war games for leadership of the right he would not become a scalp for the Redwood phalanx and settled at a relatively high figure.[43]

Clarke's conviction had grown that the government was at last winning back the electorate's trust, lost since Black Wednesday, over its management of the economy. As the autumn wore on, he thus argued that the budget had to be applauded by the City and by financial commentators if the government was credibly to attack Labour as the party of tax and spend.

It was a laudable objective, but one that found no great favour with Tory backbenchers as they sat listening glumly to his polished performance in the chamber that Tuesday afternoon. A leak of the tax changes to the *Daily Mirror* and thence to the *Sun* meant that there were few surprises. Income tax was cut by 1 per cent, while spending on schools, health, law and order and transport was increased. Clarke achieved this, while still reducing the government's deficit, by bringing in several billions of extra revenue from industries considered undertaxed, such as insurance, and by moving against VAT underpayments and profit-related pay. The package overall was to cost

£800 million over three years, but he estimated that he would recoup £6.7 billion over the same period by reducing fraud.

Dolly Parton-esque expectations had indeed been placed on the budget as the secret weapon to revive Tory fortunes. Once the shot had been fired, the Party was forced to realise that that was it. Rather than live with reality and obey the leadership, however, key actors continued to 'pull the bricks away'. Eurosceptic backbenchers – too numerous to mention by name – continued to put pressure on the government to toughen its European policy. The Howard and Portillo camps continued to manoeuvre for position and to vie with Redwood and his entourage as the centre-right front-runner in any post-election leadership contest. But were their masters egging on their backers? Number Ten were never sure what the truth was, though they tended to absolve Portillo and Howard of personal responsibility,. Shephard was coming to realise her moment was passing, and while Hague and Lilley were not themselves planning, their supporters were sniffing the air. The right, mean-while, thought Heseltine was manoeuvring. It did not make for a quiet life, especially with Tebbit threatening to 'destroy' the Tory Party if Britain joined the single currency. Clarke continued, in the eyes of Eurosceptics as well as senior figures at Number Ten and Central Office, though less Major, to be the 'unguided missile', oblivious to them of any greater end than the con-sistency of his position.[44] Still others continued to blame less the bosses than their special adviser *eminences grises*, with Anthony Teasdale (Clarke), Hywel Williams (Redwood) and David Hart (Portillo) particular subjects, in the highly volatile and charged atmosphere, of suspicion.

Many Tory MPs remained largely unaware of how their decisions were being viewed from the outside. When Tory MPs threw out by 306 to 281 a post-Dunblane amendment banning all hand guns, public perception of their action, in the highly charged atmosphere of the time, was reflected in the front page of the *Daily Mirror* the next day. Carrying the pictures of the sixteen children killed at Dunblane, it pointed the finger at Major with the headline 'He betrayed them all'.[45] Not even the long-feared death of ailing Tory MP Barry Porter on 3 November brought a sense of danger; a Cabinet minister said 'it was past danger – it was fatalism and despair'.

All these tensions might have been containable had the leadership suc-ceeded in asserting its authority over the Party. The high hopes once pinned on EDCP, the coordinating committee set up in July 1995, to ensure uni-formity in the planning and presentation of government policy, had all but dissipated, as its inability to instil order in such an unruly mob became clear as 1996 wore on. Heseltine, the most experienced and toughest operator in Cabinet, was simply unable to master events: from the autumn onwards, he was no longer the consistently energetic performer of old. EDCP's morning sessions began to resemble the torpid Number Twelve Committee it had replaced, though the Wednesday evening forward planning meetings retained their vitality. The core problem with EDCP was that politicians from Cabinet downward were unwilling to follow its instructions, nor were the civil servants and Party officials able to implement and chase up all that had been decided. 'Too much time is spent sounding off about some department for making an announcement without telling us, rather than actually coordinating events proactively,' complained one attender.[46]

Labour's superior and quick-footed leadership and presentation skills only underlined the government's difficulties. The lack of a big-hitting media chief at the centre of Tory operations to match Campbell and Mandelson came increasingly to be felt. Though Jonathan Haslam, Christopher Meyer's successor as Chief Press Officer at Number Ten, was a good performer, several rued their failure to achieve a combined post of head of government and Party media after Meyer left Number Ten in early 1996, bound for Bonn and eventually Washington. Major considered the idea, but deemed it constitutionally improper.[47]

With the weeks before a general election rapidly diminishing, the self-destructive tendencies of the Party were about to become even more febrile.

Open Cabinet Divisions: December

Major and Blackwell had breakfast at Number Ten in November with Charles Moore, the staunch Eurosceptic editor of the *Daily Telegraph*, to discuss an article Major had written for the newspaper. In the run-up to the general election, it was never more important that the leader of the Tory Party and the editor of the prime Tory daily newspaper were in step; Major and Moore both hoped they were entering a new era of cooperation. The meeting went well, and Major was encouraged. According to Blackwell, Major spoke frankly about his doubts whether a Conservative government would take Britain into the single currency, and in particular that he believed it unlikely it would happen in the next Parliament.[48] Subsequently a close Major aide told Moore that he felt Major was on the verge of announcing he would rule Britain out of joining the single currency in the next Parliament.[49]

Moore had every reason to believe that this intermediary – thought wrongly to be Norman Blackwell – was speaking with the authority of the Prime Minister. Encouraged by further conversations between his newspaper and senior Conservatives, he decided to run a story on Monday 2 December, trailed by the *Sunday Telegraph* the day before, that Major now believed it would be against Britain's interests to join a single currency in the next Parliament and wanted to persuade Clarke that the moment had come to ditch Cabinet's April 'wait and see' agreement before the general election.[50]

Major was toying with some hardening of the April agreement, not least to keep the Conservatives, as the more Eurosceptic party, following Labour's own deft pledge to hold a referendum. He also saw Clarke as a principal stumbling block, though he was aware other Cabinet Europhiles, such as Gummer and Young, as well as Heseltine, would need persuasion. But did the *Telegraph* story go beyond what Major said?

Moore claims he acted in good faith and on best authority, but that the story caught Number Ten on the wrong foot.[51] Some in Number Ten and the Cabinet saw Moore's patience cracking, and that he seized an opportunity to try to bounce Major into confronting Clarke. Major himself put it down to a simple misunderstanding, and did not suspect foul play.[52] The truth is difficult to establish, though Major was wont to muse on the politically difficult in private in order to tease out reactions, only to be drawn up short when his comments appeared in public as hard fact. He was, without question, taken aback when he saw what the *Daily Telegraph* had written.[53]

With Clarke in Brussels for a finance ministers' meeting, the article was faxed out to him. When the Chancellor read it he was puzzled at what the 'wretched *Telegraph*' had written, and decided he would crush the story, using a BBC *Today* interview that morning as his platform.[54] 'Quite preposterous' was his comment that anyone would want to change the agreed Cabinet policy, least of all just six weeks after 'the Prime Minister and I' united the Tory Party Conference behind 'a sensible policy'.[55] Clarke believed at first that Mawhinney, for whom on Europe (alone) he had a deep personal mistrust, had been responsible for the story, and only learned later of Number Ten's contacts with Moore. Clarke's unequivocal riposte on *Today* neatly, he hoped, would slam the door in the face of any possible modification of Cabinet's April policy position, a copy of which he carried around in his briefcase wherever he went.[56]

At that Monday morning's EDCP meeting, Heseltine decreed that the *Daily Telegraph* story had to be 'killed'. The Number Ten Press Office promptly put out a statement that they believed would do so, but their text proved sufficiently ambiguous for Tory Eurosceptics, as well as Labour's briefing team and the media, to claim that the Number Ten denial had been half-hearted, and still left the door ajar to abandoning 'wait and see'. With Major at a security conference in Lisbon, it was left to Blackwell to telephone around newspaper editors to tell them that the April policy had indeed not changed 'one jot'.[57] Tuesday's newspapers, however, kept alive the story of a possible pre-election policy change.

The normally sober *Financial Times* now predicted that Major would soon signal that Britain would not join the single currency at its scheduled launch in 1999. This was too much for Heseltine, who told attenders at that morning's EDCP meeting that he was fed up with this issue, and that he himself was going to go out and 'do some media'.[58] At lunchtime he strutted into the BBC's Millbank studios and, on *The World at One*, categorically ruled out any change of government policy from the agreed April statement, not just during the remainder of the Parliament but during the election campaign also.[59]

Like Clarke's *Today* interview, it appeared to scotch the hope that increasing numbers in the Party clung to, that Major would abandon 'wait and see' in the run-up to the election, maximising the electoral impact while minimising the risk that Clarke, so close to polling day, would risk a public row and resign. It also destroyed the fiction believed by many on the right, that it was Clarke alone who was blocking a change of policy on the single currency. Within moments of Heseltine's interview ending, David Hill, Labour's chief media spokesman, had rung Alastair Campbell in the Opposition Leader's office and both agreed that Blair would ask Major at Prime Minister's Questions that afternoon whether or not he agreed with his Deputy Prime Minister's statement.[60]

Back from an unsatisfying Lisbon summit, Major now experienced the first of two difficult PMQs in succession. On cue on Tuesday afternoon, Blair quoted Heseltine's lunchtime comments and asked whether Major supported them. Major's terse reply did not conceal his frustration: 'My Right Honourable friend said that: that is our position.' The predominant mood on the Tory backbenches as they listened to their leader was one of cold hostility. Major's own anger with the whole affair was made very apparent when he spoke to Tory MPs in the Commons Tea Room subsequently, where he responded sharply to questions about why he had replied to Blair as he had.[61] An editorial in *The Times* the next day summed up the disillusion the Eurosceptics felt at his Commons endorsement of Heseltine: 'Mr Major's surrender to the unrepresentative views of the two men closest to him makes him look weak to the outside world while increasing dissent within his party.'[62]

On Wednesday, however, the affair appeared to be dying down. At that point Clarke, to Major's fury, was involved in a gaffe which brought the divisions at the top of the Party straight back into the headlines. Clarke was being entertained at a fashionable Park Lane restaurant, Chez Nico, by two middle-ranking BBC journalists, Mark Mardell and Jon Sopel. Clarke spoke freely, as was his style, airing his views on recent events, believing what he said to be on the usual off-the-record terms. At a nearby table, in view but out of earshot, sat Robin Oakley, the journalists' boss at the BBC, and Labour's Frank Dobson.[63] Clarke confided to Mardell and Sopel that he believed Major's alleged remarks to Moore had been a 'boomerang laden with high explosives' that had now rebounded in his face.

Details of Clarke's words duly appeared in a long and sensational report by Sopel on Thursday's *The World at One*.[64] Clarke reacted in disbelief, shocked at what he believed was not only a breach of confidence but also highly selective quotation from 'a relaxed, wide-ranging conversation'. Sopel's report claimed that the Chancellor had 'told friends' about his frustration with the Prime Minister for his attempt to harden the government's stance against the single currency, and quoted Clarke's boomerang analogy. The Chancellor, moreover, would resign, as would a number of middle-ranking and junior ministers and some MPs, Sopel claimed, were the government to change the policy on the single currency before the general election. Clarke had also, according to 'friends', confronted Mawhinney and said, 'Tell your kids to get their scooters off my lawn.' The 'kids' was taken as a reference to the senior Central Office staff, Finkelstein and Lewington, as well as more junior Eurosceptic officials like Andrew Cooper and Michael Simmonds, whom he saw as *agents provocateurs* in the battle over the single currency, and who, he also believed, had coined a mischievous telling phrase 'new Chancellor, new chance'.

Clarke was furious at the story, but matters worsened when he and Central Office issued a statement denying that he had *threatened* to resign. A Chancellor denying a threat to resign became at once a high-grade media story. His denial only fuelled speculation about his intentions, and as he did not question the rest of Sopel's report, it appeared to be confirming that the rest of it was true.[65] A joint statement with Mawhinney, denying that the two were at loggerheads, failed similarly to alter perceptions, while Frank Dobson, who had gained more than a free BBC lunch out of the episode, lost no time telling the media that the so-called 'friends of' the Chancellor was none other than Clarke himself.[66]

Major, already in despair over the damage the government was inflicting on itself, then learned that Thursday lunchtime about the Sopel radio report. It distracted his normally sacrosanct preparation for Question Time, and he arrived in the House flustered and less well briefed than usual. Blair, on his best form, embarrassed and humbled Major with questions based on leaks to the *Guardian* that morning outlining budget savings of up to £50 million on war pensions. Major thought Blair's questions dishonest, but was angry with himself for not having the rebuttal information at his fingertips, and his response was unconvincing.[67] He followed it up that evening with an angry letter to Blair complaining about Labour's 'shameless scaremongering' over war pensions and demanding an immediate apology for causing 'needless alarm' to thousands of war veterans. In a week of denials and angry statements, the letter failed to make much impression other than to broadcast how rattled Major had become.[68]

That evening also witnessed a more than usually acrimonious 1922 Committee meeting in which backbenchers railed against Clarke for appearing to be dictating government policy on the one issue they all cared about above others – Europe. The single currency was colourfully, and apparently without contradiction, labelled at the meeting as 'the greatest threat to British democracy for a thousand years'. Described by some as the worst 1922 Committee meeting of their careers, MPs failed to heed the plea from the veteran Tom King that, with the election so close, they put their differences behind them or see them all commit collective suicide.[69] So feverish and clouded had the atmosphere become that voices such as King's carried no force.

Major had left for Huntingdon on the evening of Thursday 5 December before he heard about the tone of the 1922 meeting. The next day brought even less reason for cheer: a Gallup poll gave Labour a 35-point lead, and the decision by backbench MP John Gorst to withdraw cooperation from the Party whips in protest at alleged failures to honour commitments to a hospital in his Hendon North constituency. Gorst's decision was portrayed as of great symbolic importance, with the media declaring portentously that, at 2.40 p.m. on Friday 6 December, the government officially became the first minority government since Callaghan's in 1979.[70] The technicality that Gorst did not withdraw his support from the government was widely overlooked. Comparisons with the dying days of the Callaghan government, and with the latter period of Mrs Thatcher's administration when she clashed with Lawson and Howe, now became commonplace in the media.[71]

So volatile was the atmosphere that Major decided to be interviewed on that Sunday's *On the Record* television programme, filmed at The Finings, to try to calm the atmosphere. With time to rest, and to prepare, he came across far more convincingly than during the week before. Inflamed by those backbenchers he thought were exploiting the parliamentary predicament, he castigated them for claiming their 'moment of fame'.[72] This phrase caused particular resentment in the breasts of those who, like John Gorst and Hugh Dykes, felt themselves under fire.

To many bemused observers of the Tory Party, watching it tearing into itself, it seemed that the whole behaviour of MPs was irrational and inexplicable: like 'turkeys voting for Christmas', to use the analogy current at the time.[73] Why should Tory MPs care so much about what exactly the government's policy was on the single currency when all polls pointed to the fact that they could not conceivably win the election, and hence would not themselves be taking any of the decisions on the future of the single currency? Moreover, they would let in a far more Europhile government. Rationality dictated that they all cling together in an effort to minimise the scale of the defeat and preserve their own seats. It was a symptom of the strange short-sighted psyche of the dog-end of the Parliament that backbenchers and ministers had become more concerned about ideological purity – and personal positioning – than about the fortunes of their party as a whole.

Part of the reason for the reopening of the Europe divide in November and December, however, was, on one level, rational. The fifteen-month IGC that had opened in Turin in March 1996 was not, as the British government initially thought, proving a minor affair. Its belief, or hope, had been that it would amount to a '5,000-mile service' for the EU, with little significant further integration. But it became increasingly obvious as 1996 wore on that Britain's EU partners, above all France (on defence) and Germany (on political institutions) were pressing for a range of further measures of integration and that a policy of resistance would have been formulated, without it being clear exactly what the government would be resisting, as the proposals were developing incrementally. All that year, Major worked to try to ensure that the various European Councils did not take premature decisions, leaving it all to the post-general election Amsterdam summit in June 1997.

The single currency issue, however, could not be swept under the carpet.[74] Lilley had spent part of the summer recess thinking about the single currency, and on his return wrote to Rifkind, with copies to Major and Clarke, to express his concern. He asked what decisions would have to be taken and on what timetable under the Maastricht Treaty, assuming Britain was to join the single currency in the first wave in 1999. Lilley believed that there was a possibility that the issue could blow up during the election and, even at the risk of reopening wounds, that it had to be the subject of a full Cabinet discussion before the end of 1996.[75] A confidential Treasury paper concluded that there would have to be serious thinking about EMU and the position of the Bank of England before the election, not least because the Maastricht Treaty required Britain to notify its intention to join by 1 January 1998, and legislation, which should be signalled in the election manifesto. Clarke toned down the paper, making it more relaxed on timing.[76]

Major, Clarke, Heseltine and Mawhinney were not anxious to have the matter raised in Cabinet, but several Cabinet ministers, notably Howard and Lilley, pressed hard for the single currency to be aired. Lilley asked Rifkind tersely why he had still received no reply to his letter. The pro-Europeans considered that the issue had been superseded by the 'negotiate and decide' refinement of the April referendum pledge, which had emerged at the Party Conference. On 28 November Major nevertheless duly held a discussion on the convergence criteria for a single currency. Adopting his usual style to avoid divisions within Cabinet meetings, he agreed that the Treasury should make a detailed study of timing and convergence, and explore whether other EU countries, and the Commission, were trying to 'fudge' the economic rules for joining the single currency (the last a particular concern of Howard's). Cabinet would then revisit the subject after Major returned from the European Council at Dublin on 13 December, when he hoped the sting would have been removed.[77]

Discussions on the single currency did indeed feature in the arguments at Dublin. The government lobbied intensively before it to ensure that decisions were delayed until Amsterdam. The Irish government produced a text for the IGC, which was debated, but Major did not become engaged in heated disputes. Other EU leaders had now largely forgiven him after the BSE rows, and accepted the reality of his domestic position with the election imminent. Major left pleased by what he had achieved.[78] He did sign up to the stability pact, in which countries to enter the single currency agreed to keep their budget deficits under control, but managed to ensure this would be non-binding on Britain if it did not join. While the significance and even content of the stability pact that so excited the Eurosceptics baffled many Tories, some asked whether it was not the very stability of the Tory government that ought to receive higher priority.

As promised, Cabinet returned to the single currency at its last meeting of the year, on 19 December. The Treasury paper provided the springboard for ministers to argue about whether developments in Europe now dictated a toughening of the Cabinet's April policy. The numbers on each side were nicely balanced, and in line with the description above of Cabinet ministers' positions on Europe. With Mawhinney observing his rule of silence on matters European in Cabinet, ministers lined up eleven to ten against further change to the policy, Clarke argued trenchantly against Howard and Lilley, the most vocal exponents of alteration. But Major was not happy to settle for ruling out any change at that point, which would have left nearly half his Cabinet dissatisfied. So when he summed up at the end of the discussion, he said he would like a further paper from Clarke to be discussed in Cabinet after Christmas.[79]

Clarke was not at all pleased at the postponement, which he interpreted as designed so pressure could be brought to bear on those resisting change. 'Me, by that time, not in a good mood', he later reflected, because 'I couldn't believe that a party that looked like it was heading for shattering electoral defeat precisely because of disunity was having no serious political discussion at Cabinet except on the one ridiculous subject of how they could get Ken to agree to a change of Cabinet's policy on a single currency.'[80]

Events in mid-December failed to bring anything to give Major cheer. At an unsatisfactory meeting with Bruton on 9 December, the Irish Prime Minister brought him under pressure to allow Sinn Fein to enter negotiations almost immediately after the declaration of an IRA ceasefire. Major – critics insisted because of his need to maintain Ulster Unionist support in Parliament – held out that 'definite proof' was needed that violent activities by the IRA had been halted.[81]

David Willetts resigned on 11 December after the Commons Committee on Standards and Privileges accused him of dissembling. 'Sensation! Tory minister does the decent thing,' was the jaded headline in the *Independent*, followed by 'but then David Willetts' colleagues always thought he was a little odd'.[82]

On 12 December the Barnsley East by-election produced a Labour victory and saw the Conservatives' minority status further entrenched. Reports appeared the following week that 147 out of 402 Tory MPs and parliamentary candidates would mention in their addresses their rejection of the 'wait and see' Cabinet policy and declare their opposition to a single currency in the coming Parliament.[83] Relief that a European fishing vote on 16 December was won by eleven votes disappeared when Labour and the Liberal Democrats brought the integrity issue back into centre stage when they accused the Tories of cheating over parliamentary 'pairing' arrangements. Major privately thought his whips' 'high jinks' indefensible. The opposition parties announced that in future, they would be withdrawing from duly pairing, opening the prospect of all-out war in the Commons in the New Year.[84]

A Political Cabinet before a full Cabinet on 19 December provided the chance for ministers to refocus on the election, although Europe spilled over again into discussions. Central Office polling since the Party Conference suggested that the three slogans then current – 'New Labour, New Danger', 'Life's Better with the Conservatives' and 'Opportunity for All' – needed to be honed down to one single message. Polling pointed firmly in the direction of attention being turned on Labour rather than on anything positive the Party could offer itself. As it was put: 'If *we* were the issue, we would definitely lose. If they were the issue, we stood a chance of doing better.'[85] This conclusion opened the door for Maurice Saatchi to rush in again waving his 'big D' message, the European danger now specifically the Social Chapter.

At a Chequers dinner the month before, Bell, Gummer and Saatchi had joined Major, Mawhinney and the senior Central Office team. Saatchi had argued passionately that the 'New Labour, New danger' campaign was right, but they failed to identify a clear propaganda line for the period up to the election. No further 'New Dangers' were publicised. The Chequers meeting was perhaps the last opportunity when a unified message could have emerged, but such were the discordant individuals and ideals they held, that for a consensus to emerge on the election message and what exactly was to be promoted as the Party's core appeal was but a pipedream.[86]

This much should already have been apparent from a series of disagreements over slogans and advertisements. Saatchi had been keen on an advertisement on the day of the England–Germany 'Euro 96' football semi-final on 26 June. His idea was to have photographs of Blair and Major and to pose the question 'Which person would Germany sooner tackle?' It did not run. A one-off advertisement appeared at the start of the TUC's annual conference, with the three outside consultants having argued for it developing into a campaign inviting trade unionists disillusioned with Labour to join the Tories.[87] It stopped after one outing.

Saatchi then became enthused by the idea of an 'advent calendar campaign' with a series of windows opening on attacks on Labour in the run-up to Christmas. Major could see it being found offensive, while Mawhinney – a practising Christian – also said this would be considered distasteful. As one close to him said of Saatchi: 'Maurice had no understanding of religious sensitivities: he thought Christmas was a promotional vehicle devised by retailers to advance their commercial interests.'[88] The idea suffered the same fate as the football and trade union proposals.

Disagreements over strategies and advertisements were kept away from departmental ministers, who listened attentively in Political Cabinet on 19 December as Finkelstein ran over the various themes and messages for the New Year, Lewington outlined the work on which Bell, Gummer and Saatchi had been engaged and Garrett took ministers through the election map, discussed how far the Party was behind in the polls, and told ministers that a serious leap forward was necessary in the New Year if a heavy defeat was to be avoided.[89]

Major had recovered from his disappointment at seeing the Party Conference optimism evaporate, and he returned to his belief that an outright Labour victory could be thwarted. He had taken to holding regular conversations with Garrett, whose judgement on the Party's electoral position he trusted implicitly. Ever since the autumn of 1992, Garrett had been saying that, because of the likelihood of increased tactical voting, the Party would need to win at least 43 per cent of the poll just to stand still in terms of seats, rather than the 41.9 per cent in the 1992 general election. This accorded with Major's gut feeling. He knew that this goal was unrealistic, but accepted Garrett's advice that a result of 38 to 39 per cent was just achievable, which made a hung Parliament the best feasible result.[90] If he were to lose, Major at all costs wanted to avoid a heavy defeat, and an election fought in bad taste.

The Christmas period saw a welcome lift in fortunes. Major made an effective attack on Labour's European policy at Birmingham Chamber of Commerce on 20 December. The speech had been drafted by George Bridges, but on the train Major turned to Howell James and said, 'I don't want to give this', and spoke more or less off-the-cuff.[91] Only the proximity of Christmas prevented it receiving wider attention. On the same day the jobless total fell below two million for the first time in six years. He spent a quiet Christmas and New Year at Chequers, and was greatly heartened to have come top in the Radio 4 *Today*'s 'Personality of the Year' competition. As he later confessed, accusations that it had been rigged, emanating he thought from Labour, spoilt much of his pleasure in the accolade.[92] To the end, personal popularity, and the sense that he was esteemed, mattered greatly to him.[93]

When to Go? January

Major mused over election timing over Christmas and the New Year. The economic arguments for holding out until 1 May were as strong as ever, as was the opportunity it would afford for having the planned six weeks of the campaign. Heseltine remained a consistent and influential advocate of playing it long to maximise the benefit of economic recovery. The benefit of holding the election on 1 May, the same day as the county council elections, was also clear, maximising canvassing and the support of the Party faithful. If defeat were to come, then rebuilding could begin at once on the back of the almost certain improved county council election results. But the attraction of catching Labour on the hop, and going in March, blossomed in Major's mind over the Christmas holiday. He disliked the jibe of 'hanging on', and did not want to stretch the electorate's patience. A March election would also mini-mise the risk of a parliamentary defeat in a 'no-confidence' motion, an eventuality he was anxious at all costs to avoid.[94] Over the holiday, the Number Ten Private Office drafted a speech for him to deliver should such a no-confidence debate, which officials regarded as a serious possibility, transpire.[95]

Howell James and Norman Blackwell, Major's two most trusted and loyal personal lieutenants, came to The Finings to see him on Thursday 2 January. To their surprise, Major told them he wanted to call the general election on 6 March, and dispense with the need to call the Wirral South by-election.[96]

The timing of the by-election had been hotly debated in the weeks after Barry Porter's death on 3 November. Central Office's strong advice was either to hold it on 12 (or 19) December – the last practical date that year – or avoid holding it altogether. Major was against the latter option because –

as with Staffordshire South East – he was unwilling to breach the convention that the writ for a by-election must be moved within three months of the vacancy, even though the original guidelines were more flexible during the fifth year of a Parliament.[97] In late November Major and Mawhinney decided, on the advice of the whips, that it would be folly to rush through the by-election that year, which would almost certainly be lost.[98]

Blackwell and James had not anticipated Major's new thinking, but made clear their willingness to back a March election. Finalising the manifesto became an even higher priority, and they settled down to a long conversation about its contents. Blackwell had given Major a draft to read over Christmas: at over 25,000 words it was too long (they had planned to have a 'slim' document), and much work still needed to be done. With a campaign starting perhaps within four weeks, Blackwell was authorised to send round discrete sections of the manifesto to Cabinet ministers for their clearance, and to agree the contents with Heseltine and Mawhinney.[99] After the 2 January meeting, an excited Major phoned George Bridges, telling him to start working on speeches for an early election,[100] and Mawhinney, who saw that the attraction would be dispensing with the Wirral South by-election.

Major was in chipper mood for his annual *Breakfast with Frost* television interview that weekend, telling David Frost that his aim for the new year would be to 'remain cool, calm and elected'.[101] On Monday 6 January the Party launched the first phase of a £7 million advertising campaign, with a thousand poster sites displaying a giant teardrop attached to aspects of the 'dangers' of voting Labour, to be followed by a lion – Heseltine's favourite advertisement – and a further series saying 'delivered as promised' to bolster the impression of a successful government which had honoured its policy pledges.[102]

Initial soundings suggested that the January campaign was making an impact.[103] On Tuesday, Major gave the first of his new presidential-style press conferences, in which he said he would serve a full parliamentary term if elected, and went on to hit out at Labour. His only slip, in the eyes of the Central Office strategists, came when he attacked Blair for stealing his ideas – the jackdaw tendency – on this occasion on the improbable subject of not being too nice to beggars over which Labour had attacked him in 1994.[104]

Major left the next day, 9 January, in good spirits for a five-day tour to India and Pakistan. The trip, with no obvious election tie-up, caused some concern to the election strategists. A polite memo from Number Ten's political staff was written to him just before he left hoping that he would take the opportunity of talks with the political editors to point out flaws in Labour's pre-election arguments.[105] The FCO meanwhile thought that if he was prepared to give up five days for an overseas trip, there were places of even more importance for him to visit, for example the United States, which would also have pleased Central Office as it would have made far more electoral impact. But Major did not want to go to America.[106] He had not been to the Indian subcontinent since 1993, and had taken trouble to strengthen the bond between both countries in the intervening period, beginning with the Indo–British partnership agreement, which led to trade almost doubling.[107] His enthusiasm for Indians and for the country was real and deep, and he was particularly keen to travel there at the beginning of the year marking the fiftieth anniversary of the independence of both India and Pakistan in 1947. With him went sixty businessmen, and Ian Lang, anxious to see trade with the subcontinent, which was already promising, boosted still further.

Major was enormously happy throughout the trip, and did not bother when the occasional slip occurred, notably the photographs of him looking slightly ill at ease wearing a traditional hat placed smartly on his head – as was the custom for visitors to the Khyber Pass – an image splashed ubiquit-ously across the British media. He spent a day in Calcutta, to address the annual conference of the Confederation of Indian Industry, taking the chance also of watching Lancashire beat India's 'B' cricket team in the final over. During the match, he was invited to stand on the edge of the pitch, where his presence was announced. The huge stadium, with some 40,000 spectators, erupted and Major was taken towards the centre of the pitch, where he was mobbed by television crews, journalists and the crowds. Though little of this was reflected by the British media, it spoke of an especial affection Indian people had for him, regarding him as a friend.[108]

The trip also included Major's first visit to Bangladesh, and he saw Benazir Bhutto in Pakistan. But, overall, it was not a trip where there was political capital to be made. Sensing he might not have much longer as Prime Minister, Major wanted to make one final trip to India and try to entrench Anglo–Indian relations further while he still had the power.[109] On the flight home, he obliged his Political Office staff by holding a press conference in which he rounded on Blair, but took away with the other hand by going 'off-message' and once again accusing Labour of stealing many of his best policies.[110] The press, on this his last full overseas trip, responded very positively, in part because they sensed he was on the way out, but also because they responded to his relaxed and jokey handling of them. He would have wished it ever thus.

He returned to London refreshed and contented, and keener than ever on going to the country in March, still a matter of greatest secrecy. Only the most intimate colleagues knew his intention, and then none of them knew exactly whom else he had told. He arrived back in time for a crucial budget vote on the evening of Monday 13 January, the day MPs returned to Westmin-ster. With Ulster Unionist support, the government won its first test in the 'non-cooperation' era (without pairing) by a convincing 322–287.

The general election was not the only election in the minds of some of the Cabinet. The fact of a Labour victory, and a Major departure soon after, was generally, if covertly, admitted by all. The new year opened with several figures seen by the media to be positioning themselves for the leadership election. Dorrell had spectacularly, if unwittingly, 'launched' the leadership race in 1997 when remarks he had made some weeks before were suddenly published on New Year's Day, calling for a renegotiation of the relationship with Brussels. On 11 January reports appeared, strenuously denied, of Howard signalling his intention to stand as a post-Major leadership candidate. He was seen to be working hard to project himself as a more experienced, populist and less ideological right-wing leader than either Portillo or Redwood,[111] while being one of several Cabinet ministers to invite parliamentary candidates to meet him for 'briefings' – innocent, he claimed (with some justice); currying support in the event of an election, said others. With Peter Riddell and other commentators concluding that Howard was the frontrunner, it made some of the other possible candidates, and still more their backers, more concerned to position themselves.[112] Dorrell and Rifkind were both seen to be reinventing themselves as sound Eurosceptics to appeal as centre-right challengers.

Worries from Number Ten of a different kind came from threats from Max Clifford, the publicist, to expose Tory MPs for 'sleaze' in the run-up to the general election. But after naming his first target, flamboyant Tory backbencher Jerry Hayes, concern began to ease when no further allegations emerged and Clifford's activities were dismissed as a freelance pro-Labour stunt.[113]

With the money-rich Referendum Party launching its poster attack on the Tories in mid-January, saying, 'Why not John? Why can't we have a proper referendum on Europe Mr Major?', and its literature being sent to every home in the UK, Major was under no illusions about the difficulties that lay ahead. Some of his anger spilled over in the House in his response to Blair, who claimed the Tories were planning to impose VAT on food: 'What you are seeking to do is smear our plans for the next Parliament. It simply won't wash.'[114]

The India trip had sparked off a flurry of panic about the ethnic minority vote. Labour, who traditionally worried about the Tories playing the 'race card' in the run-up to general elections to pander to racist tendencies in the electorate, were now worried about the very opposite – an appeal to the ethnic vote. It was thus delighted when Bill Morris, the black general secretary of the TGWU, accused the government of having often 'pandered to racism', such as with Howard's 'notorious' Asylum and Immigration Bill.

Major was set to give a speech on ethnicity at a 'One Nation' rally on Saturday 18 January at the Commonwealth Institute in London. His speech writers were uncertain whether he would want to make a 'politically correct' race speech or, as they hoped, one where he said that Britain gave equal opportunity for all races to be unequal.[115] In one of the most personal speeches of his premiership, he veered towards the latter, and spoke simply of his non-racist views, his belief that race relations had worked well in Britain, and his vision of a multi-cultural Britain. 'I've never been a victim of racial discrimination,' he said, 'but any decent person would agree that those kinds of acts are utterly repugnant ... They have no place in our country – and never, never in our Party.'

The speech attracted scant attention. The right-wing press found the subject uncongenial, while the centre-left newspapers did not want to make much of it beyond portraying it as a straight bid for the ethnic vote. Jon Sweeney in the *Observer* was an exception. He wrote that he went to the speech to mock Major but came away impressed because he had behaved 'too decently' for cynicism to be appropriate.[116] In truth, almost everyone had difficulty placing the speech, from his party's senior strategists to the Labour Party. Appealing to Asian voters, as with the Indian trip, was of course a factor; but there was much more to it than that. There would be other occasions in the next three months when he spoke from the heart and would cause similar bewilderment.

The key political event for Major the following week was the conclusion in Cabinet of the debate on the single currency on 23 January. Positions had been evolving slowly in the five weeks since their last discussion in Cabinet, as the pressure to see a hardening of policy became even more intense. Clarke, armed with his new Treasury paper setting out the basis on which Britain would decide to join a single currency, was adamant that he would not be bounced, especially as the remaining Europhiles in Cabinet were becoming less vocal in their support, and the 'Prime Minister's party' in the middle more sceptic. Ministers seized on an interview some days earlier in which Clarke had spoken of his long-standing view that the single currency would not necessarily go ahead on time, in January 1999. At the Cabinet, he suspected that some ministers had met beforehand to discuss how to outflank him and that he was being ambushed. Clarke insisted at the meeting that they had agreed in April 1996, and had confirmed many times since, that they would not change the policy. But, the Eurosceptics responded, some firming up of the policy would be to their advantage.[117]

Their view had been anticipated by Major and Clarke who – as the Eurosceptics suspected – had met before Cabinet and agreed there should be a change of 'nuance': that the government now deemed it 'very unlikely' that the single currency would start in 1999.[118] It was not everything the sceptics would have liked, but it was movement, and approval was registered in Cabinet.

Clarke and Rifkind, after the meeting, went out into Downing Street and announced the change in 'nuance', which Major repeated to enthusiastic Tory cheers in the House that afternoon: 'On the basis of information currently available, it is very unlikely but not impossible that the single currency can proceed safely on 1 January 1999, but if it did proceed with unreliable convergence we would not of course be part of it.'[119] Clarke continued to maintain in public that Britain could still join in the first wave in 1999, with the government introducing legislation to permit it later in 1997, even though it would have been omitted from the Queen's Speech. But he was beginning to clutch at straws. The argument in Cabinet was moving away from him. Most commentators agreed that the new Commons statement marked the Cabinet's 'most sceptical stance yet' towards EMU.[120]

The episode also marked the low point of Clarke's relationship with Major:

the Chancellor no longer blamed Mawhinney for exerting pressure behind the scenes to change the policy, but saw Major himself, under the guise of neutrality, as covertly siding with the Eurosceptics. To Clarke, they were all 'behaving like a barrel-load of monkeys'.

The anger many in the government, Central Office and on the backbenches felt in turn towards Clarke was fierce, for now almost single-handedly preventing the Cabinet from unequivocally ruling out joining the single currency during the life of the next Parliament.[121] Of the three other Europhiles, Gummer remained solid, Young did not carry the weight, and Heseltine appeared no longer so determined. Clarke did at least acknowledge the box Major was in. 'I am sure his view of me was that I was stubborn and arrogant,' he said, 'and how could he possibly manage the Party with me on one side and those bloody Eurosceptics on the other?' At the same time, however, Clarke was adamant he was not going to yield: 'I had no intention of allowing the Party to be captured by the sceptics. I was simply not going to let them roll policy in a more Eurosceptic direction. That was the point.'[122] With Clarke clinging to his belief that Cabinet had said they would not budge – apart from a change in 'nuance', not 'policy' – from the 'done deal' of April 1996, his tussle with the Eurosceptics and increasingly those in the middle was becoming a dialogue of the deaf.

A less significant but still damaging issue was discussed that week: the royal yacht. A small group, Major, Clarke, Rifkind, Heseltine, Lang and Portillo, decided that Britain commissioning a new royal yacht to replace *Britannia*, at a cost of £60 million, would make sound political and possibly even commercial sense.[123] Clarke found himself a lone voice in opposing the replacement, which he thought the 'silliest' decision in which he had ever been involved. He cited the public criticism after the Windsor Castle fire, when it had been announced that public money would be spent on repairs.[124] Clarke lost the argument. Portillo's subsequent boast that the announcement of a new yacht had 'wrong-footed Labour' was criticised for drawing royalty into the political arena, and was then shown to be foolhardy after another Labour propaganda coup, when they announced that they themselves would build the royal yacht, but with money from private enterprise. Redwood, delighted to see his rival worsted, joined Heath in an unlikely pairing to rebuke Portillo.[125]

Political Cabinet at Chequers on Monday 27 January was to be the occasion when ministers would be told about the imminent March election and when final clearance would be given to the manifesto. But with the Party's polling still showing Labour's lead unassailable, and with the January advertising campaign failing to dent it, it was decided to postpone the announcement.[126] It was a big turnout at the first-floor Great Parlour room – all the Cabinet, with a further ten senior Party figures from Number Ten and Central Office, but not Bell, Gummer and Saatchi. With a central purpose of the meeting removed, it was a torpid occasion ('ghastly' said one present), with ministers wondering why they had all been summoned out of London for another meeting.[127]

Some useful discussion, however, took place. Agreement was reached that London Underground would be privatised, with complex and disputed implications for fares, and ministers debated subjects such as further help for home ownership.[128] Waldegrave kept probing the costing of various manifesto proposals. But ministers were not told about certain core items, such as on family tax allowance, on education and law and order, for one reason only: certain of their number, and more particularly some of their special advisers, were considered insufficiently trustworthy not to leak the news to the media.[129] The impression of the meeting's gravitas was not enhanced by the Sunday newspapers recounting – accurately – that several ministers had dozed off, having eaten too much Chequers lunch.[130]

One story that came immediately out of the meeting, to make the headlines, and which angered Major, stemmed from a briefing by Lewington. Believing it to be primarily the meeting to finalise the manifesto, Lewington invited senior lobby journalists to a briefing at a public house in nearby Great Missenden, only to find that there was little manifesto news to tell them. Not knowing that a March election was a likelihood, and in response to a question, he repeated the agreed line that it was still the intention to call the election on 1 May. The media concluded that the main story of the day was that the Cabinet had resolved to end the speculation of an early election and go long.[131] Then, when the government was defeated by one vote in the House that night on the Education Bill – on account of some ministers arriving back late from Chequers, and Labour forcing a division one hour earlier than expected – the headline story changed to Major's hopes of lasting until 1 May being dealt a 'death blow' by the defeat in the House.[132] Later that evening, the inner group of Major, Heseltine, Mawhinney, Clarke, Cranborne, Newton and Blackwell undertook the task full Cabinet had not been entrusted to do, going through the various manifesto proposals, deciding to keep or chop over three-quarters of them, and leaving the remainder for further costing and exploration.[133]

To avoid further embarrassments, Mawhinney obtained Major's permission to bring Lewington into the net of those informed about March.[134] 6 March was now looking less likely than 20 March (13 March was ruled out as the anniversary of Dunblane), although Cranborne and Goodlad favoured the first date, as did Garrett in Central Office, to maximise surprise. Central Office was promptly moved onto election footing, with extra staff and computing facilities brought in.[135] Days passed with still no firm decision. The Wirral South by-election proved to be a real stumbling block. Major continued to insist, to the annoyance of Central Office, that the Speaker's Convention be observed of the writ for the Wirral by-election being served within three months of a death. Major was concerned to avoid the opposition parties' attacks on the government's integrity, claiming that convention was being flouted and, more particularly, the likelihood of Labour themselves

moving the writ ('prissy and quite unnecessary' was an indicative comment
of a Central Office young Turk on Major's concern).[136]

Major held the second of his 'presidential-style' press conferences on 31
January, announcing – as part of the strategy of rolling disclosure of manifesto
proposals – an expansion of share ownership and greater scope for personal
pensions.[137]

In Limbo: February

Still Major clung to the hope in February of an election on 20 March. There
was now an awkward vacuum to fill before the election was announced.
Neither of the main parties had much new to offer and the month of February
had an atmosphere of a 'phoney war'. Behind the scenes, Blackwell was
joined by Willetts, and periodically by Finkelstein and Bridges, to finalise the
manifesto. Following the 27 January Political Cabinet, Willetts was rehabilitated when given a dormant title, 'Chairman' of the Research Department,
to polish and edit Blackwell's text.[138] Central Office, meanwhile, worked
frantically, finalising plans for the campaign. On 3 February – three months
to the day after Barry Porter's death – it was announced that the Wirral South
by-election would be held on 27 February. In the unreal atmosphere, the
local campaign absorbed a large part of the political interest and discussion
over its three-and-a-half-week duration, not least because both parties used
it as a proxy for the general election. Mawhinney gave the experienced Tim
Collins the task of helping manage the campaign locally. Labour, meanwhile,
campaigned on mainly national issues, 'minded' their candidate, Ben
Chapman, to an exceptional degree, and signalled the importance they
attached to the contest by bringing Blair up to the constituency on three
occasions.

Whilst much of the election planning had been put in place, including
programmes of action for Cabinet ministers, and objectives for different
stages of the campaign, the Conservatives' propaganda message remained
the problem that it had been over the last year. Decisions were either not
taken at the lengthy meetings at Central Office or, less frequently, they were
taken, to be vetoed by Number Ten. Frustration grew, Mawhinney at odds
with Maurice Saatchi, while Saatchi felt insufficient headway was being made
towards a more Eurosceptic campaign and, with Bell, felt a sense growing
that opportunities were being lost because of indecision and changes of tack.
While Mawhinney, and to some extent Heseltine and Major, felt that the
'three musketeers', above all Saatchi, were exceeding their brief and trying
to dictate not just the media campaign but the overall message the Party
should be putting across, there was some feeling that the outsiders' advice
was being inappropriately challenged by 'non-experts'. Said one spectator
from the PR side: 'You have the world's best advertising and two of the
world's best PR people, but their views were not well used. It was like asking

Picasso to make a violin or Stradivarius to paint a picture.'[139] 'The campaign was run not by marketing criteria but by mere political considerations' was a frequent, and revealing, complaint from the agency side.[140]

Saatchis produced 120 advertisements which were vetoed or not presented.[141] One of the more controversial not to receive the go-ahead was 'Euro Labour, Euro Danger', dropped due to complaints from Clarke and Heseltine, mediated by Mawhinney, who disliked the word 'Euro' being employed in a pejorative manner. Clarke said plainly, as he had on 19 December, that he was not prepared to endorse a 'petty, nationalist campaign'.[142] Saatchi's were, however, allowed to attack Labour's endorsement of the Social Chapter, as part of a moderate – no one defined the lines precisely – Eurosceptic stance. As part of this campaign, Major travelled to Brussels to deliver a speech attacking the Social Chapter for being a route to the dole queue: 'First stop Social Chapter, next stop social security,' he said. In its place, the Tories offered an 'enterprise' model with a deregulated EU.[143] A rise of half a million in unemployment in Germany helped to underline Major's message, with Central Office focus groups reporting that this was a good card for the Tories to play.[144]

The tussles between the politicians, principally Mawhinney, and the outside consultants, mainly Saatchi, and to a lesser extent also among the politicians, largely between Central Office, Number Ten and the Chancellor's office, were never satisfactorily resolved. It meant that whatever cohesion the advertising campaign may have had in July, October and January was lost, and a series of differing messages appeared on posters, which confused the electorate. A subject all agreed on was that the strongest line of attack on New Labour was on Blair himself. But this brought about another disagreement, on this occasion with the outside advisers and Central Office on one side and Number Ten, and specifically Major, on the other. He was adamant that he did not want an over-personalised campaign. If he was to lose, he wanted to go down well.[145] This disagreement led to some bad blood, and the beginning of unpleasant leaks that Major was more concerned by his personal place in history than by the fortunes of the Tory Party.[146]

Sensing the campaign approaching, Major's spirits and self-confidence rose. To bolster his election team, and to help bring the right into line, he appointed Cranborne to be his chief of staff. The hero of the leadership contest in 1995 and with a proven track record of success, his appointment seemed a smart move. But Cranborne's role was never clearly defined. It overlapped with those of Mawhinney and Blackwell (who wanted the same central position Sarah Hogg had enjoyed in 1992) and it would have been a recipe for confusion and strife had the parties involved not handled it better.

The day after Cranborne's appointment was announced, Major gave his strongest performance of the year at Prime Minister's Questions when he made fun in a good-natured way of it being Dennis Skinner's sixty-fifth birthday, offering him congratulations of reaching his age but adding that he would probably accuse him of fiddling the figures. He also gave a strong performance at the Welsh Conservative Conference on Friday 14 February, attacking Labour's plans for the constitution and accusing Blair of trying to precipitate an early election because Labour was 'running scared' in the face of the success of the Conservatives' economic policy.[147] Major again displayed his recidivist 'off-message' tendency when he made a joke about Blair sending him a Valentine's card that day with the inscription 'Everything I stand for, everything I believe in, I owe to you', although on this occasion the 'policy police' had approved the joke.[148]

The chief excitement the following week was a censure motion against Douglas Hogg for his conduct of the BSE crisis. John Prescott, the originator of the idea, returned from a trip to Brussels with, he imagined, telling evidence of Hogg's mishandling of the affair. To attack an unpopular minister on a subject which most agreed had not been well handled seemed a surefire way of producing a defeat that would lead to a no-confidence motion and a forced general election – Major's nightmare scenario.[149] Major was, however, relieved that Labour had chosen to make it a personal attack on Hogg, believing, as happened, that this would help the Tory Party to unify.[150] When the debate came on 17 February, the Labour challenge was duly seen off, defeated by 320 votes to 307.[151]

The Ulster Unionists all abstained, amid talk that a secret deal had been done. The public position of both the DUP and UUP was that they would continue to support the government as long as it was in the interests of Northern Ireland for them to do so. On the censure vote, their opinion was that they did not want to support either the government or Labour, so they abstained. Number Ten categorically denied any deal, and blamed not just Labour for spreading the talk, but also Hume who, they thought, had his own Party management reasons for backing the rumours.[152] Victory in the debate meant there would not be a no-confidence motion. The Number Ten Private Office put their draft speech for Major, which Major knew they had prepared over the Christmas holiday, but did not want to read, back in the drawer.[153]

The Cabinet's agreed position on Europe was now given an absurd twist, prompted by a statement from Rifkind on 19 February that he was 'hostile to a single currency'. Clarke responded hours later, puckishly, that the Foreign Secretary's comments were of course 'obviously a slip of the tongue under pressure from a very skilful interviewer' rather than a contradiction of government policy. Howe weighed in on 20 February, saying he would find it very hard to back a government 'that is in principle hostile to the concept of a single currency'. Major came under heavy pressure from Blair later the same day at Prime Minister's Questions, being asked whether he supported his Foreign Secretary or Chancellor. Major's response was that the government was 'not hostile in its attitude to a single currency – the position remains that we have an open option'.[154] The government was relieved that the death of veteran Chinese leader Deng Xiao-ping pushed the news of the spat, which could have erupted into a full-scale row, down the broadcasters' schedules and down or off many newspapers' front pages.[155]

The Wirral by-election result could not, however, be so easily sidelined. With a high turnout of 73 per cent, the Conservative share of the vote fell by 17 per cent compared to 1992, with several thousand voters switching their votes directly from Conservative to Labour. If repeated nationally, the result would have given Labour an overall majority in the general election of 296. It was a stinging result, and gave many Tory MPs a deep scare.[156] Major had not expected such a heavy defeat. He had not stayed up to hear it, but was told first thing next morning. Tory strategists at Central Office were disappointed that he only perfunctorily mouthed the Central Office line – that the result was merely a symptom of 'by-election culture', and voters would return in the general election. Instead of doing a frantic round of media interviews, as he had done after the bad local election results in May 1996, he retreated to his tent.[157] Inevitably, the news leaked out of Central Office that the by-election had only taken place when it did at his behest, and he was thus to blame.[158]

At this time, Major also finally decided against a 20 March general election. An announcement, calling it, was due to have been made on 24 February. But following a meeting with Mawhinney, Heseltine, Newton, Goodlad and Cranborne at the end of the week before, Major said that he had finally decided against it, blaming, as was Number Ten's belief, Central Office for being insufficiently ready. 'That was news to me,' said one senior Party official, who says the Party machine was ready to go for a March election.[159]

A decisive factor in deciding against March was that Labour had elaborate plans ready in the event of the election being called for that month. 'At a stroke, it turned the decision from appearing strong and brave to cutting and running,' recalled one senior figure. 'It undermined both the elements of bravado and surprise.'[160] Not only most of the senior staff at Central Office, but also the backbenchers and the voluntary party all believed they stood their best chance on 1 May. An additional factor for MPs was the extra severance pay available if Parliament was dissolved in the new financial year in April. Major also realised that if, on his insistence, the election went ahead on 20 March and the Party was defeated badly, his own standing would be badly damaged.[161] Few decisions had caused him such agonising. The truth was that, worn down by months of fatigue, he found great difficulty making up his mind on what he realised would probably prove the last key decision of his political career.

It was a disappointing end for Major to an unsatisfactory February, in which the Party only partially succeeded in controlling the agenda, and during which its strategy appeared tentative and uncertain. Towards the end of the month, the Tory voices of dissent, mostly quiescent since the New Year, began again to sound forth – an ominous sign. Edward Heath declared his support for a range of Labour's policies, including devolution and the minimum wage; Tebbit attacked Heseltine as being 'tasteless, tacky . . . and

self-centred beyond even the call of his profession', while Redwood said
Major needed to provide stronger leadership because 'sometimes confusing
messages were being given'. After the by-election, Major realised that any
hopes he harboured that the general election could be won were not sustainable.

To the Wire: 1–17 March

Major's spirits had recovered quickly after the shock of the by-election result.
In Glasgow on Sunday 2 March his response to Blair's urging 'for heaven's
sake, in the interests of the country, stop dithering' was to warn, 'Britain
could be just weeks away from a midsummer nightmare.'[162] That was more
like it, thought Central Office.[163] Major returned to London on the Monday
in confident form. The midweek announcement of radical new pension
proposals, which had been worked up by Peter Lilley, gave the Party the
initiative, and some welcome positive press coverage.[164] The announcement
was the latest instalment of the rolling disclosure of choice manifesto proposals, and was to be the most far-ranging fresh policy in the document.[165]

No sooner had the climate improved than the Party, in time-honoured
tradition, inflicted wounds on itself. Reports appeared that some ministers,
such as Tom Sackville and David Maclean, were to defy, in their constituency
election addresses, the government line on the single currency. The report,
in the *Sunday Times*, was a harbinger of what became a recurrent election
difficulty.[166] Major privately blamed the Eurosceptic press, especially *The
Times* and the *Daily Telegraph* for whipping up concern over election
addresses, subjecting them to close textual scrutiny to cause embarrassment
over the single currency.[167] How to handle candidates' election addresses had
been the subject of disagreement.

Heseltine favoured either refusing to let Central Office print any addresses
that disagreed with 'wait and see', or to prevent their authors standing as
candidates. Less radically, Rifkind favoured offering candidates a choice of
acceptable sentences that they could use on the single currency. Advice from
Central Office was strongly against adopting either of these tacks. Mawhinney
thus counselled that only ministers should be told to abide by collective
responsibility and support 'wait and see', and leave MPs and candidates a
free vote. Major agreed, but they knew that the issue would almost certainly
blow up during the campaign.[168]

David Evans, the populist right-wing MP for Welwyn and Hatfield, next
described his Labour opponent, Melanie Johnson, as 'a single girl, lives with
her boyfriend, three bastard children . . . never done a proper job'.[169] These
comments, and others in a similar vein, spoken to a meeting of sixth formers,
were emblazoned across the national headlines. Major did not like Evans, not
least since he had been Redwood's campaign manager in the leadership
election. He condemned his remarks unreservedly at a press conference the
next day.[170]

Budgen was similarly firmly handled when he asked at Prime Minister's Questions on 4 March whether Major agreed that 'strict control of immigration' was the key to good race relations. Major felt himself being pointed towards delivering a tough line on immigration. He told the House he was 'certainly not going to lend my voice or my policy' to do anything 'to damage the improvement in race relations in Britain'.[171] Blair was moved to say, 'I think the Prime Minister deserves credit for that answer.'

Now another right-winger for whom Major had contempt, George Gardiner, was to cause waves. Deselected eventually by his Reigate constituency at the end of January for repeated disloyalty, he announced his defection to the Referendum Party, adding, for good measure, that Tory seats would 'go down the pan' at the general election.[172] Sleaze returned centre stage with allegations by the lobbyist Ian Greer that Neil Hamilton and Michael Brown both received money on commissions that were never declared in the MPs' register. All eyes began to turn to the work of Gordon Downey, asked to investigate the entire cash-for-questions affair.[173]

The Number Ten Political Office developed a gallows' humour about Tory MPs. George Bridges joked they should issue a statement that all Tories who planned to do or say anything stupid should get together in one room and say or do it together.[174] Comments from two figures, however, defeated any attempts at levity. On the eve of Major's Central Council speech at Bath, on 15 March, Edwina Currie said that if the Party was defeated, 'Please John, please don't hang around. Don't make us wait.' Mawhinney lashed out, 'If you don't have something to say that will help us to win, don't say anything at all.'[175] More damaging, Lady Thatcher was reported to have told Peter Stothard, editor of *The Times*, that Blair 'won't let Britain down'.[176]

Major's aides immediately phoned her office to find out what was going on. Their response was contrite, and they denied that she had uttered those words.[177] Major was in two minds about whether she had. He had no doubts at all that her decision before the Party Conference to be loyal and to be seen to campaign actively still stood. But equally he knew she was capable of speaking the words, and he assumed that she thought them.[178] The suggestion that the great architect of the Tory project should have said Blair was now 'safe', even when denied, was considered deeply damaging to the entire 'new danger' mission.

The party's strategists had further worries about Major's Bath speech. They knew he planned to deliver an intensely personal message. This would almost certainly be 'off-message' too. They were comforted by the conventional wisdom that Saturday speeches rarely attracted much media attention. To try to ensure some Tory headlines, Party officials fed the press with stories that Major would be going to the Palace on Monday, and that he planned to have a television debate with Blair (about which he had doubts). Both stories, not the Bath speech, duly captured the headlines in Sunday's press.[179]

The speech itself was preceded by a warm-up film, portraying images of the 1992 pre-election headlines predicting defeat. The audience cheered. Major then took to the stage, and opened with an attack on Labour for its policies on education and devolution. The campaign slogan, he told delegates, to a subdued reaction, was to be 'You can only be sure with the Conservatives'. The personal material was certainly the most deeply felt. 'I dream of a people's Britain', in which he would like 'to see the have-nots become the haves'. His vision for Britain over the next five years, now that the economy was strong and money was becoming available, was to build a country not just for the strong and self-confident, but 'for everyone, for those for whom life is a struggle, for those who don't have the best education, don't have a decent home, don't have a safe neighbourhood, don't have a job'. He said it was 'what I have always wanted to do'. He identified himself squarely with the underdog, those for whom life is a struggle: 'I come from them. I care for them all. I long to see them have their fair share of the good things in life.'[180]

As he sipped champagne afterwards, he told aides: 'This was one of the speeches I felt most comfortable delivering.'[181] Here indeed, on the verge of the end of his political career, was the authentic voice of John Major.

THIRTY-NINE

The End of a Premiership:

March–May 1997

John Major's relief that at long last the election campaign had begun was tempered by the size of the hurdle before him. The Tories' 1997 election campaign laboured under four handicaps: the press was less supportive, the Party was more divided, victory was less likely and the Party's moral authority was more in question than for any general election since 1945.

The Battle for the Press

A deep wariness had characterised John Major's view of the media throughout his premiership. As Number Ten and Central Office believed, for election victory to occur the Tory press now had to be won back, although they always exaggerated the extent that the press shaped rather than merely followed public opinion. The broadcasters – television, radio and satellite – at least had a statutory obligation to be impartial, and a sympathetic impartiality was the most that could be achieved, by employing a mixture of lightly buttered carrots – offers of exclusive stories and interviews – and heavy-handed sticks, angry phone calls and letters, and ultimately threats on licence fees and unfavourable legislation, which lacked some conviction from a party heavily tipped to lose. As it transpired, the broadcast media during the campaign were to be regarded by Number Ten and Central Office as broadly fair, although Sky Television, owned by Murdoch and run by his daughter Elizabeth as general manager, was felt to have become hostile over the preceding months.[1]

But it was the press to which most thought was given. Traditionally, the Tory Party could count on favourable coverage from the majority of national newspapers in a campaign. But no longer. From his accession in November 1990 to the autumn of 1992, the Tory press had, indeed, been generally favourable. Dislike of Major personally, for alleged weak leadership and for not being sufficiently Thatcherite, above all on Europe, surfaced in various quarters, but was kept in check by the imminence of the general election and by a greater dislike of Kinnock. From Black Wednesday in September 1992 until the leadership election in the summer of 1995, there was a rapid slide in the Tory press towards outright hostility. Britain's ejection from the ERM was the turning point. Editors either felt vindicated (like Charles Moore, then of the *Sunday Telegraph*) because they had never rated Major, or betrayed (like Max Hastings, Moore's predecessor as editor of the *Daily Telegraph*). Conrad Black, the *Telegraph*'s proprietor, had been pushing Hastings to attack Major much earlier: Hastings continued to support Major longer than any other senior journalist on his paper, holding on until Black Wednesday, but never trusted Major again after it.[2] The absence of an apology or any admission of responsibility from Number Ten for the ERM, and for the economic hardship that followed Britain's departure, antagonised many other editors and journalists also.

The unprecedented loss of support from the Tory press cannot be explained, however, by Black Wednesday alone. Changes of editor were significant. Those either positive or neutral about Major were steadily replaced by those who did not rate him, notably Peter Stothard succeeding Simon Jenkins at *The Times* in 1992, Max Hastings replacing Stewart Steven at the London *Evening Standard* in 1995 and Richard Addis taking over from Nicholas Lloyd at the *Daily Express* in 1995. Steven and Lloyd were both suspected by the Eurosceptic right of running with stories deliberately damaging to their cause.[3] If true, Major still had a less partisan press prepared to help him out than most premiers. Editors not unnaturally followed their commercial interest: as Conservative support fell after Black Wednesday to an average of 30 per cent, and as Labour under Blair became much more friendly to the middle classes and to advertisers, support for the Conservatives made less obvious economic sense. Boredom with the same old Tory faces, the lack of star players (Clarke and Heseltine were exceptions) or exciting fresh policies inclined several papers in the same direction. Only the *Daily Express* backed Major in the leadership election. Had Redwood won, the Tory press would have returned far more whole-heartedly to the fold.

Victories for the press in helping bring down Mellor, Mates and Lamont, and in the abandonment of back to basics, encouraged several newspapers into bold, oppositional stances. Once they sensed their ability to make or break politicians and policies, the press's power, much written about this century but mostly overstated, was turned to the relentless pursuit of Major's head. Proprietors, Rupert Murdoch, Conrad Black, Lord Stevens and Lord Rothermere, were happy to watch and even to encourage this stag hunt, none of them believing Major much good as premier. In their different ways, they all admired Thatcher, and disapproved of Major's European policy and his failure to look after their predominantly middle-class readership, above all because of raising taxes. A clique of right-wing, Eurosceptic journalists – notably Simon Heffer, Paul Johnson, Boris Johnson and Charles Moore – mixed freely with the dispossessed Thatcher court, and with disaffected backbenchers and ministers such as Redwood, Lilley and Portillo. The journalists lapped up stories from those close to them. The days when the government was in charge of the leaking and story-spinning agenda were over: they now competed for top news slots and headlines with the 'alternative government', the anti-Major faction reaching right up to Cabinet ministers. In an unequal race, it was the latter that usually won.[4]

After the leadership election, serious thought began to be put into winning back the Tory press before the general election. When Meyer took over as Number Ten Press Secretary from O'Donnell in early 1994, he rapidly formed the view that little positive relationship existed between Number Ten and a large number of proprietors and editors. The lack of respect between lobby journalists and Number Ten also alarmed him, and he set to work building up Major into a more prime ministerial figure.

Major was, he believed, too promiscuous with journalists, especially on foreign trips, and needed to be more detached and to wait for them to come to him. Having established this change of culture, he set to work on the editors. Every fortnight on a rolling programme one would be invited to Downing Street for a drink at 6 p.m. with just Major and himself. They would be free to print unattributably whatever they wished based on what they heard. None refused to come, though Paul Dacre of the *Daily Mail* proved the most elusive. For proprietors, Meyer persuaded Major to make greater use of Chequers. Several dinners were also held at Number Ten attended by Murdoch; Rothermere and Black came to the dinner for Clinton in November 1995, while Stevens attended the dinner for Chirac.[5] Major went along with the strategy, but without great enthusiasm, or belief that good would come out of it.[6] Gone was the Major of old, consorting happily with selected journalists: his experience at Number Ten had destroyed the trust and faith he once placed in the media. 'He didn't want to prostitute himself by running after people for whom he had little regard' said one aide.

The leadership election over, it was the Conrad Black group that Number Ten was most anxious to court. Moore at the *Daily Telegraph* had decided to give Major a fresh chance. Though he still thought him lacking in ideas ('I think he has no actual views at all') and without the qualities he wanted in a Tory leader, he did at least think him less bad than some recent Tory leaders, notably Macmillan and Heath.[7] But by the spring of 1996 Moore had lost patience, and penned his stinging 'get off your knees' editorial on Major's uncertain leadership. Only very slowly did the newspaper accommodate itself again to Major, but by the election was back firmly on side. Its commercial interest always dictated that it would support the Tories, but the pleasant surprise for Central Office was how strongly they backed them. Not only Moore's editorials, but the news pages were also firmly pro-Tory and anti-Labour, and the newspaper was also happy to be used by the Party to give publicity for the Tory cause, notably on trade union recognition. Robert Shrimsley, on the political staff, and George Jones, the political editor, were regarded by Number Ten as two of the most pro-Major journalists.[8]

The *Sunday Telegraph* also backed the Tories during the campaign, though neither Dominic Lawson nor Matthew d'Ancona, editor and deputy editor, developed any higher a regard for Major. On 12 March, on the eve of the campaign opening, the senior *Sunday Telegraph* team had lunch with him.

They were not impressed, in particular by what he said on the single currency and by his responses on why he did not sack 'incompetent' ministers such as Hogg (BSE), Lamont (ERM) and Soames (Gulf War syndrome).[9] ('I do not believe they did anything dishonest. Am I to sack them because the public or the press want their blood?' he replied.[10]) Their verdict after the lunch was that he was more concerned by his place in history than by his party's electoral interests. The *Spectator*, acquired by Black in 1990, had changed from its virulent anti-Major stance in the early 1990s to being tolerably positive after Frank Johnson became editor in 1995 and Bruce Anderson a regular columnist. It ceased to be the journal about which Major would be openly scornful and say he never read (though he occasionally did), and 'Franco' (as Johnson was known) was made welcome at Number Ten.[11]

As the election approached, Murdoch's News International group was to prove far less biddable than Black's empire. Number Ten used to debate how far Murdoch directed his editors – no one was exactly sure. When Stothard was appointed editor by Murdoch in 1992, he was given no advice on the line to take on Major, and he asserts that his proprietor subsequently did not try to interfere with his editorial decisions.[12] Not that Stothard needed any prompting to take an anti-Major line: like Murdoch, his mind was made up. Stothard, a convinced Eurosceptic, was determined to take *The Times* in a fresh direction and, he says, 'never saw a successful day of the Major government' while he was editor, having taken over shortly after Black Wednesday.[13] As the election approached, Major convinced himself that the newspaper would come out for Blair, despite Norman Blackwell and Maurice Saatchi having good relationships with Stothard, and working hard to show him how far in a sceptical direction the government was moving on Europe.[14]

Stothard's senior leader-writing team debated the options at a meeting at the Reform Club in January 1997. Michael Gove, Portillo's biographer, put the Tory case and Mary-Ann Sieghart argued for Labour. No decisions were taken.[15] Riddell, who had been one of the most fair-handed journalists in Fleet Street towards Major's government, recognised the case for a change, but fell short of endorsing Blair.[16] Rather than commit itself to one party, however, *The Times* eventually pronounced the advice that its readers should back the most Eurosceptic candidate in their constituency.[17] The response from Central Office, to highlight the inconsistency of the position in supporting Alan Clark and at the same time the left-wing Labour MP Jeremy Corbyn, disguised their relief that the paper had not come out in favour of Labour. Said one senior figure: 'Its equivocation was a welcome relief.'[18] *The Times*, in common with the *Daily Telegraph*, published daily lists of Conservative candidates defying the government line on the single currency but, unlike its fellow newspaper, was open-minded to Labour in both its news and editorial pages.

The *Sunday Times* had been courted assiduously by Central Office and Number Ten, though its importance in setting the agenda, in common with other Sunday papers, diminished considerably once the campaign started, when attention focused on the daily papers. Under Andrew Neil's editorship until 1994, the newspaper had swung from pro-Thatcher in the 1980s to virulently anti-Major in 1992–4, motivated in significant part by Neil's widely-trumpeted dislike of the government's European and economic policies.[19] John Witherow, the new editor, and Martin Ivens, deputy editor, were wooed by Mawhinney and Lewington, while the latter ensured that the paper's Andrew Grice and Michael Prescott were always fed with quality inside information for their weekly in-depth articles. Michael Jones, the associate editor, was regarded as a powerful ally, and the most pro-Major of all the senior staff on the newspaper.[20] The *Sunday Times*'s eventual decision to declare for the Tories caused relief, but paled into insignificance besides the decision of the *Sun* to take the opposite course.

While Murdoch's influence on the two *Times* titles was sketchy, it was profound on his daily tabloid. Stuart Higgins and Trevor Kavanagh, editor and political editor, kept telling Number Ten that they were working hard to put Murdoch off deciding the paper should back Labour. Higgins was more pro-Major than had been his predecessor Kevin MacKenzie, and Major felt he had re-established a good personal relationship with Kavanagh after a difficult passage in 1993–4. A lunch with the *Sun*'s senior staff in early 1996 went well. Major received nods of approval when he told them he had not fought for the National Lottery for the money 'to go to men in tights' and other offbeat causes.[21] But Higgins and Kavanagh also warned that it would be Europe that would weigh most heavily on the newspaper's decision.[22] The *Sun* ran a phone-in in December 1996 which revealed 100,000 readers were apparently anti-single currency,[23] a statistic that puzzled some journalists who were doubtful whether that many *Sun* readers had informed views on the matter. Driving back from a lunch with Higgins and Kavanagh in February 1997, Major was gloomy and uttered 'I have a very bad feeling' about whether they would back the Tories.

Comfort came from Tim Bell, who assured them that the *Sun* would come over to their cause,[24] employing the argument that it would want to position itself differently from the *Daily Mirror*. In fact, commercial interests supported the *Sun*'s three-page ringing endorsement of New Labour on 18 March: MORI found 56 per cent of *Sun* readers backed Labour.[25] Labour's wooing of the *Sun* had paid off. Major put a brave face on the news, which broke on 17 March, the day he called the election. When he addressed his final meeting to the 1922 Committee on 19 March, he began by parodying the *Sun*'s boast after the 1992 general election when he told backbenchers, 'It's the *Sun* wot blew it!'[26] To lose the newspaper that had championed Thatcherism in the 1980s and which claimed it had won the 1992 general election for the Tories was a powerful blow, above all psychologically. The *News of the World*, the final national newspaper in Murdoch's group, was similarly susceptible to the Murdoch line and supported Labour.[27]

Rothermere's Associated Newspapers group, also traditionally Tory, equally saw its titles split on whom to back. Rothermere himself was won over by Blair, describing him as 'very charming, very acute ... extremely *sympatico*'.[28] His flagship was the *Daily Mail*, edited since 1992 by the dour Paul Dacre, an admirer of Mrs Thatcher but not of Major, who he felt was weak on Europe and who had not done enough for family values. Dacre's assaults on the government had damaged the Tories more than the critical stance any other newspaper.[29] Mawhinney and Lewington tried to persuade Dacre of Tory merits, a difficult task given the editor's dislike of personal contacts. They offered the *Daily Mail* an exclusive on the 'lion' advertisement, and told Dacre 'the family' would be emphasised in Tory election policies. The transferable family allowance owed much of its success at being included in the manifesto to the argument that it was exactly the type of policy *Daily Mail* readers favoured and might tip Dacre into backing the Party.[30]

Europe was the factor that led Dacre to place a Union Jack on its front cover and to say 1,000 years of history were about to be undone in the run-up to election day.[31] Although his election leader urged readers only reluctantly to stick with Major, the *Daily Mail*'s news pages became a guaranteed home for anti-Labour stories offered by Central Office or initiated by their own news and political reporters.[32] On 25 March it gave prominence to a report about Labour's alleged plans to boost union power, and on 3 April it reported that there had been a deal to gag the trade unions. But Labour considered the attacks tame compared with 1992.[33] The softer, less ideological *Mail on Sunday*, edited by Jonathan Holborow, returned to the Tory fold during the election campaign after a period in 1995 and 1996 when it had been critical, and was regarded in Central Office as the most supportive Sunday newspaper. Its sister paper, the London *Evening Standard*, backed Labour.[34] Its editor Max Hastings said he personally would be voting Tory, on whose success he had placed a bet, not out of any regard for Major but because he opposed Labour's anti-fox hunting proposals.[35] But Londoners' interests, he thought, would be best served by a Labour victory.

Stevens's United Newspapers, the final traditional Tory group, taken over by the conglomerate MAI in 1996, endured similar agonising before reaching its decisions. At the *Daily Express* Addis was told by Stevens that he would be happy for him to be more independent and to move the newspaper away from being seen as a mouthpiece of Central Office, as it had been under Lloyd. Major sensed the danger of losing such a stalwart. Not enjoying the experience, over a drink at Number Ten in January 1996, Major told Addis that the *Daily Express* had been his family newspaper and that he always felt very attached to it.[36] But Addis had to battle to increase the newspaper's flagging circulation, which partly dictated his flirting with non-Tory positions in a search for new readers. Central Office and Number Ten came to the conclusion that they had few hopes of many favours from the newspaper, believing that Addis would not only be governed by commercial considerations, but by thinking about his own position after the election. The Labour peer Lord Hollick had become the group's new owner and chief executive in 1996 with the MAI takeover, and naturally inclined the group in a Labour direction. The *Express*, as the paper was renamed in October 1996, nevertheless was to endorse the Tories during the campaign, as did the *Sunday Express*, but both did so only tepidly, as if they were giving a speech at a farewell party for someone they disliked. Neither paper was well disposed to run pro-Tory or anti-Labour stories, but both provided a platform for damaging reports and articles, notably Edwina Currie's prediction of a Labour landslide victory.[37]

Little effort was expended by Number Ten or Central Office on other national newspapers, all considered more or less lost causes. The Mirror Group papers were solidly Labour, as expected. The *Independent on Sunday*, half-owned by the group, supported Blair, as did Andrew Marr's *Independent*. Alan Rusbridger's *Guardian* and Will Hutton's *Observer* remained virulently anti-Tory, the former causing the sleaze issue to retain its high profile for so long into the campaign. The *Financial Times* was, however, one newspaper that the Tories had hoped they might win over. Major was considered by the newspaper's editorial staff to have performed impressively when he was interviewed by them at the start of the campaign. Major was himself pleased by the impact he made on Richard Lambert and Philip Stephens, editor and political columnist, and on the rest of their staff.[38] But it was insufficient to persuade them to back him, and at the end of the campaign they backed Labour, as they had done in 1992.

The loss of great swathes of the press, after all the efforts expended since 1995 to win them over, was both harbinger and part cause for the eventual scale of the defeat.

The Battle Over Sleaze: 17–31 March

At 12.35 p.m. on 17 March, on his return from Buckingham Palace, Major walked out of Number Ten to announce that the general election would be held on 1 May. As he stood facing the media he told them that there had been a 'dramatic change in the lifestyle of the people of this country ...' and that '... people are looking for change'. To combat at the very outset what was seen as Labour's strongest card, he bounced straight back with: 'But we are the change, and we will carry forward what we have been doing for the last eighteen years ... I believe this election is winnable ... I think we are going to win.'[39] But as we have seen, even from the outset he did not think the election winnable: if he could have restricted it to a Labour majority of only twenty to thirty, he would have been delighted.

The six-week campaign would provide the opportunity to hack into Labour's lead, which in mid-March, depending on the poll, varied between 18 and 25 percentage points. Labour's divisions, policy inconsistencies and spending uncertainties would be heavily probed, while a series of good economic news, scheduled to come out during the campaign, would help a bandwagon to begin to roll towards the Conservatives. As the polls started to move the Tories' way, the Party would see the folly of any further disloyalty, and would pull hard together.[40] That, anyway, was the hope. To bring all guns to bear on Labour was regarded as essential, while making Major himself the centre of attention. 'We want to do what he is comfortable doing,' was a common wish expressed by senior staff at Number Ten and Central Office. What he felt happy doing was travelling around the country, meeting voters, and giving a series of speeches where he was free to speak his mind.[41]

Major was to travel the country in a British Midland Boeing 737 jet, lent by Michael Bishop, the airline's chairman, and in the Wallace Arnold battlebus, modified from 1992 by the addition of a mobile side platform from which he could speak. This technical device was kept very 'hush-hush', and felt to have almost certain prospects of success. Those with jaundiced senses of humour in the Party compared the confidence placed in it to that of Hitler's secret weapons (the flying bombs) when it was clear the Second World War had been lost.[42]

During the six weeks, he clocked up 10,000 miles, visiting fifty-six constituencies. Travelling with him on his personal staff for the marathon were Howell James and John Ward from Number Ten, Sheila Gunn, appointed his Personal Press Secretary, Shirley Stotter, the tour's organiser, and periodically Lord Cranborne, the chief of staff. Norman Blackwell worked as a liaison between the battlebus and operators at the centre. Working on speeches at Number Ten were Blackwell and George Bridges, joined by the veteran trio of Ronnie Millar, Nick True, and Jonathan Hill on interviews. Tim Bell, Peter Gummer and Maurice Saatchi were very regular visitors at Central Office, where operations were directed by Brian Mawhinney and Michael Trend. It was an experienced crew, and they were reasonably confident that their plans, which had been fifteen months in the formulation, would, despite their differences over some of the advertisements, prove effective.

From the start, however, little went to plan, and during the first two weeks the Party rarely held the initiative. On his trip to Luton on 17 March, where he had gone to tell the nation about the general election mounted on his soapbox, he learned about the *Sun*'s defection to Blair. But it was 'sleaze' that overshadowed the first two weeks. The opening shot was first the Liberal Democrats and then Labour accusing Major of proroguing Parliament deliberately early to avoid the publication of Sir Gordon Downey's cash-for-questions inquiry into Neil Hamilton and other MPs. The charge succeeded in capturing the headlines, and undercutting government 'good news' stories, primarily that unemployment had fallen by 60,000. Downey was almost ready to deliver his report to the Commons Standards and Privileges Committee, but as Parliament was to be imminently prorogued, he would be unable to do so. The opposition parties' case was given added credence when they argued that several government Bills were being lost or amended in the haste to prorogue Parliament at the end of the week on Friday 21 March.

At Question Time, wittily on Tuesday and angrily on Thursday, Major denied that the prorogation had anything to do with trying to avoid the publication of Downey's report.[43] The prorogation decision was taken in line with the six-week campaign planned since the summer of 1996, to allow as long as possible for the focus to move away from Westminster out into the country, which the Tory leadership believed it could control more easily, and for Labour's supposed contradictions to manifest. Major further felt that if the report were to have been handed to the Commons Standards and Privileges Committee, it would have been leaked, resulting in trial of the accused by media, and justice not being done fairly. Heseltine's view was that it would have been a 'kangaroo court'.[44]

Labour and the Liberal Democrats succeeded in disrupting the first week of the campaign, and in conveying a widespread impression that the Tory leadership itself was now guilty of sleaze by obstructing the truth coming out into the open. When the *Guardian* published four pages of evidence submitted to the Downey Inquiry reportedly showing that a number of MPs standing for re-election took money from Mohamed Al Fayed in return for asking questions in Parliament, further support was given to the belief that the cover-up was to avoid the Party being damaged at the election.[45]

Major was angered and upset by the first week of the campaign. By its end, he, Heseltine and Mawhinney were no closer to deciding how to rebut the sleaze accusations. When they realised how badly the campaign had been derailed, the tack shifted over the weekend from stonewall defence to blaming both the MPs concerned for not resigning, and their associations for backing their MPs, a line that found itself into a headline in the *Sunday Express* on 23 March, 'Major wants the sleaze MPs out'.[46] By letting such stories get into the press, the Party's high command raised the expectation that tough action would – and could – be taken, with charges of indecision when it was not. The ambivalence reflected yet again the limited room for manoeuvre under which Major operated, where 'megaphone diplomacy was the only strategy we had left', according to one Central Office source.[47]

Sleaze continued to dominate into the second week. Even the Prime Minister's tour was dogged by ill-luck: to the delight of Labour, on 24 March he was photographed near a sign advertising 'Slee's' hardware shop' in Barnstaple, Devon. The next day, Allan Stewart quit the safest Tory seat in Scotland following press allegations about an affair, which overshadowed publication of the best current account trade figures since 1985. Another MP, Tim Smith, resigned on 25 March after confessing he had accepted £25,000 from Mohamed Al Fayed, and another good Tory story, a row over trade union rights, was swamped. The next day, the *Sun* splashed a story about Piers Merchant, the Beckenham MP, allegedly having an affair with a seventeen-year-old 'Soho nightclub hostess'.

By now, Major, Heseltine and Mawhinney were losing their self-possession, imagining that the entire campaign might be overshadowed by sleaze stories. The leadership made attempts to suggest Merchant stand down, only to be soundly rebuffed by his constituency association, as were similar attempts in public and private to suggest Hamilton step aside by his Tatton association.

Major had so often felt let down by the behaviour of his MPs that he ceased to be surprised by anything they did, but Hamilton's failure to step aside and instead to fight on brazenly left him speechless, above all because his failure to come up with a satisfactory answer to the Hamilton saga was portrayed successfully by Labour both as a sign of his weak leadership and of Tories' poor moral standards. Two days after Merchant's headlines, Michael Hirst, the Party's Scottish chairman, resigned in Scotland over a personal indiscretion. Reports appeared of unsavoury infighting in the Scottish Conservative Party surrounding his decision to stand down. At the end of the second week, MORI put Labour 21 points ahead, while Harris showed Labour 24 points above the Conservatives. It was the biggest lead at the comparable stage of the campaign for any party since the beginning of polling.[48]

As Major returned to The Finings for his last birthday as premier, and for the Easter weekend over 29 to 31 March, some lessons were plain. With all the dominance of sleaze the Party's advertising, with 'Britain is booming. Don't let Labour blow it', was becoming swamped. Nor was the Party's media operation, for all its industry and skill, a match for Labour's far stronger team. The Prime Minister's tour, a subject of heated prior debate, was better planned than in 1992, with an eye to having different news stories and pictures on the lunchtime, early evening and late evening news broadcasts. But it was proving less attention-grabbing and exciting for the media than than Blair's. Journalists travelling on the Major tour might have found it more friendly, and that they were less bossed about than on Blair's heavily stage-managed party, but it was the reporting that mattered.

Another casualty just before Easter was the idea of the television debate between the Party leaders. On 19 December, the BBC had written to all parties with proposals for such a face-to-face event, discussed for many years in Britain, but unlike in the United States, not yet realised. The ITN put forward their own proposals at the end of February. The briefing at Bath from Lewington on 15 March that Major wanted a debate produced a flurry of discussions during the following week, with Michael Dobbs representing the Tories, Lord Irvine Labour and Lord Holme the Liberal Democrats. Dobbs fought hard, believing that in a head-to-head debate Major, with his greater experience and command of detail, could beat Blair. Mawhinney was also keen, and twice, with Major's agreement, unreservedly accepted ITN's proposal for the debate.[49] Labour, with their overwhelming lead, however, had more to lose. On 26 March, the BBC thought they were close to a deal, but talks finally broke down the next day amidst mutual recrimination. Accommodating third parties in the debate, above all the Liberal Democrats, who threatened legal action unless their demands were met, was a major hurdle. Having two television companies competing to stage the debate did not help. But the chief reason for failure was that neither Major nor Blair fought hard for it, fearing that such a debate might overshadow the entire election campaign.[50] Both Party leaders, to an extent the broadcasters never fully seemed to grasp, used the discussion as a political football.[51]

The Battle Against Labour: 1–11 April

An early fruit of the rethink over Easter was a letter Major sent to all constituency chairmen in the country warning them that, if misconduct was proved against any MP, he would back their expulsion from Parliament and from the Tory Party,[52] pointedly referring to the honourable behaviour of Michael Hirst.

Tuesday 1 April was the official launch day of the campaign, and the date of the Party's first press conference. In addition to some discussion of the wisdom of opening the campaign on April Fool's Day (the *Independent* ran a spoof story about Blair planning to appoint Lady Thatcher Ambassador in Washington), the subject to lead on was changed in the days immediately before.

The economic record, in tune with the 'Britain is booming' message, was to have been the theme, but several senior figures counselled that if they introduced any topic other than sleaze, the media would ignore it, and fire in with questions about Hamilton, Merchant, *et al*, and then claim that the Tories were unable to dominate the agenda. Much better, it was decided, to allow the media to ask about sleaze, and let the questions play themselves out. Those who wanted the Party to stick with the positive economic theme were overruled,[53] and Major duly spoke in favour of tough action from the Standards and Privileges Committee. While his argument that constituency associations had a right to field MPs not yet found guilty of any offence may have appeared to be fence-sitting, it was still an answer that took the Party off the hook, and had an undeniable justice to it. The strategy worked.[54] Sleaze slowly receded as an issue during the third week; having dominated the first two weeks of the campaign, it faded out, with only the bizarre and isolated campaign, reminiscent of a by-election, in Tatton.

Wednesday 2 April was launch day of the manifesto. Boasting a photograph of Major on the front cover, and another on the first page, the document was the climax of over two years' planning and consultation, and was very much the fruit of Norman Blackwell's labour. It was the culmination of his meticulous analysis of what Conservatism entailed at the end of the twentieth century, as well as one of the most widely grounded policy statements that the Party had produced since 1945. But even this failed to receive the widespread support in the Party it deserved.[55] On 10 March, draft sections of the manifesto were sent out to departmental ministers for final approval. At Political Cabinet on the morning of 20 March, ministers were shown an almost complete draft, with some of the more sensitive passages again edited out to avoid leaking. That afternoon, the inner group of Major, Heseltine, Clarke, Mawhinney, Cranborne, Waldegrave and Goodlad met a final time to settle outstanding issues. Forsyth and Hague came in for the part of the discussion dealing with their separate Scottish and Welsh manifestos.[56]

The core dilemma of the manifesto was how to align it with the theme of the 'safety' of the Tories against the risk of Labour, which dictated a consolidating manifesto, while also offering fresh ideas, to combat the charge that Sarah Hogg had also battled with in 1992, that the government had run out of steam. The manifesto met the challenge by offering both consolidation and new ideas.

Several of the proposals had already been made public as part of the 'rolling programme' strategy, or had already been foreshadowed by policy statements, such as no legislation on the single currency in the first Queen's Speech, and cutting public spending to less than 40 per cent of national income. Income tax was to have a goal of a 20 pence basic rate. The two principal proposals were Lilley's 'basic pension plus', and Blackwell's transferable family tax proposals. The latter had to be forced past a reluctant Clarke, who had successfully resisted other tax changes. By restructuring the transferable allowances to husbands and wives only when they were caring for a child or relative, the overall cost was reduced from £3 billion to less than half that.[57]

The manifesto was generally well received, *The Times* saying it was 'more coherent' and the *Daily Telegraph* 'more clear' than its 1992 counterpart.[58] Selective briefings were given to the *Daily Mail* and the *Financial Times*, which helped ensure good coverage; Labour's leaks the same day of parts of its own manifesto to the *Guardian* (on education) and the *Daily Telegraph* (of Eurosceptical passages) did not prevent Thursday's newspapers being dominated by the Tory manifesto.[59]

In contrast to Mandelson's tightly controlled day-to-day programme of events, Central Office adopted a looser formula. The party had a day-to-day as well as a week-to-week 'grid' of events drawn up in advance, but did not follow it slavishly, due in part to the difficulty of persuading the media to follow its agenda. Though some in Number Ten thought Central Office still too rigid and insufficiently robust, pouncing on opportunities as they arose, in general the structure allowed the Party to react to the rapidly changing climate, as seen in the third week.

The battleground between the parties during that third week was for the floating voter, with both Conservatives and Labour claiming to be the true 'One-Nation' party, uniquely appealing to all classes. Blair announced at Labour's manifesto launch on 3 April that 'we are a broad-based movement for progress and justice ... Not a party of narrow class or sectional interest', while Major returned to the theme of the Bath Central Council: 'In the tradition of one-nation Conservatism, we wish to make haves of the have-nots, to bring wealth and welfare hand in hand.' At the Albert Hall at the Party's first rally on 4 April, in an unscripted passage, he told his audience of Party faithful that his kind of Conservatism was 'not just for the privileged but for the underprivileged as well, not just for the confident but for those who have doubts ...'[60] In an interview published in the *Sunday Times* on 6 April but recorded shortly before he left for the Albert Hall, he said he had always been a 'One-Nation' Tory, and not the right-winger Thatcherites thought initially he was.[61]

To convince the electorate that New Labour was truly 'One Nation', it was necessary to distance itself from the trade unions. Here the Tories saw a main chance, scoring points with claims of secret deals between Labour and unions, over trade union recognition rights promised by Labour and over new legal rights to workers. The Tories pressed the attack hard on a broad front, on Labour's past failure to support the Anti-Terrorism Act, on whether the Party would hold up the IGC in defence of British fishing interest, and on Labour's pledge to sign the EU Social Chapter as a threat to jobs as well as a further entrenchment of trade union rights. Then Blair, who clumsily stated that if an English council had tax-raising powers then a Scottish parliament should too, was forced into semantic debates over Scottish devolution. Gaining the initiative for the first time in the campaign, the Tories by the end of the third week were forcing Labour into rebuttals and shifts in policy which conveyed the impression of incompetence and lack of grip. Labour's strategists were firmly on the defensive, and worked hard to try to avoid the trade union theme spilling over into the fourth week.[62]

IRA bomb threats causing the Grand National to be postponed on 5 April now gave Major an opportunity to display himself prominently. He was determined that the race should go ahead, and that he would attend the rescheduled event on Monday 7 April. It meant a punishing day – his most hectic of the campaign: police motorcade to Northolt airport in West London (12 miles), British Midland flight to Manchester (185 miles), battlebus to Bury to see an opt-out school (17 miles), helicopter to a factory in Andover (195 miles), helicopter to Aintree for the Grand National (213 miles), helicopter to Cheltenham to visit an out-of-town Tesco store (142 miles). The energy expended was impressive, but apart from the opportunity to display Major's calm and fortitude in the face of the IRA's attempts to intimidate and cause havoc, some asked how far Major's tours were succeeding in convincing voters?

Far greater impact was being made from the heat on Labour. A story in the *Sunday Times* on 6 April about Labour's U-turns on trade union rights and privatisation of air traffic control threatened to keep the pressure simmering.[63] News breaking that day about Martin Bell, the BBC war correspondent, standing as 'anti-sleaze' candidate against Hamilton at Tatton meant that on Monday the threats to both parties vied for domination of the media – a return to sleaze, or Blair's manoeuvrings to avoid appearing as pro-national-isation, pro-trade union Old Labour? To the relief of Central Office, the latter became more dominant. Major decreed there were to be no personal attacks on Bell, and he waved the issue aside when confronted by it in Bury on 7 April.[64]

Fresh charges kept Labour on the defensive. Accusations began to appear that Blair promised peerages to long-serving backbenchers to make way for approved New Labour candidates. The Tories attacked on an alleged £1.5

billion 'black hole' in Labour's spending programmes. Blair came under heavy pressure from David Dimbleby on BBC television's *Panorama* on 7 April, in particular for his *volte-face* over air traffic control. It brought to the fore strongly the question about what Labour principles Blair was not prepared to abandon for electoral advantage.[65] The *Daily Mail* kept air traffic control privatisation high on the agenda with a leaked letter on Labour's change of policy, causing Mandelson to snap at the BBC's John Sergeant, 'You're on the *Daily Mail* agenda ... it's what we expect of you.'[66]

Feeling the heat, Labour's Millbank organisation sent a plea to every constituency for its workers to sniff out and send in election material embarrassing to the Tories to provide material for a counterattack. The trawl produced information that Angela Browning, the junior Treasury minister, said that if Britain joined the single currency, it would be 'the end of sovereignty of the nation state' and 'I will not support it'.[67] This piece of bounty allowed Labour to play the 'Euroschism card' for the first time in the election campaign. By doing so, Labour was able to reclaim the initiative; for the remainder of the campaign they were never to lose it. The battle with Labour was over. Major's battle to hold his party together, fittingly over Europe, was about to begin.

The Battle Over Europe: 11–21 April

Major and Mawhinney knew that their compromise formula over election addresses, allowing candidates and backbenchers to speak out against the single currency, but insisting that ministers accept their collective responsibility to abide by the government line of 'wait and see', was bound to create problems at some point during the campaign. Privately, they were exasperated by the incitement to disloyalty fermented by various figures such as George Gardiner who, during the previous summer, canvassed a common line for MPs and candidates to adopt in their addresses against the single currency, and then was joined by John Townend who had written a circular in the autumn to gauge the level of opposition to the single currency among candidates.[68] Outside their control altogether was Paul Sykes, a multimillionaire businessman, who wrote to all Eurosceptic candidates offering to pay their election expenses.[69] But when Angela Browning's views failed to ignite the media after a softly-softly response from the Party's leadership, Major and Mawhinney thought that they might be spared a showdown.

Major watched the London Marathon on Sunday 13 April, bringing his daughter Elizabeth and her boyfriend, Luke Salter, into the election limelight for the first time.[70] It made one of the most arresting photographs of him during the election, drink in hand, with his arm round his daughter's shoulder enjoying watching what he loved, sport. Mawhinney and others had been pressing him for weeks to attend, believing that many people would be watching the race and he sensed that it would portray him in a good light.[71]

On Monday and Tuesday he travelled to the West Country, still confident. He spoke toughly to crowds in the Cornish fishing port Newlyn about stopping EU fleets 'quota hopping' to net the British catch. Later, at a rally in Plymouth, he gave his strongest speech to date attacking Blair, not least for his 'shameless hypocrisy' in sending his children to a grant maintained school.[72] That night, he spent one of the most convivial evenings of the campaign in a remote hotel, Glazebrook House, in the countryside between Plymouth and Exeter. Major's tour party and the detectives took over the entire ten bedrooms in the hotel, the only anxiety coming when the latter realised their mobile phones were out-of-range. On Tuesday the party visited marginal seats in Devon, including Emma Nicholson's former seat of Torridge and West Devon, before flying back to London for interviews and briefings for his appearance that evening at the *Sunday Times*'s open forum at Westminster Central Hall.

Jonathan Hill, ensconced in Number Ten, was to look back on these three or four days as the 'one crucial moment' of the campaign. Central Office should have cancelled Major's West Country trip, he believed, and all weekend, and again on the Monday and Tuesday, have kept up the pressure on Labour over privatisation, rather than letting them, as he sees it, get off the hook and into the attack themselves.[73]

Warning bells were already ringing when Angela Rumbold's election address – 'No to more power for Brussels. No to a single currency' – was given widespread attention on Monday 14 April. As Vice-Chairman at Central Office in charge of the Party's candidates, her views carried a certain *ex cathedra* authority. On BBC's *Newsnight* that evening, she sought to downplay any damage the disclosure of her address had caused by saying that she was merely sharing her private opinions with her constituents, and cited Major's view that he was not worried about what candidates said to their own electorates. Central Office brushed it off by saying that only current ministers – not former ministers like Rumbold – had to follow the government line.[74] That formulation, it hoped, would draw the sting. Alas for Central Office, Browning was not the only current minister to deviate from it. The hope of gaining a few extra votes by appearing Eurosceptic was too much for some.

While Major addressed an audience of 1,100 readers of the *Sunday Times* on Tuesday evening, a political squall was brewing. Central Office learned that John Horam, the former Labour minister and now a junior Health minister, had written an election address disagreeing with 'wait and see'. Central Office had not identified Horam as a potential ministerial hazard, and had only learned of the problem that evening at 8 p.m. Lewington tried to phone him, but was told he would be out canvassing until 9.30 p.m. When he returned the call, Mawhinney asked whether he would be willing to go on television and, though he might not like it much, say that he backed the 'wait and see' policy? Horam replied that he had already recorded an interview for that evening's *Newsnight*, to be televised at 10.30 p.m., defending his thinking on the single currency.[75]

Horam convinced Mawhinney that he had not realised that what he had written – 'I am opposed to replacing the pound sterling' – was in breach of government policy which, if true, displayed a certain naïveté. Lewington briefed ITN's Michael Brunson that Horam would probably be sacked, and several senior figures, including Blackwell and Finkelstein, favoured dismissing him. Mawhinney, anxious to avoid martyrs, opted for forgiveness.[76] Horam agreed to repeat in future some words dictated to him by Mawhinney, as did James Paice, another junior minister, whose election address was also 'outed' in *The Times* on 16 April.[77]

Blair spent the night of 15–16 April at the Grand Harbour Hotel, Southampton. When Campbell went into Blair's room and told him the news about Horam, Blair replied, according to Campbell, 'They can't come back from this. They're becoming a joke.'[78] After two difficult weeks, when Blair had often felt himself on the defensive, this was the moment he thought he was going to be Prime Minister.[79] Ninety miles away in Downing Street, Major felt far less sanguine. That night he churned over in his mind how to respond to the government's collapsing policy on EMU. Adding to his apprehensions was the knowledge that next morning's *Daily Mail* would suggest that as many as 150 Tory candidates in winnable seats were ruling out a single currency.[80]

Before 7.30 a.m., Major was on the telephone to Cranborne and Mawhinney, who had already spoken that morning to Rifkind. They concluded that they had to scrap their plans to lead on the latest economic statistics at that morning's press conference. Mawhinney readily agreed that he should step aside and let Major chair the conference, to heighten the drama for a bold statement by the Prime Minister of his policy on the single currency, the subject which was leading all the news bulletins that morning. Major told aides he would give his personal credo 'hot and strong', in an attempt to calm nerves and restore his authority.

At that morning's meeting that preceded the press conference, Major walked in announcing that in every election, sooner or later, there comes a defining moment. You can't predict it, but it comes, he said, and 'this is it'. Maurice Saatchi was asked if he could film Major's statement, as he wanted to scrap the Party election broadcast they had planned to go out that evening (on the shallowness of Labour, depicted by a tree without roots) to substitute one of him talking direct to camera giving the same message on the single currency. As when the Framework Document on Northern Ireland leaked, Major's instinct was always to make a direct appeal to the nation in times of crisis. Saatchi agreed, and filmed Major during the press conference, judged by journalists present to be as fine a public performance as he delivered as premier.

Even the most battle-weary of journalists sat up agog. Major said that he would negotiate on EMU in the interests of the UK as a whole, not on the 'convenient party political interests of the Conservative party', and made the dramatic gesture of clasping both hands together in an appeal to his backbenchers: 'Like me or loathe me, do not bind my hands when I am negotiating on behalf of the British nation.' He proceeded to give a lucid exposition of the case for and against Britain joining the single currency.[81]

Three takes were filmed of Major upstairs talking direct to camera, all without a script. It was decided to use the final one, and Saatchi and Mawhinney supervised cutting it to length. Broadcast that evening, it was not nearly as fine a piece of political theatre as that morning's stunning press conference. One observer described it as akin to a video made of a jaded hostage filmed by their captors.[82] But it was still an eloquent and clear case of 'wait and see', or, as Party officials kept trying, but largely failing, to describe it, 'negotiate and decide'.[83] The *Daily Telegraph* described the broadcast, accurately, as 'a presidential appeal over the heads of his party'.[84]

The motorcade was an hour late leaving Central Office that morning for Northolt. Waiting for his plane to land at Teesside airport was Lady Thatcher, due to spend the day with him on the trail. True to her word, she had campaigned hard for the Tories during the election, visiting Central Office on 26 March with Major to address parliamentary candidates, and making trips, including to Dorset and Hampshire on 9 April.[85] There were no more slips of the tongue nor any actions that could be construed as disloyal. She was not even bad-tempered because she had been kept waiting, and sympathised with his plight when she learned of the reason for his late arrival. 'I do want to be helpful, John,' she told him. It was an extraordinary meeting of two powerful figures who, between them, had held the premiership for nearly a fifth of the century, yet had never enjoyed each other's company, nor indeed valued each other's gifts.

They spent the day campaigning together, meeting local candidates and workers, unveiling a plaque, planting a tree, and revisiting the now regenerated urban site of famous images of her in 1987 amid post-industrial wasteland. When press photographers failed to take sufficient pictures of a shot they particularly wanted, they put in a request whether Major and Thatcher, now back on the battlebus, would mind coming off again to walk side by side. 'Come on John, let's do the walk again,' she responded. Behind the bonhomie, the atmosphere remained tense and awkward. Major had no doubts about the damage she had inflicted on him during his premiership, nor had Norma, who spent most of her time on board the coach pointedly looking out of the window. The atmosphere tangibly lightened when Lady Thatcher left them.[86] They were pleased by how it had gone and the wine flowed freely.

On 17 April, while Blair announced at his morning press conference, 'There are two Conservative parties fighting this election. John Major is in charge of neither of them', Major, exhausted from the travails of the last thirty-six hours, let a change in policy slip out at his. The previous week, at a pre-press conference meeting, Major had suggested granting a free vote to all MPs if a Tory Cabinet decided to recommend Britain join a single currency, but after discussion decided against advocating it during the campaign for fear of opening wounds.[87] At the Thursday press conference on 17 April, however, in response to a question from Channel 4's Elinor Goodman, he let out that he would allow a free vote on EMU when it came before the House of Commons. Close aides of Major were 'pretty certain' that he had not meant to say what the election's historians described as 'the most memorable unpremeditated news break' of the campaign.[88] The Party's planners were certainly caught by surprise by the announcement: they had no time to forewarn Heseltine, or Clarke, who admitted on radio to not having been consulted beforehand.[89]

At this point, the Europhiles began to become restless. Major had already ruffled feathers by announcing in an interview early in the campaign that he 'made errors in his choice of language' and was 'careless' in describing Britain as being at 'the very heart of Europe' in March 1991,[90] and then partly apologised on BBC's *Newsnight* for the problems caused by Britain's ejection from the ERM.[91] Now Europhiles had to swallow two further perceived slights on top of his free vote promise at the 17 April press conference. When accused of making policy on the hoof over the free vote, Major responded to reporters by saying that he did not have to consult 'Ken Clarke or Joe Bloggs' every time he wanted to make up his mind on key decisions. Clarke's aides reported that he was 'not pleased' by the free vote announcement, nor by Major's riposte.[92]

Worse, in the eyes of many Europhiles, was a Saatchi advertisement of Blair sitting on Kohl's knee. The Deputy Prime Minister, fired by his memories of an early 1960s image by the cartoonist Vicky of Macmillan sitting on President Kennedy's knee, had, during a strategy meeting a month before, sketched a doodle of Blair sitting on Kohl's knee. Those present laughed at the idea of Blair being the German Chancellor's ventriloquist's dummy or puppet, but thought little more of it until Saatchi brought into Central Office just after the Horam affair a finished advert of Blair on Kohl's knee, with another of Blair on Mandelson's knee for good measure.

The Party's strategists vetoed the latter, but approved of the former, which ran in three national newspapers on Friday 18 April with the caption 'Labour's position on Europe'. Heseltine, hugely enjoying his throwaway idea proving so successful, said he wanted the name of the agency changed to M. M. and C. Saatchi – Michael, Maurice and Charles Saatchi.[93] Some on the Eurosceptic right did not share the humour. Several, like Redwood, believe that the leaking of Heseltine's authorship of the advertisement was deliberately engineered to prove his credentials to the Party's Eurosceptics as a way of launching his campaign for the leadership.[94] 'From that point on', another sceptic said, 'there were two campaigns: one about schools, hospitals etc and the other about who would lead what was left of the Tory Party.'[95]

The harmony between some senior Party figures and Maurice Saatchi was soon, too, to return to rancour, as tensions resurfaced during the last two weeks of the campaign. The crunch came in week five. Saatchi had a script for a Party election broadcast – which became known as 'Faust' after the mythical character who sold his soul to the devil for short-term gain – and which had as its main character a figure in shadow, who sounded very like Blair. His voice says that his party had lost many times in a row but he was hoping to win this time. Another figure appears in shadow at the door – the likeness is to Mandelson – and says, 'I'll show you how to win.' The Blair-figure listens while the standing figure says, 'Tell them you won't put up taxes.' The Blair figure replies, 'I can't do that', and the standing figure says, 'I didn't say you shouldn't put up taxes, but you have got to tell them that you won't.' And so it goes on, with the Mephistopheles figure goading the sitting figure into making all kinds of pledges. At the end, with Faust's eyes glowing red, newspapers are shown, with headlines like, 'Blair promises not to put up taxes', etc.[96]

The devil metaphor was too much for Mawhinney, who rejected the idea completely. Maurice Saatchi, however, kept trying to secure agreement that he should film it. After a meeting with Mawhinney in his room in the Commons, at which a Number Ten aide shouted at him that Major was also not interested in accepting it and he should drop the matter, Saatchi still went ahead and had the film commissioned. When he heard not only that Saatchi had made the film, but was showing it to senior figures to gain their support behind his back, Mawhinney exploded. Upon seeing the film, Blackwell and Cranborne, however, became converts, and tried to convince Major of the merits of the Party election broadcast.

It was decided that a screening should take place in front of Heseltine, with Mawhinney remaining the final arbiter. Arranged at Central Office for 24 April, Saatchi and Peter Gummer spoke passionately in its defence. The assembled company then saw the video. Some present thought it the most chilling and effective Party election broadcast they had ever seen, but Heseltine did not like it, he said, for three reasons: Major was against it; second, so was Mawhinney; and third, he himself thought it would prove counter-productive politically. Mawhinney was so angry that he insisted that Saatchi's bear the cost of making the film.[97] The frustration of the Saatchi team was expressed by one close to them who said: 'There were two ways we could have approached the 1997 election. Be a gentleman, as if one were on the *Titanic*, and avoid being ungentlemanly as you go down, which is a perfectly respectable position. Or you could say, we are going to win come hell or high water, we'll do anything we need to win, as long as it is legal. The Tory high command could never quite decide which route they wanted to follow.'[98]

The 'Faust' episode was the nadir of the relationship between Saatchi and Mawhinney. A showdown between the two men, both immensely proud and stubborn, was inevitable before long.[99] Their differences had come over the harshness of the attacks on Labour and over making Europe an election issue. Mawhinney thought further negative advertising would lose votes. On Europe, Saatchi remained convinced until the very end that a strong attack on the 'European social model' was the key to success. Mawhinney's reticence on both issues was in part his personal conviction, but was also a strong reflection of Major's thinking. Major, for example, vetoed the advertisement showing 'devil eyes' peering out from a pair of smiling plastic lips, invoking Blair's ubiquitous grin. The caption was to have been, 'What lies behind the smile?'[100] While unhappy with personalised attacks in advertising, it should be noted that Major was himself content to hit Blair hard in his own speeches. Major, however, never lost his suspicion of Saatchi, and indeed of the various campaign strategies devised by the 'three musketeers'.[101]

Labour's conviction that the Tories had finally lost all hopes of winning due to their battles over Europe grew as the fifth week drew on. The official line at Labour's Millbank Tower was that the Tories were imploding and Major was losing control.[102] Credence was given to that view as both ministers and backbenchers nonchalantly brushed Major aside after his 'don't bind my hands' plea. Eric Forth's election leaflet in which he rejected EMU was released within hours of the broadcast. Redwood repeated what Eurosceptic Cabinet ministers had been saying for several months, that 'wait and see' was a case of 'the Emperor's new clothes', an empty device designed purely to hold the Conservative Party together; all the negotiating over the single currency had already taken place, so nothing was left to 'see' preventing an imminent decision on whether Britain should join.

Marcus Fox, who had annoyed vocal sections of the backbenches with his loyalty to Major as chairman of the 1922 Committee, now rocked the cart by saying that nine out of the ten officers of his executive shared his belief that Britain should not join. Lady Thatcher weighed in at this point, breaking her vow of non-controversy, although she had been caught off-guard. Stopped in a supermarket in Essex on 18 April, and asked about whether she supported the single currency, she fired back, 'Good heavens. No! I was the one who invented the answer, no, No, NO!' When *The Times* declared on 19 April that only twenty-five Tory candidates in Conservative-held seats, excluding ministers, had rejected financial support from the millionaire Paul Sykes for printing anti-single currency election addresses, Eurosceptics felt convinced that events were at last flowing their way. Teddy Taylor described it as a 'mini revolution' against European federalism.[103] The revolt, in fact, was achieving little more than increasing the size of Labour's electoral support.

The Europhiles' anger now burst out into the open. While Heseltine masked his irritation about not being informed of the change on the free vote, and remained fiercely loyal to Major up to the end, Clarke let rip on 19 April calling the idea that the EU posed a threat to Europe 'paranoid nonsense'. Heath and Howe, and more worryingly Ian Taylor, a junior minister, joined a chorus of disapproval in Westminster and Fleet Street against the Kohl advertisement.[104] The first was nonplussed when, having called on BBC's *Newsnight* for Major to sack 'the whizz-kid who dreamed up that poster', he was told it was none other than his former Minister for Aerospace, Michael Heseltine.[105] At least Heath was not himself positioning for the coming leadership contest, which several other senior figures were increasingly suspected of doing, notably Howard, who warned that the 'very survival of Britain as an independent nation state' was at risk from the EU.[106]

The Battle With Himself: 20 April–1 May

Major saw more clearly than ever that 'Europe' had been a totem around which the right could rally to attack him, and further that it had now become the central issue not just – as he said in the press conference on 16 April – in the general election, but in the ensuing leadership election also. He had been obsessed since 1992 with keeping the Conservative Party together, and now saw it visibly breaking up before his eyes. The election, he realised over the weekend of 19–20 April, was going to be a serious defeat. It began to alarm his lieutenants that he was becoming defeatist.[107] The next ten days were a battle for him to rally himself to accept the first big election reverse of his lifetime. He clung to the hope that the defeat would be fifty to sixty seats at worst, and that opposition would allow the Party a chance to rebuild. But he realised it would be a much bigger defeat than the twenty to thirty seats which he had settled in his mind as the figure which might induce him to stay on as leader of the Party.[108] His mood found an echo in a strange episode that occurred on Sunday, 20 April.

There was an eerie silence in Number Ten, where George Bridges was finishing a speech and became aware that he was almost the only person in the building. He put on the television and found the film *Zulu*. As he watched, he felt as if Major and his closest aides were like the British soldiers isolated at Rorke's Drift, surrounded and vastly outnumbered by enemies. But on this occasion there was to be no miraculous rescue. Several of Major's political staff commented that they found themselves lingering in the building, knowing in their hearts that they would probably never enter it again.

An interview in *The Times*, published on Monday 21 April, gave the impression of Major being resigned to defeat. Rather than displaying a gung-ho belief in Tory victory and his enthusiasm for a new lease of office, he came across as world-weary and wanting to offer Blair advice on how not to be hoodwinked in his relations with the EU.[109] Concern felt by his close aides and by senior figures in Central Office at his low morale was scarcely abated when he was in Yorkshire on Monday and in Scotland on Tuesday. But his spirits rose significantly when, on Tuesday evening, news was received of an ICM poll in the *Guardian* which put the Labour lead down to five points (42 to 37 per cent). Major for the first time was also placed ahead of Blair as the better leader. Although those around Major were almost ecstatic at the first solidly good poll news of the campaign, Major was more controlled. To him it only confirmed the Party's private polling, also conducted by ICM, which had for several days been showing the Labour lead cut.[110]

Hopes were cruelly crushed when a Gallup poll in the *Daily Telegraph* just afterwards put the Labour lead at 21 per cent. After a day campaigning in marginal Scottish constituencies on Wednesday, Major's conviction grew that, as he was to lose the general election, he would make a heartfelt statement of his beliefs that evening at an election rally in Aberdeen. This meant tearing up his planned script, to the bemusement of the media, who had been given the intended text at 3 p.m. that afternoon, and some of whom had already filed their reports based on it.[111]

Placing side-by-side the planned script and a transcript of his actual talk gives a fascinating insight into the state of his mind in his last days as Prime Minister. The planned version was an attack on Labour's policy on devolution and on Europe, and contained an italicised passage:

I appeal to you. Don't let whatever doubts you may have had about the Conservative Party in the past weigh with you, when the future of the United Kingdom may be at stake. Think about it. Think seriously. Think again. Look in my eyes and know this. I will always deal fair and true by this great nation.[112]

The *Independent* boasted a front-page cartoon, of the red eyes transposed onto Major, based on his words about his eyes.[113] But he did not utter them in his speech. He spoke instead of his mission to bring the economic prosperity that had come to Britain to 'the circle of . . . people who are still locked outside it'. There was humour too: 'Let us suppose that I said to you this evening that I had decided for national security reasons to invade Mars ... By tomorrow morning, Mr Blair would have decided to invade Mars as well! Not only that, he would say "Why has it taken the Conservatives eighteen years?" ... From their point of view, Mars today, Cadbury's tomorrow, Bournville the day after – heaven alone knows where they'll go!'

The threat from the EU and Scotland still dominated the middle part of his speech, but then he veered back onto his own themes again, including the spectacularly 'off-message' idea that few of Labour's leaders deep down believed in New Labour ideas. 'Margaret Beckett – I can just see her enthusiasm for things like privatisation, deregulation, those intimate little meetings with the CBI and the IoD.'[114]

Major was pleased by his extempore speech. His entourage was not. Neither were the media, alienated by the script change, nor the organisers, by his abandoning the podium and speaking from the front of the stage.[115] The Party's strategists back in London that Wednesday, however, had their minds on different matters. Their concern was to maintain the pressure on Labour, who were clearly rattled by the news of the ICM *Guardian* poll. A Blair speech in Luton failed to attract much attention; after it Alastair Campbell snapped at journalists for constructing a 'wall of cynicism' around Blair's creation of a 'new Labour' Party.[116]

On Wednesday morning, Mawhinney decided that the moment had come to lay down his ace – information about Labour's 'war book', leaked to Central Office in December. It consisted of a flow-chart style document listing possible campaign approaches, including Labour playing on the electorate's fears of a new Tory government, and setting out the strengths and weaknesses of both parties. The document said: 'You will pay to visit your school, you will pay for your books, there will be guns and knives, you will pay for water through a meter.' Early in the New Year, Labour's senior staff had begun to suspect that the Tories had obtained some high-grade intelligence on their election thinking, because some of the language used in the Tories' propaganda bore a strong resemblance to what was in the war book, and because of hints during a dinner-party conversation uttered by Saatchi which had been passed on to Mandelson.[117]

Mawhinney hoped the war book would show how negative Labour had planned to be in the election as a disguise for their lack of positive policies. His only concern was how to inject the news of his find into the media's veins: the route selected was via a letter written to each Tory candidate telling them about it. On Wednesday, while Major was travelling down the west coast of Scotland, Mawhinney and Tim Bell drafted the letter and sent it out, having first alerted the BBC to its substance.[118] The Tories overall gained less from their acquisition of the document than might have been expected, its primary value being its use in Major's and Mawhinney's New Year messages.[119]

Blair's senior team immediately went into a huddle in the middle of the large campaign room in their Millbank office to debate their response. Gordon Brown favoured caution, but Mandelson and Campbell counselled going on the offensive.[120] Blair agreed with a tough line. Campbell gave dozens of photocopies of the war book to the Press Gallery at the Commons, and briefed journalists that it showed Labour were delivering a strategy whereas the Conservatives were merely reacting to Labour's agenda. Campbell later thought the ICM poll and the leaked war book played into Labour's hands, as it encouraged the media to focus on what a fifth Tory term might be like, which Labour had failed largely to make the media do because of its unlikelihood.[121]

Labour had its own ace up its sleeve – Lilley's basic pension plus scheme, which they argued could be portrayed as the Tories seeking to scrap the state pension. They asked John Denham, their spokesman on pensions, to announce that in their fifth term the Tories planned to abolish state pensions. That night, to Central Office horror, and the surprise and delight of Labour's team at the speed of their success, the television news bulletins highlighted the Labour story.[122] Labour's ace was of a higher suit, and media interest in Labour's war book rapidly dwindled.

Blair decided the time had come to go for the jugular. At his morning press conference, he strode away from the podium and delivered a passionate speech without notes about his fitness to be Prime Minister, and went through a list of his own pledges and what the Tories would do if re-elected. The last on the list was 'abolishing the state pension'. Blair said there was 'no doubt' that the aim of the Tories' plan was to replace it by a private pension scheme.

While Major's initial response to Blair's performance, relayed on television screens at Central Office, was 'New Labour, New Crap', both he and the Tory strategists knew they had to come back strongly against Labour's 'gross misrepresentation' of their pension plans.[123] The media was accordingly reminded of an article Blair wrote in *The Times* on 7 March acknowledging that Lilley's pension proposals were bold and provided the opportunity for the debate to be conducted 'more sensibly'. In what seems with hindsight to have been an overreaction, Mawhinney decided to hold a special press conference that afternoon to answer the charge, while Dorrell was deputed to denounce Blair for 'telling bare-faced, despicable lies'.

The old guard at Number Ten – Hill, True and Bridges – held their counsel but felt strongly nevertheless that the Labour assault on pensions need never have occurred. Two weeks before, Blair had met a group of pensioners in London. They drafted a rebuttal to put out that warned that it had the potential to become the 'Jennifer's Ear' of the 1997 election. But neither Lilley, as Social Security Secretary, nor indeed Major, was anxious to make an issue of it. Had they made a fuss at the time, and put their case across firmly on pensions, Labour rather than the Tories would have been placed on the back foot, and the issue might indeed have faded away.[124]

Thursday was to be 'inward investment day'. Major spent it visiting Jaguar in Coventry (where he sat in the driving seat beside Norma in the car manufacturer's new sports car, remembering he had not driven a car since before he became premier), and on to Siemens in Newcastle. While on the flight northwards, Mawhinney spoke by telephone to Howell James, and it was agreed that Major himself would use the 'L-word' (i.e. calling Blair a 'liar') during the visit to Siemens. Labour reacted by deciding further to intensify the attack. Advice was sent out from Millbank to all Labour candidates in the field to press home the issue on the doorsteps. The line candidates should deliver was, 'Your pension's not safe with the Tories. Only Labour guarantees security in retirement.'[125] It was the most unedifying episode in a campaign which, despite the usual dire predictions, saw no more mud-slinging than in 1992. It was a measure of the erosion of trust in the Tories over the previous five years that Labour's largely cynical attack on pensions struck so far home.

The pensions attack damaged the Tories both psychologically and in poll support: their polling showed their lead among pensioners, especially among women aged fifty-five and over, one of Labour's weakest segments, disappeared almost overnight.[126] Major's own mood became deflated as a succession of further polls, including Channel 4's Harris poll, showed the ICM *Guardian* poll to have been a rogue response. As one Number Ten aide admitted, 'By the end of the week, it became obvious that we had nothing left to offer.'[127]

Major kept himself busy on the Friday, visiting a mosque in East London, where he was mobbed, travelling on the Docklands Light Railway, and going up Canary Wharf tower. The party tried to keep their spirits high by talking about the 20 per cent who had not yet decided how to cast their vote. But not even the wildest optimists among them believed any more that they could win. Major had been given to making melancholic forecasts about the election result and said at the end of the week that 'this is the day I know that the election is lost'; but he had been thinking it and even admitting the thought in private for the previous few days.[128] When it was suggested that the result might be as bad as in 1945, when the Party was reduced to 213 seats, he looked deeply pained and replied, 'Oh, my God, you don't think it will be that bad, surely?'[129]

Major's mood over the weekend was thoughtful. He did not speak much as he inwardly prepared himself for what he knew was going to be on any reckoning a very testing week. On Saturday he went to The Finings to lose himself watching football on television and in the privacy of his own home and garden, relieved to be no longer surrounded by people and clamour.

On Sunday afternoon, he was driven down to London for press interviews and to record a Party election broadcast. His mood was not helped by being told that the Party's support was still haemorrhaging, especially in marginals.[130] The Sunday press offered little comfort. Edwina Currie predicted that Labour was heading for a landslide victory, while the headline in the *Sunday Telegraph* was, 'It's all over, admit top Tory aides.'[131]

Arriving back in Downing Street for what he knew would be his last few days at Number Ten heightened his feeling of emotion. Close colleagues who had worked with him since his earliest days said they had never seen him as restless or as irritable.[132] He let off some of his frustration in an interview with one of his favourite journalists, George Jones, reserving his harshest words for Blair's conduct during the campaign and for his own backbenchers for ignoring the manifesto statement on the single currency. One of the few topics he spoke to Jones about with pride was race relations. On 25 March, he had rebuked Budgen for raising the question of immigration controls, and he discouraged Howard from making a speech in which he referred to immigration, or to assent to his highlighting the difference between parties on the issue. 'I am not going ... to play dirty' on race, he told his interviewer.[133]

Technical problems with the lighting caused long delays to the Party election broadcast. More time-consuming was Major's dissatisfaction with the script that led him – as his own text of the broadcast reveals – to far more than his usual crossings out and additions. At one point he disappeared up to the Number Ten flat with Mawhinney to make further revisions. Several references to Blair were removed. The tone overall was avuncular and reassuring. Only with the Conservatives could voters 'be sure' of protecting their country and prosperity. Although this was a reference to the campaign slogan and manifesto title, Major's uncertainty about exactly what he wanted to say in his final broadcast was a reminder that uncertainty over the substance and tone of the Party's appeal to the electorate continued up to the very last days of the campaign. Shortly after midnight, Major was still dissatisfied with the filming, and insisted on one more take. Mawhinney put his foot down and said that the takes were getting steadily worse, and that the time had come for him to go to bed. Reluctantly he obeyed his Party chairman, and sauntered off down the corridor a troubled and dissatisfied man.[134]

The sheer business of the programme on Monday 28 April kept him absorbed. This was his 1,000-mile, 'four corners of the kingdom' trip, designed to display the unity of the United Kingdom. First port of call was Belfast, where Central Office boasted he was the first Prime Minister to make a campaign visit to the province. The solid ring of RUC officers in their flak jackets kept him mostly away from the crowds, but he was pleased to make the symbolic visit to a part of the country on which he had devoted so much effort.

Scotland was next on the agenda. Landing at Edinburgh, he addressed voters from the battlebus parked on the Mound, with Edinburgh Castle in the background. He flew next to the Isle of Anglesey in northwest Wales, where he was photographed with William Hague, with the Menai Bridge in the background. Some mirth was caused by Rifkind's praise for Major visiting 'all four capitals in one day'. When it was pointed out that Anglesey was not the capital of Wales, he replied swiftly 'I'm only the Foreign Secretary!' Finally, with Big Ben chiming six o'clock, Major stood in front of Parliament and warned voters, 'You have seventy-two hours to save the Union, seventy-two hours to make sure our Government is not changed irrevocably for the worst.'[135]

Major rallied himself bravely for his set-piece speeches during the day, but they lacked the vim and self-confidence of his earlier campaign appearances. 'Major found it hard to dispel the sense of gloom that surrounds his campaign,' was James Blitz's comment in the *Financial Times* on the 'four corners' trip.[136] The photographs from the final days of the campaign, contrasting the tired-looking Major with the exultant Blair, now confident of victory, were all too clear. The tour meant that Major, alone of the three Party leaders, could not participate that day in television's *ITV 500* panel discussion. Heseltine, who deputised for him, exploded when a member of the audience suggested Major was a coward for not going on the programme. 'If you think that the Prime Minister going to Northern Ireland is "chicken",' he replied, 'you haven't the first idea what a brave and courageous man is all about.'[137]

Major would no doubt have preferred to have appeared before the panel to being interviewed by David Dimbleby on BBC's *Panorama* that evening. Dimbleby was unyielding and direct, as he questioned Major on some of the most sensitive subjects of his premiership – why he had changed his mind over Europe, given away pre-election 'bribes' in 1992 to secure election only to increase taxes later, and ignored the poor. After early faltering, Major regained his composure, but did not enjoy the experience.[138]

Major's sense of impending doom was heightened at a meeting at Central Office on Tuesday morning, with just Mawhinney, James and Garrett present. It was a much shorter meeting than the comparable meeting – forty-eight hours before polling began – in 1992. Major turned to Garrett and said, 'How many?' Garrett responded, '260 to 280 seats.' 'Are you sure?' Major asked. Garrett replied that all the evidence at his disposal suggested that he was.[139] Asked at the morning conference whether Blair would win, Major replied baldly, 'He does not deserve to win.'

With the prospect of a heavy defeat, the search for scapegoats began. Was Major to blame, above all for failing to take a strong line on Europe, as the right thought, or was the campaign, and Mawhinney in particular, responsible, as some at all levels of the Party also believed? The campaign had certainly not been without its problems. The tactics were based largely on the successful earlier precedents of the four campaigns from 1979, and in many ways the 1997 campaign was better planned than in 1992. The seven rallies in 1997 however achieved little national attention, and the regional tours were often upstaged by more arresting Labour stunts. The 'long' campaign was a last shot in the Conservatives' locker: as Major told businessmen in a closed meeting, he would use the six weeks to 'wear down' Labour. He did not realise that several present had switched allegiance and promptly told Blair's office of the Tory thinking. The reliance on Major himself placed an intolerable strain on him once the vital adrenalin supplies that come with success failed to materialise. Just as Heseltine had increasingly failed to impose a central diktat on the Party over the previous twenty-one months, so Mawhinney, also not for want of trying, could not master all the various pungent players under his command, nor could Blackwell ensure that the Party adopt his five core Tory themes, above all when the polls failed to improve. If the prospect of success encourages unity, the likelihood of defeat creates dissent, as Mrs Thatcher found fleetingly on just one day, 'wobbly Thursday' in 1987. When facing almost certain defeat, almost any new idea, or individual, can appear more attractive than sticking by the status quo.

Maurice Saatchi blamed Mawhinney rather than Major himself, whom he liked, for the problems, but the fact was that Maurice Saatchi's and John Major's ideas on how to run an election campaign and the images of Conservatism they wished to portray, were poles apart. Mawhinney loyally backed Major throughout, even though the latter was not always clear or consistent during the long campaign in the message he wanted to deliver. It was not entirely his fault. As Major lamented to one aide: 'Everyone says I'm the Party's best asset and have good ideas, but I'm not allowed to say what I want to say.' The addition of Cranborne as chief of staff created too many leaders, and further institutionalised friction. Failure to reach agreement over election timing, advertisements, slogans, election addresses and Party election broadcasts were all symptoms of a much wider malaise: a party that had lost a belief in victory and willingness to put divisions behind it and bind together even – amazingly – in the final days before a general election. For only ten days, from 1 to 11 April, was the Party able to command the agenda, outlining its own proposals and bringing its fire onto Labour. The election was not lost as badly as it was because of the campaign, which had its bright moments, plenty of bright ideas, and through all the prodigious difficulties maintained coherence. Without valuable days and authority being lost over sleaze and in-fighting over Europe, the defeat would not have been so large, and many

Tory MPs would have retained their seats. The Conservatives ultimately lost because the country had become bored by them and their divisions, since the late 1980s, and because nothing that it was able to do in the campaign could dent that fact.

By the final Tuesday, cracks within the Party's high command now began to break into the open. Stories appeared in the morning's broadsheets about divisions between Number Ten and Central Office, and between Mawhinney and Saatchi.[140] It all contributed to a depressing day, which Major spent in Brighton wandering around, almost aimlessly, before going to London Docklands for the seventh and final rally of the campaign. The mood in Number Ten that evening was funereal, though by the rally it was upbeat in rather a manic way. As the final strains of 'Land of Hope and Glory' rose and fell, and the waving flags stilled, it was clear that underneath the mood was sombre, as it was on Wednesday, the last full day of campaigning. At Stevenage, in the constituency shortly to be won by Barbara Follett, he was mobbed by an ugly crowd of hecklers, and turned his back on them. It was, said one aide, a 'sad day'.[141] At an anonymous lay-by near Bedford, Major bade farewell to his personal campaign team, who had been with him on the battlebus throughout. As they made their way back to London, he returned to The Finings for what he knew would be his last full night's sleep as Prime Minister. He felt let down by almost everyone in his party at Westminster, and his treatment in Stevenage had appeared like a metaphor for the isolation he now felt.

When Major woke up on 1 May, he still hoped that Labour's lead could be kept down to eighty or ninety seats. Over the previous few days he had discussed with Alex Allan the arrangements for the almost inevitable defeat, including the time for his audience with the Queen on the Friday morning, and the mechanics of how he and Norma, and their possessions, could leave Number Ten in a dignified way. Panic set in at Number Ten when a removal van turned up, but it transpired that it had been summoned by the Cabinet Office, seizing the chance to move some of their equipment. At least he was spared a photograph of a removal van in Downing Street. Major spent the morning of 1 May touring his Huntingdon constituency with John Bridge, his chairman, and Peter Brown, his agent. Norma and James toured the committee rooms in the opposite direction. After lunch at The Finings with the family and Party workers, he set out again on the trail. He was reasonably cheery until a call came through on his phone in the car at 5 p.m. It was from Tony Garrett at Central Office. Exit polls suggested his revised prediction of the Tory Party winning 240 seats had been a grave over-estimation. It suggested that the result would be much worse than he ever dared to imagine. Major went very, very quiet.

EPILOGUE

The Verdict

JOHN MAJOR SLIPPED swiftly from public view after 2 May 1997, as the media and country turned their attention to Tony Blair and his new government, which made such a confident start.

The first time I saw Major again after the general election was on Thursday 19 June, to spend part of the morning together finishing off our discussions on the biography. It was his last day as leader, and to mark the occasion the *Daily Mail* had invited his critic Paul Johnson to write an article assessing the place of his premiership in history. He wrote, 'Almost everyone in the higher ranks of the party' (apparently) came to consider Major 'a hopeless leader' who 'should never have been made Prime Minister'. His personality did not escape Johnson's pen: there was 'virtually nothing there' and there were significant reasons – which will emerge, he said, when the memoirs, diaries and letters appear – for believing he was 'not a nice man at all'.[1]

Whatever Major's faults as premier, I thought Johnson's piece as ungenerous as it was ill-balanced. I also knew it would cause Major great pain if he read it. I hoped no one had shown it to him. As I entered his room in the Commons, I saw the *Daily Mail* lying on his table. He was even more chewed up than I had expected, and the article cast a cloud over our two hours together.[2] Later that day, he spoke at the Party meeting which anointed William Hague as new leader. Echoing the manner of his farewell from Number Ten seven weeks before, he spoke with modesty, and without rancour.

The day highlighted several core themes: Major's continued vulnerability and lack of inner confidence, which dated back fifty years and more; the extreme and personally unpleasant press criticism, a feature of the previous five years; and his inner strength and humanity, which allowed him for his last time as leader to rally during the day and, regardless of what he felt inside, to bless the new leader's period of office without a trace of bitterness or regret.

Five Critiques

Five distinct critiques of Major's premiership rapidly crystallised. Although several of the criticisms appear in more than one, each nevertheless approaches him from a different political perspective.

Paul Johnson is firmly in the first school of criticism, which alleges that Major betrayed Tory principles and the Thatcherite revolution by seeking to place Britain 'at the very heart of Europe' and by failing to stand firm on the union with Northern Ireland, which showed how little regard he had for the integrity of Britain as a sovereign nation state. His inability to hold down public spending meant that the tax cuts the electorate demanded could not occur, and revealed how little understanding he possessed of another core Tory principle, minimum government. A weak and vacillating leader, he was seen as pandering to offensive social minorities like gays and feminists, while chasing the foolish and profoundly un-Conservative notion of a 'classless society'. Janet Daley wrote in another historical evaluation of Major:

His was the cleverness of the dedicated anti-intellectual: the sort of politician who believes that real life has little connection with ideas and is all to do with relations between personalities. So he struggled on hopelessly trying to reconcile the factions in his party by appealing or threatening on a personal basis. When this failed he was hurt and reproachful.[3]

Failure to be sufficiently Tory, or to provide a clear lead for his party, this school asserts, accounted for the catastrophic decline in popularity of the Party, turning the three Thatcherite general election victories into the greatest defeat of the century in 1997.

The left of the Tory Party were never as public, but felt as strongly that he had failed to save the Conservative Party from itself: in his indulgent approach to faction and ideology, they believe, he was the Tories' Harold Wilson. He pandered to an irrational frenzy of nationalism and fears of the European 'superstate' from the right, which could have been calmed by a display of authoritative leadership. Further, he all but abandoned 'One Nation' traditions of progressive law and order policies and gradualist reform of the constitution, and did little or nothing to halt the decline of political pluralism, notably in the form of local government.

A liberal approach provides the third critique, and sees Major failing to deliver his classless society or living up to his early promise on a positive agenda for ethnic minorities, women, gays and the underprivileged. Too much under the influence of the vocal in his party, and the establishment, he compromised too many of his beliefs because he did not want to upset his party and because he became absorbed into the establishment power structure, hence his opposition to constitutional change. He defended the indefensible in his attitude to the Nolan and Scott Reports, and insufficiently stood up against 'sleaze'. His Bosnian policy showed that, for all his advocacy of a tough policy, he was insufficiently prepared to do more to stand up for those suffering from Serb aggression. Personal survival, this approach has it, was ultimately more important to him than acting on his undoubted liberal instincts.

A fourth critique, from the left of centre, sees Major's government as doing no more for the social fabric of Britain than Mrs Thatcher's. He presided over more benefit cuts, widening inequality and division in society, and showed favour to 'fat cats' in the utilities and the newly privatised industries. He handed over functions of government to unaccountable quangos packed with his political allies who could not get elected to local bodies. His was a particularly cynical and incompetent government, which lied about taxes and shrugged off responsibility for its errors by failing to demand the resignation of those condemned by the Scott Inquiry, or those responsible for Black Wednesday.

A final line of attack was from those who focused on Major's alleged weaknesses as a leader and manager. He condemned Britain to years of drift, simply because he was insufficiently clear about what he was wanting to achieve on an ideological or even an administrative level. He was unable to separate tactics from long-term strategy, resulting in humiliating U-turns on matters such as European Council voting rights (March 1994), and retreats on back to basics (February 1994) and BSE (June 1996). He was obsessed with his personal image and press coverage to an extent that damaged his ability to provide a consistent direction. His leadership was littered with missed opportunities and failures to grasp nettles – acting decisively on sterling in the ERM, delaying the Maastricht Bill in the early summer of 1992, capitalising on the opportunities of his mandates at the general election in 1992 and the leadership election of 1995, providing an effective response to the saga of Neil Hamilton. Loyalty to flawed friends is an admirable feature in a person, although when it meant having departments of state run by people unfit to do so, it was an irresponsible indulgence.

Each of these approaches contains some truth, though more untruth, about him and his premiership. But does that mean there is no more to be said about his period in office? I think that there is. First, the right of the Party – for all the rewriting of history – voted for Major rather than Heseltine or Hurd in November 1990, and if they did not like what they got, they must share some of the blame. Mrs Thatcher by 1990 was widely regarded, even by the right in the Party, as out of touch, aloof, and relying on too few favourites. The Party as a whole wanted a change to a more collegiate, inclusive and unideological leader, and that is exactly what Major proved to be. His brief ministerial career – in which his most important decision was for Britain to join the ERM – and his statements during the 1990 leadership election, suggest that if the right claim to believe they were electing one of their own, they were short on common sense. In time, his very qualities, of emollience, pragmatism, wanting to hold all factions together, evoked scorn and then widespread contempt. If these very qualities are bad as unusual or unadmirable in a prime minister as some believe, nor indeed that a Thatcherite 'leadership from the front' style would have worked any better during 1992–7, then the blame must be shared. And – an interesting historical game – might a Hurd, a Heseltine or a Redwood premiership have proved much more successful? Would the much-vaunted 'strong leadership' have succeeded when the Party was so fundamentally divided?

Major's Style of Leadership

Having led the Party only when in government, it is harder than with most to place Major as a Tory leader, because he had no record as leader of the Party in opposition. To the end, he loved the Party in the country, and he was regarded with real affection by many constituency activists. But he did not love his parliamentary party, nor they him, and neither did his Cabinet, and to that extent there is some truth in Paul Johnson's statement above. Major belonged to no single school of Conservatism, had no mentors among past Tory leaders or theorists, and had no interest in redefining Toryism – though in articulating some of his homespun personal beliefs he did chime with some of its essential propositions. Of the Party organisation, he was a gradual reformer, encouraging consultation with members and overseeing an overhaul of Central Office under Fowler and Mawhinney. But his grand plans for making the Party more democratic, on which he spoke at length on his final day as Party leader, were left unacted upon.[4] If the balance at the end of his leadership of the Tory Party is negative, with a reduced and ageing membership and with the Party at an historic low ebb in electoral success, although seeing some revival on 1 May 1997 in local government, one can say it was not for want of his caring or trying to arrest the long-term decline in the Party's appeal to activists or voters, which predated his arrival at Number Ten. He also carried the centre of the Party mostly with him and played a key role in the 1992 general election which killed off 'old Labour'.

Major by temperament and choice was a conciliator. Before he became Prime Minister, he had found Mrs Thatcher's style of 'macho leadership' personally distasteful. His chairmanship of Cabinet and Cabinet committees, in contrast, allowed ministers to express their views, and guided them to a conclusion in line with his intentions. Rather than have dissent in Cabinet, he preferred to delay decisions until he could reconcile differences. He presided over a regular and more public system of Cabinet committees, with less recourse to pressurising decisions in bilaterals than most of his predecessors. Though he had close allies in Cabinet, principally Chris Patten (1990–92), Michael Heseltine (1995–7), and Tony Newton throughout, he did not have a 'kitchen Cabinet' of regular close aides and resorted to an *ad hoc* inner Cabinet only in the run-up to both general elections and during particularly difficult periods, such as late 1994.

During his term he tried to improve institutional coordination by innovations such as the Number Twelve Committee (1991–5) and EDCP (from 1995). Although his government was rarely sure-footed in coordination and presentation, at least the machinery was there, and the situation might have been even more fraught without it. The worst that can be said of his unassertive style of leadership was that it may have encouraged divisions to grow, whereas a strong line earlier might have resolved some issues sooner.

Major's consensual style extended, again in marked contrast to his predecessor, towards the Civil Service. Major had always enjoyed extremely good relations with his personal civil servants, continuing after he became Prime Minister with officials such as Alex Allan (Principal Private Secretary 1992–7), Stephen Wall (Foreign Affairs Private Secretary 1991–3) and his successor Roderic Lyne (1993–6), and Gus O'Donnell (Chief Press Secretary 1990–94). Apart from Number Ten, where he was clear which officials he wanted to serve him, he was content to offer advice but ultimately to leave judgements on senior civil service appointments to the mandarins. He expressly said he rejected Mrs Thatcher's test of whether an official was 'one of us', an active 'go-getter', and would want to see such officials given preferment.[5] A very rare occasion on which Major did interfere was when Howard, as Home Secretary, refused to accept the first choice of the senior mandarins under Robin Butler for his new Permanent Under-Secretary. The mandarins wanted John Chilcot of the Northern Ireland Office. Howard wanted Richard Wilson. With Major's backing, he achieved his wishes.

Many of the harsher criticisms levelled against Major by commentators, his own Party and others are also intellectually limited, because they have little regard for the circumstances under which Major served his premiership from 1990 to 1997.

Difficult Circumstances

Great leaders throughout history have been made by great opportunities – war, depression, or a widespread shift in public mood that the leader can articulate. The historical opportunity for *any* leader who succeeded Mrs Thatcher in November 1990 was, in contrast, unusually restricting. The environment in which any historic figure acts needs to be considered under four headings: individuals, ideas, circumstances and interests.[6]

The scope for strong, assertive, leadership in the 1990s was less than in the 1980s. Not just was Major, as we have seen, a collegiate leader, and such leaders do not make the weather, but he also faced far tougher Labour leaders than did Mrs Thatcher. She served opposite James Callaghan on his way out, Michael Foot, and a young but improving Neil Kinnock; Major faced Kinnock in his prime, John Smith, and Tony Blair, the most effective Labour leader in opposition since Ramsay MacDonald. Unlike Mrs Thatcher, and after the departure of Chris Patten, he never found a senior figure such as Whitelaw to underpin his position: Hurd was preoccupied on foreign business; Cranborne rose spectacularly for the big occasion, notably the leadership election, but faded; Heseltine was ever loyal from July 1995 but was past his prime. Neither did Major have, like Mrs Thatcher, a côterie of sympathetic interpreters of his policies and position in the media and intellectual life – the *sine qua non* for a successful modern premiership. Instead, he had the opposite, with obvious results. No Conservative leader this century has had to contend with a predecessor so overtly and covertly questioning their premiership. I leave it to readers to judge her actions and their effect.

While he was served by some outstanding officials and very able ministers, not least Lamont and Clarke, the pool of political talent at his disposal after eleven years in office, and still more so after many able Tories lost their seats in 1992, however, was restricted. The seventy former ministers on the backbenches were often bitter and unbiddable. Those who knew they would not receive jobs – including many hardened Eurosceptics – saw little reason for being either loyal to Major, or understanding of his plight.

The ideological background for Major in the 1990s was similarly unpromising. Mrs Thatcher was able to adopt an intellectually coherent platform developed in universities and among thinkers dating back to Hayek's *Road to Serfdom* (1944) and before, and packaged for her in the 1970s and 1980s by friendly think-tanks, such as the Institute for Economic Affairs, Centre for Policy Studies and Adam Smith Institute. While large elements of her party, the 'wets', did not accept the anti-*dirigiste* analysis, and she showed considerable courage and persistence in winning through with these ideas, the point is that a coherent body of ideas was at least there for her to take off the peg. By the time Major became Prime Minister, the battle for ideas had been won, as had the Cold War, and the 1990s offered fewer certainties. The demand was still there for a big idea – 'what is Majorism?' – but Blair's adoption of much of the Thatcherite, and Majorite, agenda shows that in the 1990s fresh portmanteau ideas, certainly on the right, were not to be had. Major and his government received little credit for his completion of the Thatcherite agenda in economic and social policy, taking it into areas from which she had shrunk; it tended to be seen as almost cheating, a mere footnote or coda to her premiership.

Major served at a time when circumstances were especially difficult. Few premiers enjoy favourable inheritances; none claim them. Major's in 1990, however, was unusually bleak. In the in-tray was the Gulf crisis, deepening recession, the poll tax, and a party already deeply unpopular and divided over Europe. It also contained unexploded bombs such as arms trading with Iraq, the Pergau Dam, and the growth of shady lobbying companies. He felt peculiarly strongly the lack of a ready understanding of the problems he inherited from Thatcher, so reluctant was the press to admit to her having any faults. His first years were overshadowed by the recession and the consequent problems in the public finances (which he could have done more to master). His later years suffered because of a small and dwindling parliamentary majority at the mercy of eccentric backbenchers, and the mischance of having to steer the Maastricht Treaty through in 1993 in very different circumstances from the acclaim that had greeted his original deal in 1991.

Sleaze, neither initiated nor encouraged by Major, and which was one of the defining issues of his premiership, proved a daunting subject to confront. Major responded by establishing Scott and Nolan, to the fury of his right, and then, when parliamentary pressures prevented him endorsing their reports to the full, he was castigated by the centre and left. The Hamilton affair, over which he had to battle with both an angry right and Hamilton's Tatton constituency, proved equally evasive of an early solution. How might Mrs Thatcher, or Blair, have managed the issue? Yet again, many more condemned Major over sleaze than came forward with practical and workable solutions. The irony remained: an honest man crippled by sleaze.

He did not have room in 1990–97 to pursue a real Majorite agenda, nor did he have the time to develop his admittedly inchoate ideas. Where Heath had five years in opposition to plan, Mrs Thatcher four years and Blair three, Major had barely one month, after it seemed likely he would win in November 1990, to plan his policies and the personnel he wanted to serve him. Once in office, he again lacked the time to develop his ideas. For a cricketer, he was placed from the outset on the back foot, and only rarely did he have the chance to play forward.

In electoral terms, Major suffered from the emergence of New Labour, which stole the Tories' true secret weapon, not loyalty, but adaptability. In place of the Labour Party of old, for whom ideological purity often meant difficulties in adapting to changing voter preference, Major faced the supreme 'flexi-party', willing to adopt almost any policy and position to appeal to centre-ground voters. Labour was no longer frightening to many Tory voters. 'New Labour New Danger' ultimately failed because too few believed in the danger.

Tory hegemony this century has depended in significant part on the backing of the powerful interests in the country – the City, business and the press, as well as the professions. The last was alienated by Mrs Thatcher and never fully returned. Significant elements of the first three flew in the 1990s. In contrast, the interests that in electoral terms had handicapped Labour since the 1970s, the trade unions, were distanced from them. There were no powerful interests for Major to slay, or the equivalent to those whose vanquishing added so greatly to Mrs Thatcher's stature – a bloated state sector, inefficient nationalised industries, overmighty trade unions. If Major's equivalent of the Falklands War was the Gulf War, which did not end in such conclusive fashion, the equivalent of the 1980s victory in the Cold War, where the popular forces of liberal democracy triumphed over corrupt statism, was Bosnia in the 1990s, without such clear moral absolutes, and where the Tory Party was itself torn down the middle, as was the West, on how to respond.

A truly considerable leader might have been able to rise above the unfavourable background of individuals, ideas, circumstances and interests. Major could not. But then no one, least of all this author, has ever claimed he was such a first-order leader.

I do not seek to make excuses for Major; nor did I believe that he played the hand he was dealt to best advantage. But I do believe that it would be shallow to judge a premier without balancing such factors as described above. The most difficult problem of all that he faced was that, with polls and by-elections pointing continually to the likelihood of a heavy defeat, there was little incentive for his own parliamentary party to follow his lead when an alternative – any alternative – offered the prospect of a revival in fortunes.

Major's premiership, moreover, was not without its achievements. While others were also responsible in part for them, if he was such a 'hopeless leader' as 'almost every' senior Tory apparently thought – and I do not believe they thought in such simplistic terms – then the government would have been as devoid of positive results as the governments of A. J. Balfour (1902–5), Eden (1955–7), Heath (1970–74) or Callaghan (1976–9). But Major's cupboard is not bare, nor even sparsely stocked.[7]

Major's Record

The Major government's agenda consolidated Thatcherism, succeeding in privatising coal (1994) and rail (1996–7 sale of Railtrack and franchises), as well as pursuing other radical policies such as the sale of the nuclear industry (1996) and traditional state organisations like HMSO (1996). The Deregulation and Contracting Out Act 1994 produced a significant clearout of regulations that had survived the 1980s. The government introduced welfare reforms which, for the first time since 1945, meant that welfare costs fell as a proportion of national income. The march of reform continued through institutions such as the Stock Exchange and the army, and through a mini-revolution in education. Many of the reforms, such as reforms to the Civil Service or the steady pace of administrative reform carried out by his ministers, received scant attention because of the government's propensity to score 'own goals' and the media's interest being otherwise engaged. Yet even in 1997 the government was still producing policies that followed a radical Conservative approach, such as basic pension plus.

In hard, measurable terms the government produced a strong economic record. The Major years – after the recession of 1990–92 – saw consistently low inflation (below 4 per cent for four years); steady economic growth at 2–3 per cent which showed no sign of overheating or slackening; and repeated praise from international organisations such as the OECD. There has been a renaissance of culture and sport through National Lottery funding (1994), and unsung improvements to public services through the Citizen's Charter (1991). In foreign and defence policy the Major government adapted surprisingly smoothly to the post-Cold War world, with a clear appraisal of priorities and capabilities. A steady and resolute leader over Iraq, in Bosnia, against a majority of his Cabinet, he argued for increasing British troops and, though still too cautious for some, he helped pave the way for the coming of peace. It was a better legacy than many governments leave.

Major's leadership style could be argued to have been exactly what was required for the times. Conservative unity on Europe, which fractured in the mid- to late 1980s, showed that Mrs Thatcher's style of leadership and negative stance on the EC was no longer tenable. Major had the difficult task of managing strong and complex trends of parliamentary and public opinion which moved decisively in a Eurosceptic direction in the 1990s. Across a range of other policy issues, his undoctrinaire approach suited the tenor of the times. Instead of, like the right, wishing that the public sector would go away or, like much of the centre-left of his party, considering it sacrosanct, he took a case-by-case approach to reform. The same applies to privatisation: rail privatisation and the Private Finance Initiative have involved innovative ways of mixing public and private sectors. Major's pragmatic and humane approach offered a real way forward in Northern Ireland, as will be acknowledged if and when a lasting peace comes to the province. Ireland is a prime example where the accusation of Major lacking all principles or consistency falls apart.

Failed leaders see little of their policy survive. This will not happen with Major. What, then, will last of the Major years? A consensus on the role of the state in the economy; the National Lottery; public service reform; and possibly stable economic growth with low inflation, perhaps the fabled 'end of inflation'. On the last point more hindsight is required before accepting any propositions about 'the best performance for generations', rather than regarding the current state of affairs as just a point on the cycle. A further possible legacy is a consensus on what makes for the desirable characteristics of state provision in health and welfare; a consensus on taxation and distributive justice; and a European policy based around the principles of his 1994 Leiden lecture. Ironically, these latter three points have been consolidated by the election of a Labour government. A Conservative victory could have resulted in further pressure to drag the agenda to the right. Major's legacy is relatively secure because Labour have taken most of it on board and the scale of the Conservative defeat should give pause to those who suggest that rejecting the Majorite equilibrium is the path back to power.

A Conclusion

Major was neither non-entity nor failure. His will be judged an important if unruly premiership at the end of the Conservative century, completing some parts of an earlier agenda while in some key respects helping to define a Conservatism for the twenty-first century.

His weaknesses date back in part to his childhood insecurities. He did not happily assert himself nor like to be unpopular, and would sooner say 'yes' than 'no'. His track record on public spending in 1989–93 which led to the loss of the tax card, saw this vulnerability displayed at its most acute. But as he later admitted, 'I followed Keynesian policies. If I had not let government spending increase, unemployment would have been much higher.' His insecurity, coupled with his lack of grounding in Tory philosophy, made him often appear to be lacking in consistency. His lack of time to prepare for office, and disappearing parliamentary majority, prevented him pushing ahead further with his deeply felt instincts, on constitutional reform, modernisation of his party, and reforms to help the underprivileged and dispossessed, not least in the inner cities. There is a tragic poignancy that in some of the final speeches of his premiership he spoke of his deep concern to help 'ordinary people', which his party's high command treated with either amused tolerance or irritation, but rarely comprehension.

As a human being, he was often sorely tested. Much of his pleasure in being Prime Minister was taken away by the barrage of criticism, and the difficulty he found in making an appropriate response. Yet he remained a dignified and polite premier, lacking arrogance or disdain for people in his personal dealings, even after more than six years in Downing Street. He was perhaps the first Conservative premier to believe in race and sex equality, and in progress towards homosexual equality. His command of detail enabled surprisingly positive negotiating outcomes, for instance at Edinburgh in December 1992. He showed occasional, perhaps under-used, political courage and a gambler's nerve, as in his defying his 'handlers' in the 1992 and 1997 general elections and in launching the 1995 leadership election.

Some memoirists will no doubt say that Major was a nasty and ineffective man. Some are already preparing their texts, and one can expect much more of the mantras that echoed throughout his premiership – no ideas, feeble leader, vain and self-serving, hopeless on Europe. All of which are, as I hope I have shown, baleful, intellectually boring and plain inadequate. I myself agree with the writer who, throughout his premiership, best understood Major's complex personality, Matthew Parris. John Major is not an unpleasant man, which does not mean he could not be petty or barbed. I would judge him a better man and – dare I say – the possessor of a sharper intellect than many of his detractors.

In history, Major is not a towering figure like Churchill or Gladstone, nor even a significant new departure such as Attlee, Lloyd George or Mrs Thatcher. On the other hand, he was not a failure like Balfour or Eden, nor a footnote in the Party's evolution like Bonar Law or Home. If circumstances had been different, Major might have been a Baldwin, presiding over a new deal between Party and mass electorate. His place, nevertheless, in a league table (on which his government was so keen), and when considering the opportunity open to a leader in 1990, would be in the second quartile from the top.

NOTE ON SOURCES

The core of the book is based on a series of over 500 interviews, mostly conducted by Anthony Seldon with people who have known John Major at all stages of his career. The frequency of the footnote 'Private interview', which includes references to several private diaries and other documents, is a reflection of the balance between the candid accounts that off-the-record status can produce and the need to protect one's sources. In a journalistic account, it is easier to blend the product of such interviews into a narrative. The interview records and supporting research materials form an historical archive of Major's years in power. Subject to the agreement of those interviewed, records will be kept and made available for study in 2027, well within the Radcliffe guidelines. A full record has been kept of the identity of the private interview sources: should anyone still be interested, these will become available, with all other supporting material not destroyed at the request of those who created it, also in 2027.

Interview records are supported by references from the press, which in the 1990s has produced an ever-increasing range and depth of political coverage. Each broadsheet Sunday newspaper now carries a regular piece of well-informed instant political history. The contemporary historian is therefore immensely in the debt of David Hughes, Andrew Grice, Michael Prescott, Michael Jones, Nicholas Wapshott, Andy McSmith, Anthony Bevins, Patrick Wintour, David Wastell, Toby Helm and Stephen Castle, among several others, for developing this form of journalism. As these pieces cumulatively form an invaluable historical archive, not least for this book, the most informative articles are listed in the bibliography.

There have been four biographies already written about John Major; without the valuable spade work by Bruce Anderson, Penny Junor, Edward Pearce and Nesta Wyn Ellis in trying to disentangle a chequered early life and political career, this project would have been much harder.

NOTES

ONE: AN UNPREPOSSESSING START

1. Anderson (1991), p. 196. Anderson gives Tom's date of birth as 18 May 1879. According to his marriage certificate with Gwen, he was only forty-eight in 1929, i.e. he was not born until 1881.
2. Major-Ball (1994). This is the most informative account of Major's family and his early years.
3. Major-Ball (1994), p. 38.
4. They were married at the North Harborne parish church in Staffordshire. Marriage certificate.
5. Major-Ball (1994), p. 43.
6. John Major birth certificate, registered in the Merton and Carshalton sub-district of Surrey on 4 May 1943.
7. Joanna Seldon, diary, 26.4.95.
8. Major-Ball (1994), p. 44.
9. Ibid., p. 45; interview 2, Pat Dessoy, 3.12.95.
10. Anderson (1991), p. 201.
11. Junor (1993), p. 13.
12. Major-Ball (1994), pp. 51–2.
13. Junor (1993), p. 13.
14. Interview 2, Pat Dessoy.
15. Major-Ball (1994), p. 51.
16. Ibid., p. 52.
17. Gilbert (1989), p. 416.
18. Ibid., p. 539.
19. Junor (1993), p. 13.
20. Interview 2, Pat Dessoy.
21. Junor (1993), p. 14; Pearce (1991), p. 4.
22. Major-Ball (1994), p. 60.
23. Ibid., pp. 65–6.
24. Interview 2, Pat Dessoy.
25. Ibid.
26. Anderson (1991), p. 201.
27. Interview 1, Pat Dessoy, 24.8.95;
   interview 2, Pat Dessoy.
28. Interview, John Brand, *Panorama*, 1991, p. 10.
29. Interview 4, Pat Dessoy, 21.5.96. She said Gwen received a small amount from social security after she finished working.
30. Interview 1, Pat Dessoy.
31. Interview 2, Pat Dessoy.
32. Interview 1, Pat Dessoy.
33. John Brand, *Panorama*, p. 9.
34. Ibid., p. 2.
35. Interview 2, Pat Dessoy.
36. Interview, Christopher Spencer, 5.9.95.
37. Junor (1993), p. 19.
38. John Brand, *Panorama*, pp. 19–20.
39. Major-Ball (1994), p. 60.
40. John Brand, *Panorama*, p. 19.
41. Interview 2, Pat Dessoy.
42. Major-Ball (1994), p. 65.
43. Interview 2, Pat Dessoy.
44. Interview 2, John Major, 17.1.95.
45. Interview, Colin Brock, 2.2.96; interview, Stewart Wild, 26.3.96.
46. Interview, Stewart Wild; letter, John Preuveneers, 27.8.96.
47. Private interview.
48. Ibid.
49. Interview, Stewart Wild.
50. Interview, Derek Esterson, *Panorama*, March 1991.
51. Interview 2, Pat Dessoy.
52. *Rutlishian*, 1959.
53. Interview 2, Pat Dessoy.
54. Ibid.
55. Anderson (1991), pp. 207–8.
56. Interview, John Preuveneers, 22.11.95; letter, John Preuveneers, 26.7.96.

57. *Rutlishian*, 1952–61.
58. Junor (1993), p. 31; Cal McCrystal, *Independent on Sunday*, 21.4.91, p. 9.
59. Junor (1993), p. 32.
60. Interview 2, Pat Dessoy; interview 2, John Major; Nicholas Wapshott, *Observer*, December 1990.
61. John Major quoted in Nicholas Wapshott, *Harpers and Queen*, November 1990.
62. Junor (1993), p. 22.
63. Major-Ball (1994), p. 68.
64. John Major, Wapshott, *Harpers and Queen*.
65. Ibid., pp. 68–9.
66. Anderson (1991), p. 206.
67. Interview 2, John Major.
68. Ibid.
69. Interview 2, Pat Dessoy.
70. Mike Spacey (Rutlish pupil) interview by Tom Bower and Nicholas Farrell, *Sunday Telegraph*, 2.12.90.
71. John Brand, *Panorama*, pp. 13–14.
72. Junor (1993), p. 26.
73. John Major, Wapshott, *Harpers and Queen*.
74. Ibid., p. 29.
75. Interview 2, John Major.
76. Letter, Anthony Storr to author, 19.7.97.

TWO: ESCAPING THE CHRYSALIS

1. John Major, as quoted by Wyn Ellis (1991), p. 73.
2. Junor (1993), p. 36.
3. Interview, Derek Stone, 21.1.95.
4. Anderson (1991), p. 216.
5. Junor (1993), pp. 39–40.
6. Letter from London Electricity, 1995, but they do confirm that they employed him from 3 December 1962 to May 1965.
7. Crick interviews. Michael Crick was at the forefront of uncovering details about Mrs Kierans, and other aspects of Major's early political life.
8. Crick interviews.
9. Anderson (1991), p. 212; Wapshott, *Harpers and Queen*.
10. Interview 2, John Major.
11. Ibid.
12. Interview 1, Clive Jones, 25.1.95. John Major himself believes this version to be correct. An effort was made to track down YC records, but to no avail. Some say they were destroyed.
13. Interview, Derek Stone.
14. Interview, Marion Standing Wright, 21.4.95.
15. Interview, Derek Stone.
16. A Central Office press release about Major dated June 1976 says he was successively Treasurer, Vice-Chairman, political officer, before becoming Chairman of Brixton Young Conservatives. In practice, these titles mean little.
17. Interview 2, John Major.
18. M. Crick, 'John Major and the older woman', *Esquire*, March 1995.
19. Interview 2, Peter Golds, 24.4.96.
20. Crick, *Esquire*; private interview.
21. Private interview.
22. Letter, Michael Crick to author, 13.5.96.
23. Election address, Larkhall ward, May 1964. The 'R.' (Roy) disappeared in the 1970s: he never liked the name. Interview, Peter Golds, 21.5.96.
24. Interview 2, John Major.
25. Interview 1, Ken Payne, 2.10.95.
26. Interview 2, John Major.
27. Interview, Derek Stone.
28. Ibid.
29. Anderson (1991), p. 216.
30. Junor (1993), pp. 42–3.
31. Interview, John Rennie, 29.9.95; Westminster electoral registers 1967, 1968.
32. Lynda Lee-Potter, *Daily Mail*, 14.2.95.
33. Dixon's notes recall canvassing using 'John Major's scheme' in June 1965. Interview, Dixon, *Panorama*, 11.4.91.
34. Interview 2, John Major; StanChart, Standard Chartered Bank magazine, December 1990.
35. St James's, Camberwell parish magazine spring 1967; with thanks to Pat Dessoy. Major knew the vicar through family and political connections. He was not an assiduous attender at church.
36. Interview, John Rennie.

37. Pearce (1991), p. 10, quoting *Guardian* (Jos), 24.12.90.
38. Interview, Peter Golds, *Panorama*, April 1991.
39. Interview 2, John Major.
40. Ibid.
41. Ibid.
42. Interview, John Rennie.
43. Ibid. Accounts in Pearce (1991), p. 11, Junor (1993), pp.45–6 and Anderson (1991), p. 225 differ markedly, and exonerate Cockeram of drinking heavily. I was unable to track down Cockeram to get his side of the story. Jean Kierans, *Daily Mail*, 14.2.95, says Cockeram had drunk a lot.
44. Private interview.
45. Jean Kierans, *Daily Mail*.
46. Interview, John Rennie.
47. Peter Golds, *Panorama*.
48. Charles Oulton and Tim Kelsey, 'The Life of Major', *Profile*.
49. Interview 2, John Major; interview, Alan Orsich, 20.4.95.
50. Private interview.
51. Cited in Crick, *Esquire*.
52. Private information.
53. Letter, John Major to James Wray MP, 23.4.91, cited in Crick, *Esquire*.
54. Interview, Marion Standing Wright.
55. Interview 2, Peter Golds.
56. Interview 1, Clive Jones.
57. Interview 2, Peter Golds.
58. Interview 2, John Major; interview, Jean Lucas, 5.12.94.

THREE: FIRST RUNG ON THE LADDER

1. Ferndale Ward Conservative Election Address, published by Mrs D. Dickson (election agent), 1968.
2. Gallup Poll findings, D. and G. Butler (1994).
3. Lambeth election result table, 1968; interview 1, Clive Jones.
4. The themes appear in all Conservative candidates' election addresses.
5. *Brixton Advertiser*, 17.5.68.
6. Ibid., 4.68 and 5.68 *passim*.
7. Interview 1, Clive Jones.
8. Pearce (1991), p. 28. In 1970, as the candidate for Vauxhall, Jones, with Major, made a statement distancing themselves from a local Monday Club with which Jones had previously had some dealings.
9. Pearce (1991), p. 28.
10. Junor (1993), p. 57.
11. Butler and Pinto-Duschinsky (1971) draw attention to this result.
12. Major had become Treasurer of the Brixton Conservative Association in 1968. Precise dates of Major's promotion through the ranks of the association are difficult to pin down as papers have been lost or burned. Interview 3, Peter Golds, 2.5.96.
13. Interview 2, Peter Golds.
14. James Harkess, *Evening Standard*, 2.11.92.
15. James Harkess, 1970 General Election Address, published by Martin Stannard, 1970.
16. Interview 1, Clive Jones.
17. Pearce (1991), p. 23.
18. Interview 1, Barbara Wallis, 27.9.95.
19. Interview 2, John Major.
20. Private information.
21. Interview 1, Barbara Wallis.
22. Lambeth Borough Council Minutes, 1969/70, pp. 103, 244.
23. Lambeth Borough General Purposes Committee Minutes, 18.6.69, p. 103, 14.1.70, p. 505.
24. Lambeth Borough Council Minutes.
25. Interview 5, Barbara Wallis.
26. Interview 5, John Major, 5.6.96.
27. Junor (1991), p. 51. She speculates that Simpson in this period became like a father to Major. The closeness of the Major–Simpson relationship can be seen by Simpson's wife, also a close friend, becoming godmother to the Majors' daughter and first child, Elizabeth.
28. Interview 2, John Major.
29. Ibid.
30. Interview, John Major, Anthony Seldon, *Sunday Telegraph*, 30.3.97.

31. Lambeth Borough Council Minutes, 1970/71, 5.5.71, p. 783.
32. The Moorlands Estate reached the Housing Committee on 23.2.70. Labour approved the principle of the Stockwell Park Estate in March 1968, but the tender was agreed in June 1969.
33. Lambeth Borough Council Minutes, 27.4.92.
34. Lambeth Borough Council Housing Committee Minutes, p. 357.
35. Major to Penny Junor, in Junor (1993), p. 55.
36. Loans were increased from £280,000 in 1968/9 to £678,000 in 1969/70. Minutes 1970/71, p. 302.
37. Junor (1993), p. 54.
38. Lambeth Borough Council Housing Committee Minutes, pp. 358, 577.
39. Walker (1991), p. 139.
40. *ROOF* magazine, Nov./Dec. 1991.

41. Interview 2, John Major.
42. Annual Abstract of Greater London Statistics, 1974.
43. Private interview.
44. Letter, Clive Jones, 24.7.96.
45. Junor (1993), p. 54.
46. Annual Abstract of Greater London Statistics, 1973/4.
47. Harloe, Issacharoff and Minns (1974).
48. Quoted in Pearce (1991), p. 24.
49. Interview, Andrew Beadle, 18.9.95.
50. Ibid.
51. Interview 2, John Major.
52. Private information.
53. Interview, Ian Cameron Black, 24.2.95. He said Major found the incident 'very disturbing'.
54. Interview 1, Clive Jones. The two *South London Press* journalists were Alistair Ephraim and Pat Hellicar.

FOUR: SECURING THE FOUNDATION

1. Private information.
2. Details of Norma Major's life can be found in Walker (1993). An excellent account is given in Junor (1993), pp. 61–6.
3. Junor (1993), p. 65.
4. Major-Ball (1994), pp. 134–5.
5. Junor (1993), p. 67.
6. Interview 1, Clive Jones; letter, Clive Jones, 24.7.96.
7. Interview 1, Clive Jones.
8. Private information.
9. Interview 1, Peter Golds, 3.1.95.
10. Interview, David Rodgers, 7.3.95. James Major, their second and last child, was born when the family was at West Oak.
11. Fisher (1973), p. 261.
12. Interview, David Rodgers.
13. John Major, summary of a career with Standard Chartered Bank, 1990.
14. Private interview.
15. Interview, Alan Orsich.
16. Ibid.
17. John Major, summary of a career with Standard Chartered Bank, 1990.
18. *Standard Chartered Bank: A Story Brought Up To Date* (Standard Chartered Bank, 1980), p. 17.

19. Private interview.
20. *StanChart*, Standard Chartered Bank magazine, December 1990.
21. Interview, Norma Major, 14.9.95.
22. Interview, Geoff Ledden, 20.1.97.
23. Since 1979 BIFU (Banking, Insurance and Finance Union).
24. *NUBE News*, September 1973.
25. Interview, Stan Hurn, 24.4.96.
26. Interview, John Jennings, 13.3.96.
27. Interview, Geoff Ledden.
28. Roth (1984).
29. Interview, Sir Peter Graham, 2.5.95.
30. Interview, Stan Hurn.
31. Interview, Sir Peter Graham.
32. Interview 2, John Major.
33. Interview, Jean Lucas.
34. Interview 2, John Major.
35. Junor (1993), p. 72.
36. Letter, Jean Lucas to David Mitchell, area agent for Greater London, 20.7.71.
37. Interview 1, Peter Golds.
38. Records of St Pancras North Conservative Association.
39. Interview 2, John Major.
40. St Pancras North Executive Committee Minute, 19.6.73.
41. *Camden Journal*, 7.7.72.

42. Ibid., 2.2.73.
43. Interview 2, Sue Winter, 4.3.96.
44. Interview, Roland Walker, 25.1.95.
45. John Major's February 1974 election address, published by agent J. De Ath, 37 Leighton Road, NW5.
46. John Major, *Hampstead and Highgate Express*, 22.2.74.
47. Records of St Pancras North Conservative Association.
48. *Camden Journal*, 15.2.74.
49. Interview, Roland Walker.
50. Butler and Kavanagh (1974).
51. Interview 3, Peter Golds. It is difficult to be precise about the names and timing of constituency searches by Major. Peter Golds's testimony is relied upon in the absence of other documentation.
52. *Hampstead and Highgate Express*, 13.9.74.
53. Interview 2, Sue Winter.
54. Steve Grant, 'The Night I Went Out Canvassing With a Candidate', *Camden Gazette*, 4.10.74.
55. *Hampstead and Highgate Express*, 4.10.74.
56. Interview 2, Sue Winter.
57. John Major, October 1974 election address, published by agent Sue Winter.
58. *John Major Answers Your Questions*, P. and P. S. Winter, 37 Leighton Road, 1974.
59. Interview 2, Sue Winter.
60. *Hampstead and Highgate Express*, 22.8.74.
61. Interview 2, Sue Winter.
62. James Major was born in 1975. Norma's presence, though she was in evidence, was much less than in February 1974.

63. Interview 2, Sue Winter. He took the time he spent at St Pancras North out of his Standard Chartered holiday entitlement. Interview, Ian Cameron Black.
64. Interview 2, Sue Winter.
65. Interview 5, John Major.
66. Interview, Stan Hurn; interview 3, Peter Golds.
67. Robert Atkins quoted in Walker (1993), p. 40; private interview.
68. Interview, Robert Hughes, 22.2.95.
69. Private information.
70. Interview 2, John Major.
71. Interview, John Reveley Major, *Panorama*, April 1991.
72. Interview 2, John Major.
73. Both Forman and Mellor went on to become ministers under Major's premiership. Mellor believes that Putney would have selected Major above him. Interview 1, David Mellor, 23.12.94.
74. Interview, Nicholas Bennett, 27.9.95.
75. Interview 5, John Major.
76. Interview, Derek Pinks, 28.9.95.
77. Interview, Sir Peter Graham.
78. Interview, Ian Cameron Black.
79. Ibid.
80. Interview, Sir Peter Graham.
81. Interview, Norma Major. She added, however, 'I know now that it wouldn't have stopped him. He would have carried on and on until he got somewhere.'

FIVE: INTO PARLIAMENT

1. Anderson (1991), p. 244, says 280; Junor (1993), p. 82, says nearly 300. Interview, Roger Juggins, 7.2.96. Renton announced his retirement in August 1976, *Hunts Post*, 5.8.76.
2. Interview 2, John Major.
3. Andrew Thomson became Margaret Thatcher's agent for Finchley in 1985.
4. Interview 2, John Major.
5. Jock Bruce-Gardyne became MP for Knutsford in March 1979; Alan Haselhurst became MP for Saffron Walden in July 1977; Charles Douro became Euro MP for Surrey in 1979.

6. Anderson (1991), pp. 246–7; Junor (1993), p. 85.
7. *Hunts Post*, 25.11.76.
8. Interview, Lord Renton, 16.4.96.
9. Private information.
10. *Hunts Post*, 31.5.79; private interview.
11. Interview, Lord Renton; interview, Roger Juggins.
12. Interview, Roger Juggins.
13. Interview, Derek Holley, 7.2.96.
14. Anderson (1991), p. 249.
15. Interview, Lord Renton.
16. Interview, Roger Juggins.
17. Junor (1993), p. 89.

18. Private information, 54.
19. Ibid.
20. Ibid.
21. John Major, summary of career with Standard Chartered Bank.
22. Private interview.
23. John Major, summary of career with Standard Chartered Bank.
24. Interview 2, Sir Graham Bright, 31.8.95. Graham Bright became his PPS at Number Ten, 1990–94, and Mellor a Cabinet minister, 1990–93.
25. Interview, John Watson, 9.11.95.
26. Interview, Peter Cropper, 1.12.94.
27. *Hunts Post*, 31.3.79.
28. Interview 1, Peter Brown, 7.2.96.
29. Interview, Norma Major.
30. Renton's majority in October 1974 had been 9,200.
31. 'Make Your Mind Up Day', *Hunts Post*, 3.5.79. The swing to the Conservatives in the election was 5.1 per cent.
32. John Major, election address, 1979.
33. Interview 2, John Major.
34. Joint with Butcher for the first two years.
35. Interview 1, Barbara Wallis.
36. Interview, John Watson.
37. Interview 2, John Major.
38. HC Debs, 5th Series, vol. 968, cols 519–26.
39. Interview 2, John Major.
40. Interview, John Watson.
41. HC Debs, 5th Series, vol. 996, cols 1210–13.
42. Interview 2, John Major.
43. HC Debs, 6th Series, vol. 9, cols 888–91.
44. Ibid., vol. 22, cols 313–33.
45. Ibid., vol. 974, cols 890–944.
46. Ibid., vol. 12, cols 66–70.
47. Ibid., vol. 31, cols 65–70.
48. Ibid., vol. 12, cols 66–70.
49. Ibid., vol. 31, cols 779–87.
50. Ibid., vol. 982, cols 1249–54.
51. Interview 1, Ian Lang, 25.10.95.
52. Interview, Sir Anthony Durant, 19.12.94.
53. In opposition, the frontbench spokesmen are officers of the committee. In government, they become more low key, though in some areas, like Foreign Affairs, they can be important.
54. Interview, Sir Anthony Durant.
55. Interview, John Drew, 1.5.96.
56. HC Debs, 6th Series, vol. 8, cols 740–60; Pearce (1991), p. 78.
57. Ibid., vol. 13, cols 672–5.
58. Ibid., vol. 31, cols 63–70.
59. Private interview.
60. Interview 1, Chris Patten, 29.5.95.
61. Interview, John Watson.
62. Thatcher (1993), p. 422.
63. Pearce (1991), pp. 79–81.
64. Interview, Ken Weetch, 20.3.96; *Hunts Post*, 8.4.82.
65. Interview, John Watson.
66. Private information.
67. Butler and Kavanagh (1980). As 'secondary only', Major was one of only twenty-eight Tories – compared to fifty-one Old Etonians.
68. Interview 1, Matthew Parris, 23.11.94.
69. Interview 2, Sir Graham Bright.
70. Private information.
71. Interview, John Watson.
72. Annotated Members' Dining Room menu, 14.4.81; John Watson's papers.
73. The appointment was announced in *The Times*, 14.1.81.
74. Chris Patten was appointed PPS to Patrick Jenkin, Secretary of State for Social Services.
75. Interview, Sir Patrick Mayhew, 2.11.95.
76. Interview, Michael Jopling, 20.2.95.
77. Interview, Lord Whitelaw, 9.5.95.
78. Interview, Sir Timothy Raison, 20.12.94.
79. Ibid.
80. Interview, Sir Patrick Mayhew.
81. Interview 2, Sir Graham Bright.
82. Interview, Norma Major.
83. Interview 1, Robin Squire, 8.11.95.
84. Private information.
85. Anderson (1991), p. 257.

SIX: WHIP AND SOCIAL SECURITY

1. *Financial Times*, 15.1.83.
2. *Private Eye*, 29.1.83.
3. Interview 2, John Major.
4. Interview, Michael Jopling. The Chief

Whip, however, is appointed by the Prime Minister, and the Deputy Chief Whip nominated by the Chief Whip.

5. Interview, Michael Jopling.

6. Thatcher (1993).

7. Incredibly, there is still no satisfactory account published on the Whips' Office and *modus operandi* of the chief and other whips.

8. Interview 1, Lord Wakeham, 20.12.94.

9. Ibid.

10. Private interview.

11. Interview 1, Robert Hayward, 1.3.95.

12. Interview, John Maples, 20.2.95.

13. Interview 1, Lord Wakeham.

14. Interview, Alan Howarth, 18.3.96.

15. Interview 1, Francis Maude, 21.12.94.

16. Interview, Roger Bright, 19.7.95.

17. Interview, Ian Lang.

18. Interview, Sir Nicholas Lyell, 21.2.95.

19. Interview 1, Robert Hayward.

20. Interview 1, Peter Riddell, 21.11.94.

21. Interview 1, Tristan Garel-Jones, 28.2.95; interview, Alan Howarth.

22. Interview, Alan Clark, 16.4.95.

23. *Hunts Post*, 31.5.79, 31.1.80, 28.2.80, 8.7.82.

24. Ibid., 6.12.79.

25. Ibid., 19.6.80, 26.6.80, 3.7.80, 24.7.80, 13.11.80.

26. Ibid., 20.8.81.

27. Interview, Roger Juggins. Major could drive by the end of the 1970s, but did not enjoy it.

28. Interview, Derek Holley.

29. Interview, Mike Bloomfield, 26.2.96.

30. *Hunts Post*, 5.2.81.

31. Interview, Derek Holley.

32. Crewe and Fox (1984).

33. Interview, Stan Hurn.

34. Interview, Sir John Cope, 19.12.94.

35. Interview 1, Tristan Garel-Jones.

36. Interview, Peter Cropper.

37. Interview, Lord Lawson, 19.12.94.

38. Interview, Peter Cropper.

39. Interview, Lord Moore, 21.12.94.

40. Interview, Howard Davies, 20.2.96.

41. Interview 1, Jeremy Hanley, 31.1.96.

42. Interview 2, John Major.

43. Interview 1, Lord Wakeham. Mrs Thatcher's account, Thatcher (1993), p. 422, says it was a lunch at Downing Street.

44. Interview 1, Lord Wakeham.

45. Private information.

46. Mrs Thatcher says she started talks on the reshuffle with Wakeham and Whitelaw in May 1985. Thatcher (1993), p. 418.

47. Thatcher (1993), pp. 422–3.

48. Private interview.

49. See Glennerster in Catterall (1995), pp. 180–87.

50. Interview 3, John Major, 4.9.95.

51. Lewis Carter-Jones, Labour MP for Eccles until 1987, who had a special interest in the disabled, said that Major was the first Conservative minister who understood what social security was all about; interview 2, Sir Graham Bright.

52. Interview, Sir Geoffrey Otton, 16.10.95.

53. Fowler (1991), p. 271.

54. Private interview.

55. Ibid.

56. Ibid.

57. Ibid.

58. Interview 3, Nick True, 8.3.95.

59. Private interview.

60. Ibid.

61. Interview, Sir Norman Fowler, 24.10.95.

62. Ibid.

63. *The Times*, 11.9.86.

64. *Financial Times*, 11.9.86.

65. Interview, Sir Nicholas Lyell.

66. Conservative Party Annual Conference Reports, 1986, pp. 38–9.

67. *Financial Times*, 11.12.86; *Guardian*, 16.12.86.

68. *Sunday Times*, 11.1.87.

69. Quoted in the *Sunday Times*, 11.1.87.

70. HC Debs, 6th Series, vol. 102, cols 388–95.

71. Private interview.

72. Interview 3, John Major; private interview. The evidence conflicts slightly, with officials tending to believe it was Mrs Thatcher who persuaded Major, rather than vice versa.

73. Interview 3, John Major.

74. Private interview.

75. Ibid.

76. Brian Deer, 'Major sits tight on aid to the disabled', *Sunday Times*, 25.1.87. Major defended the government's record on the elderly in an article 'Care for the old and cold', *Sunday Times*, 1.2.87.

77. Interview 1, Matthew Parris.
78. Reported in *Sunday Times*, 23.1.87.
79. Interview, Lord McColl, 2.4.96; private interview.
80. Interview 3, John Major.
81. Private interview.
82. *Daily Telegraph*, 15.1.87.
83. Private interview.
84. Ibid.
85. *The Times*, 8.10.86.
86. Private interview.
87. Interview 3, John Major.
88. Interview, Sir Norman Fowler.

89. Interview 1, Matthew Parris.
90. Interview, Sir Bernard Ingham, 5.4.95. Mrs Thatcher was Joint Parliamentary Secretary at the Ministry of Pensions and National Insurance 1961–4.
91. Interview, Sir Charles Powell, 21.4.95.
92. Interview 3, Nick True.
93. Interview 1, Andrew Tyrie, 20.2.95; interview 8, Nick True, 10.5.96.
94. Private interview.
95. Ibid.
96. Interview 3, John Major.

SEVEN: CHIEF SECRETARY

1. Interview, Lord Lawson.
2. *Guardian*, 15.6.87.
3. *Daily Telegraph*, 15.6.87.
4. Moore had to retire from politics with stress-related ill-health in July 1989.
5. Interview, Norma Major.
6. Interview 1, Lord Wakeham. He had written to Mrs Thatcher and said the only job he wanted to do was to become Leader of the House of Commons.
7. Lawson (1992), pp. 710–12.
8. Interview, Lord Lawson.
9. Interview, Peter Cropper. Rees had not been a successful Chief Secretary and MacGregor took over from him in September 1985.
10. Lawson (1992), p. 711; interview, Peter Cropper.
11. Private interview.
12. Ibid.
13. Interview, Sir Norman Fowler.
14. Private interview.
15. Interview, Lord Lawson.
16. Lawson (1992), p. 719.
17. Interview 1, Andrew Tyrie.
18. Private interview; interview, Norma Major.
19. Interview 1, Sir Peter Middleton, 21.12.94.
20. Interview, Stan Hurn.
21. She read PPE at Somerville College, Oxford, 1975–8. Awarded a first class degree, she entered the Treasury. She became Press Secretary to the Chancellor in 1995–6.

22. Private interview.
23. Lawson sets out the factors running in Major's favour in Lawson (1992), p. 720.
24. Private interview.
25. Ibid.
26. Interview 2, Norman Lamont, 22.2.95.
27. Private interview.
28. Interview 1, Sir Peter Middleton.
29. *The Times*, 15.6.87.
30. Ibid.
31. 'Major cracks whip against big spenders', *Guardian*, 23.6.87.
32. *The Times*, 29.6.87.
33. Christopher Huhne, *Guardian*, 29.6.87.
34. Ibid.
35. Ibid., 8.7.87.
36. James Naughtie, 'Baker Lines up with Ridley to fight the Treasury', *Guardian*, 23.6.87.
37. Ibid.
38. *The Times*, 29.7.87.
39. Ibid.
40. This facet of his background was to be found commonly across the press in June and July 1987. An interesting, and not hostile, portrait of Major is given by Robin Oakley, *The Times*, 21.7.87.
41. Craig Brown, *The Times*, 9.7.87.
42. *Daily Telegraph*, 9.7.87.
43. *Guardian*, 29.6.87.
44. Interview 3, John Major.
45. Interview 1, Chris Patten.
46. Walker (1993), p. 203.
47. Private interview.

48. Private interviews.
49. Tuesday 19 January 1988, Clark (1994), p. 197.
50. Interview, Lord Parkinson, 23.2.95.
51. Lawson (1992), p. 720.
52. Private interview.
53. As attributed to 'Whitehall sources', *Sunday Times*, 20.9.87.
54. Lawson (1992), p. 720.
55. *The Times*, 3.10.87, said Mrs Thatcher was impressed by the way he had conducted the expenditure round.
56. Interview, Lord Parkinson.
57. *The Times*, 5.2.88.
58. 'The Major not so minor', *Guardian*, 6.2.88.
59. Ingham (1991), p. 184.
60. Interview, Sir Bernard Ingham.
61. Gordon Brown, HC Debs, 6th Series, vol. 129, cols 929–1118.
62. John Major, HC Debs, 6th Series, vol. 132, cols 214–26.
63. HC Debs, 6th Series, vol. 125, cols 542–9.
64. *The Times*, 25.2.88.
65. Ibid., 16.3.88.
66. See Lawson (1992), pp. 612–19; Thatcher (1993), pp. 606–17. The Thatcher camp expected Lawson to challenge the Thatcher account when published. Private interview.
67. Private interview.
68. Ibid.; Glennerster in Seldon (1994), pp. 203–8.
69. Cm 555, London, HMSO.
70. James Naughtie, 'Premier sees Major as key to reshuffle', *Guardian*, 11.7.88.
71. Private interviews.
72. Interview, Sir Michael Quinlan, 16.8.95.
73. Private interviews.
74. Private interview.
75. Lawson (1992), pp. 725–7. *The Times* on 7.10.88 said, 'It is thought unlikely that child benefit will be held down for the second year running.'
76. Interview, Lord Parkinson.
77. Lawson (1992), pp. 726–7.
78. Private interview.
79. Ibid.
80. Lawson (1992), pp. 724–5. Private interview.
81. Interview, Lord Lawson.
82. *The Times*, 27.9.88.
83. Ibid., 10.9.88.
84. *Guardian*, 13.12.88.
85. *The Times*, 14.12.88.
86. *Sunday Times*, 11.11.89.
87. Private interview.
88. Robin Oakley, *The Times*, 14.12.88.
89. *The Times*, 13.10.88.
90. Interview 3, John Major.
91. *The Times*, 10.2.89.
92. Lawson (1992), pp. 874–87.
93. Junor (1993), pp. 153–5.
94. Private interview.
95. Interview, Sir Charles Powell.
96. Interview, Lord Whitelaw.
97. Interview 1, Norman Lamont, 17.5.94.
98. Interview, Lord Lawson.
99. *The Times*, 22.6.89; interview, Howard Davies.
100. *The Times* leader on 23.6.89 said his views in the speech had much in common with the prospectus set out in the past by David Owen of the SDP.
101. Interview 1, Francis Maude.
102. Private interview.
103. Interview, Sir Nicholas Lyell.
104. Interview 3, Peter Riddell, 23.8.95.
105. Interview, Lord Lawson.
106. Private interview.
107. Ibid.
108. *Daily Telegraph*, 5.10.87.
109. *The Times*, 20.7.89.

EIGHT: FOREIGN SECRETARY

1. Interview, Lord Howe of Aberavon, 20.12.94; interview, Lord Parkinson.
2. Private interview.
3. Interview, Lord Wright, 18.7.95.
4. Interview 1, Francis Maude.
5. Interview, Sir Charles Powell; interview, Lord Lawson.
6. Private interview.
7. Interview, Sir Charles Powell.
8. Private interview.

9. *Sunday Times*, 23.7.89.
10. *Daily Telegraph*, 25.7.89; Thatcher (1993), p. 756.
11. Private interview.
12. George Jones, *Daily Telegraph*, 25.7.89; Lawson (1992), p. 936.
13. Interview, Norma Major.
14. Interview 3, John Major.
15. Interview, Jean Lucas.
16. Interview, Carys Evans, 20.10.95.
17. Interview 3, John Major.
18. Private interview.
19. Interview, Carys Evans.
20. Interview 3, John Major; private interview.
21. Interview, Carys Evans.
22. Interview 1, Sir Stephen Wall, 12.10.95.
23. Hella Pick in the *Guardian*, 26.7.89.
24. Private interview.
25. Interview 1, Francis Maude.
26. Howe (1995), p. 596.
27. Ibid.
28. Interview 1, Anthony Teasdale, 1.12.94.
29. Interview 2, Douglas Hurd, 1.6.95.
30. Interview, Sir Charles Powell.
31. Private interview.
32. Ibid.
33. Interview, Sir Charles Powell.
34. Interview 1, Francis Maude.
35. Private interview.
36. Interview 1, Sir Rodric Braithwaite, 20.2.96.
37. Private interview.
38. Ibid.
39. Ibid.
40. Ibid.
41. Ibid.
42. Interview, Lord Wright.
43. Private interview.
44. Ibid.
45. Ibid.
46. Interview, Lord Wright.
47. Reported in *The Times*, 1.8.89.
48. Letter to author, 2.9.96.
49. Private interview.
50. Ibid.
51. Letter to author, 2.9.96.
52. 'China's Inglorious Army', *The Times*, 1.8.89.
53. Dimbleby (1997).
54. Interview 2, Francis Maude, 22.5.95.
55. Interview 2, Tristan Garel-Jones, 31.1.96.
56. Interview 1, Tristan-Garel Jones.
57. Interview 5, John Major.
58. Private interview.
59. Interview, Robert Atkins, 6.12.95; Home (1989), pp. 193–8.
60. Interview, Robert Atkins; interview 2, Tristan Garel-Jones.
61. Interview 3, John Major.
62. Interview, Lord Wright.
63. Interview 3, John Major.
64. Interview, Sir Antony Acland, 23.11.95.
65. *The Times*, 13.9.89.
66. Private interview.
67. Interview, Sir Antony Acland; private interview.
68. Interview, Francis Cornish, 29.5.95.
69. *New York Times*, 14.2.89.
70. *The Times*, 13.9.89.
71. Ibid.
72. Private interview; letter to author, 2.9.96.
73. Peter Stothard, *The Times*, 13.9.89; Thatcher (1993), p. 792.
74. Interview 1, Raymond Seitz, 24.4.96.
75. Private interview.
76. *The Times*, 28.9.89.
77. Private interview.
78. Interview 3, John Major; private interview.
79. Private interview.
80. Interview 5, John Major.
81. Interview 1, Francis Maude.
82. Private interview.
83. Nicholas Wood, *The Times*, 13.10.89.
84. Interview 1, Maurice Fraser, 15.9.95.
85. Private interview.
86. Ibid.
87. Junor (1993), p. 167.
88. Major to Ed Pearce, quoted in Pearce (1991), p. 121.
89. Private interview.
90. Letter to author, 2.9.96.
91. Interview, Sir Charles Powell.
92. Ibid.; Thatcher (1993), pp. 530–31.
93. Private interview.
94. Interview, Lord Wright.
95. Thatcher (1993), pp. 530–31.
96. See, for example, *Daily Mail* and *Daily Telegraph*, 23.10.89.
97. 'Major Wins on Sanctions', *Sunday Times*, 22.10.89.
98. Private interview.
99. *The Times*, 26.10.89.
100. HC Debs, 6th Series, vol. 158, cols 1051–2.

101. Interview 1, Chris Patten.
102. Private interview.
103. Interview 1, Francis Maude.

104. Interview, Sir David Hannay, 23.10.95.
105. Private interview.
106. Ibid.

NINE: CHANCELLOR OF THE EXCHEQUER

1. Interview, Lord Lawson; Lawson (1992), pp. 955–65.
2. *Financial Times*, 18.10.89.
3. Private interview.
4. Interview, Lord Waddington, 28.8.95.
5. Howe (1995), p. 605.
6. Interview, Sir Charles Powell.
7. Interview, Alan Clark.
8. Private interviews.
9. Interview 5, John Major.
10. Interview, Lord Howe of Aberavon.
11. *The Times*, 27.10.89.
12. Private interview.
13. Lawson (1992), pp. 950–51.
14. Private interviews.
15. 'The Chancellor's Options', *The Times*, 28.10.89.
16. *The Times*, 28.10.89.
17. Ibid.; private interview.
18. See *Financial Times, Daily Telegraph*, 27 and 28.10.89.
19. *Guardian*, 28.10.89.
20. Ian Aitken, *Guardian*, 27.10.89.
21. Thatcher (1993), p. 718.
22. Howe (1995), pp. 606–8.
23. 'Panic Over', *The Times*, 1.11.89.
24. Private interview.
25. Ibid.
26. Private interview; Mrs Thatcher wrote, 'It seemed strange to me that ... he did not feel more at home with tackling the difficult issues he now faced when he returned to the Treasury.' Thatcher (1993), p. 675.
27. Private information.
28. Lawson (1992), p. 385.
29. Private interview.
30. Chaplin, diary, 3.9.90.
31. Private interview. Chaplin's first husband had been a member of the House of Lords.
32. Interview 2, Sir Peter Middleton, 18.7.95.
33. Private interview.
34. HC Debs, 6th Series, vol. 160, cols 357–61.

35. David Smith and David Hughes, *Sunday Times*, 19.11.89.
36. Simon Jenkins, *Sunday Times*, 19.11.89.
37. Ibid.
38. Chaplin, diary, 29.11.89.
39. Interview 2, Norman Lamont.
40. Private interviews.
41. Chaplin, diary, 12–13.11.90.
42. Smith (1992), pp. 160–62.
43. Private interview.
44. Interview 2, Sir Peter Middleton.
45. Chaplin, diary, 12–13.11.90.
46. Private interview.
47. Interview 2, Sir Peter Middleton.
48. Smith (1992), pp. 161–2.
49. Chaplin, diary, 20.3.90.
50. Private information.
51. HC Debs, 6th Series, vol. 169, cols 1009–26.
52. Chaplin, diary, 20.3.90; Butler, Adonis and Travers (1994), p. 151.
53. Private interview.
54. Rodney Lord, *The Times*, 21.3.90.
55. Quoted in *The Times*, 21.3.90.
56. Tim Congdon in *The Times*, 21.3.90.
57. Butler, Adonis and Travers (1994), p. 151.
58. Chaplin, diary, 23.3.90.
59. Thatcher (1993), p. 719.
60. Smith (1992), pp. 162–3.
61. Private interview.
62. Interview, Albert Reynolds, 25.7.95.
63. Interview, Sir David Hannay.
64. Ibid.
65. Thatcher (1993), p. 759.
66. Private interview.
67. Ibid.
68. Ibid.
69. Stephens (1996), pp. 161–2.
70. Focus, *Sunday Times*, 24.6.90.
71. Howe (1995), p. 630.
72. Private interview.
73. Chaplin, diary, 8–9.9.90.
74. Lord Cockfield said the hard ecu plan was 'ten years out of date', House of Lords, 18.7.90.

75. Focus, *Sunday Times*, 24.6.90.
76. Leigh (1995).
77. Interview 1, Andrew Lansley, 23.12.94; Baker (1993), p. 345.
78. Smith (1992), pp. 173–9.
79. Major said at the IMF on 22.9.90 that the economy was not in recession so no interest rate reduction was imminent. *Sunday Times*, 24.9.90.
80. Tim Congdon quoted in Smith (1992), p. 177.
81. HC Debs, 6th Series, vol. 178, cols 195–202.
82. Private interview.
83. Ibid.
84. Ibid.
85. Ibid.
86. Interview, Sir Charles Powell.
87. *Spectator*, 13.7.90.
88. Private interview.
89. Smith (1992), p. 166.
90. Ibid., pp. 166–7.
91. Chaplin, diary, 17.4.90.
92. Thatcher (1993), p. 721.
93. Ibid., p. 722.
94. Interview 2, Sir Peter Middleton.
95. Private interview.
96. Interview, Sir Charles Powell.
97. Interview, Lord Parkinson.
98. *The Times*, 19.7.90.
99. *Wall Street Journal*, 30.5.90.

100. Smith (1992), p. 168.
101. Ibid., p. 167.
102. Ibid., p. 170.
103. Graham Searjeant, *The Times*, 24.9.90; letter, Peter Riddell to author, 23.10.96.
104. Private interview.
105. Smith (1992), p. 171.
106. Stephens (1996), p. 172. Philip Stephens's is by far the best account of the episode. See also Connolly (1995), pp. 1008–9 on ERM entry.
107. Interview 1, Sir Peter Middleton.
108. Interview, Lord Kingsdown (formerly Robin Leigh-Pemberton), 4.1.96.
109. Stephens (1996), pp. 171, 175.
110. Private interview.
111. Interview 1, Andrew Lansley.
112. Private interview.
113. Smith (1992), p. 172; Lawson (1992), p. 1009.
114. *The Economist*, 13.10.90.
115. *The Times*, 6.10.90.
116. *Observer*, 7.10.90.
117. *The Times*, 8.10.90.
118. Stephens (1996), p. 178.
119. HC Debs, 6th Series, vol. 178, cols 195–291.
120. Cited in the David Lipsey profile, *The Times*, 11.10.90.

TEN: LEADERSHIP ELECTION

1. The newspaper column inches and television and radio programmes on the events in November 1990 are of daunting size. Among the Major biographies, the fullest account is in Anderson (1991), pp. 98–194. Watkins (1991) is devoted to the election.
2. Chaplin, diary, 12.10.90.
3. *The Times*, 12.10.90.
4. Ibid.
5. *Daily Telegraph*, 12.10.90.
6. Chaplin, diary, 12.10.90. The speech was written by Major, Chaplin and Tyrie. Interview 1, Andrew Tyrie.
7. Stephens (1996), p. 179.
8. *Guardian*, 19.10.90.

9. The debate on the ERM took place on 23.10.90, in which eleven Conservative MPs voted against the government.
10. *The Times*, 29.10.90.
11. HC Debs, 6th Series, vol. 178, cols 869–90.
12. Howe (1995), pp. 645–68. He says he decided to resign on 31 October, the trigger being Mrs Thatcher's report on the Rome summit.
13. *Observer*, 4.11.90; 'Out Come the Knives', *Sunday Times*, 4.11.90.
14. *Observer*, *Sunday Telegraph*, 11.11.90.
15. Baker (1993), pp. 382–3.
16. *Daily Telegraph*, 9.11.90.
17. *Guardian*, 5.11.90.

18. Headline in the *Guardian*, 9.11.90.
19. *The Times*, 9.11.90.
20. *Daily Telegraph*, 9.11.90.
21. Howe (1995), pp. 663–8.
22. *Guardian*, 14.11.90.
23. Thatcher (1993), p. 840.
24. Chaplin, diary, 12.9.90.
25. Ibid., 16.11.90.
26. Profile, *Observer*, 7.10.90; interview, Sir Antony Acland.
27. Interview 1, Barbara Wallis.
28. Anderson (1991), pp. 115–16.
29. *Observer; Sunday Telegraph; Sunday Times*, 18.11.90.
30. Interview 2, Francis Maude.
31. *Guardian*, 19.11.90.
32. Anderson (1991), p. 116; Crick (1995), p. 386.
33. Interview 1, Lord Archer, 3.11.95.
34. *Daily Telegraph*, 21.11.90; Thatcher (1993), pp. 843–4.
35. Private interview.
36. Thatcher (1993), p. 846.
37. Ibid., pp. 850–55.
38. Private interview.
39. Interview 3, John Major.
40. Private interview.
41. Chaplin, diary, 28.1.91 (sic).
42. *The Times*, 19.11.90.
43. Chaplin, diary, 9–10.3.91 (sic).
44. *The Times*, 23.11.90.

45. Interview, Lord Tebbit, 14.8.95; letter to author, 3.3.97.
46. *Daily Telegraph*, 23.11.90.
47. Chaplin clearly thought the reason Lamont supported Major was in the hope of becoming Chancellor. Diary 25.1.91.
48. Interview 2, Francis Maude.
49. Interview 1, Robert Hayward.
50. Interview 2, Francis Maude.
51. Private interview.
52. *Independent*, 24.11.90.
53. Private interview.
54. Interview 1, Douglas Hurd, 5.4.95.
55. *Sunday Times*, 25.11.90.
56. Thatcher (1993), pp. 860–62.
57. Private interview.
58. Interview, Nicholas Bennett.
59. *The Times*, 26.11.90.
60. *Sunday Telegraph*, 25.11.90.
61. Philip Cowley, 'How did he do that? A systematic analysis of the 1990 Conservative leadership election', University of Hull, September 1995.
62. Interview 3, John Major.
63. Interview 1, Francis Maude.
64. Private interview.
65. Interview 1, Sir Tim Bell, 24.4.96.
66. Private interview.
67. Interview 1, Andrew Tyrie.

ELEVEN: THE NEW PRIME MINISTER

1. Chaplin, diary, 27.11.90.
2. Interview, David Wilshire, 19.6.96.
3. Interview 1, Sir Tim Bell.
4. Interview 1, Gus O'Donnell, 20.4.95.
5. Alan Hamilton, *The Times*, 28.11.90.
6. Hogg and Hill (1995), p. 3.
7. *Financial Times*, 29.11.90.
8. Private interview.
9. Interview, Norma Major.
10. Interview 1, Barbara Wallis.
11. *Daily Telegraph*, 28.11.90.
12. Ibid.
13. Ibid.
14. *The Economist*, 1.12.90, 8.12.90.
15. *Guardian*, 29.11.90.
16. Ibid.
17. Ibid., 28.11.90.

18. Norman Stone, *Sunday Times*, 9.12.90; Catherine Bennett, *Guardian*, 30.11.90.
19. Private interview. In fact, after the IRA ceasefire in 1994, he would walk across to the House of Commons via St James's Park.
20. Interview 3, John Major.
21. Letter, Major to Neville Sandelson, 25.5.89; interview, Neville Sandelson, 29.8.95. .
22. Interview 1, Maurice Fraser.
23. John Major, 'Radicalism and the Conservative Party', Radical Society Speech, 11.10.89.
24. Neville Sandelson believes he did use the phrase 'classless society', but press reports are inconclusive.

25. Quoted in a revealing David Lipsey profile, *The Times*, 11.10.90.
26. *Daily Telegraph*, 12.10.90.
27. *Guardian*, 27.11.90.
28. Interview 3, John Major.
29. Interview 1, Gus O'Donnell.
30. Hogg and Hill (1995), p. 8.
31. Interview, Lord Waddington.
32. Private interview.
33. *Guardian*, 29.11.90.
34. Interview 2, Chris Patten, 30.5.95.
35. Private interviews.
36. Hogg and Hill (1995), pp. 8–11. John Cole discussed Patten as a possible successor.
37. Interview 1, Kenneth Clarke, 22.5.96.
38. Interview 2, Chris Patten.
39. Ibid.
40. Interview, Kenneth Baker, 24.4.96.
41. Hogg and Hill (1995), p. 10.
42. Private interview.
43. Interview, Lord Waddington.
44. Interview 2, Sir Graham Bright.
45. Interview 2, Chris Patten.
46. Interview, Lord Waddington.
47. Interview, Lord Parkinson.
48. Interview 2, Chris Patten.
49. Hogg and Hill (1995), p. 11.
50. HC Debs, 6th Series, vol. 181, cols 1012–16.
51. *Guardian*, 30.11.90.
52. Private interview.
53. Ibid.
54. Profile, Sarah Hogg, *Sunday Times*, 9.12.90.
55. Interview 1, Lady Hogg, 16.2.95.
56. Private interview.
57. *The Times*, 29.11.90.
58. Private interview.
59. Interview, John Mills, 10.8.95.
60. Ibid.; interview, Carolyn Sinclair, 7.4.95; Hogg and Hill (1995), p. 27; *Guardian*, 29.11.90.
61. Private interview.
62. Interview, Robin Harris, 3.4.96.
63. *Guardian*, 29.11.90.
64. Interview 3, Nick True.
65. Interview 3, Jonathan Hill, 14.3.95.
66. Private interview.
67. Interview, John Mills.
68. Private interview.
69. Interview, Howell Harris Hughes.
70. Ibid.
71. Interview, Sir Charles Powell.
72. Private interview.
73. Interview, Sir Bernard Ingham.
74. Interview 1, Gus O'Donnell.
75. Private interview.
76. 'Economist with a popular touch', *Guardian*, 29.11.90.
77. *The Economist*, 2.11.91; *New Statesman and Society*, 2.8.91; *Guardian*, 4.3.91.
78. Chaplin, diary, 10.12.90; private interview.
79. Interview, Michael Chaplin, 22.12.95.
80. Interview 1, Tim Collins, 30.8.95.
81. Interview, David Cameron, 28.3.96.
82. Chaplin, diaries.
83. Interview 1, Andrew Lansley.
84. Interview 2, Graham Bright.
85. Interview 1, Barbara Wallis.
86. Interview, Debbie de Satge, 15.8.95.
87. Interview, Sir Percy Cradock, 15.4.96.
88. Ibid.
89. Interview, Sir Robin Catford, 16.8.95.
90. Private interview.
91. Thatcher (1993), p. 828.
92. Interview, Sir Charles Powell.
93. Interview, Lord Wright.
94. Interview, Sir Percy Cradock.
95. Ibid.
96. Interview 1, Nick True, 21.4.94.
97. Interview 2, Chris Patten.
98. *Sunday Times*, 30.12.90.
99. Interview, Debbie de Satge.
100. Interview, Sir Charles Powell.
101. Hogg and Hill (1995), pp. 12–13.
102. Major, sensitive to slighting remarks about his tendency for bathos, was later to regret uttering those words, even though they had defused tension at a difficult time. Interview, Jonathan Holborow, 1.5.96.
103. Hunt, diary, 29.11.90.
104. Hogg and Hill (1995), p. 13.
105. Ibid., p. 31.
106. HC Debs, 6th Series, vol. 181, cols 1012–16.
107. Hogg and Hill (1995), p. 32.
108. *Daily Telegraph*, 30.11.90.
109. Butler and Kavanagh (1992), p. 320.

TWELVE: WAR IN THE GULF

1. Hogg and Hill (1995), p. 37.
2. Interview, James Baker, 19.12.95.
3. Interview, Brent Scowcroft, 17.12.95.
4. Interview, Lord Craig, 17.7.95.
5. Interview 1, Raymond Seitz.
6. Interview, James Baker.
7. Interview 1, Raymond Seitz.
8. Interview, Sir Charles Powell.
9. Interview, George Bush, 19.12.95.
10. Interview, Brent Scowcroft.
11. Interview, George Bush.
12. Interview, John Major, Hugh Scully, 19.4.95.
13. Interview, Sir Antony Acland.
14. Private interview.
15. Interview, Sir Charles Powell.
16. Major, Scully.
17. Interview, Sir Antony Acland; *Sunday Times*, 23.12.90.
18. *The Times*, 31.12.90.
19. Private interview.
20. De la Billière (1992), p. 138.
21. Interview, Tom King, 11.1.96; de la Billière (1992), p. 125.
22. Private interview.
23. Ibid.
24. Interview 2, Gus O'Donnell, 8.8.95.
25. Major, Scully.
26. De la Billière (1992), pp. 185–91.
27. Interview, Sir Charles Powell.
28. Cited in Junor (1993), p. 222.
29. Hunt, diary, 17.1.91.
30. Interview, Lord Craig.
31. The Wakeham Committee was known as OPDG(MH) as opposed to the War Cabinet, known as OPDD(G). Hogg and Hill (1995), p. 41.
32. Major, Scully.
33. Private interview.
34. Major, Scully.
35. Michael Jones, *Sunday Times*, 3.3.91; interview, Neil Kinnock, 19.2.96.
36. Interview, Sir Charles Powell.
37. *Financial Times*, 22.1.91.
38. *Observer*, 13.1.91.
39. Interview, James Baker.
40. Freedman and Karsh (1991), pp. 272–4.
41. HC Debs, 6th Series, vol. 183, cols 734–825.
42. *Guardian*, 16.1.91.

43. Private information; *Guardian*, 18.1.91.
44. Hunt, diary, 17.1.91.
45. Hogg and Hill (1995), p. 42.
46. Hunt, diary, 17.1.91.
47. *Guardian*, 18.1.91.
48. Ibid., 19.1.91.
49. Hogg and Hill (1995), pp. 42–3; interview 1, Lady Hogg.
50. *Sunday Times*, 3.3.91; Chaplin, diary, 17.1.91.
51. Interview, Sir Patrick Hine, 12.2.96.
52. Hogg and Hill (1995), pp. 44–7.
53. Hunt, diary, 7.2.91.
54. Freedman and Karsh (1991), p. 385.
55. Hogg and Hill (1995), p. 48.
56. *Guardian*, 1.3.91.
57. HC Debs, 6th Series, vol. 186, col. 1120.
58. Interview, Brent Scowcroft.
59. Interview, Sir Percy Cradock.
60. Interview, Sir Patrick Hine.
61. Interview, Brent Scowcroft.
62. Interview, Sir Patrick Mayhew.
63. Major, Scully.
64. Interview, Sir Patrick Hine.
65. Chaplin, diary.
66. Interview, Alan Clark.
67. *Guardian*, 16.2.91.
68. Interview 3, Douglas Hurd, 13.9.95.
69. De la Billière (1992), pp. 321–2.
70. Hogg and Hill (1995), p. 48; Junor (1993), p. 227; *The Times*, 7.3.91.
71. Hunt, diary, 21.3.91.
72. William Wallace described the 'safe haven' idea as Major's 'distinctive' contribution to the Gulf crisis, in Kavanagh and Seldon (1994), p. 288.
73. Major, Scully.
74. Private interview.
75. *Guardian*, 10.4.91.
76. Interview 2, Michael Jay, 31.5.96.
77. Ibid.; interview, Sir David Hannay.
78. Private interview.
79. Interview, Sir Antony Acland.
80. Hunt, diary, 11.4.91.
81. Freedman and Karsh (1991), pp. 422–5.
82. Kavanagh and Seldon (1994), p. 288.
83. Chaplin, diary, 18.4.91; *Guardian*, 18.4.91.
84. Profile of Patrick Robertson, *Daily Telegraph*, 10.1.91.

85. Interview, Sir Christopher Mallaby, 21.2.96.
86. Interview, Sir John Kerr; interview 1, Douglas Hurd.
87. *Daily Telegraph*, 15.12.90.
88. Interview 1, Michael Jay, 22.5.96.
89. Ibid.
90. *Le Monde*, 17.12.90.
91. *Sunday Telegraph*, 6.1.91.
92. Interview 2, Lady Hogg, 18.10.95.
93. *Guardian*, 12.2.91.
94. Interview, Sir Christopher Mallaby.
95. Private interview.
96. Edward Llewellyn acted as Patten's assistant in drafting.
97. Patten had established contacts with the CDU as Director of the Conservative Research Department in the late 1970s. He had given an interview with Martin Jacques in *Marxism Today* (Feb. 1991) in which he had praised Christian democracy. Patten gleaned from Number Ten that his expressed enthusiasm for Christian Democrats was not welcomed. Interview 2, Chris Patten, 30.5.95.
98. Interview, Sir Charles Powell.
99. Interview 4, John Major; *Daily Telegraph*, 22.11.95.
100. Speech as reported in the *Guardian*, 12.3.91.
101. *Daily Telegraph*, 22.11.95.
102. *The Times*, 12.3.91.
103. *Sunday Times*, 10.3.91.
104. HC Debs, 6th Series, vol. 189, col. 805.
105. *Guardian*, 13.3.91.
106. *The Times*, 16.3.91.
107. *European*, 15.3.91.
108. *Guardian*, 16.3.91.
109. Thatcher (1995), p. 475.
110. Letter to author.
111. *Guardian*, 13.3.91.

THIRTEEN: REVERSING THE CHARGE

1. Butler, Adonis and Travers (1994) is a full study of the episode.
2. Lawson (1992), pp. 561–85.
3. Interview 3, David Hunt, 3.1.96.
4. Butler, Adonis and Travers (1994), p. 289.
5. Hunt, diary, 29.11.90.
6. Interview 1, Lord Wakeham.
7. Hogg and Hill (1995), p. 59. Their chapter on the poll tax (pp. 55–70) is a particularly informative section of their book.
8. Hogg and Hill (1995), pp. 63–5.
9. *Independent*, 17.1.91.
10. Chaplin, diary, 25.2.91.
11. Hogg and Hill (1995), p. 64.
12. Private interview.
13. Interview, Bill Robinson, 20.6.95.
14. Interview 1, David Hunt, 24.10.95.
15. Interview, John Mills.
16. HC Debs, 6th Series, vol. 188, cols 182–7.
17. Smith (1992), p. 200.
18. Michael White, *Guardian*, 20.3.91.
19. Private information.
20. Butler, Adonis and Travers (1994), p. 175.
21. Standing for the eighth 'General' or *ad hoc* Cabinet committee to be set up under Major. It was shadowed by a back-up group entitled 'GEN 14'. Hogg and Hill (1995), p. 60.
22. Private interview.
23. Private interview.
24. Private information; Butler, Adonis and Travers (1994), p. 173.
25. Interview, Michael Portillo, 18.7.97.
26. Crick (1997), p. 364.
27. Private interview.
28. Private information. Mrs Thatcher's Policy Unit had been heavily involved in bringing in the tax in the first place.
29. Interview, Roger Bright.
30. Private information.
31. Ibid.
32. Chaplin, diary 19.2.91.
33. Private interview.
34. *Independent*, 4.3.91.
35. *Guardian*, 11.3.91.
36. Ibid., 13.3.91.
37. Hogg and Hill (1995), p. 62.
38. Butler, Adonis and Travers (1994), p. 174.
39. *Financial Times*, 11.3.91.

40. *Guardian*, 18.3.91.
41. Lawson (1992), p. 1005.
42. HC Debs, 6th Series, vol. 188, cols 630–37.
43. Chaplin, diary, 24.3.91.
44. HC Debs, 6th Series, vol. 188, cols 761–2.
45. Michael Jones, *Sunday Times*, 31.3.91; Joe Rogaly, *Financial Times*, 28.3.91.
46. Hogg and Hill (1995), p. 66.
47. *Time* magazine, 20.5.91.
48. *Spectator*, 23.3.91.
49. Private information.
50. HC Debs, 6th series, vol. 188, cols 401–5.
51. *The Economist*, 30.3.91.
52. Hogg and Hill (1995), pp. 68–70.
53. Butler, Adonis and Travers (1994), p. 178.
54. Ken Young in Kavanagh and Seldon (1994), p. 87.
55. Patten himself felt that the loss of his seat in Bath was due to a combination of the local unpopularity of the poll tax and the uniform business rate.
56. McLean and Smith in Heath et al. (1994) calculate that this factor might have been worth nine seats in the 1992 election, reducing the Conservative majority to three.
57. Butler, Adonis and Travers (1994), p. 180.
58. Ridley (1991), pp. 134–5; Thatcher (1993), p. 667; Butler, Adonis and Travers (1994), pp. 287–8.
59. Butler, Adonis and Travers (1994), p. 182.
60. Private interview.
61. HC Debs, 6th Series, vol. 200, cols 244–5.
62. *The Times*, 10.5.90.
63. Butler, Adonis and Travers (1994), p. 170.
64. Crick (1997), p. 362.
65. Hogg and Hill (1995), p. 59.
66. Private interview.
67. Ibid.
68. Interview 9, Nick True, 14.12.96.
69. Private information.
70. HC Debs, 6th Series, vol. 188, cols 401–5.
71. Private information.
72. Interview 2, Lord Wakeham, 15.5.96.
73. Young (1990), pp. 90–94.
74. Interview, Alan Howarth. Major told Howarth that he agreed in devolving responsibility to local government, but it would be difficult to get the Treasury to agree.

FOURTEEN: A MAJORITE AGENDA

1. Private information.
2. Ibid.
3. Ibid.
4. Scott, in Kavanagh and Seldon (1994), p. 338.
5. Interview 1, Kenneth Clarke.
6. Alan Smithers in Peter Catterall (1992), p. 333.
7. *The Times*, 31.1.91.
8. Private information.
9. The text of this, and several other Major speeches of 1990–91, is in Major (1991).
10. Smithers in Catterall (1992), p. 333.
11. Hogg and Hill (1995), p. 89.
12. Private information.
13. Hogg and Hill (1995), p. 90.
14. *Guardian*, 21.5.91.
15. Private information.
16. Ibid.
17. Interview, Sir John Caines, 24.6.95.
18. Private information.
19. Interview, John Mills; letter, 6.11.96.
20. Major (1991), pp. 53–61.
21. *Guardian*, 4.7.91.
22. *Financial Times*, 5.7.91.
23. *Times Educational Supplement*, 16.7.91; cited by Smithers in Catterall (1992), p. 337.
24. Interview 1, Lady Hogg.
25. See Chapter 7.
26. Willman in Kavanagh and Seldon (1994), p. 64.
27. Interview 4, Nick True, 1.6.95.
28. *Independent*, 4.3.91.
29. Memo, True to Hogg, 12.3.91; interview 4, Nick True.
30. Hogg and Hill (1995), p. 94.

31. Ibid., p. 94, n. 3.
32. *Observer*, 24.3.91.
33. *Sunday Telegraph*, 24.3.91; *Sunday Times*, 24.3.91.
34. *Guardian*, 26.3.91.
35. *Spectator*, 23.3.91; *Independent on Sunday*, 24.3.91.
36. Interview 4, Nick True.
37. Interview 1, Lady Hogg.
38. Record of Chequers meeting, 24–25.3.91.
39. Memo, PM's office to departmental ministers, 26.3.91; interview 4, Nick True.
40. *Independent*, 11.5.91.
41. Policy Unit Memo, 7.5.91; private information.
42. Private interview.
43. Interview 2, Francis Maude.
44. Private interview.
45. Interview 2, Francis Maude.
46. Minute, True to PM, 13.5.91; interview 4, Nick True.
47. Interview 4, Nick True.
48. Interview 1, Madsen Pirie, 12.4.95.
49. Interview 1, John Redwood, 24.10.95.
50. Hogg and Hill (1995), pp. 96–7.
51. *Guardian*, 7.6.91.
52. Hogg and Hill (1995), p. 97.
53. Interview 2, Francis Maude.
54. Interview 4, Nick True.
55. Note to Nick True, 11.5.91; private information.
56. Interview 2, Francis Maude.
57. Hogg and Hill (1995), pp. 100–101.
58. Willman in Kavanagh and Seldon (1994), pp. 64–5.
59. Interview 1, Tim Collins.
60. Junor (1993), p. 308.
61. Blyth had spent five years in Whitehall as Head of Defence Sales, 1981–5, and believes the combination of senior positions in the private and public sectors explain his selection; interview, Lord Blyth, 19.2.96.
62. Interview, Howard Davies.
63. Private interview.
64. Kavanagh in Kavanagh and Seldon (1994), pp. 3–17.
65. *The Times*, 25.1.91.

FIFTEEN: A NEW STYLE?

1. Private interview.
2. Sir Charles Powell to Penny Junor, Junor (1993), p. 209.
3. Interview 2, Sir Graham Bright.
4. Interview 3, Jonathan Hill.
5. Hogg and Hill (1995), p. 19.
6. Interview, John Holroyd, 23.2.96.
7. Interview 3, John Hill.
8. Interview 2, Sir Graham Bright.
9. Private interview.
10. Ibid.
11. Hogg and Hill (1995), p. 35.
12. Interview 1, Douglas Hurd.
13. Interview, Debbie de Satge.
14. Interview, Sir Robin Catford; interview, John Holroyd.
15. *The Times*, 27.1.92.
16. Interview 1, Chris Patten.
17. Interview 2, Tristan Garel-Jones.
18. Private interview.
19. Interview, Steve Bell, 12.2.97.
20. *Guardian*, 7.3.91; interview, George Jones, 19.4.96.
21. Bell (1994).
22. The diaries have been compiled and published in several volumes. For Harris's opinion, see *Sunday Times*, 5.4.92.
23. *Sunday Times*, 4.4.91; *Guardian*, 3.12.91; *Independent on Sunday*, 10.5.92.
24. *Sunday Times*, 15.8.93.
25. *Guardian*, 7.3.91.
26. Interview 1, Barbara Wallis.
27. *Guardian*, 7.3.91.
28. *Sunday Times*, 31.3.91.
29. *Daily Telegraph*, 3.1.56.
30. *Daily Telegraph*, 27.3.91.
31. *Guardian*, 17.4.91.
32. Chaplin, diary, 18.3.91.
33. Ibid., early April 1991.
34. Ibid., 21.4.91.
35. *The Times*, 17.4.91.
36. Interview, Norma Major.
37. Major (1996), pp. 259–60.
38. Interview 4, Peter Golds, 12.6.96.
39. Interview 1, Peter Golds.
40. Junor (1993), p. 209; Baker (1993), p.

427. I admit to have modified my earlier view in Kavanagh and Seldon (1994), p. 166.
41. Private interview.
42. Ibid.
43. Seldon in Kavanagh and Seldon (1994), pp. 161–2.
44. Chaplin, diary, 16.1.92.
45. Kavanagh and Seldon (1994), p. 166; private information.
46. Hennessy (1992), p. 15.
47. Interview 1, John Redwood.
48. Lewis Baston and Anthony Seldon in Ball and Seldon (1996), pp. 64–5.
49. Interview 4, John Major.
50. Interview 2, Chris Patten.
51. Private interview.
52. Ibid.
53. Interview 1, Kenneth Clarke.
54. Interview 2, Kenneth Clarke, 19.6.97.
55. Botham was a briliant but mercurial cricketer, a prominent figure in England sides in the 1980s. Joseph Chamberlain was the pivotal figure in late-Victorian party politics.
56. Interview 2, Peter Brooke, 23.10.95.
57. Interview 1, William Waldegrave, 4.5.94.
58. June Burnham and G. W. Jones with Robert Elgie, BJ Pol. Sci. 5, 25, pp. 551–63.
59. HC Debs, 6th Series, vol. 238, cols 162–3; cited in Burnham et al., p. 555.
60. Burnham et al., pp. 556–7.
61. Peter Riddell in Seldon and Kavanagh (1994), p. 59.
62. Public Information Office Factsheet 46, House of Commons (1994).
63. Interview, William Chapman, 22.5.96; interview, Roy Stone, 24.4.96.
64. R. L. Borthwick in Franklin and Norton (1993), p. 89.
65. Derek Draper, Sunday Times, 27.7.97.
66. Interview, Neil Kinnock.
67. Interview, David Cameron.

68. Hogg and Hill (1995), p. 33; Burnham et al., p. 553.
69. Interview, Dominic Morris, 21.9.95.
70. Burnham et al., p. 553.
71. Franklin and Norton (1993).
72. Norton in Catterall (1993), p. 44.
73. HC Debs, 6th Series, vol. 194, cols 436–8.
74. Ibid., vol. 195, cols 1028–9.
75. Ibid., vol. 189, col. 566.
76. Interview, Neil Kinnock.
77. HC Debs, 6th Series, vol. 198, cols 23–4.
78. See Chapter 17.
79. Interview 1, Robin Squire.
80. Interview, Sir Ian McKellen, 8.3.96; Sunday Times, 29.9.91.
81. Private information.
82. Text for meeting with Major, Sir Ian McKellen papers.
83. HC Debs, 6th Series, vol. 195, col. 474.
84. Note of meeting, Major and McKellen, 24.9.91, McKellen papers.
85. Interview, Sir Ian McKellen; Daily Telegraph, 25.9.91.
86. Private information.
87. Letter, Major to McKellen, 16.10.91, McKellen papers.
88. Private papers.
89. The Times, 25.9.91.
90. Independent, 25.9.91.
91. Though Thatcher herself showed tolerant attitudes to gay men she knew personally.
92. The Times, 25.9.91.
93. Daily Telegraph, 25.9.91.
94. Guardian, 25.9.91.
95. The Times, 25.9.91; letter, McKellen to Major, 28.9.91, McKellen papers.
96. Interview, Sir Ian McKellen.
97. See Chapter 27.
98. Major's record on equal opportunities came under withering criticism shortly after this event from Paul Johnson, Spectator, 9.11.91.
99. Private information.
100. Private interview.

SIXTEEN: HIGH SUMMER, LOW SUMMER

1. Interview 2, Chris Patten.
2. Interview 1, Andrew Lansley.
3. Private interview.
4. Hogg and Hill (1995), p. 106.
5. Chaplin, diary, 11–12.1.91.
6. Hogg and Hill (1995), p. 107.

7. Private information.
8. Interview 2, Chris Patten.
9. Chaplin, diary, 1.2.91.
10. Interview 2, Chris Patten; interview 1, Sir Tim Bell.
11. Chaplin, diary, 27.1.91.
12. Interview 2, Chris Patten.
13. Chaplin, diary, 23.3.91.
14. Ibid.
15. Ibid., 22.4.91; Hogg and Hill (1995), p. 109.
16. Hogg and Hill (1995), p. 103.
17. Chaplin, diary, 26.4.91.
18. Hogg and Hill (1995), p. 221.
19. Chaplin, diary, 29.4.91.
20. Ibid., 26.4.91; Hogg and Hill (1995), p. 221.
21. Hogg and Hill (1995), p. 109.
22. *Guardian*, 4.2.91.
23. *Daily Telegraph*, 4.2.91.
24. *The Times*, 4.2.91.
25. Private information.
26. Hogg and Hill (1995), pp. 109–10.
27. Chaplin, diary, 3.5.91.
28. Ibid., 9.5.91.
29. Private information.
30. *The Times*, 23.5.91.
31. Hogg and Hill (1995), p. 112.
32. Chaplin, diary, 23.5.91.
33. *Guardian*, 15.6.91.
34. Interview 2, Robert Hayward, 10.4.95.
35. Baker (1993), pp. 433–6.
36. Private interview.
37. Interview 7, Nick True, 22.2.96.
38. Private information.
39. Interview, John MacGregor, 6.12.95.
40. Morris (1994), p. 309.
41. Interview 7, Nick True; interview 1, Kenneth Clarke.
42. Private information.
43. Private interview.
44. Private information. Douglas Hogg attended for the Foreign Office when Hurd was abroad.
45. *The Times*, 25.4.91, 29.4.91.
46. *Independent*, 25.4.91.
47. Interview, Lord Kingsdown.
48. HC Debs, 6th Series, vol. 195, cols 1028–9.
49. Private interview.
50. *Daily Telegraph*, 12.6.91.
51. *European*, 15.3.91.
52. Chaplin, diary, 10–15.6.91.
53. Hogg and Hill (1995), pp. 79–80.

54. *The Economist*, 22.6.91.
55. HC Debs, 6th Series, vol. 194, cols 21–41.
56. Interview 2, Tristan Garel-Jones; interview, Sir John Kerr.
57. Hogg and Hill (1995), pp. 81–2.
58. *Guardian*, 16.7.91.
59. Bush (1994), p. 420.
60. HC Debs, 6th Series, vol. 195, cols 662–81.
61. *Wall Street Journal*, 18.7.91.
62. Private interview.
63. Interview, Sir Rodric Braithwaite.
64. Ibid.
65. Ibid.
66. Private interview.
67. Ibid.
68. Ibid.
69. Ibid.
70. Interview, Sir Percy Cradock.
71. Hill in Catterall (1992), p. 137.
72. Interview, Sir Rodric Braithwaite.
73. Ibid.
74. Private interview.
75. Hogg and Hill (1995), pp. 51–3.
76. *The Times*, 30.8.91.
77. *New York Times*, 21.8.91.
78. Interview, President Bush.
79. Interview 2, Sir Robin Renwick, 10.1.96.
80. Interview, President Bush.
81. Private interview.
82. Cradock (1994), pp. 240–45.
83. Interview, Sir Percy Cradock.
84. *Far Eastern Economic Review*, 12.9.91.
85. Interview, Francis Cornish.
86. Cradock (1994), pp. 244–5.
87. Interview 1, Sue Tinson, 21.12.95.
88. Private interview.
89. Interview 1, Sir Andrew Turnbull, 12.4.95.
90. Interview 3, Sir Andrew Turnbull, 9.7.96.
91. Interview 3, Maurice Fraser, 28.11.95.
92. Interview, Sir Tim Lankester, 19.2.96.
93. Chaplin, diary, 2.9.91.
94. *The Economist*, 7.9.91.
95. Private information.
96. Interview, Edward Llewellyn; interview, Lord Kingsland, 4.7.96; private information.
97. Chaplin, diary, 15.9.91.
98. Hunt, diary, 26.9.91.
99. Chaplin, diary, 26.9.91.

100. *Independent*, 27.9.91.
101. Chaplin, diary, 26.9.91.
102. Ibid.
103. Interview 1, Lady Hogg.
104. Melinda Wittstock, *The Times*, 2.10.91.
105. *The Times*, 1.10.91.
106. Ibid., 2.10.91.
107. *Guardian*, 5.10.91.
108. *Daily Telegraph*, 5.10.91.
109. *The Times*, 10.10.91.

110. Hogg and Hill (1995), pp. 133–4.
111. *Sunday Express*, 13.10.91.
112. Interview 2, Lord Wakeham.
113. Chaplin, diary, 7.10.91.
114. Millar (1993), pp. 365–9.
115. Chaplin, diary, conference week.
116. *The Times*, 12.10.91.
117. Chaplin, diary, conference week.
118. *Independent*, 12.10.91.
119. *Daily Telegraph*, 10.10.91.

SEVENTEEN: MAASTRICHT AUTUMN

1. Stephens (1996), p. 189.
2. HC Debs, 6th Series, vol. 188, cols 164–6.
3. Ibid., vol. 191, col. 413.
4. Ibid., vol. 195, cols 1194–1202.
5. Hogg and Hill (1995), pp. 187–8.
6. Private interview.
7. Ibid.
8. Ibid.
9. Ibid.
10. Interview, Alastair Ross Goobey, 1.8.97.
11. Interview 2, Francis Maude; interview, Stephen Dorrell, 20.6.96.
12. Interview, Kenneth Baker.
13. Private interview.
14. Interview 2, David Mellor, 23.10.95.
15. Interview 3, John Major.
16. Interview 1, Norman Lamont, 17.5.94.
17. HC Debs, 6th Series, vol. 198, col. 31.
18. *The Times*, 1.11.91.
19. Alexander Eadie, HC Debs, 6th Series, vol. 198, col. 27.
20. Chaplin, diary, 30.10.91.
21. Ibid., 17–18.11.91.
22. Ibid., 22.11.91.
23. Ibid., 15.9.91.
24. Ibid.
25. Private interview.
26. *The Times*, 27.9.91.
27. *Independent*, 12.11.91.
28. *Guardian*, 12.11.91.
29. *Independent*, 16.11.91.
30. *Guardian*, 16.11.91.
31. *Independent*, 21.11.91.
32. HC Debs, 6th Series, vol. 199, cols 269–81.
33. *Guardian*, 21.11.91.
34. HC Debs, 6th Series, vol. 199, cols 293–8.

35. Thatcher (1995), pp. 479–80.
36. Chaplin, diary, 20.11.91.
37. HC Debs, 6th Series, vol. 199, col. 385.
38. Chaplin, diary, 21.11.91.
39. *Guardian*, 23.11.91.
40. Tories voting against were Biffen, N. Winterton, Browne, Shepherd, Body and Fairbairn. Abstainers were Tebbit, Taylor, Cran, Jessel, Gill, Cash, A. Winterton, Favell. There were also two Tory amendments, for a referendum and rejecting the principle of EMU. Over thirty MPs signed, including Aitken, Boyson, Gorman, Butcher, Lawrence, Bonsor and Carlisle.
41. Chaplin, diary, 25.11.91.
42. Letter, Hurd to author, 8.11.95.
43. Interview, Kenneth Baker; Baker (1993), pp. 439–45.
44. Private interview.
45. Letter, Hurd to author, 8.11.95.
46. Interview 1, David Mellor.
47. Chaplin, diary, 27.11.91.
48. Ibid., 2–6.12.91.
49. Hogg and Hill (1995), p. 147.
50. Interview, Sir Christopher Mallaby.
51. Minutes, Maastricht Conference, 9.12.91.
52. Hogg and Hill (1995), p. 140.
53. Ibid., pp. 150–54.
54. Private interview.
55. Hogg and Hill (1995), pp. 150–56.
56. Private interview.
57. Interview 4, Lady Hogg, 22.2.96.
58. *The Times*, 12.12.91.
59. Hogg and Hill (1995), p. 157, n. 7, say Major always disliked the phrase

'game set and match', which 'crept into the briefing'.

60. Private interview.
61. Butler and Westlake (1995), p. 34.
62. Interview, John Kerr.
63. *Daily Telegraph*, 11.12.91.
64. Interview 4, Douglas Hurd, 25.10.95.
65. *Independent*, 11.12.91.
66. HC Debs, 6th Series, vol. 200, col. 862.
67. *Independent*, 9.12.91.
68. *Daily Telegraph*, 13.12.91.
69. *Independent*, 12.12.91.
70. *Daily Telegraph*, 12.12.91; *The Economist*, 14.12.91.
71. Private information.
72. *The Times*, 20.12.91.
73. Bill Walker and John Browne also voted with Tebbit against the government. *The Times*, 20.12.91.
74. Hogg and Hill (1995), pp. 161–2.
75. Interview 3, Sue Tinson, 20.6.96.
76. *Spectator*, 14.12.91.
77. Chaplin, diary, 9–10.12.91.
78. Even Wallace, no arch Eurosceptic, wrote that 'substantial concessions were made on the Europeanisation of security and defence policy, and on the formalisation of cooperation among police and intelligence services: significant inroads into British sovereignty, successfully concealed from the British press and the Conservative backbenches and unnoticed by an ineffective

parliamentary opposition'. Wallace in Kavanagh and Seldon (1994), pp. 291–2.
79. *Independent*, 13.12.91; private information.
80. Thatcher (1995), p. 480.
81. Private interview.
82. Thatcher (1993), pp. 720–21.
83. Private interview.
84. Ibid.
85. Chaplin, diary, 3.1.91.
86. George Urban, *The Times*, 24.9.96.
87. The rumours did not reach print at the time.
88. Chaplin, diary, 25.1.91.
89. Private interview.
90. *The Times*, 9.3.91.
91. *Daily Express*, 9.3.91.
92. *The Times*, 4.4.91.
93. Private interview; Carol Thatcher (1996), pp. 275–6.
94. Private interviews.
95. *The Times*, 19.6.91.
96. Ibid.
97. Private interview.
98. *The Times*, 21.8.91.
99. Private interview.
100. Interview, Lord Parkinson.
101. Private interviews.
102. *The Times*, 23.11.91.
103. Private interview.
104. *Newsweek*, 27.4.92.
105. Private interview.
106. Ibid.
107. Ibid.

EIGHTEEN: THE LONG CAMPAIGN

1. Chaplin, diary, Jan. 1992.
2. Butler and Kavanagh (1992), pp. 77–86.
3. Hogg and Hill (1995), p. 165.
4. Butler and Kavanagh (1992), p. 85.
5. Ibid.
6. Private information.
7. Hogg's attitude to Central Office can be seen in Hogg and Hill (1995), pp. 164–8.
8. Interview 1, Lord Archer.
9. Private information.
10. Butler and Kavanagh (1992), pp. 30–31, 174–5.
11. Interview 1, John Major.
12. Ibid.
13. Hogg and Hill (1995), pp. 168–73; private information.
14. Chaplin, diary, 7–8.1.92.
15. Interview, Neil Kinnock.
16. Interview, Sir David Hannay.
17. Private information.
18. Ibid.
19. Ibid.
20. HC Debs, 6th Series, vol. 203, col. 21.
21. Ibid., col. 25.
22. Hogg and Hill (1995), pp. 191–3.
23. Chaplin, diary, 27.1.92.

24. Ibid., 2.3.92.
25. Private interview.
26. Hogg and Hill (1995), pp. 176–82.
27. Chaplin, diary, 9.1.92.
28. Interview 2, Chris Patten; private interview.
29. Chaplin, diary, 10.1.92.
30. Ibid., early Feb. 1992.
31. Ibid., 17.2.92.
32. Ibid.
33. Ibid., 11.3.92.
34. Hogg and Hill (1995), p. 180.
35. Interview 1, Ian Lang.
36. Ibid.
37. *The Times*, 22.2.92.
38. *Guardian*, 11.2.92.
39. Interview 2, Alistair Cooke, 23.12.94.
40. Interview, Lord Fraser, 5.6.96; letter, Ian Lang, 20.10.96.
41. Interview 1, Ian Lang.
42. Gamble in Kavanagh and Seldon (1994), pp. 386–7.
43. Interview 1, Lord Archer.
44. Interview 1, John Major.
45. Interview 5, John Major.
46. Interview 2, Peter Brooke.
47. Mallie and McKittrick (1996), p. 106.
48. Arthur and Jeffrey (1996), p. 129.
49. Mallie and McKittrick (1996), p. 126.
50. *Independent*, 10.12.91.
51. Mallie and McKittrick (1996), p. 111.
52. Interview, James Molyneaux, 27.9.95.
53. Private interview.
54. Ibid.
55. Interview 2, Peter Brooke.
56. Mallie and McKittrick (1996), pp. 115–17.
57. Ibid., pp. 114–15.
58. Interview 2, Peter Brooke.
59. Ibid.
60. Private interview.
61. Ibid.
62. *The Times*, 11.1.92.
63. *Daily Telegraph*, 18.1.92.
64. *Guardian*, 7.2.92.
65. *Sunday Telegraph*, 19.1.92.
66. Private interview.
67. *Guardian*, 12.2.92.
68. Private interview; Ryan (1994), p. 196.
69. Interview, Albert Reynolds.
70. Interview, Dick Spring, 12.10.95.
71. Interview, Albert Reynolds.
72. Ibid.
73. Chaplin, diary, 2.3.92.
74. Interview 2, Chris Patten; Hogg and Hill (1995), pp. 178–82.
75. Interview, John Mills.
76. Interview 5, Andrew Lansley, 24.6.96.
77. Chaplin, diary, 2.3.92.
78. Hogg and Hill (1995), p. 182.
79. Interview 1, Lady Hogg.
80. Private interview.
81. Hogg and Hill (1995), p. 182.
82. Interview 5, Andrew Lansley.
83. Interview 2, Andrew Lansley, 21.2.95.
84. Interview 4, Lady Hogg.
85. *Independent on Sunday*, 15.3.92; Hogg and Hill (1995), pp. 194–7.
86. Private information.
87. *Sunday Times*, 15.3.92.
88. Chaplin, diary, 17–21.2.92.
89. Interview, Bill Robinson.
90. Stephens (1996), p. 196.
91. Chaplin, diary, 10.3.92.
92. *Guardian*, 11.3.92.
93. Anatole Kaletsky, *The Times*, 11.3.92; *The Economist*, 14.3.92; see also *Financial Times*, 11.3.92.
94. *Sunday Times*, 15.3.92.
95. Interview 2, Norman Lamont.
96. Hogg and Hill (1995), p. 197.
97. Butler and Kavanagh (1992), p. 86.
98. Stephens (1996), p. 197.
99. Private information.
100. Butler and Kavanagh (1992), p. 100.
101. *Guardian*, 12.3.92.

NINETEEN: GENERAL ELECTION

1. Interview 1, John Major.
2. Private interview.
3. *Observer*, 15.3.92.
4. BBC Poll of Polls, *Daily Telegraph*, 12.3.92.
5. *The Times*, 12.3.92.
6. *Sunday Times*, 15.3.92.
7. *The Times*, 12.3.92.
8. Chaplin, diary, 12.3.92.
9. HC Debs, 6th Series, vol. 205, col. 968.
10. Layton-Henry in Catterall (1993), pp. 405–7.

11. *Observer*, 15.3.92.
12. Major (1992), p. 16.
13. The speeches are set out in Major (1992), compiled by Alistair Cooke.
14. Interview 1, John Major; Millar (1993), pp. 369–71.
15. Hogg and Hill (1995), pp. 209–10; Butler and Kavanagh (1992), p. 102.
16. *Guardian*, 16.3.92.
17. Norma Major, *Sunday Express*, 22.3.92.
18. *Daily Telegraph*, 17.3.92.
19. Interview, Debbie de Satge.
20. Butler and Kavanagh (1992), p. 109.
21. Hogg and Hill (1995), p. 211.
22. Butler and Kavanagh (1992), p. 103.
23. Ibid., p. 105.
24. Interview 5, Andrew Lansley; *Independent*, 18.3.92. The irony on timing was that Labour advanced its shadow budget fearing it would be overshadowed by the Conservative manifesto.
25. *Independent*, 19.3.92.
26. Hogg and Hill (1995), pp. 218–21.
27. Interview 1, Chris Patten.
28. Interview 1, John Major.
29. Hogg and Hill (1995), pp. 224–5; interview 1, John Major.
30. Butler and Kavanagh (1992), p. 114.
31. *Daily Telegraph*, 21.3.92.
32. Philip Webster and Robin Oakley, *The Times*, 21.3.92.
33. *Daily Telegraph*, 20.3.92.
34. Interview 1, John Major.
35. *Sunday Times*, 22.3.92.
36. *Sunday Telegraph*, 22.3.92.
37. *Guardian*, 23.3.92.
38. *Daily Telegraph*, 23.3.92.
39. Butler and Kavanagh (1992), pp. 122–7.
40. Major (1992), pp. 36–43.
41. George Jones, *Daily Telegraph*, 28.3.92.
42. Interview 1, John Major.
43. *Sunday Times*, 29.3.92.
44. Hogg and Hill (1995), p. 228.
45. Stephen Sherbourne, who had worked in Number Ten under Mrs Thatcher, returned to help out during the general election. Interview, Stephen Sherbourne, 12.3.96.
46. Private information; *Daily Express*, 30.3.92.
47. *The Times*, 31.3.92.
48. *Sunday Times*, 5.4.92.
49. *Evening Chronicle*, 31.3.92.
50. Hogg and Hill (1995), p. 241.
51. Interview, Alastair Ross Goobey.
52. Butler and Kavanagh (1992), p. 125.
53. *Sunday Times*, 5.4.92.
54. Anthony Howard, *Guardian*, 3.4.92.
55. *Guardian*, 6.4.92.
56. Letter, Peter Riddell to author, 23.10.96.
57. Interview 1, John Major.
58. Ibid.
59. Hogg and Hill (1995), p. 251.
60. Butler and Kavanagh (1992), pp. 130–31.
61. Ibid., p. 130.
62. Hogg and Hill (1995), pp. 251–2.
63. *Sunday Telegraph*, 12.4.92.
64. *Financial Times*, 9.4.92.
65. Interview 1, Lord Archer.
66. Ibid.
67. Interview 1, Peter Brown.
68. Interview 1, John Major.
69. Ibid.
70. Hogg and Hill (1995), pp. 256–7.
71. Interview 1, John Major.
72. Hogg and Hill (1995), p. 258.
73. Interview 1, Peter Brown.
74. Ibid.
75. Private interview.
76. Hogg and Hill (1995), p. 259; private interview.
77. Interview 1, John Major.
78. Butler and Kavanagh (1992), p. 108.
79. Ibid., pp. 110–11.
80. Interview, Patrick Rock, 14.3.96.
81. Riddell in Seldon and Kavanagh (1994), p. 50.
82. Interview 2, Tristan Garel-Jones.
83. *Sunday Times*, 12.4.92.
84. *Daily Telegraph*, 11.4.92.
85. *Sun*, 11.4.92; *Daily Mail*, 10.4.92.
86. Interview 1, John Major.
87. Interview, Neil Kinnock.
88. Private interview.
89. Interview 2, Chris Patten.
90. Interview 1, John Major.
91. Interview 2, Peter Brooke.
92. Interview 1, Chris Patten.
93. Interview, Sir Percy Cradock.
94. Private interview.
95. Interview 2, Peter Brooke.
96. Interview 2, Tristan Garel-Jones.
97. Interview, Sir Patrick Mayhew.
98. Interview, Keith Hampson, 22.7.96.
99. Private interview.

TWENTY: INDIAN SUMMER

1. Interview 5, Nick True, 30.10.95.
2. Interview 6, Jonathan Hill, 20.12.95.
3. Private information.
4. *Newsweek*, 27.4.92.
5. *The Times*, 22.4.92.
6. Interview, Sir Bernard Ingham.
7. HC Debs, 6th Series, vol. 207, col. 64.
8. *The Times*, 7.5.92.
9. HC Debs, 6th Series, vol. 207, cols 70–71.
10. Robin Oakley, *The Times*, 7.5.92.
11. *Guardian*, 8.5.92.
12. *The Times*, 9.5.92.
13. Interview 2, Andrew Lansley.
14. Private interview.
15. Thatcher (1995), p. 491.
16. HC Debs, 6th Series, vol. 208, cols 265–6.
17. Stephens (1996), p. 204.
18. Private interview.
19. Ibid.
20. *Spectator*, 13.6.92.
21. Interview, John Major, *Poisoned Chalice*.
22. Private interview; *The Times*, 3.6.92.
23. Interview 1, Sir Rodric Braithwaite.
24. Interview 4, Douglas Hurd.
25. Interview, Bill Robinson.
26. Stephens (1992), p. 205.
27. Interview, John Major, *Poisoned Chalice*; Stephens (1996), pp. 206–7.
28. HC Debs, 6th Series, vol. 208, cols 827, 830.
29. Private interview.
30. Interview 1, Michael Jay.
31. Interview, Michael Gove, 2.4.96.
32. Gorman (1993), pp. 54–5.
33. Stephens (1996), p. 204.
34. Private interview.
35. Interview 4, Douglas Hurd.
36. *The Times*, 12.6.92.
37. Baker, Gamble and Ludlam (1993).
38. Stephens (1996), pp. 205–6.
39. Private interviews.
40. Private interview.
41. Interview 2, Chris Patten.
42. Interview 2, Andrew Lansley.
43. A symbolic blow to economic optimism came in May, when the developers of Canary Wharf went into receivership. The development's tall tower rising from reclaimed dockland in east London had become an icon of Thatcherism, being 'topped out' in the week she was overthrown. Major refused to bail out the developers, an affirmation of free market faith that impressed David Poole, a new recruit to the Policy Unit. Interview 2, Lord Poole, 22.5.96.
44. Stephens (1996), p. 207.
45. *Guardian*, 20.7.92.
46. Ibid., 23.7.92.
47. Ibid., 15.7.92, 16.7.92; *Independent on Sunday*, 29.7.92.
48. Stephens (1996), pp. 211–19.
49. Interview, Philip Stephens, 3.4.96; *Daily Mail*, 17.7.92.
50. Interview, Michael Jones, 6.3.96.
51. *Sunday Times*, 2.8.92.
52. Neil (1996), pp. 1–11, discusses this episode in considerable detail.
53. Interview, Max Hastings, 2.4.96.
54. Private interview.
55. Ibid.
56. Interview 3, Sir Stephen Wall, 4.7.97.
57. *People*, 19.7.92.
58. *The Times*, 21.7.92.
59. Ibid., 26.4.92.
60. *Independent*, 27.5.92.
61. *The Times*, 29.5.92.
62. Serialisation began in the *Sunday Times*, 7.6.92.
63. *The Times*, 11.6.92.
64. Private interview.
65. Hogg and Hill (1995), p. 53, n. 10.
66. Private interviews.
67. Interview 2, Sir Robin Renwick.
68. Ibid.
69. Interview, Patrick Rock; private interview.
70. HC Debs, 6th Series, vol. 209, cols 649–64.
71. Interview, Sir David Hannay.
72. *Guardian*, 6.7.92.
73. *Independent*, 30.6.92.
74. *Guardian*, 29.6.92.
75. Ibid., 8.7.92.
76. *Independent*, 9.7.92.
77. *Guardian*, 11.7.92.
78. Private interview.
79. Interview, Sir Percy Cradock.

80. Private interview.
81. Vulliamy (1994) is the account of a journalist who went to Omarska.
82. Interview, Norman Stone, 21.1.96.
83. Private interview.
84. *New York Times*, 6.8.92, cited in Thatcher (1995), pp. 515–16.
85. Interview 1, Raymond Seitz.
86. Private interview.
87. Ibid.

88. *The Times*, 19.8.96; Owen (1995), pp. 14–29.
89. Private interview.
90. Interview, Dick Cheney, 19.12.95.
91. *The Times*, 27.8.92.
92. *Daily Telegraph*, 28.8.92.
93. *The Times*, 28.8.92.
94. Bennett (1995), p. 193.
95. Malcolm (1994), pp. 244–7.
96. Interview 3, John Major.

TWENTY-ONE: BLACK SEPTEMBER

1. Interview 3, John Major.
2. Stephens (1996), p. 226.
3. Interview 3, John Major.
4. Private interview.
5. Connolly (1995), pp. 144–6.
6. Stephens (1996), p. 229.
7. Ibid., pp. 233, 229.
8. Ibid., pp. 146–7.
9. Interview, Lord Kingsdown.
10. Private interview; Stephens (1996), pp. 231–2.
11. Private interview.
12. Interview 3, John Major.
13. Private interview.
14. *Guardian*, 1.12.92.
15. *Financial Times*, 11.9.92.
16. Ibid.; *The Times*, 11.9.92.
17. Reported in the *Daily Telegraph*, 11.9.92.
18. Private interview.
19. Private interview.
20. The motive supplied by Connolly (1995), p. 145.
21. Private interview.
22. Ibid.
23. Ibid.
24. Ibid.
25. Junor (1993), pp. 258–9.
26. Ibid., p. 259.
27. Stephens (1996), pp. 236–8.
28. Private interview.
29. Private information; Stephens (1996), pp. 239–40.
30. *Financial Times*, 15.9.92.
31. *Daily Telegraph*, 16.9.92.
32. Stephens (1996), p. 242.
33. Interview 3, John Major.
34. *Sunday Times*, 20.9.92.
35. Stephens (1996), p. 243.
36. Private interview.

37. Stephens (1996), p. 247.
38. Private diary, 16.9.92.
39. Stephens (1996), pp. 247–9.
40. Interview, Stephen Milligan, *Panorama*, October 1992.
41. *Sunday Times*, 20.9.92.
42. Private information; Stephens (1996), pp. 249–51.
43. Interview 2, Lord Wakeham.
44. Private interview.
45. Ibid.
46. Stephens (1996), pp. 245–6.
47. *Guardian*, 17.9.92.
48. Fowler, *Express*, 4.5.97.
49. Private interview.
50. Ibid.
51. Ibid.
52. Ibid.
53. Interview 2, Jonathan Hill, 30.1.95.
54. Interview, Lord Kingsdown.
55. *Daily Telegraph*, 17.9.92.
56. Interview, Max Hastings.
57. Stephens (1996), p. 262.
58. Interview 3, Norman Lamont, 21.7.97.
59. *The Times*, 17.9.92.
60. Interview, Alastair Ross Goobey.
61. *Independent*, 17.9.92.
62. *Daily Telegraph*, 17.9.92.
63. *The Times*, 17.9.92.
64. *Sunday Times*, 20.9.92.
65. *The Times*, 18.9.92.
66. Private interviews; *Financial Times*, 18.9.92.
67. *Independent*, 18.9.92.
68. *The Times*, 18.9.92.
69. Gallup survey, *Daily Telegraph*, 19.9.92.
70. Gorman (1993), p. 71.
71. *Daily Telegraph*, 18.9.92.

72. John Wilkinson, HC Debs, 6th Series, vol. 212, col. 3.
73. Private diary, 20.9.92.
74. Private interview.
75. Fowler, *Express*, 4.5.97.
76. Private interview.
77. For a vivid Eurosceptic perspective on the debate, see Gorman (1993), pp. 71–81.
78. HC Debs, 6th Series, vol. 212, col. 4.
79. Ibid., col. 10.
80. Ibid., col. 12.
81. *The Times*, 26.9.92.
82. Crewe (1994), pp. 107–10.
83. Letter, Edmund Dell to author, 8.5.97.
84. Stephens (1996), pp. 252–7.
85. *Sunday Times*, 13.9.92.
86. *The Times*, 23.9.92.
87. Interview 2, David Mellor.
88. *The Times*, 25.9.92.

TWENTY-TWO: 'THE WORST PERIOD BY FAR'

1. Interview 3, John Major.
2. *Sunday Times*, 4.10.92.
3. Neil (1996), p. 9.
4. *Daily Telegraph*, 2.10.92.
5. *Independent*, 1.10.92.
6. *Daily Mail*, 29.9.92.
7. *Independent*, 1.10.92.
8. *Sunday Times*, 4.10.92.
9. *Independent on Sunday*, 11.10.92.
10. *The Times*, 7.10.92.
11. Private interviews.
12. Letter, Douglas Hurd to author, 25.4.97.
13. *Independent*, 7.10.92.
14. *Independent on Sunday*, 11.10.92.
15. *Daily Telegraph*, 7.10.92.
16. Michael Jones, *Sunday Times*, 11.10.92; private interview.
17. *Sunday Times*, 11.10.92.
18. *European*, 8.10.92.
19. *Independent*, 8.10.92.
20. *Guardian*, 8.10.92.
21. Private interview.
22. *The Times*, 8.10.92.
23. *Independent on Sunday*, 11.10.92; letter, Peter Riddell to author, 23.10.96.
24. Interview 1, Sir Ronald Millar, 21.12.95.
25. *The Times, Sun, Daily Mail*, 10.10.92.
26. *Daily Telegraph*, 6.10.92.
27. *Sunday Telegraph*, 11.10.92.
28. Interview 2, John Major.
29. Interview 2, Lord Wakeham.
30. Private interview.
31. *Sunday Times*, 25.10.92.
32. Private interviews.
33. Ibid.
34. *Sunday Times*, 25.10.92.
35. Junor (1993), p. 274.
36. Interview 2, Andrew Lansley.
37. Interview, Keith Hampson.
38. *Sunday Times*, 18.10.92.
39. *The Times*, 16.10.92.
40. Ibid., 16, 17.10.92.
41. *Independent on Sunday, Sunday Express*, 18.10.92.
42. *Independent*, 17.10.92; *The Economist*, 24.10.92.
43. Private interview.
44. *Sunday Times*, 25.10.92.
45. Private interview.
46. *Independent on Sunday, Sunday Times*, 25.10.92; private interview.
47. *Guardian*, 22.10.92.
48. Interview 2, Chris Patten.
49. Graham Paterson and Andrew Pierce, *The Times*, 21.10.92.
50. *Guardian*, 22.10.92.
51. Interview, Simon Jenkins, 10.2.97.
52. *European*, 22.10.92.
53. Interview, Robert Hughes.
54. Interview 1, Lord Poole, 8.2.96; letter, Lord Poole to author, 7.2.97.
55. Private interview.
56. Private interviews.
57. Private interview.
58. Ibid.
59. Ibid.
60. *Independent on Sunday*, 25.10.92.
61. *Independent*, 21.10.92.
62. Private interview.
63. *Sunday Times*, 25.10.92.
64. Private interview.
65. *Guardian*, 30.10.92.
66. Private interview.
67. Interview 2, Norman Lamont.
68. *Sunday Times*, 18.10.92.
69. Private interviews.
70. Interview 3, Norman Lamont.
71. Private interviews.

72. Private information.
73. *Daily Telegraph*, 17.10.92.
74. *The Times*, 23.10.92.
75. Private interview.
76. *Sun*, 24.10.92.
77. Interview, Andrew Neil, *Panorama*, 2.10.92.
78. Private interview.
79. Interview, Andrew Neil, *Panorama*; *Sunday Times*, 25.10.92.
80. *Independent*, 27.10.92.
81. Interview, Don Macintyre, 17.12.96.

82. Private interviews.
83. *Independent*, 27.10.92.
84. Ibid., 30.10.92.
85. Baker, Gamble and Ludlam (1993), pp. 151–66.
86. Ibid., p. 163.
87. *Independent*, 5.11.92.
88. Private interview.
89. *Spectator*, 31.10.92; *The Times*, 28.10.92.
90. *Guardian*, 5.11.92.
91. *Sunday Times*, 8.11.92.

TWENTY-THREE: DEEP WINTER

1. Interview 2, Peter Brooke.
2. Private interview.
3. Ministerial Committees of the Cabinet, Membership and Terms of Reference, Cabinet Office, 10.2.94; Seldon in Seldon and Kavanagh (1994), p. 164.
4. Gove (1995), p. 226.
5. *Sunday Times*, 8.11.92.
6. *Financial Times*, 13.11.92.
7. Catterall (1993), p. 11.
8. *The Times*, 10.11.92.
9. Private interviews.
10. Llewellyn in Catterall (1993), pp. 195–7.
11. Private interview.
12. Ibid.
13. Ibid.
14. *Independent*, 13.11.92.
15. *Sunday Times*, 15.11.92.
16. Interview 1, Lord Mackay, 23.6.97.
17. *Sun*, 26.11.92; *The Times*, 30.11.92; Barnes in Catterall (1995), pp. 160–68.
18. Private interview.
19. Interview 2, Andrew Lansley.
20. Hennessy in Catterall (1993), p. 33.
21. Private interviews.
22. Private information.
23. Catterall (1993), p. 2.
24. Private interview.
25. Interview 3, Sir Graham Bright, 30.11.95.
26. Private interview.
27. HC Debs, 6th Series, vol. 215, col. 845.
28. Peter Riddell, *The Times*, 10.12.92.
29. Hennessy in Catterall (1993), pp. 33–4.
30. *Independent*, 27.11.92.

31. *The Times*, 22.12.92.
32. Private interview.
33. Private information. Major visited Brussels (23 November), Rome and Athens (27–8 November), Luxembourg, Madrid and Lisbon (30 November–1 December), Copenhagen (2 December), The Hague (6 December) and Dublin (7 December).
34. *Guardian*, 14.12.92.
35. *The Times*, 12.11.92.
36. *Sunday Times*, 13.12.92.
37. Private interview.
38. *Independent*, 30.11.92.
39. *Guardian*, 14.12.92.
40. Private interview.
41. *The Times*, 14.12.92.
42. Interview 3, Douglas Hurd.
43. *Spectator*, 12.12.92.
44. *Daily Telegraph*, 14.12.92.
45. Baker himself denies he led the vote of congratulations in Cabinet after Maastricht. Private information.
46. Private interviews; *The Times*, 19.12.92.
47. Private interview.
48. Interview, Jonathan Powell, 5.2.96.
49. Interview 2, Raymond Seitz, 16.5.96.
50. Private interview.
51. *The Times*, 21.12.92.
52. US State Department, Press Release, 28.12.92, vol. 3, no. 52.
53. Vulliamy (1994), p. 246.
54. Private interview.
55. *New York Times*, 21.12.92.
56. Interview, President Bush.
57. Interview 2, Robin Renwick.

58. *The Times*, 21.12.92.
59. Ibid., 23.12.92; Stewart (1993), p. 175.
60. Interview, Robert Atkins.
61. *Financial Times*, 18.12.92.
62. Junor (1993), p. 185.
63. *Observer*, 16.8.92, 23.8.92; *Evening Standard*, 28.7.92, 4.8.92.
64. Private interview.
65. *The Times*, 22.1.93.
66. Interview, Howard Davies.
67. Private interview.
68. *Guardian*, 26.1.93.
69. *New Statesman and Society*, 29.1.93.
70. Interview, Steve Platt, 11.6.96.
71. *New Statesman and Society*, 29.1.93.
72. *Daily Express*, 28.1.93.
73. Interview, Steve Platt.
74. Private diary, 23, 28.1.93.
75. Connolly (1995), p. 221; *The Times*, 22.1.93.
76. Connolly (1995), pp. 221–2.
77. Private interview.
78. Interview 6, John Major, 17.1.97.

TWENTY-FOUR: BROKEN SPRING

1. Private interviews; *Sunday Times*, 20.12.92.
2. *Sunday Times*, 27.12.92.
3. Ibid.
4. *Independent*, 4.1.93.
5. Paul Johnson, *Sunday Times*, 20.12.92.
6. *Daily Express*, 2.1.93.
7. *The Times*, 31.12.92.
8. *Sunday Times*, 27.12.92.
9. Private information; *Daily Telegraph*, 11.1.93.
10. *The Times*, 25.1.93.
11. Interview 5, Lady Hogg, 23.10.96.
12. Interview 4, Lady Hogg.
13. Private interviews.
14. Private interview.
15. Interview, Iain McWhirter, 20.8.96.
16. *The Times*, 25.1.93.
17. Private interview.
18. Private information.
19. Private interview.
20. *The Times*, 25.1.93.
21. *Guardian*, 22.1.93.
22. HC Debs, 6th Series, vol. 217, col. 495.
23. *Daily Telegraph*, 4.2.93.
24. Independent, 5.2.93.
25. Ibid.
26. *Guardian*, 5.2.93.
27. Private information; *Financial Times*, 18.2.93.
28. Peter Riddell, *The Times*, 2.2.93.
29. *Financial Times*, 23.2.93.
30. *The Times*, 25.2.93.
31. Interview 2, Sir Robin Renwick.
32. *Daily Telegraph*, 2.1.93; private interview.
33. Private interview.
34. Interview 3, Lady Hogg, 24.10.95.
35. Private interview.
36. Interview 2, Raymond Seitz.
37. Private interview.
38. Official report of press conference, 24.2.93, *Congressional Quarterly, Weekly Report*, 51:9, 27.3.93.
39. Interview 2, Raymond Seitz.
40. Private interview.
41. Ibid.
42. Private diary.
43. Vulliamy (1994), p. 212.
44. Interview, Sir David Hannay.
45. Andrew Grice, *Sunday Times*, 28.2.93.
46. Letter, Peter Riddell to author, 23.10.96.
47. Private interview.
48. *Daily Telegraph*, 25.2.93; *Sunday Telegraph*, 28.2.93.
49. *Guardian*, 27.2.93.
50. Private information.
51. *Guardian*, 5.3.93; *Daily Telegraph*, 5.3.93.
52. *Independent*, 4.3.93.
53. Interview, Andrew Marr, 4.4.96.
54. *Guardian*, 5.3.93.
55. Private interview.
56. Interview, Bill Robinson.
57. Hogg and Hill (1995), pp. 200–2; Stephens (1996), pp. 282–3.
58. *The Best Future for Britain*, Conservative Central Office, 1992.
59. Stephens (1996), p. 283.
60. Private interview.

61. *Independent*, 17.3.93.
62. Private interview.
63. Baker, Gamble and Ludlam (1994), pp. 56–7.
64. Private interview.
65. Alderman (1993), p. 502.
66. Interview, Bill Cash, *The Major Years*, Sky Television, September 1997.
67. *Independent*, 23.4.93.
68. *Guardian*, 23.4.93.
69. Baker, Gamble and Ludlam (1994), p. 59; Alderman (1993), p. 503.
70. *Daily Telegraph*, 6.3.93.
71. Interview, Michael Chaplin.
72. Interview 3, John Major.
73. *Independent on Sunday*, 4.4.93.
74. *Independent*, 8.4.93; *The Times*, 8.4.93.
75. *Sunday Times*, 11.4.93.
76. *The Times*, 10.5.93.
77. *Guardian*, 10.5.93.
78. *Daily Telegraph*, 15.5.93.
79. Private interview.
80. Owen (1995), pp. 102–3.
81. *Sunday Telegraph*, 18.4.93.
82. Private interview.
83. Interview 2, Sir Robin Renwick.
84. Interview 1, Raymond Seitz.
85. Private interview.

86. Private interview and diary; *Guardian*, 21.5.96.
87. Private interview.
88. Jay in Seldon and Kavanagh (1994), p. 192.
89. Private interviews.
90. Private interview.
91. Ibid.
92. Stephens (1996), p. 184.
93. *The Economist*, 15.5.93.
94. *Sunday Times*, 30.5.93.
95. Private interview.
96. Ibid.
97. Interview 2, Norman Lamont.
98. Interview, Alastair Ross Goobey.
99. Private interviews; *Sunday Times*, 30.5.93.
100. *Daily Telegraph*, 28.5.93.
101. Private interview.
102. Ibid.
103. Baker (1994), pp. 255–9.
104. Interview, Michael Portillo.
105. Private interview.
106. Peter Riddell, *The Times*, 28.5.93.
107. HC Debs, 6th Series, vol. 226, cols 284–5.
108. *Guardian*, 3.6.93.
109. HC Debs, 6th Series, vol. 226, col. 305.
110. *The Times*, 10.6.93.

TWENTY-FIVE: PYRRHIC VICTORY

1. George Jones, *Daily Telegraph*, 5.6.93.
2. *Independent*, 5.6.93.
3. *The Times*, 6.6.93.
4. David Wastell and Toby Helm, *Sunday Telegraph*, 13.6.93.
5. Ibid.
6. Letter, Douglas Hurd to author, 8.11.95.
7. Private interview.
8. Dimbleby (1997), p. 247.
9. *Guardian*, 11.6.93.
10. *Daily Telegraph*, 15.6.93.
11. Private interview.
12. *The Times*, 9.6.93.
13. HC Debs, 6th Series, vol. 226, col. 141.
14. *Sunday Telegraph*, 27.6.93.
15. Private interview.
16. Interview, Michael Mates, 30.11.95.
17. *Daily Telegraph*, 21.6.93.
18. Ibid., 22.6.93.
19. *Guardian*, 23.6.93.

20. *Sunday Telegraph*, 27.6.93.
21. Ibid.
22. *The Times*, 26.6.93.
23. *Los Angeles Times*, 20.6.93.
24. Alderman (1993), p. 505.
25. *Independent*, 8.6.93.
26. *Financial Times*, 15.7.93.
27. Peter Riddell, *The Times*, 6.9.93.
28. *Daily Telegraph*, 19.7.93.
29. *Sunday Times*, 25.7.93.
30. Ibid.
31. *Independent*, 20.7.93.
32. Private interview.
33. *Sunday Times*, 25.7.93.
34. *The Times*, 16.7.93.
35. Private interview.
36. Private information.
37. Interview, James Molyneaux.
38. Private interview.
39. *Guardian*, 24.7.93.

40. *Sunday Times*, 25.7.93.
41. Private interview.
42. *Sunday Times*, 25.7.93.
43. *Guardian*, 24.7.93.
44. Private information.
45. *Sunday Times*, 25.7.93.
46. Michael Jones, *Sunday Times*, 25.7.93.
47. *The Economist*, 31.7.93.
48. See, for example, Paul Johnson, *Daily Mail*, 19.6.97.
49. *The Times*, 26.7.93.
50. *Guardian*, 27.7.93.
51. Interview, Michael Brunson, 30.11.95. Brunson wrote about the incident in the *Guardian*, 31.7.93.
52. *The Times*, 26.7.93.
53. Letter, John Redwood to author, 31.7.97.
54. Gorman (1993), p. xv.
55. Private interview.
56. Interview 2, Robert Hayward.
57. *The Times*, 3.7.93.
58. Private interview.
59. *The Times*, 3.7.93.
60. *Guardian*, 9.7.93; *The Times*, 10.7.93.
61. *The Times*, 7.7.93.
62. Ibid., 12.8.93.
63. Ibid., 16.8.93. Irma died in March 1995.
64. Ibid., 23.7.93.
65. Private interview.
66. Ibid.
67. Interview 3, Lady Hogg.
68. Private interview.
69. *The Economist*, 25.9.93.
70. Private interviews.
71. Interview 4, Douglas Hurd.
72. Private interview.
73. Ibid.
74. *Financial Times*, 10.9.93.
75. *Sunday Times*, 12.9.93.
76. Private interview.
77. *Independent*, 14.9.93.
78. Interview, Tessa Keswick, 19.4.96.
79. *Guardian*, 17.9.93.
80. *Sunday Times*, 19.9.93.
81. *Guardian*, 17.9.93.
82. Ibid.
83. Interview, John Sergeant, 18.4.96; private interviews.
84. *The Times*, 20.9.93.
85. Private interviews; *Independent*, 21.9.93.
86. Private interviews.
87. *The Times*, 22.9.93.
88. Bilsborough in Catterall (1994), pp. 296–306.
89. *Guardian*, 27.9.93.
90. Private information; *Sunday Times*, 26.9.93.
91. *Daily Telegraph*, 15.9.93; *Financial Times*, 18.9.93; *Guardian*, 21.9.93.

TWENTY-SIX: REGAINING THE INITIATIVE

1. Private interview.
2. Scott in Kavanagh and Seldon (1994), p. 345.
3. Private interview.
4. Interview 4, Nick True.
5. Private interview.
6. Interview 3, Lady Hogg.
7. *Sunday Times*, 25.7.93.
8. *Guardian*, 11.9.93; interview 2, Tim Collins, 12.11.95.
9. Private interview.
10. Ibid.
11. Ibid.
12. Private information.
13. Interview 2, Tim Collins.
14. Gorman (1993); Thatcher (1993).
15. Private information; Thatcher (1993), p. 721.
16. *Daily Mirror*, 5.10.93; *The Times*, 6.10.93.
17. *The Times*, 8.10.93.
18. Private interview.
19. *Christian Century*, 27.10.93.
20. Interview 2, Tim Collins.
21. Interview 1, Sir Ronald Millar.
22. Interview 7, Nick True.
23. Private letter to author, 7.4.97.
24. Private information; *Financial Times*, 15.10.93.
25. *National Review* (US), 13.12.93.
26. *Financial Times*, *Independent*, *The Times*, 29.10.93.
27. Baylis in Catterall (1994), p. 137.
28. *Independent*, 29.10.93; private information.
29. *The Times*, 9.11.93.
30. Interview, Sir Peter Harding, 25.10.95.
31. Private interviews.

32. *The Times*, 13.10.93.
33. Private diary, 30.9.93.
34. *The Times*, 26.10.93.
35. Ibid., 30.10.93.
36. Ibid., 13.10.93.
37. *Sunday Times*, 7.11.93.
38. Private interviews.
39. *The Times*, 15.11.93.
40. *Independent*, 15.11.93.
41. Private interview.
42. *Guardian*, 18.11.93.
43. *The Times*, 11.11.93.
44. *The Economist*, 20.11.93.
45. Private interview.
46. Ibid.

47. *Financial Times*, 14.5.93.
48. *Independent on Sunday*, 21.9.93.
49. Private information.
50. Interview 2, Andrew Lansley.
51. Private interview.
52. Stephens (1996), p. 292.
53. *The Economist*, 4.12.93.
54. Baker (1994), p. 276.
55. *Financial Times*, 1.12.93.
56. *Guardian*, 13.12.93; *Independent*, 11.12.93.
57. *Guardian*, 13.12.93.
58. Ludlam in Catterall (1994), p. 67.
59. Private interview.
60. Interview 3, Lady Hogg.

TWENTY-SEVEN: A BREAKTHROUGH IN IRELAND

1. Arthur (1996), p. 509.
2. Mallie and McKittrick (1996), p. 153.
3. Arthur (1996), p. 509.
4. Interview, Sir Patrick Mayhew.
5. Arthur (1996), p. 508.
6. Mallie and McKittrick (1996), pp. 148–9.
7. Private interview.
8. Interview, Sir Patrick Mayhew.
9. Arthur (1996), p. 511.
10. The term 'back-channel' was used by most of those involved, although some called it 'the link'.
11. Private interview.
12. The principal accounts are in the *Observer*, 5.12.93 and Mallie and McKittrick (1996), pp. 232–55.
13. *Observer*, 5.12.93.
14. Arthur (1996), p. 402.
15. Private interview.
16. Mallie and McKittrick (1996), p. 249.
17. *Observer*, 5.12.93.
18. Mallie and McKittrick (1996), pp. 249–52.
19. Private information.
20. *Observer*, 5.12.93.
21. Mallie and McKittrick (1996), p. 252.
22. Private interview.
23. Ibid.
24. Mansergh (1995b), p. 11.
25. Private interview.
26. Mansergh (1995b), p. 17.
27. Mallie and McKittrick (1996), p. 178.
28. Private interview.

29. Quoted in Mallie and McKittrick (1996), p. 187.
30. *The Times*, 27.9.93.
31. Private interview.
32. Mallie and McKittrick, p. 193.
33. Arthur (1996), pp. 403–4.
34. Private interview.
35. *Independent on Sunday*, 19.12.93.
36. Private interview.
37. Ibid.
38. Ibid.
39. Ibid.
40. Mallie and McKittrick (1996), pp. 226–7.
41. Private interview.
42. *The Times*, 16.11.93.
43. Private interview.
44. Mallie and McKittrick, pp. 232–7.
45. Interview, James Molyneaux.
46. Private interview.
47. *Sunday Telegraph*, 5.12.93.
48. Private interview.
49. Interview, Albert Reynolds.
50. Mallie and McKittrick (1996), p. 256.
51. Private interview.
52. Letter, Major to Reynolds, 25.11.93, cited in Mallie and McKittrick (1996), pp. 228–9.
53. Sean Duigan, diary, quoted in Mallie and McKittrick (1996), p. 230.
54. *Independent on Sunday*, 19.12.93.
55. Private interview.
56. Ibid.
57. Mallie and McKittrick (1996), p. 259.

58. Private interview.
59. Ibid.
60. Ibid.
61. Mrs Geoghegan-Quinn, Irish Justice Minister, in Mallie and McKittrick (1996), p. 262.
62. Private interview.
63. Ibid.
64. *Sunday Times*, 19.12.93.
65. Quoted in Mallie and McKittrick (1996), p. 265.
66. Private interview.
67. Quoted in Mallie and McKittrick (1996), p. 265.
68. *Independent on Sunday*, 19.12.93.
69. HC Debs, 6th Series, vol. 234, col. 1076.
70. *Guardian, Independent*, 16.12.93.
71. 'The Joint Declaration', verbatim quotations, 15.12.93.
72. Private interview.
73. Interview, James Molyneaux.
74. Ibid.
75. Private interview.
76. *Independent*, 23.12.93.
77. Mallie and McKittrick (1996), pp. 269–73.
78. Mansergh (1995a), p. 27.
79. Interview, Albert Reynolds; interview, Sir Patrick Mayhew.
80. *Independent*, 28.12.93.

TWENTY-EIGHT: BACK TO THE BAD TIMES

1. Toby Helm, *Sunday Telegraph*, 9.1.94; private interview.
2. *Sunday Times*, 9.1.94.
3. *The Times*, 6.1.94.
4. *Sunday Times*, 9.1.94.
5. *Sunday Telegraph*, 9.1.94.
6. Private interview.
7. Ibid.
8. Ibid.
9. *Spectator*, 8.1.94.
10. Ibid., 1.1.94.
11. *Sun*, 14.1.94.
12. Sunday Telegraph, 9.1.94.
13. *Sunday Times*, 16.1.94.
14. *Daily Telegraph*, 11.1.94.
15. *The Times, Daily Telegraph*, 10.1.94.
16. Private diary, 13.1.94; *Daily Telegraph*, 14.1.94; *Financial Times*,14.1.94.
17. *Sunday Times*, 16.1.94.
18. *The Times*, 15.1.94.
19. Private interview.
20. *Sunday Times*, 16.1.94.
21. Private diary, 13.1.94.
22. Private interview.
23. *Guardian*, 18.1.94.
24. Private diary, 20.1.94.
25. Evidence from interview, Sir Tim Lankester and the *Guardian*, 18.1.94, 21.7.94 and 11.11.94.
26. Private diary, 23.3.94.
27. Peter Riddell, *The Times*, 17.1.94.
28. Tunstall (1996), pp. 277–80; *Sunday Times*, 16.1.94; private interviews.
29. Ginny Douglas interview article, *The Times* magazine, 29.1.94.
30. *Sunday Times*, 3.1.94.
31. *Yorkshire Post*, 31.1.94.
32. Private interview.
33. 'Heirs Unapparent', *Sunday Times*, 30.1.94.
34. Anthony Bevins, *Observer*, 30.1.94.
35. Andrew Rawnsley, *Observer*, 30.1.94. The article is one of a vast number that reveals how far even Major's allies were content to talk to the press.
36. *The Times*, 21.1.94.
37. *Sunday Times*, 30.1.94.
38. Ibid.
39. *Daily Telegraph*, 3.2.94.
40. Lecture by Sir Bernard Ingham, St Dunstan's College, 3.2.94; Martin Fletcher profile of Meyer, *The Times*, 31.1.94.
41. Private interview.
42. *Sunday Telegraph*, 6.2.94.
43. *The Times*, 8.2.94.
44. *Daily Telegraph*, 8.2.94.
45. Ibid., 14.2.94.
46. *Sunday Telegraph*, 13.2.94; *Sunday Times*, 20.2.94.
47. *Sunday Times*, 20.2.94.
48. Private interviews; *The Times*, 15.2.94.
49. Private interview.
50. *Daily Telegraph*, 16.2.94.
51. Private interview.
52. Ibid.; *Guardian*, 17.2.94.
53. Private diary, 17.2.94.
54. *Daily Telegraph*, 18.2.94.

55. Private interview.
56. *The Times*, 18.2.94.
57. Interview 7, Nick True.
58. Interview 4, Lady Hogg.
59. Private interview.
60. Interview, Patrick Rock.
61. *The Times*, 22.2.94.
62. 'Neither one thing nor the other', *Guardian*, 22.2.94.
63. Interview 2, Andrew Lansley.
64. *Sunday Times*, 20.2.94.
65. Interview 1, William Waldegrave.
66. *Daily Telegraph*, 18.2.94.
67. Private interview.
68. Mallie and McKittrick (1996), p. 282.
69. Private interview.
70. Interview 2, Raymond Seitz.
71. Private interview.
72. Interview 2, Raymond Seitz.
73. Nancy Soderberg, quoted in Mallie and McKittrick (1996), p. 285.
74. Private interview.
75. Private diary, 3.2.94.
76. *Sunday Times*, 6.2.94.
77. See also Woodward (1994), pp. 323–4.
78. *US News and World Report*, 14.2.94.
79. Private interview.
80. *The Times*, 21.2.94.
81. Interview, Anthony Lake, 18.12.95.
82. *Washington Post*, 21.2.94.
83. Weekly Compilation of Presidential Documents, 7 March 1994, V30 N9, pp. 396–8.
84. Private interviews.
85. *Guardian*, 28.2.94.
86. Private interview.
87. Interview, Anthony Lake.
88. *The Times*, 2.3.94.
89. *Guardian*, 2.3.94.
90. *Sunday Times*, 6.3.94.
91. Private diary, 3.3.94.
92. *Sunday Times*, 6.3.94.
93. Private interview.
94. *The Times*, 18.3.94.
95. *Daily Telegraph*, 19.3.94.
96. Private interview.
97. *The Times*, 9.3.94.
98. *Sunday Times*, 13.3.94.
99. Mallie and McKittrick (1996), pp. 287–8.
100. *Sunday Times*, 13.3.94.
101. Ibid.
102. *Independent*, 12.3.94.
103. *The Times*, 15.3.94.
104. Butler and Westlake (1995), pp. 52–4.
105. Private interviews.
106. *Daily Telegraph*, 29.3.94.
107. *Sunday Telegraph*, 20.3.94.
108. *Financial Times*, 18.3.94.
109. Private diary, 23.3.94.
110. Ibid.
111. *Sunday Telegraph*, 20.3.94; Butler and Westlake (1995), p. 56.
112. HC Debs, 6th Series, vol. 240, col. 134.
113. Ibid.
114. Private interview.
115. Ibid. The same thinking can be gleaned in Riddell's article, *The Times*, 26.3.94.
116. Peter Riddell, *The Times*, 23.3.94.
117. Letter, Peter Riddell to author, 25.7.97.
118. *Guardian*, 25.3.94.
119. *Daily Telegraph*, 25.3.94; *Guardian*, 26.3.94.
120. Butler and Westlake (1995), p. 58.
121. *Sunday Telegraph*, 3.4.94; *Guardian*, 26.3.94.
122. Interview 4, Douglas Hurd.
123. *Daily Telegraph, Daily Mail*, 28.3.94.
124. Butler and Westlake (1995), pp. 55–9.
125. *Sunday Times*, 27.3.94.
126. *Observer, Independent on Sunday*, 27.3.94.
127. *Sunday Times*, 3.4.94.
128. *Independent*, 30.3.94.
129. Private diary, 23.3.94.
130. *The Times*, 28.3.94.
131. *Sunday Times*, 3.4.94.
132. *The Times*, 29.3.94.
133. George Jones, *Daily Telegraph*, 29.3.94.
134. Private interview.
135. Ibid.
136. Ibid.
137. Private diary, 29.3.94.
138. *Sunday Times*, 3.4.94.
139. *The Times*, 30.3.94; Seldon in Seldon and Kavanagh (1994), p. 166.
140. *Sunday Times*, 3.4.94.
141. HC Debs, 6th Series, vol. 240, col. 802.
142. Private interview.
143. *Independent*, 30.3.94.
144. *Sunday Telegraph*, 3.4.94.
145. Private interview.
146. Ibid.
147. *The Times, Daily Express, Daily Mail*, 30.3.94.
148. *The Times*, 31.3.94; *Sunday Telegraph*, 3.4.94.

149. *The Times*, 7.4.94.
150. *Sunday Times*, 3.4.94.
151. Ibid.; Butler and Westlake (1995), pp. 60–61.
152. Butler and Westlake (1995), p. 62.
153. Interview 4, Douglas Hurd.
154. Private interview.
155. *The Times*. 21.1.94; *Daily Telegraph*, 25.2.94; *Financial Times*, 24.2.94.
156. *Independent on Sunday*, 3.4.94.
157. *Daily Telegraph*, 5.4.94.
158. Interview 2, George Bridges, 9.1.97.
159. *Financial Times*, 7.4.94.
160. *The Times*, 7.4.94.
161. Butler and Westlake (1995), pp. 64–5.
162. Private interview.
163. *Daily Telegraph*, 29.4.94.
164. Butler and Westlake (1995), pp. 66–7.
165. Andrew Grice, *Sunday Times*, 7.8.94.
166. *The Times*, 4.5.94.
167. Ibid., 28.4.94.
168. Ibid.
169. *Independent*, 3.5.94.
170. *The Times*, 25.4.94.
171. Butler and Westlake (1995), p. 68.
172. Private interview.
173. *Guardian*, 7.5.94.
174. Private interview.
175. *Daily Telegraph*, 7.5.94.
176. *Sunday Telegraph*, 8.5.94.
177. *Observer*, 8.5.94.
178. *Independent on Sunday*, 3.4.94.
179. *Sunday Times*, 7.8.94.
180. *Spectator*, 7.5.94.
181. *Sunday Times*, 8.5.94.
182. Ibid.

TWENTY-NINE: A KINDER SUMMER

1. Private interview.
2. Ibid.
3. McSmith (1994), pp. viii–ix.
4. Private interview.
5. Private diary, 12.5.94.
6. HC Debs, 6th Series, vol. 243, col. 429.
7. Ibid.
8. *The Times*, 13.5.94.
9. *Guardian*, 13.5.94.
10. Private interviews.
11. Private interview.
12. Ibid.
13. Interview 1, Damian Green, 4.1.95.
14. *The Times*, 14.5.94.
15. Interview 2, Andrew Lansley.
16. *Guardian*, 14.5.94.
17. *The Times*, 14.5.94.
18. Private interview.
19. Interview 6, John Major.
20. Interview 4, Lady Hogg; interview 4, Douglas Hurd.
21. Butler and Westlake (1995), pp. 99–102.
22. Interview, Paul Judge, 27.11.95.
23. Interview 3, Maurice Fraser; Butler and Westlake (1995), p. 105.
24. Interview 2, Maurice Fraser, 23.10.95.
25. Interview 3, Maurice Fraser; *The Times*, 29.4.94; *Independent on Sunday*, 1.5.94.
26. Private interview; *Financial Times*, 6.5.94.
27. Butler and Westlake (1995), p. 106.
28. *Independent*, 29.4.94.
29. Interview 4, Douglas Hurd.
30. Interview 6, John Major.
31. *Daily Telegraph*, 28.5.94.
32. *Bristol Evening News*, 27.5.94.
33. Private interview.
34. *Sunday Telegraph*, 29.5.94.
35. Butler and Westlake (1995), p. 179.
36. *Independent*, 30.5.94.
37. Private information.
38. Ibid.
39. Butler and Westlake (1995), pp. 179–80.
40. *Independent*, 2.6.94.
41. *Financial Times*, 2.6.94.
42. *Independent*, 2.6.94.
43. Interview 1, Anthony Teasdale.
44. Butler and Westlake (1995), p. 183.
45. Private interview.
46. Interview 4, Lord Cranborne, 18.7.97.
47. *Observer*, 5.6.94.
48. Private interview.
49. Ibid.
50. Ibid.
51. Ibid.
52. *The Times*, 8.6.94.
53. *Financial Times*, *Guardian*, 9.6.94.
54. *Sunday Times*, 12.6.94.
55. *Guardian*, 11.6.94. Marcus Fox, however, told Alastair Campbell in

the *Spectator* on 11.6.94 that the 1922 Committee was behind Major.

56. *Sunday Times*, 12.6.94.
57. Private interview.
58. Ibid.
59. Unless one counts the Liberals in the 1920s.
60. *Sunday Telegraph*, 12.6.94.
61. *Daily Telegraph*, 14.6.94.
62. See, for example, Anthony King, *Daily Telegraph*, 11.6.94 and Peter Kellner, *Sunday Times*, 12.6.94.
63. Interview 6, John Major.
64. Private interview.
65. Ibid.
66. Colin Brown, *Independent*, 14.6.94.
67. Andrew Marr, *Independent*, 14.6.94.
68. *Daily Express*, 2.6.94.
69. Private interview.
70. Private diary, 11.6.94.
71. Private interview.
72. *Sunday Telegraph*, 26.6.94.
73. Private interview; *Guardian, Daily Telegraph*, 24.6.94.
74. *Financial Times*, 25.6.94.
75. Christopher Lockwood, *Daily Telegraph*, 24.6.94.
76. *Independent on Sunday*, 26.6.94.
77. Andrew Grice, *Sunday Times*, 26.6.94.
78. *Independent on Sunday*, 26.6.94.
79. David Wastell and Christopher Lockwood, *Sunday Telegraph*, 26.6.94.
80. Boris Johnson, *Sunday Telegraph*, 26.6.94.
81. Private interview.
82. Private diary, 30.6.94.
83. *Sunday Times*, 26.6.94.
84. *Daily Telegraph*, 29.6.94.
85. *The Times*, 1.7.94.
86. Philip Webster, *The Times*, 27.6.94.
87. *Daily Telegraph*, 30.6.94.
88. *The Times*, 1.7.94.
89. *Daily Telegraph*, 30.6.94.
90. *Financial Times*, 4.7.94.
91. *Daily Telegraph*, 8.7.94. Michael Jones in the *Sunday Times*, 10.7.94, said his sources recounted just a double 'repeated'.
92. Don MacIntyre, *Independent*, 8.7.94.
93. *Independent*, 9.7.94.
94. *Observer*, 10.7.94.
95. *Sunday Times*, 10.7.94.
96. *The Times*, 6.7.94.
97. Ibid., 11.7.94.

98. Interview 2, George Bridges.
99. Private interview.
100. Ibid.
101. *Guardian*, 9.7.94.
102. Private interview.
103. Ibid.
104. *Sunday Times*, 10.7.94.
105. Private interview.
106. *The Times*, 12.7.94.
107. Ibid., 7.7.94.
108. *Daily Telegraph*, 13.7.94.
109. Ibid., 14.7.94.
110. *Financial Times*, 16.7.94.
111. *Daily Telegraph*, 20.7.94.
112. Private interview.
113. Interview 6, John Major.
114. *Independent*, 21.7.94.
115. Dimbleby (1997), pp. 200–202, 247–8.
116. Interview 4, Jonathan Hill, 18.7.95.
117. Interview 1, Jeremy Hanley.
118. Interview 2, Michael McManus, 27.11.95.
119. Private interview.
120. Ibid.
121. Peter Riddell, *The Times*, 21.7.94.
122. *Daily Telegraph, Independent*, 21.7.94.
123. Private interview.
124. Ibid.
125. Interview, John Ward and Lord McColl.
126. George Gardiner, 'Tories Yearn for a Message', *The Times*, 28.7.94.
127. *Daily Telegraph*, 28.7.94.
128. Ibid.
129. *Independent*, 28.7.94; Hugo Young, *Guardian*, 28.7.94.
130. *Guardian*, 2.8.94.
131. Private interview.
132. *Independent*, 3.8.94.
133. Private interview.
134. Mallie and McKittrick (1996), p. 290; private interview.
135. Private interview.
136. Ibid.
137. Mallie and McKittrick (1996), p. 291.
138. Interview, Albert Reynolds.
139. Private interview.
140. Interview, Albert Reynolds.
141. Private interview; Mallie and McKittrick (1996), p. 327.
142. Mallie and McKittrick (1996), p. 341.
143. *Sunday Telegraph*, 31.7.94.
144. Private interview.
145. Ibid.
146. Ibid.

147. *Financial Times, Independent,* 17.9.94.
148. Private interview.
149. Ibid.
150. Ibid.
151. *Daily Telegraph,* 8.9.94.
152. *Independent,* 10.9.94.
153. Interview 2, Maurice Fraser.
154. Private interview.
155. Interview 2, Douglas Hurd.
156. Private interview.
157. *The Times,* 6.5.93.
158. Private interview.
159. Ibid.
160. *Guardian,* 20.9.94.
161. Private interview.
162. *Daily Telegraph,* 20.9.94.
163. Private interviews.
164. Private interview.
165. *Financial Times,* 21.9.94.

166. *Guardian,* 21.9.94.
167. Private interview.
168. Ibid.
169. Ibid.
170. Interview, John Ward and Lord McColl.
171. *The Times, Independent,* 22.9.94.
172. *Guardian,* 22.9.94.
173. Interview 3, Douglas Hurd.
174. Interview 6, John Major.
175. *The Times,* 22.9.94.
176. *Daily Telegraph,* 22.9.94; private interview.
177. *Daily Telegraph,* 23.9.94.
178. *Sunday Telegraph,* 25.9.94.
179. Interview, Pik Botha, 22.8.95.
180. Interview, F. W. De Klerk, 22.8.95.
181. *Sunday Times,* 25.9.94; *The Times,* 26.9.94.

THIRTY: THE LIEUTENANTS FALL

1. Seldon in Kavanagh and Seldon (1994), pp. 30–34; Whiteley, Seyd and Richardson (1994), pp. 227–38.
2. Whiteley et al. (1994), p. 228.
3. *Guardian, Independent,* 21.6.94. The Fowler chairmanship was written about very dismissively by Eric Chalker, *Independent,* 17.6.94.
4. Rallings, Thrasher (1996).
5. Interview, Sir Norman Fowler.
6. In addition to Whiteley et al. (1994), see Stuart Ball, 'Vanishing Tories', *Guardian,* 10.10.94, Michael Pinto-Duschinsky's research, reflected in *The Times,* 11.10.94, and Simon Heffer in the *Daily Telegraph,* 11.9.94.
7. This view is also supported by survey evidence in Whiteley et al. (1994).
8. The exercise is discussed by Andrew Marr, *Independent,* 19.8.94, and Martin Jacques, *Sunday Times,* 21.8.94.
9. Private interview.
10. Interview 1, Jeremy Hanley.
11. Private interview.
12. *Daily Telegraph,* 12.9.94.
13. *Independent,* 10.9.94.
14. Cm 2614, 'The Future of Postal Services'.
15. Interview, Tim Rycroft, 21.12.95.

16. *The Times,* 12.9.94.
17. Private interview.
18. *Financial Times,* 12.9.94.
19. *Independent,* 12.9.94.
20. Interview 1, Jeremy Hanley.
21. Ibid.
22. *Financial Times,* 21.11.94; private interview.
23. Private interviews.
24. *The Times,* 11.10.94.
25. Ibid., 19.9.94.
26. *Sunday Times,* 18.9.94.
27. *Independent,* 25.9.94.
28. Interview 3, Andrew Lansley, 8.6.95.
29. *Daily Telegraph,* 6.10.94.
30. Interview 3, Andrew Lansley.
31. *Observer,* 9.10.94.
32. Hugo Young, *Guardian,* 11.10.94; diary, Anthony Seldon, 1.10.94; Robert Rhodes Jones, *Evening Standard,* 10.10.94.
33. *Sunday Times,* 9.10.94.
34. Interview 2, Jeremy Hanley, 22.2.96.
35. *Independent,* 11.10.94.
36. Ibid., 13.10.94.
37. *Sunday Times,* 16.10.94.
38. *Sunday Telegraph,* 16.10.94.
39. *Independent,* 13.10.94.
40. *Observer,* 16.10.94; *Independent,* 13.10.94.

41. Interview 1, Sir Ronnie Millar; interview 2, George Bridges.
42. *Guardian*, 15.10.94.
43. John Major, 'Prime Minister's Speech', Conservative Party Press Release.
44. *Observer*, 16.10.94.
45. Interview, Michael Gove.
46. Gove (1995), pp. 303–11.
47. *Guardian*, 29.1.94.
48. Ibid., 5.2.94.
49. *Daily Telegraph*, 25.2.94.
50. See, for example, Peter Riddell, 'Power goes to their heads', *The Times*, 21.4.94. See also David Rose, 'A dangerous state of irresponsibility', *Observer*, 30.1.94.
51. Leigh and Vulliamy (1997), pp. 173–7.
52. *Guardian*, 20.10.94.
53. *Daily Telegraph*, 10.10.94.
54. Private interview; *Daily Telegraph*, 26.10.94.
55. Leigh and Vulliamy (1997), pp. 180–83.
56. *Sunday Times*, 30.10.94.
57. Private interviews.
58. Private interview.
59. Ibid.
60. *Daily Telegraph*, 26.10.94.
61. Interview, Michael Gove.
62. See Boris Johnson, *Spectator*, 29.10.94; Simon Heffer, *Daily Telegraph*, 26.10.94.
63. HC Debs, 6th Series, vol. 248, cols 1002–3.
64. Cm 2101.
65. Private diary, 13.5.93.
66. *The Times*, 19.5.93.
67. *Financial Times*, 25.5.93.
68. Private interview.
69. *The Times*, 18.5.94.
70. Ibid., 5.5.94.
71. *Sunday Times*, 8.5.94; *The Times*, 18.5.94.
72. *Financial Times*, 11.5.94.
73. Private diary, 19.5.94.
74. Green Paper info.
75. *Financial Times*, 20.5.94.
76. Interview 1, John Redwood.
77. HC Debs, 6th Series, vol. 243, col. 973.
78. Interview 6, John Major.
79. *Sunday Times*, 6.11.94.
80. Private interviews.
81. Private interview.
82. Interview 1, David Hunt; Interview 5, David Hunt, 20.2.96.
83. Private interview.
84. *Independent on Sunday*, 6.11.94.
85. *Sunday Times*, 6.11.94.
86. Private diary, 3.11.94.
87. Interview 1, John Redwood.
88. Peterborough, *Daily Telegraph*, 5.11.94. By all accounts, however, Major's lunch with Dehaene was extremely convivial.
89. Private diary, 3.11.94.
90. *Sunday Times*, 6.11.94; private diary, 3.11.94.
91. Interview 1, Kenneth Clarke.
92. *Daily Telegraph*, 4.11.94, 7.11.94.
93. *Guardian*, 4.11.94.
94. *Sunday Times*, 6.11.94.
95. Private interview.
96. Interview 6, John Major.
97. *The Times*, 10.11.94; *Guardian*, 11.11.94; *Sunday Times*, 13.11.94.
98. *Financial Times*, 4.11.94.
99. *Independent*, 15.11.94.
100. Private interview.
101. *Financial Times*, 17.11.94.
102. HC Debs, 6th Series, vol. 250, col. 30.
103. *The Times*, 17.11.94; Don MacIntyre, *Independent*, 17.11.94.
104. *The Times*, 15.11.94.
105. *Independent*, 15.11.94.
106. Private interview.
107. *Financial Times*, 19.11.94.
108. Andrew Grice, *Sunday Times*, 27.11.94.
109. *Sunday Telegraph*, 20.11.94.
110. Private interview.
111. Ibid.
112. Ibid.
113. *Sunday Times*, 27.11.94.
114. *The Times*, 24.11.94; *Sunday Times*, 27.11.94.
115. Interview 1, David Willetts, 25.10.95.
116. *Financial Times*, 21.11.94; private interview.
117. Profile of Marcus Fox, *Independent on Sunday*, 27.11.94.
118. *Financial Times*, 23.11.94.
119. *Daily Mail*, 23.11.94.
120. *Sunday Times*, 27.11.94.
121. Private interview; *Independent*, 25.11.94; *Sunday Times*, 27.11.94.
122. Private diary, 27.11.94.
123. Interview 1, John Redwood; private interview.
124. *Guardian*, 25.11.94; *Sunday Times*, 27.11.94.

125. Private interview.
126. *The Times*, 25.11.94.
127. HC Debs, 6th Series, vol. 250, col. 725.
128. *Daily Mail*, 24.11.94.
129. *Daily Telegraph*, 24.11.94.
130. *Independent*, 25.11.94; *Independent on Sunday*, 27.11.94.
131. Private interview.
132. John Major admitted that he had considered triggering a leadership election before 1995. Interview 4, John Major.
133. Private interview.
134. *Sunday Times*, 27.11.94; *The Times*, 24.11.94.
135. *Daily Telegraph*, 28.11.94.
136. Private interview.
137. Clarke was talking about the net *increase* in Britain's contribution as a result of the Bill, Cash was talking about the *absolute level* of the contribution. Peter Riddell, *The Times*, 16.11.94.
138. Leader, *Independent*, 26.11.94.
139. *Guardian*, 29.11.94.
140. Interview 1, David Willetts.
141. *Financial Times*, 29.11.94.
142. *Daily Telegraph*, 29.11.94.
143. Interview 1, Jeremy Hanley.
144. Private interviews.
145. *The Times*, 24.11.94.
146. Interview, John Maples.
147. Private interviews.
148. Interview 5, Lady Hogg.
149. Private interview.
150. Ibid.
151. *Independent*, 2.12.94.
152. Interview, Michael Portillo.
153. Stephen Castle, Paul Routledge, *Independent on Sunday*, 27.11.94.
154. *Guardian*, 7.12.94.
155. *Sunday Times*, 11.12.94.
156. *Observer, Sunday Times*, 11.12.94.
157. Interview 1, Jeremy Hanley.
158. *The Times*, 6 and 7.12.94; *Daily Telegraph*, 7.12.94; *Financial Times*, 6.12.94.
159. *The Times*, 7.12.94.
160. *Daily Telegraph*, 7.12.94.
161. *Sunday Times*, 11.12.94; *The Times*, 8.12.94.
162. *Observer*, 11.12.94.
163. *Financial Times*, 7.12.94.
164. *Guardian*, 8.12.94.
165. *The Times*, 8.12.94.
166. *Independent, Financial Times*, 7.12.94.
167. *Daily Telegraph*, 9.12.94.
168. *The Times*, 8.12.94.
169. *Sunday Telegraph, Observer*, 11.12.94.
170. *The Times*, 12.12.94.
171. *Sunday Telegraph*, 11.12.94.
172. Private interview.
173. *Mail on Sunday*, 11.12.94.
174. *Sunday Times*, 11.12.94.
175. Ibid.
176. *Independent*, 27.12.94.
177. *Sunday Times*, 20.12.92.
178. Ibid., 6.11.94.
179. Interview 5, Lady Hogg.
180. Interview 4, Lady Hogg.
181. Private interviews.
182. Private interview.
183. Ibid.
184. *Independent*, 29.12.94; *The Times*, 31.12.94.

THIRTY-ONE: GOVERNING WITHOUT A MAJORITY

1. Private interview.
2. *Daily Telegraph*, 16.11.94; *Sunday Times*, 22.1.95.
3. Interview 3, Howell James, 30.8.95.
4. Interview 2, George Bridges.
5. Ibid.
6. Interview 2, Tim Collins.
7. Interview, Tim Rycroft; interview 3, Howell James.
8. Private interview.
9. *Independent*, 9.1.95.
10. Leader, *The Times*, 9.1.95.
11. *The Times*, 9.1.95.
12. *Financial Times*, 12.1.95.
13. *Daily Telegraph*, 13.1.95.
14. *The Times*, 13.1.95; Simon Heffer offered a critical view of the policy groups, *Daily Telegraph*, 18.1.95.
15. *The Times*, 14.1.95.
16. *Independent*, 14.1.95; interview 3, Douglas Hurd.
17. Private interview.
18. HC Debs, 6th Series, vol. 252, col. 276.
19. *Daily Telegraph, The Times*, 18.1.95.

20. HC Debs, 6th Series, vol. 252, col. 579.
21. *Daily Telegraph*, 18.1.95.
22. Diary, Anthony Seldon, 17.1.95.
23. *The Times*, 17.1.95.
24. Ibid., 14.1.95.
25. *Guardian*, 19.1.95.
26. Private diary, 19.1.95.
27. *The Times*, 27.1.95.
28. Andrew Rawnsley, *Observer*, 8.1.95.
29. *Sunday Times*, 8.1.95; *Daily Telegraph*, 16.1.95; private diary, 12.1.95.
30. An edited version of the speech appeared in *The Times*, 7.1.95.
31. *Sunday Times*, 1.1.95.
32. *Guardian*, 20.1.95. Michael Carttiss had decided to operate as a freelance.
33. *The Times, Daily Telegraph*, 20.1.95.
34. *Observer*, 22.1.95; *Daily Telegraph*, 20.1.95.
35. Leaders, *Daily Telegraph, The Times*, 20.1.95.
36. *Sunday Times*, 22.1.95.
37. *The Times*, 23.1.95.
38. Private interviews; *The Times*, 26.1.95.
39. *The Times*, 27.1.95.
40. Private interview.
41. *The Times*, 27.1.95; *Sunday Telegraph*, 29.1.95; *The Times*, 31.1.95.
42. *The Times*, 31.1.95.
43. Private interview.
44. Private interviews.
45. Ibid.
46. Interview, James Molyneaux.
47. Private interview.
48. Mallie and McKittrick (1996), p. 343.
49. Private interviews.
50. Interview 1, Peter Stothard, 25.5.95.
51. Private interview.
52. Toby Helm, David Wastell, *Sunday Telegraph*, 5.2.95.
53. Private interview.
54. Interview 1, Peter Stothard.
55. Private interview.
56. Interview 1, Matthew d'Ancona, 19.3.96.
57. Private interview.
58. Ibid.
59. Arthur Leathley, *The Times*, 2.2.95; *Sunday Telegraph*, 5.2.95.
60. Interview, Sir Patrick Mayhew.
61. *The Times*, 1.2.95.
62. Ibid., 2.2.95.
63. Private interview.
64. *The Times*, 2.2.95.

65. *Daily Telegraph*, 2.2.95.
66. Interview 1, Matthew d'Ancona.
67. Interview, Sir Patrick Mayhew.
68. Private interview.
69. Interview 1, Matthew d'Ancona.
70. Interview, James Molyneaux.
71. *Sunday Times*, 26.2.95.
72. Private diary, 21.2.95.
73. Private interview.
74. Ibid.
75. *Independent*, 25.2.95.
76. *The Times*, 23.2.95.
77. HC Debs, 6th Series, vol. 255, col. 362.
78. *Independent*, 23.2.95.
79. Ibid., 25.2.95.
80. Private interview.
81. Ibid.
82. Ibid.
83. *Guardian, The Times*, 4.2.95.
84. *Guardian*, 4.2.95.
85. Private interview.
86. *Daily Telegraph*, 4.2.95.
87. Ibid., 7.2.95; *Guardian*, 6.2.95.
88. Private interviews.
89. Private interview; *The Times*, 8.2.95.
90. *Guardian*, 8.2.95.
91. Private interview; *Guardian, The Times*, 13.2.95.
92. Andrew Marr, *Independent*, 15.2.95.
93. *Independent*, 15.2.95.
94. Private interview.
95. Ibid.
96. *Financial Times*, 10.2.95.
97. *Sunday Telegraph*, 19.2.95.
98. Private interview.
99. Interview, Tessa Keswick.
100. Private Interview; *Sunday Telegraph*, 19.2.95.
101. Private interview.
102. Ibid.
103. *Sunday Telegraph*, 19.2.95.
104. Private diary, 16.2.95. Even details of the dressing down were leaked to the press: *The Times*. 17.2.95, for example.
105. *Independent on Sunday*, 19.2.95.
106. *Sunday Telegraph*, 19.2.95.
107. *Independent*, 17.2.95.
108. See Lamont profiles, *Sunday Times, Observer*, 5.3.95.
109. *Daily Telegraph*, 2.3.95.
110. Private interview; *The Times*, 2.3.95.
111. Interview 3, Douglas Hurd.
112. Interview, Lord Greenbury, 23.2.96.

113. *The Times*, 13.3.95.
114. *Jewish Chronicle*, 10.3.95.
115. *The Times*, 15.3.95.
116. Private interview.
117. Ibid.
118. Interview, John Sergeant.
119. *Daily Telegraph*, 13.3.95.
120. *Today*, 14.3.95.
121. Interview, Lord Greenbury.
122. Interview, Sir Martin Gilbert, 22.11.95. When Gilbert accompanied Major to the US in early April, some started reading a greater intimacy than existed in practice. See 'Major's Muse', *The Times*, 4.4.95; David Rennie, *Evening Standard*, 10.4.95.
123. Private interview.
124. Ibid.
125. Ibid.
126. Ibid.
127. *Facts on File*, 23.3.95, USS, no. 2834, p. 215.
128. Private interview.
129. *The Times*, 16.3.95.
130. *Guardian*, 13.3.95.
131. *The Times*, 15.3.95.
132. *Financial Times*, 17.3.95.
133. Private interview.
134. *Facts on File*, 23.3.95, USS, no. 2834, p. 215.
135. *The Times*, 3.4.95.
136. Ibid., 5.4.95.
137. Private interview.
138. *The Times*, 5.4.95.
139. *Independent*, 3.4.95.
140. Private interview.
141. Ibid.
142. Interview 2, Maurice Fraser.
143. Private interview.
144. *Independent*, 30.3.95.
145. *Daily Telegraph*, 17.3.95.
146. *Guardian*, 17.3.95.
147. *New Statesman and Society*, 17.3.95.
148. Interview, Lord McAlpine, 16.1.97.
149. *Daily Telegraph*, 17.3.95.
150. HC Debs, 6th Series, vol. 256, col. 1025.
151. David Wastell, *Sunday Telegraph*, 19.3.95; Michael Prescott, Andrew Grice, *Sunday Times*, 19.3.95; Ivor Crewe, *Observer*, 19.3.95.
152. Interview 4, Howell James, 20.10.95.
153. Paul Vallely profile, *Independent*, 2.2.95.
154. *Financial Times*, 19.11.94.
155. Michael White profile, *Guardian*, 1.2.95.
156. Interview 2, Norman Blackwell, 23.2.96.
157. Ibid.
158. Private interviews.
159. *Daily Telegraph*, 29.3.95.
160. *Daily Mail*, 1.4.95.
161. *The Times*, 1.4.95.
162. *Observer*, 2.4.95.
163. *Sunday Times*, 2.4.95.
164. Interview 2, Norman Blackwell.
165. Private interviews.
166. *Financial Times*, 7.4.95.
167. Andrew Marr, *Independent*, 4.4.95.
168. Private interview.
169. *The Times*, 7.4.95.
170. *Independent*, 8.4.95.
171. *Guardian*, 5.4.95.
172. *Daily Telegraph*, 11.4.95.
173. *Independent*, 25.4.95.
174. Private interview.
175. Ibid.
176. Ibid.
177. Ibid.
178. Ibid.
179. Ibid.
180. *Independent*, 25.4.95.
181. Private interview.
182. Ibid.
183. *The Times*, 26.4.95; HC Debs, 6th Series, vol. 258, col. 656.
184. *The Times*, 26.4.95.

THIRTY-TWO: 'BACKS TO THE WALL'

1. Private interview.
2. Private letter to author, 8.4.95.
3. *Daily Telegraph*, 15.3.95.
4. *Sunday Times*, 2.4.95.
5. Private interview.
6. Ibid.
7. Ibid.
8. *Sunday Times*, 2.4.95; *The Times*, 26.4.95.
9. Private interview.

10. *The Times, Independent,* 27.4.95.
11. Matthew d'Ancona, *The Times,* 27.4.95.
12. 'Our Future Homes: Opportunity, Choice, Responsibility', Cm 2901.
13. Interview with John Major, *Sunday Telegraph,* 30.3.97.
14. *Sunday Times,* 30.4.95;. Michael Jones, *Sunday Times,* 30.4.95.
15. Private interview.
16. Letter, Alastair Campbell to author, 30.7.97.
17. *Sunday Times,* 30.4.95.
18. *The Times,* 2.5.95.
19. *Independent,* 2.5.95.
20. Toby Helm, *Daily Telegraph,* 7.5.95.
21. *Independent,* 4.5.95.
22. Ibid., 5.5.95.
23. *Daily Telegraph,* 6.5.95.
24. *Sunday Telegraph,* 7.5.95.
25. Interview, Sir Rhodes Boyson, 18.4.96.
26. *Observer,* 7.5.95.
27. *The Times,* 6.5.95.
28. *Independent on Sunday,* 7.5.95.
29. Private interview.
30. Ibid.
31. Ibid.
32. Ibid.
33. *The Times,* 9.5.95.
34. Ibid., 10.5.95.
35. Interview 4, Howell James.
36. *Sunday Times,* 16.4.95.
37. Private interview.
38. Ibid.
39. Ibid.
40. Ibid.
41. Ibid.
42. *Independent on Sunday,* 7.5.95.
43. Andrew Marr, *Independent,* 16.5.95; *Daily Telegraph,* 17.5.95.
44. Private interview.
45. *Daily Telegraph,* 15.4.95; Michael White, *Guardian,* 5.5.95.
46. Private interview.
47. Ibid.
48. *Daily Telegraph,* 13.5.95.
49. *The Times,* 13.5.95. He elaborated on the speech in an article in the *Sunday Express,* 14 and 21.5.95.
50. *Sunday Telegraph,* 14.5.95.
51. *Daily Telegraph,* 13.5.95.
52. *Sunday Telegraph,* 14.5.95.
53. *Daily Telegraph,* 13.5.95.
54. Private interview.
55. *The Times,* 19.5.95.
56. *Spectator,* 20.5.95.
57. Anthony Seldon, diary, 18.5.95; private interview.
58. Private interview.
59. *Guardian,* 11.4.95.
60. Robert Shrimsley, *Daily Telegraph,* 20.5.95.
61. Interview 6, David Hunt, 17.3.97.
62. *The Times,* 12.5.95.
63. Private diary, 11.5.95; *The Times,* 12.5.95; *Sunday Telegraph,* 21.5.95.
64. *Guardian,* 12.5.95.
65. Robert Shrimsley, *Daily Telegraph,* 20.5.95.
66. *Daily Telegraph,* 17.5.95.
67. HC Debs, 6th Series, vol. 260, col. 506.
68. *The Times, Independent,* 19.5.95.
69. *The Times,* 19.5.95.
70. *Independent,* 23.5.95.
71. David Wastell, *Sunday Telegraph,* 21.5.95.
72. *The Times,* 18.5.95.
73. Ibid.
74. Private interview; *Observer,* 21.5.95; see also Andrew Marr's mordant piece, *Independent,* 24.5.95.
75. *The Times,* 26.5.95.
76. *Sunday Telegraph,* 28.5.95.
77. *The Times,* 29.5.95.
78. *Mail on Sunday,* 28.5.95.
79. *Daily Telegraph,* 29.5.95.
80. Private interview.
81. Interview, Sir Peter Inge, 22.5.96.
82. Private interviews.
83. *The Times,* 31.5.95.
84. HC Debs, 6th Series, vol. 260, col. 1005.
85. Ibid., col. 1006.
86. Andrew Marr, *Independent,* 1.6.95.
87. Private interview.
88. Private diary, 8.6.95.
89. *Sunday Telegraph,* 30.3.97.
90. Andrew Grice, *Sunday Times,* 11.6.95.
91. *Sunday Telegraph, Observer,* 11.6.95.
92. Private interview.
93. Ibid.
94. Ibid.
95. *Sunday Times,* 21.5.95.
96. Ibid.
97. *The Times,* 22.5.95.
98. Ibid., 15.6.95.
99. *Daily Telegraph,* 29.5.95.
100. *The Times,* 29.5.95.
101. *Guardian,* 9.6.95.
102. Private information.

103. Private interview.
104. *The Times*, 12.6.95.
105. *Sunday Times*, 18.6.95.
106. Excellent accounts of the meeting appeared in *The Times*, 16.6.95, *Sunday Times*, *Sunday Telegraph*, 18.6.95.
107. Toby Helm, *Sunday Telegraph*, 18.6.95.
108. Private interview.
109. Nicholas Wood and Arthur Leathley, *The Times*, 16.6.95.
110. *Sunday Times*, *Sunday Telegraph*, 19.6.95.
111. Private interview.
112. *The Times*, 26 and 27.5.95.
113. *The Times*, 13.6.95; *Observer*, 11.6.95.
114. Private interview.
115. Leader, *Daily Telegraph*, 13.5.95; *The Times*, 9.5.95; Clarke profile, *Sunday Telegraph*, 14.5.95.
116. Quoted in *Sunday Telegraph*, 13.5.95; Stephen Castle, *Independent on Sunday*, 7.5.95.
117. Private interview.
118. Ibid.; Boris Johnson, *Spectator*, 1.4.95.
119. Private interviews.
120. *The Times*, 12.6.95; private interview.
121. Interview 1, John Redwood.
122. *Independent*, 19.6.95.
123. Interview 3, Sir Graham Bright.
124. Private interview.
125. Interview 4, John Major; Junor (1996), p. 301.
126. Private interview.
127. Interview 2, Sir Graham Bright.
128. Junor (1996), p. 301.
129. *The Times*, 17.6.95.
130. *Independent*, 17.6.95.
131. *The Times*, 17.6.95.
132. *Daily Telegraph*, 17.6.95.
133. Private interview.
134. Janet Bush, *The Times*, 17.6.95; private interview.
135. Private interview.
136. Ibid.
137. *The Times*, 17.6.95.
138. *Guardian*, 16.6.95.
139. Private interview.
140. *Financial Times*, 21.6.95.
141. Private diary, 22.6.95.
142. Private interview.
143. *The Times*, 19.6.95; private interview.
144. Interview 3, John Major.
145. Interview 4, Douglas Hurd.
146. Interview 3, John Major.
147. *Independent on Sunday*, 25.6.95.
148. Interview 2, Sir Graham Bright.
149. *Sunday Times*, 25.6.95.
150. Hogg and Hill (1995), p. 267.
151. *Daily Telegraph*, 19.6.95.
152. Interview 3, John Major; Hogg and Hill (1995), pp. 267–8.
153. *Sunday Times*, 25.6.95.
154. *The Times*, 22.6.95.
155. Private interview.
156. Private interview.
157. Interview 2, Lord Cranborne, 15.5.96.
158. Ibid.
159. Private interview.
160. Ibid.
161. Ibid.
162. Hogg and Hill (1995), p. 269.
163. Matthew Parris, *The Times*, 23.6.95; Andrew Marr, *Independent*, 23.6.95.
164. Private diary, 22.6.96.
165. Private interview.
166. Interview 1, John Redwood; Don MacIntyre, *Independent*, 24.6.95.
167. *Sunday Times*, 25.6.95.
168. Stephen Castle, Paul Routledge, *Independent on Sunday*, 25.6.95.
169. Interview, Michael Brunson.
170. *The Times*, 22.6.95.

THIRTY-THREE: LEADERSHIP ON THE LINE

1. Interview 5, John Major.
2. Interview 4, Jonathan Hill.
3. Private interview.
4. *The Times*, 23.6.95.
5. *Guardian*, 24.6.95.
6. Private interview.
7. Ibid.
8. Private information.
9. Interview 7, Howell James, 23.4.96.
10. Interview 3, Lord Cranborne, 3.6.97.
11. Private interview.
12. Ibid.; *Independent on Sunday*, 2.7.95.
13. *Sunday Times*, 25.6.95.
14. Interview 2, Damian Green, 19.2.96.

15. Private interview; Hogg and Hill (1995), pp. 271–2.
16. Private interviews.
17. Ibid.; Hogg and Hill (1995), p. 272.
18. Interview, Edward Leigh, 10.3.97.
19. *The Times*, 23.6.95.
20. Hogg and Hill (1995), p. 272.
21. *Daily Express*, 23.6.95.
22. Private interview.
23. *Daily Telegraph*, *The Times*, 24.6.95.
24. Private interview.
25. Ibid.
26. Gove (1995), pp. 318–24.
27. *Sunday Times*, 2.7.95.
28. Interview 2, John Redwood, 1.7.97.
29. Hogg and Hill (1995), p. 273.
30. Private interview.
31. *Independent*, 26.6.95; *Observer*, 25.6.95.
32. Interview 1, John Redwood.
33. Private interview.
34. Interview 2, Ian Lang, 9.6.97.
35. Private interview.
36. Interview, Michael Portillo.
37. Interview, Lord Harris of Peckham, 7.7.97.
38. Michael Prescott, *Sunday Times*, 25.6.95; *Daily Telegraph*, 26.6.95.
39. Private interview.
40. Hogg and Hill (1995), p. 274.
41. Interview 3, Lord Cranborne.
42. Interview 2, Ian Lang.
43. Private interview.
44. Interview 2, Ian Lang.
45. Interview 2, Maurice Fraser.
46. Interview 4, Douglas Hurd.
47. Andrew Marr, *Independent*, 24.6.95; Hogg and Hill (1995).
48. *Sunday Times*, 25.6.95.
49. Crick (1997), pp. 413–17; Gove (1995), pp. 319–24.
50. *Sunday Times*, 2.7.95.
51. Private interview.
52. Interview 2, Damian Green.
53. *Sunday Telegraph*, 2.7.95.
54. Interview 2, John Redwood.
55. Private interview.
56. *Independent*, 27.6.95; Stephens (1997), p. 326.
57. Private interview.
58. Interview 2, John Redwood.
59. Interview, Robin Harris.
60. Interview, Lord McAlpine.
61. Private interview.
62. Ibid.; *Daily Telegraph*, 27.6.95.
63. Private interview.
64. Interview 4, Jonathan Hill.
65. Interview 4, Howell James; interview 4, Jonathan Hill.
66. *Evening Standard*, 27.6.95; Hogg and Hill (1995), p. 275.
67. Private interview.
68. *Independent*, 27.6.95.
69. Hogg and Hill (1995), p. 276.
70. Private interview.
71. *Sun*, 29.6.95.
72. *Sunday Times*, 2.7.95.
73. Private interviews.
74. HC Debs, 6th Series, vol. 262, col. 1078.
75. *Guardian*, 30.6.95.
76. Interview 2, Damian Green.
77. *Observer*, 2.7.95.
78. *Sunday Telegraph*, 2.7.95.
79. *Daily Telegraph*, 3.7.95.
80. David Wastell, *Sunday Telegraph*, 2.7.95.
81. Private interview; Hogg and Hill (1995), p. 280.
82. Ibid., pp. 278–9.
83. *Sun*, 29.6.95.
84. *The Economist*, 30.6.95.
85. *Sunday Times*, *Sunday Telegraph*, 2.7.95.
86. *Sunday Express*, 2.7.95.
87. *Daily Telegraph*, 3.7.95.
88. Pendennis, *Observer*, 9.7.95.
89. *Independent*, 30.6.95.
90. Private interview.
91. Stephens (1997), pp. 327–8.
92. *Financial Times*, 1.7.95.
93. *Daily Telegraph*, 4.7.95.
94. *Daily Mail*, 4.7.95.
95. See Riddell, *The Times*, 3.7.95, and Parris, *The Times*, 26.6.95.
96. Private interview.
97. Hogg and Hill (1995), p. 279.
98. Private interview; David Wastell, *Sunday Telegraph*, 26.11.95; Heseltine interview with Riddell and Webster, *The Times*, 2.12.95.
99. Private interviews.
100. Crick (1997), pp. 417–20. Crick, a shrewd investigative journalist, pooh-poohed the idea of a 'deal'. Gove (1995), pp. 338–9, asserts there was a deal. The *Sunday Times*, 9.7.95, was one of many press accounts speaking of the deal.
101. Hogg and Hill (1995), p. 281.
102. Private interview.
103. Interview 5, Howell James, 5.12.95.

104. Private interview.
105. Hogg and Hill (1995), p. 282. The abstentions rose later to twenty-two. For a discussion of what figure would constitute a victory, see Cowley (1996).
106. Interview 4, Jonathan Hill.
107. Interview 3, Lord Cranborne.
108. Interview 2, Damian Green.
109. Interview 1, Ian Lang.
110. *Sunday Times*, 9.7.95.
111. Interview 1, Lord Archer.
112. Private interview.
113. Ibid.
114. Interview 2, Ian Lang.
115. Interview, Norma Major.
116. *Independent*, 5.7.95.
117. Private interview.
118. Hogg and Hill (1995), p. 283.
119. Interview 5, Howell James.
120. Interview, Jonathan Holborow.
121. *Daily Telegraph*, 5.7.95.
122. *The Times*, 5.7.95; *Sunday Times*, 9.7.95. A lucid analysis of the Tory press's stance on Major can be found in Andrew Neil, *Sunday Times*, 9.7.95.
123. Private interview, 316.
124. *The Times*, 6.7.95.
125. *Guardian*, 5.7.95.
126. *The Times*, 6.7.95.
127. Leader, ibid.
128. Private interview.
129. *Daily Telegraph, Independent*, 6.7.95.
130. Private interview.
131. Private letter; private interview.
132. Private interview.
133. Interview 1, Jeremy Hanley.
134. Private interview.
135. Ibid.
136. Ibid.
137. Toby Helm, *Sunday Telegraph*, 9.7.95; Leader, *The Times*, 6.7.95.
138. *Sunday Times, Sunday Telegraph*, 9.7.95.
139. *Sunday Telegraph*, 9.7.95.

THIRTY-FOUR: BACK IN COMMAND

1. A common belief expressed in interviews with centre-left Cabinet ministers.
2. Andrew Rawnsley, *Observer*, 9.7.95.
3. Interview 7, Howell James.
4. Peter Riddell, *The Times*, 5.7.95.
5. *Guardian, The Times*, 12.7.95; Xhudo (1996), p. 141.
6. Private interview.
7. *Independent*, 15.7.95.
8. *The Times*, 15.7.95.
9. *Guardian*, 18.7.95; *The Times*, 15.7.95.
10. Private interview.
11. Interview 2, Sir Robin Renwick.
12. Private interview.
13. Interview 2, Sir Robin Renwick.
14. *Financial Times*, 22.9.95.
15. Private interview.
16. Ibid.
17. Ibid.
18. Private interviews.
19. *The Times*, 15.7.95.
20. Ibid., 14.7.95; *Independent on Sunday*, 16.7.95.
21. *Guardian*, 11.7.95; *The Times*, 14.7.95.
22. *Financial Times*, 28.7.95.
23. *The Times, Guardian*, 17.7.95.
24. Private interview.
25. Ibid.
26. Private interviews.
27. Private interview.
28. Ibid.
29. Ibid.
30. *Daily Telegraph*, 19.8.95.
31. *The Times*, 24.8.95.
32. Private interview.
33. Ibid.; *The Times*, 5.7.95.
34. Private interview.
35. *The Times*, 24.8.95; interview 2, Norman Blackwell.
36. Interview 3, Norman Blackwell, 11.6.97.
37. Interview, Bruce Anderson, 25.10.95.
38. Private interview; Norma Major (1996), p. 259.
39. *Observer*, 10.9.95.
40. John Clare, *Daily Telegraph*, 13.9.95.
41. Interview, Sir Tim Lankester.
42. Private interview.
43. *The Times*, 15.9.95.
44. Private interview.
45. Interview 3, Norman Blackwell, 6.6.97.
46. Private interview.
47. Ibid.

48. Ibid.
49. *Sunday Times*, 8.10.95.
50. *Guardian*, 21.9.95; *Daily Telegraph*, 23.9.95.
51. *Independent on Sunday, Sunday Telegraph*, 24.9.95.
52. *The Times*, 26.9.95; *Daily Telegraph*, 27.9.95.
53. Private interview.
54. *Sunday Times*, 17.9.95.
55. *The Times*, 29.9.95.
56. Interview 7, Nick True.
57. Anthony Bevins, *Observer*, 9.7.95.
58. Crick (1997), pp. 421–2.
59. Private interview.
60. Interview 1, Damian Green.
61. Interview 1, David Hunt.
62. Private interview; interview 1, David Hunt.
63. Private interview.
64. Interview 1, David Hunt.
65. Private interview.
66. Ibid.
67. Interview 6, Jonathan Hill.
68. Interview 7, Howell James.
69. Interview 6, Danny Finkelstein, 6.6.97.
70. *Sunday Times*, 8.10.95; *Daily Telegraph*, 7.10.95.
71. Interview, Alan Howarth.
72. Anthony Bevins, *Observer*, 8.10.95.
73. Letter, Alastair Campbell to author, 30.7.97.
74. *Observer*, 8.10.95.
75. Interview, Alan Howarth.
76. Private interview.
77. *Independent*, 9.10.95.
78. *Sunday Telegraph*, 15.10.95.
79. *Guardian*, 9 and 10.10.95.
80. *Sunday Times*, 15.10.95; *The Economist*, 13.10.95.
81. *Independent*, 11.10.95.
82. *The Times*, 11 and 12.10.95.
83. Private interview.
84. *Financial Times*, 12.10.95.
85. *Daily Telegraph*, 13.10.95.
86. *Sunday Times*, 15.10.95.
87. Private interview.
88. Interview 1, Sir Ronald Millar.
89. Interview 2, Tim Collins.
90. Private interview.
91. *The Times*, 14.10.95.
92. Interview 5, Howell James.
93. Private interview.
94. *Daily Telegraph*, 14.10.95.
95. *Independent*, 14.10.95.
96. *Guardian*, 14.10.95.
97. Toby Helm, David Wastell, *Sunday Telegraph*, 15.10.95.
98. Interview 1, Norman Blackwell, 24.8.95.
99. *Sunday Times*, 15.10.95.

THIRTY-FIVE: INTO A BOX

1. The issue is discussed in Lewis (1997), pp. 105–8, 116–23, 188–213.
2. Letter, Ann Widdecombe to author, 25.6.97.
3. Private interview.
4. *Financial Times*, 18.10.95.
5. *Guardian*, 19.10.95.
6. *Sunday Telegraph*, 22.10.95.
7. *The Times*, 23.10.95.
8. *Independent*, 24.10.95.
9. *The Times*, 24.10.95.
10. Ibid., 25.10.95.
11. Interview 1, Roderic Lyne, 9.1.96.
12. Private interview.
13. *Daily Telegraph*, 31.10.95.
14. *Independent*, 1.11.95.
15. Private interview.
16. *Sunday Times*, 5.11.95.
17. Interview, Iain McWhirter.
18. Private interview.
19. Ibid.
20. Nicholson (1996), pp. 9–15.
21. *Sunday Times*, 12.11.95. An editorial in the *Daily Telegraph*, 6.11.95, said, 'By putting the Nolan Committee above the authority of Parliament, Mr Major was guilty not just of a constitutional impertinence but a tactical error.'
22. Private interview.
23. Ibid.
24. *Independent*, 5.11.95.
25. Private interview.
26. *The Times*, 7.11.95.
27. *New Zealand Herald*, 1 and 2.11.95; *Financial Times*, 9.11.95.
28. Private interview.
29. *The Times*. 9.11.95.

30. Private interview.
31. *Daily Telegraph*, 10 and 11.11.95.
32. Private interview.
33. *The Times*, 9.11.95.
34. Private interview.
35. *Daily Telegraph*, 11.11.95.
36. *The Times*, 13.11.95.
37. *Sun*, 9.11.95.
38. *Sunday Times*, 12.11.95.
39. *Sun*, 9.11.95.
40. *Sunday Telegraph*, 12.11.95.
41. *Sunday Times*, 12.11.95.
42. *Evening Standard*, 14.12.95.
43. Interview 6, Danny Finkelstein.
44. *Independent*, 16.12.95.
45. Private interview.
46. Ibid.
47. Ibid.
48. Ibid.
49. Ibid.
50. *Daily Telegraph*, 16.11.95.
51. Private interview.
52. Robert Peston, *Financial Times*, 16.11.95.
53. *Daily Telegraph*, 16.11.95.
54. HC Debs, 6th Series, vol. 267, col. 22.
55. *Financial Times*, 16.11.95.
56. Private interview.
57. Ibid.
58. *Guardian*, 21.11.95.
59. *The Times*, 1.11.95.
60. *Evening Standard*, 2.11.95; *Guardian*, 3.11.95.
61. *Financial Times*, 16.11.95.
62. *Sun*, 29.11.95.
63. *The Times*, 29.11.95.
64. *Sunday Times*, 3.12.95.
65. *Sunday Telegraph*, 3.12.95.
66. Interview 2, Tim Collins.
67. *Independent on Sunday*, 12.11.95.
68. Interview 6, Howell James, 2.4.96.
69. Interview, *Daily Telegraph*, 27.11.95.
70. Ian Jack, *Independent on Sunday*, 26.11.95; Toby Helm, *Sunday Telegraph*, 26.11.95; Simon Heffer, *Observer*, 26.11.95.
71. *The Times*, 14.12.95.
72. *Daily Telegraph*, 22.11.95.
73. *Sunday Times*, 3.12.95.
74. *Sunday Telegraph*, 3.12.95.
75. *Observer*, 10.12.95.
76. Private interview.
77. *Daily Telegraph*, 13.12.95.
78. Ibid., 13, 15 and 21.12.95.
79. *Sunday Times*, 24.12.95.
80. Mallie and McKittrick (1996), pp. 364–5.
81. *Observer*, 10.9.95; *Independent*, 11.9.95.
82. Private interviews; Mallie and McKittrick (1996), p. 351.
83. Private interview.
84. *Sunday Telegraph*, 24.9.95.
85. Private interview.
86. *Guardian*, 25.11.95; *Sunday Times*, 26.11.95.
87. *The Economist*, 2.12.95.
88. Private interview; *The Times*, 29.11.95.
89. *Independent, Daily Telegraph*, 28.11.95.
90. *Daily Telegraph*, 29.11.95.
91. *Independent*, 4.12.95.
92. *The Economist*, 2.12.95.
93. *Independent*, 30.11.95.
94. Michael Jones, *Sunday Times*, 3.12.95; *Observer, Independent on Sunday*, 3.12.95.
95. Private interview.
96. *Independent*, 22.12.95.
97. Private interviews.
98. *Independent*, 25.1.96.
99. Private interview.
100. Mallie and McKittrick (1996), pp. 361–2.
101. Private interview.
102. Private interviews.
103. Private interview; *Observer, Sunday Times*, 11.2.96.
104. *Independent, Daily Telegraph*, 13.2.96.
105. Private interview; *Daily Telegraph*, 20.2.96.
106. *Sunday Times*, 15.10.95.
107. Interview 6, Danny Finkelstein.
108. Ibid.
109. Interview 3, Norman Blackwell; interview 6, Danny Finkelstein.
110. Private interview.
111. Interview 3, Norman Blackwell.
112. Private interview.
113. *Daily Telegraph*, 1.1.96; Nicholson (1996), pp. 211–15.
114. Private interview.
115. *Independent*, 1.1.96.
116. Private interview.
117. *Independent*, 8.1.96.
118. *Daily Telegraph*, 10.1.96.
119. Private interview.
120. *The Times, Independent*, 12.1.96.
121. Private interview.

122. David Wastell, *Sunday Telegraph*, 14.1.96.
123. *Guardian*, 8.1.96.
124. Andrew Grice, *Sunday Times*, 14.1.96; Iain McWhirter, *Observer*, 21.1.96.
125. *The Times*, 18.1.96; *Sunday Times*, 21.1.96.
126. Interview 2, Lord Cranborne.
127. HC Debs, 6th Series, vol. 270, cols 140–41.
128. *Sunday Telegraph*, 28.1.96.
129. *Guardian*, 30.1.96; *Daily Telegraph*, 31.1.96.
130. *Independent*, 2.2.96.
131. *Guardian*, 1.2.96.
132. Private interview.
133. Negrine (1997), p. 35.
134. Thompson and Ridley (1997), p. 4.
135. Interview, Max Hastings.
136. Private interview.
137. Ibid.
138. Ibid.
139. Ibid.
140. Ibid.
141. Lewis Baston, 'Getting Off Scott Free', Background paper, June 1997.
142. Philip Stephens, *Financial Times*, 16.2.96, quoted in Negrine (1997), p. 36.
143. Private interview.
144. Norton-Taylor, Lloyd and Cook (1996), p. 170.
145. *The Times*, 16.2.96.
146. *Financial Times*, 16.2.96.
147. *Daily Telegraph*, 21.2.96.
148. Private interview.
149. Private papers.
150. Norton-Taylor, Lloyd and Cook (1996), pp. 170–87.
151. Hennessy (1996), pp. 214–15; Bogdanor (1997), p. 85.

THIRTY-SIX: MAD COWS AND A NEW PARTY

1. Private interview.
2. Ibid.; *Independent*, 1.3.96.
3. *The Times*, 4.3.96.
4. Private interviews.
5. Private information.
6. Ibid.
7. *Sunday Telegraph*, 10.3.96.
8. *The Times*, 4.3.96.
9. Ibid., 4, 5 and 6.3.96.
10. Stephens (1996), p. 336; *Daily Telegraph*, 19.1.96.
11. Private interview.
12. Ibid.
13. Stephens (1996), pp. 336–7.
14. *The Times*, 21.10.95; *Daily Telegraph*, 16.12.95; private interview.
15. Private interview.
16. Ibid.; Stephens (1996), pp. 337–8.
17. Private interview; *Sunday Times*, 17.3.96.
18. Private interview.
19. Stephens (1996), pp. 340–41; *Daily Telegraph*, 8.3.96.
20. HC Debs, 6th Series, vol. 273, col. 450.
21. Private interview.
22. Ibid.; Stephens (1996), p. 342; Andrew Marr, *Independent*, 14.3.96; Sarah Hogg, *Daily Telegraph*, 18.3.96.
23. Private interview.
24. Ibid.
25. Private interviews.
26. *The Times*, 16.3.96.
27. Private interview.
28. Interview 2, Kenneth Clarke.
29. *Daily Telegraph*, 5.4.96.
30. Private interview.
31. *The Times*, 5.4.96; Stephens (1996), p. 345.
32. Private interview.
33. Stephens (1996), p. 345.
34. Private interview.
35. Ibid.
36. *Independent on Sunday*, 24.3.96.
37. *Observer*, 24.3.96.
38. Private interview.
39. *Daily Mirror*, 20.3.96.
40. *Sunday Telegraph*, 24.3.96.
41. Interview 1, Kenneth Clarke.
42. *Sunday Times, Independent on Sunday*, 24.3.96.
43. *Independent*, 21.3.96.
44. *The Times*, 23.3.96.
45. *Daily Telegraph, The Times*, 23.3.96.
46. Interview 3, Norman Blackwell; *Guardian*, 26.3.96.
47. Private interview.

48. Ibid.
49. Ibid.
50. *Daily Telegraph*, 29.3.96.
51. Private interview.
52. Private interviews.
53. *The Times*, 30.3.96.
54. Ibid., *Daily Telegraph*, 30.3.96.
55. *Independent*, 30.3.96.
56. Interview 3, Norman Blackwell.
57. Andrew Grice, *Sunday Times*, 31.3.96; *Sunday Telegraph*, 24.3.96.
58. *Financial Times*, 12.4.96.
59. Private interview.
60. *Sunday Times*, 14.4.96.
61. *Independent on Sunday, Sunday Times*, 14.4.96.
62. *Guardian*, 12.4.96.
63. *Independent*, 16.4.96.
64. *Daily Telegraph*, 13.4.96.
65. Private interview.
66. Private interview; *Daily Telegraph*, 18.4.96.
67. Private interview.
68. Interview 8, John Major, 23.8.97.
69. *Daily Telegraph*, 17.4.96.
70. *Independent*, 18.4.96.
71. *The Times*, 19.4.96.
72. *Daily Telegraph*, 18.4.96.
73. Private interview.
74. *Sunday Telegraph*, 21.4.96.
75. *Daily Telegraph*, 14.4.96.
76. *The Times*, 25.4.96.
77. Interview 3, John Redwood, 19.7.97.
78. Private interview.
79. Ibid.
80. Interview, Lord McAlpine.
81. Private interview.
82. Andrew Grice, *Sunday Times*, 28.4.96; Anthony Bevins, *Observer*, 28.4.96.
83. Private interview; *The Times*, 25.4.96.
84. *Daily Mail*, 25.4.96.
85. *Independent*, 1.5.96.
86. *Observer*, 5.5.96; *The Times*, 19.4.96.
87. *The Times*, 25.4.96.
88. *Daily Telegraph*, 30.4.96.
89. *Sunday Times*, 28.4.96.
90. *Sunday Times*, 5.5.96.
91. Interview 8, Howell James.
92. *Guardian*, 4.5.96.
93. *Independent on Sunday, Sunday Times*, 5.5.96.
94. *Evening Standard*, 3.5.96.
95. Michael Jones, *Sunday Times*, 5.5.96.
96. David Wastell, *Sunday Telegraph*, 5.5.96.
97. *Sunday Times*, 7.4.96.
98. Julie Kirkbride, David Wastell, *Sunday Telegraph*, 26.5.96.
99. Private interview.
100. *Sunday Telegraph*, 26.5.96.
101. *Daily Telegraph*, 22.4.96.
102. *Sunday Times*, 28.4.96; *Sunday Telegraph*, 26.5.96.
103. *Sunday Times, Independent on Sunday*, 5.5.96.
104. Private interview.
105. *Observer*, 12.5.96.
106. *Sunday Telegraph*, 26.5.96; private interview.
107. Private interview: *Independent on Sunday*, 26.5.96.
108. *Sunday Times, Sunday Telegraph*, 26.5.96.
109. Matthew d'Ancona, *Sunday Telegraph*, 26.5.96.
110. *Daily Mail*, 22.5.96.
111. Private interview.
112. *Sunday Times*, 26.6.96.
113. *Independent on Sunday*, 26.5.96; *The Times*, 27.5.96.
114. Stephens (1996), p. 346; *Independent on Sunday*, 26.5.96.
115. *Sunday Telegraph*, 16.6.96.
116. Andrew Grice, Michael Prescott, *Sunday Times*, 16.6.96; *Independent*, 14.6.96.
117. *The Times*, 1.5.96.
118. *Guardian*, 15.6.96.
119. Patrick Wintour and Stephen Bates, *Observer*, 23.6.96.
120. *Financial Times*, 22.6.96.
121. *Sunday Times*, 23.6.96.
122. *The Times*, 20.6.96.
123. *Independent, The Times*, 20.6.96.
124. *Sunday Times*, 23.6.96.
125. *Guardian*, 21.6.96.
126. *Sunday Times*, 23.6.96.
127. *Independent*, 22.6.96.
128. Private interview.
129. *Independent*, 17.11.95.
130. Interview, Lord Strathclyde, 24.6.97.
131. Interview, Douglas Slater, 24.6.97.
132. Interview 3, Lord Cranborne.
133. Private letter to author.
134. Conservative Party News, CPS Lecture, 26 June 1996.
135. *Daily Telegraph*, 29.2.96.

136. *Observer*, 10.3.96.
137. *Independent*, 29.2.96.

138. Private interview.
139. Ibid.

THIRTY-SEVEN: 'WE'LL WIN'

1. *Sunday Times*, 7.7.96.
2. *Independent*, 20.5.96; *Guardian*, 22.5.96; *The Times*, 28.8.96; *Sunday Times*, 26.5.96.
3. *The Times*, 15.5.96
4. Interview 6, Danny Finkelstein.
5. Interview 1, Brian Mawhinney, 24.6.97.
6. Interview 3, Danny Finkelstein.
7. Interview 3, Norman Blackwell; *The Times*, 2.7.96.
8. Private interview.
9. Private interview.
10. *Daily Telegraph*, 3.7.96.
11. *The Times*, 3.7.96.
12. Interview 6, Danny Finkelstein.
13. Interview 3, Norman Blackwell.
14. Ibid.
15. Memo, Blackwell to Major and Clarke, 12.7.96.
16. *Sunday Times*, 13.10.96.
17. *Observer*, 2.6.96.
18. Private interview.
19. *Daily Telegraph*, 1.7.96.
20. Private interview.
21. *Independent*, 29.6.96.
22. *The Times*, 8.7.96.
23. Private interview.
24. *Independent*, 13.7.96.
25. *The Times*, 13 and 15.7.96; Paul Routledge, Stephen Castle, *Independent on Sunday*, 14.7.96.
26. *Daily Telegraph*, 23.7.96.
27. *Independent*, 17.7.96.
28. Private interview.
29. *Independent*, 19.7.97.
30. *The Times*, 29.6.96.
31. Private interview.
32. *The Times*, 11.7.96.
33. *Guardian*, 19.7.96.
34. *Independent*, 19.7.96.
35. *Daily Telegraph*, 23.7.96.
36. *The Times*, 23.7.96.
37. Private interviews.
38. *The Times*, 25.7.96.
39. *Sunday Telegraph*, 28.7.96.
40. *The Times*, 20.7.96.
41. Ibid., 4.7.96, 6.8.96.

42. *Daily Telegraph*, 4.7.96.
43. *Independent*, 6.7.96.
44. *The Times*, 30.7.96; *Independent on Sunday*, 28.7.96.
45. Private interview.
46. Ibid.
47. *The Times*, 24.7.96.
48. Private interview.
49. *New Statesman and Society*, 9.8.96.
50. Tom Baldwin, *Sunday Telegraph*, 18.8.96.
51. Interview 1, Brian Mawhinney.
52. *Sunday Telegraph*, 18 and 25.8.96.
53. Ibid., 18.8.96.
54. Private interview.
55. *The Times*, 21.8.96.
56. *New Statesman and Society*, 30.8.96.
57. *Daily Telegraph*, 26.9.96.
58. *The Times*, 1.8.96, 30.9.96.
59. *Sunday Telegraph, Mail on Sunday*, 8.9.96; Elizabeth Grice, *Daily Telegraph*, 26.9.96.
60. Private interview.
61. *The Times*, 5.9.96.
62. *Sunday Times*, 15.9.96.
63. Ibid., 8.9.96.
64. Private interview.
65. *The Times*, 14.9.96.
66. Private interview.
67. Ibid.
68. *Independent*, 12.9.96.
69. *Guardian*, 16.9.96.
70. *The Times*, 7.9.96.
71. *Guardian*, 6.9.96; private interview.
72. Interview 6, Danny Finkelstein.
73. Interview 2, Charles Lewington, 29.5.97.
74. Interview 3, Norman Blackwell.
75. Interview 6, Danny Finkelstein.
76. Interview 4, George Bridges, 3.7.97; private letter to author, 23.7.97.
77. Interview 3, Charles Lewington, 28.6.97.
78. Ibid.
79. Private letter to author, 29.7.97.

80. Interview 6, Danny Finkelstein.
81. Private interview.
82. Interview 6, Danny Finkelstein.
83. *Daily Telegraph*, 19.9.96.
84. *Independent*, 19.9.96.
85. Private interview.
86. Ibid.
87. *Independent*, 20.9.96.
88. *Sunday Times*, 22.9.96.
89. *Independent*, 19.9.96; Stephens (1996), p. 355.
90. Private interview.
91. *The Times*, 17.9.96.
92. *Daily Telegraph*, 29.9.96.
93. *Independent*, 25.9.96.
94. Private interview.
95. Ibid.
96. *Guardian*, 31.8.96.
97. *The Times*, 24.9.96.
98. Interview 2, Charles Lewington; interview 1, Brian Mawhinney.
99. *Sunday Telegraph*, 13.10.96.
100. Private interview.
101. Ibid.
102. Private interview; *The Times*, 4.9.96.
103. Private interview.

104. *The Times*, 7.10.96.
105. Private interview.
106. *The Times*, 7.10.96; *Observer*, 6.10.96; *The Times*, 5.10.96.
107. *Sunday Telegraph*, 6.10.96.
108. Private interview.
109. *The Times*, *Daily Telegraph*, 7.10.96.
110. *Daily Telegraph*, 8.10.96.
111. Private interview.
112. Private interview.
113. *Sunday Times*, 13.10.96.
114. *Daily Telegraph*, 10.10.96.
115. Private interview.
116. Ibid.
117. Ibid.
118. *The Times*, 11.10.96.
119. David Wastell, Tom Baldwin, *Sunday Telegraph*, 13.10.96.
120. Private interview.
121. Conservative Party News, Prime Minister's Speech, 11.10.96.
122. *Guardian*, 12.10.96.
123. *Daily Mail*, *Express*, 12.10.96.
124. Private interview.
125. *Sunday Telegraph*, 13.10.96.
126. *Daily Telegraph*, 11.10.96.

THIRTY-EIGHT: CAN THE CENTRE HOLD?

1. Anthony Seldon, diary, 2.10.96.
2. *Sunday Times*, 20.10.96.
3. Private interview.
4. *Sunday Times*, 13.10.96.
5. Private interview.
6. *Sunday Telegraph*, 13.10.96.
7. Ibid., 7.4.96.
8. Ibid., 2.10.96; extract from *Belief in Politics* (1996)
9. *Independent on Sunday*, 1.11.96; private interview.
10. Private interview; *Independent on Sunday*, 3.11.96.
11. *Sunday Times*, 20.10.96.
12. *Daily Telegraph*, 25.10.96.
13. Private interview.
14. Private interview.
15. Ibid.
16. *Daily Telegraph*, 31.10.96.
17. Private interview.
18. *Sunday Times*, 3.11.96.
19. *Sunday Telegraph*, 24.11.96; private interview.

20. Private interview.
21. Private interview.
22. Interview 2, Kenneth Clarke.
23. *The Times*, 19.10.96.
24. *Guardian*, 8.11.96; *The Times*, 9.11.96.
25. *Independent*, 14.11.96.
26. *Observer*, 24.11.96.
27. Jones (1997), pp. 78–9.
28. *Sunday Times*, 24.11.96.
29. Private interview.
30. *Sunday Telegraph*, 24.11.96.
31. *Observer*, *Sunday Times*, 24.11.96.
32. Interview 3, John Redwood.
33. *Sun*, 22.11.96.
34. *Sunday Telegraph*, 24.11.96.
35. *Sunday Times*, 24.11.96.
36. Jones (1997), pp. 56–60.
37. *The Times*, 26.11.96.
38. Private interview.
39. Ibid.
40. Interview 2, Kenneth Clarke.
41. Ibid.

42. Private interview.
43. *The Times*, 26.7.96; private interview.
44. Private interview.
45. *Daily Mirror*, 19.11.96.
46. Private interview.
47. Interview 8, John Major.
48. Interview 5, Norman Blackwell, 19.7.97.
49. Interview 2, Charles Moore, 7.7.97.
50. *Sunday Telegraph*, 1.12.96; *Daily Telegraph*, 2.12.96; private interviews.
51. Interview 3, Charles Moore.
52. Interview 8, John Major.
53. Private interview.
54. Interview 2, Kenneth Clarke.
55. Private interview.
56. Excellent accounts of the week are to be found in the *Sunday Times*, *Sunday Telegraph*, *Observer*, *Independent on Sunday*, 8.12.96.
57. *Sunday Times*, 8.12.96.
58. *Sunday Telegraph*, 8.12.96.
59. *Independent*, 4.12.96.
60. *Observer*, 8.12.96.
61. *Sunday Telegraph*, 8.12.96.
62. *The Times*, 4.12.96.
63. *Observer*, 8.12.96.
64. Private interview.
65. *The Times*, 5.12.96; *Sunday Times*, 8.12.96.
66. *Observer*, 8.12.96.
67. Interview 8, John Major.
68. *Sunday Telegraph*, 8.12.96.
69. *Independent on Sunday*, *Observer*, 8.12.96.
70. *Guardian*, 7.12.96.
71. *Sunday Times*, 8.12.96; Peter Riddell, *The Times*, 6.12.96.
72. *The Times*, 9.12.96.
73. *Independent on Sunday*, 8.12.96.
74. Private interview.
75. Ibid.
76. Stephens (1996), p. 352.
77. Private interview; *Sunday Telegraph*, 8.12.96.
78. Private interview.
79. *Daily Telegraph*, 20.12.96; private interviews.
80. Interview 2, Kenneth Clarke.
81. *The Times*, 10.12.96; private interview.
82. *Independent*, 12.12.96.
83. *Daily Telegraph*, 16.12.96.
84. *The Times*, 17.12.96; *Observer*, 22.12.96.
85. Interview 6, Danny Finkelstein.
86. Private interview.
87. Ibid.
88. Ibid.
89. Interview, Tony Garrett, 3.7.97.
90. Ibid.
91. Interview 5, George Bridges.
92. Interview 8, John Major.
93. Private interviews; *Guardian*, 21.12.96.
94. Private interview.
95. Ibid.
96. Ibid.
97. Letter, Speaker to Prime Minister, 26.11.73.
98. Private interviews.
99. Private interview.
100. Interview 3, George Bridges, 20.6.97.
101. *The Times*, 6.1.97.
102. Patrick Wintour, *Observer*, 5.1.97.
103. Interview 1, Brian Mawhinney.
104. *Sunday Telegraph*, 12.1.97.
105. Memo, Bridges to Major, 8.1.97.
106. Private interview.
107. Editorial, *Independent*, 10.1.97.
108. Interview 2, Ian Lang.
109. Private interview.
110. Ibid.; *The Times*, 15.1.97.
111. Andy McSmith, *Observer*, 9.2.97.
112. *The Times*, 14.1.97; *Independent on Sunday*, 12.1.97.
113. *The Times*, 7.1.97; interview 3, George Bridges.
114. *Independent*, 17.1.97.
115. Private interview.
116. *Independent on Sunday*, *Observer*, 19.1.97.
117. Private interviews.
118. Private interview.
119. *Independent*, 24.1.97.
120. *Daily Telegraph*, *The Times*, 24.1.97.
121. Private interview.
122. Interview 2, Kenneth Clarke.
123. *The Times*, 24.1.97.
124. Private interview.
125. *Observer*, 9.2.97.
126. Private interview.
127. Ibid.
128. Ibid.
129. Ibid.
130. Williams (1997), p. 12.
131. Interview 2, Charles Lewington.
132. *Daily Telegraph*, *Daily Mail*, 28.1.97.
133. Private interview.
134. Ibid.

135. Ibid.
136. Ibid.
137. *The Times*, 1.2.97.
138. Ibid., 31.1.97.
139. Private interview.
140. Ibid.
141. Ibid.
142. Ibid.
143. *The Times*, 5.2.97.
144. Interview 2, Charles Lewington.
145. Private interview.
146. Ibid.
147. *The Times*, 15.2.97.
148. *Daily Telegraph*, 15.2.97.
149. *Sunday Times*, 16.2.97.
150. Private interview.
151. *The Times*, 18.2.97.
152. Private interview.
153. Ibid.
154. *Independent*, 21.2.97.
155. David Wastell, Tom Baldwin, *Sunday Telegraph*, 23.2.97.
156. *Sunday Telegraph*, 2.3.97.
157. Private interview.
158. *The Times*, 1.3.97.
159. Private interview.
160. Private interview.
161. Private interview.
162. *Independent*, 1.3.97.
163. Private interview.
164. *The Times, Daily Telegraph*, 6.3.97; *Sunday Times*, 9.3.97.
165. *Independent*, 28.2.97.
166. *Sunday Times*, 2.3.97.
167. Private interview.
168. Private interviews.
169. *Guardian*, 5.3.97.
170. Ibid., 6.3.97.
171. *Daily Telegraph*, 5.3.97; private interview.
172. *Sunday Times*, 9.3.97; *The Times*, 10.3.97.
173. *Observer*, 9.3.97.
174. Interview 5, George Bridges.
175. *Independent*, 15.3.97.
176. Williams (1997), p. 19.
177. Private interview.
178. Ibid.
179. Ibid.; *Sunday Times, Sunday Telegraph, Independent on Sunday*, 16.3.97.
180. Williams (1997), pp. 20–21.
181. *Sunday Times*, 16.3.97.

THIRTY-NINE: THE END OF A PREMIERSHIP

1. Private interview.
2. Interview, Max Hastings.
3. Private interview.
4. Ibid.; Siklos (1995), pp. 226–33.
5. Private interview.
6. Interview 8, John Major.
7. Interview 1, Charles Moore, 19.2.96.
8. Private interviews.
9. Interview, Dominic Lawson, 13.3.97.
10. Private interview.
11. Ibid.
12. Interview 3, Peter Stothard, 7.6.96.
13. Private interviews.
14. Ibid.
15. Private interview.
16. Ibid.
17. *The Times*, 29.4.97.
18. Letter, Brian Mawhinney to author, 5.8.97.
19. Neil (1996); interview, Michael Jones.
20. Private interviews.
21. Interview 2, Charles Lewington.
22. Private interview.
23. *Sun*, 4.12.96.
24. Private interview.
25. Roy Greenslade, *Guardian*, 19.3.97.
26. Major's notes of speech to the 1922 Committee, private papers.
27. *News of the World*, 27.4.97.
28. Andy McSmith, *Observer*, 2.2.97.
29. The view also of John Lloyd, *New Statesman and Society*, 15.11.96.
30. Private interview.
31. *Daily Mail*, 30.4.97.
32. Private interview.
33. Letter, Alastair Campbell to author, 30.7.97.
34. *Evening Standard*, 29.4.97.
35. Steven Glover, *Daily Telegraph*, 30.4.97.
36. Interview, Richard Addis, 20.6.95.
37. *Sunday Express*, 27.4.97.
38. Private interview.
39. Butler and Kavanagh (1997); Williams (1997), p. 24.
40. Private interview.
41. Ibid.

42. Ibid.
43. *Observer*, 23.3.97.
44. Private interview.
45. *Guardian*, 21.3.97.
46. *Sunday Express*, 23.3.97.
47. Private interview.
48. *Guardian*, 29.3.97.
49. Private interview.
50. Butler and Kavanagh (1997); Tony Hall and Anne Sloman, *Independent*, 2.7.97.
51. Private interview.
52. *The Times*, 1.4.97.
53. Interview 7, Danny Finkelstein, 7.7.97.
54. Patrick Wintour, *Observer*, 6.4.97.
55. Interview 2, David Willetts, 9.7.97.
56. Interview 4, Norman Blackwell, 30.6.97.
57. Private interview.
58. *The Times, Daily Telegraph*, 3.4.97.
59. *Observer*, 6.4.97.
60. Michael Jones, *Sunday Times*, 6.4.97.
61. *Sunday Times*, 6.4.97.
62. *Sunday Telegraph*, 6.4.97.
63. *Sunday Times*, 6.4.97.
64. Ibid., 13.4.97.
65. *Daily Telegraph*, 8.4.97; *Sunday Times*, 13.4.97.
66. *Sunday Times*, 13.4.97.
67. Ibid.
68. Private interview.
69. *Observer*, 20.4.97.
70. *The Times*, 14.4.97.
71. Private interview.
72. *Guardian*, 15.4.97.
73. Interview 6, Jonathan Hill.
74. *Guardian*, 15.4.97.
75. *Sunday Times*, 20.4.97.
76. *Observer*, 20.4.97.
77. Private interview.
78. Letter, Alastair Campbell to author, 30.7.97.
79. Williams (1997), p. 80.
80. *Observer*, 20.4.97.
81. *Guardian*, 17.4.97.
82. Karen Baston, Lewis Baston diary, 17.4.97.
83. *Sunday Telegraph*, 1.6.97; *Sunday Times*, 30.4.97; private interviews.
84. *Daily Telegraph*, 17.4.97.
85. Butler and Kavanagh (1997).
86. Private interviews.
87. Interview 8, Danny Finkelstein, 9.7.97.
88. Butler and Kavanagh (1997); private interview.

89. *Observer*, 20.4.97.
90. Anthony Seldon interview with John Major, *Sunday Telegraph*, 30.3.97.
91. *Independent*, 6.4.97.
92. *Sunday Times*, 20.4.97.
93. Private interview; *Sunday Times*, 20.4.97.
94. Private interview.
95. Ibid.
96. Private interviews.
97. Ibid.
98. Private interview.
99. Ibid.
100. *Sunday Times*, 13.4.97.
101. Private interview.
102. *Sunday Times*, 20.4.97.
103. *Sunday Times*, 20.4.97; *The Times*, 19.4.97.
104. Riddell wrote very critically of the Kohl advertisement in *The Times*, 19.4.97; see also Leader, *Independent*, 19.4.97.
105. *Observer*, 20.4.97.
106. *Sunday Telegraph*, 21.4.97.
107. Private diary, 24.4.97.
108. Private interviews.
109. *The Times*, 21.4.97.
110. Interview 2, Brian Mawhinney, 6.7.97.
111. Rian Malan, *Observer*, 27.4.97.
112. Planned Prime Minister's speech to Conservative Party Rally, Aberdeen, 23.4.97.
113. *Independent*, 24.4.97.
114. Transcript of Prime Minister's actual speech, Aberdeen, 23.4.97.
115. Private interview.
116. *Sunday Times*, 27.4.97.
117. *Independent on Sunday*, 27.4.97.
118. Private interview.
119. Ibid.
120. *Sunday Times*, 27.4.97.
121. Private interview.
122. *Independent on Sunday*, 27.4.97.
123. Private interview.
124. Ibid.
125. *Sunday Times*, 27.4.97.
126. Private interview.
127. Interview 11, Howell James, 1.7.97.
128. Private diary, 24.4.97.
129. Private interview.
130. Ibid.
131. *Sunday Telegraph*, 27.4.97.
132. Private interview.
133. *Sunday Telegraph*, 27.4.97.
134. Private interviews.

135. *Daily Telegraph, Guardian*, 29.4.97.
136. *Financial Times*, 29.4.97.
137. *The Times*, 29.4.97.
138. *Daily Telegraph*, 29.4.97.
139. Interview, Tony Garrett.
140. *The Times, Financial Times*, 29.4.97.
141. Private interview.

EPILOGUE: THE VERDICT

1. *Daily Mail*, 19.6.97.
2. Anthony Seldon, diary, 19.6.97.
3. *Daily Telegraph*, 5.5.97.
4. Interview 7, John Major.
5. Interview 8, John Major.
6. I developed this analysis first in Marquand and Seldon (1996), pp. 257–89.
7. I argued similarly in *Churchill's Indian Summer* that if Churchill had been 'gaga' during 1951–5, his government would not have achieved so much.

BIBLIOGRAPHY

BOOKS AND PAPERS

Anderson, B., *John Major*, London, Weidenfeld & Nicolson, 1991

Arthur, P. and Jeffrey, K., *Northern Ireland Since 1968*, Oxford, Blackwell, 1996

Baker, J., *The Politics of Diplomacy*, New York, Putnam, 1995

Baker, K., *The Turbulent Years*, London, Faber & Faber, 1993

Balen, M., *Kenneth Clarke*, London, Fourth Estate, 1994

Bell, S., *For Whom Bell Tolls*, London, Methuen, 1994

Bell, S. and Hoggart, S., *Live Briefs*, London, Methuen, 1996

Blackstone, T. and Plowden, W., *Inside the Think Tank*, London, Heinemann, 1988

Bonefeld, W., Brown, A. and Burnham, P., *A Major Crisis?*, Aldershot, Dartmouth, 1995

Brock, C., *Rutlish School: The First Hundred Years*, Merton, Rutlish School, 1995

Bush, B., *Barbara Bush: A Memoir*, New York, St Martin's Press, 1995

Butler, D., Adonis, A. and Travers, T., *Failure in British Government*, Oxford, OUP, 1994

—— and Kavanagh, D., *The British General Election of 1992*, London, Macmillan, 1992

—— and Kavanagh, D., *The British General Election of 1997*, London, Macmillan, 1997

—— and Pinto-Duschinsky, M., *The British General Election of 1970*, London, Macmillan, 1971

—— and Westlake, M., *British Politics and European Elections 1994*, London, Macmillan, 1995

Catterall, P. (ed.), *Contemporary Britain 1991*, Aldershot, Dartmouth, 1991

——, *Contemporary Britain 1992*, Aldershot, Dartmouth, 1992

——, *Contemporary Britain 1993*, Aldershot, Dartmouth, 1993

——, *Contemporary Britain 1994*, Aldershot, Dartmouth, 1994

——, *Contemporary Britain 1995*, Aldershot, Dartmouth, 1996

Clark, A., *Diaries*, Weidenfeld & Nicolson, London, 1993

Cole, J., *As It Seemed to Me*, Weidenfeld & Nicolson, London, 1995

Connolly, B., *The Rotten Heart of Europe*, London, Faber & Faber, 1995

Conservative Party, *The Best Future for Britain*, London CCO, 1992

——, *You Can Only Be Sure With the Conservatives*, London, CCO, 1997

Cowley, P., *How Did He Do That?*, Hull, University of Hull, 1995

Cradock, P., *Experiences of China*, London, Routledge, 1993

Crewe, I. and Fox, A., *British Parliamentary Constituencies, A Statistical Compendium*, London, Faber, 1984.

Crick, M., *Jeffrey Archer: Stranger Than Fiction*, London, Penguin, 1995

——, *Michael Heseltine*, London, Hamish Hamilton, 1997

De la Billière, P., *Storm Command*, London, HarperCollins, 1992

Dell, E., *The Chancellors*, London, HarperCollins, 1996

Dimbleby, J., *The Last Governor*, London, Little, Brown, 1997

Fisher, N., *Iain Macleod*, London, Deutsch, 1973

Fowler, N., *Ministers Decide*, London, Chapman, 1991

Franklin, M. and Norton, P. (eds), *Questions,*

Oxford, Clarendon, 1993

Freedman, L. and Karsh, E., *The Gulf Conflict 1990–91*, London, Faber & Faber, 1991

Gorman, T., *The Bastards*, London, Pan, 1993

Gove, M., *Michael Portillo*, London, Fourth Estate, 1995

Harloe, M., Issacharoff, R. and Minns, R., *The Organization of Housing: Public and Private Enterprise in London*, London, Heinemann Educational, 1974

Heath, A., Jowell, R., Curtice, J. et al., *Labour's Last Chance?*, Aldershot, Dartmouth, 1994

Hennessy, P., *The Hidden Writing*, London, Gollancz, 1996

Hogg, S. and Hill, J., *Too Close to Call*, London, Little, Brown, 1995

Howe, G., *Conflict of Loyalty*, London, Macmillan, 1994

Hutton, W., *The State We're In*, London, Jonathan Cape, 1995

Jenkin, J. (ed.), *John Major: Prime Minister*, London, Bloomsbury, 1990

Jones, N., *Campaign 92*, London, BBC, 1992

——, *Soundbites and Spin Doctors*, London, Cassell, 1995

——, *Campaign 97*, London, Indigo, 1997

Junor, P., *The Major Enigma*, London, Michael Joseph, 1993

——, *John Major: From Brixton to Downing Street*, London, Penguin, 1996

Lawson, N., *The View from Number 11*, London, Bantam, 1992

Leigh, D. and Vulliamy, E., *Sleaze: The Corruption of Parliament*, London, Fourth Estate, 1997

Lewis, D., *Hidden Agendas*, London, Hamish Hamilton, 1997

Major, J., *The Power to Choose: The Right to Own*, London, Conservative Political Centre, 1991

——, *Trust the People*, London, Conservative Political Centre, 1992

Major, N., *Chequers*, London, HarperCollins, 1996

Major-Ball, T., *Major Major*, London, Duckworth, 1994

Malcolm, N., *Bosnia: A Short History*, London, Macmillan, 1994

Mallie, E. and McKittrick, D., *The Fight for Peace*, London, Heinemann, 1996

Marr, A., *The Battle for Scotland*, London, Penguin, 1994

McCloughry, R. (ed.), *Belief in Politics*, London, Hodder & Stoughton, 1996

McSmith, A., *Kenneth Clarke*, London, Verso, 1994

——, *John Smith: A Life*, London, Minerva, 1994

Millar, R., *A View from the Wings*, London, Weidenfeld & Nicolson, 1993

Neil, A., *Full Disclosure*, London, Macmillan, 1996

Nicholson, E., *Secret Society*, London, Indigo, 1996

Norton-Taylor, R., Lloyd, M. and Cook, S., *Knee-deep in Dishonour*, London, Gollancz, 1996

Owen, D., *Balkan Odyssey*, London, Gollancz, 1995

Pearce, E., *The Quiet Rise of John Major*, London, Weidenfeld & Nicolson, 1991

Ridley, N., *My Style of Government*, London, Hutchinson, 1991

Ryan, T., *Albert Reynolds: The Longford Leader*, Dublin, Blackwater, 1994

Seldon, A. and Ball, S. (eds), *The Heath Government*, London, Macmillan, 1996

Seldon, A. and Kavanagh, D. (eds), *The Major Effect*, London, Macmillan, 1994

Siklos, R., *Shades of Black*, London, Heinemann, 1995

Silber, L. and Little, A., *The Death of Yugoslavia*, London, Penguin, 1995

Smith, D., *From Boom to Bust*, London, Penguin, 1992

Standard Chartered Bank, *Standard Chartered: A Story Brought Up to Date*, London SCB, 1980

Stephens, P., *Politics and the Pound*, London, Macmillan, 1996

——, *Politics and the Pound*, 2nd edn, London, Papermac, 1997

Stewart, R., *Broken Lives*, London, HarperCollins, 1993

Thatcher, C., *Below the Parapet*, London, Chivers Press, 1997

Thatcher, M., *The Downing Street Years*, London, HarperCollins, 1995

Thompson, B. and Ridley, F. (eds), *Under the Scott-light: British Government Seen Through the Scott Report*, Oxford, OUP, 1997

Tonge, J. and Geddes, A., *Labour's Landslide: The British General Election 1997*, Manchester, Manchester University Press, 1997

Tunstall, J., *Newspaper Power*, Oxford, OUP, 1996

Urban, G., *Diplomacy and Disillusion at the Court of Margaret Thatcher*, London, I. B. Tauris, 1996

Vulliamy, E., *Seasons in Hell*, London, Simon & Schuster, 1994

——, *Bosnia: The Secret War*, London, The Guardian, 1996

Walker, T., *Norma*, London, Fourth Estate, 1993

Watkins, A., *A Conservative Coup*, London, Duckworth, 1991

Whiteley, C. et al., *True Blues*, Oxford, OUP, 1994

Williams, J., *Victory*, London, Bookman Projects, 1997

Woodward, B., *The Agenda*, London, Simon & Schuster, 1994

Wyn Ellis, N., *John Major*, London, Futura, 1991

Xhudo, G., *Diplomacy and Crisis Management in the Balkans*, Basingstoke, Macmillan, 1996

ARTICLES

Baker, S., Gamble, A. and Ludlam, S., 'Whips or Scorpions?', *Parliamentary Affairs* 47.1, 1993

Burnham, J. and Jones, G. W., *British Journal of Political Science* 5.25, 1996, pp. 551–63

Cowley, P., 'The Mystery of the Third Hurdle', *Politics* 16(2), 1996

Mansergh, M. (a), 'The Background to the Peace Process', address to the International Committee of the Royal Irish Academy, 22.5.95

Mansergh, M. (b), 'Building the Bridge to Peace', paper given to symposium on Irish republicanism, University of Rennes, 16.9.95

SUNDAY TIMES FOCUS

14 Jan. 1990   Grice, Smith, Hughes, 'Back to the bad old days?'

24 June 1990   Jones, Smith, 'Quids out!'

7 Oct. 1990   Jones, Smith, 'Inside the snake'

18 Nov. 1990   Hughes, Driscoll, 'The duel for the crown'

25 Nov. 1990   Hughes, 'Tory three ring circus'

2 Dec. 1990   Hughes, 'The people's champion'

20 Jan. 1991   Gulf War Team, 'War: the first three days'

10 Feb. 1991   Chittenden, Leppard, Rayment, 'The day John Major missed his lunch'

24 March 1991   Jones, Grice, Hughes, ' "Big Bertha" heaves the poll tax into history'

21 April 1991   Cassidy, Hughes, Adams, Driscoll, 'Haven from the hell-holes'

5 May 1991   Grice, 'Open verdict'

12 May 1991   Grice, 'Under starter's orders'

19 May 1991   Jones, Smith, Hughes, 'Nightmare at Number 10'

23 June 1991   Grice, Hughes, Cassidy, 'The Tory family at war'

8 Sept. 1991   Hughes, Grice, 'November . . . ?'

13 Oct. 1991   Jones, 'Back to the old time religion'

17 Nov. 1991   Hughes, Leishman, 'Hit the road, Jock'

22 Dec. 1991   Jones, 'Norman's Christmas lament'

12 Jan. 1992   Smith, Hughes, Grice, 'Yes it's begun'

8 March 1992   Hughes, Grice, 'Neck and neck, the race begins'

15 March 1992   Jones, Hughes, Grice, 'Week one: Budget blues'

22 March 1992   Jones, Hughes, Grice, 'Tory tremors'

29 March 1992   Jones, Hughes, Grice, 'Major's big gamble'

5 April 1992   Jones, Hughes, Grice, Furbisher, 'All to play for'

12 April 1992   Jones, Hughes, Grice, Furbisher, 'Victory'

7 June 1992   Miller, Grice, Jenkins, 'Falling apart'

14 June 1992   Hughes, Grice, 'Crisis, what crisis?'

19 July 1992   Smith, Hughes, 'Can he tough it out?'

2 Aug. 1992   Fallon, 'Major's dream'

20 Sept. 1992   Fallon, Smith, Hughes, Grice, Lynn, Miller, Jenkins, Wavell, Johnson, 'John Major's days of pain'

27 Sept. 1992   Jones, 'The Major mess'

4 Oct. 1992   Jones, 'Going for Broke'

11 Oct. 1992   Jones, 'Conservatives in Brighton: civil war'

18 Oct. 1992 Fallon, Grice, Jones, Lorenz,
Prescott, Smith, 'Depression Britain:
Major's road to nowhere'

25 Oct. 1992 Jones, Prescott, 'What a
shambles!'

1 Nov. 1992 Jones, Prescott, 'The battle of
Maastricht'

8 Nov. 1992 Jones, Grice, Prescott, Devine,
'The crisis continues'

7 Feb. 1993 Grice, Smith, 'Major's rollercoaster'

14 Feb. 1993 Grice, 'Make or break?'

28 Feb. 1993 Grice, 'Mr Major goes to
Washington'

21 March 1993 Jones, 'Jitters, not
judgement'

18 April 1993 di Giovanni, Grice, Adams,
'Bosnia in agony'

9 May 1993 Jones, 'The voters' revenge'

16 May 1993 Jones, Millar, 'Daylight
snobbery'

30 May 1993 Smith, Prescott, 'Norman
Lamont: the final days'

13 June 1993 Jones, Prescott, Grice,
'Major's little local difficulty'

27 June 1993 Rufford, Leppard, Wavell,
Grice, Prescott, Burrell, Swain, 'Funny
money'

27 July 1993 Grice, Prescott, Janmohamed,
Miller, Fowler, Clarke, 'Treachery dressed
up as principle'

19 Sept. 1993 Grice, 'Major crossroad
ahead'

26 Sept. 1993 Grice, Prescott, 'The invisible
man'

5 Dec. 1993 Jones, Clarke, Hadfield, 'High
wire act'

9 Jan. 1994 Grice, Wavell, 'Basic instinct'

16 Jan. 1994 Jones, Grice, Prescott, 'Never
had it so bad'

30 Jan. 1994 Jones, Grice, Prescott, 'Heirs
unapparent'

6 Feb. 1994 Adams, 'Kneecapped!'

27 Feb. 1994 Davison, Rufford, 'Breach in
the dam'

3 April 1994 Grice, Prescott, 'Not if, but
when'

8 May 1994 Grice, Prescott, 'Out ... for the
count'

15 May 1994 Grice, Prescott, 'Who will
carry the torch?'

5 June 1994 Grice, Prescott, 'Through the
looking glass'

17 July 1994 Chittenden, Skipworth,

Calvert, Ramesh, 'Dishonourable
members?'

24 July 1994 Grice, Prescott, 'First past the
post'

16 Oct. 1994 Grice, Prescott, 'Divided we
stand'

23 Oct. 1994 Chittenden, Skipworth, Grice,
Calvert, Oldfield, 'Welcome to the House
of sleaze'

30 Oct. 1994 Jones, Chittenden, Skipworth,
Prescott, Calvert, Oldfield, 'Whipping a
crisis out of a drama'

6 Nov. 1994 Grice, Prescott, 'Man of straw'

27 Nov. 1994 Grice, 'Press Major to self-
destruct'

4 Dec. 1994 Adams, Davison, Prescott,
'Ties that unwind'

11 Dec. 1994 Jones, 'The disease of dissent'

31 Dec. 1994 Jones, Prescott, 'Out of the
blue'

22 Jan. 1995 Grice, Prescott, 'Dancing to
the spin doctors'

5 Feb. 1995 Jones, Grice, Prescott, Clarke,
Burns, 'Too much to lose'

19 Feb. 1995 Grice, Prescott, 'The week
that unravelled Major'

12 March 1995 Stephen, Adams, 'So long,
nice while it lasted'

19 March 1995 Grice, Prescott, 'The call of
the wilderness'

2 April 1995 Grice, Prescott, 'With friends
like these'

16 April 1995 Grice, Davison, 'Looking for
a showdown'

30 April 1995 Jones, Grice, 'No more Mr
Nice Guys'

7 May 1995 Grice, Prescott, 'Okay, John,
what do we do now?'

21 May 1995 Jones, 'From doubt to despair'

18 June 1995 Grice, Prescott, Jones, Smith,
Hamilton, 'Scent of blood starts civil war'

25 June 1995 Jones, Grice, Prescott, Smith,
Hamilton, 'Waving or drowning'

2 July 1995 Jones, Grice, Prescott, Smith,
Hamilton, 'Praying for a knockout'

9 July 1995 Grice, Prescott, 'The end game'

16 July 1995 Grice, Prescott, 'Enter the lion
king'

17 Sept. 1995 Grice, Prescott, 'Many a
slip ...'

8 Oct. 1995 Jones, 'The remaking of John
Major'

15 Oct. 1995 Grice, Prescott, 'Flags
unfurled: battle is joined'

5 Nov. 1995   Grice, Prescott, 'MPs panic at peek into their pockets'

11 Feb. 1996   Grice, Jones, Prescott, 'Day of judgement'

3 March 1996   Prescott, Clarke, Godson, 'Bombed to the table?'

14 April 1996   Prescott, Grice, Syal, 'End game'

5 May 1996   Grice, Prescott, 'In defeat, defiance'

19 May 1996   Grice, Prescott, 'Blair bloodied'

16 June 1996   Grice, Prescott, 'Blackmail, backbiting, betrayal'

23 June 1996   Grice, Prescott, Conradi, 'Who blinked first?'

21 July 1996   Smith, Grice, 'Thinking the unthinkable'

22 Sept. 1996   Grice, Prescott, 'Divided they fall'

13 Oct. 1996   Grice, 'Honest John v the middle-class Messiah'

24 Nov. 1996   Grice, Prescott, 'Another fine mess'

8 Dec. 1996   Grice, Prescott, 'Divided we fall'

16 Feb. 1997   Grice, Prescott, 'The long goodbye'

OBSERVER ARTICLES

4 March 1990   Wapshott, Keegan, 'Now the Tories start to panic'

18 March 1990   Keegan, 'Major's no-win Budget'

7 Oct. 1990   Wapshott, Keegan, 'The Pound in Europe: Why Maggie bit the bullet'

4 Nov. 1990   Wapshott, 'Conservative Crisis: The spectre quits the stage'

18 Nov. 1990   Wapshott, 'Tory Leadership: She will be winged and bleeding'

25 Nov. 1990   Wapshott, 'How the Tories toppled Maggie'

2 Dec. 1990   Raphael, Smart, 'Tears, fears, plots . . . and toothache'

10 Feb. 1991   Keegan, 'The alarm bells ring'

23 June 1991   Wapshott, 'Conservative row: Thatcher's long shadow'

24 Nov. 1991   Wapshott, 'Maggie goes to war'

1 Dec. 1991   Wapshott, 'Road to Maastricht: How Major really sees the battle of Europe'

8 Dec. 1991   Leonard, Catterall, Hooper, 'Maastricht: Last hand in the biggest game in town'

29 Dec. 1991   Keegan, 'Economic crisis: The nightmare scenario'

26 Jan. 1992   Wapshott, 'Tories opt for power of the bribe'

15 March 1992   Wapshott, 'Wobbly Tory starts down the yellow brick road'

22 March 1992   Wapshott, 'Reality intrudes into the spin-doctors' company'

29 March 1992   Wapshott, 'A nasty attack of sickness and health'

5 April 1992   Wapshott, 'Tories sharpen knives after horror of Red Wednesday'

13 April 1992   Wapshott, 'John Major's discreet charm to the British bourgeoisie'

7 June 1992   Wapshott, 'Whoops and rebel yells back no quick fixes'

13 Sept. 1992   Routledge, 'Chelsea fan vs the tabloids'

20 Sept. 1992   Hoggart, Keegan, Routledge, 'Major's wager: Heads you win, tails we lose'

27 Sept. 1992   Hoggart, 'Major's sea of troubles'

4 Oct. 1992   Hoggart, 'Major moves into minor'

11 Oct. 1992   Hoggart, 'Masque of the Blue Death'

18 Oct. 1992   Hoggart, Routledge, 'Blackout Britain'

25 Oct. 1992   Hoggart, 'A whiff of defeat in the air'

15 Nov. 1992   Sweeney, 'How Britain armed Saddam'

14 Dec. 1993   Hoggart, 'Maastricht Muddle: Blunders that could wreck Euro dream'

30 May 1993   Hoggart, 'Why Norman just had to go'

13 June 1993   Routledge, 'Major on trial: He is hurt and down but not out – yet!'

20 June 1993   Harrison, Routledge, 'Funding the Tories: who pays for the party?'

25 July 1993   Hoggart, Routledge, 'Major's Crisis Week: How long can he survive?'

21 Nov. 1993   Bevins, 'Search for peace in Ireland: Orange still means peril'

24 July 1994   Bevins, Hillmore, 'New men in search of a mandate'

4 Sept. 1994   Holland, Mallie, 'The Irish
Question: Did 3,500 people have to die?'

22 Jan. 1995   Bevins, 'The tail wagging the
Tory dog'

19 March 1995   Crewe, 'Felled by the feel-
bad factor'

7 May 1995   Bevins, 'Towards oblivion'

25 June 1995   Rawnsley, 'The Gambler'

2 July 1995   McSmith, Sweeney, Bevins,
'The Rollercoaster'

9 July 1995   Bevins, McSmith, 'A Battle
Won'

27 Aug. 1995   Hugill, Nelson, 'Peace for one
year but the war is not over'

3 Dec. 1995   Holland, Bevins, Nicoll, 'Inch
by Inch towards peace'

11 Feb. 1996   Ferguson, Rose, Connett,
Nelson, Harrison, Eagar, Mills, Ribbans,
'A Shot Across the Bows'

18 Feb. 1996   Bevins, Ghazi, 'Duplicity'

25 Feb. 1996   Bevins, 'Major in the Dock'

28 April 1996   Bevins, 'The Lion and the
Eunuch'

5 May 1996   Bevins, Kellner, 'Black and
blue – and on the ropes'

26 May 1996   Bevins, McSmith, Bates,
'Who do you think you are kidding Mr
Major?'

23 June 1996   Wintour, Bates, 'How the beef
war was lost'

18 Aug. 1996   Cohen, 'Tories go to the
Devil'

5 Jan. 1997   Wintour, 'Can Major move the
earth?'

5 Jan. 1997   Kellner, 'Blair's bedrock vote is
solid'

2 Feb. 1997   Rayner, 'Two buildings: one
election metaphor'

9 Feb. 1997   Leadbeater, 'Life after death'

2 March 1997   McSmith, 'An end in sight
and a new beginning'

23 March 1997   Rawnsley, 'Going, going . . .'

23 March 1997   Wintour, McSmith,
'Starting pistol shoots Tories in foot'

6 April 1997   McSmith, 'Mark Anthony'

6 April 1997   Wintour, 'Fighting back with
tax (and chickens)'

13 April 1997   Sweeney, 'Decency v deceit'

13 April 1997   Wintour, McSmith,
'Labour's week of trouble at Millbank'

20 April 1997   Hill, 'Liars don't win'

20 April 1997   Wintour, McSmith, 'A single
issue that gave John Major 186 problems'

INDEPENDENT ON SUNDAY
ARTICLES

7 Oct. 1990   Huhne, Castle, 'Why Mrs
Thatcher did her biggest U-turn'

25 Nov. 1990   Castle, Judd, 'Blood, sweat
and double-dealing'

2 Dec. 1990   Oulton, Helsey, 'Our unknown
PM: The life of Major'

10 March 1991   Macintyre, 'Norman
Lamont: A very complex innocent'

17 March 1991   Macintyre, Castle, 'Death
of Thatcherism'

24 March 1991   Macintyre, Hulme, 'How
Major staged his budget coup'

22 March 1992   Hilton, 'The Media Party'

29 March 1992   Hilton, 'It's Scotland the
Grave'

19 April 1992   Macintyre, Castle, 'The
victors: What may we expect from them?'

20 Sept. 1992   Huhne, Macintyre,
Eisenhammer, 'The Breaking of the
Pound'

4 Oct. 1992   Castle, 'Would the real Norman
Lamont please stand up?'

11 Oct. 1992   Leith, 'On the Rocks at
Brighton'

11 Oct. 1992   Macintyre, 'Winner by a short
head'

18 Oct. 1992   Bouen, Castle, Warner,
Macintyre, Faith, Cathcart, 'Who killed
King Coal?'

23 Oct. 1992   Macintyre, Castle, 'Walking
over the viper pit?'

15 Nov. 1992   Macintyre, Castle, 'Don't tell
the public'

4 April 1993   McCrystal, 'Disappointment
in the "nowhere man" '

30 May 1993   Macintyre, Castle, 'Firing
Lamont'

13 June 1993   Macintyre, 'A Norman
Conquest?'

20 June 1993   Castle, Cohen, 'Who pays the
piper?'

27 June 1993   Macintyre, Cohen, 'Sleaze,
smears, Saudis, leaks and dodgy money'

25 July 1993   Macintyre, Castle, 'Where
does Major go from here?'

28 Aug. 1993   Thomson, Macintyre, 'The
story of a bad idea'

26 Sept. 1993   Castle, Cathcart, 'All got up
by the press'

21 Nov. 1993   Castle, Routledge, 'Bastards

vs The Rest'

28 Nov. 1993   McCrystal, 'Back to Basics'

27 March 1994   Castle, 'Wrapped in the Flag'

8 Jan. 1995   Castle, 'The new shape of Britain?'

18 Feb. 1995   Macintyre, 'Prince Rupert at a dangerous gallop'

31 March 1995   Macintyre, Rentoul, 'High anxiety in the Tory heartlands'

2 April 1995   Hellier, 'MP saw no evil'

7 May 1995   Judd, Waterhouse, Cohen, Hosking, Sheridan, Wolmar, 'Things are bad ... but they'll get worse'

18 June 1995   Castle, 'Britain's New Right'

25 June 1995   Cathcart, 'I have seen the future. Its name is Portillo'

2 July 1955   Castle, Routledge, 'Will they both be dumped?'

2 Dec. 1995   Castle, Routledge, 'Some Hope'

18 Feb. 1996   Castle, 'It's not over yet'

18 Feb. 1996   Cathcart, 'Death by a thousand cuts'

24 March 1996   Castle, Watts, Cohen, Routledge, Cathcart, 'How ministers had to eat their words'

5 May 1996   Castle, Routledge, 'Doomed to split?'

26 May 1996   Castle, Lichfield, 'His very own stampede'

23 June 1996   Judd, Abrams, 'Time to bring back grammar schools?'

6 Oct. 1996   Calvert, Gillard, Leigh, 'The Minister for corporate catering'

3 Nov. 1996   Castle, 'This time it's personal'

8 Dec. 1996   Castle, Routledge, 'Will they count him out?'

APPENDIX I
John Major's Cabinets 1990–97

Bold indicates a minister moved in a reshuffle.
Bold italics indicate a minister joining the Cabinet in a reshuffle.

Dates in the first table are the dates when ministers not moved in Major's first reshuffle were put in charge of that department under Margaret Thatcher.

In the reshuffle of 29–30 November 1990, Margaret Thatcher and Cecil Parkinson left the government, while Lord Belstead and Tim Renton were given non-Cabinet appointments.

John Major's first Cabinet 30 November 1990–11 April 1992

Prime Minister	**John Major**	
Chancellor of the Exchequer	**Norman Lamont**	
Foreign Secretary	Douglas Hurd	26 Oct. 1989
Home Secretary	**Kenneth Baker**	
Lord Chancellor	Lord Mackay of Clashfern	26 Oct. 1987
Scotland	*Ian Lang*	
Wales	David Hunt	4 May 1990
Northern Ireland	Peter Brooke	24 July 1989
Leader of the Commons	John MacGregor	2 Nov. 1990
Leader of the Lords	**Lord Waddington**	
Trade and Industry	Peter Lilley	14 July 1990
Defence	Tom King	24 July 1989
Health	William Waldegrave	2 Nov. 1990
Social Security	Tony Newton	24 July 1989
Environment	*Michael Heseltine*	
Transport	**Malcolm Rifkind**	
Employment	Michael Howard	3 Jan. 1990
Education and Science	Kenneth Clarke	2 Nov. 1990
Agriculture	John Gummer	24 July 1988
Energy	John Wakeham	24 July 1989
Duchy of Lancaster (Party Chairman)	**Chris Patten**	

Chief Secretary to the Treasury	*David Mellor*
Chief Whip (non-Cabinet)	*Richard Ryder*

John Major's second Cabinet 11 April 1992–24 September 1992

Kenneth Baker, Lord Waddington, Tom King and Chris Patten left the government, as did Peter Brooke for a time.

The Department of Energy was abolished and its functions subsumed in the DTI under a Minister of State, Tim Eggar. A new Department of National Heritage was created. The Office of Public Service and Science was established, athough its minister, Waldegrave, sat in Cabinet as Chancellor of the Duchy of Lancaster. Chris Patten continued as Party Chairman until May 1992. Education changed title, losing Science to the OPSS, and Michael Heseltine sat in Cabinet as President of the Board of Trade while running the DTI.

Prime Minister	John Major
Chancellor of the Exchequer	Norman Lamont
Foreign Secretary	Douglas Hurd
Home Secretary	**Kenneth Clarke**
Lord Chancellor	Lord Mackay of Clashfern
Scotland	Ian Lang
Wales	David Hunt
Northern Ireland	*Patrick Mayhew*
Leader of the Commons	**Tony Newton**
Leader of the Lords	**Lord Wakeham**
Board of Trade (DTI)	**Michael Heseltine**
Defence	**Malcolm Rifkind**
Health	*Virginia Bottomley*
Social Security	**Peter Lilley**
Environment	**Michael Howard**
Transport	John MacGregor
Employment	*Gillian Shephard*
Education	*John Patten*
Agriculture	John Gummer
National Heritage	**David Mellor**
Duchy of Lancaster (OPSS)	**William Waldegrave**
Chief Secretary to the Treasury	*Michael Portillo*
Party Chairman (non-Cabinet)	*Norman Fowler*
Chief Whip (non-Cabinet)	Richard Ryder

John Major's third Cabinet 25 September 1992–27 May 1993

David Mellor left the government.

Prime Minister	John Major
Chancellor of the Exchequer	Norman Lamont
Foreign Secretary	Douglas Hurd
Home Secretary	Kenneth Clarke
Lord Chancellor	Lord Mackay of Clashfern
Scotland	Ian Lang
Wales	David Hunt
Northern Ireland	Patrick Mayhew
Leader of the Commons	Tony Newton
Leader of the Lords	Lord Wakeham
Board of Trade (DTI)	Michael Heseltine
Defence	Malcolm Rifkind
Health	Virginia Bottomley
Social Security	Peter Lilley
Environment	Michael Howard
Transport	John MacGregor
Employment	Gillian Shephard
Education	John Patten
Agriculture	John Gummer
National Heritage	*Peter Brooke*
Duchy of Lancaster (OPSS)	William Waldegrave
Chief Secretary to the Treasury	Michael Portillo
Party Chairman (non-Cabinet)	Norman Fowler
Chief Whip (non-Cabinet)	Richard Ryder

John Major's fourth Cabinet 27 May 1993–20 July 1994

Norman Lamont left the government.

Prime Minister	John Major
Chancellor of the Exchequer	**Kenneth Clarke**
Foreign Secretary	Douglas Hurd
Home Secretary	**Michael Howard**
Lord Chancellor	Lord Mackay of Clashfern
Scotland	Ian Lang
Wales	*John Redwood*
Northern Ireland	Patrick Mayhew
Leader of the Commons	Tony Newton
Leader of the Lords	Lord Wakeham
Board of Trade (DTI)	Michael Heseltine
Defence	Malcolm Rifkind
Health	Virginia Bottomley

Social Security	Peter Lilley
Environment	**John Gummer**
Transport	John MacGregor
Employment	**David Hunt**
Education	John Patten
Agriculture	**Gillian Shephard**
National Heritage	Peter Brooke
Duchy of Lancaster (OPSS)	William Waldegrave
Chief Secretary to the Treasury	Michael Portillo
Party Chairman (non-Cabinet)	Norman Fowler
Chief Whip (non-Cabinet)	Richard Ryder

John Major's fifth Cabinet 21 July 1994–6 July 1995

Peter Brooke, John MacGregor, John Patten and Lord Wakeham left the government.

Prime Minister	John Major
Chancellor of the Exchequer	Kenneth Clarke
Foreign Secretary	Douglas Hurd
Home Secretary	Michael Howard
Lord Chancellor	Lord Mackay of Clashfern
Scotland	Ian Lang
Wales	John Redwood
Northern Ireland	Patrick Mayhew
Leader of the Commons	Tony Newton
Leader of the Lords	*Lord Cranborne*
Board of Trade (DTI)	Michael Heseltine
Defence	Malcolm Rifkind
Health	Virginia Bottomley
Social Security	Peter Lilley
Environment	John Gummer
Transport	*Brian Mawhinney*
Employment	**Michael Portillo**
Education	**Gillian Shephard**
Agriculture	**William Waldegrave**
National Heritage	*Stephen Dorrell*
Duchy of Lancaster (publicity)	**David Hunt**
Chief Secretary to the Treasury	*Jonathan Aitken*
Minister without Portfolio (Party Chairman)	*Jeremy Hanley*
Chief Whip (non-Cabinet)	Richard Ryder

John Redwood resigned as Welsh Secretary on 26 June 1995. During the leadership election David Hunt was acting Welsh Secretary.

John Major's sixth Cabinet 6 July 1995–2 May 1997

Douglas Hurd, David Hunt, Richard Ryder and Jonathan Aitken left the government, John Redwood already having resigned. Jeremy Hanley moved to a non-Cabinet post.

The Department of Employment was abolished and most of its functions taken over by the Department for Education. The office of Deputy Prime Minister and First Secretary of State was established, working from the Cabinet Office.

Prime Minister	John Major
Deputy Prime Minister	**Michael Heseltine**
Chancellor of the Exchequer	Kenneth Clarke
Foreign Secretary	**Malcolm Rifkind**
Home Secretary	Michael Howard
Lord Chancellor	Lord Mackay of Clashfern
Scotland	*Michael Forsyth*
Wales	*William Hague*
Northern Ireland	Patrick Mayhew
Leader of the Commons	Tony Newton
Leader of the Lords	Lord Cranborne
Board of Trade (DTI)	**Ian Lang**
Defence	**Michael Portillo**
Health	**Stephen Dorrell**
Social Security	Peter Lilley
Environment	John Gummer
Transport	*George Young*
Education and Employment	Gillian Shephard
Agriculture	*Douglas Hogg*
National Heritage	**Virginia Bottomley**
Duchy of Lancaster (OPSS)	*Roger Freeman*
Chief Secretary to the Treasure	**William Waldegrave**
Minister without Portfolio (Party Chairman)	**Brian Mawhinney**
Chief Whip (non-Cabinet)	**Alastair Goodlad**

APPENDIX II

John Major's Principal Staff 1990–97

Principal Private Secretary

Andrew Turnbull	Nov. 1990–May 1992
Alex Allan	May 1992–May 1997

Chief Press Secretary

Gus O'Donnell	Nov. 1990–Jan. 1994
Christopher Meyer	Jan. 1994–Jan. 1996
Jonathan Haslam	Jan. 1996–May 1997

Political Secretary

Judith Chaplin	Dec. 1990–March 1992
Jonathan Hill	March 1992–Nov. 1994
Howell James	Nov. 1994–May 1997

Head of Policy Unit

Sarah Hogg	Dec. 1990–Jan. 1995
Norman Blackwell	Feb. 1995–May 1997

Parliamentary Private Secretary

Graham Bright	Nov. 1990–July 1994
John Ward	July 1994–April 1997
Lord McColl	July 1994–April 1997

APPENDIX III

The Prime Minister's Day 1990–1997

1 December 1990 – 31 March 1997

	1990	1991	1992	1993	1994	1995	1996	1997	Total
Cabinet	2	37	43	45	44	44	45	11	271
Cabinet Committees	7	60	30	26	22	16	25	3	189
Meetings: individual Ministers	8	143	121	137	151	184	143	24	911
Meetings: individual MPs	7	90	82	121	112	102	84	11	609
British visitors/hosts *[meetings & formal meals]*	18	177	220	271	215	252	176	30	1359
Foreign visitors *[meetings & formal meals]*	14	115	140	99	104	90	81	19	662
Official overseas visits *	2	20	18	14	14	14	11	3	96
Days spent overseas *	6	49	48	42	34	39	25	8	251
House: Questions	–	–	–	–	–	–	–	–	334
Statements/speeches/tributes	–	–	–	–	–	–	–	–	71
HM The Queen: Audiences	3	21	17	22	16	18	19	5	⎫
Windsor	–	2	1	1	1	1	1	–	⎬ 138
Balmoral	–	1	1	1	1	1	1	–	⎪
Overseas	–	1	1	1	–	–	–	–	⎭

The above figures do not include Personal, Party or Constituency engagements   * excluding holidays

APPENDIX IV

John Major's Dwindling Majority 1992–7

Date	Event	Majority	Whipped majority
9 April 1992[1]	Election	21	21
19 Feb. 1993	Death of Judith Chaplin (Con)	20	20
6 May 1993	LD gain Newbury	19	19
13 May 1993	Death of Robert Adley (Con)	18	18
23 July 1993	Whip withdrawn from Rupert Allason (Con)	18	16
29 July 1993	LD gain Christchurch	17	15
25 Jan. 1994	Death of Jimmy Boyce (Lab)	18	16
1 Feb. 1994	Death of Jo Richardson (Lab)	19	17
7 Feb. 1994	Death of Stephen Milligan (Con)	18	16
28 Feb. 1994	Death of Ron Leighton (Lab)	19	17
12 April 1994	Death of Bob Cryer (Lab)	20	18
5 May 1994	Lab hold Rotherham	19	17
12 May 1994	Death of John Smith (Lab)	20	18
16 May 1994	Resignation of Bryan Gould (Lab)	21	19
9 June 1994	LD gain Eastleigh Lab hold 4 seats	16	14
30 June 1994	Lab hold Monklands E	15	13
28 July 1994	Whip restored to Allason	15	15
12 Oct. 1994	Death of John Blackburn (Con)	14	14
28 Nov. 1994	Whip withdrawn from 8 MPs; Richard Body resigns whip	14	−4
15 Dec. 1994	Lab gain Dudley W	13	−5
19 Jan. 1995	Resignation of Neil Kinnock (Lab)	14	−4
16 Feb. 1995	Lab hold Islwyn	13	−5

[1] The election of Betty Boothroyd (Labour) as Speaker in April 1992 boosted the government's apparent majority to 22, although this did not count because of the usual abstention of the Deputy Speakers drawn from the Conservative side.

19 Feb. 1995	Death of Nicholas Fairbairn (Con)	12	−6
20 March 1995	Death of Jim Kilfedder (UPUP)[2]	13	−5
24 April 1995	Whip restored to 8 rebels	13	11
17 May 1995	Death of Geoffrey Dickens (Con)	12	10
25 May 1995	SNP gain Perth & Kinross	11	9
15 June 1995	UKU gain North Down	10	8
27 July 1995	LD gain Littleborough & Saddleworth	9	7
7 Oct. 1995	Alan Howarth (Con) defects to Lab	7	5
31 Oct. 1995	Death of Derek Enright (Lab)	8	6
12 Dec. 1995	Death of David Lightbown (Con)	7	5
29 Dec. 1995	Emma Nicholson (Con) defects to LDs	5	3
17 Jan. 1996	Whip restored to Body	5	5
1 Feb. 1996	Lab hold Hemsworth	4	4
22 Feb. 1996	Peter Thurnham (Con) becomes Independent	2	2
11 April 1996	Lab gain Staffordshire SE	1	1
11 Oct. 1996	Death of Terry Patchett (Lab)	2	2
12 Oct. 1996	Thurnham (Ind) joins LDs	2	2
3 Nov. 1996	Death of Barry Porter (Con)	1	1
6 Dec. 1996	John Gorst (Con) withholds support[3]	1	1
12 Dec. 1996	Lab hold Barnsley E	0	0
16 Jan. 1997	Death of Ian Mills (Con)	−1	−1
20 Jan. 1997	Death of Martin Redmond (Lab)	0	0
27 Feb. 1997	Lab gain Wirral S	−1	−1
8 March 1997	George Gardiner (Con) defects to Referendum	−3	−3

The column 'Majority' counts whipless Conservatives in the majority, but the column 'Whipped majority' supposes that the whipless were in opposition, as the Commons authorities assumed after November 1994.

[2] Kilfedder was a fairly reliable pro-Conservative vote, although he was technically an Opposition member. His replacement by the pro-Labour Robert McCartney in the North Down by-election had, therefore, a similar effect on the Commons arithmetic to a Lab gain from Con although it is not counted as such.

[3] Gorst did not technically resign the whip, but he did not promise to back the government in any confidence vote. It is therefore ambiguous as to whether he could count towards the government's majority. He stood as an official Conservative candidate in the election.

ACKNOWLEDGEMENTS

This book took three years to research and write, during which I was Deputy Headmaster and at the very end Acting Head of St Dunstan's College. It could not have been written without a huge amount of support.

My principal debt is to my researcher, Lewis Baston, to whom I have spoken daily, often several times, throughout that period. He is a man of prodigious intellectual power and determination. Our *modus operandi*, in brief, was that we jointly discussed the book's structure, I conducted most of the 550 interviews, he prepared the chapter briefs based on those interviews and other sources, I wrote the chapters and with his help, I revised them, while leaving all judgements (with which he was not always in agreement) as my own.

My long-suffering and highly able secretary-cum-editorial assistant on nearly ten books, Anne Marie Weitzel, typed every word of the book and most of the interviews. Ian Gerrard (ex-Whitgift) was deputy chief researcher for two years, happily working through the night to meet deadlines and always intelligent and utterly calm. Daniel Collings (ex-Tonbridge) and Peter Snowdon (ex-St Dunstan's College) showed a persistence and intellectual rigour which I would not expect in most postgraduates. At the time of writing, both are waiting to go up to university.

Further valuable research work was done by Alex Card, William Gelling, Karen Grudzien, Michael Harley, Valerie Holford, Timothy Merritt, Jessica Nierenberg, Matthew Pendered, Katharine Raymond, Joanna Seldon, Ed Smith, Stuart Thomas and Chuka Umunna.

At Weidenfeld and Nicolson, Ion Trewin, my editor, shows me again why he is the best editor of political and contemporary books working in London. Rachel Leyshon was an admirable editorial assistant, not least in assembling pictures. Lesley Baxter was a tenacious copy editor. My thanks to Sarah Eirera for the index. Rebecca Salt dealt with publicity.

At the Institute of Contemporary British History I always find a warmth and stimulation free from the tensions and petty jealousies that dog too much of academic life. I would especially like to thank my fellow founder of the Institute, Peter Hennessy, and those associated with the ICBH or who work in allied fields, particularly Peter Catterall, Virginia Preston, Paul Nicholson, Roger Langley, John Barnes, Brian Brivati, Ben Pimlott, Kathy Burk, David

Butler, John Campbell, David Marquand, Stuart Ball, Peter Middleton, Frank Cooper, Olive Wood, David Severn, Edmund Dell, John Ramsden, Hugo Young, Harriet Jones, Robert Taylor, Dennis Kavanagh, Richard Cockett, Denys Blakeway, Michael Kandiah, Stephanie Maggin and Peter Riddell.

I was fortunate to have so many stimulating and supportive colleagues at the three schools at which I have taught, and to whom, with my former pupils, the book is dedicated. At the excellent St Dunstan's College, I would especially like to thank my fellow historians Tony Sharp, Gary Hunter, Brett Harrild, my senior colleagues Tim Pratt, Norrie Wallace, Martin Blocksidge, Margaret Lipton, Simon Thorogood, John Gaskell, Rick Bodenham, and my politics and economics colleagues, Peter Ruben and Hilary Moffatt, and quasi politics colleague Chris Muller. For intellectual upbraiding and reading of some scripts, my admiration and thanks to an extraordinary school teacher who has inspired many creative students, David Norris. For support and understanding I would like to thank the Governors under Sir Roger Cork, and Head David Moore. My outstanding pastoral team made my life both easier and much more pleasant: Gerry Pickett, Liz Emes, Kerry Pitcher, Michael Punt, Liz Gray, Buster Price and Alistair Dickson. Norma Thompson was a constant source of wit as my secretary, and my thanks to the secretariat, Sue Letchford, Carol Dodds, Pat Russell and Maura Bacca for constant friendship and encouragement.

I would like to thank all my colleagues at my two earlier schools. At Tonbridge my history colleagues: Joe Davies, David Walsh, Francis Cazalet, Michael Bushby, Paul Taylor, Anthony Wallersteiner; economics and politics – Russell Tillson, Ian MacEwen, John Gibbs, John Maynard; English – Jonathan Smith, Andrew Edwards, John James, Sharon Jennings, polymath-in-residence, Geoff Allibone, and the head, Martin Hammond. At Whitgift, I would especially like to thank Brian Griffiths, David Fletcher, Bob McGrath, David Vanstone, Stephen Howarth, John Clarke, Peter Sutherland, Andrew Halls, Anthony Ridley and the then Head, David Raeburn.

Among other institutions I would particularly like to thank Standard Chartered Bank for donating a helpful sum to the ICBH towards the cost of transcribing the interviews, and for the assistance from broadcasting organisations working on related matters, including particularly Blakeway Productions, the BBC, Sky television and Michael Crick. The public libraries of Kensington & Chelsea (particularly James Hamilton at Chelsea reference), Camden, Westminster, Bromley, Haringay, Croydon, City of London, Kent, Cambridgeshire and last but by no means least Lambeth were mines of information for the research team and I am grateful for the help the staff of these institutions have offered this project. Other libraries used included the unique British Library, the Bodleian Library, Nuffield College, the National TV archive and the library of Baker College of Mount Clemens, Michigan. The ICBH and the Social Market Foundation were generous with office space for Lewis Baston, and Nuffield College gave him a many times extended leave of absence to assist me. Sevenoaks Preparatory School were gracious hosts to Daniel Collings in the course of his research. Brighton College, especially Bob Alexander, Rosemary Hands, John Spencer and Tony Smith, helped smooth the final stages. The marvellous Number Ten switchboard were always a pleasure to deal with. Holborn and St Pancras Conservative Association and Roland Walker were kind enough to open their files from the early 1970s, and other people who have provided help through documents include Michael Chaplin and the Chaplin family, Michael Crick, Nicholas Bennett, Pat Dessoy, John Pank, Philip Cowley, Ken Payne, John Watson and Sir Martin Gilbert, as well as many people who would prefer not to be thanked in public. Sarah King was particularly helpful with photographs.

I inflicted embryonic thoughts about John Major on sixth formers and/or parent groups at many schools, and would like to thank them for their forbearance: Alleyn's, Birkenhead; Canford; Kings School, Canterbury; Eastbourne College; Jane Allen's Girls' School; Monmouth; Portsmouth Grammar School; RGS Guildford; RGS Worcester; St John's Leatherhead; Trinity, Tonbridge; and Whitgift.

Friends with whom I stayed while researching or writing, or have had to live with the book during family holidays together, include Richard and Adrienne Alder, Nick and Sarah Dibb, David and Debbie Fletcher, Andrew and Hilary Grant, John and Louise James, John and Sue Mitchell, Jonathan and Gillie Smith, Paul and Amanda Taylor, and Buck and Dinah Waranch. Martin and Godelieve Westlake and Matthew Happoid hosted Lewis Baston. Finally, to Charlie Percy and his excellent staff at the Hotel San Lucianu, Corsica, not to say the guests, who had to put up with a mad Englishman in their midst sweating under a canopy revising this book.

Jonathan Hill and Howell James deserve particular thanks for their part in opening doors and liaising with me throughout the project. There not being a set ruling on which office within Number 10 deals with biographers, the duty fell to the Political Secretaries, both of whom were constantly burdened with issues of more pressing magnitude yet found time to talk and help. Others among John Major's non-civil service staff whom I can mention by name, include Nick True, Baroness Hogg, Norman Blackwell, George Bridges, Arabella Warburton and Sheila Gunn.

Peter Hennessy, John Major and Sir Robin Butler deserve credit for, between them, helping to open up Whitehall to the contemporary historian. I would particularly like to thank the many people who have seen events from the vantage point of the Number 10 Private Office and struck such a fair balance between the confidentiality their position entails and the interests of open government. Because of the rules regarding attributed interviews with officials, I offer a general acknowledgement to all serving and retired officials, whose interviews were in many cases the most perceptive and informative. I hope that those who gave hours of help understand why I am not thanking them by name. I am also deeply indebted to my other interviewees.

The vast majority of John Major's Cabinet ministers agreed to give interviews for the book, as did many of his parliamentary colleagues and political opponents inside and outside the Conservative Party. The following people are among those who helped provide information for my research: Anthony Acland, Richard Addis, Bruce Anderson, Jeffrey Archer, Robert Atkins, James Baker, Kenneth Baker, John Banham, Andrew Beadle, Steve Bell, Tim Bell, Nicholas Bennett, Anthony Bevins, Guy Black, Norman Blackwell, Emily Blatch, Mike Bloomfield, Hartley Booth, Pik Botha, Virginia Bottomley, Rhodes Boyson, George Bridges, Graham Bright, Colin Brock, Peter Brooke, Peter Brown, Michael Brunson, George Bush, Jonathan Caine, David Cameron, Ian Cameron Black, Hugh Chambers, Michael Chaplin, Dick Cheney, Alan Clark, Kenneth Clarke, Tim Collins, Alistair Cooke, Andrew Cooper, John Cope, Colin Cowdrey, Robert Cranborne, Michael Crick, Peter Cropper, Matthew d'Ancona, F. W. De Klerk, Debbie de Satge, Pat Dessoy, Terry Dicks, Peter Dobbie, Stephen Dorrell, John Drew, Roland Dumas, Anthony Durant, Danny Finkelstein, Marcus Fox, Maurice Fraser, Peter Fraser, George Gardiner, Tristan Garel-Jones, Tony Garrett, Martin Gilbert, Peter Golds, Alastair Goodlad, Paul Goodman, Michael Gove, Peter Graham, Damian Green, Richard Greenbury, Peter Guilford, John Gummer, Peter Gummer, Sheila Gunn, Claire Haddock, Ronald Hampel, Keith Hampson, Jeremy Hanley, David Hannay, Philip Harris, Ralph Harris, Robin Harris, Max Hastings, Robert Hayward, Sarah Hogg, Jonathan Holborow, Derek Holley, Michael Howard, Alan Howarth, Geoffrey Howe, Robert Hughes, Trevor Humber, David Hunt, Douglas Hurd, Stanley Hurn, Bernard Ingham, Oliver James, John Jennings, Paul Johnson, Clive Jones, George Jones, Michael Jones, Michael Jopling, Paul Judge, Roger Juggins, Trevor Kavanagh, Tessa Keswick, Sarah King, Tom King, Robin Kingsdown, Neil Kinnock, Tony Lake, Norman Lamont, Ian Lang, Andrew Lansley, Dominic Lawson, Nigel Lawson, Geoff Ledden, Edward Leigh, Charles Lewington, Warwick Lightfoot, Peter Lilley, Edward Llewellyn, Nicholas Lloyd, Jean Lucas, Nicholas Lyell, John MacGregor, James Mackay, Norma Major, Martin Mansergh, John Maples, Andrew Marr, Francis Maude, Brian Mawhinney, Patrick Mayhew, Alastair McAlpine, Ian McColl, Don Macintyre, Ian McKellen, Michael McManus, Iain McWhirter, Douglas McWilliams, David Mellor, Ronnie Millar, Kenneth Minogue, James Molyneaux, Charles Moore, John Moore, Roy Mortimer, Lucy Neville-Rolfe, Barbara Oakley, Alan Orsich, Cecil Parkinson, Matthew Parris, Chris Patten, Ken Payne, Derek Pinks, Madsen Pirie, Steve Platt, David Poole, Michael Portillo, Charles Powell, John Preuveneers, James Prior, Christopher Prout, Tim Raison, John Redwood, Jonathan Rees, William Rees-Mogg, John Rennie, Robin Renwick, Albert Reynolds, Peter Riddell, Bill Robinson, Patrick Rock, David Rodgers, Alan Rosling, Guy Rowlands, Tim Rycroft, Neville Sandelson, Richard Scott, Brent Scowcroft, Hugh Seckleman, Raymond Seitz, John Sergeant, Gillian Shephard, Stephen Sherbourne, Michael Simmonds, Jeremy Sinclair, Douglas Slater, Christopher Spencer, Michael Spicer, Dick Spring, Robin Squire, Marion Standing Wright, Philip Stephens, Derek Stone, Norman Stone, Anthony Storr, Peter Stothard,

Shirley Stotter, Thomas Strathclyde, Raman Subba Row, Peter Sutherland, Anthony Teasdale, Sue Tinson, Michael Trend, Nick True, David Waddington, John Wakeham, William Waldegrave, Roland Walker, Stephen Wall, Arabella Warburton, John Ward, David Wastell, John Watson, Ken Weetch, Michael White, William Whitelaw, Dafydd Wigley, Stuart Wild, David Willetts, David Wilshire, Sue Winter, Patrick Wright, George Young and Hugo Young. Many of the people above, and others, have read over sections of the book and provided many helpful comments in the interests of accuracy. Peter Riddell, Vernon Bogdanor and William Waldegrave here may be singled out for seeing the entire draft.

Particular thanks to John Major, who has been a considerate subject in an intrusive process, and has given me what time he could find in his punishing schedule. He obviously has strong views on the contents of the book but never sought to influence unduly what I wrote.

Many people who have given interviews or helped in other ways would prefer me not to mention them in the acknowledgements. You know who you are, and I am extremely grateful. The errors, of fact and judgement, that remain are wholly my own.

I would like to thank Karen Grudzien Baston for allowing her husband to devote weekends, holidays and, not least, countless evenings to this book, and always with a cheerful, not to say resigned, smile. My parents, Arthur and Marjorie Seldon, were a constant source of wisdom and support. Finally, I would like to thank my own wife Joanna, and my young family Jessica, Susannah and Adam. Truth to tell, none of them liked my writing this book which took me so much away from them. Yet their total love carried me through some rocky passages. Joanna has proved yet again that she is the finest wife in the world. I can only hope that, though it may well have put my children off politics, it has not put them off books.

INDEX

(Generally, titles have not been included)